lonely planet

Caribbean Islands

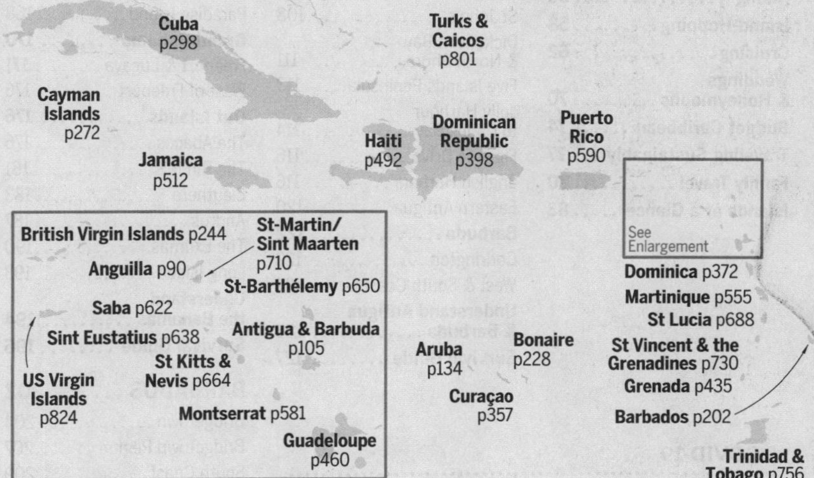

Paul Clammer, Stephanie d'Arc Taylor, Marc Di Duca, Alex Egerton, Sarah Gilbert, Michael Grosberg, Paul Harding, Ashley Harrell, Mark Johanson, Anna Kaminski, Tom Masters, Brendan Sainsbury, Andrea Schulte-Peevers, Polly Thomas, Wendy Yanagihara

PLAN YOUR TRIP

COVID-19

We have re-checked every business in this book before publication to ensure that it is still open after 2020's COVID-19 outbreak. However, the economic and social impacts of COVID-19 will continue to be felt long after the outbreak has been contained, and many businesses, services and events referenced in this guide may experience ongoing restrictions. Some businesses may be temporarily closed, have changed their opening hours and services, or require bookings; some unfortunately could have closed permanently. We suggest you check with venues before visiting for the latest information.

ON THE ROAD

Contents

ON THE ROAD

EL MORRO, HAVANA P310

Contents

SURVIVAL GUIDE

SPECIAL FEATURES

Welcome to the Caribbean Islands

From forest-clad volcanoes to shimmering reefs, spicy salsa rhythms to deep reggae bass, pirate hideouts to sugar-sand beaches, the Caribbean is a thrillingly diverse region.

A Caribbean Mosaic

The Caribbean is a joyful mosaic of islands, an explosion of color, fringed by beaches and soaked in rum. It's a lively and intoxicating profusion of people and places spread over 7000 islands and cays. But, for all they share, there's also much that makes them different. Can there be a greater contrast than between bustling Barbados and its neighbor, the seemingly unchanged-since-colonial-times St Vincent? Revolutionary Cuba and its next-door banking capital, the Caymans? Or between booming British-oriented St Kitts and its sleepy, Dutch-affiliated neighbor Sint Eustatius, just across a narrow channel?

Island Colors

Azure seas, white beaches, green forests so cool they soothe the eyes – there is nothing subtle about the landscapes of the Caribbean. Dive below the waters for a color chart of darting fish, coral and wrecks. Feel the sand between your toes at any one of a thousand holiday-brochure-ready beaches. Hike into emerald wilderness and spot the accents of red orchids and yellow parrots. Outdoor-adventure enthusiasts make a beeline for unspoilt islands such as nature-lovers' Dominica and St Lucia's iconic, lush Piton mountains, which send out a siren call to climbers.

Sunlit Culture

The tropical sunlight is infectious. Like birds shedding dull adolescent plumage, visitors leave their wardrobes of gray and black behind when they step off the plane and don the Caribbean palette. Even the food is colorful, with rainbows of produce brightening up the local markets. You'll also see every hue at intense, costume-filled festivities like Carnival, celebrated throughout the region but particularly in Trinidad. Glorious, crumbling Cuba, reggae-rolling Jamaica, and Vodou-loving Haiti top the wish lists for travelers seeking unique cultural experiences and Unesco heritage havens.

Tropical Adventures

You can find any kind of island adventure here. With so many islands, beaches, cultures, flavors and waves to choose from, how could this not be vacation paradise? You can do nothing on the sand, party at a resort, explore a new community, hop between islands, discover wonders under the water or catch a perfect wave above, revel in a centuries-old culture (and sway to some of the world's greatest music while you're at it), and then run off to find your inner pirate… Just about anything is possible in the Caribbean.

Why I Love the Caribbean

By Paul Clammer, Writer

I was on a beach, taking a break from research. Had I been out to the island on the edge of the bay, a fisherman asked. There was a ruin there, stories of pirates. Did I want to see? His boat was beaten up and its sail made from old plastic sheets, but in we got and dipped over the waves, then waded ashore to a tumble of buildings overgrown with roots and lianas. It felt like *Treasure Island* and I wondered if guidebooks should come with maps telling you 'X marks the spot.' This could only be the Caribbean...

For more about our writers, see p896.

Above: Natural Pool, Arikok National Park, Aruba (p144)

Caribbean Islands

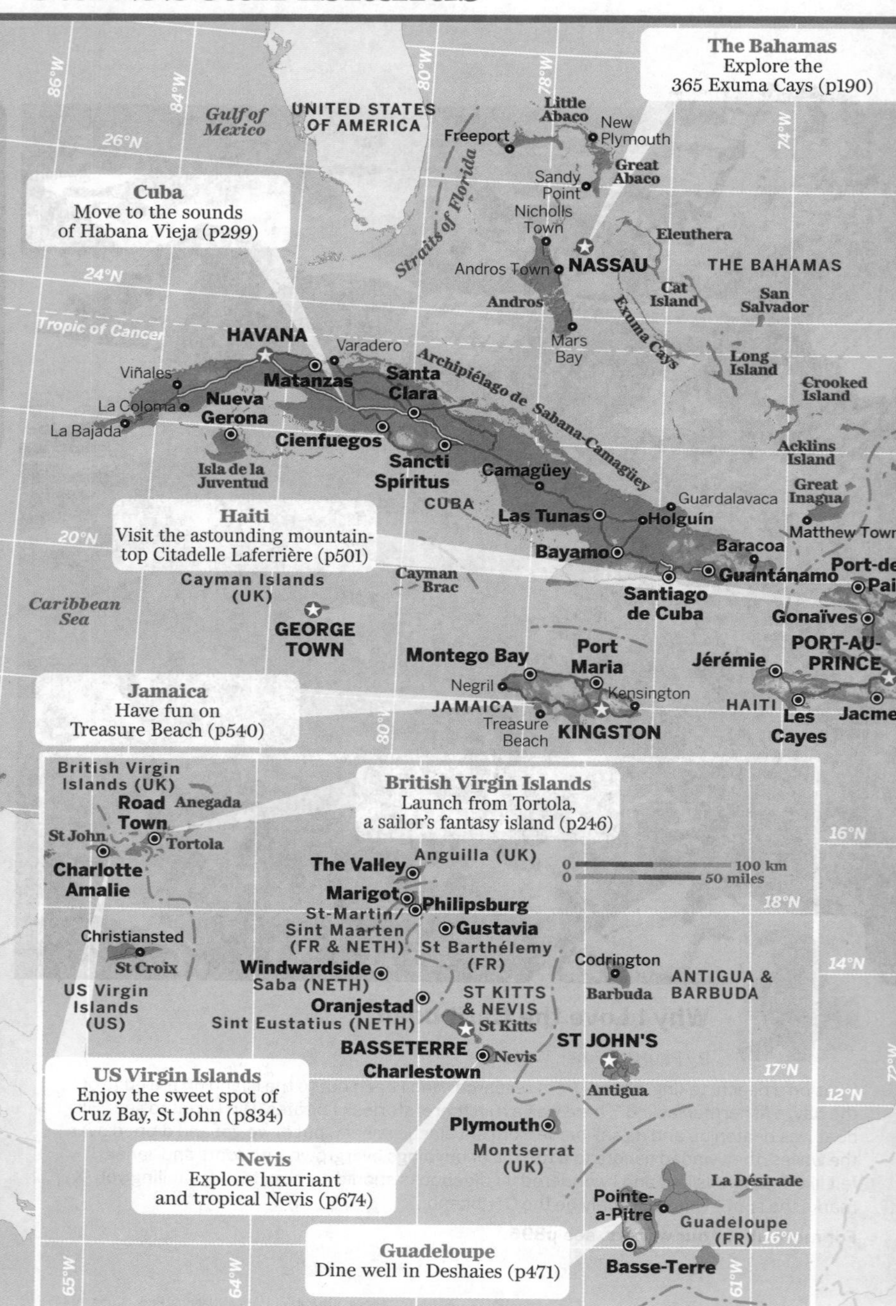

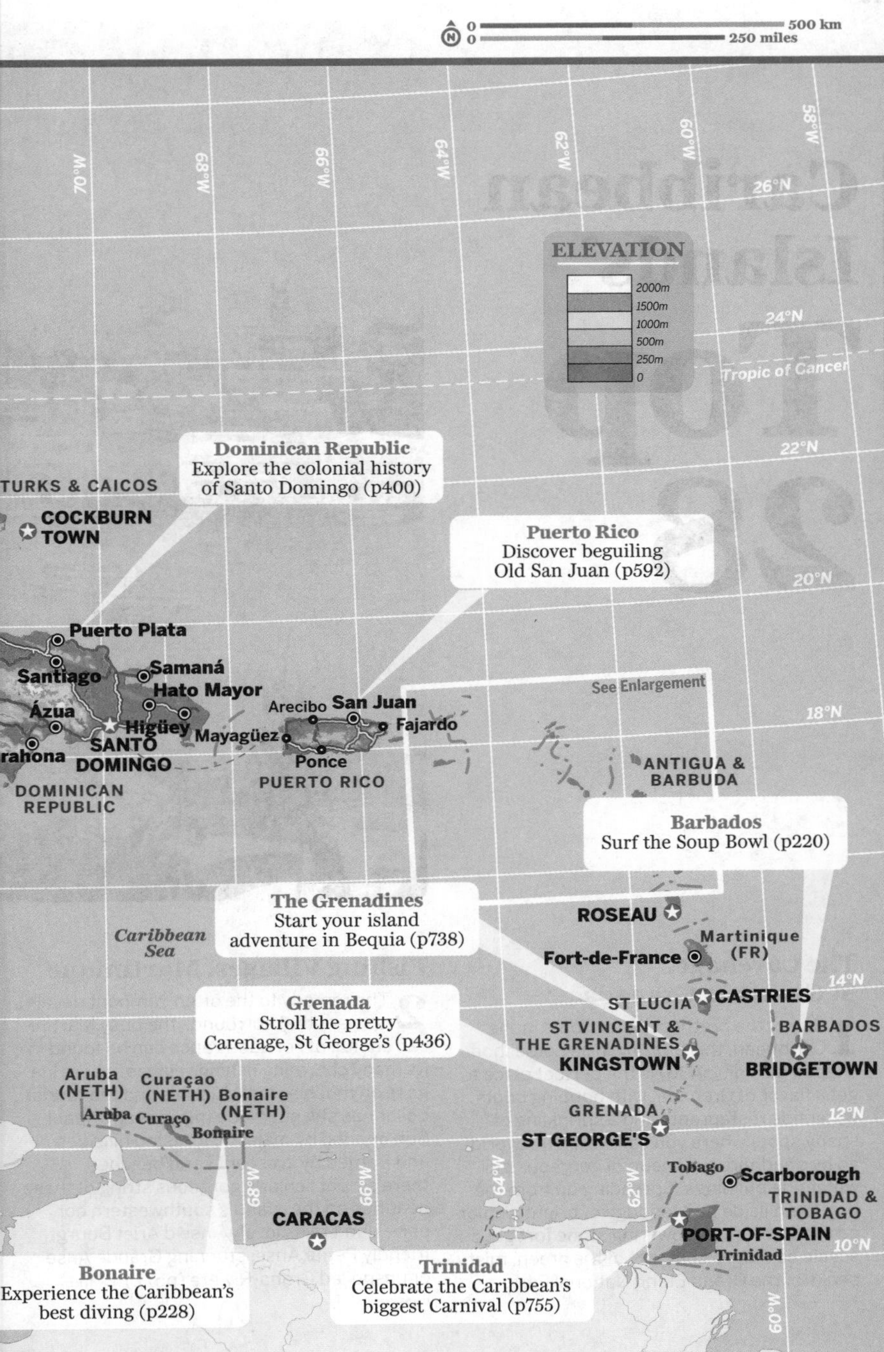

0 500 km
0 250 miles
ELEVATION
2000m
1500m
1000m
500m
250m
0
Tropic of Cancer
Dominican Republic
Explore the colonial history of Santo Domingo (p400)
Puerto Rico
Discover beguiling Old San Juan (p592)
Barbados
Surf the Soup Bowl (p220)
The Grenadines
Start your island adventure in Bequia (p738)
Grenada
Stroll the pretty Carenage, St George's (p436)
Bonaire
Experience the Caribbean's best diving (p228)
Trinidad
Celebrate the Caribbean's biggest Carnival (p755)
TURKS & CAICOS
COCKBURN TOWN
Puerto Plata
Santiago
Samaná
Hato Mayor
Ázua
Higüey
SANTO DOMINGO
Barahona
DOMINICAN REPUBLIC
Arecibo
San Juan
Fajardo
Mayagüez
Ponce
PUERTO RICO
See Enlargement
ANTIGUA & BARBUDA
ROSEAU
Martinique (FR)
Fort-de-France
ST LUCIA
CASTRIES
ST VINCENT & THE GRENADINES
KINGSTOWN
BARBADOS
BRIDGETOWN
GRENADA
ST GEORGE'S
Tobago
Scarborough
TRINIDAD & TOBAGO
PORT-OF-SPAIN
Trinidad
Caribbean Sea
Aruba (NETH)
Aruba
Curaçao (NETH)
Curaçao
Bonaire (NETH)
Bonaire
CARACAS
70°W
68°W
66°W
64°W
62°W
60°W
58°W
26°N
24°N
22°N
20°N
18°N
14°N
12°N
10°N

Caribbean Islands' Top 28

The Carenage, St George's, Grenada

1 One of the prettiest waterfronts in the Caribbean, this buzzing little horseshoe-shaped harbor (p436) is the perfect place to get a flavor of Grenada, with bobbing boats, waterside restaurants and a sprinkling of shady spots where you can watch the world go by or admire the lineup of gorgeous old waterside buildings. Spreading up from the bay, the hillside hodgepodge of brightly colored rooftops and a glowering stone fort get a scenic backdrop courtesy of the green, misty peaks of the Grand Etang National Park.

Fishing Villages, Martinique

2 The remedy to the often-rampant development that surrounds the busy Martinican capital of Fort-de-France can be found in its many charming fishing villages, where life goes on much as it always has and the tourist dollar has still not made much of an impact. Surrounded by majestic forested hillsides and framed by crescent sand beaches, there's a particularly gorgeous string of these beauties on the island's southwestern corner – don't miss lovely Anse d'Arlet Bourg, friendly Petite Anse, stunning Grande Anse or unspoiled Grand-Rivière (p572). Grand-Rivière

FRANK FELL/ROBERTHARDING/GETTY IMAGES ©

BRUNO DE HOGUES/GETTY IMAGES ©

Tiny Islands, St Vincent & the Grenadines

3 It's heard in office cubicles the world over daily: 'I'm chucking it all in and going to tramp around tropical islands!' In a world of package tourism, huge cruise ships and mega-resorts, the very idea seems lost in another, simpler time. Until, that is, you reach the Grenadines. Starting with Bequia (p738), multiple tiny islands stretch south, linked by regular ferries. Jump aboard or hitch a ride on a passing yacht to feel the wind in your face and head off to adventure. Port Elizabeth, Bequia

Music & Culture, Havana, Cuba

4 Few come to Cuba without visiting Havana (p299), a hauntingly romantic city, ridden with ambiguity and imbued with shabby magnificence. A stroll around the atmospheric if sometimes rundown streets of Habana Vieja reveals rusting American Buicks, kids playing stickball with rolled-up balls of plastic, and a tremendous mish-mash of architectural styles that mirrors the nation's diverse history. Underlying it all is the musical soundtrack for which Cuba is famous: rumba, salsa, *son*, reggaeton and *trova*.

3

JOHN SEATON CALLAHAN/GETTY IMAGES ©

ISABELLE KUEHN/SHUTTERSTOCK ©

Surfing the Soup, Barbados

5 Like a monster wave breaking, Barbados has crashed onto the world surf scene. Although long the haunt of surf-happy locals, only recently has Barbados' east-side surf break, called the Soup Bowl (p220), gone supernova. Swells travel thousands of miles across the rough Atlantic and form into huge waves that challenge the world's best. From September to December, faces found in surfing magazines stare wistfully out to sea from the very mellow beach village of Bathsheba. A slight calming from January to May brings out the hopefuls.

Shore Diving, Bonaire

6 Almost the entire coast of Bonaire is ringed by some of the healthiest coral reefs in the region. Sometimes it seems like half the population of the island are divers – and why shouldn't they be? The Unesco-recognized shore reefs (p232) can be reached right off your room's back deck at oodles of low-key diver-run hotels. All-you-can-breathe-in-a-week tank specials are common. Beyond the exquisite shore diving (more than half of the 100 named sites are right off the beach) are more challenging sites for advanced divers. Manta ray

Willemstad, Curaçao

7 Colorful Willemstad (p359) feels like a city in the old country, albeit with sunny skies and Caribbean views. This cosmopolitan capital is a cultural treasure trove, complete with unique museums, street art and vibrant nightlife. On both sides of the Sint Annabaai shipping channel, the city streets are lined with Dutch-colonial architecture, here with a citrus-hued, tropical twist. The historic districts are being restored and re-energized, especially Pietermaai, now housing boutique hotels, fine restaurants and cool cafes.

USS Kittiwake, Grand Cayman

8 Off the coast of Seven Mile Beach, the 250ft (76m) submarine USS *Kittiwake* (p277) has found her final resting place in 60ft (18m) of water. The former rescue sub was purposely sunk to create an artificial reef and dive site. The doors and windows were removed, allowing in light and making for easy exploration of the decks and interiors. In fact, when conditions are clear, even snorkelers and free divers can investigate the ship's upper reaches, which are only about 15ft (5m) below the surface.

Treasure Beach, Jamaica

9 Down in Treasure Beach (p541), miles from the urban chaos of Kingston, you'll find a quiet stretch of sand where visitors, expats and Jamaican locals kick back every evening. Beers are passed around, reggae cracks over the air and a supreme sense of chilled-out-ness – oh, let's just say it: 'irie' – descends onto the crowd. Music, food, Red Stripe, smiles – it all comes together here to create the laid-back Jamaican scene that many travelers dream of. Come for a day, stay for a week.

English Harbour, Antigua

10 English Harbour flaunts its heritage at one of the pre-eminent historic sites in the Caribbean: Nelson's Dockyard (p117). Travel back to the 18th century as you wander along cobbled lanes and past meticulously restored old buildings, with superb views to nearby beaches and fortresses. Still a working marina, it's one of the world's key yachting centers and attracts an international flotilla to its regattas. It's also Antigua's biggest foodie destination, with a truly international choice of cuisines and dozens of excellent restaurants vying for your custom.

JOHN BRYDEN/500PX ©

Carnival, Trinidad

11 Home to one of the world's biggest and best Carnivals (p754), Trinidad is party central, and its two days of festival fabulousness have inspired the most creative and dynamic music and dance culture in the Caribbean. Visit a panyard and let the rhythmic sweetness of steel pan vibrate through your body, check out the fireworks and drama of a soca concert or, best of all, don a spangly, feathery masquerade band costume and learn to 'wine your waist' like the locals during the two-day street parade.

French-flavored St-Barthélemy

12 It's easy to dismiss St-Barthélemy (p650) as the Caribbean's capital of jet-setterdom, but there's so much more to this hilly island. Cradled within its craggy coves are small towns with stone walls that look as though they've been plucked directly from the French countryside. This counterpoint of cultures plays out in the local cuisine as well – scores of world-class restaurants dish out expertly crafted meals that meld the savoir faire and mastery of French cuisine with vivid bursts of bright island flavors.

Volcanic Splendor, Montserrat

13 The tiny island of Montserrat (p581) has seen a disproportionate amount of drama: the hundreds of eruptions of Soufrière Hills Volcano in the late 1990s led to the abandonment of the capital Plymouth, as well as some two thirds of the rest of the island. But visiting this slice of the past today is a wonderful experience, with no cruise crowds or resorts to contend with and instead a vibrant slice of old Caribbean culture, where everyone knows everyone else and where the volcanic landscapes never cease to amaze.

Tortola, British Virgin Islands

14 Endowed with steady trade winds, tame currents and hundreds of protected bays, the British Virgin Islands are a sailor's fantasyland. Many visitors come expressly to hoist a jib and dawdle among the multiple isles, trying to determine which one serves the best rum-pineapple-and-coconut Painkiller. Tortola (p246), known as the charter-boat capital of the world, is the launching pad, so it's easy to get geared up. Don't know how to sail? Learn on the job with a sailing school.

LEONARD ZHUKOVSKY/SHUTTERSTOCK ©

15

16

Old San Juan, Puerto Rico

15 Even those limited to a quick visit find it easy to fall under the beguiling spell of the cobblestone streets, pastel-painted colonial buildings and grand fortresses of Old San Juan (p592). Atop the ramparts of El Morro, the allure of this place is evident in every direction – from the labyrinth of crooked lanes to the endless sparkle of the Atlantic. By day, lose yourself in historical stories of blood and drama; by night, tap in (and tap along) to the condensed cluster of bars and clubs constituting the neighborhood's nightlife.

Amazing Hiking, Saba

16 Rising dramatically out of the ocean, tiny Saba's volcanic peak (p624) can only be fully appreciated in person. Even the craftiest photographers can't correctly capture its beauty. Sign up for a trek with Crocodile James and wend your way through fascinatingly different climate zones as you make your way from the crashing waves up into the lazy clouds. From the top, you can stare out over the island's traditional gingerbread-trimmed, red-roofed white cottages in the valleys below.

Cruz Bay, US Virgin Islands

17 Nowhere embodies the territory's vibe better than Cruz Bay (p834), St John. As the gateway to Virgin Islands National Park, it has trails right from town that wind by shrub-nibbling wild donkeys and drop onto secluded beaches prime for snorkeling. All the activity can make a visitor thirsty, so it's a good thing Cruz Bay knows how to host a happy hour. Hippies, sea captains, retirees and reggae devotees all clink glasses at daily parties that spill out into the street.

Sint Maarten

18 Most island-goers would consider huge careening jets and large tracts of concrete runway to be noisy eyesores, but not on St-Martin/Sint Maarten (p710). Clustered around Juliana International Airport – the area's transportation hub – you'll find a handful of bumpin' bars that cling to the sides of the runway while also abutting the turquoise waters. At Sunset Beach Bar, arrival times are posted in chalk on a surfboard and aircraft landings are awaited with much anticipation as beach bums get blown into the blue from the backlash of jet propulsion.

Zona Colonial, Dominican Republic

19 Take a walk through history in the oldest European city in the Americas. With its cobblestone streets and beautifully restored mansions, churches and forts – many now converted into evocative museums, hotels and restaurants – it's easy to imagine Santo Domingo's landmark quarter (p400) as the seat of Spain's 16th-century empire. But the past and present coexist gracefully here: follow in the footsteps of pirates and conquistadores one moment, then pop into a 4D movie theater the next. Museo Alcázar de Colón (p400)

Deshaies, Guadeloupe

20 This Basse-Terre village strikes just the right balance between working fishing port and sophisticated dining destination to keep its well-heeled visitors happy. The setting is like a colonial-era painting, with wooden houses lining the tidy sand beach and colorful fishing boats bobbing up and down in the turquoise waters. Only the odd yacht in the distance gives you any indication of the smart crowd that flocks to Deshaies (p471) for its great restaurants, lively bars and fabulous nearby beaches.

ANOUCHKA/GETTY IMAGES ©

PLUSONE/SHUTTERSTOCK ©

Wild Wonder, Dominica

21 One of the least developed and most traditional islands in the region, Dominica (p372) is covered almost entirely by thick, virgin rainforest and soaring mountain peaks. Stagger into beautiful scenes of misty waterfalls, chilly and boiling lakes, hot sulfur springs steaming through the earth, and valleys and gorges chiseled by time and the elements. It's a natural mosaic that will appeal to anyone wanting to get back to nature, and it may not remain as it is if a long-promised new airport is finally built. Emerald Pool (p380)

Historic Cockburn Town, Turks & Caicos

22 Look no further for the old Caribbean than Cockburn Town (p814), the tiny capital of the Turks and Caicos, where brightly painted colonial buildings line the roads and life goes on at a wonderfully slow pace miles away from the resorts of Providenciales. Wander down Duke St and Front St and pass whitewashed stone walls, traditional streetlamps and creaking old buildings, some of which have miraculously survived both hurricanes and modern urban development.

Party Beaches, Aruba

23 Hit the beach with 10,000 of your new best friends on Aruba. Two legendary beaches, Eagle and Palm, stretch for miles and fulfill the sun-drenched fantasies of shivering hordes every winter. Wide, white and powdery, they face water that has enough surf to be interesting but not so much you'll be lost at sea. The beaches are backed by shady palms, and cheery holidaymakers stay at the long row of resorts just behind. The scene here is pulsing, vibrant and happy, with action that extends well into the night. Palm Beach (p139)

JOHN SEATON CALLAHAN/GETTY IMAGES ©

Citadelle Laferrièrre, Haiti

24 Haiti doesn't always rate as high on the Caribbean tourism meter as it should, but there's one reason above all others to consider a visit: it's called the Citadelle Laferrière (p501). The largest fort in the Americas, it was built more than 200 years ago on a thickly forested mountaintop to hold 5000 soldiers and defend a nation – one created by the modern world's first successful enslaved people's revolution – against French invasion. It's one of the Caribbean's most staggering Unesco World Heritage sites, and you'll have it almost entirely to yourself.

Beach Time, Anguilla

25 It's hard to go past the spectacular white sandy coast and glistening turquoise waters of Anguilla. The ultimate way to while away days under the bright tropical sun on the beach is lazing on sun loungers, splashing in the sea and licking your fingers after gorging on ribs grilled over smoky barbecues. On weekends especially, find local artists jammin' at their favorite seaside haunts, such as the world-famous Bankie Banx's Dune Preserve (p99), built from driftwood and old boats. Rendezvous Bay (p97)

Island Hopping, the Bahamas

26 With nearly 700 islands spread across 100,000 sq miles of ocean, The Bahamas (p153) has enough deserted beaches, people-free cays, blue holes and snorkeling spots for several lifetimes of exploration. Each island has its own character. For ethereal rosy-hued sands, ferry to Eleuthera and Harbour Island, where beaches are tinted pink by crushed coral. The 365 Exuma Cays are a wonderland of cerulean waters and uninhabited islets, while the Abacos offer luscious sands fringed by teeming reefs and a dose of loyalist history. The Exumas (p190)

Soufrière, St Lucia

27 Swim-up bars, lavish spas, infinity pools, gourmet restaurants... When it comes to upscale resorts, St Lucia is hard to beat and there's something for everybody. Some venues are straight from the pages of a glossy magazine, with luxurious units that ooze style and class, such as Ladera, Hotel Chocolat and Jade Mountain, near Soufrière (p699), while others specialize in all-inclusive packages. You don't need to remortgage the house to stay in one of them; special rates can be found on the hotels' websites or on booking sites.

Oranjestad Ruins, Sint Eustatius

28 Like monuments to fallen empires, the ruins scattered throughout Sint Eustatius' capital and sole town, Oranjestad (p640), are whispers of a forgotten age, when rum, gold and pirates moved around the world with great alacrity. Sint Eustatius' naturally deep harbor was the doorway to the Americas, and at the height of the colonial period there were over 10,000 inhabitants representing a diverse spread of cultures and religions. Today, all that's left of this time are vestiges of imposing forts, mansions, a synagogue and a church.

27

28

Need to Know

For more information, see Survival Guide (p857).

Main Currencies

US dollar (US$), euro (€), Eastern Caribbean dollar (EC$)

Languages

Spanish, English, French

Money

ATMs are generally common on all but small islands; credit cards are widely accepted. US dollars are often accepted in lieu of local currency (and in some cases are the local currency).

Cell Phones

Most cell phones work in the Caribbean; avoid roaming charges with easily bought local SIM cards. Puerto Rico and the US Virgin Islands are included in US plans.

Time

Eastern Standard Time (EST; five hours behind GMT/UTC): Turks & Caicos, Jamaica, Cayman Islands, Dominican Republic. Atlantic Standard Time (AST; four hours behind GMT/UTC): all other islands.

When to Go

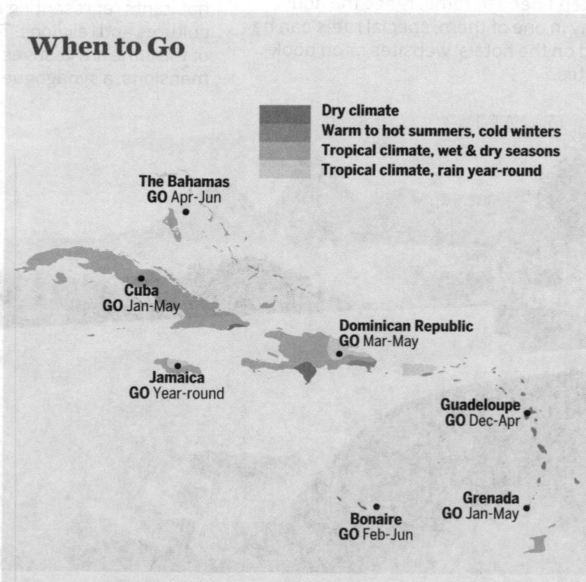

High Season (Dec–Apr)

- People fleeing the northern winter arrive in droves and prices peak.
- The region's driest time.
- Can be cold in the northern Caribbean from Cuba to the Bahamas.

Shoulder (May, Jun & Nov)

- The weather is good, rains are moderate.
- Warm temperatures elsewhere reduce visitor numbers.
- Best mix of affordable rates and good weather.

Low Season (Jul–Oct)

- Hurricane season; odds of being caught are small, but tropical storms are like clockwork.
- Good for the Eastern Caribbean's surf beaches, eg Barbados.
- Room prices can be half or less than in high season.

Visas

Requirements vary from island to island. Citizens of Canada, the EU and the US don't need visas for visits of under 90 days throughout the region (Cuba is one exception; most nationalities require a Tourist Card, which can be bought online ahead of travel).

Opening Hours

Opening hours vary across the region, although Sunday remains sacrosanct, with businesses and offices firmly shut throughout the Caribbean. Note that small and family-run businesses may close for a period between August and November.

Top Tips

- The US dollar is king. Credit cards are widely accepted in most destinations, but it's always useful to carry some extra in cash.
- Hiring a car can be a great way to explore an island.
- Islanders tend to dress smartly when they can – keep the beachwear for the beach. Topless/nude swimming is never allowed unless in specially designated areas.
- Don't plan on getting much done on a Sunday: many sights and restaurants shut for the day.
- When snorkeling or scuba diving, *never* touch coral, which can be easily damaged.
- Book accommodation and car rental in advance to save money. High-season prices particularly apply in December and January.
- Much of the Caribbean is poor – use common sense about flashing around expensive smartphones and jewellery.

Daily Costs

Budget: Less than US$150

- Room away from the beach: under US$100
- Meal at a locally popular restaurant: US$10
- Local buses: US$3

Midrange: US$150–300

- Double room in the action: US$200
- Bikes or snorkel rental: US$10
- Rental car for exploring: US$40–60

Top End: More than US$300

- Beautiful rooms at the best resorts in high season: US$400 and over
- Activities in beautiful places: US$100 and up
- World-renowned meals: US$100 per person and more

Useful Websites

Caribbean Journal (www.caribjournal.com) Regional news and travel features.

LargeUp (www.largeup.com) Lively website dedicated to Caribbean music, arts and culture.

Lonely Planet (www.lonelyplanet.com/caribbean) Destination information, hotel bookings, traveler forum and more.

Pree Lit (www.preelit.com) Showcasing the best in contemporary Caribbean writing.

Arriving in the Caribbean Islands

Every airport will have taxis waiting for flights.

Many hotels and resorts will meet your flight, usually for a modest fee.

Car rental is easily arranged in advance, either through major firms or small local outfits. Don't expect that cars will be available for walk-up rental in high season.

Public transit that's convenient for arriving visitors at airports is uncommon.

Getting Around

Air Flights between islands within sight of each other; flying may require long detours and connections.

Bicycle A good choice on flatter, quieter islands.

Walk Some islands are so small, you can easily walk everywhere.

Rental car Always available from somebody; note variations in local road rules. Road conditions are usually bad; travel can be very slow, despite seemingly short distances.

Public minivan or bus Cheap; can be found in some form on most islands, get info by asking locals.

Charter taxi On all islands, taxi drivers will give custom tours and arrange for cross-island transfers; agree to a fee in advance.

Ferry Not common, only operating on some routes.

For much more on **getting around**, see p865.

What's New

With over 7000 islands and cays, there's always a lot happening in the Caribbean. From islands bouncing back from hurricane damage to environment-friendly initiatives, and new luxury hotels to restored colonial ruins, the Caribbean has plenty on offer for first-time and repeat visitors alike.

Best in Travel

Aruba was awarded fourth place in Lonely Planet's list of top 10 countries in 2019. The hub of San Nicolas is relishing a colorful and creative revival, with international and local artists adorning street walls and pop-up carnival experiences extending the happy vibes beyond the annual festivities. Also worth celebrating are the country's ambitious sustainability efforts. Aruba has offered the island as a testing hub for other countries' renewable energy solutions and is working to implement a ban on all single-use plastics and reef-destroying sunscreens in 2020.

The Bahamas

Since 2017 Nassau, the Bahamas, has finally seen the opening of several backpacker hostels where travelers can share a dorm for as little as US$30.

Barbados

Restored and once again open to visitors, Morgan Lewis Windmill (p219), one of the Caribbean's few remaining working colonial-era windmills, stands on a remote hillside in western Barbados, working the Atlantic breezes.

British Virgin Islands

The relatively new Anegada Lobster Festival (p261) is emblematic of the BVI's recent push to promote the far-off Virgin (and its seafood) as one of its greatest assets.

LOCAL KNOWLEDGE

WHAT'S HAPPENING IN THE CARIBBEAN ISLANDS

Paul Clammer, Lonely Planet writer

The Caribbean isn't just rum cocktails – it's as interesting, complex and engaging as anywhere on the planet.

Long at the forefront of globalization, the region is now on the frontline of climate change. Since 2016 the Caribbean has taken a bruising from a succession of Category 5 hurricanes. Haiti, Barbuda, the British and US Virgin Islands, the Bahamas and the island of Puerto Rico have all taken a battering in recent years.

Political winds have also buffeted the Caribbean. From the north, President Trump has aimed insults at Puerto Rico and shut down détente with Cuba, while from the south Venezuela's political crisis has washed over into Haiti, Trinidad and Curaçao.

Fairer breezes have blown in support of renewable energy booms in the Dutch Antilles, region-wide moves against single-use plastic, LGBT communities increasingly demanding their rights, moves to decriminalize marijuana in Jamaica and beyond, and of course the business, fashion and musical empires of Barbados's world-conquering Rihanna.

Cayman Islands

Experienced, in-the-know rock climbers have been frequenting Cayman Brac and scaling its craggy limestone cliffs for years. Now Rock Iguana (p288) offers superb tours so that all levels can get in on the action.

Cuba

After six years of renovations, Havana's emblematic Capitolio Nacional (p305) reopened in time for the city's 500th anniversary celebrations in 2019. Guided tours unlock the wonders of its grandiose interior.

Dominica

Dozens of hotels and restaurants have reopened since the devastation of Hurricane Maria. Particularly noteworthy is Secret Bay (p384), the island's first true luxury property.

Grenada

Full luxury has finally landed on Grenada: Silver Sands (p440) is built around the longest infinity pool in the Caribbean.

Jamaica

The decriminalization of marijuana has led to the opening of several medical ganja dispensaries, such as Kaya (p524) near Ocho Rios.

Martinique

Fort St-Louis (p556) in Fort-de-France is not new as such – it's an 18th-century French fortress – but it has finally been restored and is now open to the public to explore for the first time.

Puerto Rico

With full recovery from the 2017 hurricanes, tourism in Puerto Rico is back. Drop in on San Juan's up-and-coming Santurce district for great bars, cafes and the brilliant Museum of Art & Design Miramar (p593).

Saba

Join in the Pride at the Saba Rainbow Festival (p628) in November, the Caribbean's first LGBT+ celebration.

LISTEN, WATCH & FOLLOW

For inspiration and up-to-date news, visit www.lonelyplanet.com/caribbean/articles and www.lonelyplanet.com/news/region/caribbean.

Twitter @caribjournal Region-wide news feed with an emphasis on events affecting tourism.

Insta @uncommoncarib Caribbean travel by travelers from the Caribbean.

Large Up (www.largeup.com) The latest in music, culture and style from across the Caribbean.

Pree Lit (www.preelit.com) Caribbean voices from the best in contemporary fiction and nonfiction writing from across the region.

FAST FACTS

Food trend Farm-to-table eating

Top-selling music artists Bob Marley (Jamaica), Ricky Martin (Puerto Rico), Rihanna (Barbados)

Number of active volcanoes 19

Pop 44.4 million

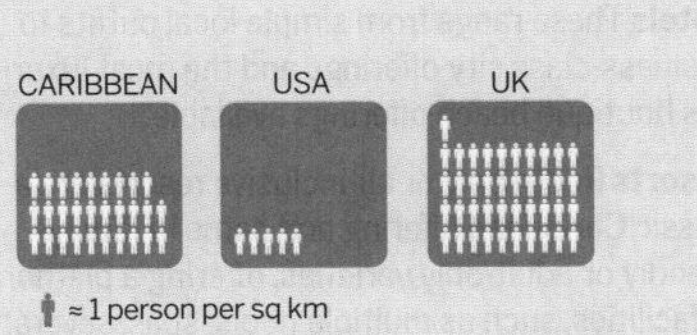

Trinidad & Tobago

Chocolate tourism is taking off in Trinidad and Tobago, with walking tours and 'Tree to Bar' experiences run by community-based collectives, including ARCTT Chocolate Tours (p757).

US Virgin Islands

Frederiksted is pushing to become the gay capital of the Caribbean with St Croix Pride and new hotels such as Fred (p848) catering to the LGBT+ community.

Accommodations

Find more accommodation reviews throughout the On the Road chapters (from p89).

Accommodation Types

Accommodations in the Caribbean range from simple camping spots to exclusive high-end resorts catering mainly to the rich and famous.

Camping Camping is limited in the Caribbean, and on some islands wild camping is either illegal or discouraged. A few destinations offer more organized camping opportunities, including Puerto Rico and the US Virgin Islands.

Guesthouses Most guesthouses are inexpensive and are good places to mix with the locals. Breakfast is often included. Some are homely houses, while others are almost indistinguishable from hotels.

Hotels These range from simple local outfits to business-class city offerings and the most luxurious boutique beach offerings available.

Resorts Room only or all-inclusive resorts are a classic Caribbean offering and come in family-friendly or adult-only varieties, offering a plethora of facilities, such as multiple pools, spas, several restaurants, water sports and more. There are often minimum-stay requirements, such as for three nights.

Villas Private rentals are popular in the Caribbean, especially for groups, and can be found for most budgets. Book as far in advance as possible during high season; at low season rates can fall dramatically.

Price Ranges

Accommodation prices vary greatly across the Caribbean. See individual destinations for price ranges.

Best Places to Stay

Best of the Caribbean

You can stay in some of the most idiosyncratic and luxurious accommodation in the Caribbean. The house where James Bond was created? Check. Art deco luxury or Afrocuban architecture? Rustic romance with sea-view infinity pools or gingerbread fantasias? The region has all this covered and more.

➡ Jake's Hotel, Jamaica (p542) Perfectly formed boutique accommodations sitting at the heart of super-chilled Treasure Beach.

➡ Malecón 663, Cuba (p312) An impossible-to-classify hotel stuffed to the rafters with the best of Havana creativity.

➡ L'Impératrice, Martinique (p556) With its perfectly preserved art deco facade it's a Fort-de-France institution.

➡ Coral Reef Club, Barbados (p216) Elegant gingerbread fantasy in acres of grounds.

➡ Casa El Paraíso, Dominican Republic (p419) This bed-and-breakfast in Las Galeras is the most romantic on the island.

Best Boutique Beach Stays

Hit the Caribbean in style. The region has a rich variety of decadent lodgings, independently owned and keen to offer a stay to remember. From historic houses to designer architecture, think splashy tropical style, sea views, sundowner cocktails and intimate dinners.

➡ Anegada Beach Club, British Virgin Islands (p261) On the furthest flung island, with flamingos and wind-whipped beaches.

➡ Ti' Paradis, Martinique (p566) Boutique hotel on Gros Raisin beach.

➡ Malliouhana, Anguilla (p96) Mediterranean-style grand hotel with three white-sand beaches.

➡ Barbuda Cottages, Barbuda (p125) Brightly painted villas on stilts right on the beach.

➡ Cotton House Mustique, St Vincent & the Grenadines (p742) Villas with plunge pools and access to Mustique's loveliest beach.

Best for Colonial Style

The Caribbean has a rich (and often difficult) history, which is reflected in some of its most interesting accommodations. Think along the lines of 19th- and early-20th-century townhouses, gingerbread decoration, Georgian stonework and plenty of period detail balanced with modern amenities.

➡ Scuba Lodge, Curaçao (p361) A rainbow-colored row of converted colonial houses in Petermaai.

➡ Hotel Saratoga, Cuba (p313) Architectural work of art in Old Havana.

➡ Admiral's Inn, Antigua (p118) Charmingly old-school and romantic hotel in 18th-century Georgian stone.

➡ Old Gin House, Sint Eustatius (p641) Stately hotel in a 17th-century cotton-seed ginning station.

➡ Gingerbread House, Trinidad (p759) A fretworked 1920s house with bags of character and breezy veranda.

Best for Getting Close to Nature

The Caribbean is green! Why stay in a beach resort when you can get away from everything and immerse yourself in the natural world. There are plenty of opportunities for environmentally friendly living and wildlife spotting in the region's green guesthouses.

➡ La Maison Rousse, Martinique (p571) Gorgeous retreat amid thick jungle in the heights of Fonds St-Denis.

➡ Tendacayou Ecolodge & Spa, Guadeloupe (p472) Treehouse hideaway in the green mountains.

➡ Aruba's Little Secret, Aruba (p144) Cosy cottages in a cactus-dotted national park.

➡ Fond Doux Plantation & Resort, St Lucia (p701) Bijou hideaway with its own chocolate plantation.

POPPY HOLLIS/GETTY IMAGES ©

Jake's Hotel, Treasure Beach, Jamaica (p542)

➡ Citrus Creek Plantation, Dominica (p381) Total seclusion on the banks of a river surrounded by thick forest.

Booking

A wide range of accommodations awaits travelers in the Caribbean. Advance booking is always a good idea, especially if you're planning to visit in high season or stay in a resort. Airbnb has a selection of private accommodations across the region. The following booking services all specialize in luxury Caribbean villas:

➡ **CV Villas** (www.cvtravel.co.uk)

➡ **Villas of Distinction** (www.villasofdistinction.com)

➡ **Wimco Villas** (www.wimcovillas.com)

You can also find recommendations and bookings at Lonely Planet (lonelyplanet.com/caribbean/hotels).

If You Like...

Beautiful Scenery

The Caribbean has a lot more than beaches. Green volcanic peaks rise out of the ocean, valleys are cleaved by waterfalls, and palm trees and flowers are everywhere you look.

Dominica A lake that boils, the aptly named Valley of Desolation and waterfalls splashing down everywhere. (p372)

Montserrat One of the most dramatic islands in the Caribbean, it surges out of the water covered in dense forest with smoking volcanoes above. (p581)

Cascada El Limón, Dominican Republic This 170ft-high waterfall is rough, rugged and surrounded by forest-covered peaks. (p415)

Northern Range, Trinidad & Tobago This chain of small coastal mountains hosts rich rainforests and stunning beaches. (p771)

Les Saintes, Guadeloupe This mountainous chain of tiny islands is almost impossibly scenic. (p476)

The Pitons, St Lucia Majestic twin peaks emerge vertical and proud from the lush green foliage as if admiring their reflection in the crystal clear sea below. (p699)

Music

Reggae, calypso, salsa, soca and more – the music of the Caribbean is as ingrained in perceptions of the region as beaches and fruity drinks. Vibrant and ever changing, the Caribbean's beat is its soul and reason alone to make the trip.

Jamaica The island that comes with a soundtrack, Jamaica is unbeatable for reggae and dancehall parties. (p512)

Trinidad & Tobago Electrifying, mesmerizing and embodying the creativity of Trinidad and Tobago, the islands' soca and steel-pan music styles are infectious. (p756)

Santiago de Cuba Cuba's most Caribbean city grinds to its own rhythm in sweaty bars and open-air *trova* and rumba clubs. (p340)

Dominican Republic Test out your merengue moves with seriously talented dancers at one of Santo Domingo's nightclubs. (p398)

Puerto Rico Music and dance are part of daily life from the smallest village to the streets of San Juan. (p590)

Romantic Getaways

With 7000 islands, the Caribbean has no shortage of places to get away to and shut out the world. People have been flocking here for steamy, sultry times for decades and everybody's in on it.

Golden Rock Inn, Nevis Fall asleep to a tree frog serenade amid the tropical gardens on the edge of the rainforest. (p679)

The Grenadines Pick a tiny island like Bequia, Mustique or Canouan and let love blossom. (p730)

Anguilla Many of Anguilla's luxurious villas have amenities such as private butlers and direct beach access. (p90)

St Lucia Magnificent open-air villas that cling to mountainsides offer privacy and panoramic views. (p688)

Historic Towns

French, British and Spanish ships carrying explorers and colonizers once prowled the Caribbean waters. They established some of the hemisphere's most enduringly charming towns.

Top: Rafting the Martha Brae River, Jamaica (p531).

Bottom: Museo de las Casas Reales, Santo Domingo, Dominican Republic (p401)

Havana A vast and crumbling metropolitan time capsule, the Cuban capital can steal days of your life. (p299)

Willemstad Little changed in a century, this 300-year-old Dutch city in Curaçao is being beautifully restored. (p359)

Sint Eustatius Once the busiest seaport in the world, it's littered with archaeological sites and ruins. (p638)

Cockburn Town The real old Caribbean, Turks and Caicos' Cockburn Town is undeveloped and absolutely charming. (p814)

Old San Juan Like a scrubbed-up Havana in Puerto Rico, perfectly preserved cobbled streets and pretty plazas are lined with pastel-colored mansions. (p592)

Santo Domingo The Dominican Republic's capital is home to the Caribbean's biggest and oldest colonial district. (p400)

Outdoor Adventure

The biggest problem with getting outside for an adventure in the Caribbean is choosing a location: you can surf the waves, hike a volcano, mountain bike the trails and more.

Rafting, Jamaica Take to a bamboo raft and cruise your way downriver through the Rio Grande Valley. (p530)

Windsurfing, Barbados The southern surf isn't too rough, the wind blows well and one of the world's great windsurf shops is here. (p224)

Hiking, Martinique Hike along the base of the still-smoldering Mont Pelée, a volcano that wiped out Martinique's former capital in 1902. (p570)

Cycling, St Lucia The purpose-built cycling tracks are some of the best you'll find anywhere. (p701)

Chasing waterfalls, Trinidad & Tobago From easy-access Avocat and Marianne to remote Paria and Rio Seco, T&T offers fabulous freshwater swims. (p772)

Nightlife

Sipping a glass of wine on a beach with someone special while yachts gently clank offshore, making a hundred new friends at a raucous strip of bars, losing yourself in intoxicating island culture: all ways you'll relish the hours after dark.

Havana, Cuba A music and culture scene unmatched in the Caribbean – cabarets, rumba, jazz, cutting-edge ballet and more. (p320)

Frigate Bay South, St Kitts Compare the potency of the rum punches poured at the string of funky beach bars making up the 'Strip.' (p668)

San Juan, Puerto Rico Calle San Sebastian is the heart of nightlife in Old San Juan – a lively mix of tourists and locals out for their evening stroll. (p601)

Kingston, Jamaica Check out an all-night dancehall street party or the coolest reggae and dub vibes on the planet. (p520)

Port-au-Prince, Haiti Few Caribbean nights are as memorable as seeing the Vodou rock-and-roots band RAM at iconic Hotel Oloffson. (p496)

Shopping

Ports of call filled with stores selling luxury items and souvenirs at duty-free prices, local crafts and artwork, and wonderful specialty items are all part of the region's shopping scene.

Nassau, Bahamas Bay St is lined with some of the best duty-free stores in the Caribbean. (p167)

San Juan, Puerto Rico Old San Juan has some great arts and crafts; head to Santurce's Calle Loíza for local and Latin American designers. (p602)

Castries, St Lucia Find quality silk-screen paintings, batik and wood carvings in the artisan workshops in the hills surrounding Castries. (p691)

Charlotte Amalie, US Virgin Islands There are plenty of the jewelry and electronics shops that cruisers love. (p830)

Havana, Cuba Two legendary items to seek out when in Havana: rum and cigars. (p323)

Jacmel, Haiti This arty town is a celebrated crafts center, famous for its colorful papier-mâché sculptures. (p502)

Watching Wildlife

We don't mean the folks partying one bar over. When it comes to watching wildlife, divers don't have all the fun. There's plenty to spot above the water in some of the remote corners of the Caribbean.

Frigate Bird Sanctuary, Barbuda Observe magnificent birds up close in one of the world's largest frigate bird colonies. (p125)

South End, Bonaire Huge salt pans are home to flocks of pini Caribbean flamingos. (p235)

Salt Cay, Turks & Caicos One of the best places on earth to see whales during the annual humpback migration. (p816)

Parque Nacional Los Haitises, Dominican Republic Watch birds and manatees from a boat cruising through a mangrove forest. (p414)

Grande Riviere, Trinidad Up to 500 leatherback turtles lumber up the beach nightly in peak laying season to deposit their eggs in the sand. (p772)

Remembrance

Mémorial ACTe, Guadeloupe State-of-the-art museum about slavery and colonialism housed (with defiant irony) in a former sugar factory. (p464)

Underwater Sculpture Park, Grenada Sunken figures clasping hands are now a touching memorial to those lost to the transatlantic slave trade. (p436)

Museum Kura Hulanda, Curaçao This excellent museum in a 19th-century merchant's house documents the brutal history of slavery. (p359)

Seville Great House, Jamaica Superbly presented plantation house, with a strong focus on remembering the enslaved who labored there. (p525)

Mémorial Cap 110, Martinique Haunting memorial overlooking the sea commemorating the scores of enslaved people who perished in a shipwreck here. (p562)

Month by Month

TOP EVENTS

Fiestas de la Calle San Sebastián, Puerto Rico, January

Carnival, Trinidad, February

Jacmel Carnival, Haiti, February

Reggae Sumfest, Jamaica, July

Crop-Over Festival, Barbados, July

January

New Year is celebrated with huge gusto in the Caribbean. Resorts are full, and people are partying. Weather across the region is balmy, although there is the odd cool day in the north.

Triumph of the Revolution

Cuba celebrates the New Year, the revolution and the nation's birth. Sure there are speeches – often long ones – but this is really an excuse for people to take to the streets with a passion.

Festival San Sebastián

Puerto Rico's famous street party, Fiestas de la Calle San Sebastián, draws big crowds to Old San Juan for a week in mid-January. There are parades, dancing and much more. (p596)

February

Carnival is a huge event in many Caribbean countries, where it is tied to the Lenten calendar (so sometimes held in March). No country has a bigger Carnival than Trinidad, which prepares all year for its exuberant explosion.

Bob Marley Birthday Bash

The love for the sound that plays in beach bars worldwide brings fans to the Bob Marley Museum in Jamaica on Bob Marley's birthday, February 6, and kicks off Jamaica's reggae month.

Republic of Fun

The Dominican Republic celebrates its Carnival with great fervor every Sunday in February, culminating in a huge blowout in Santo Domingo on the last weekend of the month or the first weekend of March. Santiago hosts an international *careta* (mask) competition. (p403)

ABCs of Carnival

Aruba, Bonaire and Curaçao's Carnivals all begin right after New Year and culminate with parades during the weekend before Ash Wednesday. (p230 & p361)

Haiti Unmasked

Jacmel in Haiti is known for its fantastic papier-mâché masks, which are made for the wild street theater performed at one of the Caribbean's best Carnivals. (p503)

Trinidad Carnival

Simply the biggest party in the Caribbean. Trinidad spends all year gearing up for its legendary, pre-Lent street party, with steel-pan bands, blasting soca and calypso music and outrageous costumes. Ecstatic revelers indulge their most hedonistic inclinations as they welcome in Carnival. (p764)

Carriacou Carnival

A vibrant Grenadian event featuring street parades, live bands and the quirky 'Shakespeare Mas' – like a rap battle but with men dressed in bright garb reciting verses by the Bard. Get ready to be covered in paint and party. (p448)

March

It's high season throughout the Caribbean. On Barbados, American college students invade for spring break. The late-winter influx of visitors is greeted by lovely weather everywhere.

St Patrick's Week

It's not a day, it's a week on Montserrat. There's a lot of Irish heritage here so the day o' green has always been huge. Costumes, food, drink, dance and concerts by the much-lauded Emerald Community Singers are highlights. (p584)

April

Easter signals more Carnivals. High season continues but the winds of change are blowing. Rates begin to fall at resorts. Temperatures are climbing in the south but the Caribbean is mostly dry.

Simadan

Bonaire's harvest festival is held in the small town of Rincon in early April, only proper as Rincon was the historic home of the enslaved people who were brought to the island to make salt and harvest food. The celebrations include traditional dance and food.

Antigua Sailing Week

The Caribbean's largest regatta, Antigua Sailing Week follows the Antigua Classic Yacht Regatta and involves a range of sailing and social events around Nelson's Dockyard and Falmouth Harbour.

Oistins Fish Festival

On the southern coast of Barbados, the Oistins Fish Festival commemorates the signing of the Charter of Barbados and celebrates the skills of local fishermen. It's held over Easter weekend and features boat races, fish-filleting competitions, local foods and dancing. (p212)

Sint Maarten Carnival

The two-week Sint Maarten Carnival, on the Dutch side, outclasses its counterpart on the French side. Activities begin in the second week after Easter. (p712)

Carriacou Maroon & String Band Festival

Held late in the month, this music festival draws hordes of partiers from Grenada for big-drum music and dancing, string bands, Shakespeare Mas, and every other Carriacou tradition at venues around the tiny island. (p448)

May

May sees the last of the Caribbean's carnivals, as the temperatures start to get hotter and hotter.

Cayman Batabano

Cayman Islands' answer to Carnival is a week-long festival of music and masquerade parades – for adults and children alike – during the first week in May.

June

June remains dry and relatively storm-free. Like May, it's not a peak time for visitors, except the savvy ones who value dry, sunny days and low hotel rates.

St Kitts Music Festival

Top-name calypso, soca, reggae, salsa, jazz and gospel performers from throughout the Caribbean pack into Basseterre's Warner Park during this three-day music festival. Reserve a room way in advance. (p667)

July

A busy month! Summer holiday crowds start arriving, as do the very first tropical storms of the hurricane season. There's another tranche of Carnivals and other special events.

Crop-Over Festival

Beginning in mid-July and running until early August, the Crop-Over Festival is Barbados' top event and features fairs, activities and a parade. (p211)

Reggae Sumfest

The big mama of all reggae and dancehall festivals, held in late July in Montego Bay, Jamaica, this event brings top acts together for an unforgettable party. Even if you're not attending, you're attending – the festivities tend to take over MoBay. (p531)

Top: Junkanoo festival, Bahamas (p161).

Bottom: Carnival, Santo Domingo, Dominican Republic (p403)

Vincy Mas

St Vincent's Carnival and biggest cultural event for the year, Vincy Mas, is held in late June and early July. (p734)

Cuban Carnaval

Santiago de Cuba throws Cuba's oldest, biggest and wildest celebration in the last week of July. (p342)

Santo Domingo Merengue Festival

Santo Domingo hosts the Dominican Republic's largest and most raucous merengue festival. For two weeks at the end of July and the beginning of August, the world's top merengue bands play for the world's best dancers, all over the city. (p403)

August

The summer high season continues and you can expect the first real storms of the hurricane season, although mostly that means heavy rains as opposed to big blows.

Anguilla Summer Festival

Anguilla's 10-day-long Summer Festival takes place around the first week of August and is celebrated with boat races, music, dancing and more. (p97)

Antigua Carnival

The famous Antigua Carnival celebrates the country's emancipation from slavery during 10 days of merriment starting in late July, culminating with a grand parade on the first Tuesday in August. Calypso music, steel bands, masked merrymakers, floats and street parties all add to the excitement.

September

Crowds are down and the weather tends to be wet. This is the low season and it might be a good time to rent a beach house for a month and write that book.

Martinique Heritage Days

Martinique's Journées du Patrimoine (Heritage Days) celebrate local culture and history principally through the opening of buildings to the public that are normally closed.

October

Dominica comes to the rescue of what is otherwise a quiet month (other than a few passing squalls). Some family-run businesses close for the month.

World Creole Music Festival

Dominica's ode to Creole music attracts big-name Caribbean music and dance acts, and food vendors sell much spicy goodness. (p375)

Sea & Learn

Throughout October Saba becomes a learning center as scientists and naturalists give nightly presentations and anyone is welcome to take part in field and research activities. (p628)

November

Hurricane season has mostly blown itself out and Christmas decorations are going up. Baseball season arrives in the Dominican Republic.

Pirates Week

This wildly popular, family-friendly extravaganza on Grand Cayman features a mock pirate invasion, music, dances, costumes, games and controlled mayhem. Book hotels in advance or you'll be out on your booty.

St Kitts Carnival

Carnival is the biggest event on St Kitts. It starts in mid-November, kicking into high gear for two weeks of music, dancing and steel pan from December 26. (p667)

December

High season begins midmonth and incoming flights are full. Rates are up and everything is open. Down backstreets Carnival prep is reaching fever pitch on many islands.

Junkanoo

The Bahamas' national festival starts in the twilight hours of Boxing Day (December 26). It's a frenzied party with marching 'shacks,' colorful costumes and music. Crowds prepare much of the year for this Carnival-like happening. (p161)

Rastafari Rootzfest

A three-day gathering near Negril, Jamaica, celebrating the best of Rastafari culture, from reggae and I-tal food to the Ganjamaica Cup (the latter sponsored by the Jamaican Ministry of Tourism). (p538)

Itineraries

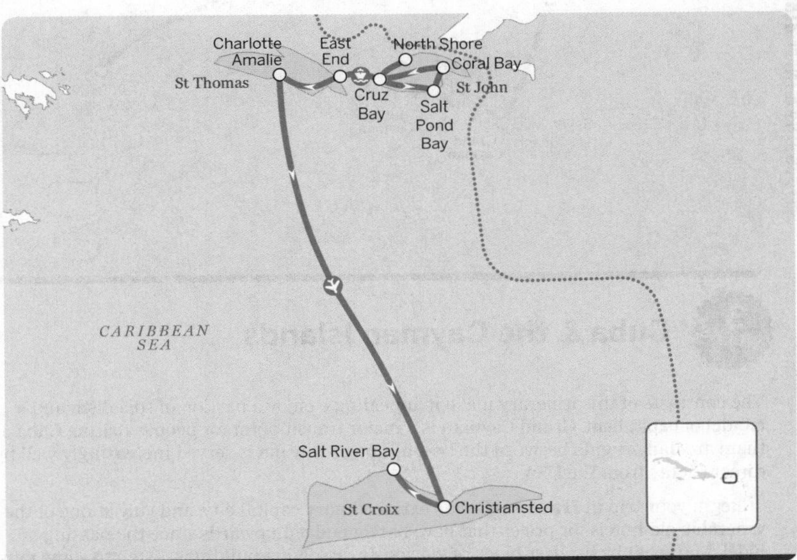

Easy-to-Access Virgin Islands

Scads of nonstop flights put the US Virgin Islands in easy reach of the US and Canada. One week gives the ideal overview of this small but perfectly formed cluster of islands.

Start on **St John**. Spend day one at the **North Shore** beaches: Cinnamon Bay, with windsurfing and trails through mill ruins; Maho Bay, where sea turtles swim; or Leinster Bay/Waterlemon Cay, where snorkelers can jump in among rays and barracuda. Raise a toast to your beach in rollicking **Cruz Bay**.

Spend day two at **Salt Pond Bay**, where cool hikes, beachcombing and turtle snorkeling await. Drink, dance and dine with the colorful characters in **Coral Bay** afterward.

Devote day three to the Reef Bay Hike, kayaking along coastal reefs or another favorite activity. Hop on a ferry on day four to check out **St Thomas' East End**, with its resorts and marine park.

Spend part of day five in the popular cruise-ship stop of **Charlotte Amalie**, **St Thomas**, then take the seaplane to **Christiansted**, **St Croix**. Over the next two days drink at old windmills turned gin mills, dive its barrier reef and paddle through the glowing waters of **Salt River Bay**.

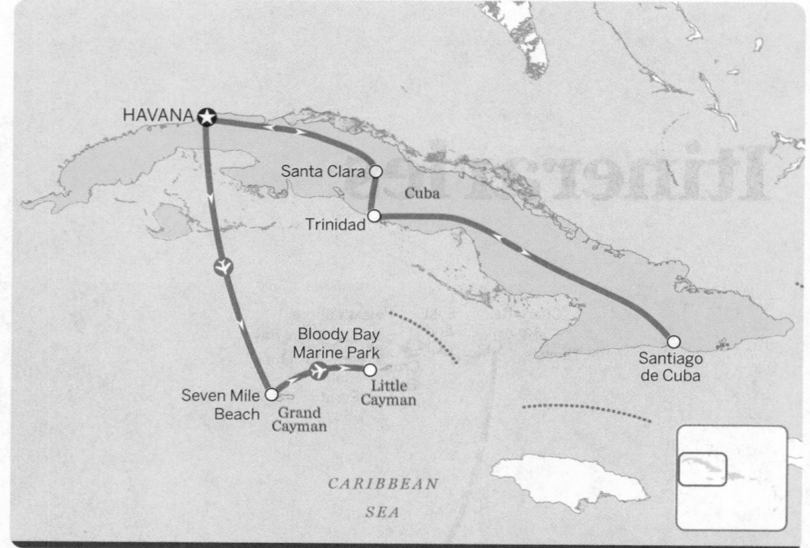

Cuba & the Cayman Islands

The contrasts of this itinerary make it appealing – enjoy a bastion of socialism and a citadel of capitalism. Grand Cayman is a major transit point for people visiting Cuba and there are daily flights between the two, although Havana is served increasingly well by direct flights from the USA.

Begin your trip in **Havana**, Cuba's extraordinary capital city, and stay at one of the venerable old hotels for prices that have barely nudged upwards since the passing of Fidel. Marvel at block after block of gloriously dissolving buildings, listen to some music and drink with locals. Just wander around: every block holds a surprise and the seawall is world-famous. Head to **Santa Clara** and the venerable monument to Ernesto Che Guevara, the city's adopted son, then plunge into the city's youth-oriented culture. Push on from here to **Trinidad**, a Unesco World Heritage site. You can easily spend a week in this perfectly preserved Spanish colonial town, hiking in Topes de Collantes, horseback riding in Valle de los Ingenios or lazing at Playa Ancón. Head east to **Santiago de Cuba** and its many attractions, including the Castillo de San Pedro de la Roca del Morro, the Cuartel Moncada and, of course, the vibrant music scene.

Return to Havana and fly on to Grand Cayman. Head straight to **Seven Mile Beach** and do purely fun things such as snorkeling at Bio Bay. Grand Cayman is known for its commercialism, but you can see another side to the islands if you carry on with an excursion to **Little Cayman**, where the 120 or so residents will be happy to see you. Laze on its deserted beaches and consider a world-class wall dive at **Bloody Bay Marine Park**. There's great birdwatching on Little Cayman and if you're feeling energetic you can cycle around the whole island in a single day.

Top: St Croix, US Virgin Islands (p840)
Bottom: Sea huts, Canouan, Grenadines (p743)

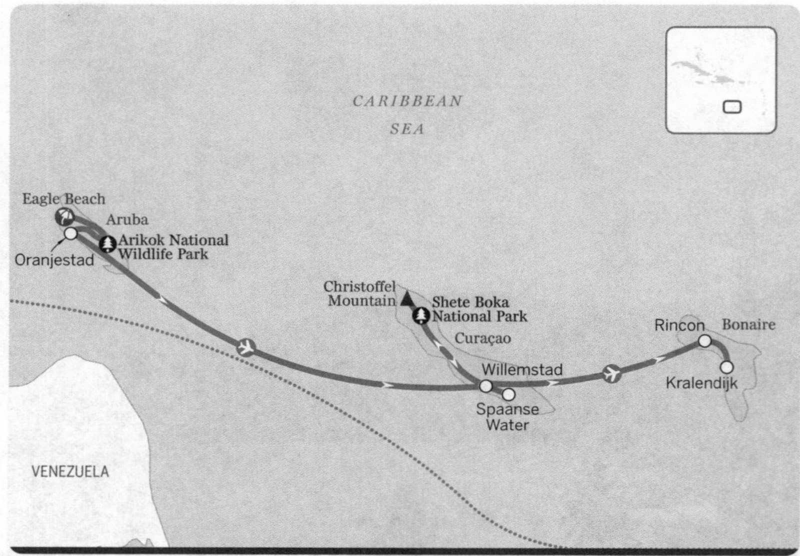

Aruba, Curaçao & Bonaire

The small size of all three islands, Aruba, Bonaire and Curaçao, means that even the most peripatetic vacationer will require little time for complete explorations, so there'll be plenty of time to simply plop down and relax.

Most places to stay, eat and even play on **Aruba** are in the north. Stay on relaxed **Eagle Beach**, Aruba's best. Assuming you're here for the sand – that's Aruba's real charm – then besides a day to explore the wet and wild northeast coast, **Arikok National Wildlife Park**, which has some nice hiking trails, and colorful **Oranjestad** (which hops when the cruise ships are in port), you should just play on the beach. And given the vast stretches of sand on the island, it won't be too hard to find the ideal plot for your beach blanket.

From Aruba, it's quick hop over to **Curaçao**. This is an island to take your time exploring. Stay in colonial **Willemstad**, which is one of the region's most interesting towns, then wander the coasts to the north, where national parks, restored plantations and a bevy of hidden beaches await. Count on three days at least to enjoy it all at a leisurely pace, including climbing Christoffel Mountain and exploring **Shete Boka National Park**. You might even want to try some snorkeling or head to **Spaanse Water**, where the windsurfing will blow you away.

Fly from Curaçao to **Bonaire**. Once you're there, you may not see much of the island above sea level as you'll be underwater a lot of the time. One of the world's great diving locations, Bonaire's underwater splendor and 100 named dive sites will keep you busy. Exploring the island, which has stark beauty and flamingo-spotting, and learning about an easily accessed past will take about a day. The island's second city – a village really – **Rincon**, has a slow and inviting pace, while at the horizon-spanning salt flats in the south you can see the evidence of slavery and colonial trade. In the middle of it all, cute little **Kralendijk** combines eating, sleeping and fun.

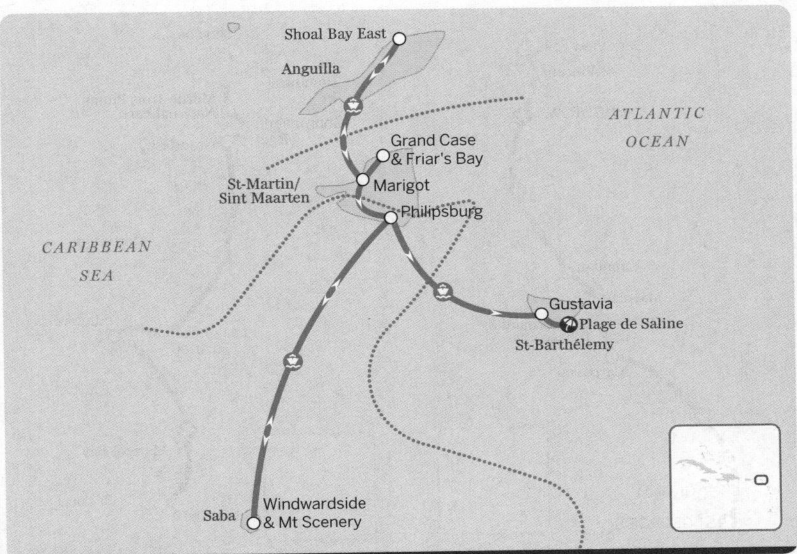

Sint Maarten & Neighboring Islands

Once off the plane in St-Martin/Sint-Maarten, you can hop your way around some of the Caribbean's cutest islands by ferry and never see another plane until it's time to go home.

Head to the French side of the island and hang out in **Grand Case**, where your dining choices range from beach-shack casual to fine French bistro. For beach time try the local favorite **Friar's Bay**, then from Marigot, make the 25-minute ferry run to Anguilla. Once there, spread your towel on popular **Shoal Bay East** or or catch the boat to uninhabited **Sandy Island**.

Back on St-Martin/Sint Maarten, head down to **Philipsburg** for some retail therapy. Get a ferry to Saba, and enjoy views of its splendid volcano. Explore the small town of **Windwardside**, then head out for a hike up **Mt Scenery**. Rent some diving gear – waters here teem with turtles and nurse sharks.

Back in Philipsburg, take the ferry to St-Barthélemy. Have lunch at the gorgeous French capital of **Gustavia**, and then sun yourself on white-sand **Plage de Saline**. Although St-Barth is fabled as a playground of the rich and famous, the beauty of the island is that this matters little once everybody's in T-shirts and shorts.

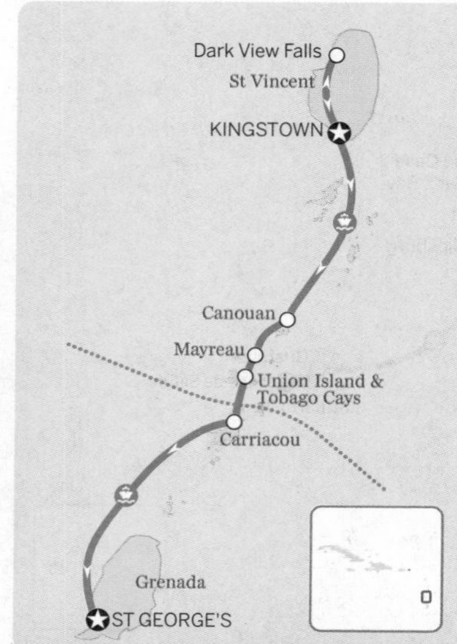

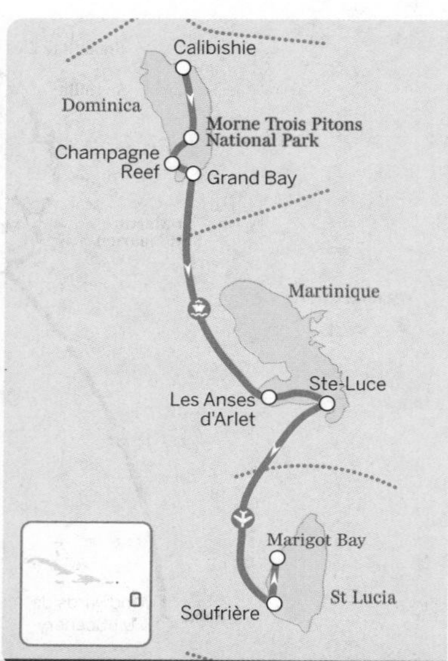

St Vincent to Grenada

You can add the **Dominica to St Lucia itinerary** to this one for a real island-hopping adventure that explores the best of the Windward Islands. Just get a connecting flight from St Lucia to St Vincent and the Grenadines.

St Vincent is an island of boundless energy. Market days in **Kingstown** are joyfully chaotic as the streets teem with people. The scenes have changed little in decades. Explore some of the island's unexplored lush countryside and enjoy panoramic vistas on a hike to **Dark View Falls**.

Jump on the slow boat down through the Grenadines, stopping at one of the pretty islands of **Canouan**, **Mayreau** or **Union Island**. Take a day trip to snorkel the amazing **Tobago Cays**. Catch a mail boat or hire a fishing boat and cross the aquatic border to **Carriacou**, the pint-sized sister island to Grenada, which you will reach by ferry. Once there, immerse yourself in **St George's**, one of the Caribbean's most charming capital cities, and smell the local nutmeg in the air.

1 WEEK

Dominica to St Lucia

Hopscotch your way south through some of the least-visited, least-developed Caribbean islands.

Begin in Dominica, which many consider the wildest and most natural of the bunch. Start at the comfy properties of **Calibishie**, with some of Dominica's best beaches, then lose yourself in the rainforest at **Morne Trois Pitons National Park**. The half-day walk in the park to Middleham Falls is splendid. Celebrate with a glass of bubbly, or maybe the natural bubbles that tickle you while diving at **Champagne Reef**.

Head to Grand Bay for quick hop to Martinique, where you should hit the beaches and restaurants of **Les Anses d'Arlet**, followed by diving and drinking in the lively fishing village of **Ste-Luce**.

Take the scenic ferry to St Lucia, which emerges like a virescent monolith from the Caribbean. Stay in **Soufrière**, dramatically located shadowed by the iconic peaks of the Pitons. You can hike these in the morning and dive in the afternoon. For a jaunt, head over to **Marigot Bay**, with its small beach and beautiful surrounds.

Plan Your Trip

Diving & Snorkeling

Whether you're an experienced diver or slapping on fins for the first time, few places offer such perfect conditions for underwater exploration. The Caribbean Sea is consistently warm and spectacularly clear waters mean great visibility. Professional dive operators are plentiful, helping you get under the waves quickly and safely.

Learning to Dive

With warm, calm, crystalline waters, the Caribbean is an excellent place to get scuba certified. If you want to experience diving for the first time, most operators offer a short beginner course for nondivers, commonly dubbed a 'resort course,' which includes brief instructions, followed by a shallow beach or boat dive. Depending on the island (and whether a boat is used), the cost generally ranges from US$80 to US$150.

For those who want to jump into the sport wholeheartedly, a number of operators offer full open-water certification courses. The cost generally hovers around US$420, equipment included, and the course takes the better part of a week.

Where to Dive

Anguilla

Anguilla is ringed by seven marine parks and visibility is usually excellent. Wreck diving is big here with several intentionally sunk vessels and the pièce de résistance: a massive colonial-era Spanish galleon called *El Buen Consejo*. Offshore, Sandy Island and Prickly Pear Cays are practically untouched and are excellent spots

Top Sites

Best All-Round Dive Sites

Réserve Cousteau (p473), Guadeloupe

Little Cayman (p290), Cayman Islands

Bonaire (p236)

Saba Marine Park (p632), Saba

St Croix (p840), US Virgin Islands

Best Snorkeling

Réserve Cousteau (p473), Guadeloupe

Grand Cayman (p294), Cayman Islands

Little Tobago (p790), Trinidad and Tobago

Tobago Cays (p747), St Vincent & the Grenadines

Soufrière (p700), St Lucia

Best for Wreck Diving

Martinique (p555)

Sint Eustatius (p647)

Aruba (p143)

US Virgin Islands (p824)

Grenada (p456)

Cayman Islands (p272)

RESPONSIBLE DIVING

- Never use anchors on the reef and take care not to ground boats on coral.
- Avoid touching or standing on living marine organisms, or dragging equipment across the reef. Polyps can be damaged by even the gentlest contact. If you must hold on to the reef, only touch exposed rock or dead coral.
- Be conscious of your fins. Even without contact, the surge from fin strokes near the reef can damage delicate organisms. Take care not to kick up clouds of sand, which can smother organisms.
- Practice and maintain proper buoyancy control. Major damage can be done by divers descending too fast and colliding with the reef.
- Take great care in underwater caves. Spend as little time within them as possible as your air bubbles may be caught within the roof and thereby leave organisms high and dry. Take turns to inspect the interior of a small cave.
- Resist the temptation to collect or buy corals or shells or to loot marine archaeological sites (mainly shipwrecks).
- Ensure that you take home all your rubbish and any litter you may find. Plastics, in particular, are a serious threat to marine life.
- Do not feed fish.
- Minimize your disturbance of marine animals. Never touch, chase or otherwise harass sea turtles.

for both diving and snorkeling. Sea turtles are often around in abundance, while rays roam across the ocean floor and tropical fish flitter among the coral.

Antigua & Barbuda

Antigua has excellent diving, with coral canyons, wall drops and sea caves hosting a range of marine creatures, including turtles, sharks and barracuda. Popular sites include the 2-mile-long (3km) Cades Reef and Ariadne Shoal. A fun spot for divers and snorkelers is the wreck of the *Jettias,* a 310ft (94m) steamer that sank in 1917 and now provides habitat for fish and coral.

And Barbuda? It's still a secret, word-of-mouth destination, with scores of shipwrecks along its surrounding reef.

Aruba

There is fine diving and snorkeling around the southern shores, with elaborate, shallow reefs and coral gardens ablaze with colorful critters. Wreck fans will love it here too, with a series of plane- and shipwrecks, some of which were sunk intentionally as artificial reefs. Of particular interest is the large German WWII freighter *Antilla*.

The Bahamas

This is Caribbean diving heaven. The Bahamas' great success as a diving hub is due to its unbeatable repertoire of diving adventures. Pristine reefs, shipwrecks, blue holes, vertigo-inducing drop-offs, abundant tropical fish, rays, sharks and dolphins are the reality of diving here. Where else in the world can you join a shark feed, then mingle with dolphins, visit movie-set shipwrecks, descend along bottomless walls and explore a mysterious blue hole – all in the same area? A bonus is state-of-the-art dive operations.

Almost all islands offer diving, from Walker's Cay in the north down to Long Island in the south.

Barbados

Barbados cannot compete with its neighboring heavyweights, but it boasts excellent diving nonetheless. The west coast is blessed with lovely reefs, wreathed with soft corals, gorgonians and colorful sponges. There are also a dozen shipwrecks. The largest and most popular, the 364ft (111m) freighter *Stavronikita,* sits upright off the central west coast in 138ft (42m) of water, with the rigging reaching to within 20ft (6m) of the surface. In Bridgetown's Carlisle Bay, a series of coral-encrusted wrecks

Top: Stingrays at Stingray City (p277), Cayman Islands
Below: Flamingo tongue snail

BEARCREATIVE/SHUTTERSTOCK ©

BEST DIVING BOOKS

- *Best Dives of the Caribbean* (1994) by Joyce Huber
- *The Complete Diving Guide: The Caribbean* (1998) series by Colleen Ryan and Brian Savage
- *Reef Fish Identification: Tropical Pacific* and *Reef Creature Identification: Florida, Caribbean Bahamas* (2010) by Paul Humann

lies in only 23ft (7m) of water, making for good snorkeling as well as diving.

Bonaire

Bonaire is one of the most charismatic dive areas in the Caribbean. Since 1979 the crystal-blue canvas that wraps around the island has been a protected haven. Dive boats are required to use permanent moorings and popular dive sites are periodically closed to let the reefs recover. With the exception of Klein Bonaire sites, most dive sites are accessible from shore. Diving is absurdly easy: drive up, wade in, descend, explore. The gently sloping reefs are positively festooned with hard and soft corals, sponges, gorgonians and a dizzying array of tropical fish. A couple of wrecks, including the *Hilma Hooker,* spice up the diving.

British Virgin Islands

The islands huddle to form a sheltered paradise of secluded coves, calm shores and crystal-clear water, which in turn provide outstanding visibility, healthy coral and a wide variety of dive and snorkeling sites. Conservation is taken seriously, and there are lots of permanent mooring buoys.

Salt Island offers one of the Caribbean's best wreck dives: the monster-sized RMS *Rhone* – with a 310ft (94m) length and 40ft (12m) beam – sunk in 1867. Amazingly, it's still in good shape and is heavily overgrown with marine life.

Another drawcard is the seascape – expect giant boulders, canyons, tunnels, caverns and grottoes.

Cayman Islands

With more than 250 moored sites, and plenty of shore diving and snorkeling possibilities, diving is the most popular activity in the Cayman Islands. Little Cayman has the finest Caribbean wall diving – along Bloody and Jackson's Bays, sheer cliffs drop so vertically they'll make you gasp in your regulator. The snorkeling here can be fantastic. Coral and sponges of all types, colors and sizes cascade downward as you slowly descend along the wall.

For wreck sites, few come better in the Caribbean than the USS *Kittiwake.*

Cuba

Improving diving facilities and abundant coral make Cuba a great destination for divers The best diving can be found at the Bay of Pigs, María la Gorda, the Península de Guanahacabibes and the Isla de la Juventud. For snorkelers, there are several fine swim-out reefs.

Curaçao

Curaçao was once a secret escape for savvy divers, but the news has spread; so the island now ranks among the best diving destinations in the region. There's a slew of rewarding dive sites along the southern lee coast. Some of the most popular sites are accessible from the beach, including Alice in Wonderland at Playa Kalki (Curaçao/West End), Mushroom Forest near Boka Pretu and the double reef at Playa Porto Mari (Curaçao/Willbrordus). South of Mambo Beach, the coast and reefs have been protected as part of the National Underwater Park. *Tugboat* is a popular wreck dive east of the Spaanse Water.

Dominica

The strength of Dominica is its underwater topography. The island's rugged scenery continues below the surface, where it forms sheer drop-offs, volcanic arches, massive pinnacles, chasms, gullies and caves.

Many top dive sites are in the Soufriere Bay marine reserve. Scotts Head Drop-Off, the Pinnacle and the Soufriere Pinnacle are favorites. Champagne Reef, popular with beginners and snorkelers, is a subaquatic hot spring off Pointe Guignard where bubbles rise from underwater vents.

The central west coast is another premier diving area, though the topography is not as unusual as in the southwest, making the dives less challenging.

Reef life, Bonaire (p228)

Dominican Republic

The Dominican Republic is mostly famous for its kitesurfing and windsurfing, but diving here shouldn't be sneezed at. There's a wide choice of easy dives lurking off the Península de Samaná on the northeastern coast. Facing the Atlantic, the water there is cooler and visibility is somewhat reduced but the terrain is varied and you'll find a few shipwrecks to keep you happy. All the main dive spots have shallow reefs where nondivers can snorkel, but Cayo Arena offers the best snorkeling on the island: the water is crystal clear and the reef there is absolutely flourishing.

Grenada

With extensive reefs and a wide variety of marine life, the waters around Grenada offer excellent diving. The southwest coast has the majority of dive sites, with the wreck of the *Bianca C* ocean liner one of the most popular. Other good log entries for wreck buffs include the *King Mitch,* the *Rum Runner* and the *Hema 1.*

Molinière Point, north of St George's, has some of Grenada's best snorkeling and is also an access point for the underwater sculpture park, a swim-through gallery of sunken monuments.

Guadeloupe

Guadeloupe's top diving site is the Réserve Cousteau, at Pigeon Island off the west coast of Basse-Terre. This is a protected area, so you can expect myriad tropical fish, turtles and sponges, and a vibrant assemblage of hard- and soft-coral formations. There are also two superb wrecks in the vicinity. The Réserve Cousteau is a magnet for snorkelers, with scenic spots in shallow, turquoise waters.

For those willing to venture away from the tourist areas, there's Les Saintes. This area is a true gem with numerous untouched sites, striking underwater scenery and a diverse fish population – not to mention the phenomenal Sec Pâté, which consists of two giant pitons in the channel between Basse-Terre and Les Saintes.

Jamaica

So, you want variety? Jamaica's your answer. Sure, nothing is really world-class, but Jamaica offers an assortment of diving experiences. Treasures here include shallow reefs, caverns and trenches, walls, drop-offs and wrecks just a few hundred meters offshore. This is especially true on the north coast from around Ocho Rios, where diving and snorkeling conditions are exceptional. Tip: if you're after less-crowded dive sites, opt for Runaway Bay.

Martinique

Wrecks galore! St-Pierre is a must for wreck enthusiasts. Picture this: more than a dozen ships that were anchored in the harbor when the 1902 volcanic eruption hit now lie on the seabed, at depths ranging from around 30ft to 280ft (10m to 85m).

To the southwest, Grande Anse and Diamant also deserve attention, with a good balance of scenic seascapes, elaborate reef structures and dense marine life.

Montserrat

Tiny Montserrat punches well above its weight with some excellent diving at over 50 sites, where you're unlikely to ever encounter other divers. One amazing experience is to dive in the pristine waters of Redonda Island, a dramatic but uninhabited island off the coast of Montserrat proper. The waters teem with marine life thanks to the fact that few fishermen come here.

Puerto Rico

You will find good snorkeling reefs off the coasts of Vieques, Culebra, Fajardo and the small cays east of Fajardo. The cays off the south and east coasts also have good shallow reefs. There's good diving off Rincón and Fajardo, as well as spectacular wall dives out of La Parguera on the south coast.

Saba

This stunning volcanic island might even be more scenic below the ocean's surface. Divers and snorkelers can find a bit of everything (except wrecks): steep wall dives just offshore, submerged pinnacles and prolific marine life, including nurse sharks, stingrays and turtles. The Saba Marine Park has protected the area since 1987 and offers many untouched, buoy-designated diving spots.

Sint Eustatius

The island's last volcanic eruption was in AD 400 but you can still see evidence of the lava flow on the seabed, in its deep trenches and fissures. Vestiges of 18th-century colonial Sint Eustatius are also found beneath the surface, such as portions of quay wall that have slipped into the sea. Old ballast stones, anchors, cannons and ship remains have become vibrant coral reefs, protected by the Statia Marine Park.

A collection of ships has also been purposefully sunk in recent years.

St-Barthélemy

St-Barth has healthy, expansive reefs in shallow water with mostly smaller marine life like lobsters, rays, sea urchins, reef and nurse sharks, sponges and coral. The best sites lie just off the various islets that are scattered off the island. St-Barth also features one major wreck dive, the *Kaïali,* in 100ft (30m) of water.

St Kitts & Nevis

Both islands have excellent diving, with healthy reefs and lots of caves and wrecks to explore. The best cave diving is at Devil's Cave off Nevis, where divers navigate overhangs in a series of exciting grottoes where sharks are often seen. The most popular and accessible wreck dive is the *River Taw,* off the coast of St Kitts, a 144ft (44m) freighter that sank in 1985.

St Lucia

If you think the above-ground scenery is spectacular in St Lucia, you should see it under the sea. The area near Soufrière boasts spectacular, near-shore reefs, with a wide variety of corals, sponges, fans and reef fish. It's excellent for both diving and snorkeling. Wreck enthusiasts will enjoy *Lesleen,* a 165ft (50m) freighter that was deliberately sunk in 1986.

St-Martin/Sint Maarten

St-Martin/Sint Maarten has about 17 dive sites, mostly in the waters south and southeast of the island. Other prime dive sites include the Maze, where you can go cave diving and spot turtles, angelfish, sponges and corals; Turtle Reef, a deep dive of up to 60ft (18m) with octopuses, eels, lobsters and namesake turtles; and

DIVING IN THE CARIBBEAN: AN OVERVIEW

ISLANDS	MAIN DIVE AREAS	WRECK DIVES	FISH LIFE	COSTS (2-TANK DIVE)
Anguilla	Off-shore cays	YY	YY	US$65-100
Antigua & Barbuda	Reef, Great Bird Island	YY	YY	US$60-120
Aruba	South and northwest coasts	YYY	YY	US$75-100
The Bahamas	All major islands	YY	YYY	US$90-150
Barbados	West coast	YY	YY	US$70-120
Bonaire	West coast & around Klein Bonaire	Y	YYY	US$25-50
British Virgin Islands	Out Islands, south of Tortola, Virgin Gorda	YY	YY	US$130-145
Cayman Islands	Seven Mile Beach, West Bay, Little Cayman, East End	YYY	YYY	US$105-120
Cuba	Bay of Pigs, María la Gorda, Isla de la Juventud	YY	YYY	US$25-50
Curaçao	Willemstad, Playa Lagún	Y	YY	US$100-110
Dominica	Soufriere-Scott's Head Marine Reserve, Douglas Bay, Salisbury	Y	YY	US$60-80
Dominican Republic	Península de Samaná	Y	YY	US$50-100
Grenada	Southwest coast	YYY	YY	US$80-130
Guadeloupe	Réserve Cousteau, Les Saintes	Y	YY	US$70-110
Haiti	Côte des Arcadins, Môle Saint-Nicolas	YY	Y	US$90-110
Jamaica	Ocho Rios, Runaway Bay	Y	YY	US$60-110
Martinique	St-Pierre, Grande Anse, Diamant	YYY	YY	US$70-110
Montserrat	West coast, Redonda Island	YY	YY	US$100-130
Puerto Rico	Vieques, Culebra, Fajardo, Rincón, La Parguera	Y	YY	US$60-90
Saba	South and west coasts	None	YYY	US$65-135
Sint Eustatius	South and west coasts	YYY	YY	US$60-110
St Kitts & Nevis	Peninsula St Kitts, West Nevis	YYY	YY	US$120-150
St Lucia	Soufrière, Pigeon Island	Y	YY	US$80-120
St-Martin/Sint Maarten	South and southeast coasts	YY	Y	US$65-100
St Vincent & the Grenadines	St Vincent, Canouan, Bequia, Tobago Cays	None	YYY	US$80-140
Trinidad & Tobago	Crown Point, Speyside, Little Tobago	Y	YYY	US$55-95
Turks & Caicos	Salt Cay, Grand Turk	Y	YYY	US$125-175
US Virgin Islands	St Thomas (south coast, northern cays), St John (south coast), St Croix (north coast)	YYY	YY	US$110-145
Y = good	YY = great	YYY = awesome		

One Step Beyond, which has large schools of fish along with barracudas, morays, lobsters and sharks. The best snorkeling is at Creole Rock between Grand Case and Anse Marcel on the French side.

St Vincent & the Grenadines

The sparsely inhabited islands and bays shelter thriving offshore reefs. You'll find steep walls decorated with black coral around St Vincent, giant schools of fish around Bequia, and a coral wonderland around Canouan. There's also pure bliss in

The Baths beach, British Virgin Islands (p254)

the Tobago Cays: these five palm-studded, deserted islands surrounded by shallow reefs are part of a protected marine sanctuary and offer some of the most pristine reef diving in the Caribbean. Snorkeling is also superlative.

Trinidad & Tobago

Tobago is most definitely a diving destination. Situated on the South American continental shelf between the Caribbean and Atlantic, the island is massaged by the Guyana and North Equatorial Currents. Also injected with periodic pulses of nutrient-rich water from the Orinoco River, Tobago's waters teem with marine life, including pelagics (read: hammerhead sharks). The variety of corals, sponges and ancient sea fans make this a top destination.

Speyside is the launching pad for Little Tobago island, which is famous for its large brain corals and is also a mecca for snorkelers.

Turks & Caicos

Salt Cay is a diving highlight, where you can dive with humpback whales during their annual migration. Grand Turk has pristine reefs and spectacular wall diving, while the exceptional diving on rarely visited South Caicos is worth the hassle of getting there. There is also diving off Provo, where you can get the chance to see dolphins and numerous reef species.

US Virgin Islands

The sister islands of St Thomas and St John offer top-notch diving and snorkeling conditions, with a combination of fringing reefs and a contoured topography (arches, caves, pinnacles, tunnels and vertical walls). St Croix features a fascinating mix of wreck (Butler Bay shelters no fewer than five wrecks) and wall dives; the Cane Bay Wall is the most spectacular, dropping from 40ft (12m) to more than 3200ft (975m).

Plan Your Trip
Water Sports

The Caribbean has plenty to get you active, and with water everywhere it's no wonder aquatic sports are a big draw for many vacationers. There are great breaks for surfers, myriad opportunities for exploring with sea kayaks and paddleboards, stiff breezes off the Atlantic to attract kitesurfers, or you can become the captain of your own adventure by getting under sail in a yacht.

Boating & Sailing

The Caribbean is a first-rate sailing destination. On many public beaches and at resorts, water-sports huts rent out Hobie Cats or other small sailboats for near-shore exploring. Many sailboat charter companies run day trips to other islands and offer party trips aboard tall ships or sunset cruises on catamarans.

The region is one of the world's prime yachting locales, offering diversity, warm weather and fine scenery. The many small islands grouped closely together are not only fun to explore but also form a barrier, providing relatively calm sailing waters.

Anguilla Prickly Pear Cays is a super-secluded mini-Anguilla with 360 degrees of flaxen sand reachable only by boat.

Antigua & Barbuda Yachting base. Dickenson Bay is a popular anchorage with resorts ashore and a good beach, while English Harbour is a historic and premier yacht harbor.

The Bahamas Yachting base. The Abacos is the self-proclaimed 'Sailing Capital of the World' so take time to tool around the Loyalist Cays with a rental boat. The Biminis are a yachties' haven only 80 miles (130km) from Florida. Explore the 365 Exuma Cays at your leisure with a rental boat.

British Virgin Islands Sailing here is a top Caribbean activity thanks to steady trade winds, hundreds of protected bays and an abundance of charter boats. Tortola is the charter-boat capital of the Caribbean.

Best Activities on the Water

Boating & Sailing With islands everywhere, being under sail is understandably the purpose of many trips. The Bahamas, Caymans, Antigua and Barbuda and both Virgin Islands are all top yachting destinations.

Fishing Hemingway made Caribbean fishing famous, and casting your rod in the blue waters continues to challenge many. Head to the Bahamas, Caymans, St Lucia and the Turks and Caicos for great fishing.

Kayaking & Paddleboarding This is the best way to see hidden coves and beaches or wildlife-rich mangroves, often with transparent canoes to see what lies below. You'll find kayaks everywhere, we particularly enjoy the tours in Aruba, Bonaire and Grenada.

Surfing The Caribbean Sea sounds gentle, but strong Atlantic swells offer great breaks on many islands. Northern Barbados has great surfing, while Rincón in Puerto Rico has been famous since the Beach Boys sang its praises.

Windsurfing & Kitesurfing It blows a lot in the islands and there's plenty of ways to catch the wind. The Dominican Republic in particular is a great destination to catch the breeze and the waves alike.

Dominica Experience the watery side of the jungle on a silent glide by boat on the Indian River.

Dominican Republic Parque Nacional Los Haitises operates boat trips. Take a whale-watching tour around Bahía de Samaná to see 30-tonne humpbacks or visit Bahía de Las Águilas, best reached by boat. Catamaran sailing trips frequently travel between Cabarete and Sosúa.

Grenada A popular base with loads of marinas throughout the south of the island. Fewer storms means cheaper insurance too.

St Kitts Has a superyacht harbor at Christophe Harbour in southern St Kitts.

St Lucia Yachting base. Popular ports and anchorages are Rodney Bay and Marigot Bay. Take a day trip by boat up the beautiful west coast of the island.

St-Martin/Sint Maarten Yachting base. Popular ports include Marigot and Philipsburg.

St Vincent & the Grenadines Yachting base. Sailing the Grenadines is a top Caribbean activity. Bequia is one of the Caribbean's best small islands and a lovely anchorage for yachts. Union Island is a popular anchorage with a busy harbor.

Trinidad & Tobago Trinidad's Chaguaramas peninsula is lined with yacht harbors and full-service marinas that are popular refuges during hurricane season.

Turks & Caicos These little islands are popular stops between the Bahamas and the Eastern Caribbean.

US Virgin Islands Sailing here is a top Caribbean activity.

Fishing

There's good deep-sea fishing in the Caribbean, with marlin, tuna, wahoo and barracuda among the prime catches. Charter fishing-boat rentals are available on most islands. Expect a half-day of fishing for four to six people to run to about US$400. Boats are usually individually owned and, consequently, the list of available skippers tends to fluctuate.

The Bahamas The Biminis were good enough for Hemingway!

Cayman Islands There are many charter boat operators on Grand Cayman; blue marlin is a big catch.

Cuba Cayo Guillermo boasts more Hemingway-standard fishing.

Dominican Republic Resorts in Bávaro and Punta Cana organize trips and cook the catch.

Jamaica Montego Bay, Negril and Ocho Rios resorts organize trips and cook the catch.

Puerto Rico La Parguera Fishing Charters runs out to some of the world's best marlin and *mahimahi* runs.

St Lucia Billfish, marlin and yellowfin tuna can be caught from November to January, and wahoo and dorado from February to May. Vigie is a good place to get on a boat.

Trinidad & Tobago From Tobago's Crown Point, charter boats offer deep-sea fishing in waters rich with tarpon and other big-game fish.

Turks & Caicos The country's biggest fishing competition, the Grand Turk Game Fishing Tournament, gets underway at the end of July. Providenciales is the center for sport-fishing.

US Virgin Islands Deep-sea fishing charters depart from the St Thomas port of Red Hook.

Kayaking & Paddleboarding

You can rent kayaks and paddleboards across the Caribbean. Explore beach-dotted coasts, wildlife-filled mangroves and more. Many tour companies now offer kayak adventures, some at night in bioluminescent waters.

Antigua & Barbuda Kayak and paddleboard around the Robinson Crusoe islands off the east coast of Antigua.

Aruba Kayak through mangroves and old pirate sites with Aruba Kayak Adventure.

The Bahamas The Exuma Cays offer endless exploration for kayakers. Lucayan National Park on Grand Bahama has mangrove swamps and blue holes; Grand Bahamas Nature Tours offers tours with naturalist guides.

Bonaire The Mangrove Info & Kayak Center offers highly recommended tours through mangroves.

Cayman Islands Kayak tours depart from the North Side to explore the mangrove swamps, Starfish Point, and/or the magically luminescent Bio Bay.

Dominica The Soufriere/Scotts Head Marine Reserve is popular for excursions.

Grenada Conservation Kayak explores Grenada's shores and mangroves.

Montserrat The only white-sand beach, at Rendezvous Bay, is best reached by kayak.

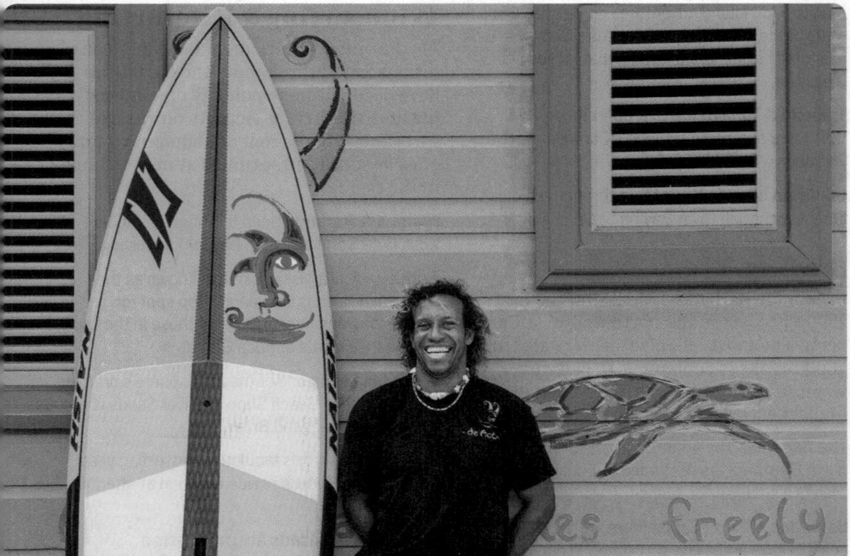

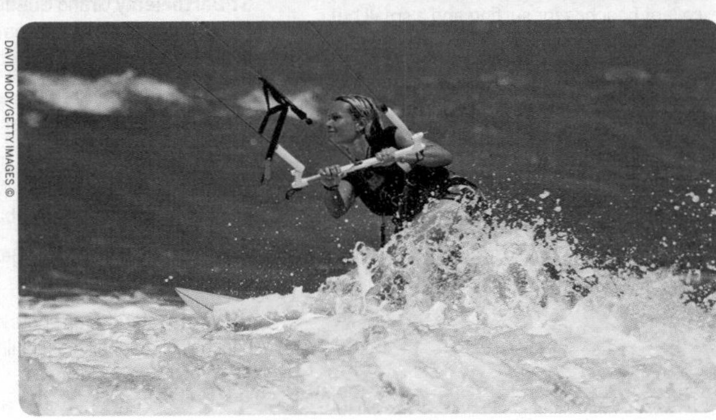

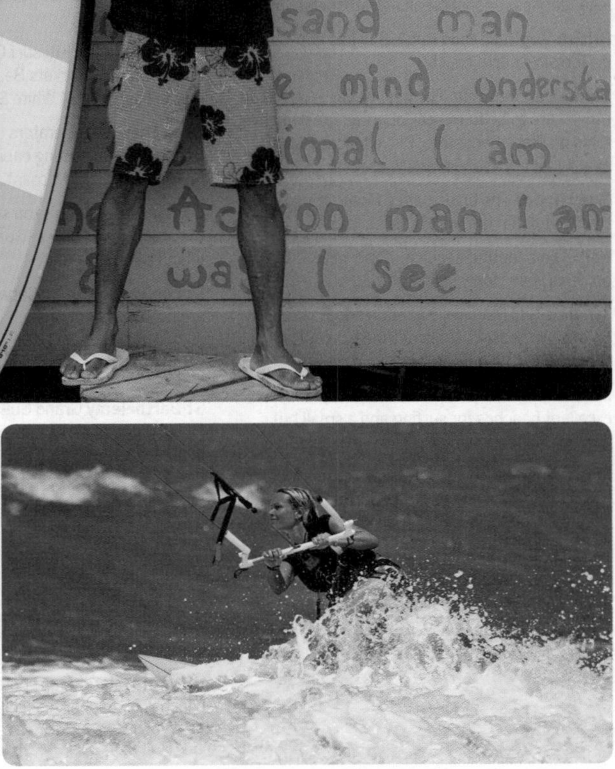

Top: Local surfing icon Brian Talma, Silver Sands, Barbados (p213)
Bottom: Kiteboarding, Dominican Republic (p398)

DAVID MODY/GETTY IMAGES ©

Puerto Rico Island Adventures on Vieques leads tours of the bay; Vieques Adventure Company has totally transparent kayaks that let you see the action.

Trinidad & Tobago Kayak around Tobago with SUP Tobago; explore Trinidad's Caroni or Nariva Wetlands with Paria Springs.

US Virgin Islands Night tours through the bioluminescent Salt River Bay on St Croix.

Surfing

Except for Barbados, you'll find the best surfing coasts in the north and west Caribbean. The most reliable time for catching good breaks is September to November, when Atlantic swells arrive to create the highest waves and best surfing conditions.

The Bahamas The Atlantic-ocean surf beaches on north Eleuthera are renowned but uncrowded and there's a small surfer scene.

Barbados At Silver Sands there are good south-coast breaks and a fine surf school. Soup Bowl is a legendary east-coast break at Bathsheba.

British Virgin Islands Apple Bay has good surfing on Tortola's north coast.

Dominican Republic The best waves – up to 13ft (4m) – are to be found at Cabarete, breaking over reefs on Playa Encuentro. Playa Macao, a surf beach just north of Bavaro, is another good option.

Guadeloupe The breaks at Le Moule are so good that it's hosted the world surf championships.

Haiti The beautiful beach at Kabic near Jacmel is home to Haiti's only surf school.

Jamaica Bull Bay near Kingston and Boston Bay on the northeast coast boast the best surfing in Jamaica.

Martinique Presqu'île de Caravelle has several excellent beaches for surfing and a small but growing surfer presence on its north coast.

Puerto Rico Rincón is well known for perfect tubes and a Beach Boys song; Surfing Puerto Rico in Luquillo offers lessons for all ages and abilities.

Trinidad & Tobago Tobago's Mt Irvine has a mini surf scene; Trinidad's Sans Souci and Blanchisseuse are popular with local surfers.

US Virgin Islands Hull Bay is St Thomas' most popular break.

Windsurfing & Kitesurfing

The favorable winds and good water conditions found throughout the Caribbean have boosted the popularity of windsurfing and kitesurfing. Activity outfits, resorts and vendors rent out equipment and offer lessons to first-timers at many islands in the region.

Antigua & Barbuda Head to Antigua's Jabberwock Beach and Nonsuch Bay for kitesurfing.

Aruba Hadicurari Beach, better known as the Fisherman Huts, is the island's top spot for windsurfing and kitesurfing, but those in the know escape the crowds at Boca Grandi.

Barbados Set on one of the hemisphere's premier spots, deAction Beach Shop at Silver Sands is run by windsurfing legend Brian Talma.

Bonaire Lac Bay has fabulous windsurfing year-round, while kitesurfers ride the wind at Atlantis Kite Beach.

British Virgin Islands Anegada hosts a kitesurfing school for novices and experienced enthusiasts alike.

Cayman Islands Kitesurf Cayman sets up its operation near Barkers Beach on Grand Cayman; on the East End try White Sands Water Sports.

Cuba There are operators in Varadero, but the undoubted kitesurfing capital is Cayo Guillermo on the central north coast.

Curaçao The island's top spot for windsurfing is the smooth and breezy Spaanse Water, a large inland bay.

Dominican Republic Cabarete and Las Terrenas are both excellent areas.

Martinique Pointe du Bout offers top conditions and a good school.

St-Barthélemy Grand Cul-de-Sac's sandy beach is one of the island's top spots for water sports including windsurfing and kitesurfing.

St Vincent & the Grenadines Budget-friendly Union Island is the epicenter of kitesurfing in the Grenadines.

Trinidad & Tobago Radical Watersports at Pigeon Point is where you'll find Tobago's kitesurf experts.

Turks & Caicos Long Bay Beach is a prime kitesurfing destination.

US Virgin Islands Top spots are at the North Shore beaches on St John, especially Cinnamon Bay.

Plan Your Trip

Hiking

The Caribbean is an unexpectedly rich hiking destination. You can thank the slow shifts of ancient geology for this – rising tectonic plates and active volcanoes have produced islands dominated by forest-clad mountains and rolling coastlines that will have you itching to get your walking boots on.

Hiking Conditions

Hiking in the tropics is different to hiking in temperate zones, and conditions may come as a surprise. Treks up mountains and volcanoes are often muddy and you may walk for a lot of the time over slippery tree roots – always a hiker's favorite – and in mist. Rain is common and the air remains humid even below 68°F (20°C), but you may also need to be prepared for cool pre-dawn starts. Take plenty of water, sunscreen, a hat, waterproofs, swimwear and food.

Most hikes listed range between a half and a full day in length. Walking up to an island's highest point is a popular hike in many destinations. The Caribbean has relatively few multi-day hikes – exceptions include the ascent of Pico Turquino in Cuba, Pico Duarte in the Dominican Republic, and Dominica's epic Waitukubuli National Trail, which runs the entire length of the island.

Finally, bad weather (and especially hurricanes) can regularly close hiking routes. Always check with a local tourist office or guiding operator that the route you intend to take is actually accessible.

Best Hikes

Dominica

Take a day trek to Boiling Lake (p396), or tackle the epic, island-wide Waitukubuli National Trail (p379) through rainforests.

Martinique

Hike along the base of the still-smoldering Mont Pelée (p570), a volcano that wiped out the island's former capital in 1902.

Cuba

Take a guided hike up Cuba's highest peak, **Pico Turquino**, a mountain imbued with revolutionary history.

Barbados

The National Trust's weekend hikes (p204) are a great way to get some exercise and learn more about the island's rich history.

St Vincent

Soufrière volcano dominates the northern part of the island and a hike to its summit (p737) is a highlight for adventurous travelers.

Jamaica

Trek past coffee plantations to climb Blue Mountain Peak (p521), or get deep and wild on the **Troy-Windsor Trail** in Cockpit Country.

Where to Hike

Barbados

Barbados lacks the dramatic scenery of many Caribbean islands, but it's a surprisingly good walking destination. The Barbados National Trust leads guided hikes in the countryside, with hike leaders sharing insights into local history, geology and wildlife.

A good self-guided hike is along the old railroad bed that runs along the east coast from Belleplaine to Martin's Bay. The whole walk is about 12 miles (20km), but it can be easily broken into shorter stretches.

Cuba

The best areas for day hikes are Topes de Collantes in the Sierra del Escambray near Trinidad, with its waterfalls and rich plant and birdlife; around the forest-engulfed plantation ruins of Las Terrazas; and Viñales, where local guides can take you around caves, tobacco plantations and ecofarms.

There is only one multi-day hike – to the top of Pico Turquino, Cuba's highest mountain. It's easy to organize and usually done over two or three days. Hiking guides are usually pretty good.

Dominica

Dominica is home to the Caribbean's first long-distance hiking trail. Over its 115-mile (185km) length, it links Scotts Head in the far southwest with Cabrits National Park in the northwest. The trail is broken into 14 sections of varying length and difficulty, but along its way takes in the island's most scenic spots, including Boiling Lake and Emerald Pool. In 2019, some sections of the route were still awaiting reopening after being damaged by Hurricane Maria.

Shorter (but equally worthwhile) hikes include Middleham Falls, and the charming Syndicate Nature Trail.

Dominican Republic

The Dominican Republic has quite a few challenging trails around Jarabacoa, many of which lead to dramatic waterfalls. The Península de Samaná has some beautiful hikes near Las Galeras, with picturesque deserted beaches as your reward at the end. In the southwest, there are some decent half-day and full-day hikes just outside Paraíso, though they are best visited as part of a tour.

The most famous hike in the DR is the ascent of Pico Duarte (10,125ft/3098m), the tallest peak in the Caribbean. It's a tough multi-day hike, supported by mules.

Grenada

Grand Etang National Park is a natural wonderland of misty landscapes centered around a lovely lake. There are many hiking trails within the park, varying in duration and difficulty. Some are well maintained while others are overgrown and require the use of a local guide, which can easily be arranged at the park visitor center.

Guadeloupe

La Soufrière, Guadeloupe's active volcano, usually gets top billing for its rainforest hiking trails. However, reaching the summit depends very much on how lively the volcano is – the trails were temporarily closed in summer 2019 for safety reasons. The nearby hike to the double waterfalls of Chutes du Carbet is a good alternative.

The Parc National de la Guadeloupe offers good walking and, if you're self-sufficient, you can extend your trek by overnighting in the basic refuges en route.

Haiti

Within easy reach of Port-au-Prince, the Parc National la Visite is a mountainous park offering good hiking through pine forests, with views to the Caribbean Sea. You walk from Kenscoff through the woods, and slowly descend through wild rock formations towards the coast, where you arrive a short drive from the town of Jacmel. It's possible to break the hike with an overnight stay at a lodge in Seguin.

Jamaica

The hike through coffee country to Blue Mountain Peak, Jamaica's highest mountain, is the most popular walk in the country. It's easily accessible from Kingston, but most hikers start from Penlyne Castle where you can overnight, as an early start allows you to enjoy dawn rising over the Caribbean from the mountaintop.

For those craving something remote, head for Cockpit Country in the center of the island, where the Maroon guides will help you hack your way along the green and tough Troy-Windsor Trail.

Martinique

Martinique is an excellent hiking destination. Head to Grand-Rivière for one of the Caribbean's top walks – the hike to the top of Mont Pelée, Martinique's active (though currently slumbering) volcano.

Notable coastal routes include the network of paths at the end of the Presqu'île de Caravelle, the dramatic Chemin de la Crabière, the Chemin des Anses du Nord between Anse Couleuvre and Grand-Rivière, and the Trace des Caps in Martinique's far southeast.

Puerto Rico

Puerto Rico offers excellent DIY adventures, even if routes are not always brilliantly marked. The big draw is the green and misty El Yunque National Forest, which has trails to suit all hikers. In 2019 some of the trails were closed for repair and maintenance following Hurricane Maria.

The island's highest peak, Cerro la Punta, has a network of virtually untrammeled forest trails. For a complete contrast, walk the weird cactus-strewn landscapes of Bosque Estatal de Guánica.

Saba

Tiny but craggy Saba is very organised when it comes to hiking, with 17 marked trails cut across seven ecosystems, including coastal meadows and cloud forests. The most popular hike is the rugged hike up Mt Scenery, for sweeping Caribbean views.

Other options include the moderately strenuous Sulphur Mine Trail, which offers views of Saba's dramatic cliffside landing strip; the Spring Bay Trail to Windwardside; and the long but easy Sandy Cruz Trail from Upper Hell's Gate to The Bottom.

St Kitts & Nevis

Mt Liamuiga is St Kitts' highest volcano, and the hike up here is very rewarding if you're fit enough. It's steep and the trail is often quite overgrown (a guide is recommended), but the crater at the summit, which has its own seasonal lake, is more like something from a science fiction landscape than the chilled out Caribbean.

St Lucia

Modest St Lucia punches well above its weight when it comes to hiking opportunities. The Pitons mountains offer the chance to trek through dense forest up Gros Piton. It's a steep ascent (and a guide is required) but the reward is tremendous views of southern St Lucia. Petit Piton is suited to experienced scramblers.

High in the mountains above Soufrière you'll find the trailhead for the Edmund Rainforest Trail, while the little-visited Des Cartiers Rainforest Trail offers the chance to spot the rare St Lucian parrot.

St Vincent & the Grenadines

The sulfur-spitting Soufrière volcano dominates northern St Vincent, and a hike to the summit is a big draw for adventurous visitors. There are two trails up its slopes – the windward and leeward trails, depending on your fitness. The former is a more moderate hike, but the latter rewards walkers with great views of both sea and volcano for the entire hike.

US Virgin Islands

The low-lying US Virgin Islands offer some welcome surprises for hikers. Virgin Islands National Park on St John has 20 trails, including ones that lead to petroglyphs, plantation ruins and isolated beaches. On St Croix, the St Croix Hiking Association runs several guided hikes a month, which are a great way to learn about the island and meet locals at the same time.

Plan Your Trip
Island-Hopping

The Caribbean lends itself easily to island-hopping. Planes and/or boats link all the main islands with their neighbors. Because tickets are priced for the local market, with advance planning you can find airline tickets for about US$150 to US$200 or less.

Need to Know

Best Ways to Island-Hop

Airplane Airlines link every island with an airport to its neighbors.

Ferry Not comprehensive but, where they exist, the most scenic links.

Sailboat Aboard a rental yacht, you have the ultimate freedom to island-hop.

What You Need

Time With two weeks you can see a lot of a region; with a month you'll live the fantasy.

Sense of adventure Unexpected experiences will be the most memorable.

Money Perhaps not as much as you think as you'll be traveling like a local.

The Ultimate Itinerary

It's possible to get from Aruba in the far south to the Bahamas in the north, stopping at every major island on the way.

Getting Around

Air

Regional airlines, large and small, travel around the Caribbean. A certain level of patience and understanding is required when you island-hop. Schedules can change at a moment's notice or there may be delays without explanation. Your best bet is to embrace island time, relax and enjoy the ride.

Regional planes are sometimes like old buses, seemingly stopping at every possible corner to pick up passengers – a boon for island-hoppers! You'll sometimes get stuck on what you could call the 'LIAT shuffle,' where your plane touches down and takes off again from several different airports. For example, if you're flying from St Thomas to Trinidad, you might stop in Antigua, St Lucia and St Vincent before arriving.

There are many airlines operating within the Caribbean. There are some good local carriers with dozens of connections, which will give you ideas for itinerary building:

Caribbean Airlines (www.caribbean-airlines.com) Hubs: Port of Spain, Trinidad; Kingston, Jamaica

Intercaribbean (www.intercaribbean.com) Hub: Providenciales, Turks and Caicos

LIAT (www.liat.com) Hubs: St John's, Antigua; Bridgetown, Barbados

Seaborne Airlines (www.seaborneairlines.com) Hub: San Juan, Puerto Rico

Sunrise Airways (www.sunriseairways.net) Hub: Port-au-Prince, Haiti

WinAir (www.fly-winair.sx) Hub: Sint-Maarten

Ferry

For a place surrounded by water, the Caribbean doesn't have as many ferries as you'd think. However, there are regional ferries, which travel between several island groups. These can be a nice change of pace after cramped airplanes, smelly buses and dodgy rental cars. Ferries are a good way to get around the Leeward Islands.

When available, ferries tend to be reasonably modern and a great travel option.

Yacht

The Caribbean is a prime locale for yachting. The many small islands grouped closely together are not only fun to explore but also provide calm sailing waters.

It's easiest to sail down-island, from north to south, as on the reverse trip boats must beat back into the wind. Because of this, several yacht-charter companies only allow sailors to take the boats in one direction, arranging for their own crews to bring the boats back to home base later.

Yacht charters are the ultimate Caribbean fantasy, sailing in a large boat from idyllic island to idyllic island. And it's a surprisingly achievable – albeit not cheap – fantasy.

Start by choosing from two basic types of yacht charter: bareboat or crewed.

On a bareboat charter, you skipper a fully equipped sailboat after you've proved your qualifications; sail where you want, when you want. With a crewed charter, you sip a drink on deck while the rental boat's crew swabs the poop deck and does everything else (usually including cooking and bringing you that drink). You can either make your own detailed itinerary or provide a vague idea of the kind of places you'd like to visit and let the captain decide where to anchor.

The cost of a bareboat charter for a week for four people begins at about US$3000 and goes up from there. Crewed options are much more and all prices vary hugely by season, type of boat, crew etc. The British Virgin Islands are the top destination for renters.

The following charter companies offer both bareboat and crewed yacht charters in the Caribbean:

Catamaran Company (www.catamarans.com)

Horizon Yacht Charters (www.horizon yacht charters.com)

Moorings (www.moorings.com)

Sunsail (www.sunsail.com).

For those who don't want to be bothered shopping around, charter-yacht brokers work on commission, like travel agents, and they match you to a rental boat. Better-known charter-yacht brokers include **Ed Hamilton & Co** (www.ed-hamilton.com) and **Nicholson Yacht Charters** (www.nicholsoncharters.com).

Island Links

The following list shows *direct* links between neighboring islands.

Anguilla Air: Puerto Rico, St-Barthélemy, St-Martin/Sint Maarten; Sea: St-Martin/Sint Maarten

Antigua and Barbuda Air: Dominica, Guadeloupe, Montserrat, St Kitts and Nevis, St-Martin/Sint Maarten, Trinidad; Sea: Montserrat

Aruba Air: Bonaire, Cuba, Curaçao

The Bahamas Air: Cayman Islands, Cuba, Jamaica, Turks and Caicos

Barbados Air: Dominica, Grenada, St Lucia, St Vincent and the Grenadines, Trinidad and Tobago

Bonaire Air: Aruba, Curaçao

British Virgin Islands Air: Puerto Rico, US Virgin Islands

Cayman Islands Air: The Bahamas, Cuba, Jamaica

Cuba Air: Aruba, The Bahamas, Cayman Islands, Dominican Republic, Haiti, Jamaica, Trinidad

Curaçao Air: Aruba, Bonaire, Dominican Republic, St-Martin/Sint Maarten, Trinidad

Dominica Air: Antigua, Barbados, Guadeloupe, Puerto Rico; Sea: Guadeloupe, Martinique, St Lucia

Dominican Republic Air: Cuba, Curaçao, Guadeloupe, Haiti, Puerto Rico, Turks and Caicos; Land: Haiti

CARIBBEAN GEOGRAPHY 101

You will hear the Caribbean islands referred to in numerous ways – the Leewards, the Windwards, the West Indies etc. It can get confusing, so here's a quick primer in Caribbean geography.

Caribbean islands An archipelago of thousands of islands that stretch from the southeast coast of Florida in the USA to the northern coast of Venezuela. The largest island within the Caribbean Sea is Cuba, followed by the island of Hispaniola (shared by the nations of Haiti and the Dominican Republic), then Jamaica and Puerto Rico. The Bahamas, to the north, are technically outside of the Caribbean archipelago.

Greater Antilles Consists of the large islands, such as Hispaniola, Cuba and Jamaica at the top of the Caribbean and extends east as far as Puerto Rico. It also includes the Cayman Islands, due to their western location.

Lesser Antilles The archipelago that extends east and southeastward from the Virgin Islands down to Trinidad and Tobago, just off the northern coast of Venezuela. Also called the Eastern Caribbean Islands, the Lesser Antilles are further divided into the Leeward Islands and the Windward Islands.

Leeward Islands From north to south: the US Virgin Islands (USVI), the British Virgin Islands (BVI), Anguilla, St-Martin/Sint Maarten, St-Barthélemy, Saba, Sint Eustatius (Statia), St Kitts and Nevis, Antigua and Barbuda, Montserrat, and Guadeloupe.

Windward Islands From north to south: Dominica, Martinique, St Lucia, St Vincent and the Grenadines, and Grenada. Barbados and Trinidad and Tobago are often geographically considered part of the Windwards, but do not belong to the Windward Islands geopolitical group.

Grenada Air: Barbados, St Vincent and the Grenadines, Trinidad and Tobago; Sea: St Vincent and the Grenadines

Guadeloupe Air: Antigua, Dominica, Dominican Republic, Haiti, Martinique, St-Barthélemy, St-Martin/Sint Maarten; Sea: Dominica, Martinique, St Lucia.

Haiti Air: Cuba, Dominican Republic, Guadeloupe, Turks and Caicos; Land: Dominican Republic

Jamaica Air: The Bahamas, Cayman Islands, Cuba, Trinidad, Turks and Caicos

Martinique Air: Guadeloupe, St Lucia; Sea: Dominica, Guadeloupe, St Lucia

Montserrat Air: Antigua; Sea: Antigua

Puerto Rico Air: Anguilla, British Virgin Islands, Dominica, Dominican Republic, St-Barthélemy, St Kitts and Nevis, Turks and Caicos, US Virgin Islands

Saba Air: Sint Eustatius, St-Martin/Sint Maarten; Sea: St-Martin/Sint Maarten

Sint Eustatius Air: Saba, St-Martin/Sint Maarten; Sea: St-Martin/Sint Maarten

St-Barthélemy Air: Anguilla, Guadeloupe, Nevis, St-Martin/Sint Maarten, St Thomas, Puerto Rico; Sea: St-Martin/Sint Maarten

St Kitts and Nevis Air: Antigua, Puerto Rico, St-Martin/Sint Maarten, US Virgin Islands

St Lucia Air: Barbados, Martinique, St Vincent and the Grenadines, Trinidad; Sea: Dominica, Guadeloupe, Martinique

St-Martin/Sint Maarten Air: Anguilla, Antigua, Curacao, Guadeloupe, Saba, Sint Eustatius, St-Barthélemy, St Kitts and Nevis, St Thomas, Trinidad; Sea: Anguilla, Saba, Sint Eustatius, St-Barthélemy

St Vincent and the Grenadines Air: Barbados, Grenada, St Lucia, Trinidad; Sea: Grenada

Trinidad and Tobago Air: Antigua, Barbados, Cuba, Curaçao, Grenada, Jamaica, St Lucia, St-Martin/Sint Maarten, St Vincent

Turks and Caicos Air: The Bahamas, Dominican Republic, Haiti, Jamaica, Puerto Rico

US Virgin Islands Air: British Virgin Islands, Puerto Rico, St Kitts and Nevis

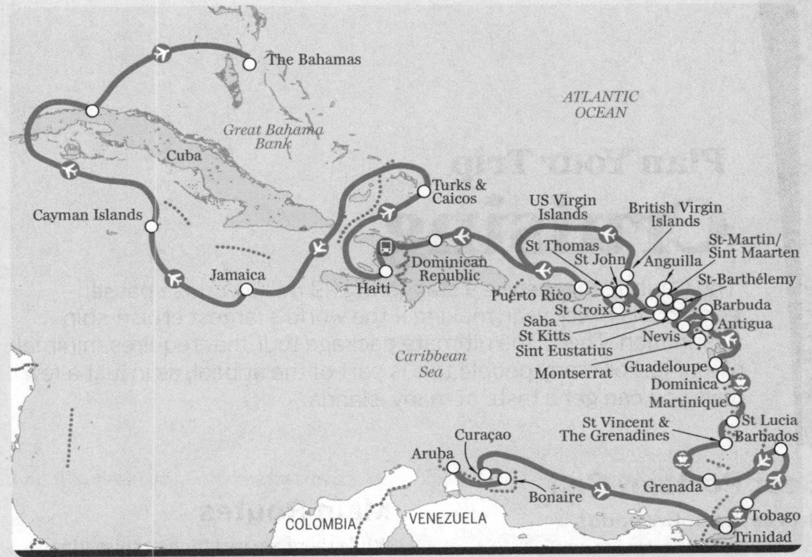

Ultimate Island-Hopping Itinerary

This trip lets you see all the main regions, starting in the south. Ferries are used when possible, supplemented by planes. Don't have the time or cash for this mammoth adventure? Cut off a chunk and do just that part. A full tour could take from three weeks to one month.

Start in the resorts of **Aruba**, then fly to **Bonaire** for diving and then to **Curaçao** for old Willemstad. Now it's a flight to Port of Spain, **Trinidad**, followed by a ferry trip to the natural beauty of **Tobago**. From here fly to lovely beaches and even better surfing in **Barbados**, then take a flight to surprising **Grenada**. Here you can take boats (ferries and mail boats) island-hopping up through **St Vincent and the Grenadines**. Don't miss Bequia.

A quick flight to **St Lucia** and you are again island-hopping. Going north, make the ferry voyages to *très française* **Martinique** and on to the waterfalls and wilds of **Dominica** and then the twin cones of **Guadeloupe**. You are back on a plane to **Antigua**, from where you can take a boat round-trip to beautiful **Barbuda** before making the 20-minute flight round-trip for plucky **Montserrat** and its active volcano.

Leave the Antigua hub by plane for **Nevis**, followed by the chance to get spray in your face on a ferry to the volcanic perfection of **St Kitts**. From here it's 30 minutes by air to the transport hub of **St-Martin/Sint Maarten**, with its awesome runway beach and bar.

Do round-trip ferry visits to upscale **Anguilla**, tiny **Saba** and very French **St-Barthélemy**, and a hop by air to volcanic **Sint Eustatius** and its ruins. Now fly to St Thomas in the **US Virgin Islands** and escape by boat to lovely St Croix. Get a ferry to the **British Virgin Islands** and then a flight to **Puerto Rico** and beautiful Old San Juan. Fly to the **Dominican Republic** and then go for a bus adventure to **Haiti** (or fly). Another plane takes you to the **Turks and Caicos**, where you can continue by air to reggae-licious **Jamaica**. See stingrays in the **Cayman Islands**, and continue on to amazing, intoxicating and confounding **Cuba**. From here it is a short flight from Havana across to Nassau in the **Bahamas**, where you can lose yourself among hundreds of islands.

Plan Your Trip

Cruising

The Caribbean receives a staggering 29 million cruise passenger arrivals every year, making it the world's largest cruise-ship destination. This is the ultimate package tour that requires minimal planning. For many people this is part of the appeal, as in just a few days you can get a taste of many islands.

Best Ports of Call

Bridgetown, Barbados

A vibrant, modern Caribbean capital with loads of shops popular with locals and cruisers alike. Plus you can walk to a great beach.

Tortola, British Virgin Islands

Port of fancy for yachties, this lovely spot handles visitors with aplomb, never hitting a false note.

Havana, Cuba

Begin exploring the endlessly fascinating old parts of the city as soon as you step off the gangplank.

St George's, Grenada

A beautiful old port town with interesting shops and top-notch strolling.

Old San Juan, Puerto Rico

Cruisers blend right into this ever-surprising, vast and historic neighborhood of tiny bars, cafes, shops and ancient buildings.

Main Routes

While there are variations, cruise itineraries tend to concentrate on three main areas.

Eastern Caribbean

Cruises can last three to seven days; the profusion of port calls means that there are few days during which you're at sea all day. Some itineraries may venture south to Barbados or even to Aruba, Bonaire and Curaçao; there is much overlap between the eastern and southern itineraries. Islands in the eastern area: Antigua, Bahamas, British Virgin Islands, Dominican Republic, Guadeloupe, Puerto Rico, St Kitts and Nevis, St-Martin/Sint Maarten, Turks and Caicos, US Virgin Islands.

Southern Caribbean

Itineraries are usually at least seven days due to the distance from the main departure ports. There is often some overlap with the Eastern Caribbean islands, with stops at the US Virgin Islands common. Islands in the southern area: Aruba, Barbados, Bonaire, Curaçao, Dominica, Grenada, Martinique, St Lucia, St Vincent and the Grenadines, Trinidad and Tobago.

Western Caribbean

Often only five days in length, the western itineraries usually also include Mexican ports, such as Cancun. There are often stops at Puerto Rico and other eastern ports. Longer itineraries may include southern stops. Islands in the western area: Cayman Islands, Jamaica and Dominican Republic.

Cuba's return to cruise itineraries is subject to the changing political winds blowing from the USA. Many companies added Cuba to their routes following the Obama-era thaw, but as of June 2019 US ships are barred from visiting Cuba. Havana remains a highlight for non-US cruise ships.

Ports of Departure

Main departure ports for Caribbean cruises are Fort Lauderdale and Miami, Florida; and San Juan, Puerto Rico. All three cities are well equipped to deal with vast numbers of departing and arriving cruise-ship passengers and are closest to the Caribbean.

Secondary departure ports are typically set up for local markets and won't see the line's biggest or flashiest ships (though some veteran cruisers like that). These include Galveston, Texas; New Orleans, Louisiana; Port Canaveral and Tampa, Florida and even as far north as Baltimore, Maryland and New York City. Cruises from these ports need more time at sea to travel to and from the Caribbean.

Ports of Call

There are many choices of where to visit on a cruise. Note that some cruise lines stop at 'private islands,' which are beaches that function as an extension of the shipboard experience. A prime example is 'Labadie,' used by ships under the Royal Caribbean umbrella and which is really a private resort on Haiti's north coast.

Choosing a Cruise

There are six main things to consider when booking a cruise:

Budget How much can you spend? Can you trade a cabin with a balcony (the most common kind now) for a cheaper, windowless room on a nicer ship for a longer voyage?

Style A mass-market, upscale or specialist cruise? Consider your budget, whether you prefer numerous formal evenings or keeping things casual, and any special interests you have.

Itinerary Where do you want to go and what ports of call appeal? Do you like the idea of days spent just at sea?

Size The megaships are geared for various budgets, so the important decision is how many people you want to sail with. On large ships, you can have 6000 potential new friends and also have the greatest range of shipboard diversions. Small ships, while sometimes exclusive and luxurious, are not always so, and usually lack the flashier amenities (such as climbing walls). However, smaller ships also call at smaller ports on islands that are less visited but more interesting.

Season High season for Caribbean cruising is the same as at resorts in the islands: mid-December to April. The largest number of ships sail at this time and prices are at their highest. At other times there are far fewer voyages but prices drop. Storms are more likely to cause itineraries to suddenly change during the June to November hurricane season.

Demographics Different cruise lines, and even ships within cruise lines, tend to appeal to different groups. Although cruisers in general tend to be slightly older, some ships have quite a party reputation; others are known for their art auctions and oldies music in the lounges. Also consider if you're looking for a family- or singles-oriented cruise.

CRUISING RESOURCES

A good source for general cruise information, news and reviews before you book is **Cruise Critic** (www.cruisecritic.com). Some specialist websites for cruising have spectacular deals as lines dump trips at the last moment that otherwise would go unsold. Some recommended sites:

Cruise411 (www.cruise411.com)

Cruise.com (www.cruise.com)

Cruise Outlet (www.thecruiseoutlet.com)

Vacations to Go (www.vacationstogo.com)

Also check out Lonely Planet's *Cruise Ports Caribbean*, with advice on what to see and what to skip.

POPULAR PORTS OF CALL

Unless otherwise noted, ships dock at ports located in or very near town.

PORT	DESCRIPTION	EXCURSIONS
Antigua: St John's	Busy, vibrant capital with lots of daily life & shopping at markets	Rainforest canopy tours, catamaran sail, English Harbour, beaches, market, kayaking
Aruba: Oranjestad	Commercial hub divided between a zone of malls (some quite tired) serving cruisers & a regular shopping area	Natural sites on the east coast, beaches
The Bahamas: Nassau	The country's busy main cruise-ship port; passengers can walk to the sights of downtown, which revolves around cruisers	Aquaventure Waterpark, diving & snorkeling at Stuart Cove
The Bahamas: Lucaya	The Lucayan Harbour cruise port is a few miles from Freeport & Lucaya – cruise-ship passengers have to take a bus or taxi to town	Trips to Garden of the Groves, hanging out on Lucaya Beach
Barbados: Bridgetown	Attractive capital with plenty of locally owned shops; it's big so copes well with crowds	Beaches, rum distilleries, nature & wildlife
Bonaire: Kralendijk	Tiny with only a few shops, so large ships bring a tsunami of people; it's best to get a driver & leave	Diving, windsurfing, sightseeing, flamingo spotting
British Virgin Islands: Road Town	Vibrant place that accepts cruisers with aplomb, but gets crowded	Taxi to Cane Garden Bay, ferry to Virgin Gorda
Cayman Islands: George Town	Has a busy, compact center with a mix of local- & tourist-oriented businesses; ships don't dock, tenders are used	Seven Mile Beach, Stingray City, Cayman Turtle Center
Cuba: Havana	This is one place you don't need an excursion. It's a fascinating city perfect for wandering, especially the old Habana Vieja area near the port	Exploring the old city, shopping, museums
Curaçao: Willemstad	The harbor cleaves the city in two – it's a spectacular place to arrive by ship; most central shops are geared toward cruisers	Tours of historic Willemstad, museums, beaches, snorkeling
Dominica: Roseau	Scruffy but charismatic city center with busy markets, bars & historic sights	Boiling Lake, Morne Trois Piton National Park, Titou Gorge, snorkeling
Dominican Republic: Samaná	Unsophisticated old port town with sparse waterside restaurants; hops during whale season; ships don't dock, tenders are used	Beaches of Cayo Levantado, Cascada El Limón waterfall, whale watching (in season)
Dominican Republic: Santo Domingo	Has two ports: one basically in Zona Colonial, the other directly across the river	Walking tour of the remarkable Zona Colonial to absorb its culture
Grenada: St George's	One of the Caribbean's most beautiful old cities – a mini San Francisco; it has interesting local shops hidden about	Touring the town, Grand Anse Beach, Grand Etang hikes
Guadeloupe: Pointe-à-Pitre	Slowly growing as a cruise stop, Pointe-à-Pitre may be rather dilapidated, but it has the excellent Mémorial ACTe museum, which rightly attracts crowds	Hiking in Parc National de la Guadeloupe is worth the effort

PORT	DESCRIPTION	EXCURSIONS
Jamaica: Montego Bay	Bustling city that many cruisers miss; the trendy areas get packed when many ships arrive; dock is 2.5 miles (4km) south of town	Doctor's Cave Beach (walkable from town), exploring downtown Montego, shopping, diving
Jamaica: Ocho Rios	Very sleepy place when cruise ships aren't in port; doesn't get crowded	Dunn's River Falls, Turtle Beach, Blue Hole
Martinique: Fort-de-France	Following a massive cleanup, Fort-de-France is a popular destination & now has two cruise terminals within easy walking distance of the center	Take a ferry from the port to the beaches at Pointe du Bout or explore colonial Fort Louis, which also has its own beach
Nevis: Charlestown	A small, historic & lovely capital; tenders are used to bring passengers to the port in town	Touring the plantation inns, rainforest hiking, beach time
Puerto Rico: Old San Juan	Has the region's best combination of historic, cultural, drinking & shopping spots; gets crowded with cruisers	City tour, Casa Bacardí, El Yunque, snorkeling & diving, horseback riding
St Kitts: Basseterre	Compact, working Caribbean port town interesting for about an hour's wander beyond the non-alluring port shops	Cockleshell Bay, Brimstone Hill Fortress, Mt Liamuiga volcano, St Kitts Scenic Railway
St Lucia: Castries	Has two ports; feel the modern Creole vibe while taking a stroll through the large covered market	Reduit Beach (Rodney Bay), Pigeon Island National Landmark, zip-lining
St-Martin/Sint Maarten: Philipsburg	Has a large duty-free shopping area near the dock on Front St in Philipsburg & boisterous daytime beach bars; gets crowded with cruisers	Catching a cab to remote beaches, island-wide food tours, shopping
St Vincent: Kingstown	Seems little changed in 150 years; the streets teem with locals out shopping for staples while socializing	Visit Dark View Falls or the Montreal Gardens, ferry to beautiful Bequia
Tobago: Scarborough	An interesting small town where you can browse stores & markets – most quite authentic	Pigeon Point Beach, Tobago Forest Reserve, Argyle Falls
Trinidad: Port of Spain	Pulsing city that moves to the beat of beloved local music; port is in the lively & somewhat seedy downtown area	Asa Wright Nature Centre, Caroni Bird Sanctuary, Maracas Bay
Turks & Caicos: Grand Turk	Small Grand Turk has a cruise center with beaches & a range of facilities; port is 3 miles (5km) south of town	Snorkeling & diving trips, wandering charming Cockburn Town, whale-watching (in season)
US Virgin Islands: Charlotte Amalie	An old town filled with new duty-free megastores & good local food; there are two ports, each 1.4 miles (2.3km) from town; it gets crowded with cruisers	Magens Bay beach, strolling downtown Charlotte Amalie, ferry to St John's beaches
US Virgin Islands: Frederiksted	A tiny, uncrowded place that seems empty when no cruise ships are visiting	Cruzan Rum Distillery, Estate Whim Plantation Museum, Christiansted

SUSTAINABLE CRUISING?

Although all travel comes with an environmental cost, by their very size, cruise ships have an outsize effect.

Main Issues

Air pollution According to UK-based Climate Care, a carbon-offsetting company, cruise ships emit more carbon per passenger than airplanes – nearly twice as much – and that's not including the flights that most passengers take to get to their point of departure. Most ships burn low-grade bunker fuel, which contains more sulfur and particulates than higher-quality fuel. The US and Canada are phasing in new regulations to require ships to burn cleaner fuel when they are close to land; however, the industry is fighting this. Small nations in the Caribbean are also being pressured into not adopting these regulations.

Water pollution Cruise ships generate enormous amounts of sewage, solid waste and gray water. While some countries and states have imposed regulations on sewage treatment (with which the cruise lines comply), there's little regulation in the Caribbean. Since 2016, Carnival's subsidiary Princess has been given fines topping $60 million for illegally dumping oil, plastic and other waste in the region.

Cultural impact Although cruise lines generate money for their ports of call, thousands of people arriving at once can change the character of a town and seem overwhelming to locals and noncruising travelers. In Bonaire, for example, 7000 cruisers can arrive in one day – half the country's population.

What You Can Do

If you're planning a cruise, it's worth doing some research. Email the cruise lines and ask them about their environmental policies: wastewater treatment, recycling initiatives and whether they use alternative energy sources. Knowing that customers care about these things has an impact. There are also organizations that review lines and ships on their environmental records. These include the following:

Friends of the Earth (www.foe.org/cruisereportcard) Grades given annually in their Cruise Ship Report Card to cruise lines and ships for environmental and human health impacts.

World Travel Awards (www.worldtravelawards.com) Annual awards for the 'World's Leading Green Cruise Line.'

Accessible Cruises

Many cruise lines make efforts to make their ships and excursions accessible to those with disabilities. For specialist advice, Accessible Caribbean Vacations (www.accessiblecaribbeanvacations.com) has a particular emphasis on cruising, and its website has comprehensive accessibility information for region-wide ports of call and shore excursions.

Theme Cruises

Old TV shows, science fiction, computers, musicians, (very) minor celebrities, soap operas, sports teams, nudism... What these all have in common is that they're all themes for cruises.

Cruise lines sell group space to promoters of theme cruises but typically no theme is enough to fill an entire ship. Rather, a critical mass of people will occupy a block of cabins and have activities day and night just for them, including lectures, autograph sessions, costume balls and performances.

No theme or interest is too obscure or improbable. To find one, simply search your phrase with 'cruise.'

LGBT Cruises

One of the largest segments of special-interest cruises are those aimed at the LGBT+ community. So popular are these cruises that often an entire ship will be devoted to catering for LBGT+

Top: *Oasis of the Seas* departing Nassau, Bahamas (p156)

Bottom: Cruise ships at Philipsburg, Sint Maarten (p712)

RUTH PETERKIN/SHUTTERSTOCK ©

WHAT TO PACK

Clothes and personal items such as toiletries and medications are the important things to pack. Sundries can be bought at high prices on board or at regular prices in ports of call. Don't forget the following:

➡ comfortable, casual cotton wear

➡ comfortable, cool walking shoes for shore excursions

➡ waterproof sandals for around the pool and active shore excursions

➡ khakis, a dress/shirts with collars for evening dining

➡ outfits for cruises with formal nights (men can often rent tuxes in advance through the cruise line).

passengers. Start by checking out the following operators:

Olivia (www.olivia.com) Organizes lesbian-only cruises.

RSVP Vacations (www.rsvpvacations.com) Good for active travelers, RSVP has trips on both large cruise ships and smaller yachts.

Booking a Cruise

There are several options for researching and booking a cruise. A cruise line's own website will offer deals or upgrades not found elsewhere and there are big discounts for booking with them up to a year in advance. Large travel-booking sites often have last-minute discounts.

Cruise Lines

Cruising is huge business and the major players earn billions of dollars a year. Many lines are actually brands owned by one of the two big players: between them, Carnival and Royal Caribbean control 90% of the market in the Caribbean.

There are also nontraditional cruises, where you can feel the wind at your back on large sailing ships equipped with modern technology.

Popular Cruise Lines

The following cruise lines sail large vessels on numerous itineraries in the Caribbean:

Carnival Cruise Lines (www.carnival.com) The largest cruise line in the world. Its enormous ships offer cruising on myriad Caribbean itineraries.

Celebrity Cruises (www.celebritycruises.com) An important brand of Royal Caribbean, it has huge ships that offer a more upscale experience than many other lines.

Costa Cruises (www.costacruises.com) Owned by Carnival, Costa is aimed at European travelers: bigger spas, smaller cabins and better coffee. Ships are huge, similar to Carnival's megaships.

Crystal Cruises (www.crystalcruises.com) Luxury cruise line with ships carrying about 800 passengers – small by modern standards. Attracts affluent, older clients who enjoy a wide range of cultural activities and formal evenings.

Cunard Line (www.cunard.com) Owned by Carnival, Cunard Line operates the huge *Queen Elizabeth*, *Queen Mary II* and *Queen Victoria*. The focus is on 'classic luxury' and the ships have limited Caribbean sailings.

Disney Cruise Line (www.disneycruise.com) Disney's large ships are like floating theme parks, with children's programs and large staterooms that appeal to families.

Holland America (www.hollandamerica.com) Owned by Carnival, Holland America offers a traditional cruising experience, generally for older passengers.

Norwegian Cruise Line (www.ncl.com) Offers 'freestyle cruising' on large cruise ships, which means that dress codes are relaxed and dining options more flexible than on other lines. There are lots of extra-fee dining choices.

Regent Seven Seas Cruises (www.rssc.com) Smaller ships (maximum 750 passengers) with a focus on luxury cabins and excellent food. All shore excursions are included in the price.

Royal Caribbean International (www.royalcaribbean.com) The arch-rival to Carnival has a huge fleet of megaships (some carry over 6000 people), aimed right at the middle of the market. It has itineraries everywhere in the Caribbean all the time and offers lots of activities for kids.

Nontraditional Cruise Lines

Sail Windjammer (www.sailwindjammer.com) Cruises around the Leeward Islands under sail on the three-masted *S/V Mandalay*, a 236ft (72m) sailing yacht built in 1923.

Sea Cloud Cruises (www.seacloud.com) Cruise by tall ship in a fleet that includes *Sea Cloud*, a four-masted, 360ft (110m) windjammer dating from 1931; its modern sibling *Sea Cloud 2;* and three-masted *Sea Cloud Spirit*. On all three, the sails are set by hand. This German-American company operates luxury cruises in the Eastern Caribbean.

Star Clippers (www.starclippers.com) These modern four-masted clipper ships have tall-ship designs and carry 180 passengers. Itineraries take in smaller islands of the Eastern Caribbean.

Windstar Cruises (www.windstarcruises.com) Windstar's luxury four-masted, 440ft (134m) vessels have high-tech, computer-operated sails and carry under 400 passengers. Note that the sails are the main means of propulsion only part of the time.

Costs

The cost of a cruise can vary widely, depending on the season and vacancies. While it will save you money to book early, keep in mind that cruise lines want to sail full, so many will offer excellent last-minute discounts – sometimes as much as 50% off the full fare.

You'll pay less for an inside room deep within the ship, but study the deck plans as the cheapest rooms are often claustrophobic and poorly located. Some packages provide free or discounted airfares to and from the port of embarkation (or will provide a rebate if you make your own transportation arrangements).

Most cruises end up costing US$200 to US$600 per person, per day, including airfare from a major US gateway city. Port charges and government taxes typically add on another US$150 per cruise. Be sure to check the fine print about deposits, cancellation and refund policies, and travel insurance.

Shore Excursions

Numerous guided tours and activities are offered at each port of call, each generally costing US$40 to US$100 or more. These tours are also a major profit earner for the cruise lines so there is great pressure for passengers to join – some reported heavy-handed tactics include people who booked tours with third parties being left behind in port.

Note the following:

- There is no requirement to book tours via the cruise lines.
- By going outside of the cruise line's shore excursions, travelers can set their own itinerary, avoid less-appealing mandatory stops (for shopping) and save money.
- Find activities and tours in advance and book over the web.
- Local drivers waiting at cruise-ship ports offer their services to popular and offbeat sights and activities. Cruise forums are often filled with recommendations of locals with great reputations.

Tipping

Tipping is usually expected and can add 20% or more to your shipboard account. Many lines have gotten around the discretionary nature of tips (which are the primary wages for the crew) by automatically putting them on your bill in the form of 18% to 20% gratuity fees.

Note, however, that there's often no transparency about how much of these 'gratuities' actually reach the crews, many of whom work 12-hour days, seven days a week.

Extras on Board

Alcoholic drinks Usually not included in the price of the cruise; a profit center for the lines.

Activities Spas, adventure sports, classes; the lines are always looking for new things they can sell to passengers.

Meals You can still get free and abundant food but ships now have a range of extra-cost restaurants where for, say, US$20 you can get a steak dinner in an exclusive setting. But even fancy coffees now often come with a fee.

Plan Your Trip

Weddings & Honeymoons

The Caribbean is a world-class destination for love. If you're getting married, you'll join the numerous couples who've exchanged vows in one of these beautiful places. Because the region is so popular for weddings, most hotels and resorts can offer plenty of planning advice, from arranging the event to getting your license.

The Perfect Caribbean Wedding

Caribbean weddings come in all flavors and sizes. Try on these different options while picking out your dress and suit:

Big Adventure

Enjoy one of the Caribbean's off-the-beaten-path locations where you can hike, kayak or dive. These are good choices for couples who want a nontraditional ceremony.

Intimate Luxe

Live large in a small exclusive resort. These can be expensive, so it could limit the number of guests. Luxury boutique resorts will usually handle all details and customize anything according to your needs.

Resort Ball

Group rates at a large resort mean that you can send out invitations far and wide for an event that isn't out of reach. Resorts can be expert in organizing a traditional ceremony and reception.

Wedding Destinations

Intimate

Boutique hotels and resorts can create an intimate setting for the perfect day.

Anguilla One of the Caribbean's poshest islands is bound to offer everything you'd want for an exclusive and expensive event. Go ahead, rent your own villa with a butler.

Antigua and Barbuda A big range of upscale resorts means this is the place for an exquisite event. It's a popular destination for Brits due to good air links and its colonial history. Isolated Barbuda is great for honeymoons.

Barbados A full array of top-end services for any style of wedding; good UK connections make this popular with Brits. The many long-time-open resorts and hotels mean they know just what to do, although the smaller sizes favor more intimate affairs.

St-Barthélemy Excels at small, top-end weddings. Rent a villa with staff for your special day. Also the place to go for a top-end honeymoon.

St Kitts and Nevis Bliss-inducing pampering on Nevis plus the island's own intimate beauty make this a natural choice for a small and special event.

St Lucia A score of small, luxurious boutique hotels in the gorgeous south are ideal, both for the wedding and the honeymoon.

Grand

Go big with a wedding party to remember hosted by a resort that can handle a lot of guests.

Aruba There are plenty of resorts specializing in big weddings. In fact any of the resorts at Palm Beach will easily handle affairs with hundreds of guests. Good air links make access easy.

Cayman Islands There are plenty of resorts that offer good group rates on Seven Mile Beach. Lots of flights make it easy to invite people from all over.

Dominican Republic Big resorts by the dozen mean you have many choices when planning a big event. Try Punta Cana; flights can be cheap, easing the fiscal pain on guests.

Jamaica One of the top Caribbean wedding destinations. Some major resorts offer free ceremonies if you book enough rooms, so invite everyone you know. Negril is especially popular for its romantic sunsets over the sea.

Puerto Rico All those huge resorts right on the beach in San Juan and beyond are perfect for large ceremonies. Americans will find the marriage legalities are extra simple, plus there are lots of good venues for subsidiary events such as rehearsal parties.

St-Martin/Sint Maarten Dutch and French resorts are well versed in hosting fabulous weddings. You can literally choose the kind of accent you want.

Turks and Caicos The large resorts on Grace Bay beach will easily absorb scores of friends and family, yet the scale is not so vast that everyone will get lost. The smaller islands offer complete honeymoon escapes.

US Virgin Islands A good place for Americans wary of red tape or of requiring that all their guests have passports. Large resorts have decades of experience with nuptials, yet you can find tiny, intimate places for the honeymoon.

Adventurous

These islands are great for weddings with a touch of the great outdoors as only the Caribbean can provide.

Bonaire Perfect for outdoor nuptials with a twist: get married at a small waterfront resort, then go diving with the bridal party, or say 'I do' underwater.

British Virgin Islands Tortola is the center of Caribbean yachting; it's great for boat-based weddings or for honeymoons. Get a few of your favorite couples and laze your way through the islands on a chartered yacht.

LGBT-FRIENDLY WEDDING DESTINATIONS

Not all Caribbean islands are created equal when it comes to recognizing marriage for same-sex couples. Homosexuality is still illegal in some countries, including Jamaica and Barbados. Destinations where it's possible to get married and that are known for their LGBT-friendly resorts include the US Virgin Islands, St-Barthélemy, St-Martin/Sint Maarten, Aruba, Bonaire, Saba, Martinique and Guadeloupe.

Grenada Small, secluded lodges with warm hospitality make good choices for smaller events. Choose Anse La Roche for splendid isolation or Calabash Hotel for waterside luxury.

St Vincent and the Grenadines From chartering a yacht to finding an intimate setting on a small island such as Bequia, SVG is good for adding a dash of adventure to your event.

Wedding Paperwork

It is vital that you confirm in advance what you'll need for a marriage license. It varies greatly by country. Get info from the national tourism authority or a resort that specializes in weddings and then double-check it all.

Here are just some of the bureaucratic hoops you may need to bound through:

- original birth certificates
- legal proof of divorce or death of previous spouse
- legal proof of the marriage officiant's status
- a local marriage license (up to US$300 or more in some places)
- blood tests.

There can also be delays in processing: some islands need 48 hours or more to process a license request; others require that you be on the island 48 hours or more in advance of the ceremony.

If the red tape proves too much, you can always have the unofficial ceremony of your dreams in the Caribbean while saving the legal ceremony for your home country.

ROMANCE NEEDS NO EXCUSE

ISLANDS	BEST FOR	DESCRIPTION	RECOMMENDATIONS
Anguilla	Intimate luxe, big adventure	Exclusive and expensive for something exquisite and exotic	Rent your own villa with a butler
Antigua & Barbuda	Intimate luxe, big adventure	A popular destination for Brits thanks to good air links and colonial history	Rendezvous Bay, Antigua; Jumby Bay Resort, Antigua
Aruba	Resort ball	Plenty of resorts specializing in weddings	Any of the resorts at Palm Beach
The Bahamas	Big adventure, intimate luxe, resort ball	Private islands where you can indulge in almost anything	Kamalame Cay, Andros; The Cove, Atlantis, Paradise Island; Harbour Island, Eleuthera
Barbados	Big adventure, intimate luxe, resort ball	A full array of services for any style of wedding; good UK connections make this popular with Brits	Coral Reef Club, Holetown; Crane Beach Hotel, Crane Beach; Eco Lifestyle Lodge, Bathsheba
Bonaire	Big adventure	Perfect for outdoor nuptials with a twist	Get married at a small waterfront resort, then go diving with the bridal party
British Virgin Islands	Big adventure	Tortola is the center of Caribbean yachting; great for boat-based weddings or for honeymoons	Get a few of your favorite couples and laze your way through the islands on a chartered yacht
Cayman Islands	Resort ball	Plenty of resorts that offer good group rates	Seven Mile Beach, Grand Cayman
Cuba	Big adventure	A great adventure; don't count on legally recognized marriage certificates	Postnuptial drive in a classic convertible past clapping throngs on the streets of Havana
Dominica	Big adventure	Great for outdoors activities alongside your ceremony	Secret Bay, Portsmouth; Pagua Bay House, Pagua Bay
Dominican Republic	Big adventure, resort ball	Big resorts or more intimate options.	Resorts at Punta Cana, or Playa Bonita and Playa Coson outside Las Terrenas
Grenada	Big adventure	Small, secluded lodges with warm hospitality	Anse la Roche; Green Roof Inn, Hillsborough

ISLANDS	BEST FOR	DESCRIPTION	RECOMMENDATIONS
Jamaica	Big adventure, intimate luxe, resort ball	One of the top Caribbean wedding destinations. Some major resorts offer free ceremonies if you book enough rooms	Treasure Beach; Negril
Puerto Rico	Big adventure, resort ball, intimate luxe	Large resorts or hidden retreats; marriage legalities simple for Americans	Vieques; Culebra; Isla Culebrita
Saba	Big adventure	An island so small that a wedding party would almost take it over	No beaches but plenty of outdoorsy fun
St-Barthélemy	Intimate luxe	Excels at small, top-end weddings	Rent a villa with staff for your special day
St Kitts & Nevis	Intimate luxe, resort ball	Bliss-inducing pampering on Nevis and a resort vibe on St Kitts	Four Seasons or Golden Rock Inn, Nevis; Belle Mont Farm, St Kitts
St Lucia	Big adventure, intimate luxe	Boutique options with a French accent	Fond Doux Plantation; Ladera; Pink Plantation House, Castries
St-Martin/Sint Maarten	Resort ball	Dutch and French resorts that host fabulous weddings	Get a group together and take over a resort
St Vincent & the Grenadines	Big adventure, intimate luxe	Plenty of accommodations options for groups; also offers top-end luxury hidden away from the paparazzi	Palm Island Resort; Petit St Vincent Resort
Trinidad & Tobago	Big adventure	Relaxed hideaways – a quirky, offbeat option	Tobago's Pigeon Point Beach has a purpose-built wedding gazebo
Turks & Caicos	Intimate luxe	Small resorts and one of the longest and most beautiful beaches in the Caribbean	Parrot Cay; the resorts at Grace Bay
US Virgin Islands	Big adventure, intimate luxe, resort ball	Everything from lavish resorts to secluded eco-escapes	Take your pick of Honeymoon Beaches – one by St Thomas, the other on St John

Plan Your Trip

Budget Caribbean

The Caribbean isn't always the cheapest destination, but there are ways to get the most bang for your buck with a little forward planning and some savvy choices. All islands are not created equal in the budget department – some can be much more affordable than others.

Best Budget Tips

Here are some of the best ways to save money:

Travel in groups Bring your friends along with you and rent a villa.

Book far in advance For high-season deals.

Book at the last minute For incredible deals as hotels dump empty rooms.

Follow the divers They demand great value near beautiful waters.

Ride buses and ferries You meet folks and may have an adventure.

Live like a local Save money while having a more authentic visit.

Travel sustainably It's the right thing to do and it saves you money.

Travel in low season Prices can drop 40% or more.

Great-Value Islands

These islands are least likely to break the bank.

Bonaire Excellent budget choice. Small resorts on the water cater to divers who are value-conscious.

Dominica One of the Caribbean's best bargains: everything is much cheaper than the region's averages, especially lodging and eating; public transportation is comprehensive.

Montserrat Definitely a budget island: great value and high standards, even at guesthouses. Local eateries are cheap and excellent. Limited public transportation; taxis are not too expensive.

Puerto Rico In San Juan there's an abundance of hotels: look for internet deals and good rates for apartment rentals. Culebra and Vieques have fine budget options. Good public transportation.

Saba A tiny island with few accommodations but some nice ones for around US$100.

Sint Eustatius Although choices are few, limited tourism except for value-conscious divers means accommodations are good value, even January to March.

Trinidad Not particularly tourist-oriented, so many good-value options. Inexpensive in comparison to other islands. Public transportation and street food are cheap and good.

Tobago As in Trinidad, there are many good-value options. Crown Point has the majority of places to stay, and competition keeps prices low.

A simple fried fish dish, Dominican Republic (p398)

LIVE LIKE A LOCAL

Take time to meet the locals by doing what they do – you'll enjoy a more affordable and authentic experience. Some simple, common-sense tips:

➡ Eat at lunch wagons or stalls. The local fare is cheap and often incredibly good.

➡ Drop by a local bar – often the de facto community center. Besides a drink, you'll get all sorts of useful – or wonderfully frivolous – advice.

➡ Look for community fish fries or barbecues in the Eastern Caribbean.

Islands for All Budgets

You can spend a lot or, well, less on these islands.

Antigua Expensive island: mostly higher-end resorts; few guesthouses and those are not appealing. Rent an apartment and self-cater. Vacation rentals have become more prevalent – try along the southwest coast near Cades Bay. Public transportation is OK in developed areas but rare to the remote east and southeast.

Aruba The beaches are lined with mostly top-end resorts but Eagle Beach – our favorite – does have some good midrange options. Stay 10 minutes' walk from the beach and you can get a good room with a kitchen for about US$100 a night. Public transportation is excellent.

Barbados The west coast with its old-money resorts and mansions can be pricey, although there are good-value apartments 10 minutes from the beaches; the south is filled with budget and midrange choices close to the sand. Excellent public transportation but eating out can be expensive.

British Virgin Islands Tortola is the secret to budget travel in the BVI. It has a good range of guesthouses and moderate resorts.

Cuba Super-economical private homestays make your money go further among the expensive historic hotels and all-inclusives.

Curaçao Budget accommodations in beautiful Willemstad are often not worth the cheap prices, but some better midrange options are opening. Holiday apartments on north-coast beaches are good value. Public transportation is OK.

Dominican Republic The central highlands are better value than elsewhere; there are uniquely charming midrange guesthouses and boutique hotels in the Península de Samaná and fabulously upscale all-inclusives in Bavaro and Punta Cana. Buses cover the country.

Grenada Budget accommodations are thin on the ground on Grenada island although there are some modest resorts around St George's. Eating out on a budget is fairly good and local buses will get you to most places. On Carriacou, Hillsborough has a few good budget accommodations options.

The Grenadines Some islands are quite expensive (eg Mustique) but others such as Bequia have excellent good-value choices. You can walk where you want to go.

Guadeloupe Good budget and midrange options are available – think US$50 per night – but no hostels. Good buses; ferries to the tiny offshore islands are cheap and fun.

Jamaica Treasure Beach, Port Antonio and Kingston are all good for backpackers, while the resorts on the north coast offer plenty of opportunities for a blowout.

Martinique Budget and cheap midrange options are available throughout the country for around

Hiker looking over Gros Piton, Soufrière, St Lucia (p701)

QUICK GETAWAYS

With competitive airfares from the US and Canada, and resorts offering great deals online, several Caribbean islands are well suited to a quick, affordable getaway. Consider the following:

Montego Bay, Jamaica Famous resort town with a huge range of beachside accommodations.

Old San Juan, Puerto Rico Explore forts and beaches by day; wander lively streets by night.

St-Martin/Sint Maarten The choice of a French frolic or Dutch treat.

US$70 per night. Ferries provide good links but bus services are poor.

St Lucia Consider staying in midrange places such as inns and guesthouses that are not directly on the beach. Travel in low season.

St-Martin/Sint Maarten Post-Irma inventory is still low, and bargains are rare. Try some of the older hotels on the Dutch side or rent an apartment on the French side. For food, pick up groceries at the big supermarkets or stop at *lolos* (local barbecues). Public transportation is unreliable.

St Vincent There are some good modest resorts near Kingstown, which also has a good inn in town. Public transportation just OK.

Turks and Caicos Expensive beachfront resorts; the best value is at diving resorts in Providenciales and Grand Turk.

US Virgin Islands Rates are very seasonal, falling 40% or more outside high season. Resorts tend to be pricey; look for holiday apartments online.

Top-End Islands

These are the posh islands of the Caribbean; still, there are ways even these can fit a budget.

Anguilla One of the most exclusive and expensive islands in the Caribbean; not a budget option.

Cayman Islands Most of the accommodations are on beautiful Seven Mile Beach and are quite expensive. There are more-affordable options off-beach. Public transportation is excellent.

Nevis Stay in Charlestown, which has some reasonably priced eateries. The rest of the island is very expensive but actually good value given the high standards.

St-Barthélemy Prohibitively expensive in high season; other times you might find an affordable villa rental online. Splurge at the luxury restaurants with their €29 'value' meals.

St Kitts Expensive island. Look for online specials at the resorts. Use the decent public transportation and get a room with a kitchen.

Plan Your Trip

Traveling Sustainably

Tourism pays the bills in most of the Caribbean, and the impact on the environment and the culture is huge. Most islands are still putting economic development ahead of the environment because poverty is so widespread, but luckily there are some 'green' trail-blazers worth supporting.

Steps for Sustainability

You can do your part and make a difference. Here are a few pointers for minimizing your impact on the environment.

Turn off the tap Fresh water is an extremely precious commodity on all of the islands, where desalination plants work overtime converting saltwater to fresh. Many islanders depend only on rainwater collected in cisterns. Keep in mind that winter – peak tourism time – is the driest time of year.

Skip bottled water If the water is safe to drink, use it to fill containers so you can skip bottled water and its transport and refuse costs.

Turn off the air-con Rarely is it so hot in the Caribbean that you need air-con at night; turn it off and let the breezes in.

Ride the bus Instead of renting a car, immerse yourself in local culture while you save gas. Islands such as Aruba, Barbados and Grand Cayman have excellent bus networks.

Return the car early Decide if you need a rental car for your entire stay. You might only need it for a day or two of exploration.

Say no to plastic On Barbados and some other islands, stores will ask you if you want a plastic bag rather than just giving you one. Straws are also best avoided because they float around for years.

Sustainable Seafood

Many fish and shellfish species in the Caribbean are at risk due to overfishing. Try to order dishes that use sustainable catches – preferably wild-caught from managed stocks of local fish, rather than imported, farmed fish. Many fish and crustaceans also have a 'closed' season to allow them to breed and maintain stock levels. Don't be afraid to ask questions about where your seafood comes from.

Good Seafood Choices

Barramundi (farm-raised)

Conch (farm-raised)

Lionfish (an invasive species)

Shrimp

Tilapia (farm-raised)

Yellowtail snapper

Mahimahi

Crab

Seafood to Avoid

Atlantic salmon

Conch (wild-caught)

Florida pompano

Grouper

Spiny lobster

Swordfish

Wild turtle

Bathsheba, Barbados (p219)

Go green Look for hotels and resorts that carry an audited green certification.

Ask questions Ask your hotel or tour operator about its green practices. Even if they have none, it'll tell them it matters to customers.

Travel globally, shop locally Not only will buying local products infuse the local economy, it will also help to save you money. Local beer is always fresher than imported.

Avoid coral Don't touch it in the wild and don't buy it in shops or from vendors. Also avoid any souvenirs made of seashell or turtle shell. Buying goods made with any of these only encourages environmental destruction and hunting.

Don't litter You may see locals do it (especially with KFC boxes), but don't do it yourself. Almost everything discarded on land makes its way to the sea, where it can wreak havoc on marine life. Carry your trash off beaches, trails and campsites.

Consider the dolphins Be aware that wild dolphins are often captured to be used in enclosed swim-with-dolphins tourist attractions, a practice that has been condemned by wildlife conservationists.

Eco-Conscious Establishments

Environmental awareness is ever-growing in the Caribbean. Here are some of our favorite green businesses in the region.

Anguilla

Zemi Beach House (p99) Ecofriendly motion-sensor air-con is just one hi-tech hack at this smart resort.

Antigua & Barbuda

Barbuda Cottages (p125) Solar-powered villas on stilts.

Aruba

Bucuti & Tara Beach Resort (p141) The first carbon-neutral resort in North America.

The Bahamas

Small Hope Bay Lodge (p189) This laid-back ecoresort takes a genuine interest in sustainability, composting food and making drinking glasses from old wine bottles.

Barbados

Eco Lifestyle Lodge (p220) Excellent green cred not far from the most natural beach in Barbados.

Bonaire

The entire coast of the island is a marine reserve and conservation is taken seriously.

Captain Don's Habitat (p231) Resort leading the way in local environmental causes.

British Virgin Islands

Ocean Spa BVI (p258) Floating spa built from lumber salvaged from the 2017 hurricanes.

Cayman Islands

Central Caribbean Marine Institute (p290) Recreational divers can participate in the 'Dive on the EDGE' program, identifying and cataloging different species of coral and sea life.

Cuba

El Olivo (p329) You can eat at this farm-to-table restaurant in Viñales, then visit the farm owned by the restaurateur's family.

Curaçao

Ocean Encounters (p364) After undergoing specialized PADI training to become a coral restoration diver, volunteers can help maintain coral nurseries.

Dominica

Cocoa Cottage (p378) A cluster of ecocottages; serves organic meals around communal tables.

Dominican Republic

Tubagua Plantation Eco-Village (☎809-696-6932; www.tubagua.com; El Descanso; dm/s/d US$30/100/135; P 📶) Simple, low-impact wooden cabins on a mountaintop.

Grenada

Maca Bana (p443) Luxury ecovillas scattered along a hillside.

Guadeloupe

Tendacayou Ecolodge & Spa (p472). A green treehouse hideaway in the mountains above Deshaies.

Jamaica

Stush in the Bush (p524) A hillside vegan farm-to-table experience.

Montserrat

Aqua Montserrat (p584) Locally-run outfit taking visitors on adventure tours showing off Montserrat's secret nooks and crannies above and below the water.

Puerto Rico

Hix Island House (p611) This groundbreaking hilltop eco-retreat was the first in the Caribbean to be entirely off the grid.

Saba

Kakona (p629) Pick up items crafted both from indigenous plants and recycled materials by local artists and artisans.

Sint Eustatius

Scubaqua Dive Center (p640) One of the only dive operators permitted in Sint Eustatius National Marine Park.

St-Barthélemy

Shankar Juice (☎0590-87-78-03; www.facebook.com/shankarjuicebar; Passage de la Crémaillère; medium/large €8/10; ⏱8:30am-6pm Mon-Fri, 9am-noon & 3-6pm Sat; 📶) Detox at this green juice bar.

St Kitts & Nevis

St Kitts Eco-Park (Map p670; ☎869-465-8755; Sir Gillies Estate, Sandy Point Town; adult/child US$10/5; ⏱9am-4pm Mon-Sat) This greenhouse and garden complex showcases local flora and also serves as a place to teach young locals about sustainable horticulture and agriculture.

St Lucia

Boucan (p702) Set in a cocoa plantation, this resort prides itself on the contribution it makes to the local community.

St-Martin & Sint-Maarten

Loterie Farm (p720) A must for hikers and foodies, oasis-like Loterie Farm is on the way up Pic Paradis.

Trinidad & Tobago

Grande Riviere Nature Tour Guide Association (p773) Community-run nature and hiking tour operation.

Turks & Caicos

Big Blue Collective (p806) Ecofriendly adventure sports operator that also runs cultural tours and whale-watching in season.

US Virgin Islands

Virgin Islands Campground (p827) Solar-powered and rainwater-fed campsite.

Plan Your Trip
Family Travel

Taking the kids on their first-ever boat ride, building sandcastles, wandering rainforest trails or meeting local children – it's simple adventures like these that make the Caribbean such a great region for families, with islands offering attractions and facilities to cater from tinies to teenagers.

Best Islands for Kids

Aruba Plenty of family-friendly resorts with great beaches and soft waves, with lots of organised activities and water sports.

Barbados Head to the south and west for the best beaches and resorts; the east-coast surf is too powerful for novice swimmers of any age.

Cayman Islands Seven Mile Beach is ideal for families, as it's lined with resorts offering child-friendly activities, and the water is calm.

Puerto Rico An island hosting brilliant resorts, while its old colonial forts and historic parks bring out the inner pirate.

US Virgin Islands The islands offer a mix of kid-friendly beaches, shallow water, minimal waves and water-sports centers, plus a host of old cannon-clad forts.

Children's Highlights

Exciting Critters

Zoo de Martinique (p568) This privately run zoo in an old botanic garden is one of the best in the region.

Maho Bay, St John (p838) Lots of seagrass means lots of enormous sea turtles nibbling close to shore.

Donkey Sanctuary, Aruba (p145) Befriend these former beasts of burden at this child-friendly center.

Bioluminescent Bay, Grand Cayman (p294) Go for an incandescent night snorkel with glow-in-the-dark plankton.

Turtle-watching, Trinidad (p773) Witness hundreds of huge leatherbacks laying eggs on Grande-Rivière beach (March–August).

Amazing Adventures

Antigua Rainforest Zip Line Tours (p116) Make like mini Tarzans and Janes while roaring on a wire through the treetops.

Dunn's River Falls, Jamaica (p523) Popular child-friendly attraction that has you swimming and climbing up a series of beautiful waterfalls.

Tanamá River Adventures, Puerto Rico (☎787-462-4121; www.tanamariveradventures.com; Hwy 111; tours US$59-79) Tubing and rappelling through caves on family-designed tours.

Atlantis submarine (Map p206; ☎436-8929; www.barbados.atlantissubmarines.com; Shallow

KIDS IN THE CARIBBEAN

The following islands all offer something for children. Kids will never want to leave islands rated 1, while those rated 2 have some interesting diversions.

Island	Rating	Description
Antigua & Barbuda	2	Good beaches for playing plus several fun activities: Antigua Rainforest Zip Line Tours, Antigua Donkey Sanctuary
Aruba	1	Large resorts with kids' activities, excellent beaches, mostly calm seas & lots of adventure activities, including water sports
The Bahamas	1	New Providence (Nassau) has active beaches, wildlife parks & the waterparks of Paradise Island, while the Abacos is laid-back, with great snorkeling & easy island-hopping.
Barbados	2	Lots of family-friendly beaches in the south & west & popular surfing lessons for kids, but few large resorts with kids' programs
Bonaire	2	Good for older kids who want to learn how to dive & windsurf, but limited beaches
Cayman Islands	1	Seven Mile Beach is great for families; large resorts have kids' programs; Bio Bay is always a hit, as is spotting sea stars at Starfish Point, snorkeling with sea turtles at Spotts Beach & exploring Crystal Caves.
Dominican Republic	2	The resorts of Punta Cana & Bávaro cater to kids, where they can make friends with other young holidaymakers from around the world.
Jamaica	2	Montego Bay & Ocho Rios have resorts good for families, but some resorts are aimed at adults-only partying. Dunn's River Falls is the stand-out family-friendly attraction.
Puerto Rico	1	Old San Juan has resorts nearby that are good for kids; top attractions include the Museo del Niño de Carolina, amazing forts with pirate history & the Observatorio de Arecibo; Playa Flamenco in Culebra is one of the world's best beaches & has lifeguards.
St Marten/Sint Maarten	2	Many resorts cater to families, plus there are lots of kid-friendly activities, such as zip-lining, hiking & horseback riding.
St-Barthélemy	2	Water sports galore & gourmet children's menus
US Virgin Islands	1	One of the best destinations for kids; highlights are abundant & include resort fun, tourist towns with child-friendly allure on all three islands, lifeguard-patrolled Magens Bay beach, & Maho Bay's sea turtles.

Draught; adult/child US$109/57; ⌚8am-4pm) Enter the world of Captain Nemo, and get close to the reefs and fishes in this submarine adventure.

St Kitts Scenic Railway, St Kitts (p673) This scenic ride around the island in a cheery historic train is perfect for children.

Pirates!

Faro y Parque Histórico de Arecibo, Puerto Rico (Arecibo Lighthouse and Historical Park; ☎787-880-7540; www.arecibolighthouse.com; Rte 655; adult/child US$12/10; ⌚9am-6pm Mon-Fri, 10am-7pm Sat & Sun) Capture young imaginations at this pirate-themed historical amusement park.

Pirates of Nassau museum, Bahamas (p157) Explore a full-scale replica pirate ship at this brilliant interactive museum.

Pirates Week, Grand Cayman Mock pirate invasions and more keep scurvy dogs entertained in this popular festival.

Planning

➡ Changing facilities, cots, high chairs, kids' menus and all the other niceties of family travel are best found at large international resorts. Look for ones with kids clubs and the like.

➡ The larger islands will have complete health facilities. They will also have large supermarkets with diapers, familiar treats from home etc.

Castillo San Felipe del Morro, San Juan, Puerto Rico (p592)

Where to Stay

Resorts offer scores of kid-friendly amenities, but some families prefer staying in simpler places closer to island life. Before booking any lodging, ask for details to assess its appropriateness. For example:

➡ Does it welcome kids or accept them grudgingly?

➡ If it's a resort, what sort of kids' activities does it offer?

➡ Does the room have a DVD player and wi-fi?

➡ Is there a kitchen or at least a refrigerator, so you can avoid the expense of always eating out?

➡ Are there safe places where kids can play?

➡ Even if the beach is nearby, is it across a heavily trafficked street?

➡ Does it provide cribs, change tables and other baby supplies?

➡ Does it offer on-site babysitting?

Staying Safe

To help kids acclimatize to the Caribbean heat, take it easy at first and make sure they drink plenty of water. Children should wear a high-protection sunscreen and cover up whenever they're outside to avoid sunburn and heatstroke.

Bring insect repellent formulated for children and whatever medication you normally use to treat insect bites.

What to Pack

Be prepared for lots of time in the sun and sea. Most lodgings provide beach towels, chairs and umbrellas. You can buy sand pails, snorkel masks and anything else you forget at beach shops in resort areas. Elsewhere you'll need to bring what you want in the diversions department. Bring the following:

➡ snorkel gear (especially masks) that you've tested for leaks and proper fit

➡ water wings and other flotation devices

➡ pails and shovels

➡ sturdy reef shoes

➡ underwater camera

➡ car seat if driving a lot.

Islands at a Glance

The Caribbean is staggeringly diverse. Of course, you'll find great climate and fab beaches across the region, but there are plenty of local characteristics that set each island apart from the next, allowing you zero in on those that best suit you. Whether your interests are history, music, food or diving, there are islands that will meet your travel needs. If your idea of pleasure is a night dancing to local rhythms or simply taking time to smell the flowers, you can find that here too.

Anguilla

Beaches
Food
Water Sports

This scrubby limestone bump may not be as visually striking as its neighbors, but Anguilla's ethereal beaches make up for it. Neon-blue waves crash against powder-white shores where you'll find locals barbecuing succulent local fare.

p90

Antigua & Barbuda

Beaches
History
Activities

Antigua is the place to frolic on the beach, play golf, indulge in a fancy meal or explore Britain's naval history, whereas Barbuda, with its pearly-white beaches, is a remote, unspoiled place where winged creatures outnumber people.

p105

Aruba

Resorts
Beaches
Party

Choose from beachside resorts great and small, from flashy to funky, from high-rise to low-rise. Hit the beaches by day, then hit bars, restaurants and clubs as you would at home if it was warmer.

p134

The Bahamas

Diving
Beaches
Fishing

This watery wonderland, with its 700 islands, hundreds of miles of white sand and innumerable hidden coves, is paradise for beach bums, history buffs, diving enthusiasts, sailors, anglers and, well, pretty much everybody else.

p153

Barbados

Water Sports
Resorts
Dining

From surfing the waves and windsurfing the shallows to snorkeling the reefs, you may never dry off. But if you do, this genteel island's many fine restaurants ensure you'll never have to eat in the same place twice.

p202

Bonaire

Diving
Outdoor Adventure
History

Bonaire is a diver's paradise, with dozens of easily accessible dive sites. The adventure continues above the surface, with kayaking, windsurfing on Lac Bay, miles of mountain-biking trails and a fascinating history to discover.

p228

British Virgin Islands

Sailing
Islands
Beaches

Tortola lets its hair down with sailing, surfing and full-moon parties, while Virgin Gorda offers boulder-studded beaches and yacht havens for billionaires. Jost Van Dyke is the 'barefoot island.'

p244

Cayman Islands

Beach
Diving
Islands

Seven Mile Beach is the most famous and fabulous beach in the Cayman Islands, but these islands are lined with stunning stretches of sand. Underwater, the reef is rich with sealife and dotted with shipwrecks.

p272

Cuba

Music
Architecture
Beaches

Cuba's musical prowess is no secret – the whole archipelago rocks to an eclectic pot of live sounds – and the nation's 50-year political time warp has unwittingly led to benefits such as period architecture and unblemished beaches.

p298

Curaçao

History
Nightlife
Beaches

The Dutch-colonial legacy is hundreds of beautiful old buildings in Willemstad neighborhoods dripping with character. Join the raucous music culture that practices for Carnival year-round or explore the coast and discover a hidden beach.

p357

Dominica

Nature
Adventure
Hiking

With thundering waterfalls, a boiling lake, bushy jungle, hot sulfur springs, secret swimming holes, sprightly rivers, teeming reefs and dramatic coastline, this untamed and mass-tourism-free 'nature island' promises adventure.

p372

Dominican Republic

History
Beaches
Outdoor Adventure

The country's coastline offers windswept conditions for water sports. Roaring rivers and mountain peaks draw active travelers, while Santo Domingo's Zona Colonial transports you back in time.

p398

Grenada

Beaches
Nature
Diving & Snorkeling

White sand, turquoise sea, palm trees and no crowds make Grenada's beaches truly sublime. Go for a rainforest-shaded hike on the island's interior or dive among shipwrecks and the Underwater Sculpture Park just offshore.

p435

Guadeloupe

Hiking
Beaches
Diving

Guadeloupe offers world-class hiking in Basse-Terre, superb beaches with some of the Caribbean's best diving on Grande-Terre, and a selection of remote and virtually pristine islands perfect for the ultimate getaway.

p460

Haiti

History
Art
Adventure

Location of the modern world's only successful slave revolution, Haiti has the richest visual-arts tradition in the Caribbean and its most spectacular fortress. It's also the region's most rugged destination.

p492

Jamaica

Music
Food
Outdoors

Jamaica and music are inseparable, and its cuisine pits spice rub against delicious Jamaican jerk. Raft Black River to find Jamaica's jungly interior or dance all night at a Kingston street party.

p512

Martinique

Beaches
Hiking
Eating

Southern Martinique has great beaches, friendly fishing villages and lots of activities to keep you busy, while the north, with its mountains and botanical gardens, is perfect for hikers and nature lovers.

p555

Montserrat

Volcanoes
Nature
Wildlife

Stand in awe of the damage done by the mean-but-majestic Soufrière Hills Volcano, the key attraction of this tranquil and charming island. Exhilarating diving, birdwatching and nature walks also beckon.

p581

Puerto Rico

Nightlife
History
Nature

Discover tangible history in Old San Juan, lounge on world-class beaches, hike the rainforest, snorkel pristine reefs, feast on farm-to-table fare washed down with a craft beer or creative cocktail and sway to sensuous late-night rhythms.

p590

Saba

Diving
Hiking
Crafts

Dive deep to cavort with sharks in the colorful playground of reefs that encircles doll-house-sized Saba. On land, traverse rainforest, elfin forest and other ecosystems while traipsing to the top of its soaring volcano.

p622

Sint Eustatius

Diving
Hiking
History

Crowned by a lonely volcano and filled with colonial-era architecture, this tiny island was once the world's busiest seaport as cargo passed between Europe and the American colonies.

p638

St-Barthélemy

Beaches
Food
Water Sports

A brilliant tapestry of arid, cactus-clad cliffs and sparkling azure waters sets the scene on this idyllic isle, which lures celebrities and discerning travelers with top-notch fusion cuisine and miles of silky sands.

p650

St Kitts & Nevis

History
Beaches
Heritage

Wander in the footsteps of Nelson, Hamilton and enslaved Africans while exploring these verdant twin islands dotted with historical plantation inns, ringed by beautiful beaches and lorded over by a cloud-fringed (dormant) volcano.

p664

St Lucia

Outdoors
Village Life
Beaches

Take an enticing coastline, add rainforest and mountains, then sprinkle in attractive coastal towns. Next, pepper this island with history and culture, spike it with an array of outdoor activities, and there you have St Lucia.

p688

St-Martin/Sint Maarten

Beaches
Food
Nightlife

St-Martin/Sint Maarten is a kaleidoscope of Caribbean clichés: postcard-worthy beaches, superb local restaurants and roaring bars that spill over every crevice – even right up to the airport's main runway.

p710

St Vincent & the Grenadines

sland-Hopping
Adventure
Beauty

Hike the impossibly green jungles of St Vincent and then set off by slow boat to the beautiful beach-ringed islands of the Grenadines, starting with perfect little Bequia. Take time to explore wonders underwater.

p730

Trinidad & Tobago

Music & Nightlife
Birdwatching
Hiking

Trinidad and Tobago's party mentality leaks into every walk of life, and there's tip-top birdwatching, too. Trinidad's wild Northern Range and Tobago's ancient protected rainforest are laced with trails and swimmable waterfalls.

p756

Turks & Caicos

Diving
Beaches
Wildlife

With some of the whitest beaches, the clearest waters and the most varied marine life in the Caribbean, Turks and Caicos will thrill anyone who likes to spend time in or by the water.

p801

US Virgin Islands

Food
Parks
Diving

St Thomas sets the table with fungi, callaloo (spicy soup) and West Indian fare. St John goes green with hiking, snorkeling and kayaking in Virgin Islands National Park. St Croix offers divers the 'wall' and drinkers the rum factories.

p824

On the Road

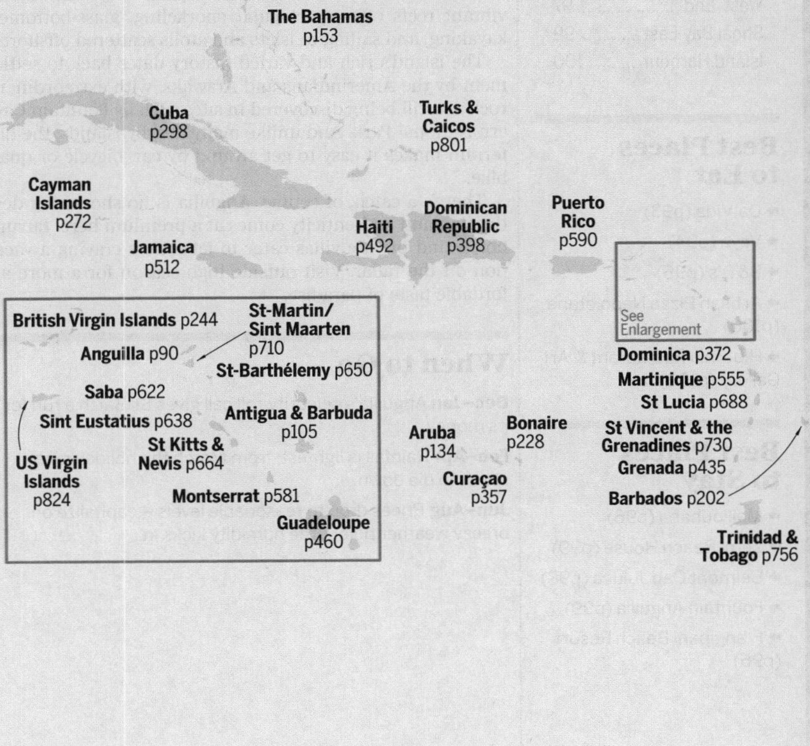

The Bahamas p153
Cuba p298
Turks & Caicos p801
Cayman Islands p272
Jamaica p512
Haiti p492
Dominican Republic p398
Puerto Rico p590
See Enlargement

British Virgin Islands p244
St-Martin/ Sint Maarten p710
Anguilla p90
St-Barthélemy p650
Saba p622
Sint Eustatius p638
Antigua & Barbuda p105
US Virgin Islands p824
St Kitts & Nevis p664
Montserrat p581
Guadeloupe p460

Aruba p134
Bonaire p228
Curaçao p357

Dominica p372
Martinique p555
St Lucia p688
St Vincent & the Grenadines p730
Grenada p435
Barbados p202
Trinidad & Tobago p756

Anguilla

1-264 / POP 16,045

Includes ➡

Best Places to Eat

- ➡ Da'Vida (p93)
- ➡ Veya (p94)
- ➡ B&D's (p96)
- ➡ Artisan Pizza Napoletana (p100)
- ➡ Hibernia Restaurant & Art Gallery (p100)

Best Places to Stay

- ➡ Malliouhana (p96)
- ➡ Zemi Beach House (p99)
- ➡ Belmont Cap Juluca (p98)
- ➡ Fountain Anguilla (p99)
- ➡ Frangipani Beach Resort (p96)

Why Go?

Fringed by shimmering white-sand beaches shaded by coconut palms and sea-grape trees, and filled with colorfully painted, open-sided beach bars serving sizzling barbecues, feisty rum punches and live reggae tunes, Anguilla is the Caribbean dream come true. Its crystal-clear waters and vibrant reefs offer spectacular snorkeling, glass-bottomed kayaking, and sailing to islets and atolls scattered offshore.

The island's rich and varied history dates back to settlement by the Amerindians and Arawaks, with extraordinary rock art still being discovered in sites such as Fountain Cavern National Park. And unlike many nearby islands, the flat terrain makes it easy to get around by car, bicycle or quad bike.

There's a catch, of course. Anguilla is no shoestring destination and authenticity comes at a premium here. Luxury hotels and private villas cater to jet-setters craving a vacation off the radar. Visit outside high season for a more affordable taste of paradise.

When to Go

Dec–Jan Anguilla's celebrity roll call gives St-Barth a run for its money.

Feb–Apr Rainfall is lightest; from March the holiday rush starts to die down.

Jun–Aug Prices drop to reasonable levels – capitalize on breezy weather before the humidity kicks in.

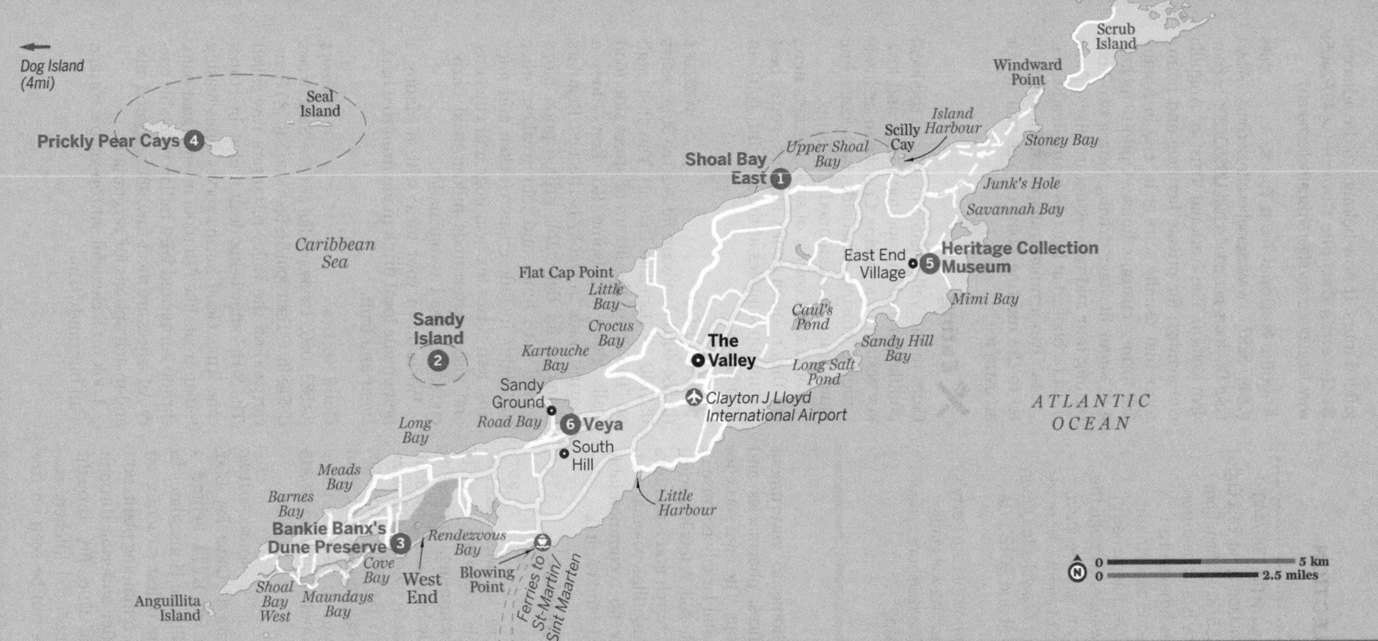

Anguilla Highlights

1 **Shoal Bay East** (p99) Snorkeling, lazing on the sand or hanging out at a beach bar on the island's best beach.

2 **Sandy Island** (p95) Catching a quick shuttle boat for a day of tranquil bliss in a pint-size island paradise.

3 **Bankie Banx's Dune Preserve** (p99) Tapping into Anguilla's music scene at reggae-legend Bankie Banx's beachside Dune Preserve.

4 **Prickly Pear Cays** (p95) Sailing to this super-secluded mini-Anguilla with 360 degrees of flaxen sand and mellow waves.

5 **Heritage Collection Museum** (p92) Learning about the island's fascinating history from the Arawaks onward at Anguilla's only museum.

6 **Veya** (p94) Treating yourself to a gourmet dinner at this top kitchen with soft live music nightly.

WORTH A TRIP

HERITAGE COLLECTION MUSEUM

Anguilla's lone **museum** (☎235-7440; petty@anguillanet.com; Liberty Rd, East End Village; adult/child US$5/3; ⏰10am-5pm Mon-Sat) is curated by island historian Colville Petty who has amassed an astonishing and eclectic assortment of artifacts to chronicle milestones in Anguillan history. A wander through the different rooms lets you experience a well-curated timeline of events, from the settling of the ancient Arawaks to Queen Elizabeth II's 1994 visit and 2018's Calypso King.

Perhaps most memorable are Petty's personal stories, which he will gladly share with visitors. The museum is near the East End Salt Pond.

The Valley

Anguilla's capital is home to government buildings, medical offices, pharmacies and most of the island's shops. The area was chosen as the colonial capital largely because of the abundance of arable soil. A few historical buildings, including a church and a planter's house, are vestiges of Anguilla's colonial past.

There are currently no recommendable lodging options in the island capital.

Sights & Activities

★Little Bay BEACH

Among Anguilla's more secluded beaches, west-facing Little Bay is a sublime sliver of sand with excellent swimming, snorkeling and sunsets. It can only be reached by boat. Drop by **Da'Vida Bayside** (☎498-5433; www.davidaanguilla.com; Crocus Bay Rd, Crocus Bay; ⏰10am-5pm) in Crocus Bay and ask for Calvin or whoever else is around to take you there. The round-trip fare should be around US$15 per person.

Wallblake House HISTORIC BUILDING

(☎497-2944; www.wallblake.ai; Carter Rey Blvd; ⏰tours 10am-noon Tue & Fri) FREE Behind a white picket fence, Wallblake House dates to 1787. It's considered the oldest structure on Anguilla and is the only remaining plantation house on the island after suffering through the French invasion of 1796, fire, drought and hurricanes. The restored kitchen, stables and slave quarters can be seen on free guided tours. It now belongs to the adjacent **St Gerard's Catholic Church** (☎497-2405; www.facebook.com/stgerardscatholicchurch).

Anguilla National Trust Tours TOURS

(☎497-5297; www.axanationaltrust.com; Albert Lake Dr; tours per adult/child US$50/20; ⏰8am-4pm Mon-Fri) The National Trust of Anguilla can arrange for private heritage and nature tours that usually start at its HQ in Anguilla's former customs house. Options include a 2½-hour heritage driving tour, a two-hour birding tour and various nature hikes. Tours must be booked at least 48 hours in advance.

Staff can arrange transport from your hotel to the meeting point or pick you up for an extra fee.

Eating

Cafes in the Valley cater mostly to the local population and include food vans and low-key restaurants serving Caribbean or international cuisine. Roadside barbecues line Landsome Rd, nicknamed 'The Strip'.

There are a couple of supermarkets here, but they're often poorly stocked; you're best picking up supplies at the Best Buy (p97) in Meads Bay.

★Ken's BBQ BARBECUE $

(☎584-4053; Landsome Rd, aka The Strip; dishes US$1-10; ⏰11am-2am Thu-Sat) The first stall on 'The Strip,' the lineup of street-side food stalls along Landsome Rd, Ken's does a roaring trade in smoky barbecues. Regulars swing by for delectable grilled pork chops served with limes and johnnycakes; other highlights include crispy chicken and juicy ribs. Ken raises his own hogs and chickens, and also masterminds mild-to-wild barbecue sauces used as marinades.

Wash down your meal with a Mauby, a homemade local drink made from tree bark, sugar and fruit.

Good Korma INDIAN $

(☎583-7066; Landsome Rd, aka The Strip; mains US$10-16; ⏰11am-3pm & 6-9pm Mon-Sat; 🌶) Reincarnated on the Valley restaurant row called 'The Strip' after being dealt a blow by Hurricane Irma, Good Korma serves sinus-teasing Indian treats like fish tikka masala, goat balti, shrimp korma and West Indian vegetable curry. All sauces are meat-free, offering good mix-and-match options for vegetarians.

Look for a cheerful saffron-yellow cottage with burgundy trim.

Roti Hut CARIBBEAN $
(☎548-2390; www.facebook.com/voilet19; Valley Rd; roti US$7-10, sides US$2-3; ⏰10am-9pm or later) Heavenly aromas waft from this adorable cinnamon-colored cottage with kelly-green trim, which cooks up chicken, beef, goat, shrimp and vegetarian rotis, plus occasional island specials like bull-foot or pig-tail soup. It's popular for takeout but plane-spotters might want to grab a table on its covered deck to keep an eye on the airport landing strip opposite.

Hungry's Good Food CARIBBEAN $
(☎235-8907; www.hungrysgoodfood.com; Carter Rey Blvd, cnr Parliamentary Dr; dishes US$5-18; ⏰noon-10pm Mon-Sat) Their famous food truck is history but chefs Irad and Papi, who have helmed some of Anguilla's top kitchens, still dish up honest-to-goodness fare in their brick-and-mortar lair opposite St Gerard's Church. Regulars swear by their quesadillas, pastas and soups (including bull-foot, conch and lobster-and-corn) but mains like snapper and chips or curried goat give the menu extra bandwidth.

Eat at the bar, or do as locals do and get it as takeout and devour your loot on a beach.

★**Da'Vida** FUSION $$$
(☎498-5433; www.davidaanguilla.com; Crocus Bay Rd, Crocus Bay; mains US$26-50; ⏰5-10pm Tue-Sat; P 📶) A canopied deck with linen-bedecked tables, eye-candy decor and a bar-lounge area with pillow-strewn teak furniture, Da'Vida is an island of sophistication overlooking sensuous Crocus Bay beach. The aroma of stunning Asian-Caribbean creations wafting from the kitchen may include conch carpaccio, green-curry tofu or the signature grilled lobster. Finish with a digestif as the moon rises over the calm water.

Information

Princess Alexandra Hospital (☎497-2551; Queen Elizabeth Ave; ⏰24hr) Princess Alexandra Hospital has a 24-hour emergency room.

Sandy Ground

Sandy Ground sits between the impossibly clear waters of the bay and a shallow salt pond out back, which was commercially harvested until the 1970s. Though sleepy in the daytime, its row of small bars and restaurants along the beach roar into action in the evening, especially on weekends.

Sights & Activities

Sandy Ground BEACH
(Sandy Ground Rd) Fronting bobbing yachts and a couple of small piers, this golden-sand beach is calm, shallow and free from coral, making it a good spot to splash about. Snorkeling is best at the rocky northern end – keep an eye out for sea turtles; Scuba Shack rents gear. The beach bars and restaurants here draw plenty of punters, especially on weekends, when live bands often play.

The boat tender for sweet little Sandy Island launches off this beach.

Scuba Shack DIVING
(Shoal Bay Scuba; ☎235-1482; www.scubashackaxa.com; 2-tank boat dive US$100, with full gear US$130; ⏰8am-5pm Mon-Sat) This PADI-affiliated diving operation has high-quality equipment, good boats and professional dive masters familiar with every underwater crack and crevice and can take you out to seven wrecks and over 30 reefs. An introductory dive course costs US$150; PADI open water certification starts from US$445. Snorkeling equipment rents from US$20.

Sleeping

Sea View Apartments APARTMENT $
(☎497-2427; www.inns.ai/seaview; Sandy Ground Rd; 1-/2-bedroom apt US$87/170; P 📶) A hop, skip and jump from the beach, bars and restaurants, these one- and two-bedroom apartments make a fine, if old-school, base. Each has a kitchen, cable TV and ceiling fan. A cleaner swings by regularly. You'll be downstairs from a local family who can help arrange diving and sightseeing adventures.

La Vue Boutique Inn INN $$
(☎497-3000; www.lavueanguilla.com; Back St, South Hill; 1-/2-bedroom ste from US$200/300; ⏰reception 8am-6pm Mon-Sat & by appointment; P ❄ 📶 🏊) It's well worth spending the extra money for an ocean-facing unit to enjoy lavish views of Sandy Ground Bay from your balcony, perhaps while enjoying a drink or snack prepared in your kitchen or kitchenette. Units in this family-run hotel have modern if minimal decor, king-size beds and sleep up to six people.

Ambia Villa VILLA $$$
(☎498-2741; www.ambiavilla.com; South Hill Rd; 2-bedroom villa US$550; P ❄ 📶 🏊) On a scrubby hillside, this Zen-like villa flanked by smooth wooden balusters and bursts

of bamboo sleeps up to eight people. It's only rented in its entirety, so privacy is guaranteed. Asian-inspired rooms incorporate shoji screens and offer views of Sandy Ground's distant moorings. Amenities include a gas barbecue, beautiful pool, and washing machine and dryer. Four-day minimum rental.

Eating

Village Bakehouse BAKERY $

(☎498-5050; www.facebook.com/pg/villagebakehouseanguilla; Rendezvous Bay Rd; treats US$2-8, breakfast US$6-17, roti US$7.50-13; ⏰7am-2:30pm Wed-Fri, to 1pm Sat, to noon Sun; P) In a contemporary whitewashed building next to a wine shop, this French bakery is the place to stop for baguettes, croissants and pains au chocolat, artistic cakes and other mouthwatering carb-bombs. Also has cooked breakfast, sandwiches, charcuterie (cold meat) platters and roti.

E's Oven CARIBBEAN $$

(☎498-8258; www.facebook.com/esoven; South Hill Rd, South Hill; mains US$14-28; ⏰11:30am-10:30pm Wed-Mon Nov-Aug; P 📶) Named in honor of owner-chef Vernon Hughes' late mom, this charismatic cottage is a sure bet for Caribbean specialties at competitive prices. Insiders phone ahead to call dibs on the famous oven-roasted chicken, but when that's gone, coconut-encrusted grouper with banana-rum sauce, curried goat or Creole conch are tasty alternatives – and best enjoyed with an E's Smile (rum punch).

All mains come with a choice of rice or mash and veggies or plantains.

SandBar INTERNATIONAL $$

(☎498-0171; www.facebook.com/sandbaranguilla; tapas US$9-15; ⏰5:30-9:30pm Mon-Sat; P 📶) Presided over by California transplants Darren and Alicia, this chic yet laid-back beachside lair offers exquisite tapas and an inspired cocktail menu. Kick off at sunset sipping its signature SandBar, a frozen rum punch whipped through a frozen yogurt machine, before picking your fave small plates, ranging from garlic shrimp and pulled-pork sliders to some of the islands's best fries.

Happy hour runs from 4:30pm to 6:30pm.

Tasty's Restaurant CARIBBEAN $$

(☎584-2737; www.facebook.com/tastysrestauranttanguilla; South Hill Rd, South Hill; mains US$18-45; ⏰5-9:30pm; P 📶) Chef Dale Carty puts an upscale spin on Caribbean classics amid a cheerful setting of shells and tropical paraphernalia. Standout dishes include coconut-encrusted fish with spicy banana-rum sauce, conch fritters and sautéed shrimp in coconut-curry sauce. Look for the cute cottage drenched in lilac and turquoise.

Don't miss the Grand Marnier French toast at Sunday brunch (US$24).

Roy's Bayside Grill INTERNATIONAL $$

(☎584-2390; www.roysbaysidegrill.com; Sandy Ground; mains US$12-37; ⏰10am-9pm, bar to late; 📶) This easygoing seaside shack packs plenty of culinary joy onto its plates. You can't go wrong with England-born Roy's lightly battered fish-and-chips, although the build-your-own burgers, Angus steaks and lobster pasta are equally tasty standard bearers. The most rollicking time to drop by is happy hour on Fridays and live music on Sundays.

★**Veya** FUSION $$$

(☎498-8392; www.veya-axa.com; off Sir Emile Gumbs Dr; mains US$30-60; ⏰6:30-10pm Mon-Sat Nov-May, Mon-Fri Jun-Oct) The food-obsessed on Anguilla name Veya among their favorite restaurants. Hidden amid tropical gardens with a koi pond and waterfalls, the rambling upstairs lair exudes an ambience that feels both mysterious and sophisticated. The perky Caribbean-Asian fare (jerk-spiced tuna, lobster with passion-fruit sauce) dutifully follows suit while mellow live jazz or blues is piped in from the stage below.

Its casual Moroccan-inspired sibling Meze, with tapas, craft cocktails and live music, is downstairs.

Drinking & Nightlife

★**Johnno's** BAR

(☎497-2728; www.facebook.com/johnnosbeachstop; ⏰11am-midnight Tue-Sun; 📶) No shirt and no shoes still gets you service at this funky been-here-forever (since the '80s!) beach shack where Johnno's 'famous rum punch,' piña coladas, fresh-fruit daiquiris and classic cocktails flow freely. Live jazz and reggae bands usually kick into gear from 8pm to midnight Thursday to Saturday and from 1pm to 4pm Sunday.

Beach-bar fare (mains US$15 to US$35) includes the signature steamed whole snapper.

Meze COCKTAIL BAR

(☎498-8392; www.meze-axa.com; off Sir Emile Gumbs Dr; ⏰6-11pm Mon-Sat) Heed the call of the casbah in this Moroccan-themed tent, with sultry lighting and cushion-strewn sofas, to munch on Mediterranean tapas (US$5 to US$22) and sip artisan cocktails, including the bourbon-rye-cherry potion named 'Prince of Darkness' after local reggae icon Bankie Banx. There's live jazz, reggae and blues from 8pm to 10pm, often featuring Bankie's son Omari.

Elvis' Beach Bar BAR

(www.elvisbeachbar.org; Sandy Ground Rd; 11am-1am or later Tue-Sat, to midnight Sun, closed Tue Sep & Oct;) The beer is ice-cold, the margaritas are strong and the rum punch is laced with amaretto at Elvis' salty beach bar, which also has a feisty menu of Mexican food (dishes US$10 to US$35). Hang out at the 16ft-boat-turned-bar or rock out to DJs or live bands during high-octane beach parties that often stretch into the wee hours.

Beach chairs are free if you order food.

Shopping

SeaSpray Boutique & Ice & Easy Smoothies ARTS & CRAFTS

(South Hill Roundabout, South Hill; 10am-5pm Mon-Sat;) Ice-cream-colored shades of pink, yellow and blue adorn the facade of this adorable shop, where artist Pamela Miller sells reasonably priced handmade jewelry, handicrafts, Christmas ornaments, pottery and local music as well as art, including her own works, which you'll often see her crafting on the porch. Her attached smoothie bar is a great stop for fresh-fruit concoctions.

Blowing Point

If you're coming to Anguilla by ferry, Blowing Point is the first community you encounter. Since there's just a smattering of shops and services, you'll likely be blowing through Blowing Point.

Tours

Freedom Rentals & Tours ADVENTURE SPORTS

(498-2830; www.freedomrentalsaxa.com; Blowing Point Village; per day incl temporary drivers' license US$100; 9am-5pm Mon-Sat) For an intrepid exploration of the island, rent an ATV quad bike accommodating one or two people, or sign up for a two-hour guided off-road tour taking in historic and cultural sights (US$180). ATVs can also be delivered for an extra US$30.

Sleeping & Eating

Ferryboat Inn APARTMENT $$

(497-6613; www.ferryboatinn.ai; Cul De Sac Dr; apt US$286; P) Owners Marjorie and Christian quickly make strangers feel like

WORTH A TRIP

SANDY ISLAND & PRICKLY PEAR CAYS

A trip to tiny solar-powered **Sandy Island** (476-4104; www.mysandyisland.com; shuttle boat return US$10; shuttle boat 10am-4pm Nov-Jul) is the quintessential Anguilla dream experience. Picture a pure white-sand beach fringed by palm trees, with translucent waters for snorkeling amid the turtle- and grouper-filled coral. The on-site restaurant runs hourly boat shuttles from the second pier in Sandy Ground (p93) and cooks up delicious barbecued lobster, chicken, ribs and other tasties. The bar serves island-inspired cocktails including potent JoJo rum punch. Buy tickets at the office in Sandy Ground (reservations requested but not necessary).

The ride is about 10 minutes but the captain often slows down the boat in the bay to point out sea turtles coming up for air. Food is only served from noon to 3pm, so it's best to order as soon as you get to the island since it takes the tiny crew a while to cook. Staff also rents sun loungers (US$5 with lunch, US$10 without) but no snorkeling gear. If needed, pick some up at Scuba Shack in Sandy Ground.

Perhaps topping even Anguilla's tiara of beaches, the twin island of **Prickly Pear Cays** (www.pricklypearanguilla.com; shuttle round-trip adult/child under 12yr US$40/20; boat shuttle 11am & 12:30pm, restaurant 11am-4pm Tue-Sun Nov-Jul), some 6 miles (10km) northwest of Sandy Ground, seduces with its pristine white-sand beach and some of the region's best snorkeling and diving. On land, a restaurant-bar feeds hungry tummies with grilled foods, salads and sandwiches (mains US$18 to US$50) and also rents beach chairs, umbrellas, kayaks, SUP and snorkeling gear. A shuttle operated by **Calypso Charters** (584-8504; www.calypsochartersanguilla.com) leaves Sandy Ground at 11am and 12:30pm, returning at 2pm and 4pm.

family at this inn steps from the ferry pier. Nicknamed 'FBI,' the Ferryboat Inn's quaint apartment-style rooms with basic kitchens look out over the jagged volcanic peaks of St-Martin/Sint Maarten nearby. Views of the water are partially obscured by the four-person beach house (US$375), the in-house restaurant and its parking lot.

Rates include all taxes and fees.

Ferryboat Inn Restaurant INTERNATIONAL $$
(☎497-6613; www.ferryboatinn.ai; Cul De Sac Dr; mains US$20-40; ⊙noon-3pm & 6:30-9:30pm Mon-Sat;) Next to the eponymous hotel, this waterfront restaurant has uninterrupted views across to mountainous St-Martin/Sint Maarten. It does dependable salads, burgers, fish and steaks but truly shines on Wednesdays when the community comes to gobble up US$1 wings on 'Wings Night.' Monday's 'Burger Night' stars changing patty-and-bun combos, including KFC (Korean Fried Chicken) and blackened *mahimahi*.

Meads Bay

Meads Bay's majestic beach gets busy around the big resorts but has plenty of quiet spots further east to unwind.

Sights

★Meads Bay BEACH
(John Hodge Rd) This long majestic white-sand beach exudes sultry languor and is a lovely spot to swim or take a sunset stroll. It's bookended by the Four Seasons and Malliouhana luxury hotels and also home to great restaurants like Blanchard's and Straw Hat.

Sleeping

★Malliouhana LUXURY HOTEL $$$
(☎USA 844-229-9004, USA toll-free 877-733-3611; www.aubergeresorts.com/malliouhana; John Hodge Rd; d incl breakfast from US$900;) On a low cliff at the eastern end of Meads Bay, iconic Malliouhana is a class act from the grand, art-filled lobby to each of the 44 stately suites whose yellow-turquoise palette echoes the colors of sun and sea. In between are two serene pools, including a spectacular two-tiered infinity pool, an open-air restaurant, gym, spa and children's playground.

Originally built in 1984 and renovated twice since, Malliouhana's 25 acres of Mediterranean-style architecture and fragrant frangipani- and bougainvillea-filled gardens are within strolling distance of three white-sand beaches. In the afternoon, complimentary tea and infused rum are served in the lobby.

Meads Bay Beach Villas VILLA $$$
(☎476-1469; www.meadsbaybeachvillas.com; John Hodge Rd; villas from US$550;) Each of this quartet of unrelentingly pretty and posh villas has two bedrooms, full kitchen, a spacious living area, wooden cathedral ceilings, West Indian tiling and private pool. There's enough privacy to make them a favorite with honeymooners, though anyone with enough cash will feel like they've found their own pocket of paradise.

Frangipani Beach Resort HOTEL $$$
(☎497-6442; www.frangipaniresort.com; John Hodge Rd; d/ste incl breakfast from US$450/995;) With its pale-pink-painted exterior, red-tile roofs and Juliet balconies, this 19-suite boutique resort evokes an Italian palazzo-by-the-sea. Rooms, though, have Caribbean flair, with wicker furniture, tiled floors and colorful art. Even the cheapest rooms facing the gravel car park have cool 'cave showers' with massage jets. Rates include all water sports (SUP, wakeboarding and snorkeling).

It's home to the popular Straw Hat restaurant.

If money's no object, ask about the private four-bedroom beachfront villa with private pool, personal chef and butler service (from US$6000 per week). Eco-kudos for the solar paneling next to the car park.

Carimar Beach Club APARTMENT $$$
(☎497-6881, USA 866-270-3764; www.carimar.com; John Hodge Rd; 1-/2-bedroom apt from US$470/620; ⊙mid-Oct–Aug;) The six two-story Spanish-style haciendas with bougainvillea-draped balconies flank a tropical garden that spills into the powdery white beach. Each of the 24 units has different decor but all come with modern kitchen and dining area. Only the beachfront villas are fully air-conditioned. Extras include private tennis courts, free bicycles and snorkeling gear, and a laundry room. The priciest suites open directly onto the beach.

Eating & Drinking

★B&D's BARBECUE $
(John Hodge Rd, Long Bay Village; mains US$9-22, lobster US$30; ⊙6-9pm Fri, from noon Sat) An Anguilla institution, this family-run roadside barbecue next to chef Bernice's private home dishes up heaping platters of chicken,

ribs, fish and lobster accompanied by sides such as rice, pasta salad, fries or coleslaw to a cult following of islanders and clued-in visitors seated on lawn chairs under an open tent. The johnnycakes are the biggest and flakiest around.

Blanchard's Beach Shack INTERNATIONAL $
(☎498-6100; www.blanchardsrestaurant.com; John Hodge Rd; dishes US$7-18; ⏰11:30am-8:30pm Mon-Sat; 📶👶) 🍃 Along a flowery garden path, this charismatic barefoot beach bar is an island budget favorite. Wriggle your toes in the sand while devouring satisfying snacks from tacos, burgers and salads to sandwiches, bowls and hot dogs, all made to order with local, organic produce. Only compostible plates, cups and cutlery are used.

Rum punch aside, the bar serves sangria, piña coladas and mojitos, as well as fresh fruit smoothies and ice-cold milkshakes. There's also a small kids' menu. Blanchard's restaurant next door serves grown-up dinners (small plates US$7 to US$18, mains US$36 to US$62) amid romantic ambience after 6:30pm.

Best Buy Supermarket SUPERMARKET $
(☎497-4444; Albert Hughes Dr; ⏰7:30am-9pm Mon-Fri, 8am-10pm Sat, to 9pm Sun) If you're self-catering, you absolutely need to know about this supermarket, which is the best stocked on the island (you'll often see Anguilla's top chefs shopping here), with fresh meats, fruits, vegetables, premade meals and salads, and artisan bread from its own ovens, along with homewares and drugstore and pharmacy items.

Ocean Echo INTERNATIONAL
(☎498-5454; www.oceanechoanguilla.com; John Hodge Rd; mains US$15-50; ⏰11am-10pm; 📶👶) Don't be fooled by the casual look – the menu at Ocean Echo is ambitious and laced with international influences. In the daytime, take a break from the sun lounger to feast on lobster salad or sip their signature 'rumzie.' Prime time is on Sunday afternoons when a lively band makes the cross-cultural crowd dance off those calories.

Straw Hat INTERNATIONAL $$$
(☎497-8300; www.strawhat.com; John Hodge Rd, Frangipani Beach Resort; mains lunch US$14-35, dinner US$27-37, lobster US$51; ⏰7-11am, noon-3pm & 6-9pm; P📶👶) This breezy charmer pairs a feet-in-the-sand atmosphere with high-end cooking. Straw hats filled with homemade bread precede sophisticated evening meals such as grilled lobster or crayfish; lunch is a more casual affair (pastrami Reuben sandwiches, seafood pasta, conch fritters). Good kids' menus, too.

> **ANGUILLA FESTIVALS**
>
> **Moonsplash** (Dune Preserve, Rende[...] Bay; ⏰Mar) Anguilla reggae icon Ba[...] Banx invites his old reggae friends along with emerging artists to the Dune Preserve (p99) under the first full moon before Easter for jamming until late into the night. Guests have included Third World, the Wailers, and Toots and the Maytals.
>
> **Anguilla Summer Festival** (www.anguillasummerfestival.com; ⏰late Jul-early Aug) Anguilla's Carnival is its main festival. The 10-day celebration starts on the weekend preceding August Monday (the first Monday in August) and continues until the following weekend. High-spirited events include traditional boat racing, costumed parades, a beauty pageant and calypso competitions with continuous music and dancing.
>
> **Livin in the Sun** (www.facebook.com/litsfestival; ⏰late Nov) Some of the hottest DJs from around the planet hit the decks at locations across Anguilla and out on Sandy Island during this three-day beat-filled festival.

West End

Stunning beaches at Anguilla's rugged west end include Rendezvous Bay, which is home to the island's only golf course. On undeveloped Cove Bay you can canter along the sands on horseback. Further along, Shoal Bay West has fabulous snorkeling and nearby dive sites, while sublime Maundays Bay is almost entirely taken up by a ritzy resort.

👁 Sights

Rendezvous Bay BEACH
(Willow Lane) Cradled by calm, crystal-clear waters, this pearly white crescent is idyllic for an extended stroll with a rum-punch stop or live music at Bankie Banx's Dune Preserve. The sprawling CuisinArt Resort and its golf course dominate the western end of the bay. There are several restaurants

…re although, for local flair, drop by Sunshine Shack.

Shoal Bay West BEACH
(end of Rupert Carty Dr) The island road ends at this divine and often deserted south-facing sweep of white powdery sand with views of St-Martin/Sint Maarten and great sunsets. There's some good offshore snorkeling but no gear rental places, so bring some with you.

Cove Bay BEACH
(Anderson Fleming Dr) Sea grapes hem in this fairly narrow sliver of sand along Cove Bay, a refreshingly undeveloped beach that's great for whiling away an afternoon in tranquility, at least if you keep your distance from the inflatable water park at the east end. The water is quite shallow and usually calm. Nearby Seaside Stables offers horseback rides along the beach.

Activities

Anguilla Aqua Park WATER PARK
(☎584-1204; www.anguillawatersports.com; off Anderson Fleming Dr, Cove Bay; half/full day US$40/50; ⊙10am-6pm Nov-Sep) Kids adore splashing around on this interconnected island of trampolines, slides and climbing structures. Floating on Cove Bay's warm, clear waters, it sports Anguilla's national colors (orange, white and sky-blue) and is monitored by lifeguards. Anguilla's only kitesurfing academy is here (lessons from US$150 per hour), plus SUP rentals (US$80/100 per three hours/day) and glass-bottomed kayak rentals (per day US$120). It also runs 1½-hour SUP/kayak tours (US$125).

Seaside Stables HORSEBACK RIDING
(☎235-3667; www.seasidestablesanguilla.com; Paradise Dr, Cove Bay; 30min/1hr private beach ride US$75/125, minimum 2 people; ⊙by appointment) Seaside Stables offers horseback rides along the beach that have you and you horse cooling off together in the sea – an exhilarating experience. Kids' pony rides cost US$50 per 30 minutes.

Sleeping

The poshest part of the island is largely the domain of upscale resorts and frill-packed villas.

Anguilla Great House Beach Resort HOTEL $
(☎497-6061, USA 800-583-9247; www.anguillagreathouse.com; Willow Lane, Rendezvous Bay; d from US$310; P❄📶≋) Dwarfed by vast surrounding resort properties, this venerable cluster of West Indian–style cottages has been lovingly restored after suffering severe Hurricane Irma damage. Rooms offer plenty of elbow room, quality furniture, a sunny color scheme and the gamut of mod-cons, including a fridge.

It's right on glorious Rendezvous Bay beach and a stroll from cool hangouts such as Bankie Banx's Dune Preserve and Sunshine Shack.

Paradise Cove Resort HOTEL $$
(☎497-6603; www.paradisecoveanguilla.com; Paradise Dr, Cove Bay; ste from US$232; P❄📶≋) Set amid flowering gardens anchored by a vast pool, Paradise Cove is a comfy, well-priced enclave of spacious rooms with private terraces located some 500m from Cove Beach. Rooms have traditional furnishings that capture the island's easygoing magic. On request, the super-friendly proprietor Sherille will happily have your in-room kitchenette stocked prior to arrival.

Anguilla's best supermarket, Best Buy, is nearby.

★ **Belmond Cap Juluca** LUXURY HOTEL $$$
(☎497-6666, USA 800-183-0781; www.capjuluca.com; off Samuel Fleming Rd, Maundays Bay; d incl breakfast from US$1100; ⊙Nov-Aug; P❄📶≋) With its domed Moroccan villas and three on-site restaurants stretching along a white sandy arc, Belmont Cap Juluca is easily one of Anguilla's most seductive, exclusive resorts. Each suite has direct access to the sand and comes with four-poster bed, seagrass armoire and bathroom entirely clad in marble; some have private pool and full kitchen.

CuisinArt Golf Resort & Spa RESORT $$$
(☎498-2000; www.cuisinartresort.com; Sisal Rd, Rendezvous Bay; ste from US$1100; P❄📶≋) This top-notch whitewashed golf resort is again sitting pretty on a divine stretch of beach after undergoing an involuntary makeover following merciless Hurricane Irma. It's back with giant suites sporting a breezy-cool aesthetic, all mod-cons plus unexpected features like outdoor showers, detangling brushes and mosquito repellent. Three restaurants compete for your attention, and the spa is the island's best.

Resort guests get heavily discounted rates at the **golf club** (☎498-5602; 9/18 holes US$225/299, club rental from US$50).

Eating & Drinking

High-end restaurants are located in the resorts, with more casual cafes dotted along the beaches.

Sunshine Shack BARBECUE **$$**
(476-0649; www.sunshineshack.net; Rendezvous Bay; mains US$17-45; 10:30am-5:30pm Wed-Mon; P) Live up, love it, live on! is the motto of this ultrafunky sandy chill zone decorated with old license plates and fronted by a flotilla of beach umbrellas in Rasta red, yellow and green. Chicken, ribs, snapper and lobster get a workout on the barbecue before being served on plastic plates. Beware Garvey's wicked rum punch. Live music on Sunday.

Picante MEXICAN **$$**
(498-1616; www.picante-restaurant-anguilla.com; Albert Hughes Dr; mains US$14-23; 6:30-9pm Mon-Sat Nov–mid-Aug; P) In a romantically lit, open-air, tin-roofed space, this longstanding spot run by a Californian couple turns out sophisticated Mexican fare: chipotle shrimp burritos, chili-crusted tuna tacos and lime-marinated steak quesadillas. The house margarita, by the glass or pitcher, is a must.

★**Bankie Banx's Dune Preserve** BAR
(729-4215; www.bankiebanx.net/dunepreserve; Botanic Rd, Rendezvous Bay; 11:30am-11:30pm Thu-Tue, hours may vary) Legendary reggae star Bankie Banx transformed huge piles of driftwood and old boats into what's essentially a giant tree house on the beach. Phenomenal live music plays regularly; with luck, you'll catch Bankie or his musician/cricketer son Omari Banks performing. After knocking back a signature Dune Shine (ginger, pineapple juice, white rum and bitters), you'll never want to leave.

Bankie has jammed and limed in this Rendezvous Bay spot for decades, founding Moonsplash, one of the Caribbean's top music festivals, in 1991.

Shopping

Cheddie's Carving Studio ARTS & CRAFTS
(497-6027; cheddie@anguillanet.com; Albert Hughes Dr; 8:30am-4:30pm Mon-Fri, 9:30am-3pm Sat) Drop by the studio of local artist Cheddie Richardson to watch him carve driftwood into masterful sculptures. You'll find him near the Sol gas station but do call ahead to confirm he's around.

Shoal Bay East

A quintessential Caribbean stretch of white sand, glorious Shoal Bay East is a 2-mile-long beach with swaying coconut palms and sea-grape trees, reefs ideal for snorkeling and luminous turquoise water.

Sights

★**Shoal Bay East** BEACH
Idyllic Shoal Bay East – a shimmering stretch of brilliant pinkish-white sand strewn with tiny crushed shells – is still miraculously blight-free. There's a handful of small-scale resorts and villas as well as a string of laid-back beach bars along the sand, but it's surprisingly quiet, even in high season. Bring your snorkeling gear (or rent some on-site), as the glassy turquoise waters are perfect for underwater observation.

Sleeping

Fountain Anguilla APARTMENT **$$**
(US 615-216-5600, US 866-376-7077; www.fountainanguilla.com; off Brimegin Dr; studio from US$225, 1-/2-bedroom apt from US$275/395; P) Stylishly designed studios and one- and two-bedroom apartments at this welcoming, well-kept complex have oversized bathrooms with rain showers, cable TV and kitchens kitted out with everything you need to whip up a gourmet meal. The best have private terraces overlooking Shoal Bay East beach a 100m stroll away; garden apartments fan around the landscaped pool.

★**Zemi Beach House** RESORT **$$$**
(584-0001; www.zemibeach.com; Brimegin Dr; d/ste from US$795/2650; P) Tiptoeing between hip and haute, this contemporary property overlooks a swoon-worthy beach and has two infinity pools, restaurants and even a bar specializing in premium rums. Special kudos for the many thoughtful touches, including the ecofriendly motion-sensor air-con, the svelte Frette linens and the personalized minibar. The kids' club keeps youngsters entertained.

Serenity Cottages HOTEL **$$$**
(497-3328; www.serenity.ai; Bay View Rd; studio US$350, 1-/2-bedroom apt US$450/550;

(P❄📶🏊) This cluster of cottages dotted amid bougainvillea and coconut palms is a tranquil retreat. Well-kept units exude homey flair thanks to mahogany and rattan furniture, heavy drapes and floral sofas. All have kitchenette and balcony. The hotel beach is a little cove with a nifty beach bar. Grand Shoal Bay East is about 400m away at low tide (1km by road).

Eating & Drinking

Beach bars serving food – from smoky barbecue fare to Caribbean staples such as fish soup as well as burgers and sandwiches – scatter along the length of the beach. High-end hotels here also have excellent restaurants open to the public.

★Gwen's Reggae Bar & Grill BARBECUE $$
(Brimegin Rd, Lower Shoal Bay East; mains US$12-30; ⏲10am-5pm Mon-Sat, to 7pm Sun; 📶) After the sand was washed away from under her original place, the 'new' Gwen's is as vibrant as ever and one of Anguillas's most beloved beach bars. Order at the bar, then salivate as Gwen chargrills fish, chicken, ribs and lobster. It's jumping on Sundays when Anguilla's famous Scratch Band performs reggae favorites and *super*-strong rum punch fuels barefoot dancing.

Uncle Ernie's CARIBBEAN $$
(☎497-3907; www.uncleerniesbeachbar.com; Shoal Bay East beach; dishes US$8-22; ⏲10am-6pm) After splashing in Shoal Bay East's translucent water, refuel on casual fare at this beach shack, founded in 1984 by the late Ernie and now run by his daughters. The no-nonsense menu includes mostly barbecued chicken and ribs, burgers and local fish but may have such specials as lobster or conch stew. Beers and cocktails are decently priced. Cash only.

★Rhum Room BAR
(☎584-0001; www.zemibeach.com; Zemi Beach House; rum from US$30, flights US$100) Dedicated rum lovers should not skip this sophisticated bar wallowing in clubby coziness thanks to dark wood and heavy chairs draped in brown leather and blue velvet. Ask the rummelier (yes, there is such a thing) to find your match from among the 100 or so small-batch single-estate rums or embark on a rum flight featuring five premium pours.

Island Harbour

Anguilla's quiet eastern seascape is a narrowing strip of breezy coves dotted by casbah-like villas and hidden cafes. Island Harbour is a working fishing community, not a resort area, and its beach is lined with brightly colored fishing boats rather than umbrella-shaded sun loungers.

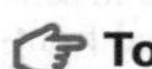

Tours

Liquid Glow KAYAKING
(☎582-5820; www.anguillakayak.com; night tour US$75; ⏲tours daily) Lynn Morancie's eureka moment came after renting a glass-bottom kayak on a trip to Dubai. How cool would it be to outfit transparent kayaks with LED lights and paddle around in the dark, she thought. Find out for yourself on her one-hour moonlit evening tours while keeping an eye out for turtles, rays and other sea life.

Lynn also offers daytime kayak tours to Little Bay (US$85) and all-day rentals (US$120).

Eating

Falcon Nest Bar & Grill CARIBBEAN $$
(☎497-1127; Nashville Webster Rd; mains US$7-48; ⏲noon-9pm Mon-Sat) Honest-to-goodness food prepared with panache and served with a smile is the winning formula at this beach grill. Chicken, burgers and pasta all make menu appearances but it's the seafood (lobster in particular), caught right offshore and served steamed, grilled or fried, that will have you lickin' your fingers.

Artisan Pizza Napoletana PIZZA $$
(☎235-6116; Nashville Webster Rd, Webster's Yard; pizza & pasta US$14-25; ⏲5-10pm Mon, Tue & Thu-Sat; P📶) This enchanting pizza parlor with candlelit terrace and outdoor lounge is proudly certified by the Associazione Verace Pizza Napoletana, Italy's standard-bearer for authentic Neapolitan-style pizzas. Soft-crust pies topped with imported Italian ingredients get their perfect tan in an imported mosaic-tiled wood-fired oven.

★Hibernia Restaurant & Art Gallery FUSION $$$
(☎497-4290; www.hiberniarestaurant.com; Harbour Ridge Dr; mains US$36-49; ⏲noon-1:30pm & 6:30-8:30pm Tue-Sat Nov-Jun; P) Raoul and Mary hail from France and Ireland and regularly visit Asia. Their Caribbean-Zen culinary retreat harmonizes these influences in com-

plex and sublime dishes like lobster tail with miso black-garlic sauce, chicken pumpkin soup with lemongrass-bamboo charcoal, and freshly smoked local fish. This care extends to the decor, with a tranquil Balinese-style reflection pool and Asian art gallery. Reservations required. Island-wide transport to and from the restaurant can be arranged (from US$35 for two people). If you're driving, see the website for detailed directions.

UNDERSTAND ANGUILLA

History

First settled by the Amerindian peoples from South America about 4000 years ago, then by a succession of tribes and cultures including the Arawaks, Anguilla was called 'Malliouhana,' meaning arrow-shaped sea serpent. The Arawaks remained on the island for millennia, as evidenced by many cave sites with petroglyphs and artifacts such as shell axes, flint blades and conch-shell drinking receptacles still visible today.

Columbus sailed by in 1493, but didn't land on the island (probably because he didn't notice it since it's extremely flat compared with St-Martin/Sint Maarten next door). Britain sent a colony in 1650 to take advantage of soil that was hospitable to growing corn and tobacco. However, it wasn't hospitable to much else, and the plantation colonies that bloomed on nearby Caribbean islands, such as St Kitts and Nevis, never defined Anguilla.

When the sugar plantations were abandoned due to a lack of viable soil and insufficient rain, small-scale industries, such as sailing, fishing and private farming, began to crop up on the island. In 1834 Britain abolished slavery in its colonies, and many formerly enslaved Anguillians took up positions as farmers, sailors and fishers.

In 1958, Anguilla formed a federation with St Kitts and Nevis, which was disliked by most of the ex-slave population. Anguilla was allowed only one freeholder representative to the House of Assembly on St Kitts and was largely ignored, eventually culminating in the Anguilla Revolution in 1967. Anguilla Day marks May 30, 1967, the day Anguillans forced the Royal St Kitts Police Force off the island for good.

As a result of its revolt against St Kitts, Anguilla returned to Britain and once again became an overseas territory. Under the Anguilla constitution, which came into effect in 1982, one queen-appointed representative acts as the British governor and presides over the Executive Council and an elected Anguilla House of Assembly.

Anguilla has seen its share of devastating hurricanes, including the mother of all storms, Hurricane Irma, that roared through in 2017, leaving a path of destruction from which much of the island has recuperated.

People & Culture

Anguillan culture is a blend of West Indian, British and African influences. Anguilla's local population is almost entirely descended from African slaves brought to the Caribbean several centuries ago. Since 2006, many Chinese, Mexican and Indian workers have been employed on the island to build Anguilla's surge of new resorts.

Sailboat racing is the national sport and a vital part of everyday life. Races are a common occurrence and are a great way to hang out with the community. Road biking is also popular thanks to the island being pancake-flat. The John T Memorial Cycling Race, hosted by the Anguilla Cycling Association every July, is one of the biggest cycling races in the Caribbean.

Upscale tourism drives the economy and today almost three-quarters of the island's inhabitants work in hospitality or commerce. Anguillans take pride in maintaining the balance between tourist development and the preservation of a thriving local society.

Protestant churches, Anglican and Methodist in particular, are the main religious affiliations, followed by Roman Catholicism.

Landscape & Wildlife

Anguilla, an arid island shaped like an eel, lies 5 miles north of St-Martin/Sint Maarten. Its 33 white-sand beaches have prompted countless imaginations to linger over whether one could subsist on a diet of coconuts well enough to take an early retirement here.

Some 160 bird species have been recorded here, one quarter of which are considered regionally or globally threatened. Species include the Antillean crested hummingbird, frigate, brown pelican, snow egret and black-necked stilt. Anguilla's 20 wetlands are a key habitat both for resident birds and for migratory species traveling on the Atlantic Flyway.

Endangered sea turtles, such as the hawksbill, can be spotted offshore in seven protected marine parks: Dog Island, Little Bay, Prickly Pear, Sandy Island, Seal Island Reef System, Shoal Bay–Island Harbour Reef System and Stoney Bay. The most commonplace creatures on the island are the many roaming goats and sheep as well as lizards, geckos and iguanas. (If you see a slightly fuzzier-looking goat with its tail down, not up, it's actually a Caribbean sheep.)

Like many Caribbean islands, Anguilla desalinates much of its water. Be mindful of letting the water run needlessly.

SURVIVAL GUIDE

Directory A–Z

ACCESSIBLE TRAVEL

Anguilla's flat terrain makes getting around somewhat easier for travelers with disabilities or limited mobility compared to other Caribbean islands. In addition, many hotels and villas have rooms equipped for wheelchair users. Wheelchair-friendly bathroom facilities at bars and restaurants are rare, however – confirm when booking.

ACCOMMODATIONS

Anguilla offers the gamut of accommodations from simple guesthouses to self-catering apartments and lavish resorts and villas. Overall, it is an expensive destination in high season (December 15 to April 15) with rates peaking around Christmas and New Year's. Most properties charge significantly less in low season.

Accommodations charge a 10% government tax, 10% service charge and daily US$3 per-person tourism fee. These are not included in rates unless stated.

Booking Services

Island Dream Properties (☎498-3200; www.islanddreamproperties.com) Offers villa rental (from US$3000 per week for a one-bedroom property); can also organize private chefs, provisioning, car rental, babysitting and boat charters.

Ricketts Luxury Properties (☎497-6049; www.rickettsluxury.com; Rendezvous Rd, Lower South Hill; ⏰9am-5pm Mon-Fri, to noon Sat) Rents everything from one-bedroom villas to fully staffed three-villa estates with 22 bedrooms. Rates per week for a one-bedroom villa start at around US$4000. Some properties require a 10-day minimum stay.

> **SLEEPING PRICE RANGES**
>
> The following price ranges refer to a double room with bathroom in high season (mid-December to mid-April).
>
> **$** less than US$200
>
> **$$** US$200–400
>
> **$$$** more than US$400

CHILDREN

Anguilla is a very family-friendly destination. Many of the larger resorts have kids' clubs. Children will also adore the island's opportunities for water sports, beach combing and activities such as horseback riding. Supermarkets stock baby-care items including diapers (nappies).

ELECTRICITY

110-120V; North American–style sockets are common.

EMBASSIES & CONSULATES

There are no embassies or consulates on Anguilla.

EMERGENCY NUMBERS

Ambulance, fire, police ☎911

FOOD

Global flavors abound on Anguilla, along with some exquisite fusion creations, while local specialties include seafood (lobster, crayfish and snapper in particular), barbecue and Creole cuisine. Beach bars are popular dining spots throughout the day; many higher-end restaurants only open at night.

If you're self-catering in an apartment or villa, be aware that supermarkets are often poorly stocked. Anguilla's best supermarket by far is Best Buy Supermarket in Meads Bay.

HEALTH

Clinics and the hospital are all located in the Valley but have limited emergency facilities. Patients needing specialized care are taken to hospitals in Sint Maarten or Puerto Rico. Private doctors are expensive, so be sure to have health insurance with comprehensive coverage.

Princess Alexandra Hospital (p93), located in the Valley; has a 24-hour emergency room.

INTERNET ACCESS

Anguilla has reliable wi-fi across the island; most beach bars, restaurants, cafes and accommodations have free access.

LGBT+ TRAVELERS

Generally speaking, Anguillans are socially conversative and do not have an open-minded approach to LGBT travelers, so it's best to avoid public displays of affection. While homosexuality has been legal on Anguilla since 2000, same-sex marriage or civil partnerships are not, and there are no nondiscrimination laws. Hotels, however – especially larger and/or high-end establishments – are generally welcoming to all, so sharing a double room is unlikely to pose any problems.

MONEY

Local currency is the Eastern Caribbean dollar (EC$). US dollars are preferred and often required. Many smaller establishments don't accept credit cards.

ATMs

Banks with ATMs are located in the Valley and dispense both US and EC dollars. Keep cash on hand, as ATMs won't work for all foreign cards. ATMs sometimes run out of cash on weekends, so it's best to make withdrawals by Friday.

Scotiabank Anguilla (497-3333; www.scotiabank.com; Cosely Dr; 8am-2pm Mon-Fri)

Exchange Rates

Australia	A$1	US$0.67
Canada	C$1	US$0.75
Euro zone	€1	US$1.12
Japan	¥100	US$0.94
New Zealand	NZ$1	US$0.64
UK	UK£1	US$1.20

For current exchange rates, see www.xe.com.

Tipping

Hotels A 10% service charge is added to the bill. Tip bellhops US$1 or US$2 per bag and cleaning staff the same per person per day for good service.

Restaurants Most restaurant bills include a 15% service charge. Additional tipping is at your discretion.

Taxi Tip 10% or 15%.

POST

Post office (497-2528; www.aps.ai; Carter Rey Blvd; 8am-3pm Mon-Fri)

PUBLIC HOLIDAYS

New Year's Day January 1

James Ronald Webster Day March 2

Good Friday March/April

Easter Monday March/April

Labor Day May 1

Whit Monday mid-May

Anguilla Day May 30

Queen's Birthday mid-June

August Monday (Emancipation Day) First Monday in August

August Thursday First Thursday in August

Constitution Day early August

National Heroes & Heroines Day December 19

Christmas Day December 25

Boxing Day December 26

EATING PRICE RANGES

The following price ranges refer to a main course.

$ less than US$15

$$ US$15–35

$$$ more than US$35

TELEPHONE

- Anguilla's country code is 1-264, which is followed by a seven-digit local number.
- To call the island from North America, dial 1 + 264 + the local number.
- From elsewhere, dial your country's international access code + 1 + 264 + the local number.
- If you are calling locally, simply dial the local number.
- If you are calling internationally from Anguilla, unless you are dialing a landline within the North American Numbering Plan (NANP), you need to dial the international exit code 011.

Cell Phones

Check with your home provider about roaming capabilities and costs. If you have an unlocked phone, you can buy a prepaid SIM card with a local number for around US$10 from the main local provider, **Flow** (498-2422; www.discoverflow.co; Carter Rey Blvd; 8am-5pm Mon-Fri, to 1pm Sat) or its competitor **Digicel** (461-3444; www.digicelgroup.com; Rock Farm; 8am-5:30pm Mon-Fri, 8:30am-1pm Sat), both with branches in the Valley (bring your passport). Top up credit online, at supermarkets or gas stations.

TIME

Anguilla is on Atlantic Time (GMT/UTC minus four hours). Daylight saving is not observed.

TOURIST INFORMATION

Anguilla doesn't have a walk-in tourist office, but brochures and maps are available at most hotels. Alternatively, you can contact the **Anguilla Tourist Board** (497-2759; www.ivisitanguilla.com).

PRACTICALITIES

Smoking Smoking is banned inside enclosed spaces including hotel rooms and restaurants. Outdoor areas, including some open-air dining areas, are often not smoke-free.

Weights & measures Anguilla uses the imperial system.

DRINKING WATER

Most of the island's water is collected in cisterns, so it's advisable to drink bottled water.

com) by phone or via its comprehensive website for information about the island.

Getting There & Away

Anguilla has regular regional flights, particularly to St-Martin/Sint Maarten's Princess Juliana International Airport, and frequent ferries to St-Martin/Sint Maarten. No cruise ships dock in Anguilla.

AIR

There are no direct international flights to Anguilla. Passengers must transfer in St-Martin/Sint Maarten, Antigua or Puerto Rico.

Only small aircraft service Anguilla's tiny **Clayton J Lloyd International Airport** (AXA; 497-3510), located just south of The Valley, the island's capital.

Anguilla Air Services (498-5922; www.anguillaairservices.com; Clayton J Lloyd International Airport) serves St-Martin/Sint Maarten's Princess Juliana International Airport (Dutch side) and St-Barthélemy, while **Seaborne Airlines** (Puerto Rico 787-946-7800; www.seaborneairlines.com) and **Tradewind Aviation** (USA 203-267-3305; www.flytradewind.com) fly to San Juan (Puerto Rico).

SEA

The **ferry terminal** (Blowing Point Rd) in Blowing Point has boats to both the French and Dutch sides of St-Martin/Sint Maarten. The cheapest connection is the public ferry to Marigot (French side). However, if you need to catch a flight at Princess Juliana International Airport, taking a ferry straight to Simpson Bay (Dutch side) saves considerable time compared with taking a taxi from Marigot to the airport (US$20, 30 to 40 minutes).

The port of entry for yachts is at Sandy Ground. Before arriving, contact **Customs & Immigration** (497-2451; Sandy Ground Rd; 8am-noon & 1-4pm) on VHF channel 16.

Getting Around

Anguilla has no public transportation and taxis are expensive, so it's best to rent a car for a few days. Some resorts and hotels have bicycles for their guests' use.

BICYCLE

Anguilla's flat terrain makes cycling easy in theory, but be mindful of distances, heat and narrow, rough and potholed road conditions.

Epic Ride (729-1664; Back St, South Hill Village; per day US$25; noon-5pm Tue-Sat)

Freedom Rentals (p95)

CAR & MOTORCYCLE

Driving is on the left-hand side of the road, but steering wheels can confusingly be on either the left or the right side of the car. The official speed limit is 30mph unless posted otherwise.

Anguilla is totally flat and there is rarely traffic – it takes quite a while to go through a tank of gas. If you need to fill up, you'll find Sol gas stations in **Meads Bay** (Albert Hughes Dr) and in **The Valley** (Albert Lake Dr) and **Anguilla Gases** (Main St, Blowing Point Village) in Blowing Point.

Car Rental

Car-rental companies issue the compulsory local driving permit for US$15 for 72 hours or US$25 for three months. Compact cars start from US$45 per day (usually US$5 cheaper in summer).

Most companies don't have physical offices open to the public; book in advance to arrange pickup and drop-off.

Andy's Auto Rentals (584-7010; www.andyrentals.com; Blowing Point Rd, ferry terminal; per day from US$35)

Apex/Avis (497-2642; www.avisanguilla.com; per day from US$38)

Island Car Rental (497-2723; www.islandcar.ai; per day US$50-95)

Junie's Car Rental (235-6114; www.juniescarrental.com; per day from US$35)

Triple K Car/Hertz Rental (497-2934; www.hertz.com; per day from US$44; 8am-5pm)

TAXI

Anguilla is divided into 10 taxi zones with fares depending on how many zones you travel through (ie one zone US$10, 10 zones US$36). Fares are for two persons with each additional person charged at US$5.

Two pieces of luggage are free, additional ones are US$1 each. There is also US$4 surcharge for rides between 6pm and midnight and US$10 for rides between midnight and 6am. Two-hour island tours for one or two people cost US$55. Drivers only accept US dollars.

Recommended drivers include Wendell Connor's Taxi Service (497-6894) and Frank's Anguilla Taxi Service (497-4238).

DEPARTURE TAX

Departure tax is US$20.

Antigua & Barbuda

1-268 / POP 102,000

Includes ➡

Best Places to Eat

- ➡ Le Bistro (p113)
- ➡ Cecilia's High Point Cafe (p113)
- ➡ Catherine's Cafe Plage (p120)
- ➡ Colibri (p120)
- ➡ Papa Zouk (p110)

Best Places to Stay

- ➡ Admiral's Inn (p118)
- ➡ Blue Bay Antigua B&B (p121)
- ➡ Buccaneer Beach Club (p112)
- ➡ Waterfront Hostel (p118)
- ➡ Barbuda Cottages (p125)

Why Go?

Antigua's corrugated coasts cradle hundreds of perfect little coves lapped by beguiling enamel-blue water, while the sheltered bays have provided refuge for everyone from Admiral Nelson to buccaneers and yachties. If you can tear yourself away from that towel, you'll discover that there's a distinct English accent to this island. You'll find it in the bustling capital of St John's, in salty-glamorous English Harbour, and in the historical forts and other vestiges of the colonial past. Yet, Antigua is also quintessential Caribbean, full of candy-colored villages, a rum-infused mellowness and engaging locals who'll greet you with wide smiles.

Antigua's smaller sister island Barbuda was devastated by Hurricane Irma in 2017 and is still busy rebuilding, though its extraordinary beaches were unaffected, meaning that travelers wanting to lounge on white sand, snorkel around pristine reefs and watch the famous frigate birds nesting should not hesitate to make the journey here.

When to Go

Dec–Apr Peak season. Daily highs average 81°F (27°C); nighttime temperatures drop to 72°F (22°C).

Jul & Aug Slightly hotter (86°F/30°C high and 77°F/25°C low); can get humid. Hurricane season starts July (to November).

May–Nov Prices drop and crowds thin.

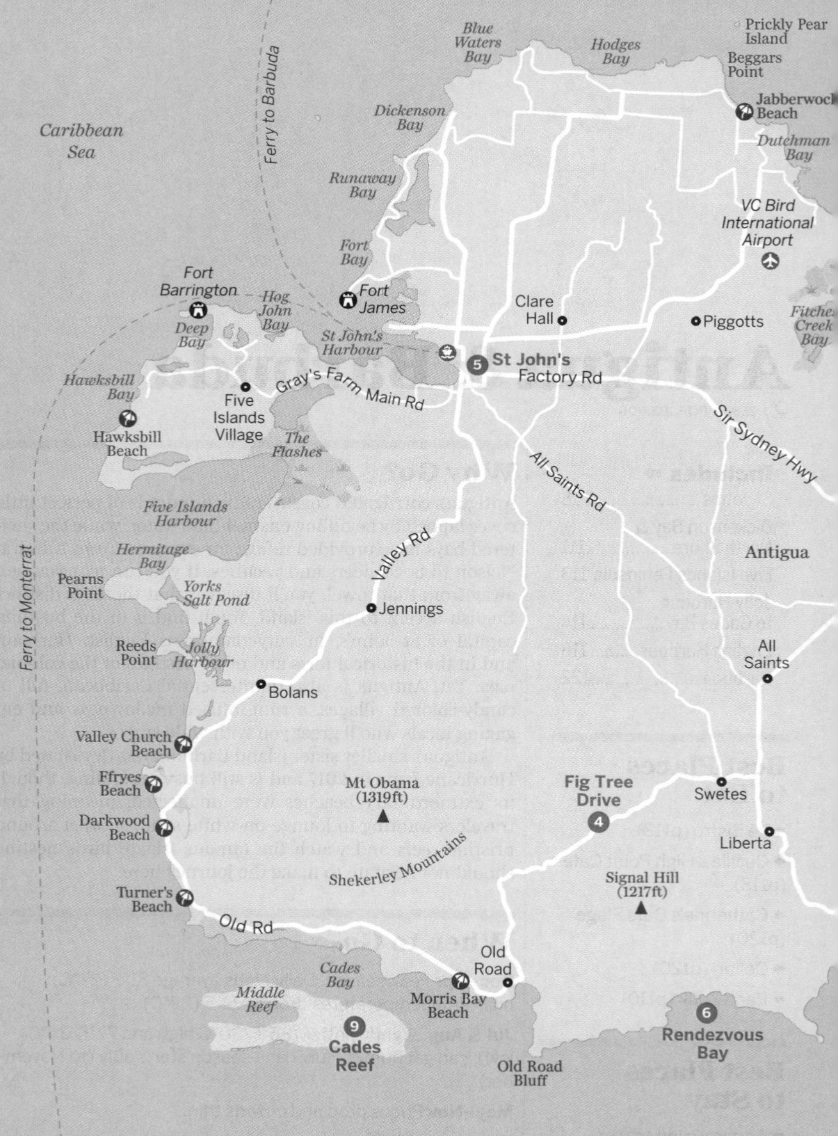

Antigua & Barbuda Highlights

❶ **Half Moon Bay** (p120) Playing in the waves of Antigua's most beautiful beach.

❷ **Frigate Bird Sanctuary** (p125) Marveling at the magnificent birds off Barbuda's northwest coast.

❸ **Shirley Heights Lookout Restaurant** (p120) Swaying to steel drum and reggae at the Sunday-afternoon barbecue

❹ **Fig Tree Drive** (p116) Tasting the sweetness of a black pineapple at a fruit stand along this rainforest road.

❺ **St John's Public Market** (p108) Putting together a

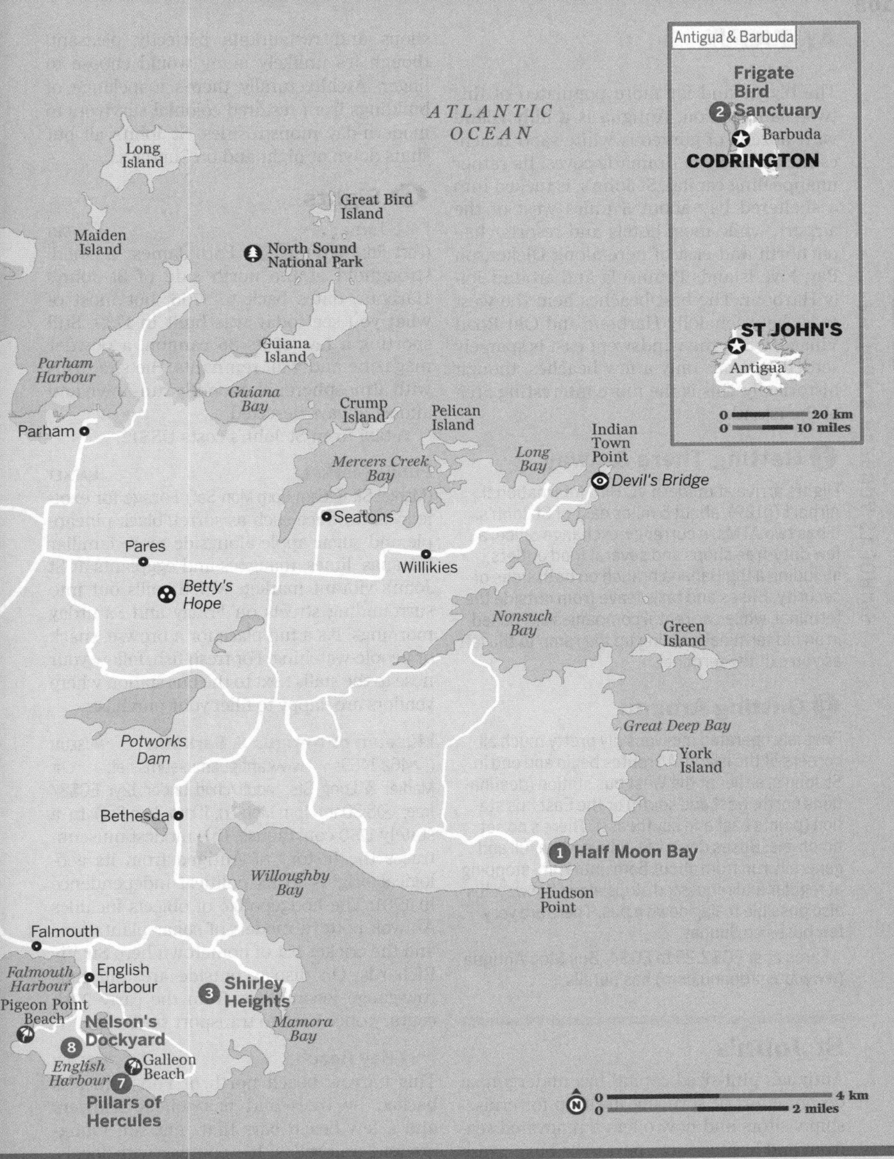

beach picnic from the colorful wheel of exotic bounty.

6 **Rendezvous Bay** (p117) Traipsing through thick rainforest to deserted shimmering sands.

7 **Pillars of Hercules** (p117) Scrambling over rocks or taking a boat ride to these whimsically eroded cliffs.

8 **Nelson's Dockyard** (p117) Flashing back to colonial times at this restored 18th-century naval base.

9 **Cades Reef** (p109) Diving in Antigua's watery underbelly.

ANTIGUA

POP 100,400

The bigger and far more populated of this two-island nation, Antigua is a hilly island with dozens of gorgeous white-sand beaches tucked away in dramatic coves. Its rather unappealing capital, St John's, is tucked into a sheltered bay about 5 miles west of the airport, while most hotels and resorts cluster north and east of here along Dickenson Bay, Five Islands Peninsula and around Jolly Harbour. The best beaches hem the west coast between Jolly Harbour and Old Road Village, while the windswept east is sparsely settled and has only a few beaches, though historically, this is the more interesting area of the island.

Getting There & Away

Flights arrive at modern VC Bird International Airport (p129), about 5 miles east of St John's. It has two ATMs, a currency-exchange office, a few duty-free shops and several food outlets, including a Big Banana branch on both sides of security. Buses and taxis leave from outside the terminal, while car-rental companies are based in an old terminal building up the ramp to the left as you exit the terminal.

Getting Around

Privately operated minivans ply pretty much all corners of the island. All routes begin and end in St John's, either at the West bus station (destinations north, west and south) or the East bus station (points east and southeast). There's no set timetable. Buses depart St John's when full and generally run from about 6am until 7pm, stopping at regular and requested stops along the way. It's also possible to flag down a bus. There are very few buses on Sunday.

Fares cost EC$2.25 to EC$4. Bus Stop Antigua (www.busstopanu.com) has details.

St John's

Antigua's pint-sized capital has undergone a decent effort at sprucing itself up for cruise-ship visitors and now offers a renovated seafront and heritage area next to its busy cruise terminal. But let's face it, nobody comes to Antigua to see St John's, which is fairly run-down and often rather dirty, with dilapidated buildings, chaotic traffic and disintegrating sidewalks likely to be your main impression if you visit. That said, cruise passengers have to pass through St John's, and many find a few hours exploring its modicum of sights, shops and restaurants perfectly pleasant, though it's unlikely many would choose to linger. Architecturally there's a melange of buildings from restored colonial survivors to modern-day monstrosities. St John's all but shuts down at night and on Sundays.

Sights

Fort James FORT

(Fort Rd; 17) FREE Fort James, a small stronghold at the north side of St John's Harbour, dates back to 1706, but most of what you see today was built in 1739. Still sporting a few of its 36 cannon, a powder magazine and wall remnants, the site drips with atmosphere: it's moodily run-down and almost always deserted.

A taxi from St John's costs US$12.

Public Market MARKET

(Market St; 6am-6pm Mon-Sat) Forage for exotic local produce such as sorrel, black pineapple and sugar apple alongside more familiar bananas, limes, mangoes and eggplants at St John's vibrant market, which spills out into surrounding streets on Friday and Saturday mornings. It's a fun place for a browse, snack or people-watching. For fresh fish, follow your nose to the stalls next to the bus station where vendors are happy to fillet your purchase.

Museum of Antigua & Barbuda MUSEUM

(462-1469; www.antiguamuseums.net; cnr Market & Long Sts; adult/child under 12yr EC$8/free; 8:30am-4pm Mon-Fri, 10am-2pm Sat) In a stately 1750 courthouse, this modest museum traces the history of Antigua from its geological origins to its political independence in 1981. The hodgepodge of objects includes Arawak pottery, models of sugar plantations and the cricket bat of hometown hero Sir Viv Richards. On display outside are four narrow-gauge locomotives from the early 20th century once used to transport sugarcane.

Fort Bay Beach BEACH

This narrow beach north of Fort James is backed by trees and has toilets, showers and a few beach bars that rent sun loungers and umbrellas. It's popular with locals, but is also popular with cruise-ship visitors because of its proximity to the pier; it's best avoided on cruise days.

Tours

★**Adventure Antigua** ADVENTURE

(726-6355; www.adventureantigua.com) Eli Fuller, a former Olympian and third-generation

St John's

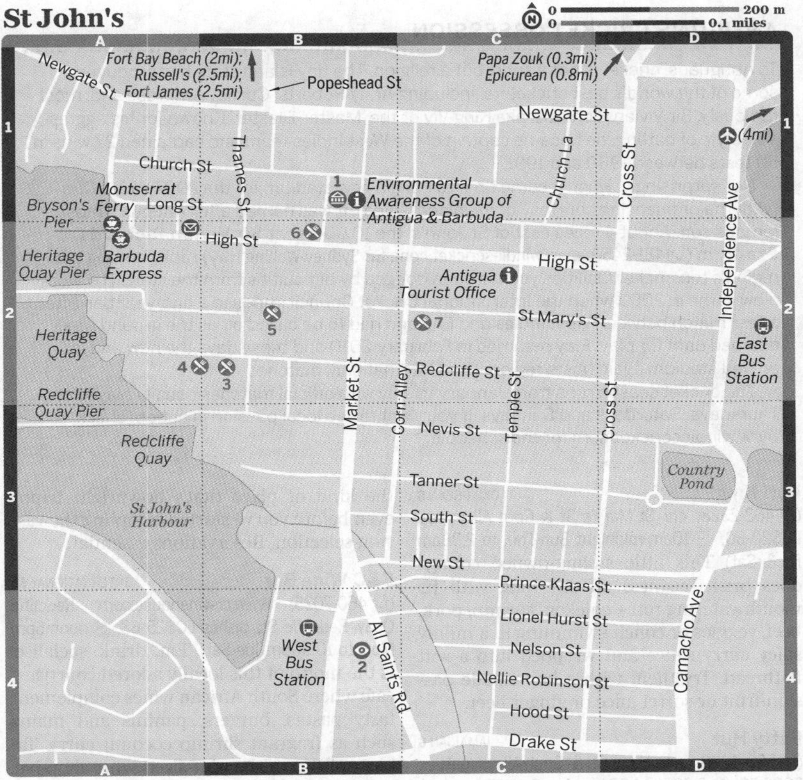

St John's

Sights

1 Museum of Antigua & Barbuda B1
2 Public Market B4

Eating

3 Big Banana B2
4 C&C Wine Bar A2
5 Hemingways Caribbean Cafe B2
6 Patty Hut B2
7 Roti King C2

Antiguan, offers educational and fun tours. His signature trip is the all-day Eco-Tour (US$115), which involves boating, swimming and snorkeling in the waters of North Sound National Park. The Xtreme Circumnav (US$170) aboard a 45ft speedboat includes a snorkel trip, a stop at a stingray marine park and a swim at Rendezvous Bay

Book online for a 10% discount.

Treasure Island Cruises BOATING

(☎461-8675; www.facebook.com/TreasureIslandCruises) Denzil and Brian take small groups of people out on boat trips aboard a 70ft catamaran that combine sailing, snorkeling, entertainment and a barbecue. Options include the Circumnavigation tour (US$120), the Cades Reef tour (US$120) and the Bird Island tour (US$100).

Eating

There's no reason to stay in St John's unless you're here for business. Almost everyone heads to the coast for lodging, where there are beaches and far more choice in both dining and sleeping options.

St John's has several excellent restaurants as well as plenty of street food in the downtown area and near the market, which is busiest on Saturday mornings.

ANTIGUA'S CRICKET OBSESSION

To Antiguans, cricket is not a sport but a religion. The tiny island state has produced some of the world's best cricketers, including Andy Roberts, Curtley Ambrose and, most famously, Sir Vivian Richards, aka King Viv or the 'Master-Blaster.' Known for his aggressive style of batting, he became captain of the West Indies team and captained 27 wins in 50 tests between 1980 and 1991.

Not surprisingly, when it came time to build a new stadium for the 2007 World Cup (with major financing courtesy of mainland China), it was named after Antigua's most famous son. About 4 miles east of St John's, the 10,000-seat **Sir Vivian Richards Stadium** (☎481-2450; www.windiescricket.com; Sir Sydney Walling Hwy) ranks among the region's top cricket facilities yet has been dogged by difficulties from the start. The worst blow came in 2009 when the International Cricket Council imposed a one-year ban after a Test match between West Indies and England had to be called off as the ground was deemed unfit for play. Play resumed in February 2010 and these days the new and improved stadium again hosts regional and international matches.

The cricket season runs from January to July with official matches usually played on Thursdays, Saturdays and Sundays. If you want to see local passion in action, check www.windiescricket.com for the schedule.

Roti King CARIBBEAN $

(☎462-2328; cnr St Mary's St & Corn Alley; roti EC$20-30; ⏰10am-midnight Sun-Thu, to 2:30am Fri & Sat) This little sibling-owned cottage does brisk business all day long with its mouthwatering roti – chicken, shrimp, pork, beef, veggies or conch swimming in a mildly spicy curry sauce and wrapped into a soft flatbread. Try them with a homemade passion-fruit or sorrel juice or ginger beer.

Patty Hut JAMAICAN $

(☎562-4098; cnr High St & Soul Alley; patties EC$6.50; ⏰8:30am-4:30pm Mon-Sat) This local institution in a shingled cottage dressed in cheerful blue and green doles out delicious Jamaican beef, chicken and vegetable patties to adoring local crowds.

Epicurean SUPERMARKET $

(☎484-5400; www.epicureanantigua.com; Friars Hill Rd; ⏰7am-11pm; P) This upscale market is Antigua's best and has a wide selection of fresh local foods, imported international foods (especially from the UK and the US), as well as a pharmacy, a hot-food counter and ATMs.

★ **Papa Zouk** SEAFOOD $$

(☎464-6044; www.facebook.com/Papazouk; Hilda Davis Dr; mains EC$50-100; ⏰7pm-midnight Mon-Sat; wi-fi) This high-energy joint is a local institution, famous for its Antiguan-style bouillabaisse and fresh fish – *mahimahi* to butterfish – served grilled or fried. With zouk on the sound system, crazy murals, Christmas lights and a nautical decor, it's the kind of place that's downright trippy even before you've started sampling the vast rum selection. Reservations essential.

C&C Wine Bar INTERNATIONAL $$

(☎460-7025; www.ccwinehouse.com; Redcliffe Quay, Redcliffe St; dishes EC$25-68; ⏰noon-5pm Mon, to 10:30pm Tue-Sat) 'Eat, drink, socialise' is the motto of this locally adored courtyard cafe where South African wines complement tasty pastas, burgers, paninis and mains such as fragrant shrimp coconut curry. Tables spill from the pint-sized wine shop-bar onto a romantic courtyard, and fill to capacity crowd during 'Lasagne Thursdays' and 'Karaoke Saturdays' – book ahead.

The name, by the way, stands for Cutie and Claudine, the charming hosts.

Big Banana PIZZA $$

(☎480-6985; www.bigbanana-antigua.com; Redcliffe Quay; pizzas EC$25-81; ⏰7am-11pm Mon-Sat; wi-fi, family-friendly) This airy, cool space on Redcliffe Quay is always reassuringly packed full of locals, some of whom have been coming to this buzzy former rum warehouse for more than 30 years. Indeed, so irresistible are its pizzas that on weekends you may have to elbow your way inside. There's a kids' menu and breakfast is served daily until 10am.

Russell's SEAFOOD $$

(☎462-5479; www.facebook.com/russellsbarandrestaurant; Fort James; mains EC$45-60; ⏰10am-8pm Tue-Sat; wi-fi) In the reconstructed officers' quarters of Fort James, one of Antigua's main citadels, bluff-top Russell's offers drinks and sea-to-table fish with awesome ocean views from its wide verandas. Sunsets can be achingly beautiful and there's live music on some nights, usually Fridays. The menu changes daily depending on the catch; the snapper is rightly famous.

Hemingways Caribbean Cafe CARIBBEAN **$$**
(☎462-2763; Lower St Mary's St; mains lunch EC$24-65, dinner EC$50-85; ⏲9:30am-10pm Mon-Sat; 📶) You can have a fine meal upstairs at this deeply unpretentious 1820s Creole cottage with gingerbread trim. Skip the international choices and go for local flavors such as spicy chicken curry, coconut-rum-flambéed lobster and the off-menu blueberry bread pudding with rum-butter sauce.

The veranda tables are great for people watching.

Shopping

Duty-free shops cluster in Heritage Quay just off the cruise-ship pier, but don't expect major bargains except on booze and cigarettes. It segues into the **Vendors' Mall**, a cacophonous maze of trinkets and T-shirts (bargaining advised). Adjacent Redcliffe Quay (the former site of the St John's slave market) has more upscale galleries and boutiques. For local color, skip over a block or two to Market, Thames and St Mary's streets.

Information

Antigua Tourist Office (☎562-7600; www.visitantiguabarbuda.com; 3rd fl, ACB Financial Centre, High St; ⏲8am-4pm Mon-Fri) Has a small selection of pamphlets, maps and brochures available to people who drop into its offices in St John's.

Mt St John's Medical Centre (☎484-2700; www.msjmc.org; Michael's Mount, off Queen Elizabeth Hwy; ⏲24hr) This modern 185-bed hospital also operates a 24-hour emergency room.

Police (☎462-0045; cnr Newgate & Market Sts) Main downtown police station.

Post Office (cnr High St & Heritage Quay; ⏲8:15am-3:30pm Mon-Thu, to 2pm Fri)

Getting There & Around

East bus station (Independence Ave) For destinations east and southeast of town such as Betty's Hope, Long Bay and Seatons.

West bus station (Market St) Minivans headed to points north, west and south (eg Jolly Harbour, the beaches and English Harbour) leave from this station next to the public market. Buses depart when full and stop at regular and requested stops en route. Fares cost EC$2.25 to EC$4.

There's a taxi stand adjacent to the West bus station, and taxi drivers also hang around Heritage Quay.

Dickenson Bay & North Shore

North of St John's, the middle market of Antigua's holidaymakers is concentrated in the resorts along Dickenson Bay, a long crescent of yellow sand on the northwest coast. The swimming is good and there's no shortage of aquatic activities to keep visitors busy.

The beach can get crowded, not least due to the hordes of fun-seekers from the massive Sandals resort, but the pervasive strains of reggae set the mood for a quintessential Caribbean beach vibe.

East of here, all the way to the airport, are some of Antigua's poshest residential areas, with a golf course, fancy restaurants and surf sports off Jabberwock Beach.

Sights

Runaway Bay BEACH
If you're keen on escaping the all-inclusive crowds at busy Dickenson Bay, head south beyond a small bluff to Runaway Bay, where the beach is just as white but tranquil and facility-free.

Jabberwock Beach BEACH
(Hodges Bay) This long white sandy beach is largely the domain of windsurfers and kitesurfers thanks to its excellent cross-onshore winds and shallow waters. Conditions are mostly likely to be ideal between January and June.

Dickenson Bay BEACH
(🚌50) Antigua's busiest beach is backed by a long line of low-rise hotels and resorts, most notably the vast all-inclusive Sandals resort. Naturally, there's no shortage of beach bars and water-sports facilities. The calm waters are good for kids and the beach is wide except toward the southern end, but this is also one of Antigua's most crowded strips of sand.

Activities

Kite Antigua KITESURFING
(☎720-5483; www.kitesurfantigua.com; Jabberwock Rd) This pro outfit has taught kitesurfing to the curious for some two decades,

with a vibe that's convivial and supportive. It's right on northeast-facing Jabberwock Beach, which has ideal wind conditions for the sport.

A four-hour introductory course starts at US$240, a 10-hour clinic at US$650, and equipment rental (experienced riders only) costs US$100 per day. Prebooking advised.

Tony's Water Sports WATER SPORTS
(☎462-6326; www.tonyswatersports.com; next to Sandals resort, Dickenson Bay; ⏰8am-5pm; 🚌50) Run by the son of local calypso great King Short Shirt, well-respected Tony's gets you waterborne with Hobie Cats, jet skis, banana boats and water skis (about US$50 each per session). Hooking a tuna on a chartered deep-sea fishing expedition will set you and up to five of your friends back US$700 for the five-hour trip.

Windsurf Antigua WINDSURFING
(☎461-9463; www.windsurfantigua.net; Jabberwock Beach, Hodges Bay; rental per hr/day US$30/80) Local windsurfing guru Patrick Scales guarantees to get beginners up and onto the water in one session (US$90 for two hours). Boards can be delivered island-wide. Prebooking advised.

Sleeping

The Dickenson Bay area has the largest concentration of properties on Antigua, from cute apartments to the mega-sized Sandals resort. The more affordable places are often just a short walk away from the beach.

Wind Chimes Inn B&B $
(☎728-2917; windchimesinn@gmail.com; Sir George Walter Hwy; s/d incl breakfast US$85/95; P❄📶🏊; 🚌42) Plane-spotters will cherish the runway views at this modern inn 2 miles from the airport terminal, but anyone can enjoy the spotless, spacious rooms where the pillow-top mattresses, small kitchenettes and patio belie the modest price. Rates include continental breakfast brought to your room. Airport transfers are free, making it a smart choice if you need to overnight between flights.

Siboney Beach Club HOTEL $$
(☎462-0806; Marina Bay Rd, Dickenson Bay; ste from US$180; P❄📶🏊; 🚌50) This low-key, 12-unit beachfront retreat on busy Dickenson Bay has smart suites with kitchenettes in shades of beige that offset the riot of color of the tropical garden and the intense blue of the ocean. Watch hummingbirds flutter among the frangipani trees from your patio or let the in-house massage therapist work out your kinks beneath the palm trees.

Dickenson Bay Cottages APARTMENT $$
(☎462-4940; www.dickensonbaycottages.com; Trade Winds Dr; 1-/2-bedroom apt US$180/225; ❄🏊; 🚌50) A good option if you want to be close to the beach without paying beachfront prices, this hillside charmer is a complex of gleaming white houses built around a good-sized pool with friendly staff, decent kitchens and tropical gardens. There's a supermarket nearby. Small units are priced for two; large ones for up to four people.

★**Buccaneer Beach Club** VILLA $$$
(☎562-6785; www.buccaneerbeach.com; Marina Bay Rd; villas US$275-650; ❄📶🏊; 🚌50) This serene cluster of cottages alongside a large pool is perfect for families and self-caterers. It sits amid a lovely palm-and-orchid garden on a tiny sugary beach on the quiet end of Dickenson Bay with easy access to the restaurants and water-sports facilities of the adjacent resorts. Cottages have full kitchens.

Ocean Point Resort & Spa HOTEL $$$
(☎562-8330; www.oceanpointantigua.com; Hodges Bay Main Rd, Hodges Bay; d all-inclusive from US$449; P❄📶🏊) This rambling adults-only property is an all-inclusive that's very popular with Italians. Pastel-colored rooms come with a balcony, preferably one overlooking the huge pool and the two lovely secluded beaches that rarely get busy. The breezy Italian restaurant serves buffet-style meals.

Jumby Bay Resort RESORT $$$
(☎484-6072; www.jumbybayisland.com; ste all-inclusive from US$2995; ❄📶🏊) There's a virtual 'Do Not Disturb' sign attached to this ultra-exclusive luxury resort set on its own private island reached by shuttle boat from Dutchman's Bay. You need a reservation for one of the 40 guest rooms to be taken here.

Eating

From a food truck to fine French dining, there's some excellent eating in this area. The better options are right on the beach.

Chippy Antigua SEAFOOD $
(☎724-1166; www.caribya.com/antigua/chippy.antigua; Marina Bay Rd; mains EC$25-40; ⏰4-9pm Wed & Fri; 🚌50) Dave and Jane's food truck enjoys cult status among local British-style fish-and-chips devotees, but the succulent shrimp, spicy sausages and Indian curries

also deserve a mention. There's a full bar and you can enjoy it all at plastic tables under the stars. The truck parks on the road next to Buccaneer Beach Club. Cash only.

Ana's on the Beach ITALIAN **$$**

(☎562-8562; www.anas.ag; Marina Bay Rd; mains EC$50-100; ⏱11am-10pm Tue-Sun; 📶; 🚌50) With its hot-pink, white and black color scheme, wispy cabanas and attached art gallery, breezy Ana's mixes urban sophistication with a relaxed vibe that matches its beachfront setting. The menu is big on Mediterranean staples including Caprese salad, seafood risotto and salmon tagliatelle, but also does a range of tasty curries.

Being hemmed in by resorts puts it largely off the radar of locals.

★Cecilia's High Point Cafe MEDITERRANEAN **$$$**

(☎562-7070; www.highpointantigua.com; Texaco Dock Rd, Dutchman's Bay; mains EC$55-110; ⏱noon-4pm Fri-Mon and 6-9pm Fri & Mon; 📶; 🚌42) With gorgeous views of the azure sea, this fabulous beachfront find is presided over by a former Swedish model and her host of animal friends. It strikes the perfect balance between informality and professionalism. Perennial top menu picks include the lobster ravioli and the beef tenderloin, although the regularly changing blackboard specials also beckon mightily. Reservations advisable.

★Le Bistro FRENCH **$$$**

(☎462-3881; www.lebistroantigua.com; Hodges Bay; mains EC$80-160; ⏱6:30-10:30pm Tue-Sun; 📶; 🚌42) Le Bistro is straight out of a foodie's daydream with a kitchen that has consistently wowed diners with meticulously prepared classic French cuisine. No matter if you fancy *escargots* or *canard,* you'll find the ingredients top flight, the presentation exquisite and the service immaculate. Reservations are essential.

Coconut Grove CARIBBEAN **$$$**

(☎462-1538; www.coconutgroveantigua.com; Marina Bay Rd; mains EC$65-125; ⏱7am-11pm; 📶; 🚌50) This beachy daytime hangout beneath the palm trees at Siboney Beach Club morphs into an elegant candlelit affair for dinner. The lobster thermidor medallions in mustard-brandy sauce is a top menu pick among regulars who also invade for beers and rum punch, and not only during the daily happy hour (5pm to 7pm).

ℹ Getting There & Away

Bus 50 leaves St John's West bus station for Dickenson Bay, while bus 55 heads to Hodges Bay from the East bus station. A one-way taxi ride from St John's costs US$15 to anywhere in the area. From the airport, the fare costs US$15 to US$18.

Five Islands Peninsula

A single road connects this attractive and dramatic peninsula with St John's. Five Islands Village itself is a fairly scruffy place giving way to a string of lovely and unhurried turquoise coves and white-sand beaches, dotted with mostly all-inclusive resorts. One of the beaches is clothing optional – it's the only one on Antigua – while the main sightseeing attraction in the area is the colonial-era Fort Barrington, from which there are superb views.

Sights

Deep Bay BEACH

Lorded over by the ruins of Fort Barrington, this curvy little – and often deserted – bay is backed by a large salt pond and has a beach with gray-yellow sand and calm, protected waters. The coral-encrusted *Andes* wreck, a cargo boat from Trinidad that sank in the middle of the bay some 100 years ago, is just a short swim away and great for snorkeling.

Hawksbill Bay BEACH

(Gray's Farm Rd, Five Islands Village; 🚌61) Named for a landmark rock formation, this bay has a string of four blissful beaches that are rarely crowded. The turnoff for the first one is before you get to Hawksbill by Rex Resort, but the other three must be accessed through the property. The furthest one (Eden Beach) is Antigua's only official clothing-optional beach.

Fort Barrington FORT

FREE Fort Barrington was built by the British in 1779 atop Goat Hill to protect the entrance to St John's Harbour from French attack. Those who tackle the brief but steep climb up here can clamber around the partly overgrown ruins and enjoy panoramic views of the harbor, Deep Bay and the wide open sea.

ℹ Getting There & Away

Bus 61 travels to the peninsula from St John's West bus station as far as Five Islands Village. A taxi to the hotels or beaches costs US$15 from St John's.

Jolly Harbour to Cades Bay

Jolly Harbour is a busy marina and dockside condominium village with a big supermarket, a bunch of other shops and facilities and a few restaurants and bars. South of here, the coastal road wears a necklace of some of Antigua's best beaches, which are popular with cruise-ship passengers and, on weekends, with locals but otherwise often deserted. Down in Cades Bay, the road passes a pineapple farm before turning inland and cutting through rainforest and Fig Tree Dr, which culminates in Swetes. From here, you're back in St John's in a 20-minute drive.

Sights

Mt Obama MOUNTAIN
(Mt Obama Rd, off Old Rd; 22) Antigua's 'Everest' rises a modest 1319ft in the island's southwestern corner as part of the Shekerley mountain range. Known as Boggy Peak until 2009 (Mt Obama is definitely an improvement), the mountain is crowned by dense trees and locked up telecommunications towers. This makes views only so-so unless you can get inside the compound.

During the colonial area, escaped African slaves, called 'maroons,' hid out in the surrounding hills. The entire area is now a national park and a growing number of trails are being developed from the northern side via Christian Valley. For now, the easiest access is from Cades Bay in the south. The turnoff for partly paved Mt Obama Rd (best with a 4WD) is from Old Rd, just east of the village of Urlings. Drive as far as you can, then walk the rest to the top. A bus can drop you at the turnoff.

Ffryes Beach BEACH
(Valley Rd, Bolans; 22) This long, sea-grape-shaded sandy ribbon has barbecue facilities, showers and toilets, and is popular with local families on weekends. Grab a cocktail in time for sunset from Dennis Cocktail Bar & Restaurant on the hillside to the north of the beach. Sadly, two large new developments behind the beach threaten its idyllic atmosphere.

Hermitage Bay BEACH
(off Valley Rd, Jennings) This dreamy secluded arc punctuates the end of a 2½-mile-long road (the last two are graded dirt road). Wave-tossed shells litter the white sand that remains largely crowd-free despite being next to the ultra-posh Hermitage Bay resort. A huge new luxury residential development being built on the peninsula nearby may change this end-of-the-road feeling somewhat.

Valley Church Beach BEACH
(Valley Rd, Valley Church village; 22) This pretty palm-lined beach has calm, shallow aquamarine waters and powdery white sand. It's a popular excursion for cruise-ship guests, for whom water sports are laid on and loungers serviced by fleets of bar staff. Most cruisers gather around popular beach restaurant the Nest, so if you're looking for a quiet spot, head to the south end of the beach.

The gate to the beach is open from dawn to sunset. If it's closed, park on the street and walk in.

Darkwood Beach BEACH
(Valley Rd; 22) This road-adjacent swath of beige sand makes for a convenient swimming and snorkeling spot. The eponymous cafe here has a shower (US$1), changing rooms and also rents beach chairs. It's popular with locals on weekends.

Morris Bay Beach BEACH
(Valley Rd, Old Road Village; 22) Hemmed in by coconut palms, Morris Bay is locally beloved for its calm waters and stretches all the way to the posh Curtain Bluff Resort, which has water-sports facilities. You'll find grazing animals, refreshment vendors on weekends and shaded picnic tables.

Activities

Jolly Dive DIVING
(462-8305; www.jollydiveantigua.com; Jolly Harbour Dr; 2-tank dive incl equipment & wetsuit US$150; 8am-4pm Mon-Fri, to 2pm Sat; 22) This dive shop has been in business for more than 30 years and has built up excellent local knowledge and tons of experience. Boat dives hit nearby reefs, wrecks and dropoffs, bringing you close to corals, sharks, rays and lobsters. Also does PADI certifications. It's on the beach next to Castaways Beach Bar and the Tranquility Bay resort.

Sleeping

This part of the island has some of the best places to stay, from exclusive all-inclusives scattered among the hillsides to boutique hotels and self-catering apartments. No matter where you stay, you'll never be far from a superb beach, though the area feels far from Antiguan.

South Coast Ocean View Apartments APARTMENT $$
(☎560-4933; www.scova-antigua.com; Cades Bay; apt US$165-190; closed mid-May to end Oct; ; 22) A steep road deposits you at Rudi and Wilma's hilltop complex of four spotless one-bedroom apartments with subdued tropical decor, a tranquil vibe and breezy terraces. Each has its own fully equipped kitchen, making self-catering a cinch.

Sugar Ridge Resort BOUTIQUE HOTEL $$$
(☎562-7700; www.sugarridgeantigua.com; Valley Rd, Jolly Harbour; r incl breakfast US$336-550; ; 22) This sophisticated yet relaxed boutique charmer has stunning views from its 60 colonial-meets-contemporary rooms, the most impressive of which have big verandas, four-poster beds and a private plunge pool. Extra diversion can be had at the two restaurants, Aveda spa and three further pools. A stellar beach is only a short ride away on a free shuttle (or bicycle).

Cocobay Resort RESORT $$$
(☎562-2400; www.cocobayresort.com; Little Ffryes Beach, Bolans; all-inclusive per person cottage US$595-975; ; 22) This all-inclusive 49-unit resort offers stylish and romantic villas including many with their own plunge pool. All rooms come with espresso machines, hammocks and 100% Egyptian-cotton sheets; some have outdoor bathtubs. A great choice if you want to split your time between the infinity pool and nearby Valley Church Beach.

Eating

Jolly Harbour itself has a few pleasant eateries but there are plenty more interesting and atmospheric spots along the highway and on the beaches.

Dennis Cocktail Bar & Restaurant CARIBBEAN $$
(☎462-6740; www.dennis-antigua.com; Valley Rd, Ffryes Beach; mains EC$50-100; 10:30am-10pm, closed Mon Apr-Oct; ; 22) Local boy Dennis Thomas creates magic on the plate with his mom's recipes and produce from his own garden. Tuck into such soulful dishes as creamy conch curry or pungent shrimp-and-chicken medley while taking in the sublime beach views from the breezy terrace. Those in the know come Fridays for the reggae barbecue or Sundays for the suckling pig roast.

Happy hour runs from 4pm to 6:30pm, perfect for wrapping up a day in the sand with a coconut-rum-based Caribbean Sunset.

Miracle's CARIBBEAN $$
(☎732-1682; www.miraclessouthcoast.com; Valley Rd, Jolly Harbour; mains EC$30-100; 11am-1am; ; 22) What was once a humble roadside cottage has evolved over the years into a cozy restaurant with linen-bedecked tables and a sophisticated island vibe. Catch of the day varies from *mahimahi* to tuna and even shark, while shrimp and lobster can be ordered in numerous ways and are served with a choice of two sides. Reservations recommended.

Most dishes take a while to prepare, giving you plenty of time to nurse your beer on the wooden deck.

OJ's Beach Bar & Restaurant CARIBBEAN $$
(☎460-0184; www.facebook.com/ojsbeachbar; Valley Rd, Crabb Hill Village; sandwiches EC$25-30, mains EC$45-100; 10am-11pm; ; 22) Driftwood, conch shells, fishing nets and whatever else the sea washes up get worked into the salty decor of this sun- and rum-soaked beach-bum hangout. It's an Antigua institution. Top menu picks include the grilled snapper and lobster salad, but it's also worth stopping by for a swim and the cinnamon-scented rum punch. Live entertainment on Friday and Sunday nights.

Carmichael's FUSION $$$
(☎562-7700; www.sugarridgeantigua.com/dining/carmichaels; Sugar Ridge Resort, Valley Rd, Jolly Harbour; mains EC$40-100; 6-10pm; ; 22) The chefs at this fine-dining outpost create a blend of Carib-continental cuisine, to be enjoyed with stunning views from the top of Sugar Ridge Resort. Bring a swimsuit for a sunset dip and cocktail in the infinity pool, then settle into a stylish rattan chair on the wooden deck while waiting for dishes such as Caribbean bouillabaisse and fresh lobster.

Getting There & Away

From St John's West bus station (p130), bus 22 travels south along Valley Rd via Jolly Harbour and the beaches as far as Old Road Village. A taxi costs US$20 to Jolly Harbour, about US$25 to the beaches and US$26 to Old Road Village.

Fig Tree Drive

Old Road, a village that juxtaposes scruffiness with two swank resorts, marks the southern start of the 5-mile-long Fig Tree Dr, which winds through rainforest teeming with big old mango and giant-leaved banana trees (called 'figs' locally). Roadside stands sell fruit, jam, juices and the local black pineapple, unique to Antigua. A number of enjoyable hiking trails start at the historical Wallings Dam, including one to Signal Hill and another to wonderful Rendezvous Bay.

Sights & Activities

Wallings Dam & Reservoir HISTORIC SITE

(off Fig Tree Dr; 24hr) FREE Built by the British around 1900, this Victorian-style dam originally created a reservoir holding 13 million gallons of water and supplied it to surrounding villages. In 1912, after three years of drought, it was drained and the area was reforested; it's now teeming with mahoe, ironwood, locust, mango, white cedar and other tree species.

Birdwatchers might be able to spot banana quits, broadwinged hawks and redstars, among others. The reservoir is also the starting point for hikes up Signal Hill and to secluded Rendezvous Bay.

★ Footsteps Rainforest Hiking Tours HIKING

(773-2345; www.hikingantigua.com; Fig Tree Dr; adult/under 16yr US$45/25, minimum 2 people; tours 9am Tue, Thu & by arrangement) Charismatic local guide Dassa shares his extensive knowledge of the island's flora, fauna and history on fun and educational hikes. His signature two- to 2½-hour Signal Hill loop trail tour goes through the rainforest and past the historical Wallings Reservoir to the top for 360-degree island views. Other routes, including treks to secluded Rendezvous Bay, can be customized.

Tours depart from the Fig Tree Studio Art Gallery.

Antigua Rainforest Zip Line Tours ADVENTURE SPORTS

(562-6363; www.antiguarainforest.com; Fig Tree Dr, Wallings; from US$59; tours hourly 9am-noon Mon-Sat) One of Antigua's most enjoyable activities is to roar over the treetops suspended on zip lines. The 2½-hour full course includes 12 zips, short hikes between suspension bridges and a challenge course. Reservations are a must.

Sleeping

Carlisle Bay HOTEL $$$

(866-502-2855; www.carlisle-bay.com; Old Road; ste incl breakfast from US$900; P ❄ 🛜 ≋; 🚌22) Ultra-posh and contemporary, the Carlisle courts style-conscious global nomads who like to trade the beach lounger for the tennis court, the gym, the trail or the yoga mat. All rooms face the calm bay, where you can engage in a full range of complimentary water sports. The kids' club keeps children aged six months to 12 years entertained all day.

Shopping

Fig Tree Studio Art Gallery ART

(460-1234; www.figtreestudioart.com; Fig Tree Dr; 9am-5:30pm Mon-Sat Nov-May; 🛜) For quality regional art and crafts, drop by this lovely gallery in a cottage cradled by rainforest and run by local artist Sallie Harker. The British expat handpicks an ever-changing roster that might showcase boldly pigmented Caribbean scenes, engraved calabashes, bright screen prints and Harker's own woodcuts, oils and watercolors.

Getting There & Away

There is no bus service right along Fig Tree Dr. You can get close by taking either bus 13 from St John's West bus station to Swetes near the northern end, or bus 22 to Old Road on the southern end. From there you'll have to either walk, call a cab or hitch a ride. Hitching is never entirely safe, and we don't recommend it. Travelers who hitch should understand that they are taking a small but potentially serious risk.

English Harbour

Nowhere does Antigua flaunt its maritime heritage more than in English Harbour, a rather stylish and exclusive town sitting on two sheltered bays, where salty fishing boats and ritzy yachts bob side by side in the water. The era when the British Navy was based here is still encapsulated in the beautifully restored Nelson's Dockyard, the island's top historical attraction. For superb views, make your way up to the top of Shirley Heights, and don't miss the gorgeous beaches or the fabulous eating opportunities this upmarket yachtie town has to offer.

Sights

★Nelson's Dockyard National Park HISTORIC SITE

(☎481-5021; www.nationalparksantigua.com; Dockyard Dr, English Harbour; adult/child under 12yr US$8/free; ⏲8am-6pm; 🚌17) Continuously in operation since 1745, this extensively restored Georgian-era marina is Antigua's top sightseeing draw and was made a Unesco World Heritage site in 2016. Today its restored buildings house restaurants, hotels and businesses, the most important of which is the **Dockyard Museum**, which features information on Antigua's history, the dockyard and life at the forts. Among the many trinkets on display is a telescope once used by Nelson himself.

Admission to the Dockyard area is also good for Shirley Heights and the Dow's Hill Interpretation Centre.

★Rendezvous Bay BEACH

After a 90-minute walk through the rainforest (or by a far shorter stony path from Springhill Riding Stables in Falmouth) you'll arrive at one of Antigua's loveliest beaches. Because of its remoteness, you'll usually be alone here, or sharing with a couple of other adventurous romantics. The rainforest path starts near the Wallings Reservoir off Fig Tree Dr but is not signposted, so ask for directions locally. From Falmouth, follow the road past the stables uphill and just keep going.

Follow the signs to the stables and either park here or continue to the end of the road and park just outside a gated compound, then follow the dirt road on your left down to the beach.

Shirley Heights HISTORIC SITE

(☎481-5028; www.nationalparksantigua.com; Shirley Heights Rd, English Harbour; adult/child under 12yr US$8/free) This restored military lookout and gun battery was named after Sir Thomas Shirley (1727–1800), who became the first Governor of the Leeward Islands in 1781. Get some historical background at the small interpretive center, then head uphill to explore the grounds for crumbling ruins and enjoy sweeping views. Admission includes entry to Nelson's Dockyard and the **Dow's Hill Interpretation Centre** (☎481-5021; US$8; ⏲9am-5pm).

As you drive uphill, the road forks with the left lane leading to the **Blockhouse**, where you can see the vestiges of officers' quarters and a powder magazine as well as enjoy superb views southwest, including Eric Clapton's vast Crossroads drug rehab center. If you turn right at the fork, the road dead ends at the **Shirley Heights Lookout**. The former guardhouse is now home to a restaurant-bar (p120) that hosts a famous Sunday-afternoon barbecue party with live bands. Views take in English Harbour and, on clear days, Montserrat and Guadeloupe. The moderate 1.5-mile Carpenters Trail runs from Galleon Beach up to Shirley Heights.

Pillars of Hercules NATURAL FEATURE

(off Galleon Beach; 🚌17) FREE The entrance to English Harbour is guarded by this phalanx of rock soldiers eroded by the relentless wind, rain and crashing waves. The formation is best appreciated from a boat but it's also possible to get close-ups by hiking to the end of Galleon Beach and then scrambling over large boulders. They're slippery, so watch your footing and don't go during high tide.

Pigeon Beach BEACH

(Falmouth; 👪; 🚌17) This tree-shaded community beach has showers, bathrooms, a playground and several cafes and bars, but only so-so snorkeling. The water is remarkably tranquil though, meaning it's a good beach for families. The access road turns off just before the Nelson's Dockyard parking lot.

Galleon Beach BEACH

(English Harbour; 🚌17) The beach closest to the entrance of English Harbour, Galleon borders a resort and thus has plenty of facilities, calm waters and a snorkeling reef close to shore. Take the turn-off from Shirley Heights Rd or catch the water taxi (p120) from the Copper & Lumber Store Hotel.

The beach is also the departure point for several trails up to Shirley Heights and to the Pillars of Hercules eroded cliff formations.

Activities

Middle Ground Trail HIKING

(Pigeon Beach; 🚌17) This popular 1-mile trail connects Pigeon Beach with Nelson's Dockyard and is popular with joggers in the morning and evening hours. From the trailhead near Bumpkins beach bar, it climbs steeply at first, then levels out and follows the ridge of Windward Bay before descending down toward Fort Berkeley and the dockyards.

Desmond Trail HIKING

(off Galleon Beach Rd; 🚌17) This short moderate walk starts just before Galleon Beach and culminates near the Shirley Heights Lookout Restaurant (p120) and offers nice views of English Harbour in the course of the half-hour climb.

Carpenters Trail HIKING

(Galleon Beach; 17) This moderate 1.5-mile-long trail up Shirley Heights starts at the far end of Galleon Beach, skirts ruined Fort Charlotte, and treats you to breezy views of the rugged coastline and rock formations. It's easily combined into a loop route with the Desmond Trail.

Watch out for cactus thorns, which can pierce right through shoe soles; bring a pocketknife or pliers to remove them right away.

Springhill Riding Stables HORSEBACK RIDING

(773-3139; www.antiguaequestrian.com; Falmouth; 1hr lesson & ride US$65; tours 8:30am Mon-Sat) Offers riding lessons as well as a variety of morning tours, including a two-hour ride to Rendezvous Bay (US$125). If you want to swim with your horse, it's an extra US$45. Advanced reservations are required.

Soul Immersions Dive Centre DIVING

(727-8314; www.soulimmersions.ag; Dockyard Dr, Falmouth Harbour; 2-tank dive with equipment US$125; 17) This well-respected dive center offers PADI certification as well as one- and two-tank dives for certified divers to sites in the southern part of the island. You'll get to poke around coral-covered boulders and reefs teeming with rays, sharks and other creatures.

Dockyard Divers DIVING

(729-3040; www.dockyard-divers.com; Nelson's Dockyard, English Harbour; 2-tank dive US$99, snorkeling trip US$45; 17) This well-established outfit offers diving and snorkeling trips to caves, reefs and sunken wrecks. Snorkeling gear rents for US$13 per day.

Sleeping

English Harbour is a justifiably popular place to be based in Antigua. Instead of big resorts, options range from a convivial waterfront hostel to genteel colonial gems and smart boutique hotels.

★ Waterfront Hostel HOSTEL $

(721-2164; www.thewaterfronthostel.com; Compton Bldg, Dockyard Dr, English Harbour; dm/s/d/tr US$30/45/65/95; ; 17) Easily one of the best-value sleeping options in Antigua and certainly the cheapest spot in English Harbour, Waterfront boasts 10 rooms that sleep up to three people and come with sink and shower; shared toilets are down the hall. Make new friends at the harbor-view bar over home-cooked breakfast or cold beers. Restaurants and a supermarket are nearby.

Lodge Antigua HOTEL $

(562-8060; www.thelodgeantigua.com; Dockyard Dr, English Harbour; d/apt/cottage US$95/120/140; P; 17) This perky budget pick at the National Sailing Academy comes with a restaurant-bar overlooking the harbor and a clutch of compact but nicely furnished units surrounded by leafy grounds. Apartments and cottages sleep up to four and come with cooking facilities. Gracious hosts Peter and Elizabeth also rent sailing dinghies, kayaks and SUP boards. Minimum stay is three nights.

Copper & Lumber Store Hotel HOTEL $$

(460-1160; www.copperandlumberhotel.com; Nelson's Dockyard, English Harbour; ste US$165-365; P; 17) Dripping with colonial character, this gracious hotel was built in the 1780s to store the copper and lumber needed for ship repairs. It now has 14 studios and suites, each named after one of Nelson's ships. All open onto a flowery courtyard and burst with vintage flair courtesy of four-poster beds, brick walls, wooden beams and mock gas lamps.

Weekends are rung in with the legendary 'Seafood Friday,' a tasty barbecue on the hotel lawn that brings out locals and visitors in droves.

Ocean Inn B&B $$

(463-7950; www.theoceaninn.com; English Harbour; d incl breakfast US$147-270; ; 17) For reasonably priced five-star views of English Harbour, secure a room at Robert's hillside hideout with 12 units cradled by flowery, terraced grounds. The very best value are the cottages with private verandas; the cheapest are the breezy 'ocean view budget' rooms with shared bathroom. Avoid the windowless room 5.

★Admiral's Inn HISTORIC HOTEL $$$
(☎460-1027; www.admiralsantigua.com; Dockyard Dr, English Harbour; r US$270-392, ste US$495-620; P❄📶🏊) This intimate inn with 23 rooms spread over four Georgian stone buildings is charmingly old-school and romantic with lots of design touches and service that lend character and a deep sense of place. The most impressive rooms are the Gunpowder Suites with four-poster beds, modern bathrooms, and views of the harbor and the infinity pool. There are two restaurants on site.

Inn at English Harbour BOUTIQUE HOTEL $$$
(☎460-1014; www.theinnantigua.com; Freeman's Bay, English Harbour; ste from US$979, 3-night minimum; ❄@📶🏊) Enjoy sublime sunsets, cold glass of wine in hand, from the private terrace of your lusciously furnished suite or beach *cabaña* at this peaceful and romantic retreat from reality. Though it has a colonial style in looks and flair, all the expected 21st-century amenities are accounted for, both in rooms and public areas, and its white sand beach is heavenly.

South Point Hotel DESIGN HOTEL $$$
(☎562-9600; www.southpointantigua.com; English Harbour; ste incl breakfast from US$699; P❄📶🏊; 🚌17) Urban cool meets Caribbean chic at this classy port of call where you can enjoy front-row views of sailing yachts from sleek one- or two-bedroom suites with kitchens, big terraces, and walk-in showers and closets. Fresh flowers add bright accents to the subdued white-and-gray color scheme, and staff fall over themselves to ensure you have everything you need.

Eating

English Harbour has by far the most interesting and innovative dining options in Antigua, and you'll find some great eats down by the waterfront and along the main road. Sunday-afternoon barbecues at Shirley Heights Lookout Restaurant are legendary.

Dockyard Bakery BAKERY $
(☎460-1474; Nelson's Dockyard; baked goods EC$5-10; ⏲8am-4pm Mon-Sat; 🚌17) Behind the museum at Nelson's Dockyard, the fresh bread and delectable baked goods such as cinnamon rolls and chocolate cake will draw you in like a sailor to rum.

Incanto ITALIAN $$
(☎562-9130; www.incantoantigua.com; Antigua Slipway; mains EC$54-93; ⏲noon-3pm & 6-10pm Wed-Mon; 📶) A mother and son team from Milan have created one of Antigua's best dining experiences, complete with fabulous views of the bay. Just getting to this strip of land opposite Nelson's Dockyard is an adventure; take the free boat across the bay or wander through a working shipyard past dry-docked yachts. The menu includes lobster linguine and seared pistachio tuna.

Flatties Flame Grill PORTUGUESE $$
(☎726-4440; www.facebook.com/Flatties-Flame-Grill; Dockyard Dr, English Harbour; mains EC$30-75; ⏲6pm-midnight Tue-Sun; 📶; 🚌17) A local institution, Mark and Amanda's roadside grill sees quality meats and spices get orchestrated into culinary symphonies, mostly of Portuguese origin. The signature dish is the peri-peri chicken, a succulent half or whole bird bathed in a marinade before getting grilled to perfection. Look for South African specials such as *boerewors* (sausage) or biltong (dried meat).

Trappas INTERNATIONAL $$
(☎562-3534; www.facebook.com/Trappas; Dockyard Dr, English Harbour; mains EC$60; ⏲6-10pm Mon-Sat; 📶; 🚌17) It's often standing-room only in this dining room with tropical murals and a big bar. Expats, locals and yachties descend upon this long-time hangout for upscale comfort food such as breaded calamari with garlic dip, burgers with blue cheese, and creative seafood curries bathed in an aromatic balm of local spices.

Bumpkins CARIBBEAN $$
(☎562-2522; islandpropertiesag@live.com; Pigeon Beach; mains EC$30-70; ⏲11am-sunset, dinner Thu-Sun Dec-Mar; 📶; 🚌17) Punctuating the north end of lovely Pigeon Beach, Bumpkins is the go-to place for sublime banana piña coladas, but also feeds fans of unfussy local fare with garlic shrimp, barbecued ribs, jerk chicken, pulled pork and other tasty treats. On Saturday afternoons, tap your feet to the smooth rhythms of a reggae band. Also famous for its full-moon parties.

DON'T MISS

SHIRLEY HEIGHTS SUNDAY BARBECUE

For more than three decades, the place to be in Antigua on a Sunday afternoon has been the **Shirley Heights Lookout Restaurant** (☎728-0636; www.shirleyheightslookout.com; Shirley Heights Rd, English Harbour; mains EC$25-80; ⏰9am-10pm; 📶) with killer views of English Harbour. A steel band gets everyone in the mood from around 4pm during the afternoon barbecue before a reggae band hits the stage at 7pm and the wicked rum punches flow ever more freely. Admission is US$10, and so is the one-way cab ride to or from English Harbour.

Abracadabra ITALIAN $$
(☎460-2701; www.abracadabra-antigua.com; Dockyard Dr, English Harbour; mains US$15-35; ⏰dinner Mon-Sat; 📶; 🚌17) Fondly known as 'Abra,' Salvatore's outpost has been all things to all people since 1984: a little slice of Italy where you can devour homemade pastas or the signature suckling pig; a chilled bar and lounge; and, on weekends, an energetic open-air club with a white-sand dance floor in a tropical garden setting.

Caribbean Taste CARIBBEAN $$
(☎562-3049; off Dockyard Dr, English Harbour; mains US$10-25; ⏰11am-8pm Mon-Sat) For authentic local food cooked with soul, point your compass to this cheerily painted cottage just off the main road to Nelson's Dockyard. The chalkboard menu lists such flavor-packed staples as conch stew and goat curry along with changing specials that might include octopus ceviche or Creole snapper.

★Catherine's Cafe Plage FRENCH $$$
(☎460-5050; www.facebook.com/CatherinesCafe; south end, Pigeon Beach; mains EC$80-135; ⏰noon-3pm daily, 6-9pm Wed-Fri; 📶👪; 🚌17) Downright fancy for a beachside restaurant, delightful Catherine's overlooks the boats of Falmouth Bay and Pigeon Beach's shimmering sands. Hosts Claudine and Guillaume regale expats, yachties and locals with mouthwatering French fare from a stylish-casual cottage with a long bar and lounge chairs in the sand. It's a great lunch spot and especially busy for Sunday brunch. Reservations recommended.

★Colibri FRENCH CARIBBEAN $$$
(☎460-3434; www.colibri-antigua.com; Dockyard Dr, English Harbour; mains EC$70-85; ⏰5pm-midnight Tue-Sat, 11am-7pm Sun; 📶) The most talked-about recent addition to English Harbour's fine slew of dining options, Colibri is the brainchild of French transplant Didier, who helms a professional team working hard to bring its diners a superlative experience, either in the garden under the trees or in the stylish main dining room. Don't miss the excellent lobster risotto or the line-caught wahoo. Reservations advisable.

Information

Eastern Caribbean Amalgamated Bank (☎480-5300; www.ecabank.com; Nelson's Dockyard; ⏰8:30am-1:30pm Mon-Thu, to 3:30pm Fri; 🚌17) Has an ATM.

Nelson's Dockyard Post Office (Dockyard Dr; ⏰8:15am-3pm Mon-Thu, to 1pm Fri; 🚌17)

Getting There & Around

English Harbour is about 13 miles south of St John's via All Saints Rd. Bus 17 makes the trip from the West bus station (EC$3.75). A taxi costs US$25 from St John's and US$35 from the airport.

Water taxis (one way EC$10-15; ⏰9am-6pm) to Galleon Beach or other points in the harbor can be hired near the Copper & Lumber Store Hotel (p118) in Nelson's Dockyard. Most rides are EC$10 to EC$15.

Eastern Antigua

Flat and windswept, Antigua's eastern side is dotted with a small number of quiet villages and gets far fewer visitors than other parts of the island. Those that stay are drawn to the Atlantic-side beaches at Long Bay and Nonsuch Bay, which have great conditions for windsurfing and kitesurfing. Most people, though, come on day trips to explore historical sites including Betty's Hope, the rugged splendor of Devil's Bridge or the gorgeous crescent of white sand at Half Moon Bay.

Sights

★Half Moon Bay BEACH

(near Freetown) Water the color of blue curaçao laps this white crescent in the remote southeast. Bodysurfers head to the south end, snorkelers to the calm waters north, and everyone meets at the two beach bars for grilled-fish lunches and rum cocktails. A new resort being built on the hillside above the south end of the beach may change it forever, though.

Scrambling over the bluff at the far end takes you to another beach backed by an exclusive villa resort with views of uninhabited offshore Smith Island.

Long Bay BEACH

A favorite beach with locals, Long Bay has clear-blue, kid-friendly waters and a gorgeous white-sand beach that's reef-protected and good for snorkeling. Two resorts bookend the beach, which is lined with souvenir shops, a water-sports concession and a couple of bars.

Betty's Hope HISTORIC SITE

(269-462-1469; off Pares Village Main Rd, Pares; site 24hr, interpretive center 9am-4pm Mon-Sat; 33) FREE Ponder Antigua's colonial past while poking around a restored stone windmill, as well as remnants of the Great House, the distillery and other buildings of the island's first sugar plantation, established in 1674 by Christopher Codrington and named for his daughter. An interpretive center demystifies the sugar-making process and provides glimpses into the hardship of daily life on the plantation, which had around 400 slaves at its peak.

Devil's Bridge NATURAL FEATURE

(Pares Village Main Rd, past Willikies, Long Bay) Just before reaching Long Bay, a rough 1-mile dirt road veers off the main highway toward this windswept bluff ringed by rugged cliffs shaped by the relentless crashing of powerful waves. Views are fabulous and especially rewarding at sunset. If the tide is right, you can see the powerful blowhole at the far end in action. A new adults-only resort being built here does seem set to rather change the overall atmosphere, however.

Antigua's Donkey Sanctuary ZOO

(461-4957; www.antiguaanimals.com/donkey; near Bethesda; donations appreciated; 10am-4pm Mon-Sat;) FREE Meet Charley, Chrissy, blind Stevie or any of the other 150 or so stray donkeys that have found a loving home in this sanctuary operated by the Antigua & Barbuda Humane Society. Dedicated staff are happy to introduce visitors to the friendly animals and let them brush them and take pictures with them.

For a mere US$25 donation you can even adopt one of the donkeys. The facility is about 0.9 miles off the highway via an unpaved road.

Activities

40 Knots Kitesurfing & Windsurfing School KITESURFING

(788-9504; www.40knots.net; Nonsuch Bay Resort, near Freetown; kitesurfing lessons 1hr/half-day/2 half-days US$89/225/550; Oct-Aug) If you've always wanted to 'fly' over water, this friendly and dedicated international team will get you up and going with individual lessons or in groups of up to three. The reef-enclosed bay offers ideal learning conditions for kite-flying, windsurfing and SUP. Experienced surfers can rent equipment and catch a lift to nearby idyllic Green Island.

Sleeping & Eating

★Blue Bay Antigua B&B B&B $$

(785-2877; www.bluebayantigua.com; Seatons; d incl breakfast US$150;) Proud citizen of the world Cecilia has created a quite atypical 'eco B&B' on this delightful hilltop overlooking the eponymous blue bay below. This is a place for travelers interested in sustainable travel and getting off the grid, but who enjoy doing so comfortably and affordably in a charming three-room villa complete with swimming pool, garden and on-site goats.

★Road House CARIBBEAN $

(764-8090; Main Rd, New Field Village; mains EC$10-35; 6:30am-3pm Mon-Thu, 6:30am-late Fri & Sun) A popular stop for a cold beer and local lunch (goat water, seafood chowder, grilled fish) en route to Half Moon Bay, this place kicks into high gear on Fridays when all dishes cost EC$5 after 5pm, and even more so on Sunday afternoons when villagers arrive in droves to ring out the weekend with barbecue and a reggae band.

Smiling Harry's CARIBBEAN $
(☎460-4084; www.facebook.com/smilingharrys; Half Moon Bay, near Freetown; mains EC$20-40; ⊙11am-sunset Sat & Sun) The eponymous owner, Harry Thomas, has passed on, but his smiling spirit still hovers over this rustic beach shack famous for its 'Thirst Quenchers' and unfussy Antiguan fare. There's no set menu, so just ask what's cooking. Gets busy with local families at Sunday lunchtime.

Beach Bum Bar & Grill CARIBBEAN $$
(Half Moon Bay; mains EC$26-70; ⊙9am-5pm; 📶) The most popular of the two beach restaurants at Half Moon Bay, Beach Bum wins with its views of the sea, fun atmosphere and friendly staff. Meals of fresh fish and seafood are no frills but delicious, served up on packed wooden tables that enjoy a party atmosphere on the weekend.

Getting There & Away

This sprawling area is best explored by vehicle, either in your own rental car or by taxi. Gas stations are scarce, so be sure to have plenty in the tank. The drive from English Harbour to Half Moon Bay takes about 30 to 45 minutes and presents you with spectacular views of Willoughby Bay. A taxi from St John's costs US$18 to Betty's Hope, US$27 to Long Bay and Devil's Bridge, and US$30 to Half Moon Bay.

From St John's East bus station, bus 33 runs east past Betty's Hope as far as Willikies (close to Long Bay and Devil's Bridge).

OFF THE BEATEN TRACK

BARBUDA'S CAVES

Two Foot Bay National Park (east coast) FREE, on the northeastern coast, consists of coastal scrub forest hemming in the cliff-lined waterfront. It's famous for its caves, most importantly the **Indian Cave** (Highland Rd, Two Foot Bay National Park) FREE, which has the only known petroglyphs on Barbuda. You need your own transportation or preferably a guide to make the most of visiting here. On weekends, the park is a popular camping site with locals.

Darby Sink Cave (northeast coast) FREE is not a true cave but a 300ft-wide, 70ft-deep sinkhole with tall palm trees growing out of it and mighty ferns and lianas dangling down from the rim, creating a miniature rainforest ecosystem. Look for lizards, hermit crabs, iguanas and other critters among the dense foliage.

BARBUDA

Antigua's tiny sister island took a devastating direct hit from Hurricane Irma in 2017. The population was evacuated and a year-long shutdown of its small but significant tourism industry followed. Almost every roof on the island was torn off by the storm, and many houses and businesses were completely flattened. The island's only town, Codrington, is still in the earliest stages of rebuilding, with international aid agencies present to help with reconstruction.

With this in mind, it may seem like a bad time to visit Barbuda, but locals are very keen to see travelers return. Businesses are slowly reopening, even if hurricane damage will be visible for years. The island's two biggest attractions – its extraordinary white-sand beaches and its fascinating Frigate Bird Sanctuary – were both largely unaffected by the storm, and while there's only a handful of hotels open, Barbuda is doubtless coming back from the brink.

Getting There & Around

Barbuda is reached by the Barbuda Express (p130) ferry, which normally leaves St John's daily except Sunday, as well as by daily flights on SVG Air (p129) from Antigua's VC Bird International Airport. For those in a hurry, helicopter charter to the island is another way to get there.

Barbuda has no public transportation. There are only a few private rental cars available; book ahead (try Barbuda Rentals (p124)) to ensure you can get one. Most visitors get around by taxis or arrange for tours with a guide who drives.

Codrington

Barbuda's only town, lagoon-front Codrington is home to most of the island's residents and a minuscule airstrip. It's a fairly ho-hum place, all the more so since Hurricane Irma tore through it in 2017, destroying many of its older houses and leaving many of its

Barbuda

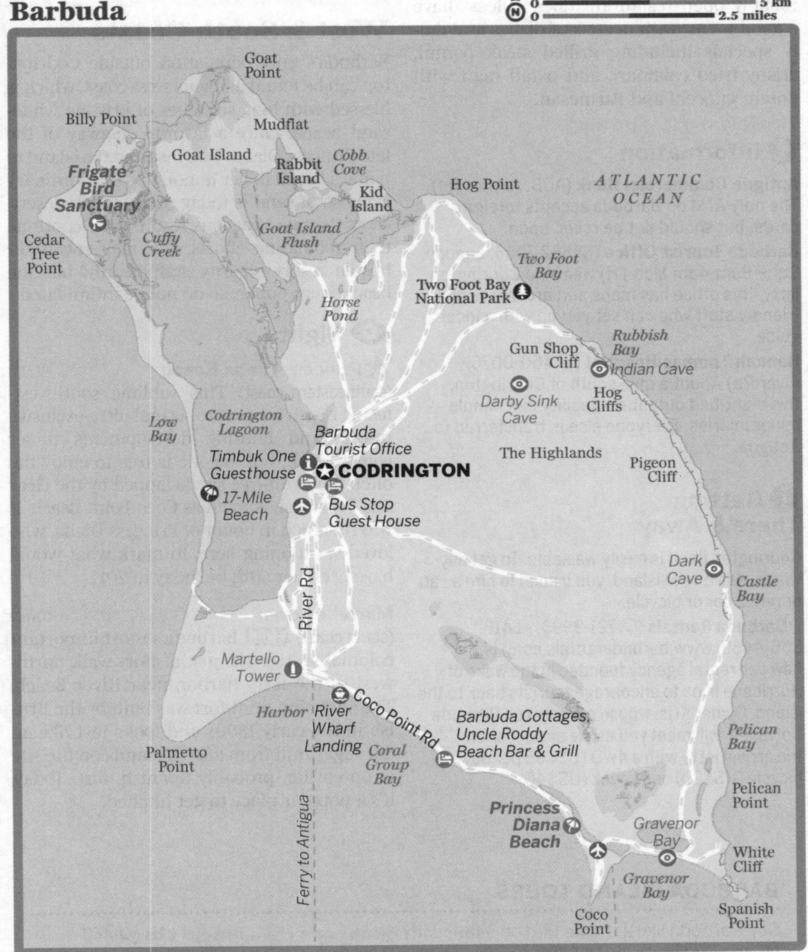

structures – including its church – roofless. Aid agencies are hard at work helping locals rebuild, though many houses have been abandoned and very few businesses are working. Despite this, Codrington has a friendly atmosphere and welcomes visitors with a wave.

Sleeping & Eating

Timbuk One Guesthouse GUESTHOUSE $
(722-8085; Timbuk St; r with/without bathroom US$110/85;) The best guesthouse in Codrington at present is also where you'll find its most reliable restaurant. The seven rooms upstairs share bathrooms, while the seven downstairs have en suite facilities, as do the three new rooms built in front. Rooms are simple but clean, though wi-fi is charged.

Timbuk One CARIBBEAN $
(Timbuk St; mains EC$20-50; 8am-9pm Mon & Tue, to midnight Wed-Sat, 3-10pm Sun;) You'll be sharing this rather unappealing space with dozens of one-armed bandits and their occasional punters, but Codrington's most

reliably open restaurant does at least have a good menu with dozens of dishes and daily specials including grilled steak panini, crispy fried calamari, and oxtail ragu with potato gnocchi and Parmesan.

Information

Antigua Commercial Bank (ACB; Airport Rd) The only ATM on Barbuda accepts foreign cards, but should not be relied upon.

Barbuda Tourist Office (562-7066; Lagoon St; 8am-4pm Mon-Fri) Near the Codrington jetty, this office has maps and brochures and friendly staff who can set you up with a local guide.

Hannah Thomas Hospital (460-0076; River Rd) About a mile south of Codrington, this eight-bed outpatient facility can handle minor injuries. Everyone else is transferred to Antigua.

Getting There & Away

Codrington itself is easily walkable. To get anywhere else on the island, you'll need to hire a cab or rent a car or bicycle.

Barbuda Rentals (721-9993, +1 416-856-4469; www.barbudarentals.com) is a new car-rental agency founded in the wake of Hurricane Irma to encourage tourists back to the island. Owner Kris, whose parents run Barbuda Cottages, will meet you at the airport or on the arrival jetty with a 4WD (US$65 per day), a bicycle (US$20) or a kayak (US$40).

West & South Coasts

Barbuda's only population outside Codrington can be found along its west coast, which is blessed with long stretches of pristine white-sand beach. Once a favorite getaway of the late Princess Diana, who inspired the island to name a beach in her honor, this extraordinary expanse of sand is today pretty much deserted as the two luxurious resorts here continue their rebuilding efforts. You may encounter hostile resort security staff nearby, but the beaches are public, so do not be intimidated.

Sights

★Princess Diana Beach BEACH

(southeastern coast) This sublime southwest-facing beach is home to several ultra-exclusive resorts and housing developments under construction, but anyone is free to enjoy the often footprint-free sands lapped by the clear sea. Previously known as Coco Point Beach, it was renamed in honor of Princess Diana, who loved vacationing here, to mark what would have been her 50th birthday in 2011.

Martello Tower TOWER

(south coast) FREE Barbuda's most important colonial vestige sits just a short walk northwest of the ferry harbor, near River Beach. The 56ft-high mini-fort was built by the British in the early 1800s and looks just like an old sugar mill from afar. It stands on the site of an earlier, probably Spanish, fort. Today, it's a popular place to get hitched.

BARBUDA ISLAND TOURS

See Barbuda like a frigate bird on a tour with **Caribbean Helicopters Ltd** (460-5900; www.flychl.com; US$385, 4-passenger minimum, 6-passenger maximum; tours 9am, 9:45am & 10:30am), departing from Antigua. Price includes flight and a beachside lobster lunch at Low Bay. The entire trip takes 4½ hours and includes time to swim and explore the bird sanctuary. Note that these tours target the cruise-ship market. Private tours can also be arranged (US$1315 for up to six people).

The **Barbuda Day Tour** (560-7989; www.barbudaexpress.com; adult/child 3-12yr US$164/100; tours 9am-4pm Mon, Tue, Thu & Fri, 6am-2pm Wed), operated by Barbuda Express, includes a 90-minute ferry ride and visits to the bird sanctuary and the caves, as well as a lobster lunch and a beach-splashing session at Princess Diana Beach.

John Taxi Service (788-5378; www.facebook.com/JohnTaxiServiceTours; per person US$75; tours 11am-3pm Tue-Fri) specializes in guided minibus tours targeted at day-trippers arriving by ferry. In four hours, Levi John will take you to the caves, the bird sanctuary and to a lobster lunch, making this a great deal.

WORTH A TRIP

FRIGATE BIRD SANCTUARY

Codrington Lagoon National Park protects a vast estuary that supports one of the world's largest colonies of frigate birds at the **Frigate Bird Sanctuary** (☎480-1225; sea taxi US$50, 4 people maximum, national park US$2). More than 2500 of these black-feathered critters roost among the scrubby mangroves. The birds' nesting sites are abuzz with squawking, and the sight of all those blood-red inflating throat pouches is mesmerizing. The lagoon can only be visited by licensed sea taxi from the Codrington jetty. Make arrangements at least a day in advance through the tourist office.

17-Mile Beach BEACH
(Palm Beach) This epic stretch of silky smooth, unblemished sands separates the ocean from the Codrington Lagoon. It's possible to walk for hours but note that there's no shade and no vendors, so bring everything you need.

Gravenor Bay BAY
(southeast coast) The pristine waters of Gravenor Bay between Coco Point and Spanish Point are a popular yacht anchorage and have reefs offering excellent snorkeling. Near the heart of the bay is an old dilapidated pier, while the ruins of a small tower lie about a half-mile away to the east.

Sleeping & Eating

★ **Barbuda Cottages** APARTMENT $$$
(☎722-3050; www.barbudacottages.com; Coral Group Bay; 1-/3-bedroom cottage US$375/525, 3-night minimum; ⊙closed Aug-Oct;) At this little slice of paradise you'll fall asleep to the ocean breezes in one of three solar-powered, brightly painted villas on stilts right on Coral Group Bay beach. Each of the three stylish cottages has a full kitchen and a breezy veranda with great views. The on-site restaurant-bar makes tempting culinary treats.

Uncle Roddy Beach Bar & Grill CARIBBEAN $$
(☎722-3050; www.barbudacottages.com; next to Barbuda Cottages, Coral Group Bay; mains EC$30-100; ⊙11am-10pm Mon-Sat;) Badly damaged during Irma and now expanded, this solar-powered beach bar is perfect for spending a relaxing day with grilled lobster and the signature Barbuda Smash. Make reservations 24 hours in advance as Roddy only buys supplies as needed. Bring bug spray to combat pesky sand flies.

Getting There & Away

If you happen to have your own yacht, you can drop anchor for easy access. Everyone else will have to get here by taxi or rental car, on foot or by bike or kayak.

UNDERSTAND ANTIGUA & BARBUDA

History

Wadadli

The first permanent settlers on Antigua were an Amerindian tribe called Siboney who came to the area around 2900 BC. They were followed by the Arawaks who arrived around the 1st century AD and called Antigua 'Wadadli,' a name still used today. Around AD 1200 the Arawaks were forced out by invading Caribs, who used the islands as bases for their forays in the region, but apparently didn't settle them.

Columbus sighted Antigua in 1493 and named it after a church in Seville, Spain. In 1632 the British colonized Antigua, establishing a settlement at Parham, on the east side of the island. The settlers started planting indigo and tobacco, but a glut in the supply of those crops soon drove down prices, leaving growers looking for something new.

Colonialism & Sugarcane

In 1674 Sir Christopher Codrington arrived on Antigua and established the first sugar plantation, Betty's Hope. By the end of the century, a plantation economy had developed, huge numbers of enslaved people were imported and the central valleys were deforested and planted with cane. Britain had annexed Barbuda in 1628 and granted it to the Codrington family in 1680. After the slave trade was abolished in 1807, the Codringtons established a 'slave breeding farm' on Barbuda, which remained in operation until slavery as such was abolished in 1834. In 1860 Barbuda reverted back to the Crown and became a dependency of Antigua.

As Antigua prospered, the British built numerous fortifications around the island, turning it into one of their most secure bases in the Caribbean. The most heavily fortified area was English Harbour, where the Caribbean fleet of the British Royal Navy was based from 1725 until 1854. What is today's Nelson's Dockyard was continually expanded and improved throughout the 18th century. Other forts were Fort James and Fort Barrington, both of which protected the harbor of St John's.

With the abolition of slavery, the plantations went into a steady decline. Unlike on some other Caribbean islands, the land was not turned over to formerly enslaved people when the plantations went under, but was instead consolidated under the ownership of a few landowners. Many former slaves moved off the plantations and into shantytowns, while others crowded onto properties held by the church.

Road to Independence

A military-related construction boom during WWII, and the development of a tourist industry during the postwar period, helped spur economic growth. A first step in Antigua's road to independence was the West Indies Act of 1967 in which Britain granted the island control over domestic issues while retaining responsibility for external issues and defense. Finally, on November 1, 1981, Antigua and Barbuda became an independent state within the British Commonwealth with Vere Cornwall Bird as its first prime minister.

People & Culture

Away from the resorts, Antigua retains its traditional West Indian character. It's manifested in the gingerbread architecture found around the capital, the popularity of steelpan (steel-band), calypso and reggae music, and in festivities, such as Carnival. English traditions also play an important role, as is evident in the national sport of cricket.

Many Barbudans originally come from or have spent time living on their sister island, Antigua, and favor the quieter pace of life on the more isolated Barbuda. In fact, many Barbudans working in tourism are happy with the trickle of tourists that the remote island attracts, and have been reluctant to court the kind of development Antigua has seen.

Approximately 90% of Antiguans are of African descent. There are also small minority populations of British, Portuguese and Lebanese ancestry. The population of Barbuda is approximately 1600, with most of African descent.

Beside the Anglican Church, Antiguans belong to a host of religious denominations, which include Roman Catholic, Moravian, Methodist, Seventh Day Adventist, Lutheran and Jehovah's Witness. On Sundays, services at the more fundamentalist churches draw such crowds that roads are blocked and drivers pray for divine intervention.

Landscape & Wildlife

Unlike Montserrat, its (at times) smoking neighbor to the southwest, neither Antigua nor Barbuda is dominated by a dramatic volcano. However, the southwest corner of Antigua is volcanic in origin and quite hilly, rising to 1319ft at Mt Obama (known as Boggy Peak until 2009), the island's highest point. The rest of the island, which is predominantly of limestone and coral formation, is given to a more gently undulating terrain of open plains and scrubland.

FRIGATE BIRDS: AERIAL PIRATES

Frigate birds skim the water's surface for fish, but because their feathers lack the water-resistant oils common to other seabirds, they cannot dive into water. Also known as the man-of-war bird, the frigate bird has evolved into an aerial pirate that supplements its own fishing efforts by harassing other seabirds until they release their catch, which the frigate bird then swoops up in mid-flight.

While awkward on the ground, the frigate bird, with its distinctive forked tail and 6ft wingspan, is beautifully graceful in flight. It has the lightest weight-to-wingspan ratio of any bird and can soar at great heights for hours on end – making it possible for the bird to feed along the coast of distant islands and return home to roost at sunset without having landed anywhere other than its nesting site.

Antigua's land area is 108 sq miles. The island is vaguely rounded in shape, averaging about 11 miles across. The coastline is cut by numerous coves and bays, many lined with white-sand beaches.

Barbuda, 25 miles north of Antigua, is nearly as flat as the surrounding ocean. A low-lying coral island, Barbuda's highest point is a mere 145ft above sea level. The west side of Barbuda encompasses the expansive Codrington Lagoon, which is bound by a long, undeveloped barrier beach of blindingly white sand.

As a consequence of colonial-era deforestation for sugar production, most of Antigua's vegetation is dryland scrub. The island's marshes and salt ponds attract a fair number of stilts, egrets, ducks and pelicans, while hummingbirds are found in garden settings. Codrington Lagoon has one of the largest frigate-bird colonies in the world.

SURVIVAL GUIDE

Directory A–Z

ACCESSIBLE TRAVEL

Generally speaking, Antigua and Barbuda are not very progressive when it comes to meeting the needs of the disabled. The big resorts usually have rooms that can accommodate the mobility-impaired; some provide beach wheelchairs.

In most villages, sidewalks are in poor condition or nonexistent. In St John's, many of the shops and toilets adjacent to the cruise-ship terminal (ie at Heritage Quay and Redcliffe Quay) are accessible.

Neither buses nor taxis are equipped to transport wheelchair-bound travelers. The nonprofit Antigua & Barbuda Association of Persons with Disabilities is working toward improving the situation.

ACCOMMODATIONS

Accommodations on Antigua and Barbuda are expensive, and besides a few locally run guesthouses in the inland villages, older hotels and moderately priced apartments, the market is dominated by high-end (often all-inclusive) resorts. On Antigua, properties cluster on Dickenson Bay, around Jolly Harbour and in English Harbour. Many close for a few weeks between August and October.

CHILDREN

The Antigua and Barbuda tourism industry generally caters more to grown-up visitors, with some resorts even being restricted to 'adults only.' If traveling with children, check if your resort has a children's pool, organized activities or day-care/babysitting services.

West-coast beaches tend to be calmer. Water-sports activity is best on Dickenson Bay.

A great place to visit with animal-loving tots is Antigua's Donkey Sanctuary (p121). Older children will enjoy the Antigua Rainforest Zip Line Tours (p116).

> **SLEEPING PRICE RANGES**
>
> The following price ranges refer to a double with bathroom during peak season (December to April). Unless otherwise stated, breakfast is not included. In most cases, listed room rates do not include the 12.5% value-added tax (VAT) and 10% service charge.
>
> **$** less than US$100
>
> **$$** US$100–300
>
> **$$$** more than US$300

ELECTRICITY

220V, 60 cycles. Some places provide 110V, 60 cycles, some provide both. American two-pin sockets dominate; UK sockets are rare.

EMBASSIES & CONSULATES

Consular affairs for US citizens are handled by the **US Consular Agent** (☎726-6531, mobile 463-6531; Jasmine Crt, Ste 2, Friars Hill Rd; ⏲9am-noon Mon & Fri, 1:30-4:30pm Wed) in St John's. There are no foreign embassies in Antigua and Barbuda – most countries handle Antigua through their embassies in Bridgetown, Barbados.

EMERGENCY NUMBERS

Ambulance, fire, police ☎911 or 999

FOOD

From roadside barbecues to rustic beach bars and gourmet temples, feeding your tummy is no tall order in Antigua, although on Barbuda the selection is far more limited. Opening hours are erratic and subject to change at any time; some places close from August to October. Menu prices may not include tax (15%) and a service charge (10%).

Essential Food & Drink

Pepperpot Antigua's national dish is a hearty stew blending meat and vegetables, such as okra, spinach, eggplant, squash and potatoes. It's often served with fungi, which are not mushrooms but cornmeal patties or dumplings.

EATING PRICE RANGES

The following price ranges refer to a main course.

$ less than US$10

$$ US$10–25

$$$ more than US$25

Black pineapple The local pineapple was first introduced by the Arawaks and is smaller than your garden variety. It's known as 'black' because it's at its sweetest when kind of dark green. It grows primarily on the southwest coast, near Cades Bay.

Rock lobster This hulking crustacean has a succulent tail but no claws and is best served grilled. (And you'll be forgiven if after a few rum punches you're humming a tune by the B-52s while digging in.)

Wadadli Antigua Brewery makes this local brew, a fresh pale lager, with desalinated seawater.

Cavalier and **English Harbour** Locally produced rums best mixed with fruit juice.

HEALTH

For minor illnesses, hotels and resorts will be able to help you find medical assistance. Healthcare is expensive and the standard of the care and equipment not as high, modern or comprehensive as you might be used to. The nearest hyperbaric chambers are in Saba, St Thomas and Guadeloupe.

Hannah Thomas Hospital (p124) Tiny outpatient facility on Barbuda.

Mt St John's Medical Centre (p111) Main hospital with 185 beds and 24-hour emergency room; on Antigua.

INTERNET ACCESS

Hotels, restaurants, cafes, bars and many other businesses provide free wi-fi for their customers.

LEGAL MATTERS

Antigua and Barbuda's legal system is based on British common law. In case of legal difficulties, you have the right to legal representation and are eligible for legal aid if you can't afford to pay for private services. Foreign nationals should receive the same legal protections as local citizens.

Drunk driving, drug or gun possession, cross-dressing, prostitution, public cursing and wearing camouflage clothing are among the offenses that can get you in trouble on Antigua and Barbuda.

The police have the right to arrest anyone suspected of committing a crime without a warrant. Suspects must be brought before a court within 48 hours of arrest or detention.

LGBT+ TRAVELERS

There is no real gay scene on Antigua and Barbuda but no overt discrimination either. However, homosexuality is on the books as illegal and is theoretically punishable with jail time, although enforcement is nonexistent. Just be discreet and avoid public displays of affection, especially outside the international resorts, and you're unlikely to run into any problems. Most locals meet online.

MONEY

ATMs can be found all over Antigua, including at the airport, in downtown St John's, in English Harbour and in major supermarkets including Epicurean. All dispense Eastern Caribbean dollars; some also dispense US dollars. Barbuda presently has only one ATM (p124) (in Codrington).

Credit cards are widely accepted.

Exchange Rates

Australia	A$1	EC$1.94
Canada	C$1	EC$2.03
Euro Zone	€1	EC$3.05
Japan	¥100	EC$2.41
New Zealand	NZ$1	EC$1.81
UK	UK£1	EC$3.52
US	US$1	EC$2.71

For current exchange rates, see www.xe.com.

Taxes & Refunds

Antigua and Barbuda levies a 15% sales tax (called ABST) on most goods and services. Basic foods, medicine, education and other services are exempt.

At hotels, the rate is 12.5%. It's not always factored into quoted prices at restaurant and hotels, so ask and/or read the small print.

Visitors are not eligible to reclaim VAT upon leaving Antigua and Barbuda.

Tipping

Hotels US$0.50 to US$1 per bag is standard; gratuity for cleaning staff is at your discretion.

Restaurants If the service charge is not automatically added to the bill, tip 10% to 15%.

Taxis Tip 10% to 15% of the fare.

POST

When mailing a letter to the islands, follow the addressee's name with the town and 'Antigua, West Indies' or 'Barbuda, West Indies.'

Post Office English Harbour (p120)

Post Office St John's (p111)

PUBLIC HOLIDAYS

New Year's Day January 1
Good Friday/Easter Monday March/April
Labour Day First Monday in May
Pentecost/Whit Monday 40 days after Easter
Carnival Late July to first Tuesday in August
Independence Day November 1
VC Bird Day December 9
Christmas/Boxing Day December 25/26

SAFE TRAVEL

Most visits to Antigua, and especially Barbuda, are trouble-free.

- Theft is a possibility, so lock your valuables at your hotel and don't carry too much cash or flaunt expensive jewelry.
- Through rare, violent crimes such as sexual assault and armed robbery do occur, so take the usual precautions. Women especially should avoid potentially dangerous situations, such as hiking or going to deserted beaches alone.
- If you're driving, be extra careful at night due to unlit roads, poor or complete lack of signage, and potholed narrow roads.

TELEPHONE

- The country code for Antigua and Barbuda is 268.
- To place a call to Antigua and Barbuda, dial your country's international access code + 268 + local number.
- To call abroad, dial 011 + country code + area code + local number.
- If making a call within or between Antigua and Barbuda, you only need to dial the seven-digit local number if dialing from a landline.
- For directory assistance, dial 411.
- In hotels, local calls are often free but international ones are charged at exorbitant rates.

Cell Phones

The two main networks in Antigua and Barbuda are Digicel (www.digicelgroup.com/ag) and Flow (https://discoverflow.co/antigua). You can only get a SIM card for either network at their offices in St John's, Antigua, but can top up credit almost anywhere, including online.

TIME

Clocks in Antigua and Barbuda are set to Eastern Caribbean Time (Atlantic Time), which is four hours behind GMT. The islands do not observe daylight savings time.

TOURIST INFORMATION

For advance planning, check www.antigua-barbuda.org, www.visitantiguabarbuda.com or www.barbudaful.net.

Antigua Tourist Office (p111) Maintains an information kiosk at Heritage Quay on cruise-ship days.

Barbuda Tourist Office (p124) Small office in Codrington offering information about Barbuda.

> **PRACTICALITIES**
>
> **News Sites** Key local news sites are www.antiguaobserver.com and https://caribbeanchronicle.org
>
> **Radio** Popular local stations include NiceFM (104.3FM) and Observer Radio (91.1FM). The BBC is on 89.1FM.
>
> **Smoking** Officially permitted everywhere except in government buildings. However, most hotels and restaurants prohibit guests from smoking indoors. Some have designated outdoor areas for smokers.
>
> **Weights & Measures** The imperial system is used.

VOLUNTEERING

Antigua's Donkey Sanctuary (p121) Operated by the Antigua & Barbuda Humane Society, this outfit needs volunteer help to take care of stray donkeys.

Environmental Awareness Group of Antigua & Barbuda (EAG; ☎462-6236; www.eagantigua.org; cnr Market & Long Sts; ⏰9am-4pm Mon-Fri) Needs help with a wide variety of programs, from turtle protection to bird censuses and fern conservation.

ℹ Getting There & Away

AIR

VC Bird International Airport (☎484-2300; www.vcbia.com; Sir George Walter Hwy, Antigua; 📶), about 5 miles east of St John's, is a modern terminal that opened in 2015.

Delta, US Airways, United Airlines, WestJet, JetBlue, CanJet and Air Canada have direct flights from various North American gateway cities to Antigua.

British Airways and Virgin Atlantic operate direct flights from the UK, while Condor has a direct flight from Frankfurt.

LIAT (☎480-5582; www.liat.com) and **Caribbean Airlines** (☎800-744-2225; www.caribbean-airlines.com; ⏰office 8am-4pm Mon-Fri) are the main regional carriers. **Fly Montserrat** (☎664-491-3434; www.flymontserrat.com) and **SVG Air** (☎784-457-5124; www.flysvgair.com) fly to Montserrat. **BMN Air** (☎562-7183;

www.antigua-flights.com) offers charter services between Antigua and Montserrat.

Getting to Neighboring Islands

Montserrat is served by air (Fly Montserrat, SVG Air) and by **ferry** (☎778-9786; return adult/child 2-12yr EC$300/150) from Antigua.

Antigua is the hub of regional airline LIAT, and has frequent flights to St Kitts, Nevis, St-Martin/Sint Maarten and other islands. Winair has connections to its base in St-Martin/Sint Maarten as well as to St Kitts and Dominica. Caribbean Airlines flies to Antigua from Jamaica and Trinidad. Trans Anguilla Airways connects Antigua to Anguilla via Nevis, and Seaborne Airlines operates flights from San Juan, Puerto Rico.

SEA

Cruise Ship

Antigua is a major port of call for cruise ships. The cruise-ship pier, at Heritage Quay in St John's Harbour, segues into a duty-free shopping mall, and is within easy walking distance of St John's main sights.

When several behemoths are docked on the same day, beaches and other attractions can get very busy. Independent travelers might want to check the cruise-ship schedule (eg at www.cruisetimetables.com/cruises-to-st-johns-antigua.html) if they wish to avoid the crowds.

By contrast, Barbuda has no cruise-ship terminal and is completely off the radar of cruise travelers.

Ferry

The Barbuda Express ferry connects Antigua and Barbuda in both directions daily except Sunday. There is also a ferry service with Montserrat Ferry between Antigua and Montserrat. Montserrat's tourist office site (www.visitmontserrat.com/sea) also posts the latest schedule. The round-trip fare is EC$300 (EC$150 for children aged two to 12).

Yacht

Antigua's many fine, protected ports make it one of the major yachting centers of the Caribbean. Full-service marinas are at English Harbour, Falmouth Harbour, Jolly Harbour and Parham Harbour. If you're going on to Barbuda, ask for a cruising permit, which will allow you to visit without further formalities. Bring everything you'll need from Antigua, as there are no yachting facilities on Barbuda.

> **CAR RENTAL WARNING**
>
> Because of the poor road conditions, most vehicles have dents and scratches. Make sure that the car-rental agent records all damages and hands you a copy before taking over the car. In addition, take detailed photographs of your vehicle when you receive it.
>
> If the agent is not present when you return the car, take another set of photographs before leaving it. Some companies, including presumably reputable international ones, may claim that you added additional damage and charge your credit card for bogus repairs. With your photographs, you should be able to prove the scam.

Getting Around

AIR

Scheduled air service between Antigua and Barbuda is offered by SVG Air and Fly Montserrat. Transfers and tours may also be arranged through **Caribbean Helicopters** (CHL; ☎460-5900; www.flychl.com; VC Bird International Airport, Antigua).

BICYCLE

Check with your hotel, as many have a small fleet of bikes available for their guests. A reliable bike shop with rentals is **Bike Plus** (☎462-2453; Camacho Ave; bike rental per day US$20; ⏰8am-5pm Mon-Sat) in St John's. On Barbuda, rentals are available from Barbuda Rentals (p124).

BOAT

Bumpy 90-minute catamaran rides operated by **Barbuda Express** (☎560-7989; www.barbuda-express.com; return adult/7-12yr/3-6yr/0-2yr US$85/75/45/15; ⏰office 9am-6pm daily, ferry daily except Sun) link St John's with the **River Wharf Landing** in southern Barbuda. Schedules change, but in general boats leave Antigua early in the morning and return from Barbuda in the late afternoon.

In peak season, it's best to make reservations or buy tickets in advance. Inclement weather may cancel service, so call ahead to confirm departure times and take precautions if you're prone to seasickness.

The company also operates guided day tours to Barbuda (from US$129).

BUS

Antigua has a decent network of private minivans traveling along the main roads. Buses to the south, northwest and west leave from the **West bus station** (Market St) opposite the Public Market in St John's; buses to the northeast, the east and southeast leave from the **East bus station** (Independence Ave). Fares cost EC$2.25 to EC$4, with a small surcharge between 10pm and 5am. Bus Stop Antigua (www.busstopanu.com) has details.

Buses don't leave until full and generally run from about 6am until 7pm; there are very few buses at night and on Sunday. Buses to English Harbour may run as late as midnight, but do confirm this with the driver.

CAR & MOTORCYCLE

Driving is on the left, the steering wheel is on the right. The speed limit is generally 20mph in built-up areas and 40mph on highways.

If you have an accident, call the police and don't move the vehicle.

Car Rental

International car-rental companies with outlets at the Antigua airport include Avis, Dollar and Hertz. **Big's Car Rental** (☎562-4901; www.bigscarrental.net; English Harbour; vehicles per day from US$40) is a local outfit in English Harbour. Car rentals on Barbuda are all local and very limited as much of the fleet was destroyed by Hurricane Irma. Ask at your hotel for a referral.

Most agencies will deliver cars to your hotel free of charge. Daily rates start at about US$40 for a compact. Gas stations are scattered around Antigua, including a handy one for refueling just outside the airport. There is just one gas station on Barbuda.

Driver's License

A local driving permit, available from car-rental agencies, is required for driving on Antigua or Barbuda. It costs US$20 or EC$50 and is valid on both islands for three months.

Road Conditions

Antigua's roads range from smooth to rough to deadly. You'll be cruising along when suddenly a hubcap-popping pothole or a speed bump appears. Smaller roads are often narrow with poor visibility, particularly on curves. If you plan to get off the beaten track (especially in the remote eastern part of Antigua), it's best to hire a 4WD.

DEPARTURE TAX

All passengers who have spent more than 24 hours in Antigua must pay a US$22 departure tax, though this is sometimes included in your ticket price.

Driving at night is challenging since roads are narrow, street lights or reflector posts are nonexistent and most people use their blinding brights. Also be aware of people, donkeys, dogs, goats and other animals by the side – or on – the road.

Road signage is rare – a GPS navigator is essential.

TAXI

Antigua

Taxis on Antigua have number plates beginning with 'TX.' On both Antigua and Barbuda, fares are government regulated with one tariff applying to up to four passengers. However, it's best to confirm the price before riding away.

Airport to St John's	US$15
Airport to Dickenson Bay	US$18
Airport to English Harbour	US$32
St John's to Dickenson Bay	US$14
St John's to English Harbour	US$25
St John's to Half Moon Bay	US$30

Private island tours are charged at US$25 per hour with a two-hour minimum. Waiting times cost US$5 per 30 minutes.

Barbuda

Taxis wait at the airport or the ferry dock, but you may prefer to prearrange a transfer or an island tour through your hotel, the Barbuda tourist office (p124) or by contacting a driver directly. There is usually a minimum charge of US$20, no matter where you're going.

IMAGE SOURCE TRADING LTD/SHUTTERSTOCK ©

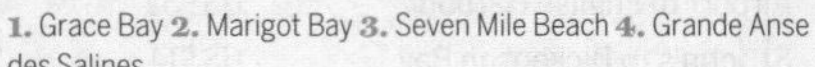

1. Grace Bay **2.** Marigot Bay **3.** Seven Mile Beach **4.** Grande Anse des Salines

LUCIA PITTER/SHUTTERSTOCK ©

Caribbean Beaches

Like Paris and art or Arizona and canyons, when you think of the Caribbean, you think beaches. Alluring beaches in Jamaica, perfect beaches in Grand Cayman, lost beaches in the Bahamas and unspoiled beaches in the Grenadines all await.

Grace Bay, Caicos Islands

This stretch of snow-white sand is perfect for relaxing, swimming and forgetting about home. Though it's dotted with resorts, its sheer size means that finding your own square of paradise is a snap.

Marigot Bay, St Lucia

Marigot Bay is a stunning example of natural architecture. Sheltered by towering palms and surrounding hills, the narrow inlet hid the British fleet from French pursuers. Today it hides a fabulous beach.

Seven Mile Beach, Grand Cayman

Walk the length of this beach, straight out of central casting, and see if it measures up – literally. Enjoy swimming, sunbathing and water sports galore on Grand Cayman's superb stretch of white sand.

Shoal Bay East, Anguilla

Got a fantasy of an idyllic white-sand beach? You've just pictured Shoal Bay East, a 2-mile-long beach with pristine sand, reefs ideal for snorkeling, and glassy turquoise water.

Grande Anse des Salines, Martinique

Les Salines is probably Martinique's finest beach. The gorgeous long stretch of golden sand lures French tourists and local families alike, but it never seems crowded.

Aruba

☎297 / POP 105,530

Includes ➡

Best Places to Eat

- ➡ Papiamento (p141)
- ➡ Zeerover (p147)
- ➡ Madame Janette (p142)
- ➡ Taste My Aruba (p137)
- ➡ Flying Fishbone (p147)
- ➡ Pelican Nest (p141)

Best Places to Stay

- ➡ Beach House Aruba (p143)
- ➡ Bucuti & Tara Beach Resort (p141)
- ➡ Aruba Ocean Villas (p147)
- ➡ Aruba's Little Secret (p144)
- ➡ Boardwalk Hotel (p141)

Why Go?

North Americans fleeing winter make Aruba the most touristed island in the southern Caribbean. The draws are obvious: miles of glorious white-sand beach, plenty of all-inclusive resorts, and a cute, compact capital, Oranjestad, which is well suited to the short strolls favored by cruise-ship passengers. It's all about sun, fun and spending money.

Venture away from the resorts and you're in for a real treat. At the island's extreme ends are rugged, windswept vistas and uncrowded beaches – perfect for hiking and horseback riding. Crystal-clear waters are bursting with sea life and shipwrecks (and an airplane wreck or two), providing incredible opportunities for snorkeling and diving. And nonstop breezes create near-perfect conditions for windsurfing and kiteboarding.

So whether you're longing to lounge on a beach or delve into the great outdoors, Aruba has you covered. One happy island, indeed!

When to Go

Dec–Apr High season: accommodations fill up and prices climb.

Jan & Feb Carnival means it's party time in Aruba; expect lively crowds.

Sep–Dec The island sees a bit of rain; prices plummet.

Aruba Highlights

❶ **Diving and snorkeling** (p143) Exploring the amazing underwater world, such as the wreck of the *Antilla*.

❷ **Natural Pool** (p144) Hiking or horseback riding through Arikok National Wildlife Park, then cooling off in this geological wonder.

❸ **Eagle Beach** (p139) Lounging on the powdery sand at this most beautiful beach.

❹ **Savaneta seafood** (p147) Devouring the local catch with your toes in the sand at a fish shack.

❺ **Street murals** (p146) Discovering hidden art and talent in revitalized San Nicolas.

❻ **Boca Grandi** (p146) Riding the wind on Aruba's best kitesurfing beach.

❼ **California Dunes** (p143) Catching a glorious sunset from the dunes at the island's desolate northern tip.

Oranjestad

Aruba's capital city is also its largest municipality, and wandering its streets is usually a low-key, even languid affair offering sporadic encounters with local life. Or, if a cruise ship's in port, thousands of passengers descend on the shops and restaurants, transforming the vibe into one of high-pitched frenzy.

Regardless of when you visit, main drag Caya GF Betico Croes is lined with a mix of mom-and-pop stores and international chains, and the surrounding blocks offer colorful Dutch colonial buildings sprinkled amid shiny newer shopping malls. A lovely linear park follows the waterfront from the airport, past the city's finest beaches, and all the way to downtown Oranjestad and its almighty cruise-ship terminal.

Sights

Surfside Beach BEACH

(Lloyd G Smith Blvd; inflatable water park per person US$17;) Surfside is a pretty pleasant place to spend an afternoon if you're hankering after some sun, surf and sand. It's the best, most swimmable beach in Oranjestad proper, with plenty of shade and a handful of excellent bars. Kids will love the **inflatable water park** just offshore, which offers swings, slides, monkey bars, climbing walls and a free-floating catapult.

Fort Zoutman FORT

It's not much to look at, but this 18th-century fort was built to defend the port against pirates. The attached Willem III Tower was added later, serving as both lighthouse and clock tower until 1963. The complex now houses the small **Aruba Historical Museum** (588-5199; US$5; 9am-6pm Mon-Fri, 10am-2pm Sat & Sun) and the weekly **Bonbini Festival** (US$10; 6-8:30pm Tue).

Dr Eloy Arends House HISTORIC BUILDING

(Wilhelminastraat 8) A local landmark – and no wonder, it's a beauty. Dating to 1922, the elegant, emerald-green, white-trimmed house is now part of the city-council complex.

Activities

SE Aruba Fly 'n' Dive DIVING

(588-1150; www.se-aruba.com; Lloyd G Smith Blvd 1a; 2-tank dive from US$90) This highly recommended shop is located just north of the airport, which explains the name. Trips to local dive sites depart every morning at 9am, with transportation available from area hotels or the cruise-ship terminal. Fly 'n' Dive is unique in that it caters to divers and snorkelers, so there's no need to leave your nondiving friends behind.

Festivals & Events

★Carnival CARNIVAL

(www.arubacarnival.com; Jan or Feb) Carnival is a big deal on the islands, where a packed schedule of fun begins shortly after New Year's Day. Aruba's parades are an explosion of sound and color.

Sleeping

★Wonders Boutique Hotel B&B $$

(593-4032; www.wondersaruba.com; Emmastraat 63; r US$120-150;) It calls itself a boutique hotel, but it's really more of a B&B, with its warm welcome and intimate atmosphere (adults only). The 11 stylish rooms are decorated with understated elegance and stocked with local aloe-vera products. They overlook a lush garden and a swimming pool fed by natural springs. It's a 15-minute walk south to downtown Oranjestad.

Aruba Surfside Marina HOTEL $$

(583-0300; www.arubasurfsidemarina.com; Lloyd G Smith Blvd 7; d from US$170;) This gem has only five suites, each with plenty of living space, plus kitchenette, private balcony and fabulous ocean view. A spacious private garden overlooks the waves or, upon request, staff will kindly set up chairs on the sand at nearby Surfside Beach. It's a 20-minute walk to Oranjestad center. Great value.

Talk of the Town BOUTIQUE HOTEL $$

(524-3300; www.tottaruba.com; Lloyd G Smith Blvd 2; r from US$240;) The guest rooms, swimming pool and sun garden have been revamped, and this small hotel is looking its tropical best. Expect citrus colors, contemporary furnishings and private balconies. Right on the highway, the location can be noisy, but it's only a few steps to Surfside Beach.

Eating

Some of Aruba's finest dining is in Oranjestad. Take a break from predictable resort restaurants and sample the city's excellent, eclectic local dining scene. In addition to bricks-and-mortar restaurants, snack trucks are an island institution, serving up a wide range of street food from sunset into the wee hours.

Central Oranjestad

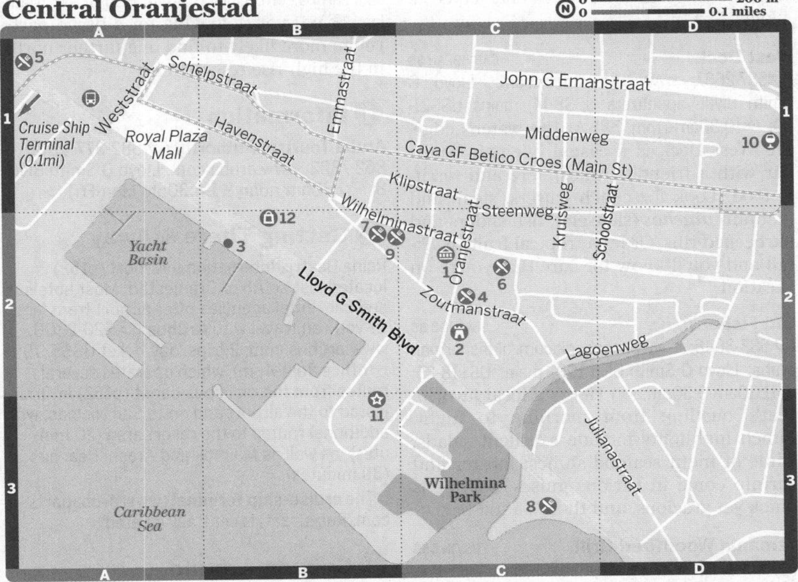

Central Oranjestad

Sights
- Aruba Historical Museum ....(see 2)
- 1 Dr Eloy Arends House C2
- 2 Fort Zoutman C2

Activities, Courses & Tours
- 3 Atlantis Submarines B2

Eating
- 4 Italy in the World C2
- 5 Old Fisherman A1
- 6 Qué Pasa C2
- 7 Taste My Aruba B2
- 8 West Deck C3
- 9 Yemanja Woodfired Grill B2

Drinking & Nightlife
- 10 @7 Club D1

Entertainment
- 11 Renaissance Marketplace B3

Shopping
- 12 Renaissance Mall B2

★ Taste My Aruba CAFE $$

(☎749-1600; http://tastemyaruba.com; Zoutmanstraat 1; mains US$13-18; ⊙noon-10pm Mon-Sat) In quaint digs behind the **Renaissance Mall** (Lloyd G Smith Blvd 82; ⊙10am-7pm Mon-Sat), this little cafe offers big rewards for those who stumble upon it. Inventive and affable owner-chef Nathaly is passionate about her menu, and scrawls it on a chalkboard each day based on what's fresh. Expect the likes of tuna tataki, local wahoo and tender filet mignon, along with cashew cake, a classic island treat.

Qué Pasa INTERNATIONAL $$

(☎583-4888; www.quepasaaruba.com; Wilhelminastraat 18; mains US$21-34; ⊙5-11pm; 📶🍸) The accent is Spanish but the language global at this effusive spot. The vibrant, sunshine-yellow cafe is just the place to settle in for cocktails, conversation and exotic flavors (kangaroo tenderloin, anyone?). The on-site art gallery is also internationally inspired.

Italy in the World ITALIAN $$

(☎585-7958; Oranjestraat 2; mains US$19-26; ⊙3-10pm Mon-Fri, from 4pm Sat, from 5pm Sun; 🍸) At first appearance this looks like a well-stocked Italian deli and wine shop, but slip into the back to discover the stash of wine, plus a handful of tables and a daily-changing menu scrawled on a blackboard. A tantalizing selection of handmade pastas is paired with the chef's favorite wines and served to a lucky few.

West Deck CARIBBEAN **$$**
(587-2667; www.thewestdeck.com; Lloyd G Smith Blvd; appetizers US$8-14, mains US$21-30; 10:30am-11pm;) At the water's edge, the West Deck is a casual open-air beach bar with a friendly atmosphere and terrific food. Look for conch fritters, steak and plantain *pinchos* (skewers), fish sliders and barbecued ribs. Order a tropical fruity cocktail and you'll know for sure that you're on vacation.

Old Fisherman SEAFOOD **$$**
(588-3648; www.facebook.com/oldfishermanaruba; Lloyd G Smith Blvd 100; mains US$18-25; 11:30am-9:30pm;) Here's a local favorite that's bustling from morning to night. Lunch highlights include excellent salads, while at night seafood shines: lobster and shrimp come in various guises. Service is quick yet gracious, and there's a full bar.

Yemanja Woodfired Grill FUSION **$$$**
(588-4711; www.yemanja-aruba.com; Wilhelminastraat 2; mains US$26-49; 5:30-10:30pm Mon-Sat;) Two colorful colonial-era buildings have been transformed into one of Aruba's most stylish eateries, which grills most of its menu items over a fire fueled by wood from the local Watapana tree, adding a rich flavor to the seafood, steaks and veggies. While meats and seafood are the specialty, folks with dietary restrictions (including vegetarians) won't go hungry.

Pinchos SEAFOOD **$$$**
(583-2666; www.pinchosaruba.com; Lloyd G Smith Blvd 7; mains US$24-52; 5pm-midnight) Pinchos is one of Aruba's most romantic spots. Set on a pier jutting into the ocean, the restaurant is surrounded by twinkling stars and lapping waves. The food isn't nearly as special as the setting, involving mostly bland and uninspired fish and steak dishes, and service is on the slow side. Reservations recommended. The restaurant is located behind the Aruba Surfside Marina.

Drinking & Entertainment

Oranjestad is pretty quiet after dark, but there are a few respectable drinking establishments with live music on weekends and there's always some action around the **Renaissance Marketplace** (www.shoprenaissancearuba.com; Lloyd G Smith Blvd 82; 10am-late;). If you're looking for a beach party, you're more likely to find one further north, in the high-rise resort area.

Information

Aruba Tourism Authority (582-3777, 800-862-7822; www.aruba.com; Lloyd G Smith Blvd 8; 7:30am-noon & 1-4:30pm Mon-Fri)

Getting There & Away

Reina Beatrix International Airport (p152) is located just south of Oranjestad. Most hotels and car-rental agencies offer airport transfers. Or you can travel with **Arubus** (520-2300; www.arubus.com; 2 trips/day ticket US$5/10; office 8am-4pm), which operates several routes from the main bus depot (p152) in Oranjestad to the airport and on to San Nicolas, with additional routes to the resort area (20 minutes), as well as Malmok and Arashi Beaches (30 minutes).

The **cruise-ship terminal** (www.arubaports.com; Ruizstraat) is centrally located.

Getting Around

The easiest way to get around Oranjestad is to walk, as most of the sights and attractions are within an area of a few square miles. There's also a free, single-track electric **trolley** (trips free; 10am-5pm) that runs from the cruise-ship terminal, through downtown Oranjestad and along Caya GF Betico Croes before looping back to the port. It runs every 20 to 30 minutes.

Aruba Resort Area

Here is the Aruba that you see in the tourist brochures. Beginning just north of Oranjestad, the western coastline is a 10km chain of wide, wonderful fine-sand beaches, fronted by gorgeous turquoise waters. Most island accommodations are located along this coast – generally clustered in two areas known as the low-rise resort area and the high-rise resort area – which gives you a good idea of the backdrop.

The resorts provide the lush landscaping, which – along with the lounge chairs, the towel service, the beach bars and the water aerobics – fools many a tourist into forgetting that this is a desert. And if there's anything the resorts don't provide, many tour operators do: from snorkel tours to sunset cruises, there's no shortage of ways to experience the Caribbean blue.

Sights

★ Eagle Beach — BEACH

Fronting a line of low-rise resorts just northwest of Oranjestad, Eagle is a long stretch of white sand that regularly makes lists of the best beaches in the world. There are shade trees in some areas and you can obtain every service you need, from a lounger to a cold drink.

Eagle Beach is a leatherback-turtle nesting area, so parts of it may be closed from March to July.

Manchebo Beach — BEACH

Just south of Eagle, this large beach reaches out to a point. It was once a destination for topless sunbathers, but that's frowned upon these days. Still, this beach offers the best chance on the strip to get away from the crowds.

Butterfly Farm — GARDENS

(☎586-3656; www.thebutterflyfarm.com; JE Irausquin Blvd; adult/child US$16/8.50; ⏲8:30am-4:30pm) Tucked between the low-rise and high-rise resort areas, this place will make your heart go aflutter, as the gorgeous gardens are teeming with butterflies and moths of all sizes and colors. Guided tours walk you through the lepidoptera life cycle, and the habitat provides for tropical dry forest and rainforest species. The variety is impressive.

Palm Beach — BEACH

A classic white-sand beauty – but only for those who enjoy the company of lots of people, as it fronts the high-rise resorts. During high season the sands can get jammed, but for some that's part of the scene.

Activities & Tours

Palm Beach is a hub for all sorts of watery activities, including sailing and snorkeling tours, diving, stand-up paddleboarding, Jet Skiing, parasailing, tubing and flyboarding. If none of that gets you excited, you're in a perfect spot for sunbathing and sandcastle building. So take your pick.

Red Sail — WATER SPORTS

(☎523-1600; www.redsailaruba.com; Opal; sailing adult/child from US$55/29, snorkeling from US$30, 1-/2-tank dive from US$52/82; ⏲8am-6pm Mon-Sat) Large, recommended Red Sail offers diving, catamaran trips, deep-sea fishing, kitesurfing, windsurfing and an array of other outdoor pursuits. It runs an especially good dive trip to the Antilla, as divemasters can point out frogfishes living on the wreck. The company has tour desks and retail boutiques at numerous hotels in the resort area and beyond.

Native Divers Aruba — DIVING

(☎565-4090, 593-3960; www.nativedivers.com; Palm Beach; 2-tank dive US$100) Located on the beach in front of the Marriott Surf Club, this is one of the island's smaller dive operations, which makes for a more personal experience. It offers custom trips and certification training.

Tanks and weights are included. Other rental equipment costs extra.

Roberto's — SNORKELING

(☎592-2859; www.robertoswatersports.com; Palm Beach; per person US$40) Climb aboard Roberto's trimaran for a three-hour sail-and-snorkel tour. The two snorkel stops usually include the Antilla wreck (p143), a local favorite. Sandwiches, snacks and drinks (alcoholic and non) are included.

Festivals

Soul Beach Music Festival — MUSIC

(www.soulbeach.com; ⏲May) On Memorial Day weekend Aruba becomes a hot spot (even more than usual) for music, comedy and beach parties. This three-day event attracts an impressive lineup of artists: in the past Alicia Keys, Boyz II Men, Chaka Khan, Estelle, Lauryn Hill, Mary J Blige and Robin Thicke have performed.

Sleeping

The vast majority of places to stay lie along the beach north of Oranjestad. The low-rise resorts front Eagle and Manchebo Beaches. Further north, the high-rise resort area runs the length of Palm Beach, which is lined with huge hotels run by international chains. Inland, especially in the district of Bubali, you'll find some smaller lodgings that cater to travelers on a more modest budget.

Coconut Inn — HOTEL $

(☎586-6288; www.coconutinn.com; Noord 31, Riberostraat; incl breakfast r US$90-95, apt US$110; ⏲reception 8:30am-8:30pm; ❄@≋) You'll want a car if you stay at this budget-friendly place, which has 40 dated rooms surrounding a large rectangle of aqua joy. It's not much more than a place to sleep, but the rooms do have private balconies and kitchenettes. There's a hearty homemade breakfast.

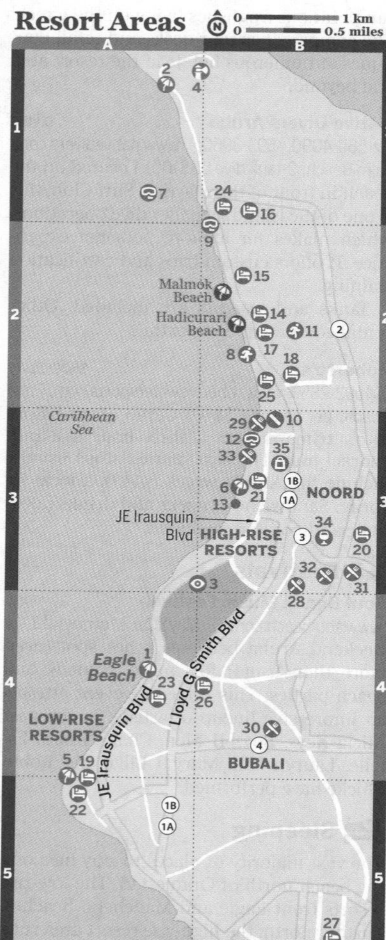

Resort Areas

Top Sights
1 Eagle Beach A4

Sights
2 Arashi Beach A1
3 Butterfly Farm B3
4 California Lighthouse A1
5 Manchebo Beach A4
6 Palm Beach B3

Activities, Courses & Tours
7 Antilla Wreck A1
Aruba Active Vacations .... (see 8)
De Palm Tours .... (see 13)
8 Fisherman Huts B2
Island Yoga .... (see 31)
9 Malmok Beach B2
10 Native Divers Aruba B3
11 Red Sail B2
12 Roberto's B3
13 Seaworld Explorer B3

Sleeping
14 Aruba Beach Villas B2
15 Aruba Sunset Beach Studios B2
16 Bananas Resort B1
17 Beach House Aruba B2
18 Boardwalk Hotel B2
19 Bucuti & Tara Beach Resort A5
20 Coconut Inn B3
21 Hyatt Regency Aruba Resort B3
22 Manchebo Beach Resort A5
23 MVC Eagle Beach Aruba A4
24 OceanZ B1
25 Ritz-Carlton Aruba B2
26 Sasaki Apartments B4
27 Wonders Boutique Hotel B5

Eating
28 Gasparito Restaurant B3
29 Hadicurari B3
30 Madame Janette B4
31 Nourish B3
32 Papiamento B3
33 Pelican Nest B3
Senses .... (see 19)

Drinking & Nightlife
34 Local Store B3

Shopping
35 Paseo Herrencia B3

From Lloyd G Smith Blvd, drive east on Rte 3, turn left onto Washington and continue on Riberostraat until you reach the Coconut Inn.

MVC Eagle Beach Aruba HOTEL $$
(☎587-0110; www.mvceaglebeach.com; JE Irausquin Blvd 240, Eagle Beach; d/q from US$202/272; ❄@≋) Thank Dutch taxpayers for this excellent deal right across from Eagle Beach (p139). Frequented by members of the Dutch Navy, it's a basic two-story block with 19 small, bright rooms facing a postage-stamp-size pool. Although beefy sailor types do stay here, it's open to everyone, and guests enjoy the best value on Aruba for the location.

Sasaki Apartments HOTEL $$
(☎587-7482; www.sasakiapts.com; Bubali 143; r from US$135; ❄@📶≋) The price is right for these studio apartments, located just a couple of busy roads away (400m) from Eagle

Beach (p139). The 24 spiffy apartments are spare in decor but have kitchenettes and other standard amenities. Conveniently, a giant supermarket is right across the road.

★Bucuti & Tara Beach Resort RESORT **$$$**
(☎583-1100; www.bucuti.com; Lloyd G Smith Blvd 55b, Eagle Beach; r/ste from US$507/750;) With its white-stucco edifice and red-tile roofs, Bucuti & Tara is among the classiest of the low-rise resorts. It's also the first carbon-neutral resort in North America, meaning your lavish stay is also guilt free. The adults-only facility is all about exclusivity and romance: massive rooms have chic contemporary interiors and sunset-view balconies.

There's also a strong emphasis on wellness, with a 'healthy hour' involving free smoothies, a yoga program and a tranquil spa. Still more perks include movies under the stars and two excellent restaurants onsite, along with private dining on the beach.

★Boardwalk Hotel BOUTIQUE HOTEL **$$$**
(☎586-6654; www.boardwalkaruba.com; Bakval 20; d from US$305; ⏲reception 9am-5pm Mon-Sat;) Located on a former coconut plantation, this delightful boutique hotel is just a short block from Palm Beach (p139), where beach service is available at the **Ritz-Carlton** (☎527-2222; www.theritzcarlton.com; Lloyd G Smith Blvd 107; r from US$539), but miles from the tourist madness. In 2019 a sweeping revamp welcomed 32 new casitas and upgraded the original 12, with all accommodations featuring well-equipped kitchens, spacious living areas hung with local artwork, and private terraces kitted out with hammocks and grills. The expansion also introduced new water features, including a second pool and overwater hammocks, along with ecofriendly solar panels, LED lighting and green building materials.

Three- to five-night minimum depending on the season.

Manchebo Beach Resort RESORT **$$$**
(☎582-3444; www.manchebo.com; JE Irausquin Blvd 55, Manchebo Beach; r US$380-505, ste US$585;) Facing the eponymous beach, this crescent-shaped boutique resort will make you feel pampered. It's all understated luxury, where rooms renovated in 2018 feature cherrywood furniture, new marble bathrooms and a color palette to match the sea and sand. There's an explicit focus on wellness, with daily yoga classes, special fruit-smoothie menus and the glorious Spa del Sol.

Eating

Close to the high-rise resorts is a plethora of development thick with international chains and other tourist-oriented restaurants. A short walk or drive inland, in Noord, there's a range of privately owned places, serving local fare, international cuisine and, of course, tons of seafood.

Nourish HEALTH FOOD **$**
(☎280-0025; https://islandyoga.com/cafe; Noord 19a; mains US$8-12.50; ⏲8:30am-2:30pm Mon-Sat;) A cheerful Bali-inspired cafe serving healthy vegetarian and vegan treats, smoothie bowls, cold-pressed juices, organic coffee, yummy breakfasts and salads. Along with the attached **yoga studio** (☎280-0025; https://islandyoga.com; Noord 19a; drop-in yoga class US$20, SUP yoga class US$50; ⏲hours vary), this place is owned by Rachel Brathran (aka Yoga Girl), a local Instagram celebrity. Plop down on a beanbag chair inside or at a table in the relaxing garden.

★Pelican Nest SEAFOOD **$$**
(☎586-2259; www.pelican-aruba.com; Pelican Pier, Palm Beach; mains US$15-25; ⏲11am-10pm) Pelican Pier juts into the Caribbean, offering sea breezes, salty air and – if you time it right – gorgeous sunset views. The full menu of local seafood includes such delicacies as ceviche (a specialty of the Peruvian chef) and perfectly grilled shrimp. A reservation (or an early arrival) is essential if you want to catch that sunset.

Hadicurari SEAFOOD **$$**
(☎586-2288; www.hadicurari.com; Berea di Piscado 96; breakfast items US$10-15, lunch & dinner mains US$23-45; ⏲8am-11pm;) A solid, reasonably priced Palm Beach restaurant dishing up all three meals, with friendly service and a lovely ambience. Feast on Dutch pancakes or filet-mignon Benedict at breakfast, a mouthwatering grouper sandwich at lunch, and pasta or surf and turf in the evening. There's also an impressive vegan menu, with items such as soy fish tempura and yam-based scallops.

★Papiamento INTERNATIONAL **$$$**
(☎586-4544; https://papiamentoaruba.com; Washington 61; mains US$29-48; ⏲6-9:30pm Mon-Sat) Aruba's most atmospheric restaurant occupies a century-old manor filled with antiques from Europe, with tables

in elegant rooms and surrounding a large courtyard pool. A go-to for locals celebrating special occasions, it has a vast international menu inspired by Caribbean flavors. Favorites include stone-cooked specials such as wahoo and rock lobster, coconut-curry shrimp, and Aruban specialty *keshi yena* (cheese casserole).

The *keshi yena* is prepared according to an old family recipe, with minced tenderloin and chicken stewed with raisins, olives and cashews, and flame-broiled with Dutch cheese. Pair it with the cocktail of the day. Reservations recommended.

★Madame Janette INTERNATIONAL **$$$**

(☎587-0184; www.madamejanette.info; Cunucu Abou 37; mains US$27-45; ⏰5:30-10pm Mon-Sat) An 'international restaurant with a Caribbean touch,' Madame Janette offers an enticing menu of seafood, steaks and schnitzels, such as sweet and spicy 'Bang-Bang Shrimp,' a popular grouper amandine, and the decadent 'Gianni Versace' – filet mignon topped with spinach, portobello mushrooms and lobster medallions. Twinkling with lights, the lush garden makes a delightful dining room.

Madame Janette also promises the biggest selection of craft beers in the Caribbean (which is about 160, if anybody's counting).

Senses INTERNATIONAL **$$$**

(☎586-0044; www.sensesaruba.restaurant; Bucuti & Tara Beach Resort, Lloyd G Smith Blvd 55b; 8-course tasting menu per person US$105; ⏰seating at 7pm) Newly established within the Bucuti & Tara Beach Resort (p141), this intimate and elevated chef's table features eight eclectic courses and a delightful wine list. The menu changes each month, with inventive and frankly awe-inspiring concoctions based on French tradition and influenced by Dutch, Norwegian and Indonesian cooking techniques.

The maître d' is a superb entertainer, as is the chef, who has picked up lots of ideas (and exotic ingredients) on distant travels. He prepares the food in full view of diners, describing each dish thoroughly.

Gasparito Restaurant CARIBBEAN **$$$**

(☎594-2550; www.gasparito.com; Gasparito 3, Noord; mains US$23-38; ⏰6-9pm Mon-Sat; 🍷) If you can find this family-run favorite, you're in for a treat: it'll give you a taste of delectable, down-home Aruban cuisine. Old family recipes include goat stew and *keshi yena*. Dine in the *cunucu* (country house) or on the candlelit patio. Check the website for specials.

Drinking & Nightlife

If you're looking for a beach party, you're sure to find it on Palm Beach. If you prefer a local spot where you can make friends and let the evening drift away, head to the amiable bars and rum shops further inland.

Local Store BAR

(☎586-1414; www.localstorearuba.com; Palm Beach 13a, Rte 3; ⏰11am-midnight Mon-Fri, from 8am Sat & Sun) Do you love a local dive bar? Then you'll love the Local Store with its beer-keg bar stools, bare light bulbs and tin ceiling. This is the place for excellent burgers, wings and beer (with a surprising selection of North American craft brews). There's occasional live music as well.

Getting There & Away

To reach the resort area from Oranjestad or from the airport, drive north on Lloyd G Smith Blvd (Rte 1). About 3km north of the city, turn left at JE Irausquin Blvd to reach the low-rise resorts, or continue north to the high-rise resort area and watch for the turnoff to your destination.

The taxi fare from the airport to the low-rise and high-rise resort areas is US$25 and US$30, respectively. The resort area is also accessible by Arubus (p138); it runs every 10 to 15 minutes from Oranjestad.

Northwest Coast

If high-rise hotels and crowded casinos aren't your thing, that's OK: just take the coastal road north – all the way north – to where it's lined with gracious homes and small but stellar beaches. This stretch is perfect for snorkeling, bodysurfing and sunset viewing, giving way eventually to a magnificent, awe-inspiring landscape of sand dunes and wild waves.

These stunning natural surroundings are your destination for windsurfing at the Fisherman Huts, snorkeling at Malmok Beach, swimming at Arashi Beach or hiking in the California Dunes. Yet it's only a few miles north of Palm Beach – so when you get bored or tired or hungry or thirsty, it's a quick trip to the comforts and conveniences of the resort area.

Sights

Arashi Beach BEACH

Near the island's northwestern tip, this is a favorite with locals and popular with families. There's good bodysurfing, some shade and just a few rocks right offshore.

California Lighthouse LIGHTHOUSE
Up the hill from Arashi Beach, this tall sentinel is named for an old wrecked ship called the *California*, which is *not* the ship of similar name *(Californian)* that stood by ineffectually while the *Titanic* sank, despite much local lore to the contrary. The views are great and the wind is strong, especially at the top. This is a popular spot to catch the sunset.

Activities

California Dunes HIKING
The northern tip of Aruba is wild. Wind and waves pound the landscape, which consists of endless sand dunes, enormous boulders and little else. A network of trails crisscrosses the area, eventually arriving at the sea. This is a romantic sunset spot – but don't linger, as darkness comes quickly. Water and sunblock are essential during the day.

Like the lighthouse, the dunes are named for a shipwreck that lies offshore. Driving on the dunes is prohibited, so leave your car in one of the parking areas that are visible from the lighthouse road.

Fisherman Huts WATER SPORTS
(Hadicurari Beach) Hadicurari is easy to recognize from the old fishing shanties that line the shore. Sandy beach, shallow water and strong trade winds make this a prime spot for boarding: windsurfers set up at the northern end of the beach, while kitesurfers take over the southern part. Several operators give lessons and rent gear, including Aruba Active Vacations (p152).

Malmok Beach SNORKELING
North of the Fisherman Huts, narrow, rocky Malmok Beach lies close to the road. The coral shoreline attracts ample sea life, making this an excellent snorkeling site. The water is clear and calm, with an easy entry from the beach. Many snorkel tours come here, so arrive early in the morning or late in the afternoon to avoid the crowds.

Sleeping & Eating

Apart from one high-end restaurant at OceanZ (p144), there's no place to eat in the north of the island (which is why all hotel rooms have kitchenettes). That said, it's less than 2 miles to Palm Beach – in some cases, much less – so you don't have to cook if you don't want to.

DON'T MISS

ANTILLA WRECK

The USS **Antilla**, a WWII US Navy ship that was sunk near Malmok Beach, is a popular destination for snorkelers and divers. The 400ft wreck is lying on its side in about 60ft of water. What's unique about the Antilla is that the masts, bow and forward deck are shallow enough that they're mostly visible to snorkelers.

The ship is turning into an artificial reef: it's covered with coral and home to ample sea life, including a few rarely seen frogfish. It's a cool site, but be aware that the water is often choppy and currents are strong. Do not try to swim out to the wreck; book a trip with Roberto's (p139) or Red Sail (p139).

★ **Beach House Aruba** HOTEL $$
(☎593-3991; www.beachhousearuba.com; Lloyd G Smith Blvd 450; garden view r US$115-160, ocean view r/ste US$220/250;) This charming collection of beach huts is the perfect antidote to the generic resorts that dominate the island. The eight apartments and surrounding gardens are littered with conch shells, driftwood, handmade furniture and unusual artwork, creating an atmosphere of intimacy and eclecticism. A tiny plunge pool and shady gardens face the ocean, so everyone can enjoy the breeze.

Bananas Resort APARTMENT $$
(☎586-2858; www.bananasaruba.com; Malmokweg 19; apt from US$120;) Here's one of the island's best bargains. Bananas has spacious, comfortable apartments with tile floors, wicker furniture, well-equipped kitchens and private terraces. They surround a large pool with lush gardens. Your gracious hosts (including two small dogs) are always on hand. The residential location is delightfully peaceful, but it's only half a mile to Malmok Beach. What's not to love?

Aruba Sunset Beach Studios HOTEL $$
(☎586-3940; www.arubasunsetbeach.com; Lloyd G Smith Blvd 486; studios US$155-265;) Right across the coastal road from rocky Malmok Beach, this 10-room property has an excellent location and an easygoing

WORTH A TRIP

ARIKOK NATIONAL WILDLIFE PARK

Arid and rugged, Arikok National Wildlife Park is a vast, desolate stretch of desert wilderness that covers much of the east coast (nearly 20% of the island's total area). It's a fascinating contrast to the heavily developed and lushly landscaped west coast. Even the ocean is different over here: midnight blue, it smashes against the rocky shore with a fury not evident on the other side of the island.

As you explore the park and its 45 miles of hiking trails, you'll notice the peculiar flora: the iconic and bizarrely twisted divi-divi; the *kwihi* with its tasty, sweet-sour long, yellow beans; and the *hubada*, which has sharp, tough thorns. Spiky aloe plants abound, as do some seven varieties of cactus. Also keep your eyes peeled for wild donkeys and goats, Aruban whiptail lizards and a few dozen species of bird.

Stop at the **Visitors Center** (☎585-1234; www.arubanationalpark.org; adult/child US$11/free; ⊙ticket sales 8am-4pm) to pay your park admission fee, pick up a map, and browse the displays on the park's flora and fauna. The center also has a small cafe.

Powerful wave action has worn a depression into the coastal limestone ridge at **Natural Pool** (Conchi). The surrounding rocks break the surf, so – with waves crashing all around – you can take a peaceful, cooling dip. Bring your mask and snorkel and commune with the fish hiding out in here. You'll want water shoes for the sharp rocks.

The road to the Natural Pool is not passable in a regular car. You can reach it by 4WD or via a 3.5-mile walk from the visitors center. The scenery is stunning, but the journey is hot and windy. Bring plenty of water and start early. Along the way you'll reach the summit of Sero Arikok, Aruba's second-highest peak, yielding marvelous views of the coast and the island.

Hidden among cacti-dotted hills, far removed from anything resembling tourism, **Aruba's Little Secret** (☎594-6562; www.aruba-secret.com; Bringamosa 3e; casitas incl breakfast US$108-165; P ❄ ☜ ≋) consists of six delightful casitas which undoubtedly represent the island's most laid-back stay. Four colorful one-bedroom abodes (each with outdoor kitchen) comprise one complex, along with shared pool, hammock, barbecue grill and open-air gazebo. The second, more private complex features two spacious one-bedroom houses perched by a chic lounging area and pool.

Snorkel gear is provided by expat owner John Dubois, who has comprehensive knowledge of the island and its offerings. Be sure to ask him about deals on rental cars. There's a five-night minimum and you'll probably want to stay longer.

The park's principal road is about 5 miles long and links the western entrance with the southern one near San Nicolas, allowing a circular tour. With the exception of the Natural Pool, all sites can be reached in a budget rental car.

atmosphere. The studios are modern and comfortable, with cool tile floors, darkwood furniture, private terraces and well-equipped kitchenettes. Swimming pool, hot tub and blooming gardens are on-site, and snorkel gear, beach chairs and barbecue grills are available for guest use.

Aruba Beach Villas HOTEL **$$**

(☎586-1072; www.arubabeachvillas.com; Lloyd G Smith Blvd 462; r with/without ocean view from US$238/178; ⊙reception 9am-5pm; ❄ @ ☜ ≋) Nicely located near Hadicurari Beach, the 32 units here are basic but bright, with kitchenettes and private patios. The ocean units have wide decks with comfy lounge chairs and lovely views. Windsurfing gear is available in high season for those with considerable experience. This place is ideal for the self-sufficient traveler who prefers independence to indulgence.

OceanZ BOUTIQUE HOTEL **$$$**

(☎586-9500; www.oceanzaruba.com; Lloyd G Smith Blvd 526; ste US$380-1198; ❄ ☜ ≋) Venezuelan architect Óscar Enrique Bracho Malpica designed this South Beach–style stunner facing Malmok Beach (p143). Thirteen guest rooms exude understated luxury, with plush white linens, open-air showers and enormous windows. Rates include champagne on arrival, a gourmet breakfast in the oceanfront dining room, and transport to Arashi Beach (p142) along with an ice-filled cooler, beach chairs and umbrellas.

Service is exceptional, so prepare to be pampered. The hotel's international, seafood-focused **restaurant** opened in 2019.

Getting There & Away

The best way to reach the north of the island from the resort area is to walk or cycle along the coastal road (it's about 2 miles from Palm Beach to Arashi Beach). Arubus (p138) also plies this route: line 10 goes to Malmok, line 10A all the way to Arashi and line 10B to the Fisherman Huts.

East Coast

Aruba may be small, but you'll feel as though you've left the island behind on its remote and rugged east coast, where wind and wave add atmosphere to the desolation. Geology is the star attraction here, with fantastic cliffs, beaches and pools carved out of the coastline, and mysterious rock formations studding the desert further inland. It's worth taking a day or two to marvel at the geological wonders, relax on desolate beaches, explore the remains of the gold-mining industry and discover the surprising life inhabiting the island's biggest national park.

Sights & Activities

★Andicuri Beach BEACH

Limestone cliffs, crystal-clear waters and crashing waves make this beach experience different from all others on the island. This east-coast beauty is popular with surfers and boogie-boarders. Otherwise, you might have the place to yourself (note that swimming is treacherous).

It can be a challenge to find Andicuri. If you come from the north – via the **Natural Bridge** – you'll need a 4WD (or two strong legs to do the rough 1-mile hike); a regular car can get closer by coming through Ayo.

Donkey Sanctuary WILDLIFE RESERVE

(☎593-2933; www.arubandonkey.org; Bringamosa 2-Z; donations appreciated; ⏰9am-4pm) FREE Make an ass of yourself doting on these winsome critters, who will follow you around for attention and snacks. Donkeys were brought to Aruba by the Spaniards, but many animals went rogue when they were no longer needed on farms. Unfortunately, they didn't fare well after automobile traffic increased on the island. The donkeys at the sanctuary are well taken care of: they are named, treated, fed, protected and loved. You won't be able to resist them!

Gold Mine Ranch HORSEBACK RIDING

(☎586-4954; www.thegoldmineranch.com; Matividiri 60; per person US$85; ⏰tours 9am & 4pm) Explore the eastern side of Aruba on horseback, visiting the island's most remote beaches and most spectacular countryside, as well as the Natural Bridge. The two-hour tour is billed not as a trail ride but as a 'horseback adventure.' Confident riders have the chance to run the horses on the beach and in the water.

Getting There & Away

There is no public transportation on the eastern side of the island, but plenty of tours bring visitors to see the sights. Most sights are accessible with a regular vehicle, but a 4WD is required to reach some parts of Arikok National Wildlife Park.

Three major east–west roads cut across the island: Rte 3 from Palm Beach, Rte 4 from Eagle Beach and Rte 7 from Oranjestad. Rte 6 is the main north–south road on the east side of the island.

San Nicolas

A small town near the island's southern tip, San Nicolas preserves Aruba's former rough-and-ready character, long since banished from Oranjestad. The centerpiece of the town is the Valero oil refinery, which has waned in importance and doesn't make for the most picturesque scenery. But this is an authentically Aruban town where locals abound, the beaches are blissful and a new art movement is making a colorful splash.

More than 40 murals depicting Aruba's people, traditions, wildlife and more can be seen on the town's walls, and visitors can learn more by attending the vibrant art fair, taking the mural tour or visiting the craft center. Kitesurfers will definitely want to spend some time here: nearby Boca Grandi offers the most consistent wind on the island.

Sights & Activities

Baby Beach BEACH

At the island's far southern tip, Baby Beach is a nice curve of sand with gentle waters and some decent snorkeling spots. It's popular with locals but not nearly as crowded as the west-coast beaches. The beach bar at the eastern end is a hoot for *Flintstones* fans. Nearby, Rodger's Beach is also quite lovely, if you don't mind the oil refinery towering above.

Boca Grandi KITESURFING

Boca Grandi is the island's top destination for experienced kitesurfers, as the winds are more consistent and the beach less crowded than at the Fisherman Huts (p143) up north. As is typical of windward beaches, conditions are hazardous for swimming. The beach is accessible from San Nicolas or Arikok.

★ **Aruba Mural Tours** WALKING

(☎593-4475; https://arubamuraltours.com; Bernard van de Veen Zeppenfeldstraat 14; per person US$15-35; ⏲9am-5pm Mon-Fri) Led by charismatic local Tito Bolivar, these highly engaging tours introduce visitors to the growing artistic movement in the island's one-time capital. Left drab and depressing after its oil refinery closed, San Nicolas developed a reputation for rampant prostitution. Now its walls are graced by more than 40 vibrant murals, each telling a unique story about Aruba and its inhabitants.

The murals are giving the youth of San Nicolas ideas about trying out art – and ideas in general. Every time the Aruba Art Fair rolls around, there will be new murals to admire and ponder.

Bolivar's definitely the one you want to hear this story from. He has spearheaded all of the art-related projects in San Nicolas, involving everybody from school kids to international artists to big-time donors to sister cities. He's a gifted and passionate 34-year-old with serious vision. Don't be surprised if one day he becomes prime minister.

Festivals & Events

Aruba Art Fair ART

(https://arubaartfair.com; ⏲Sep) Artists and visitors from all over the world come to town for the purpose of 'painting the forgotten city of San Nicolas,' as founder Tito Bolivar puts it. The whimsical and ever-transforming event has involved pop-up fine dining, dance performances in the streets, poetry readings, fashion shows and, of course, murals (for which the town is now known).

The 2018 event drew 12,000 visitors to San Nicolas, lighting up its residents and beautifying its streets. If you aren't in town during the festival, you can walk the streets, witness the revitalization and learn the story with Aruba Mural Tours.

Eating

San Nicolas isn't packed with eateries as the more touristy parts of Aruba are, but it's not difficult to find somewhere for a meal. In addition to the bars around Baby Beach, there are some worthwhile restaurants in town – not to mention Charlie's Bar, which should be a required stop for all visitors.

Big Mama Grill GRILL **$$**

(☎568-5688; www.facebook.com/bigmamagrill; Baby Beach; mains US$6-25; ⏲9:30am-7pm) The view and the cocktails are the main draws at this bar and grill steps from Baby Beach (the *Flintstones* theme is taken a bit too far, however: employees are dressed like characters). The food's decent; go for a sandwich, some seafood or a local favorite such as goat curry or johnnycakes (deep-fried dough filled with cheese, meat or vegetables).

Charlie's Bar BAR

(☎584-5086; www.facebook.com/charliesbar aruba; Zeppenfeldstraat 56; ⏲11:30am-7pm Mon-Sat) An island institution, Charlie's has been serving up cold beers and good times to tourists and locals alike since 1941. The walls are plastered with old photos, flags, pennants, posters, newspaper clippings and license plates that recount a characterful history of the restaurant, town and island. The food's pretty good and service is tops.

Charlie's is located just west of the oil refinery.

Getting There & Away

At the southern tip of the island, San Nicolas is a straight shot 20km south from Oranjestad on Rte 1. Arubus (p138) runs regular buses into town and all the way to Baby Beach.

Spanish Lagoon & Savaneta

About 10km south of Oranjestad, Savaneta is an old Aruban town, settled in 1816 and since forgotten. Compared to their counterparts on the northwestern coast, the beaches aren't as wide and glorious, and the attractions and amenities are fewer and further between – and tourists are scarce. And that contrast is precisely what makes this area so appealing. Besides its yet-to-be-discovered status, Savaneta boasts excellent onshore snorkeling and a few restaurants that defy comparison.

Just north, Spanish Lagoon is a narrow inlet fringed by mudflats and mangroves that makes an atmospheric spot for kayaking and snorkeling. Although you're unlikely to encounter one now, this was one of the few places on the island that pirates were known to visit.

Activities & Tours

Aruba Bob's Snorkel Tours SNORKELING
(☎745-7459; www.arubabob.com; Club Arias, Savaneta 123k; per person US$100) Not your typical snorkel tour. Aruba Bob provides each client with an underwater 'scooter,' which allows you to cover a lot more ground (nearly a mile of reef in a 1½-hour tour) and makes it easier to dive down for an up-close look at the sea creatures. Tours enter the water from the beach at Mangel Halto.

Mangel Halto SNORKELING
(Pos Chiquito) Just south of Spanish Lagoon, Mangel Halto is a small sandy beach with clear, calm waters and a few palm umbrellas for shade. The beach is unique for its cluster of mangroves at the southern end. The beachfront is protected by a reef, which makes Mangel Halto an excellent and accessible snorkeling spot.

Strong swimmers can enter the water on the southern side of the mangroves and allow the current to carry them north to the main beach. This is a good way to see the outside of the reef, where the coral is more vibrant and the marine life more varied.

Aruba Kayak Adventure KAYAKING
(☎582-5520; http://arubakayak.com; Ponton 90; from US$83; ⏲tours 8:30am) Both novices and pros enjoy a fascinating circuit of the mangroves and shoreline near Spanish Lagoon on the south coast. Transportation, gear and lunch are included in the price. Both tour options include a snorkel stop at Mangel Halto or **De Palm Island** (☎522-4400; www.depalmisland.com; adult/child US$104/79; ⏲9am-5pm).

Sleeping & Eating

Club Arias B&B $$
(☎593-3408; www.clubarias.com; Savaneta 123k; ste US$120-200;) This small resort is a sweet retreat well off the beaten tourist track. The place has 10 enormous suites surrounding a fantastic bedrock-style swimming pool and swim-up bar. Other perks include outdoor showers and a pizza joint on-site. It's a five-minute walk to the beach.

★**Aruba Ocean Villas** VILLA $$$
(☎594-1815; www.arubaoceanvillas.com; 356a Savaneta; bungalows US$400-950;) When guests arrive at this collection of dazzling and eclectic overwater bungalows, they often wonder if somehow they've been transported to the Maldives, or perhaps Tahiti. Truth be told, the place isn't like anything on those islands or elsewhere – it's a figment of an exceptional Aruban artist's wild imagination that's been brought vividly to life.

★**Zeerover** SEAFOOD $
(☎584-8401; www.facebook.com/zeerovers; Savaneta 270a; mains US$6-15; ⏲11am-9pm Tue-Sun) Folks come from all around the island to dine at this fisherfolk cooperative by the water. The menu is short and sweet, featuring the catch of the day and shrimp, all of it fresh caught and deep-fried. Wait in line to place your order, then grab a drink from the side window. Cash only.

There's ample seating at picnic tables overlooking the water, though the prime spot is out on the dock.

★**Flying Fishbone** INTERNATIONAL $$$
(☎584-2506; www.flyingfishbone.com; Savaneta 344; mains US$28-45; ⏲5-10pm) The ultimate romantic beach-dining experience. Kick off your shoes and sink your toes into the sand – or dip them in the water – as you feast on fresh seafood and prime-cut steak. The setting is spectacular, and only enhanced by sunset or starlight, but the food presentations are also inspired. Reservations essential.

Getting There & Away

Savaneta is 10km south of Oranjestad along Rte 1. Arubus (p138) runs north to the capital and south to San Nicolas and Baby Beach.

UNDERSTAND ARUBA

History

Caquetío History

Aruba's earliest inhabitants were the Caquetíos – a branch of the Arawak – who were hunter-gatherers (and fishers) along the northwestern coast from as early as 2500 BC. Evidence of their civilization is still visible today in the piles of conch shells that were discarded around the salina near Malmok Beach. From AD 1000 to 1500, the Caquetíos settled in five villages around the island, where they crafted pottery and practiced agriculture, growing corn and yucca. Artifacts from this Ceramic Period are on display at the Aruba Archaeological Museum. The cave paintings in Fontein Cave also date to this period.

Spain claimed the island in 1499, but its inhospitable arid landscape provoked little colonial enthusiasm, even earning Aruba its status as *una isla inutíl* (a useless island). Eventually, most of the indigenous population was enslaved and taken to work on plantations in Hispaniola.

From Colony to Autonomy

In 1636 the Netherlands claimed Aruba to ameliorate its other nearby acquisitions: Curaçao (base of the West India Trading Co) and Bonaire (center of its salt industry). The colony of Aruba served a strategic purpose with the establishment of a naval base. Aruba would remain in Dutch hands for most of the next three centuries. In 1954 the islands formed the autonomous Netherlands Antilles.

The ABC islands (Aruba, Bonaire and Curaçao) have never been chums, and Aruba was able to leverage its affluence to break away from the rest of the Netherlands Antilles and become an autonomous entity within the Netherlands in 1986 (in 2006 the Netherlands Antilles dissolved and Curaçao also achieved *status aparte* – special status). Talk of achieving full independence in Aruba has thus far not become anything more than that: talk.

Economics: Oil & Tourism

Prosperity came to the island in the form of the huge refinery built to process Venezuelan crude oil in the 1920s. This large complex occupies the southeastern end of Aruba and still dominates the blue-collar town of San Nicolas. Jobs at the plant contributed to the development of a local middle class, and the island thrived.

Midcentury the industry began to modernize and many oil workers lost their jobs. The Dutch government established a tourist commission to promote the nascent holiday sector as an alternative source of employment. In 1959 the first multistory hotel, the Caribbean Hotel, opened on the island and tourism has been booming ever since.

People & Culture

The population of Aruba hovers at around 100,000 and includes some 90 nationalities. Most islanders have mixed ancestry, with Caquetío, African and European roots. About 20% of the population consists of Dutch and American expats.

Most Arubans speak Dutch, English and Spanish, but the native language is Papiamento, an Afro-Portuguese creole. The predominant religion is Catholicism.

This mélange of peoples has created a colorful fusion of cultures that blends the best of Caribbean, African and European influences. This cultural mix is on full display during Carnival, a month-long pre-Lenten celebration. Dancers don extravagant costumes; steel and brass bands play; and the city streets are alive with parades, music and lights.

Landscapes & Wildlife

Despite the lush landscaping that surrounds the resorts, Aruba has an arid climate, with less than 500mm of rainfall per year. Its indigenous plants are hardy desert species, including seven kinds of cactus, as well as the beloved aloe plant and the iconic divi-divi tree. Native animals are mostly reptiles, including a large variety of iguanas and lizards. Birdlife abounds, including the ubiquitous banana quit and the striking troupial. Donkeys and goats run wild on the island's eastern side.

Historically, Aruba's most visible environmental woe was the puffing stacks of the oil refinery in San Nicolas. (In 2019 the Venezuelan state oil company's plans to upgrade and reopen the facility were indefinitely on hold.) Smog also comes from one of the world's largest desalination plants, south of the airport, which roars away 24/7. (In fairness, the water on the island is safe and delicious to drink.)

Meanwhile, the island has set a goal of using 100% renewable energy resources by 2020. Toward this goal, the Vader Piet Windmill Farm has been constructed on the southeastern coast, with more wind farms in the works. Other proposals have included an airport solar park, a waste-to-energy plant, and microgrid technology that would integrate solar and wind systems. There's been talk of making tourist destinations more walkable and accessible, but time's running short and the goal is starting to look unrealistic.

The need to balance the island's healthy economy with its limited water and energy resources has been a major point of discussion, as locals have pressed for growth controls. This has slowed – but certainly not stopped – the rampant development of hotels and condos on the long strip in the island's north.

In addition to its goal of becoming fossil-fuel free by 2020, Aruba has lately made several new rules to protect its environment. In 2017 the government decided to ban plastic shopping bags. Before the ban, the island was going through an estimated 30 million single-use carry-out bags per year. People felt pretty good about putting an end to that, and as of January 1, 2019, plastic straws, single-use plastic cups and foam plates were also prohibited (with a one-year transition period for businesses to come fully into compliance).

In 2018 the island's Ministry of the Environment jumped on the bandwagon and announced that sunscreens containing oxybenzone would also be made illegal in Aruba. Oxybenzone is known to alter the DNA of coral, preventing it from recovering from bleaching or other damage. The phase-out for the chemical began in 2019, with a full ban set for 2020. Meanwhile, some local companies have started coming out with biodegradable 'reef-safe' sunscreens made from natural ingredients. Of course, the best way to protect the reef (and your skin) is to skip all lotions and wear a rash guard or a wetsuit.

SURVIVAL GUIDE

Directory A–Z

ACCESSIBLE TRAVEL

It's not perfect, but Aruba is a relatively friendly destination for travelers with disabilities.

- Many resorts offer accessible rooms and beach *palapas* (open-sided thatched dwellings), including the **Hyatt** (☎586-1234; www.hyatt.com; JE Irausquin Blvd 85, Palm Beach; r from US$400; ❄ @ 📶 ≈). Many restaurants and casinos around the island are also wheelchair accessible.
- Other services such as beach-wheelchair rental and medical transportation can be arranged through specialty suppliers such as **Offroad Wheelchair Aruba** (☎565-0393; www.facebook.com/pg/offroadwheelchairaruba), **Essential Health Supplies** (www.essentialaruba.com), **Lite Life Medicab** (www.litelifemedicab.com) and **Labco** (www.labcoaruba.com).

Accessible Caribbean Vacations (www.accessiblecaribbeanvacations.com) offers sightseeing tours and beach excursions for wheelchair-bound travelers.

De Palm Tours (☎522-4400; www.depalm.com; Palm Beach; adult/child from US$40/29) has one wheelchair-accessible bus, which may be requested for airport transportation or sightseeing tours.

Wheelchair-accessible sights include the Butterfly Farm (p139).

The downside is that there are no wheelchair-accessible boats or taxis, which makes transportation and boat tours a challenge.

In Oranjestad, the cruise-ship pier has a wheelchair ramp, as do many sidewalks around town. But once you leave Oranjestad or the immediate resort area, sidewalks are practically nonexistent.

> **SLEEPING PRICE RANGES**
>
> The following price ranges refer to the cost of a double room with private bathroom, not including taxes.
>
> **$** less than US$100
>
> **$$** US$100–250
>
> **$$$** more than US$250

ACCOMMODATIONS

Most of Aruba's sleeping options are among the 'high-rise resorts' and 'low-rise resorts' along Palm Beach and Eagle Beach, respectively. On a smaller scale, there's a new breed of classy boutique hotel and a few B&Bs in the less touristy areas. You'll also find more modestly priced places off the main strip, both to the east (inland) and to the north.

High-season prices usually run mid-December to mid-April. Prices do not include taxes, which include a 9.5% hotel tax and a US$3-per-day environmental levy. Many resorts also tack on a service fee of 11% (or more).

CHILDREN

Aruba is an ideal destination for families, as there are sights and activities for kids of all ages. Many resorts, shopping malls and other facilities cater especially to families.

All of Aruba's west-coast beaches are protected from the strongest surf, making them ideal for kids to frolic, swim and build sandcastles. There are some waves at Arashi Beach (p142), where older children will enjoy bodysurfing. Mangel Halto (p147) is a perfectly calm, protected place for snorkeling. Aruba Bob's (p147) can teach kids as young as five years old to snorkel.

Even if they're not ready for snorkeling, children can get a peek at the underwater world with **Atlantis Adventures** (☎522-4500; www.depalmtours.com; Lloyd G Smith Blvd 82; adult/child US$115/84; ⏲departs 11am & noon) and **Seaworld Explorer** (☎522-4500; www.depalmtours.com; Palm Beach; adult/child US$44/29) boat tours.

When they need a break from the beach, kids will be delighted by the Donkey Sanctuary (p145), where they can befriend the well-cared-for residents, and the Butterfly Farm (p139), for up-close looks at these beauties. De Palm Island (p147) has activities of all kinds, including a zip line and a water park.

Some resorts are for adults only, but most are very family-friendly. Swimming pools are often designed with kids in mind, and most larger resorts offer kids' clubs, game rooms and other kinds of programming to keep the little ones busy. Family-style rooms and suites are common, as are kitchenettes.

Public restrooms are few and far between, and practically nonexistent at beaches (with the exception of some portable toilets). Changing tables are not common. Sidewalks are super in some dedicated areas, such as the high-rise resort area (JE Irausquin Blvd) and the coastal road (Lloyd G Smith Blvd) along the northwestern shore, but once you leave these specific stretches, sidewalks are practically nonexistent, making it dangerous to walk with children or push a stroller.

ELECTRICITY

Power is 110V to 120V, 60Hz; Aruba uses outlet and plug types A and B.

EMERGENCY NUMBERS

Ambulance	☎911
Fire	☎911
Police	☎911, 100
Road Service	☎165

FOOD

Food is one of the joys of Aruba, although eating out is pricey. If you're on a budget, take advantage of your kitchenette. Generally, the most creative cooking takes place outside the resort area. Look for interesting, innovative cuisine in inland Noord and in Oranjestad. You'll certainly eat well on Palm Beach, though: it's lined with seafood restaurants, beach bars and snack shacks – some with very tasty dishes indeed.

EATING PRICE RANGES

The following price ranges refer to the cost of a main course.

$ less than US$10

$$ US$10–25

$$$ more than US$25

HEALTH

Dr Horacio Oduber Hospital (☎527-4000; www.arubahospital.com) is a large, well-equipped facility off Lloyd G Smith Blvd, near the low-rise resorts. Emergency care is available.

Tap water in Aruba is safe to drink.

INTERNET ACCESS

All of Aruba's resorts and hotels offer wireless internet access, as do many restaurants and cafes. Some accommodations also have computers for guest use.

LEGAL MATTERS

The police do not maintain a particularly visible presence in Aruba, but they are here. And they stringently enforce the island's laws:

➡ Unlike in the Netherlands proper, all drugs are illegal. Violating these laws can lead to arrest and imprisonment.

➡ Littering laws are strictly enforced, so pick up after yourself on the beach and do not leave your cigarette butts around.

As always, if you get arrested, your embassy can help you contact an attorney but cannot do not much else.

LGBT+ TRAVELERS

The 2016 civil code allows 'registered partnerships' for both same-sex and opposite-sex unions. For visitors, Aruba is an open and welcoming island, no matter your sexual orientation: resorts and hotels welcome all comers. That said, there's not much of an LGBTQ scene, other than a **gay bar** (☎582-2550; www.7aruba.com; Windstraat 32; ⏲7pm-2am Wed & Thu, to 4am Fri & Sat) or two in Oranjestad.

MONEY

Although Aruba's official currency is the florin (Afl), prices are often quoted in US dollars and you can pay for just about everything with US currency. Sometimes you will get change back in US dollars, at other times in Aruban florins.

ATMs are widely available, dispensing US dollars and Aruban florins. Credit cards are accepted at most hotels and restaurants.

Exchange Rates

Australia	A$1	Afl1.27
Canada	C$	Afl1.34
Curaçao	NAf1	Afl0.96

Euro zone	€1	Afl2.02
Japan	¥100	Afl1.62
New Zealand	NZ$1	Afl1.20
UK	UK£1	Afl2.35
US	US$	Afl1.80

For current exchange rates, see www.xe.com.

Tipping

Bars and restaurants For good service, tip 15% to 20% (minus the service charge that is sometimes included in the bill).

Resorts If service charge not included on the bill, tip US$1 to US$3 per day for housekeeping.

Taxis A 10% tip is usual.

Tour guides Tip US$10 for a half-day outing.

OPENING HOURS

Many offices, shops and even restaurants are closed on Sunday.

Banks 9am to 4pm Monday to Friday.

Restaurants 11am to 10pm.

Shops 9am to 6pm Monday to Saturday (in tourist areas to 8pm daily).

POST

Post Aruba provides reliable international service. Expect mail to reach the US or Canada in a week or two and Europe in two or three weeks. The main **post office** (☎528-7678; www.postaruba.com; Irausquin Plein 9; ⏰7:30am-4:30pm Mon-Fri) is located in downtown Oranjestad, but there's also an outlet in the Palm Beach Plaza, which is next to the **Paseo Herrencia mall** (www.paseoherencia.com; JE Irausquin Blvd 382a, Palm Beach; ⏰10am-10pm Mon-Sat, 5-10pm Sun).

PUBLIC HOLIDAYS

New Year's Day January 1

GF (Betico) Croes Day January 25

Carnival Monday Monday before Ash Wednesday

National Day March 18

Good Friday Friday before Easter

Easter Monday Monday after Easter

King's Birthday April 27

Labor Day May 1

Ascension Day Sixth Thursday after Easter

Christmas Day December 25

Boxing Day December 26

SAFE TRAVEL

Aruba is one of the safest islands in the Caribbean, with low rates of petty and violent crime. But the typical precautions are still valid.

- Do not leave valuables unattended on the beach or in the car.
- Be wary of overly friendly strangers.

PRACTICALITIES

Newspapers The main English-language newspaper is *Aruba Today* (www.arubatoday.com), which focuses on international news.

Television Local channels generally broadcast in Dutch and/or Papiamento.

Smoking Permitted at all restaurants, bars and casinos, although they usually have nonsmoking sections, too. Hotels usually have specific smoking and non-smoking rooms.

Weights & measures The metric system is used.

TELEPHONE

Aruba's country code is 297.

To call locally, dial the seven-digit number with no area code. To call internationally, dial the international access code (00), plus the country code, plus the number.

Cell Phones

GSM cell (mobile) phones are compatible with local SIM cards. There's also 3G service. The main operators are **Digicel** (www.digicelaruba.com) and **Setar** (www.setar.aw).

TIME

Aruba runs to Atlantic Standard Time (AST), which is four hours behind Greenwich Mean Time. Daylight saving is not observed.

TOURIST INFORMATION

The Aruba Tourism Authority (p138) is a well-funded entity with a comprehensive and useful website. It has an Oranjestad office, part of a trio of buildings that comprise the Aruban tourism complex, with helpful staff.

VOLUNTEERING

Aruba is one of the more prosperous islands in the Caribbean, and volunteer opportunities are scarce. That said, a few organizations depend on the efforts of dedicated volunteers:

Aruba Animal Shelter (www.arubaanimalshelter.com; Planterust; ⏰8am-noon Mon-Fri, to 3pm Sat) Give some love to the island's homeless dogs and cats.

Aruba Reef Care Foundation (☎740-0797; arubareefcare@gmail.com) For 20-plus years this group has sponsored an annual cleanup of the island's beaches and dive and snorkel sites.

Donkey Sanctuary (p145) Entirely volunteer-run sanctuary caring for donkeys without a home.

FLYING TO THE US

Passengers flying to the US absolutely must check in at least three hours before flight time. This is not your typical international departure: US-bound passengers clear US customs and immigration *before* leaving Aruba, so don't underestimate the time required.

Most flights to the US leave around the same time, and the US-staffed immigration facilities are often mobbed. If possible, try to avoid going on a weekend, when things are at their worst. In any case, allow plenty of time: three hours is the minimum.

Special Olympics Aruba (www.specialolympics.org/programs/north-america/aruba; Piedra Plat 86b) Volunteers help with coaching, event planning, publicity and more.

Getting There & Away

You can reach Aruba by air or sea (cruise ships). Flights, cars and tours can be booked online at lonelyplanet.com/bookings.

AIR

Reina Beatrix International Airport (AUA; ☎524-2424; www.airportaruba.com) is a busy, modern airport with services to North and South America as well as daily flights to Amsterdam and weekly flights to the UK. It's just south of Oranjestad.

The most popular regional carriers include:

Aruba Airlines (☎583-8300; www.arubaairlines.com) Daily flights to and from Curaçao, with frequent connections to and from Bonaire.

Avianca (☎582-5484; www.avianca.com) Services South and Central America, via Bogotá, Colombia.

Divi Divi (www.flydivi.com) Regular flights between Aruba, Bonaire, Curaçao and Sint Maarten.

Winair (www.fly-winair.sx) Connects Aruba with Curaçao, Bonaire and Sint Maarten.

SEA

The island of Aruba is accessible by cruise ship. Despite the proximity of the ABCs (Aruba, Bonaire and Curaçao) to each other, no ferries run between them. Plans for this seem perpetually afoot, but it hasn't worked out yet.

The ABCs are part of cruise-ship itineraries that cover the southern Caribbean, often on longer 10-day and two-week trips. When the biggest ships are in port, it's not unusual to have more than 10,000 passengers descend on the island in a day. Boats dock at the port in the middle of Oranjestad.

Getting Around

BICYCLE

Although there are no bike lanes on Aruba, many people enjoy riding along the mostly flat roads. You can easily rent bikes at many resorts. **Aruba Active Vacations** (☎741-2991, 586-0989; www.aruba-active-vacations.com; Hadicurari Beach; rental per hour/day US$25/60, lesson from US$50) rents mountain bikes.

North of Palm Beach, Lloyd G Smith Blvd runs along the coast all the way up to Arashi Beach (it's about 2 miles). This is a popular route for cyclists, as traffic is light and the setting is lovely.

BUS

Arubus (p138) operates several routes running from the **main bus depot** (Lloyd G Smith Blvd) in Oranjestad south to the airport and on to San Nicolas, with additional routes to the Fisherman Huts, Malmok Beach and Arashi Beach (all via the resort areas). Buses run every 10 to 20 minutes.

CAR & MOTORCYCLE

European road rules and signs are used. Driving is on the right-hand side, seat belts are required and motorcyclists must use helmets.

You'll know other visitors not only by the V-registrations of their rental cars but also by their actual use of turn signals. All the major car-rental companies have offices at the airport. It's worth comparing prices with local outfits, including **Carvenience** (☎568-0383; https://carvenience.rentals; Sabana Berde 16d; ⏰7am-7pm), **Optima** (☎582-4828; www.optimarentacar.com; Camacuri 8; ⏰8am-5pm Mon & Tue, 6am-7pm Wed-Sun) and **Wheels 2 Go** (☎586-8632; www.wheels2goaruba.com; ⏰8am-5pm Mon-Sat).

TAXI

Taxis are safe and reliable, and easy to flag down at hotels and resorts. Fares are set for fixed distances; for example, from the airport to the high-rise resort area costs US$31.

The Bahamas

☎242 / POP 395,000

Includes ➡

Best Places to Eat

- Chat & Chill Bar & Grill (p193)
- Fish Fry (p164)
- Café Matisse (p165)
- Stuart's Conch Stand (p182)

Best Places to Stay

- HumesHouse@Hillcrest (p163)
- Pineville Motel (p189)
- Graycliff Hotel (p163)
- Pink Sands Resort (p184)
- BahaSea Backpackers (p164)

Why Go?

Spangled between the depths of the North Atlantic and Florida's eastern coast, the Bahamas – not technically part of the Caribbean – comprises more than 700 stunning subtropical islands and 2400 cays, most uninhabited, and all fringed by spectacular coral and fathomless ocean trenches. From the grit and bustle of Nassau to the vast mangroves of Andros, there's an astonishing array of beaches, reefs, forests and historic towns to be discovered, all within the compass of an hour's flight.

The Bahamas is an inescapably pricey destination but whether sailing around the Abacos' history-filled Loyalist Cays, partying at Paradise Island's Atlantis resort, swimming with wild pigs or lounging on Eleuthera's pink-sand beaches, there's likely a Bahamian island to match every water- and sand-based compulsion, all framed by a backdrop of gorgeous, mesmerizing blue.

The Bahamians are a laid-back lot and a night spent at a local fish fry is not to be missed.

When to Go

Mid-Dec–mid-Apr High season, when hotel prices are highest.

Jun–Sep Daytime temperatures average a perfect 80°F (26°C) but this is also hurricane season.

Mar Spring break means Nassau and Grand Bahama crawl with rum-fueled revelers.

The Bahamas Highlights

1. **Nassau** (p156) Enjoying the beaches, museums, nightlife and Paradise Island excesses in the Bahamas' gritty but fun-filled capital.
2. **Diving** (p160) Plunging into one of the world's great underwater playgrounds.
3. **Fish Fry** (p164) Chowing down at Nassau's premiere spot for conch salad, blackened grouper and sky-juice-fueled parties.
4. **Bimini** (p182) Snorkeling geometric Bimini Road and visiting eccentric Dolphin House.
5. **Harbour Island** (p183) Losing yourself in the ramshackle streets and top-drawer resorts of this perfect Bahamian microcosm.
6. **Exuma Cays** (p190) Exploring this string of island paradises and meeting the original swimming pigs.
7. **Loyalist Cays, Abacos** (p176) Visiting these beautiful islands will help with the economy and recovery after the destruction of Hurricane Dorian.

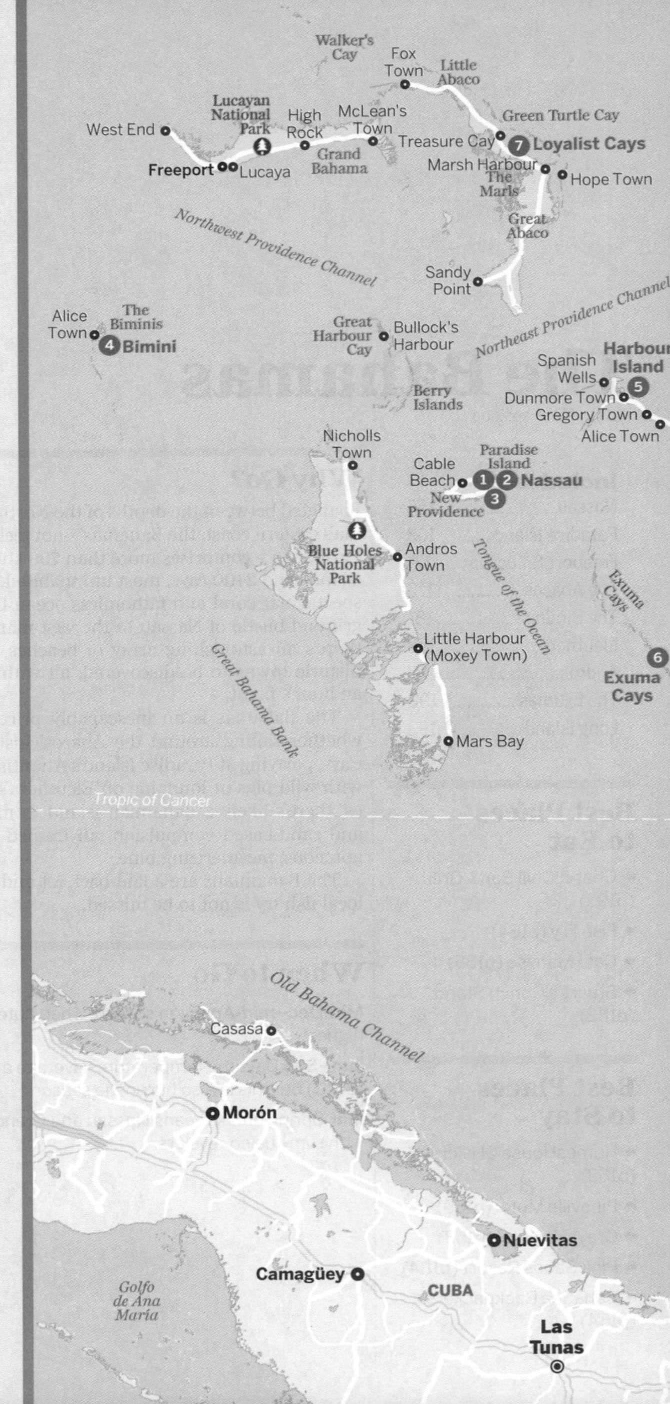

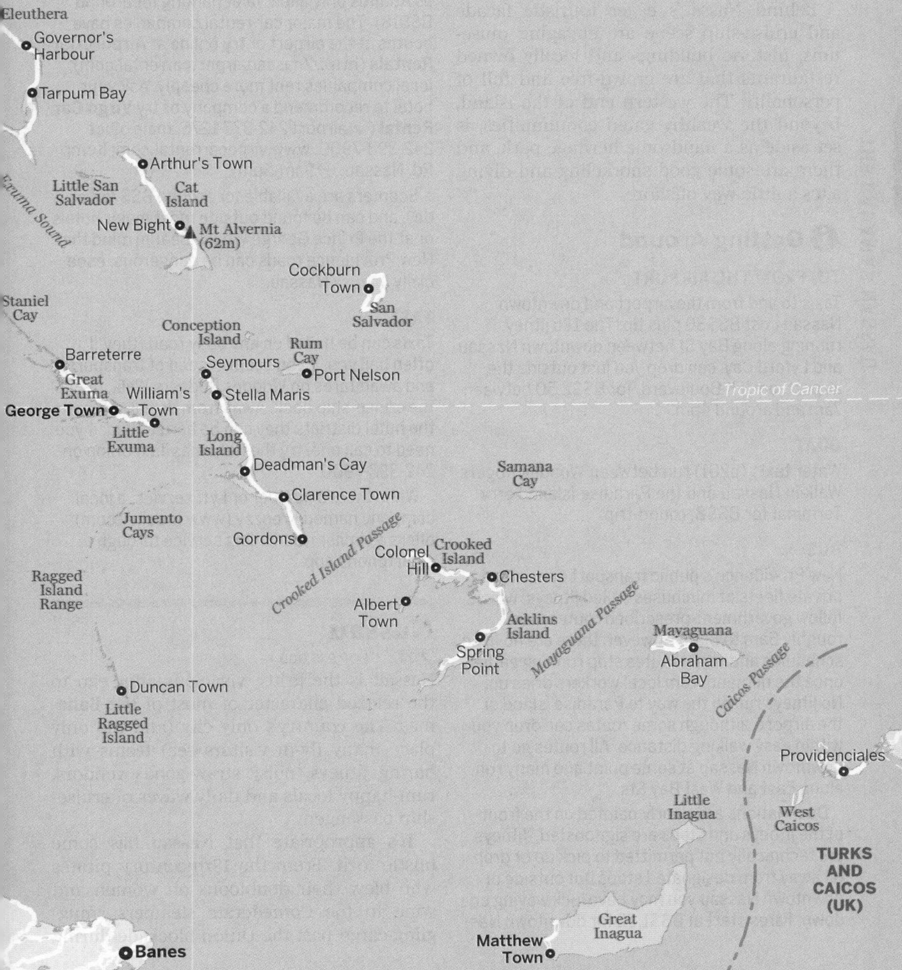

N
0 100 km
0 50 miles
ATLANTIC OCEAN
THE BAHAMAS
Eleuthera
Governor's Harbour
Tarpum Bay
Arthur's Town
Little San Salvador
Cat Island
Exuma Sound
New Bight
Mt Alvernia (62m)
Cockburn Town
San Salvador
Staniel Cay
Conception Island
Rum Cay
Barreterre
Seymours
Port Nelson
Great Exuma
William's Town
Stella Maris
Tropic of Cancer
George Town
Little Exuma
Long Island
Deadman's Cay
Samana Cay
Clarence Town
Jumento Cays
Gordons
Crooked Island Passage
Colonel Hill
Crooked Island
Chesters
Ragged Island Range
Albert Town
Acklins Island
Mayaguana Passage
Mayaguana
Abraham Bay
Spring Point
Caicos Passage
Duncan Town
Little Ragged Island
Providenciales
Little Inagua
West Caicos
TURKS AND CAICOS (UK)
Great Inagua
Matthew Town
Banes

NEW PROVIDENCE

POP 274,000

Most travellers and locals use Nassau (the capital city) and New Providence (the island it occupies) interchangeably. Undoubtedly the hub and nerve centre of the Bahamas, what New Providence/Nassau lacks in size, it more than makes up for in energy, attitude and devil-may-care spirit. This 34km-long powerhouse of an island is a perfect fit for the extroverted tourist with money to burn. Plummet down a 15m waterslide, puff on a hand-rolled stogie, place your bets on a high-stakes hand and carouse like a pirate into the wee hours – it's all there for the grabbing.

Behind Nassau's eager touristic facade and cruise-ship scene are engaging museums, historic buildings and locally owned restaurants that are crowd-free and full of personality. The western end of the island, beyond the wealthy gated communities, is set aside as a handsome heritage park, and there are some good snorkeling and diving sites a little way offshore.

Getting Around

TO/FROM THE AIRPORT

Taxis to and from the airport and downtown Nassau cost BS$30 plus tip. The 12b jitney, running along Bay St between downtown Nassau and Lyford Cay, can drop you just outside the airport, on JFK Boulevard, for BS$2.50 between 7am and around 4pm.

BOAT

Water taxis (p201) run between Woodes Rogers Walk in Nassau and the Paradise Island Ferry Terminal for BS$8, round-trip.

BUS

New Providence's public transport consists of private fleets of minibuses called jitneys, which follow government-prescribed routes from roughly 6am to 8pm. However, there are no fixed schedules and many routes stop running earlier, once the demand from local workers dries up. No jitneys run all the way to Paradise Island or the airport, although some routes can drop you within easy walking distance. All routes go to downtown Nassau at some point and many run along East and West Bay Sts.

Destinations are clearly painted on the front of the jitneys and stops are signposted. Jitneys are technically not permitted to pick up or drop off away from designated stops but outside of downtown Nassau you may have luck waving one down. Fares start at BS$1.25 for downtown Nassau and rise to BS$2.50 depending on distance. Some useful routes:

10 & 10A Running through Cable Beach, Sandyport Bay and Lyford Cay, this is the busiest route, and the cheapest way to get a tour of the island.

1, 7 & 7A Paradise Island bridges.

12b Love Beach and close to the airport.

CAR & SCOOTER

You don't need a car to explore downtown Nassau or to get to the beaches, but you will if you intend to explore New Providence (taxi fares would quickly outweigh rental costs). Parking can be a problem in downtown Nassau and Paradise Island – it's either difficult to find a spot during the day or expensive (large hotels such as Atlantis only allow valet parking for around BS$18). The major car-rental companies have booths at the airport or try online at **Airport Car Rentals** (http://nassauairportcarrental.com); local companies rent more cheaply. Ask your hotel to recommend a company or try **Virgo Car Rental** (☎ airport 242-377-1275, main office 242-393-7900; www.virgocarrental.com; Kemp Rd, Nassau; ⏱9am-5pm).

Scooters are available for around BS$75 per day, and can be found outside most major hotels or at the Prince George Wharf. Bear in mind that New Providence roads can be dangerous, especially in busy Nassau.

TAXI

Taxis can be hailed on any busy road (they'll often hail you, if you seem in need of transport) and await fares on Woodes Rodgers Walk, near the cruise-ship dock. Away from downtown or the hotel districts they can be hard to find: if you need to call one, try the Bahamas Taxi Union on 242-323-7900.

While there's no Uber or Lyft service, a local company named Kroozzy (www.kroozzy.com) offers a similar ride-hailing service through a smartphone app.

Nassau

☎242 / POP 275,000

Nassau is the gritty, vivacious alter ego to the relaxed character of most of the Bahamas. The country's only city (and the only place many fly-in visitors see) teems with haring jitneys, noisy straw-goods vendors, rum-happy locals and daily waves of cruise-ship passengers.

It's appropriate that Nassau has some hustle to it. From the 18th-century pirates who blew their doubloons on women and wine to the Confederate steamers smuggling cargo past the Union blockade during the American Civil War, the city has long sheltered daring dodgers on the make. The make-a-buck spirit of this global tax haven animates the duty-free shops and cigar salesmen of Bay St, while the historic wealth of the ruling classes finds tangible expression in grand, Georgian government buildings and homes. Whether you come to shop, eat, party or sightsee, Nassau is *the* place for a dose of urban excitement.

Sights

Downtown Nassau and Bay St largely consist of modern commercial buildings dedicated to the cruise-ship market, although some historic buildings remain. Other sights are dotted throughout Nassau, most in walkable proximity to each other, especially to the landward side of Bay St.

★ National Art Gallery of the Bahamas MUSEUM

(Map p166; ☎242-358-5800; www.nagb.org.bs; cnr West & West Hill Sts; adult/child BS$10/free; ⏰10am-5pm Tue-Sat, from noon Sun) Anchoring the West Hill St tourist enclave, the National Art Gallery is a welcome oasis inside the stately 1860s-era Villa Doyle and one of the gems in the Bahamian cultural crown. The permanent collection focuses on modern and contemporary Bahamian artists, from renowned sculptor Antonius Roberts to folk painter Wellington Bridgewater. There are also pieces by artists of the wider Caribbean, and temporary exhibits on ecological, cultural and historical themes relevant to the islands.

★ Graycliff Cigar Co FACTORY

(Map p166; ☎242-302-9150; www.graycliff.com; Graycliff Hotel & Restaurant, West Hill St; ⏰9am-5pm) FREE Wandering into this cigar factory is like falling into 1920s Cuba. In a narrow, smoke-yellowed room with old-fashioned mosaic floors, *torcedores* (cigar rollers) are busy at work, their fingers a blur as they roll hand-dried tobacco leaves into premium stogies. You can wander through and take photos for free, or a guided factory tour is BS$10. Book ahead for a cigar-rolling lesson (BS$75) or a cigar-rolling demo with rum tasting (BS$150).

Graycliff's head *torcedor* was the late Avelino Lara, former personal cigar roller for Fidel Castro.

★ Junkanoo Beach BEACH

(Map p166) Between downtown Nassau and Arawak Cay, Junkanoo is popular with locals and visitors alike, with beach-shack bars, volleyball nets, sky-juice vendors and friendly Bahamians in ample supply.

★ John Watling's Distillery DISTILLERY

(Map p166; ☎242-322-2811; www.johnwatlings.com; 17 Delancy St; tour free, tastings from B$10; ⏰10am-6pm; P) Watling's, relatively new to the Bahamian rum-distilling game, has found a home in the beautifully restored 18th-century Buena Vista Estate, its extensive tiki-lit gardens patrolled by fluffy-legged bantams and staff in colonial-era costumes. Take a free 15-minute tour of the house and distillery – named for a 17th-century pirate – then adjourn to the stylish bar for a tasting of the pale, amber and buena vista rums.

Pirates of Nassau MUSEUM

(Map p166; ☎242-356-3759; www.piratesofnassau.com; cnr King & George Sts; adult/child BS$13.50/6.75; ⏰8:30am-5pm Mon-Sat, 9am-2pm Sun; 👪) It's hard to ignore the pirate pacing outside and posing for selfies on the pedestrianized strip off George St. The walk-through exhibition space trades entirely on Nassau's history as a haven and republic for pirates and has some interesting displays, from the scale replica of the pirate ship *Revenge,* and semi-animatronic pirates to accessible exhibits on everything from marooning to pirate Hall-of-Famers. In a modern age it feels decidedly dated but there's some historical pirate education for kids and parents.

Graycliff Chocolatier FACTORY

(Map p166; ☎242-302-9190; www.graycliff.com; 8-14 West Hill St; tours BS$11.20; ⏰9am-4pm) Completing the Graycliff's Heritage Village trifecta (wine, chocolate and cigars), this boutique chocolate factory uses Caribbean cacao to produce a wide range of chocolate products (including chocolate cigars), all on display and for sale. Short tours include tastings in liquid form as well as the final product.

Fort Fincastle & the Queen's Staircase FORT

(Map p166; ☎242-322-7500; Elizabeth Ave; BS$3; ⏰8am-4pm) Set on a small hill just south of downtown Nassau, this small fort was built by Lord Dunmore in 1793 to guard the harbor against invaders. Never used, it was eventually converted into a lighthouse. The fort itself is not particularly fascinating, but it's worth the trip for the sweeping panoramic views from the top. Leading up from Elizabeth Ave is the Queen's Staircase: built from solid limestone carved by slaves, it's one of the island's most enduring landmarks.

New Providence

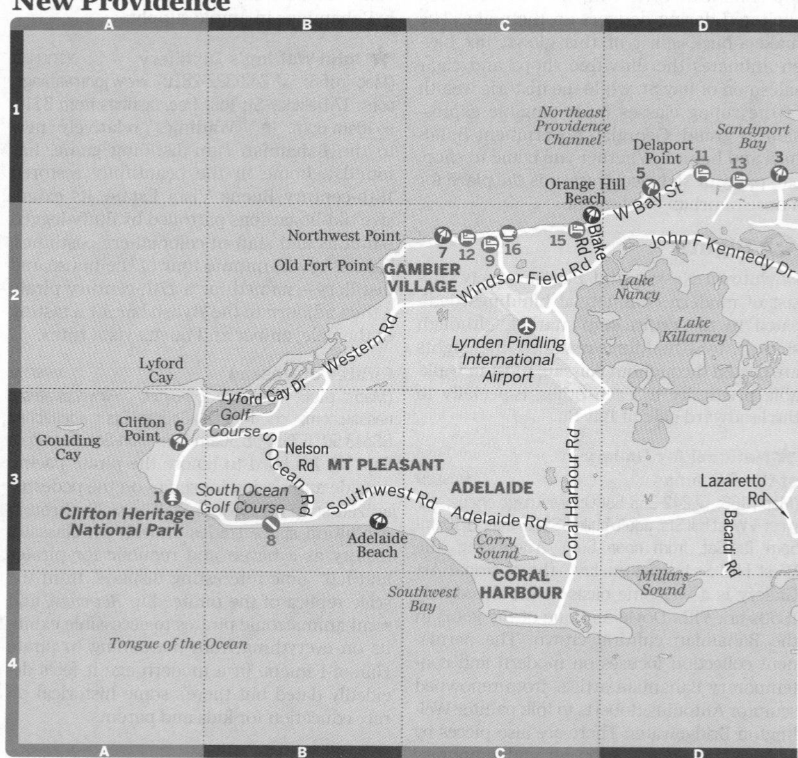

THE BAHAMAS NASSAU

New Providence

Top Sights
1 Clifton Heritage National Park.............. A3

Sights
2 Blue Lagoon Island.............................. H1
3 Cable Beach.. D1
4 Cove Beach... G1
5 Delaporte Beach.................................. D1
6 Jaws Beach... A3
7 Love Beach... C2

Activities, Courses & Tours
8 Stuart Cove's Dive & Snorkel Bahamas.. B3

Sleeping
9 A Stone's Throw Away......................... C2
10 Baha Mar.. E2
11 BahaSea Backpackers......................... D1
12 Compass Point Beach Resort.............. C2
13 Marley Resort..................................... D1
14 Meliá Nassau Beach............................ E1
15 Orange Hill Beach Inn......................... C2

Drinking & Nightlife
16 Louis & Steen's New Orleans Coffee House... C2
17 Sky Bar... E2

Government House NOTABLE BUILDING
(Map p166; 242-322-1875; Duke St; 9am-5pm Mon-Fri) FREE This splendid Georgian mansion, residence of the governor-general, surmounts Mount Fitzwilliam (central Nassau's low hill) like a festive pink cake. Sitting on the site of a predecessor built in 1737, the 1803 structure was badly damaged by a hurricane in 1929, leading to extensive repairs and remodeling (1932), and lavish redecoration during the Duke of Windsor's time as governor (1940–45). Below, the statue of

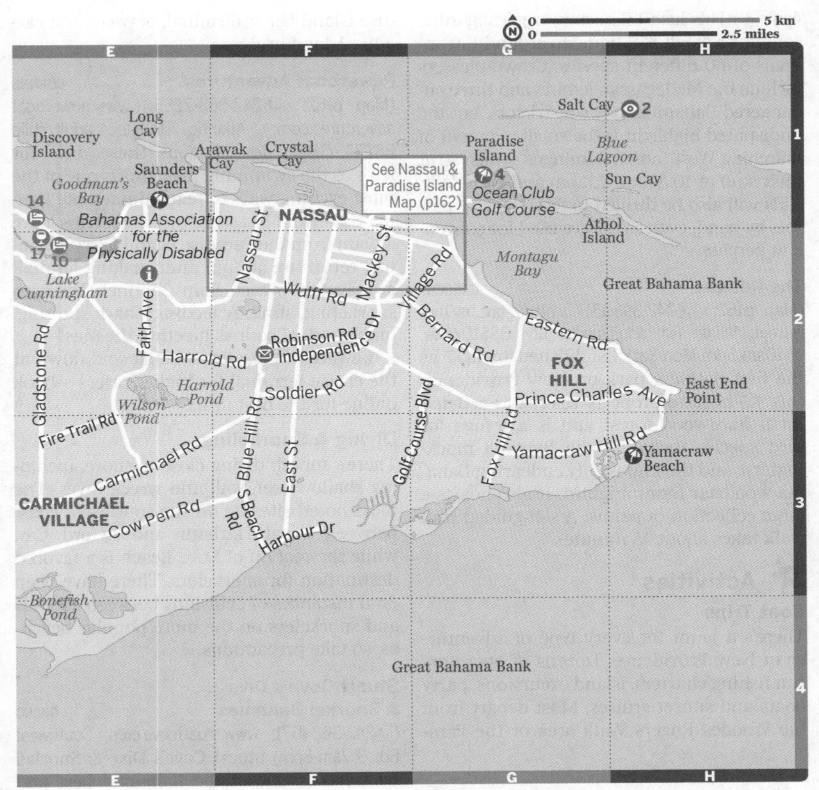

Christopher Columbus has maintained a jaunty pose on the steps overlooking Duke St since 1830.

Heritage Museum of the Bahamas MUSEUM
(Map p166; ☎242-302-9150; 8-14 West Hill St; BS$11.20 with audio guide; ⏰9am-5pm) Mostly comprising a substantial private collection of antiques and artifacts relating to the history of the Bahamas, this small museum covers a lot of ground, from fossils and a meteorite to pirate-era relics. The self-guided audio tour helps bring it to life. The museum is upstairs in the restored 19th-century Mountbatten House.

Pompey Museum of Slavery & Emancipation MUSEUM
(Map p166; ☎242-356-0495; Bay St; adult/child BS$3/1; ⏰9:30am-4:30pm Mon-Sat) Located in the Vendue House – a queen-conch-pink building from the 1760s in which slave auctions were once held – this one-room museum features exhibitions detailing the story of slavery and emancipation in the Bahamas. The name derives from Pompey, leader of an 1830 slave revolt on Exuma, who successfully resisted transfer to neighboring Cat Island.

Doongalik Studios GALLERY
(Map p162; ☎242-394-1886; www.doongalik.com; 18 Village Rd; ⏰10am-4pm Mon-Wed, 9am-1pm Sat) FREE Offering an eclectic window into modern Bahamian art, Doongalik runs exhibitions on solo artists' work, and everything from quilts to straw crafts and island life. Book launches, musical performances and other events are also frequent. It's set in the lovely two-storied building and the surrounding gardens, and there's a farmers market every Saturday morning.

Ardastra Gardens, Zoo & Conservation Center GARDENS
(Map p162; ☎242-323-5806; www.ardastra.com; Chippingham Rd; adult/child/under 3yr BS$18.75/9.50/free; ⏰9am-5pm, last admission

4pm;) This lush 1.6-hectare tropical garden contains a small zoo, home to around 180 animals of 60 different species. Crowd-pleasers include the Madagascan lemurs and three endangered Bahamian boa constrictors, but the undisputed highlight is the small regiment of marching West Indian flamingos, which strut their stuff at 10:30am, 2:15pm and 4pm daily. Kids will also be thrilled to feed the lory parrots by hand, even as they're used for convenient perches.

The Retreat GARDENS
(Map p162; 242-393-1317; http://bnt.bs/the-retreat; Village Rd; adult/under 12yr BS$10/free; 10am-5pm Mon-Sat) Established in 1977 as the first national park on New Providence, this 4.5-hectare property re-creates a Bahamian hardwood forest and is a refuge for bird species including the Bahama mockingbird, and the impossibly endearing Bahama woodstar hummingbird. It also boasts a large collection of palms. A self-guided trail walk takes about 45 minutes.

Activities

Boat Trips

There's a jaunt for every type of adventurer in New Providence. Dozens of operators run fishing charters, island excursions, party boats and sunset cruises. Most depart from the Woodes Rogers Walk area or the Paradise Island Ferry Terminal, between the Paradise Island bridges.

Powerboat Adventures BOATING
(Map p162; 242-363-2265; www.powerboatadventures.com; Atlantic Bridge; adult/child BS$245/180) Most famous these days for trips to the swimming pigs, this is one of the most exciting ways to reach the remote Exuma Cays from Nassau. Powerboat trips leave at 9am from the Paradise Island Ferry Terminal, returning at 5pm after making landfall at privately owned Ship Channel Cay, with snorkeling, stingray feeding, shark-spotting, lunch and, of course, meeting the pigs.

Beware of these trips being sold down at the cruise terminal for higher prices – book online for the best deals.

Diving & Snorkeling

There's superb diving close to shore, including shallow-reef, wall and wreck dives. The most noted sites lie off the southwest coast between Coral Harbour and Lyford Cay, while the reef off of Love Beach is a favored destination for snorkelers. There have been fatal instances of collisions between Jet Skis and snorkelers on the more popular beaches, so take precautions.

Stuart Cove's Dive & Snorkel Bahamas DIVING
(242-362-4171; www.stuartcove.com; Southwest Rd; 7am-8pm) Stuart Cove's Dive & Snorkel Bahamas is one of the Bahamas' best and largest dive operators. It offers a range of diving, PADI certification and snorkeling choices, including a buttock-clenching shark wall and shark-feeding dive (BS$182); a two-tank dive trip (BS$134); and a three-dive 'Seafari' trip to the blue holes and plunging walls of Andros island (by prior arrangement).

Bahama Divers DIVING
(Map p162; 242-393-5644; www.bahamadivers.com; East Bay St; 1-/2-tank dive from B$100/134; 8am-6pm) Bahama Divers has a regular schedule of morning and afternoon dives to sites including the Lost Blue Hole, Stubbs Wall and De La Salle wreck, as well as night dives and snorkeling trips. See the website for the dive schedule.

Fishing

Nassau is a great base for fishing, with superb deepwater sites just 20 minutes away. Game species include blue marlin, sailfish, yellowfin tuna, *mahimahi* and wahoo. Charters can be arranged at most major ho-

---

GRAYCLIFF'S VILLAGE

West Hill St, one of the oldest streets in downtown Nassau, is little more than 100m long but it has developed into a tourist hot spot thanks to the ever-growing Graycliff's Heritage Village. Anchored by the historic Gray Cliff Hotel and its high-end restaurants, the 'village' includes a cigar factory, chocolatier, boutique **winery** (Map p166; 242-302-9150; West Hill St; 9am-5pm), heritage museum and **artists' studio**, where you can meet local artists and admire their work. The central area, where you'll find the Drawbridge Cafe and Chillin' fish fry, is sometimes decoratively shaded by multihued umbrellas suspended above the street.

Nearby, but not connected to Graycliff's, are the National Art Gallery of the Bahamas (p157) and John Watling's Distillery (p157).

DON'T MISS

JUMPING AT JUNKANOO

You feel the music before you see it – a frenzied barrage of whistles and horns overriding the *ka-LICK-ka-LICK* of cowbells, the rumble of drums and the joyful blasts of conch shells. Then the costumed revelers stream into view, whirling and gyrating like a kaleidoscope in rhythm with the cacophony. This is Junkanoo, the national festival of the Bahamas; a mass of energy and color that starts in the twilight hours of Boxing Day.

Junkanoo is fiercely competitive and many marchers belong to 'shacks': groups who vie to produce the best performance, costumes, dancing and music. The most elaborately costumed performers are one-person parade floats, whose costumes can weigh over 90kg (200lb) and depict colorful scenes adorned with glittering beads, foils and rhinestones.

Junkanoo, which had its origins in West African secret societies, evolved on the plantations of the British Caribbean among slaves who were forbidden to observe their sacred rites and hid their identity with masks.The name is thought to come from a West African term for 'deadly sorcerer'; others say it's named for John Canoe, the tribal leader who demanded that his enslaved people be allowed to enjoy a festivity.

In Nassau, the first 'rush,' as the parade is known, is on Boxing Day (December 26); the second occurs New Year's Day and the third in summer, when teams practice. Parades begin at about 3am. Elbow into a viewing spot along Shirley St or Bay St, where crowds can be thick and rowdy. For a less hectic bleacher seat, contact the Ministry of Tourism (p201) for information on obtaining tickets.

tels or by calling a charter company, which typically charge two to six people BS$550 to BS$700 per half-day, or BS$1000 to BS$1500 per full day.

★Chubasco Charters FISHING
(Map p162; ☎242-324-3474; www.chubasco charters.com; Paradise Island Ferry Terminal; half-/full-day charter from BS$580/1160; ⊙departures 8am & 1pm) Chubasco swaggeringly offers a 'no splash, no cash' guarantee: if you book a full-day fishing charter and don't catch a thing, your trip is free. Chubasco runs four boats, from 11m to 14.5m long, taking its fleet into the deep waters just 15 to 30 minutes out of Nassau Harbour to chase down tuna, marlin, wahoo and *mahimahi*.

Born Free Charter Service FISHING
(Map p166; ☎242-698-1770; www.bornfree fishing.com; ⊙departures 8am & 1pm) Captain Pinder has uncanny knowledge of Bahamian waters, taking anglers to where the big game - sailfish, tuna, marlin - are most likely to bite. Chartering one of his five vessels, together with all that know-how, will set you back at least BS$650/1300 (half-/full day). Pickups are from behind the Straw Market or by the tollbooth on Paradise Island.

Tours

Tru Bahamian Food Tours FOOD
(Map p166; ☎242-601-1725; www.trubahamian foodtours.com; cnr George & Bay Sts; adult/child from BS$69/49; ⊙8am-9pm Mon-Sat, to 6pm Sun) This outfit's **Bites of Nassau** tour is a three-hour excursion around the best of Bahamian food, stopping off at six local kitchens to meet the chefs and sample the good stuff. The **Old Nassau Dining Stroll** on Sunday (adults-only BS$79) matches food with cocktails and local food history.

Nassau Jeep Adventures TOURS
(☎242-676-8541; www.nassaujeepadventures.com; adult/child B$90/85) These three-hour open-top jeep tours cover off some of the city's offbeat sights and include food and drink tasting, with an emphasis on fun.

Festivals & Events

RumBahamas FOOD & DRINK
(Fort Charlotte, West Bay St; ⊙late Feb) Rum producers from across the Caribbean and Latin America descend on Nassau each February for this three-day celebration of food, culture and cane spirit. Held behind the doughty ramparts of 18th-century Fort Charlotte, it features rum tastings and classes, competitive cocktail mixing, live music, fire dancing, a Junkanoo party and, naturally, Bahamian food aplenty.

Sleeping

Nassau hotel rooms can be very expensive, and quality varies widely. Guest charges and taxes can push daily rates up by 20% to 30%, yet web rates are often dramatically lower than official listed prices - it pays to shop

Nassau & Paradise Island

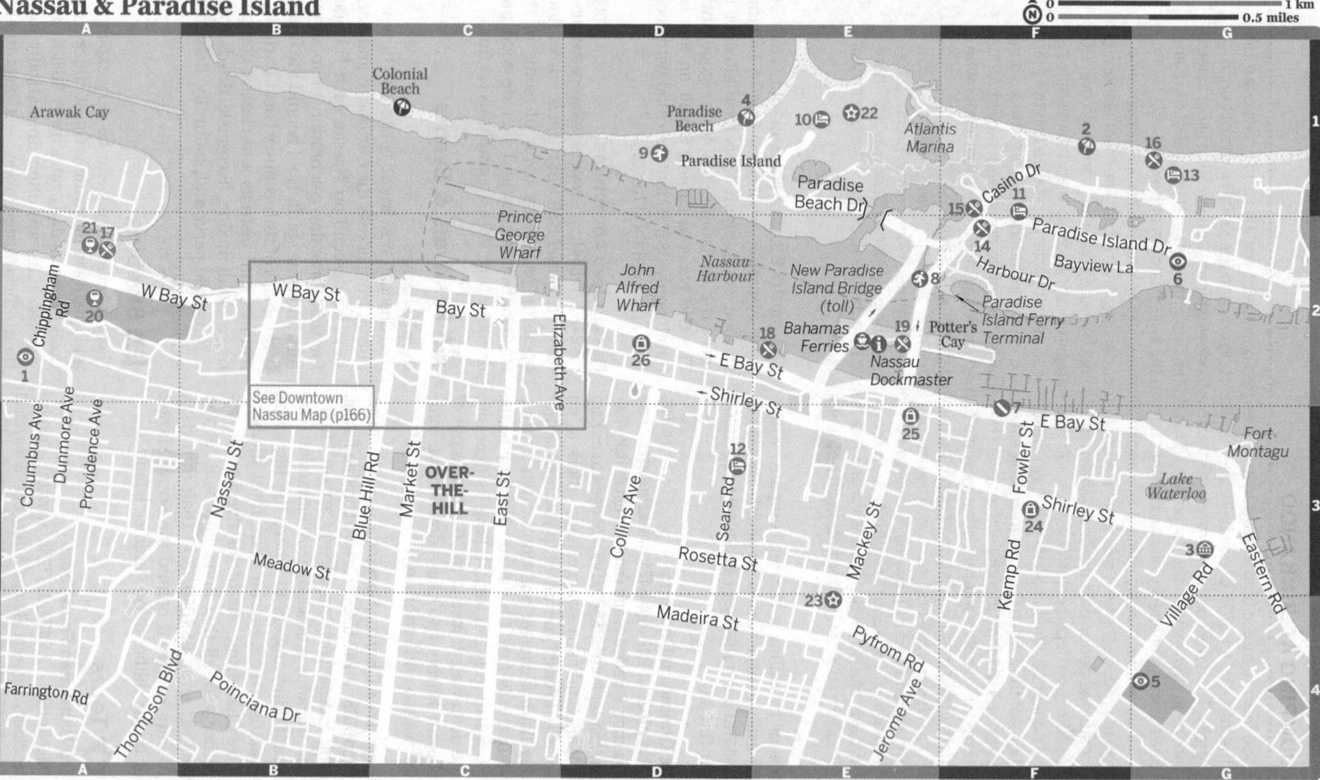

Nassau & Paradise Island

around. A growing trend in backpacker hostels is a bonus for budget travelers.

Downtown

★HumesHouse@HillCrest HOSTEL $
(Map p162; 242-525-5189; www.humeshouse.com; Sears Rd; dm BS$32, d without/with bath BS$81/87;) Nassau local Edward Humes started this, the first backpacker hostel in town, in 2017 and it's a godsend to budget travelers. The older-style house is in a quiet neighborhood about a 20-minute walk to downtown or Paradise Island. With a single communal lounge, kitchen, two dorms (non-air-con) and two private rooms, it's cozy, sociable and excellent value.

El Greco HOTEL $
(Map p166; 242-325-1121; elgrecohotel@gmail.com; West Bay St; d from BS$150;) Central location opposite Junkanoo Beach and affordable rates are the chief advantages of this welcoming 'Spanish-style' hotel. Some of the (interior) rooms can be a bit gloomy – ask for a sunny end room with gracefully arched entranceways and a view over the bougainvillea-draped balconies, and you'll be happy with your bargain.

Towne Hotel HOTEL $
(Map p166; 242-322-8450; www.townehotel.com; 40 George St; d BS$122-170;) For the location it doesn't get much cheaper than this long-running hotel in downtown Nassau. Friendly management and a kitschy Junkanoo-themed bar make an otherwise ordinary 46-room motel-style place feel a bit cheerful and the lobby's resident macaw is something of a legend. Rooms are small (not as small as the pool) but clean enough; better rooms have shared balconies.

British Colonial Hilton HOTEL $$
(Map p166; 242-322-3301; www3.hilton.com; 1 Bay St; d BS$270-340;) Built in 1922, this seven-story grand dame is a downtown Nassau institution. The hotel was a location for two James Bond movies, and it's easy to see why – with its gleaming marble lobby, private beach and sleek graphite-and-mahogany common spaces, it has the timeless international elegance of 007 himself. Outside, a garden and pool overlook a private stretch of beach.

★Graycliff Hotel BOUTIQUE HOTEL $$$
(Map p166; 242-302-9150; www.graycliff.com; West Hill St; d from BS$550;) Nassau's most characterful hotel is this 260-year-old home, built by a wealthy pirate. Hidden above town on West Hill St, the Georgian main house is filled with high-ceilinged rooms, musty antiques, mismatched oriental rugs and intriguing nooks and corners begging further exploration. Huge gardenside cottages, arrayed around an extraordinary Spanish-tiled pool, are equally alluring.

West of Downtown

★ BahaSea Backpackers HOSTEL $
(242-426-0688; https://bahasea.com; 560 West Bay St, Sandy Port; dm BS$45-75, d BS$145-195; P ❄ 📶 🏊) Perched right on the ocean opposite Sandy Port marina complex, this is flashpacking at its best. BahaSea has two pools, kayaks and bikes for rent, yoga classes, a small gym, kitchen and lots of social common areas where travelers gather over beers and shared experiences. Rooms and dorms are clean and well equipped with lockers and aircon.

Although 12km west of downtown, jitney (bus) No 10 stops outside and there are lots of restaurants and a supermarket nearby.

★ A Stone's Throw Away B&B $$
(242-327-7030; www.astonesthrowaway.com; Tropical Gardens Rd, Gambier Village; d/ste BS$268/358; P ❄ 📶 🏊) Talk about dramatic entrances: getting to this extraordinary B&B requires climbing steep stone stairs through a cliffside tunnel, after which you emerge in a tropical garden that's like something out of a Merchant Ivory film. Burnished wood, worn oriental rugs, a rock grotto swimming pool: just lovely. Pet-friendly.

Marley Resort BOUTIQUE HOTEL $$
(242-702-2800; www.marleyresort.com; West Bay St, Cable Beach; ste BS$245-355; ❄ 📶 🏊) Formerly the governor's house, then Bob Marley's Bahamian bolt-hole, this shaded coastal retreat is now a boutique hotel, run by Rita Marley and her daughters. Rooms, each named after a Marley song, are spare-no-expense luxurious, with hand-carved mahogany furniture and original Africana art. Down a rum punch in the Stir It Up bar or relax at the 'Natural Mystic' Spa.

Compass Point Beach Resort RESORT $$
(242-327-4500; www.compasspointbeachresort.com; West Bay St, Gambier Village; d BS$315-475; ❄ 📶 🏊) Founded by Island Records supremo Chris Blackwell, this jumble of crayon-bright, 'Junkanoo-inspired' luxury huts is an automatic mood enhancer. They're on the small side, but hip furniture, surround-sound systems, cute porches, an excellent restaurant and astounding views make up for that. There's a poolside bar and monthly house parties draw the revelers, as does the daily happy hour.

Orange Hill Beach Inn GUESTHOUSE $$
(242-327-7157; www.orangehill.com; West Bay St; d BS$193-230; ❄ 📶 🏊) Divers and international backpackers adore this homey hillside guesthouse, with its Fawlty Towers sign and just-like-family staff. The sprawling property has a wide range of rooms, from basic motel units and more appealing upper-floor rooms to full apartments. At night, everyone congregates in the funky main house, with its self-serve bar and shelves full of used books.

Baha Mar LUXURY HOTEL $$$
(242-788-8000; https://bahamar.com; Baha Mar Blvd; d BS$360-855; ❄ 🏊) This luxury resort complex in New Providence's Cable Beach area finally opened its gilded doors in 2017. It features three high-rise hotels, the Grand Hyatt, Rosewood and SLS, along with a casino that puts Atlantis in the shade, 22 restaurants, 17 bars and the Bond nightclub. It's luxury all the way from lobby to ocean-view rooms and expansive pools.

Meliá Nassau Beach RESORT $$$
(242-327-6000; www.melia.com; West Bay St; d BS$599-930, ste from BS$1560; ❄ 📶 🏊) With three pools, slick rooms, a fitness center, seven restaurants, a kids' club, live entertainment and even bingo, this all-inclusive Cable Beach resort has most things a leisure-loving family (or couple) could want. It's part of a growing luxury hotel-resort complex near Cable Beach, and downtown Nassau is just 15 minutes away by jitney.

Eating

Options are rich in Nassau, from a BS$5 breakfast of tuna and grits served through plexiglass to a three-course meal at a fine-dining establishment. For a splurge, try one of the resort hotels on Paradise Island or at Baha Mar. Many places in downtown close after 6pm.

★ Fish Fry BAHAMIAN $
(Map p162; 242-425-7275; Arawak Cay, off West Bay St; mains BS$12-25; 7am-midnight) The colorful village of conch stands, bars, jerk joints and seafood restaurants at Arawak Cay, known collectively as the 'Fish Fry', is one of Nassau's great experiences. Come for conch salad, fried chicken wings, fritters, blackened snapper, 'sky juice', Rake'n'scrape bands, reggae DJs, Junkanoo dances and friendly chatter.

The fish fry restaurants are open most days but Friday to Sunday evening are most popular and Sunday is the big locals night, when crowds gather after spending the day with family. **Twin Brothers** and **Drifters** are two of the more popular joints and have inside seating, but to be honest everywhere is good at the Fish Fry, and the semipermanent vans sell cheaper food. Maybe just follow the locals' lead and plump for the place with the longest line.

Bahamian Cookin' BAHAMIAN **$**

(Map p166; ☎242-328-0334; Trinity Place; mains BS$12-31; ⏲11:30am-4pm Mon-Sat) For no-nonsense traditional Bahamian dishes in a no-frills setting, head to this busy downtown kitchen. Naturally conch features heavily, from chowder to fritters, along with other seafood, pork chops and sides such as peas 'n' rice and fried plantain. Serves cold beer (BS$5) and cheap cocktails.

Potter's Cay BAHAMIAN **$**

(Map p162; East Bay St; mains BS$12-20; ⏲6am-11pm) Less popular than the Fish Fry and a bit seedy-feeling at times, this lively food and drink market sits beneath the Paradise Island Exit Bridge. Fishing boats from the Out Islands arrive daily, carrying the sea's harvest, as well as fruit, herbs, pepper sauces and vegetables, and the Bahamas Ferries and mail boats dock just to the north.

You can meet locals over a Kalik beer, conch salad or sheep's-tongue *souse* (stew) here, but it's not a great place to hang around alone at night.

Green Parrot INTERNATIONAL **$$**

(Map p162; ☎242-322-6900; www.greenparrotbar.com; East Bay St; mains BS$15-40; ⏲7am-midnight) Looking over the harbour towards Paradise Island, this waterfront restaurant impresses with location and is popular with visitors and locals alike for consistently good food, ranging from pizzas, burgers and quesadillas to Bahamian-influenced seafood such as lobster ravioli and fish tacos. Nightly happy hours midweek and occasional live music.

Tiki Bikini Hut BAHAMIAN **$$**

(Map p166; ☎242-432-9995; West Bay St, Junkanoo Beach; mains BS$14-35; ⏲8am-1am Sun-Thu, to 2am Fri & Sat) The only place on Junkanoo Beach that regularly stays open after the cruise-ship crowds depart, Tiki Bikini is an open-sided *palapa*-style thatch place with an island bar, cold beer, cocktails and a monster menu of seafood, pizza and Bahamian staples – the generous conch salad comes with the shell.

The bar has expanded over the years into a happening evening venue with open-mic nights, karaoke, soca and, on weekends, live music. Cocktails from BS$10.

Athena Cafe GREEK **$$**

(Map p166; ☎242-326-1296; www.athenacafenassau.com; cnr Bay & Charlotte Sts; mains BS$15-38; ⏲9:30am-5:30pm Mon-Sat) This authentic family-run Greek taverna above a Bay St jewelry store does very solid renditions of the Hellenic classics, such as dolmades, grilled seafood, moussaka and gyro (BS$15-18). It can be very pleasant to eat on the veranda over a plate of saganaki, watching the duty-free shoppers mill around below.

★Café Matisse ITALIAN **$$$**

(Map p166; ☎242-356-7012; Bank Lane; mains BS$35-45; ⏲noon-3pm & 6-11pm Tue-Sat; 📶) Cloaked among downtown Nassau's historic government buildings, this dignified Italian is a delightful alternative to the standard cruise-ship scene. Grab a terrace table and let professional, crisp-shirted waiters serve you rack of wild boar with red-wine sauce, delicate pasta dishes, *mahimahi* or even plain old pizza. Fine wine list.

Prices drop by around BS$14 per dish at lunch.

Graycliff Restaurant INTERNATIONAL **$$$**

(Map p166; ☎242-302-9150; www.graycliff.com; Graycliff Hotel, West Hill St; mains BS$45-72; ⏲noon-2:30pm Mon-Fri, 6:30-10:30pm daily; 📶) Colonial elegance hangs heavily at this atmospheric fine-diner in the 18th-century Graycliff Hotel (p163). The predominantly European menu deploys a lot of imported ingredients but also makes use of Bahamian lobster and other local treasures. The wine cellar is legendary, with precious vintages such as an 1865 Château Lafite among its 250,000 bottles. Dress code is elegant: no shorts or sandals.

Humidor Churrascaria BRAZILIAN **$$$**

(Map p166; ☎242-302-9150; www.graycliff.com; Graycliff Hotel, West Hill St; prix fixe BS$56; ⏲6:30-10:30pm Mon-Sat; 📶) Carnivores will love the wafting smoking aromas at this Brazilian steakhouse attached to the Graycliff Hotel complex. Hunks of dripping pork loin, lamb, beef and spicy sausages are carved tableside from wicked-looking metal skewers, and the prix fixe includes a salad bar stuffed with seafood appetizers, veggies and pastas.

If this isn't your thing, you can order pizza from the adjacent **Giotto Pizzeria** for around BS$15. The attached beer garden is a casual place for a drink.

Downtown Nassau

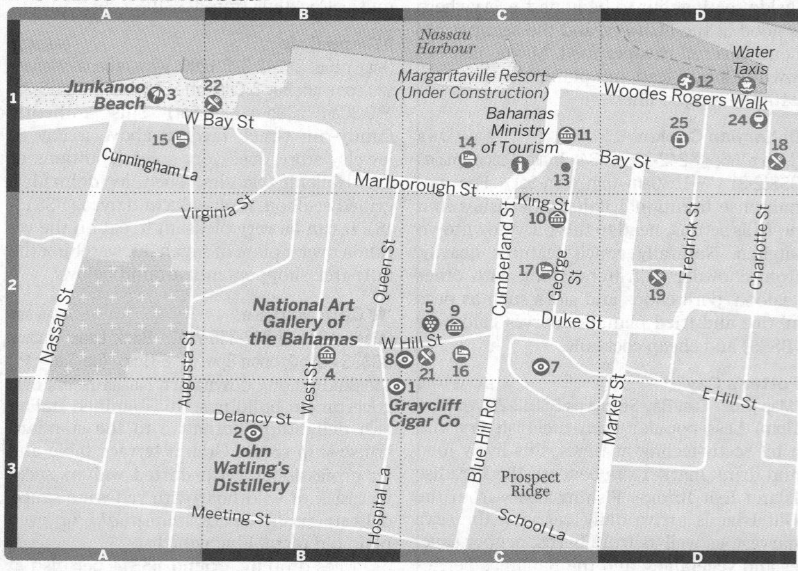

Drinking & Nightlife

Nassau is the undisputed nightlife capital of the Bahamas but it's still pretty low-key outside the resorts of Paradise Island and Baha Mar. Downtown Nassau's bars cater mainly to tourists, but the further you move from the cruise-ship dock toward Junkanoo Beach and Arawak Cay (for instance), the more local places and sociable Bahamians you'll find.

★Fish Fry BAR
(Map p162; West Bay St; ⌚5pm-midnight) The unmissable nightly Fish Fry is certainly not just about eating. Sky-juice trailers, wooden beer shacks and more substantial establishments keep everyone oiled and easy, as multiple DJs compete for the most bowel-shuddering bass line. Sunday night is the big locals night.

Crew Pub BAR
(Map p166; ☎242-698-0603; 3 East St North; ⌚1pm-2am) If you're wondering where the locals go to drink in downtown Nassau, this is it. The combination of fun-loving Bahamians, backpackers, in-the-know tourists and supercheap draft beer make this one of the few places near the cruise-ship port worth being after 10pm. Beer pong and loud music are guaranteed.

Sky Bar ROOFTOP BAR
(Baha Mar Bld; ⌚5pm-1am) The views are hard to beat from this suave rooftop bar atop SLS Baha Mar. Cocktails start at BS$18 plus tax. Dress up.

Pirate Republic MICROBREWERY
(Map p166; ☎242-328-0612; www.piraterepublicbahamas.com; Woodes Rogers Walk; ⌚11am-11pm; 📶) The bar staff are dressed as buccaneers and the tap handles are pistols but you come to Pirate Republic, the Bahamas first craft brewery, more to sample the beers than for the atmosphere or a big night out. Signature brews include the Island Pirate Ale IPA and Blackbeer'd stout – try a tasting paddle for BS$10.

There are tours of the brewery next door at 11am and 2:30pm (BS$10 including beer tasting and a pretzel).

Bahamas Cricket Club PUB
(Map p162; ☎242-326-4720; http://bahamascricket.com; West Bay St; ⌚8am-11pm) Ravaged by Hurricane Matthew in 2016, this historic cricket pavilion-pub overlooking the Haynes Oval immediately got back on its feet, a sign of how much it means to those who water and wield the willow here. It's a great place to eat Bahamian (or British) food and knock back a beer while watching a game from the 1st-floor veranda.

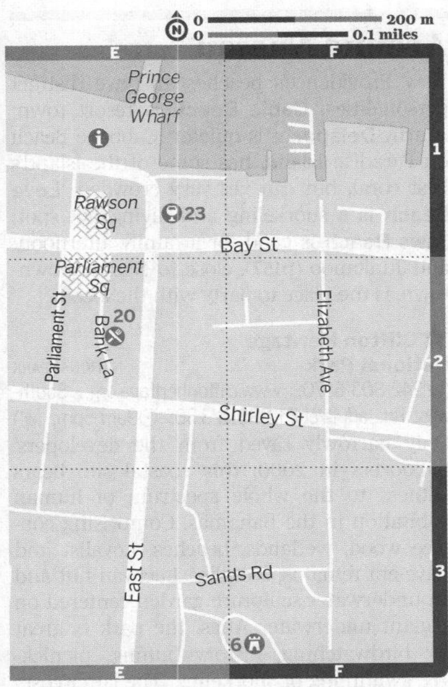

Downtown Nassau

Top Sights
1 Graycliff Cigar Co....B3
2 John Watling's Distillery....B3
3 Junkanoo Beach....A1
4 National Art Gallery of the Bahamas....B2

Sights
5 Bahama Barrels....C2
6 Fort Fincastle & the Queen's Staircase....F3
7 Government House....C2
8 Graycliff Chocolatier....C2
9 Heritage Museum of the Bahamas....C2
10 Pirates of Nassau....C2
11 Pompey Museum of Slavery & Emancipation....C1

Activities, Courses & Tours
12 Born Free Charter Service....D1
13 Tru Bahamian Food Tours....C1

Sleeping
14 British Colonial Hilton....C1
15 El Greco....A1
16 Graycliff Hotel....C2
17 Towne Hotel....C2

Eating
18 Athena Cafe....D1
19 Bahamian Cookin'....D2
20 Café Matisse....E2
Graycliff Restaurant....(see 16)
21 Humidor Churrascaria....C2
22 Tiki Bikini Hut....B1

Drinking & Nightlife
23 Crew Pub....E1
24 Pirate Republic....D1

Shopping
25 Straw Market....D1

Louis & Steen's New Orleans Coffee House COFFEE

(☎242-601-9907; http://louisandsteens.com; West Bay St; ⏰7am-3pm Mon-Fri, 8am-5pm Sat, 10am-5pm Sun) If you're after good coffee, head to this colourful cafe about 16km west of downtown, where single-origin beans are roasted, brewed and served as espresso, pour overs, iced lattes and cold brews. Atmosphere is relaxed with jazz music and terrace seating with ocean views. New Orleans–inspired Creole-Cajun food is served alongside sweets such as pecan pie.

☆ Entertainment

Dundas Centre for the Performing Arts PERFORMING ARTS

(Map p162; ☎242-393-3728; www.dundascentre.org; 103 Mackey St; ⏰office 10am-4pm Mon-Fri) Comedy, drama, dance, live music, kids' shows, spoken word: the Dundas Centre is a haven for many forms of expression under-represented in the Bahamas. Ticket prices depend on the show, but generally start at around BS$10; check the website or Facebook page for what's coming up.

Shopping

Visitors flock to Bay St for duty-free liquor, jewelry, perfume and cigars, but savings are not guaranteed; check prices at home before your trip. Most stores close at night and on Sunday. Bahamian-made products are sold at booths throughout **Festival Place** at Prince George Wharf.

Bahama Art & Handicraft ARTS & CRAFTS

(Map p162; ☎242-394-7892; East Shirley St; ⏰9am-4:30pm Tue-Sat) If you're interested in picking up traditional Bahamian handicrafts from around the islands, this shop makes it easy. The paintings, jewelry, driftwood sculptures, handmade baskets and other pieces are the work of many different producers from across the archipelago.

Bahama Handprints CLOTHING
(Map p162; ☎242-394-4111; www.bahamahand prints.com; Island Traders' Bldg, Ernest St; ⏲10am-4pm Mon-Fri, 9am-2pm Sat) Just behind the main Island Traders' Building on Ernest St, this boutique and factory outlet sells lovely, handmade interior-design fabric, clothes, bags, accessories and furnishings. It's possible to tour the factory by arrangement.

Bahamas Rum Cake Factory FOOD
(Map p162; ☎242-328-3750; https://thebahamasrumcakefactory.com; 602 East Bay St; ⏲10am-5pm Mon-Sat, to 3pm Sun) Thoroughly marinated in Ole Nassau Bahamian rum, these buttery little bundt cakes sell for BS$7, and up to BS$19 for large ones in decorative tins. Pineapple, pecan and piña colada vie with the original, but they're all dependably moist, delicious and a tiny bit boozy.

Straw Market MARKET
(Map p166; ☎242-363-2000; West Bay St; ⏲7am-7pm) Fronted by touts directing the cruise-ship crowds inside, this frenetic market has long been the go-to place for knock-off purses, souvenir T-shirts, and cheap, made-in-China straw goods. It's tacky and fun for a browse, but can't rival **Festival Place** at Prince George Wharf for Bahamian-made products and straw goods.

ℹ Information

MEDICAL SERVICES

Pharmacies can be found in all shopping malls, but mainly keep standard shop hours. For medical attention, visit **Princess Margaret Hospital** (☎242-322-2861; www.pmh.phabahamas.org; Shirley St; ⏲emergencies 24hr) or the **Doctor's Hospital** (☎242-302-4600; www.doctorshosp.com; 1 Collins Ave; ⏲emergencies 24hr).

POST

Main post office (Town Center Mall, Baillou Hill Rd; ⏲8:30am-5:30pm Mon-Fri)

TOURIST INFORMATION

Tourist office (Map p162; ☎242-323-3182; www.bahamas.com; Welcome Centre, Festival Pl, Prince George Wharf; ⏲8am-11pm) The tourist office is currently at the 'welcome desk' for cruise-ship passengers. You can pick up the usual pamphlets, maps and advice, and book 45-minute guided walking tours of historic Nassau, leaving between 10am and 1pm depending on demand (BS$10 per person).

Around Nassau

New Providence's beaches all have distinct personalities: **Cable Beach** is resort town; nearby **Delaporte** is quieter; Cabbage Beach on Paradise Island, has some of the island's best coral, but can get very crowded; **Love Beach** is a snorkeling and diving hot spot; **Jaws Beach** is good for a family afternoon; and Junkanoo (p157), close to Nassau downtown, is the place to party with the locals.

★Clifton Heritage National Park NATIONAL PARK
(☎242-803-6870; www.cliftonheritage.org; Southwest Rd; adult/child BS$11/3.30; ⏲9am-5pm; 👪) Only narrowly saved from the developers' bulldozers in 2000, this coastal site bears witness to the whole spectrum of human habitation in the Bahamas. Comprising coppice wood, wetlands, beaches, Loyalist and slave-era remains, a replica Lucayan hut and an underwater sculpture garden centered on a giant underwater Atlas, the park is great for birdwatching, history buffing, picnicking, swimming or snorkeling. The latter costs BS$22.50 (or BS$50 if you need to hire gear) and heritage tours are BS$11/5.50 for adults/kids.

While the underwater sculpture garden is a big attraction, there's a large oil refinery right next to the site; check with reception that the water is clear of oil spills before going in.

Blue Lagoon Island ISLAND
(☎242-363-1003; www.bahamasbluelagoon.com; Salt Cay; day trip adult/child B$69/45) Also called Salt Cay, this small island north of Paradise Island has been developed into a day-trip beach destination with tours, water sports or just lounging on the beach. Packages include lunch and boat transfers from Paradise Island.

Paradise Island

Privileged Paradise Island – linked to Nassau by two great arcs that may as well be bridges to another world – is unashamedly built for profit and pleasure. Its landscape is mostly artificial: vast hotels straight from the covers of fantasy paperbacks, hangar-sized casinos, ersatz 'villages' in which to shop and eat, a superb golf course and the lushest lawns in the Bahamas.

Before the 1960s, PI was 'Hog Island' – flat and undistinguished. A&P supermarket heir Huntington Hartford II renamed it in 1959, resolving to build the next Monte Carlo here. He clearly had some success: over the years it became a bolt-hole for Howard Hughes, Richard Nixon and the deposed shah of Iran. But it was the 1998 opening of the vast resort, casino and shopping complex Atlantis that did the most to realize Hartford's dream. It's now synonymous with Bahamian luxury for families, honeymooners, high-stakes gamblers and bachelor partiers.

Sights

Atlantis' central hotel, the Royal Towers, is a sight in and of itself, with shops, a casino, and faux archaeological excavation and giant aquarium windows in its lower lobby. The adjacent Marina Village is a popular shopping and eating destination.

Public access beaches on the island include **Cabbage Beach** (Map p162), **Paradise Beach** (Map p162) and **Cove Beach**.

Discover Atlantis Tour AQUARIUM
(Map p162; ☎242-363-3000; www.atlantisbahamas.com; Atlantis, 1 Casino Dr; per person BS$44; ⏰9am-5pm; 👪) Strolling through a glass tunnel while sharks glide overhead is awesome. This thrill is found in the Predator's Lagoon, one of the exhibits on this walking tour of Atlantis' Marine Habitat aquariums and faux-archaeological sites. Look for manta rays, spiny lobsters, striped Nemos, translucent jellyfish and thousands of other sea creatures in the underground Great Hall of Waters.

Versailles Gardens GARDENS
(Map p162; Paradise Island Dr) This hushed, symmetrical formal garden is the last thing you expect to find on bling-lovin' Paradise Island, but here it is. The terraced landscape is lined with statues depicting great men throughout the ages, including Napoleon, Franklin D Roosevelt and a 12th-century Hercules. The garden's big photo op is the **Cloisters**, a rectangular stone colonnade built by Augustinian monks in 14th-century France. Huntington Hartford purchased it from newspaper magnate William Randolph Hearst and had it shipped piece-by-piece to the Bahamas.

Now owned by the upscale Ocean Club, the gardens are technically off-limits, but nobody seems to mind respectful visitors ignoring the 'No Tresspassing' signs.

Activities

★**Aquaventure Water Park** WATER PARK
(Map p162; ☎888-877-7525; www.atlantisbahamas.com; Suite 42, 1 Casino Dr, Atlantis Resort; adult/child/hotel guests BS$157/103/free; ⏰9am-5pm) Kids and adults alike will hyperventilate at the sight of this astonishing 57-hectare water park, an Indiana Jones–style vision of the ruins of the Lost City of Atlantis. The vast park – one of the largest in the hemisphere – is centered on a five-story Mayan temple, with multiple waterslides shooting guests into a variety of grottoes and caves.

Sivananda Yoga Ashram YOGA
(Map p162; ☎416-479-0199; www.sivanandabahamas.org; Paradise Island) The backyard of the Atlantis megaresort is perhaps not the place you'd expect to find a yoga ashram in the Indian tradition of Sivananda. On a heavily forested 2.2-hectare patch of Paradise Island, Sivananda Yoga Ashram has been attracting yoga devotees since 1967. You can drop in for a single yoga class (BS$10), a full-day pass (BS$50) or an extended program with accommodations from tents to ocean-front rooms.

Sleeping & Eating

The number of visitors that flock to the big resorts of Paradise Island outweighs those staying in Nassau proper but it comes at a price – rooms are around 50% more here than in downtown Nassau or Cable Beach and there's not much in the budget category.

Comfort Suites HOTEL **$$**
(Map p162; ☎242-363-2588; www.comfortsuitespi.com; Paradise Island Dr; d incl breakfast BS$327-520; ❄📶🏊) Though this above-average hotel is not part of Atlantis, guests here get full pool and water-park privileges at the neighboring megaresort. The 200-plus rooms are clean and modern, with bright tropical appeal, and the on-site restaurant (Crusoe's) and bar (Bamboo Lounge) are good for lazy days.

★**Atlantis** RESORT **$$$**
(Map p162; ☎954-809-2100; www.atlantisbahamas.com; 1 Casino Dr; d BS$275-2800; ❄📶🏊) If Disneyland, Vegas and Sea World birthed a love child, this watery wonderland would be its pricey but irresistible spawn. The Lost World of Atlantis–themed megaresort has five separate hotels, all within walking distance of one another. The mothership is the Royal Towers – 23-story conch-pink towers linked by an enormous central arch.

The Royal Towers (from BS$410) are the most heavily invested in the Atlantis portfolio – aquarium windows in the lobby, faux hieroglyphics everywhere, and a replica of King Triton's throne – and the nexus of all resort activity. There's a massive casino, an indoor shopping mall gleaming with Versace and Cartier, and multiple celebrity-chef restaurants. Set at a tasteful distance, the Cove (from BS$570) is Atlantis' most adult property – all koi ponds and minimalist chandeliers, and an adults-only pool area with wandering masseuses. The Reef (from BS$500) is a stylish condo-style hotel perfect for families. Beach Towers (from BS$275) and Coral Towers (from BS$290) are, relatively speaking, less flashy, more affordable options. Minimum two-night stay on all rooms.

Ocean Club RESORT **$$$**
(Map p162; 242-363-2501; www.fourseasons.com/oceanclub; 1 Casino Dr; d BS$1480-1970;) Paradise Island's most elite hotel and now owned by Four Seasons, this is the kind of place where people with marquee names come to get away from it all, in lush gardens surrounded by high walls and gates. Rooms come with personal butlers, who will sprinkle rose petals on your bed or bring you your afternoon champagne. Minimum stays (three to four days) sometimes apply.

Anthony's Grill INTERNATIONAL **$$**
(Map p162; 242-363-3152; www.anthonysgrill paradiseisland.com; Paradise Island Shopping Center, Paradise Dr; mains BS$20-45; 8am-10pm;) One of Paradise Island's few non-hotel restaurants, this Caribbean-bright diner is a favorite with families for its big menu of burgers, pizzas, pastas and big American-style breakfasts. There's a BS$10 kids' menu and happy hour every day from 4pm to 6pm (BS$9 appetizers and two-for-one drinks).

★**Nobu** JAPANESE **$$$**
(Map p162; 242-363-3000; www.atlantisbahamas.com; Royal Towers, Atlantis, 1 Casino Dr; mains BS$24-125, sushi rolls from BS$11; sushi bar 5:30-10pm, dinner to 11pm Fri & Sat;) Like every outpost of Nobu Matsuhisa's empire, this restaurant deals exclusively in immaculately sourced and prepared Japanese food with modern twists. Sushi and noodles are impeccable, but why not create enduring memories, with Matsuhisa's signature miso black cod, or Bahamian lobster in truffled panko? The decor is very *Lost in Translation*: a wistful, stylish collision of Japanese and Western ideas.

Children of six and under are welcome at the night's very first sitting, but not beyond.

★**Dune** FUSION **$$$**
(Map p162; 242-363-2501; www.fourseasons.com/oceanclub; Ocean Club, 1 Casino Dr, Paradise Island; mains BS$34-77; 7-11am, noon-3pm & 6-10pm) French-American celebrity chef Jean-Georges Vongerichten created the menu at this ultrapopular (and ultrapricey) fusion restaurant, floating atop a dune in front of the genteel Ocean Club hotel. The menu globe-hops with agility: Asian fish dishes, Australian lamb, Bahamian lobster and truffle pizza.

Café Martinique FRENCH CARIBBEAN **$$$**
(Map p162; 888-526-0386; www.atlantisbahamas.com; Atlantis, 1 Casino Dr; mains BS$50-68; 6-10pm;) A homage to the long-gone original featured in the 1965 Bond flick *Thunderball,* this upscale French-fusion restaurant in Atlantis bears the imprimatur of French-American celebrity chef Jean-Georges Vongerichten. Alongside Mediterranean classics such as seafood Provençal you'll find classy renditions of more Bahamian seafood fare, such as sea bass cartoccio.

☆ Entertainment

Atlantis Casino CASINO
(Map p162; 242-363-3000; www.atlantisbahamas.com; Royal Towers, Atlantis, 1 Casino Dr; slots 24hr, tables 9am-4am Sun-Thu, 24hr Fri & Sat) The nerve center of the Atlantis complex, suspended over the 'lagoon' by the bridge between the towers, this 2.8-hectare casino has 85 game tables and 700 slot machines tinkling away incessantly. Dangerously, you can use your room key on tables and slots to 'begin earning points toward promotional giveaways'.

ℹ Getting There & Away

There's no road public transport to Paradise Island but you can drive (US$2 tollway), take a taxi or walk across the bridge. Note that parking is at a premium on the island.

Water taxis leave every half-hour, on the hour, from Nassau's cruise-ship terminal to Paradise Island. A round-trip is BS$8, one way is BS$4.

GRAND BAHAMA

POP 51,800

Despite the name, Grand Bahama has always run second to bigger, more glamorous Nassau (New Providence). Yet if you're looking for a laid-back, accessible getaway with a minimum of fuss and more infrastructure than the Out Islands, Grand Bahama has some good beaches, water sports, diving and golf courses. The streets of Freeport, its main city, and Lucaya are wide and traffic is light. Its golden beaches and aquamarine waters are rarely overcrowded, even in high season. The frequent cruise-ship arrivals ensure that just enough amenities – dive shops, restaurants, pubs, boutiques – are all open for business and centrally located. A high-speed ferry from Florida makes Grand Bahama accessible for weekend breaks or even day trips for US visitors.

Outside the city, the 137km-long island is a little-explored expanse of mangrove swamps, sea caves and sandy cays. There's world-class diving and snorkeling, great kayaking and fishing.

Grand Bahama was badly damaged by destructive Hurricane Dorian in September 2019 but at the time of writing most of the island's businesses, including hotels, restaurants and tour or boat operators, were open for business. Cruise ships and flights were also back to approaching normal schedules.

Getting There & Away

The 35-minute flight from Nassau is easily the most convenient way to reach Grand Bahama; there are multiple flights every day. **Flamingo Air** (242-351-4963; www.flamingoairbah.com) also connects Grand Bahama with Marsh Harbour on Great Abaco, and South Bimini.

Balearia Caribbean (866-699-6988; www.baleariacaribbean.com; one way US$88-104) has a direct high-speed ferry service between Fort Lauderdale (USA) and **Freeport Cruise Terminal** (Freeport Harbour) departing Fort Lauderdale at 8am (2½ hours) and returning at 6.30pm.

There's no longer a Bahamas Ferry passenger service from Nassau but you may be able to get on the mail boat. There are daily ferries – maximum 20 people – from McLean's Town, Grand Bahama, to Crown Haven, Little Abaco, run by **Pinder's** (242-353-3062) and **Barry's** (242-443-5293; McLean's Town) ferry services. But these are mostly used by locals and the difficulty is in getting between the ferry dock and the main towns (Freeport or Marsh Harbour). There are two scheduled but unreliable bus services daily, otherwise you'll need to hire a car or charter a taxi for around BS$100.

Getting Around

You'll need your own wheels to explore Grand Bahama. There are a number of car-rental agencies at the airport. The local companies are cheaper than the international chains, with daily hire from BS$55.

You can rent a scooter in the parking lot of the Port Lucaya Marketplace for about BS$50 to BS$70 per day, plus a deposit.

Freeport & Lucaya

Freeport, Grand Bahama's only urban settlement, was built seemingly overnight in the 1950s to serve as a duty-free tourist destination for Rat Pack–era pleasure-seekers. Half a century and several major hurricanes later, it's now an uninspiring grid of banks, strip malls and government buildings, with little appeal for travelers.

Lucaya, a modern coastal suburb of Freeport, is where most of the vacation action takes place. Its tidy marketplace of shops and restaurants appeals to a largely cruise-ship-based tourist contingent, who appreciate its safety and walkability, and the marina here is a launching place for a range of water-based activities and cruises. On warm nights, when the music is thumping at the Port Lucaya Marketplace bandstand, this is the place to be.

Sights

★Garden of the Groves GARDENS

(242-374-7778; www.thegardenofthegroves.com; cnr Midshipman Rd & Magellan Dr, Freeport; adult/child BS$17/12; 9am-4pm) This 5-hectare botanical garden is a lush tropical refuge on an island that's otherwise mostly scrub pine and asphalt. A walking trail meanders through groves of tamarind and java plum trees, past cascading (artificial) waterfalls, a placid lagoon and a tiny 19th-century hilltop chapel. The spiritually minded will enjoy a meditative stroll through the limestone labyrinth, a replica of the one at Chartres Cathedral in France. Kids will dig the raccoon habitat, where trapped specimens come to retire.

The gardens are several kilometers east of Freeport on Midshipman Rd; a minibus will take you there for about BS$5 if you request. There's a good **cafe** on-site.

Activities

Undersea Explorers' Society (UNEXSO) DIVING

(242-373-1244; https://unexso.com; 1 Seagorse Rd, Port Lucaya Marina, Lucaya; 8am-6pm) Founded in 1965, UNEXSO is a highly regarded dive center offering multiple dive and snorkel packages, and other marine activities in the warm, abundant waters around Grand Bahama. Two-tank dives are BS$107, introductory packages are BS$134, diving with

Grand Bahama

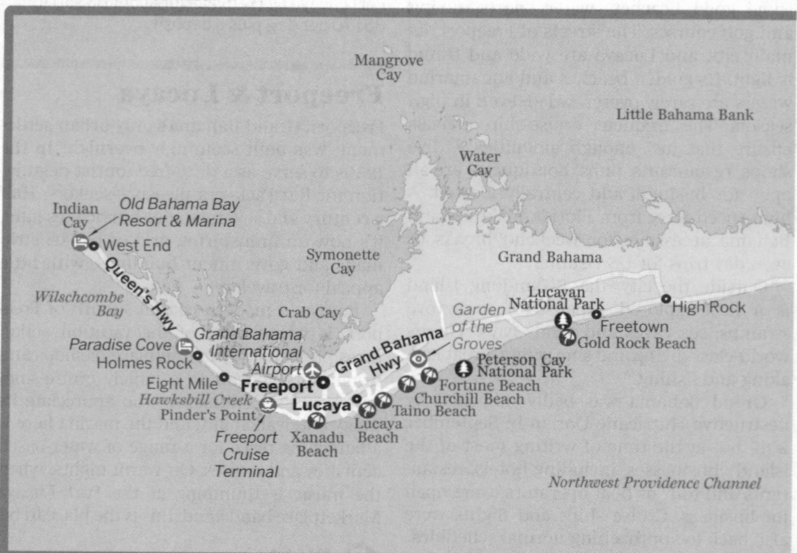

wild dolphins is BS$245, and with sharks BS$117. Plate Reef and Theo's Wreck are two of its more popular destinations.

Note there is a captive dolphin show here.

Sunn Odyssey DIVING
(242-373-4014; www.sunnodysseydivers.com; 30 Beachway Dr, Freeport; 8am-5pm Mon-Sat, from 1pm Sun) Sunn Odyssey offers personalized dive tours, taking small groups on the kind of adventures they're most interested in. Two-tank dives are BS$110 with tax, and night dives are BS$91. The PADI Open Water course (four days) is B$435.

Pirate's Cove OUTDOORS
(242-373-2683; Taino Beach; adult/child BS$5/3; 9am-5pm) Combining a beach club with water park (BS$10/25 per hour/day) and ziplining course (BS$55 to BS$95), this is Lucaya's latest adventure activity, popular with cruise-ship arrivals. Water sports on Taino Beach include Jet Ski hire, parasailing, snorkeling tours and stand-up paddleboarding or you can just lounge on the beach and make use of the restaurants and sun loungers.

Exotic Adventures BOATING
(242-374-2278; www.exoticadventuresbahamas.com; half-/full day BS$95/139, child under 12yr half price; 10am-5pm) Captain AJ runs rum-fueled deep-sea and bottom-fishing trips, as well as reef-snorkeling excursions, dolphin encounters and other watery diversions. Call to organize collection, and to arrange overnight trips to the Biminis and Abacos.

Reef Course & Country Club GOLF
(242-350-5466; Tarrytown St; 18 holes BS$99) This 6.3km championship course, part of the partially closed Grand Lucayan Hotel, is conveniently tucked close to the beach, marketplace and hotels.

Tours

Grand Bahama Nature Tours OUTDOORS
(242-373-2485; www.facebook.com/grandbahamanaturetours; tours from BS$89) To truly appreciate Grand Bahama's natural beauty take a full-day kayak tour of Lucayan National park with this experienced local outfit. Also cycling, jeep, all-terrain vehicle (ATV) and birdwatching safaris.

Bahamian Brewery BREWERY
(242-352-4070; www.bahamianbrewery.com; Queen's Hwy, Regency Park; tours 10am-4pm Mon-Sat) Brewer of Sands, Strong Back stout and Bush Crack among others, locally owned Bahamian Brewery opened in 2007 and now produces beer for sale all over the Bahamas. Brewery tours are available, followed by tastings at Jimmy's Tap Bar, and

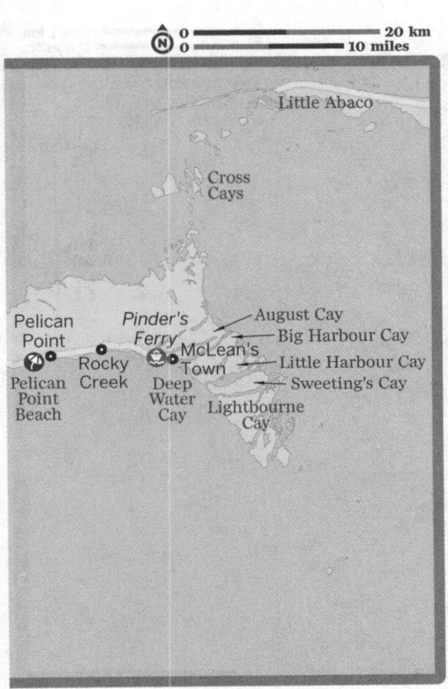

there's a gift store and beer garden on-site for further sampling.

CocoNutz Cruisers CYCLING
(☎242-808-7292; www.coconutzcruisers.com; Seahorse Rd, Port Lucaya Marketplace; tours BS$120; ⏰10am Mon-Sat) Tour the island by electric bicycle on these fun guided five-hour day tours, visiting beaches and other places of interest.

Reef Tours BOATING
(☎242-373-5880; www.reeftoursfreeport.com; Port Lucaya Marketplace, Lucaya;) Introducing visitors to the delights of the Grand Bahamas since 1978, Reef Tours offers a wine-and-cheese-fueled Enchanted Evening Sail (BS$40), a glass-bottomed-boat tour (adult/child BS$30/18), a snorkel and fish-feeding trip (adult/child BS$40/20) and more. It's great value compared to many Bahamian tourist operations.

Festivals & Events

New Year's Day Junkanoo Parade PARADE
(⏰Jan 1) A highlight of the social calendar, the parade takes over East Mall in Freeport, with extravagant costumes, music, dancing and rum.

Sleeping

Most accommodations are concentrated in Lucaya or around the marinas south of Freeport, with a few beach resorts to the west and little else for long stretches heading east.

Island Hideaway HOMESTAY $
(☎242-727-0400; Spanish Cay Rd; d BS$50) This well-appointed modern apartment just south of downtown Freeport is run by a lovely local family and is a real bargain, with a spacious main room and full kitchen. You can book online.

Bell Channel Inn MOTEL $
(☎242-373-1053; www.bellchannelinn.com; King's Rd, Port Lucaya Marina; d BS$110; P ❄ 📶 🏊) On the far side of Bell Channel from the Port Lucaya Marketplace, this slightly faded pink hotel is popular with divers, who can book very reasonable room-and-scuba packages with the on-site dive center. Rooms, all facing the marina, are surprisingly spacious and well-equipped.

WORTH A TRIP

LUCAYAN NATIONAL PARK

This 16-hectare **national park** (☎242-352-5438; http://bnt.bs/lucayan-national-park; adult/child BS$5/free; ⏰8:30am-4:30pm) is Grand Bahama's natural treasure. About 40km east of Ranfurly Circle, the park is known for its underwater cave system, which is one of the longest in the world. Visitors can easily check out two of the caves – Ben's Cave and Burial Mound Cave – via a short footpath. Ben's Cave provides a refuge for tiny buffy flower bats, while bones of the island's earliest inhabitants, the Lucayans, were discovered in Burial Mound Cave in 1986.

The park is also unique because it's home to all six of the Bahamas' vegetation zones. Mangrove trails spill out onto the secluded and beautiful Gold Rock Beach, definitely worth a stop if you're out this way. You'll see more raccoons and seabirds than people, but watch your food at the picnic area near the beach – the raccoons are unabashed (but harmless) scavengers.

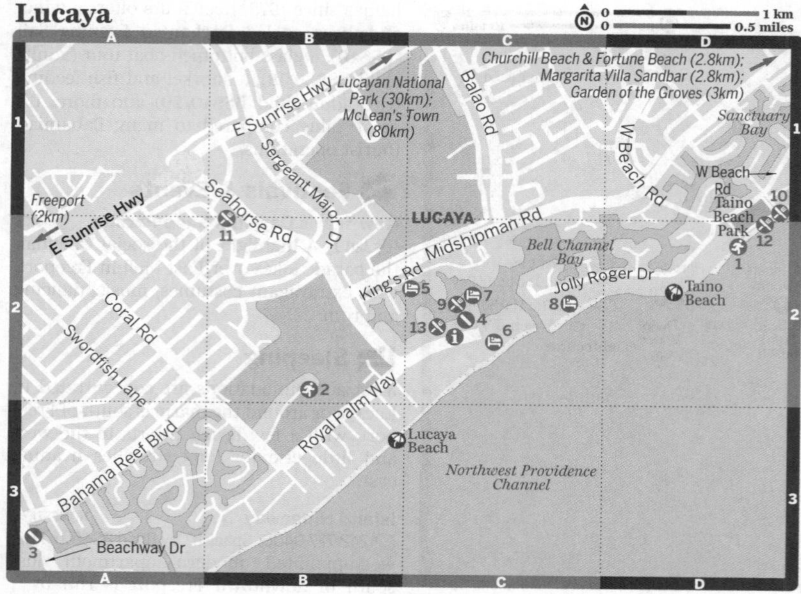

Lucaya

Activities, Courses & Tours
- CocoNutz Cruisers .... (see 13)
- 1 Pirate's Cove D2
- 2 Reef Course & Country Club B2
- Reef Tours .... (see 13)
- 3 Sunn Odyssey A3
- 4 Undersea Explorers' Society (UNEXSO) C2

Sleeping
- 5 Bell Channel Inn C2
- 6 Grand Lucayan Lighthouse Pointe C2
- 7 Pelican Bay Hotel C2
- 8 Taino Beach Resort & Club C2

Eating
- 9 Sabor C2
- 10 Smith's Point Fish Fry D1
- 11 Solomon's B2
- 12 Tony Macaroni's Conch Experience D2
- 13 Zorba's C2

Drinking & Nightlife
- Rum Runners .... (see 13)

Shopping
- Port Lucaya Marketplace .... (see 13)

Royal Islander Hotel HOTEL $
(☎242-351-6000; www.royalislanderhotel.com; East Mall, Freeport; d/tr/q BS$102/110/120; P❄📶🏊) For a budget stay in downtown Freeport, it's hard to beat this central hotel. It's all very 1980s-motel decor, with flowery bedspreads, but it's clean and there's a sociable pool area with bar and jacuzzi.

Grand Lucayan Lighthouse Pointe RESORT $$
(☎242-373-1333; www.grandlucayan.com; 1 Sea Horse Rd, Lucaya; d from BS$320; P❄📶🏊) Only the Lighthouse Pointe wing of this large hotel complex and golf resort is presently open but it's still one of the most impressive stays on Grand Bahama, with simple but spacious beachfront rooms, several restaurants, swimming pools, a spa and competitive all-inclusive packages.

Taino Beach Resort & Club HOTEL $$
(☎242-350-2200; www.tainobeach.com; Jolly Roger Dr, Taino Beach; d from BS$180; ❄📶🏊) On the far end of pretty Taino Beach, this low-key resort complex encompasses the upscale Marlin, the midrange Coral and the dated but budget-friendly Ocean. The all-suite set-up is good for families, with a long list of activities such as bonfires, Bahamian Night,

beach volleyball and bingo lending a cheery communal touch.

Pelican Bay Hotel HOTEL **$$**
(☎242-373-9550; www.pelicanbayhotel.com; Sea Horse Rd, Port Lucaya Marina; d BS$235-270; P❄📶🏊) Pelican Bay's retro-Bahamian colonial exterior contains 186 marina-side suites with private balconies. The interiors continue the theme, with lots of dark wood and canopy beds. Though the hotel isn't oceanfront, the views of Bell Channel from the pool deck are lovely at sunset.

Eating & Drinking

As with accommodations, most of the eateries worth visiting are in Lucaya. Port Lucaya Marketplace draws crowds with dozens of restaurants and bars. Head further afield along the beach for authentic fish fries and Bahamian cafes.

Self-caterers should head to **Solomon's** (Seahorse Rd, Lucaya Shopping Center; ⏰7:30am-8pm Mon-Wed, to 9pm Thu-Sat, to 5pm Sun), a well-stocked supermarket in the Lucaya Shopping Center.

★**Smith's Point Fish Fry** BAHAMIAN **$**
(Taino Beach; mains BS$12-15; ⏰5pm-2am Wed, to 11pm Sat) Wednesday night at the Fish Fry is like a giant neighborhood party. Several beachfront shacks fire up oil-drum cookers and fry turbot, lobster and conch fritters for crowds of locals, who gossip the night away eating and drinking cold Kaliks and rum punch. The scene heats up after 9pm, when the live music gets rolling.

Tony Macaroni's Conch Experience BAHAMIAN **$**
(☎242-533-6766; Taino Beach; mains BS$11-24; ⏰noon-10pm Wed-Sun) Tony Macaroni, the self-proclaimed 'most unique man in the Bahamas' and proprietor of this famed Taino Beach conch shack, is a bit of an acquired taste. Be prepared for nonstop teasing and (if you're female) flirting along with your roast conch or conch salad. The conch is good.

Zorba's GREEK **$$**
(☎242-373-6137; Port Lucaya Marketplace; mains BS$18-28; ⏰7am-11pm; 📶👪) Locals know the food at Zorba's is some of the best on Grand Bahama, and will frequently recommend it to visitors. There's a smattering of Bahamian and American dishes (conch chowder, hamburgers) but the highlights are the straight-shooting Hellenic classics: saganaki, gyro, moussaka, Greek salad and the like.

Sabor INTERNATIONAL **$$**
(☎242-373-5588; http://sabor-bahamas.com; Pelican Bay Hotel, Port Lucaya Marina; mains BS$10-42; ⏰11am-10pm; 📶) With a marina-side location that can be spectacular at sunset, Sabor is a perfectly pleasant place for a cocktail and meal at day's end. The food is international, with 'Asian-fusion' dishes sharing carte space with inexpensive burgers and blackened grouper.

★**Margarita Villa Sandbar** BAR
(☎242-373-4525; www.sandbarbahamas.com; Churchill Beach, Mather Town; ⏰11:30am-midnight; 📶) Down a few winding backroads to the beach east of Lucaya, this funky little timber beach shack is an under-the-radar classic with sandy floor and beachfront decks. It's the best place on Grand Bahama for NFL addicts to get their Sunday fix.

Rum Runners BAR
(☎242-373-4550; Port Lucaya Marketplace; ⏰9am-1am) The best bar in Port Lucaya's busy marketplace, Rum Runners draws you in with its two-for-one happy hour drink deals, friendly staff and close proximity to the marketplace bandstand

Shopping

Port Lucaya Marketplace MARKET
(☎242-373-8446; www.portlucaya.com; Sea Horse Rd; ⏰9am-midnight) At Lucaya's heart, this tidied-up pastel version of a traditional Bahamian marketplace has the majority of the area's shopping, dining and entertainment options. Haggle for tote bags and batik cloth at the **straw market**, peruse duty-free emeralds at one of the many jewelry shops or have a cocktail overlooking the Bell Channel waterway.

Information

Grand Bahama Vacations (www.grandbahamavacations.com) Florida-based travel agency with a useful website.

Tourist office (☎242-373-8988; www.bahamas.com; Port Lucaya Marketplace, Sea Horse Rd; ⏰9am-5pm) Useful visitor centre in Port Lucaya Marketplace. There's also a tourist desk at the airport (often unstaffed).

Getting There & Around

Bus fares from Freetown's **bus station** (W Mall Dr) include Port Lucaya Marketplace (BS$1.50), East End (BS$10, twice daily) and West End (BS$5, twice daily). Though drivers are meant to stick to their circuit, they'll often function as impromptu taxis, taking you wherever you want for a fee. Just ask.

Free shuttles also run between most downtown hotels, the beach and town.

West of Freeport

Head west out of Freeport, over the Freeport Harbour Channel and past the docks, and the island narrows into a slender, scrub- and mangrove-covered peninsula. Two resorts attract snorkelers, sailors and sunseekers, but there's not much beyond those, and a few workaday settlements, to see.

Old Bahama Bay Resort & Marina RESORT **$$**
(☎242-602-5171; www.oldbahamabayresorts.com; Bayshore Rd, West End; ste BS$330-440; P❄🛜🏊) Just 90km from Florida, this multihued beachfront resort and marina on Grand Bahama's western extremity is a favorite with the American yachting fraternity. Facilities include walking and snorkeling trails, a 372 sq-meter heated swimming pool, a gym, spa, restaurant, bar and helipad. Tennis, massages, deep-sea fishing and other activities await.

Paradise Cove RESORT **$$**
(☎242-349-2677; www.deadmansreef.com; Deadman's Reef; 1-/2-bedroom cottages BS$196/252; ❄🛜) This friendly beach club is a popular day-trip resort thanks to blooms of psychedelic coral just offshore offering fabulous snorkeling (day trip including transport and gear, adult/child BS$50/30). Other activities include lounging on the beach, kayaking, volleyball or just enjoying a grouper sandwich and a draught Kalik at the resort's Red Bar. Accommodations consist of two modern, two-bedroom beachfront villas.

OUT ISLANDS

Often known as the 'Family Islands', a term coined to make them seem more inviting and to recognise that many Bahamians originally hail from outside New Providence and Grand Bahama, the original 'Out Islands' term is still very much in currency, and you'll hear both used interchangeably. The essence and geography is still the same: the Out Islands – everywhere in the Bahamas beyond New Providence and Grand Bahama – include hundreds of stunning islands and cays, and have a growing and enviable reputation for peace, beauty, unrivalled beaches, a relatively small tourism footprint and natural splendor. And families.

It's trite to say this is the 'real' Bahamas, but it's certainly a contrast to Nassau and if you're seeking solitude, world-class diving and a laid-back, crime-free welcoming culture then you'll probably say it anyway.

The Out Islands Promotion Board (www.myoutislands.com) is the place to begin planning.

ℹ Getting There & Away

Planes connecting with Nassau are the inevitable conveyance of those who wish to explore the Out Islands, but have yet to acquire a yacht. Bahamas Ferries (p200) has scheduled services from Nassau to Andros, the Abacos, Grand Bahama, Long Island, and Eleuthera and Harbour Island, but they don't operate daily and you'll need to allow more time if traveling by sea.

The Abacos

POP 17,100

The Abacos – Great and Little Abaco, and their offshore cays – are among the jewels of the Bahamas: a 320km crescent of sand that's a sailor's paradise, a history-buff's delight, a seafood-lover's dream and a bold entry in any diver's wish list.

Tragically, the islands bore the brunt of devastating Hurricane Dorian in September 2019, with the majority of buildings in Marsh Habour, the main settlement, and the outlying cays partially or completely destroyed and many lives lost. A massive relief effort and rebuilding operation was still underway at the time of writing, with many residents still displaced and power, communications and transport connections gradually being restored.

From Marsh Harbour or Treasure Cay regular ferries will take you to the **'Loyalist Cays'** – Elbow, Great Guana, Man O' War and Green Turtle. Named after the 18th-century settlers who came here after backing the wrong side in the American Revolution, they're special places graced by clapboard homes (many now in ruins), historic lighthouses, lush mangroves and a unique culture. Offshore, the warm and bounteous Sea of Abaco is studded with stunning coral, and overflowing with marine life.

Getting There & Away

The Abacos have two airports: **Leonard M. Thompson International Airport** (242-367-5500), formerly known as Marsh Harbour Airport, and Treasure Cay International Airport. You're most likely to be scheduled into the former; taxis at Leonard M. Thompson International Airport charge BS$15 to take you into town.

There are multiple flights between Nassau and Marsh Harbour and between Marsh Harbour and Florida in the US.

Pinder's Ferry (242-365-2356) operates four to five times daily between Grand Bahama (McLean's Town) and Little Abaco (Crown Haven; BS$50, one hour). There's also a mail boat between Nassau and Abaco.

Getting Around

BOAT

Schedules for the regular ferries between Great Abaco and the Cays can be found on maps, in the weekly *Abaconian* newspaper or on the website for **Albury's Ferry Service** (242-367-3147; www.alburysferry.com; round-trip/one way BS$30/19, child BS$17/11). You can set your watch by the latter – get to the departure dock 10 minutes early.

CAR, MOTORCYCLE & GOLF CART

You'll need to hire a car to explore Great Abaco: Marsh Harbour has places renting cars from around BS$75 per day, but it's wise to book something in busy periods. Try **Rental Wheels** (242-367-4643; www.rentalwheels.com; Bay St; 8am-5pm Mon-Fri, 9am-1pm Sat & Sun) or **U Save Auto Rentals** (242-699-3346; https://usaveautorentalsbs.com; Don MacKay Blvd). Motorcycles and scooters are slightly cheaper. Golf carts are the wheels of choice on the compact cays, and can be hired on the docks for around BS$50 per day but again you'll need to book ahead, especially on Elbow Cay.

TAXI

A taxi between Leonard M. Thompson International Airport and most hotels in the marina area costs BS$20 for two people. Taxis run up and down Marsh Harbour's broad main roads and are easy to flag down. The fare from Marsh Harbour to Treasure Cay is BS$80 – you might as well rent a car.

Marsh Harbour

POP 4638

Believe it or not, this one-stoplight town is the third-largest city in the Bahamas and the capital of the Abacos. Marsh Harbour was effectively ground zero for the destruction of Hurricane Dorian's catastrophic winds and storm surges, with the majority of buildings destroyed. At the time of writing only a few businesses were fully operational, but as the main population center and launching point for most of the nearby Loyalist cays, locals have vowed to rebuild their little marina town.

Sleeping & Eating

Marsh Harbour's accommodations and restaurants, especially those around the central marina, were decimated by Hurricane Dorian in 2019. Rebuilding here will be a lengthy process but it's hoped that long-running places like **Conch Inn Hotel** (242-367-4000; www.moorings.com/hotels/conch-inn-bahamas; East Bay St; d BS$213;) and **Lofty Fig Villas** (242-367-2681; http://lofty-fig.com; East Bay St; d BS$213;) can rebuild quickly.

Abaco Beach Resort & Boat Harbour RESORT **$$$**

(242-367-2158; www.abacobeachresort.com; East Bay St; d BS$410-585, ste from BS$760;) Down a gated drive, Marsh Harbour's only true resort is a self-contained retreat fronted by a private beach and marina with views to the distant cays. At the time of writing parts of the resort were back up and running following Hurricane Dorian. There are also two pools (one with swim-up bar) kayaks, paddleboards, tennis courts and plenty of opportunities for boating and diving.

The Angler's restaurant here (mains BS$28-59) is one of the fanciest in Marsh Harbour.

Blackfly Lodge LODGE **$$$**

(242-577-5577, USA 1-904-997-2220; www.blackflylodge.com; off Great Abaco Hwy, Schooner Bay, South Abaco; 3-night trip BS$2925; mid-Sep–mid-Aug;) Only for serious (and seriously well-heeled) fly-fishing enthusiasts, Black Fly is an all-inclusive fishing lodge that takes guests into the Marls – the vast mangroves that cloak the western shore of the Abacos. Equipment, booze, expert guidance and excellent food are all laid on to make the experience of fighting the prehistoric fish in the shallows as pleasurable as possible.

Maxwell's Supermarket SUPERMARKET **$**

(242-367-2601; Stratton Dr; 8am-7pm Mon-Thu, to 8pm Fri & Sat, to 4pm Sun; P) Stock up for off-island trips at this supermarket, the most complete in the Abacos.

HURRICANE DORIAN

Hurricane Dorian hit the northern Bahamas in 1 September 2019 with Category 5 ferocity and sustained winds of almost 300kmh. Passing directly over the populated islands of the Abacos and Grand Bahama, it is considered the worst natural disaster in Bahamian modern history. The official death toll was put at more than 70, but the true toll may never be known with dozens missing, hundreds evacuated and thousands of homes destroyed.

The Atlantic storm developed in late August and gathered intensity before making landfall on the Abacos, obliterating much of Elbow Cay and Marsh Harbour and causing widespread damage to Great Guana Cay, Man o War Cay, Great Turtle Cay and Treasure Cay. The hurricane continued northwest to Grand Bahama, where it slowed and continued to wreak prolonged havoc before moving towards the mainland US.

The human cost of Dorian was enormous. Apart from the loss of life, thousands were left homeless and either struggling without power, fresh water and communications or evacuated to shelters on Nassau. Many were Haitian immigrants living in shanty towns around Marsh Harbour, some of whom would later be deported. The financial cost was estimated at more than US$3 billion. A number of relief funds were set up in the aftermath and aid organisations worked hard to provide food, water and building materials, while tonnes of debris was shipped off the islands. For more information see www.bahamas.com/relief. Meanwhile, visiting Grand Bahama and the Abacos will be the best way to help rebuild the tourism economy.

Wally's Fine Dining INTERNATIONAL **$$$**
(☎242-367-2074; Bay St; mains BS$21-40; ⏲11am-3:30pm & 6-10pm Mon-Sat) Long-running Wally's is Marsh Harbour's fine-dining option and what it lacks in harbour views, it makes up for in the sophisticated setting and exquisitely prepared seafood and Bahamian and international dishes. The conch fritters and key lime pie are legendary, as is the *mahimahi* Provençal. Lunch is more relaxed (and cheaper), with salads, burgers and pasta dishes.

Getting There & Away

Leonard M. Thompson International Airport – formerly Marsh Harbour Airport – is a short BS$15 taxi ride south of town. It has daily connections with Nassau, Miami, Fort Lauderdale and several other US cities. A taxi from Treasure Cay International Airport to Marsh Harbour is BS$85.

Elbow Cay

Separated from Marsh Harbour by 10km of clear, shallow sea, historic Elbow Cay is one of the prettiest islands in the Bahamas. Though many of its historic brightly painted timber cottages were destroyed by Hurricane Dorian, the landmark candy-striped lighthouse still stands strong and the broad sheltered harbor is still studded with sails and framed by low greenery. Hope Town, founded in 1785 by Loyalists fleeing the fledgling United States, is home to many of their descendants to this day. Strict building controls and a ban on cars make it a delightful village to perambulate and commune with locals at harbourside cafes. The reefs off the Atlantic side of the cay are excellent for diving and snorkeling. The waters near Hope Town and the northern tip of the cay are calmer and easily reached by swimming from shore.

Sights & Activities

★**Wyannie Malone Museum** MUSEUM
(☎242-366-0293; www.hopetownmuseum.com; Back St; adult/child BS$5/2; ⏲9:30am-5pm Mon-Sat Nov-Aug) Wyannie Malone, a South Carolina Loyalist whose husband was killed during the American Revolution, fled to Elbow Cay with her four children and helped found Hope Town. Today, the Malone name is spread across the Bahamas, and Wyannie is considered the spiritual matriarch of Hope Town. Her story, and that of Elbow Cay, including rum runners, pirates, shipwrecks and independence. is told at this small but engaging museum.

Elbow Reef Lighthouse LIGHTHOUSE
(☎242-577-0542; www.elbowreeflighthousesociety.com; ⏲9am-6pm Mon-Sat) **FREE** Lit by a hand-pumped kerosene burner (the last of

its kind still in operation), this candy-striped lighthouse was erected in 1863, despite the attempts of local wreckers to sabotage its construction. Featured on the Bahamian $10 bill, it's now a much-loved icon. You can check out views from the top via a 101-step climb, but will need to ask the ferry to drop you at (and collect you from) the lighthouse marina or the Hope Town Inn & Marina.

Tahiti Beach BEACH
This small sand bar disappears at high tide and is surrounded by exquisitely clear, warm waters. At the sheltered southern end of Elbow Cay, it's ideal for kids, and is reached by a road through private property that the locals routinely use without issue. For the best views, go round the peninsula on foot.

Sundried T's SURFING
(242-366-0616; 9.30am-5.30pm Mon-Sat) Rents boards for BS$35 per day.

Sleeping & Eating

Sadly, the majority of buildings in Hope Town and elsewhere on Elbow Cay – many of them vacation rentals – were damaged or destroyed by Hurricane Dorian. Established resorts such as **Hope Town Harbour Lodge** (242-366-0095; www.hopetownlodge.com; Queen's Hwy) and **Hope Town Inn & Marina** (242-366-0003; www.hopetownmarina.com) were closed for repairs at the time of writing but were expected to reopen some time in 2020.

To check what vacation rentals are available, contact **Elbow Cay Properties** (242-366-0035; http://elbowcayproperties.com; Front St, Hope Town; 8am-4pm Mon-Fri, 9am-1pm Sat) or **Hope Town Hideaways** (561-656-9703; www.hopetown.com; Queen's Hwy).

Abaco Inn HOTEL $$
(242-366-0133; www.abacoinn.net; Old White Sound Rd; d BS$320-476;) Location location! Straddling the bluff that forms the island's narrowest point, the Abaco Inn has killer views of two gorgeous, but very different, beaches. The 20 rustic cottages have painted wood paneling, postage-stamp-sized bathrooms and private hammocks. A lively tiki bar, dramatically situated oceanfront pool and generous touches such as kayaks and snorkel gear tie things together.

Cap'n Jack's BAHAMIAN $
(242-366-0247; www.capnjackshopetown.com; Front St, Hope Town; mains BS$14-23; 8:30am-9pm Mon-Sat;) Elbow Cay's wood-planked watering hole is the local pub and top spot for value bar food. Although badly damaged by Hurricane Dorian it should be rebuilt and returned to its status as a go-to place for burgers, salads, fish sandwiches and Bahamian staples. Everyone heads here in the evenings for live music on Wednesdays, trivia on Thursdays, and happy hour at 5pm weekdays.

Getting There & Around

In normal conditions Albury's Ferry Service (p177) runs up to nine services a day from Marsh Harbour to Hope Town on Elbow Cay, though it was running on a reduced timetable at the time of writing. The 20-minute ride is BS$30/17 return for adults/kids, and BS$19/11 one way.

G&L Transportation (242-359-6208; one way/return BS$13/20) is also running scheduled trips on this route.

Island Cart Rentals (242-366-0448; www.islandcartrentals.com; per day BS$55; Mon-Sat) Meets ferries and delivers carts to accommodations, by arrangement. Book ahead.

The Bike Shop (www.hopetowncanvas.com/bikes; Bay St; per 24hr BS$12-18; 9am-5pm Mon-Sat, 10am-3pm Sun) Quality single-speed and 7-speed cruisers for rent on a 24-hour basis. No bookings (or phone). The entrepreneurial people here also manufacture bags and belts out of sail canvas.

Great Guana Cay

Surrounded by shallow, coral-filled seas, ringed with gorgeous beaches and home to some of the most convivial bars and resorts in the country, Great Guana is a fortunate little stretch of sand. A short hop from Marsh Harbour, it's quiet and only modestly populated: the only thing you need to watch out for wandering its streets are the golf carts that zip hither and thither on hushed tires.

Activities

Dive Guana DIVING
(242-365-5178; www.diveguana.com; Front St) This experienced all-rounder offers two-tank dives (BS$145), snorkeling trips (BS$62), PADI courses, island-hopping trips and boat rental (from BS$250 a day). This is also the place to rent a bike (BS$15 a day) or golf cart (BS$57) – call ahead to book.

Sleeping & Eating

Although devastated by Hurricane Dorian, both Grabbers and Nippers, long-running local stalwarts were busy rebuilding at the time of writing.

Grabbers Bed, Bar & Grill RESORT $$
(☎242-365-5133; www.grabbersatsunset.com; d BS$225-250; ❄📶) Descended from the first resort on Guana Cay, Grabbers is a charmingly relaxed little pleasure compound that sprawls in primary colors along its own small slice of beach. If fishing, diving, swimming and other active diversions don't appeal, you could always just laze in a hammock sipping an eponymous Guana Grabber, first mixed here in the 1960s. Two-night minimum.

Mama's BAHAMIAN $
(☎242-475-1007; breakfast BS$8-15, lunch BS$15; ⏱7-11am & noon-3pm) Tucked away between the harbour and the beach, Mama offers a great-value BS$15 changing menu that might feature blackened fish, teriyaki ribs or lobster quesadillas. Breakfast is coffee, sandwiches, bagels and the like, all served in Mama's lovely garden terrace.

★**Nipper's Beach Bar & Grill** BAHAMIAN $$
(☎242-365-5111; www.nippersbar.com; mains BS$18-40; ⏱11am-10pm; 📶) This candy-bright beachside Shangri-la can rock like a spring-break party, which may not be everyone's cup of tea, but it is undeniably Great Guana's most famous destination. The Sunday afternoon pig roast is legendary, drawing locals and tourists from across the Abacos. It's backed by 9km of stunning white sand, with a couple of swimming pools if you get hot.

WORTH A TRIP

TREASURE CAY

Treasure Cay, about 40km northwest of Marsh Harbour, is considerably more than just a resort. It's a community, village, marina, golf course and holiday playground fringing a string of some of the most beautiful powder-soft beaches in the Abacos. Like elsewhere in the islands, Treasure Cay was subject to a destructive battering by Hurricane Dorian in 2019, with many of the buildings, homes, restaurants and shops badly damaged.

At the time of writing, rebuilding of the resort hotel and shopping centre was well underway, and direct flights from the US and Nassau had resumed to Treasure Cay airport, 11km north.

The beaches alone make Treasure Cay worth a day trip, and the Green Turtle Cay ferry is nearby.

Getting There & Away

Only charter services were operating at the time of writing, but Albury's Ferry Service (p177) normally runs up to five services a day to/from Great Guana and Scotland Cays. The 30-minute ride costs BS$30/19 return for adults/kids and BS$17/11 one way, and leaves from Marsh Harbour's marina – not the main Albury dock on the eastern end of the island.

Green Turtle Cay

The northernmost of the Loyalist Cays, Green Turtle takes a little more effort to get to from Marsh Harbour (the ferry departs from near Treasure Cay airport), but is in many ways the most interesting of all the Abaco cays. Rich with tangible Loyalist history, harboring dense emerald mangroves and surrounded by exceptional diving, fishing and sailing opportunities, it's also a delightfully friendly place where slipping into conversation with the locals is the most natural thing in the world. The island and its only town, New Plymouth, were severely battered by Hurricane Dorian but the islanders are steadfastly rebuilding. Golf carts can be hired from several operators near the docks: try **Kool Karts** (☎242-365-4176; www.koolkartrentals.com; per day BS$56).

Sights & Activities

New Plymouth's small grid of streets is worth wandering to see what remains of the quaint pastel cottages and grand waterfront houses in the wake of 2019's Hurricane Dorian. On Victoria St you'll find the pink ruins of **Ye Olde Jail** and, nearby, a small, windswept **cemetery** where the headstones have spectacular views of Great Abaco. On Parliament St is the strangely touching **Loyalist Memorial Sculpture Garden**.

★**Albert Lowe Museum** MUSEUM
(☎242-365-4094; https://albertlowemuseum.com; Parliament St; BS$5; ⏱9am-noon & 1-4pm Mon-Sat; 👪) This 1825 house was created as the Bahamas' first museum in 1976, when local Alton Lowe opened it in honor of his father Albert. It was severely damaged by Hurricane Dorian in 2019 but locals were hoping to salvage the majority of the collection and reopen. The home-museum features a fine collection of locally crafted model ships (Mr Lowe was himself a model-ship builder), Lucayan artifacts, paintings by Alton Lowe and old photographs highlighting the cay's history.

Brendal's Dive Center DIVING
(☎242-365-4411; www.brendal.com; White Sound) This well-established and highly regarded diving outfit offers two-tank dives (BS$130), night dives (BS$100), open-water certification courses (from BS$650) and snorkel trips (BS$70). Ask about meeting the divers' wild 'pets': groupers Junkanoo and Calypso, who cuddle up like dogs, and Goombay the grinning green moray eel. Specialty trips include diving with stingrays and the local swimming pigs.

Reel Serious Charters BOATING
(☎242-365-4019; www.reelseriouscharters242.com; fishing charters half-/full day B$450/600) Captain Thom Sawyer is an experienced operator who can take you out on fishing charters or to No Name Cay to swim with the pigs (BS$70 to BS$150 depending on numbers) and further afield to see stingrays and sharks

Sleeping & Eating

★**Green Turtle Club & Marina** RESORT **$$**
(☎242-365-4271; www.greenturtleclub.com; White Sound; d BS$340, 1-/2-bedroom villas BS$507/670; ❄📶🏊) This peaceful cluster of cottages exudes good taste and attention to detail. Sage-green linens and British-colonial-style dark wood furniture are common touches in the villas and waterfront rooms. The lobby has a tropical-ski-lodge feel, with a fireplace and charmingly dim pub, and its Caribbean-flavored restaurant, The Club, is one of the island's top dining spots.

McIntosh Restaurant & Bakery BAHAMIAN **$**
(☎242-365-4625; Parliament St; mains BS$10-18; ⏲8am-4pm & 5-9pm) It could be 1955 inside this humble New Plymouth cafe, with plastic-covered tables, carpeted floors and delectable Bahamian dishes such as coconut-crusted lobster, tropical conch salad and sweet chilli grouper wrap. It's worth saving room for the key lime pie and other homemade cakes and desserts.

Drinking & Nightlife

★**Miss Emily's Blue Bee Bar** BAR
(Victoria St; ⏲11am-10pm) Green Turtle Cay's most beloved bar was badly damaged in Hurricane Dorian but was being rebuilt at the time of writing. That's not surprising as it's been a local institution since the 1960s when original owner, Miss Emily, created her signature drink, the goombay smash (BS$8).

The potent concoction is poured straight from a plastic gallon jug into your cup. Violet, Miss Emily's daughter and the current patron, keeps the exact ingredients secret but you can bet one of them is rum.

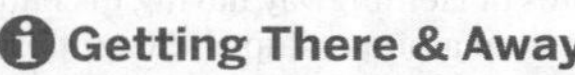

Getting There & Away

The only scheduled service to the cay is the **Green Turtle Ferry** (☎242-365-4166; Treasure Cay Airport dock, SC Bootle Hwy; adult/child return BS$20/12, one way BS$14/8; ⏲8am-6.30pm), which leaves from the Treasure Cay Airport dock, around 10km north of Treasure Cay. There are eight trips per day.

The Biminis

On the edge of the Gulf Stream, closer to Miami than Nassau, this pint-sized paradise comprises North, South and East Bimini and a scattering of private and uninhabited islets. Naturally stunning, culturally relaxed and boasting excellent diving and unsurpassed deep-sea fishing, Bimini is well worth the 30-minute flight from Nassau. Once home to Prohibition-era rum runners and one of Papa Hemingway's legendary haunts, it's now a favorite destination of serious fisherfolk and sunseekers from the States and beyond. The arrival of the slick Resorts World complex has transformed North Bimini but beyond its gates, tiny Alice Town and other settlements retain a sleepy tropical-village vibe.

The latest development is the Bimini Beach Club, another high-end resort which at time of writing was set to open in 2020 and owned by the Virgin group. Virgin Voyager cruise ships are also due to start weighing anchor from 2020, bringing a whole new crowd to the island.

Sights & Activities

★**Dolphin House** HOUSE
(☎242-347-3201; www.facebook.com/dolphinhouse242; Saunders St, Alice Town, North Bimini; per person BS$5; ⏲10am-6pm) Looking like Gaudí's tropical hobby, this astonishing house is the lifelong labor of Bimini historian and poet Ashley Saunders. Born on the site (all the surrounding houses belong to the Bimini Saunders), Ashley was touched after swimming with wild dolphins, and has been building this 'tribute' piece by piece since 1993. Plastered with dolphin mosaics, sea glass, shells, Lucayan artifacts, coconut-rum bottles, pickled-sausage jars and every conceivable

type of flotsam and jetsam, it's absolutely unique and arrestingly beautiful.

Downstairs you'll find a museum filled with salvaged ephemera such as a brass naval cannon from an 18th-century British wreck, photos of Hemingway having his hair cut, copper from a pirate ship and countless other random pieces. There's also a gift shop, where you can get both volumes of Ashley's history of Bimini. Ashley is currently building an upper level with plans to turn it into a fully functioning two-room guesthouse.

★Bimini Road DIVE SITE

Five and a half metres below the waves and stretching for 0.8km, this bizarrely symmetrical limestone formation was discovered in 1968. Its precision seems unnatural, giving rise to the perhaps inevitable interpretation that Plato's mythical city of Atlantis had finally been located. Nothing else of the 'city' remains, but it's an evocative dive site, often blessed with abundant sea life.

Neal Watson's Bimini Scuba Center DIVING

(242-473-8816; www.biminiscubacenter.com; Bimini Big Game Club, King's Hwy; 9am-5pm) Operating out of the Bimini Big Game Club, Neal Watson's has an 18m glass-bottomed boat that serves divers, snorkelers and sightseers equally well. Destinations include Bimini Road, Hawksbill Reef and various wrecks. A two-tank dive is BS$134, a snorkel safari with wild dolphins is BS$145, the hammerhead shark dive is $335 and a PADI Open Water referral course is BS$560.

Sleeping

Sea Crest Hotel HOTEL $

(242-347-3071; www.seacrestbimini.com; Queen's Hwy, Alice Town, North Bimini; d BS$130-155, ste BS$260-360;) It's nothing fancy, but this pale-yellow two-story hotel in the southern part of Alice Town is one of the few budget places left. The rooms are spare and clean, with larger one-, two- and three-bedroom suites, and there's a marina, should you need somewhere to park your yacht.

Bimini Big Game Club RESORT $$

(242-347-3391; http://biggameclubbimini.com; Kings Highway, Alice Town, North Bimini; d BS$283-345;) If you want to indulge your inner Hemingway, then the Big Game Club is where it's at. But it's not only about deep-sea fishing: there's also reef fishing, diving, snorkeling, and the usual resort pastimes of massage, wining and dining. Dating back to 1954, the resort nonetheless has modern, cheerfully decorated and thoroughly comfortable rooms and cottages.

Hilton at Resorts World HOTEL $$$

(242-347-8000; www.hilton.com; Resorts World, King's Hwy, North Bimini; d BS$310-360, ste from BS$930;) Crowning the Resorts World complex (built in 2013) on North Bimini, this gleaming multistorey hotel is typical Hilton, complete with six restaurants, a casino, rooftop pool and slick, luxuriously appointed rooms with king-sized beds, marble bathrooms and picture-windows.

Eating

★Stuart's Conch Stand BAHAMIAN $

(242-347-2474; King's Hwy, Bailey Town; mains BS$8-14; 4pm-midnight) Slicing up super-fresh and tangy plates of the Bahamas' favorite sea-snail snack, this renowned conch stand stands by Porgy Bay in North Bimini's Bailey Town. Conch and lobster salads (or combinations of the two) is all Fabian (Stuart) does, and he does it very well – check out the piles of discarded conch shells next door. Cold beers are only $3.

Edith's Pizza PIZZA $

(242-347-2800; King's Hwy, Porgy Bay; pizzas BS$12-30; 1-8pm) The deep-dish pizzas and Bimini bread are delicious at this open-sided waterfront place. Build your own pizza from the list of toppings; also Bahamian staples such as conch fritters and cold beer.

Nate's Bimini Breads BAKERY $

(242-347-2414; Hill Top St; baked goods BS$5-8; 8am-8pm) Nate's bakes fresh Bimini bread every other day, as well as takeaway deep-dish pizza.

My Three Daughters BAHAMIAN $

(242-347-2119; Queen's Hwy, Bailey Town, North Bimini; mains BS$12-29; 9am-11pm Mon-Sat;) Perhaps the best local Bahamian dining on the island, this welcoming little family affair does great things with lobster, ribs and conch, and the sweet Bimini bread is very more-ish. They also have a food truck that's often parked in Alice Town. No alcohol. There are air-con rooms for rent upstairs for BS$130.

CJ's Deli BAHAMIAN $$

(242-347-3295; Queen's Hwy, Alice Town; mains $12-20; 7am-8pm Sun-Wed, to 11pm Thu-Sat) This simple clapboard shack fronting the beach in Alice Town is a local favorite for eggs and grits, *souse,* stew fish, conch and other Bahamian comfort foods. Go inside to order and collect, then eat on the wooden tables overlooking the Atlantic.

Information

Tourist office (☎242-347-3528; www.bahamas.com; King's Hwy; ⏲9am-5pm Mon-Fri)

Getting There & Around

Several daily flights connect South Bimini International Airport with Nassau, Miami and Fort Lauderdale. From the airport a bus and ferry combination (BS$5) whisks you to Alice Town on North Bimini.

Golf carts are available to rent from the dock in Alice Town for BS$50 a day. It's around 3.5km from the dock to Resorts World.

Eleuthera

POP 11,000

A painfully skinny 175km-long crescent of pink-sand beaches, Atlantic-battered reefs, weather-warped rock and dense subtropical scrub, lovely Eleuthera also harbors boutique hotels, revered surf breaks and some fabulous restaurants. Depending on where you wander, whom you meet and (in some cases) how fat your wallet is, this is a place you're sure to extemporize one of the most diverse and memorable experiences possible on any Bahamian island. Regular ferries and flights between the capital and boutiquey Harbour Island make this the Bahamas' most popular short-trip destination outside of Nassau.

Getting There & Away

AIR

There are three airports spaced along skinny Eleuthera:

Governor's Harbour Airport (☎242-332-2321; Queen's Hwy) Halfway down the island about 13km north of the capital.

North Eleuthera International Airport (☎242-335-1242) The busiest, and the easiest to reach Harbour Island.

Rock Sound Airport (☎242-334-2177; 📶) Another 45km south of Governor's Harbour town, this is only really used by those staying in southern resorts.

BOAT

Bahamas Ferries (p200) fast boats (BS$84 one way, three hours) and mail boats (BS$30, five hours) run to Harbour Island, Spanish Wells and Governor's Harbour from Nassau. From Harbour Island, water taxis run between the Government Dock and North Eleuthera (BS$5).

Harbour Island

'Briland', as locals and repeat visitors call it, is renowned as one of the loveliest, most stylish and enjoyable islands in all of the Bahamas, if not the Caribbean. Just 5km long and 2km wide, this photogenic bric-a-brac of pink-sand beaches and colonial houses once served as the national capital but these days it's a tourist-brochure-designer's delight: humble pastel cottages abut BS$1000-a-night boutique hotels, chickens peck the dust in front of sleek French bistros, and local fishers and millionaires wave as they speed past each other in identical golf carts.

Quaint **Dunmore Town**, on the harbor side, harks back 300 years: it was laid out in 1791 by Lord Dunmore, governor of the Bahamas (1787–96), who had a summer residence here. The clip-clop of hooves may have been replaced with the whir of golf carts, but the daily pace since Dunmore's time hasn't changed all that much.

Sights & Activities

The broad and alluring **Pink Sands Beach** on the eastern shore is Harbour Island's main attraction. Architecturally, the white-washed Loyalist Cottage (1797) on Bay St, just west of Princess St, is the finest local example of the style.

The funky side of things is to be found at the corner of Dunmore and Clarence Sts, where a mishmash of signs, international license plates and driftwood relics are displayed, painted with humorous limericks and aphorisms.

Harbour Island is surrounded by superb snorkeling and dive sites, highlighted by the Devil's Backbone. The pristine reefs are littered with ancient wrecks. **Valentine's Dive Center** (☎242-333-2080; www.valentinesdive.com; Bay St; ⏲8am-7pm Mon-Sat, shorter hours Sun), the island's biggest and best diving operation, offers two-tank dives (BS$174) and snorkeling (BS$110).

Michael's Cycles (☎242-464-0994; www.michaelscyclesbriland.com; Colebrook St; ⏲8am-5pm Mon-Sat, to 4pm Sun) rents bikes (BS$15 per day) and golf carts (BS$55).

Sleeping

Both prices and quality are high at Harbour Island's hotels and resorts, though a few cheaper guesthouses can still be found. Most accommodations are in Dunmore Town.

BEACHES & A BRIDGE IN ELEUTHERA

Lighthouse Beach The harrowing drive down the impossibly rutted 5km road will feel worth it when you emerge onto this dazzling stretch of South Eleuthera beach.

Tay Bay Beach Beyond Preacher's Cave, this utterly secluded strip has pinkish sands and calm waters.

Ten Bay Beach South of Palmetto Point; the waters are shallow and perfect for beachcombing.

Glass Window Bridge Here Eleuthera narrows dramatically to a thin span straddling the divide between pounding deep blue Atlantic and the tranquil turquoise shoals of the Bight of Eleuthera.

Royal Palm MOTEL **$**

(242-333-2738; http://royalpalmhotel.com; cnr Dunmore & Clarence St; d BS$115-176;) One of the few budget options on Harbour Island, the Royal Palm has plain but tidy and spacious motel-style rooms only a block back from Bay St. Deluxe rooms have kitchenettes and all have cable TV and aircon.

Tingum Village HOTEL **$**

(242-333-2161; http://tingumvillage.com; Colebrook St; d BS$150-210;) Operating since 1969, Tingum Village is pleasingly low-key and low-priced, compared to much of Briland's accommodations. Spick-and-span suites are arranged around a tranquil picket-fenced garden; the cheaper ones are simple, tiled and dim, while the fancier have stylish touches such as stone accent walls and in-room tubs. All have patios and basic kitchens.

★**Pink Sands Resort** RESORT **$$$**

(242-333-2030; www.pinksandsresort.com; Chapel St; cottages from BS$1040;) This delightful resort, rambling over 8 hectares of landscaped foliage behind the impossibly photogenic Pink Sands Beach, may be Harbour Island's loveliest accommodations. Arriving in the impeccably tasteful lobby under the shade of ancient fig trees you realize why this place is beloved by celebrities, models and the super-rich. Rooms are in individual cottages with garden or ocean views.

Rock House BOUTIQUE HOTEL **$$$**

(242-333-2053; www.rockhousebahamas.com; cnr Bay & Hill Street Sts; d from BS$470;) This lovely 1940s harbourside home has been skilfully redeveloped as an upmarket hotel. The 10 rooms are smallish but luxe, with top-notch king-size beds, private *cabañas* and crisp white decor broken up with designer touches such as vintage birdcages and orchids. There's also a small gym, umbrellas, chairs and snorkeling gear for the beach, and one of Briland's best restaurants.

Runaway Hill BOUTIQUE HOTEL **$$$**

(242-333-2150; www.runawayhill.com; cnr Colebrook St & Love Lane; d BS$630-756; Dec-Jul;) A Harbour Island icon, this 1940s private estate is now a hotel on an unimprovable bluff setting overlooking the Atlantic, and is lavishly blessed with WWII-era features such as the checkerboard lobby and dark-wood library. Rooms and villas are distinguished by subtle whites, Cuban tiles and vintage woods, and the pool deck overlooks the sea. Children are welcome.

Eating

Harbour Island probably has more fine-dining options than all the other Out Islands combined. And if you're not hankering for haute cuisine, some of the island's best meals are served at the waterfront shacks lining Bay St. Expect the better restaurants to impose a 20% service fee on top of VAT.

Arthur's Bakery BAKERY **$**

(242-333-2285; cnr Crown & Dunmore Sts; mains BS$7-13; 8am-2pm Mon-Sat;) Locally famous for its donuts, fresh bread, cakes and assorted baked good, this cornerside nook is the place to catch up on gossip and relax over coffee and croissants. Owner Robert Arthur is a one-time screenwriter and well-known man-about-town; his baker wife, Anna, makes a mean key lime pie.

Angela's Starfish Restaurant BAHAMIAN **$**

(242-333-2253; Nesbit St; mains BS$14-15; 9am-8pm) Grandmotherly Angela will cook you a heaping plate of conch with peas and rice at this cozy local joint, decorated in beachy kitsch including old street signs and tiki dancer dolls. Never refuse a slice of her homemade pineapple cake.

★Sip Sip INTERNATIONAL **$$**

(242-333-3316; www.sipsiprestaurant.com; Court St; mains BS$16-26; 11:30am-4pm Thu-Mon;) Good luck getting a table on the deck at this uber-popular and convivial lime-green cafe at lunchtime (no reservations). The cosmopolitan Bahamian menu ranges from lobster quesadillas to curried chicken salad. It's a blissfully sited beachfront place to linger over a plate, enjoy pink-sand views and indulge in a little 'sip sip' – the local term for gossip.

Da Vine SUSHI **$$**

(242-333-2950; www.davinewine.com; 1 Bay St; sushi rolls BS$16-35, platters from BS$65; noon-3pm & 5-10pm Tue-Sat, dinner only Mon) Exquisitely prepared sushi and sashimi is the specialty at this classy wine bar, where you can sink into a chesterfield couch with a glass of Napa Valley red and a tasting plate. Complementing the sushi are Japanese small plates such as shrimp gyozo, black cod miso and pork ramen. There's a lengthy international wine list and killer cocktails.

Queen Conch BAHAMIAN **$$**

(242-333-3811; Bay St; mains BS$19-34; 11am-3pm & 5-9pm Mon-Sat) The overwater deck here is a fabulous place to savour typical Bahamian dishes and seafood with none of the airs and graces of Harbour Island's fancier restaurants. It's a great place for a cold beer and an appetizer of conch chowder (BS$10), smoked *mahimahi* dip or grouper fingers.

Ma Ruby's BAHAMIAN **$$**

(242-333-2161; Tingum Village, Colebrook St; mains BS$10-35; 8am-midnight;) Ma Ruby MBE sadly passed away in 2016, but the secret to her 'cheeseburger in paradise' has been passed on to Michael, the chef at this family-run patio restaurant. Cooked to order and served smothered with gooey cheese on thick slices of toasted brioche, it has earned legions of fans from across the globe.

★Malcolm 51 INTERNATIONAL **$$$**

(242-333-2030; www.pinksandsresort.com; Pink Sands Resort, Chapel St; mains BS$60-70, prix fixe BS$110; 6:30-9pm;) This serious, grown-up's restaurant brings the luxury that Pink Sands' pampered guests expect. The menu shows plenty of Mediterranean touches (pancetta bucatini) alongside 'island cuisine' (lobster bisque or roasted *mahimahi*). The terraced gardens and inviting furnishings create an atmosphere commensurate with the food.

Rock House Restaurant INTERNATIONAL **$$$**

(242-333-2053; www.rockhousebahamas.com; cnr Bay & Hill Sts; mains BS$43-61; noon-2pm & 6:30-9pm;) With a cracking view overlooking Dunmore Town's harbor, this two-storied colonial building serves some of Harbour Town's most upmarket fare. Expect lavish use of ingredients such as lobster, New Zealand lamb and grass-fed beef on a menu that throws some Bahamian touches into its generally French-inspired international dishes.

Drinking & Nightlife

Bahamas Coffee Roasters COFFEE

(242-470-8015; www.bahamascoffeeroasters.com; Dunmore St; 7am-3pm Sat-Thu, to 11pm Fri) Blended and roasted on Eleuthera using arabica beans, the strong organic coffee here is brewed with love. It's also a great spot for breakfast or a light lunch on the terrace.

Gusty's Bar BAR

(242-333-2342; Coconut Grove Ave; 9:30pm-1am) Jimmy Buffet has been known to jam at this ramshackle north-end cottage, with its pink-sand dance floor and harbor views. No singlets (tank tops) or political attire allowed.

Shopping

Harbour Island is a hot spot for boutique shopping with some fabulous little designer stores. Although Nassau has a greater range, Harbour Island is definitely a more enjoyable high-end shopping experience.

Most stores are in central Dunmore Town and almost all are closed on Sundays.

Sugar Mill Trading Company FASHION & ACCESSORIES

(242-333-3558; Bay St; 9am-5pm Mon-Fri, from 10am Sat) Owned by India Hicks, socialite designer and cousin to Prince Charles, this upscale boutique has an impeccably edited selection of men's and women's clothes, island-inspired gifts and children's toys.

Blue Rooster FASHION & ACCESSORIES

(242-333-2240; King St; 9am-5pm Mon-Fri) Visit this boutique, handsomely established in a blue-shuttered house from 1840, for stylish sundresses, wraps, hats and accessories.

Information

Post office (242-332-2215; Gaol St; 9am-5pm Mon-Fri)

Tourist office (☎242-333-2621; www.bahamas.com; Bay St; ⏲9am-5pm Mon-Fri) Up some stairs opposite the harbour.

Getting There & Away

Most visitors fly to North Eleuthera International Airport (p183), which connects with Nassau, Atlanta, Miami, Orlando and Fort Lauderdale. From the airport, it's a short taxi ride (BS$5 per person) to Three Island Dock, then another five minutes by water taxi (BS$5) to Dunmore Town.

Bahamas Ferries (p200) fast boats (BS$84 one way, two hours) and (slow) mail boats (BS$30, five hours) run to Harbour Island from Nassau. From Harbour Island, water taxis run between the Government Dock and North Eleuthera (BS$5).

Getting Around

While distances are negligible, Briland is a mini-LA – no one walks if they can help it and the walk between harbourside and oceanside is further than it looks. You can rent golf carts from agencies based at the dock, beginning at $50 per day. Try **Johnson's Rentals** (☎242-332-2376; Bay St) or Michael's Cycles (p183), which also rents bikes.

For a taxi, call **Major's** (☎242-470-5065; www.majorsrentals.com).

Gregory Town

POP 646

Quiet six nights out of the week, this low-key village is 40km north of Governor's Harbour and 8km south of the Glass Window Bridge. Once famous for its thriving pineapple industry, it sits on a compact, deep harbor in a cove once used by pirates. These days it's renowned for its Atlantic surf beaches and local surfer scene.

Sights & Activities

Surfer's Beach BEACH

The long left-hand break at this secluded Atlantic-facing beach has been popular with surfers since the 1970s. It's a little difficult to access (the 'road' is deeply pitted rock) but that only makes it more likely you'll have it largely to yourself.

Hatchet Bay Cave CAVE

The rough-stone entrance to this 1.5km-long cave is between Gregory Town and Alice Town, on the southwestern side of the Queen's Hwy. Several chambers bear charcoal signatures dating back to the mid-19th century, and there are some impressive stalagmites and stalactites. If exploring beyond the first few chambers, you'll need a headlamp, long pants and local guide.

Gaulding Cay BEACH

(Queen's Hwy) This beautiful yet often-empty beach just south of Glass Window Bridge has shallow, gin-clear water and great snorkeling around a small rocky island in the middle of the bay. Lovely for a picnic or unscheduled nap, too.

★**Bahamas Out-Island Adventures** WATER SPORTS

(☎242-809-4653; www.bahamasadventures.com; Surfer's Beach; kayak/snorkel tours from BS$109) Tom Glucksmann (based at Surfer's Haven guesthouse) runs ecominded kayaking, surfing, snorkeling and nature trips. The man knows his birds and is a passionate advocate for preserving **Lighthouse Point** at the southern tip of the island. Surf lessons are BS$100 per person in a group, or BS$150 for one or two people. Board hire is BS$25 to BS$30 per day.

A highlight is the kayak/snorkel day tour (BS$109 per person in a group, BS$129 if two people) with some of the best drift snorkeling on Eleuthera. Tom also runs an annual surf camp in late June/early July.

Festivals & Events

Pineapple Festival FOOD & DRINK

(⏲early Jun) The area's long history of pineapple cultivation is celebrated every June, with a long weekend of competitions, games, demonstrations and (of course) eating, drinking, music and dancing.

Sleeping & Eating

Surfer's Haven GUESTHOUSE $

(☎242-335-0349; Surfer's Beach; d BS$55; ❄📶) This wonderful laid-back budget guesthouse is found down a rugged dirt road only 10 minutes' walk from Surfer's Beach. The two rooms next to the owners' house have aircon and wifi and share a timber deck with lovely sea views, a covered outdoor kitchen and tiki hut. Surfboards and other gear are available for hire (BS$25 to BS$30). Bargain.

This is also the home of Bahamas Out-Island Adventures.

Surfer's Manor MOTEL $

(☎242-335-5300; www.surfersmanor.com; off Queen's Hwy, Gregory Town; d BS$130-150) The floral bed spreads and aging carpets create a

1980s motel feel, but this lemon-yellow hotel is a reasonable deal within walking distance of Surfer's Beach. There's a restaurant and bar, car rental and surfboard rental (BS$30).

Rainbow Room INTERNATIONAL **$$**
(☎242-335-0294; www.rainbowinn.com; Queen's Hwy, Rainbow Bay; mains BS$22-37; ⊙noon-3pm & 5-10pm Mon-Sat, 3-10pm Sun;) Local seafood and imported steak are two of the menu mainstays at this ever-popular octagonal timber restaurant overlooking Rainbow Bay, 15km south of Gregory Town. Monday, Thursday and Friday are popular wood-fired pizza nights (BS$7-24), and there's live rock music on Mondays. The Rainbow's a bit of a community hub for Eleuthera's middle section, and the bonhomie can be infectious.

Governor's Harbour

POP 700

Eleuthera's sleepy island 'capital' overlooks a broad and handsome harbor that runs west to Cupid's Cay, apparently the original settlement of the Eleutheran Adventurers, English Puritans who emigrated here in 1648. It has some faded architectural reminders of its official stature, and is an ideal base for exploring Eleuthera in either direction.

Over the hill (follow Haynes Ave) from the harbor brings you to the Atlantic Ocean side with some gorgeous beaches and resorts as you follow Banks Rd to Palmetto Point.

Leon Levy Native Plant Reserve (www.levypreserve.org; Banks Rd; adult/child BS$10/6; ⊙9am-5pm) is a 10-hectare Bahamas National Trust–run park alive with native plants reached by meandering walking trails, including a mangrove boardwalk and wetland environments. There's a strong educational focus with signs identifying native flora, guided tours available and a research centre for traditional bush medicine.

Sleeping & Eating

Pineapple Fields RESORT **$$**
(☎242-332-2221; www.pineapplefields.com; Banks Rd, Palmetto Point; 1-/2-bed apt BS$330/460;) This impressive luxury resort is regularly touted as one of the best in the Bahamas and has one and two-bedroom condos with full kitchens set in a tropical garden overlooking a broad pink-sand Atlantic Ocean beach. It's also home to Tippy's Bar & Beach Restaurant.

Anchor Bay Fish Fry BAHAMIAN **$**
(☎242-332-2467; Anchor Bay; BS$12-15; ⊙6pm-midnight Fri) Music, singing, dancing, conch, lobster, Kalik: this has all the prerequisites of a classic Bahamian fish fry.

★Tippy's Bar & Beach Restaurant INTERNATIONAL **$$**
(☎242-332-3331; Banks Rd, North Palmetto Point Beach; mains BS$23-36; ⊙11am-midnight Tue-Sun;) This beach bar has a delightful ocean-facing deck and eclectic, welcoming timber decor inside its individual huts. The restaurant specializes in globally influenced seafood dishes – coconut shrimp, Bahamian bouillabaisse, homemade lasagna – presented on a giant chalkboard menu that's carried to your table with a flourish. Jam-packed even in low season, it gets totally wild on busy weekend nights.

Buccaneer Club INTERNATIONAL **$$**
(☎242-332-2000; www.hwadventures.com; cnr Haynes Ave & New Bourne St; mains BS$15-25;) With an inviting deck beneath a spreading Lebbek tree, a whitewashed interior lit by radiantly colorful local art and subtle tunes piped throughout, this restaurant-bar is the most relaxing place in Governor's to kick back for a drink or meal. The chef is equally at home with Bahamian, American and pan-Asian flavors.

Information

Tourist office (☎242-332-2142; www.bahamas.com; Queen's Hwy; ⊙9am-5pm)

Getting There & Away

Governor's Harbour Airport (p183) has connections to Nassau and Fort Lauderdale; 15km north of town.

In theory there's a twice-weekly Bahamas Ferries (p200) boat between Nassau and Governor's Harbour but it's a slow overnight sailing and doesn't always take passengers. It's easier to take the ferry to Spanish Wells or Harbour Island and drive from there.

Andros

POP 7500

Known as 'the Big Yard,' Andros is the country's largest but most sparsely populated major island – 5960 sq km of mangroves, palm savannas and eerie pine forests full of wild boar and (as legend has it) an evil man-bird known as the chickcharnie. It's largely uninhabited – considerable distances separate tiny settlements dotting the east coast, while the entire western side is an uninhabited patchwork of swampland known, appropriately, as 'the Mud.' Most travellers come here for the world-renowned bonefishing in the shallows, or scuba diving further afield.

Off the east shore lies a 225km-long coral reef, and beyond that the 3000m-deep Tongue of the Ocean, making diving and fishing equally exceptional. Then there are the many blue holes: vast, water-filled caves found both on- and offshore.

Public transport is nonexistent: to get around, it's just you, your rental car and some long expanses of empty, potholed road.

Getting There & Away

AIR

Of Andros's four airports, you're most likely to use either **San Andros Airport** (242-329-4224; Queen's Hwy, North Andros;), 15km south of Nicholls Town, **Andros Town Airport** (242-368-2030; Queen's Hwy), near Fresh Creek or **South Andros Airport** (242-369-2640; Queen's Hwy, Congo Town), near Congo Town on the island of the same name.

BOAT

Bahamas Ferries (p200) runs a 7am Saturday service from the Potter' Cay dock in Nassau to Fresh Creek on Central Andros. It's a three-hour journey, returning the same day at 12:30pm and costs BS$112/62 return/one way for adults, and BS$71/39 for children.

Getting Around

Andros is divided into three discrete islands: North and Central Andros (connected by road bridge) and South Andros, which is estranged from its northern brethren by a maze of mangroves, channels and cays. The largest of these, Mangrove Cay, connects to South Andros via a twice-daily government **ferry** (242-357-2926; Lisbon Creek, Mangrove Cay), but that's it for interisland transport. To get from the southern extremity of Central Andros to Mangrove Cay (and then on to South Andros by ferry), you'd need to pay a willing Behring Point local to boat you across. Or you could fly back to Nassau, and double back to South Andros by plane.

Whether you fly or get the ferry, you'll need to hire a car to get anywhere once you're in the Big Yard. If arriving in Fresh Creek, try **Adderley's** (242-357-2149); in San Andros, try **Gaitor's** (242-329-4052). Rentals start from around BS$75 per day, with discounts for three or more days.

North & Central Andros

Geographically one island, North and Central Andros are two separate administrative districts. Sleepy Nicholls Town (population 645) is the closest settlement to San Andros Airport and the center of activity for much of North Andros. Outside of town are some extraordinary hidden beaches and coves. Northeast of here, poor settlements such as Lowe Sound were hit hard by hurricanes in 2016 and 2017 and need a great deal to rebuild their lives. Heading south across Stafford Creek and into Central Andros, the mostly empty roads are bordered by whispering forests of Caribbean pine and the glorious Blue Holes National Park. Settlements begin to emerge as you veer toward the coast, eventually reaching the largest center on these islands: Fresh Creek/Andros Town.

Sights & Activities

★**Blue Holes National Park** NATIONAL PARK
(http://bnt.bs/blue-hole-national-park) Blue Holes – deep vertical 'caves' formed by karst limestone subsidence that fill with rain and seawater, forming unique ecosystems – are more abundant on Andros than anywhere else. This 40,000-acre national park comprises vast tracts of Caribbean pine and coppice forest pitted with these phenomena. Trails and info boards introduce you to the flora, fauna and geology. The most accessible is **Captain Bill's** hole, with a swimming platform, toilets and parking area.

The access road for the park heads west off the Queen's Hwy along Leroy Hanna Dr from the settlement of Love Hill.

Androsia Ltd FACTORY
(242-376-9339; www.androsia.com; Androsia St, Andros Town; 9am-4.30pm Mon-Fri, to 2:30pm Sat) FREE This factory has been hand-producing the gorgeous batiks sold throughout the Bahamas since 1973. Watch workers create fabric with age-old wax techniques (Monday to Friday), then buy some for yourself at the adjacent shop. Turn east off the Queen's Hwy immediately after taking the Fresh Creek Bridge south into Andros Town, and you'll see the sign on your right.

Uncle Charlie's Blue Hole LANDMARK
A few kilometers south of Nicholls Town, this unfathomed blue hole, hidden in the pine forest, was made famous by Jacques Cousteau when he explored it in the 1960s. Today, local kids use a dangling rope swing to splash their

way into the hole's black waters. To get here, follow the signs from Queen's Hwy and drive down a short dirt road.

Small Hope Bay Lodge DIVING
(☎242-368-2013; www.smallhope.com; Small Hope Bay) This highly acclaimed dive outfit, based in a lovely, laid-back resort, offers one-/two-tank dives (BS$90/110), night dives (BS$100) and shark dives (BS$100), as well as snorkeling safaris (BS$40). Ask about specialty trips, including blue-hole dives and wall dives to 56m. Rates fall when you dive for three or more days.

Andros Island Bonefish Club FISHING
(☎242-368-5167; www.androsbonefishing.com; Queen's Hwy, Behring Point) Fly-fishing devotees will be in clover at this dedicated bonefishing club, offering all-inclusive packages bundling bed and board in its 29-room lodge with guided trips to the vast mudflats of Western Andros, one of the meccas of the sport. Three nights, with two days' fishing, is BS$1452 per person, on a twin-share basis (B$2040 for a single).

Sleeping & Eating

Accommodations are few and far between on Andros and are generally vacation rentals, fishing lodges or intimate resorts. Nicholls Town and Fresh Creek have a handful of accommodations. Small Hope is about 10km north of Fresh Creek on the Queen's Hwy, while further north the Davis Creek and Staniard Creek areas have some options.

★Pineville Motel MOTEL $
(☎242-329-2788; Queen's Hwy; d/ste from BS$72/154; ❄📶) There aren't many reasons to stay in the Nicholls Town area, but Pineville is definitely one of them. The ebullient creator, Eugene, has put creativity, imagination, community-mindedness and inspirational industriousness into his motel and community hub. It includes a petting zoo, two live-music stages with regular performances, garden and cinema. There's usually something happening, and rooms are cheap and comfy.

The Pineville is tucked away behind Scotia Bank on the road into Nicholls Town, 11km north of San Andros airport.

Dream Villas VILLA $$
(☎242-357-2108; www.dreamvillasbahamas.com; Davis Creek; villas BS$280-450; ❄📶) These immaculate and thoughtfully furnished one- and two-bedrooms villas have full kitchens, dining and living areas and are a great alternative to the island's fishing lodges. Each has a beachfront location, with deck or balcony, in a quiet spot about 5km north of Fresh Creek and is wheelchair accessible.

★Small Hope Bay Lodge RESORT $$$
(☎242-368-2013; www.smallhope.com; Small Hope Bay; d from BS$660; ❄📶🏊) These 21 luxurious yet unfussy units on a quiet, mangrove-backed stretch of Small Hope Bay are a lovely place to linger. Always convivial and beloved by divers, it's a barefoot holiday-mode kind of place that continues to lead the way for ecotourism in the Bahamas. All meals and drinks are included and the bar and restaurant are exclusive to guests.

★Kamalame Cay RESORT $$$
(☎242-368-6281; www.kamalame.com; villas from BS$630; ❄📶🏊) A ferry whisks lucky guests across the water to a 162-sq-km private island, home to this exquisite luxury resort. Discrete, delightful villas are tucked away down paths lined with kamalame trees, wild dilly, casuarina and love vine, inland from kilometers of perfect beach. Don't miss a massage at the spa on stilts above the sea. Access near Staniard Creek.

Brigadier's BAHAMIAN $
(☎242-368-2106; Davis Creek; mains BS$8-25; ⊙7:30-11am, noon-3pm & 4-9pm; 📶) Brigadier's is a step up from the usual shack restaurants with its gracious dining room and bar and long overwater deck offering views up and down the coast. The Bahamian dishes include conch chowder, boiled crab, chicken *souse* and the local catch of the day. This is Andros' best outside of the resorts.

Information

Tourist office (☎242-368-2286; www.bahamas.com; Mayeu Plaza, Queen's Hwy, Andros Town; ⊙9am-5pm Mon-Fri) Helpful office across the bridge from Fresh Creek.

Mangrove Cay & South Andros

Mangrove Cay and South Andros are pretty much the wildest and most isolated areas of one of the Bahamas' wildest and most isolated islands. Virgin Caribbean-pine forests, vibrant reefs, uncluttered beaches of pink-and-silver sand, eerie blue holes and abundant, lush mangroves make it a nature-lover's dream. Add to that its inaccessibility, sparse population and minimal development, and it could hardly be a better place to drop off the grid.

★Seascape Inn RESORT $
(☎242-369-0342; www.seascapeinn.com; Mangrove Cay; d cabañas incl breakfast BS$175-195;) New Yorkers Mickey and Joan McGowan escaped city life to run this *Swiss Family Robinson*-like colony of beach *cabañas*, and their friendliness has earned them a loyal following. Snorkel, kayak, fish, borrow a bike, commune with the dogs on the beach, or just shoot the breeze with other guests in the small on-site restaurant and pub.

Tiamo RESORT $$$
(☎242-225-6871; www.tiamoresorts.com; South Andros; villas from BS$945; ⊙7am-8pm;) Accessible only by water, this all-inclusive resort caters to couples seeking intimacy and exclusivity. Ten cottages have a luxe ecochic vibe – all pale wood, slate tiles and textured linens. Guests lounge on private porches, swim in the placid, protected beach or sip cocktails on the poolside terrace. Everything but liquor is included, and the minimum guest age is 14.

The Exumas

POP 6928

More than 300 islands and cays scattered across the central Bahamas, the Exumas are renowned for blissfully isolated beaches, world-class diving, and serene resorts. The main islands are Great Exuma and Little Exuma, wonderful in their own right, and then there's the stunning Exuma Cays: a string of mostly uninhabited ocean outposts surrounded by blooming reefs and astonishing ecological bounty. The jewel in that crown is the Exuma Cays Land and Sea Park, a huge expanse of islands, water and reef founded as the world's first land-and-sea reserve in 1958.

Great and Little Exuma support historic ruins, lively settlements, blissful beaches and some exceptional resorts and restaurants. In recent years the aquatic pigs marooned on uninhabited 'pig island' have put the Exumas on the tourist map, but you may find the rest of Exumas will be a highlight of your Bahamian adventure.

George Town

Great Exuma's major center, the capital of the island group, is where you'll find the sugar-pink-and-white neoclassical **Government Administration Building**, housing the **post office** (⊙9am-4pm Mon-Fri) and jail. Just south, the small **straw market** (☎242-336-2584; Queen's Hwy; ⊙8am-6pm Mon-Sat) sells Bahamian-made straw goods, while to the north is the white-stoned Georgian **St Andrew's** Anglican Church, straddling a bluff above Lake Victoria, the circular saltwater lagoon in the middle of town.

South of George Town

The first major settlement south of George Town is **Rolle Town**, recalling the Loyalist planter who lends his name to the estimated 60% of native Exumans descended from his emancipated slaves. Follow the main road, Queen's Hwy, to the town's hilltop crossroads. Here, turn north and drive along a short ridge for panoramic views – you might see a parasailer catching gusts off **Man O' War Cay**.

South of the crossroad, follow the signs a short distance to the **Rolle Town Tombs**.

Next up is a keep-you-on-your-toes **one-lane bridge** linking Great and Little Exuma at the town of **Ferry**. Further on down the Queen's Hwy is the town of **Forbes Hill**; beyond it, two stunning **beaches** await. After passing the 'Leaving Forbes Hill' sign, there's a dangerous curve, then a beach access sign on your left (sometimes the signs disappear). Park, then follow the dirt track past an old stone building to the glimmering, usually shallow, turquoise water.

About 4km past the Leaving Forbes Hill sign is a series of dirt roads on the left. Take one of them – if you get to the 'Lonesome Conch' cottage on Queen's Hwy you've gone too far. These 'roads' lead to poorly marked Ocean Rd, running parallel to the spectacular white-sand **Tropic of Cancer Beach** (Ocean Rd, Moore Hill). Turn right on Ocean Rd and follow it to a wooden beachside hut with a small parking area. Stand on the Tropic of Cancer – there's a faded blue line marking the spot. The *Pirates of the Caribbean II* and *III* crew loaded gear onto boats here before heading to southern cays.

Keep driving down the Queen's Hwy from Forbes Hill and you'll soon reach lonely **William's Town**. Just past Santanna's Grill (p193) is the overgrown ruins of the **Hermitage Estate** (William's Town) FREE, a cotton plantation once run by local bigwigs the Rolles. On the roadside, look out for the prominent **Salt Beacon** (Queen's Hwy, Williams Town), a 10m-high Tuscan-style pillar erected on a hill to guide ships to collect salt during the salt production heyday of the late 18th century. A boardwalk leads up to the pillar, affording great views of the *salina* (salt pond) and Exuma Sound.

Stocking Island

This 240-hectare slip of an island beckons about 1.5km off the coast, separated from George Town by the turquoise beauty of Elizabeth Harbour. For a day trip appealing to adventurers and beach bums alike, grab a water taxi from the Government Dock in George Town to the island (BS$15 to BS$20), where you can snorkel, stroll over talcum-fine sand or bushwhack up a nature 'trail' to the island's highest point. Don't miss the short hike across the island to the Atlantic for more deep-blue views. The Chat & Chill's (p193) Sunday-afternoon pig roast (BS$20) is a don't-miss affair.

Two services leave from George Town Government Dock for various points on Stocking Island: **Elvis Water Taxi** (242-464-1558; one-way/return BS$10/15; hourly 10am-6pm) and **Martin Ferry**. Both charge BS$15 to BS$20 return, depending on which part of Stocking Island you're headed to. They operate from roughly 10am to 6pm daily, leave hourly (or when full) and will collect you for the return trip at your preferred time.

Exuma Cays

The Exuma Cays are a world unto themselves and the stuff of Caribbean fantasy. Tantalizingly inaccessible (you'll need to have your own boat or charter one to make it to most places), they begin at the barren Sail Rocks, nearly 60km southeast of New Providence, and continue in a long line of some 360 islets to Great Exuma. Most are uninhabited, and all are part of the same oceanic mountain range, yet each is distinct, and many are privately owned.

If you're in your own boat and island-hopping at your leisure, visiting picturesque **Staniel Cay** is recommended. Here you can explore wonderful **Thunderball Grotto** (appearing in the eponymous 1965 Bond flick), and snorkel around pristine reefs for an unbeatable Bahamas experience.

The first marine 'replenishment nursery' in the world, created in 1958, the **Exuma Cays Land & Sea Park** (242-225-6402; http://eclsp.com; office 9am-noon & 1-4pm Mon-Sat, 9am-noon Sun) boasts 283 sq km of protected islands and surrounding seas. All fishing and collecting is banned – including plants and shells – and the diving is accordingly out of this world.

Activities

The Exumas offer a plethora of activities, including diving, snorkeling, boat trips, fishing, kayaking and kitesurfing. Call or stop by Exuma's tourist office (p193) for a list of fishing guides. Naturally there are numerous operators running tours to see Exuma's famous swimming pigs and rock iguanas.

Dive Exuma DIVING
(242-336-2893, 242-357-0313; www.dive-exuma.com; Government Dock, George Town; 9am-3pm Mon-Fri, or by appointment) The most highly recommended (and only PADI) operation in town, Dive Exuma offers one-/two-tank dives for BS$90/145 (includes tanks and

SWIMMING PIGS OF THE BAHAMAS

Swimming pigs? It may sound strange but one of the big attractions in the Bahamas is a bunch of aquatic wild pigs marooned on a remote island in the far-flung Exumas. And they're not the only island pigs: a small drift also lives on uninhabited No Name Cay (aka Piggyville) in the Abacos and another on Meeks Patch Island near Spanish Wells in Eleuthera.

Local boatmen, charter operators and even powerboat companies based in Nassau have found that taking tourists to see, feed and photograph the pigs is a lucrative endeavour.

It's thought the pigs on uninhabited Major Cay in the remote Exuma Cays have been living there for well over a decade but the tourism interest really began when *National Geographic* published an article on this porcine phenomenon in 2015. The pigs have certainly become adept swimmers, usually paddling out to boats in search of food. Animal rights groups say wild pigs shouldn't be hand-fed or exploited for tourism, while some locals counter that the pigs would likely not survive without being fed or given fresh water. A bigger concern is that other islanders might plant pigs on islands to cash in on the tourism interest.

If you do decide to visit the pigs, ensure your boat stays a respectful distance, don't touch them (they can bite) and use natural plant-based food scraps or bread.

weights, gear rental extra), full PADI courses from BS$700 and snorkeling trips.

Exuma Kitesurfing KITESURFING
(242-524-7099; www.exumakitesurfing.com; Beach Access Rd, Rolle Town; 9am-5pm) Offers a dizzying array of packages, including 2½-hour beginner lessons from BS$260 and four-hour 'kiteventures' from BS$180 (BS$310 with gear provided). Also offers stand-up paddleboarding (three hours, with gear and instruction, from BS$130) and accommodations (cottages and bungalows BS$259 to BS$359 per night).

Minn's Water Sports BOATING
(242-336-3483; www.mwsboats.com; Queen's Hwy, George Town; 8:30am-5pm) Rents out boats from BS$198 per day, with reduced rates for bookings over two days. The boats, which aren't licensed for waters beyond Elizabeth Harbour, vary in size from 4.5m to 6.5m. A BS$200 to BS$300 cash deposit is required.

Tours

Out Island Explorers SAILING
(242-542-8246; www.outislandexplorers.com; George Town) Out Island Explorers' six-day-five-night all-inclusive guided sailing trips (B$1895 per person) are one of the loveliest ways to see the Exuma Cays. For something more low-key it also runs guided kayaking trips and rent out kayaks.

Off Island Boat Tours BOATING
(242-524-0524; http://offislandboattours.com; George Town) Off Island specializes in charter boat trips exploring the sights and sites close to George Town and Elizabeth Harbour. Tours start from BS$350 for three hours' snorkeling and exploring Stocking Island's blue hole and beaches, and go all the way to an eight-hour, BS$1200 trip to remote White Cay. The boat takes up to eight people.

Festivals & Events

Bahamian Music & Heritage Festival CULTURAL
(Regatta Point, Georgetown; noon-midnight Fri-Sun early Mar) This annual celebration of Bahamian food, music, crafts and other cultural traditions turns Regatta Point into a night party from Friday to Sunday. Watch out for competitive conch cracking and sugarcane peeling.

Sleeping

Marshall's Guest House MOTEL $
(242-551-6820; Queen's Hwy, George Town; d BS$95-110;) This drab-looking motel next to the Shell gas station in the middle of town isn't much to look at but it has the cheapest rooms around and they're pretty clean and spacious with TV and air-con. Cash only.

Staniel Cay Yacht Club RESORT $$
(242-355-2024; www.stanielcay.com; Staniel Cay; d BS$300-545;) On tiny picturesque Staniel Cay, this resort offers waterfront bungalows, smaller double rooms and all-inclusive packages including sailing, meals, snorkeling, kayaks and more. Spacious verandas make soaking in the sensational views a pleasure, and the cool and comfortable rooms are available at reduced weekly rates. Book ahead. This is the closest island to the famous swimming pigs.

Sandy Palms RENTAL HOUSE $$
(www.sandypalmsbahamas.com; Queen's Hwy; d/apt per week B$1450/2065; P) The beachfront location at this rental house is outstanding, with a jetty leading out to the calm waters of Hooper Bay and free kayaks available. There are decent-value studios and a two- and four-bedroom apartment, all with kitchen. It's available for six nights minimum, which can work out well for groups. No phone – book online.

Regatta Point GUESTHOUSE $$
(242-336-2206; www.regattapointbahamas.com; Regatta Point, George Town; d BS$220-290; P) Perfectly located on the peninsula sheltering Kidd Cove, these guesthouses manage to be both tucked away and close to the center of George Town. All six enjoy full kitchens and casuarina-shaded gardens leading to a rocky private beach. TV and wi-fi are deliberately absent, rooms are fan-cooled, hot water is solar-powered and the welcome is genuinely warm.

Club Peace & Plenty HOTEL $$
(242-336-2551; www.peaceandplenty.com; Queen's Hwy, George Town; d BS$250-345;) Built on the location of an old slave market and plantation, this friendly hotel in the middle of George Town has 32 bright rooms (renovated in 2019), a small pool, a bar (the former plantation cookhouse) and a seaside deck with views to Stocking Island. The in-house Italian restaurant is worth a splurge.

Eating

Fish Fry BAHAMIAN
(Queen's Hwy, George Town; ⏲1am-1pm) The collection of clapboard shacks with names like Charlie's and Shirley's is the best place on the island to meet locals and indulge in typical Bahamian seafood staples. Friday and Saturday are the big nights when there's music and the rum is flowing but at least one shack is open each day. It's 2.5km northwest of George Town

Karijava Coffee House CAFE $
(☎242-524-2738; Queen's Hwy, George Town; snacks BS$3-7; ⏲7:30am-4pm; 📶) The best place in Grand Exuma for an espresso coffee and a cinnamon roll or light breakfast, welcoming Karijava also encourages you to linger with free wi-fi.

★**Chat & Chill Bar & Grill** BAHAMIAN $$
(☎242-336-2700; www.chatnchill.com; Stocking Island; mains BS$15-25; ⏲11am-7pm; 📶👪) Located on the low sand spit bordering Stocking Island's shallow 'harbor', the Chat & Chill Bar & Grill combines a bar, broad casuarina-shaded beaches, volleyball court, gift shop, conch shack and more into one beachside pleasure complex. Sunday's pig-roast (BS$20, beginning from noon) is an Exuma institution, and you should make sure to bring swimwear to fraternize with the friendly stingrays beneath the conch shack.

★**Tropic Breeze** BAHAMIAN $$
(☎242-345-4100; Queen's Hwy, William's Town; mains BS$14-28; ⏲11:30am-6pm Tue-Sat) With superb ocean views and some of the best Bahamian seafood in the Exumas, this relaxed but efficient restaurant-bar is a killer spot for a long, lazy lunch.

Santanna's Grill BAHAMIAN $$
(☎242-345-4102; Queen's Hwy, William's Town; mains BS$15-30; ⏲10:30am-5pm Mon-Sat) Run by the formidable Denise Rolle, this superbly situated shack restaurant offers the best-value fresh lobster in the Exumas, and its many regulars often entertain diners with increasingly tall stories from the *Pirates of the Caribbean* shoot, part of which took place at nearby Sandy Point. There's also a great (if rocky) beach just a few meters from the bar.

Information

Tourist office (☎242-336-2430; www.bahamas.com; Queen's Hwy, George Town; ⏲9am-5pm Mon-Fri)

Getting There & Away

There are regular flights connecting Nassau and Exuma. Bahamas Ferries no longer has scheduled passenger ferries to Georgetown, but Nassau-based operators run day trips to the Exumas by powerboat.

Thompson's Rental (☎242-345-0058; http://exumacars.com; Exuma International Airport; ⏲7:30am-5pm Mon-Sat) and **Airport Car Rental** (☎242-345-0090; www.exumacarrental.com; Exuma International Airport; ⏲7am-7pm) both have offices at Exuma International Airport, renting cars from BS$75 per day.

Long Island

Straddling the Tropic of Cancer, Long Island is one of the most scenic Out Islands, a slender 130km north–south expanse of sand with stunning white-and-sky-blue churches, lush greenery, elaborate cave systems and bougainvillea-draped villages. The lone highway leads to magnificent bays, blue holes and kilometers of empty beaches, and some delightful resorts help you make the most of this Eden, without sacrificing comfort.

Sights & Activities

Dean's Blue Hole CAVE
Not only is this the second-deepest blue hole in the world at 203m (after the more recently discovered Dragon Hole in the South China Sea), but it's accessible right off the beach. This remarkable vertical cave teems with sea life and is globally renowned as a free-diving location. There's easy swimming in shallow waters from the sand bank. It's about 7km west of Clarence Town.

Conception Island Wall DIVE SITE
Some 20km northeast of Long Island lies Conception Island, an uninhabited land-and-sea nature reserve. The lavish coral heads, warm currents and unmolested marine life to be found in the waters off its leeward shore offer some of the most spectacular diving in the Bahamas.

Bahamas Discovery Quest OUTDOORS
(☎242-472-2605; https://bahamasdiscoveryquest.com; Long Island) This experienced local

adventure tour operator can arrange custom fishing, snorkeling, hiking, birdwatching and round-island tours to hot spots such as Dean's Blue Hole.

Sleeping & Eating

★Cape Santa Maria RESORT **$$**
(☎1-800-663-7090; www.capesantamaria.com; 1327 Beach Dr, Stella Maris; bungalows BS$300-350; ❄📶) A string of bungalows and villas along the gleaming-white Cape Santa Maria Beach, this resort brings to life what many have in mind when seeking untrammeled Bahamian coastal relaxation. There are gazebos and daybeds for enjoying the island air, the usual suite of sea-based activities on offer, and half- and full-board packages available. Minimum seven-night stay in high season.

Stella Maris Resort RESORT **$$**
(☎242-338-2050; www.stellamarisresort.com; s/d BS$225/254, cottages from BS$254/320; ❄📶🏊) Hotel-style rooms and beach cottages at this delightfully situated resort invite relaxed satisfaction, with patios or verandas, quality bedding, three swimming pools and unspoiled Atlantic views. Activities on offer are mainly marine (including scuba diving) and the on-site beach bar and restaurant are no afterthoughts (full-board packages are available).

Chez Pierre INTERNATIONAL **$$**
(☎242-338-8809; www.chezpierrebahamas.com; Queen's Hwy, Miller's Bay; mains BS$20-45; ⊙7-9am, 11.30am-2pm & 5-8pm; reservations expected; 📶) The eponymous French-Canadian Pierre produces food that treats good produce with love and skill, all in a delightfully scenic setting by the sea. Global crowd-pleasers such as pizza and pasta are augmented by more refined French and European fare and, naturally, Bahamian seafood. It's down a rugged dirt road off the Queen's Hwy at Sam McKinnon's Settlement.

Information

Tourist office (☎242-338-8668; Queen's Hwy, Salt Pond; ⊙9am-5pm Mon-Fri)

Getting There & Away

Long Island has two airports: Southern Air flies twice daily from Nassau to **Stella Maris** (☎242-338-2006; Queen's Hwy) in the north, and Bahamas Air flies at least six times a week to **Deadman's Cay** (Queen's Hwy), north of Clarence Town.

UNDERSTAND THE BAHAMAS

History

The original inhabitants of the Bahamas were a tribe of Arawaks, the peaceful Lucayans, who arrived near the turn of the 9th century. Christopher Columbus arrived in 1492, and shortly thereafter the Spanish began shipping out the Lucayans as slaves.

Infamous pirates such as Blackbeard and Calico Jack took over New Providence in the 1600s, establishing a pirates' paradise lined with brothels and taverns for 'common cheats, thieves and lewd persons.' With the aid of Woodes Rogers, the Bahamas' first Royal Governor and a former privateer, the British established order, and an administration answerable to the English Crown, in 1718. The Bahamas' new motto was *Expulsis Piratis – Restituta Commercia* (Pirates Expelled – Commerce Restored).

Following the American Revolution, Loyalist refugees – many quite rich or entrepreneurial – began arriving, giving new vigor to the city. These wealthy landowners lived well and kept slaves until the British Empire abolished the slave trade. During the American Civil War the islands were an exchange center for blockade runners transferring munitions and supplies for Southern cotton.

While Nassauvians illicitly supplied liquor to the US during Prohibition, Americans flocked to Nassau and its new casinos. When Fidel Castro spun Cuba into Soviet orbit in 1961, the subsequent US embargo forced revelers to seek their pleasures elsewhere; Nassau became *the* new hot spot.

Tourism and finance bloomed together. The government promoted the nascent banking industry, encouraging British investors escaping onerous taxes.

This upturn in fortunes coincided with the evolution of party politics and festering ethnic tensions, as the white elite and a growing black middle class reaped profits from the boom. Middle-class blacks' aspirations for representation coalesced with the pent-up frustrations of their impoverished brothers, leading to the victory of the black-led Progressive Liberal party and leader Sir Lynden Pindling in 1967. On July 10, 1973, the Bahamas officially became a new nation – the Independent Commonwealth of the Bahamas – ending 325 years of British rule. The

Queen remains head of state, represented by the governor general (Cornelius Alvin Smith since 2019). In 2017 the centre-right Free National Movement formed government, with Hubert Minnis as prime minister.

Devastating hurricanes ravaged various islands between 1999 and 2019, wreaking havoc on tourism. Hurricanes Maria and Irma both made landfall in the Bahamas, causing evacuations and scattered damage. The worst of the local destruction, however, was caused by Hurricane Dorian, which utterly ravaged the Abacos and Grand Bahama in September 2019. Despite these storms, development continues with massive resorts and cruise ports on New Providence and Out Islands such as Bimini chugging toward completion.

People & Culture

Contemporary Bahamian culture still revolves around family, church and the sea, but cable TV and the proximity of North America have had a profound influence on contemporary life and material values.

In Nassau and Freeport, most working people are employed in banking, tourism or government work and live a nine-to-five lifestyle.

The citizens inhabiting the islands outside of New Providence and Grand Bahama, called the Out Islands or Family Islands, are a bit more neighborly and traditional. Thus the practice of Obeah (a form of African-based ritual magic), bush medicine, and folkloric songs and tales still infuse their daily lives. Though tourism is bringing change to the Out Islands, many people still live simple lives centered on fishing, catching conch and lobster, and raising corn, bananas and other crops.

The Arts

The Bahamas rock to the soul-riveting sounds of calypso, soca, reggae and its own distinctive music, which echoes African rhythms and synthesizes Caribbean calypso, soca and English folk songs into its own goombay beat.

Goombay – the name comes from an African word for 'rhythm' – derives its melody from a guitar, piano or horn instrument, accompanied by any combination of goatskin goombay drums, maracas, rhythm sticks, rattles, conch-shell horns, fifes, flutes and cowbells, to add a *kalik-kalik-kalik* sound.

Rake 'n' scrape is the Bahamas' downhome, working-class music, usually featuring a guitar, an accordion, shakers made from the pods of poinciana trees, and other makeshift instruments, such as a saw played with a screwdriver.

Landscape & Wildlife

The Land

The Bahamian islands are strewn in a linear fashion from northwest to southeast. Several of them – Great Abaco, Eleuthera, Long Island and Andros – are more than 160km in length. Few, however, are more than a few kilometers wide. All are low-lying, and the highest point in the Bahamas – Mt Alvernia on Cat Island – is only 62m above sea level.

Virtually the entire length of these shores is lined by white- or pinkish-sand beaches – about 3540km in all – shelving into turquoise shallows. The interiors are generally marked by scrub-filled forests and, on some of the more remote islands, the plants found here are still used in bush medicine.

The islands are pocked by blue holes – water-filled circular pits that open to underground and submarine caves and descend as far as 182m.

Wildlife

The islands are a birdwatcher's paradise, with about 300 recorded species of birds. Only a few are endemic, including the Bahama swallow, the endangered Bahama parrot, and the Bahama woodstar hummingbird, a pugnacious bird weighing less than 3g. The West Indian (Caribbean) flamingo – the national bird – inhabits Crooked Island, Long Cay and the sanctuary of Great Inagua.

Iguanas inhabit some outlying isles and cays, and are protected. The archipelago's largest native land animal, they can reach 1.2m in length.

The region's marine life is as varied as its islands and coral reefs. Depending on who you believe, the Bahamas have between 2330 sq km and 6992 sq km of coral reef, and countless species of fish, such as bonito, stingrays, sharks, kingfish, jewelfish and deep-blue Creole wrasse.

Humpback whales pass through the waters windward of the Bahamas and blue whales are also frequently sighted.

Environmental Issues

The Bahamas National Trust maintains 26 national parks and reserves, including large sections of the barrier reef, but outside of the national park system, inappropriate development, pollution and overexploitation increasingly threaten wildlife and marine resources. Although the Bahamas was the first Caribbean nation to outlaw long-line fishing, the islands' stocks of grouper, spiny lobster and conch all face the consequences of overfishing.

Today, local groups are leading environmental awareness and action. The Abacos' Friends of the Environment (www.friendsoftheenvironment.org) organizes community-wide projects and passes the message along in schools. In Eleuthera, the Eleuthera School (www.islandschool.org) is earning kudos as an environmental learning center, drawing US high schoolers as well as adult 'students' looking to become environmentally engaged global citizens.

The Bahamas banned hunting and eating of sea turtles, an endangered species, in 2009.

The islands are a popular cruise-ship destination and the issue of ships polluting the waters has long been a contentious one. In 2019 Carnival, the largest cruise company, was fined US$20 million after pleading guilty to dumping waste and pollutants in the Caribbean. This followed an earlier conviction in 2016.

SURVIVAL GUIDE

Directory A–Z

ACCESSIBLE TRAVEL

Travelers with disabilities will need to plan their vacation carefully, as few allowances have been made for them in the Bahamas. The larger hotels and resorts are generally well set up for accessibility, but beyond their gates, things get tough. Tourism boards can provide a list of hotels with wheelchair ramps, as can the **National Commission for Persons With Disabilities** (242-397 8600; www.disabilitiescommissionbahamas.org) and the **Bahamas Association for the Physically Disabled** (242-322-2393; Dolphin Dr; 9am-5pm Mon-Fri). While these organizations don't have offices open to the public, you can call them or contact them online for help hiring equipment and organizing accessible holiday options.

In 2014 the government passed the Persons With Disabilities (Equal Opportunities) Act, which required all publicly used buildings in the country to be easily accessible to those who are visually- or hearing-impaired, use a wheelchair or have other disabilities, and to have sufficient accessible parking spaces by 2017. Some places have been slow to act and there are still many challenges in areas such as public transport.

ACCOMMODATIONS

The Bahamas are known for their resorts, from basic family places to no-expense-spared enclaves of extreme privilege. But there are alternatives: most inhabited islands offer villas and hotels and (with a little more effort) a few hostels and campsites can be found. Bear in mind that some places close annually around September and October, and that booking ahead is strongly advised in peak periods (US summer and college holidays).

ACTIVITIES

The Bahamas are an outdoor-lover's paradise: swimming, snorkeling, diving, fishing, kitesurfing, sailing, hiking and birdwatching are just some of the activities most islands offer.

Diving & Snorkeling

With gin-clear, often-shallow waters and high visibility, the Bahamas is one of the richest marine realms in the Caribbean for divers and snorkelers. Its warm tropical waters hold one of the greatest varieties of sea life found in the region. You can mingle with Caribbean reef sharks, nurse sharks, barracuda, bottlenose dolphins and spotted dolphins, as well as loads of reef fish, including angelfish, snapper, jacks, grunts, parrotfish, lobsters, cardinal fish, damselfish, Nassau groupers, stingrays and moray eels.

Typical prices: one/two tanks BS$70/130 with only tank and weights supplied (more for a specialty dive, such as shark dives or dolphin dives), Discover Scuba BS$130-150, PADI certification from BS$600.

SLEEPING PRICE RANGES

Nearly all hotels change their rates at least twice a year between low and high season. Prices quoted here are for the high season and include the 12% VAT. During low season (June to November) prices may drop between 20% and 60%.

$ less than BS$200

$$ BS$200–500

$$$ more than BS$500

All of the islands offer numerous dive sites within a short boat ride. Popular choices:

New Providence Shark Wall (p160) Shark dives, plunging walls and wreck off the west coast of Bahamas' main island.

The Biminis Bimini Road (p182) is an evocative limestone formation; the wreck of Henry Ford's concrete yacht *Sapona* makes for a classic shallow-water dive.

The Exumas The protected Land and Sea Park (p191) is bursting with life; also 28m-deep Angelfish Blue Hole off Stocking Island.

Andros Famous for its Ocean Blue Holes (p188), the 'Big Yard' was popularized by M. Costeau himself.

Long Island The Conception Island Wall (p193) justifiably tops many divers' bucket lists, while Dean's Blue Hole (p193) is the world's second-deepest.

Grand Bahama Dive the Theo wreck or with sharks and dolphins with UNEXSO (p171).

The Abacos Teeming reefs such as Fowl Cay Preserve and Tiloo Cay, and numerous wrecks.

ELECTRICITY

Electrical outlets are 120V/60 cycles, which is compatible with US appliances. Plug sockets are two- or three-prong US standard: appliances may require an adapter and 220V converter.

EMBASSIES & CONSULATES

Most countries are represented by honorary consuls and most consulates are located in Nassau, New Providence. These include the following:

Australian Consulate (242-327-8301; http://dfat.gov.au; Lyford Manor, Lyford Cay; 9am-5pm Mon-Fri)

Canadian Consulate (242-393-2123; Shirley St Plaza; 9:30am-noon Mon-Thu)

French Consulate (242-302-5001; Lyford Cay House, Western Rd; 8am-4pm Mon-Fri)

German Consulate (242-357-3633; Suite 115, Lagoon Ct, Olde Towne Sandyport)

UK Consulate (242-225-6033)

US Embassy (242-322-1181; https://bs.usembassy.gov; 42 Queen Street; 8:30am-5:30pm Mon-Thu, to 1pm Fri)

EMERGENCY NUMBERS

Ambulance, fire, police 911 or 919

FOOD

Bahamian food reflects the bounty of the seas and the islands' mixed European, African and South American heritage. Chilies, bay leaves, allspice and lime are common. The islands aren't especially fertile, and many staples must be imported. If it grows in sandy tropical soils (coconut), or it swims in the surrounding seas (lobster, grouper), it's usually the best thing on the menu.

EATING PRICE RANGES

The following price categories represent the cost of a main dish or equivalent.

$ less than BS$20

$$ BS$20–30

$$$ more than BS$30

Essential Food & Drink

Conch Roasted, cracked (fried), chopped into salads or dipped in dough and fried into fritters, this chewy sea snail is ubiquitous in the Bahamas. Think calamari. Starchy side dishes like peas 'n' rice (rice with beans), mac 'n' cheese and potato salad round out the menu.

Boil fish A breakfast dish of grouper stewed with lime juice, onions and potatoes. Usually served with johnnycake, a sweetish type of flat cornbread.

Spiny Caribbean lobster The Bahamas' native lobster, often served sautéed with onions and pepper, minced and even curried.

Souse A thick stew of chicken, sheep's head, pig's trotter or other 'leftover' meats.

Guava duff Boiled pastry filled with sweet guava paste and topped off with rum or cream sauce.

Beer Wash everything down with a cold Kalik or Sands beer.

Rum cocktails Try goombay smash or a Bahama mama.

Switcher A refreshing lime-based drink, sometimes available as an alcoholic version.

Sky Juice Gin and coconut milk.

HEALTH

Nassau and Grand Bahama have modern hospitals with emergency rooms open 24/7, but free care is only provided to legal residents. The Out Islands are serviced by small government clinics, usually found off the Queen's Hwy in the major settlements and open 9am to 5pm Monday to Friday. All will have 24-hour emergency numbers posted outside, although serious conditions will have to be treated in one of the major centers.

LEGAL MATTERS

The Bahamian legal system bears traces of UK common law and the US constitutional model. Innocence is presumed, and arrests must follow prescribed legal limits.

Recreational drugs are strictly prohibited in The Bahamas. There are reports of cruise-ship passengers in possession of small amounts of marijuana and cocaine being faced with either

PRACTICALITIES

Newspapers Daily New Providence newspapers include the *Nassau Guardian* (https://thenassauguardian.com), the *Tribune* (http://www.tribune242.com) and the *Bahama Journal* (http://jonesbahamas.com). Grand Bahama offers the daily *Freeport News* (http://thefreeportnews.com), and on Abaconians there's the weekly *Abaconian* (http://www.theabaconian.com).

TV & radio The government-owned Bahamas Broadcasting Corporation operates ZNS-13 and the radio stations ZNS-1, ZNS-2AM, ZNS-2FM and ZNS-3AM. Commercial radio stations include Love 97FM, More 94.9FM and Jam 100FM. Most hotels also offer American cable TV.

Smoking The Bahamas have been slow to implement smoking legislation, and restrictions are often at the discretion of individual businesses and organizations. That said, public tobacco use isn't widespread on the islands and it's rare to see anyone smoking indoors.

Weights & measures The imperial and metric systems are both in use.

paying a BS$500 to BS$800 on-the-spot fine, or being sent to jail for three months.

The legal limit for blood-alcohol content when driving is 0.06%; breaching this can attract penalties of up to BS$3000, or time in jail.

If you are arrested, authorities are obliged to contact your embassy or consulate on request. There is no automatic public-defense provision for foreigners in lower courts, and any representation must be self-funded.

LGBT+ TRAVELERS

Homosexuality is legal in the Bahamas (for those 18 and over). There's not much public support for LGBT+ populations across the largely Christian and conservative islands, and discretion is advised. Gay bars and clubs are very subterranean.

There are currently few gay-rights groups with a high profile in the Bahamas; the best source of information is through the Facebook page of Bahamas LGBT Equality Advocates (www.facebook.com/myBLEA).

MONEY

Bahamian dollars (BS$) and US dollars (US$) are equal and interchangeable throughout the country.

There are plenty of banks with ATMs in the major tourist centers, though they can be rare to nonexistent on the Out Islands. ATMs near the Nassau cruise-ship dock offer either BS$ or US$.

Exchange Rates

Australia	A$1	BS$0.69
Canada	C$1	BS$0.76
Europe	€1	BS$1.11
Japan	¥100	BS$0.92
New Zealand	NZ$1	BS$0.66
Switzerland	Sfr1	BS$1.00
UK	UK£1	BS$1.24
USA	US$1	BS$1

For current exchange rates, see www.xe.com.

Taxes & Refunds

Value-added tax (VAT) of 12% (controversially increased from 7.5% in 2018) is imposed on all goods and services in the Bahamas. Some businesses list the pretax price, some the final price, and some both prices. Hotels and restaurants usually list just the pretax price.

The introduction of a VAT Free Shopping Scheme in 2016 has enabled participating merchants to sell goods tax-free to tourists.

Tipping

Hotels BS$2 per bag is routine for porters.

Restaurants A tip of 15% or so is standard, but it's often added to your bill automatically – check before you pay.

Taxis About 15% is the norm.

OPENING HOURS

Exceptions to the following business hours are noted in specific listings. Banks on smaller Out Islands and cays may be open only once or twice a week.

Banks 9am to 4pm Monday to Friday.

Businesses 9am to 5pm Monday to Friday.

Post offices 9am to 5pm Monday to Friday, 9am to noon Saturday.

Restaurants breakfast 7am to 10am, lunch noon to 2pm, dinner 6pm to 9pm.

Shops 9am to 5pm Monday to Friday, 9 or 10am to 5pm Saturday.

Tourist information 9am to 5pm Monday to Friday.

PUBLIC HOLIDAYS

Bahamian national holidays that fall on Saturday or Sunday are usually observed on the previous Friday or following Monday.

New Year's Day January 1

Majority Rule Day January 10

Good Friday March/April

Easter Monday March/April
Whit Monday Seventh Monday after Easter
Labour Day First Friday in June
Independence Day July 10
Emancipation Day First Monday in August
National Heroes Day Second Monday in October
Christmas Day December 25
Boxing Day December 26

SAFE TRAVEL

- The Bahamas is generally safe, but crimes against people and property have increased since 2010, principally in certain neighborhoods of Nassau. Drug- and gang-related crime is on the increase and is highest in the suburbs south of downtown, known collectively as 'Over the Hill.'
- On Nassau's main beaches such as Junkanoo, female bathers may be approached by smooth-talking men – more an annoyance than a danger.
- Although very rare, shark attacks do occur and there have been a number of fatalities in Bahamian waters, the most recent in 2019.

TELEPHONE

The Bahamian country code is 242. You need to dial this when making interisland calls from landlines, but not from cell phones. To call the Bahamas from the US and Canada, dial 1-242. From elsewhere, dial your country's international access code + 242 + the local number. Most US toll-free numbers can't be accessed from the Bahamas. Usually you must dial 1-880, plus the last seven digits of the number. There are no area codes.

Mobile Phones

The main carrier is **BTC Bahamas** (☎ 242-302-7700; www.btcbahamas.com; cnr Cumberland & King St; ⏲ 9am-5pm Mon-Fri, 8am-3pm Sat) with offices or stores in Nassau, Freeport and most Out Islands. Unlocked mobile (cell) phones can be used with Bahamian SIM cards. Locked phones can only be used when roaming.

Prepaid mobile plans vary but start at BS$15 for seven days validity and 3GB of data. Service is poor outside of towns on many of the Out Islands. A new carrier, Aliv (www.bealiv.com) is gradually extending its coverage and offers very competitive prepaid plans online.

TIME

All of the Bahamas falls within the Eastern Standard Time Zone. It switches to Daylight Saving Time (DST) at the same time as the USA and Canada.

VOLUNTEERING

Volunteering options aren't rich in the Bahamas, outside of missionary organizations. Hurricane season does bring its opportunities, sadly, as there can be huge cleanup and reconstruction efforts to be undertaken. Organizations such as Volunteer Match (www.volunteermatch.org) can help you find a way to make a difference in the wake of a particularly violent storm.

Marine monitoring and conservation is, however, an area in which volunteer programs are well established in the Bahamas. Programs lasting several weeks to several months and involving volunteers in reef monitoring, turtle tagging, dolphin tracking and similar activities can be found through Earthwatch Institute (www.earthwatch.org) and Oceanic Society (www.oceanicsociety.org). The Bahamas National Trust (http://bnt.bs) also invites volunteers for conservation programs in the 8100 sq km of habitat it manages throughout the islands.

ℹ Getting There & Away

The Bahamas have six international airports, with major hubs at Nassau and Freeport. The two cities are also popular stopovers for cruise ships.

AIR

The Bahamas' proximity to Florida means regular, relatively inexpensive flights from Miami, Fort Lauderdale and Orlando, as well as other East Coast gateways. A few airlines and charter companies fly directly to airports on the larger Out Islands (such as Abaco), but the majority of flights arrive in Nassau or Freeport where passengers will connect to another flight before continuing to the Out Islands. For a brief summary of airlines and flight schedules by island, check www.bahamas.com.

The national airline Bahamasair (p200) has an unblemished safety record and its pilots have an excellent reputation (see www.airsafe.com for details). Delays, however, are regular occurrences and flights may be canceled without warning. Bahamians like to say, 'If you have time to spare, fly Bahamasair.'

Lynden Pindling International Airport (Nassau; http://nassaulpia.com) The Bahamas' number-one entry point, with direct services to the USA, Canada, the UK, the Cayman Islands, Cuba, Jamaica, Panama, and Turks and Caicos.

Grand Bahama International Airport (Freeport) Direct flights to the US and Canada.

SEA

Numerous cruise ships dock in Nassau and Grand Bahama, most originating in Florida. Among the most prominent are **Carnival** (☎ US 1-800-764-7419; www.carnival.com), **Costa** (☎ US 1-800-462-6782; www.costacruise.

INTERISLAND FLIGHTS

Interisland flights offer the only quick and convenient way to travel within the Bahamas; islanders ride airplanes like mainlanders use buses. Private charter flights can be an affordable option for those traveling in a group – or they might be the only option for some more remote destinations.

Regular scheduled flights from Nassau (one-way prices are approximate and include taxes):

DESTINATION	AIRLINE	PRICE, DURATION, FREQUENCY
Abaco (Marsh Harbour)	Bahamasair , SkyBahamas	BS$110, 30min, 3 daily
Andros (San Andros)	Western Air	BS$87, 20min, 2 daily
Biminis (South Bimini)	Western Air	BS$110, 35min, 2 daily
Eleuthera (North Eleuthera)	Pineapple Air, Southern Air	BS$104, 20min, 6 daily
Exuma (George Town)	Bahamasair, SkyBahamas	BS$132, 40min, 4 daily
Grand Bahama (Freeport)	Bahamasair, SkyBahamas, Western Air	BS$115, 40min, frequent
Inagua	Bahamasair	BS$163, 1½hr, 3 weekly
Long Island (Deadman's Cay)	Bahamasair, Southern Air	BS$127, 55min, 1-2 daily
San Salvador	Bahamasair	BS$123, 1hr, 1 daily

com), **Norwegian** (www.ncl.com) and **Royal Caribbean** (☎UK 0844-493-4005; www.royal-caribbean.com).

The sheltered waters of the archipelago attract thousands of yachters each year. Winds and currents favor the passage south, and sailing conditions are at their best in summer, though hurricanes can be a threat throughout the season (June to November).

Private boats arriving in the Bahamas must clear customs and immigration at an official port of entry, of which there are around 50 across the islands. Until clearance is given, the yellow quarantine flag must be flown, and only the captain can come ashore. All aboard must fill out immigration forms, and there's an entry fee for each vessel (BS$150 for vessels of less than 10.5m, BS$300 for anything larger), which includes cruising and fishing permits and departure tax for three people.

Getting Around

Perusing a map, it's tempting to think that island-hopping down the chain is easy. Unfortunately, it's not – that is, unless you have your own boat or plane. Interisland air travel is unavoidably centered on Nassau, and getting between the islands on scheduled flights or ferries usually requires backtracking. Even the mail boats are Nassau-centric. An exception is the flights from Grand Bahama direct to Abaco and the Biminis.

AIR

In the Bahamas, charter services fill the gaps that scheduled flights can't profitably address. Flamingo Air (p171) is one of the main charter companies, flying to South Andros, Cat Island, Exuma Cays, Inagua and San Salvador, while **Southern Air** (☎242-323-6833, 242-323-7217; www.southernaircharter.com) flies to Long Island and Eleuthera.

Regular scheduled flights are operated by the following:

Bahamasair (☎242-702-4140; www.bahamasair.com)

Pineapple Air (☎242-702-7133; www.pineappleair.com)

SkyBahamas (☎242-702-2600; www.skybahamas.net)

Southern Air

Western Air (☎242-329-4000; www.westernairbahamas.com)

BICYCLE

Cycling is not particularly popular in the Bahamas. It's not safe in traffic-clogged Nassau, though can be pleasant on Paradise Island, Grand Bahama and the Out Islands. Many hotels rent cruiser bikes for about BS$15 a day; some let guests use them for free.

BOAT

Ferry

The only major interisland ferry operator in the Bahamas is **Bahamas Ferries** (Map p162; ☎242-394-9700, 242-323-2166; www.bahamasferries.com; Potter's Cay Dock), though passenger services have been wound back in recent years (cargo services still operate to major islands). High-speed services run between Nassau and Eleuthera (Harbour Island, Spanish Wells and Governor's Harbour), with less frequent services to Andros, Grand Exuma and Long Island. Considering the cost and frequency of flights, only the Nassau–-Harbour Island/Spanish Wells ferry is worth using. Services (one-way fares, tax included) from Nassau:

DESTINATION	PRICE, DURATION, DEPARTURES
Fresh Creek (Andros)	BS$61.50, 4hr, 7am Sat
George Town (Exuma)	BS$74, 14hr, 2 weekly
Governor's Harbour (Eleuthera)	BS$61.50, 8-14hr, 2 weekly
Simms (Long Island)	BS$74, 19hr, 1 weekly
Harbour Island (Eleuthera)	BS$84, 3hr, daily except Sun

Ferries leave from the Potter's Cay Dock in Nassau.

Mail Boat & Water Taxi

Mail boats (www.mailboatbahamas.com) sail under government contract to most inhabited islands, delivering post, freight and passengers. They regularly depart Potter's Cay for Grand Bahama and all the Out Islands. Traditionally sailing overnight, mail-boat journeys last between five and 24 hours; comforts are minimal, and fares between BS$30 and BS$45. Always call the **Nassau Dockmaster** (Map p162; ☎242-393-1064; Potter's Cay) and check with the **Bahamas Ministry of Tourism** (Map p166; www.bahamas.com) for the latest schedules and prices.

In New Providence, **water taxis** (Map p166; ☎242-363-1030; ⏰9am-6pm) zip back and forth between Prince George Wharf, Nassau and Paradise Island every half-hour between 9am and 6pm. Other offshore islands and their neighboring cays are served by private water taxis, such as the services between George Town and Stocking Island, Exuma.

Government-run water taxis link islands that are a short distance apart, such as North and South Bimini, Mangrove Cay and South Andros, and Crooked and Acklins Islands.

CAR & MOTORCYCLE

Road conditions Driving in busy downtown Nassau can be a pain due to narrow streets, heavy traffic and one-way street systems, but nothing citizens of busy cities aren't accustomed to. A danger in the Out Islands can be potholes: you can be cruising for ages on smooth road, then suddenly encounter an axle-cracking crater. Stay vigilant.

Rental Major international car-rental companies have outlets in Nassau, Freeport and other tourist centers, and there are a host of local firms and individuals to choose from. It can be as casual as arriving at the airport and asking around for someone who knows someone, especially in the Out Islands. Ask at your hotel or look for display boards at the airport. Renters must be 21 (some companies rent only to those 25 or older), and collision damage waiver insurance is around BS$15 per day (smaller local companies may not offer insurance). Rates start at around BS$55 per day. Golf carts are popular on the smaller islands and cays, and rent for about BS$50 to BS$70 per day.

Road rules In order to drive you must have a current license from your home country or state. A visitor can drive on their home license for three months. Drive on the left-hand side. At traffic circles (roundabouts), remember to circle in a clockwise direction, entering to the left. You must give way to traffic already in the circle. It's compulsory to wear a helmet when riding a motorcycle or scooter.

TAXI

There's no shortage of licensed taxis in Nassau and Freeport, where they can be hailed on the streets (many will actually hail you, if you seem in need of a lift). Taxis are also the main local transportation in the Out Islands, where they meet all incoming planes and ferries in the larger settlements.

All taxi operators are licensed. Taxi fares are fixed by the government according to distance, and rates are usually for two people (each additional person is charged a flat rate of BS$3). Fixed rates have been established from airports and cruise terminals to specific hotels and major destinations, and should be displayed in the taxi or at the airport/ferry terminal.

Barbados

☎1-246 / POP 285,000

Includes ➡

Best Places to Eat

- ➡ Fisherman's Pub (p217)
- ➡ Champers (p210)
- ➡ India Grill (p209)
- ➡ Nishi (p217)
- ➡ Castaway (p212)

Best Places to Stay

- ➡ Crane Beach Hotel (p214)
- ➡ Tamarind Hotel (p215)
- ➡ Little Arches Hotel (p212)
- ➡ Surfer's Point Guest House (p213)
- ➡ Coral Reef Club (p216)
- ➡ Eco Lifestyle Lodge (p220)

Why Go?

While it's justifiably famed for its fantastic beaches, Barbados is an island that has plenty more to offer. In addition to fine powdery sand and brilliant turquoise bays, you'll find smashing nightlife, a Unesco World Heritage–listed capital, a beautiful interior dotted with gardens, and wild surf on the lonely east coast, all inhabited by a proud, welcoming and extremely laid-back populace. It seems tailor-made for fun and relaxation.

Most visitors come to Barbados, check into one of the island's many comfortable resorts and barely leave the sun loungers. And it's hard to blame them. The gentle warm waters are the most picturesque in the region and make the perfect backdrop for an Instagram-worthy vacation.

But the island also holds wonderful surprises for those who get out and explore the Bajan culture – its very Caribbean take on traditional British traits is endlessly endearing.

When to Go

Nov–Mar The island's driest, hottest months from February to April are the most popular. Resorts tend to be full but there's still plenty of sand around.

Apr–May Plenty of dry weather but fewer crowds, accommodations tend to be cheaper.

Jun–Oct The wet season see fewer visitors and lower prices but some business closes up shop. In August the Crop-Over Festival reaches its climax.

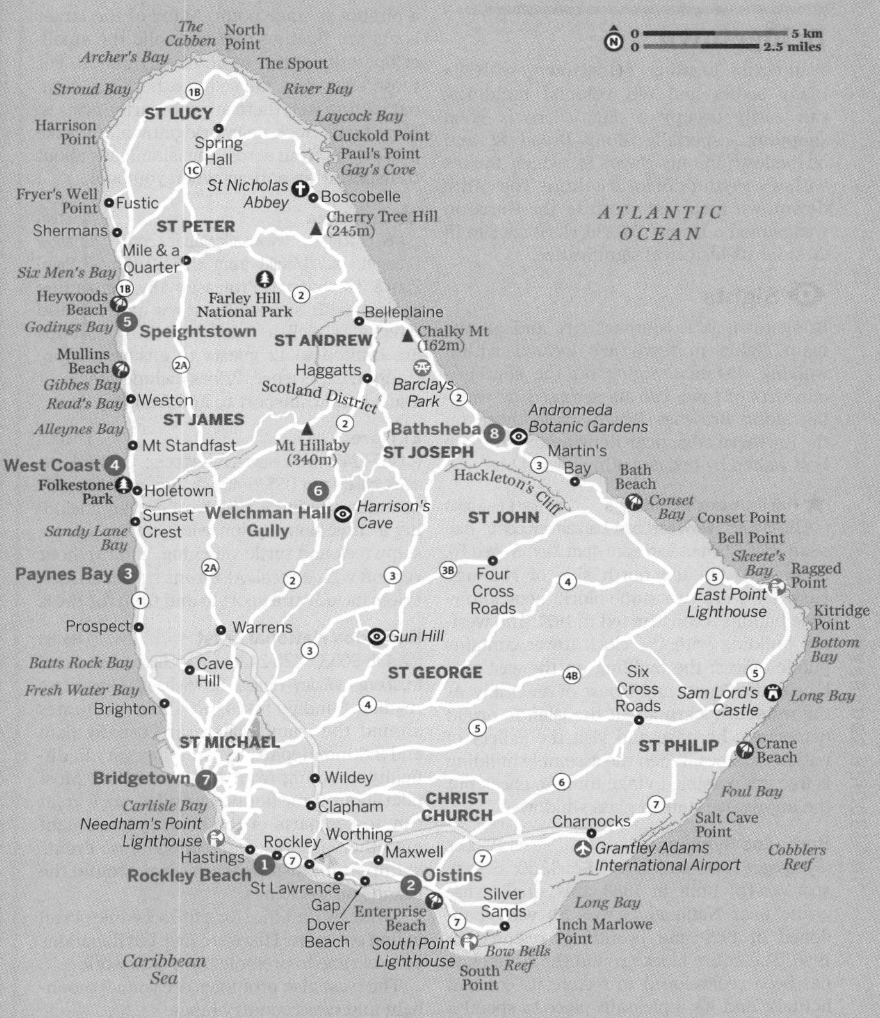

Barbados Highlights

1 Rockley Beach (p209) Unwinding on one of the island's most blissful beaches.

2 Oistins Fish Fry (p214) Dancing the night away at one of the Caribbean's great parties.

3 Paynes Bay (p215) Snorkeling with majestic sea turtles in warm tranquil waters.

4 West Coast (p214) Exploring the region in style aboard a sailing boat.

5 Speightstown (p217) Strolling the streets of this charismatic old port town.

6 Welchman Hall Gully (p219) Enjoying the lush beauty of the island's rich floral wonders.

7 Bridgetown (p205) Sampling Barbados' most popular meal, a flying-fish dish

8 Bathsheba (p219) Taking a road trip to the wild side to explore rugged shores.

Bridgetown

Wandering bustling Bridgetown, with its many sights and old colonial buildings, can easily occupy a day. There is good shopping, especially along Broad St and on pedestrian-only Swan St, which buzzes with the rhythms of local culture. The entire downtown area and south to the Garrison was named a Unesco World Heritage site in 2012 for its historical significance.

Sights

Bridgetown is a compact city and all the main sights in town are located within walking distance. Sights on the southern outskirts of town can be accessed by walking along Brownes Beach while those on the northern edge near Kensington Oval are best visited by taxi or taking a local bus.

★Parliament Buildings NOTABLE BUILDING
(☎310-5400; www.barbadosparliament.com; museum B$10; ⊙museum 9am-4pm Mon & Wed-Fri, to 3pm Sat) On the north side of National Heroes Sq are two stone-block, neo-Gothic-style buildings constructed in 1871. The western building with the clock tower contains public offices; the building on the east side houses the Senate and House of Assembly. At the **museum** learn about the island's proud democratic heritage and visit the gallery of national heroes. When the assembly building is free, it's possible to take tours to check out the impressive stained-glass windows.

Barbados Synagogue SYNAGOGUE
(Synagogue Lane; adult/child B$25/12.50; ⊙9am-4pm Mon-Fri) Built in 1833, this small synagogue near National Heroes Sq was abandoned in 1929 and beautifully restored in 1986. The entire block around the synagogue has been redeveloped to restore its colonial heritage and it's a pleasant place to spend a couple of hours. There's a little cafe in the old fire-station building.

Nidhe Israel Museum MUSEUM
(☎822-5421; Synagogue Lane; adult/child B$25/12.50; ⊙9am-4pm Mon-Fri) Housed in a restored 1750 Jewish community center, this museum documents the fascinating story of the Barbados Jewish community. Admission ticket also provides access to the synagogue.

Activities & Tours

Day cruises are a popular way to explore the island, especially the west coast, from a pirate's vantage point. Many of the larger boats are floating parties, while the smaller operations tend to be more tranquil. For those who want the scuba experience without getting wet, there are submarine cruises. Most boats dock near Bridgetown, but take passengers from across the island; ask about transportation options when you book.

★Calabaza BOATING
(☎826-4048; www.sailcalabaza.com; Shallow Draught; adult/child from US$110/90; ⊙9am-2pm & 2:45-6:15pm) Professionally run sailing cruises with snorkeling stops at reefs and wrecks as well as turtle-watching. Groups are limited to 12 guests to ensure a more tranquil experience. Prices include snacks or a meal and transport to and from the dock.

El Tigre BOATING
(☎417-7245; www.eltigrecruises.com; Cavans Lane; adult/child from US$75/40) A fun and friendly operator offering a variety of cruises, including a three-hour option with snorkeling at a shipwreck and turtle-watching, and five-hour version with a meal. Also runs sunset cruises. Prices include transport to and from the dock.

Barbados National Trust HIKING
(☎436-9033, 426-2421; www.barbadosnationaltrust.org; Wildey House, St Michael) Organizes regular Sunday hikes on different routes around the island. There are usually 6am and 3:30pm departures and they vary in difficulty, covering from 10km to 20km. Most take about three hours. The hikes are a great way to see parts of the country you might not otherwise. Also runs open-house events at important historical buildings around the islands on weekends.

Swing by the office for a full schedule or call to find out more. Hikes are free, but donations are welcome to promote the trust's work.

The trust also promotes occasional moonlight and cross country hikes.

Festivals & Events

Barbados Food & Rum Festival FOOD & DRINK
(www.foodandrum.com; ⊙Oct) Local chefs and mixologists join forces with international invitees at this constantly expanding culinary festival with events all over the island and plenty of opportunities to sample the best local rums.

Sleeping & Eating

Few visitors stay in Bridgetown and there aren't many accommodations available.

Aquatic Gap, just south of town, is the first spot with any hotels to speak of, though it's worth heading the few minutes further to Hastings, Rockley, Worthing, St Lawrence Gap or beyond for a more relaxed beach atmosphere.

Bridgetown is the best place to enjoy genuine local food and genuine local prices. You can find cheap eats at any of the markets around town, which are generally open from 7am to late afternoon Monday to Saturday.

★Mustor's Restaurant CARIBBEAN **$**
(McGregor St; lunch B$14-20; ⌚10am-3:45pm Mon-Fri) Climb the stairs to a large, plain dining room. Choose from staples such as baked pork chops and flying fish. Then select the sides – we love the macaroni pie. Finally, hope for an open balcony table.

Pink Star Bar CARIBBEAN **$**
(Baxters Rd; cutters from B$5; ⌚7pm-6am) Located on rough-and-ready Baxters Rd, Pink Star is famous among locals for being the cheapest place in town to fill your stomach. It opens in the evenings and runs through to dawn serving liver cutters (sandwiches), fried chicken necks and steppers (chicken feet) to the drunk and hungry masses. It's the Caribbean version of an all-night greasy-kebab spot.

Waterfront Cafe CAFE **$$**
(☎427-0093; www.waterfrontcafe.com.bb; Careenage; sandwiches B$30-35, mains B$42-89; ⌚9am-6pm Mon-Wed, to 10pm Thu-Sat) Always packed, especially the breezy tables on the river. Lunches include a fine version of a flying-fish sandwich; dinners are more elaborate and have Mediterranean color and flair. There's live music ranging from steel pan to jazz – check out the web page to find out what's on.

Lobster Alive SEAFOOD **$$$**
(☎435-0305; www.lobsteralive.net; Bay St; lobster mains B$105-195; ⌚noon-4pm & 6-9pm Wed-Sat, noon-5pm Sun) The name is only true until you order. Lobster bisque and grilled lobster are just some of the choices on the menu at this cute joint on the beach. A huge tank holds hundreds of the namesake critters at any given time – all flown in from the Grenadines. At lunch there's steel-pan music while in the evening it's smooth jazz.

Drinking & Nightlife

On the south side of town, along Bay St, there is a collection of rum shops and bars, but stick to the main drag because one block back you'll be among shady Nelson St's brothels. For a daylight drink, check out the beach bars right on the sand at the northern end of Carlisle Bay.

Bridgetown's many rum shops are patronized by local regulars, though visitors are not unwelcome. Although women will not be turned away, be warned that rum shops are a macho haunt.

Pirate's Cove BAR
(☎832-7413; Lower Bay St, Carlisle Bay; ⌚8am-8pm) On the closest stretch of sand to Bridgetown, this beach bar is less than a 10-minute walk from downtown but feels far from the bustle. The sand is soft and white, the water brilliantly blue and the drinks are cold. It pulls in a fun, mixed crowd of Bajans and visitors. Beach chairs and snorkeling tours are available for a fee.

Well-priced meals are served.

Shopping

Broad St, in the city center, is the place for higher-end shopping, while Swan St, one block back, is more blue collar with plenty of shops hawking cheap products.

Pelican Craft Village ARTS & CRAFTS
(Princess Alice Hwy; ⌚10am-5pm Mon-Sat) This ever-evolving complex of galleries, souvenir stands and workshops, between downtown and the cruise-ship terminal, features the works of many local artists. You'll find paintings, jewelry, pottery and some particularly well-crafted woodwork among the crafts on sale. There are also a couple of bars and spas for relaxation between purchases.

Information

Post office (Cheapside; ⌚7:30am-5pm Mon-Fri) Next to the Cheapside Market.

Queen Elizabeth Hospital (☎436-6450; www.qehconnect.com; Martindale's Rd; ⌚24hr)

Getting There & Away

The main bus stations are inconveniently located on opposite sides of town and there's no service between them, so if you're traveling from north to south, or vice versa, you'll either need to cross town on foot (15 minutes) or take a taxi (B$10). Terminals include the following:

Bridgetown

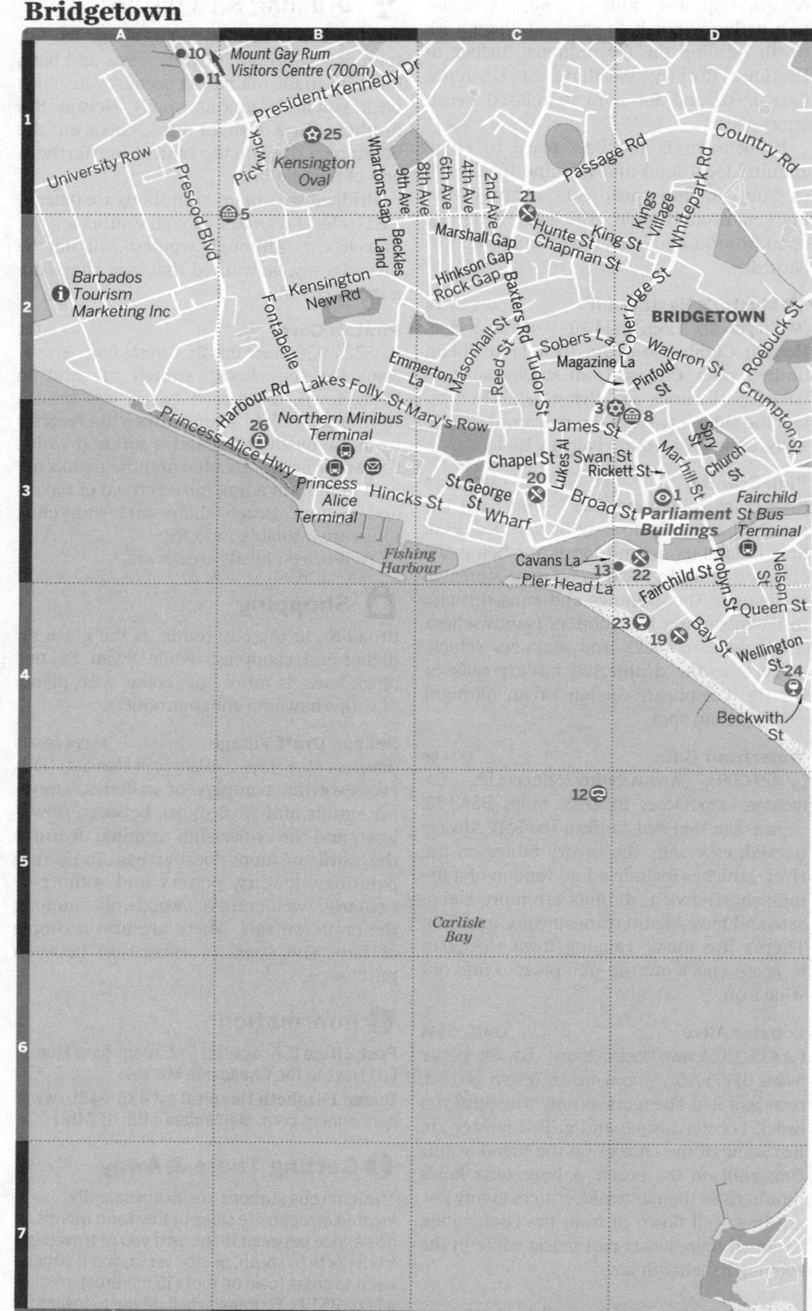

A
B
C
D
1
2
3
4
5
6
7
10
11
Mount Gay Rum Visitors Centre (700m)
President Kennedy Dr
Country Rd
University Row
Pickwick
25
Kensington Oval
Prescod Blvd
Whartons Gap
9th Ave
8th Ave
6th Ave
4th Ave
2nd Ave
Passage Rd
Whitepark Rd
Kings Village
21
5
Hunte St
King St
Chapman St
Marshall Gap
Beckles Land
Hinkson Gap
Rock Gap
Barbados Tourism Marketing Inc
Kensington New Rd
Fontabelle
Baxters Rd
Coleridge St
BRIDGETOWN
Roebuck St
Masonhall St
Reed St
Tudor St
Sobers La
Magazine La
Waldron St
Pinfold St
Emmerton La
Crumpton St
Harbour Rd
Lakes Folly
St Mary's Row
26
Princess Alice Hwy
Northern Minibus Terminal
3
8
James St
Spry St
Church St
Marhill St
Chapel St
Swan St
Rickett St
Lukes Al
20
Princess Alice Terminal
Hincks St
St George St
Wharf
Broad St
1
Parliament Buildings
Fairchild St Bus Terminal
Fishing Harbour
Cavans La
13
22
Pier Head La
Fairchild St
Probyn St
Nelson St
Queen St
23
19
Bay St
Wellington St
24
Beckwith St
12
Carlisle Bay

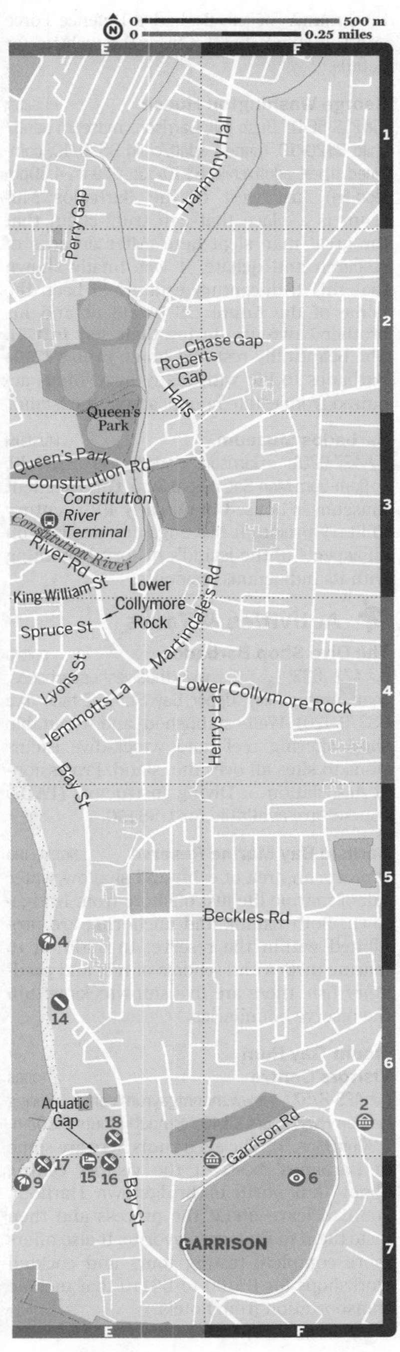

Bridgetown

Top Sights
1 Parliament Buildings ... D3

Sights
2 Barbados Museum ... F6
3 Barbados Synagogue ... D3
4 Brownes Beach ... E5
5 Cricket Legends of Barbados ... B1
6 Garrison Savannah Area ... F7
7 George Washington House ... F7
8 Nidhe Israel Museum ... D3
9 Pebbles Beach ... E7

Activities, Courses & Tours
10 Atlantis ... A1
11 Calabaza ... A1
12 Carlisle Bay Marine Reserve ... C5
13 El Tigre ... D3
14 The Dive Shop Barbados ... E6

Sleeping
15 Island Inn Hotel ... E7

Eating
16 Brown Sugar ... E7
17 Cuz's Fish Shack ... E7
18 India Grill ... E6
19 Lobster Alive ... D4
20 Mustor's Restaurant ... C3
21 Pink Star Bar ... C1
22 Waterfront Cafe ... D3

Drinking & Nightlife
23 Pirate's Cove ... D4
24 Smith Corner Pub ... D4

Entertainment
25 Barbados Cricket Association ... B1

Shopping
26 Pelican Craft Village ... B3

Constitution River Terminal (Nursery Rd) Yellow medium-sized buses and white vans south, central and east.

Fairchild St Bus Terminal (Bridge St) Public buses south and east.

Northern Minibus Terminal (Princess Alice Hwy) Minibuses north.

Princess Alice Terminal (Princess Alice Hwy) Public buses north.

Bridgetown Region

There are many worthwhile sights within 5km of Bridgetown's center, especially to the south where you'll find the Garrison Savannah Unesco World Heritage site.

You don't have to travel far to reach good beaches either. Carlisle Bay, just a 10-minute walk from town, has a couple of first-class stretches of sand.

Sights

Cricket Legends of Barbados MUSEUM

(☎227-2651; Herbert House, Fontabelle; B$20; ⊙10am-4pm Mon-Fri) A must for cricket fans, this museum is the best of its kind in the Caribbean. The walls are plastered with press clippings and there are many interesting artifacts from the game. The rear wall downstairs features an impressive roll call of Barbados' many great cricketers. Large groups can even get one of the legends to show them around.

Brownes Beach BEACH

(Hwy 7) A fine beach close to downtown Bridgetown (a 10-minute walk) that makes a good break before and after lunch and shopping. A long white crescent of sand bends along with the brilliant waters of Carlisle Bay. Lots of parking and shade trees plus shacks selling drinks.

Pebbles Beach BEACH

(Aquatic Gap) Running between two high-end hotels, this lovely stretch of sand is really just an extension of Brownes Beach. It has soft sands and calm waters and is home to water-sports outfitters. It offers a lively ambience rather than island tranquility and can get a bit crowded, but is a fine place to hang out.

Garrison Savannah Area HISTORIC SITE

(www.barbadosgarrison.org) About 2km south of central Bridgetown and inland from Carlisle Bay, the Garrison is part of the World Heritage area and was the home of the British command in the 1800s. A focal point is the oval-shaped Savannah, which was once parade grounds and is now used for cricket games, jogging and Saturday horse races.

Standing along the west side of the Savannah are some of the Garrison's more ornate colonial buildings, where you'll find the world's largest collection of 17th-century cannons. A network of tunnels built by British armed forces have been discovered beneath the Garrison and it's possible to visit one stretch beginning at George Washington House. The Garrison administration runs a number of interesting tours through the area – including a Thursday-morning tour for military buffs that includes the tunnels and access to normally restricted forts on the grounds of the Barbados Defence Force and the Hilton hotel. Check the website for details.

George Washington House MUSEUM

(☎228-5641; Bush Hill, Garrison; museum adult/child B$20/10, tunnels adult/child B$20/10, combined ticket adult/child B$30/15; ⊙9am-4:30pm Mon-Fri) Just west of the Barbados Museum is a place that can truly claim that the great man slept here. After decades of research and debate, it was finally shown that this 18th-century estate had been the home of the future US president and his brother Lawrence during their stay in 1751. The beautifully restored home brings 1750s Barbados to life with many furnishings acquired from estate houses across the island.

Barbados Museum MUSEUM

(☎427-0201; Garrison; adult/child B$20/10; ⊙9am-5pm Mon-Sat, 2-6pm Sun) This excellent museum is housed in an early 19th-century military prison. It has engaging displays on all aspects of the island's history, beginning with its indigenous residents.

Activities & Tours

The Dive Shop Barbados DIVING

(☎422-3133; www.thediveshopbarbados.com; Ameys Alley, Upper Bay St; 1-/2-tank dive US$70/120) Well-established and reputable shop offering reef- and wreck-dive excursions to sites all over the island. Professional Association of Diving Instructors (PADI) courses are available for US$450.

Carlisle Bay Marine Reserve SNORKELING

Protects an area of calm and shallow water full of marine life just offshore from Bridgetown. Both fishing and anchoring are prohibited within the reserve. In addition to marine turtles and schools of reef and predatory fish, there are five shipwrecks within the reserve boundaries.

Mount Gay Rum Visitors Centre TOURS

(☎425-8757; www.mountgayrum.com; Spring Garden Hwy; tours B$40; ⊙hourly tours 9:30am-2:30pm Mon-Fri) The aged rums here are some of Barbados' best. At the visitors centre, about 1km north of Bridgetown Harbour, you can learn about the process and then taste them to find your favorite. It also offers more complete tasting tours and cocktail workshops for B$100 to B$140 that include transportation from hotels.

Sleeping & Eating

There are a couple of good hotels and midrange resorts on the southern edge of the Garrison, particularly around Aquatic Gap and on the road towards Hastings. A number of big-chain hotels can be found at Needhams Point.

Island Inn Hotel RESORT $$$
(☎436-6393; www.islandinnbarbados.com; Aquatic Gap; s/d from US$360/435; ❄@📶≋) This 24-room, all-inclusive hotel is partially built in a restored 1804 garrison building that was originally a military rum store. It is near the beach off Bay St and close to town. It has been completely renovated and boasts elegant decoration with muted island-chic motifs.

India Grill CARIBBEAN $
(☎436-2361; Bay St; roti B$14-25; ⏲11am-3:45pm Mon-Sat) Ask serious roti connoisseurs the best place on the island to indulge and they'll point you to this simple hole-in-the-wall restaurant at the entrance to Aquatic Gap. It also does curry and rice, but the rotis are where it's at.

Cuz's Fish Shack SEAFOOD $
(Pebbles Beach; sandwiches B$9-10; ⏲10am-4pm) Doles out stupendously juicy fish cutters from a beachside food truck. Add cheese and hot sauce and you have some of the Caribbean's best fast food.

Brown Sugar CARIBBEAN $$
(☎426-7684; www.brownsugarbarbados.net; Aquatic Gap; lunch buffet B$69, mains B$42-95; ⏲noon-2:30pm Sun-Fri, 6-9:30pm daily) The much-loved Brown Sugar at Aquatic Gap is a lush paradise inside and out. The excellent West Indian buffet includes a variety of starters, half a dozen mains, salads and sweet delights. Dinner is off a menu that includes shrimp Creole, lobster, flying fish and much more. The Bajan bread pudding is a rummy delight. Book for dinner.

Getting There & Away

You can walk from downtown Bridgetown to the Garrisson Savannah area; walking along Brownes Beach is far nicer than along the busy road. Alternatively, hop on any Oistins-bound van or bus.

South Coast

The south coast is the island's midrange-tourism epicenter. This virtually uninterrupted stretch of development – and beach – runs from the outskirts of Bridgetown all the way to the airport.

Hastings, Rockley and Worthing are part of one long commercial strip. St Lawrence Gap and Dover Beach is a surprisingly appealing area off the main road. Next up is the more relaxed pace of Maxwell and the fishing community of Oistins. East of here, development begins to thin out until the end of the road at Silver Sands, a residential area popular for wind sports. The entire area is within Christ Church Parish.

Getting There & Away

All of the south-coast towns are linked by the main road along the coast, which, while designated Hwy 7, is never actually called that, rather taking on a variety of names depending on the town it is passing through.

Frequent minibuses from the Route Taxi Terminal in Bridgetown run along Hwy 7 down to Silver Sands and link all the south-coast villages. Less frequent large blue buses leave from the Fairchild St Terminal and run the same route before continuing on to the southeast coast, ending at Sam Lord's Castle. There's also a blue bus service from the south coast all the way up to Speightstown that bypasses Bridgetown.

Private taxis are fairly easy to find throughout this area. Expect to pay B$20 to B$25 to travel between south-coast villages while a taxi into Bridgetown will run B$30 to B$35.

Hastings & Rockley

Hastings and Rockley are home to some attractive, popular beaches. Commercialism rules here, although there's an attractive boardwalk on the waterfront east of Hastings. There are plenty of shops, banks and ATMs along the main road, Hwy 7.

Sights

★**Rockley Beach** BEACH
(Accra Beach; Rockley Main Rd) The largest beach in the area, Rockley is a picture-perfect crescent of sand. Backed by shade trees, there's moderate surf. The new boardwalk allows you to walk west for more than 3km to Hastings.

Sleeping & Eating

Coconut Court Beach Resort HOTEL $$$
(427-1655; www.coconut-court.com; Main Rd, Hastings; r US$290-359;) A five-story, beachfront, 112-room hotel filled with package tourists that's fairly good for families. In the right light, the institutional green paint can take on a turquoise hue from the azure waters out front. There are different room categories, the cheaper ones are actually bigger but don't have as good a view. Avoid rooms across the road in the annex.

All rooms have balconies or terraces plus minimal kitchen facilities, but if you want to prepare anything more complex than toast you'll want one of the studio apartments.

Punchline VEGETARIAN $
(Hastings Main Rd; smoothies B$12-13, mains B$11-32; 11am-8pm Mon-Thu, to 9pm Fri & Sat;) Vegetarians, vegans and pescatarians can all get their fill at this awesome little eatery on the main road in Hastings that serves a variety of delicious light meals. There are many varieties of veggie burger as well as wraps, salads and awesome smoothies. On the fish front there are great cutters alongside fish and salad plates.

Champers SEAFOOD $$$
(434-3463; www.champersbarbados.com; Skeetes Hill, Rockley; dinner mains B$54-99; 11:30am-3pm Sun-Fri, 6-9:30pm daily) This longtime favorite has a dreamy location overlooking Rockley Beach. Elegant meals include the usual range of grilled seafood plus fresh pasta. Brits will understand the name means 'Champagne' – drink some in the lower-level lounge. At lunch there's a three-course menu for B$89.

Worthing

Worthing is a good base if you're on a tight budget but still want to be near the action. It has a pretty, uncrowded beach and good transportation links.

The area was hit by a sewage crisis in 2017/18 when waste waters continually bubbled up into the streets, shuttering commerce and decimating tourism, and creating a mountain of negative headlines for an island that depends greatly on tourism.

However with the infrastructure now sorted Worthing is bouncing back.

Sights

Sandy Beach BEACH
This wonderful strip of white powdery sand was hit hard by the sewage failures of 2017/18 when it was closed to visitors after waste from nearby roads washed into the sea, making waters unsafe for swimming and the sands an unpleasant place to be. It has now been officially reopened and government scientists report that the brilliant turquoise waters are completely safe.

Sleeping

Crystal Waters GUESTHOUSE $
(435-7514; 1st Ave; s/d from US$61/79;) With a fantastic location right on Sandy Beach, this traditional guesthouse has plenty of character. The simple but elegant fan-cooled rooms have polished hardwood floors and classic furniture, while the breezy common room opens onto a fantastic veranda overlooking the turquoise Caribbean. The shared breakfast downstairs is a social affair that's a great place to meet partners for sightseeing trips.

House Cleverdale GUESTHOUSE $
(826-0772; info@barbados-rentals.com; 4th Ave; r from US$65;) Set back just a bit from Sandy Beach and away from the main road, this large wooden home is a popular budget spot. The three rooms and two apartments are clean and some boast split air-con units and flatscreen TVs. Some rooms have shared bathrooms and there's a large communal kitchen.

It's not fancy, but if you want to meet other travelers in the common rooms and never, ever wear shoes, you'll love it. The owner has other cheap places nearby.

Maraval Guesthouse & Apartments GUESTHOUSE $
(435-7437; www.maravalbarbados.com; 3rd Ave; r from US$40, apt US$100-150;) On a tiny lane near Sandy Beach, Maraval is a fantastic budget choice with simple but spotless rooms in a vintage beach house. Don't be put off by the decidedly rickety 2nd floor which is not part of the guesthouse; downstairs there's a spacious kitchen, a pleasant common room and an appealing communal vibe.

Coral Mist Beach Hotel HOTEL $$
(435-7712; www.coralmistbarbados.com; Worthing Main Rd; r US$213-353;) This fairly compact and traditional beachfront hotel

wins plaudits for its ideal beachfront location. All 32 rooms have kitchen facilities, balconies and views of the blinding-white beach. You can walk to much nearby.

Eating & Drinking

Carib Beach Bar CARIBBEAN $$
(2nd Ave; mains B$30-45; ⏲10am-11pm) This open-air bar/restaurant right on Sandy Beach is a local hot spot at all hours. It's good for traditional local fare and drinks either on the deck or at tables on the sand under coconut palms. On Sunday evenings it hosts a regular party night with live music and local DJs that draws a good mixed crowd and goes on until late.

Mojo BAR
(Hwy 7; ⏲11am-late) A real bar in a big old house by the side of the road, Mojo has a wide open-air veranda plus all sorts of nooks inside for nuzzling your companion or listening to the excellent music. Monday is open-mic night. Good burgers.

St Lawrence Gap & Dover Beach

Blink and you'll miss the tiny village of St Lawrence, which pretty much gets lost among the urban development on Hwy 7 south of Worthing. The real action here lies along a 1.6km-long spur road that runs close to the beach and is lined with hotels, bars, restaurants and shops. The west end is known as St Lawrence Gap; the east end carries the Dover Beach moniker.

It's Barbados' most famed nightlife zone and is mostly free of traffic, allowing nighttime strolling.

Dover Beach itself is worth a visit while the sun is out. It has a nice, broad ribbon of white sand that attracts swimmers, bodysurfers and windsurfers although some parts have quite a lot of rocks in the water.

Courses

Barry's Surf Barbados SURFING
(☎256-3906; www.surfing-barbados.com; Salt Ash Apts, Dover) A long-running outfit that transports beginners and experienced surfers to the breaks that best suit their needs. Beginners classes cost US$75 for the first class and US$60 for additional classes. Includes free rental for the rest of the day to practice so it's worth taking morning lessons. Also rents boards.

DON'T MISS

CROP-OVER FESTIVAL

The island's top event, the **Crop-Over Festival** (www.barbadoscropoverfestival.com; ⏲Jul & Aug) originated in colonial times as a celebration to mark the end of the sugarcane harvest. The main festivities stretch over a three-week period, beginning in mid-July with spirited calypso competitions, fairs and other activities. The festival culminates with a Carnival-like costume parade and fireworks on Kadooment Day, a national holiday, in August.

Thousands cavort, dance and strut their stuff in a madcap procession where the air pulses with music and is alive with wafting feathers.

Sleeping

Rio Guest House HOSTEL $
(☎428-1546; St Lawrence Gap; s/d from US$35/45; ❄@📶) This family-run backpacker special has nine unpretentious, fan-cooled rooms. Singles share a bathroom and some rooms have optional air-con and kitchens. It's in a tranquil location, off the main drag but about one minute from the beach and nightlife.

Yellow Bird Hotel HOTEL $$
(☎418-8444; www.yellowbirdbarbados.com; St Lawrence Gap; r US$237, 2-bed apt US$363; ❄📶🏊) This modern, four-story block sits right at the west entrance to the Gap. Excellent modern studios have kitchens and all the mod cons, but the best part is the sunset views from the balconies. It's across a narrow street from the water and there's a small pool in front. Larger apartments are also available.

Dover Beach Hotel HOTEL $$
(☎428-8076; www.doverbeach.com; Dover Rd; r US$180-255; ❄@📶🏊) You go down a tiny lane to reach this gracious, secluded and older beach hotel, tucked into a corner at the east end of the Gap. The main three-story building surrounds a good-sized pool and large oceanfront terrace with access to a stretch of white sand that lies to the side.

Southern Palms Beach Club RESORT $$$
(☎428-7171; www.southernpalms.net; St Lawrence Gap; r US$325-550; ❄@📶🏊) A traditional beach resort that stays in the pink, literally

– the various blocks of rooms are decked out in a cheery pink tone. It is a large place, but still has plenty of character and is fronted by a fine stretch of white sand.

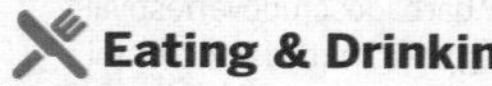

Eating & Drinking

Castaway CARIBBEAN $$$
(☎420-7587; St Lawrence Gap; mains B$48-90; ⏰5pm-1am Mon-Thu, 11am-1am Fri-Sun; last meal orders 9:45pm) Set right on the water at the entrance to the Gap, this fantastic open-air bistro has a good selection of mains and great pizzas – order the 'Bajan Style' with grilled chicken, plantain, bacon and local hot sauce. The fun, relaxed atmosphere makes it an excellent place to stick around for drinks after the plates are cleared away.

Harlequin INTERNATIONAL $$$
(☎420-7677; www.harlequinrestaurant.com; St Lawrence Gap; mains B$38-109; ⏰6-10pm;) The deck at this relaxed open-air bistro doesn't back onto the water like some of its neighbors, but it makes up for the lack of view with an excellent varied menu of carefully prepared dishes and professional service. In addition to Bajan classics you'll also find pastas, Thai-spiced dishes and imported steaks and lamb. Reservations recommended.

Old Jamm Inn BAR
(☎428-3919; St Lawrence Gap; ⏰6pm-3am) This spacious bar is popular with both locals and visitors and plays a somewhat frustrating mix of good dancehall and bad pop. There's an air-con dance floor out the back where plenty of simulated loving goes on, but the best seats in the house are the bar stools on the deck at the front overlooking the Gap's comings and goings.

Oistins

This decidedly local yet modern town, a few kilometers east of St Lawrence, is best known as the center of the island's fishing industry. Oistins' heart is the large, bustling seaside fish market, which on Friday hosts the island's most popular party.

Sights & Activities

★Miami Beach BEACH
(Enterprise Beach; Oistins Bay) A somewhat hidden gem that is the antithesis of its American namesake. Small, shady and intimate, it's well removed from the often frenetic south-coast pace. The beach is divided into two sections by a rock breakwater. The west side is one of the premier swimming spots on the island, with deep, calm and crystal-clear waters, while the east side has a wide recreation area featuring picnic tables under shady evergreen pines and almond trees.

Ride the Tide SURFING
(www.ridethetidebarbados.com; Enterprise Dr; group/private lessons B$150/190) With a small office across the road from the Freights Bay break, this is one of the more organized surf schools on the island. Offers classes at points all over the island depending on swell and skill level. Free board hire included after classes.

Festivals & Events

Oistins Fish Festival CULTURAL
The largest community-based festival in the country commemorates the signing of the Charter of Barbados and celebrates the skills of local fisherfolk. It's a seaside festivity with events focusing on boat races, fish-filleting competitions, local foods, crafts and dancing. Held over the Easter weekend.

Sleeping & Eating

There are few hotels in Oistins town itself but just to the north in Maxwell, or to the south in the Enterprise area, there's a variety of options.

★Little Arches Hotel BOUTIQUE HOTEL $$$
(☎420-4689; www.littlearches.com; Enterprise Beach Rd, Miami Beach; r US$340-580;) Possibly the best boutique hotel on the south coast. Once a Mediterranean-style mansion, the hotel now has 10 rooms in a variety of shapes and sizes, some with private whirlpool baths and plunge pools. The decor combines bright Caribbean colors with restrained luxury, such as deeply comfortable wicker chairs. It's on the quiet Miami Beach access road.

Golden Sands CARIBBEAN $$
(☎428-8051; Maxwell Main Rd; pudding & souse from B$10, mains B$20-45; ⏰6:30am-10pm) This unassuming restaurant out the back of a hotel is a great place to try some traditional Bajan dishes, especially on Saturday when it serves souse – pickled pieces of pork served cold with steamed potato and blood pudding. It includes all parts (ears and feet are highly prized), but if you're feeling squeamish you can order 'steam and lean', the all-meat version.

Getting There & Away

Minivans running along the south coast from Bridgetown stop right in the heart of Oistins village, in front of the fish fry. Vans get fairly crowded on Fridays so you might have to squeeze in by the doorway or hop on another passenger's lap.

If you want to go further south to the airport, or beyond to the southeast, blue-and-yellow buses pass through on their way to Sam Lord's Castle.

You'll find plenty of taxis circulating on the main road.

Silver Sands

At the southernmost tip of the island, between Oistins and the airport, is the sleepy suburban area of Silver Sands. It's a sun-baked corner of the island that doesn't get that many visitors. The real action here is out on the water, where the regular winds attract serious kitesurfing enthusiasts.

Activities

Surfing, whether powered by waves, kite or sail, is the huge draw here.

★deAction Beach Shop KITESURFING
(☎428-2027; www.briantalma.com; Round the Rock; 6hr course US$450, 2hr rentals US$60; ⌚8am-dusk) Run by board legend Brian Talma, this shop is set on one of the hemisphere's premier spots for windsurfing and kitesurfing. With a cold Banks at the cafe, watch huge kites twirl about the sky while riders hop the waves below. It also rents surf and stand-up paddle (SUP) boards.

Zed's Surfing Adventures SURFING
(☎428-7873; www.zedssurftravel.com; Surfer's Point; board rental per 2hr/day/week US$25/40/160, lessons from US$80; ⌚9am-5pm Mon-Sat) An experienced outfit offering tours and classes island-wide. Board hire for the week is thrown in If you take three lessons. Beginners classes are usually run on the local beach or at Freight's Bay.

Sleeping & Eating

Many kitesurfers and windsurfers stay a night or two in a hotel and then, through word of mouth, find a shared house or apartment nearby (simple doubles for around US$50 a night can be found in high season – ask at the activity shops).

★Surfer's Point Guest House GUESTHOUSE $$
(☎428-7873; www.zedssurftravel.com; Surfer's Point; apt US$150-250; ❄@📶) The HQ of Zed's Surfing Adventures is on a pretty little point just steps from the sand and a very good break. The seven comfortable units here surround well-maintained grounds and come in various sizes; some have balconies with views, all have kitchens and wi-fi. Friendly staff hit the perfect balance of efficiency and tranquility.

Moonraker Beach Hotel HOTEL $$
(☎262-5483; www.moonrakerbarbados.com; Landsdown; r US$130, apt from US$160; ❄📶🏊) Simple modern rooms with tiled floors and small balconies open onto grounds with a small pool just steps from the waves. It's remote and service can be a bit lax but it's peaceful and good value.

Ocean Spray Beach Apartments APARTMENT $$
(☎428-5426; www.oceansprayapartments.com; Inch Marlow; r US$135-175; 📶) Salt spray from the pounding surf mists the air at this attractive and modern 25-unit apartment complex. Balconies on rooms with views offer a captivating spectacle of the famous local surf. Relax with a cranberry juice and vodka. The excellent on-site restaurant does healthy breakfasts and brunches using local farm-fresh ingredients.

Surfer's Bay CARIBBEAN $$
(☎262-5483; Landsdown; mains B$26-59; ⌚noon-9pm) Set on a slightly ramshackle wooden deck overlooking the waves below, this low-key spot really does nail the island hideaway vibe. The menu – written on the board above the bar – is small but it's all pretty tasty. Don't expect fast service – that would go against everything this place stands for.

Getting There & Away

Silver Sands is the end of the line for minivans running along Hwy 7 from Bridgetown. Service is frequent, but they don't all go down to the water's edge, so you may have to walk a couple of blocks up to the main road.

Southeast Coast & Crane Beach

St Philip, the diamond-shaped parish east of the airport, is sparsely populated, with a scattering of small villages. It's a great place to escape the crowds and explore the island's wilderness. Along the coast are a couple of resort hotels and fine beaches including long and wild Crane Beach and the beautiful tiny sheltered cove at Shark Hole.

Sights

★Shark Hole BEACH
Well off the beaten track, the pint-sized Shark Hole is one of those special places for which your selfie will not do justice. Down a short flight of steps, a small stretch of delicate white sand is totally enclosed by rocks that wrap around 300 degrees, forming a perfect secluded cove. A reef just offshore calms the water, creating a perfect natural saltwater swimming pool.

★Bottom Bay BEACH
On an island blessed with beautiful stretches of sand, Bottom Bay is up there with the best. With translucent turquoise waters framed by rocks and windswept palms, it's a remote piece of paradise where you won't have to share the sands with hordes of visitors. The only downside is the strong currents that make swimming tricky.

Crane Beach BEACH
Crane Beach, 7km northeast of the airport, is a hidden beach cove backed by cliffs and fronted by aqua-blue waters. An adventurous trail over rocks along the water provides access to the beach from the end of a small road about 700m east of the Crane Beach Hotel. Parking is competitive, only three vehicles fit at the trailhead, but the sands are simply wonderful. Bring a picnic and make a day of it.

Sleeping & Eating

Crane Beach Hotel RESORT $$$
(☎423-6220; www.thecrane.com; Crane Main Rd; r from US$895;) Dating to 1887, the roots of this gracious resort can still be found in the lovely restaurants set in classic buildings that overlook the beach and ocean. Much of the complex is quite modern, with hundreds of luxurious condos decked out with high-end furnishings and mod cons. Some have fantastic views and all have access to the lavish resort facilities.

Delon's Roti & Bar CARIBBEAN $
(Remora Ave, Crane; items B$2-9; ⌚6-8pm Mon-Fri, to 9pm Sat & Sun) An authentic little place set in the pebbled driveway of a suburban house just north of the Crane complex, Delon's is a great choice for a cheap meal or a cold beer. Food is tasty and unpretentious – choose from rotis, cutters, bakes and more filling mains and pull up a table while the resident DJ belts out the tunes.

Getting There & Away

Large blue buses and midsized yellow buses from the Fairchild St Bus Terminal in Bridgetown run through St Philip to Sam Lord's Castle, dropping visitors within walking distance of many of the area's beaches.

West Coast

Barbados' west coast has lovely tranquil beaches that are largely hidden by the majority of the island's luxury hotels and walled estates. It's known to some as the Platinum

DON'T MISS

OISTINS FISH FRY

The legendary **Oistins Fish Fry** (Oistins Main Rd; mains B$25-40; ⌚food 6-10:30pm Fri & Sat) attracts masses of tourists but locals still like to come down for a fish meal and a beer, especially on Friday night, which is significantly more hectic than the fish fry's other main night, Saturday. It's held in a complex of low-rise modern buildings next to the fish market.

Most of the stalls serve the same menu: grilled fish and shellfish, pork chops, ribs and chicken. Sides include macaroni pie, chips, plantain, grilled breadfruit, garlic bread and more. Unless you specify, you'll get a bit of each side with your main. Just because there are more than 30 vendors serving the same menu doesn't mean all are created equal, however. Go with the crowds; they know. Buy a cheap and icy bottle of Banks and plunge in.

There's a large stage in the middle of the complex where DJs belt out high-volume sets while dancers show off their moves to the crowd – don't expect much conversation during your meal.

While most of the action is on the weekends, if you're not into partying with the crowds – which can involve long lines and crammed minibuses – you can usually find a couple of places serving meals and snacks, including tasty fish cakes, during off-peak moments.

Coast, a moniker earned either from the color of the sand or the color of the credit cards.

In colonial times, the area was a popular holiday retreat for the upper crust of British society. These days the villas that haven't been converted to resorts are owned by the wealthy and famous. That's on the water side, of course. On the *other* side of Hwy 1 are modest huts and simple vacation retreats. Although the beaches are all public, the near-constant development means you only get a few coastal glimpses.

Getting There & Away

The west coast is served by both the large blue buses and midsized yellow vehicles that depart from the Princess Alice Terminal in Bridgetown, running up to Speightstown. Minivans do not run along this route.

If you're coming or going to the south coast there are direct blue buses that run between Oistins and the west coast without entering Bridgetown.

For points further north, buses and minibuses run up the west coast from the Speightstown terminal, passing through Weston, Mt Standfast, Shermans and Moon Town.

Paynes Bay

Chic Paynes Bay in St James boasts one of the best beaches on the island. The village itself is little more than a collection of high-end hotels and luxury homes, along with a couple of places to eat and a fish market at the southern end.

Sights

Paynes Bay Beach BEACH

Fringed by a fine stretch of sand, gently curving Paynes Bay is endlessly popular and its calm waters make it one of the west coast's best spots for swimming and snorkeling (if you're patient enough there's a very good chance of seeing sea turtles).

There are three public access points. The easiest is next to the fish market on the south side, where there are a couple of parking spots, but the bay is more picturesque further north. The middle access is a narrow alley between houses about 200m north of the Tamarind Hotel – blink and you'll miss it, there's no sign.

The northernmost access is just alongside the north wall of the ultra-exclusive Sandy Lane hotel and resort – right next to Rhianna's villa. Have your paparazzi moment on the celebrity-studded beach in front.

Sleeping & Eating

Angler Apartments APARTMENT $

(☎537-0278; www.anglerapartments.com; Clarke's Rd 1, Derricks; r from US$80; ❄📶) An unpretentious place with 12 basic and well-worn apartments. Studios in an adjacent older house are similar but smaller and less airy. There's a little patio bar and nice gardens. It's at the south end of Paynes Bay, off a road east of the main road. Good value for the area.

Tamarind Hotel RESORT $$$

(☎432-1332; www.eleganthotels.com/tamarind; Hwy 1; r from US$599; ❄@📶🏊) Everything is discreet about this understated luxury resort, which has a hacienda motif, right on the beach at Paynes Bay. The 100 units are decked out in a restful palette of beachy pastels. All have balconies or patios and views of either one of the three pools or the ocean. The lushly landscaped grounds boast many fountains.

Sandy Lane RESORT $$$

(☎444-2000; www.sandylane.com; Hwy 1; r from US$1845; ❄📶🏊) Right on the best part of Paynes Bay, the ultra-luxurious Sandy Lane is the most prestigious resort on the island. Everything is top of the line, and you get access to an exclusive guest-only golf course carved out of an old quarry.

Roti Den CARIBBEAN $

(Hwy 1; rotis B$17-35; ⏰10am-8pm) Step inside the bright-yellow house right by the road to find a full selection of great rotis – take your pick from vegetable, chicken, pork, shrimp, lamb or beef, or mix it up. They are filled to bursting, so it's easier to eat in on a plate than try to keep it in one piece outside.

Daphne's ITALIAN $$$

(☎432-2731; www.daphnesbarbados.com; Hwy 1; mains B$73-108; ⏰noon-3pm & 6-10pm Tue-Sun) In an elegant open-air dining room right next to one of the island's best stretches of sand, Daphne's serves good contemporary Italian dishes in a semi-formal environment. The lunch menu is lighter and cheaper.

Getting There & Away

Regular Bridgetown–Speightstown buses will drop you at Paynes Bay. For the beach ask to be let off at either the fish market or Sandy Lane.

Holetown

The first English settlers to Barbados landed at Holetown in 1627. Long a bastion of understated luxury, Holetown has exclusive shops and a charming little nightlife area near the beach. There's lots of good snorkeling in the mellow waters and reefs here.

Holetown is the center for all services north of Bridgetown, with banks, ATMs and a large supermarket.

Sights & Activities

Mt Standfast Beach BEACH

A narrow but pretty stretch of sand just north of Holetown with good swimming. The real reason to come here is the marine life. The waters are inhabited by hawksbill turtles, which come to feed on sea grasses just offshore. Many snorkeling tours stop here, but you can also rent snorkel gear along the beach and go it alone.

Hightide Watersports DIVING

(☎432-0931; www.divehightide.com; Coral Reef Club; 1-/2-tank dive US$80/142) One of the better dive shops on the west coast. Also runs PADI open-water courses for US$450.

Folkestone Marine Park SNORKELING

(Folkestone Beach) Spanning several kilometers along the midwest coast, this marine reserve was set up to preserve coral and shallow areas inhabited by turtles. There are four reserve zones: two sport areas where motorized aquatic sports are permitted, a scientific zone and a recreation zone where you can snorkel in peace free of Jet Skis and speedboats.

There is no entry fee or permit required to enter the reserve and if you're staying in the area there's a good chance that the waters in front of your hotel are part of it. In front of the **reserve office** (☎422-2314; Folkestone Park; museum adult/child B$5/2; ⏲9am-5pm Mon-Fri) there's a large area protected by buoys that's good for snorkeling.

Festivals & Events

Holetown Festival CULTURAL

(www.holetownfestivalbarbados.org) This festival celebrates February 17, 1627 – the date of the arrival of the first English settlers on Barbados. Holetown's weeklong festivities include street fairs, concerts, lectures, a beauty pageant, a road race and even a tattoo show.

Sleeping

Tropical Sunset Hotel HOTEL $$

(☎432-2715; www.tropicalsunsetbarbados.com; Hwy 1; r US$233; P ❄ 🛜 🏊) Right on the water in the center of Holetown, this popular hotel has clean and spacious rooms all offering views over the pool to the Caribbean. The attached waterfront bar/restaurant serves decent meals and is a fine place for a drink at sunset. Good value for this area.

★**Coral Reef Club** RESORT $$$

(☎422-2372; www.coralreefbarbados.com; Hwy 1; r US$584-3146; P ❄ @ 🛜 🏊) This family-owned 88-unit luxury hotel has 12 acres of gorgeous landscaped grounds surrounding an elegant gingerbread fantasy of a main building. Unlike some other top-end accommodations in the area, this place oozes character. Rooms are spacious and elegant, especially the suites, which have private porches overlooking the sea.

Lone Star Hotel BOUTIQUE HOTEL $$$

(☎629-0599; www.thelonestar.com; Hwy 1, Mt Standfast; r from US$790; ❄ 🛜) Built right on the sands, this new low-rise boutique hotel has supremely comfortable rooms with stained wooden floors, vaulted ceilings and full-length sliding glass doors that afford tremendous sea views. It doesn't have the spacious grounds, and hence the privacy, that some of the nearby resorts offer but on the plus side you'll hear the waves from bed.

Eating

Just Grillin' CARIBBEAN $

(Hwy 1; mains B$22-44; ⏲11am-10:30pm Mon-Sat, 5:30-10:30pm Sun) For a reasonably priced meal, head to this unpretentious place next to the Chatel village. It serves up good sandwiches and grilled plates of everything from catch of the day to jerk chicken. Portions aren't huge, but it's all tasty. There is another branch in Rockley.

Lemongrass THAI $$

(☎271-8265; www.lemongrassbarbados.com; Limegrove Mall; mains B$35-50; ⏲11:30am-9:30pm) OK, so the atmosphere is far removed from a dingy alley in Bangkok, but this Thai restaurant in an upmarket mall knocks out some tasty dishes and is great value for Holetown.

Tides CARIBBEAN $$$

(☎432-8356; www.tidesbarbados.com; Hwy 1; mains B$88-118; ⏲noon-2:30pm Sun-Fri, 6-9:30pm daily) You'll need to make a reservation well in advance to get a table at Holetown's flashiest restaurant but the fine views from the waterside dining room and sophisticated flavors make it well worth the effort. Local ingredients are seamlessly mixed with international flavours to create interesting plates and there are dedicated menus for non-carnivores. Theres a decent wine list too.

Nishi FUSION $$$
(☎ 432-8287; www.nishi-restaurant.com; 2nd St; mains B$57-101; ⏲ 6-10pm) Holetown's hippest eatery doesn't feel particularly Caribbean – there's a gold Buddha in the garden and a house-music soundtrack – but locals love it, giving it a lively atmosphere. The food, which spans the gamut from burgers and curries to sushi, is all carefully prepared and full of flavor.

Beach House INTERNATIONAL $$$
(☎ 432-1163; www.thebeachhousebarbados.com; Hwy 1; dinner mains B$39-98; ⏲ 11am-10pm) Anchored by a vast terrace right on the water, the Beach House fulfills all your holiday dining fantasies. The drinks and wine list is encyclopedic. The menu segues from comfy lunch food (burgers, salads) to steak and seafood at night.

Ragamuffins CARIBBEAN $$$
(☎ 432-1295; www.ragamuffinsbarbados.com; 1st St; mains from B$49-72; ⏲ 6-10pm) Ragamuffins is in a 60-year-old chattel house (a simple wooden dwelling placed on cement or stone blocks) now filled with personalities. Dishes are all Caribbean with some added attitude. It fills up on Sunday for the famous drag show – reservations are essential.

Getting There & Away

Buses running between Bridgetown and Speightstown stop at several places along the main road in Holetown.

There's a taxi rank outside the Massy Stores supermarket.

Speightstown

Easily the most evocative small town on Barbados, Speightstown combines old colonial charms with a vibe that has more rough edges than the endlessly upscale precincts to the south. The settlement was once dubbed 'Little Bristol' as, thanks to its maritime connection to that English town, many of the first settlers originated from there, and it still has a classic nautical vibe.

Since the main road was moved to the charmless bypass east, traffic is modest, so take time strolling to look up at the battered old wooden facades.

Sights & Activities

Arlington House HISTORIC BUILDING
(☎ 422-4064; arlington@caribsurf.com; Queen St; adult/child B$25/12.50; ⏲ 8:30am-4:30pm Mon-Fri, to 3pm Sat; 👪) A radiant vision in white stucco, this 18th-century colonial house now has an engaging museum run with love by the National Trust. It's divided into various sections, with interactive displays covering local commerce, town history, plantations and the nautical trade with some displays specifically tailored for younger visitors.

Mullins Beach BEACH
A popular and family-friendly beach along Hwy 1 between Holetown and Speightstown with waters that are usually calm and good for swimming and snorkeling. It's a fine place for a west-coast sunset. Unfortunately the once buzzing beach bar has been taken over by a nearby luxury housing development and is now a private members club frequented by bored-looking homeowners who must surely miss the good old times with the local characters.

Heywoods Beach BEACH
One of the best strands on the west coast for day-trippers from elsewhere on the island, Heywoods Beach offers good parking, a location well off Hwy 1 and lots of uncrowded sand (especially on weekdays). It's about 500m north of the road into Speightstown.

Reefers & Wreckers DIVING
(☎ 422-5450; www.scubadiving.bb; Ascot House, Gibbes; 1-/2-tank dive US$70/125; ⏲ 9am-5pm) A family-owned dive shop based on the west coast but offering dives all over the island.

Eating

★ **Fisherman's Pub** CARIBBEAN $
(☎ 422-2703; Queen St; mains from B$15; ⏲ 11am-late Mon-Sat, noon-4pm Sun) This waterfront cafe is a local institution that serves up fish from the boats floating off the side deck. On Wednesdays there is steel-pan music and a buffet. As the evening wears on, the scene gets more Bajan. Line up for the ever-changing and excellent fare.

PRC Bakery BAKERY $
(Sand St; items B$2.50-6; ⏲ 8am-8pm) One of the best traditional Caribbean bakeries on the island. Take your pick from sweet and savory delights. We love the unadvertised currant rolls – delicious layers of buttery pastry filled with sweet currants – but everything is

good. Best time to come is between 2pm and 4pm when most things come out hot from the ovens.

De Sweet Pot CARIBBEAN $
(Hwy 1B; mains from B$23; ⏲1-9:30pm Wed-Sun) Offering some of the best value in the north, this friendly open-air diner in front of the bus station serves great Bajan-style ribs, fish and chicken in healthy portions. The quality here puts many more expensive places to shame.

Orange Street Grocer CAFE $$
(Sand St; breakfast B$15-30, mains B$44-47; ⏲8am-6pm Mon-Thu, to 10pm Fri & Sat) A bright, modern cafe that opens out onto a lovely shaded deck right by the water. It offers a wide variety of scrumptious dishes with Caribbean and Mediterranean flavors featuring prominently. There's also great wood-fired pizzas, bruschetta, baguette sandwiches and tasty breakfast options. Finish up with real coffee from the Italian machine.

Juma's CARIBBEAN $$$
(☎432-0232; www.jumasrestaurant.com; Queen St; mains B$55-115; ⏲8am-8pm) An atmospheric 2nd-floor eatery under a thatched roof right by the water serving good modern Caribbean cuisine, including pan-roasted duck breast and a variety of fish plates. There is a lighter lunch menu (B$20 to B$55) that offers baguettes, salads, curries and burgers. Also a fine place for breakfast out on the deck.

Getting There & Away

Speightstown is the main transport hub for the west coast, with regular bus services running south to Bridgetown, through the interior to Bathsheba and north to St Lucy via the villages of the northern west coast. Buses leave from the **terminal** (Major Walk) just off Hwy 1.

Minivans to St Lucy depart from outside the small market near the entrance to town on Hwy 1.

North Barbados

The remote parish of St Lucy covers the northern tip of the island. While it was once considered a backwater, the wilderness here is slowly being tamed as new housing projects go up on cheap land. However, it still remains a wonderfully raw and rarely visited destination, with a rugged coastline that boasts towering cliffs that shelter tiny bays.

St Lucy remains mostly off the radar and tourism has yet to take much of a hold here. Accommodations options are thin on the ground although there are a couple of apartment hotels; fortunately it's close enough to easily visit from the west coast, where there's a good selection of hotels.

Sights & Activities

Animal Flower Cave CAVE
(☎439-8797; www.animalflowercave.com; adult/child B$25/10; ⏲9am-4:30pm) At the northern tip of the island, near where the Caribbean and Atlantic meet, you'll find this large waterside cave carved into a cliff face. It is accessed by a set of stairs that have been carved into a blowhole – there's no other way down the cliffs – and there's a pool inside for paddling. You'll be accompanied by a guide into the cave. Bring reef shoes if possible, but any old tennis shoes will also do the trick.

North Point SURFING
Drive in past the ruins of a once-grand resort to find one of the best surf breaks on the north side. The eerie shells of buildings on the clifftop add to the epic end-of-the-world atmosphere. It's a complicated wave – not for beginners.

The area is also known for its sharks (rumor has it that local chicken farmers throw their dead birds off the cliffs here), and many dive operators make trips up this way to see various species in a challenging swim-through.

The road in is full of crater-sized potholes – go slow, especially if you're in a rental.

Getting There & Away

There are a few direct buses to St Lucy each day from the Princess Alice Terminal in Bridgetown, but they depart in the evening and are not convenient. The best way to access the island's northern reaches is to make your way to Speightstown, from where regular buses and minivans ply the roads of St Lucy.

Central Barbados

Several roads cross the rolling green hills of the island's interior. There's a wealth of historic and natural sights here and you can spend days winding around small roads far from the crowds.

Surprises abound – you'll round a corner and discover a huge 19th-century stone church or a fascinating plantation-era signal tower, which was how the colonials once communicated. The rolling hills in the interior are also home to the island's best gardens and some wonderful old mansions.

Sights

★Welchman Hall Gully NATURE RESERVE
(☎438-6671; www.welchmanhallgullybarbados.com; Hwy 2, Welchman Hall; adult/child B$28/14; ⊙9am-4pm) Once part of a large estate that covered the area, this National Trust property contains some rare tracts of original Barbados tropical rainforest, although there are also several introduced species present. A trail leads from the car park through a narrow canyon lined with diverse tree species and rocks covered in moss past some wonderful shallow caves draped in vines.

★St Nicholas Abbey HISTORIC SITE
(www.stnicholasabbey.com; adult/child B$46/20, train adult/child B$60/30; ⊙10am-3:30pm Sun-Fri) St Nicholas Abbey is a Jacobean-style mansion that is one of the oldest plantation houses in the Caribbean and a must-see stop on any island itinerary. The grounds include the Great House, various gardens and a very traditional rum distillery. A cafe serves light lunches (B$30 to B$42) on a platform overlooking a lush valley full of trees.

A fully functioning steam train complete with smartly attired conductors runs a loop round the property and up to Cherry Tree Hill.

Farley Hill National Park PARK
(☎422-3555; Hwy 2; per car B$6; ⊙vehicle access 9am-5pm) A tree-covered hillside set around the ruins of an old estate home. Climb to the top and sit on one of the benches in front of the pagoda for a fresh breeze and phenomenal views down to the Atlantic. Bring a book and a picnic lunch. If you arrive in a vehicle you pay admission, but if you walk up from the public bus it's free.

Hunte's Gardens GARDENS
(☎433-3333; www.huntesgardens-barbados.com; Castle Grant St, St Joseph; B$30; ⊙9am-5pm) These gardens at the home of famed local horticulturalist Anthony Hunte already have a magical aura. Set mostly within the confines of a collapsed cave, all kinds of plants and shrubs line crisscrossing paths beneath majestic cabbage palms, while hummingbirds, lizards and monkeys frolic around. Classical music combined with the extravagant colors and harmonious birdsong make it a full-on sensory experience. Make use of the benches at key points on the trail to sit back and take in the beauty.

Harrison's Cave CAVE
(Hwy 2) This cave is promoted as one of the island's premier attractions, but how much you enjoy it will depend on which tour you choose. The main 'tram tour' involves sitting on a vehicle and being driven through the interior, but the one you really want is the rather pricey 'adventure tour' where you'll crawl, swim and duck through the cave's smaller passageways. Wear old clothes.

Morgan Lewis Windmill WINDMILL
(☎622-4039; B$5, tour B$10; ⊙10am-5pm) The largest complete windmill in the Caribbean, this impressive stone structure sits proud on a hilltop north of Belleplaine. It was used to grind sugarcane from the area throughout the 18th and 19th centuries. The enthusiastic site manager will show you inside and give a full rundown of the history of the area.

Eating

Many of the major sights in the interior have restaurants that are usually only open for lunch, and morning and afternoon tea. If you're driving, bring a picnic or a couple or rotis to enjoy in one of the many scenic spots along the way.

Brighton Farmers Market MARKET $
(☎262-1901; ⊙6-10am Sat) Early on Saturdays, foodies, chefs, artisans and more converge on the Brighton Farmers Market in the heart of the fertile St George Valley on Hwy 4B. It's a festival of the finest produce, prepared foods and crafts and is a good place to get off the traveler trail and mingle with the locals.

Grab a cup of coffee, enjoy some local gab and see what treasures you root out. Make sure to arrive early – by 10am it's all over.

Getting There & Away

There are numerous roads crisscrossing the interior of the island. Public buses run on the main interior highways, but many of the attractions are off spur roads and you'll lose plenty of time waiting for a passing service.

In order to maximise your experience, it's highly recommended to hire a vehicle to explore the region. A good map is essential or, even better, work with a GPS.

Bathsheba

The wild Atlantic waters of the east coast are far removed from the rest of the island – the population is small, the coast craggy and the waves incessant. Bathsheba is prime surfing country, and it's also good for long beach walks that leave you feeling like you've reached the end of the world. It's an idyllic image of sand, sea and palm trees.

If you're not a great swimmer, this is not really the place to go into the water; rather, enjoy the wave-tossed scenery on long beach walks. Note the iconic Mushroom Rock, one of several rocks carved into shapes that will cause mycologists to swoon.

Sights & Activities

Andromeda Botanic Gardens GARDENS
(433-9384; www.andromedabarbados.com; Hwy 3; adult/child B$30/15; 9am-5pm, last admission 4:30pm) The island's original botanic gardens, this lovely spot has two exploratory paths that wind their way through a wide collection of tropical plants, including orchids, ferns, water lilies, bougainvillea, cacti and palms.

There's a cafe on-site that serves good light meals and refreshments. It's best to come just before closing time, when the birds and monkeys are at play. As long as you are in before the bell, they won't hurry you out. Discounts for international national trust members.

Bathsheba Beach BEACH
A wild stretch of golden sand that's framed by rough headlands and punctuated by magnificent rock formations standing defiant in the shallows against the constant pounding of the waves. The waters here are not suitable for swimming.

Soup Bowl SURFING
The world-famous reef break known as the Soup Bowl is right off the beach and is one of the best waves in the Caribbean islands. Don't underestimate the break just because the region is not known for powerful surf – Soup Bowl gets big. The best months are August to March.

Sleeping

There are a couple of great hotels on the outskirts of Bathsheba, but there's not a lot of quality options for budget travelers in the area.

★**Eco Lifestyle Lodge** BOUTIQUE HOTEL $$
(433-9450; www.ecolifestylelodge.com; Tent Bay; r US$139-218;) Rebranded with a holistic slant, the former Sea-U Guesthouse remains a wonderful option with charming wooden buildings and a very appealing porch looking out to sea from the hillside location. A pleasant restaurant pavilion rounds out the verdant site. The higher-end rooms have air-con and kitchens and there is a new path down to the water's edge.

Santosha HOTEL $$
(422-7999; www.santoshabarbados.com; Belleplaine, St Andrew; r US$165-297;) Filling a gap for a quality midrange hotel on this side of the island, this inviting new offering is set in an elegant three-story wooden building overlooking the beach at Belleplaine, north of Bathsheba. It offers bright modern rooms and an excellent pool area. Go for one of the upstairs rooms with polished wood floors, high ceilings and panoramic views.

It's pretty remote and there are not many places to eat close by – fortunately the food at the attached restaurant is excellent.

Atlantis Hotel HOTEL $$$
(433-9445; www.atlantishotelbarbados.com; Tent Bay; r from US$418-473;) One cove south of Bathsheba, Atlantis was the original hotel in the area. It is centered around a carefully renovated period building facing the sea. The views are sweeping and you have a choice of one-bedroom suites in the original building, or apartments in a new wing by the small pool.

Eating & Drinking

You can get local-style meals at some of the bars around town. Note that most eateries close very early; after 8pm you'll often be hard pressed to find anything more than a snack.

Roundhouse Restaurant CARIBBEAN $$
(433-9678; breakfast B$20-30, mains B$34-74; 8am-9pm) Set in a dramatic stone building up on the hillside at the north end of town, this excellent restaurant has customers throughout the day who sit around, sip cocktails and savor the fresh breeze and fine views south over Soup Bowl. You can enjoy banana bread with your breakfast, sandwiches and salads at lunch and local specials and pastas at dinner.

Getting There & Away

A taxi can be negotiated for about B$80 from Bridgetown or the south coast. Alternatively take bus 6 from the Fairchild St Terminal in Bridgetown, or catch one of the regular vans from the River Bus Terminal. The trip takes about 45 minutes.

Bus 1E travels from Bathsheba to Speightstown along Hwy 2, passing by Farley Hill.

Bathsheba South to Christ Church Parish

Few people take the time to follow the coast south of Bathsheba. They should. The road curves around hillsides above the rugged Atlantic, passing tiny villages populated by friendly locals who eke out a living from the sea. This is another Barbados, far removed from the glitzy resorts of the west, a place where tradition is still strong and nature remains wild.

The road runs south from Bathsheba along the Atlantic past Martin's Bay and Bath before turning inland through cane fields. Look for the iconic Anglican St Philip Church from where, if you turn south, you'll reach the historic Sunbury Plantation House. Continuing south will take you to the busy village of Six Cross Roads, where your route options live up to the promise of the name. You can head southeast to Crane Beach, southwest to Oistins or west to Bridgetown.

Sights & Activities

Bath BEACH

This wonderful long and remote stretch of golden sand is usually totally empty. It is one of the few places on this coast where it's safe to swim, thanks to the offshore reef that tames the wild currents. There are picnic tables, but bring your own meal because the kiosk has gone out of business. Alternatively, at the far southern end of the beach there is a seaside club that serves meals and rents out kayaks.

Sunbury Plantation House NOTABLE BUILDING

(☎423-6270; Sunbury, St Philip; tours adult/child B$25/12.50; ⏱9:30am-4:30pm) Built between 1660 and 1670, the handsome Sunbury Plantation House was painstakingly restored after a 1995 fire. The house has 60cm-thick walls built of local coral blocks and ballast stones, the latter coming from the ships that set sail from England to pick up Barbadian sugar. It's the only one of Barbados' great houses where visitors are able to get inside all the rooms.

★**Ocean Echo Stables** HORSEBACK RIDING

(☎834-0783, 433-6772; www.barbadoshorseriding.com; Newcastle, St John; B$160) Run by a nature loving and affable local woman, this stables just south of Bathsheba offers 90-minute horse rides on fit and healthy animals through the spectacular wilderness surrounding Bath beach. There are morning and afternoon excursions.

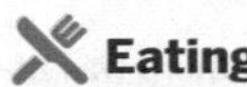

Eating

Bay Tavern CARIBBEAN $

(mains B$25-40; ⏱11am-6pm Fri-Wed, to 8pm Thu) Home to the Martin's Bay fish fry, the east coast's more tranquil answer to Oistins, the Bay Tavern has lost a lot of its charm since being redeveloped from a simple shack into a three-floor modern structure, but is still a good place to dig into plates of fresh-from-the-boat marlin or snapper and macaroni pie.

Take it to go and cross the road to one of the picnic tables on the water's edge for the old-school experience. The 'big' day is Thursday, but they cook all week so come on another day – the food is better and the nature is louder.

Getting There & Away

Public transport is very thin on the ground south of Bathsheba. The best way to explore this area is in a rental vehicle.

UNDERSTAND BARBADOS

History

The original inhabitants of Barbados were Arawaks, who were driven off the island around AD 1200 by Caribs from South America. The Caribs, in turn, abandoned (or fled) Barbados close to the arrival of the first Europeans. The Portuguese visited the island in 1536, but Barbados was uninhabited by the time Captain John Powell claimed it for England in 1625. Two years later, a group of settlers established the island's first European settlement, Jamestown, at present-day Holetown. Within a few years, the colonists had cleared much of the forest, planting tobacco and cotton fields. In the 1640s they switched to sugarcane. The new sugar plantations were labor intensive, and the landowners began to import large numbers of enslaved Africans. These large sugar plantations – some of the first in the Caribbean – proved immensely profitable, and gave rise to a wealthy colonial class. A visit to a plantation estate, like the one at St Nicholas Abbey (p219), will give some idea of the money involved.

The sugar industry boomed during the next century, and continued to prosper after the abolition of slavery in 1834. As the planters owned all of the best land, there was little choice for the freed slaves other than to stay on at the cane fields for a pittance.

Social tensions flared during the 1930s, and Barbados' black majority gradually gained more access to the political process. The economy diversified through international tourism and gave more islanders the opportunity for economic success and self-determination. England granted Barbados internal self-government in 1961 and it became an independent nation on November 30, 1966, with Errol Barrow as its first prime minister. While not flawless, Barbados has remained a stable democracy.

Owen Arthur and the Barbados Labour Party were in power from 1993 to 2008. In a campaign that saw 'change' as the popular theme, David Thompson and the left-leaning Democratic Labour Party (DLP) won election in 2008. But in late 2010 Thompson died suddenly, which was a traumatic event for a nation used to political stability. He was succeeded by Deputy Prime Minister Freundel Stuart.

In mid 2017 Barbados' failing infrastructure meant raw sewage began bubbling up into the streets in Worthing on the south coast, closing beaches and reducing commerce in the area. Despite the crisis taking place in one of the most important tourism regions of Barbados – just a few hundred meters from the island's main dining strip – the government was unable to bring it under control.

In the lead up to the 2018 elections, criticism of the government continued to grow, the main issues being economic stagnation and infrastructure issues, along with murmurs of corruption.

The DLP were absolutely destroyed in the polls, with the Barbados Labour Party winning every single seat across the country, meaning for the first time there would be no opposition in parliament. Following the victory, labour leader Mia Mottley was sworn in as Barbados' first female prime minister.

The new government got off to a fast start, rapidly resolving the waste-water crisis on the south coast that the previous government had been unable to sort out. But once the scale of the country's economic problems was uncovered, the government was forced to make a series of unpopular moves to balance the books including raising taxes and increasing bus fares by 75%. While the government remains popular – most Barbadians understand the necessity of getting the country back on track – the increases have led to the first real protests against Mottley's leadership.

Unlike other Caribbean islands, Barbados maintains its sugar industry, although the majority of the economy is now based on tourism and offshore banking. Condos are being built as fast as the concrete dries.

People & Culture

Bajan culture displays some trappings of English life: cricket, polo and horse racing are popular pastimes, business is performed in a highly organized fashion, gardens are lovingly tended, older women often wear prim little hats and special events are carried out with a great deal of pomp and ceremony.

However, on closer examination, Barbados is very deeply rooted in Afro-Caribbean tradition. Family life, art, food, music, architecture, religion and dress have more in common with the Windward Islands than with London. The African and East Indian influences are especially apparent in the spicy cuisine, rhythmic music and pulsating festivals.

Like other Caribbean cultures, Bajans are relatively conservative and the men are macho, but the ongoing bond with a cosmopolitan center such as London has made Barbados slightly more socially progressive than its neighbors.

Bajan youth are fully within the media orbit of North America. The NBA and New York hip-hop fashion are as popular in Bridgetown as in Brooklyn. Another similarity to the US is the suburban sprawl around Bridgetown. Traffic is often a problem and you can join the masses shopping at some large air-conditioned malls.

Sports

The national sport, if not national obsession, is cricket. Per capita, Bajans boast more world-class cricket players than any other nation. One of the world's top all-rounders, Bajan native Sir Garfield Sobers, was knighted by Queen Elizabeth II during her 1975 visit to Barbados, while another cricket hero, Sir Frank Worrell, appears on the B$5 bill.

In Barbados you can catch an international Test match, a heated local First Division match, or even just a friendly game on the beach or grassy field. Although international matches are less common here now that they are being spread more widely around the Caribbean, when it is Barbados' turn, thousands of Bajans and other West Indians pour into matches at Kensington Oval. For schedules and tickets, contact the Barbados Cricket Association (www.bcacricket.org).

Horse races and polo are at their peak during the tourist season.

Music

Bajan contributions to West Indian music are renowned in the region, having produced such greats as the Mighty Gabby, a calypso artist whose songs on cultural identity and political protest speak for emerging black pride throughout the Caribbean. These days Bajan music leans toward the faster beats of soca (an energetic offspring of calypso), *rapso* (a fusion of soca and hip-hop) and dancehall (a contemporary offshoot of reggae with faster, digital beats and an MC). Hugely popular Bajan soca artist Rupee brings the sound of the island to audiences worldwide.

The massively popular singer Rihanna has achieved worldwide fame while being idolized at home. Her reggae-style rap has won many Grammy awards, including best rap song and best dance recording.

Landscape & Wildlife

The Land

Barbados lies 160km east of the Windward Islands. It is somewhat pear-shaped, measuring 34km from north to south and 22km at its widest. The island is composed largely of coral accumulations built on sedimentary rocks. Water permeates the soft coral cap, creating underground streams, springs and limestone caverns.

Most of the island's terrain is relatively flat, rising to low, gentle hills in the interior. However, the northeastern part of the island, known as the Scotland District, rises to a relatively lofty 340m at Barbados' highest point, Mt Hillaby. The west coast has white-sand beaches and calm turquoise waters, while the east side of the island has turbulent Atlantic waters and a coastline punctuated with cliffs. Coral reefs surround most of the island and contribute to the fine white sands on the western and southern beaches.

Two good places to enjoy the island's lush natural beauty are Andromeda Botanic Gardens (p220), in a gorgeous setting above Bathsheba with a huge range of beautifully displayed local flora; and Welchman Hall Gully (p219), off the highway from Bridgetown to Belleplaine, which has examples of the island's ancient forests.

Wildlife

The majority of Barbados' indigenous wildlife was overwhelmed by agriculture and competition with introduced species. Found only on Barbados is the harmless and elusive grass snake. The island also shelters a species of small, nonpoisonous, blind snake, plus whistling frogs, lizards, red-footed tortoises and eight species of bat.

Hawksbill turtles regularly come ashore to lay their eggs, as does the occasional leatherback turtle. As elsewhere, the turtles face numerous threats from pollution and human interference. The **Barbados Sea Turtle Project** (☎230-0142; www.barbadosseaturtles.org; University of the West Indies, Bridgetown) is working to restore habitat and populations.

Most, if not all, mammals found in the wild on Barbados have been introduced. They include wild green monkeys, mongooses, European hares, mice and rats.

More than 180 species of birds have been sighted on Barbados. Most of them are migrating shorebirds and waders that breed in North America and stop over on Barbados en route to winter feeding grounds in South America.

Environmental Issues

The forests that once covered Barbados were long ago felled by British planters. One of the knock-on effects is that the country now has a problem with soil erosion. This loose dirt, along with pollution from ships and illegally dumped solid wastes, threatens to contaminate the aquifers that supply the island's drinking water.

Masses of sargassum seaweed washing up on the island's Atlantic shores is an environmental issue that has come to the fore. Caused by an excess of nutrients and warming of the oceans out in the Atlantic, the outbreaks are becoming bigger and more frequent.

Following the lead of some of its greener neighbors, Barbados has begun to pay far more attention to green policies, with a ban on the importation and use of single-use plastic items and styrofoam coming into effect in early 2019 for businesses across the island. Paper straws and cardboard food containers are now the norm in restaurants and food vans. From 2020 plastic bags will also be banned.

SURVIVAL GUIDE

Directory A–Z

ACCESSIBLE TRAVEL

Barbados is one of the better-equipped destinations in the eastern Caribbean for travelers with disabilities, though it still has some way to go.

Many areas still have uneven sidewalks, or don't have any at all. Furthermore, public transport is generally not conditioned for wheelchair access.

The excellent Barbados Council for the Disabled (http://barbadosdisabled.org.bb) is working with local businesses to make them accessible through the 'Fully Accessible Barbados' program. They provide a number of services to travelers, including beach wheelchairs, accessible transportation and travel-planning assistance.

ACCOMMODATIONS

You can find some place to stay at every price point on Barbados, although there are more places at the top end. The west coast is home to the most exclusive resorts while the southwest features large hotels, all-inclusive and family-friendly resorts, and independent budget accommodations around Worthing and Dover.

Camping is generally not allowed on public lands.

Rates decline by as much as 40% outside of high season.

SLEEPING PRICE RANGES

The following price ranges refer to a double room with bathroom.

$ less than US$100

$$ US$100–250

$$$ more than US$250

ACTIVITIES

Hiking

The Barbados National Trust (p204) leads guided hikes in the countryside. Hike leaders share insights into local history, geology and wildlife.

A nice hike to do on your own is along the old railroad bed that runs along the east coast from Belleplaine to Martin's Bay. The whole walk is about 20km, but it can be broken into shorter stretches.

Kitesurfing & Windsurfing

Barbados has good windsurfing and kitesurfing, with the best winds from December to June. Silver Sands, at the southern tip of the island, has excellent conditions for advanced practitioners, while Maxwell, just to the west, is better for intermediates. There are also good breaks for surfers in the area.

Surfing

Barbados has gained international fame for its east-coast breaks. Ground zero is the Soup Bowl (p220), off Bathsheba, and another spot called **Duppies**, up the coast.

South Point, Silver Sands and Rockley Beach (p209) on the south coast are sometimes good, as is Brandon's, which is next to the Hilton Hotel at Needham's Point. There are some 30 other named breaks.

Freights Bay south of Oistins is one of the best places for beginners and a number of surf schools operate there.

There are local guys renting out boards on the beach at most of the popular surf spots. Prices are negotiable depending on the quality of the board, but even the nicest board shouldn't be much more than B$20 per hour, or B$60 for daily rental. It's worth noting that the locals are generally nice and welcoming to outsiders.

There are several good surf schools of note: Zed's Surfing Adventures (p213), based at Silver Sands, and Barry's Surf Barbados (p211) at Dover, which transports clients to various spots, depending on conditions.

CHILDREN

Barbados is generally a family-friendly destination. A number of resorts have organized children's activities or in-house day care and babysitting.

Most beaches are safe for children to play on and many of the southern and western beaches are calm enough for younger swimmers. The east-coast surf is too powerful for novice swimmers of any age. Older kids enjoy surfing lessons.

Public transport can be crowded but drivers and assistants are generally helpful. Large public buses are generally less full than the private minivans and hence it's easier to get seats together.

ELECTRICITY

Electrical outlets are 110V, 50Hz. US-style two-pin plugs are used; you may find the occasional UK-style three-pin sockets as well.

EMERGENCY NUMBERS

Ambulance	☎511
Fire	☎311
Hyperbaric chamber	☎436-5483
Police	211

FOOD

Eating in Barbados is a rewarding experience at all budget levels. Whether you're hitting up humble waterside fry shacks or fine-dining restaurants, you'll find plenty of outstanding fresh seafood. But Bajan cuisine is about more than just fried fish and there are many richly spiced local specialties to try out. Most restaurants in areas popular with travelers offer menus featuring both traditional plates and international cuisine.

Essential Food & Drink

Bananas Local varieties are green even when ripe (look for them in markets).

Banks The island's crisp lager is refreshing after a day in the hot sun.

Barbadian rum Considered some of the finest in the Caribbean, with Mount Gay being the best-known label.

Conkies A mixture of cornmeal, coconut, pumpkin, sweet potato, raisins and spices, steamed in a plantain leaf.

Cou-cou A creamy cornmeal-and-okra mash.

Cutters Meat or fish sandwiches in a salt-bread roll.

Fish cakes There are myriad Bajan recipes, made from salt cod and deep-fried.

Flying fish Served fried in delicious sandwiches all over the country. It's a mild white fish that is great sautéed or deep-fried.

Jug-jug A mixture of cornmeal, green peas and salted meat.

Roti A curry filling rolled inside flat bread.

HEALTH

Barbados' health care is the best in the region, and around Bridgetown you'll find modern hospitals and medical centers.

For minor illnesses, nearly all hotels will have a doctor on call or will be able to help you find assistance.

LEGAL MATTERS

Barbados is an ordered place and the local police force is friendly but professional. It is highly unlikely that you'll be shaken down or approached for a bribe by law enforcement.

> **EATING PRICE RANGES**
>
> The following price ranges are for the cost of a main course.
>
> **$** less than B$30
>
> **$$** B$30–60
>
> **$$$** more than B$60

The island has a British legal system. If you find yourself in legal difficulties you have the right to legal representation and are eligible for legal aid if you can't afford to pay for private services.

LGBT+ TRAVELERS

Barbados is a conservative and religious place that has traditionally been opposed to homosexuality. It has some of the most extreme anti-gay laws in the region but in reality these are not enforced.

Attitudes are changing slowly, but since Barbados is a busy transit point with active links to UK attitudes, it is perhaps slightly ahead of other nearby islands. There are a few openly gay Bajan couples, although they still tend to be discreet.

Gay visitors to Barbados will need to be judicious outside of international resorts, and especially in smaller, more traditional towns, but are unlikely to run into any major problems.

MONEY

You'll certainly want some Barbadian dollars on hand, but larger payments can be made in US dollars, frequently with a major credit card. Hotels and guesthouses quote rates in US dollars (as do many dive shops and some restaurants), although you can use either US or Bajan currency to settle the account.

Exchange Rates

The exchange rate is fixed at B$2 to US$1.

Australia	A$1	B$1.49
Canada	C$1	B$1.48
Eastern Caribbean	EC$1	B$0.74
Euro zone	€1	B$2.22
Japan	¥100	B$1.90
New Zealand	NZ$	B$1.42
UK	£1	B$2.47
US	US$1	B$2.00

Tipping

Hotels While a service charge is usually added to the bill, a tip of B$2 per bag for porters is appreciated; gratuity for cleaning staff is at your discretion.

PRACTICALITIES

Newspapers Barbados has two daily newspapers, the *Barbados Advocate* and the *Daily Nation*. Some UK papers are sold in touristy areas for those who need a dose of Middle England.

TV The government-owned TV station CBC broadcasts on Channel 8.

Radio Government broadcaster CBC broadcasts on AM 900 and has three FM stations on 94.7FM, 98.1FM and 100.7FM. Local commercial talk radio is on 92.9FM while popular music is on 95.3FM and the BBC on 92.1FM. Gospel music is broadcast on 102.1FM.

Smoking Smoking is prohibited in public places. In effect this means in enclosed spaces. It's permitted to smoke in nonenclosed spaces, including beaches and parks.

Weights & measures Barbados uses the metric system, though many islanders still give directions in feet and miles and sell produce by the pound.

Restaurants Most restaurants add a service fee to the bill; if it's not automatically included in the bill, tip 10% to 15%; if it is, it's up to you to leave a small additional tip.
Taxi Tip 10% to 15% of the fare.

PUBLIC HOLIDAYS

In addition to those observed throughout the region, Barbados has the following public holidays:
Errol Barrow Day January 21
Heroes' Day April 28
Labor Day May 1
Emancipation Day August 1
Kadooment Day First Monday in August
UN Day First Monday in October
Independence Day November 30

SAFE TRAVEL

Crime, including assaults on tourists, is not unknown on Barbados. Most crimes are simple tourist scams – normal precautions should suffice. Truth be told, the greatest risk is bad sunburn.

➡ Beware of pickpockets in Bridgetown – keep your valuables secure around the bustling center on Swan and Broad Sts.

➡ Sidewalks are narrow or nonexistent and roads are curvy, so use caution even while walking along quiet streets.

➡ Portuguese man-of-war jellyfish are occasionally encountered in Bajan waters (although they are large, slow and usually easy to spot), and poisonous manchineel trees grow along some beaches.

TELEPHONE

Barbados' country code is 1; the area code is 246. To call any other country with a country code of 1 (most of North America and the Caribbean), just dial 1 and the 10-digit number. For other countries, dial the international access code 011 + country code + number.

TIME

Atlantic Standard Time (GMT/UTC minus four hours).

ℹ Getting There & Away

AIR

Grantley Adams International Airport (BGI; www.gaia.bb) is on the island's southeast corner, about 16km from Bridgetown. It's the largest airport in the Eastern Caribbean and the major point of entry for the region.

Barbados is served by major airlines flying from North America and the UK. Airlines include the following:

Caribbean Airlines (☎429-5929; www.caribbean-airlines.com; Grantley Adams International Airport)

LIAT (☎434-5428; www.liat.com; Grantley Adams International Airport)

SEA

Cruise Ship

About 800,000 cruise-ship passengers arrive in Barbados each year as part of Eastern Caribbean itineraries. Ships dock at Bridgetown Harbour, about 1km west of the city center. The harbour has the usual duty-free shops and a branch office of the **Barbados Tourism Authority** (BTMI; Cruise Ship Terminal).

Yacht

The Windward Islands are among the most popular places to sail in the world. Yacht harbors and charters abound. Barbados, however, is the one exception – its easterly position and challenging sailing conditions keep it well off the main track for most sailors.

ℹ Getting Around

BICYCLE

Barbados offers interesting riding for the adventurous. It's hilly, but roads are not usually steep (excepting parts of the east). However, most roads are quite narrow and many are in poor condition. Traffic is a constant bother in the west and south with many drivers not showing much respect to two-wheeled road users.

Most shops require a credit card or B$100 deposit for rentals. Your hotel can hook you up with a rental.

BOAT

With its good networks of roads, water taxis are not common in Barbados (unlike some other parts of the Caribbean), although on the west coast there are a couple of operators running between local businesses.

BUS

It's possible to get to virtually any place on the island by public bus. There are three kinds of bus:

Government-operated public buses Large and blue with a yellow stripe.

Privately operated minibuses Midsized buses painted yellow with a blue stripe.

Route taxis Individually owned minivans that have 'ZR' on their license plates and are painted white.

All types of bus charge the same fare: B$3.50 to any place on the island. You should have exact change when you board the government bus, but minibuses and route taxis will make change.

Most buses transit through Bridgetown, although a few north–south buses bypass the city. Buses to the southeast part of the island generally transit through Oistins.

Bus stops around the island are marked with red-and-white signs printed with the direction in which the bus is heading ('To City' or 'Out of City'). Buses usually have their destinations posted on or above the front windshield.

Buses along the main routes, such as Bridgetown to Oistins or Speightstown, are frequent, running from 6am to around midnight. You can get complete schedule information for public buses on any route from the **Transport Board.** (☎436-6820; www.transportboard.com)

CAR & MOTORCYCLE

In Barbados, you drive on the left. At intersections and narrow passages, drivers may flash their lights to indicate that you should proceed.

Driver's License

Visitors must obtain a temporary driving permit (US$5) from their car-rental agency; you'll need to show a valid driving license from your home country. The permit is valid for two months from issue.

Car Rental

Barbados doesn't have many major international rental chains. There are, instead, scores of independent car-rental companies, some so small that they're based out of private homes. A couple of local companies at the airport do have cooperation agreements with international brands.

Despite the number of companies, prices don't seem to vary much. The going rate for a small car is about B$130 to B$150 a day, including unlimited mileage and insurance.

Previously it was common for companies to rent out strange, small convertible cars called 'mokes' (they look like the odd car in *Fantasy Island*), which don't have doors. These are an acquired taste and small economy cars are more common now. Rental cars are marked with an 'H' on the license plate.

While many car-rental companies don't have booths at the airport, most will deliver your car there or to your hotel.

Agencies include the following:

Courtesy Rent-A-Car (☎431-4160; www.courtesyrentacar.com; Grantley Adams International Airport)

Stoutes Car Rental (☎416-4456; www.stoutescar.com; Grantley Adams International Airport)

Top Class Car Rentals (☎228-7368; www.topclassrentals.com)

Road Conditions

Highways are not very well marked, although landmarks are clearly labeled, as are some roundabouts (traffic circles) and major intersections. The most consistent highway markings are often the low cement posts at the side of the road showing the highway number and, below that, the number of kilometers from Bridgetown.

All primary and main secondary roads are paved, although some are a bit narrow and smaller highways in the middle of the island can be in fairly poor condition. There are plenty of gas stations around the island, except on the east coast. Some stations in the Bridgetown area are open 24 hours.

Expect rush-hour traffic on the roads around booming Bridgetown.

TAXI

Taxis have a 'Z' on the license plate and usually a 'taxi' sign on the roof. They're easy to find and often wait at the side of the road in popular tourist areas.

Although fares are fixed by the government, taxis are not metered and you will have to haggle for a fair price. The rate per kilometer is around B$4, but short trips cost more. Sample fares from Bridgetown include Bathsheba B$76, Oistins B$40 and Speightstown B$60.

Bonaire

☎599 / POP 19,550

Includes ➡

Best Places to Eat

- ➡ Mezze (p232)
- ➡ Hang Out Beachbar (p236)
- ➡ Kite City (p236)
- ➡ Capriccio Ristorante (p232)
- ➡ Posada Para Mira (p235)

Best Places to Stay

- ➡ Harbour Village Beach Club (p231)
- ➡ Bellafonte (p236)
- ➡ Carib Inn (p230)
- ➡ Coco Palm Garden & Casa Oleander (p236)
- ➡ Sorobon Beach Resort (p236)
- ➡ Coral Paradise (p230)

Why Go?

A small island with a desert landscape, Bonaire is not for everyone – but it *is* for divers and snorkelers who want to immerse themselves in that vibrant world under the sea. The beauty of Bonaire is that the coral reef, designated a national park, is just a few feet from the shoreline. Dozens of exceptional dive sites are easily accessible from the shore and teeming with life, making this island an independent diver's (and snorkeler's) paradise.

Above the surface there's world-class windsurfing on Lac Bay and excellent kayaking among the mangroves. Biking trails wind through the arid hills, while driving routes show off the island's historical and natural sights. Classy but low-key resorts and a few enticing restaurants complete the picture – perfect for travelers who prefer their adventure with some amenities.

When to Go

Dec–Apr High season: accommodations fill up and prices are higher.

Jan & Feb Carnival *(Karnaval)* is Bonaire's biggest celebration – a week of music and costumes, parades and parties.

Sep–Dec Bonaire is below the hurricane belt, but it sometimes rains and the temperature drops.

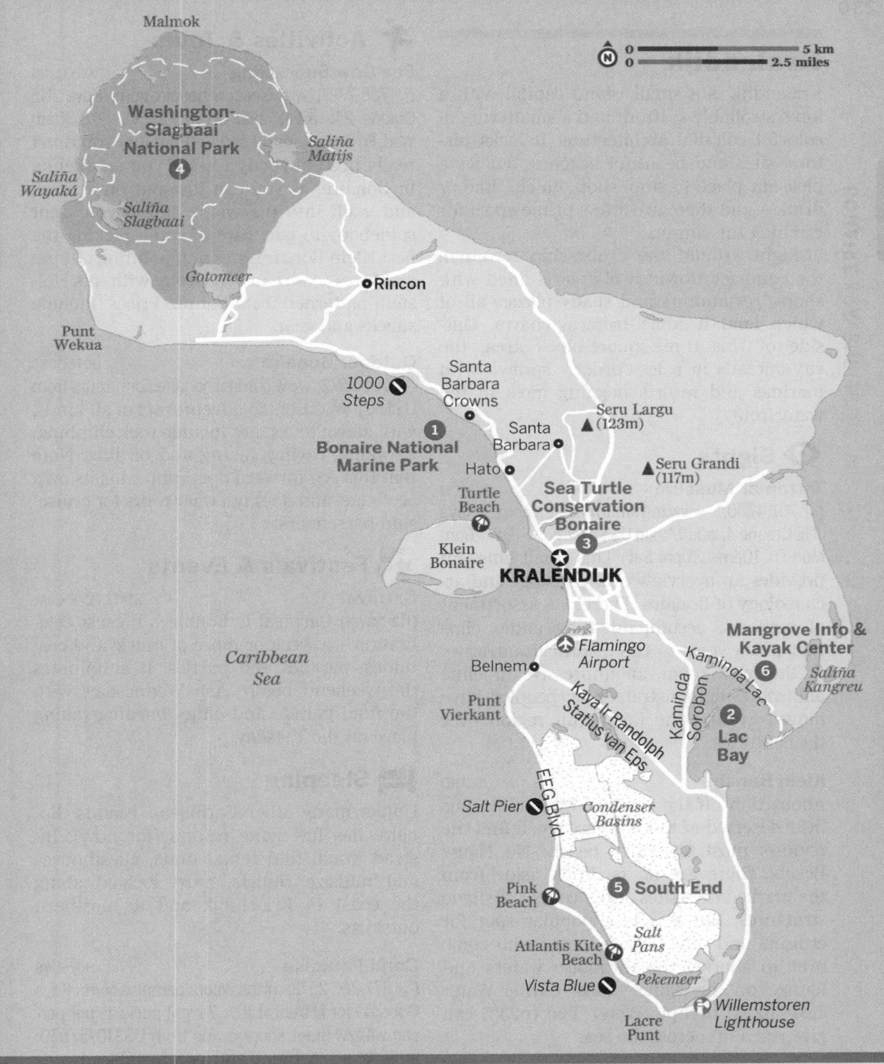

Bonaire Highlights

1 **Bonaire National Marine Park** (p232) Donning a mask and discovering the incredible underwater world that lies right offshore.

2 **Lac Bay** (p237) Windsurfing at one of the world's premier destinations for beginners and pros alike, or observing from the beach bar.

3 **Sea Turtle Conservation Bonaire** (p240) Keeping the beaches safe for sea turtles – and maybe even ushering some newborn *tortuguitas* safely into the sea.

4 **Washington-Slagbaai National Park** (p233) Exploring the island's remote northern tip by car or bicycle or on foot.

5 **South End** (p235) Seeing pink (flamingos!) while driving or cycling through the salt pans.

6 **Mangrove Info & Kayak Center** (p237) Kayaking and snorkeling in the ecologically rich 'reef nursery.'

Kralendijk

Kralendijk is a small island capital with a long, strollable seafront and a smattering of colorful colonial architecture. It lacks historic sites and beautiful beaches, but it's a pleasant place to stop, shop, lunch, dine or drink – and there are a few prime spots for catching the sunset.

Right around the cruise-ship terminal, the compact 'downtown' area is lined with shops, restaurants and shady plazas, all of which lend it some tropical charm. Outside of this three-square-block area, the city spreads in a less orderly sprawl, with marinas and resorts hogging most of the waterfront.

Sights

Terramar Museum MUSEUM

(☎701-4700; www.terramarmuseum.com; Kaya JNE Craane 4; adult/child US$10/free; ⏲9am-6pm Mon-Fri, 10am-1:30pm Sat) This small museum provides an overview of the history and archaeology of Bonaire. There's an assortment of artifacts, accompanied by audio clips that put a voice to the historical narrative. In the front room, an impressive timeline and video demonstrate how peoples have moved around the Caribbean region over the centuries.

Klein Bonaire ISLAND

About 1km off the coast of Kralendijk, this little deserted island is where you'll find the region's most attractive beach: No Name Beach. There are no facilities, aside from the marked dive sites and a couple of shade structures. But this is a popular spot for cruisers and other beach bums, who come over to snorkel the turquoise waters and lounge on the white sands. Caribe Water Taxi (p233) or Epic Water Taxi (p233) can give you a lift across the sea.

Fort Oranje FORT

FREE Follow the cannons south along the waterfront to a small bastion that was built by the Dutch in 1639 and served as the governor's mansion until 1837. The defensive cannons were scavenged from a British warship that ran aground on the south shore in the early 1800s. Although the British gained control of Bonaire several times during the Napoleonic Wars, the island (and thus the fort) never saw any action.

Activities & Tours

Sea Cow Snorkeling SNORKELING

(☎785-7727; www.seacow-bonaire.com; Kaya JNE Craane 24; adult/child US$55/27.50; ⏲8:30am Wed, Fri & Sun, sunset snorkel 6pm Tue) You don't really need anybody to take you snorkeling in Bonaire, as you can just put on a mask and walk into the water. But if you want somebody to take care of you – picking the best Klein Bonaire sites and pointing out the creatures – you can't go wrong with this Holstein-patterned catamaran. Prices include snacks and gear.

Outdoor Bonaire OUTDOORS

(☎791-6272; www.outdoorbonaire.com; tours from US$50) Caters to adventurers of all kinds, with active tours that include rock climbing, kayaking, caving, hiking and birding. Note that this eco-forward operation runs its own ecolodge, and does not offer tours for cruise-ship passengers.

Festivals & Events

Carnival STREET CARNIVAL

(Karnaval) Carnival is Bonaire's biggest celebration – a week or more of music and costumes, parades and parties. It culminates the weekend before Ash Wednesday, with the final parade and effigy burning taking place on the Tuesday.

Sleeping

Unlike many other Caribbean islands, Bonaire has few large resorts (for now). Instead, you'll find rental units, guesthouses and midsize resorts, most located along the coast in Kralendijk and its northern outskirts.

Coral Paradise HOTEL **$$**

(☎877-267-2572; https://coralparadise.com; Kaya Gobernador N Debrot 107; 7-night package per person with/without shore diving from US$1075/850; P ❄ ☜ ≋) A quiet and comfortable diver's haven, with outstanding service and a convenient location for some excellent shore diving. Guests return year after year, and are especially jazzed to receive a rental truck as part of their vacation packages, along with rinse tanks, drying racks, personal dive lockers and mobile phones with a few dollars' credit.

Carib Inn GUESTHOUSE **$$**

(☎717-8819; www.caribinn.com; Julio A Abraham Blvd; r/apt/houses from US$129/149/199; ❄ ☜) Long-time resident Bruce Bowker extends

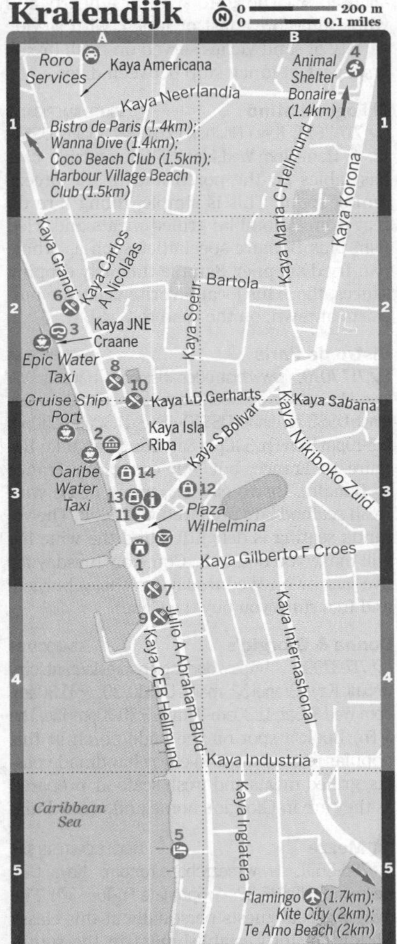

a warm and personable welcome at his waterside compound on the southern side of town. Surrounding a small pool, the rooms are quirky, cozy and comfortable. The on-site dive shop offers occasional trips to Klein Bonaire, as well as equipment rental, guided shore dives and various training programs.

Captain Don's Habitat RESORT **$$**

(☎717-8290; www.habitatbonaire.com; Kaya Gobernador N Debrot 103; s/d US$169/221, ste from US$192; ❄@📶🏊) Captain Don's Habitat is set on lushly landscaped grounds 3km north of town, with 85 units surrounding a large swimming pool. The rooms are

Kralendijk

Sights

1 Fort Oranje A3
2 Terramar Museum A3

Activities, Courses & Tours

3 Sea Cow Snorkeling A2
4 Sea Turtle Conservation Bonaire B1

Sleeping

5 Carib Inn A5

Eating

6 Bobbejan's Take-Away A2
7 Capriccio Ristorante A4
8 Donna & Giorgio's A2
9 Mezze A4
10 Pasa Bon Pizza A3

Drinking & Nightlife

11 Cuba Compagnie A3

Shopping

12 Buddy Dive Watersports A3
13 Cadushy Shop A3
14 Salt Shop A3

spacious, clean and comfortable, without too many frills. Always at the forefront of environmental technologies, the place uses solar water heaters and a state-of-the-art water-treatment system. The on-site restaurant, Rum Runners, is an obligatory stop.

Captain Don will go down in the Bonaire history books, as he was instrumental in setting up the island's infrastructure for shore diving, personally marking and naming most of the sites so that they would be accessible to all.

Buddy Dive Resort RESORT **$$**

(☎717-5080; www.buddydive.com; Kaya Gobernador N Debrot 85; studios from US$185, 1-/2-bedroom apt from US$212/336; ❄@🏊) North of town, this place is a diver's delight. With more than 70 studios and apartments in 10 sunny yellow buildings, this is one of the larger resorts on the island. All facilities are here, including two restaurants, two swimming pools, truck rental, a dive shop and – for your convenience – a drive-through filling station.

★**Harbour Village Beach Club** RESORT **$$$**

(☎717-7500; www.harbourvillage.com; Kaya Gobernador N Debrot 71; r from US$400; ❄@📶🏊) A colonial beauty with impeccable service, Harbour Village is set on a postcard-worthy white-sand beach and yacht harbor 2km north of town. It has elegantly decorated

BONAIRE NATIONAL PARK

Bonaire National Marine Park (☎717-8444; www.stinapabonaire.org; Park Headquarters, Barcadera 10; diving/snorkeling US$45/25; ⊙headquarters 8am-4pm Mon-Fri) is the island's star attraction, a unique and precious resource that allows divers and snorkelers to explore miles of pristine coral reef. The protected area covers the entire coast of the island, including Klein Bonaire, to a depth of 200ft (60m). Between the two islands there are now more than 100 named dive sites, many of which are accessible from the shore. Look for the painted yellow rocks.

lodgings in wide two-story blocks lined with tropical gardens. Amenities include large balconies and luxury foam mattresses, and as you climb the rate card you gain kitchenettes, Jacuzzis, marina and beach views and more.

Eating

Bonaire's top restaurants are clustered in Kralendijk, mostly along the waterfront or on the main drag, Kaya Grandi. The larger resorts all have restaurants, some of which are counted among the island's culinary highlights.

Bobbejan's Take-Away BARBECUE $
(☎717-4783; Kaya Albert Engelhardt 2; mains US$10-15; ⊙6-10pm Fri & Sat, noon-2pm & 6-10pm Sun) Don't let the name fool you: there are tables here, out back under a nice tree. But getting one is a challenge, as *everybody* turns up for the super-tender ribs and the velvety peanut sauce on the plate of Indonesian-style chicken satay.

Pasa Bon Pizza PIZZA $
(☎780-1111; Kaya LD Gerharts 3; pizzas US$6-31; ⊙5-11pm Wed-Sun) The only stoplight on Bonaire is part of a sign over the newly relocated Pasa Bon Pizza. The joint is famous for its pizza topped with lionfish, which allows you to do good by eating well (the invasive lionfish is a threat to the reef). Even without the specialty topping, the American-style pizza is tasty and the atmosphere is fun.

Between 2 Buns SANDWICHES $
(☎717-1723; www.facebook.com/between2bunsbonaire; Kaya Gobernador N Debrot 74; sandwiches US$13-16; ⊙7am-5pm Mon-Fri, 8am-4pm Sat; 📶) The go-to spot for a hearty and wholesome breakfast or lunch, with a wide variety of sandwiches served on fresh bread. It's a perfect lunch stop between dives.

El Fogon Latino SOUTH AMERICAN $
(☎717-2677; Kaya Nikiboko Zuid 88; mains US$6-12; ⊙11am-11pm Wed-Mon) This roadside cafe has tables on the porch and in the breezy dining room. This is simple, filling fare direct from Colombia: grilled meats and fried fish, plus Bonaire specialties such as whole pan-fried snapper. Sample the tasty dipping sauces, too. This local favorite is on the outskirts of town, on the road to Lac Bay.

Bistro de Paris FRENCH $$
(☎717-7070; www.bistrodeparis.com; Harbour Village Marina, Kaya Gobernador N Debrot 71; mains lunch US$8-16, dinner US$10-48; ⊙11:30am-2:30pm & 5-10pm Mon-Fri, 5-10pm Sat) You can't take Bonaire to France, but you can bring France to Bonaire. Bistro classics, many made with fresh seafood, are prepared with skill. The veranda seating is delightful, and the wine list will make you ooh-la-la. Come on Tuesday for live jazz or on Wednesday for cheap burgers and free rum (you buy the Coke).

Donna & Giorgio's SEAFOOD $$
(☎717-3799; https://donnagiorgiorestaurant.jouwweb.nl; Kaya Grandi 52; mains US$10-30; ⊙11:30am-3pm Wed & Sat, 11:30am-3pm & 6:30-10pm Tue, Thu & Fri) Book a spot on the wide porch at this popular restaurant, and enjoy handmade pastas, grilled meats and fresh seafood, prepared as they are in Giorgio's homeland of Sardinia.

★**Mezze** MIDDLE EASTERN $$$
(☎786-8631; www.mezzebonaire.com; Kaya CEB Hellmund; US$25-32; ⊙6pm-late Fri-Tue; 🖉) The owner greets guests personally at this classy Middle Eastern establishment in the southern stretch of Kralendijk, and shortly thereafter a marvelous homemade flatbread with hummus arrives. The rest of the journey is up to you, but the Istanbul-style shrimp, beetroot and goat-cheese salad and the *muhammara* (made with Syrian pepper, walnuts, cumin and breadcrumbs) are exquisite.

★**Capriccio Ristorante** ITALIAN $$$
(☎717-7230; www.capricciobonaire.com; Kaya CEB Hellmund 5; pasta US$18-25, mains US$25-30; ⊙6:30-10pm Wed-Mon) Direct from Italy, this *ristorante* and boutique is sophisticated and stylish. Begin with one of the tempting *cicchetti* (small bites), then sample an exquisite handmade pizza or pasta (the pumpkin ra-

violi is superb). Classic main dishes include the likes of slow-cooked veal shank and oven-baked chicken. It's all accompanied by a thoughtful wine list and lots of love.

Drinking & Nightlife

★Coco Beach Club BAR

(☎717-1171; www.cocobeachbonaire.com; Kaya Gobernador N Debrot 75; ⏲10am-11pm) Bonaire's pretty people seem to have chosen this relatively new double-decker beach bar as their natural habitat – throughout the day they can be spotted on nearby lounge chairs sipping tropical cocktails. They stay put thanks to the plentiful food: there are sandwiches, salads and finger food for lunch, and heaping plates of noodles, seafood and steak for dinner.

Cuba Compagnie BAR

(☎717-1822; www.cubacompagniebonaire.nl; Kaya Grandi 1; ⏲5:30pm-late) The capital's hottest spot is this sultry Cuban cafe, especially on Thursday night, when salsa dancers strut their stuff. Any night of the week the place is packed with happy patrons sipping mojitos and feasting on fusion fare. The atmospheric interior is adorned with eclectic artwork and old photographs, but the outdoor seating area is the place to be.

Shopping

Salt Shop COSMETICS

(www.bonairesaltshop.com; Kaya Grandi 9; ⏲8am-6pm Mon-Sat) What could be a better Bonaire souvenir than something made from sea salt? This little shop carries sea salt for cooking (plus grinders and shakers), as well as bath and body products.

Information

Bonaire Tourist Office (☎717-8322; www.tourismbonaire.com; Kaya Grandi 2; ⏲8am-noon & 1:30-5pm Mon-Fri) Staff here can answer questions about accommodations, tours and more, as well as offer a good selection of brochures.

Hospital San Francisco (Fundashon Mariadal; ☎715-8900; Kaya Soeur Bartola 2; ⏲24hr) Provides emergency care.

Post office (www.fxdc-post.com; Plaza Wilhelmina 11; ⏲8am-4pm Mon-Fri) Reliable postal service is provided by Flamingo Express Dutch Caribbean.

Getting There & Away

Flamingo Airport (p240) is just south of town, about 3km from the center of Kralendijk.

Although most resorts do not offer airport transfers, it's easy enough to arrange a taxi to your hotel (destinations in and around Kralendijk cost between US$10 and US$20).

The cruise-ship port is centrally located.

Getting Around

The city is small enough that you can explore most of it on foot, though you'll want a vehicle (or at least a bicycle) to get around the island. Boats to Klein Bonaire operated by **Caribe Water Taxi** (Karel's Water Taxi; ☎700-8080; www.caribewatersport.com; adult/child US$15/10; ⏲departs 10:15am, 12:15pm & 2:15pm Mon-Sat) and **Epic Water Taxi** (Kantika di Amor; ☎786-9490, 777-2668; www.watertaxikleinbonaire.com; round-trip US$20; ⏲departs 10am, noon & 2pm) depart from Karel's Beach Bar and the small marina across from It Rains Fishes, respectively.

Roro (☎717-6787; www.rorobonaire.com; Kaya America 21; ⏲6am-7pm) offers wheelchair- and accessible-transportation services.

North End

You'll likely make your way to the North End on a quest to dive at one site or another. Even so, it's also worth spending a day or more on land – exploring the national park and hiking in the hills, visiting Rincon, the island's oldest town, and discovering some of the small-scale, grassroots ecological and agricultural initiatives in the area.

Bonaire's second town, Rincon, is rather sleepy and very old – even older than Kralendijk. More than 500 years ago, Spaniards chose this valley to establish their settlement because it was relatively fertile, and because it was hidden from passing pirates. Rincon became the home base of the enslaved people who worked the farms and made the long trek to labor in the salt flats in the south.

Nowadays, most of the residents are descended from enslaved people, and the village maintains an authentic island atmosphere, celebrating true Bonairean culture with classic Caribbean architecture, lively cultural markets, tantalizing local cuisine and a rousing harvest festival.

Sights

★Washington-Slagbaai National Park NATIONAL PARK

(☎788-9015; www.stinapabonaire.org; visitor center US$3, day pass US$15-40, per calendar year US$20-45, with national marine-park tag free;

8am-5pm, last entry 2:45pm;) Comprising almost 20% of the island's area, this vast desert landscape is a fantastic place to explore on foot, by bike or by car (preferably 4WD). Stop at the visitor center, at the entrance, to pick up a map and see exhibits on the park's ecology and history. From here, two driving routes and two hiking trails show off the park's diversity, including salt ponds, seascapes, remote beaches, mangroves, volcanic hills and amazing desert vistas. And cacti – lots of cacti.

The two circular driving routes (24km long and 34km long) have birding stops, dive sites and hidden beaches – many ideal for swimming and snorkeling – along the way. Roads are rough but well worth the effort. Allow about two hours.

If you're hiking, it's best to get an early start. The 1½-hour Lagadishi loop takes you past ancient stone walls, a blowhole along the rugged coast, and a salt pan with congregating flamingos. The more difficult, two-hour Kasikunda trail ascends a challenging path to the top of a hill for sweeping views. A new kids' trail near the visitor center features a short loop and a swing set.

The park entrance, with restrooms and a small museum, is at the end of a good 4km concrete road from Rincon. Be sure to bring plenty of water.

Echo Parrot Sanctuary BIRD SANCTUARY

(Kunuku Dos Pos; 701-1188; www.echobonaire.org; Kaminda Goto; tour per person US$10; tour 5pm Wed) Bonaire's most beloved bird is the yellow-throated Amazon parrot, but the loquacious *lora* (as she is locally known) is threatened with extinction: there are fewer than a thousand birds living on the island. Learn about Echo's efforts to preserve the parrot's habitat, rehabilitate injured birds and save the *lora*. Located 2km west of Rincon.

Cadushy Distillery DISTILLERY

(701-7011; www.cadushy.com; Kaya Cornelis D Crestian; 10am-5pm Mon, Wed & Fri, plus when cruise ships in port) FREE Drinking a cactus sounds like a prickly affair, but it's not as scary as it sounds. Pay a visit to this small-scale distillery to see how the prickly green plant is turned into the delicious 'Spirit of Bonaire' known as Cadushy. Sample it in the shady courtyard, surrounded by blooming gardens and squawking parrots. Or visit the new **shop** (717-3456; www.cadushy.com; Kaya Grandi 11; 10am-5pm Tue, Thu, Sat & when cruise ships in port) in Kralendijk.

Mangazina di Rei MUSEUM

(786-2101; Blvd Miguel A Pourier; adult/child US$5/free; 9am-4pm Tue-Fri) Located about 1.5km east of Rincon, the second-oldest stone building on Bonaire used to be a storehouse. Every week, enslaved people made the arduous 10-hour journey from the salt pans in the south to this village in the north, to see their families and to get their provisions from the storehouse. Now it contains a small museum about the nature, geology and history of Bonaire, as well as island culture and how it evolved during and after slavery.

Bonaire Botanical Garden GARDENS

(777-0508, 770-8853; Kaminda Tras di Montana 9; adult/child US$10/5; 9am-4pm;) Everything you ever wanted to know (and more!) about organic gardening, permaculture and medicinal plants. Manuel Vargas' gardens are a delightful maze of lush greenery, flowing fountains and whimsical artwork. The 1½-hour tour is followed by a complimentary cup of herbal tea. Located about 7km southeast of Rincon.

Gotomeer LAGOON

(Kaminda Goto) At the edge of Washington-Slagbaai National Park, this large inland saltwater lagoon attracts flocks of flamingos, especially during nesting season (January to June). You can't get close to these shy feathered friends, but you can usually spot some from the observation area and even from the road. Take the paved road heading due west from Rincon for about 4km.

Eating

Rincon is the place to come to sample authentic, delicious local fare, whether you get it at the monthly **cultural market** (Mangazina di Rei; 8am-2pm last Sat of month) or at one of the charming restaurants in the village.

Thirsty & Hungry CARIBBEAN $

(782-1737; www.facebook.com/pg/thirstyandhungry; Kaya Gilberto RE Herrera 11; mains from US$5; 8am-6pm Tue-Sun) This quaint little restaurant opened in 2018 along the road to Washington-Slagbaai National Park, and is a fabulously homey spot for local specialties such as fresh lemon juice, salt fish and iguana soup. For less adventurous patrons, there are also hot dogs and hamburgers. The owners are kind and hospitable, and live on the restaurant property.

Posada Para Mira CARIBBEAN $$
(☎717-2199; Kaya Para Mira; mains US$7-20; ⌚11am-6pm Fri-Mon & Wed) At this delightful place on Rincon's western outskirts you can sample local specialties such as *sopi di yuana* (iguana soup) and *stoba di kabritu* (goat stew), as well as dishes you may find more familiar. Para Mira's definitely on island time, but the breeze is lovely, and there's live music and a view of cactus-covered hills to enjoy while you wait.

Rose Inn CARIBBEAN $$
(☎786-6420, 796-1526; Kaya Guyaba 4; mains from US$10; ⌚11am-3pm Thu-Sun) At this long-standing place a genial mix of folks enjoy plate lunches of local fare (fish stew, goat, fried chicken) at mismatched tables scattered under trees. Service can be erratic, but that's part of the charm. Located in the heart of Rincon village, with a few very simple rooms available for overnight stays.

Getting There & Away

Rincon is about 16km north of Kralendijk. Kaya Korona turns into Kaminda Gurubu: head out of town and keep driving.

South End

The southern end of Bonaire is flat and arid, with vistas that extend for many miles in all directions. The horizon is broken only by the massive mounds of sparkling-white salt. Yes, salt. This is the product of the Cargill solar salt works, and further south you'll see acres and acres of salt pans, where ocean water sits and eventually evaporates, leaving the salty residue. The landscape is oddly – startlingly – beautiful, especially as the water evaporates and with increasing salinity the pans turn 50 shades of pink. Speaking of pink, look out for flamingos flocking in the pans.

Aside from the salt works the South End is nearly deserted. But the coast is punctuated by rocky beaches, colonial-era landmarks, and lovely, windsurfer-dotted Lac Bay, making the perimeter a fascinating driving or cycling route.

Sights

Te Amo Beach BEACH
(👪) Near the airport, this beach is a local favorite for its shade trees and fine white sand, which allows easy access to the reef just offshore. It's also the location of the excellent food truck Kite City (p236), and kids will enjoy watching the planes fly in and out.

Donkey Sanctuary Bonaire WILDLIFE RESERVE
(☎560-7607; www.donkeysanctuary.com; Kaya Ir Randolph Statius van Eps; adult/child US$9/4.50; ⌚10am-4pm) Ever feel like you're surrounded by jackasses? You will in Bonaire, because the animals live free and wild on the island. The vast Donkey Sanctuary offers safe haven for 700 of the gentle creatures, along with a few rescued flamingos and tortoises. Visitors can view newborn donkeys in the special-care unit, observe the droves from the watchtower, and drive the circuit to meet resident jacks and jennies. Bring some carrots and you'll make friends for sure.

Slave Huts & Pyramids HISTORIC SITE
These stone huts served as shelter for the enslaved people who worked the salt pans in the 19th century. The four different-colored 10m pyramids along the coast are another legacy of the Dutch colonial era: colored flags matching one of the pyramids were flown to tell ships where they should drop anchor to load salt.

Activities

Pink Beach SNORKELING
Just north of the slave huts, Pink Beach is a sliver of sand that takes its color from pink coral washed ashore. It's rough for sunbathing, but the swimming and snorkeling (and diving) are prime.

Horse Ranch Bonaire HORSEBACK RIDING
(Kunuku Warhama; ☎786-2094; www.horseranchbonaire.com; Kaya Warahama 40; per person from US$125; ⌚tours depart 8am) The signature tour here is the half-day 'Ride & Swim,' which takes you riding over forested trails and along deserted beaches. The tour stops halfway at Lac Bay so both riders and horses can cool down in the water. If you love horses, you'll love the thrill of swimming with them.

Kiteboarding Bonaire KITESURFING
(☎701-5483; www.kiteboardingbonaire.com; Atlantis Kite Beach; intro lesson US$165-245, 3-lesson package US$660; ⌚lessons 10am-1pm & 2-5pm) Learn to fly on Atlantis Kite Beach, where the wind blows between 17 and 22 knots almost every day. The school operates out of a colorful bus, with beanbags, hammocks and cold drinks for when it's time to take a break. It's pretty much a one-stop shop, with air compressors for inflating kites and lockers for storing your stuff.

Sleeping

Coco Palm Garden & Casa Oleander APARTMENT $

(☎717-2108; www.cocopalmgarden.com; Kaya Ir Randolph Statius van Eps 9, Belnem; d US$66-86;) Coco Palm rents a variety of rooms and apartments in various brightly painted houses in the residential neighborhood of Belnem, just south of the airport. Beds and layouts vary, as do amenities, but you can always count on a kitchen and a hammock-strung garden. Bachelor Beach is just down the road.

Beware the additional air-con fee (US$15 per night) and cleaning fee (US$20 to US$35) that will be added to your bill.

Bellafonte APARTMENT $$

(☎717-3333; www.bellafontebonaire.com; EEG Blvd 10, Belnem; studios/ste from US$155/225;) This oceanfront property offers a collection of spacious, sparkling studios and suites, all equipped with private balconies, well-stocked kitchens and luxurious linens. Staff are on hand to ensure all needs are met (including the need for dining recommendations, since there's no restaurant on-site). A private pier juts into the Caribbean, offering a perfect spot for sunbathing, swimming and snorkeling.

Sorobon Beach Resort RESORT $$

(☎717-8080; www.sorobonbeachresort.com; Kaminda Sorobon 10; studios/apt from US$165/200;) There aren't many beaches on Bonaire, so there aren't many beach resorts. Sorobon is one of the few accommodations to front a sweet stretch of sand, complete with palm trees and tranquil waters, plus easy access to Lac Bay. The setting is gorgeous, the chalets are relaxed and cozy, and the service is excellent. Great beach bar, too!

In 2018 Sorobon added 10 apartments (located 1.5km from the beach resort) to its collection. The units vary in size, but all come with full kitchens, access to a magnesium pool and lovely views over Lac Bay.

Eating

★**Kite City** FOOD TRUCK $

(☎782-5100; www.facebook.com/kitecitybonaire; Te Amo Beach; meals US$11-15; ⊙11am-4pm;) Bonaire's best food truck is also one of the island's best lunch spots, period. There are spicy beef burgers, catch-of-the-day salads, tuna prepared every way from Sunday, and veggie wraps and quesadillas, all expertly whipped up with fresh local vegetables, oils and herbs. Grab a shaded table in the sand to feast, and wash it down with lemonade or sangria.

★**Hang Out Beachbar** BARBECUE $$

(☎717-5064; www.hangoutbeachbar.com; Kaminda Sorobon 12, Jibe City; table barbecue adult/child US$27.50/15; ⊙8am-7pm Mon-Wed, to 11pm Thu & Fri, 9am-7pm Sat, 9am-9pm Sun) WIndsurfing is the main event on Lac Bay, but chillin' with a tropical cocktail and admiring the pretty sails from this dope beach bar is a pretty close second. Thursday-night 'table barbe-

DIVING IN BONAIRE

Bonaire's dive sites are mostly strung along the western side of the island. The closeness of the reefs, the clarity of the waters and the system of marking the sites combine to make for unparalleled access for divers. You can reach more than half of the identified dive sites from shore – and many resorts claim a 'house dive site' right offshore.

Bonaire National Marine Park (p232), recognized by Unesco, covers the entire coast of the island, including Klein Bonaire, to a depth of 200ft. Between the two islands are more than 100 named dive sites; look for the painted yellow rocks. **Hilma Hooker** is the island's best-known wreck dive, while the **Salt Pier** is famous for the photo-worthy sponges and coral growing on the pillars. Sites vary greatly in terms of depth, currents and other factors, but plenty of them are ideal for beginners.

Before diving independently, all divers must pay the US$45 marine-park fee (US$25 for snorkelers) and do an orientation and check-out dive at a local dive shop to get comfortable with weights, conditions and park rules.

Recommended operators include **Buddy Dive Watersports** (☎717-5085; 6 Kaya S Bolivar; ⊙8am-6pm), **East Coast Diving** (☎717-5211; www.bonaireeastcoastdiving.com; Fishermens Pier, Kaminda Sorobon; 1-/2-tank dive US$65/120) and **Wanna Dive** (☎717-8884; www.wannadive.com; Eden Beach Resort, Kaya Gobernador N Debrot 73; boat dive from US$30, night dive from US$40; ⊙9am-5pm).

DON'T MISS

LAC BAY

On the island's southeastern side, Lac is a large inland bay that provides a critical habitat for green turtles and queen conchs – and windsurfers. Indeed, this is one of the world's premier destinations for riding the gusts, thanks to steady trade winds and warm, shallow waters.

The northern side of Lac Bay is sheltered by mangrove forests, where wetland birds breed and reef creatures mature (which explains why the mangrove is sometimes called a 'coral-reef nursery'). It's a gem for paddlers and snorkelers, who can spot young fish, sea stars and sponges in the crystal-clear waters. The Kaminda Lac – around the northern side of the bay – is a picturesque drive (and a popular cycling route), with views of flocks of flamingos and dense mangroves.

Set in the middle of the Lac Bay mangrove forest, the **Mangrove Info & Kayak Center** (☎780-5353; www.mangrovecenter.com; Kaminda Lac 140; 1hr/2hr tour US$27/46, solar boat US$27; ⊙from 8:30am Mon-Sat) offers guided kayaking trips, as well as excursions in a solar-powered boat. Stop by the information center (completely wind and solar powered, by the way) for displays about this unique ecosystem.

cue' dinners are especially popular. They involve minigrills at each table, all-you-can-eat grilled meats and tuna, baked potatoes, salad, bread and dessert.

ℹ Getting There & Away

EEG Blvd hugs the southern coast, starting just below the airport and continuing around the tip and all the way up to Lac Bay. If you're headed to Lac Bay, however, it's quicker to take the main road, Kaminda Sorobon, which comes directly from Kralendijk. It takes about 15 minutes to drive directly from Kralendijk to Lac Bay, but the longer route around the tip takes about 40 minutes.

The third and final road at the island's southern end is Kaya Ir Randolph Statius van Eps, which bisects the tip from Belnem to Lac Bay, passing the Donkey Sanctuary on the way.

UNDERSTAND BONAIRE

History

The Arawaks lived on Bonaire for thousands of years before Spain laid claim to it in 1499. A mere 20 years later there were no Arawaks left, as the Spanish sent all the indigenous people to work in mines elsewhere in the empire. The only remains of the Arawak civilization on Bonaire are a few inscriptions in remote caves – although there are some artifacts from around the region at the Terramar Museum.

The depopulated Bonaire stayed pretty quiet until 1634, when the Dutch took control, building Fort Oranje to protect the harbor. The Dutch looked to the flat land in the south and saw a future in salt production. Thousands of enslaved people were imported to work in horrific conditions. You can see a few surviving slave huts at the southern end of the island, and the Mangazina di Rei, where slaves had to go to get their provisions, in Rincon.

When slavery was abolished in the 19th century, the salt factories closed. The population – former slaves, Dutch landowners and South American transplants – lived pretty simple lives until after WWII, when the salt ponds reopened (this time with machines doing the hard work). The revived industry, coupled with the postwar booms in tourism and diving, gave a real boost to the economy.

Meanwhile relations with Curaçao, capital of the Netherlands Antilles (NA), slowly turned frosty. Locals felt ignored by their wealthier neighbor and lobbied for change. In 2008 Bonaire returned to direct Dutch rule as a rather far-flung special municipality within the Netherlands, a designation it shares with Saba and Sint Eustatius. The NA was formally dissolved in 2010.

Landscape & Wildlife

Bonaire's landscape is arid and mostly flat, with a few notable hills and valleys in the northern part of the island. Vegetation consists of cactus and scrubby trees – nothing else can really grow due to lack of water and the onslaught of goats, donkeys and other nibblers. The southern part of the island is

PLIGHT OF THE FLAMINGOS

Locally known as the *chogogo*, the Caribbean flamingo is Bonaire's darling spokes-creature and national bird. Visitors love watching the quirky, bright-pink birds forage for brine shrimp in the island's *saliñas* (salt pans), which in turn gives them their signature color. Some 3000 pairs mate dramatically each year within the Pekelmeer sanctuary, one of just four such breeding areas in the Caribbean. The season takes place in December and again for part of June, and females usually lay just one egg.

Lately, though, trouble's been afoot. In early 2019 more than 100 malnourished baby flamingos were picked up around Bonaire and delivered to Bonaire Wild Bird Rehab. The center opened in early 2018 in response to the growing numbers of ailing chicks. The exact cause is tough to pinpoint, though some islanders have speculated that stronger winds than usual have disrupted feeding patterns. Others believe that the flamingos' food source shrank during an extended drought or because of the large amount of *Sargassum* seaweed that's blown in over the last two years. Whatever the case, there are certain ways that you as a visitor can avoid exacerbating the problem – or, better still, help out.

First of all, don't approach the flamingos. There are clear markers (yellow rocks) along the roads instructing visitors not to enter the birds' habitats. When people get close the flamingos become stressed, causing them to expend crucial energy that would otherwise be used to forage and possibly to feed and care for chicks. Avoid making loud noises or bold movements. If you'd like to contribute something to nursing chicks back to health, Bonaire Wild Bird Rehab (www.mangrovecenter.com/bonaire-wild-bird-rehab) accepts and appreciates donations. You won't be able to visit, as the goal is to limit human contact and release the birds back into the wild, but the center has installed cameras that will allow you to watch the baby flamingos.

characterized by its vast salt flats and the lush mangrove swamps around Lac Bay.

Despite the seeming desolation, the island is rich in birdlife, including the iconic pink flamingo and the endangered yellow-shouldered Amazon parrot. Other species you're sure to spot include the banana quit, brown-throated parakeet, caracara, tropical mockingbird and troupial, not to mention many waterbirds.

Speaking of water, this is where Bonaire is truly replete with life. Coral reefs grow in profusion along the leeward coast, often just a few meters from the shore. Hundreds of species of fish and dozens of corals thrive in the clear, warm waters. Sea turtles, dolphins and rays are among the larger creatures swimming about.

Bonaire has historically faced few major environmental problems, thanks to a lack of industry, but there are always concerns, and according to a 2019 report the natural habitats of the island aren't as healthy as once believed. Development and overgrazing have caused deforestation on much of the island – a problem that has been exacerbated in recent years by extended drought. The reef along the coastline is protected by the marine park, but the degree of independence granted to divers makes the regulations difficult to enforce. In 2019 a report by Wageningen University in the Netherlands assessed the biodiversity of the Dutch Caribbean (Bonaire, Saba and Sint Eustatius) as 'moderately unfavorable to very unfavorable.' Top threats, according to the report, include cattle, invasive species, climate change, overfishing, coastal development, erosion and eutrophication by waste water.

Environmentalists are also concerned about the influx of tourists to the island – arrivals hit 130,000 in 2018. That figure doesn't even include cruise-ship visitors, who were estimated to number around 400,000 in 2019. Marine experts argue that the strain on the island's sewerage system and the sheer amount of sunscreen (toxic to coral reefs) that these tourists represent is not justified by what they spend on the island during their visit.

SURVIVAL GUIDE

Directory A–Z

ACCESSIBLE TRAVEL

It's not perfect, but Bonaire is a relatively friendly destination for travelers with disabilities.

Many resorts offer accessible rooms, restaurants and docks. Several resorts – including Captain Don's Habitat (p231) – have staff trained to assist disabled divers, with extensive experience training and guiding groups of disabled US veterans.

In Kralendijk, the cruise-ship terminal has a wheelchair ramp, as do many sidewalks around town. Roro Services (p233) offers wheelchair-accessible transportation and tours.

ACCOMMODATIONS

Bonaire has small guesthouses and resorts geared mostly to divers: most have in-house dive operations and some dive sites right offshore. Most accommodations are located in the northern outskirts of Kralendijk, with a few places south of the airport in Belnem. High season is from December to April, but the island doesn't see a huge spike in visitors (or prices).

The tax on accommodations is US$5.50 to US$6.50 per person per night, plus a 10% to 15% service charge.

SLEEPING PRICE RANGES

The following price ranges refer to a double room with private bathroom, not including taxes.

$ less than US$75

$$ US$75–200

$$$ more than US$200

ELECTRICITY

Power is 127V, 50Hz; A, B and F plugs and sockets are used.

EMERGENCY NUMBERS

Ambulance, fire, police ☎911

FOOD

Eat. Sleep. Dive. So goes the mantra of many a Bonaire visitor. As such, the island boasts some excellent places to eat (in addition to the places to sleep and dive). The major resorts all have decent restaurants, but downtown Kralendijk is also peppered with recommended eateries offering Caribbean, American and European cuisine with plenty of innovation. For local fare, head to Rincon.

HEALTH

Foundation Recompression Chamber (www.bonairehyperbaric.com; Kaya Soeur Bartola 7; ⏲24hr) Provides treatment for diving accidents and is staffed by diving medical professionals.

Hospital San Francisco (p233) Provides emergency care.

INTERNET ACCESS

Most resorts, hotels and rental units offer wireless internet access.

LGBT+ TRAVELERS

Bonaire is a 'special municipality' of the Netherlands, and as such, observes the same laws regarding LGBT equality. Same-sex marriage is legal (though rare) on the island.

That said, gay populations are not out or active on the island. There are no gay bars (and few bars of any type). There is no official Pride celebration and there are no gay activist groups. LGBT travelers are unlikely to encounter any discrimination, but they are also unlikely to encounter other gay folks, except by sheer coincidence.

MONEY

The local currency is the US dollar. ATMs are widely available. Credit cards are accepted at most hotels and restaurants.

Exchange Rates

Aruba	Afl1	US$0.56
Australia	A$1	US$0.70
Canada	C$1	US$0.74
Curaçao	Nafl	US$0.53
Euro zone	€1	US$1.11
Japan	¥100	US$0.90
New Zealand	NZ$1	US$0.66
UK	£1	US$1.29

For current exchange rates, see www.xe.com.

Tipping

Bars and restaurants For good service, tip 15% to 20% (minus the service charge that is sometimes included in the bill).

Dive guides Tip US$10 for a half-day outing.

Resorts Often include a 15% service charge on the bill. If not, tip US$1 to US$3 per day for housekeeping.

Taxis A 10% tip is usual.

OPENING HOURS

The following are standard business hours across the island. When cruise ships are in port, shops tend to be open. Outside tourist areas much is closed on Sunday.

EATING PRICE RANGES

The following price ranges refer to the cost of a main meal.

$ less than US$15

$$ US$15–25

$$$ more than US$25

Banks 9am–4pm Monday to Friday
Restaurants 11am–9pm
Shops 9am–noon and 2–6pm Monday to Saturday

PUBLIC HOLIDAYS

New Years Day January 1
Carnival Monday Monday before Ash Wednesday
Good Friday Friday before Easter
Easter Monday Monday after Easter
King's Birthday April 27
Labour Day May 1
Ascension Day Sixth Thursday after Easter
Bonaire Day September 6
Christmas Day December 25
Boxing Day December 26

TELEPHONE

Bonaire's country code is is 599.

To call within Bonaire, dial the seven-digit number without the code. For other countries, dial the international access code (011), then the country code, then the number.

Cell Phones

GSM cell (mobile) phones are compatible with local SIM cards. There is also 3G service. The main operator is Digicel (www.digicelbonaire.com).

> **PRACTICALITIES**
>
> **Newspapers** The *Bonaire Reporter* (www.bonairereporter.com) is a free biweekly newspaper that actually covers controversial issues on the island.
>
> **Radio** Bonaire Nu (99.9 Live99FM; www.bonaire.nu) Papiamento radio station and website featuring news and entertainment.
>
> **Smoking** Not usually restricted in bars or casinos, though restaurants tend to designate smoking and nonsmoking areas. The airport and other public buildings also have designated smoking areas. Most hotels and resorts prohibit smoking in rooms but allow it on the grounds.
>
> **Television** Tourist TV Bonaire (Telbo MiTV channel 1 and Flamingo TV channel 60) shows short documentaries on the island's history, culture and nature.
>
> **Weights & measures** The metric system is used.

TIME

Bonaire runs to Atlantic Standard Time (AST), which is four hours behind Greenwich Mean Time. Daylight saving is not observed.

VOLUNTEERING

Bonaire is one of the more prosperous islands in the Caribbean, and volunteer opportunities are scarce. That said, there are a few organizations that depend on the efforts of dedicated volunteers:

Animal Shelter Bonaire (☎717-4989; www.animalshelterbonaire.com; Kaminda Lagoen 26; ⏲9am-noon & 3-5pm Mon-Fri, 9am-3pm Sat) This beloved place depends on volunteers to help out with maintenance and promoting adoption at local markets, as well as showering some loving kindness on the resident dogs and cats.

Donkey Sanctuary (p235) Dote on the donkeys and make them feel at home.

Echo Parrot Sanctuary (p234) This bird sanctuary – working to protect the yellow-shouldered Amazon parrot – depends on volunteers for all manner of support, including population monitoring, bird care, trail maintenance and more.

Reef Renewal Foundation (Coral Restoration Foundation; ☎717-5080; https://reefrenewalbonaire.org) This inspiring organization works hard to preserve and produce endangered species of staghorn and elkhorn coral around Bonaire's reef. After undergoing specialized Professional Association of Diving Instructors (PADI) training to be a coral-restoration diver, volunteers can help maintain offshore coral nurseries and transplant healthy specimens to degraded areas.

Sea Turtle Conservation Bonaire (STCB; ☎780-0433, 717-2225; www.bonaireturtles.org; Kaya Korona 53; turtle tour US$40) Long-term volunteers undergo training to become independent 'beachkeepers,' monitoring beaches all around the island. From January to April, STCB recruits snorkelers to help with its in-water survey to count, identify and record sea-turtle species.

ℹ Getting There & Away

You can arrive in Bonaire by air or by sea (cruise ship). Flights, cars and tours can be booked online at lonelyplanet.com/bookings.

AIR

Flamingo Airport (www.flamingoairport.com) is immediately south of Kralendijk. Direct flights arrive from and depart for Amsterdam (Netherlands), Houston, Atlanta and Newark (USA) and Toronto (Canada), along with Curaçao and Aruba. Small regional airlines frequently appear and disappear, but Divi Divi Air (www.flydivi.

com) offers frequent service to/from Curaçao, as well as charters to Aruba.

SEA

Many cruise ships call at Bonaire, docking at the port in the middle of Kralendijk. On days when there's more than one ship in port, the center of town is closed and thousands of visitors swarm the island. See Info Bonaire (www.infobonaire.com) for the schedule of ships and cruises arriving in the port of Bonaire.

There are no ferries between the ABCs (Aruba, Bonaire and Curaçao).

Getting Around

There is no public transportation on Bonaire; however, tour operators and dive shops often offer transportation.

BICYCLE

Although there are no bike lanes on Bonaire, plenty of people ride along the flat roads, especially in the south. Traffic is usually light and roads are in decent condition. There are also mountain-biking routes in Washington-Slagbaai National Park and other off-road destinations in the north.

Bicycles are available at many resorts, bike shops and tour companies. **Bike Rental Delivery** (☎701-1441; www.bikerentalbonaire.com; cruiser/mountain bike per day from US$11/13, all bikes per week US$60) operates out of a van, which explains the name.

CAR & MOTORCYCLE

Branches of most international car-rental firms, including **Budget** (☎717-4700; www.budget.com; ⏰5am-10pm) and **Hertz** (☎717-7221; www.hertz.com), can be found at the airport, as can local agency **Pays-Bas Bonaire** (PB; ☎717-7424; www.totalbonaire.com). Other local agencies, including the highly recommended **AB Car Rental** (☎717-8980; www.abcarrental.com; Kaya Industria 31; ⏰7am-7pm Mon-Fri, to 8pm Sat & Sun) and **Carvenience** (☎770-0001; www.facebook.com/carveniencebonaire), are nearby.

- Main roads are mostly in good condition, but you'll want a 4WD for the rough roads in the national park and some remote spots on the east coast.
- Gasoline can only be found in Kralendijk.
- Road signs are sporadic, so you'll need a map or a GPS.
- Driving is on the right-hand side, seat belts are required and motorcyclists must wear helmets.

TAXI

Taxi service is available at the airport and near the cruise-ship terminal. Rates are set by the local government. From the airport, expect to pay US$10 to US$15 to the resorts around Kralendijk and US$18 to US$20 to resorts near Lac Bay. **Bonaire Taxi** (☎717-3964; www.bonairetaxi.net) is one of many taxi services around the island.

Roro (p233) offers wheelchair- and accessible-transportation services.

DEPARTURE TAX

The departure tax for most international flights is US$35, but it's just US$9 for flights to Aruba and Curaçao. The tax is normally included in the ticket price.

1

ISTHATITSME/BUDGET TRAVEL ©

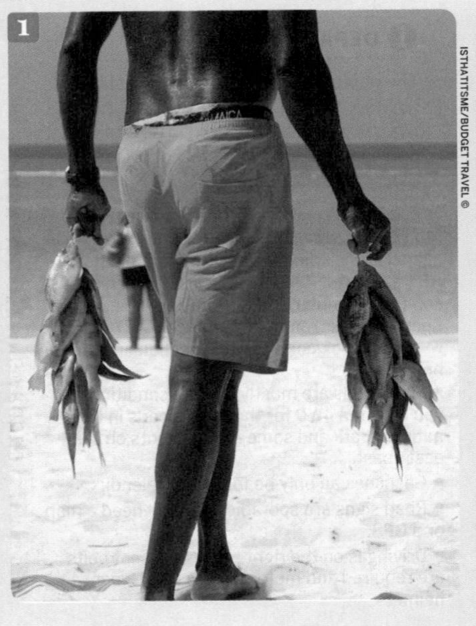

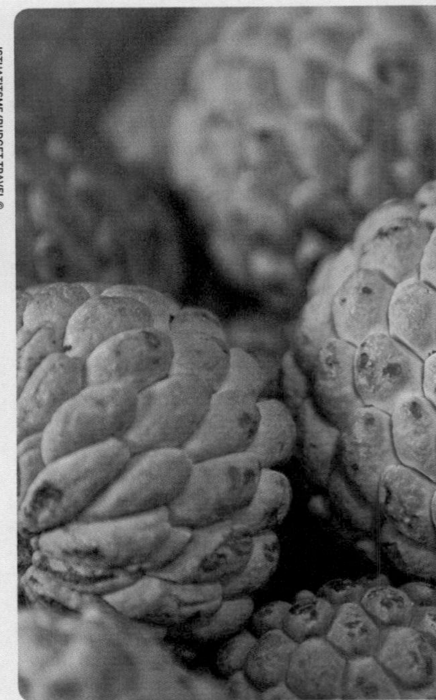

1. Fresh catch on Negril beach (p538) 2. Sugar or custard apples 3. Mofongo 4. Mojito

3

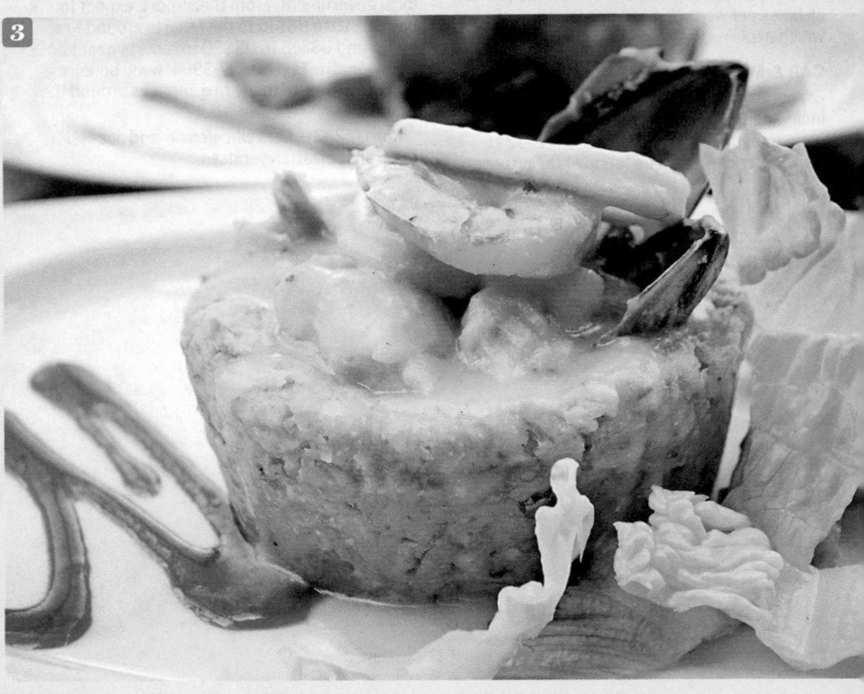

2

GWENGOAT/GETTY IMAGES ©

Island Cuisine

Seafood

A fish still dripping with saltwater, thrown on the grill and spritzed with lime, has made many a Caribbean travel memory. So too has a tasty lobster, grilled over coals then drenched in garlic butter.

Meat & Poultry

As for meat, chicken rules the roost. Mixed with rice, it's called *arroz con pollo* in the Spanish-speaking islands and *pelau* in Trinidad and St Kitts. Other favorites are *lechón asado* (roast pork), which features in Cuban and Puerto Rican sandwiches; and *cabrito* (goat).

Fruits

Tropical fruits are Caribbean icons. There are the usual suspects, like papaya, but be sure to sample sugar apple – a custardy fruit shot through with black pits – in the Bahamas (*anon* in Cuba); or *guinep,* a small lychee-like fruit, in Jamaica.

4

Drinks

Minty mojitos and lemony daiquiris in Cuba, sugary ti-punch in Martinique and the smooth and fruity goombay smash in the Bahamas are just some of the drinks on offer. It's no surprise that all of these contain rum: the Caribbean makes the world's best, and while some people venture no further than a regular old Cuba libre (rum and cola) or piña colada, a highball of exquisite seven-year-old *añejo* over ice is liquid heaven.

FOODIE FAVORITES

Jerk Jamaica's classic barbecue of spice-rubbed meat served with a fiery side sauce is found in many variations across the region.

Roti A tasty and ubiquitous South Asian–derived flat bread filled with curried meats, vegetables and more.

Mofongo A plantain crust encases seafood or steak in this Puerto Rican classic.

Callaloo Spicy soup with okra, meats, greens and hot peppers.

British Virgin Islands

☎284 / POP 28,000

Includes ➡

Best Places to Eat

- ➡ Lady Sarah's (p248)
- ➡ Hog Heaven (p256)
- ➡ CocoMaya (p255)
- ➡ D'Coalpot (p252)
- ➡ Wonky Dog (p262)
- ➡ Foxy's Taboo (p259)

Best Places to Stay

- ➡ Anegada Beach Club (p261)
- ➡ Guavaberry Spring Bay Homes (p255)
- ➡ Heritage Inn (p251)
- ➡ Oil Nut Bay (p256)
- ➡ Carrie's Island Comfort Inn (p251)

Why Go?

The British Virgin Islands (BVI) are territories of Her Majesty's land, but aside from scattered offerings of fish and chips, there's little that's overtly British. Most travelers come to hoist a jib and dawdle among the 50-plus isles. With steady trade winds, calm currents, protected bays and pirate-ship bars, this is one of the world's sailing hot spots.

Main island Tortola is known for its full-moon parties and sailing prowess. Billionaires and yachties swoon over Virgin Gorda and its magical rocks. Anegada floats in a remote reef and has a hammock waiting for those serious about unplugging. And who can resist little Jost Van Dyke, the 'barefoot island' where Main St is a calypso-wafting beach?

The islands have a quirky edge, and despite all the fancy boats and celebrity visitors, they remain relatively undeveloped.

When to Go

Mid-Dec–Apr Peak season: great weather, everything's open and the sailing scene is in full swing.

May & Jun Everything is still open, but crowds are fewer, prices decrease and winds are milder for sailors.

Nov The islands are lush from summer rains, crowds are minimal and lobster season begins anew.

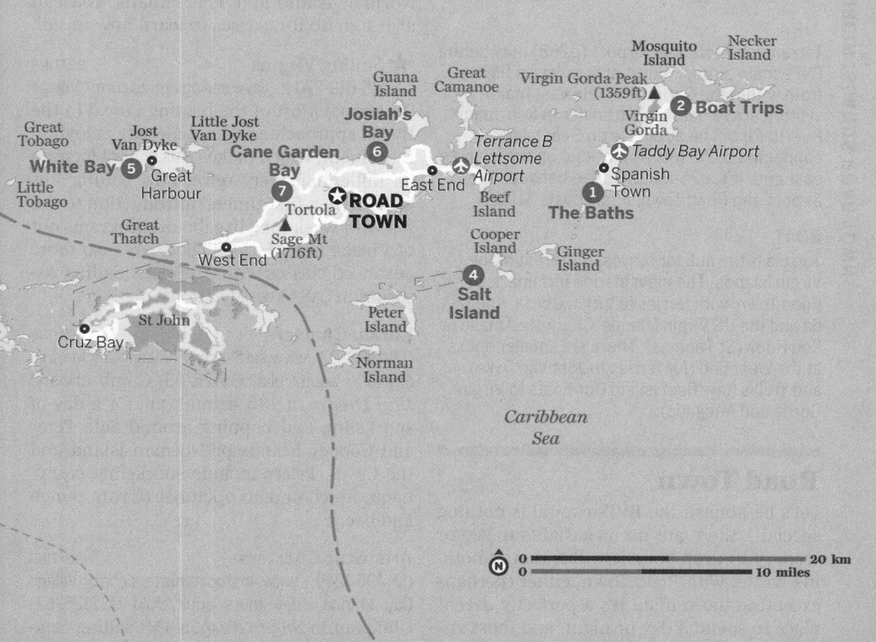

British Virgin Islands Highlights

❶ **The Baths** (p254) Wading around megaboulders and sloshing through grottoes at sunrise.

❷ **Boat trips** (p256) Sailing around the islands in a DIY charter boat or a glass-bottomed day-tour boat.

❸ **Anegada** (p260) Dining on lobsters, searching for flamingos and leaving the world behind on a far-flung island.

❹ **Wreck of the Rhone** (p263) Snorkeling or diving at the 1867 shipwreck by Salt Island.

❺ **White Bay** (p258) Drinking a rum-soaked Painkiller while learning to play the ring game.

❻ **Josiah's Bay** (p252) Kicking back on the dramatic strand of sand after a day of perfecting your surfing skills.

❼ **Cane Garden Bay** (p251) Dancing barefoot to the beat of reggae at the bustling beach bars.

TORTOLA

Among Tortola's sharp peaks and hillsides clad in bougainvillea you'll find a mash-up of play places. Take surfing lessons, join fire jugglers at a full-moon party, dive on shipwrecks, and by all means go sailing amid the festive surrounding isles.

More than 80% of the BVI's 28,000 citizens live and work on Tortola. It's the BVI's governmental and commercial center, plus its air and ferry hub. It's also the Caribbean's charter-boat capital. Beyond busy Road Town, groovy beaches and West Indian settlements full of local flavor await.

Getting There & Away

AIR

Terrance B Lettsome Airport (p268) may be the BVI's main airport, but it only receives flights from within the Caribbean. The vast majority of visitors arrive here via a transfer in San Juan, Puerto Rico. The airport is on Beef Island, connected to Tortola by a bridge on the island's east end. It's a 25-minute drive between the airport and Road Town; a taxi costs $US27.

BOAT

Tortola is the hub for ferries to the rest of the Virgin Islands. The main marine terminal is in Road Town, with ferries to Virgin Gorda, Anegada and the US Virgin Islands' Charlotte Amalie or Red Hook (St Thomas). There are smaller docks at the West End (for ferries to Jost Van Dyke) and Trellis Bay/Beef Island (for boats to Virgin Gorda and Anegada).

Road Town

Let's be honest: the BVI's capital is nothing special – there are no megasights to see or scenery to drop your jaw. But there's nothing wrong with Road Town, either (perhaps excepting the traffic). It's a perfectly decent place to spend a day or night, and most visitors do exactly that when they charter their own boat or take the ferries to the outlying islands.

Sights

Tortola Pier Park AREA

(www.tortolapier.com; Wickhams Cay 1; 9am-6pm) Located right by the cruise-ship dock, this area holds lanes of brightly painted, purple-roofed buildings filled with souvenir shops, clothing and jewelry boutiques, bars, restaurants and tour operators.

JR O'Neal Botanic Gardens GARDENS

(cnr Botanic Rd & Main St; adult/child US$3/2; 8am-4:30pm) These elegantly dilapidated 4-acre gardens provide a shady refuge from Road Town's hullabaloo and heat. Benches are set amid indigenous and exotic tropical plants, and there's also a lily pond, a small rainforest, a cactus grove and a herb garden. It's about two blocks north of the town's main roundabout.

Tours

Day-sail boats are plentiful. Most depart at around 9:30am and return by 4:30pm, calling in at some combination of the Baths, Cooper Island, Peter Island, Salt Island, Norman Island and The Indians. You can also sign up for classes to learn how to sail.

★ **Sailing Virgins** BOATING

(415-619-2704; www.sailingvirgins.com; Village Cay Marina) Most of the boating crowd in the BVI is approaching (if not already enjoying) retirement, which makes this school focused on millennials very refreshing. Sailing Virgins offers a first-timers' introduction to the sea with week-long liveaboard programs out of Village Cay Marina. There are also more advanced classes with American Sailing Association (ASA) certifications.

Kuralu Charters BOATING

(499-1313; www.kuralu.com; Village Cay Marina; day tours adult/child US$125/65) Climb aboard *Day Dream*, a 43ft catamaran, for a day of snorkeling and bopping around Salt, Peter and Cooper Islands or Norman Island and the Caves. Prices include snorkeling equipment, lunch and an open bar of rum punch and beers.

Aristocat Charters BOATING

(499-1249; www.aristocatcharters.com; Village Cay Marina; day tours adult/child US$125/62) Glide out in *Sugar Rush*, a 45ft sailing catamaran, for a day of island-hopping and snorkeling. The boat has a huge shaded cockpit and large 'trampolines' at the bow that are stellar for sun lounging. Prices include snorkeling gear, paddleboards, a buffet lunch and an open bar.

Festivals & Events

BVI Emancipation Festival CULTURAL

(www.bvitourism.com; late Jul-early Aug) This marks the 1834 Emancipation Act that abolished slavery in the BVI. Activities include everything from a beauty pageant to 'rise

Road Town

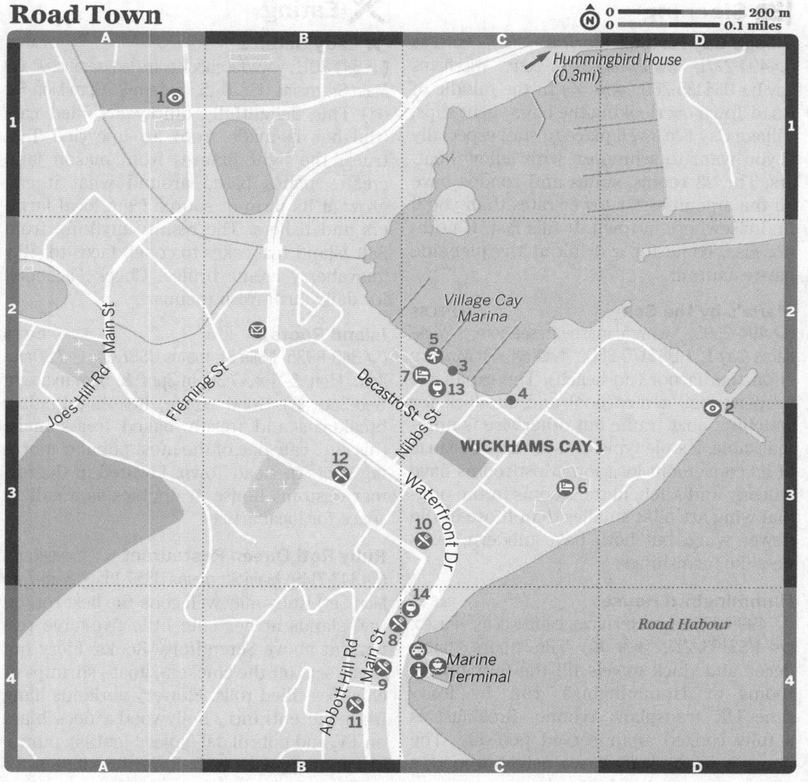

Road Town

Sights
1 JR O'Neal Botanic Gardens A1
2 Tortola Pier Park D3

Activities, Courses & Tours
3 Aristocat Charters C2
4 Kuralu Charters C2
5 Sailing Virgins C2

Sleeping
6 Maria's by the Sea C3
7 Village Cay Hotel & Marina C2

Eating
8 Capriccio di Mare B4
9 Dove B4
10 Island Roots C3
11 Lady Sarah's B4
12 Ruby Roti Queen Restaurant B3

Drinking & Nightlife
13 Dockside Bar C2
14 Pusser's Pub C4

Shopping
Pusser's Company Store .... (see 14)
Serendipity Books .... (see 12)

and shine tramps' (noisy parades led by reggae bands in the back of a truck that start at 3am). Events take place at various locations.

BVI Spring Regatta SAILING
(www.bvispringregatta.org; ⏰late Mar-early Apr) One of the Caribbean's biggest parties, with seven days of bands, boats and beer.

Sleeping

Village Cay Hotel & Marina HOTEL $$
(494-2771; www.villagecaybvi.com; Wickhams Cay 1; r US$135-260;) In the middle of Road Town overlooking the bay's yacht slips, Village Cay is a swell place to stay, especially if you want to schmooze with fellow boaters. The 23 rooms, suites and condos have all the amenities for lower rates than you'll find elsewhere in town. It fills fast. If nothing else, come for a drink at the pier-side bar-restaurant.

Maria's by the Sea HOTEL $$
(494-2595; www.mariasbythesea.com; Wickhams Cay 1; r US$170-260;) Maria's is on the harbor (no beach). The expansive property has a nice pool and sundeck for watching boat traffic but otherwise is unremarkable. People typically stay here because of its convenient location. Most rooms have balcony and kitchenette. Rooms in the original wing are a bit smaller than those in the newer wing, but both have modern, businesslike furnishings.

Hummingbird House B&B $$
(499-4326; www.hummingbirdbvi.com; Pasea; s/d US$193/217;) Tile floors, batik decor and thick towels fill the four breezy rooms at Hummingbird, run by longtime UK transplant Yvonne. Breakfast is a fully cooked affair served poolside. The house is in the leafy Pasea neighborhood, a 25-minute walk or US$5 cab ride northeast from town. It's near the Moorings, so many boaters stay here.

Eating

★**Lady Sarah's** CAFE $
(541-8011; www.facebook.com/ladysarahsbvi; 60 Main St; mains US$10-15; 8am-3:30pm Mon-Fri;) This delightfully quirky art-filled cafe (the bar is made from an upcycled Tata truck, the light fixtures from mason jars) creates plates based around what it can grow at its farm or source from local farmers and fishers. The result: anything from Salt Island fish cakes to conch tacos to silky guavaberry crème brûlée. Check Facebook for daily farm-fresh menus.

Island Roots CAFE $
(343-8985; Main St; mains US$8-14; 7:30am-3pm Mon & Tue, 7:30am-3pm & 5pm-midnight Wed-Sat;) Good coffee, heaping English breakfasts and freshly baked treats make this cute cafe one of the most popular morning spots in Road Town. Located in the former customs house, it doubles as a gallery space for local artists.

Ruby Roti Queen Restaurant CARIBBEAN $
(343-7149; Main St; mains US$7-15; 8am-7pm Mon-Sat) Ruby may well cook the best roti on the islands at her cute little five-table restaurant above Serendipity Books. Fiery hot sauce sets off the chicken-, goat-, shrimp- or chickpea-filled rolls. Flowery garlands hang from the entrance, Bollywood videos blare on TV, and pots of dal (spiced lentils), pumpkin and eggplant waft from the kitchen for additional sustenance.

WORTH A TRIP

NANNY CAY

Just west of Road Town the highway hugs the shoreline, dipping past marinas and resorts that tuck into the bays and offer several wet and wild activities. The area's main attraction is Nanny Cay, a small island made up of three cays originally known as Big Cay, Little Cay and Miss Peggy Cay.

These were consolidated in the 1970s to form a single landmass now helmed by the **Nanny Cay Resort & Marina** (394-2512; www.nannycay.com; r US$155-200;). Despite the 'resort' title, Nanny Cay is used more by boaters and business people than pleasure-seeking holidaymakers. The 40-room hotel has serviceable chambers with kitchenettes and balconies, as well as two restaurants, a marina, a beach, and a minimarket that nonguests can take advantage of.

Blue Water Divers (494-2847; www.bluewaterdiversbvi.com; Nanny Cay Marina; 2-tank dive US$130, discover scuba US$140; 8am-5pm) is a Professional Association of Diving Instructors (PADI)–certified dive shop here with three boats to get you to the good spots. It also does PADI courses such as discover scuba lessons for beginners. A taxi between town and Nanny Cay costs US$15.

Capriccio di Mare ITALIAN **$$**
(494-5369; Waterfront Dr; mains US$10-18; 8am-9pm Mon-Sat) Set on the porch of a classic West Indian house across from the ferry dock, this Italian cafe draws both locals and travelers. Breakfast includes pastries and cappuccino. Lunch and dinner feature salads, pasta dishes and pizza, with plenty of wines to wash it all down.

★**Dove** FRENCH **$$$**
(494-0313; http://dove-restaurant.com; 67 Main St; mains US$28-42; lunch noon-3pm, happy hour 4-6pm, dinner 6-10pm Mon-Fri;) The cozy, French-flaired Dove, set in a historic house, is pretty much the top address in town. The menu changes, but you might see pistachio-crusted duck, seared scallops, charcuterie platters, even foie-gras parfait. For something lighter, head upstairs to the **Dragonfly Lounge** for tapas. And then there's the wine: the list at the Dove is supposedly the BVI's largest.

Drinking & Nightlife

Dockside Bar BAR
(494-2771; www.villagecaybvi.com; Village Cay Marina; 7am-9:30pm) The expansive open-air bar-restaurant at Village Cay Marina is an amiable spot for a drink among charter-boat crews and networking local business people. There's live music on Friday and Saturday nights.

Pusser's Pub PUB
(494-3897; www.pussers.com; Waterfront Dr; mains US$12-24; 11am-10pm) Pusser's English-style, nautical-themed pub gets lively with travelers swilling the signature rum and whooping it up at brass-ringed tables. The menu of burgers, sandwiches, and fish and chips helps soak up the alcohol.

Pusser's Company Store GIFTS & SOUVENIRS
(494-2467; www.pussers.com; Main St; 9am-7pm Mon-Sat, to 5pm Sun) Adjoining Pusser's Pub, this shop sells logo clothing and accessories, as well as bottles of Pusser's Rum – the blend served on Her Majesty's Royal Navy ships for more than 300 years.

Information

Peebles Hospital (494-3497; www.bvihsa.vg; Main St; 24hr) Has complete emergency services.

Post office (468-5160; James Walter Francis Hwy; 9am-3:30pm Mon-Fri, to noon Sat)

Tourist office (www.bvitourism.com; Main St; 8am-7pm) Drop by the tiny office at the ferry terminal for a free road map and *BVI Welcome Guide*.

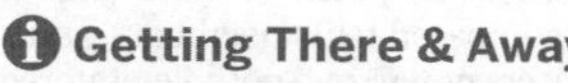

Terrance B Lettsome Airport (p268) is a 25-minute drive east of Road Town. A taxi costs US$27.

BOAT

Road Town's marine terminal is a busy hub for ferries to/from the following locations:

Anegada Twice daily on Monday, Wednesday and Friday (round-trip US$55, 1½ hours), via Road Town Fast Ferry (p269).

Charlotte Amalie, St Thomas Three or four times daily (one way US$40, one hour), via Road Town Fast Ferry and Native Son (p269).

Red Hook, St Thomas One or two daily (one way US$40, 45 minutes), via Native Son.

Virgin Gorda Roughly every hour (one way US$20, 30 minutes), via Smith's (p269), Speedy's (p269) and Sensation (p270).

All nonresidents entering the BVI have to pay a US$10 'environmental and tourism levy' on arrival.

CAR

Rates start at US$50 per day. **Itgo Car Rental** (494-5150; www.itgobvi.com; Wickhams Cay 1; 8:30am-5pm Mon-Sat) is a well-used independent company located at Wickhams Cay 1. **Avis** (494-4169; www.avis.com), **Hertz** (495-6600; www.hertz.com) and **National** (495-2626; www.nationalcar.com) also have branches around town.

TAXI

Taxis queue at the marine terminal and by the Crafts Alive Market. Otherwise, call the BVI Taxi Association (p271). The following are set, per-person rates from downtown:

Apple Bay US$27
Cane Garden Bay US$24
Nanny Cay US$15
Wickhams Cay 2 US$5

West End

The West End is known mostly for its sleepy little ferry terminal with vessels going to and from Jost Van Dyke. The action has historically centered on Soper's Hole, the site of a 16th-century pirates' den. It's now a major anchorage, with a marina and a pastel-colored building complex that once housed several bars and restaurants but has been painfully slow to recover after the 2017 hurricanes.

Sights & Activities

Smuggler's Cove BEACH

Near the island's northwestern tip, Smuggler's is a gorgeous patch of sand that is lightly trod compared to its neighbors, as access is via a crazy-narrow, pothole-cratered road. That said, cruise-ship groups do make their way here on occasion. Nigel's snack stand sells beer and rents beach chairs. The only other amenity is a portable bathroom. Snorkeling is fair.

Island Surf & Sail WATER SPORTS

(☎345-0123; www.bviwatertoys.com; Soper's Hole Marina) Rents all kinds of boards (surfboards, stand-up paddleboards), fishing gear, snorkeling equipment and even acoustic guitars for beachside *jammin'*. It's best to contact it online as the Soper's Hole location was in flux at the time of research.

Eating & Drinking

Omar's Fusion INTERNATIONAL **$$**

(☎495-8015; https://omarfusion.com; Soper's Hole; mains US$17-28; ⏲11am-10pm Nov-Aug) The newer (and nicer) sister of nearby **Omar's Cafe** (www.omarscafebvi.com; Soper's Hole; mains US$7-14; ⏲7am-2pm; 📶), this more upmarket eatery specializes in a fusion of Caribbean and Indian cuisine that goes well beyond the standard roti. You might dine on a lamb vindaloo while your neighbor chows down on a jerk-chicken pizza. It's a good place to hobnob with the yachting crowd.

Nigel's Boom Boom Beach Bar BAR

(www.facebook.com/Nigelboomboom; Smuggler's Cove; ⏲10am-5pm) This tarp-shaded shack on the white sands of Smuggler's Cove sells beer, booze and hot dogs, as well as two daily platters (usually with chicken or shrimp; US$17 to US$22). You can also rent snorkels (US$13 per day) and paddleboards or kayaks ($50 per hour). Bring a marker to write a message on the driftwood walls like everyone else.

Getting There & Away

The **ferry dock** (https://bviports.org/facilities/west-end; Sir Francis Drake Hwy) at Soper's Hole took a beating during the 2017 hurricanes and now only has boats running to and from Jost Van Dyke. There are still customs and immigration facilities for boaters, but there's little else here (no shops, no food – not even a shaded waiting area). Ferries to Cruz Bay and Red Hook in the USVI may return in 2020 or 2021.

New Horizon Ferry (p269) runs to Jost Van Dyke (one way US$20, 25 minutes, five daily); cash only.

You can no longer rely on taxis waiting around at the ferry terminal, so it's best to call the West End Taxi Association (p271) in advance. **Denzil Clyne Jeep & Car Rentals** (☎495-4900; www.denzilclynerentals.com; Sir Francis Drake Hwy; ⏲8am-4:30pm) is nearby for DIY drivers. **Ocean Dreams Water Taxi** (☎340-998-6720, 345-1242; www.oceandreamswatertaxi.com; Soper's Hole) can shuttle groups between the West End and the USVI.

Cane Garden Bay Area

A turquoise cove ringed by steep green hills, Cane Garden Bay is exactly the kind of place Jimmy Buffett would immortalize in song – which he did in the 1978 tune 'Mañana.' The area's perfect 1-mile beach and throngs of rum-serving bars and restaurants make it Tortola's most popular party zone.

South of Cane Garden Bay is a series of picturesque bays. Speckled amid clumps of shoreside holiday villas are small West Indian settlements. When you stay out here you're living among locals.

Sights

★**Sage Mountain National Park** PARK

(Sage Mountain Rd; ⏲sunrise-sunset) At 1716ft, Sage Mountain rises higher than any other peak in the Virgin Islands. Seven trails crisscross the surrounding 92-acre park, including the main path that leaves from the parking lot and moseys up through the greenery to a picnic spot. From there, you can head onward on the central trail and return on the north trail for a good loop (be prepared for mud). There's a US$3 entrance fee, but nobody's been around to collect it for years.

The park is humid and damp, populated by bo-peep frogs and lizards. The 20ft fern trees and other flora look as though they're straight out of the age of the dinosaurs. Allow two hours for your rambles. Or say to heck with hiking, and simply make your way to the viewing platforms off the parking lot for vistas of the USVI and BVI.

Jim Cullimore, owner of **Mountain View** gift shop and restaurant (open 9am to 3pm) at the trailhead, is a fount of park knowledge. He'll set you up with a map and tips on how to navigate the trails if you purchase something.

★Cane Garden Bay BEACH

Cane Garden Bay is probably on the postcard that drew you to the British Virgin Islands. The gently sloping crescent of sand hosts plenty of beachside bars and water-sports vendors renting kayaks and paddleboards. It's a popular yacht anchorage, and becomes a full-on madhouse when cruise ships arrive in Road Town and shuttle passengers over for the day. It's the island's main party beach, but you can't deny its beauty and good-time vibe. Live bands often rock the bars.

Brewers Bay BEACH

(👪) Shady, tree-lined Brewers has decent snorkeling and a more tranquil scene than you'll find at nearby Cane Garden Bay – possibly because getting here involves a brake-smoking drive down steep switchbacks. **Nicole's Beach Bar** (⏲ 10am-10pm) has restrooms, rents chairs and snorkels (no fixed price; bargain hard), and offers food and drinks. All other establishments here were destroyed by the 2017 hurricanes and hadn't returned at research time.

Brewers gets moderately crowded with families if a cruise ship is in; otherwise it's blissfully empty.

Apple Bay BEACH

Apple Bay is long and narrow, and is known as the 'surfing beach,' especially from late December to March, when the consistent swells roll in. It's not a traditional beach with lounge chairs, swimming and people lolling on the sand. Rather it's a spot to watch ripped folks catch waves. Sadly, many of the area's ramshackle beach bars, including the famed Bomba Shack, were destroyed in the 2017 hurricanes and haven't returned.

On many maps, Apple Bay includes Cappoons Bay.

North Shore Shell Museum MUSEUM

(☎343-7581; Carrot Bay; by donation; ⏲hours vary) It's more a folk-art gallery and junk shop than a museum, but it's funky however you describe it, with a hodgepodge of shells and signs painted with cryptic local sayings filling the shelves. The hours vary depending on when the proprietor, Egbert Donovan, is around to show you through. He'll also encourage you to buy something.

Long Bay BEACH

Long Bay is an attractive 1-mile stretch of white sand well used by joggers and walkers. A top-end resort sits on the eastern portion, where you can get food and drinks.

Sleeping

Cane Garden Bay has the mother lode of options and is home to the cheapest rooms in the BVI, though the party noise at night can ruin the tranquility. You could feasibly stay at Cane Garden Bay's beachside digs without a car, but you'll need wheels to stay at any of the lodgings at Brewers Bay, Carrot Bay or Apple Bay.

★Carrie's Island Comfort Inn INN $

(☎542-1092; www.stanleycomfort.com; Cane Garden Bay; r US$65-100; ❄📶) Each of the 16 units in this lavender-colored building has full kitchen, spacious living room and private balcony with sublime views over Cane Garden Bay (a quick walk down and a hard slog back up). Sure, the beds are a bit stiff, but you won't find a better value in the BVI.

★Heritage Inn HOTEL $$

(☎494-5842; Windy Hill; 1-/2-bedroom ste US$180/380; ❄📶🏊) High on Windy Hill between Cane Garden Bay and Carrot Bay, this property has nine spacious rooms that seem to hang out in thin air. If you like the feel of a self-contained oasis with pool, sundeck, and bar-restaurant with awesome views, the Heritage Inn is for you. Each unit has a full kitchen.

★Ke Villas HOTEL $$

(☎496-8991; www.kevillasbvi.com; Carrot Bay; r US$150-210; ❄📶) Pronounced 'key,' this place has 12 great-value, recently built, spick-and-span waterfront rooms. Each offers wi-fi, comfy bed, kitchenette with dishware, and big walk-in rain shower. The 1st-floor rooms have a patio and the 2nd-floor rooms a balcony, both prime for watching pelicans dive-bomb fish out front. Ke's hospitable and knowledgable owners really set this property apart.

Sebastian's on the Beach HOTEL $$

(☎544-4212; www.sebastiansbvi.com; Little Apple Bay; r US$188-298, villas US$330-360; ❄📶) Well known for its pretty stretch of beachfront, Sebastian's has 26 banana-yellow rooms in a wide range of sizes and locations (some on the beach, some not). Take a good look around before deciding: room decor and brightness vary even within the same price bracket. There are also nine hilltop villas with kitchens, and balconies practically over the water.

★**Sugar Mill Hotel** BOUTIQUE HOTEL $$$
(☎495-4355; www.sugarmillhotel.com; Apple Bay; r incl breakfast US$295-495;) In a league of its own for ambience, intimacy and customer service, this boutique hotel rises from the ruins of the Appleby Plantation that gave Apple Bay its name. Guests stay in the 24 studios and suites that hide on the steep hillside among mahogany trees, bougainvillea and palms. All rooms have balconies and sea views.

Eating

The most concentrated scene is at Cane Garden Bay, where all the bars also serve seafood and Caribbean dishes. Move beyond to the area's further-flung communities, and you'll find stellar hotel restaurants and local eateries that cook up authentic West Indian fare.

★**D'Coalpot** CARIBBEAN $$
(☎545-6510; www.dcoalpotbvi.com; Carrot Bay; mains US$18-29; ⊙5-10pm Mon-Fri, from noon Sat & Sun;) D'Coalpot's casual outdoor tables under strings of lights are a local favorite. Spicy jerk meats, curries, rotis, grilled fish and other West Indian staples emerge from the kitchen in heaping portions. Staff are friendly, prices are reasonable – what's not to love?

Sugar Mill Restaurant CARIBBEAN $$$
(☎495-4355; www.sugarmillhotel.com; Apple Bay; mains US$30-45; ⊙7-8:30pm) Mod Caribbean concoctions such as creamy lobster ravioli and coconut-crusted chicken with lime chutney hit the Sugar Mill's polished tables. It's hard to beat for romance, with meals served in the restored, candlelit boiling house of the plantation's rum distillery. Wines, fizzy cocktails and decadent desserts complete the sensory experience. Reservations are a must.

Bananakeet INTERNATIONAL $$$
(☎494-5842; Windy Hill; mains US$20-40; ⊙4-9:30pm;) What more can you ask for than stellar Caribbean and international cuisine, a refreshing breeze and soaring views across three Tortola bays? Try the jerk pork with banana-mango chutney and you will experience the tropics on a plate.

Drinking & Nightlife

★**Paradise Club** BAR
(www.facebook.com/paradiseclubvi; Cane Garden Bay; ⊙10am-1am;) The most buzzing beach bar on Tortola is ready-made for your Instagram account, with swings in the sea and an 'I heart BVI' sign on land. Paradise lights up by night with tiki torches, firepits and psychedelic glow lights. It also serves pub-style lunches and dinners at picnic tables in the sand.

★**Quito's Gazebo** BAR
(☎495-4837; www.facebook.com/quitosgazebo; Cane Garden Bay; ⊙10am-11pm) This beachside bar-restaurant almost always has a crowd of boozy revelers. It takes its name from owner Quito Rymer, whose band has toured with Ziggy Marley. You can dance up a storm to Quito's reggae rhythms, and people flock in to do just that. Check Facebook for when he's playing (usually Wednesdays). Live music fills the air every happy hour, too.

Getting There & Away

Cane Garden Bay is a 25-minute drive over the mountainous route from Road Town; a taxi costs US$24. It's the same price from Road Town to Brewers Bay, and a few dollars more to Apple Bay and Cappoons Bay (US$27). Cane Garden Bay has a taxi stand, but otherwise you'll need a car to get around.

East End

Tortola's East End is a mix of steep mountains, remote bays and thickly settled West Indian communities. Art and surfing take pride of place. The BVI's main airport welcomes travelers here.

The hurricanes of 2017 destroyed all East End hotels. Not one had reopened at research time. A resort at Lambert Beach should be fixed up by 2020, and there are a few rental villas scattered atop the hills. Otherwise, the closest lodgings are luxe properties on the offshore islands of Guana and Scrub.

Sights

★**Josiah's Bay** BEACH
An undeveloped gem at the foot of a valley on the north shore, Josiah's Bay is a dramatic strand that has excellent surf with a point break in winter. Many say it offers Tortola's best surfing. A beach bar serves snacks and cold beers. Surf School BVI has a facility on-site from which it rents boards and offers lessons.

Aragorn's Studio ARTS CENTER
(☎542-0586; www.aragornsstudio.com; Trellis Bay; ⊙9am-6pm) Local metal sculptor Aragorn Dick-Read started his studio under the sea-grape trees fronting Trellis Bay, the broad beach just east of the airport. It grew to include space for potters, coconut carvers and batik makers, many of whom you can see at work in the now-sprawling arts center. Aragorn also hosts family-friendly full-moon parties.

Activities

★Tortola Sailing & Sights BOATING
(☎340-7594; www.tortolasailingandsights.com; Penn's Landing Marina; ⊙9am-5pm) Perfect for an educational vacation learning to sail or captain a boat in one of the best classrooms in the world. IYT- and ASA-approved courses include the two-day Learn to Sail, the five-day Powerboat Captain and the week-long Liveaboard Fast-Track to Bareboat Cruising.

Surf School BVI SURFING
(☎343-0002; www.surfschoolbvi.com; Josiah's Bay; 1½hr lessons from US$65, full-day rental US$35; 👪) Excellent instructors teach you how to hang 10 at Josiah's Bay. Beginners and children welcome. Board rentals for experienced surfers available, too.

Festivals & Events

★Fireball Full Moon Party CULTURAL
(Trellis Bay; 👪) Aragorn's Studio and the surrounding businesses combine to put on the Fireball Full Moon Party each month. It's an artsy, family-friendly event, unlike the island's other moon bashes. The party kicks off around 8pm with calypso music, stilt walkers and fire jugglers. At midnight Aragorn sets his steel 'fireball sculpture' ablaze on the ocean – a must-see.

Eating

Trellis Bay Market Bar & Grill CARIBBEAN $
(www.trellisbaymarket.com; Trellis Bay; mains US$10-15; ⊙11am-9pm) Sit at the lime-green picnic tables and dine on jerk pork, grilled pig tail, lobster pasta or a veggie roti at this popular beachfront dive. By night the string lights flicker on and the party rages, especially when there's a full moon.

Red Rock INTERNATIONAL $$
(☎442-1646; www.bviredrock.com; Penn's Landing Marina; mains US$15-35; ⊙3-10pm Tue-Thu & Sun, from 11am Fri & Sat; 📶) Mingle with the boating crowd at the East End's top restaurant, which deftly manages a world of cuisines from pad Thai to chicken schnitzel to plantain gnocchi. The service is hit or miss, but the breezy marina setting is superb.

Getting There & Away

Terrance B Lettsome Airport (p268) is technically on Beef Island, connected via bridge to Tortola. It's a 25-minute drive to Road Town. A small dock lies within walking distance of the airport at Trellis Bay. Speedy's (p269) ferries depart for Virgin Gorda (US$20 one way, 20 minutes, seven daily), while Anegada Express (p269) ferries depart for Anegada (US$35 one way, one hour, 7:30am and 3:30pm Tuesday, Thursday, Saturday and Sunday).

For a taxi, try Beef Island Taxi Association (p271).

VIRGIN GORDA

Virgin Gorda is the BVI's rich, plump beauty. The otherworldly granite megaliths at the Baths put on the main show, but gorgeous beaches unfurl all around the island. Movie stars live here (oh hey, Morgan Freeman), and billionaires own the isles floating just offshore (lookin' at you, Richard Branson). Somehow, Virgin Gorda keeps a level head and remains a slowpoke, chicken-dotted destination without rampant commercialism.

Getting There & Away

AIR

Taddy Bay Airport (VIJ; www.bviaa.com) is on the Valley's east side, about 1 mile from Spanish Town. A taxi into town costs US$5. The airport is teeny, though it's well used by small regional airlines.

BOAT

The main dock is in Spanish Town. Ferries sail between here and Road Town in Tortola almost every hour during the day (one way US$20, 30 minutes) via three companies: Sensation Ferries (p270), Smith's Ferry/Tortola Fast Ferry (p269) and Speedy's.

Speedy's also provides direct service between Spanish Town and Charlotte Amalie, St Thomas (in the US Virgin Islands), on Tuesday and Saturday (one way US$40, 1½ hours) and to Beef Island, Tortola (by the airport), several times daily (one way US$20, 20 minutes).

Both Road Town Fast Ferry and Anegada Express call at Virgin Gorda on their way from Tortola to Anegada (one way US$35, one hour).

The former stops at the main dock, while the latter picks up at Yacht Harbour.

Spanish Town & the Valley

Spanish Town isn't a town so much as a long road with businesses strung along it. While it may be the commercial center of Virgin Gorda, it's a sleepy place where roosters and goats dodge the occasional traffic. The mix of islanders, yachties and land travelers eating and drinking together creates a festive vibe.

'The Valley' is the long rolling plain that covers the island's southern half, including Spanish Town.

Sights

★The Baths PARK

(US$3; sunrise-sunset;) This collection of sky-high boulders marks a national park and the BVI's most popular attraction. The rocks – volcanic-lava leftovers from some 70 million years ago – form a series of grottoes that flood with seawater. The area makes for unique swimming and snorkeling, but the coolest part is the trail through the 'Caves' to Devil's Bay. During the 20-minute trek, you'll clamber over boulders, slosh through tidal pools, squeeze into impossibly narrow passages, then drop onto a sugar-sand beach.

While the Baths and environs stir the imagination, they're often overrun with tourists. By 9am each morning fleets of yachts have moored off the coast, and visitors have been shuttled in from resorts and cruise ships. All you have to do, though, is come at sunrise or late in the day and you'll get a lot more elbow room.

The Baths' beach has bathrooms with showers, a snack shack and snorkel-gear rental (US$10). Taxis run constantly between the park and the ferry dock in Spanish Town.

Spring Bay BEACH

FREE An excellent beach with national-park designation, Spring Bay abuts the Baths to the north. The beauty here is having a Baths-like setting but without the crowds. Hulking boulders dot the fine white sand. There's clear water and good snorkeling off the area called 'the Crawl' (a large pool enclosed by boulders and protected from the sea). Sea-grape trees shade a scattering of picnic tables, but that's the extent of the facilities.

Copper Mine National Park PARK

(sunrise-sunset) FREE You'll drive down a winding, boulder-avoiding road to reach this forlorn bluff at Virgin Gorda's southeastern tip, but it's worth it to see the impressive stone ruins (including a chimney, a cistern and a mine-shaft house) that comprise the park. Cornish miners worked the area between 1838 and 1867 and extracted as much as 10,000 tons of copper, then abandoned the mine to the elements. The blue sea pounds below, and a couple of paths meander through the ruins.

Activities & Tours

Dive BVI DIVING

(541-9818; www.divebvi.com; Yacht Harbour; 1-/2-tank dives US$95/130; 8am-5pm Mon-Fri, 10am-3pm Sat) This shop has three fast boats that can take you diving at any of the BVI sites. It also offers full-day boating/snorkeling trips (from US$120 per person) aboard a catamaran.

Double 'D' BOATING

(499-2479; www.doubledbvi.com; Yacht Harbour; day trips US$125) Glide to Jost, Anegada, Cooper or Norman islands aboard a 40ft yacht or 30ft powerboat. Trips include time for snorkeling, hiking and general island shenanigans.

Festivals & Events

Virgin Gorda Easter Festival CARNIVAL

(www.facebook.com/virgingordaeasterfestival; late Mar-Apr) Spanish Town around the yacht harbor comes alive with mocko jumbies (costumed stilt walkers representing spirits of the dead), a fishing competition, a food fair, a full lineup of live music and parades for the Easter Fest, held Saturday through Monday.

Sleeping

Lodgings here tend to be smaller and more low-key than up north. A couple of options are walkable from the ferry dock; everything else is within a 10-minute drive.

★Bayview Vacation Apartments APARTMENT $$

(499-0755; www.bayviewbvi.com; apt from US$120;) Each of these two-floor apartments near the ferry dock, off Lee Rd, has two bedrooms with balconies, a full kitchen, dining facilities and an airy living room. It's the best deal on Virgin Gorda, especially if you have three or four people, though you'll have to drive to the nearest beach.

Fischer's Cove Beach Hotel HOTEL $$
(☎495-5253; www.fischerscove.com; d/apt from US$165/245; ❄📶) Fischer's Cove took a beating in the 2017 hurricanes and, while open, was still a work in progress at research time. There were eight beachfront apartments with full kitchens and a garden-facing hotel block of six no-frills studios with kitchenettes. More units were forthcoming. The restaurant has an enviable view over the sea. The complex is off Lee Rd.

★Guavaberry Spring Bay Homes COTTAGE $$$
(☎544-7186; www.guavaberryspringbay.com; apt US$288-525; @📶) A short walk from the Baths and plopped amid similar hulking boulders off Tower Rd, Guavaberry's circular cottages have one to three bedrooms, full kitchen, dining area and sun porch. The setting is amazing. There's a common area with games and books, and a commissary stocked with alcohol, snacks and meals to cook in your cottage.

Little Dix Bay HOTEL $$$
(☎214-880-4320; www.littledixbay.com; ❄📶🏊) This is the resort that rocketed Virgin Gorda to glory, and it remains the island's swankiest, most celebrity-favored digs. Though closed at the time of research due to extensive hurricane damage, it should be open again by the time you read this.

Eating

Spanish Town Cafe CARIBBEAN $
(☎542-8188; www.facebook.com/spanishtowncafe; Little Rd; mains US$12-18; ⏲6am-9pm) Virgin Gorda has a strong Dominican community, and this family-run open-air cafe on the road leading away from the ferry dock offers dishes that reflect the community's fusion of Latin flavors with West Indian ingredients. Daily lunch specials are some of the best budget meals in town and might include stewed oxtail or steamed snapper with rice and beans.

Mad Dog SANDWICHES $
(☎544-2681; Tower Rd; mains US$8-12; ⏲10am-6pm; 📶) Expatriates and tourists alike gather at this airy little pavilion set among the rocks where the road ends at the Baths. They can't resist the toasted sandwiches – the turkey and bacon wins particular plaudits – to help take the edge off the killer, secret-recipe piña coladas.

★CocoMaya INTERNATIONAL $$
(☎495-6344; www.cocomayarestaurant.com; Tower Rd; mains US$18-36; ⏲noon-3pm & 5-10pm Tue-Sun; 🖉) Slick CocoMaya seems more suited to the city than the beach. But on the sand it is, creating dishes with an Asian and Latin twist. Small plates include hoisin-sauced duck tacos and beer-battered snapper sliders, while large plates bring pork belly and pad Thai. There are more vegetarian and gluten-free choices than you usually see in these parts. Inventive, gingery cocktails add pizzazz.

Top of the Baths INTERNATIONAL $$
(☎495-5497; Tower Rd; mains US$14-23; ⏲8am-6pm) Yes, it sits above the Baths and yes, it's touristy. But the hilltop view kills and the comfort food (such as Amaretto French toast for breakfast or coconut shrimp for lunch) is decent. Plus there's a little swimming pool to dip into.

ℹ Getting There & Around

The **ferry dock** (Little Rd) sits next to the Yacht Harbour, both abuzz with boats. Sensation Ferries and Smith's Ferry/Tortola Fast Ferry run services to Road Town, Tortola (30 minutes). Speedy's runs ferries to Road Town as well as to Beef Island, Tortola (20 minutes), and to Charlotte Amalie, St Thomas (1½ hours). Both Road Town Fast Ferry and Anegada Express call at Virgin Gorda on their way from Tortola to Anegada (one hour).

Taxis queue outside the terminal. Rental-car companies will usually meet you here.

North Sound

Steep mountain slopes rise on Virgin Gorda's midsection, culminating at hike-worthy Gorda Peak. Beyond lies North Sound, a little settlement whose job is to serve the hotels and myriad yachts anchored in the surrounding bays. A mini-armada of ferries tootle back and forth from the Sound's

Gun Creek dock to the luxurious resorts along the remote northeastern peninsula. Kiteboarding, glass-bottom-boat tours and lengthy beach walks are also on tap.

Sights

★Savannah Bay — BEACH

A short distance north of the Valley, Savannah Bay features more than a mile of white sand. Except for the beaches of Anegada, no other shore provides such opportunities for long, solitary walks. Sunsets here can be fabulous. The water is calm and typically there are very few people about. There are no facilities and not much shade, so come prepared. A small sign off North Sound Rd points the way to a little parking area.

The Dogs — ISLAND

This clutch of five little islands lies 2.5 miles off the northwestern coast of Virgin Gorda. Partly protected by the BVI National Parks Trust, the Dogs are sanctuaries for birds and marine animals. The unusual name is due to the barking noises early sailors heard here, which came not from canines but from Caribbean monk seals, later hunted to extinction. The diving and snorkeling here are excellent. Book a trip with a Spanish Town-based dive or charter outfit.

Gorda Peak National Park — PARK

(sunrise-sunset) FREE At 1359ft, Gorda Peak is the island's highest point. Two well-marked trails lead to the summit off North Sound Rd, and make a sweet hike. If you're coming from the Valley, the first trailhead you'll see marks the start of the longer trail (about 1.5 miles). It's easier to begin at the higher-up trailhead, from where it's a 20-minute, half-mile walk to the crest.

Activities & Tours

★Sea It Clear Tours — BOATING

(343-9537; www.seaitcleartours.com; Gun Creek dock; prices vary) This outfit is also known as Gumption's Tours (after amiable owner Gumption Creque). Gumption takes you out in his glass-bottom boat to see shipwrecks and creatures swimming on the local reef. He also runs nature tours to Sir Richard Branson's Necker Island (Branson loaned Gumption the money to start his company). See the website for the changing schedule.

Heaven Spa & Wellness — SPA

(499-0102; www.heavenspaworld.com; massage from US$100, yoga US$10) A friendly young Indian couple runs this small spa (with sweeping views) by Hog Heaven. It specializes in Ayurveda treatments and massages, and there are also yoga classes at 6:15am on Monday, Wednesday and Friday (or by request).

Sleeping

Most North Sound lodgings are fairly isolated resorts, some accessible by ferry only. They're great places for active couples or families who like to spend their days on the water.

Note that most resorts were badly damaged by the 2017 hurricanes; many remained closed at the time of research.

Gordian Terrace — GUESTHOUSE $$

(499-6045; www.gordianterrace.com; North Sound Rd, Little Hill; d/q US$240/350) This eight-unit guesthouse up the road from the Gun Creek ferry dock has spacious rooms with distant sea views, full kitchens and even grills on the balconies for barbecues. Delightful Lauralee runs the place and is great for a chat, particularly about Caribbean art.

★Oil Nut Bay — RESORT $$$

(393-1000; www.oilnutbay.com; ste/villas from US$750/1250; @) Virgin Gorda is known for its high-end resorts, but Oil Nut Bay takes the cake for over-the-top luxury. Between the manicured hills and the powdered-sugar beach is an ever-growing collection of fabulous villas, more affordable suites (with dreamy infinity pools), plenty of water sports, a spa and wellness center, a kids club, a nature center and more.

If you didn't roll up in your own yacht or helicopter, access is via the hourly ferry from Gun Creek.

Bitter End Yacht Club & Resort — RESORT $$$

(800-872-2392; www.beyc.com; @) This iconic resort at the east end of North Sound has a collection of well-appointed hillside villas and bountiful equipment for sailing, windsurfing, kayaking and much more. Though largely destroyed in the hurricanes of 2017 (and closed at the time of research), it planned to reopen.

Eating

★Hog Heaven — BARBECUE $$

(547-5964; mains US$16-20; 10am-10pm) Off-the-beaten-path Hog Heaven is located way up on a hill that unfurls spectacular views. Tender, tangy, ginger-touched barbecue ribs are the house specialty, and the crunchy fried chicken, potato salad and conch chowder are terrific. There are banquet-hall-like indoor tables, but most people throng the outdoor bar and deck, from where you can see Moskito, Necker and other islands glimmering offshore.

It can be windy up here, so bring a jacket.

Sugarcane Restaurant INTERNATIONAL **$$**
(www.nailbaysportsclub.com; Nail Bay; mains US$14-20; ⌚8am-11pm Wed-Mon; 📶) Come to this beautifully manicured hilltop property above Nail Bay for chic poolside dining and Instagrammable features such as curvaceous sun loungers and tables set in a sand pit. Inventive mains include a grilled lobster-and-cheese sandwich and a shaved-kale caesar with mahi. Bring your swimsuit for a post-meal dip!

Getting There & Away

Ferries depart from Gun Creek to nearby resorts. Due to hurricane damage (and the temporary closure of many properties), only the Oil Nut Bay boat was operating at the time of research. It departs roughly every hour on the 45 (eg 10:45) and returns on the 15.

A taxi from the ferry in Spanish Town to Gun Creek or Leverick Bay costs US$30. Unless you're headed onward to a resort that's only accessible by sea, you're better off renting a car.

JOST VAN DYKE

Jost (pronounced 'yoast') is a little island with a big personality. It may only take up 4 sq miles of teal-blue sea, but its reputation has spread thousands of miles beyond. A lot of that is due to calypsonian and philosopher Foxy Callwood, the island's main man.

In the late 1960s, free-spirited boaters found Jost's shores, and Foxy built a bar to greet them. Soon folks such as Jimmy Buffett and Keith Richards were dropping by for a drink.

Despite its fame, Jost remains an unspoiled oasis of green hills fringed by blinding white sand. There's a small clutch of restaurants, beach bars and guesthouses, but little else.

Getting There & Away

Most visitors arrive by yacht. Landlubbers can get here by ferry from Tortola's West End via New Horizon Ferry (p269; US$30 round-trip, 25 minutes, five daily) or from St John and St Thomas (US Virgin Islands) via Inter Island (p269; US$130 round-trip, 30 minutes, twice daily Friday, Saturday and Sunday). Ferries arrive at the pier by Great Harbour.

Dohm's Water Taxi (☎340-775-6501; www.dohmswatertaxi.com) and Foxy's Charters offers a customized, much pricier way to get between Jost and St John or St Thomas.

Taxis wait by the ferry dock. Fares are set. Taxis charge per person, and fares go down considerably the more passengers there are.

Great Harbour

In Jost's foremost settlement, Main St is a beach lined with hammocks and open-air bar-restaurants, which might give you a hint as to the vibe here. Most folks just hang out, though active types can arrange kayaking, snorkeling and boating trips.

Activities & Tours

Foxy's Charters BOATING
(☎441-1905; www.foxyscharters.com) Based at Foxy's (p258). Arrange day trips to neighboring islands on a 37ft or 31ft motorboat. Also runs water taxis between the BVI and St John or St Thomas in the US Virgin Islands.

JVD Scuba OUTDOORS
(☎443-2222, 287-2731; www.jostvandykescuba.com; ⌚8am-6pm Sun-Fri) The one-stop shop for activities on Jost. It can set you up for hiking and snorkeling ecotours, paddleboard rentals, and diving and fishing trips.

Endeavor II BOATING
(☎496-0861; www.jvdps.org; per person US$125) Head out for a day sail to remote cays for snorkeling and an education about Jost's ecology. Locals – led by the legendary Foxy Callwood – built the 32ft wooden sloop by hand, then rebuilt it after the 2017 hurricanes. The JVD Preservation Society sponsored the project to teach the island's youth traditional boat-building skills.

Sleeping

Great Harbour has a smattering of simple rooms. White Bay offers more choices.

Sea Crest Inn APARTMENT **$$**
(☎443-5300; www.seacrestinn.net; apt US$200-230; ❄📶) Each of the six large studio apartments at this family-run property has kitchenette, TV, queen-size bed, private

bathroom and balcony. The deck overlooking the harbor is prime for cocktail sipping. It's just east of Foxy's bar, so it can be a bit noisy.

Ali Baba's GUESTHOUSE $$
(☎544-5602; r US$160-180; ❄) This popular restaurant offers three 'heavenly rooms' on its 2nd floor. One of the compact, whitewashed, wicker-furnished units faces the beach; the others have a wind-cooled balcony from which to view the action. Given the location, noise can be an issue. Patrons flock to the lazy open-air restaurant (mains US$25 to US$48; open 8am to 11pm) for fresh fish and barbecue.

Eating & Drinking

Christine's Bakery BAKERY $
(☎495-9281; mains US$3-10; ⏱8am-5pm) The scent of banana bread, coconut bread and coffee waft out of Christine's and fill the settlement by 8am. It's the local breakfast hangout.

Corsairs INTERNATIONAL $$$
(☎495-9294; www.corsairsbvi.com; mains US$25-45; ⏱8:30am-11pm) Corsairs provides a variation on the usual theme by featuring lots of pizza, pasta and calzones on its menu. Most dishes incorporate seafood in some fashion, including the popular lobster mac and cheese. The place was struggling to keep a steady chef after the 2017 hurricanes and had erratic hours at research time.

★**Foxy's** BAR
(☎442-3074; www.foxysbvi.com; ⏱8:30am-11pm) Calypso singer Foxy Callwood single-handedly put Jost on the map with this legendary beach bar. He has his own rum distillery on-site, so fresh booze fills the glasses. Rotis, seafood dishes and darn good burgers help soak it up. The best time to catch Foxy crooning is around 10am. Bands rock the stage weekend nights and there are big full-moon parties.

Getting There & Away

Ferries arrive at the pier on the west side of town. It's about a 10-minute walk to Great Harbour's center, or a steep 15-minute walk to White Bay. Taxis linger by the dock. It costs US$5 per person to White Bay, US$6 to Little Harbour.

White Bay

Home to Jost's most striking beach, and the jovial birthplace of the rum-soaked Painkiller cocktail, White Bay will draw you in at some point during your visit. It's a primo spot to hang out thanks to its highly entertaining beach bars, though two new additions – the out-of-place luxury villas bookending backpacker favorite Ivan's and the flamboyant beach shelters built to lure cruise-ship visitors – signal something of an identity crisis following the devastation of the 2017 hurricanes.

White Bay is a hilly 1-mile walk from Great Harbour, or a US$10 taxi ride.

Sights & Activities

White Bay BEACH
This gorgeous long white crescent lies pressed to the sea by steep hills. A barrier reef shelters the water from swells and waves, making for good swimming and a protected anchorage. Lots of day-trippers arrive by charter boat. The beach's main activities are drinking, wriggling your toes in the sand and people-watching.

★**Ocean Spa BVI** MASSAGE
(☎340-0772; www.oceanspabvi.com; 1hr massage US$120; ⏱9am-5pm; 👪) There are at least three reasons to love this floating spa. One: it was built using lumber salvaged from the 2017 hurricanes. Two: you reach it via a kayak on the beach in front of Ivan's. Three: you can watch colorful fish flutter on the far side of a see-through floor as the massage therapist digs into your stress points.

Sleeping

White Bay has the island's largest range of options, from low-cost camping to exclusive waterfront villas.

Ivan's White Bay Campground CAMPGROUND $
(☎US 340-513-1095; www.ivanscampground.com; campsites US$30, cabins US$150) The 2017 hurricanes obliterated Ivan's cabins, kitchen, bathhouse and bar, and also the site's foliage: you can still camp here, but it'll be a scorcher. Sea-grape trees and fixed tents are planned for coming years. At research time there was just one (inexplicably carpeted) beachfront cabin, which cost double the rate of the old ones and was only marginally better.

Perfect Pineapple GUESTHOUSE **$$**
(US 340-514-0713; www.perfectpineapple.com; ste from US$170;) Foxy Callwood's son Greg owns this property set on a steep hill back from the beach. The three one-bedroom suites each have a full kitchen and a private porch with ocean views. There are also a couple of larger two-bedroom suites and a cottage. The family owns **Gertrude's seafood restaurant** down on the beach if you don't want to cook.

White Bay Villas & Seaside Cottages VILLA **$$$**
(410-349-1851; www.jostvandyke.com; cottages/villas from US$260/390;) Here you can choose from view-tastic beachfront villas ranging from one-bedroom cottages to three-bedroom spreads. All units have kitchen and wi-fi. Rentals are typically for four or five nights in high season. Reserve far ahead, as the well-run property has loads of repeat guests. Prepare to walk up a big hill to get here.

Eating & Drinking

All of the bars and restaurants line up right on the beach. Most chefs cook Caribbean dishes, heavy on the fish and lobster, or American-style burgers and quesadillas.

Hendo's Hideout CARIBBEAN **$$**
(340-0074; www.hendoshideout.com; mains US$18-35; 10am-6pm Sun-Wed, to 9:30pm Thu-Sat;) Hendo's is a bit more refined than its competitors, starting with its handsome, reclaimed-wood decor. Bite into rum-and-Coke-marinated pulled-pork sandwiches, tender mahi tacos and lobster wraps. Sip a Delirious Donkey (citrus-infused vodka and ginger beer). Heck, stay all day playing volleyball or lazing in the loungers on the beach out front.

One Love Bar & Grill CARIBBEAN **$$**
(495-9829; mains US$17-26; 10am-6pm) Foxy's son Seddy owns this reggae-blasting beach bar. He'll wow you with his magic tricks, and certainly magic is how he gets the place to hold together – old buoys, life preservers and other beach junk form its 'walls.' Lobster quesadillas are the house specialty.

★ **Soggy Dollar Bar** BAR
(495-9888; www.soggydollar.com; 9am-7pm) The Soggy Dollar takes its name from sailors swimming ashore to spend wet bills. It's also the bar that invented the Painkiller, the BVI's delicious-yet-lethal cocktail of rum, coconut, pineapple, orange juice and nutmeg. This place is always hopping. Be sure to play the ring game and find out how addictive swinging a metal circle onto a hook can be.

Ivan's Stress Free Bar & Restaurant BAR
(US 340-513-1095; www.facebook.com/ivansstressfreebarjvd; 9am-9pm Dec-Apr, to 7pm May-Nov;) Oh, how past visitors must miss the old Ivan's, which truly was a stress-free bar strewn with shells and run on the honor system. But hurricanes come and times change. The new Ivan's has a hint of its old whimsy, but prices are fixed and you'll hear more reggaeton than reggae. As a plus: service is much improved!

Little Harbour

This is Jost's quieter side, with just a few businesses. Most visitors arrive by yacht to hike, swim and soak up the wild, sage-dotted landscape.

You'll have to head to Great Harbour or White Bay to sleep.

A taxi from Great Harbour to Little Harbour costs US$6 per person; it costs US$10 per person if you continue to Bubbly Pool.

Activities

Bubbly Pool SWIMMING
This natural whirlpool is formed by odd rock outcrops. When waves crash in, swimmers experience bubbling water like that of a Jacuzzi. Conditions vary: sometimes it's so calm that there are no bubbles (though it's still worth hopping in for a soak); at other times it can be too rough to go in, though this is rare.

Reach the site via a goat trail from Foxy's Taboo restaurant (about a 20-minute walk). Many visitors bring a picnic and stay awhile.

Eating

The handful of restaurants that dot the area are similar open-air, casual, weather-beaten, waterside spots with a penchant for lobster. Most were still struggling to rebuild and bounce back from the 2017 hurricanes at research time.

Foxy's Taboo CARIBBEAN **$$**
(441-1423; www.foxysbvi.com; mains US$15-30; 11am-8pm) Foxy Callwood teams up with

daughter Justine at Foxy's Taboo to serve breezy dishes such as Greek salads, lamb kebabs and pepper-jack cheeseburgers for lunch, and more sophisticated fare (the likes of snapper in lemon-caper sauce) at dinner, all accompanied by candy-like cocktails. It's in a scenic dockside building under a thatch of palms, overlooking the turquoise sea.

Sidney's Peace & Love CARIBBEAN **$$**
(☎344-2160; mains US$15-42; ⏰10am-9pm) The specialty here is lobster (US$50 to US$60), but Sidney's serves up plenty of West Indian fish dishes, along with burgers and barbecue. Pour your own drinks to go with the goods at the honor bar. Notes left behind by visiting revelers decorate the rafters.

Harris' Place CARIBBEAN **$$$**
(☎344-8816; www.facebook.com/harrisplacejvd; mains US$28-42; ⏰4-10pm; 📶) Amiable Cynthia Jones runs this harborside pavilion known for its barbecued pork, ribs and chicken. Oh, and lobster, too! On Monday night, feast on all-you-can-eat lobster in garlic-butter sauce.

ANEGADA

The northernmost Virgin floats just 12 miles away from its brethren, but you'll think you've landed on another planet: Anegada's pancake-flat desert landscape looks so different, and its wee clutch of restaurants and guesthouses are so baked-in-the-sun mellow. Flamingos ripple the salt ponds, and ridiculously blue water laps at beaches with whimsical names such as Loblolly Bay and Flash of Beauty.

You've probably seen 'Anegada lobster' on menus throughout the islands. Indeed, this is where it's sourced. Dinners consist of huge crustaceans plucked from the water in front of your eyes and grilled on the beach in converted oil drums.

Some travelers find Anegada to be too sleepy. But if listening to waves and walking solitary beaches rank high on your list, this is your island. It's a mysterious, magical and lonesome place to hang your hammock for a stretch.

ℹ Getting There & Away

AIR

Tiny **Auguste George Airport** (NGD) lies in the island's center and receives two daily flights from Tortola/Beef Island via VI Airlink (p269). Other than that, only charter planes from Tortola and Virgin Gorda land here. Charter companies include Fly BVI (p269) and Island Birds (p269).

BOAT

Road Town Fast Ferry (p269) sails from Road Town, Tortola, on Monday, Wednesday and Friday at 6:45am and 3:30pm; it departs Anegada at 8:30am and 5pm. Anegada Express (p269) runs from Trellis Bay (near Tortola's airport) at 7:30am and 3:30pm on Tuesday, Thursday, Saturday and Sunday, returning at 9:15am and 5:15pm. There is usually an additional midday ferry on Tuesday and Thursday.

Both boat companies make a quick stop at Spanish Town, Virgin Gorda, en route. Many travelers use these public ferries to do a day trip. It costs US$55 round-trip and takes about 75 to 90 minutes each way.

West End

Setting Point anchors the island's west end. It contains the ferry dock and a small cluster of restaurants, hotels and supply shops. To the north lies Cow Wreck Bay, one of the Caribbean's most breathtaking beaches, and the waterfront glamping tents of the Anegada Beach Club.

The Anegada Reef Hotel, by the dock, serves as the island's unofficial information center. Inquire at the hotel office about fishing, car rental or transport to the beaches.

👁 Sights

★Cow Wreck Bay BEACH
Here's what you'll find on dazzling, secluded Cow Wreck beach: the most sea-green water you've ever laid eyes on, colorful wooden beach chairs under rustling palms, roaming cows, conch shells, a delicious bar-restaurant, bathrooms and maybe even Sir Richard Branson on a kiteboard. The best way to spend the afternoon here is to swim, lounge and then lounge some more.

★Flamingo Pond NATURE RESERVE
The large salt pond at the island's west end hosts a flock of greater flamingos. They were plentiful on Anegada and other cays in the BVI until hunters seeking their tender meat and feathers decimated the population. Since being reintroduced in 1992 they've made a comeback. You can't get close, but you can often see the birds wading on the north side of the pond through the spotting

LOCAL KNOWLEDGE

ANEGADA LOBSTERS

Cracking an Anegada lobster is a tourist rite of passage. Every restaurant serves the massive crustaceans, often grilled on the beach in a converted oil drum and spiced with the chef's secret seasonings. Because the critters are plucked fresh from the surrounding waters, you must call by 4pm to place your order so that each restaurant knows how many to stock. Most places charge around US$55 to indulge in the entire creature, US$35 for half. Note that lobster fishing is prohibited from August 1 through November 1 so that stocks can replenish; thus they're not on menus (nor is conch) during that time. In fact, many restaurants simply close.

The **Anegada Lobster Festival** is a two-day culinary event typically held the last weekend of November. It lures lobster lovers to Anegada, where chefs prepare sampler-size dishes and bands ferry over to perform for the crowds.

scope at **Flamingo Pond Lookout**, or in the pond near Neptune's Treasure hotel.

Activities

Tommy Gaunt Kitesurfing SURFING
(☎344-9903; www.tommygauntkitesurfing.com; kite & board per half/full day US$90/150; ⏲10am-5pm Nov-Aug) Get your kite on at this facility located at the Anegada Beach Club. Lessons are available for all skill levels.

Danny's Bonefishing FISHING
(☎441-6334; www.dannysbonefishing.com; per half/full day US$400/600) There's world-class bonefishing year-round on the flats around Setting Point and Salt Heap Point on the south shore. Danny Vanterpool's family has been guiding in the area for decades. Gear is included in the price. Reserve ahead.

Sleeping

A couple of simple hotels are walkable from the ferry dock. More exotic options pop up along the water on the north shore.

★**Anegada Beach Club** HOTEL $$
(☎340-4455; www.anegadabeachclub.com; r US$235, glamping tents US$370; ❄📶🏊) Anegada's slickest property has two options: beachfront glamping tents (canvas-sided structures on stilts with canopy bed, heated shower, deck with hammock and romantic views of the water) and hotel rooms kitted out in blond wood and soothing pastel blues with air-conditioning and TV. A kitesurfing school is on-site, and you can rent kayaks and paddleboards, too.

ABC's restaurant – open for breakfast, lunch and dinner – makes fab food, including a BLLT (bacon, lettuce, lobster and tomato) sandwich. A free shuttle picks up at the airport and ferry dock.

Ann's Guest Houses COTTAGE $$
(☎954-600-6616; www.cowwreckbeachbvi.com; Cow Wreck Beach; cottages US$200; ❄📶) It'll just be you and the wandering bovines sharing the grounds here after the crowds leave Cow Wreck Beach Bar (p262) in the evening. While these four pastel-colored cottages don't have a direct view of the beach, they're only a few steps from the sand, and have full kitchens, high ceilings and funky maritime-themed decor.

Anegada Reef Hotel HOTEL $$
(☎495-8002; www.anegadareef.com; Setting Point; d US$180-310; ❄📶) Anegada's first hotel, this seaside lodge by the ferry dock has the feel of a classic out-island fishing camp. The property's 20 rooms (only 10 were open at research time, due to the 2017 hurricanes) are quite basic, but the fishing dock, restaurant (mains US$22 to US$52, open 8:30am to 9pm) and beach bar are Anegada's social epicenter.

A lot of yachts pull up to join the party, while fish and lobster sizzle on the grill.

Neptune's Treasure HOTEL $$
(☎495-9439; www.neptunestreasure.com; Setting Point; r US$170; ❄📶) The price is the cheapest on the island and the beachfront setting is superb – but the exceptionally grumpy owners (from the Azores via the Bahamas) can really put a black cloud over all that Anegada sunshine. Wi-fi doesn't reach most rooms. This is only worth it as a last resort.

Eating

Several open-air restaurants await along the water by Setting Point. Follow your nose toward the lobster and other meats sizzling on the grill. The restaurants also have bars if you just want a drink.

★ **Cow Wreck Beach Bar** CARIBBEAN **$$**
(☎954-600-6616; www.cowwreckbeachbvi.com; mains US$16-53; ⏲10am-8pm) This festive, open-air bar-restaurant features lobster and barbecue ribs, but most folks come to drink the day away at a picnic table in the sand or a bench along the beach. Owner Bell's hospitality (and her conch fritters) are something special.

Sid's Pomato Point CARIBBEAN **$$**
(☎547-0368; mains US$18-40; ⏲11am-late; 📶) The island's most popular bartender (the eponymous Sid) finally has his own place at isolated Pomato Point, where the sunsets are epic. Gather around the curvaceous mahogany bar, or sit at one of the breezy outdoor tables, and chow down on lobster tacos, stewed conch or baby back ribs.

★ **Wonky Dog** SEAFOOD **$$$**
(☎547-0539; www.thewonkydog.com; Setting Point; mains US$25-55; ⏲10am-11pm) The Wonky Dog is a class act, with candlelit tables on the sand, bartenders who know how to mix, and a beyond-the-norm menu that ranges from Thai red-curry mussels to tuna poke to all sorts of lobster (jerk-mango-coconut lobster, lobster Rockefeller, creamy lobster Thermidor and more). DJs entertain three nights, and there's steel-pan music on Tuesdays.

★ **Lobster Trap** CARIBBEAN **$$$**
(☎346-5055; www.facebook.com/thelobstertrap bvi; Setting Point; mains US$25-55; ⏲11am-9pm; 📶) Lobster Trap's grilled version of the namesake crustacean approaches perfection on a menu that includes the usual seafood suspects. The chef pulls the spiny critters straight from the sea out of a dockside snare. The twinkly garden setting on the main anchorage's waterfront adds to the pleasure. The Anegada Beach Club (p261) runs the Trap and offers shuttles between the two properties.

Potter's by the Sea CARIBBEAN **$$$**
(☎341-9769; http://pottersanegada.com; Setting Point; mains US$25-55; ⏲8am-midnight; 📶) Potter's is the first place you stumble into when leaving the ferry dock. Potter lived in Queens, New York, and worked in the restaurant biz there for years, so he knows how to make customers feel at home while serving them ribs, fettuccine, curried shrimp and lobster. Graffiti and T-shirts cover the open-air walls; DJs occasionally spin in the evenings.

ℹ Getting There & Away

Road Town Fast Ferry (p269) runs between Road Town, Tortola, and Setting Point twice daily on Monday, Wednesday and Friday. Anegada Express (p269) runs between Trellis Bay (near Tortola's airport) and Setting Point twice daily on Tuesday, Thursday, Saturday and Sunday.

Anjuliena's (☎495-9002; Setting Point; half-day/full day/24hr US$35/45/55; ⏲8am-5pm) rents scooters by the dock. They're a great way to get around the island. **L&H Rentals** (☎495-8002; Anegada Reef Hotel, Setting Point; Mini Moke/SUV/truck US$80/85/110; ⏲8am-6pm) offers Mini Mokes, standard SUVs and trucks. A taxi from Setting Point to Cow Wreck costs US$12 per person round-trip. Book at the Anegada Reef Hotel (p261) or with **L&M's Taxi Service** (☎443-9972, 441-0563; www.lmanegada.com).

ℹ Getting Around

Taxis wait by the ferry dock. A 2½-hour island tour costs US$35 per person. Open-air shuttles (per person round-trip US$12 to US$15) run to the beaches from the Anegada Reef Hotel. Call L&M's Taxi Service to arrange any kind of trip or tour.

Scooters are the most popular way to get around the island. Various businesses rent them by the ferry dock, including Anjuliena's. Note that the road from Pomato Point over to The Settlement and Loblolly Bay via the southern coast is entirely paved. However, the route from Loblolly over to Cow Wreck Bay on the northern coast is not, and includes long stretches of deep sands that have trapped many a scooter.

East End

The Settlement, Anegada's only town, is a wee village of boxy houses, laundry flapping in the breeze and folks feeding goats and chickens. There are a couple of teensy shops where you can buy food and supplies. The iguanas and the beaches a few miles north are the draws.

Open-air shuttles (per person round-trip US$15) make frequent runs to Loblolly from the Anegada Reef Hotel. If you plan to drink or dine at Big Bamboo, they'll provide a free transfer (just call!).

Sights

Loblolly Bay Beach BEACH

Loblolly is an idyllic stretch of sand with a few bars, fixed umbrellas for shade, a shower (US$3), and snorkel-gear rental (US$10 per day) at bar-restaurant Big Bamboo. You can swim over a widespread area with spotted eagle rays and barracudas. The water might be rough between November and March.

Flash of Beauty BEACH

Flash of Beauty is just east of Loblolly Bay Beach. With perfect white sand and deep turquoise water, it certainly lives up to its name. There's a bar-restaurant, and nifty snorkeling over a compact area of big coral and bright-hued fish.

Anegada Iguana Headstart Facility WILDLIFE RESERVE

(8:30am-4:30pm) FREE The Parks Trust started this facility because feral cats were eating the island's baby iguanas, endangering the rare species. Workers now bring the babies to the nursery's cages to grow safely. After two years they're big enough to be released back into the wild, where they'll sprout to around 5ft from tip to tail. The hatchery sits behind the government administration building; just let yourself in.

Sleeping & Eating

You find a smattering of cottages by Loblolly Bay Beach, but there's not much else out this way.

Big Bamboo CARIBBEAN **$$**

(499-1680; www.bigbambooanegada.com; mains US$12-25; 9am-6pm) Diane Levons' tiki-esque restaurant-bar is on the beach at Loblolly Bay's western end and always packs a crowd. It specializes in island recipes for lobster (US$40 to US$50), fish and chicken.

Bright-blue walkways lead from the restaurant to four circular cottages with large balconies overlooking the sea. Some cottages consist of one room (US$250), others two (US$350); all have wi-fi, air-conditioning and a full kitchen.

Flash of Beauty Restaurant CARIBBEAN **$$**

(343-8403; mains US$6-20; 10am-5pm, dinner by reservation) After you finish snorkeling the waters out front, climb onshore to Flash of Beauty's bar-restaurant, where owner Monica awaits with spicy rotis, curried conch and lobster (US$45). Staff members make a mean 'bushwhacker' – a milkshake-esque drink using seven liquors.

THE LITTLE SISTERS

The chain of small islands south of Tortola, collectively known as the Little Sisters, offers a wonderful mix of marine sanctuaries, luxurious hideaways for the rich and famous, and provisioning stops for sailors. Most islands are reachable only by charter or private boat. If you don't have your own vessel, hook up with a Tortola or Virgin Gorda day-sail tour.

Sights

Norman Island ISLAND

Since 1843, legend has told that treasure is buried on Norman Island, supposedly the prototype for Robert Louis Stevenson's *Treasure Island*. It fits the bill: Norman is the BVI's largest uninhabited landmass – though that may soon change. Plans are afoot for a US$200-million environmentally conscious luxury resort and residential property here. For now, adventurers come to visit the island's one establishment, Pirates Bight, an open-air pavilion on the beach with loud music and a party-hearty crowd.

If you don't have your own boat, call Pirates Bight and ask about the ferry (round-trip US$20).

Salt Island ISLAND

This T-shaped island is a forlorn place. The salt making (which gave the place its name) still goes on, but the **RMS Rhone** is the big attraction now. The *Rhone* crashed against the rocks off the southwest coast during a hurricane in 1867. Now a marine national park, the steamer's remains are extensive, making it one of the Caribbean's best wreck dives. The stern lies in shallower water, so snorkelers can get in on the action, too.

Cooper Island ISLAND

Lying about 4 miles south of Tortola, Cooper Island is a moderately hilly cay and is virtually undeveloped except for the Cooper Island Beach Club – its restaurant, rum bar and brewery make it a popular anchorage for cruising yachts. Snorkelers and divers also swarm the island's surrounding sites.

Peter Island ISLAND

This lofty L-shaped landmass, about 4 miles south of Tortola, is the BVI's fifth-largest island and home to the luxurious Peter Island Resort (ravaged by the 2017 hurricanes but in line to reopen). The island remains lush and wild for the most part. There are five pristine beaches, plus excellent snorkeling sites and hiking paths.

Sleeping

Cooper Island Beach Club RESORT $$

(☎345-6725; www.cooperislandbeachclub.com; Cooper Island; r US$290; ⊙closed Sep; 📶) It's not really a 'club' at all but a casual property where it's just fine to be barefoot. The 10 teak-furnished rooms each have four-poster bed, mini-fridge, balcony and rain shower. Solar panels provide 70% of the electricity and heat the water. Ceiling fans keep you cool at night.

Eating & Drinking

Cooper Island Beach Club Restaurant CARIBBEAN $$

(☎547-2002; www.cooperislandbeachclub.com; Cooper Island; mains US$16-45; ⊙noon-3pm & 5:30-8:30pm, closed Sep) This casual restaurant is a premier gathering spot for boaters. Curried-chicken rotis, jerk pork tenderloin and greenshell mussels in white-wine sauce all have exceptional flavor. The rum bar and on-site solar-powered brewery add to the pleasure. The bar stools made from recycled fishing boats are a nice touch.

Make reservations for dinner.

William Thornton BAR

(Willy T's; ☎340-8603; www.willy-t.com; Peter Island; ⊙noon-late) The original Willy T's was destroyed in Hurricane Irma. Version 2.0 of this floating bar is bigger and cleaner, though just as rowdy. Conch fritters and barbecue ribs are merely side dishes for all the booze. Body shots are de rigueur, and many a patron has been known to jump off the deck nude after a few too many.

It's moored at Great Harbour, Peter Island.

Pirates Bight BAR

(☎443-1305; www.piratesbight.com; Norman Island; ⊙11:30am-midnight) This open-air pavilion on the beach at The Bight pours an awful lot of rum (and gin, and tequila, and vodka). Chicken rotis, conch fritters and grilled *mahimahi* sandwiches help soak it up. Kick back in the waterside beach chairs and enjoy. If you don't have your own boat, call and ask about the ferry (round-trip US$20).

Getting There & Away

The majority of the Little Sisters are reachable only if you have your own boat or join a tour, but there's one exception: Norman Island runs a ferry (round-trip US$20, three daily) from a dock on the outskirts of Road Town, Tortola. Call ahead (443-1305) to verify the schedule, as it changes regularly.

UNDERSTAND THE BRITISH VIRGIN ISLANDS

History

Columbus & the Pirates

On Christopher Columbus' second trip to the Caribbean in 1493, Caribs led him to an archipelago of pristine islands that he dubbed Santa Ursula y Las Once Mil Vírgenes (St Ursula and the 11,000 Virgins), in honor of a 4th-century princess who, legend tells, was raped and murdered, along with 11,000 maidens, in Cologne by marauding Huns.

By 1595 the famous English privateers Sir Francis Drake and Jack Hawkins were using the Virgin Islands as a staging ground for making attacks on Spanish shipping. In the wake of Drake and Hawkins came French corsairs and Dutch freebooters. All knew that the Virgin Islands had some of the most secure and unattended harbors in the West Indies. Places such as Sopers Hole at Tortola's West End and the Bight at Norman Island were legendary pirates' dens.

While the Danes settled on what is now the US Virgin Islands, the English had a firm hold on today's BVI. The middle island of St John remained disputed territory until 1717, when the Danish side claimed it for good. The Narrows between St John and Tortola has divided the eastern Virgins (BVI) from the western Virgins (USVI) for more than 250 years.

The BVI after WWII

Following WWII, British citizens in the islands clamored for more independence. In 1949, BVI citizens demonstrated for a representative government and got a presidential legislature the next year. By 1967 the BVI had become an independent colony of Britain, with its own political parties, a legislative council and an elected premier (with elections every four years). Elizabeth II also made her first royal visit to the BVI in 1967, casting a glow of celebrity on the islands. Royal-family members still cruise through every few years.

In the mid-1980s the government had the shrewd idea of offering offshore registration to companies wishing to incorporate in the islands. Incorporation fees – along with tourism – now prop up the economy. Whether you call the territory an 'international financial center' or a tax haven, you have to admit it's odd that this population of 28,000 people hosts more than 422,000 active registered companies. It has created an unusual island workforce infused with foreign accountants, trust lawyers and investment brokers.

People & Culture

Despite the name, apart from little touches such as Cadbury chocolate, the culture of the British Virgin Islands is West Indian to the core. The population is a mix of professional people toiling away in financial services, folks working the tourist trade or raising livestock, and adventurers whose biochemistry is intricately tied to the seas. The ethnic breakdown is 77% black, 6% Latino, 5% white, and the remainder mixed, East Indian or other.

The BVI have one of the Caribbean's most stable economies. The per-capita GDP is US$34,200. In general, most people live comfortably.

Some visitors complain that the locals (particularly on Tortola) are unfriendly. The demeanor is not rude so much as reserved.

Landscape & Wildlife

The Land

The BVI consists of some 50 islands and cays. On most, steep hills dominate the island interiors. The exception is northernmost Anegada, which is a flat coral atoll. Sage Mountain (1716ft) on Tortola is the highest point on the islands.

Thousands of tropical-plant varieties grow on the islands, and a short drive can transport a nature lover between entirely different ecosystems. Mangrove swamps, coconut groves and sea-grape trees dominate the coast, while mountain peaks support wet forest with mahogany, lignum vitae, palmetto and more than 30 varieties of wild orchid.

Islanders also grow and collect hundreds of roots and herbs as ingredients for 'bush medicine.' Psychoactive mushrooms grow wild (and are consumed) on the islands, particularly on Tortola.

Wildlife

Few land mammals are natives; most were accidentally or intentionally introduced. Virtually every island has a feral population of cats, goats or donkeys.

More than 200 species of bird inhabit the islands, adding bright colors and a symphony of sound to the tropical environment. A few snake species (none of which are poisonous) slither around, along with a host of small and not-so-small lizards, including the 5ft-long rock iguana of Anegada and the common green iguana found throughout the islands. Anoles and gecko lizards are ubiquitous, and numerous species of toad and frog populate the islands.

Environmental Issues

Environmental concerns have resulted in the formation of the BVI National Parks Trust, which protects 21 natural and cultural areas, including the *Rhone* shipwreck, Tortola's Sage Mountain and the giant boulder formations at the Baths on Virgin Gorda.

FUNGI MUSIC

Fungi (*foon*-ghee, also an island food made of cornmeal) is the BVI's local folk music. It uses homemade percussion instruments such as washboards, ribbed gourds and conch shells to accompany a singer. You'll hear lots of it at the BVI Emancipation Festival (p246). The Lashing Dogs are popular players around the territory.

Prior years of overfishing have put conch and lobster in a precarious situation. Currently, fishing for these creatures is not allowed from August through October so that stocks can replenish.

Other issues that environmentalists keep an eye on are deforestation, soil erosion and mangrove destruction. Mangrove-replanting projects are underway at various locations around the islands.

SURVIVAL GUIDE

Directory A–Z

ACCESSIBLE TRAVEL

The BVI is not particularly accessible and does not have any specific services geared toward travelers with disabilities.

ACCOMMODATIONS

Guesthouses, hotels, apartment-like villas and resorts are common on all islands, though don't expect great value for money outside Tortola. High season is mid-December through April, when rooms are costly, advance reservations are essential and three-night minimums are common. Some lodgings close in September and October, the heart of low season.

Be aware that while air-conditioning is widely available, it is not a standard amenity, even at top-end places.

Booking Services

Purple Pineapple (343-4554; www.purple-pineapple.com; villas from US$200)

Vacation Rental by Owner (www.vrbo.com) Many BVI visitors say that VRBO provides the best results since you work out all the details with the property owners themselves.

Villas Virgin Gorda (540-8002; www.villas-virgingorda.com; villas from US$250)

Virgin Gorda Villa Rentals (542-4014; www.virgingordabvi.com; villas from US$300)

SLEEPING PRICE RANGES

The following price ranges refer to a double room with bathroom in peak season. Unless otherwise stated, breakfast is not included in the price, nor is tax (10%) or other service charges (often 8% or so).

$ less than US$100

$$ US$100–300

$$$ more than US$300

ACTIVITIES

Sailing is the BVI's main claim to fame. Clear water, shipwrecks and secluded coves make for primo diving and snorkeling. Surfing is popular at Josiah's Bay on Tortola, while kitesurfing is big on Anegada and Virgin Gorda.

CHILDREN

The islands are fairly child friendly. While baby-changing facilities and smooth pavements for prams are not ubiquitous, family-friendly resorts with kids programs are.

Virgin Gorda offers a couple of top attractions, including The Baths (p254), a splash-worthy national park where kids of all ages can tromp around enormous boulders, climb rope ladders and explore sea-filled grottoes.

Tortola's East End features Surf School BVI (p253), which teaches all ages to hang 10 but is especially good for teens. Not far away, Aragorn's Full Moon Party (p253) at Trellis Bay thrills families with fire jugglers and stilt walkers.

All the islands offer villa and apartment rentals, which have lots of space and kitchens for DIY meals. Virgin Gorda and Tortola's Cane Garden Bay Area (p250) are laden with such properties.

Most restaurants do not have a children's menu, but they often serve burgers and pizza as part of their lineup. The ambience tends to be informal and relaxed wherever you go, though Jost Van Dyke has a more party-hearty adult atmosphere.

ELECTRICITY

Power plugs and sockets are of type A and B (110V, 60 Hz).

EMERGENCY NUMBERS

Ambulance, fire, police	999
Search & rescue	767

FOOD

Restaurants are pretty similar in their fare, offering mostly Caribbean dishes such as spicy barbecue and curries, along with grilled fish and lobster (the latter being the famed, strapping crustaceans from Anegada). Virgin Gorda and Tortola's Cane Garden Bay area have concentrations of excellent eateries. Meals are expensive and customer service is typically not as good as in the neighboring USVI.

Essential Food & Drink

Anegada lobster Hulking crustaceans plucked from the water as you watch and then grilled on the beach.

Fungi (*foon*-ghee) A polenta-like cornmeal cooked with okra, often topped by fish and gravy.

Painkiller Jost Van Dyke's Soggy Dollar Bar supposedly invented this sweet mix of rum, coconut, pineapple, orange juice and nutmeg.

Pate (pah-tay) Flaky fried dough pockets stuffed with spiced chicken, fish or other meat.

Roti Spicy chutney sets off the curried chicken, beef, conch (a local shellfish) or vegetable fillings in these burrito-like flatbread wraps.

HEALTH

Tortola has a modern hospital. Virgin Gorda, Jost Van Dyke and Anegada have walk-in clinics open on weekdays. Tortola and Virgin Gorda have pharmacies. If you are dependent on a particular medication be sure to travel with it, and with a copy of your prescription. Without health insurance, care in the BVI can be costly. For any major issues you'll likely be sent to St Thomas in the US Virgin Islands or to the US mainland.

INTERNET ACCESS

Internet cafes have gone by the wayside now that wi-fi is widely available across the BVI. Most lodgings have free wi-fi in their public areas (though it's less common in-room), as do many restaurants and bars in the main towns. Service can be slow and fitful.

LGBT+ TRAVELERS

Religious taboos about gay and lesbian people are slow to crumble. You're not likely to meet many islanders who are 'out,' nor are you likely to see public displays of affection between gay couples. LGBT discrimination is illegal. Same-sex marriage is not recognized in the BVI.

EATING PRICE RANGES

The following price indicators denote the cost of a main dinner dish.

$ less than US$15

$$ US$15–35

$$$ more than US$35

MONEY

ATMs in main towns on Tortola and Virgin Gorda but not elsewhere. Credit cards accepted in most hotels and restaurants (often with a US$20 minimum).

Exchange Rates

Australia	A$1	US$0.69
Canada	C$1	US$0.74
Euro zone	€1	US$1.12
Japan	¥100	US$0.91
NZ	NZ$1	US$0.65
UK	UK£1	US$1.27

For current exchange rates, see www.xe.com.

BEST DIVING & SNORKELING

Dive Sites

RMS Rhone The famous 1867 shipwreck sits in 20ft to 80ft of water off Salt Island, making it an accessible wreck dive for all levels.

Alice in Wonderland This spot off Ginger Island has some of the best deep-water coral formations in the BVI.

The Indians Just off Pelican Island, three cone-shaped rock formations rise from 36ft underwater to 30ft above water. Lots of fish and dramatic scenery.

Chikuzen The 250ft wreck is remote and for experienced divers only. Big swimmers such as reef, bull and lemon sharks are the payoff.

Snorkel Sites

The Caves Three large caves on Norman Island feature shallow waters and many small fish, which in turn attract larger predators. Good for newbie snorkelers, as the water is usually calm.

The Indians Loads of colorful fish dart around these rock pinnacles that rise up from the water near Norman Island. It's a great spot for experienced snorkelers.

RMS Rhone Although most of the Salt Island shipwreck is in deep water, the stern section is shallow – you can see the bronze propeller, rudder and aft mast from the surface. Best for experienced snorkelers.

Cooper Island Beginners fare well here, as you can swim in from the beach, it's shallow, and you'll see lots of small fish.

PRACTICALITIES

Newspapers The *BVI Beacon* (www.bvibeacon.com) is the main newspaper; it is published weekly. BVI News (www.bvinews.com) offers free daily content online. The free, weekly *Limin' Times* (www.limin-times.com) has entertainment listings.

Radio ZBVI (780AM) airs talk and music from Tortola, including BBC broadcasts.

Smoking Banned in all restaurants, bars and other public venues.

Weights & measures The islands use imperial measurements. Distances are in feet and miles; gasoline is measured in gallons.

Tipping

Dive/tour-boat operators Tipping 15% of the fee is reasonable.

Hotels Tip US$1 per bag for bellhops; US$2 to US$5 per night for cleaning staff.

Restaurants Tipping 15% of the bill is standard and sometimes automatically added.

Taxis Tip 10% of the fare.

PUBLIC HOLIDAYS

New Year's Day January 1

HL Stoutt's Birthday First Monday in March

Commonwealth Day Second Monday in March

Good Friday and Easter Monday March or April

Whit Monday May or June (date varies)

Sovereign's Birthday Mid-June (date varies)

Territory Day July 1

BVI Festival Days First Monday to Wednesday in August

St Ursula's Day October 21

Christmas Day and Boxing Day December 25 and 26

TELEPHONE

BVI phone numbers consist of the area code (284) followed by a seven-digit local number. If you're calling from abroad, dial the country code (1), then 284 and then the seven-digit number. If you're calling locally, just dial the seven-digit number. Since the 2017 hurricanes knocked out landlines in many areas, some business were using temporary cell numbers at the time of research.

Cell Phones

You should be able to use your cell phone on the islands, but beware exorbitant roaming fees. SIM cards are available in Road Town and at large marinas. A weeklong prepaid SIM with 3GB of data costs about US$28.

CCT (www.cctbvi.com), Flow (www.discoverflow.co) and Digicel (www.digicelbvi.com) provide the local service.

TIME

The islands are on Atlantic Standard Time (GMT/UTC minus four hours). Relative to New York, Miami and Eastern Standard Time, the Virgins are one hour ahead in winter and in the same time zone in summer (due to daylight-saving time).

TOURIST INFORMATION

BVI Tourist Board (www.bvitourism.com) Official site with comprehensive lodging and activity info.

ℹ Getting There & Away

AIR

Tortola's **Terrance B Lettsome Airport** (EIS; ☎852 9000; www.bviaa.com; 📶) is the gateway to the BVI, though it only receives flights from within the Caribbean. It's a modern facility with an ATM, car-rental agencies and food concessions. The tiny airports on Virgin Gorda and Anegada are mostly for charter planes, though both receive scheduled commercial flights as well.

Flights from the US mainland and Canada usually connect via Puerto Rico, while Europeans often fly in via Antigua or St-Martin/Sint Maarten. Many visitors opt to fly to Cyril E King Airport (p855) on St Thomas in the US Virgin Islands, as it is the region's largest airport and has more flights. Visitors then complete the journey by ferry.

The following airlines are the main carriers:

Air Sunshine (☎340-9999; www.airsunshine.com) Daily flights from Tortola to San Juan and St Thomas. Less frequent flights depart Virgin Gorda for both destinations (by demand).

Cape Air (☎508-771-6944; www.capeair.com) Flies to San Juan daily from Tortola and Virgin Gorda.

InterCaribbean Airways (☎877-887-9233; www.intercaribbean.com) Direct flights link Tortola with Antigua, Dominica, San Juan (Puerto Rico), Santo Domingo (Dominican Republic) and St-Martin/Sint Maarten several times weekly.

LIAT (☎888-844-5428; www.liat.com) Flies to/from St Kitts and St-Martin/Sint Maarten daily (via Tortola only).

Seaborne Airlines (☎787-946-7800; www.seaborneairlines.com) Several daily flights to/from San Juan (via Tortola only). Code-shares with American Airlines, Delta Air Lines and JetBlue.

VI Airlink Runs scheduled services from Tortola to Anegada (twice daily) and Antigua (five times weekly).

Winair (☎495-1298; www.fly-winair.sx) To/from St-Martin/Sint Maarten daily (via Tortola only).

SEA

Cruise Ship

A big ship or two calls at Road Town almost daily during peak season. The dock is downtown, so no tenders are needed (except in rare cases when the dock is particularly busy) – passengers disembark and they're in the heart of the action.

Ferry

Ferry connections link Tortola, Virgin Gorda and Jost Van Dyke with the US Virgin Islands' St Thomas and St John. BVI Tourism (www.bvitourism.com) and BVI Welcome (www.bviwelcome.com) have schedules. For trips between the USVI and BVI, a passport is required.

Ferries between the two territories run until about 5pm only. Watch out for scheduling issues if you're trying to get from one to the other at night. Also, note that some routes in operation before the 2017 hurricanes are now no longer available.

Taxes are not included in the fees below. There is a US$20 departure tax to leave the BVI and a US$10 port fee to leave the USVI. The BVI also charges a US$10 'environmental and tourism levy' upon arrival. Checked luggage costs US$5 per bag on many ferries. Arrive at least 30 minutes before departure time to buy tickets at the terminal.

Main companies and routes:

Anegada Express (☎340-1526; www.anegadaexpress.com) Runs ferries from Beef Island, Tortola (by the airport), to Anegada via Virgin Gorda twice daily Tuesday, Thursday, Saturday and Sunday (US$35 one way, one hour).

Inter Island (☎340-776-6597; www.interislandboatservices.com) Sails between Jost Van Dyke and Red Hook, St Thomas (in the US Virgin Islands), via Cruz Bay, St John (one way US$80, 30 minutes, two daily Friday, Saturday and Sunday). Also sails between the US islands and Anegada once monthly (US$175 round-trip, 1½ hours) and between Red Hook, St Thomas, and Road Town, Tortola, twice daily (US$45 one way, 45 minutes).

Native Son (☎495-4617; www.nativesonferry.com) Sails several times daily between Road Town, Tortola, and St Thomas (both Red Hook and Charlotte Amalie; one way US$40, 30 to 45 minutes).

New Horizon Ferry (p270) Sails five times daily between Jost Van Dyke and Tortola's West End (twice in the morning, three times in the afternoon; cash only; one way US$20, 25 minutes).

Road Town Fast Ferry (☎494-2323; www.roadtownfastferry.com) Goes direct between Road Town and Charlotte Amalie three times daily (US$40 one way, 45 minutes). Also links Road Town with Anegada (via Virgin Gorda) twice daily Monday, Wednesday and Friday (US$55 round-trip, 1½ hours).

Smith's Ferry/Tortola Fast Ferry (☎494-4454; www.bviferryservices.com) It uses both names. Goes between Road Town and Charlotte Amalie three times daily (one way US$40, 45 minutes). Also connects Road Town with Spanish Town, Virgin Gorda, at least four times daily (one way US$20, 30 minutes).

Speedy's (☎495-5240; www.bviferries.com) Goes between Road Town and Spanish Town multiple times daily (one way US$20, 30 minutes). Also runs direct between Virgin Gorda and Charlotte Amalie on Tuesday and Saturday (one way US$40, 90 minutes) and to Beef Island several times daily (one way US$20, 20 minutes).

Yacht

If you're arriving by yacht – as many do! – it must be at one of the following ports, which have customs and immigration facilities:

Jost Van Dyke Great Harbour

Tortola Road Town or West End

Virgin Gorda Spanish Town or Gun Creek

ℹ Getting Around

AIR

Charter planes fly between islands. Companies making the rounds include:

Fly BVI (☎340-1747; www.flybvi.com)

Island Birds (☎495-2002; www.islandbirds.com)

VI Airlink (☎495-2271; www.viairlink.com)

BOAT

Ferry

Tortola is the BVI ferry hub, and all boats route through its various docks. The BVI Welcome Guide (www.bviwelcome.com) prints the timetables. In most cases, you can buy tickets on the spot at the ferry terminal. Sometimes credit-card machines don't work, so it's good to have cash as a backup.

Main companies:

Anegada Express

New Horizon Ferry (☎499-0952; www.newhorizonferry.com)

Road Town Fast Ferry (p269)

Sensation Ferries (☎340-2723; www.sensationferries.com)

Smith's Ferry/Tortola Fast Ferry (p269)

Speedy's (p269)

Main routes:

DEPARTURE TAX

The airport levies a US$15 departure tax, a US$5 security tax and a US$30 airport-development fee for international travel. Domestic travel only incurs a US$5 airport-development fee. Some airlines incorporate these fees into the price of the ticket, but many do not and you'll have to pay them at a counter in the airport.

There's also a US$10 'environmental and tourism levy' upon arrival.

➡ Tortola (Road Town) to Virgin Gorda (Spanish Town) – One way US$20, 30 minutes, roughly every hour; Sensation, Speedy's and Smith's

➡ Tortola (Road Town) to Anegada – Round-trip US$55, 75 minutes, Monday, Wednesday and Friday; Road Town Fast Ferry

➡ Tortola (Beef Island/Trellis Bay) to Anegada – One way US$35, one hour, Sunday, Tuesday, Thursday and Saturday; Anegada Express

➡ Tortola (Beef Island/Trellis Bay) to Virgin Gorda (Spanish Town) – One way US$20, 20 minutes, several daily; Speedy's

➡ Tortola (West End) to Jost Van Dyke – One way US$20, 25 minutes, five daily; New Horizon Ferry

Boat Charter Basics

The British Virgin Islands provides it all: a year-round balmy climate, steady trade winds, little to worry about in the way of tides or currents, a protected thoroughfare in the 35-mile-long Sir Francis Drake Channel, and hundreds of anchorages, many within sight of one another. These factors make the islands one of the easiest places to sail, which explains why more than a third of all visitors come to do just that.

If you want to sail, there are three basic options: a crewed boat, with skipper and cook; a 'bareboat' sans staff that you operate on your own; or a sailing-school vessel.

A typical weeklong itinerary involves sampling the islands while partially circumnavigating Tortola. The attraction of a sailing vacation is that you can sail or stay put as long as you want, look for quiet anchorages or head for the party spots, and add on diving, hiking or shopping trips at will.

The cost of chartering a boat depends on the vessel's size and age and the time of year. It's a misconception that sailing is prohibitively expensive; once you do a little research you might be pleasantly surprised.

Charter Companies

Charter companies depend on their reputations. Ask for references and spend time talking with the company's representatives. Most companies sail out of the Moorings at Wickhams Cay 2 in Road Town.

The following is a list of respected charter services based in the BVI. Each can arrange bareboat charters as well as a variety of crew options.

BVI Yacht Charters (www.bviyachtcharters.com) Long-standing company.

Catamaran Company (www.catamarans.com) Catamaran specialist.

Horizon Yacht Charters (www.horizon-yachtcharters.com) Smaller company.

Moorings (www.moorings.com) Started the BVI bareboat business and remains the islands' largest yacht company.

Sunsail Yacht Charters (www.sunsail.com) The BVI's second-largest company.

TMM Yacht Charters (www.sailtmm.com) Smaller company with reasonable prices.

Sailing Schools

Offshore Sailing School (www.offshoresailing.com) Venerable company offering courses out of the Moorings in Road Town.

Rob Swain Sailing School (www.swainsailing.com) Well-rated smaller school operating out of Nanny Cay, Tortola.

Tortola Sailing & Sights (www.tortolasailingandsights.com) Newer school based out of Penn's Landing Marina on the East End of Tortola.

Sailing Virgins (www.sailingvirgins.com) Road Town–based upstart geared to millennials.

CAR & MOTORCYCLE

Driving is undoubtedly the most convenient way to get around, as there is no public-transport system and taxi fares add up in a hurry.

You can drive in the BVI using a valid license from your home country. A temporary license is required if you're staying longer than 30 days; any car-rental agency can provide the paperwork.

Car Rental

To rent a car in the BVI you generally need to be at least 25 years old, hold a valid driver's license and have a major credit card.

Cars cost between US$60 and US$90 per day. If you're traveling in peak season, it's wise to reserve a couple of weeks ahead, as supplies are limited.

Road Conditions

Be prepared for challenging road conditions. Steep, winding roads are often the same width as your car, and the potholes can be outrageous.

Chickens, cows, goats and donkeys dart in and out of the roadway. Keep your eyes peeled for critters.

Road Rules

- Rule number one: drive on the left-hand side of the road!
- The steering wheel is on the left side.
- Seat-belt use is compulsory; children under five years must be in a car seat.
- Driving while using a handheld cell phone is illegal (but earpieces are permitted).
- Proceed clockwise at traffic roundabouts.

TAXI

All the islands have taxis that are easily accessible in the main tourist areas. Most vehicles are vans that carry up to 12 passengers; sometimes they're open-air pickup trucks with bench seats and awnings. Rates are set. They are usually charged on a per-person basis, and they go down a bit if more than one person takes the taxi. You can access rate sheets from the BVI Tourist Board (www.bvitourism.com).

Reliable companies:

Beef Island Taxi Association (☎495-1982)

BVI Taxi Association (☎494-3942)

West End Taxi Association (☎495-4934, 343-9576)

Cayman Islands

1-345 / POP 63,415

Includes ➡

Best Places to Eat

- ➡ Vivo (p283)
- ➡ Barry's Golden Jerk (p289)
- ➡ Kaibo Beach (p285)
- ➡ Catch (p283)
- ➡ Agua (p280)

Best Places to Stay

- ➡ Beach Suites (p279)
- ➡ Turtle Nest Inn (p284)
- ➡ Kimpton Seafire Resort (p275)
- ➡ Southern Cross Club (p291)
- ➡ Pirates Point Resort (p291)

Why Go?

Some 2.5 million tourists visit the Cayman Islands each year. Most of them are cruise-ship passengers, who spend a few hours shopping, sunbathing or swimming with stingrays before pulling out of port. Others hunker down near Seven Mile Beach, enjoying their all-inclusive resort on one of the Caribbean's most beautiful stretches of sand. And a lucky few venture further.

Cayman is an undeniably cosmopolitan place – nearly half the population is from somewhere else – but its rich local culture is alive and well, especially in Bodden Town, East End and Cayman Brac. Explore the North Side and the Sister Islands, Cayman Brac and Little Cayman, to discover lush forests, diverse birdlife, mysterious caves and pristine beaches. Beneath the waves lie amazing underwater walls and accessible shipwrecks.

Dive in. It takes only a small sense of adventure to uncover Cayman's greatest treasures: the warm hospitality and the fantastic natural phenomena above and below the sea.

When to Go

Dec–Apr High season, with amazing weather, packed hotels and high prices.

Sep & Oct Rainfall is highest; some venues close, especially on Little Cayman and Cayman Brac.

Nov Pirates Week, a super-fun island-wide event, takes place early in the month.

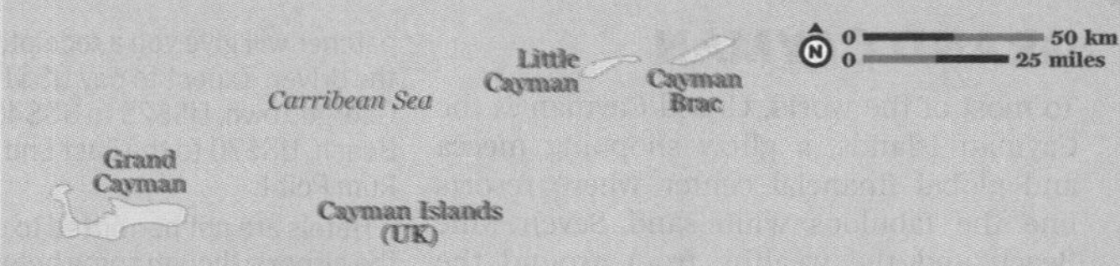

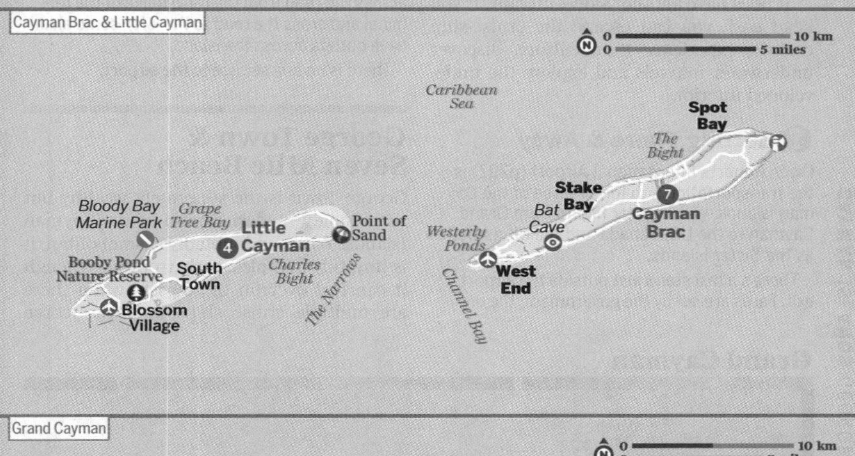

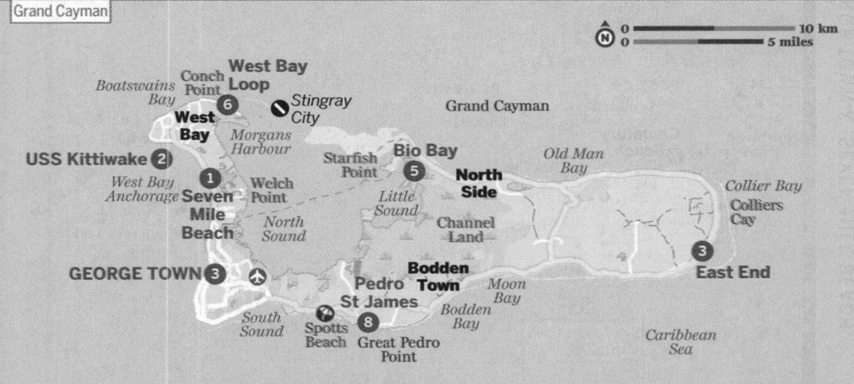

Cayman Islands Highlights

1. **Seven Mile Beach** (p275) Relaxing at this postcard-pretty white-sand beach..
2. **USS Kittiwake** (p277) Exploring this sunken US Navy ship.
3. **Dining out** (p280) Feasting in George Town or heading to the East End for local flavors.
4. **Little Cayman** (p289) Marveling at pristine coral reefs and swinging in a hammock on the smallest Cayman.
5. **Bio Bay** (p277) Swimming in the dark with millions of glowing plankton.
6. **Cycling** (p282) Enjoying the West Bay Loop's smooth roads and gorgeous scenery.
7. **Cayman Brac** (p287) Stepping back in time on this laid-back island, and hiking or scaling its epic limestone cliffs.
8. **Pedro St James** (p283) Sipping rum and pondering history.

GRAND CAYMAN

To most of the world, Grand Cayman *is* the Cayman Islands, a glitzy shopping mecca and global financial center where resorts line the fabulous white-sand Seven Mile Beach and the wealthy from around the world spend time sipping cocktails and discreetly playing with their millions.

It does have another side – literally. If you head east, you can escape the cruise-ship crowds, experience local culture, discover underwater marvels and explore the undeveloped interior.

ℹ Getting There & Away

Owen Roberts International Airport (p297) is the transportation hub for all three of the Cayman Islands, with regular flights from Grand Cayman to the US, Canada and the UK as well as the Sister Islands.

There's a taxi stand just outside the airport exit. Fares are set by the government: the dispatcher will give you a receipt, though you pay the driver. Expect to pay US$10 to US$20 to George Town, US$25 to US$45 to Seven Mile Beach, US$70 to the East End and US$80 to Rum Point.

Hotels are not permitted to collect guests at the airport, though some hotels will pay your taxi fare upon arrival.

Several car-rental agencies (p281) have offices across the road from the terminal (exit the terminal and cross the road to the left); some also have outlets across the island.

There is no bus service to the airport.

George Town & Seven Mile Beach

George Town is the supremely wealthy but surprisingly modest capital of the Cayman Islands. While undoubtedly cosmopolitan, it is tiny, tidy and pleasantly tropical – though it can feel overrun by tourists when there are multiple cruise ships in port. George

Grand Cayman

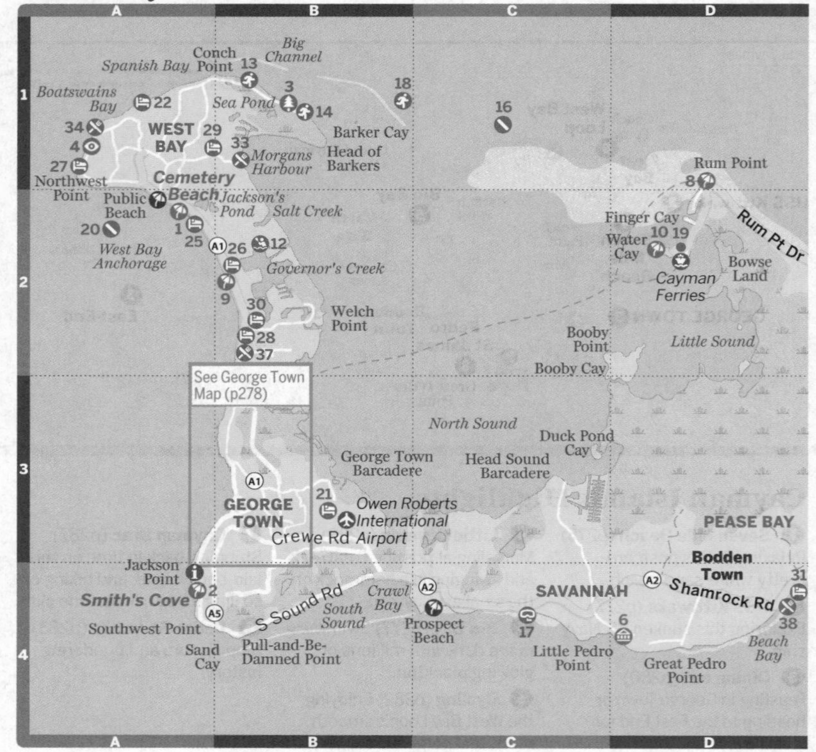

Town is a draw for dining, shopping and a few historic sights, but you'll likely spend most of your time somewhere north of here.

The focal point of Cayman's tourism industry is Seven Mile Beach, a gorgeous stretch of unbroken white sand that offers myriad opportunities for swimming, sunbathing and sunset viewing. The beach is lined with resorts and vacation properties, but there is plenty of public access to this paradise – whether you're looking for a peaceful patch of sand or a full-blown beach party.

Sights

★Smith's Cove BEACH

(Map p274) Easily one of the best snorkeling spots on Grand Cayman, this series of coves has shallow, calm water, pretty rock formations and a nice variety of sea life, including colorful fish and a resident octopus or two. The beach has a changing area and bathroom, as well as shaded picnic tables in the sand.

★Cemetery Beach BEACH

(Map p274) Ask a local where they like to spend a sunny day and they will likely direct you to this gorgeous strip of sand at the northern end of Seven Mile Beach. It's rarely crowded – not because it's haunted but because there are no big resorts in the area. You can park on the street or in the lot across from West Bay Cemetery.

Seven Mile Beach BEACH

(Map p274) Although it's really only about 5½ miles long, this gorgeous strand has flawless white sand and crystal-blue waters – it's just as pretty as a postcard. It's lined with resorts and vacation properties, but the beach itself is public. The main public beach-access point – just south of the Kimpton – has a big parking lot, a playground, beach volleyball and lounge-chair rental, with beach bars and plenty of other diversions nearby. Crowded but fun.

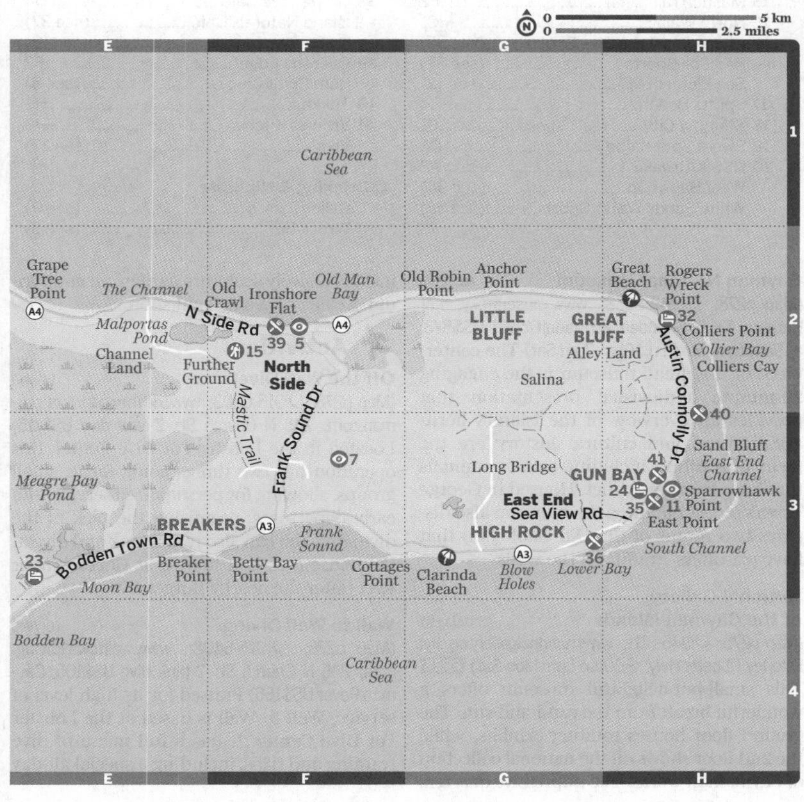

Grand Cayman

Top Sights
1 Cemetery Beach A2
2 Smith's Cove A4

Sights
3 Barkers National Park B1
4 Cayman Turtle Center A1
5 Crystal Caves F2
6 Pedro St James D4
7 Queen Elizabeth II Botanic Park F3
8 Rum Point D1
9 Seven Mile Beach B2
10 Starfish Point D2
11 Wreck of the 10 Sail Monument H3

Activities, Courses & Tours
12 Action Watersports B2
Bayside Watersports .... (see 33)
Blue Iguana Safari .... (see 7)
Blue Water Excursions .... (see 12)
13 Cayman Horse Riding B1
Cayman Kayaks .... (see 8)
Divetech .... (see 27)
14 Kitesurf Cayman B1
15 Mastic Trail F2
16 North Wall C1
Ocean Frontiers Dive Shop .... (see 35)
Red Sail Sports .... (see 37)
Sea Elements .... (see 12)
17 Spotts Beach C4
18 Stingray City B1
19 Sweet Spot Kaibo D2
20 USS Kittiwake A2
West Bay Loop .... (see 34)
White Sands Water Sports .... (see 32)

Sleeping
21 Cayman Villas B3
22 Cobalt Coast Resort & Suites A1
23 Coco Beach Villas E3
24 Compass Point Dive Resort H3
25 Discovery Point Club A2
26 Kimpton Seafire Resort B2
27 Lighthouse Point A1
Retreat at Rum Point .... (see 8)
28 Ritz-Carlton Grand Cayman B2
29 Shangri-La A1
30 Sunshine Suites B2
31 Turtle Nest Inn D4
32 Wyndham Reef Resort H2

Eating
Calypso Grill .... (see 33)
33 Catch B1
34 Cracked Conch A1
Czech Inn .... (see 23)
35 Eagle Rays H3
36 Eastern Star Fish Fry G3
37 Good Mood Food Co. B2
Grand Old House .... (see 2)
38 Grape Tree Cafe D4
Island Naturals Café .... (see 37)
Kaibo Beach .... (see 19)
39 Over the Edge F2
Rum Point Club .... (see 8)
40 Tukka H3
41 Vivine's Kitchen H3
Vivo .... (see 27)

Drinking & Nightlife
Calico Jack's .... (see 9)
Wreck Bar .... (see 8)

Cayman National Museum MUSEUM
(Map p278; ☎949-8368; www.museum.ky; cnr Harbour Dr & Shedden Rd; adult/child US$8/3; ⏲9am-5pm Mon-Fri, 10am-2pm Sat) The centerpiece of this small museum is the engaging 20-minute audiovisual presentation that provides an overview of the island's heritage. Natural and cultural history are the focus of exhibits, including one on animals that have become extinct. Housed in George Town's oldest building, the museum also displays two rooms of the Old Gaol (jail) that have prisoners' graffiti on the walls.

National Gallery of the Cayman Islands GALLERY
(Map p278; ☎945-8111; www.nationalgallery.org.ky; Esterley Tibbetts Hwy; ⏲10am-5pm Mon-Sat) FREE This small-but-delightful museum offers a wonderful break from the sand and sun. The ground floor houses rotating exhibits, while the 2nd floor shows off the national collection of Caymanian works. The impressive quarters include a lovely sculpture garden, an auditorium, a cafe and a small gift shop.

Activities

Off the Wall Divers DIVING
(Map p278; ☎916-0303; www.offthewalldivers cayman.com; 245 N Church St; 2-tank dive US$115) Located in the Lobster Pot Dive Center, this operation has two things going for it: small groups, allowing for personalized service, and early departures, promising the pick of the dive sites. You can also rent a tank and dive at the house reef, best known as Cheeseburger Reef (after the nearby Burger King).

Wall to Wall Diving DIVING
(Map p278; ☎916-6408; www.walltowalldiving.com; 245 N Church St; 2-tank dive US$105, Cayman Rover US$165) Praised for its high level of service, Wall to Wall is based at the Lobster Pot Dive Center. It has a full menu of dive training and trips, including a special all-day

trip dubbed the Cayman Rover, which visits three dive sites in the island's most remote and unspoiled corners.

Eden Rock Diving Center DIVING
(Map p278; ☎949-7243; www.edenrockdive.com; 124 S Church St; guided 1-/2-tank dives with all equipment US$70/110; ⊙guided dives 9am, 11am & 2pm) Overlooking the George Town harbor, this outfit is above two favorite shore-dive spots: Eden Rock and Devil's Grotto. Dive or snorkel with or without a guide, but be sure to bring a light to explore the underwater caverns.

Red Sail Sports WATER SPORTS
(Map p274; ☎623-5965; www.redsailcayman.com; Earth Cl; ⊙8am-5:30pm) This large water-sports center has a whole list of activities on offer, including diving, sailing, snorkeling, standup paddling, WaveRunning, wakeboarding, windsurfing and more. There are five outlets at several resorts along Seven Mile Beach and one at Rum Point (p284).

Action Watersports KAYAKING
(Map p274; ☎548-3147; www.ciactionmarine.com; Cayman Islands Yacht Club, Yacht Dr, Governor's Creek; kayak per hour US$20, WaveRunner per 30min US$75, tour per person US$75-110; ⊙8am-6pm Mon-Sat) A popular two-hour tour takes guests to Stingray City on single and double WaveRunners. Also rents kayaks and WaveRunners for independent use.

DON'T MISS

TOP DIVE SITES

USS Kittiwake (Map p274; www.facebook.com/kittiwakecayman) Cayman's top requested dive site, this is a 251ft US Navy submarine rescue ship. In 2011 the wreck was sunk deliberately to create an artificial reef and dive destination: ample entries and exits allow divers to explore the rooms, peek through windows, sit in a decompression chamber or take a turn at the steering wheel (now home to a tiny goby).

North Wall (Map p274) Grand Cayman's most famous diving destination is this magnificent underwater wall, which drops off some 6000ft into the great blue. The many dive sites offer opportunities to spot eagle rays, reef sharks and sea turtles, as well as myriad fish and coral formations. Babylon is a favorite dive site along this wall.

Tours

Stingray City WILDLIFE WATCHING
(Map p274) This stretch of shallow, sandy seafloor in the North Sound is a meeting place for southern stingrays. As soon as you enter the water a host of these prehistoric creatures will glide over in search of scraps, just as their ancestors have done from the 1930s, when fishermen cleaned their catch here. Boat tours have pretty standardized itineraries: feed squid, stroke, photograph.

Tours usually make one or two snorkel stops afterwards. Lots of operators, including Captain Marvin's Watersports, take clients here by boat and WaveRunner. Dive shops lead trips to a nearby, slightly deeper site (14ft), so divers are underwater while stroking and feeding the animals.

Before you book, though, you may want to read up on the ethical issues. Some wildlife activists say that the feedings have changed the behavior of the stingrays in undesirable ways. For example, stingrays are usually solitary creatures, but the tourist attraction brings them together, which can lead to disease transmission and aggression over food, resulting in injuries. In a large group they're also more vulnerable to predators, and the ecosystems in surrounding areas are thrown out of balance. Studies have shown that stingrays have become less healthy (they normally don't eat squid) and have developed oddball schedules (normally they're nocturnal).

Still, this is a rare opportunity to get up close and personal with a stingray. To avoid crowds, visit on a day when there are no cruise ships in port.

Sea Elements TOURS
(Map p274; ☎936-8687; www.caymanseaelements.com; Cayman Islands Yacht Club, Yacht Dr, Governor's Creek; tours adult/child from US$35/25; ⊙8am-8pm) Excellent, informative tours focus on the island's natural wonders, including swimming among the bioluminescence in Bio Bay, mangrove tours by boat or kayak, and custom trips to Stingray City. Tours depart from Cayman Islands Yacht Club in Governor's Bay. Transportation is provided.

Atlantis Adventures TOURS
(Map p278; ☎949-7700; www.caymanislandssubmarines.com; 30 S Church St; adult/child Seaworld Observatory US$49/24, Atlantis submarine US$114/59) It's possible to visit the underwater world without even mussing up your hair. The Seaworld Observatory was specially

George Town

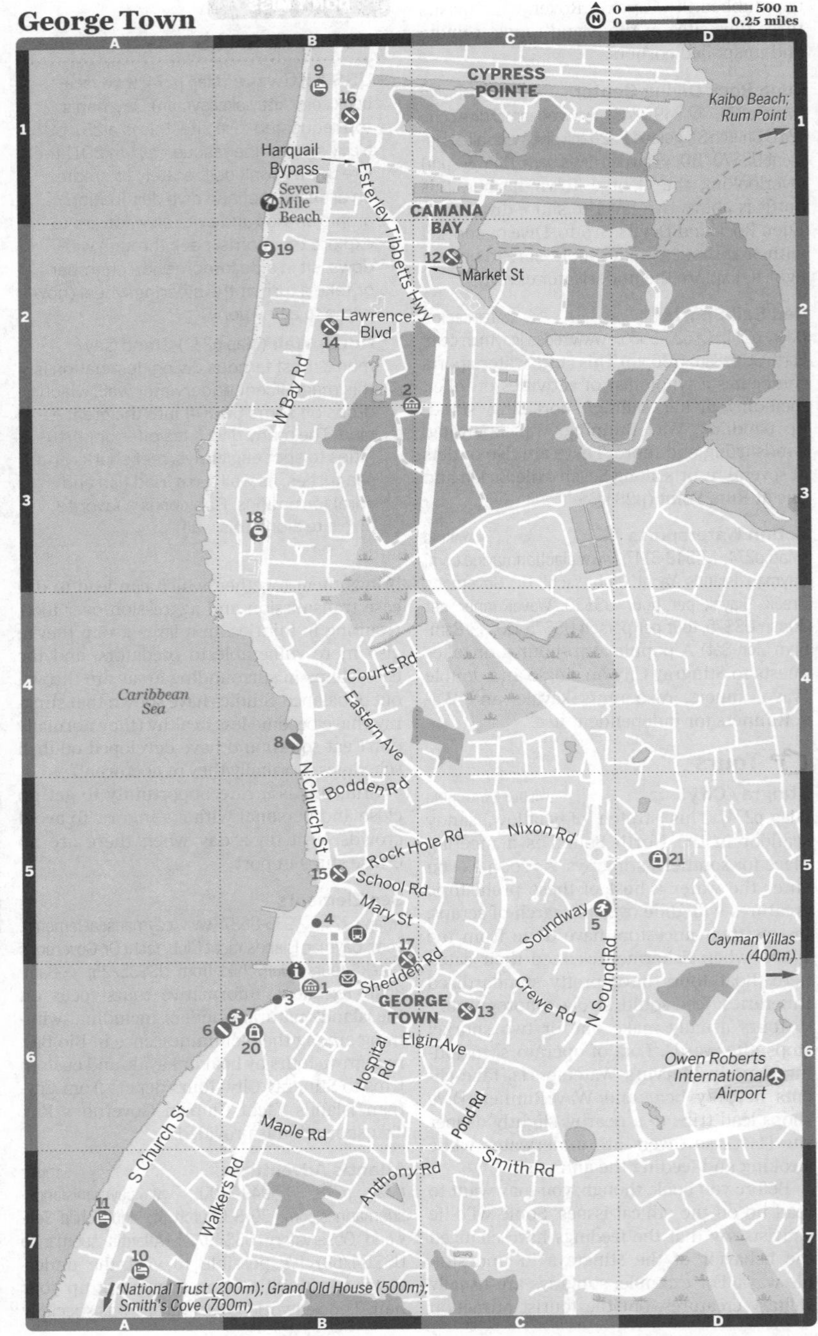

0 500 m
0 0.25 miles
CYPRESS POINTE
Kaibo Beach; Rum Point
Harquail Bypass
Esterley Tibbetts Hwy
Seven Mile Beach
CAMANA BAY
Market St
Lawrence Blvd
W Bay Rd
Courts Rd
Caribbean Sea
Eastern Ave
N Church St
Bodden Rd
Nixon Rd
Rock Hole Rd
School Rd
Mary St
Soundway
Shedden Rd
N Sound Rd
Cayman Villas (400m)
GEORGE TOWN
Crewe Rd
Elgin Ave
Hospital Rd
Owen Roberts International Airport
S Church St
Maple Rd
Pond Rd
Smith Rd
Walkers Rd
Anthony Rd
National Trust (200m); Grand Old House (500m); Smith's Cove (700m)

George Town

Sights
1 Cayman National Museum B6
2 National Gallery of the Cayman Islands B3

Activities, Courses & Tours
3 Atlantis Adventures B6
4 Captain Marvin's Watersports B5
5 Cayman Islands Humane Society C5
6 Eden Rock Diving Center B6
7 Oasis Aqua Park B6
8 Off the Wall Divers B4
Wall to Wall Diving .... (see 8)

Sleeping
9 Beach Suites B1
10 Eldemire's Tropical Island Inn A7
11 Sunset House A7

Eating
12 Agua C2
13 Brasserie C6
14 Cimboco B2
15 Greenhouse B5
16 Ragazzi B1
17 Singh's Roti Shop B5

Drinking & Nightlife
18 O Bar B3
19 Royal Palms Beach Club B2

Shopping
20 Cayman Craft Market B6
21 Tortuga Rum Co D5

designed for the shallow reefs around Grand Cayman, offering a front-row view of two shipwrecks and one fish feeding. The *Atlantis XI* submarine descends to depths up to 100ft, with options to go by day or by night.

Captain Marvin's Watersports SNORKELING
(Map p278; ✆945-6975; www.captainmarvins.com; N Church St; tours adult/child from US$40/30; ⏲tours 8:30am, 9:30am, 10am, 11:15am, 1:45pm & 2:30pm Mon-Fri, 9am, 9:30am & 1pm Sat & Sun) Captain Marvin originated this now standard tour to Stingray City, which includes two or three snorkel stops and an optional beach lunch after the main attraction. The price includes transportation from Seven Mile Beach.

Sleeping

Much of Seven Mile Beach is lined with condos, hotels and sprawling resorts. Grand Cayman caters to higher-end tourism, and places to stay are mostly top end with full services and plenty of family-friendly amenities.

Eldemire's Tropical Island Inn B&B **$**
(Map p278; ✆916-8369; www.eldemire.com; 18 Pebbles Way; r from US$139, apt US$154-186;) Here is a friendly, affordable alternative to the island's resorts and condos. For your money, you get clean, comfy quarters and minimal interference from your host. Laundry room (with coin-op machines) and communal kitchen are at your disposal; bicycles are available for rental. The quiet residential location is a short walk from the beautiful beach at Smith Cove.

Sunshine Suites HOTEL **$$**
(Map p274; ✆814-1717, 949-3000; www.sunshinesuites.com; 1465 Esterley Tibbetts Hwy, Seven Mile Beach; r from US$168;) This sunny, yellow all-suite resort is a short walk from the beach. You'll pay less for the off-beach location, but the place doesn't skimp on service (for which you'll pay a US$35-per-night 'resort fee' on top of quoted rates). Value-conscious travelers will appreciate the well-stocked kitchens and complimentary continental breakfast.

★**Beach Suites** BOUTIQUE HOTEL **$$$**
(Map p278; ✆949-1234; https://beachsuites.ky; 747 West Bay Rd; ste from US$799;) What was once an old Hyatt underwent a cool million in renovations, compliments of new owner Dart Realty Group, and reopened in 2019 as Grand Cayman's dreamiest boutique hotel. The 52 one- and two-bedroom suites feature breathtaking ocean and pool views, but guests may be lured out by the convivial vibe at the beach club.

Sunset House HOTEL **$$$**
(Map p278; ✆949-7111; www.sunsethouse.com; 390 S Church St; r from US$263;) 'For divers, by divers' is the motto here – meaning that there's terrific shore diving, morning and afternoon boat dives, and various training programs, all just a few steps from your door. Rooms are spacious, clean and comfortable, some with ocean views from the balcony. A full, hearty breakfast is included with packages.

Discovery Point Club CONDO **$$$**
(Map p274; ✆945-4724; www.discoverypointclub.com; 2043 West Bay Rd, Seven Mile Beach;

2-bedroom ste US$475-675;) This excellent condo complex is recommended for a comfortable family beach holiday. At the far north end of Seven Mile Beach (in front of a good snorkeling area), suites have superb views, balconies or patios, and kitchens. Amenities include tennis and basketball courts, along with a soothing hot tub.

Eating

There are worthwhile restaurants clustered around downtown George Town and strung out along West Bay Rd. Day-trippers will want to move beyond the immediate zone of the cruise-ship tender dock. Within walking distance there's a range of restaurants serving excellent local fare.

★Island Naturals Café VEGAN $
(Map p274; 945-2252; www.islandnaturals.ky; 12 Earth Cl; smoothies & juices US$8, mains US$10-20; 7am-8pm Mon-Fri, to 6pm Sat, to 5pm Sun;) Delicious vegan cafe featuring healthy salads, yummy soups, acai bowls, cold-pressed juice, gluten-free baked goods, and locally roasted coffee made with Brazilian beans. Main dishes such as vegan chorizo and green coconut curry will have even the staunchest carnivore salivating. The service couldn't be friendlier, and the owners also run a gift store and crystal shop upstairs.

Singh's Roti Shop CARIBBEAN $
(Map p278; 946-7684; www.singhsroti.ky; cnr Doctor Roy's Dr & Shedden Rd; mains US$7.50-10.50; 8am-10pm Mon-Thu, to midnight Fri & Sat, 9am-4pm Sun) In a city where dinner often means a three-figure check, this cheerful hole-in-the-wall place is great for some tongue-searing roti (a curry filling – often potatoes and chicken – rolled inside flatbread). Definitely one of George Town's best bargains.

Good Mood Food Co. FOOD TRUCK $
(Map p274; 926-5488; www.goodmoodfood.ky; 41 Canal Point Dr; mains US$12-17; noon-8pm Mon-Thu & Sun, to 12:30am Fri & Sat;) Grand Cayman's top food truck is beloved for its juicy burgers and inimitable sweet-and-spicy chicken sandwich. Vegetarians will be set with spring rolls or a quinoa salad, while adventurous eaters can try the crispy fried chicken feet. Kids' portions are available for grilled cheese, chicken tenders, hot dogs and all of the burgers.

Greenhouse VEGETARIAN $
(Map p278; www.greenhousecayman.com; 72 N Church St; mains US$15-18; 6am-4pm Mon-Sat;) Here's your perfect downtown lunch stop, with fresh, creative combinations of toppings and stuffings for sandwiches, salads and pizzas. Health-conscious eaters will be in heaven. Dietary restrictions pose no challenge, as the menu has plentiful gluten-free, paleo and vegetarian-friendly options.

Cimboco CARIBBEAN $$
(Map p278; 947-2782; www.cimboco.com; Marquee Plaza, Seven Mile Beach; mains US$12-22; 7:30am-10pm Mon-Fri, from 7am Sat & Sun) Despite the strip-mall setting, this all-day bistro has a showy open kitchen, a colorful dining room and a breezy charm. Artisanal pizzas, Caribbean-flavored sandwiches and various pasta dishes round out the wide-ranging menu.

Ragazzi ITALIAN $$
(Map p278; 945-3484; www.ragazzi.ky; Buckingham Sq, West Bay Rd, Seven Mile Beach; pizza US$15-20, pasta US$22-30, mains US$30-50; 11:30am-11pm) This much-loved Italian place has a sort of oddball location in a small strip mall, but the casual interior offers a warm, welcoming atmosphere. Keep it simple with crispy-crust pizza (it'll even do gluten free) or delectable pasta dishes, or take it upscale with adroitly prepared steaks and seafood.

★Agua SEAFOOD $$$
(Map p278; 949-2482; www.agua.ky; 47 Forum Lane, Camana Bay; mains US$25-52; 11:30am-3pm & 5-10pm Sat-Thu, to 10:30pm Fri) Newly ensconced on the waterfront within Camana Bay, this delightful seafood restaurant draws influence from Italian and Peruvian traditions with utterly satisfying results. The ceviche is the best on the island, available in an array of styles or even in salad form. The fresh seafood and handmade pastas are outstanding and pair well with the excellent craft cocktails.

Brasserie SEAFOOD $$$
(Map p278; 945-1815; www.brasseriecayman.com; Cricket Sq, 171 Elgin Ave; cafe US$12-16, mains US$20-30, 5-course tasting menu US$87.50, with wine pairings US$137.50; restaurant 11:30am-10pm Mon-Fri, cafe 7am-5pm Mon-Fri) The Brasserie can guarantee the freshest of seafood, because its own fishing boat goes out daily to catch it. There's also a thriving garden for produce and a beehive for honey. The result is an eclectic, innovative menu that changes frequently but is always delectable. For lighter fare including sandwiches, salads and breakfast, stop by the on-site Market Cafe.

Grand Old House CARIBBEAN $$$
(Map p274; ☎949-9333; www.grandoldhouse.com; 648 S Church St; mains lunch US$16.50-23.40, dinner US$28.50-84; ⏲11:30am-2:30pm & 5:30-10pm Mon-Fri, 5:30-10pm Sat & Sun; ✎) Set in a 1908 plantation house by the sea, Grand Old House and its gorgeous veranda offer the kind of ambience that make people want to get married there (and over 1000 local couples have). The service is excellent and the food, mostly consisting of seafood and steak, is good but not great. The extensive wine list can sometimes obscure this.

 Drinking & Nightlife

Nightlife isn't one of Cayman's main attractions, but you're never far from a tropical cocktail and a sunset view at a beach bar. Things often get grooving after dark, especially on Thursday and Friday. Draconian laws mean that clubs and bars are supposed to close at midnight on Saturday (so folks can get up and go to church on Sunday).

Calico Jack's BAR
(Map p274; www.facebook.com/CalicoJacksCayman; West Bay Rd, Seven Mile Beach; ⏲9am-1am Mon-Fri, to midnight Sat, 11am-midnight Sun) 'Calico Jack' Rackham was an English pirate who marauded around these parts in the 18th century. Nowadays he lends his name (not to mention his mug) to this classic beach bar – a place for locals, tourists and everybody who likes to dance, drink and let loose on the sand. It's high-energy fun, especially during the infamous full-moon parties.

Royal Palms Beach Club BAR
(Map p278; ☎945-6358; https://royalpalmscayman.com; 537 West Bay Rd; ⏲9am-midnight Mon & Thu, to 1:45am Tue, to 1am Wed, to 2am Fri, to 11:45pm Sat & Sun) Chill out in a private cabana or at the pool bar with live DJs fueling epic sunset dance parties and wild nights under the stars. Friday evenings are particularly well attended by the expat crowd. Bottle service available.

 Shopping

Cayman Craft Market ARTS & CRAFTS
(Map p278; www.craftmarket.ky; cnr S Church St & Boilers Rd; ⏲7:30am-5pm Mon-Fri) This local handicraft market isn't a bad place to pick up Caymanian jewelry and other handmade products, as well as local food products.

Tortuga Rum Co FOOD
(Map p278; ☎949-7701; www.tortugarumcakes.com; N Sound Way; ⏲7am-5pm Mon-Sat, 8am-4pm Sun) Some 10,000 addictive rum cakes are made here daily. Sure, you can buy them all over the island – and the region – but those at the factory are freshest and the samples the most generous.

 Information

Cayman Islands Hospital (☎949-8600; www.hsa.ky; 95 Smith Rd; ⏲24hr) Houses a state-of-the-art hyperbaric chamber.

Department of Tourism (Map p278; www.caymanislands.ky; Harbour Dr) The Cayman Islands' tourism department operates an information booth at the North Terminal cruise-ship dock at George Town harbor. It is only open when cruise ships are in port.

Main Post Office (Map p278; ☎949-2474; www.caymanpost.gov.ky; 14 Edward St; ⏲8:15am-5pm Mon-Fri, 9am-12:30pm Sat)

Police (RCIP; ☎949-4222, 911; www.rcips.ky; 69 Elgin Ave)

Getting There & Away

Cayman Ferries (Map p274; ☎345-325-7777; https://caymanferries.com; Camana Bay; adult/child round-trip to Camana Bay US$25/20, to Rum Point US$30/20) departs Camana Bay for Kaibo Bay and Rum Point at 9:30am, 11:30am, 2:30pm, 6pm and 8pm Tuesday to Friday, noon, 4pm and 6pm on Saturday, and 10am, noon and 4pm on Sunday. There's an equal number of return trips each day.

Historic George Town is compact and pleasantly walkable, but Seven Mile Beach sprawls for nearly 7 miles to the north, so it's useful to have a rental car – try **Cayman Auto Rentals** (☎949-1013; www.caymanautorentals.com.ky; N Church St; bike rental per day US$15-20; ⏲7:30am-5pm Mon-Fri), which rents not only cars but also scooters and bicycles. That said, many tour companies offer transportation from this area to the major attractions. Color-coded minibuses run from the George Town bus depot (p297) all along Seven Mile Beach and to other parts of the island.

West Bay

West Bay is on the itinerary for many visitors to Cayman, most of whom shuttle through to make obligatory stops at a few overhyped attractions. Fewer people experience the true highlights of the district – running horses on deserted beaches, diving the incredible North Wall or exploring the country roads and beach trails by bicycle.

Surrounded by the sea on three sides, West Bay offers spectacular sunrises and sunsets – not to mention excellent eating and drinking venues at which to enjoy the sea views.

Sights & Activities

Barkers National Park NATIONAL PARK
(Map p274) FREE The first national park in the Caymans, Barkers combines low scrub, dense mangroves and long, sandy beaches. There are no amenities here, or even a sign indicating that you've entered the park. But it's a beautiful spot for cycling, horseback riding or kitesurfing. The beach is often deserted. Unfortunately, beach-cleanup crews have a hard time keeping up with the trash that the tide brings in.

Cayman Horse Riding HORSEBACK RIDING
(Map p274; 916-3530; www.caymanhorseriding.com; Conch Point Rd; tours US$90-130) Nicki takes small groups (not more than five people) horseback riding on the beautiful beaches of Barkers National Park. If you're willing to pay a few bucks extra, you can even take the horses swimming. Prices include transportation from Seven Mile Beach and photographs.

West Bay Loop CYCLING
(Map p274; Northwest Point Rd) The West Bay Loop is a 9-mile cycling trail that circles the peninsula, following the spectacular coastline through Barkers National Park, through the residential areas along Spanish Bay, and around Northwest Point. Rent a bike, grab a map and start the route from the Cracked Conch.

Divetech DIVING
(Map p274; 946-5658; www.divetech.com; Lighthouse Point, 571 Northwest Point Rd; 2-tank dive from US$108; 7:30am-5pm) In addition to daily boat dives, Divetech offers some pretty excellent shore diving, which features a mini-wall, canyons and swim-throughs, as well as an underwater statue known as the Guardian of the Reef. This is one of the few shops on the island that offers lessons in tech diving and free diving. And it's got underwater scooters.

Kitesurf Cayman KITESURFING
(Map p274; 916-5483; www.kitesurfcayman.com; Barkers Beach; 2hr private lesson from US$280; 10am-5:30pm Nov-Jul) Walter, Neil and John have been offering private and group kitesurfing lessons on Cayman for nearly a decade. They use radio helmets, so they can coach you (and you can actually hear them) while you're on the board. For days when there's not quite enough wind, they also offer hydrofoil rental and lessons.

Sleeping

West Bay is a mostly residential neighborhood with plenty of rental properties as well as a few full-service resorts. It's a peaceful, pleasant place to stay that's still within striking distance of Seven Mile Beach.

Shangri-La B&B $$
(Map p274; 526-1170; www.shangrilabandb.com; 29b Sticky Toffee Lane; r US$165-219, ste US$319;) Overlooking a little lake in residential West Bay, this B&B (a rarity in Cayman) makes for a pleasant stay. Its eight rooms and one luxurious suite have abundant natural light and are individually decorated in a soothing palette. The place is renowned for its satisfying breakfasts, though the service is less than attentive and the website sometimes doesn't function properly.

Lighthouse Point CONDO $$$
(Map p274; 945-5658; www.lighthousepointdiveresort.com; 571 Northwest Point Rd; condos from US$450;) This gorgeous, green facility features nine two-bedroom condos with balconies that face the setting sun. Cayman's first eco-resort utilizes solar and wind power, a zero-discharge water-management system and custom interiors using repurposed wood. The condos are fully equipped and quite lovely, with a top-notch vegetarian restaurant and an excellent dive operation on-site.

Cobalt Coast Resort & Suites RESORT $$$
(Map p274; 946-5656; www.cobaltcoast.com; 18a Sea Fan Dr; 7-night all-inclusive dive package per person from US$1420;) This small but classy resort does its best to facilitate an amazing dive vacation. The rooms are modern and bright, the setting is dramatically beautiful, and the shore diving is phenomenal, with the North Wall (p277) just 125ft off the dock. Reef Divers, the on-site 'valet' operator, will take care of all your diving needs.

Eating

Some of the island's best restaurants are sprinkled around West Bay. They're pricey, but you can't beat the delicious seafood and beautiful seaside settings.

★Vivo VEGETARIAN $$$

(Map p274; ☎924-7804; www.vivo.ky; Lighthouse Point, 571 Northwest Point Rd; mains US$22-32; ⏰7am-8:30pm; ✎) At the forefront of Cayman's farm-to-table movement, Vivo is all about sustainability. Sit on the breezy porch and sample sandwiches, salads and other delectable innovations made with locally grown produce, farm-fresh eggs and lots of love. This place does amazing things with coconut, including irresistible coconut 'ceviche' and smoked spiced-coconut 'bacon.'

Although the menu is mostly vegan and vegetarian, Vivo is doing its part to rid the reef of its most dangerous invasive species. You can help by ordering a lionfish cake, seared Asian-style lionfish or a coconut-lionfish curry. Good for the body, good for the soul, good for the earth!

Located at Lighthouse Point condos.

★Catch SEAFOOD $$$

(Map p274; ☎949-4321; www.catch.ky; Morgan's Harbour; mains lunch US$18-25, dinner US$32-50; ⏰5:30-10pm Wed-Mon, 11:30am-3pm & 5:30-10pm Sat & Sun) Catch offers a tantalizing menu of seafood, including a daily local catch you can get cooked in one of five ways with two mouthwatering sides. Fresh ceviche and other land and sea delicacies are also on offer. The shady deck is rivaled only by the cool, contemporary decor inside. Service is utterly charming, and the mixologist is a julep genius.

Calypso Grill SEAFOOD $$$

(Map p274; ☎949-3948; www.calypsogrill cayman.com; Morgan's Harbour; mains lunch US$18-25, dinner US$35-47; ⏰11:30am-2:30pm & 6-10pm Tue-Sun) Tucked away on Morgan's Harbour, Calypso Grill is a boldly colorful and wonderfully eclectic venue. The menu is mostly seafood, but there are preparations you won't find anywhere else, such as crispy mango shrimp and – the ultimate in decadence – lobster and shrimp in champagne-cream sauce. Sticky toffee pudding is the signature dessert: don't miss it.

Cracked Conch SEAFOOD $$$

(Map p274; ☎945-5217; www.crackedconch.com.ky; 857 Northwest Point Rd; mains lunch US$18-30, dinner US$33-55; ⏰11am-3pm & 5-10:30pm Dec-May, 5-10:30pm only Jun-Nov) This oceanfront stunner has been delighting discerning diners for some three decades. Although its name makes it sound like a beach bar, this high-concept restaurant and lounge is all white tablecloths and sublime service. There's a more informal venue on the vast open-air deck. It's the perfect spot for a sunset dinner.

Getting There & Away

The sights of West Bay are about 12km north of the cruise-ship terminal in George Town. The yellow-line minibus runs from the George Town bus depot to the Cayman Turtle Center and Batabano Rd, running every 15 minutes from 6am to 11pm Sunday to Thursday, and to midnight on Friday and Saturday.

Bodden Town

Historic Bodden Town was the capital of the Cayman Islands until George Town scooped that honor in the mid-19th century. It's far removed from the bustle of the west – in atmosphere if not in distance – and maintains the appealing vibe of an authentic locals' town. A couple of historical sites and some unique dining experiences make Bodden Town a worthy stop on any drive around the island.

Sights & Activities

Pedro St James HISTORIC BUILDING

(Pedro Castle; Map p274; ☎947-3329; www.pedrostjames.ky; Pedro Castle Rd, Savannah; guided/self-guided tour US$18/12.50, child free; ⏰8:30am-5pm) The island's oldest building, this Caribbean great house was built in 1780 by one of Cayman's founding families (with enslaved people doing the heavy lifting). Over the years the structure has served as jailhouse, courthouse and parliament building. It was here in 1831 that the decision was made in favor of a public vote for elected representatives. And here, in 1835, the Slavery Abolition Act was announced. Nowadays the house is fitted with antiques and reproductions to evoke the era.

Spotts Beach SNORKELING

(Map p274; Shamrock Rd, Savannah) This pretty little public beach is the favorite feeding spot for sea turtles, who come to chow down on sea grass. Don your mask and snorkel and swim with them, but please don't touch, chase or otherwise harass these gentle creatures. Even if you don't feel like getting wet, you can usually spot them from the pier.

Sleeping & Eating

With Bodden Town as your base you might feel you're on a quiet, traditional Caribbean island, even as the bright lights of George Town shine 20 minutes to the west.

Your eating options are limited, but there are a few gems in town – it's definitely worth stopping for lunch if you're passing through.

Coco Beach Villas COTTAGE **$$**
(Map p274; ☎926-0102; www.caymanbeach villas.com; Bodden Town Rd; garden/ocean view from US$179/299; ❄📶) Here's a collection of cozy cottages facing the crystal blue. The five units – complete with modern kitchens and one or two bedrooms – sit on a private beach, strung with hammocks and kissed by Caribbean breezes. The location near the center of Bodden Town offers easy access to the island's sights.

Turtle Nest Inn GUESTHOUSE **$$**
(Map p274; ☎947-8665; www.turtlenestinn.com; Bodden Town Rd; r US$199, apt US$219-379; ❄📶🏊) Not a resort person? Located way off the tourist track, this lovely Spanish-style guesthouse offers the intimacy and authenticity that you're craving. In addition to the comfy quarters (all with kitchen facilities), there are two swimming pools, a sweet sandy beach and an onshore reef for snorkeling. Guests have access to complimentary paddleboards, kayaks and snorkeling gear.

Grape Tree Cafe SEAFOOD **$**
(Map p274; ☎324-5860; www.grapetreecafe.ky; Bodden Town Rd; mains US$10-15; ⏲noon-9pm Fri & Sat, to 8pm Sun) Right on Bodden Town beach, this simple thatched-roof shack is the hottest spot in town during its weekend fish fry. Besides the fresh fish, there are conch fritters, lobster and fried plantains, not to mention fresh tropical-fruit juices. Dine at picnic tables in the sand and enjoy unbeatable sea views.

The place is hard to see from the road: look for the Rubis gas station.

Czech Inn GRILL **$$**
(Map p274; ☎923-1986; http://czechinngrill.com; 563 Bodden Town Rd; mains US$10-28; ⏲11am-10pm, to 11pm Fri & Sat, to 7:30pm Sun) This odd roadside bar isn't a bar at all, as it serves no alcohol and you can't bring your own. But it's undeniably appealing for its kitschy decor, American oldies music, and heaping plates of European specialties and various jerk concoctions: jerk burgers, jerk-chicken quesadillas, jerk pork – you name it.

ℹ Getting There & Away

Bodden Town is about 15km east of George Town, along the south shore of the island. Both orange-line and purple-line minibuses stop in Bodden Town en route to North Side or the East End, running every 30 minutes between 6am and 11pm (and until midnight on Friday).

North Side

Windswept and uncrowded, the North Side is a region of lush greenery, secluded beaches and watery inlets, all lined with pastel-colored vacation homes with too-cute names. Here you can wander among wonderfully landscaped gardens, spot the rare blue iguana, explore mysterious caves and make a wish upon a starfish.

The only ways to get here are by boat or by driving east along the south coast and then cutting through the center of the island. It's a long, meandering journey that tends to make the North Side feel even more remote than it really is. But then again, that's part of the appeal.

👁 Sights

Crystal Caves CAVE
(Map p274; ☎949-2283; www.caymancrystalcaves.com; 69 North Side Rd; adult/child US$40/30; ⏲tours on the hour 9am-4pm) A relatively new attraction to Grand Cayman, this network of mysterious limestone caves is located deep in the island's interior. There are some 105 caves on the property, though only three are open to the public (so far). Look for impressive stalactite and stalagmite formations, lots of hidden rooms and connecting passageways, and a gorgeous interior lake. And, of course, bats. The excursion is pricey but cool.

Starfish Point BEACH
(Map p274; Water Cay Rd) Red-cushion sea stars dot this little patch of sand and sea, which can sometimes be crystal clear and sometimes murky and yellow, depending on what the current's dragging in. Soaking in a foot of water all along the beach, the starfish are easy to spot from above the surface, with or without snorkel gear. Just don't lift them out of the water, as this can kill the sensitive creatures.

Rum Point BEACH
(Map p274; www.rumpointclub.com) Swinging in hammocks and snorkeling are the main activities at this quiet beach, although the Red Sail (p277) water-sports crew also has an outlet here. Take some time to explore the trails along the reef-protected shore and mangroves, then enjoy a beachside burger at fun-filled Wreck Bar (p286).

Queen Elizabeth II Botanic Park GARDENS
(Map p274; ☎947-9462; www.botanic-park.ky; Frank Sound Dr; adult/child US$12.50/free, incl tour adult US$18.50; ⏰9am-5:30pm, tours 2pm Tue & Thu) Come here to see a veritable treasure trove of the island's native species. A series of walking trails traverses the lovely landscaped gardens, which include a rainbow-themed Color Garden, the historical Heritage Garden with a traditional Caymanian house as its centerpiece, an orchid garden (in bloom in late May and June) and the longer woodland trail. The park is also an excellent birding destination.

Activities & Tours

Mastic Trail HIKING
(Map p274; ☎749-1121; www.nationaltrust.org.ky; Further Rd; tours adult/child US$50/25; ⏰tours Tue & Thu) This surprisingly lush 2-mile-long trail meanders through old-growth forest that supplied early settlers with timber. Hikers can explore deep into Grand Cayman's wild interior, with wooden walkways traversing some of the marshy portions. Expect to see wild jasmine, wild coffee, myriad birds, land crabs and more. The **National Trust** (Map p274; ☎749-1121; www.nationaltrust.org.ky; 558 S Church St; ⏰9am-5pm Mon-Fri, 11am-4pm Sat) offers excellent guided hiking tours for groups of six or more.

The northern trailhead – on Further Rd (off North Side Rd) – is the drier, more accessible starting point, but you can also start at the southern trailhead on Mastic Rd (near the botanical garden. Bring insect repellent.

Blue Iguana Safari WILDLIFE
(Map p274; www.nationaltrust.org.ky/blue-iguana-safari; Queen Elizabeth II Botanic Park; tours adult/child incl park US$25/12.50; ⏰tours 11am Mon-Sat) Knowledgeable guides lead daily 90-minute tours of the Blue Iguana Recovery Center, where naturalists are working to restore the population of this critically endangered species. Visitors get a tour of the breeding facility as well as a guided walk around the woodland trail, where some iguanas have been released.

Cayman Kayaks KAYAKING
(Map p274; ☎926-4467; www.caymankayaks.com; Rum Point Club; kayak/boat bioluminescent tour per person US$59/69) Explore the bioluminescent Bio Bay by kayak or ecofriendly electric catamaran, both departing from Rum Point (p284) during certain windows of the lunar cycle. Transport from your hotel and back costs US$25 but is subject to availability.

Sweet Spot Kaibo KAYAKING
(Map p274; ☎925-8129; www.sweetspotwatersports.com; 585 Water Cay Rd; per person US$55) This one-stop water-sports shop rents kayaks and paddleboards, and runs a nice variety of tours. A favorite is the two-hour kayak tour that stops at Starfish Point for sunset and then in Bio Bay for some magical bioluminescence. If you don't care to paddle the 3 miles round-trip you can take the same tour in a purpose-designed 'bio boat.'

Sleeping & Eating

Rum Point and the surrounding areas are sprinkled with condominium complexes and other vacation rentals, but there are very few hotels, resorts or traditional places to stay.

There are just a few places to eat and drink on the North Side, and they are excellent. Take your pick from authentic Caymanian cooking, beach-bar fare or award-winning fine dining.

Retreat at Rum Point CONDO $$$
(Map p274; ☎947-9135; www.retreatrumpoint.com; Rum Point; condos from US$330;) A fantastic beach and an exclusive atmosphere are the draws at this waterfront complex. Amenities include tennis court, gym and luscious swimming pool. The 33 condo units – rented out by various individual owners – have modern kitchens, laundry facilities and screened-in porches to foil the 'skeeters. Five-night minimum.

★ **Kaibo Beach** INTERNATIONAL $$
(Map p274; ☎947-9975; www.kaibo.ky; 585 Water Cay Rd; mains US$19-36; ⏰11am-late, upstairs from 5:30pm) Here's a near-perfect beach bar, with tables in the sand, creative cocktails and scrumptious food ranging from conch fritters to coconut-curry fish. For a rollicking good time, come for the Tuesday-night barbecue, with live music, Caymanian cooking and dancing on the sand (US$34 per person). (Need a lift? Catch the water taxi (p281) from Camana Bay.)

Upstairs (that's the name as well as the location) is a highly lauded fine-dining restaurant by Michelin-starred chef Laurence Tham. The six-course tasting menu (US$84 per person, drink pairing US$72) is a culinary extravaganza.

Over the Edge CARIBBEAN $$
(Map p274; ☎947-9568; 312 Old Man Bay; breakfast dishes US$6-15, mains US$13-30; ⏰7:30am-9pm) This place isn't much to look at, but you can't beat it for friendly service and tasty food, served on a breezy deck facing the water. Ingredients are grown in local gardens and fished in local waters, so this is fresh, flavorful and authentic West Indian cuisine.

Rum Point Club SEAFOOD $$$
(Map p274; ☎947-9412; www.rumpointclub.com; Rum Point; mains US$28-48; ⏰5:30-10pm Tue-Sun) Rum Point Club is a locally famous foodie destination that specializes in elaborate creations of seafood as well as rare rums. The signature dish is a seafood hot pot with no fewer than five *fruits de mer*. Reservations recommended: book a table on the screened porch for maximal sea breezes.

A pleasant way to get here is to take the ferry (p281) that runs between Camana Bay, Kaibo Beach and Rum Point.

Wreck Bar BAR
(Map p274; www.rumpointclub.com; Rum Point; mains US$12-25; ⏰kitchen 10am-5pm, bar to 6pm) Beach bars don't come much more friendly than this boozy refuge, which sets up chairs on the sand. Burgers, sandwiches and cocktails are on the menu for lunch, which you can devour at a shaded picnic table. Here's your perfect spot to sample the famous mudslide (a cocktail that was apparently invented here).

Getting There & Away

It takes about 45 minutes to drive the 40km around the island to the North Side. The orange-line minibuses go as far as Old Man Bay (6am to 9pm), but you'll need a private vehicle to get to Rum Point.

A ferry (p281) departs Rum Point and Kaibo Beach at 10:30am, 12:30pm, 3:30pm, 6:30pm and 9:15pm Tuesday to Friday, 1pm, 5:15pm and 9:15pm on Saturday, and 11am, 1pm and 5pm on Sunday. There's an equal number of trips in the opposite direction.

East End

A world away from the rest of the island, the East End is a place where life goes slowly – and where the rampant development has not yet reached. Here's your chance to catch a last glimpse of traditional Caymanian living (and a taste of traditional Caymanian cooking). The area is ideal for a long bike ride or a deep dive into the sea, where canyons and caverns abound and Caribbean reef sharks can be spied on. Beyond that, the folks are friendly and the scenery is dramatic and beautiful, with avian-rich marshlands, hidden beaches and ironshore (black karst) coastline.

Sights & Activities

Wreck of the 10 Sail Monument MEMORIAL
(Map p274; Austin Connolly Dr) In 1794 a convoy of 10 British merchant ships wrecked on the reef off the East End. Local residents came to the aid of the convoy, rescuing all but eight of the passengers and crew. Legend has it that a royal prince was among the rescued, and King George was so grateful that he rewarded the islanders' bravery by forever exempting them from paying taxes and from being conscripted. (Good story, but there's no documentary evidence.)

The memorial overlooking the wreck site remembers the victims and honors the rescuers.

Ocean Frontiers Dive Shop DIVING
(Map p274; ☎640-7500; www.oceanfrontiers.com; 344c Austin Connolly Dr; 2-tank dive from US$99-129; ⏰7am-6pm) A top-notch outfit within Compass Point Dive Resort, notable for its access to 55 glorious dive sites around the East End (some frequented by Caribbean reef sharks). The shop has new boats and runs a coral-restoration program involving 18 nurseries. In addition to the usual excursions, it offers free diving, lionfish hunting, ultraviolet night dives and early-morning trips to Stingray City (p277).

White Sands Water Sports WATER SPORTS
(Map p274; ☎926-7263; www.whitesandwatersports.com; Reef Resort, 1 Queens Hwy; kitesurfing lessons per person from US$125, 1hr kayak/paddleboard rental US$20/25; ⏰9am-4:30pm) The East End's premier water-sports operation rents kayaks, paddleboards and kitesurfing gear, offers tours of all kinds and even hosts yoga classes. The glass-bottom-kayak tour to Bioluminescent Bay is highly recommended, as are the kitesurfing lessons, which take place on a wind-whipped offshore sandbar in warm, waist-deep water.

★**Eco Rides** CYCLING
(☎922-0754; www.ecoridescayman.ky; per person US$80-125) A lifelong East Ender, Shane Edwards is passionate about showing off his

end of the island – preferably on two wheels. Ranging from two to five hours, the cycling tours stop at landmarks such as the Wreck of the 10 Sail monument, the East End lighthouse and the blowholes, with a rest stop at Shane's own cozy home at Grapetree Cove.

Sleeping

For the moment, the East End feels gloriously remote, with just a few small and medium-size resorts dotting the main drag. Enjoy it while it lasts, as developer Dart Realty has recently acquired seaside property in these parts, including the beloved Barefoot Beach.

Compass Point Dive Resort RESORT $$$
(Map p274; ☎640-7500; Austin Connolly Dr; ste from US$295; P ❄ 📶 🏊) Catering to discerning divers, Compass Point offers 28 spacious and stylish units, all with balconies overlooking the beach or one of the two pools. There's a dive shop on-site, promising a quick, easy commute to the world-class sites around the East End. Snorkel gear, bicycles and kayaks are available for guest use.

Wyndham Reef Resort RESORT $$$
(Map p274; ☎640-3100; www.wyndhamcayman.com; Queen's Hwy; r US$160-458; ❄ @ 📶 🏊) All 152 rooms in these cheery yellow blocks face the sea along a gorgeous stretch of sand. Rooms are quite luxurious, service is top notch, and there's good snorkeling right off the beach. Until it sold in 2015, the Reef was celebrated as one of the island's few locally owned resorts. Wyndham has maintained the personal service and intimate atmosphere.

Eating

Come to the East End for old-fashioned Caymanian cooking. The best restaurants operate out of somebody's kitchen (or open-air grill), so you know it's pure homemade goodness.

★**Eastern Star Fish Fry** SEAFOOD $
(Map p274; ☎345-526-5945; 2550 Sea View Rd; mains US$8-15; ⏰11am-7pm Sat & Sun) Tucked into a shack behind the Rubis gas station, this local find offers some of Grand Cayman's tastiest pan-fried whole snapper, lobster tails, conch fritters and whatever else is fresh. The enormous portions can be taken to go but are best consumed at the colorful picnic tables. Wash everything down with lemonade or tamarind juice, and don't miss the cassava cake.

Vivine's Kitchen CARIBBEAN $
(Map p274; ☎947-7435; 524 Austin Connolly Dr; mains US$5-12; ⏰11am-8pm) There really is a Miss Vivine and she really does live in this roadside home with stellar views of the ocean. Local treats such as goat curry, fish and fritters, stewed beef and much more are served up home style; desserts include cassava and sweet-potato cake. Eat at a picnic table on the terrace and enjoy the scene. Cash only.

Eagle Rays INTERNATIONAL $$
(Map p274; ☎640-8888; www.eaglerays.ky; Compass Point Dive Resort, 346 Austin Connolly Dr; mains US$10-25; ⏰11:30am-9:30pm) A casual, open-air establishment that's both oceanfront and poolside, Eagle Rays attracts a lively après-diving crowd. Its lionfish tacos are second to none, and there are usually live games on the big-screen TV.

Tukka FUSION $$$
(Map p274; ☎947-2700; www.tukka.ky; 898 Queen's Hwy; mains lunch US$12-20, dinner US$28-40; ⏰11:30am-10pm Mon-Sat, from 8:30am Sun) 'Tukka' is a riff on the Australian word for food ('tucker'), and at this funky seaside restaurant Aussie Ron Hargrave serves up an eclectic assortment of Caribbean and Australian eats. Specialties include conch and croc fritters, kangaroo burgers and jerk-chicken gnocchi. The Wednesday-night walkabout, a four-course international dinner (US$47), is a highlight.

Getting There & Away

The East End is about 30km east of George Town. The purple-line bus runs from the George Town bus depot to the East End terminal every hour or so from 6am to 9pm (to midnight on Friday night).

CAYMAN BRAC

Named after the 'brac' or 'bluff' that dominates this cheese wedge of an island, the most easterly of the Cayman Islands is also the most authentically Caymanian. Tourism isn't the name of the game here. Instead, residents work in the quarries, on fishing boats and in other enterprises, as well as for the local government. While the island has (almost) all the conveniences of the modern era, it also has a laid-back, small-island atmosphere that's pretty irresistible. Visit for top-notch diving, a scenic hike or climb along the bluff, and little else.

Sights

Great Cave CAVE
(South Side Rd, East End) The island's largest, most enticing cave is at the eastern end of South Side Rd. Ascend ladders to enter a large cavern that begs to be explored. Expect bats.

Bluff NATURAL FEATURE
The limestone cliff – 140ft high at its eastern end – stretches almost the entire length of this little island and dominates the landscape. Along the north side there are several access points for hikers, including the National Trust Parrot Reserve and the Lighthouse Footpath. By car, drive up Ashton Reid Dr to Major Donald Dr, which runs across the top of the bluff.

Foots House PUBLIC ART
(South Side Rd; from 7:30am) FREE Cayman Brac sculptor Ronald 'Foots' Kynes' brightly colored oceanfront home doubles as an art museum, and he's happy to lead guests on tours. Messages pertaining to art, war and Led Zeppelin adorn surfaces and signs around the property, and provocative sculptures can be found inside and spilling into the yard and parking area. For example, there's a clay skull inside a toilet. And a couple of fake missiles. And a bunch of nude busts and a giant pair of feet.

Activities

Most people come to Cayman Brac for the diving, which is pristine and amazing. The island also has a few excellent hiking trails, some caves to explore and plenty of birds to watch. Recently, new climbing routes have made it possible for beginners to scale a bluff once reserved for experts.

Hiking & Climbing

★Lighthouse Footpath HIKING
(Major Donald Dr) With stunning vistas all around, this 2.5-mile (one way) walking trail runs along the edge of the bluff. It starts at the lighthouse, which – at 140ft – is the highest point in Cayman. The scenery is spectacular, and the bluff is an excellent vantage point for spotting the varied birdlife, including nesting brown boobies and frigate birds gliding in the updrafts.

To reach the trailhead, drive to the far eastern end of Major Donald Dr.

★Rock Iguana Ltd CLIMBING
(936-2722; http://climb.ky; South Side Rd, East End; rappelling tour/half-day rock climbing per person from US$125/185) Experienced, in-the-know climbers have been scaling Cayman Brac's limestone cliffs for years. But in 2019 this top-notch outfit for all skill levels entered the scene. Led by Angel, a rescue-trained mountaineer who used to climb in the Himalayas, the team set beginner and intermediate routes up the bluff at the southeastern end of the island and runs climbing and rappelling tours.

Diving

With crystal waters affording superb visibility and more than 40 permanent dive moorings, Cayman Brac attracts its share of diving and snorkeling enthusiasts. An artificial reef, a 315ft Russian frigate now named the *Captain Keith Tibbetts,* is popular.

Brac Scuba Shack DIVING
(925-3215; www.bracscubashack.com; West End; 2-tank dive from US$120; 8:30am-4pm) An independent dive shop that specializes in small groups and custom trips involving both shore and boat diving. Nitrox, rental gear and PADI scuba courses are all on offer.

Reef Divers DIVING
(948-1642; www.reefdiverscaymanbrac.com; West End; 2-tank dive from US$110; 7:30am-12:30pm & 1:30-5pm) Long-established dive operator based at Cayman Brac Beach Resort. Boats leave in the morning and afternoon, and night dives are offered twice a week.

Birdwatching

National Trust Parrot Reserve BIRDWATCHING
(Bight Rd; www.nationaltrust.org.ky; Major Donald Dr) Come here to spot one of about 350 remaining Cayman Brac parrots. Access to the reserve is on a hiker-only trail, Bight Rd, which crosses the Brac from north to south. The hiking is mostly on jagged ironshore, which can be challenging. The trail includes a 200m boardwalk through the dense forest that echoes with songbirds.

Westerly Ponds BIRDWATCHING
(West End) Birdwatchers should head for the Westerly Ponds at the island's western tip, where there are more than 100 species of bird nesting around the wetlands. There are viewing platforms for your birdwatching pleasure.

Sleeping & Eating

Brac Caribbean CONDO $$
(☎948-2265; www.braccaribbean.ky; West End; 1/2-bedroom condos from US$225/260;) Like its sibling, the **Carib Sands** (☎948-1121; www.caribsands.com; West End; 1/2/3-bedroom condos from US$190/243/360;), this condo complex offers understated luxury and top-notch service. The demure three-story buildings feature 16 apartments with ocean-view balconies, tropically colored interiors and easy access to the on-site **restaurant** (☎948-1418; www.facebook.com/Captains-Table-Bar-Restaurant-137029733010563; West End; mains US$12-20; ⏲11am-midnight).

Cayman Brac Beach Resort RESORT $$$
(☎948-1323; www.clearlycayman.com; West End; 7-day package incl meals & diving per person from US$1189;) A relaxed and friendly diving hotel, Cayman Brac Beach Resort occupies a charming stretch of shore. The 40 rooms, each with a small patio or balcony, are spread around a gorgeous pool. Bicycles and kayaks are available for guests, as are the nature trails, dotted with hammocks, through the grounds.

★**Barry's Golden Jerk** JAMAICAN $
(☎917-6713; West Side Rd; meals US$12; ⏲2:30-9pm Wed, Fri & Sat) Barry's roadside shack will satisfy your craving for jerk chicken and pork, served with fresh-baked bread. He's only there three days a week, but if you time it right you'll see (and smell) the spicy goodness being cooked up in the oil-drum smoker in the yard.

Star Island Restaurant CARIBBEAN $
(☎948-8406; star.island@rocketmail.com; 137 West Side Rd; sandwiches US$4-6, mains US$10-15; ⏲7am-10pm) The definitive local favorite. The menu is extensive, with well-stuffed omelets, burgers and sandwiches. But the highlight is the old-fashioned Caymanian cooking, including fish stew and shrimp curry.

Information

Cayman National Bank (Cross Rd, West End; ⏲9am-4pm Mon-Thu, to 4:30pm Fri) Has a 24hr ATM and currency exchange.

Faith Hospital (☎948-2243; 215 Dennis Foster Rd, Stake Bay) This modern hospital serves both Cayman Brac and Little Cayman.

Post Office (West End; ⏲8:30am-5pm Mon-Fri)

Getting There & Away

Charles Kirkconnell International Airport (formerly known as Gerrard Smith International Airport) is located at the western end of the island. Cayman Airways Express (www.caymanairways.com) operates several daily flights to Grand Cayman (from US$88, 40 minutes) and Little Cayman (from US$44, 10 minutes).

Getting Around

There's no public transportation on Cayman Brac, but it's not that difficult to get around without a car. Lodging providers will pick you up by prior arrangement. Bikes may be rented or borrowed from the resorts. The negligible crime rate – and the amiability of the locals – makes hitchhiking safe and easy. The mere sight of a visitor marching down the roadway occasionally results in ride offers by passing motorists.

All that said, if you intend to do extensive exploration of the island, the best way to do it is to rent a car from **B&S Motor Ventures Ltd** (☎916-5242, 948-1646; www.bandsmv.com; 126 Channel Rd SW; ⏲8am-5pm Mon-Sat, by appointment Sun) or **CB Rent-A-Car** (☎948-2424; www.cbrentacar.com; Charles Kirkconnell International Airport; ⏲8am-6:30pm). You can also call a **taxi** (☎923-5494; vanessa.carter80@yahoo.com).

LITTLE CAYMAN

The clue is in the name: Little Cayman is tiny indeed, but it abounds in birdlife, marine life and glorious natural scenery. With more resident iguanas than humans, this delightful island is the place to head for solitude, tranquility and some of the Caribbean's best diving.

Sights

The sights of Little Cayman are almost entirely natural, whether they be the birds that nest in the wetlands, the marine life populating the reef or the iguanas basking by the road.

Owen Island ISLAND
Find your inner pirate at this tiny deserted island that's a quarter-mile offshore from the Southern Cross Club (p291). The beach here is unspoiled and the vegetation thick and unexplored. Get here by kayak or paddleboard, which you can rent from the club.

Little Cayman Museum MUSEUM
(☎925-7625; www.littlecaymanmuseum.org; Guy Banks Rd, Blossom Village; ⏲1:30-4pm Mon-Thu, 2-5pm Fri, 10:30am-12:30pm Sat) FREE Housed in new quarters, this is an impressive museum for a little island. Stop by to peruse exhibits on the history of Cayman, as well as a display of wonderful underwater photography and rotating exhibits of local artwork. There's also an iguana habitat out back, which the museum attendant (an iguana expert) will happily show you.

Point of Sand BEACH
Little Cayman's best beach is a splotch of reef-protected powder that rarely has more than half a dozen people visiting at any time. There's a tiny pier, limited shade and breaking waves 200m out. It's 8 miles from the airport, which makes for a nice bike ride.

Activities

National Trust Visitors Centre BIRDWATCHING
(☎623-1107; www.facebook.com/LittleCaymanNationalTrust; Guy Banks Rd; ⏲3-5pm Mon-Fri Nov-Jun, by request Jul-Oct) The modern center backs onto Booby Pond Nature Reserve, home to one of the hemisphere's largest breeding populations of red-footed boobies and a large colony of swooping frigate birds. Spy on them from the back porch and upstairs terrace, which are always accessible, and ask to see the videos on turtles, iguanas and boobies.

Diving

Little Cayman has more than 60 dive sites marked with moorings, in addition to the many onshore sites that are accessible for snorkelers and shore divers. Almost all of the hotels and resorts have diving operations.

★Bloody Bay Marine Park DIVING
For the crystal-clear, warm waters, diversity of species and gorgeous seascapes, this marine park is widely considered to offer the Caribbean's best diving. On the island's north side, Bloody Bay includes two dozen spectacular named dive sites. And at a depth of just 18ft, Bloody Bay Wall plummets into aquamarine infinity as divers hovering over the abyss wonder whether they're hallucinating.

Central Caribbean Marine Institute DIVING
(Little Cayman Research Center; ☎948-1094; www.reefresearch.org; North Coast Rd E; Edge/Seacamp incl meals & lodging US$1688/1999) At this beautifully sited field station, CCMI works hard to study, conserve and restore coral reefs. The institute offers internships and research opportunities for scientists and students, as well as a summertime 'Seacamp' for teens.

Little Cayman & Cayman Brac

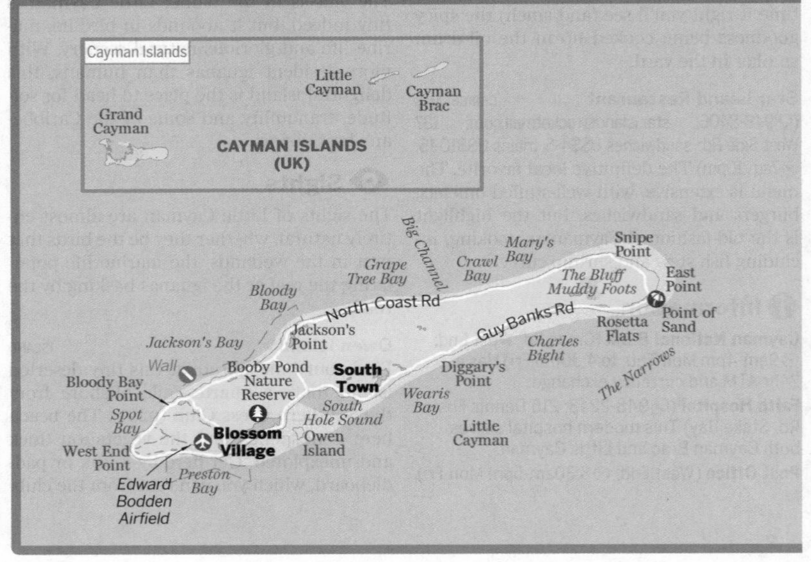

Recreational divers can participate in the weeklong 'Dive on the EDGE' program, which identifies, photographs and catalogs species of coral and sea life.

Conch Club Divers DIVING
(☎948-1026; www.conchclubdivers.com; Guy Banks Rd; 2-tank dive US$105-120) This independent dive shop is newly located next to Paradise Villas but offers top-notch valet service to anyone on the island. The 42ft *Sea-Esta* takes divers and snorkelers to Bloody Bay Wall and other excellent sites around the island.

Sleeping & Eating

It's a small island, but there's a good selection of low-key resorts, most offering decent dive packages or other all-inclusive options. Some close in September and/or October. Most prefer weeklong bookings.

There's only a handful of restaurants on Little Cayman, almost all of which are located at the resorts. You may want to take advantage of that all-inclusive option. Otherwise, you'll appreciate a kitchen in your rental unit.

Pirates Point Resort RESORT **$$**
(☎948-1010; www.piratespointresort.com; Guy Banks Rd; r per person incl meals from US$245;) Rustic Pirates Point was founded by the legendary Gladys Howard, an avid conservationist and supporter of all things Caymanian. Gladys passed away in 2015, and her daughter, Susan, now runs the resort. Fantastically located, the place is known for comfortable rooms, warm hospitality and amazing food – it's worth a visit even if you're not staying here.

Paradise Villas VILLA **$$**
(☎948-0001; www.paradisevillas.com; Guy Banks Rd, Blossom Village; r US$229-249;) Just a few steps from the airport, this friendly property is a longtime favorite for its unpretentious charm and oceanfront setting. Twelve smart cottages are right on the beach, with private verandas and swinging hammocks to catch the breeze. The property was purchased by the Dart Realty development group in 2017, but so far there haven't been any big changes.

★**Southern Cross Club** RESORT **$$$**
(☎948-1099; www.southerncrossclub.com; Guy Banks Rd; 5 nights all-inclusive per person from US$1713;) The oldest resort on the island is also the classiest: Southern Cross is a gorgeous boutique operation with an eco-conscious approach. There are 14 pastel-colored bungalows, most with private

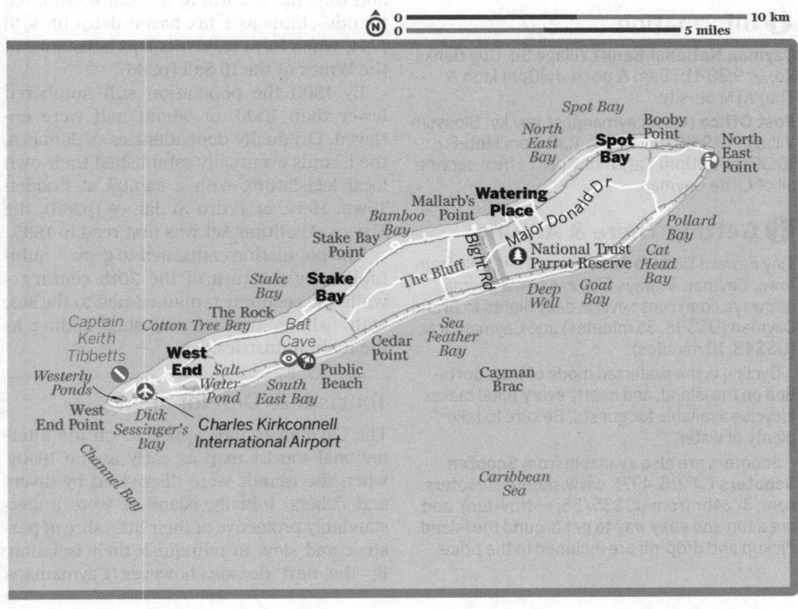

porches and outdoor showers, and all with glorious views of the sea and nearby Owen Island. Meals are excellent and the service is impeccable.

Little Cayman Beach Resort RESORT $$$
(☎948-1033; www.littlecayman.com; 1128 Guy Banks Rd, Blossom Village; 7-night dive package per person from US$1895;) The largest resort on the island (which isn't saying much) is a perfect base for your diving vacation. Some 28 stylishly tropical rooms surround the pool, while an additional dozen have private balconies facing the ocean. The property is positively dreamy, with hammocks swaying in the breeze, and the friendly, fun Beach Nuts bar keeps folks happy.

Hungry Iguana INTERNATIONAL $$
(☎948-0007; www.facebook.com/TheHungryIguana; Paradise Villas, Blossom Village; mains lunch US$15-20, dinner US$22-44; ⊙kitchen noon-2:30pm & 6-9pm Mon-Fri, 7:30-10:30am, noon-2:30pm & 6-9pm Sat & Sun, bar noon-midnight) One of the few restaurants on the island, this friendly place is on the water by the airstrip. The long lunch menu centers on burgers and sandwiches, while dinner is more elaborate, with steaks and seafood. The new owner, Dart Realty development group, has added breakfast on weekends.

Information

Cayman National Bank (Village Sq, Guy Banks Rd; ⊙9:30-11:30am & noon-4:30pm Mon & Thu) ATM on-site.

Post Office (www.caymanpost.gov.ky; Blossom Village; ⊙9:30am-noon & 1:30-3pm Mon-Fri, 10:30am-1:30pm Sat) A tiny post office serving all of Little Cayman.

Getting There & Around

Tiny Edward Bodden Airfield is a short walk from town. Cayman Airways Express (www.caymanairways.com) runs several daily flights to Grand Cayman (US$98, 35 minutes) and Cayman Brac (US$43, 10 minutes).

Cycling is the preferred mode of transportation on the island, and nearly every hotel makes bicycles available for guests. Be sure to take plenty of water.

Scooters are also available from **Scooten Scooters** (☎916-4971; www.scootenscooters.com; 3/24hr from US$35/55; ⊙Nov-Jun), and are a fun and easy way to get around the island. Pickup and drop-off are included in the price.

UNDERSTAND THE CAYMAN ISLANDS

History

Las Tortugas

For the first century after Christopher Columbus happened upon the Cayman Islands in 1503, the islands remained uninhabited by people – which may explain why the place was overrun with sea turtles, giving the islands their original Spanish name, Las Tortugas. The sun-bleached landscape languished in a near-pristine state, undisturbed but for the occasional intrusion of sailors stopping in to swipe some turtles and fill up on fresh water. No permanent settlers set up shop until well after the 1670 acquisition of the islands by the British Crown, which has held dominion over the three islands ever since.

Settlement & Growth

Once settlers started trickling in from Jamaica in the early 18th century, Caymanians quickly established their reputation as world-class seafarers. From the 1780s the Caymanian shipbuilding industry produced schooners and other seacraft used for trade and turtling. According to local legend, the islands' status as a tax haven dates back to 1794, when local residents lent assistance at the Wreck of the 10 Sail (p286).

By 1800 the population still numbered fewer than 1000, of whom half were enslaved. Originally dependencies of Jamaica, the islands eventually established their own local legislature, with a capital at Bodden Town. Here, at Pedro St James (p283), the Slavery Abolition Act was first read in 1835.

The population continued to grow – quintupling by the turn of the 20th century – while the economy remained tied to the sea, with fishing, turtling and shipbuilding as the main industries.

Tourism & Development

The Cayman Islands appeared on the international tourist map as early as the 1950s, when the islands were discovered by divers and fishers. Initially, islanders were understandably protective of their little slice of paradise and slow to relinquish their isolation. By the next decade, however, Caymanians had begun fashioning the tax structure that's made Grand Cayman an economic powerhouse – and creating the infrastructure to make it a capital of Caribbean tourism.

People & Culture

For centuries the Cayman Islands had been left to simmer undisturbed in their own juices as the rest of the world rushed headlong into modernity. As recently as 50 years ago (aside from a few adventurers and fishing nuts) there were few tourists. Electric power was provided solely by noisy generators, and most islanders did without it. What has occurred between then and now constitutes a Caymanian cultural revolution, with the advent of large-scale tourism and big-business banking.

Historically, the population is an amalgamation of British, Jamaican and African peoples, but contemporary Cayman has become even more multifaceted. Nowadays, North America is well represented, as are Europe, South America and Southeast Asia. This large influx of expatriate workers – representing more than 80 countries – means that Caymanians make up little more than half of the population in their own country.

LOCAL KNOWLEDGE

NEVER SAY THE CAYMANS

If there's one thing that gets locals' dander up, it's hearing their nation referred to as 'the Caymans.' Don't ask why: they don't know any more than a resident of San Francisco knows why they shudder at hearing 'Frisco' – it's nails on a chalkboard. Preferred terms for the entire country are 'Cayman' or 'Cayman Islands.' As a pair, Cayman Brac and Little Cayman are known as the 'Sister Islands'; the individual islands are called by their correct names.

Landscape & Wildlife

The Land

Located approximately 150 miles south of Cuba and 180 miles west of Jamaica, the Cayman Islands consist of Grand Cayman and two smaller islands – Cayman Brac and Little Cayman – 75 miles to the northeast and 5 miles apart. All three islands are low-lying, flat-topped landmasses, although Cayman Brac does have a 140ft cliff, by far the most dramatic scenery in the region. In fact, the Cayman Islands are the tips of massive submarine mountains that just barely emerge from the awesome Cayman Trench, an area with the deepest water in the Caribbean.

Encircling all three of the islands are shallow waters and a reef system harboring one of the world's richest accumulations of marine life. At Bloody Bay Wall, on the north shore of Little Cayman, the seafloor ends abruptly at a depth of only 18ft to 25ft, dropping off into a 6000ft vertical cliff. Along its sheer face grows an astonishing variety of corals, sponges and sea fans and thousands of mobile creatures going about their daily business as the occasional diver looks on, agog.

Flora & Fauna

With nearly 200 native winged species, the islands offer outstanding birdwatching. Keep your eyes open and you'll spot parrots, boobies, yellow-bellied sapsuckers, herons and egrets. Reptiles include celebrities such as green sea turtles and blue and rock iguanas, and plenty of common geckos and lizards (the latter sometimes making an appearance in the baths of luxury hotels). Cayman tries to balance protecting the environment with development – driving on beaches is against the law due to the harm this can do to turtle habitats, iguanas have the right of way, and there are plentiful marine-replenishment zones where fishing is not permitted.

The islands' landscape is dry and scrubby. Poisonous species include maiden plum (a weed with rash-causing sap), lady's hair or cowitch (a vine with fiberglass-like barbs) and the vicious manchineel tree, which produces a skin-blistering sap. Take care not to shelter under a manchineel in the rain! Other indigenous plants are cochineel, used as a shampoo as well as eaten, and pingwing, whose barbed branches were once fashioned into natural fences.

SURVIVAL GUIDE

Directory A–Z

ACCESSIBLE TRAVEL

Grand Cayman is a relatively friendly destination for travelers with disabilities:

➡ Many resorts offer accessible rooms, including the **Ritz-Carlton** (Map p274; ☎943-9000; www.ritzcarlton.com; West Bay Rd, Seven Mile Beach; r from US$720; ❄@📶🏊) and Sunshine Suites (p279). Many restaurants and shopping malls around the island are also wheelchair accessible.

➡ Other services are available, such as beach-wheelchair rental, and in 2018 Mobi-Mats were introduced at hotel beaches around the island. These allow wheelchair users to easily make their way into the sea.

➡ **Accessible Caribbean Vacations** (☎in USA 1-888-490-1280; www.accessiblecaribbeanvacations.com) offers sightseeing tours and snorkeling excursions (including to Stingray City) for wheelchair-bound travelers.

➡ Wheelchair-accessible activities include Queen Elizabeth II Botanic Park (p285) and **Cayman Turtle Center** (Map p274; ☎949-3894; www.turtle.ky; 786 Northwest Point Rd; turtle-exploration tour adult/child US$18/9, adventure tour US$45/25; ⏲8am-5pm, last entry 4:30pm).

➡ Wheelchair-accessible boats and vans facilitate transportation and boat tours.

➡ George Town and Seven Mile Beach have well-maintained sidewalks, most of which have ramps. (Outside the capital, sidewalks are not common.)

There's one major challenge that wheelchair-bound travelers may face. Cruise ships do not dock at a pier but rather shuttle passengers to shore on tenders. These smaller boats have ramps that allow wheelchairs on and off, but access may be impeded by bad weather or other factors.

ACCOMMODATIONS

Upscale resorts and vacation condominiums line the beaches of the Cayman Islands, especially Seven Mile Beach, but independent hotels and guesthouses are few and far between. Prices are high, but so are standards.

Booking Services

Cayman Villas (Map p274; ☎800-235-5888; www.caymanvillas.com; 177 Roberts Dr; ⏲9am-5pm Mon-Fri) This long-standing service offers vacation properties for rental by the night or for longer stays. There's a wide variety of sizes, styles and locations across all of the Cayman Islands, but each property is carefully inspected to guarantee high standards of quality and comfort.

SLEEPING PRICE RANGES

The following price ranges refer to the cost of a double room in high season, including tax.

$ less than US$150

$$ US$150–250

$$$ more than US$250

ACTIVITIES

Cycling

Cycling is always a fantastic way to explore a new place, and the Cayman Islands are no exception. In Grand Cayman, West Bay Loop (p282) is a popular route and tour, while Eco Rides (p286) offers informative tours of the East End. Little Cayman is also ideal for independent exploration by bicycle, and all the resorts offer bikes for their guests.

Diving & Snorkeling

Warm temperatures, amazing visibility and robust reefs make Grand Cayman a top choice for divers. Arguably, there are better, more-pristine sites on Cayman Brac and Little Cayman, but the diving around Grand Cayman is also fantastic – and unlikely to disappoint.

Several excellent resorts cater almost exclusively to divers, including Sunset House (p279), Cobalt Coast (p282), Compass Point (p287) and Lighthouse Point (p282). These offer discounts on dive packages, gear rental and storage, and excellent shore diving on-site.

There's a slew of other dive shops around the island, especially in George Town and along Seven Mile Beach. Many offer easy shore access to a 'house reef,' in addition to boat dives and gear rental. Two-tank dives usually run US$105 to US$115.

Fishing

The clear, warm waters of the Cayman Islands are teeming with blue marlin, wahoo, tuna and mahi-mahi. Charter a boat (half-day charters are US$600 to US$800, full-day charters US$900 to US$1200) with an experienced Caymanian captain and hook some real action. **Blue Water Excursions** (Map p274; ☎925-8738; www.bluewaterexcursions.com; Cayman Islands Yacht Club, Yacht Dr, Governor's Creek; ⏲half-day charter US$600-800) and **Bayside Watersports** (Map p274; ☎928-2482; www.baysidewatersports.com; Batabano Rd, Morgan's Harbour) do charters.

Kayaking

Several operators offer kayak rental and tours, including trips through the mangroves and to Bio Bay:

Action Watersports (p277)

Cayman Kayaks (p285)

Sea Elements (p277)

Sweet Spot Kaibo (p285)

CHILDREN

Cayman is a fantastic destination for families, with countless sights and activities to entertain the kids, and plenty of facilities to make life easier for parents.

The beaches of Grand Cayman are perfect for children, with warm, gentle water and sparkling-white sand. Seven Mile Beach (p275) has the most facilities, including a playground, but any beach will do. Starfish Point (p284) is a giant touch tank, with countless sea stars just waiting to be discovered. (Just don't let your kids pull them out of the water, because that will kill them.)

When your family needs a break from the sun, the Cayman National Museum (p276) features a multimedia presentation and kid-friendly exhibits on the islands' history. Crystal Caves (p284) is an awesome place for kids (and adults) to explore.

The Sister Islands are geared more to divers and less to families, although kids will get a thrill out of exploring the caves (p288) on Cayman Brac or investigating Owen Island (p289) near Little Cayman.

Your vacation in the Cayman Islands will no doubt be an active one, especially if you're traveling with children. The array of aquatic activities is seemingly endless:

- Smith's Cove (p275) Snorkeling with fish and possibly an octopus in warm, calm water.
- **Oasis Aqua Park** (Map p278; ☎323-3394; www.oasisaquaparkcayman.com; adult/child per hour US$30/25; ⊙9am-4pm Mon-Fri, to 5pm Sat & Sun; 👪) An inflatable floating playground that gets 'em every time.
- Kayaking (p277) Kids will get a kick out of paddling around Bio Bay in Grand Cayman.
- Atlantis Adventure (p277) Explore under the sea without getting wet!
- Stingray City (p277) Up-close interactions with stingrays, followed by a few stops for easy snorkeling.

On dry land, children will enjoy horseback riding in Barkers National Park (p282) or cycling the West Bay Loop (p282).

Need to Know

Condominiums are ubiquitous on Grand Cayman, so families can make themselves comfortable with multiple bedrooms, living space and kitchens. Alternatively, most resorts have plenty of rooms that sleep four people or more. Resorts and hotels also offer babysitting services or programmed activities for kids.

ELECTRICITY

Power is 120V, 60Hz; US-style two- and three-pin plugs are used.

EATING PRICE RANGES

The following price categories refer to the cost of a main course.

$ less than US$15

$$ US$15–25

$$$ more than US$25

EMBASSIES & CONSULATES

Citizens of the US should contact the embassy in Kingston, Jamaica.

UK Governor's Office (☎244-2431; www.gov.uk/government/world/cayman-islands; Government Administration Bldg, Suite 101, Elgin Ave; ⊙8am-4:30pm Mon-Thu, to 12:30pm Fri)

FOOD

You'll eat superbly almost anywhere in the Cayman Islands (though you'll pay for it). The combination of a large international community and plenty of cash sloshing about means that no effort is spared to import excellent fresh food and specialties from around the world. Plus, there's a rocketing interest in farm-to-table dining – or sea-to-table, as the case may be.

Essential Food & Drink

Caymanian cuisine centers on seafood, but look out for all of these local specialties.

Conch A popular item on restaurant menus – seek out farm-raised versions, as conch in the wild are endangered. This large pink mollusk is cooked with onion and spices in a stew, fried up as fritters, or sliced raw and served with a lime marinade.

Jelly ice Chilled coconut water sucked from the shell.

Mannish water Stewy mixture of yams plus the head and foot of a goat; *may* cure impotence.

Mudslide A creamy cocktail combining Kahlua, Baileys and vodka – apparently invented at Rum Point.

Tortuga rum cake A heavy, moist cake available in a number of addictive flavors; makes a great gift to take home.

Turtle stew The national dish may be unappetizing to some, but stewing up (farmed) green-turtle meat is a beloved tradition. Note that the stew often arrives with the meat, fat, fins and organs all mixed together.

HEALTH

Health care in Cayman is not free, though UK nationals may receive medical treatment at a reduced cost or, in some cases, for free. Health insurance is required for all Cayman residents and recommended for all visitors.There are excellent medical facilities in the Cayman Islands:

PRACTICALITIES

Smoking Prohibited in all public places, including bars, restaurants, hotels, parks and public transportation. Some open-air bars and restaurants may offer designated smoking areas. In hotels, smoking is usually allowed on balconies and terraces, but not indoors.

Weights & measures The imperial system is used.

Cayman Islands Hospital (p281) Grand Cayman's medical facility has a state-of-the-art recompression chamber.
Faith Hospital (p289) This modern hospital serves both Cayman Brac and Little Cayman.
Health City (☎640-4040; www.healthcitycaymanislands.com; 1283 Sea View Rd; ⏰24hr) An innovative hospital specializing in advanced and complex procedures and medical tourism. There's also an intensive-care unit that deals with emergencies.

INTERNET ACCESS

Cayman has good web access. Most hotels and condos offer wi-fi, as do many cafes and public buildings.

LEGAL MATTERS

The Royal Cayman Islands Police Service maintains a visible presence in Cayman, though the service has been the target of criticism for a lack of responsiveness to tourist concerns.

All drugs are illegal in the Cayman Islands, and drug laws are strictly enforced. Littering is a crime that is punishable by fines (up to CI$500) and even jail time.

Guns are strictly prohibited.

LGBT+ TRAVELERS

Gay marriage was legalized in Cayman in March 2019, but the islands remain very conservative and discretion is advised. Most hotels accommodate same-sex couples, but any kind of public display of affection is taboo. There are no gay bars or clubs in the Cayman Islands, though **OBar** (Map p278; ☎947-5691; www.facebook.com/ObarNightClub; Queens Court Plaza, West Bay Rd, Seven Mile Beach; ⏰11:30pm-4am Fri) sometimes attracts a gay clientele.

MONEY

ATMs are widely available, dispensing both US dollars (US$) and Cayman Island dollars (CI$). Credit cards are accepted by most hotels and restaurants.

Exchange Rates

Australia	A$1	CI$0.58
Canada	C$1	CI$0.62
Euro zone	€1	CI$0.93
Japan	¥100	CI$0.77
New Zealand	NZ$1	CI$0.54
UK	£1	CI$1.05
US	US$1	CI$0.83

For current exchange rates, see www.xe.com

Tipping

Tipping is an integral part of the culture. It is essential to show your appreciation with a gratuity.
Restaurants Tip of 15% to 18% usually included in the bill. If not, tip to that amount (or more, for exceptional service).
Resorts A 15% service charge is often included on the bill. Otherwise, tip $1 to $3 per day for housekeeping.
Taxis Tip 10%.
Tour guides Tip US$10 for a half-day outing.

PUBLIC HOLIDAYS

New Year's Day January 1
National Heroes' Day Fourth Monday in January
Ash Wednesday First Wednesday of Lent (usually late February)
Good Friday Friday before Easter
Easter Monday Monday after Easter
Discovery Day Third Monday in May
Queen's Birthday Second Monday in June
Constitution Day First Monday in July
Remembrance Day Second Monday in November
Christmas December 25
Boxing Day December 26

TELEPHONE

To call locally, just dial the seven-digit number with no area code or country code.

Country code	☎1
Area code	☎345

Cell Phones

GSM cell phones are compatible with local SIM cards. There is also 3G service. The main operators are Digicel (www.digicelcayman.com) and Discover Flow (www.discoverflow.ky).

TIME

The Cayman Islands run to Eastern Standard Time (EST), which is five hours behind Greenwich Mean Time. Daylight saving is not observed.

VOLUNTEERING

In addition to the following options, **Volunteer Me** (www.volunteerme.ky) maintains a database of volunteer opportunities.

Blue Iguana Recovery Program (p285) Volunteers do hard labor at the Salina Reserve and Colliers Wilderness Reserve, including trail maintenance, fence building, nest digging and iguana counting.

Cayman Islands Humane Society (Map p278; ☎949-1461; www.caymanislandshumanesociety.com; 153 North Sound Rd; ⊙11am-5pm Mon-Fri, 8am-4pm Sat, 8am-noon Sun) This organization depends on volunteers to help out with dog walking, cat care, administrative support, event planning, fundraising and more.

Central Caribbean Marine Institute (p290) Sign up to the weeklong Dive on the EDGE, which involves identifying, photographing and cataloging species of coral and sea life around Little Cayman.

National Gallery (p276) Support Cayman's most distinguished cultural institution.

Reef Environmental Education Foundation (REEF; www.reef.org) Divers and snorkelers can help protect the reef by participating in sea-life surveys, including the Great Annual Fish Count (www.fishcount.org).

Getting There & Away

Back in the day, adventurers would arrive in the Cayman Islands by pirate ship or, later, by seaplane. Nowadays, sea and air are still your only options, though the vehicles usually take the form of a cruise ship or a jet airplane.

AIR

Owen Roberts International Airport (GCM; Map p278; ☎943-7070; www.caymanairports.ky) is Cayman's main portal to the outside world, with flights from North America and the UK.

In addition to major international carriers such as American Airlines and British Airways, the local Cayman Airways (www.caymanairways.com) operates flights to Cuba, Jamaica and Honduras, as well as the US (Chicago, Dallas, Miami, New York, Tampa and Washington, DC).

SEA

Scores of cruise ships drop anchor in George Town. There are no deep-water port facilities, so passengers shuttle ship to shore using frequent tenders. Visit the Cayman Port Authority (www.caymanport.com) to determine what cruise ships will be in port when.

Getting Around

There is no ferry service within the Cayman Islands, but there is public transportation around Grand Cayman.

AIR

Each island has a small airport. Cayman Airways Express (www.caymanairways.com), a subsidiary of Cayman Airways, provides service between the three islands.

BICYCLE

Bikes are readily available on all three islands and are often included as part of an accommodations package. Flat terrain, relatively light traffic and lovely sea views make cycling a pleasure.

BUS

Minibuses run from the depot in **George Town** (Map p278; cnr Fort & Edward Sts) to other parts of Grand Cayman.

CAR & MOTORCYCLE

Driving is an essential part of life on the islands, and there's plenty of parking. While traffic on the islands is light compared with big cities, it can still be surprisingly heavy in and around George Town and Seven Mile Beach, especially during rush hour. Note that driving is on the left-hand side (as you will be frequently reminded by signs all over the islands).

Car Rental

Most rentals are automatics, although 4WDs may have manual transmissions. A variety of models at competitive rates are available in Grand Cayman; there are fewer options on Cayman Brac. Scooter rentals are available on all three islands.

You must be aged at least 21 to rent a car in the Cayman Islands, and some rental agencies' insurance will not cover renters under 25; check with your rental company in advance.

Quoted rates can be surprisingly low, but look out for the variable environmental-recovery fee (US$4 to US$8 per day) and licensing fee (US$2 to US$3.50 per day), which are tacked onto the daily rate.

Road Rules

- Driving is on the left-hand side of the road.
- Seat-belt use is mandatory.
- Speed limits are very low; 25mph is common.
- Iguanas have right of way; don't hit the endangered critters.

Cuba

☎53 / POP 11.3 MILLION

Includes ➡

Best Places to Eat

- Lamparilla 361 Tapas & Cervezas (p314)
- Doña Eutimia (p315)
- Tres Jotas (p329)
- La Redacción Cuba (p336)
- Restaurant Florida Center (p333)

Best Places to Stay

- Malecón 663 (p312)
- Hotel Ordoño (p348)
- Roy's Terrace Inn (p342)
- Hotel Iberostar Parque Central (p312)

Why Go?

Pack a sunhat and a book of José Martí's poems and get ready to uncover the buoyant, sophisticated, beautiful magic of Cuba.

Complex, contradictory and idiosyncratic, it's not easy to capture Cuba in a single sentence. That's its intrinsic beauty. It doesn't matter how many times you visit this plucky Caribbean nation with its bewildering bureaucracy and free-flowing music, you'll still return home with more questions than answers. One moment it's hot and frustrating, the next it's humbling and heart-warming. One day nothing adds up, the next day everything makes sense. From the theatrical streets of Havana to the deserted beaches of the Isla de la Juventud, Cuba jolts you with its baffling uniqueness. Welcome to a country with no precedent.

When to Go

Nov–Mar Peak season, with cooler weather, prices 30% higher and advance booking of hotels required.

Apr & Oct Look out for special deals, but prices and crowds increase with the onset of Easter.

May, Jun & Sep Smaller crowds, but some resort hotels offer fewer facilities or shut altogether.

HAVANA

7 / POP 2.1 MILLION

No one could have invented Havana. It's too audacious, too contradictory and – despite 60 years of withering neglect – too damned beautiful. How it does it is anyone's guess. Maybe it's the long history of piracy, colonialism and mobster rule. Perhaps it's the survivalist spirit of a populace scarred by two independence wars, a revolution and a US trade embargo. Or possibly it's something to do with the indefatigable salsa energy that ricochets off walls and emanates most emphatically from the people. Don't come here with a list of questions; just bring an open mind and prepare for a long, slow seduction.

Sights

Habana Vieja

★Plaza de la Catedral SQUARE

(Map p302) Habana Vieja's most uniform square is a museum to Cuban baroque, with all the surrounding buildings, including the city's beguiling asymmetrical cathedral, dating from the 1700s. Despite this homogeneity, it is actually the newest of the four squares in the Old Town, with its present layout dating from the 18th century.

On the square's eastern side, the **Casa del Lombillo** was built in 1741 and once served as a post office (a stone-mask ornamental mailbox built into the wall is still in use). Since 2000 it has functioned as an office for the City Historian. On the western side is the majestic **Palacio de los Marqueses de Aguas Claras**, completed in 1760 and widely lauded for the beauty of its shady Andalusian patio. The south side is taken up by the resplendent **Palacio de los Condes de Casa Bayona**, built in 1720, which today hosts the **Museo de Arte Colonial** (Map p302; San Ignacio No 61; CUC$2; 9:30am-4:45pm).

★Catedral de la Habana CATHEDRAL

(Map p302; cnr San Ignacio & Empedrado; 9am-4:30pm Mon-Fri, to noon Sat & Sun) FREE Described by novelist Alejo Carpentier as 'music set in stone,' Havana's incredible cathedral, dominated by two unequal towers and framed by a theatrical baroque facade, was designed by Italian architect Francesco Borromini. Construction of the church was begun by Jesuits in 1748 and work continued despite their expulsion in 1767. When the building was finished in 1787, the diocese of Havana was created and the church became a cathedral – it's one of the oldest in the Americas.

The remains of Christopher Columbus were brought here from Santo Domingo in 1795 and interred until 1898, when they were moved to Seville Cathedral in Spain.

A curiosity of the cathedral is its interior, which is neoclassical rather than baroque and relatively austere. Frescoes above the altar date from the late 1700s, but the paintings that adorn the side walls are copies of originals by Bartolomé Esteban Murillo and Peter Paul Rubens. You can climb the smaller of the towers for CUC$1.

★Museo de la Ciudad MUSEUM

(Map p302; Tacón No 1; CUC$3; 9:30am-6pm) Even with no artifacts, Havana's city museum would be a tour de force, courtesy of the opulent palace in which it resides. Filling the whole western side of Plaza de Armas, the **Palacio de los Capitanes Generales** dates from the 1770s and is a textbook example of Cuban baroque architecture, hewn out of rock from the nearby San Lázaro quarries. A museum has been here since 1968.

From 1791 until 1898 the palace was the residence of the Spanish captains general. From 1899 until 1902 the US military governors were based here, and during the first two decades of the 20th century the building briefly became the presidential palace. These days the museum is wrapped regally around a splendid central courtyard adorned with a white-marble statue of Christopher Columbus (1862). Artifacts (some of them a tad dusty) include period furniture, military uniforms and antique horse carriages, but the real history-defining highlights are the boat used by Antonio Maceo to cross the Trocha de Mariel in 1896, a cannon captured by the Mambís (Cuban Independence War soldiers) from the Spanish in 1897, and Cuba's first flag, raised by Narciso López in Cardénas in 1850. Audio guides (CUC$5) are available in Spanish and English.

Calle Mercaderes AREA

(Map p302) Cobbled, car-free Calle Mercaderes (Merchant's Street) has been extensively restored by the Office of the City Historian and is an almost complete replica of itself at its splendid 18th-century high-water mark. Interspersed with the museums,

Cuba Highlights

1 **Havana** (p299) Staying in a casa particular amid the grand splendor of the city's daily street theater.

2 **Santiago de Cuba** (p340) Discovering the revolutionary history, legendary music and seedy charm of Cuba's second city.

3 **Viñales** (p328) Cycling and hiking through some of the country's extraordinary natural landscapes.

4 **Baracoa** (p347) Visiting Cuba's oddball eastern outpost with its dense foliage and charismatic locals.

5 **Camagüey** (p338) Making an elongated pit stop in the city of earthenware pots, winding lanes and half-forgotten churches.

6 **Trinidad** (p334) Taking in the lazy colonial plazas of Cuba's most historic town.

7 **Varadero** Stretching out on one of the Caribbean's – nay world's – finest beaches.

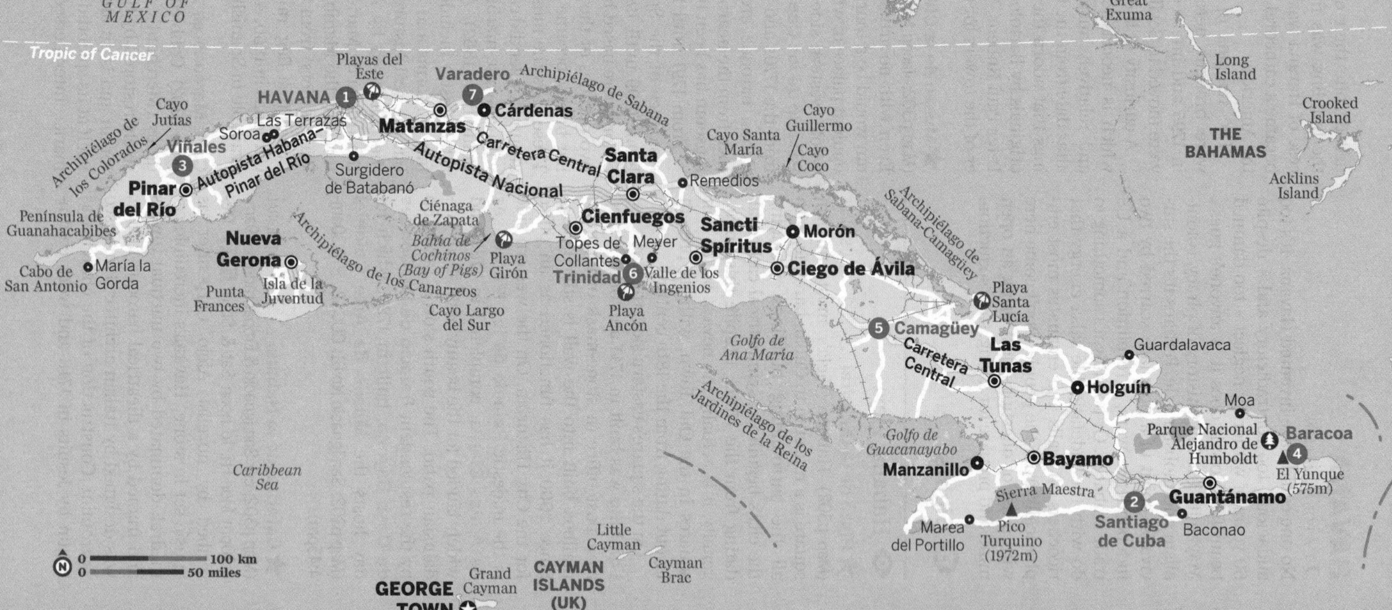

shops and restaurants are some working social projects, such as a maternity home and a paper-making cooperative.

Most of the myriad museums are free, including the **Casa de Asia** (Calle Mercaderes No 111; ⌚10am-6pm Tue-Sat, 9am-1pm Sun), with paintings and sculpture from China and Japan; the **Armería 9 de Abril** (Calle Mercaderes No 157; ⌚9am-5pm Tue-Sat, 1-5pm Mon), an old gun shop (now museum) stormed by revolutionaries on the said date in 1958; and the **Museo de Bomberos** (cnr Mercaderes & Lamparilla; ⌚10am-6pm Mon-Sat), which has antediluvian fire equipment dedicated to 19 Havana firefighters who lost their lives in an 1890 railway blaze.

Just off Mercaderes down Obrapía, it's worth slinking into the gratis **Casa de África** (Obrapía No 157; ⌚9:30am-5pm Tue-Sat, to 1pm Sun), which houses sacred objects relating to Santería and the secret Abakuá fraternity collected by ethnographer Fernando Ortíz.

The corner of Mercaderes and Obrapía has an international flavor, with a bronze **statue of Latin America liberator Simón Bolívar** (cnr Mercaderes & Obrapía); across the street you'll find the **Museo de Simón Bolívar** (Calle Mercaderes No 160; ⌚9am-5pm Tue-Sat, to 1pm Sun), dedicated to Bolívar's life. The **Casa de México Benito Juárez** (Obrapía No 116; CUC$1; ⌚10:15am-5:45pm Tue-Sat, 9am-1pm Sun) exhibits Mexican folk art and plenty of books but not a lot on Juárez (Mexico's first indigenous president) himself. Just east is the **Casa Oswaldo Guayasamín** (Obrapía No 111; ⌚9am-4:30pm Tue-Sun), now a museum but once the studio of the great Ecuadorian artist who painted Fidel Castro in numerous poses.

Mercaderes is also characterized by its restored shops, including a perfume store and a spice shop. Wander at will.

Plaza Vieja SQUARE

(Old Square; Map p302) Laid out in 1559, Plaza Vieja is Havana's most architecturally eclectic square, where Cuban baroque nestles seamlessly next to Gaudí-inspired art nouveau. Originally called Plaza Nueva (New Square), it was initially used for military exercises and later served as an open-air marketplace.

During the regime of Fulgencio Batista an ugly underground parking lot was constructed here, but this monstrosity was demolished in 1996 to make way for a massive renovation project. Sprinkled liberally with bars, restaurants and cafes, Plaza Vieja today has its own microbrewery, the Angela Landa primary school, a beautiful fenced fountain and, on its western side, some of Havana's finest *vitrales* (stained-glass windows). A number of cool bars and cafes give it a sociable buzz in the evenings.

Castillo de la Real Fuerza FORT

(Map p302; Plaza de Armas; CUC$3; ⌚9:30am-5pm Tue-Sun) On the seaward side of Plaza de Armas is one of the oldest existing forts in the Americas, built between 1558 and 1577 on the site of an earlier fort destroyed by French privateers in 1555. The imposing castle is ringed by an impressive moat and shelters the **Museo de Navegación**, which covers the history of the fort and Old Town, and its connections with the Spanish empire. Look out for the huge scale model of the *Santíssima Trinidad* galleon.

The west tower is crowned by a copy of a famous bronze weather vane called **La Giraldilla**. The original was cast in Havana in 1632 by Jerónimo Martínez Pinzón and is popularly believed to be of Doña Inés de Bobadilla, the wife of gold explorer Hernando de Soto. The original is now kept in the Museo de la Ciudad, and the figure also appears on the Havana Club rum label.

Palacio del Segundo Cabo MUSEUM

(Map p302; ☎7-801-7176; http://segundocabo.ohc.cu; O'Reilly No 4; CUC$10; ⌚9:30am-5pm Tue-Sat, to 1pm Sun; 👪) FREE Wedged into Plaza de Armas' northwestern corner, this beautiful baroque building was constructed in 1772 as the headquarters of the Spanish vice-governor. After several reincarnations as a post office, the palace of the Senate, the Supreme Court, and the National Academy of Arts and Letters, the building reopened in 2016 as a multifarious **museum** dedicated to Cuban-European cultural relations. It's masterfully done, using modern media devices to highlight various facets of Cuba and Europe's interwoven history.

Spread over two floors, the interconnecting rooms include a timeline 'tunnel,' a couple of cube-activated screens broadcasting different elements of Cuba's history, an interactive trajectory of Cuban-European musical forms, and a comparative study of the architectural development of Havana and Barcelona. Aided by EU funding, it's the best new museum in Havana for a long time.

Plazuela de Santo Ángel SQUARE

(Map p302) This lovely, intimate plaza behind the **Iglesia del Santo Ángel Custodio** (Map p302; Compostela No 2; ⌚during Mass 7:15am Tue, Wed & Fri, 6pm Thu, Sat & Sun) has benefited

Habana Vieja

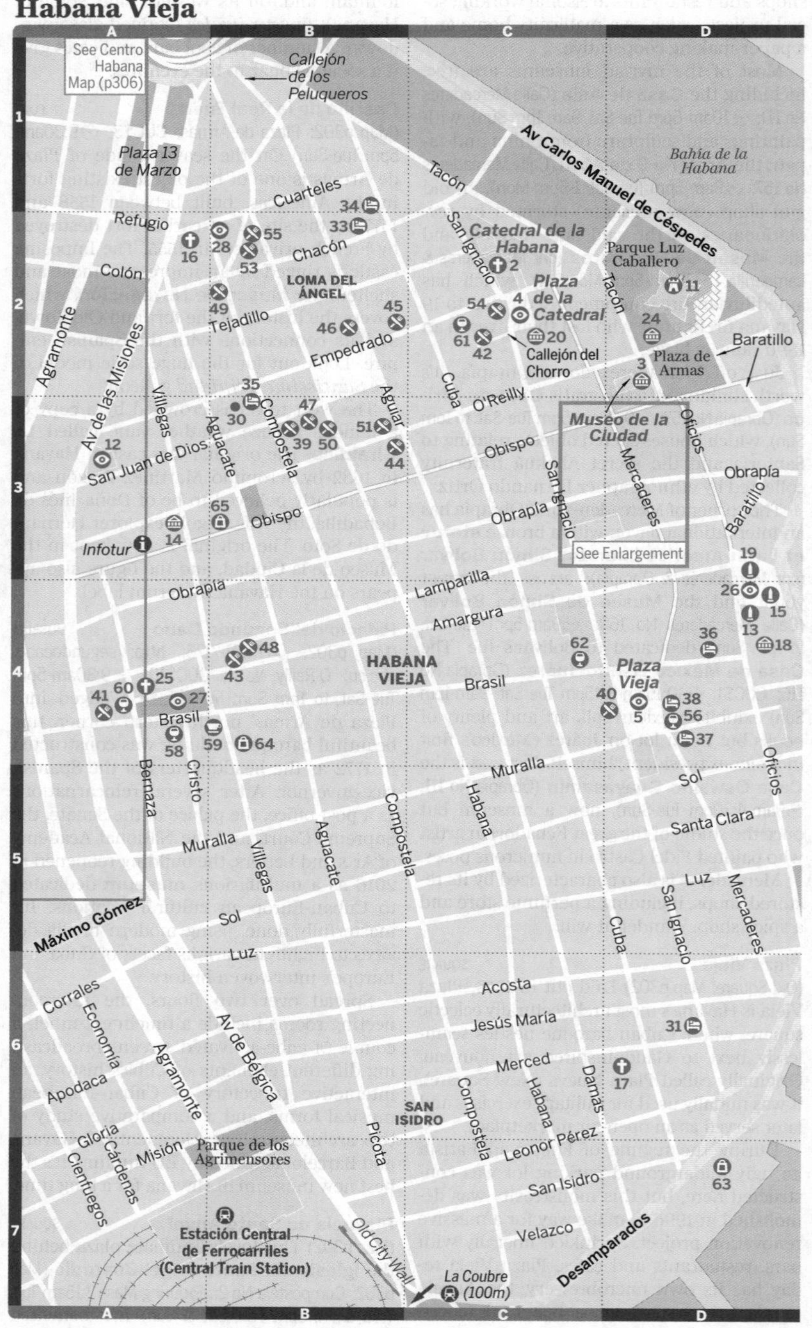

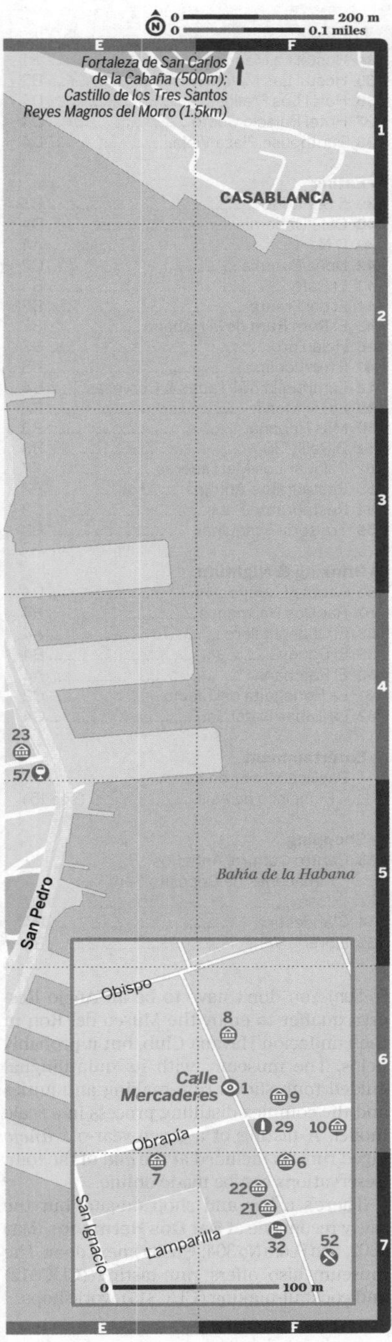

from a recent beautification project that has installed several private restaurants, along with a statue of the fictional heroine Cecilia Valdés, who is watched over by a bust of the author who created her, Cirilo Villaverde.

El Ojo del Ciclón GALLERY

(Map p302; ☎7-861-5359; O'Reilly No 501, cnr Villegas; ⏰10am-7pm) FREE Just when you think you've seen Havana's strangest, weirdest, most surreal and avant-garde art, along comes the 'eye of the cyclone' to re-stretch your imagination. The abstract gallery displays the work of Cuban visual artist Leo D'Lázaro and it's pretty mind-bending stuff – giant eyes, crashed cars, painted suitcases and junk reborn as art. Imagine Jackson Pollock sitting down for tea with JRR Tolkien and John Lennon.

Some of the art is semi-interactive: you can hit a punching bag, play a bizarre game of table football or hang your bag on a masked metal scarecrow. If that's not outlandish enough, come back for the tango classes on Friday and Sunday at 8pm.

Plaza del Cristo SQUARE

(Map p302) A little apart from the historical core, Plaza del Cristo hasn't benefited from a full restoration yet and this adds subtly to its charm. Here you can sidestep boisterous games of football, listen to the musical outpourings of several cool bars or sit down with half the neighborhood and hook up to the local wi-fi hot spot (in Cuba even the internet is a socially interactive experience!).

The square's chunkiest edifice is the **Parroquial del Santo Cristo del Buen Viaje** (⏰9am-noon), a recently renovated 18th-century church where sailors once came to pray before embarking on long voyages.

Plaza de San Francisco de Asís SQUARE

(Map p302) Facing Havana harbor, the breezy Plaza de San Francisco de Asís first grew up in the 16th century when Spanish galleons stopped quayside on their passage from the Caribbean to Spain. A market took root in the 1500s, followed by a church in 1608, though when the monks complained of too much noise, the market was moved a few blocks south to Plaza Vieja.

The plaza underwent a full restoration in the late 1990s and is most notable for its uneven cobblestones and the white-marble **Fuente de los Leones** (Fountain of Lions), a fountain carved by Italian sculptor Giuseppe Gaggini in 1836. A more modern statue outside the square's famous church depicts **El**

Habana Vieja

Caballero de París, a well-known street person who roamed Havana during the 1950s, engaging passersby with his philosophies on life, religion, politics and current events. The square's newest sculpture (added in 2012) is **La Conversación** by French artist Etienne, a modernist bronze rendition of two seated people talking.

The cruise terminal is directly opposite the square.

Museo del Ron MUSEUM
(Map p302; 7-862-4108, 7-862-3832; www.havanaclubmuseum.com; San Pedro No 262, cnr Sol; incl guide CUC$7; 9am-5pm Mon-Thu, to 4pm Fri-Sun) You don't have to be an Añejo Reserva quaffer to enjoy the Museo del Ron in the Fundación Havana Club, but it probably helps. The museum, with its quintilingual guided tour, shows rum-making antiquities and the complex distilling process in a scale model. A tasting of a seven-year-old *añejo* (aged rum) is included at the end of the tour. Reservations can be made online.

There's a bar and shop on-site, but the savvy reconvene at **Bar Dos Hermanos** (Map p302; San Pedro No 304; 24hr) next door. The museum also offers rum-tasting (CUC$12) and cocktail-making (CUC$15) workshops.

Edificio Bacardí LANDMARK

(Bacardí Bldg; Map p302; Av de las Misiones, btwn Empedrado & San Juan de Dios; ⏱hours vary) Finished in 1930, the magnificent Edificio Bacardí, once the HQ of Cuba's erstwhile rum dynasty, is a triumph of art deco architecture, with a host of lavish finishes utilizing red granite, green marble, terra-cotta reliefs and glazed tiles. Though 12 stories high, it's hemmed in by other buildings these days, so it's hard to get a panoramic view of the structure from street level. Notwithstanding, the opulent bell tower can be glimpsed from all over Havana.

Art deco aficionados can scout around the lobby, where a mediocre bar welcomes you. Note that trips up to the tower for eagle's-eye views of the city were suspended at research time.

Iglesia y Convento de Nuestra Señora de la Merced CHURCH

(Map p302; Cuba No 806; ⏱8am-noon & 3-5:30pm) Bizarrely overlooked by the tourist hordes, this baroque church in its own small square has Havana's most sumptuous ecclesiastical interior, as yet only partially restored. Beautiful gilded altars, frescoed vaults and a number of valuable old paintings create a sacrosanct mood. There's a quiet cloister adjacent.

Centro Habana

★Capitolio Nacional HISTORIC BUILDING

(Map p306; cnr Dragones & Paseo de Martí; guided tour CUC$10; ⏱10am-4pm Tue, Thu & Sun, to noon Wed & Sat) The incomparable Capitolio Nacional is Havana's most ambitious and grandiose building, constructed after the post-WWI boom ('Dance of the Millions') gifted the Cuban government a seemingly bottomless vault of sugar money. Similar to the Capitol in Washington, DC, but actually modeled on the Panthéon in Paris, the building was initiated by Cuba's US-backed dictator Gerardo Machado in 1926 and took 5000 workers three years, two months and 20 days to construct, at a cost of US$17 million.

Formerly the Capitolio was the seat of the Cuban Congress, then from 1959 to 2013 it housed the Cuban Academy of Sciences and the National Library of Science and Technology. The building underwent a massive refurbishment between 2013 and 2019, reopening in time for Havana's 500th anniversary. Guided tours leave on the hour and take in most of the main features, including the palatial hallways, the chamber of representatives and the newly established **Tumba del Mambí Desconocido (Tomb of the Unknown Soldier)**.

Constructed with white Capellanía limestone and block granite, the building has an entrance guarded by six rounded Doric columns atop a staircase that leads up from Paseo de Martí (Prado). Looking out over the Havana skyline is a 62m stone cupola topped with a replica of 16th-century Florentine sculptor Giambologna's bronze statue of Mercury in the Palazzo del Bargello. Set in the floor directly below the dome is a copy of a 24-carat diamond. Highway distances between Havana and all sites in Cuba are calculated from this point.

The entryway is accessed by a sweeping 55-step staircase guarded by two giant statues carved by Italian sculptor Angelo Zanelli: *El Trabajo* and *La Virtud Tutelar*. The main doors open into the **Salón de los Pasos Perdidos** (Room of the Lost Steps, so named because of its unusual acoustics), at the center of which is a magnificent statue of *La República*, an enormous bronze woman standing 17.6m tall and symbolizing the mythic Guardian of Virtue and Work. The 30-tonne statue is covered in gold leaf and is the third-largest indoor statue in the world. It was carved by Zanelli in Rome and shipped to Cuba in three pieces.

Gran Teatro de la Habana Alicia Alonso THEATER

(Map p306; ☎7-861-3077; Paseo de Martí No 458; guided tours CUC$5; ⏱9:30am-4pm Mon-Sat, 9:15am-12:15pm Sun) The neobaroque Gran Teatro de la Habana Alicia Alonso, erected as a Galician social club between 1907 and 1914, features highly ornate and even exuberant architectural details. It's the official stage for the Cuban National Ballet Company and the headquarters of the biennial **International Ballet Festival** (www.balletcuba.cult.cu; ⏱Oct & Nov). Dance presentations, ranging from ballet to contemporary dance to Spanish-influenced choreography by companies from all over the country and abroad, are the highlights every weekend. There are daily guided tours.

Museo Nacional de Bellas Artes MUSEUM

(Map p306; www.bellasartes.co.cu; each gallery CUC$5, combined entry CUC$8, under 14yr free; ⏱9am-5pm Tue-Sat, 10am-2pm Sun) Spread over two campuses, the Bellas Artes is arguably the finest art gallery in the Caribbean.

Centro Habana

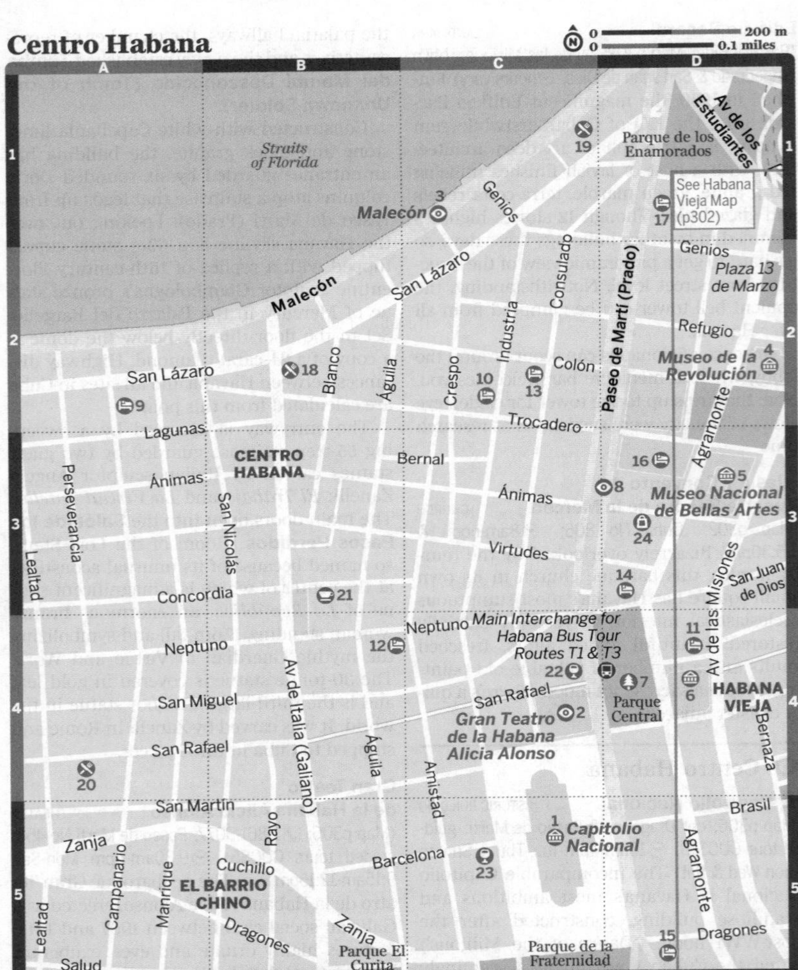

The **Arte Cubano** (CUC$5, under 14yr free; 9am-5pm Tue-Sat, 10am-2pm Sun) building contains the most comprehensive collection of Cuban art in the world, while the **Arte Universal** (CUC$5, under 14yr free; 9am-5pm Tue-Sat, 10am-2pm Sun) section is laid out in a grand eclectic palace overlooking **Parque Central** (Map p306), with exterior flourishes that are just as impressive as the international-art collections within.

Museo de la Revolución MUSEUM
(Map p306; Refugio No 1; CUC$8, guided tours CUC$2; 9:30am-4pm) This emblematic museum is set in the former **Presidential Palace**, constructed between 1913 and 1920 and used by a string of Cuban presidents, culminating in Fulgencio Batista. The world-famous Tiffany's of New York decorated the interior, and the shimmering Salón de los Espejos (Hall of Mirrors) was designed to resemble the eponymous room at the Palace of Versailles.

The museum, designed primarily to help Cubans understand their own history, descends chronologically from the top floor, focusing on the events leading up to, during and immediately after the Cuban Revolution. It presents a sometimes scruffy but always

Centro Habana

Top Sights
1 Capitolio Nacional C5
2 Gran Teatro de la Habana Alicia Alonso C4
3 Malecón C1
4 Museo de la Revolución D2
5 Museo Nacional de Bellas Artes D3
Museo Nacional de Bellas Artes – Arte Cubano .... (see 5)

Sights
6 Museo Nacional de Bellas Artes – Arte Universal D4
7 Parque Central D4
8 Paseo de Martí D3

Activities, Courses & Tours
Havana Super Tour .... (see 9)

Sleeping
9 Casa 1932 .... A2
10 Casa Colonial Yadilis & Yoel C2
11 Gran Hotel Manzana Kempinski D4
12 Hostal Neptuno 1915 .... B4
13 Hostal Peregrino Consulado C2
14 Hotel Iberostar Parque Central D3
15 Hotel Saratoga D5
16 Hotel Sevilla D3
17 Iberostar Grand Packard Hotel D1

Eating
18 Castas y Tal B2
19 Nazdarovie C1
20 San Cristóbal A4

Drinking & Nightlife
21 Café Arcángel B3
22 Rooftop Bar, Hotel Inglaterra C4
23 Siá Kará Café C5

Entertainment
Gran Teatro de la Habana Alicia Alonso .... (see 2)

Shopping
24 Memorias Librería D3

compelling story, told in English and Spanish, and tinted with *mucho* propaganda.

The palace's sweeping central staircase, guarded by a bust of José Martí, still retains the bullet holes made during an unsuccessful attack in March 1957 by a revolutionary student group intent on assassinating Batista.

The stairs take you up to the 2nd floor and several important exhibit-free rooms, including the **Salón Dorado** (decorated in Louis XVI style and once used for banquets), the **Despacho Presidencial** (President's Office, where Fidel Castro was sworn in in 1959) and the **capilla** (chapel, with a Tiffany chandelier).

In front of the building is a fragment of the former city wall, as well as an SAU-100 tank used by Castro during the 1961 Bay of Pigs battle. In the space behind you'll find the **Pavillón Granma**, containing a replica of the 18m yacht that carried Castro and 81 other revolutionaries from Tuxpán, Mexico, to Cuba in December 1956. The boat is encased in glass and guarded 24/7, presumably to stop anyone from breaking in and sailing off to Florida in it. The pavilion is surrounded by other vehicles associated with the revolution, including planes, rockets and an old postal van that was used as a getaway car during the 1957 attack.

Malecón WATERFRONT

(Map p306) The Malecón, Havana's evocative 7km-long sea drive, is one of the city's most soulful and quintessentially Cuban thoroughfares, and long a favored meeting place for assorted lovers, philosophers, poets, traveling minstrels, fishers and wistful Florida-gazers. The Malecón's atmosphere is most potent at sunset, when the weak yellow light from creamy Vedado filters like a dim torch onto the buildings of Centro Habana, lending their dilapidated facades a distinctly romantic quality.

Paseo de Martí HISTORIC SITE

(El Prado; Map p306) Construction of this stately European-style boulevard – the first street outside the old city walls – began in 1770, and work was completed in the mid-1830s during the term of Captain General Miguel Tacón (1834–38). The original idea was to create a boulevard as splendid as any found in Paris or Barcelona (El Prado bears more than a passing resemblance to Las Ramblas). The famous bronze lions that guard the central promenade at either end were added in 1928.

Callejón de Hamel STREET

(Map p316; btwn Aramburu & Hospital) There are at least four reasons that you should incorporate this community-driven back alley into any serious Havana outing: 1) it's the unofficial HQ of Havana's Afro-Cuban community; 2) it's replete with inspired street art, much of it executed with recycled materials (this is where your old bathtub gets a new life); 3) it's an essential stop for anyone trying to understand Cuba's complex syncretic religions; and 4) the denizens put on hypnotic live rumba shows (p322) every Sunday.

Vedado

★Necrópolis Cristóbal Colón CEMETERY
(Map p316; CUC$5; ⏲8am-6pm, last entry 5pm) Havana's main cemetery (a national monument), one of the largest in the Americas, is renowned for its striking religious iconography and elaborate marble statues. Far from being eerie, a walk through these 57 hallowed hectares can be an educational and emotional stroll through the annals of Cuban history. A map (CUC$1) showing the graves of assorted artists, sportspeople, politicians, writers, scientists and revolutionaries is for sale at the entrance.

Enter via the splendid Byzantine-Romanesque gateway, the **Puerta de la Paz**; the tomb of independence leader **General Máximo Gómez** (1905) is on the right (look for the bronze face in a circular medallion). Further along past the first circle, and also on the right, are the **firefighters monument** (1890) and the neo-Romanesque **Capilla Central** (1886), in the center of the cemetery. Just northeast of the chapel is the graveyard's most celebrated (and visited) tomb, that of Señora Amelia Goyri, better known as La Milagrosa (the Miraculous One), who died while giving birth on May 3, 1901. The marble figure of a woman with a large cross and a baby in her arms is easy to find due to the many flowers piled on the tomb and the local devotees in attendance. For many years after her death her heartbroken husband visited the grave several times a day. He always knocked with one of four iron rings on the burial vault and walked away backwards so that he could see her for as long as possible. When the bodies were exhumed some years later, Amelia's body was uncorrupted (a sign of sanctity in the Catholic faith), and the baby, who had been buried at its mother's feet, was allegedly found in her arms. As a result, La Milagrosa became the focus of a huge spiritual cult in Cuba, and thousands of people come here annually with gifts, in the hope of fulfilling dreams or solving problems. In keeping with tradition, pilgrims knock with the iron ring on the vault and walk away backwards when they leave.

As important as La Milagrosa among the Santería community, the **'tomb of Hermano José'** marks the grave of a woman called Leocadia Pérez Herrero, a black Havana medium known for her great acts of charity among the poor in the early 20th century. Leocadia said that she consulted with a Santería priest called Hermano José who encouraged and guided her in her generous acts. As a spiritual and superstitious person, she always kept a painting of Hermano José's image in her house, and when she died in 1962 the canvas was buried alongside her. Today followers of Santería venerate Hermano José and regularly come to Leocadia's grave to ask for charitable favors. In keeping with Santería tradition, they often leave flowers, glasses of rum, half-smoked cigars or sacrificed chickens on the grave.

Also worth looking out for are the graves of novelist Alejo Carpentier (1904–80), scientist Carlos Finlay (1833–1915), the Martyrs of Granma and the Veterans of the Independence Wars.

★Museo Napoleónico MUSEUM
(Map p316; San Miguel No 1159; CUC$3; ⏲9:30am-5pm Tue-Sat, to 12:30pm Sun) Without a doubt one of the best museums in Havana and thus in Cuba, this magnificently laid-out collection of 7000 objects associated with the life of Napoleon Bonaparte was amassed by Cuban sugar baron Julio Lobo and politician Orestes Ferrara.

Hotel Nacional HISTORIC BUILDING
(Map p316; cnr Calles O & 21; ⏲free tours 10am & 3pm Mon-Fri, 10am Sat) Far more than just a hotel, the Nacional, built in 1930 as a copy of the Breakers Hotel in Palm Beach, Florida, is a national monument and one of Havana's architectural emblems. Even if you're not staying here, reserve time to admire the Moorish lobby, stroll the breezy grounds and have a drink in the famous terrace bar overlooking the Malecón. Ask in the lobby about free tours.

Museo de Artes Decorativas MUSEUM
(Map p316; Calle 17 No 502, btwn Calles D & E; CUC$5; ⏲9:30am-4pm Tue-Sat) One of Havana's best museums dazzles like a European stately home. It's replete with all manner of architectural features, including rococo furniture, Chinese screens and an art deco bathroom. Equally interesting is the building itself, which is of French design and was commissioned in 1924 by the wealthy Gómez family, who built the Man-

zana de Gómez shopping center in Centro Habana.

Memorial a José Martí MONUMENT

(Map p316; Plaza de la Revolución; CUC$3; ⏲9:30am-4pm Mon-Sat) Center stage in Plaza de la Revolución is this monument, which at 138.5m is Havana's tallest structure. Fronted by an impressive 17m marble statue of a seated Martí in a pensive *Thinker* pose, the memorial houses a museum (the definitive word on Martí in Cuba) and a 129m lookout (reached via a small CUC$2 lift) with fantastic city views.

Playa & Marianao

★Fusterlandia PUBLIC ART

(cnr Calle 226 & Av 3, Jaimanitas) FREE Where does art go after Antoni Gaudí? For a hint, head west from central Havana to the seemingly low-key district of Jaimanitas, where artist José Fuster has turned his home neighborhood into a masterpiece of intricate tile work and kaleidoscopic colors – a street-art wonderland that makes Barcelona's Park Güell look positively sedate. Imagine maximal-impact Gaudí relocated to a tropical setting.

The result is what is unofficially known as Fusterlandia, an ongoing project first hatched around 20 years ago that has covered several suburban blocks with whimsical but highly stylized public art. The centerpiece is Fuster's own house, **Taller-Estudio José Fuster** (☎5-281-5421, studio 7-271-3028; ⏲9:30am-5pm Mon-Fri, to 4pm Sat & Sun) FREE, a sizable residence decorated from roof to foundations with art, sculpture and – above all – mosaic tiles of every color and description. The overall impression defies written description (just *go*!): it's a fantastical mishmash of spiraling walkways, rippling pools and sunburst fountains. The work mixes homages to Pablo Picasso and Gaudí with snippets of the style of Paul Gauguin and Wifredo Lam, magic realism, maritime motifs, aspects of Santería, the curvaceous lines of *modernisme*, and a large dose of Fuster's own Cubanness, which runs through almost everything. Look for the Cuban flags, a mural of the *Granma* yacht, and the words 'Viva Cuba' emblazoned across eight chimney pots.

Fusterlandia stretches way beyond Fuster's own residence. Over half the neighborhood has been given similar treatment, from street signs to bus stops to the local doctor's house. Wandering around its quiet streets is a surreal and psychedelic experience.

Jaimanitas is located just off Quinta Avenida (Av 5) in the far west of Playa, sandwiched between Club Havana and Marina Hemingway. A taxi from central Havana will cost CUC$12 to CUC$15.

DON'T MISS

HEMINGWAY'S HAVANA HOME

In 1940 American novelist Ernest Hemingway bought the Finca la Vigía, a villa on a hill in San Francisco de Paula, 15km southeast of Havana, where he lived continuously for 20 years. When he departed, tired and depressed, for the US in 1960 soon after the Castro revolution, he generously donated his house to the 'Cuban people.' It is now the **Museo Hemingway** (☎7-692-0176; cnr Vigía & Singer; CUC$5; ⏲10am-4:30pm Mon-Sat), and almost unchanged since the day he left.

To prevent the pilfering of objects, visitors are not allowed inside the house (La Casona), but there are enough open doors and windows to allow a proper glimpse of Papa's universe. Inside the house there are books everywhere (including beside the toilet), a large Victrola and record collection, and a disturbing array of trophy animal heads.

A three-story tower next to the main house contains a tiny typewriter, a telescope and a comfortable lounger, and offers suitably inspiring views north toward the distant city. In the heavily wooded grounds below you'll encounter the swimming pool where Ava Gardner once swam naked, a cockfighting ring and Hemingway's beloved fishing boat, Pilar, grounded on what was once his tennis court.

In 2019, in a rare show of Cuban-American cooperation, a restoration center was built on the site to preserve Hemingway's work.

To reach San Francisco de Paula, take metro bus P-7 (Alberro) from Parque de la Fraternidad in Centro Habana. Tell the driver you're going to the museum. You get off in San Miguel del Padrón; the house entrance is on Calle Vigía, 200m east of the main road, Calzada de Guines.

Regla, Guanabacoa & the Forts

★Castillo de los Tres Santos Reyes Magnos del Morro FORT
(El Morro; CUC$6, lighthouse CUC$2; ⊙10am-6pm) This wave-lashed fort with its emblematic lighthouse was erected between 1589 and 1630 to protect the entrance to Havana harbor from pirates and foreign invaders (French corsair Jacques de Sores had sacked the city in 1555). Perched high on a rocky bluff above the Atlantic, the fort has an irregular polygonal shape, 3m-thick walls and a deep protective moat, and is a classic example of Renaissance military architecture.

Fortaleza de San Carlos de la Cabaña FORT
(La Cabaña; before/after 6pm CUC$6/8; ⊙10am-10pm) This 18th-century colossus was built between 1763 and 1774 on a long, exposed ridge on the east side of Havana harbor to fill a weakness in the city's defenses. In 1762 the British had taken Havana by gaining control of this strategically important ridge, and it was from here that they shelled the city mercilessly into submission. In order to prevent a repeat performance, Spanish king Carlos III ordered the construction of a massive fort that would repel future invaders.

Measuring 700m from end to end and covering a whopping 10 hectares, it is the largest Spanish colonial fortress in the Americas. The impregnability of the fort meant that no invader ever stormed it, though during the 19th century Cuban patriots faced firing squads here. Dictators Gerardo Machado and Fulgencio Batista used the fortress as a military prison, and immediately after the revolution Che Guevara set up his headquarters inside the ramparts to preside over another catalog of grisly executions (this time of Batista's officers).

These days the fort has been restored for visitors, and you can spend at least half a day checking out its wealth of attractions. As well as bars, restaurants, souvenir stalls and a cigar shop (containing the world's longest cigar), La Cabaña hosts the **Museo de Fortificaciones y Armas** (free with La Cabaña ticket; ⊙10am-6pm) and the engrossing **Museo de Comandancia del Che** (free with La Cabaña ticket; ⊙10am-10pm). The nightly 9pm cañonazo ceremony is a popular evening excursion in which actors dressed in full 18th-century military regalia reenact the firing of a cannon over the harbor. You can visit the ceremony independently or as part of an excursion.

Iglesia de Nuestra Señora de Regla CHURCH
(Regla; ⊙7:30am-6pm) As important as it is diminutive, Iglesia de Nuestra Señora de Regla, which sits close to the dock in Regla, has a long and colorful history. Inside on the main altar you'll find La Santísima Virgen de Regla.

Courses

La Casa del Son DANCING
(Map p302; ☎7-861-6179; www.bailarencuba.com; Empedrado No 411, btwn Compostela & Aguacate; per hour from CUC$10; ⊙9am-7pm Mon-Sat) A highly popular private dance school based in an attractive 18th-century house. It also offers lessons in Spanish language and percussion. Very flexible with class times.

Tours

Free Walking Tour Havana WALKING
(Map p302; ☎5-818-6958; www.freewalkingtourhavana.com) These wonderfully insightful tours kick off at the Plazuela de Santo Ángel (p301) at 9:30am and 4pm daily. Look for a guide with a white umbrella. There are two options: Habana Vieja (three hours) and Centro Habana (two hours); tours are offered in Spanish or English. Reserve online or phone ahead. A well-earned tip for your guide goes a long way.

Havana Super Tour TOURS
(Map p306; ☎5-265-7101; www.campanario63.com; Campanario No 63, btwn San Lázaro & Lagunas; tours CUC$60) One of Havana's first private tour companies, Super Tour runs all its trips in classic American cars. The two most popular are the art deco architectural tour and the 'Mob tour,' uncovering the city's pre-revolution Mafia haunts. If you're short on time, the full-blown Havana day tour (CUC$150) will whip you around all of the city's key sights.

Ruta Bikes CYCLING
(Map p316; ☎5-247-6633; www.rutabikes.com; Calle 16 No 152; city tour CUC$30;) This was Havana's first decent bicycle-hire and -tour company when it started in 2013. Its cycling tours have proven to be consistently popular, particularly the three-hour classic city tour, which takes in the Bosque de la Habana, Plaza Vieja, Plaza de la Revolución and the Malecón. Book via phone or email at least a day ahead. Kids welcome.

Festivals & Events

Cañonazo Ceremony CULTURAL

(⏲9pm nightly) The *cañonazo* ceremony, held in La Cabaña fort, is a theatrical show during which actors dressed in full 18th-century military regalia reenact the firing of a cannon over Havana harbor – a ritual that used to signify the closing of the city gates.

Festival Internacional del Nuevo Cine Latinoamericano FILM

(www.habanafilmfestival.com; ⏲Dec) Widely lauded celebration of Cuba's massive film culture, with plenty of nods to other Latin American countries. Held at various cinemas and theaters across the city.

Sleeping

Habana Vieja

Greenhouse CASA PARTICULAR $

(Map p302; ☎7-862-9877; fabio.quintana@infomed.sld.cu; San Ignacio No 656, btwn Merced & Jesús María; r CUC$30-40; ❄) A fabulous Old Town casa run by Eugenio and Fabio, who have added superb design features to their huge colonial home. Check out the terrace fountain and the backlit model of Havana on the stairway. There are seven rooms in this virtual hotel, packed with precious period furnishings and gorgeous wooden beds; two rooms share a bathroom.

Hostal El Encinar CASA PARTICULAR $

(Map p302; ☎7-860-1257; www.hostalperegrino.com; Chacón No 60/Altos, btwn Cuba & Aguiar; s/d/tr incl breakfast CUC$30/40/45; ❄) This outpost of Centro Habana's popular Hostal Peregrino (p312) is like a little hotel for independent travelers. Eight rooms, all with private bathroom, approach boutique standard, with classy tile work, hairdryers, TVs and minibars. There's a comfortable lounge area and a delightful roof terrace overlooking the bay and La Cabaña fort.

Hostal Las Maletas CASA PARTICULAR $

(Map p302; ☎7-867-1623; www.hostallasmale tas.com; Empedrado No 409, btwn Aguacate & Compostela; r CUC$45-55; ❄📶) A good place to rest your *maletas* (suitcases) for a while, this private *'hostal'* has all the classic Habana Vieja calling cards: high ceilings, spiral staircases and creaky rocking chairs. It's pricier than smaller casas particulares but still a good deal cheaper than some of Havana's crappier state-run hotels – and it has much better service.

You can linger in the atmospheric communal areas, including a classic wrought-iron balcony overlooking wonderfully chaotic Calle Empedrado.

Hostal La Maestranza HOTEL $$

(Map p302; ☎5-597-7099; Cuba No 82, btwn Cuarteles & Chacón; s/d/ste CUC$100/125/150; P❄) One of several emerging private hotels in Habana Vieja, the Maestranza enjoys an excellent location practically opposite the cathedral (p299). Five rooms and one suite share a narrow atrium and small bar where an ample breakfast is laid on. While simple in design, the superclean rooms have high ceilings, original tiles and atmospheric backlighting behind the bedheads.

Penthouse Plaza Vieja CASA PARTICULAR $$

(Map p302; ☎7-801-2084; penthouseplazavieja@gmail.com; Mercaderes No 315-317, apt 16; r incl breakfast CUC$90; ❄) A private penthouse in a historic central square – this place would cost thousands anywhere else, but in Havana you can still bag it for as little as CUC$60. Fidel and Bertha's two rooms high above Plaza Vieja share a leafy terrace guarded by a Santería shrine.

Hostal Conde de Villanueva HOTEL $$$

(Map p302; ☎7-862-9293; www.gaviotahotels.com; Mercaderes No 202; s/d CUC$235/305; ❄@📶) Restored under the watchful eye of the City Historian in the late 1990s, the former residence of the Count of Villanueva, a 19th-century railway-building magnate, has been converted from a grandiose city mansion into a nine-bedroom hotel with a tobacco-growing theme. Its centerpiece is a foliage-filled inner courtyard complete with resident peacock.

Hotel Palacio Cueto HISTORIC HOTEL $$$

(Map p302; ☎7-823-4100; www.gaviotahotels.com; cnr Muralla & Mercaderes; s/d CUC$209/324; ❄@📶) After interminable renovations, Havana's finest art nouveau building once again hosts a hotel. Before you even go inside you can award five stars for the Cueto's location, at the corner of Plaza Vieja, and its facade, a rippling collection of elegant pillars and curvaceous balconies.

Hotel Los Frailes HISTORIC HOTEL $$$

(Map p302; ☎7-862-9383; www.gaviotahotels.com; Brasil No 8, btwn Oficios & Mercaderes; d/ste CUC$167/260; ❄@📶) There's nothing austere about Los Frailes (The Friars), despite the monastic theme (staff wear hooded robes), inspired by the nearby **San Francisco de Asís convent** (Map p302; Oficios, btwn Amargura & Brasil; museum CUC$2; ⏲9:30am-4:30pm). Instead, this is the kind of hotel you'll look forward to coming back to after a long day, to recline in large, historical rooms in your monkish dressing gown, with candlelight flickering on the walls.

Centro Habana

★Casa 1932 CASA PARTICULAR $
(Map p306; ☎7-863-6203, 5-264-3858; www.casahabana.net; Campanario 63, btwn San Lázaro & Lagunas; r CUC$20-60; ❄📶) Every piece of furniture has a story to tell at the carefully curated home of Luís Miguel, a cool connoisseur of art deco who offers his house as both boutique private homestay and museum to the 1930s, when his preferred architectural style was in vogue.

★Hostal Peregrino Consulado CASA PARTICULAR $
(Map p306; ☎7-861-8027; www.hostalperegrino.com; Consulado No 152, btwn Colón & Trocadero; s/d/tr/apt CUC$30/40/45/50; ❄@) Pediatrician Julio Roque and his wife, Elsa, have expanded their formerly two-room casa particular (a private home with rooms) into a web of accommodations. The HQ, Hostal Peregrino, offers five rooms and three attached apartments a block from Paseo de Martí and is one of the most professionally run private houses in Cuba.

Hostal Neptuno 1915 CASA PARTICULAR $
(Map p306; Amistad No 204, btwn Neptuno & San Miguel; r from CUC$50; ❄📶) Giving little away at street level, this new private accommodations is an island of tranquility amid the Centro Habana maelstrom. Seven delightful rooms, adorned with original art, elegant furniture and deluxe modern bathrooms, surround a small 1st-floor patio and reception-lounge. Here you can recline in tasteful comfort as the rhythms of the gritty neighborhood pulsate around you.

Casa Colonial Yadilis & Yoel CASA PARTICULAR $
(Map p306; ☎7-863-0565; www.casacolonialyadilisyyoel.com; Industria No 120/Altos, btwn Trocadero & Colón; r CUC$30-35; ❄📶) Marrying sharp professionalism and excellent service without compromising the warmth and generosity that make Cuba so special, this venerable establishment is one of the best accommodations deals in the city. Recently expanded to include two additional buildings nearby, it offers smart, clean rooms right in the middle of the city's liveliest neighborhood.

Whether you're from Croatia or Camagüey, you'll immediately feel at home.

La Casa de Concordia CASA PARTICULAR $
(Map p316; ☎7-862-5330; Concordia No 421, btwn Escobar & Gervasio; r CUC$50; ❄) A casa particular in one of Centro Habana's arterial streets, this place has grown to take on mini-hotel proportions. It now has 11 rooms, but you'll still feel as though you've joined an extended Cuban family when you stay here. Rooms marry solid 20th-century furniture with modern bathrooms and plant-filled communal areas.

The Concordia is right in the middle of Centro Habana's hectic but wonderfully theatrical 'hood and you'll really feel part of it all here.

★Malecón 663 BOUTIQUE HOTEL $$$
(Map p316; ☎7-860-1459; www.malecon663.com; Malecón No 663, btwn Gervasio & Belascoain; d CUC$210-250, ste CUC$290; ❄📶) 🍃 A work of creative genius on the Malecón, this French-run hotel is a whimsical mélange of art, recycling, comfort and sophistication. The four rooms are individually themed (art deco, vintage, contemporary and eclectic), but all are doused with Cuban flavor, from AfroCuban religions to carnivals to cutting-edge street art.

★Hotel Iberostar Parque Central HOTEL $$$
(Map p306; ☎7-860-6627; www.iberostar.com; Neptuno, btwn Agramonte & Paseo de Martí; r incl breakfast CUC$490-570; P❄@📶🏊) For over two decades the Iberostar Parque Central has been Havana's most consistent international-standard hotel, despite newer competition, with service and business facilities on par with top-ranking five-star establishments elsewhere in the Caribbean. Although the chic lobby and classily furnished rooms may lack the historical riches of Habana Vieja accommodations, the ambience is far from antiseptic.

★Iberostar Grand Packard Hotel LUXURY HOTEL $$$
(Map p306; ☎7-823-2100; www.iberostar.com; Paseo de Martí, btwn Cárcel & Genios; d/ste $250/395; P❄@📶🏊) An infinity pool overlooking the harbor is just one highlight of this 321-room hotel, centrally located at

the entrance to the bay. Accommodation is elegant and modern, with minimalist decor, open spaces, and bright white rooms and suites. Spanish-influenced gastronomy meets Cuban flavors in the hotel's six restaurants and three bars, including a tapas bar and a cigar lounge.

Gran Hotel Manzana Kempinski LUXURY HOTEL $$$
(Map p306; 7-869-9100; www.kempinski.com/en/havana/gran-hotel-kempinski-la-habana; San Rafael, btwn Av de las Misiones & Agramonte; d/ste CUC$500/800;) Swiss hotel chain Kempinski runs this self-proclaimed 5½-star hotel in the heart of Old Havana. Covering the entire block, the luxurious property features 246 large rooms and suites on five floors with views over the old city and Parque Central (p306). Facilities include a cigar lounge, a spa and fitness center, a rooftop swimming pool and a panoramic, guests-only bar-restaurant.

Hotel Sevilla HOTEL $$$
(Map p306; 7-860-8560; www.hotelsevilla-cuba.com; Trocadero No 55, btwn Paseo de Martí & Agramonte; s/d incl breakfast CUC$200/308;) Al Capone once hired out the whole 6th floor, Graham Greene used room 501 as a setting for *Our Man in Havana*, and the Mafia requisitioned the place as operations center for its pre-revolutionary North American drug racket. Nowadays the Moorish Sevilla still packs a punch, with an ostentatious lobby that could have been ripped straight out of Granada's Alhambra.

Spacious rooms with Sevillian tiles on the headboards get periodic upgrades, and the 9th-floor restaurant where you're serenaded by violin over breakfast is an 'experience,' but you're paying more for history here than modern facilities or snappy service.

Hotel Saratoga HOTEL $$$
(Map p306; 7-868-1000; www.saratogahotel-cuba.com; Paseo de Martí No 603; d/ste CUC$506/605;) The mint-green Saratoga is an architectural work of art that stands imposingly at the intersection of Paseo de Martí and Dragones, with fantastic views toward the Capitolio (p305). Sharp, if officious, service is a feature here, as are extra-comfortable beds, power showers, a truly decadent rooftop swimming pool and an exquisite hotel bar.

Vedado

Hostal Havaniko CASA PARTICULAR $
(Map p316; 7-837-4850; hostalhavaniko@gmail.com; Calle I No 457, btwn Calles 21 & 23; r CUC$40-50;) This casa particular, currently into its third owners, has had numerous incarnations, all of them good. It's located in the middle of Vedado's nightlife zone and centered on a high-walled patio with plenty of greenery and a fountain. The seven rooms are hotel standard and accented with murals, tiles and terra-cotta bricks. It was completely renovated in 2019.

Marques de Liz CASA PARTICULAR $
(Map p316; 5-264-4756; Calle 25 No 715, btwn Calles D & E; r CUC$45-60;) A handsome neoclassical house located in a quiet street, the 'Liz' has four rooms of varying configurations. All have kettles, microwaves and stocked fridges. Some have larger kitchenettes, and one has a sunny balcony overlooking Av 25. The bathrooms are large and luxuriously modern, and tempting bottles of wine and rum are left in your room (to purchase).

Marta Vitorte CASA PARTICULAR $
(Map p316; 7-832-6475; www.casamartainhavana.com; Calle G No 301, apt 14, btwn Calles 13 & 15; r CUC$40-60;) Marta has lived in this apartment block on Av de los Presidentes since the 1960s. One look at the view and you'll see why: the glass-front wraparound terrace, taking in 270 degrees of Havana's pockmarked panorama, makes it seem as though you're standing atop the Martí monument (p309). Not surprisingly, the four rooms are deluxe, with lovely furnishings, minibars and safes.

★El Candil Boutique Hotel BOUTIQUE HOTEL $$
(Map p316; 7-833-1209; www.hotelcandil.com; Calle 2 No 457, btwn 19 & 21; r CUC$150;) Boutique hotels are a new thing in Cuba, and the five-room Candil is setting a high bar, occupying a distinguished early-20th-century villa decked out with the discreet elegance of the era but with some welcome modern additions. There's a curtain-draped front porch, a sun-splashed rooftop bar and plunge pool, plus wall-mounted flat-screen TVs and air-con units in all five rooms.

★Casavana Cuba CASA PARTICULAR $$
(Map p316; 5-804-9258; www.casavanacuba.com; Calle G No 301, 5th fl, btwn Calles 13 & 15; r/ste

from CUC$130/170;) What started as a casa particular has morphed into a de facto private hotel of four-star quality. Spread over three floors (4, 5 and 11) in a residential *rascacielo* (skyscraper), Casavana's huge rooms choose modern minimalism over antique clutter, but there are elegant touches and bright common areas with floors so polished you can virtually see your face in them.

Boutique Hotel 5tay8 Vedado BOUTIQUE HOTEL $$
(Map p316; 7-881-2671; www.boutiquehotelvedado.website; Av 5, cnr Calle 8; d from CUC$115;) An exceptionally striking private hotel inhabiting a dignified villa, the 5 & 8 effortlessly mixes the modernity of Miami with the indefinable magic of Havana. The building itself is a beauty, with vines cascading down two stories from arched windows, plus a roof terrace (with illuminated bar) licked by gentle sea breezes.

★**Hotel Nacional** HOTEL $$$
(Map p316; 7-836-3564; www.hotelnacionaldecuba.com; cnr Calles O & 21; s/d/tr CUC$234/338/465;) The icing on the cake of Cuban hotels and a flagship of the government-run Gran Caribe chain, the neoclassical/neocolonial/art deco (call it eclectic) Hotel Nacional is as much a city monument as an international accommodation option. Even if you don't stay here, find time to sip at least one minty mojito in the exquisite oceanside bar.

Playa & Marianao

★**Hotel Meliá Habana** HOTEL $$$
(7-204-8500; www.meliacuba.com; Av 3, btwn Calles 76 & 80, Miramar; s/d CUC$500;) A little brutal from the outside but beautiful within, Miramar's Hotel Meliá Habana is one of the city's best-run and best-equipped accommodations options. The 409 rooms (some wheelchair accessible) are positioned around a salubrious lobby with abundant hanging vines, marble statues and extravagant water features. Outside, Cuba's largest and most attractive swimming pool lies next to a desolate, rocky shore.

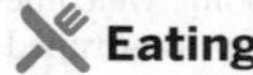

Eating

Habana Vieja

El Café BREAKFAST $
(Map p302; 7-861-3817; www.facebook.com/elcafehavana; Amargura 358, btwn Villegas & Aguacate; breakfast CUC$3-7; 9am-6pm;) There are many cafes in Havana these days, but only one *El* Café, a delicious mix of tight service, exceptional coffee and homemade sourdough sandwiches supplemented by all-day brunchy breakfasts. It's popular with indie travelers courtesy of its ample vegan and vegetarian options, including avocado and hummus varietals. Arrive early to get a seat.

D'Next CAFETERIA $
(Map p302; 7-860-5519; Brasil No 512, btwn Av de las Misiones & Bernaza; snacks CUC$3-6; 8:30am-midnight;) On the cusp of trendy Plaza del Cristo, the much-loved D'Next is ridiculously cheap, ridiculously busy and ridiculously good. Decorated sports-bar style with plastic seats and paper menus, it's particularly popular with young Cubans for its cheap burgers, icy air-conditioning and late-night cake indulgences.

Helad'oro ICE CREAM $
(Map p302; 5-305-9131; Aguiar No 206, btwn Empedrado & Tejadillo; ice cream CUC$1-4; 11am-10pm) Back when Fidel Castro was 'king,' the government had a monopoly on many things. Controlled by the legendary Coppelia, ice cream rarely strayed beyond *fresa y chocolate* (strawberry and chocolate) flavors. Then along came the economic defrosting of the 2010s, ushering in Helad'oro, with its artisan ice cream dispensed in 30-plus flavors, including mamey and *desayuno tropical* (tropical breakfast).

Café Bohemia TAPAS $
(Map p302; 7-836-6567; www.havanabohemia.com; San Ignacio No 364; tapas CUC$6-10; 10:30am-9:30pm;) Inhabiting a beautifully curated mansion on Plaza Vieja, Café Bohemia – named for a Cuban culture and arts magazine – manages to feel appropriately bohemian but also serves great cocktails, tapas and extremely addictive cakes.

★**Lamparilla 361 Tapas & Cervezas** TAPAS $$
(Map p302; 5-289-5324; Lamparilla No 361, btwn Aguacate & Villegas; tapas CUC$5-12; noon-midnight) Havana's best tapas bar might also be its finest all-round eating establishment, with food, presentation and service down to a fine art. Inside the loungy, romantically lit restaurant there's plenty to look at as you enjoy ice-cold beer, fabulous cocktails, and creative but interestingly presented tapas (on plates, slates, pans and mini-shopping trolleys).

Best of all is the sharp, discreet and multilingual service that ought to be bottled and exported all around Cuba.

You'll need more than a postcard (or tweet) to list the standout food and drink items. Could they include the tapas-size lasagna, the meatballs served freshly made in the pan, the cornbread with sweet chicken, or the daiquiri that comes with a face iced onto it? It's all epic!

★Doña Eutimia CUBAN **$$**

(Map p302; ☎7-861-1332; Callejón del Chorro 60c; mains CUC$8-12; ⊙noon-10pm) The secret at Doña Eutimia is that there *is* no secret: just serve decent-size portions of the best Cuban food. Expect the likes of *ropa vieja* (shredded beef; there's also an interesting lamb version), epic *picadillo a la habanera* (spicy beef), glorious *lechón asado* (roast pork) and beautifully rustic roast chicken, all served with ample rice, beans and fried plantains.

This is trip-defining food of the highest order, and proof that Cuba's traditional cuisine, when prepared properly, can be pretty spectacular. The restaurant is located in a cul-de-sac near the cathedral. Reserve a day ahead.

★Lo de Monik TAPAS **$$**

(Map p302; ☎7-864-4029; Compostela No 201, cnr Chacón; mains CUC$10-15; ⊙8am-9:30pm) Eschewing colonial splendor for a French bistro feel, the Monk blends seamlessly into the increasingly chic Loma del Ángel quarter, with a bright-white interior and arguably the city's friendliest and chattiest staff. Search the ever-changing blackboard menu for brunch or tapas ideas (fish tacos, well-stuffed Cuban baguettes, creamy cheesecake) and come back later for spectacular cocktails.

El del Frente INTERNATIONAL **$$**

(Map p302; ☎7-863-0206; O'Reilly No 303; mains CUC$8-13; ⊙noon-midnight) When the owners of O'Reilly 304 (p318) wanted to expand their increasingly popular restaurant a few years back, they opened another one directly across the street and amusingly called it El del Frente ('The One in Front'). It's more of the same culinary genius, with a few bonuses – a roof terrace, retro 1950s design features and heady gin cocktails.

Partake in the lobster tacos, octopus salad or drinks from what are possibly Havana's best mixologists and enjoy it all under the stars. The entrance is through a modest door in Calle O'Reilly. Book ahead; it's insanely popular.

El Rum Rum de la Habana SEAFOOD **$$**

(Map p302; ☎7-861-0806; Empedrado No 256, btwn Cuba & Aguiar; mains CUC$7-18; ⊙noon-midnight) Not every restaurant has a wine sommelier *and* a cigar sommelier, but this is Havana, and El Rum Rum (the name references both the drink and Cuban slang for 'gossip') can put you straight on every area of consumption. Everything is outstanding here, from the delicate seafood to the concert-worthy musical entertainment.

The menu's a feast of Cuban specialties full of subtle scents and sauces. There's *caldereta de mariscos* (a rich seafood stew), steak with three toppings, a paella worthy of Valencia, and about 10 ways of imbibing your mojito. Service, led by sommelier and owner Osiris Oramas, is exemplary, directing you toward the best rum and food flavors, and there are several spaces – including an air-conditioned VIP room – in which to eat.

Restaurante Antojos INTERNATIONAL **$$**

(Map p302; ☎5-277-2577; www.restauranteantojos.com; Espada, btwn Cuarteles & Chacón; mains CUC$7-12; ⊙11am-midnight) A place to satisfy your whims *(antojos)*, particularly if you're feeling whimsical about daiquiris, generously stuffed pulled-pork baguettes or chunky *tostones* (fried plantain). Wander into the dessert realm (they serve 'em any time) and you'll be equally stirred, particularly if you choose a warm bowl of cinnamon-laced *arroz con leche* (rice pudding).

5 Sentidos INTERNATIONAL **$$**

(Map p302; ☎7-864 8699; www.paladar5sentidos.com; San Juan de Dios No 67, cnr Compostela; mains CUC$10-18; ⊙noon-4pm & 6:30-11pm) The romantically named five feelings (*5 sentidos*) ought to excite at least three of yours. The open kitchen allows for the free circulation of inviting aromas, the French-bistro decor (all painted wood and elegant chandeliers) is pleasing to the eye, and your taste buds won't leave unstimulated after you've savored the ceviche, octopus or melt-in-the-mouth lamb stew.

Il Rustico ITALIAN **$$**

(Map p302; ☎5-539-4514; San Juan de Dios No 53, btwn Habana & Compostela; mains CUC$5-10; ⊙noon-10:30pm) With a Sicilian owner at the helm, furniture craftily made out of recycled wooden pallets, and a wood-fired pizza oven, Rustico can plausibly claim to serve Havana's best pizza.

The thin-crust pies – chewy, bubbled at the edges and not too busy on top – would

Vedado

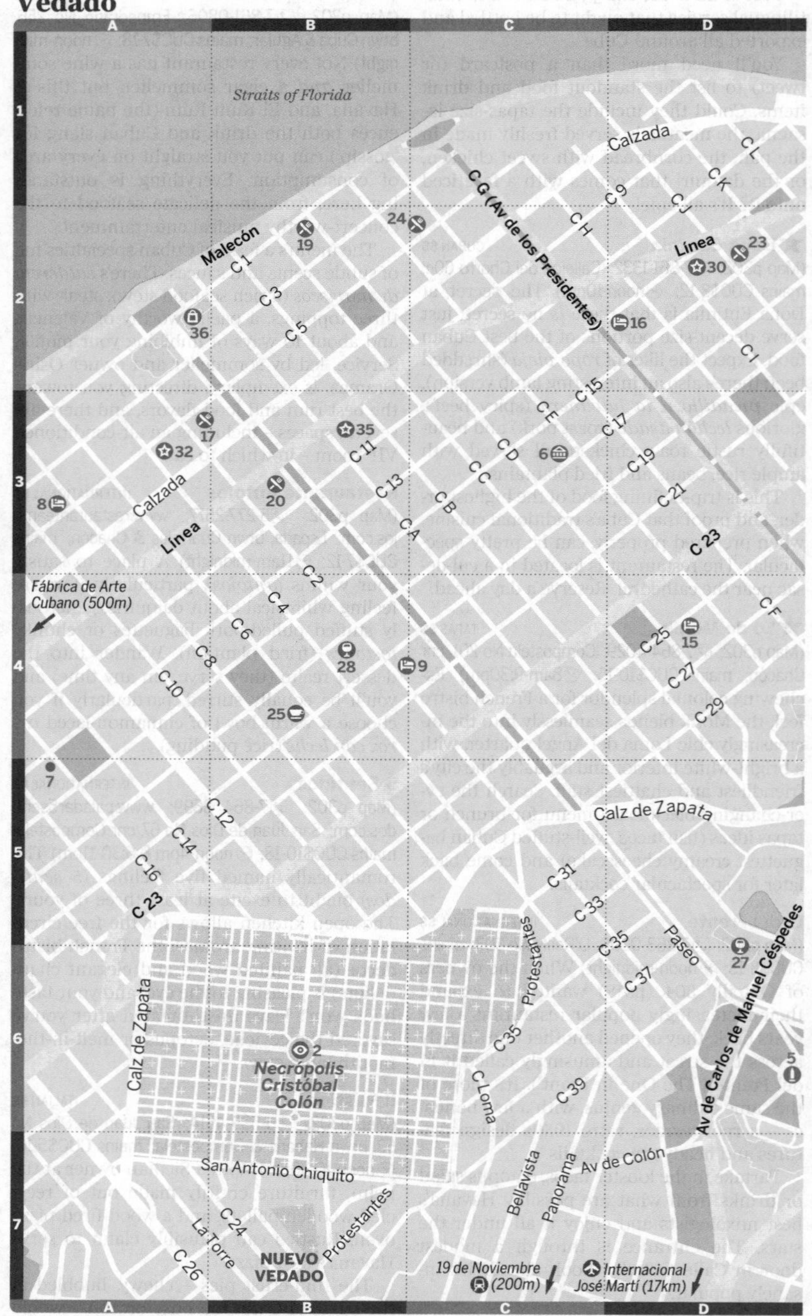
Straits of Florida
Malecón
Calzada
Línea
C G (Av de los Presidentes)
Fábrica de Arte Cubano (500m)
Calz de Zapata
Necrópolis Cristóbal Colón
San Antonio Chiquito
La Torre
NUEVO VEDADO
Protestantes
Bellavista
Panorama
Av de Colón
C Loma
Paseo
Av de Carlos de Manuel Céspedes
C 23
CF
19 de Noviembre (200m)
Internacional José Martí (17km)

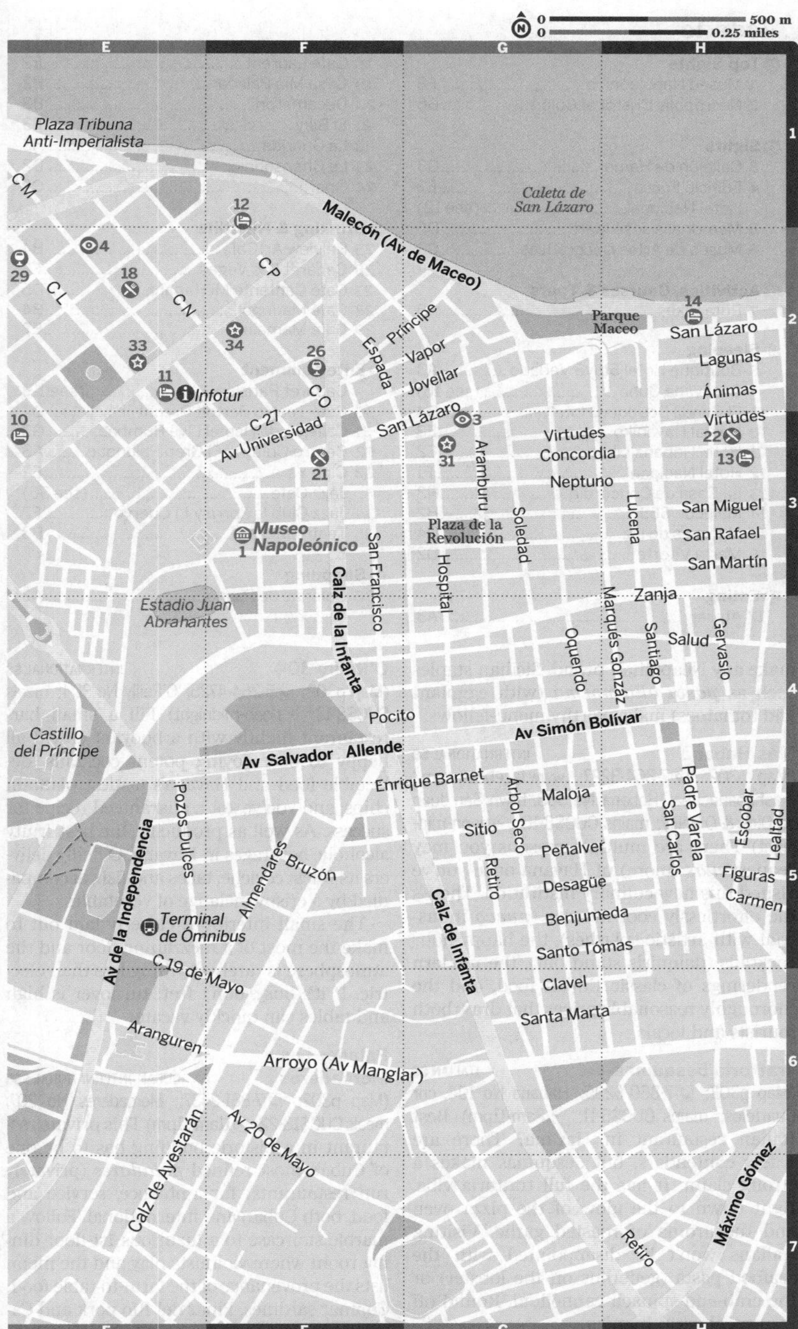
0 500 m
0 0.25 miles
Plaza Tribuna Anti-Imperialista
Caleta de San Lázaro
Malecón (Av de Maceo)
Parque Maceo
San Lázaro
Lagunas
Ánimas
Virtudes
Concordia
Neptuno
San Miguel
San Rafael
San Martín
Zanja
Salud
Infotur
Av Universidad
Museo Napoleónico
Plaza de la Revolución
Estadio Juan Abrahantes
Castillo del Príncipe
Calz de la Infanta
Pocito
Av Salvador Allende
Av Simón Bolívar
Enrique Barnet
Maloja
Sitio
Peñalver
Desagüe
Benjumeda
Santo Tómas
Clavel
Santa Marta
Terminal de Ómnibus
Av de la Independencia
C 19 de Mayo
Aranguren
Arroyo (Av Manglar)
Av 20 de Mayo
Calz de Ayestarán
Calz de Infanta
Máximo Gómez
Retiro

Vedado

Top Sights
1 Museo Napoleónico F3
2 Necrópolis Cristóbal Colón B6

Sights
3 Callejón de Hamel G3
4 Edificio Focsa E2
Hotel Nacional .... (see 12)
5 Memorial a José Martí D6
6 Museo de Artes Decorativas C3

Activities, Courses & Tours
7 Ruta Bikes A5

Sleeping
8 Boutique Hotel 5tay8 Vedado A3
Casavana Cuba .... (see 16)
9 El Candil Boutique Hotel B4
10 Hostal Havaniko E3
11 Hotel Habana Libre E2
12 Hotel Nacional F1
13 La Casa de Concordia H3
14 Malecón 663 .... H2
15 Marques de Liz D4
16 Marta Vitorte D2

Eating
17 Atelier A3
18 Café Laurent E2
19 Casa Mia Paladar B2
20 Decameron B3
21 El Biky F3
22 La Guarida H3
23 Le Chansonnier D2
24 Opera C2

Drinking & Nightlife
25 Belview ArtCafé B4
26 Cabaret Las Vegas F2
27 Café Cantante Mi Habana D5
28 Café Madrigal B4
29 Café Mamainé E2

Entertainment
Cabaret Parisién .... (see 12)
30 Café Teatro Bertolt Brecht D2
31 Callejón de Hamel Live Rumba G3
32 Centro Cultural El Gran Palenque A3
33 Cine Yara E2
Jazz Café .... (see 36)
34 Jazz Club la Zorra y El Cuervo F2
35 Teatro Mella B3

Shopping
36 Galerías de Paseo A2

make any Neapolitan proud. Sicilian staples such as *pasta alla norma* (with eggplant and tomatoes) make worthy menu-fellows.

Más Habana INTERNATIONAL **$$**
(Map p302; 7-864-3227; www.facebook.com/mashabanacuba; Habana No 308, btwn San Juan de Dios & O'Reilly; mains CUC$8-16; noon-midnight) There are multiple reasons you may request *más* (more) of Havana once you've visited this new culinary institution. There's the effortlessly cool interior (*nuevo* industrial with artistic splashes), the happy-hour cocktails (daiquiris stand out), the modern renderings of classic Cuban food, and the thoroughly reasonable prices that draw both tourists and locals.

Trattoria 5esquinas ITALIAN **$$**
(Map p302; 7-860-6295; Habana No 104, cnr Cuarteles; mains CUC$5-11; 8am-11pm) Best Italian restaurant in Havana? There are a few contenders, but 5esquinas makes a strong claim. It has the full trattoria vibe, right down to the glow of the pizza oven and the aroma of roasted garlic. Visiting Italians won't be disappointed with the seafood pasta (generous on the lobster) or the crab-and-spinach cannelloni. Round off your meal with tiramisu.

O'Reilly 304 INTERNATIONAL **$$**
(Map p302; 5-264-4725; O'Reilly No 304; meals CUC$8-13; noon-midnight) Fill a small bar-restaurant nightly with a buoyant crowd all happy to be enjoying potent cocktails, delectable food and Havana's tastiest plantain chips, and you've got a guaranteed recipe for success. As well as producing the best fruity alcoholic beverages in Havana, O'Reilly delivers its finest ceviche, tacos and fish, accompanied by a crispy mélange of vegetables.

The small interior is cleverly laid out to make the most of a mezzanine floor and the atmosphere is rarely anything less than electric. If it's busy, don't fret: turnover is high and tables can quickly vacate.

Paladar Los Mercaderes CUBAN, INTERNATIONAL **$$$**
(Map p302; 7-861-2437; Mercaderes No 207; meals CUC$18-22; 11am-11pm) This private restaurant in a historic building has to be one of Cuba's most refined *paladares* (privately run restaurants) for ambience, service and food, both Cuban and international. Follow a marble staircase to a luxurious 1st-floor dining room where violinists play and the menu lists the provenance of the farm-to-table food: Cojímar sardines, Pinar del Río pork and Camagüeyan *ropa vieja* (shredded beef).

Centro Habana

Nazdarovie RUSSIAN $$

(Map p306; ☎7-860-2947; www.nazdarovie-havana.com; Malecón No 25, btwn Prado & Cárcel; mains CUC$7-13; ⊙noon-midnight; ❄) Cuba's 31-year dalliance with bolshevism is relived in this popular restaurant in prime digs overlooking the Malecón. Upstairs, the decor is awash with old Soviet propaganda posters, brotherly photos of Fidel Castro and Nikita Khrushchev, and slightly less bombastic Russian dolls. The menu is in three languages (to get into the real spirit, try ordering in Russian).

Choices are simple but classic: beef stroganoff, chicken Kiev and borscht are all listed and they're all good. For a cocktail, try the James Bond option: a vodka martini (shaken, not stirred). From Russia with love.

Castas y Tal CUBAN $$

(Map p306; ☎7-864-2177; Av de Italia No 51, cnr San Lázaro; mains CUC$6-9; ⊙noon-midnight) Finding a balance by attracting Cubans (with economical prices and traditional recipes) and tourists (with creative 'fusion' touches), hip C&T is a bistro-style restaurant encased by the Centro Habana 'hood. High-quality, adventurous food, such as lamb with masala or chicken in orange sauce, is backed up with Cuban classics (lashings of rice and beans are served on the side).

★ **La Guarida** INTERNATIONAL $$$

(Map p316; ☎7-866-9047; www.laguarida.com; Concordia No 418, btwn Gervasio & Escobar; mains CUC$15-22; ⊙noon-4pm & 6pm-midnight) Only in Havana! The entrance to the city's most legendary private restaurant greets you like a scene out of a 1940s film noir. A decapitated statue lies at the bottom of a grand but dilapidated staircase that leads past lines of drying clothes to a wooden door, beyond which lie multiple culinary surprises.

La Guarida began to acquire its lofty reputation in the 1990s, when it was used as a location for the Oscar-nominated *Fresa y chocolate*. Regularly refined in the years since, the food is still up there with Havana's best, with the restaurant's pioneering brand of *nueva cocina cubana* driving both classic dishes and those that are unusual for Cuba (lamb tikka masala). Reservations recommended.

San Cristóbal CUBAN $$$

(Map p306; ☎7-867-9109; San Rafael, btwn Campanario & Lealtad; meals CUC$10-19; ⊙noon-midnight Mon-Sat) San Cristóbal was knocking out fine food long before the US president dropped by in March 2016, although the publicity attending Barack Obama's visit probably didn't hurt. Crammed into one of Centro Habana's grubbier streets, the restaurant has a museum-worthy interior crowded with old photos, animal hides, and a Santería altar flanked by images of Antonio Maceo and José Martí.

Vedado

El Biky CAFETERIA $

(Map p316; ☎7-870-6515; www.elbiky.com; cnr Calzada de la Infanta & San Lázaro; mains CUC$4-11; ⊙8am-midnight) Arriving like a breath of fresh air half a decade ago, Biky helped reinvent Havana's evolving brunch-lunch scene with its affordable quick-fire food, served in a modern cafe-restaurant hung with retro pre-revolution photos. It was so successful that it has since morphed into a 'gastronomic complex,' adding a cool bar and Havana's best bakery next door.

★ **Café Laurent** INTERNATIONAL $$

(Map p316; ☎7-832-6890; Calle M No 257, 5th fl, btwn Calles 19 & 21; mains CUC$8-16; ⊙noon-midnight) Talk about a hidden gem. The unsigned Café Laurent is a sophisticated fine-dining restaurant encased, incongruously, in a glaringly ugly 1950s apartment block next to the Focsa building. Starched white tablecloths, polished glasses and lacy drapes furnish the bright modernist interior, while seafood risotto and artistically presented pork sautéed with dry fruit and red wine headline the Cuban-Spanish menu.

Opera INTERNATIONAL $$

(Map p316; ☎7-831-2255; www.operahabana.com; Calle 5 No 204, btwn Calles E & F; mains CUC$9-13; ⊙noon-3pm & 7-10pm Wed-Mon; ✎) Hitting the high notes of Cuban-Italian cuisine, Opera is housed in a colonnaded villa with a billiard table in the front room and the strains of *Carmen* or *Aida* fluttering over the sound system. The food is equally dramatic and embraces the Italian 'Slow Food' philosophy, encompassing homemade gnocchi stuffed with yucca and rabbit cooked in Bucanero beer.

Casa Mia Paladar CUBAN $$

(Map p316; ☎7-832-9735; Calle 1 No 103, btwn Calles C & D; mains CUC$9-14; ⊙11:30am-11pm; ❄) Rather than blinding you with fancy decor, clean-lined Casa Mia, abutting the Malecón, saves its surprises for the food, a simple menu that rests proudly on the classic foundations of Cuban cooking. The highlight in a medley of standouts is the *cerdo* cooked Pinar del Río style, which, as locals will tell you, is the melt-in-your-mouth pinnacle of Cuban pork.

Atelier CUBAN $$$
(Map p316; ☎7-836-2025; Calle 5 No 511/Altos, btwn Paseo & Calle 2; meals CUC$15-25; ⏰noon-midnight) The first thing that hits you at Atelier is the stupendous wall art: huge, thought-provoking, religious-tinged paintings. Equally arresting is the antique wooden ceiling that might have been ripped from a *mudéjar* church, plus the terra-cotta roof terrace and old-school elegance. Eventually you'll get around to the food: Cuban with a French influence and scribbled onto an ever-changing menu.

Decameron INTERNATIONAL $$$
(Map p316; ☎7-832-2444; Línea No 753, btwn Paseo & Calle 2; mains CUC$12-18; ⏰noon-midnight; 🖉) Nondescript from the outside, but far prettier within – thanks largely to its famous collection of antique clocks (don't be late, now!) – the Decameron is a stalwart *paladar* that was always good, still is good and probably always will be good. The food is Cuban with international inflections. People rave about the savory tuna tart, risotto and swordfish.

On top of that there's a decent wine selection and powerful cocktails. The kitchen is sympathetic to vegetarians.

Le Chansonnier FRENCH $$$
(Map p316; ☎7-832-1576; www.lechansonnierhabana.com; Calle J No 257, btwn Calles 13 & 15; meals CUC$12-20; ⏰12:30pm-12:30am) A great place to dine if you can find it (there's no sign), hidden in a faded mansion turned private restaurant with a revamped interior that is dramatically more avant-garde than the neoclassical facade. Food is served in various rooms inside. French wine and French flavors shine in house specialties such as rabbit with mustard, duck terrine and spare ribs.

Playa & Marianao

El Aljibe CARIBBEAN $$
(☎7-204-1583/4; Av 7, btwn Calles 24 & 26, Miramar; mains CUC$12-15; ⏰noon-midnight) Aljibe is a legend in Havana: a restaurant whose original incarnation predated the revolution and whose second coming in the 1990s revived its most renowned dish, the obligatory *pollo asado* (roast chicken in a bitter-orange sauce), served with as-much-as-you-can-eat helpings of white rice, black beans, fried plantain, French fries and salad for only CUC$12.

★La Fontana BARBECUE $$$
(☎7-202-8337; Av 3A No 305, Miramar; mains CUC$13-28; ⏰noon-midnight) La Fontana, encased in a hard-to-find but beautiful house in Playa, is one of the best restaurants in Havana, a position it has enjoyed pretty much since its inception in 1995 (back in Cuba's culinary Stone Age). The secret: the restaurant has progressed with the times, adding space, dishes and multiple quirks such as fish ponds and live jazz.

These days there are several areas in which to drink and dine, each with a different ambience. The centerpiece is a brick-lined terrace and open grill, but there's also a trendy chill-out bar that mixes potent cocktails.

Fontana is famed for its barbecue or, more to the point, its full-on charcoal grill. Huge portions of meat and fish are served, so go easy on the starters, which include lobster ceviche, tuna tartare, and beef carpaccio with rocket.

La Cocina de Lilliam FUSION $$$
(☎7-209-6514; www.lacocinadelilliam.com; Calle 48 No 1311, btwn Avs 13 & 15, Miramar; meals CUC$15-30; ⏰noon-3pm & 7-11pm Tue-Sat) One of the oldest private restaurants in Havana (since 1994) and one that seems to have survived all the aches and pains of Cuba's economic roller coaster, entertaining illustrious guests along the way (Jimmy Carter came here in 2002).

La Esperanza INTERNATIONAL $$$
(☎7-202-4361; Calle 16 No 105, btwn Avs 1 & 3, Miramar; meals CUC$8-17; ⏰7-11pm Mon-Sat) La Esperanza recalls those old-school *paladar* days when you felt you were dining in someone's home, and here you essentially are. The interior of this vine-covered house is a riot of quirky antiques, old portraits and refined 1940s furnishings, while the food includes such exquisite dishes as *pollo luna de miel* (chicken flambéed in rum) and lamb brochettes.

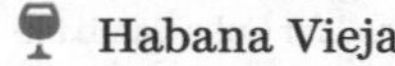

Drinking & Nightlife

Habana Vieja

★El Dandy CAFE
(Map p302; ☎7-867-6463; www.bareldandy.com; cnr Brasil & Villegas; ⏰8am-1am) More stylish man-about-town than vain popinjay, El Dandy is an unpretentious cafe by day and

a cool cocktail bar by night. A casual greeter shakes your hand at the door, efficient waitstaff take your order at the bar, and trendier-than-you customers pose like peacocks around the marble tables.

★Azúcar Lounge LOUNGE
(Map p302; ☎7-860-6563; Mercaderes No 315; ⏰11am-midnight) From a 2nd-floor balcony, high above the architectural beauty contest that is Plaza Vieja, there's no better place in Cuba to savor a piña colada than Azúcar. With its lounge-y seating, trance-y music and Ikea-meets-avant-garde decor, this is an unashamedly trendy place to hang out, but it never feels exclusive. Tourists, premillennials and self-confessed squares will all feel welcome.

★El Chanchullero BAR
(Map p302; www.el-chanchullero.com; Brasil, btwn Bernaza & Christo; ⏰1pm-midnight) *'Aqui jamás estuvo Hemingway'* (Hemingway was never here) reads the sign outside Chanchullero, with more than a hint of irony. It's a key point. Since the American author never frequented this roguish joint in Plaza del Cristo, the price of cocktails has remained refreshingly low (CUC$2.50), meaning you can get as smashed as he once did.

La Taberna del Son BAR
(Map p302; Brasil 104, btwn Cuba & San Ignacio; ⏰noon-midnight) A hurricane of Cuban energy, this tiny dive just off Plaza Vieja gives at least half of its space over to the nightly band, most of whom are older than the Rolling Stones – and just as energetic. The crowd is half Cuban, half tourist, but all are armed with a desire to sink *muchos* mojitos. Dancing quickly becomes inevitable.

El Patchanka BAR
(Map p302; ☎7-860-4161; Bernaza No 162; ⏰1pm-1am) Live bands rock the rafters, locals knock back powerful CUC$3 mojitos, and earnest travelers banter about Che Guevara's contribution to modern poster art in this gritty dive bar in Plaza del Cristo that looks comfortably lived in. Cultural interaction is the key here. By keeping prices low (lobster for CUC$9), Patchanka attracts everyone.

Centro Habana

★Café Arcángel CAFE
(Map p306; ☎5-268-5451; www.cafearcangel.com; Concordia No 57; ⏰8:15am-6pm Mon-Sat, to 1pm Sun) Excellent coffee, fine croissants, suave non-reggaeton music and Charlie Chaplin movies playing on a loop in a scarred Centro Habana apartment – what more could you want?

Rooftop Bar, Hotel Inglaterra BAR
(Map p306; Paseo de Martí No 416, btwn San Rafael & Neptuno; ⏰7pm-late) The rooms may have lost their luster, but the Inglaterra's open-air roof terrace remains one of the best free-entry bars in Havana for live music and evening libations. Turn up to watch the sunset and stick around as the resident band sends its syncopated rhythms floating over Parque Central with the baroque Gran Teatro theater sitting pretty in the background.

Siá Kará Café BAR
(Map p306; ☎7-867-4084; www.facebook.com/siakaracafecuba; Barcelona, cnr Industria No 502; ⏰noon-2am) In Starbucks-free Havana, every cafe is individual and Siá Kará exhibits its character with graffiti-covered tables, an old tie collection and a parody of the *Mona Lisa* flipping the bird. Although ostensibly a bar-cafe, it serves everything from Varadero lobster to crusty chicken sandwiches. The cushioned benches under the stairs are the perfect place to crack open a thick novel.

Vedado

★Belview ArtCafé CAFE
(Map p316; ☎7-832-5429; www.facebook.com/belviewartcafe; Calle 6 No 412, cnr Calle 19; ⏰9am-6pm Tue-Sun) Behold the backlit photo art, the sofa shoehorned into the trunk of an American car, and the globes doubling as lampshades. The Belview, bivouacked in a handsome Vedado mansion, is an explosion of thought-provoking art. Once you've worked out that you can order drinks as well as admire the graphics, you can place your order for coffee, cake, cocktails or tapas.

★Café Mamainé BAR
(Map p316; ☎7-832-8328; Calle L No 206, btwn Calles 15 & 17; ⏰8am-midnight Mon-Thu, to 3am Fri-Sun) Art and coffee go together like Fidel and Che in this wonderfully reimagined mansion with an interior that features revolving local art. Seating is arranged over a wooden mezzanine or shady side patio, the coffee is pleasantly strong, and the clientele is a mix of young students and people who look as though they've just performed at the Fábrica de Arte Cubano (p322).

Café Madrigal BAR

(Map p316; Calle 17 No 302, btwn Calles 2 & 4; 6pm-2am Tue-Sun) Vedado flirts with bohemia in this dimly lit gay-friendly bar that might have materialized from Paris' Latin Quarter in the days of James Joyce and Ernest Hemingway. Order a *tapita* (small tapa) and a cocktail, and retire to the atmospheric art nouveau terrace, where the buzz of nighttime conversation competes with the racket of vintage American cars rattling past below.

Playa & Marianao

★Café Fortuna Joe BAR

(5-413-3706; cnr Calle 24 & Av 1, Miramar; 9am-midnight) There are a lot of seriously weird (in a good way) places to drink coffee in Havana, but Café Fortuna Joe stands alone, mainly because of its original seating. Forget the mismatched chairs so beloved by hipsters elsewhere; Fortuna's places to park yourself include a horse carriage, an old car, a bed and a cushioned toilet – no kidding.

Espacios COCKTAIL BAR

(7-202-2921; Calle 10 No 513, btwn Avs 5 & 7, Miramar; noon-3am) This fabulously chilled tapas bar occupying an unsignposted villa in the diplomatic quarter is where hip *habaneros* come to consume cocktails and art. Inside, the place has the atmosphere of an informal house party, with fashionable factions of Havana's brainy and beautiful gathering in different rooms or holding court in the patio and garden.

Entertainment

★Fábrica de Arte Cubano LIVE PERFORMANCE

(7-838-2260; www.fac.cu; cnr Calle 26 & 11; CUC$2; 8pm-2am Thu-Sun;) If only every city had a cultural venue as wide-ranging, inclusive and downright revolutionary as Havana's unique art factory. The brainchild of Cuban fusion musician X-Alfonso in 2014, this gallery/live-music venue/inspirational meeting place for anyone who can afford the CUC$2 entry fee is where electrifying 'happenings' take place in a cavernous, Bauhaus-like interior.

Forget surly bouncers and elitist VIP passes. The Fábrica is a wonderfully cool yet unpretentious place where you're encouraged to meet the performers as well as applaud them. Repertoires are as flexible as they are creative. Expect everything from classical cellists to Cuban rappers to arty T-shirt designers selling their latest creations.

For the best experience, arrive at the Fábrica early (it opens promptly at 8pm) to explore the revolving art exhibits, food outlets and music stages before the crowd arrives. There are numerous bars and performance spaces. Food and drink concessions don't accept cash; instead, you must run up a bill on a stamp card and pay (in cash) when you leave.

Various performances take place throughout the evening, usually starting around 9pm – follow the sounds. Free dance lessons are sometimes offered, and artists, designers and musicians mingle with the crowd. It's more than exciting.

The Fábrica is closed for the entire months of May, September and January. It is well worth planning your trip around these times – it's that good!

★Callejón de Hamel Live Rumba LIVE MUSIC

(Map p316; from noon Sun) Aside from its funky murals and psychedelic art shops, the main reason to come to this alleyway, Havana's high temple of Afro-Cuban culture, is the frenetic rumba music that kicks off every Sunday around noon.

For aficionados, this is about as raw and hypnotic as it gets, with interlocking drum patterns and lengthy rhythmic chants powerful enough to summon the spirit of the *orishas* (Santería deities).

Due to a liberal sprinkling of tourists these days, some argue that the *callejón* (back alley) has lost much of its charm. Don't believe them. This place still rocks – and rumbas!

Gran Teatro de la Habana Alicia Alonso THEATER

(Map p306; 7-861-3077; cnr Paseo de Martí & San Rafael; tickets CUC$30; box office 9am-6pm Mon-Sat, to 3pm Sun) Havana's fabulously renovated 'great' theater is open again and offering up the best in Cuban dance and music. Its specialty is ballet (it's the headquarters of the Cuban National Ballet), but it also stages musicals, plays and opera. Check the noticeboard for upcoming events.

Cabaret Parisién CABARET

(Map p316; 7-836-3564; Hotel Nacional, cnr Calles 21 & O; entry CUC$35; 9pm) One rung down from Marianao's world-famous Tropicana, but cheaper and closer to the city center, the nightly Cabaret Parisién in the Hotel Nacional (p308) is well worth a look, especially if you're staying in or around

Vedado. It's the usual mix of frills, feathers and seminaked women (and men), but the choreography is first class and the costumes wonderfully flamboyant.

Basílica Menor de San Francisco de Asís CLASSICAL MUSIC
(Map p302; Plaza de San Francisco de Asís; tickets CUC$5; ⏲from 6pm Sat) Plaza de San Francisco de Asís' glorious church, which dates from 1738, has been reincarnated as a 21st-century museum and concert hall. The old nave hosts choral and chamber music at least once a week (check the schedule at the door) and the acoustics are famously good. It's best to bag your ticket at least a day ahead.

Tropicana Nightclub CABARET
(☎7-267-1871; Calle 72 No 4504, Marianao; tickets from CUC$75; ⏲from 10pm) An institution since its 1939 opening, the world-famous Tropicana was among the few bastions of Havana's Las Vegas–style nightlife to survive the revolution. Immortalized in Graham Greene's 1958 *Our Man in Havana*, the open-air cabaret show here has changed little since its 1950s heyday, with scantily clad *señoritas* descending from palm trees to dance Latin salsa amid bright lights.

It's easily Havana's most popular cabaret and de rigueur on the bus-tour circuit, none of which takes away from the magnificence of the spectacle.

You'll need a taxi to get here. Book tickets in advance through **Infotur** (cnr Av 5 & Calle 112, Náutico; ⏲8:30am-noon & 12:30-5pm Mon-Sat) or any top-end hotel. Prices vary depending on where you sit in relation to the stage and if you have dinner (not recommended). Most tickets include a cigar and a small measure of rum and cola.

Jazz Club la Zorra y El Cuervo LIVE MUSIC
(Map p316; ☎7-833-2402; cnr Calles 23 & O; CUC$5-10; ⏲from 10pm) One in a duo of long-standing and highly lauded jazz clubs, the Vixen and the Crow opens its doors nightly at 10pm to long lines of committed music fiends. Enter through a red British phone box and descend into a diminutive and dark basement. The scene is more hot and clamorous than the Jazz Café and leans toward freestyle jazz.

Centro Cultural El Gran Palenque DANCE
(Map p316; Calle 4 No 103, btwn Calzada & Calle 5; CUC$5; ⏲3-6pm Sat) Founded in 1962, the high-energy Conjunto Folklórico Nacional de Cuba specializes in Afro-Cuban dancing (all of the drummers are Santería priests). See them perform here, and dance along during the regular Sábado de la Rumba – three full hours of mesmerizing drumming and dancing. This group also performs at **Teatro Mella** (Map p316; ☎7-833-8696; Línea No 657, btwn Calles A & B) and internationally.

Café Teatro Bertolt Brecht LIVE MUSIC
(Map p316; ☎7-832-9359; cnr Calles 13 & I; tickets CUC$3) What pass for hipsters in Havana tend to congregate at this live-music venue known locally as No Se lo Digas a Nadie (Don't Tell Anyone) for the weekly concerts headlined by legendary music collective Interactivo (Wednesday around midnight). If you're curious about Cuban culture – and its future – roll up for an evening here. Be prepared to queue.

Jazz Café LIVE MUSIC
(Map p316; ☎7-838-3302; Galerías de Paseo, top fl, cnr Calle 1 & Paseo; cover after 8pm CUC$10; ⏲noon-2am) This upscale joint, improbably located in a **shopping mall** (Map p316; cnr Calle 1 & Paseo; ⏲9am-8pm) overlooking the Malecón, is a kind of jazz supper club, with dinner tables and a decent menu. At night the club swings into action with live jazz, *timba* (contemporary salsa) and, occasionally, straight-up salsa. It's definitely the suavest of Havana's jazz venues.

Shopping

★Clandestina CLOTHING
(Map p302; ☎5-381-4802; www.clandestina.co; Villegas No 403, btwn Brasil & Muralla; ⏲10am-8pm Mon-Sat, to 5pm Sun) Cuba's first indie design store when it opened in 2015, Clandestina makes its own T-shirts, bags and accessories out of any old junk it can find, 99% of it Cuban. It's the most progressive and coolest thing around town right now, but it's also eco-conscious and deft at working in a tough economic climate.

★Centro Cultural Antiguos Almacenes de Deposito San José ARTS & CRAFTS
(Map p302; cnr Desamparados & San Isidro; ⏲10am-6pm Mon-Sat) Havana's multifarious handicraft market sits under the cover of an old shipping warehouse in Desamparados. Check your socialist ideals at the door: herein lies a hive of free enterprise and (unusually for Cuba) haggling. Possible souvenirs include paintings, *guayaberas* (men's shirts), woodwork, leather items, jewelry and numerous apparitions of the highly marketable El Che.

MIA2YOU/SHUTTERSTOCK ©

1. Varadero Beach (p330)
One of the Caribbean's finest beaches

2. Palacio de los Capitanes Generales (p299)
Textbook example of Cuban baroque architecture

3. Street scenes, Havana (p299)
Iconic retro cars and architecture

4. Valle de Viñales (p330)
One of Cuba's most magnificent natural settings

5. Salsa, Havana (p323)
The lively dance is everywhere, even on the streets.

3

HEIKONEUMANNPHOTOGRAPHY/SHUTTERSTOCK ©

4

ORIREDMOUSE/GETTY IMAGES ©

Memorias Librería BOOKS

(Map p306; ☎7-862-3153; Ánimas No 57, btwn Paseo de Martí & Agramonte; ⏰9am-5pm) A shop full of beautiful artifacts, the Memorias Librería opened in 2014 as Havana's first genuine antique bookstore. Delve into its gathered piles and you'll find wonderful rare collectibles, including old coins, postcards, posters, magazines and art deco signs from the 1930s. Priceless!

La Casa del Habano Quinta CIGARS

(☎7-214-4737; cnr Av 5 & Calle 16, Miramar; ⏰10am-6pm Mon-Sat, to 1pm Sun) Arguably Havana's top cigar store – and there are many contenders. The primary reasons: it's well stocked, with well-informed staff, a comfy smoking lounge and a decent on-site restaurant. It also enjoys the on-off presence of many of Cuba's top cigar aficionados.

Librería Venecia BOOKS

(Map p302; Obispo No 502; ⏰10am-10pm) Wonderful little private bookshop in Calle Obispo selling yellowed secondhand tomes, esoteric film posters and other random print work that you won't find anywhere else in Havana.

Alma Shop ARTS & CRAFTS

(☎5-264-0660; www.almacubashop.com; Calle 18 No 314, btwn Avs 3 & 5, Miramar; ⏰10am-6pm Mon-Sat) Whether you're searching for jewelry, embroidered cushions or a vintage cigar humidor, this privately run shop is a great place to pick up a high-quality gift or souvenir. The owners have traveled across Cuba to carefully select pieces made by local artisans; each item is unique and handmade using natural or recycled materials.

ℹ Information

MEDICAL SERVICES

Most of Cuba's specialist hospitals offering services to visitors are based in Havana.

Havana's main hospital for foreigners is the **Clínica Central Cira García** (☎7-204-4300; Calle 20 No 4101, Miramar; ⏰9am-4pm Mon-Fri, emergencies 24hr) in Playa. There's a 24-hour emergency wing and most staff speak English.

There are 10 international pharmacies in Havana selling products priced in convertibles (CUC$). The handiest for travelers are at **Hotel Habana Libre** (Map p316; ☎7-834-6100; www.meliacuba.com; Calle L, btwn Calles 23 & 25) and Hotel Sevilla (p313).

MONEY

The quickest and most hassle-free places to exchange money are in Cadecas. There are dozens of them across Havana and they usually have much longer opening hours and quicker service than banks.

Banco Metropolitano Centro Habana (Av de Italia No 452, cnr San Martín; ⏰8:30am-7:30pm Mon-Sat), Vedado (☎7-832-2006; cnr Calles 23 & J; ⏰8:30am-7:30pm Mon-Sat), Vedado (cnr Línea & Calle M; ⏰8:30am-3:30pm Mon-Fri), Vedado (Línea, btwn Paseo & Calle A; ⏰8:30am-3:30pm Mon-Fri), Habana Vieja (cnr Cuba & O'Reilly; ⏰9am-3pm Mon-Fri)

Cadeca Centro Habana (Neptuno, btwn Industria & Consulado; ⏰8:30am-4pm Mon-Sat, to 11:30am Sun), Habana Vieja (cnr Oficios & Lamparilla; ⏰8:30am-8pm Mon-Sat, 9am-6pm Sun), Havana Vieja (Obispo No 257, btwn Cuba & Aguiar; ⏰8am-midnight), Vedado (cnr Calles 23 & J; ⏰8:30am-4pm Mon-Fri, to 11:30am Sat), Vedado (Hotel Meliá Cohiba, Paseo, btwn Calles 1 & 3; ⏰8am-11pm), Vedado (Mercado Agropecuario, cnr Calles 19 & A; ⏰8:30am-4pm Tue-Sat, to 11:30am Sun)

There are also banks and ATMs in the **Miramar Trade Center** (Av 3, btwn Calles 76 & 80, Miramar; ⏰hours vary).

TOURIST INFORMATION

Infotur offices in Havana:

Airport (☎7-642-6101; Terminal 3, Aeropuerto Internacional José Martí; ⏰24hr)

Habana Vieja (Map p302; ☎7-866-4153; Obispo No 524, btwn Bernaza & Villegas; ⏰9:30am-5:30pm)

Vedado (Map p316; Calle L, btwn Calles 23 & 25; ⏰9:30am-noon & 12:30-5pm)

ℹ Getting There & Away

AIR

Aeropuerto Internacional José Martí (p356) is at Rancho Boyeros, 25km southwest of Havana via Av de la Independencia. There are five terminals. Terminal 1, on the southeastern side of the runway, handles only domestic flights. Terminal 2 is 3km away via Av de la Independencia and receives flights and charters from the US. All other international flights use Terminal 3, a well-ordered, modern facility at Wajay, 2.5km west of Terminal 2. Charter flights, mainly to Cuban destinations, use the Caribbean Terminal (also known as Terminal 5) at the northwestern end of the runway, 2.5km west of Terminal 3. Terminal 4 handles freight. Check carefully which terminal you'll be using.

Aerogaviota (☎7-203-0668; www.aerogaviota.com) is a Cuban airline run by the government tourist agency that handles mainly domestic flights to places such as Holguín and Cayo Coco.

Most airlines, including national carrier Cubana de Aviación (p356), have offices in the **Airline**

Building (Calle 23 No 64) in Havana's Vedado district.

BUS

Víazul (www.viazul.com) covers most destinations of interest to travelers, in safe, air-conditioned coaches. Most buses are direct, except those to Guantánamo, Baracoa, Remedios and Cayo Santa María. Buses get busy, particularly in peak season (November through March), so it's wise to book up to a week ahead. You can also book online. Full schedules are available on the website. Some casa particular owners may offer help with prearranging bus tickets.

You board all Víazul buses at the **Terminal de Ómnibus** (Map p316; ☎7-878-1841; www.viazul.com; cnr Av de la Independencia & Calle 19 de Mayo), just north of the Plaza de la Revolución. This is where you'll also have to come to buy tickets. Taxis charge around CUC$5 for the ride from central Havana, or it's walkable if you have a light pack.

A newer alternative to the increasingly crowded Víazul buses is Conectando, run by **Cubanacán** (☎7-537-4090; www.cubanacan.cu), which offers six itineraries linking Havana with Viñales, Trinidad, Varadero and Santiago de Cuba. The smaller buses, which run daily, pick up from various hotels and charge similar prices to Víazul's. Tickets can be reserved via Infotur or any Cubanacán hotel rep.

VÍAZUL DEPARTURES FROM HAVANA

Check the most up-to-date departure times at www.viazul.com.

Destination	Cost (CUC$)	Duration (hr)	Frequency (daily)
Bayamo	44	13	3
Camagüey	33	9	5
Ciego de Ávila	27	7	4
Cienfuegos	20	4½	2
Holguín	44	12	3
Las Tunas	39	11½	5
Matanzas	7	2	4
Pinar del Río	11	3	3
Sancti Spíritus	23	5¾	3
Santa Clara	18	3¾	5
Santiago de Cuba	51	15	3
Trinidad	25	5-6	2
Varadero	10	3	4
Viñales	12	4	3

TAXI

Full buses are the norm in Cuba these days as they become more utilized by Cubans and Cuban-Americans, as well as tourists. To counter the shortfall, many travelers are turning to *colectivos* (shared taxis). Taxis charge approximately CUC$0.50 to CUC$0.60 per kilometer. This translates to around CUC$90 to Varadero, CUC$90 to Viñales, CUC$150 to Santa Clara, CUC$120 to Cienfuegos and CUC$160 to Trinidad. A *colectivo* can take up to four people, meaning you can share the cost. *Colectivos* can usually be organized through your casa particular, at an Infotur office or by negotiating at a standard pickup point. It's also usually pretty easy to arrange a *colectivo* at the main bus terminal.

TRAIN

Trains to most parts of Cuba depart from **La Coubre station** (Túnel de la Habana); at time of writing the **Estación Central de Ferrocarriles** (Central Train Station; ☎7-862-1920, 7-861-8540; cnr Av de Bélgica & Arsenal) was being refurbished. La Coubre is on the southwestern side of Habana Vieja; from the main station, head down Av de Bélgica toward the harbor and turn right. The ticket office is located 100m down the road on the right-hand side. If it's closed, try the Lista de Espera office adjacent, which sells tickets for trains leaving immediately. Kids under 12 travel half-price.

Cuba's railway system got a much-needed upgrade in 2019 and now utilizes modern carriages imported from China with air-con and refreshment facilities. Four scheduled trains depart from Havana several times a day. There are two classes and a limited number of seats for foreigners in each carriage. Reservations are accepted up to 30 days ahead.

Tren 1 Runs every other day between Havana and Santiago de Cuba (CUC$70, 15 hours).

Tren 3 Runs every third day to Guantánamo (CUC$75, 17 hours).

Tren 5 Runs every third day to Holguín (CUC$60, 14 hours).

Tren 7 Runs every third day to Bayamo (CUC$60, 15 hours) and Manzanillo (CUC$65, 17¼ hours).

ℹ Getting Around

BUS

The handy hop-on, hop-off **Habana Bus Tour** (Map p306) runs on two main routes: T1 and T3. The main stop is in Parque Central opposite the Hotel Inglaterra. This is the pickup point for bus T1, which runs from Habana Vieja via Centro Habana, the Malecón, Calle 23 and Plaza de la Revolución to La Cecilia at the western end of Playa; and bus T3, which runs from Centro Habana to Playas del Este (via Parque Histórico Militar Morro-Cabaña).

Bus T1 is an open-top double-decker. Bus T3 is an enclosed single-decker. All-day tickets for T1/T3 are CUC$10/5. Services run from 9am to 6pm, and routes and times are clearly marked on all bus stops. Beware: these bus routes and times have been known to change. Check the latest route maps at the bus stop in Parque Central.

Bus T2 is a shuttle that runs from La Cecilia to Marina Hemingway four times a day. It costs CUC$1 one way.

Havana's metro bus service calls on a relatively modern fleet of Chinese-made 'bendy' buses and is far less dilapidated than it used to be. These buses run regularly along 17 routes, connecting most parts of the city with the suburbs. Fares are 40 centavos (five centavos if you're using convertibles), which you deposit into a small slot in front of the driver when you enter. Cuban buses are crowded and little used by tourists. Guard your valuables closely.

TAXI

Taxis hang around outside all the major tourist hotels, outside the two main bus stations and at various city-center nexus points such as Parque Central and Parque de la Fraternidad. You're never far from a taxi in Havana.

The most common taxis are the yellow cabs of **Cubataxi** (☎7-796-6666), which are generally modern, air-conditioned and fitted with meters – but they also cost more.

Cheaper are the legal private taxis that have become more common since laws were loosened in the early 2010s. These cars are often yellow-and-black Ladas from the 1980s. You've got more chance haggling here, but agree on the fare before getting into the car.

WESTERN CUBA

Viñales

POP 29,000

When Pinar del Río's greenery starts to erupt into craggy *mogotes* (limestone monoliths) and you spy a cigar-puffing local driving his oxen and plough through a rust-colored tobacco field, you know you've arrived in Viñales. Despite its long-standing love affair with tourism, this slow, relaxed, wonderfully traditional settlement is a place that steadfastly refuses to put on a show. What you see here is what you get – a delightful rustic village where front doors are left wide open, everyone knows everyone else and a night out on the tiles involves sitting on a *sillón* (rocking chair) on a rustic porch analyzing the Milky Way.

People don't come to Viñales for the music or the mojitos, they come to dip indulgently into the natural world, hiking, horseback riding, or cycling through some of the most wonderful landscapes in Cuba. Join them.

Sleeping

★Casa Daniela CASA PARTICULAR $

(☎48-69-55-01; casadaniela@nauta.cu; Carretera a Pinar del Río; r CUC$25-30; P ❄ 📶 🏊) Run by a former doctor and nurse, who must have had formidable bedside manners if their hospitality in this surgically clean place is anything to judge by. The sunny yellow Daniela has expanded into a sizable residence without losing its local intimacy. There are six rooms, a super pool, a giant roof terrace and a shady yard.

Casa Papo y Niulvys CASA PARTICULAR $

(☎48-69-67-14; papoyniulvys@gmail.com; Rafael Trejo No 18a; r CUC$30-35; P ❄ 📶) One of the few houses in Viñales with a front garden, this place gives you room to swing on a hammock as well as rock on a rocking chair on the front porch. Rooms are small but recently decorated in a modern style. It's a dreamily tranquil spot with a wraparound porch. Book well ahead – it gets busy.

Villa El Cafetal CASA PARTICULAR $

(☎5-331-1752, 48-69-50-37; edgar21@nauta.cu; Adela Azcuy Final; r CUC$25; P ❄ 📶) The son of the owners of this foliage-draped house on the edge of town is an expert on climbing, meaning there's a shed stacked with equipment – and the best climbs in Viñales are on their doorstep. Ensconced in a resplendent garden that cultivates its own coffee (served at breakfast), you can practically taste the mountain air as you swing on the hammock.

Villa Los Reyes CASA PARTICULAR $

(☎48-79-33-17; http://villalosreyes.com; Salvador Cisneros No 206c; s/d/tr CUC$25/30/35; P ❄ @ 📶) Yoan Reyes has put huge efforts into shaping his fabulous house, which now has five modern bedrooms (some with king-sized beds), a round pool, a well-tended garden (plus vegetable patch) and a bridge-like structure linking two separate roof terraces. You're on the edge of the countryside here and the family can organize all number of excursions into the green domain.

Hotel La Ermita HOTEL $$

(☎48-79-64-11; Carretera de La Ermita Km 1.5; s/d incl breakfast CUC$60/96; P ❄ 🏊) La Ermita takes Viñales' top hotel honors for architecture, interior furnishings and all-round service. The views over town rooftops and haystack hills is equally award-worthy. The upper-floor rooms housed in handsome two-story colonial edifices overlook the misty valley. Extracurricular attractions include an excellent pool, tennis courts, a shop, horseback riding and massage.

★Hotel Los Jazmines HOTEL **$$$**
(☎48-79-64-11; Carretera a Pinar del Río; s/d incl breakfast CUC$88/138; P❄≋) Prepare yourself! The vista from this pastel-pink colonial-style hotel is one of the best in Cuba. Open the shutters of your classic valley-facing room and drink in the shimmering sight of magnificent *mogotes* (limestone monoliths), red oxen-plowed fields and palm-frond-covered tobacco-drying houses. Although the facilities are long overdue a refurbishment, the location is unrivaled and there's a gloriously inviting swimming pool.

Eating

★Tres Jotas TAPAS **$$**
(☎5-331-1658; Salvador Cisneros No 45; tapas CUC$2-6; ⏰8am-2am) One of the best restaurants in Cuba outside Havana, Tres Jotas is Viñales' original tapas bar that has since been copied by all and sundry. Its inviting polished-wood interior is the perfect place to unwind after a day in the countryside, with classy cocktails, taste-exploding tapas, and boards piled high with cured ham and manchego cheese.

★El Olivo MEDITERRANEAN **$$**
(www.olivovinalescuba.com; Salvador Cisneros No 89; pasta CUC$5-10; ⏰noon-11pm; 🖉) 🍃 Viñales' most popular restaurant, as the happy buzz of conversation will testify, serves tremendous lasagna and pasta dishes, backed up by other Med classics such as duck *à l'orange*. The salads topped with goat's cheese and dried fruits are spectacular, while the joker in the pack is the rabbit dressed with herbs in a dark chocolate sauce.

The secret? Olivo is a genuine farm-to-table affair. Most of what you eat here comes from its own **farm** (☎48-69-66-54; www.olivovinalescuba.com; Carretera al Cementerio, Km 2; ⏰10am-noon) 🍃 FREE, 3km up the road. If you liked what you ate, go and see where it came from.

Cubar INTERNATIONAL **$$**
(☎5-364-2791; Salvador Cisneros No 55; mains CUC$7-22; ⏰9am-midnight, to 2am Fri & Sat) A sophisticated new entry into Viñales' overcrowded dining scene, Cubar hits all the right notes with a smart dark-wood interior advertising the joys of Cuban rum and a menu that touts Cuban food colored with Italian and Spanish inflections. Expect fine tastes and creative presentation in dishes such as rabbit cacciatore, grilled octopus and a zesty lobster spaghetti.

Balcón del Valle CUBAN **$$**
(Carretera a Pinar del Río; mains CUC$8; ⏰noon-midnight) With three deftly constructed wooden decks overhanging a panorama of tobacco fields, drying houses and craggy *mogotes* (limestone monoliths), 'Balcony of the Valley' has food that stands up to its sensational views. The unwritten menu includes half a dozen mains, all prepared country-style with copious trimmings. It's 3km outside Viñales toward Hotel Los Jazmines.

Information

Banks in Viñales have long queues. Arrive early or consider changing money in Pinar del Río.

Banco de Crédito y Comercio (Salvador Cisneros No 58; ⏰8am-noon & 1:30-3pm Mon-Fri, 8am-11am Sat) Has two ATMs.

Cadeca (cnr Salvador Cisneros & Adela Azcuy; ⏰8:30am-4pm Mon-Sat) Quickest service.

Infotur (Salvador Cisneros No 63b; ⏰9am-6pm)

Most casas particulares (private homestays) have an abundance of information on the area and can organize excursions at short notice.

Getting There & Away

The well-ordered **Víazul ticket office** (Salvador Cisneros No 63a; ⏰8am-noon & 1-3pm) is opposite the main square in the same building as Cubataxi. Two daily Víazul buses (www.viazul.com) depart from here for Havana (CUC$12, 3¼ hours). There's also one daily bus to Cienfuegos (CUC$32, eight hours) and Trinidad (CUC$37, 9½ hours), usually leaving early in the morning. All buses stop at Pinar del Río (CUC$6, 30 minutes).

Conectando buses run by **Cubanacán** (☎48-79-63-93; Salvador Cisneros No 63c; ⏰9am-7pm Mon-Sat), and departing from outside the Cubanacán office, have daily transfers to Havana, Trinidad and Cienfuegos. Book a day ahead. Prices are the same as Víazul.

Getting Around

The Viñales Bus Tour is a hop-on/hop-off minibus that runs nine times a day between the valley's spread-out sites. Starting and finishing in the town plaza, the whole circuit takes 65 minutes, with the first bus leaving at 9am and the last at 4:50pm. There are 18 stops along the route, which runs from Hotel Los Jazmines to Hotel Rancho San Vicente, and all are clearly marked with route maps and timetables. All-day tickets cost CUC$5 and can be purchased on the bus.

Valle de Viñales

Embellished by soaring pine trees and bulbous limestone cliffs that teeter like top-heavy haystacks above placid tobacco plantations, Parque Nacional Viñales is one of Cuba's most magnificent natural settings. Wedged spectacularly into the Sierra de los Órganos mountain range, this 11km-by-5km valley was recognized as a national monument in 1979, with Unesco World Heritage status following in 1999 for its dramatic steep-sided limestone outcrops (known as *mogotes*), coupled with the vernacular architecture of its traditional farms and villages.

Viñales offers opportunities for fine hiking, rock climbing and horseback trekking. On the accommodations front, it advertises first-class hotels and some of the best casas particulares in Cuba. Despite drawing in day-trippers by the busload, the area's well-protected and spread-out natural attractions have somehow managed to escape the frenzied tourist circus of other less well-managed places, while the atmosphere in and around the town remains refreshingly hassle-free.

Sights

Gran Caverna de Santo Tomás CAVE
(CUC$15; ⌚9am-3pm) Welcome to Cuba's largest cave system and the second largest on the American continent. There are over 46km of galleries on eight levels, with a 1km section accessible to visitors. There's no artificial lighting, but headlamps are provided for the 90-minute guided tour. Highlights include bats, stalagmites and stalactites, underground pools, interesting rock formations and a replica of an ancient indigenous mural.

Activities

Cycling

Despite the sometimes hilly terrain, Viñales is one of the best places in Cuba to cycle (most roads follow the valleys and are relatively flat). Traffic on the roads is still light, and the scenery is a conveyor belt of natural beauty. Many casas particulares now offer cheap bike rentals (around CUC$10 per day). Some also offer bike tours. Ask around.

Hiking

The Parque Nacional Viñales offers around 15 official hiking routes and maps are displayed at the visitor center. It is best to go with a guide as signposting is terrible. Prices for guides are around CUC$10 per person but depend on distance and group size.

WORTH A TRIP

VARADERO

Varadero, located on the sinuous 20km-long Hicacos Peninsula, stands at the vanguard of Cuba's most important industry – tourism. As the largest resort in the Caribbean, it guards a huge, unsubtle and constantly evolving stash of hotels (over 60), shops, water activities and poolside entertainment; though its trump card is its beach, an uninterrupted 21km stretch of blond sand that is undoubtedly one of the Caribbean's finest. While these large, tourist-friendly megaresorts may be essential to the national economy, they offer little in the way of unique Cuban experiences.

Most Varadero tourists buy their vacation packages overseas and are content to enjoy a week or two of beach sloth without ever leaving their resort. For independent travelers not over-enamored with manufactured 'paradises,' Varadero has an alternative: a small Cuban town at its southwestern entrance complete with casas particulares (rooms in private homes), private restaurants and free access to that magnificent beach.

Rather than blowing hundreds of dollars on an all-inclusive, you can pay CUC$45 a night to stay at **Beny's House** (☎45-61-17-00; www.benyhouse.com; Calle 55, btwn Avs 1 & 2; r incl breakfast CUC$45; P ❄) or several other similarly priced private accommodations all within spitting distance of the beach and well-appointed private restaurants (as opposed to state-run restaurants) such as **Varadero 60** (☎45-61-39-86; cnr Calle 60 & Av 3; mains CUC$10-20; ⌚noon-midnight).

There are five daily Víazul buses between Varadero and Havana (CUC$10) and also daily connections to Santa Clara, Viñales, Trinidad and Santiago de Cuba.

You can arrange hikes at the park's visitor center or at the **Museo Municipal** (Salvador Cisneros No 115; CUC$1; ⏲8am-5pm, to 4pm Sun) in Viñales. Guided hikes leave from the museum twice a day at 8:45am and 2:30pm.

Aside from the park guides, almost every casa particular in Viñales will be able to hook you up with a private guide who can pretty much custom-build any trip you want. Eternally popular is the loop around the **Valle de Palmarito**, which starts and ends in the village and takes in a coffee plantation, tobacco house and the Cueva de Palmarito where swimming by torchlight is possible.

Other favorites are the hikes to Los Aquáticos and the Valle del Silencio.

Zip-lining

Canopy Tour ADVENTURE SPORTS
(☎5-398-8975; Carretera al Moncada, Km 6; per person CUC$8; ⏲9am-5pm) Around 6km west of town, you'll encounter one of only three canopy tours in Cuba, a fairly modest set of lines (total distance 1000m, maximum height 35m), but fun all the same and highly economical to boot. Book beforehand at the Cubanacán (p329) office in town, or just turn up and wait for the next departure.

Information

The park is administered through the highly informative **Parque Nacional Viñales Visitors Center** (☎48-79-61-44; Carretera a Pinar del Río Km 22; ⏲8am-6pm), located 3km south of the town of Viñales. Inside, colorful displays (in Spanish and English) map out the park's main features. Hiking information and guides are also on hand.

Getting Around

Bike (Salvador Cisneros No 140; bike hire per hour/day CUC$1/10), car, moped or the hop-on/hop-off bus tour departing Viñales town plaza nine times daily – take your pick.

CENTRAL CUBA

Santa Clara

POP 216,000

Sorry Havana. Santa Clara is Cuba's most revolutionary city – and not just because of its historical obsession with Argentine doctor turned *guerrillero* (guerrilla) Che Guevara. Smack bang in the geographic center of Cuba, this is a city of new trends and insatiable creativity, where an edgy youth culture has been testing the boundaries of Cuba's censorship police for years. Unique Santa Clara offerings include Cuba's only official drag show, a graphic artists' collective that produces satirical political cartoons, and the country's best rock festival: Ciudad Metal. The city's fiery personality has been shaped over time by the presence of the nation's most prestigious university outside Havana, and a long association with Che Guevara, whose liberation of Santa Clara in December 1958 marked the end of the Batista regime. Little cultural revolutions have been erupting here ever since.

Sights

★Conjunto Escultórico Comandante Ernesto Che Guevara MAUSOLEUM, MUSEUM
(Plaza de la Revolución; ⏲9:30am-4pm Tue-Sun) FREE The end point of many a Che pilgrimage, this monument, mausoleum and museum complex is 2km west of Parque Vidal (via Rafael Tristá on Av de los Desfiles), near the Víazul bus station. Even if you don't care for the Argentine guerrilla for whom many reserve an almost religious reverence, there's poignancy in the vast square that spans both sides of a wide avenue, guarded by a bronze statue of El Che atop a 16m-high pedestal.

The statue was erected in 1987 to mark the 20th anniversary of Guevara's murder in Bolivia, and can be viewed any time. Accessed from behind the statue, the respectful **mausoleum** contains 38 stone-carved niches dedicated to the other guerrillas killed in the failed Bolivian revolution. In 1997 the remains of 17 of them, including Guevara, were recovered from a secret mass grave in Bolivia and reburied in this memorial. Fidel Castro lit the eternal flame on October 17, 1997. The adjacent **museum** houses the details and ephemera of Che's life and death.

The best way to get to the monument is a 15-minute walk, or by hopping on a horse carriage on Calle Marta Abreu outside the cathedral for a couple of Cuban pesos.

Parque Vidal SQUARE
A veritable alfresco theater named for Colonel Leoncio Vidal y Caro, who was killed here on March 23, 1896, Parque Vidal was encircled by twin sidewalks during the colonial era, with a fence separating blacks and whites. Scars of more recent division are evident on the facade of mint-green **Hotel Santa Clara Libre** on the park's west side:

it's pockmarked by bullet holes from the 1958 battle for the city between Guevara and Batista's government troops.

Fábrica de Tabacos Constantino Pérez Carrodegua FACTORY
(Maceo No 181, btwn Julio Jover & Berenguer; CUC$4; ⌚9-11am & 1-3pm Mon-Fri) Santa Clara's tobacco factory, one of Cuba's best, makes a quality range of Montecristos, Partagás and Romeo y Julieta cigars. Tours here are lo-fi compared to those in Havana, and so the experience is a lot more interesting and less rushed. Buy tickets in advance at the Cubatur office. Beware, opening times can be erratic.

Museo de Artes Decorativas MUSEUM
(Parque Vidal No 27; CUC$2; ⌚9am-5pm Mon & Wed-Fri, 3-6pm Sat & Sun) Something of a sleeping beauty on Parque Vidal, this 18th-century mansion turned museum is packed with period furniture from a whole gamut of styles that seem to ape Cuba's architectural heritage. Look for baroque desks, art nouveau mirrors, art deco furniture and Veláquez' epic *Rendición de Brega* (Surrender of Brega), reproduced on a china plate. Live chamber music adds to the romanticism in the evenings.

Sitio-Museo Acción Contra El Tren Blindado MUSEUM
(CUC$1; ⌚8:30am-5pm Tue-Sat, 9am-1pm Sun) History was made at the site of this small **boxcar museum** on December 29, 1958, when Ernesto 'Che' Guevara and a band of 18 rifle-wielding revolutionaries barely out of their teens derailed an armored train using a borrowed bulldozer and homemade Molotov cocktails.

Sleeping

★Hostal Florida Terrace CASA PARTICULAR $
(☎42-22-15-80; www.hostalfloridacenter.com; Maestra Nicolasa No 59, btwn Maceo & Colón; r CUC$30-35; P❄📶) This finely decorated hotel-like place is affiliated with Restaurant Florida Center across the road and has more floors (four) than most private homestays have rooms. The smart colonial decor has art deco echoes, offering plenty to admire, and the eight rooms with antique beds are top drawer. It has an upstairs bar and *mirador* (lookout) with some of Santa Clara's best views.

★Hostal Familia Sarmiento CASA PARTICULAR $
(☎42-20-35-10; www.santaclarahostel.com; Lorda No 56, btwn Martí & Independencia; r CUC$25-35; ❄📶) The Sarmiento offers three well-appointed rooms in an attractive Cuban home in the center of town. Recently renovated bedrooms feature rain showers, graded light settings and Nespresso coffee machines. A new wing with four additional rooms was being built in the house opposite at last visit.

Casa Mercy 1938 CASA PARTICULAR $
(☎42-21-69-41; casamercy@gmail.com; Independencia No 253, btwn Estévez & Gutiérrez; r CUC$30-35; ❄📶) The name might hark back to another age, but this wonderful house has been restored to include modern comforts. The details are spectacular: an art deco–neocolonial hybrid anchored by a Seville-style fountain that sets off the central patio. The house is diligently staffed by friendly multilingual owners and comes with two large rooms and plenty of communal space – including that patio.

La Casona Jover CASA PARTICULAR $
(☎42-20-44-58; almiqui2009@yahoo.es; Colón No 167, btwn 9 de Abril & Serafín García; r CUC$30-35; ❄) The Jover is classic Santa Clara, hiding a minipalace behind a prosaic facade. Five large colonial rooms set well back from the road line a terrace stuffed with a profusion of plants and a tempting plunge pool. The Jover is also known for its restaurant, though it was only open for guests at last visit.

Authentica Pérgola CASA PARTICULAR $
(☎42-20-86-86; carmen64@yahoo.es; Luis Estévez No 61, btwn Independencia & Martí; r CUC$30; ❄📶) The Pérgola is set around an Alhambra-esque patio draped in greenery and crowned by a fountain, from where several large rooms lead off. Pretty much everything here is antique, including in the bedrooms. It's better than the town museum. There's a beautiful roof-terrace restaurant open to all called La Aldaba.

Hotel Central BOUTIQUE HOTEL $$
(☎42-20-15-85; www.cubanacan.cu; Parque Vidal; s/d incl breakfast CUC$56/102; ❄@📶) Of the dozen or so new state-run boutique hotels that have opened over the last couple of years, this is one of the best, courtesy of its Parque Vidal location, colonial furnishings and attractive streetside bar that sits opposite Santa Clara's energetic square.

Eating

Bodeguita del Medio CUBAN $

(☎42-21-54-34; Vidal No 1, btwn Colón & Maceo; mains CUC$3-7; ⊙11am-11pm; ❄) A love child of Havana's original **Bodeguita** (Map p302; Empedrado No 207; ⊙11am-midnight), this carefully branded 'dive' bar has a couple of advantages over its big-city mentor: 1) Hemingway never came here, meaning the signature mojitos only cost CUC$2; and 2) it's free of space-hogging tour groups.

However, despite the graffiti-covered streetside bar where *son*-playing musical trios roam, we're recommending this place for its food served in an air-conditioned restaurant out back. Waited on by keen young guys dressed in *guayabera* shirts, you'll be served generous meals of *comida criolla* (Creole food) that are supplemented with *mucho* bread, rice, salad and banana chips. The deep, rich *picadillo* (spicy minced beef) is highly recommended.

★ **Restaurant Florida Center** CUBAN, FUSION $$

(☎42-20-81-61; Maestra Nicolasa No 56, btwn Colón & Maceo; mains CUC$10-15; ⊙6:30-9:30pm) The Florida has been Santa Clara's best restaurant for at least a decade. The food is as good as the experience. Diners eat in a colonial, plant-festooned, candlelit courtyard full of interesting antiques. Ever-present owner Ángel is the perfect host, advising on the profusion of dishes in French, English, Italian and Spanish. The menu is simple but classic Cuban.

La Aldaba CUBAN $$

(☎42-20-86-86; Luis Estévez No 61, btwn Independencia & Martí; mains CUC$12-20; ⊙11:30am-11pm) The rooftop restaurant in the Authentica Pérgola casa particular is a great place to repose, preferably in the evening, amid potted ferns and in the company of chefs who know how to prepare good Cuban dishes with a few zings (eg curried chicken). All main dishes come with bread, soup, side trimmings and a dessert included.

Drinking & Nightlife

★ **La Marquesina** BAR

(Parque Vidal, btwn Máximo Gómez & Lorda; ⊙9am-1am) You can chinwag and neck a cold bottled beer with locals of all types in this legendary dive bar under the porches of the equally legendary Teatro la Caridad on the corner of Parque Vidal. The clientele is a potpourri of Santa Clara life – students, cigar-factory workers, off-duty taxi drivers and the odd bewildered tourist. Live music (and dancing) erupts regularly.

Cafe-Museo Revolución CAFE

(Independencia No 313; ⊙9am-11pm; 📶) You say you want a revolution... Well, Santa Clara's a good place to start. It's already had one, successfully ignited by Che Guevara in 1958. This new cafe-cum-museum pays homage to Santa Clara's (and Cuba's) revolutionary past with photos, old uniforms and other ephemera lovingly curated by the Spanish owner. The house coffee, served with syrup, meringue, milk and a shot of rum, is pretty revolutionary too.

Entertainment

★ **Club Mejunje** LIVE MUSIC

(Marta Abreu No 107; ⊙4pm-1am Tue-Sun; 👪) Urban graffiti, children's theater, LGBTQ-friendly performances, old crooners belting out *boleros*, tourists dancing salsa. You've heard about 'something for everyone,' but this is ridiculous. Welcome to Club Mejunje, set in the ruins of an old roofless building given over to sprouting greenery. It's a local – nay, national – institution, famous for many things, not least Cuba's oldest official drag show (every Saturday night).

Information

MONEY

Banco Popular de Ahorro (cnr Cuba & Maestra Nicolasa; ⊙8am-3pm Mon-Fri, to 11am Sat) Has an ATM.

Cadeca (cnr Rafael Tristá & Cuba; ⊙8:30am-7pm Mon-Sat, 9am-6pm Sun) On the corner of the main square, this is the best place to change money. Long opening hours.

TOURIST INFORMATION

Cubanacán (☎42-20-51-89; Colón, cnr Maestra Nicolasa; ⊙8am-8pm Mon-Sat) Also has a desk in Hotel Central.

Cubatur (☎42-20-89-80; Marta Abreu No 10, btwn Máximo Gómez & Villuendas; ⊙9am-noon & 1-8pm) Book tobacco-factory tours here.

Infotur (☎42-20-13-52; Cuba No 68, btwn Machado & Maestra Nicolasa; ⊙8:30am-5pm Mon-Sat) Handy maps and brochures in multiple languages.

Getting There & Away

BUS

The **Terminal de Ómnibus Nacionales** (☎42-20-34-70; Carretera Central, cnr Oquendo), which is also the bus station for Víazul (www.

viazul.com), is 2.5km west of the center, out on the Carretera Central toward Matanzas, 500m north of the Che monument. Tickets for air-con Víazul buses are sold at a special 'foreigners' ticket window at the station entrance.

Destination	Cost (CUC$)	Duration (hr)	Frequency (per day)
Cayo Santa María	13	2½	1
Havana	18	4	3
Santiago de Cuba	33	12½	4
Trinidad	8	3½	2
Varadero	11	3¼	2

TRAIN

The **train station** (Parque de los Mártires) is straight up Luis Estévez from Parque Vidal on the north side of town.

Santa Clara is on Cuba's main west–east railway line. Eight of Cuba's new trains service the town. Check at the station beforehand to find out exactly which days the trains are running.

Trinidad

☎41 / POP 76,885

Trinidad is one of a kind, a perfectly preserved Spanish-colonial settlement where the clocks stopped in 1850 and – apart from a zombie invasion of tourists – have yet to restart. Huge sugar fortunes amassed in the nearby Valle de los Ingenios during the early 19th century created the illustrious colonial-style mansions bedecked with Italian frescoes, Wedgwood china and French chandeliers.

Declared a World Heritage site by Unesco in 1988, Cuba's oldest and most enchanting 'outdoor museum' attracts busloads of visitors. Yet the cobblestone streets, replete with leather-faced *guajiros* (country folk), snorting donkeys and melodic troubadours, retain a quiet air. Come nightfall, the live-music scene is particularly good.

Trinidad is also surrounded by sparkling natural attractions. Twelve kilometers south lies platinum-blond Playa Ancón, the best beach of Cuba's southern coast. Looming 18km to the north, the purple-hued shadows of the Sierra del Escambray (Escambray Mountains) offer a lush adventure playground with hiking trails and waterfalls.

Sights

In Trinidad, all roads lead to **Plaza Mayor**, the town's remarkably peaceful main square, located at the heart of the *casco histórico* (old town) and ringed by a quartet of impressive buildings.

★Museo Histórico Municipal MUSEUM
(☎4199-4460; Simón Bolívar No 423; CUC$2; ⌚9am-5pm Sat-Thu) Just off Plaza Mayor, this grandiose mansion, Trinidad's main museum, belonged to the Borrell family from 1827 to 1830. Later it passed to a German planter named Kanter, or Cantero, for whom it's now named. The run-down exhibits could use a full makeover, but the city panoramas from the tower, reached by rickety stairs, is worth the price of admission alone.

Iglesia Parroquial de la Santísima Trinidad CHURCH
(⌚11am-12:30pm Mon-Sat) Despite its unremarkable facade, this church on the northeastern side of Plaza Mayor graces countless Trinidad postcards. Rebuilt in 1892 on the site of a church destroyed in a storm, it mixes 20th-century touch-ups with artifacts dating to the 18th century, such as the venerated Christ of the True Cross (1713), second altar from the front to the left.

Activities

★Centro Ecuestre Diana HORSEBACK RIDING
(Independencia No 39, btwn Girón & Benítez; riding CUC$26) Among the barrage of offers you'll hear in Trinidad are those for horseback rides. Booking on the street is discouraged, as you won't know the condition of the (sometimes neglected or mistreated) horses. Rest assured that with this outfit, you will enjoy a safe ride on a healthy, mild-mannered and well-cared-for horse. Book a day before at the address listed; rides depart at 9am.

Tours

Trinidad Travels TOURS
(☎5-282-3726; www.trinidadtravels.com; Antonio Maceo No 613a) One of the best private guides is English- and Italian-speaking Reinier at Trinidad Travels. He leads all kinds of excursions, including hiking in the Sierra del Escambray and horseback riding in the nearby countryside, as well as Spanish lessons. This is a safe, reputable outfit with healthy horses. He's based at **Casa de Victor** (☎4199-6444; hostalsandra@yahoo.es; Antonio Maceo No 613a; r CUC$25; ❄).

Free Walking Tour WALKING
(Parque San Francisco de Asís; ⌚10am & 4pm) A cool bunch of multilingual Cubans lead free

WORTH A TRIP

CIENFUEGOS

Cienfuegos has good pedigree. Immortalized in a song by local musical legend Benny Moré as the city he liked the best, the so-called 'Pearl of the South' has long seduced travelers from Cuba and beyond with its enlightened French airs and dreamy waterside setting. If Cuba has a Paris, this is most definitely it.

Arranged around the country's most spectacular natural bay, Cienfuegos is a nautical city founded in 1819 by French émigrés, whose homogeneous grid of elegant neoclassical architecture earned it a Unesco World Heritage site listing in 2005. Geographically, the city is split into two distinct parts: the colonnaded central zone with its stately 'Prado' boulevard and salubrious main square, and Punta Gorda, a thin knife of land slicing into the bay crowned with a clutch of outrageously eclectic palaces built by the moneyed classes in the 1920s.

Surrounding the main square, you'll find the whimsical **Teatro Tomás Terry** (☎43-55-17-72, 43-51-33-61; Av 56 No 270, btwn Calles 27 & 29; tours CUC$2; ⏲9am-6pm) with its gold-leafed mosaics and the **Palacio Ferrer** (Calle 25 No 5401; CUC$3; ⏲10am-5:30pm Tue-Sat) FREE, recently repurposed as an arts museum.

For a dash of luxury, spend the night at the **Palacio Barón Balbin** (☎43-59-60-76; www.hotelpalaciobaronbalbin.com; Av 52 No 2706, btwn Calles 27 & 29; r CUC$60-80; ❄📶) and dine at French-tinged **Doña Nora** (☎43-52-33-31; Calle 37, btwn Avs 42 & 44; mains CUC$6-10; ⏲noon-11pm).

Cienfuegos is five hours from Havana by bus (CUC$20) or less than three hours by car.

two-hour walking tours of Trinidad, daily at 10am and 4pm. This is an excellent way to familiarize yourself with the city, giving insight into historical background and local tips. Meet up at Parque San Francisco de Asís, the little plaza across from the **Museo Nacional de la Lucha Contra Bandidos** (☎4199-4121; Echerri No 59; CUC$1; ⏲9am-5pm Tue-Sun). Tip your guide!

Sleeping

Casa Muñoz – Julio & Rosa CASA PARTICULAR $
(☎4199-3673; www.trinidadphoto.com; José Martí No 401, cnr Escobar; d/tr/apt CUC$40/45/50; P❄📶) A stunning colonial home with courteous, English-speaking assistance. There are three huge rooms and a two-level apartment. Book early as it's insanely popular with licensed US people-to-people groups. Julio is an accomplished photographer offering courses and tours (CUC$25) on documentary photography, religion and life in Cuba's new economic reality.

Casa Particular El Arcangel CASA PARTICULAR $
(☎5-277-0439, 5-299-2187; arcangelmigueltvc@gmail.com; Amargura No 11; r CUC$35) The attractive, shaded porch beckons from the cobbled street, and it only gets better from there: terra-cotta floors, white stucco walls, wood-beamed ceilings and the most inclusive, welcoming atmosphere of a true home. Strongly evocative of Mexico, this refuge contains two spotless guest rooms complemented by a spiral staircase to an inviting rooftop oasis with nooks for lounging.

Hostal José & Fatima CASA PARTICULAR $
(☎4199-6682; hostaljoseyfatima@gmail.com; Zerquera No 159, btwn Frank País & Pettersen; r CUC$35; ❄📶) Highly popular casa with five rooms and colonial trimmings, including a terrace. The helpful hosts can hook you up with many local activities. There's also an adorable dachshund keen on dog lovers.

★**Casa El Suizo** CASA PARTICULAR $$
(☎5-377-2812; P Pichs Girón No 22; d CUC$50; P❄) Away from the hustle of the center and handily located for excursions by the Trinidad–Cienfuegos road, this spacious lodging feels more like an inn, with five large rooms each featuring private terraces. Installations are new, with safe and hair dryer. English and German are spoken. The only downside is longer walking distances from central attractions.

★**Iberostar Grand Hotel** BOUTIQUE HOTEL $$$
(☎4199-6070; www.iberostar.com; cnr José Martí & General Lino Pérez; d incl breakfast from CUC$400; ❄@📶) Start in the fern-filled tiled lobby and browse the courtyard surrounded by three floors of rooms in a remodeled 19th-century colonial. The five-star Grand oozes luxury. Forget the standard all-inclusive tourist formula. Instead there's

privacy, refinement and an appreciation for local history. Details shine from a cool cigar bar to 36 rooms with designer toiletries, in-room minibars, safes and coffeemakers.

Eating

★La Redacción Cuba INTERNATIONAL **$$**
(☎4199-4593; www.laredaccioncuba.com; Antonio Maceo No 463; mains CUC$8-10;) Contrasting its colonial style with a cleverly titled menu and excellent service, this French-run offering provides a dose of comfort for travelers with culinary homesickness. Think huge lamb burgers with sweet-potato fries, pasta tossed with lobster and herbs, and appealing vegetarian options. For solo travelers, there's a huge shared table in the center conducive to making friends. Otherwise, reserve ahead.

Restaurante San José CUBAN **$$**
(☎4199-4702; Antonio Maceo No 382; mains CUC$6-15; ⊙noon-10pm) Word is out on this handsome restaurant serving fresh grilled snapper, sweet potato fries and frozen limeade. It's among the town's best. Servers weave between gleaming furniture and crowded tables. Come early if you don't want to wait.

Vista Gourmet CUBAN **$$**
(☎4199-6700; Callejón de Galdos No 2f; mains CUC$13; ⊙noon-midnight;) A slick private option perched on a lovely terrace above Trinidad's red-tiled rooftops – enjoy unobstructed 360-degree views from the top terrace. Run by the charismatic sommelier Bolo, its extensive selection of wines have climatized storage. Hungry diners will love the appetizer and dessert buffet. Tender *lechón asado* (roast pork) and fresh lobster are both recommended. It has good vegetarian options.

★Esquerra CUBAN **$$$**
(☎4199-3434; Zerquera No 464; mains CUC$8-18; ⊙noon-11pm) With a prime location on the cobblestone plaza, this elegant restaurant serves well-prepared Cuban fare. It differs from the competition with specialty flavors – spicy *criollo* tomato sauce, meunière and Catalan sauces that give a boost to fish or pork. Shrimp cocktail is a standout, as is service. There's also a nice intimate courtyard option.

Drinking & Nightlife

Taberna La Botija BAR
(cnr Amargura & Piro Guinart; ⊙24hr) La Botija crams half the town into its lively corner bar without even trying. The key: a warm talk-to-your-neighbor atmosphere, cold beer served in ceramic mugs and the best house band in Trinidad (think jazz meets soul over a violin). The food ain't bad either.

Entertainment

Casa de la Música LIVE MUSIC
(Echerri; cover CUC$2) One of Trinidad's (and Cuba's) classic venues, this casa is an alfresco affair that congregates on the sweeping staircase beside the Iglesia Parroquial off Plaza Mayor. A good mix of tourists and locals take in the 10pm salsa show here. Alternatively, full-on salsa concerts are held in the casa's rear courtyard (also accessible from Amargura).

Casa de la Trova LIVE MUSIC
(Echerri No 29; CUC$1; ⊙9pm-2am) This spirited casa retains its earthy essence despite the high package-tourist-to-Cuban ratio. Local musicians to look out for here are Semillas del Son, Santa Palabra and the town's best *trovador* (traditional singer-songwriter), Israel Moreno.

Rincon de la Salsa LIVE MUSIC
(☎5-391-0245; Zerquera, btwn Rubén Martínez Villena & Ernesto; cover CUC$2; ⊙10pm-2am) A fun live-music venue aimed at those practicing their salsa steps. It can also connect travelers to dance teachers for private lessons during the daytime.

Information

MONEY

There are banking services and a currency-exchange house.

Banco de Crédito y Comercio (José Martí No 264; ⊙9am-3pm Mon-Fri) Has an ATM.

Cadeca (Antonio Maceo, btwn Camilo Cienfuegos & General Lino Pérez; ⊙8:30am-5pm) Money changers.

TOURIST INFORMATION

The agencies in Trinidad usually have a line – try to go early.

Cubatur (☎4199-6314; Antonio Maceo No 447, btwn Zerquera & Colón; ⊙8am-8pm) Good for general tourist information, plus hotel bookings and excursions. Goes to the Valle de los Ingenios (CUC$35) and Salto del Caburní in Topes de Collante (CUC$30). Snorkeling excursions go to Cayo Iguanas (CUC$45) and Cayo Blanco (CUC$50). State taxis congregate outside.

Infotur (☎4299-8258; Izquierdo No 112; ⊙9am-5pm) Useful for general information on the town, its surroundings and Sancti Spíritus Province.

Getting There & Away

The centrally located **bus station** (Piro Guinart No 224) has buses for nationals and the more reliable Víazul service aimed at foreign travelers. The **Víazul ticket office** (4199-4448; www.viazul.com; 8:30am-4pm) is further back in the station.

With Víazul, Varadero departures can deposit you in Jagüey Grande (CUC$15, three hours) with stops on request in Jovellanos, Colesio and Cárdenas. The Santiago de Cuba departure goes through Sancti Spíritus (CUC$6, 1½ hours), Ciego de Ávila (CUC$9, 2¾ hours), Camagüey (CUC$15, 5¼ hours), Las Tunas (CUC$22, 7½ hours), Holguín (CUC$26, nine hours) and Bayamo (CUC$26, 10½ hours).

The Cubanacán Conectando tourist shuttle service has direct links daily with Havana (CUC$25). There's no office. Inquire at Infotur.

VÍAZUL BUS DEPARTURES FROM TRINIDAD

Destination	Cost (CUC$)	Duration (hr)	Frequency (daily)
Cienfuegos	6	1½	6
Havana	25	6	3
Santa Clara	8	3	2
Santiago de Cuba	33	12½	1
Varadero	20	6½	2

Topes de Collantes

ELEV 771M

The **Sierra del Escambray** is Cuba's second-largest mountain range. The beautiful crenelated hills are rich in flora and surprisingly isolated. With the best network of hiking trails in Cuba, these jungle-clad forests harbor vines, ferns and eye-catching epiphytes.

In late 1958 Che Guevara camped here on his way to Santa Clara. Almost three years later, CIA-sponsored counterrevolutionary groups operated a cat-and-mouse guerrilla campaign from the same vantage point.

Not strictly a national park, Topes is a heavily protected 200-sq-km area straddling three provinces. The umbrella park contains Parque Altiplano, Parque Codina, Parque Guanayara and Parque El Cubano. A fifth enclave, El Nicho in Cienfuegos Province, is administered by the park authority.

The park name comes from its largest settlement, a 1937 health resort founded by dictator Fulgencio Batista for his sick wife. A tuberculosis sanatorium turned health 'resort' began construction in the late '30s and opened in 1954.

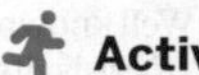

Activities

Topes has the best network of hiking trails in Cuba. Wear good, sturdy shoes. A recent relaxation in park rules means you can now tackle most of them solo, although you'll need wheels to reach some of the trailheads.

Sendero 'Centinelas del Río Melodioso' HIKING

(CUC$10, tour incl lunch CUC$47) The least accessible but the most rewarding hike by far from Topes de Collantes is this 6km round-trip hike in Parque Guanayara. The trail begins in cool, moist coffee plantations and descends steeply to **El Rocio** waterfall, where you can enjoy a bracing shower. Following the course of the Río Melodioso, pass another inviting waterfall and swimming pool, **Poza del Venado**, before emerging into the gardens of **Casa La Gallega**, a traditional rural hacienda.

Salto del Caburní HIKING

(CUC$10) The classic Topes hike, easily accessed on foot from the hotels, goes to this 62m waterfall that cascades over rocks into cool swimming holes before plunging into a chasm where macho locals dare each other to jump. Be warned: at the height of the dry season (March to May) there may be low water levels.

Information

Centro de Visitantes (8am-5pm) Near the sundial at the entrance to the hotel complexes. The best place to procure maps, guides and trail info.

Getting There & Away

Without a car, it's very difficult to get to Topes de Collantes and harder still to get around to the various trailheads. Your best bet is a taxi (CUC$40 to CUC$60 return with a wait), an excursion from Trinidad (from CUC$35) or a rental car.

The road between Trinidad and Topes de Collantes is paved but very steep. It's slippery when wet.

Camagüey

POP 331,139

Cuba's third-largest city is easily the suavest and most sophisticated after Havana. The arts shine bright here, and it's also the bastion of the Catholic Church on the island. Well known for going their own way in times of crisis, its resilient citizens are called *agramontinos* by other Cubans, after local First War of Independence hero Ignacio Agramonte, coauthor of the Guáimaro constitution and courageous leader of Cuba's finest cavalry brigade.

Camagüey's pastel colonials and warren-like streets are inspiring. Get lost for a day or two exploring hidden plazas, baroque churches, riveting galleries and congenial bars and restaurants. In 2008 the well-preserved historical center was made Cuba's ninth Unesco World Heritage site, and in 2014 the city celebrated its quincentennial. A unique motif you'll notice around the city are its *tinajones*, large clay pots used to store water, for which Camagüey is famed.

Sights

Plaza del Carmen SQUARE

(Hermanos Agüero, btwn Honda & Carmen) Around 600m west of the frenzy of República sits another sublimely beautiful square, one less visited than the central plazas. It's backed on the eastern side by the masterful **Iglesia de Nuestra Señora del Carmen**, one of the prettiest city churches.

More than a decade ago Plaza del Carmen was a ruin, but it's now restored to a state better than the original. The cobbled central space has been infused with giant *tinajones*, atmospheric street lamps and unique life-sized sculptures of *camagüeyanos* going about their daily business.

Casa de Arte Jover GALLERY

(☎3229-2305; Martí No 154, btwn Independencia & Cisneros; ⏰9am-noon & 3-5pm Mon-Sat) FREE Camagüey is home to two of Cuba's most creative and prodigious contemporary painters, Joel Jover and his wife Ileana Sánchez. Their magnificent home in Plaza Agramonte functions as a gallery and piece of art in its own right, with a slew of original pieces, resident chihuahuas and delightfully kitschy antiques on show. Guests can browse and purchase high-quality original art.

Martha Jiménez Pérez GALLERY

(☎3225-7559; www.martha-jimenez.com; Martí No 282, btwn Carmen & Honda; ⏰8am-8pm) FREE In Cuba's ceramics capital, the studio-gallery of Martha Jiménez Pérez shows the work of one of Cuba's greatest living artists. See everything from pots to paintings being produced here. The studio overlooks Pérez' magnum opus, Plaza del Carmen's alfresco statue of three gossiping women entitled *Chismosas* (gossipers). The *chismosas* also feature in many of her paintings inside.

Museo Provincial Ignacio Agramonte MUSEUM

(☎3228-2425; Av de los Mártires No 2; CUC$2; ⏰9am-5pm Tue-Fri, to 4pm Sat, to 1pm Sun) Named (like half of Camagüey) after the exalted local War of Independence hero, this cavernous museum, just north of the train station, is in a Spanish cavalry barracks dating from 1848. There's some impressive artwork upstairs, including much by Camagüey locals, as well as antique furniture and old family heirlooms.

Museo Casa Natal de Ignacio Agramonte MUSEUM

(☎3228-2425; Av Agramonte No 459; CUC$2; ⏰9am-5pm Tue-Fri, to 4pm Sat, to 1pm Sun) The birthplace of independence hero Ignacio Agramonte (1841–73), the cattle rancher who led the Camagüey area's revolt against Spain. The house – an elegant colonial building in its own right – tells of the oft-overlooked role of Camagüey and Agramonte in the First War of Independence. The hero's gun is one of his few personal possessions displayed.

Plaza San Juan de Dios SQUARE

(cnr San Juan de Dios & Ramón Pinto) Looking more Mexican than Cuban (Mexico was capital of New Spain so the colonial architecture was often superior), Plaza San Juan de Dios is Camagüey's most picturesque and beautifully preserved corner. Its eastern aspect is dominated by the Museo de San Juan de Dios, formerly a hospital. Worthwhile restaurants lurk behind the square's arresting blue, yellow and pink building facades.

Parque Ignacio Agramonte SQUARE

(cnr Martí & Independencia) Camagüey's most dazzling square in the heart of the city invites relaxation with rings of marble benches and an equestrian statue (c 1950) of Camagüey's precocious War of Independence hero, Agramonte. Stop by at 6pm to watch local youth in white campesino garb solemnly lowering the flag with great pomp, accompanied by a speaker blasting out the national anthem.

WORTH A TRIP

PLAYA ANCÓN

A ribbon of white beach on Sancti Spíritus' iridescent Caribbean shoreline, Playa Ancón is often considered the finest arc of sand on Cuba's south coast. The beach has three all-inclusive hotels and a well-equipped marina with catamaran trips to nearby coral keys. While it can't compete with the north-coast giants of Varadero, Cayo Coco and Guardalavaca, Ancón has one trump card: Trinidad, Latin America's sparkling colonial diamond, lies just 12km to the north.

Between Playa Ancón and Trinidad lies half-forgotten La Boca, a small fishing village at the mouth of the Río Guaurabo with a pebbly beach shaded by flowering acacias. If you like lazy rocking-chair tranquility, fresh lobster, raspberry-ripple sunsets and bantering in Spanish with the local fishers, it's bliss.

The one paved road crosses a tidal flat teeming with birdlife visible in the early morning. Be warned: sand fleas are famously ferocious at sunrise and sunset.

Tours

Camaguax Tours TOURS
(☎32-28-73-64, 5-864-2328; www.camaguax.com/en; República No 155, Apt 7 (altos); ⊙8:30am-5:30pm) A private agency with English- and French-speaking guides and myriad quality offerings throughout the province with a cultural or adventure focus. Hits include a city tour, sugarcane-farm visits, hiking and caving. There are excursions to Sierra del Chorrillo, Reserva Ecológica Limones Tuabaquey and Río Máximo. Uses 4WD vehicles for rough roads and has overnight options.

Sleeping

Los Vitrales CASA PARTICULAR $
(Emma Barreto & Rafael Requejo; ☎5-294-2522, 3229-5866; requejobarreto@gmail.com; Avellaneda No 3, btwn General Gómez & Martí; r CUC$30; P❄) A former convent, this enormous, painstakingly restored colonial house sports broad arches, high ceilings and dozens of antiques. Helpful owner Rafael is an architect, and it shows. Three rooms with good water pressure are arranged around a shady patio draped in lush gardens that are a highlight. There are over-the-top breakfasts and dinners with special orders available (vegetarians welcome).

Casa Láncara CASA PARTICULAR $
(☎3228-3187; aledino@nauta.cu; Avellaneda No 160; r CUC$30; ❄wifi) A dose of Seville with beautiful blue-and-yellow azulejos (tiles), this welcoming colonial is overseen by Alejandro and his wife, Dinorah. The two rooms are hung with local art, and there's a roof terrace; it's within spitting distance of the Soledad church.

El Marqués BOUTIQUE HOTEL $$$
(☎32-24-49-37; ventas@ehoteles.cmg.tur.cu; Cisneros No 222; s/d incl breakfast CUC$120/160; ❄@wifi) Simply lovely, this six-room colonial is a treasure trove of character. Rooms shoot off a central courtyard with wrought-iron furniture, each door guarded by a Martha Jiménez Pérez sculpture on a pedestal. Bedrooms feature satellite TV, safe and air-con. There's period furniture, and the place is quiet throughout. Also features a small bar with 24-hour service and hot tub.

★**Hotel Camino de Hierro** BOUTIQUE HOTEL $$$
(☎32-28-42-64; ventas@ehoteles.cmg.tur.cu; Plaza de la Solidaridad; s/d CUC$115/140; ❄@wifi) Among the best of Camagüey's boutique hotels, it occupies an attractive city-center building that was once an office for the Cuban *ferrocarril* (railway), hence the railway theme. There's also lovely colonial furniture and romantic balconies. Guests enjoy a 24-hour bar and a pleasant patio privy to all the downtown action.

Eating

★**Casa Austria** EUROPEAN $$
(☎32-28-55-80; Lugareño No 121, btwn Raúl Lamar & Matías Varona; meals CUC$4-13; ⊙11:30am-11:30pm; ❄) Locals line up for strudel and decadent cakes at this Austrian-run cafe. After so much *comida criolla*, travelers embrace the international menu featuring chicken cordon bleu, schnitzel and garbanzos stewed in tomato sauce with bacon. It's all good. The setting, stuffed with heavy colonial furniture, is a bit claustrophobic, but there's also patio dining, complete with fountain-fed pond.

El Paso INTERNATIONAL $$
(☎32-27-43-21; Hermanos Agüero No 261, btwn Carmen & Honda; meals CUC$5-10; ⊙9am-11pm) Finally, a private restaurant with all-day

hours, plus a funky interior and an enviable Plaza del Carmen location. There's flavorful *ropa vieja* (spiced shredded beef), heaping bowls of *arroz con pollo a la chorrillana* (chicken, rice, prunes and peppers in a ceramic bowl). Try *pan patato* for dessert – consisting of cassava and coconut. Good happy-hour deals from 2pm to 8pm.

Mesón del Príncipe CUBAN **$$**
(☎5-240-4598; Astilleros No 7; meals CUC$8-12; ⏰noon-midnight) This elegant restaurant offers an affordable fine-dining experience in a typically refined Camagüeyan residence. It's places like this that have put Camagüey at the cutting edge of Cuba's new culinary revolution. Bonus: it doesn't use straws – a laudable, sustainable novelty.

☆ Entertainment

Teatro Principal THEATER
(☎3229-3048; Padre Valencia No 64; CUC$5-10; ⏰shows 8:30pm Fri & Sat, 5pm Sun) If a show's on, go! Second only to Havana in its ballet credentials, the Camagüey Ballet Company, founded in 1971 by Fernando Alonso (ex-husband of number-one Cuban dancing diva Alicia Alonso), is internationally renowned, and performances are the talk of the town. Also of interest is the wonderful theater building of 1850 vintage, bedizened with majestic chandeliers and stained glass.

Casa de la Trova Patricio Ballagas LIVE MUSIC
(☎3229-1357; Cisneros No 171, btwn Martí & Cristo; CUC$3; ⏰7pm-1am) An ornate entrance hall gives way to an atmospheric patio where old crooners sing and young couples *chachachá*. One of Cuba's best *trova* (traditional poetic singing) houses, where regular tourist traffic doesn't detract from the old-world authenticity. Tuesday's a good night for traditional music. Cover includes one drink.

ℹ Information

MONEY

Bank services and money changers are plentiful.

Banco de Crédito y Comercio (☎3229-2531; cnr Av Agramonte & Cisneros; ⏰9am-3pm Mon-Fri) Has an ATM.

Banco Financiero Internacional (☎3229-4846; Independencia No 21, btwn Hermanos Agüero & Martí; ⏰9am-3pm Mon-Fri) Has an ATM.

Cadeca (☎3229-5220; República No 84, btwn Oscar Primelles & El Solitario; ⏰8:30am-8pm Mon-Sat, 9am-6pm Sun)

TOURIST INFORMATION

There are plenty of tour agencies in the city.

Cubanacán (☎3228-7879; Maceo No 67, Gran Hotel) The best place for information in the city center.

Infotur (☎3225-6794; www.facebook.com/camaguey.travel; Av Agramonte; ⏰8:30am-5:30pm) Helpful information office hidden in a gallery near Casablanca cinema.

ℹ Getting There & Away

BUS

The Estacion Ferro Omnibus is near the train station and has trucks to regional destinations (MN$20) including Playa Santa Lucía. Arrive at 5am to be ensured a spot for beach-bound trucks.

Long-distance Víazul buses depart from the **Estacion Interprovincial** (☎3227-0396; www.viazul.com; Carretera Central), 3km southeast of the center.

Víazul Bus Departures from Camagüey

Destination	Cost (CUC$)	Duration (hr)	Frequency (daily)
Havana	33	9	5
Holguín	11	3	5
Santiago de Cuba	18	6½	5
Trinidad	15	4½	1
Varadero	25	8¼	1

TRAIN

The revamped **train station** (☎3228-4766; cnr Avellaneda & Av Carlos J Finlay) is more conveniently located than the bus station, though its service isn't quite as convenient. Every other day the train leaves for Santiago at 1:25am and departs for Havana three times a week at varying times in the morning.

Schedules change frequently: check at the station a couple of days before you intend to travel.

EASTERN CUBA

Santiago de Cuba

☎22 / POP 431,272

Cuba's cultural capital, Santiago is a frenetic, passionate and noisy beauty. Situated closer to Haiti and the Dominican Republic than to Havana, it leans east rather than west, a crucial factor shaping this city's unique identity, steeped in Afro-Caribbean, entrepreneurial and rebel influences.

Trailblazing characters and a resounding sense of historical destiny define it. Diego Velázquez de Cuéllar made Santiago his second capital, Fidel Castro used it to launch his embryonic revolution, Don Facundo Bacardí based his first-ever rum factory here, and nearly every Cuban music genre from salsa to *son* first emanated from these dusty, rhythmic and sensuous streets.

Caught dramatically between the indomitable Sierra Maestra and the azure Caribbean, the colonial *casco histórico* (historical center) retains a time-worn air reminiscent of Salvador in Brazil or forgotten New Orleans. So don't let the hustlers, the speeding Chevys or the clawing heat defeat you. There's untold magic here, too.

Sights

Castillo de San Pedro de la Roca del Morro FORT

(El Morro; ☎2269-1569; CUC$5; ⏲9am-7pm) A Unesco World Heritage site since 1997, the San Pedro fort sits impregnably atop a 60m-high promontory at the entrance to Santiago harbor, 10km southwest of the city. The stupendous views from the upper terrace take in the wild western ribbon of Santiago's coastline backed by the velvety Sierra Maestra.

Multilingual guides provide invaluable historical background and color; be sure to tip.

The fort was designed in 1587 by famous Italian military engineer Juan Bautista Antonelli (who also designed La Punta and El Morro forts in Havana) to protect Santiago from pillaging pirates who had successfully sacked the city in 1554. Because of financial constraints, the building work didn't start until 1633 (17 years after Antonelli's death), and it carried on sporadically for the next 60 years. In the interim, British privateer Henry Morgan sacked and partially destroyed it.

Finally finished in the early 1700s, El Morro's massive batteries, bastions, magazines and walls got little opportunity to serve their true purpose. With the era of piracy in decline, the fort was converted into a prison in the 1800s, and it stayed that way (bar a brief interlude during the 1898 Spanish-Cuban-American War) until Cuban architect Francisco Prat Puig mustered up a restoration plan in the late 1960s.

Today, the fort hosts the swashbuckling **Museo de Piratería**, with another room given over to the US-Spanish naval battle that took place in the bay in 1898.

The fort, like Havana, has a **cañonazo ceremony** (firing of the cannon) each day at sunset when actors dress up in Mambís regalia.

To get to El Morro from the city center, take bus 212 to Ciudamar and walk the final 20 minutes. Alternatively, a round-trip taxi ride from Parque Céspedes with wait should cost no more than CUC$25.

Cementerio Santa Ifigenia CEMETERY

(Av Crombet; CUC$3; ⏲8am-6pm) Nestled peacefully on the city's western extremity, the Cementerio Santa Ifigenia is second only to Havana's Necrópolis Cristóbal Colón (p308) in its importance and grandiosity. Created in 1868 to accommodate the victims of the War of Independence and a simultaneous yellow-fever outbreak, the Santa Ifigenia includes many great historical figures among its 8000-plus tombs, notably the mausoleum of José Martí and final resting place of Fidel Castro.

Cuartel Moncada MUSEUM

(Moncada Barracks; ☎2266-1157; Av Moncada; CUC$1; ⏲9am-5pm Mon-Sat, 8am-2pm Sun) Santiago's famous Moncada Barracks, a crenelated art deco building completed in 1938, is now synonymous with one of history's greatest failed putsches. Moncada earned immortality on July 26, 1953, when more than 100 revolutionaries led by then little-known Fidel Castro stormed Batista's troops at what was then Cuba's second-most important military garrison.

After the revolution, the barracks, like all others in Cuba, was converted into a school called Ciudad Escolar 26 de Julio, and in 1967 a **museum** (CUC$2; ⏲9am-5pm Mon-Sat, to 1pm Sun) was installed near gate 3, where the main attack took place. As Batista's soldiers had cemented over the original bullet holes from the attack, the Castro government remade them (this time without guns) years later as a poignant reminder. The museum (one of Cuba's best) contains a scale model of the barracks plus interesting and sometimes grisly artifacts, diagrams and models of the attack, its planning and its aftermath. Most moving, perhaps, are the photographs of the 61 fallen at the end.

The first barracks on this site was constructed by the Spanish in 1859, and actually takes its name after Guillermón Moncada, a War of Independence fighter who was held prisoner here in 1874.

Museo de Ambiente Histórico Cubano MUSEUM
(Casa de Diego Velázquez; 22-65-26-52; Félix Peña No 602; CUC$2; 9am-5pm daily) The oldest house still standing in Cuba, this arresting early colonial abode dating from 1522 was the official residence of the island's first governor, Diego Velázquez. Restored in the late 1960s, the Andalusian-style facade with fine, wooden lattice windows was inaugurated in 1970 as a museum.

Catedral de Nuestra Señora de la Asunción CHURCH
(Heredia, btwn Félix Peña & General Lacret; Mass 6:30pm Mon & Wed-Fri, 5pm Sat, 9am & 6:30pm Sun) Santiago's most important church is stunning both inside and out. There has been a cathedral on this site since the city's inception in the 1520s, though a series of pirate raids, earthquakes and dodgy architects put paid to at least three previous incarnations. The present cathedral, characterized by its two neoclassical towers, was completed in 1922; the remains of first colonial governor, Diego Velázquez, are still buried underneath.

Museo de la Lucha Clandestina MUSEUM
(22-62-46-89; General Jesús Rabí No 1; CUC$1; 9am-5pm Tue-Sun) This gorgeous yellow colonial-style building houses a museum detailing the underground struggle against Batista in the 1950s. It's a fascinating, if bloody, story enhanced by far-reaching views from the balcony. The museum was a former police station attacked by M-26-7 activists on November 30, 1956, to divert attention from the arrival of the tardy yacht *Granma*, carrying Fidel Castro and 81 others.

Parque Alameda PARK
(Av Jesús Menéndez) Below the Tivolí quarter, this narrow park embellishes a dockside promenade opened in 1840 and redesigned in 1893. Refurbishment for the 2015 quincentennial has made it the center of the Malecón (boardwalk) in the style of Havana's, featuring a playground, palm trees and public wi-fi. The north end features the old **clock tower**, *aduana* (customs house) and cigar factory. With smart architecture, sea air and a dash of portside sketchiness, it's good for a stroll.

Jardín de los Helechos GARDENS
(22-60-83-35; Carretera de El Caney No 129; CUC$3; 9am-5pm Mon-Fri) This peaceful garden is a lush haven of 350 types of ferns and 90 types of orchids. It's the erstwhile private collection of *santiagüero* Manuel Caluff, donated in 1984 to the Academia de Ciencias de Cuba (Cuban Academy of Science), which continues to keep the 3000-sq-meter garden in psychedelic bloom. The center of the garden has an inviting dense copse-cum-sanctuary dotted with benches.

Festivals & Events

★**Carnaval** CARNIVAL
(Jul) One of the largest and most authentic in the Caribbean, Santiago de Cuba's version of Carnaval lets loose with fantastic costumes, food stalls, and music round the clock. The whole city spills out onto the streets to absorb it.

Fiesta del Fuego CULTURAL
(early Jul) The literal firing up for Carnaval, this early-July celebration includes a ceremony where the devil is burned to the glee of huge crowds on the Malecón.

Sleeping

★**Roy's Terrace Inn** CASA PARTICULAR $
(22-62-05-22; roysterraceinn@gmail.com; Diego Palacios No 177, btwn Padre Pico & Mariano Corona; r CUC$35; P) From the hanging rooftop garden to wall murals and impeccable rooms, every fiber gleams. Run by an enthusiastic team of well-traveled Cubans and local mamas who woo you with their warmth and cooking, this spot is tops. Rooms are filled with modern amenities, including TV, hairdryers and information packets. Service – in English, Spanish, French and some German – is a highlight.

Casa Terraza Pavo Real CASA PARTICULAR $
(22-65-85-89; juanmarti13@yahoo.es; Santa Rita No 302, cnr Hartmann; r CUC$25-30;) The meticulously maintained family home of Juan Martí has a palatial quality, with a riot of antique furniture, light-filtering *vitrales* (stained-glass windows) and coiled spiral staircases. The crowning glory is a huge Alhambra-esque patio with a sleep-invoking fountain and an expansive roof terrace with exotic orchids. Yet, many might feel at odds with the tropical birds and peacocks in cages.

Casa Milena CASA PARTICULAR $
(22-62-88-22, 5-319-5814; penelope1212@nauta.cu; Heredia No 306; r CUC$25-30;) Smack in the heart of the street renowned for live music, this welcoming family home features three huge rooms in a colonial home. The utterly lovely Milena and her husband maintain the colonial simplicity of her great-

grandparents' home, complete with genuine Cuban hospitality. It's very clean and central.

Hostal San Basilio BOUTIQUE HOTEL **$$**
(☎22-65-17-02; reservas@hotelversalles.co.cu; Bartolomé Masó No 403, btwn Pío Rosado & Porfirio Valiente; s/d incl breakfast CUC$30/50; ❄@) Acquired by the Encanto chain, the lovely eight-room San Basilio (named for the original name of the street on which it lies) is cozy and refreshingly contemporary – with a romantic colonial setting including a petite patio dripping with ferns. Rooms come with DVD players, umbrellas, bathroom scales and mini bottles of rum. A small restaurant serves breakfast and lunch.

★Hotel Imperial HISTORIC HOTEL **$$$**
(☎22-62-82-30; José A Saco, btwn Félix Peña & General Lacret; s/d incl breakfast CUC$89/144; ❄📶) The return of a Santiago landmark, the eclectic-style 1915 Hotel Imperial has been refurbished to sparkling condition with some welcome concessions to modernity. The 39 rooms are smartly furnished with flat-screen TVs, tall windows and glass showers. Features an elevator to an elegant roof-terrace bar with great city views and live music on weekends.

★Meliá Santiago de Cuba HOTEL **$$$**
(☎22-68-70-70; www.meliacuba.com; cnr Av de las Américas & Calle M; s/d incl breakfast CUC$107/126; P❄@📶🏊) Sleek on the inside, a blue-mirrored monster on the outside, Meliá is Santiago's only 'international' hotel with a laundry list of amenities hard to find elsewhere. Count on real bathtubs in every room, three pools, four restaurants, various shopping facilities and an elegant 15th-floor bar. The downsides are its location on the outskirts and lack of genuine Cuban charm.

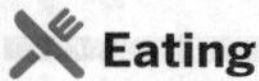

Eating

Bendita Farándula CARIBBEAN **$**
(☎22-65-37-39; Monseñor Barnada No 513; meals CUC$5-9; ⏰noon-11pm) You would probably never wander in here unbidden, but with an ambience reminiscent of a provincial French bistro, this cozy two-floored place does Santiago's only *pescado con leche de coco* (fish with coconut sauce; a Baracoan specialty), curried lamb and a nice *bistek de cerdo con jamon y queso* (pork steak with ham and cheese).

★Roy's Terrace Inn Roof Garden Restaurant CUBAN **$$**
(☎22-62-05-22; roysterraceinn@gmail.com; Diego Palacios No 177, btwn Padre Pico & Mariano Corona; meals CUC$10-15; ⏰7-9:30pm; 📶✓) If only the rest of Cuba could harness this formula: quality homemade food, caring service and excellent atmosphere. Reserve one day ahead for one of only six rooftop tables surrounded by tumbling flowers in candlelight. Cocktails deliver and family-style servings come overflowing. Fish, chicken or pork are served with sides such as crispy *tamal*es or sautéed eggplant. Vegans and vegetarians welcome.

St Pauli INTERNATIONAL **$$**
(☎2265-2292; José A Saco No 605; meals CUC$4-15; ⏰noon-11pm Mon-Thu, to midnight Fri-Sun) In a city of no great culinary tradition, St Pauli arrived like a hurricane. Walk the long, mural-decorated corridor to a bright room featuring blackboard menus and a glass-wall kitchen. Everything is consistently good, particularly the cocktail-glass gazpacho, *pulpo al ajillo* (octopus with garlic) and pineapple chicken fajitas. If you've come behind a group: patience!

Madrileño CUBAN **$$**
(☎22-64-41-38; Calle 8 No 105, Vista Alegre; meals CUC$4-15; ⏰noon-11pm) A well-respected, good-quality option, Madrileño occupies a classy colonial abode in Vista Alegre with interior patio dining with chirping birds. Contrary to the name, this is Cuban *comida criolla* (Creole food). Succulent odors waft from the kitchen. There's an extensive menu with an emphasis on grilled meats.

Thoms Yadira Restaurante CUBAN **$$**
(☎5-267-0196, 5-555-1207; General Lacret No 705 altos, btwn Heredia & Bartolomé Masó; mains CUC$4-16; ⏰10am-1:30am) This convivial upstairs restaurant just off Parque Céspedes turns out consistently high-quality seafood favorites including grilled lobster, pasta dishes and salads. A central, reliable spot for dinner before hitting Casa de la Trova; it's popular so expect a wait at peak times.

Ristorante Italiano La Fontana ITALIAN **$$$**
(Meliá Santiago de Cuba, cnr Av de las Américas & Calle M; mains CUC$6-18; ⏰noon-11pm) Pizza *deliciosa* and lasagna *formidable,* ravioli and garlic bread: this has to be the number-one option for breaking away from all that chicken and pork! Prices are jacked up on Chilean wines, but it might be worth it anyway.

Drinking & Nightlife

Casa Granda Roof Garden Bar BAR
(top fl, Heredia No 201; cover CUC$3-10; ⏰11am-1am) Slip up to the 5th-floor roof of Casa

Santiago de Cuba

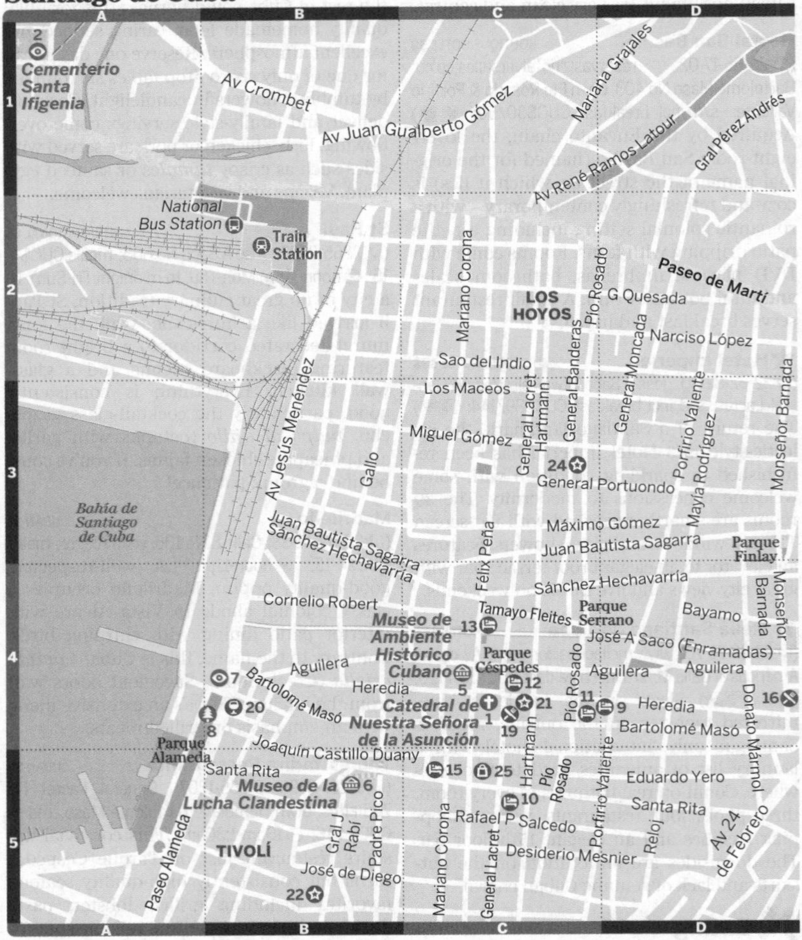

Granda for the most breathtaking sunset in Cuba. Views of the scene in Parque Céspedes and the dramatically lit cathedral are well worth the minimum consumption charge for nonguests (it increases after 7pm), which credits toward your first drink. Drinks may be double the cost of those elsewhere, but they come garnished with spectacular Santiago views.

Cervecería Puerto del Rey MICROBREWERY
(☎22-68-60-48; cnr Paseo Alameda & Aduana; ⊙noon-midnight) You know Cuba is changing when you find an actual warehouse-style brewpub filled with locals quaffing pints brewed on-site. The four beers at this noisy, fun spot range from *extra-clara* (light lager) to *negra* (black), which is as diverse an array as you'll see in Cuba. There's decent pub food, including popular *caldo del rey* (a broth with a pork-rib base).

☆ Entertainment

'Spoiled for choice' would be an understatement in Santiago. For what's happening, look for the biweekly *Cartelera Cultural*. The reception desk at **Hotel Casa Granda** (☎2265-3024; Heredia No 201, cnr General Lacret) usually has copies.

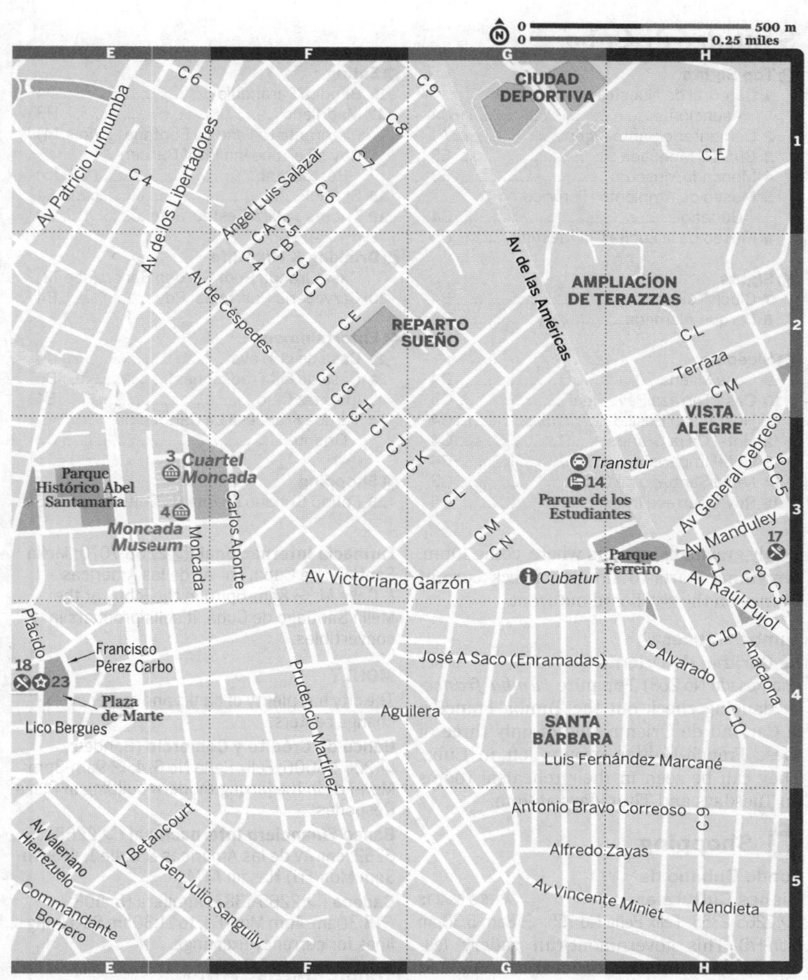

★Casa de las Tradiciones LIVE MUSIC

(☎2265-3892; General Jesús Rabí No 154; CUC$1; ⏲5pm-midnight) The most discovered 'undiscovered' spot in Santiago still retains its smoke-filled, foot-stomping, front-room feel. Hidden in the genteel Tivolí district, some of Santiago de Cuba's most exciting ensembles, singers and soloists take turns improvising. Friday nights are reserved for straight-up classic *trova,* à la Ñico Saquito and the like. There's a gritty bar and some colorful artwork.

★Iris Jazz Club JAZZ

(General Serafin Sánchez, btwn José A Saco & Bayamo; CUC$5; ⏲shows 9:30pm-2am) When Santiago gets too hot, noisy and agitated, you need a dose of Iris, one of Cuba's suavest and best jazz clubs, where you can sit in a comfy booth surrounded by pictures of puffing jazz greats and watch some incredibly intuitive exponents of Santiago's small but significant jazz scene.

Casa de la Trova LIVE MUSIC

(☎2265-3892; Heredia No 208) Santiago's shrine to the power of traditional music is still going strong five decades on, continuing to attract big names such as Buena Vista Social Club singer Eliades Ochoa. Warming up on the ground floor in the late afternoon, the action

Santiago de Cuba

Top Sights
1 Catedral de Nuestra Señora de la Asunción C4
2 Cementerio Santa Ifigenia A1
3 Cuartel Moncada E3
4 Moncada Museum E3
5 Museo de Ambiente Histórico Cubano C4
6 Museo de la Lucha Clandestina B5

Sights
7 Clock Tower B4
8 Parque Alameda B4

Sleeping
9 Casa Milena D4
10 Casa Terraza Pavo Real C5
11 Hostal San Basilio C4
12 Hotel Casa Granda C4
13 Hotel Imperial C4
14 Meliá Santiago de Cuba G3
15 Roy's Terrace Inn C5

Eating
16 Bendita Farándula D4
17 Madrileño H3
Ristorante Italiano La Fontana .....(see 14)
Roy's Terrace Inn Roof Garden Restaurant .....(see 15)
18 St Pauli E4
19 Thoms Yadira Restaurante C4

Drinking & Nightlife
Casa Granda Roof Garden Bar .....(see 12)
20 Cervecería Puerto del Rey B4

Entertainment
21 Casa de la Trova C4
22 Casa de las Tradiciones B5
23 Iris Jazz Club E4
24 Tumba Francesa La Caridad de Oriente C3

Shopping
25 Fondo Cubano de Bienes Culturales ... C5

slowly gravitates upstairs where, come 10pm, everything starts to simmer. Check current listings on the signboard out front.

Tumba Francesa La Caridad de Oriente DANCE
(Pio Rosado No 268) For pure *tumba francesa* dancing check out the Tumba Francesa la Caridad de Oriente, one of only three of these French-Haitian groups left in Cuba. They can be seen in their rehearsal rooms on Tuesdays and Thursdays at 9pm.

Shopping

Fondo Cubano de Bienes Culturales ARTS & CRAFTS
(2265-2358; Félix Peña No 755; 8am-5:30pm Mon-Fri) This government-run gallery features a good rotation of local artisans and art exhibitions, a few blocks from Parque Céspedes.

Information

MEDICAL SERVICES

Santiago has the best access to medicine and related services in the region.

Clínica Internacional de Santiago de Cuba (2271-4021, 2264-2589; cnr Av Raúl Pujol & Calle 10, Vista Alegre; 24hr) Capable staff speak some English. A dentist is also present.

Farmacia Clínica Internacional (2264-2589; cnr Av Raúl Pujol & Calle 10; 24hr) Best pharmacy in town, selling products in convertibles.

Farmacia Internacional (2268-7070; Meliá Santiago de Cuba, cnr Av de las Américas & Calle M; 8am-6pm) In the lobby of the Meliá Santiago de Cuba, it sells products in convertibles.

MONEY

The city has plenty of banks and currency-exchange centers.

Banco de Crédito y Comercio (Bandec; 2262-8006; Félix Peña No 614; 9am-3pm Mon-Fri) In the jarring modern building in Plaza Céspedes.

Banco Financiero Internacional (2268-6252; cnr Av de las Américas & Calle 1; 9am-3pm Mon-Fri) Has an ATM.

Cadeca (2265-1383; Aguilera No 508; 8:30am-4pm Mon-Fri, to 11:30am Sat) Long lines for currency exchange.

TOURIST INFORMATION

As all tour agencies are government-run, they offer overlapping services and consistent prices.

Cubanacán (2268-6412; Hotel Casa Granda, Heredia No 201; 8am-6pm) Very helpful; sells tours in the Hotel Casa Granda.

Cubatur (Heredia No 701; 8am-8pm) Sells all number of excursions, for everything from La Gran Piedra to El Cobre. There's another **branch** (2265-2560; Av Victoriano Garzón No 364, cnr Calle 4; 8am-8pm) on Av Victoriano Garzón.

Infotur (2268-6068; Félix Peña No 562; 8am-8pm) Helpful location and staff. There's also a branch in Antonio Maceo International Airport.

Getting There & Away

AIR

Antonio Maceo International Airport (☎2269-1053) is 7km south of Santiago de Cuba, off the Carretera del Morro. International flights arrive from Santo Domingo (Dominican Republic), Toronto and Montreal on Cubana (www.cubana.cu). Toronto and Montreal are also served by Sunwing (www.sunwing.ca).

Internally, Cubana flies nonstop from Havana two or three times a day.

BUS

Víazul buses (www.viazul.cu) leave from the **National Bus Station** (Paseo de Martí), opposite the Heredia Monument, 3km northeast of Parque Céspedes.

The Havana bus stops at Bayamo (CUC$7, 2¼ hours), Holguín (CUC$11, 3½ to four hours), Las Tunas (CUC$11, 5½ hours), Camagüey (CUC$18, 7½ hours), Ciego de Ávila (CUC$24, 9½ hours), Sancti Spíritus (CUC$28, 11 hours) and Santa Clara (CUC$33, 11 to 12 hours). The Trinidad bus can drop you at Bayamo, Las Tunas, Camagüey, Ciego de Ávila and Sancti Spíritus. The Baracoa bus stops in Guantánamo.

Víazul Bus Departures from Santiago de Cuba

Destination	Price (CUC$)	Duration (hr)	Frequency (daily)
Baracoa	15	4¾	1
Havana	51	15	3
Trinidad	33	11½	1
Varadero	49	15	1

TRAIN

The modern French-style **train station** (☎22-62-28-36; cnr Av Jesús Menéndez & Martí) is situated near the rum factory northwest of the center. Brand-new Chinese-made carriages replaced the deteriorating *Tren Francés* in July 2019 and depart every other day for Havana (15 hours) with stops en route.

Cuban train schedules are fickle, so always verify beforehand what train leaves when and get your ticket as soon as possible thereafter. Arrive at least an hour beforehand to confirm your seat.

Getting Around

There's a **Transtur** (☎22-68-71-60; Meliá Santiago de Cuba) taxi stand in front of Meliá Santiago de Cuba. Taxis also wait on Parque Céspedes near the cathedral and hiss at you expectantly as you pass. Hammer out a price beforehand. To the airport, costs range between CUC$8 and CUC$10 depending on the state of the car.

Bici-taxis charge about CUC$1 to CUC$2 per ride.

Baracoa

POP 79,797

Beguiling, outlandish and surreal, Baracoa's essence is addictive. On the wet and windy side of the Cuchillas del Toa mountains, Cuba's oldest and most isolated town exudes original atmosphere.

Feast your eyes upon deep green foliage that's wonderfully abundant after the stark aridity of Guantánamo's south coast. Delve into fantastical legends, and acquaint yourself with an unorthodox cast of local characters. There's Cayamba, the self-styled 'Guerrilla troubadour,' who once claimed he was the man with the ugliest voice in the world; La Rusa, an aristocratic Russian émigré who inspired a novel by magic-realist author Alejo Carpentier; and Enriqueta Faber, a French woman who passed herself off as a man to practice as a doctor and marry a local heiress in Baracoa's cathedral in 1819 – likely Cuba's first same-sex marriage. Baracoa – what would Cuba be without you?

While 2016's Hurricane Matthew hit Baracoa hard, most of the town has rebounded.

Sights

★Museo Arqueológico 'La Cueva del Paraíso' MUSEUM

(Moncada; CUC$3; ⏲9am-4pm) Baracoa's most impressive museum, La Cueva del Paraíso is a series of caves that were once Taíno burial chambers. Among nearly 2000 authentic Taíno pieces are unearthed skeletons, ceramics, 3000-year-old petroglyphs and a replica of the Ídolo de Tabaco, a sculpture found in Maisí in 1903 and considered to be one of the most important Taíno finds in the Caribbean.

Fuerte Matachín FORT

(Museo Municipal; ☎21-64-21-22; cnr José Martí & Malecón; CUC$1; ⏲8am-noon & 2-6pm) Baracoa is protected by a trio of muscular Spanish forts. This one, built in 1802 at the southern entrance to town, houses the Museo Municipal. The small but beautiful building showcases an engaging chronology of Cuba's oldest settlement, including polymita snail shells, the story of Che Guevara and the chocolate factory, and the particular strand of music Baracoa gave birth to: *kiribá*, a forefather of *son*.

OFF THE BEATEN TRACK

GIBARA

Matched only by Baracoa for its wild coastal setting, half-forgotten Gibara, with its faded pastel facades and surging ocean rollers, conspires to seduce you. Close to Holguín, there's a cultural life here that seems big for a small town. In 2008 Hurricane Ike almost wiped the town off the map.

Situated 33km from Holguín via a scenic road that undulates through villages, Gibara is a small, intimate place receiving a lift from much-needed investment. Unlike nearby Guardalavaca, development here is low-key and focused on renovating the town's beautiful but dilapidated architecture. The saddle-shaped Silla de Gibara that so captivated Columbus creates a wild, scenic backdrop.

As Gibara's specific attractions are few, rather like Baracoa, this is more a town to stroll the streets and absorb the local flavor. There are a couple of decent beaches within striking distance, including lovely **Playa Caletones** 17m to the west.

Gibara has some of the province's best options for bedding down, from regal casas particulares to the wonderful **Hotel Ordoño** (☎24-84-44-48; www.iberostar.com; J Peralta, cnr Donato Mármol; s/d incl breakfast CUC$90/140; ❄@📶), a contender for the best hotel in Cuba.

There are no reliable buses to Gibara. Travelers will need their own wheels or a taxi. Cars from Guardalavaca or Holguín cost around CUC$40.

Tours

Organized tours are a good way to view Baracoa's hard-to-reach outlying sights, and the **Cubatur** (☎6132-8342; Antonio Maceo No 181; ⏱8:30am-noon & 1-5pm Mon-Sat) and **Ecotur** (☎2164-2478; Antonio Maceo; ⏱8am-noon & 2-6pm Mon-Sat) offices on Plaza Independencia can book excursions, including to El Yunque (CUC$16 to CUC$20), Parque Nacional Alejandro de Humboldt (CUC$22 to CUC$25) and Boca de Yumurí (CUC$22).

Geovannis Steve Cardosa Matos TOURS
(☎5-530-2820; geostevecuba@nauta.cu) The ebullient, English-fluent Steve is a knowledgeable, reliable local guide with a sunny attitude and a menu of professionally led tours to the national park and cacao farm. He also does walking tours or custom adventures. Contact him directly or via **Hostal Nilson** (☎5-271-8556, 2164-3123; www.hostalnilson.baracoa.co; Flor Crombet No 143, btwn Ciro Frías & Pelayo Cuervo).

Sleeping

Casa Colonial Ykira CASA PARTICULAR $
(☎21-64-38-81; ykiram@nauta.cu; Antonio Maceo No 168a, btwn Ciro Frías & Céspedes; r CUC$25; ❄) Welcoming and hospitable, Ykira is Baracoa's premier hostess. She also serves a mean dinner made with homegrown herbs. A lovely mural lines the entrance walk, and there are two rooms set in the bosom of family life but with plenty of personal space. Guests enjoy terraces and a *mirador* (viewpoint) with sea views.

Casa Yamicel CASA PARTICULAR $
(☎21-64-11-18; neoris70@gmail.com; Martí No 145a, btwn Ciro Frías & Pelayo Cuervo; r CUC$25; ❄) Doctor-proprietors that make killer mojitos? You'd better believe it. This colonial house offers six rooms with gorgeous wooden window bars (the best are on the top floor). There's wonderful hospitality, good meals (mains CUC$6 to CUC$12) and a roof terrace with reviving sea breezes. The super-helpful owners can also hook you up with reliable professional tour guides.

Hostal La Habanera HOTEL $$
(☎2164-5273; Antonio Maceo No 126; s/d incl breakfast CUC$59/64; ❄📶) Atmospheric and inviting in a way only Baracoa can muster, La Habanera sits in a restored and regularly repainted colonial mansion. The four front bedrooms share a street-facing balcony replete with tiled floor and rocking chairs: perfect for imbibing that quintessential Baracoa ambience (street-hawkers, hip-gyrating music, and seafood a-frying in the restaurants).

Eating

Eating in Baracoa is a full-on sensory experience. Cooking here is creative, tasty and – above all – different. To experience the real deal, eat in your casa particular.

Sabor Taíno CREOLE $
(☎5-481-2622; Maravi No 114, btwn Maceo & Martí; meals CUC$5-8; ⏱10am-11pm) A lovely family-run *paladar* with the owner's paintings adding to its slightly offbeat vibe, Sabor

Taíno serves up delicious, reasonably priced Baracoan classics preceded by soup and followed by dessert. Simply homey, friendly and satisfying.

Restaurante Las Terrazas Casa Nilson CUBAN **$$**

(☎2164-3123; Flor Crombet No 143, btwn Ciro Frías & Pelayo Cuervo; meals CUC$8-15; ⊙noon-3pm & 6:30-11pm) Up above Hostal Nilson on a spectacular two-level terrace decorated in quirky Afro-Caribbean style, the chef serves some of the best authentic Baracoan food in town, and hence Cuba. Aside from the typical Baracoan delights, novelties like melt-in-your-mouth octopus with basil ink and homemade *patacon guisado* (a plantain dish), in addition to the secret house sauces, set this place apart.

El Buen Sabor CUBAN **$$**

(☎2164-1400; Calixto García No 134 altos; meals CUC$6-15; ⊙noon-midnight) Served on a spotless and breezy upstairs terrace, meals come with salad, soup and side included. You can expect the best of Baracoan cuisine at this private restaurant, including swordfish in a coconut sauce, *bacán* (raw green plantain melded with crabmeat and wrapped in a banana leaf) and chocolate-y desserts. Service is attentive.

☆ Entertainment

Casa de la Trova Victorino Rodríguez TRADITIONAL MUSIC

(Félix Ruenes No 6; CUC$1; ⊙matinee 5:30pm, 9pm-midnight) Cuba's smallest, zaniest, wildest and most atmospheric *casa de la trova* (*trova* house) rocks nightly to the Vodou-like rhythms of *changüí-son*. One night the average age of the band is 85, the next it's 22. The common denominator? It's all good. Matinees are usually free. Order a mojito in a jam jar and join in the show.

ℹ Information

MONEY

There's no shortage of banks with ATMs.

Banco de Crédito y Comercio (Antonio Maceo No 99; ⊙8am-2:30pm Mon-Fri) Has an ATM.

Banco Popular de Ahorro (☎2164-5209; José Martí No 166; ⊙8-11:30am & 2-4:30pm Mon-Fri) Has an ATM.

Cadeca (☎2164-5345; José Martí No 241; ⊙8:15am-4pm Mon-Fri, to 11:30am Sat & Sun) Short queues for currency exchange.

TOURIST INFORMATION

Tour destinations and roads may be affected by weather, so ask ahead before traveling further afield.

Cubanacán (☎2164-4383; Martí, btwn Ciro Frías & Céspedes; ⊙8am-noon & 2-6pm Mon-Sat) Sells tours, airline tickets and Conectando a Cuba shuttle tickets. Also can reserve Viazul bus tickets.

Havanatur (☎2164-2776, 2164-5358; www.havanatur.cu; Martí No 225; ⊙8:30am-noon & 1:30-4:30pm Mon-Sat) Arranges stays at campismos in Guantánamo Province, as well as other accommodations, transportation and tours.

Infotur (☎2164-1781; Antonio Maceo No 129a, btwn Frank País & Maraví; ⊙8:30am-noon & 1-4:45pm Mon-Sat) Very helpful office.

ℹ Getting There & Away

The **National Bus Station** (☎2164-3880; cnr Av Los Mártires & Martí) has service with Víazul (www.viazul.com) to Guantánamo and Santiago de Cuba. Reserve your tickets a day in advance (more in high season). **Conectando a Cuba** (Parque Martí) has a shuttle service that travels to Santiago (CUC$17) on Tuesday, Thursday and Sunday at noon, stopping in Guantanamo (CUC$12).

UNDERSTAND CUBA

Cuba Today

With new leaders taking office in both Havana and Washington, the long-running soap opera of US–Cuban relations has moved into tetchier territory since Baraka Obama and Raul Castro shook hands at a baseball game in March 2016. Faced with tightened travel restrictions, the dramatic collapse of an important economic ally (Venezuela) and the inauspicious coronation of a new, largely untested leader (Miguel Díaz-Canel), Cuba's future remains shaky and uncertain.

History

Columbus & Colonization

Columbus neared Cuba on October 27, 1492, describing it as 'the most beautiful land human eyes had ever seen.' He named it 'Juana' in honor of a Spanish heiress. But deluded in his search for the kingdom of the Great Khan, and finding little gold in Cuba's lush and heavily forested interior, Columbus quickly abandoned the territory in favor of Hispaniola (modern-day Haiti and the Dominican Republic).

The colonization of Cuba didn't begin until nearly 20 years later in 1511, when Diego Velázquez de Cuéllar led a flotilla of four ships and 400 men from Hispaniola to conquer the island for the Spanish Crown. Docking near present-day Baracoa, the conquistadors promptly set about establishing seven *villas* (towns) on the main island – Havana, Trinidad, Baracoa, Bayamo, Camagüey, Santiago de Cuba and Sancti Spíritus – in a bid to bring their new colony under strong central rule. Watching nervously from the safety of their *bohíos* (thatched huts), a scattered population of Taínos looked on with a mixture of fascination and fear.

Despite Velázquez' attempts to protect the local Taínos from the gross excesses of the Spanish swordsmen, things quickly got out of hand and the invaders soon found that they had a full-scale rebellion on their hands. Leader of the embittered and short-lived Taíno insurgency was the feisty Hatuey, an influential *cacique* (chief) and archetype of the Cuban resistance, who was eventually captured and burned at the stake, Inquisition-style, for daring to challenge the iron fist of Spanish rule.

With the resistance decapitated, the Spaniards set about emptying Cuba of its relatively meager gold and mineral reserves, using the beleaguered natives as forced labor. As slavery was nominally banned under a papal edict, the Spanish got around the various legal loopholes by introducing a ruthless *encomienda* system, whereby thousands of natives were rounded up and forced to work for Spanish landowners on the pretext that they were receiving free 'lessons' in Christianity.

The brutal system lasted 20 years before the 'Apostle of the Indians,' Fray Bartolomé de Las Casas, appealed to the Spanish Crown for more humane treatment, and in 1542 the *encomiendas* were abolished for the indigenous people. For the unfortunate Taínos, the call came too late. Those who had not already been worked to death in the gold mines quickly succumbed to fatal European diseases such as smallpox, and by 1550 only about 5000 scattered survivors remained.

The Independence Wars

With its brutal slave system established, the Spanish ruled their largest Caribbean colony with an iron fist for the next 200 years, despite a brief occupation by the British in 1792. Cuba's Creole landowners, worried about a repetition of Haiti's brutal 1791 slave rebellion, held back when the rest of Latin America took up arms against the Spanish in the 1810s and 1820s. As a result, the nation's independence wars came more than half a century after the rest of Latin America had broken away from Spain. But when they arrived, they were no less impassioned – or bloody.

Independence or Dependence?

On May 20, 1902, Cuba became an independent republic – or did it? Despite three years of blood, sweat and sacrifice during the Spanish–Cuban–American War, no Cuban representatives were invited to the historic peace treaty held in Paris in 1898 that had promised Cuban independence *with conditions*.

The conditions were contained in the infamous Platt Amendment, a sly addition to the US 1901 Army Appropriations Bill that gave the US the right to intervene militarily in Cuba whenever it saw fit. The US also used its significant leverage to secure itself a naval base in Guantánamo Bay in order to protect its strategic interests in the Panama Canal region.

Despite some opposition in the US and a great deal more in Cuba, the Platt Amendment was passed by Congress and was written into Cuba's 1902 constitution. For Cuban patriots, the US had merely replaced Spain as the new colonizer and enemy. The repercussions have been causing bitter feuds for more than a century and still continue today.

The Batista Era

Fulgencio Batista, a *holguiñero* of mixed race from the town of Banes, was a wily and shrewd negotiator who presided over Cuba's best and worst attempts to establish an embryonic democracy in the 1940s and '50s. After an army officers' coup in 1933, he had taken power almost by default, gradually worming his way into the political vacuum it left amid the corrupt factions of a dying government. From 1934 onwards, Batista served as the army's chief of staff and, in 1940 in a relatively free and fair election, he was duly elected president.

Given an official mandate, Batista began to enact a wide variety of social reforms and set about drafting Cuba's most liberal and democratic constitution to date. But neither the liberal honeymoon nor Batista's good humor were to last. Stepping down after the 1944 election, the former army sergeant handed power over to the politically inept President Ramón Grau San Martín, and corruption and inefficiency soon reigned like never before.

The Revolutionary Spark Is Lit

On March 10, 1952, Batista, hedging his bets, staged another coup. With discontent brewing, a revolutionary circle formed in Havana, with Fidel Castro and many others at its core. On July 26, 1953, Castro led 119 rebels in an attack on the Moncada army barracks in Santiago de Cuba. The assault failed when a 4WD patrol encountered Castro's motorcade, costing the attackers the element of surprise. Castro and a few others escaped into the nearby mountains, where they planned their guerrilla campaign. Soon after, Castro was captured and stood trial; he received a 15-year sentence on Isla de Pinos (now Isla de la Juventud).

In February 1955 Batista won the presidency and freed all political prisoners, including Castro, who went to Mexico and trained a revolutionary force called the 26th of July Movement ('M-26-7'). On December 2, 1956, Castro and 81 companions alighted from the Granma at Playa Las Coloradas in the Oriente. The group was quickly routed by Batista's army, but Castro and 11 others (including Argentine doctor Ernesto 'Che' Guevara, Fidel's brother Raúl,and Camilo Cienfuegos) escaped into the Sierra Maestra. In May of the next year, Batista sent 10,000 troops into the mountains to liquidate Castro's 300 guerrillas. By August, the rebels had defeated this advance and captured a great quantity of arms. Che Guevara and Camilo Cienfuegos opened additional fronts in Las Villas Province, with Che capturing Santa Clara. Batista's troops finally surrendered on December 31, 1958.

In the small hours of January 1, 1959, Batista fled by private plane to the Dominican Republic. Meanwhile, materializing in Santiago de Cuba the same day, Fidel made a rousing victory speech from the town hall in Parque Céspedes before jumping into a 4WD and traveling across the breadth of the country to Havana in a Caesar-like cavalcade. The triumph of the revolution was seemingly complete.

Post-Revolution Realities

Cuba's history since the Revolution has been a David and Goliath tale of confrontation, rhetoric, Cold War stand-offs and an omnipresent US trade embargo that has featured 11 US presidents and two infamous Cuban leaders – both called Castro. For the first 30 years, Cuba allied itself with the Soviet Union as the US used various retaliatory tactics (all unsuccessful) to bring Fidel Castro to heel, including a botched invasion, 600-plus assassination attempts and one of the longest economic blockades in modern history.

When the Soviet bloc fell in 1989–91, Cuba stood alone behind an increasingly defiant and stubborn leader surviving, against all odds, through a decade of severe economic austerity known as the Special Period. GDP fell by more than half, luxuries went out the window, and a wartime spirit of rationing and sacrifice took hold among a populace that, ironically, had prized itself free from foreign (neo)colonial influences for the first time in its history.

Enter Raúl

In July 2006, the unimaginable happened. Fidel Castro, rather than dying in office and paving the way for an American-led capitalistic reopening (as had long been predicted), retired from day-to-day governing due to poor health and passed power quietly onto his younger brother, Raúl. Inheriting the country's highest office on the cusp of a major worldwide recession, Raúl began a slow package of reforms.

It kicked off modestly in 2008 when Cubans were permitted access to tourist hotels, and allowed to purchase mobile phones and myriad electronic goods, rights taken for granted in most democratic countries, but long out of reach to the average Cuban. These moves were followed in January 2011 by the biggest economic and ideological shake-up since the country waved *adiós* to Batista. Radical new laws laid off half a million government workers and tried to stimulate the private sector by granting business licenses to 178 state-recognized professions – everything from hairdressers to disposable-lighter refillers.

By 2013, Cuba had witnessed its most dramatic economic shift in decades with nearly 400,000 people working in the private sector, 250,000 more than in 2010, though it was still far from anything like Western-style capitalism.

The Passing of Fidel

Fidel's omnipresence for the past half-century made the man seem invincible, yet on November 25th, 2016, Raúl Castro announced his brother's passing at the age of 90. His cremated remains were laid to rest in Santiago de Cuba after a cross-island procession that recalled the march of his revolutionary triumph, done in reverse. Throughout Cuba, crowds lined the streets to pay homage to their longtime leader as exiles celebrated in Miami.

Culture

Just try to understand life on this ever-contradictory island. Your first impression may be that it is solid and immutable. But the truth is that Cuba is a moving target that evades easy definition.

For starters, it's like nowhere else. For those familiar with Latin America, there's close-knit families and an ease with unpredictability. But there are differences too. Cuba's strong education system has created erudite citizens more likely to quote the classics than pop songs. They are playful, even raucous, but also intimate with hardship and austerity, skilled but as languorous as any Caribbean outport.

The best way to get to know Cuba is to reserve comment and watch it unfold before you. While long lines and poor service infuriate tourists, Cubans remain unflappable. Rushing doesn't make things happen any faster. But there are richer ways to pass the time: shooting the breeze in rocking chairs, spending Sundays with families or inviting their cousins, friends and neighbors over when a bottle of rum comes their way.

Music

Rich, vibrant, layered and soulful, Cuban music has long acted as a standard-bearer for the sounds and rhythms emanating out of Latin America. This is the birthplace of salsa, where elegant European dances adopted edgy black rhythms, and where the African drum first courted the Spanish guitar. From the down-at-heel docks of Matanzas to the bucolic villages of the Sierra Maestra, the amorous musical fusion went on to fuel everything from *son*, rumba, mambo, *chachachá*, *charanga*, *changüí*, *danzón* and more.

Aside from the obvious Spanish and African roots, Cuban music has drawn upon a number of other influences. Mixed into an already exotic melting pot are genres from France, the US, Haiti and Jamaica.

Landscape & Wildlife

Landscape

Formed by a volatile mixture of volcanic activity, plate tectonics and erosion, Cuba's landscape is a lush, varied concoction of mountains, caves, plains and *mogotes* (flat-topped hills). The highest point, Pico Turquino (1972m), is situated in the east among the Sierra Maestra's lofty triangular peaks. Further west, in the Sierra del Escambray, ruffled hilltops and gushing waterfalls straddle the borders of Cienfuegos, Villa Clara and Sancti Spíritus provinces. Rising like purple shadows in the far west, the 175km-long Cordillera de Guanguanico is a more diminutive range that includes the protected Sierra del Rosario Biosphere Reserve and the distinctive pincushion hills of the Valle de Viñales.

Lapped by the warm turquoise waters of the Caribbean Sea in the south, and the chop of the Atlantic Ocean in the north, Cuba's 5746km of coastline shelters more than 300 natural beaches and features one of the world's largest tracts of coral reef. Home to approximately 900 reported species of fish and more than 410 varieties of sponge and coral, the country's unspoiled coastline is a marine wonderland and a major reason why Cuba has become renowned as a diving destination.

As a sprawling archipelago, Cuba contains thousands of islands and keys (most uninhabited) in four major offshore groups: the Archipiélago de los Colorados, off northern Pinar del Río; the Archipiélago de Sabana-Camagüey (or Jardines del Rey), off northern Villa Clara and Ciego de Ávila; the Archipiélago de los Jardines de la Reina, off southern Ciego de Ávila; and the Archipiélago de los Canarreos, around Isla de la Juventud. Most visitors will experience one or more of these island idylls, as the majority of resorts, scuba diving and beaches are found in these regions.

Lying in the Caribbean's main hurricane region, Cuba has been hit by some blinders in recent years, notably 2012's Sandy, which caused more than US$2 billion in damage, and Hurricane Matthew, which touched down in Baracoa in 2016.

Wildlife

Cuba has an unusual share of indigenous fauna to draw serious animal-watchers. Birds are the biggest draw and Cuba has more than 350 different varieties, two dozen endemic. Head to the mangroves of Ciénaga de Zapata in Matanzas province or to the Península de Guanahacabibes in Pinar del Río for the best sightings of *zunzuncito* (bee hummingbird), the world's smallest bird. At 6.5cm, it's not much longer than a toothpick. These areas are also home to the *tocororo* (Cuban trogon), Cuba's national bird. Other popular bird species include *cartacubas* (indigenous to Cuba), herons, spoonbills, parakeets and rarely seen Cuban pygmy owls.

Flamingos are abundant in Cuba's northern keys, though the largest nesting ground in the western hemisphere located in Camagüey province's Río Máximo delta has been compromised by contamination.

Land mammals have been hunted almost to extinction with the largest indigenous survivor the friendly *jutía* (tree rat), a 4kg edible rodent that scavenges on isolated keys living in relative harmony with armies of inquisitive iguanas. The vast majority of Cuba's other 38 species of mammal are from the bat family.

Cuba harbors a species of frog so small and elusive that it wasn't discovered until 1996 in what is now Parque Nacional Alejandro de Humboldt near Baracoa. Still lacking a common name, the endemic amphibian is known as *Eleutherodactylus iberia*; it measures less than 1cm in length, and has a range of only 100 sq km.

Other odd species include the *mariposa de cristal* (Cuban clear-winged butterfly), one of only two clear-winged butterflies in the world; the rare *manjuarí* (Cuban alligator gar), an ancient fish considered a living fossil; the *polimita*, a unique land snail distinguished by its festive yellow, red and brown bands; and, discovered only in 2011, the endemic *Lucifuga*, a blind troglodyte fish.

Reptiles are well represented in Cuba. Aside from iguanas and lizards, there are 15 species of snake, none poisonous. Cuba's largest snake is the *majá*, a constrictor related to the anaconda that grows up to 4m in length; it's nocturnal and doesn't usually mess with humans. The endemic Cuban crocodile *(Crocodylus rhombifer)* is relatively small but agile on land and in water. Its 68 sharp teeth are specially adapted for crushing turtle shells. Crocs have suffered from major habitat loss in the last century though greater protection since the 1990s has seen numbers increase. Cuba has established a number of successful crocodile breeding farms *(criaderos)*, the largest of which is at Guamá near the Bay of Pigs. Living in tandem with the Cuban croc is the larger American crocodile *(Crocodylus acutus)* found in the Zapata Swamps and in various marshy territories on Cuba's southern coast.

Cuba's marine life compensates for what the island lacks in land fauna. The manatee, the world's only herbivorous aquatic mammal, is found in the Bahía de Taco and the Península de Zapata, and whale sharks frequent the María la Gorda area at Cuba's eastern tip from November to February. Four turtle species (leatherback, loggerhead, green and hawksbill) are found in Cuban waters and they nest annually in isolated keys or on protected beaches in Península de Guanahacabibes.

SURVIVAL GUIDE

Directory A–Z

ACCESSIBLE TRAVEL

Cuba's inclusive culture extends to disabled travelers, and while facilities may be lacking, the generous nature of Cubans generally compensates when it can.

However, with battered buses, potholed sidewalks and poorly maintained buildings, some of which haven't been renovated since the 1950s, independent travel can be difficult for people with physical challenges. Many older buildings in Cuba don't have elevators or, if they do, they are regularly out of order. Similarly, public buses lack facilities for the physically impaired. For comfort and reliability, modern Cubataxis are the best way of getting around.

Steps and curbs are a perennial problem. Ramps are often not available and, when they are, they can be ridiculously steep. Only the more expensive hotels offer specially designed accessible rooms with wide doors and customized bathrooms. If it's your first time in Cuba, it might be better to book into an all-inclusive resort that caters for physically challenged travelers. Start your inquiries at the part foreign-owned Meliá and Iberostar chains in places like Varadero, Cayo Coco and Guardalavaca.

Sight-impaired travelers will be helped across streets and given priority in lines. Etecsa phone centers have telephone equipment for the hearing-impaired, and TV programs are broadcast with closed captioning.

Hotels with special facilities for the physically impaired include the following:

Hotel Iberostar Parque Central (p312) Havana.

Hotel Saratoga (p313) Havana.

Meliá Internacional (☎45-62-31-00; www.melia.com; Av las Américas Km 1; s/d CUC$323/465; ❄@🛜🏊) Varadero.

Meliá Varadero (☎45-66-70-13; Carretera las Morlas; s/d all-inclusive CUC$283/405; P❄@🛜🏊) Varadero.

ACCOMMODATIONS

Cuban accommodations run the gamut from CUC$10 beach cabins to five-star resorts. Solo travelers are penalized price-wise, often paying 75% of the price of a double room. It is advisable to book your accommodations in advance in peak season (November to April).

Casas particulares Cuban homes that rent rooms to foreigners; an authentic and economic form of cultural immersion.

Campismos Cheap, rustic accommodations in rural areas, usually in bungalows or cabins.

Hotels All Cuban hotels are government-owned. Prices and quality range from cheap Soviet-era to high-flying colonial chic.

Resorts Large international-standard hotels in resort areas that sell all-inclusive packages.

SLEEPING PRICE RANGES

The following price ranges refer to a double room with bathroom in high season.

Havana

$ less than CUC$70

$$ CUC$70–150

$$$ more than CUC$150

Rest of Cuba

$ less than CUC$50

$$ CUC$50–120

$$$ more than CUC$120

EMERGENCY NUMBERS

Directory assistance	☎113
Emergency	☎108
Fire	☎105
Police	☎106

FOOD

Private restaurants Although slightly pricier than their state-run equivalents, private restaurants nearly always offer the best, freshest food and the highest-quality service.

Casas particulares Cuban homestays invariably serve a massive breakfast for around CUC$5; some also offer an equally large and tasty dinner made from the freshest ingredients.

Hotels and resorts The all-inclusives offer buffet food of an international standard but after a week it can get a bit bland.

State-run restaurants Varying food and service from top-notch places in Havana to unimaginative rations in the provinces. Prices often lower than private places.

INTERNET ACCESS

State-run telecommunications company Etecsa has a monopoly as Cuba's internet service provider. For public internet access, almost every provincial town has an Etecsa *telepuntos* (internet cafe–cum call center) where you can wait in line to enter and buy a one-hour user card (CUC$1) with scratch-off *usuario* (code) and *contraseña* (password) to use at computers onsite or in a public wi-fi area (usually the central plaza of a town). Cards can be used for multiple internet sessions.

There are no independent internet cafes outside the *telepuntos*. However, these days most hotels and a growing number of casas particulares have wi-fi (although the signal is often weak and you'll need an Etecsa scratch-card to access it). Scratch-cards can sometimes be bought in hotels and casas particulares, though often at inflated rates.

Although connections are often slow and temperamental, particularly at peak times (late afternoon and early evening), internet in Cuba has improved greatly in the last five years and is likely to continue to do so.

LGBT+ TRAVELERS

While Cuba isn't a full-blown queer destination (yet), it's more tolerant than many other Latin American countries. The hit movie *Fresa y Chocolate* (Strawberry and Chocolate; 1994) sparked a national dialogue about homosexuality. Activist Mariela Castro, the daughter of Raúl, has led the way in much-needed LGBT reforms and changing social perceptions. Today Cuba is-pretty tolerant, all things considered, and LGBT travelers shouldn't have many problems.

Same-sex marriage isn't yet legal in Cuba, although it's probably only a matter of time before it becomes so (President Díaz-Canel recently expressed his support). Discrimination on the basis of sexual orientation and gender is illegal.

Lesbianism is less tolerated and seldom discussed, and you'll see very little open displays of affection between female lovers. There are occasional *fiestas para chicas* (not necessarily all-girl parties but close); ask around at the **Cine Yara** (Map p316; cnr Calles 23 & L) in Havana's gay cruising zone.

The best gay nightlife scenes are in Havinternet accessana and Santa Clara, where drag shows are weekly occurrences in **Cafe Cantante Mi Habana** (Map p316; ☎7-879-0710; cnr Paseo & Calle 39; cover CUC$10; ⏲8pm-3am), **Cabaret Las Vegas** (Map p316; Calzada de la Infanta No 104, btwn Calles 25 & 27; entry CUC$5; ⏲10pm-4am) and Club Mejunje (p333). Countrywide, many of Cuba's best casas particluares have gay owners.

MONEY

Cuba has two currencies – convertibles (CUC$) and pesos (*moneda nacional;* MN$). One convertible is worth 25 pesos. Non-Cubans deal almost exclusively in convertibles.

ATMs & Credit Cards

Cuba is primarily a cash economy. Credit cards are accepted in resort hotels and some city hotels. There are a growing number of ATMs.

US debit and credit cards, or cards connected to US banks, cannot be used.

While services can still be booked with credit cards from the USA on the internet, inside Cuba it's another story. Residents of the US can wire money via Western Union, though this requires help from a third party and hefty fees.

When weighing up whether to use a credit card or cash, bear in mind that the charges levied by Cuban banks are similar for both (around 3%). However, your home bank may charge additional fees for ATM/credit-card transactions. An increasing number of debit cards work in Cuba, but it's best to check with both your home bank and the local Cuban bank before using them. 'Visa debit' is usually the best bet.

Ideally, it pays to arrive in Cuba with a stash of cash and a credit and debit card as backup.

Almost all private business in Cuba, such as at casas particulares, is still conducted in cash.

Cash advances can be drawn from credit cards, but the commission is the same. Check with your home bank before you leave, as many banks won't authorize large withdrawals in foreign countries unless you notify them of your travel plans first.

EATING PRICE RANGES

It will be a very rare meal in Cuba that costs over CUC$25. The following price brackets are for main-course dishes.

$ less than CUC$7

$$ CUC$7–15

$$$ more than CUC$15

ATMs are becoming more common. This being Cuba, it is wise to only use ATMs when the bank is open, in case any problems occur.

SAFE TRAVEL

Cuba is safer than most Latin American countries. Indeed, in 2018, it was voted the safest country in the world for tourists at a conference in Madrid. Violent attacks are extremely rare and city streets are generally chilled, even after dark. Be aware of the following.

- Petty theft and pickpockets
- Short-changing in bars and restaurants
- Street hustlers selling cigars
- Dual currency scams
- For women, sexist banter and unwanted attention from men

TELEPHONE

- To call Cuba from abroad, dial your international access code, Cuba's country code (53), the city or area code, and the local number.
- To call internationally from Cuba, dial the international access code '00,' followed by the country code, the area code and the number; to call the US, just dial 119, then 1, the area code and the number.
- To call cell phone to cell phone or cell phone to landline just dial the eight-digit number (which always starts with a '5').
- To call cell phone to landline (or landline to landline) dial the provincial code plus the local number.

Cell Phones

- Check with your service provider to see if your phone will work (GSM or TDMA networks only). International calls are expensive. You can buy services from the state-run phone company, Cubacel.
- You can use your own GSM or TDMA phones in Cuba with a local SIM card, though you'll need to ensure your phone is unlocked first. Buy a SIM card (CUC$40 including CUC$10 worth of data) at an Etecsa *telepunto*. Bring your passport.

VISAS

- Regular tourists who plan to spend up to two months in Cuba do not need visas. Instead, you

LICENSES FOR VISITORS FROM THE USA

The US government issues two sorts of licenses for travel to Cuba: 'specific' and 'general.' Specific licenses are considered on a case-by-case basis and require a lengthy and sometimes complicated application process; their application should start at least 45 days before your intended date of departure.

Most visitors will travel under general licenses. General licenses are self-qualifying and don't require travelers to notify the Office of Foreign Assets Control (OFAC) of their travel plans. Travelers sign an affidavit stating the purpose of travel and purchase a Cuban visa at check-in when departing the US via flights. Visas cost between US$50 and US$85 depending on which airline you fly with. Note that the Trump administration eliminated travel under the 'educational purpose' license category.

You might need supporting documentation to back up your claim when you book your flight ticket. Check with the US Department of the Treasury (www.treasury.gov/resource-center/sanctions/Programs/pages/cuba.aspx) to see if you qualify for a license.

get a *tarjeta de turista* (tourist card) valid for 30 days, which can be extended once you're in Cuba (Canadians get 90 days plus the option of a 90-day extension).

- Package tourists receive their card with their other travel documents. Those going 'air only' usually buy the tourist card from the travel agency or airline office that sells them the plane ticket, but policies vary (eg Canadian airlines give out tourist cards on their airplanes), so you'll need to check ahead with the airline office via phone or email.
- In some cases, you may be required to buy and/or pick up the card at your departure airport, sometimes at the flight gate itself some minutes before departure.
- Once in Havana, tourist-card extensions or replacements cost another CUC$25. You cannot leave Cuba without presenting your tourist card.
- You are not permitted entry to Cuba without an onward ticket.

Getting There & Away

AIR

Cuba has 10 international airports. The largest by far is **Aeropuerto Internacional José Martí** (www.havana-airport.org; Av Rancho Boyeros, Rancho Boyeros) in Havana. The only other sizable airport is **Juan Gualberto Gómez International Airport** (VRA; ☎45-61-30-16, 45-24-70-15) in Varadero.

Cubana de Aviación (☎7-649-0410; www.cubana.cu; Airline Bldg, Calle 23 No 64, Vedado, Havana; ⏲8:30am-4pm Mon-Fri, to noon Sat), the national carrier, grounded half its fleet after a crash in May 2018. At the time of writing it was still working at half capacity, operating flights to Bogotá and Buenos Aires and a handful of Caribbean destinations. Its airfares are usually among the cheapest, though overbooking and delays are nagging problems. Overweight baggage is strictly charged for every kilogram above the 20kg allowance. If you have the option, book with another airline.

For safety recommendations, check the latest at www.airsafe.com.

SEA

With US–Cuban cruises off the menu since June 2019, you're once again limited to mainly European-based cruise lines if you want to visit Cuba by ship. German-run Hapag-Lloyd Cruises (www.hl-cruises.com) runs an interesting 12-day 'Best of Cuba' cruise out of Mexico that calls at Havana, La Isla de la Juventud and Santiago de Cuba. UK-run Marella Cruises (www.tui.co.uk/cruise) has a seven-night 'Flavours of the Caribbean' trip that starts and finishes in Jamaica but does a loop around Havana, the Cayman Islands and Mexico. British-Norwegian Fred Olsen Cruise Lines (www.fredolsencruises.com) runs a comprehensive two-week trip from Barbados to the Dominican Republic that calls at both Santiago de Cuba and Havana.

Getting Around

Bus The most efficient and practical option. State-run Víazul links most places of interest to tourists on a regular daily schedule. Cubanacán runs a less comprehensive service. Local buses are crowded and have no printed schedules.

Car Rentals are quite expensive and driving can be a challenge due to the lack of signposts and ambiguous road rules. Cars are often in short supply.

Taxi *Colectivos* (shared taxis) are a good option over longer distances if you are traveling in a small group. Fares can be split four ways, meaning *colectivos* are almost as cheap as buses.

Train Cuba's extensive rail network was recently upgraded with new carriages from China. Trains are still slow, but at least they're now more comfortable.

Curaçao

5999 / POP 160,010

Includes ➡

Best Places to Eat

- ➡ Pop's Place (p364)
- ➡ Jaanchie's (p367)
- ➡ Caña Bar & Kitchen (p362)
- ➡ Fishalicious (p363)
- ➡ Old Market (p362)

Best Places to Stay

- ➡ Scuba Lodge (p361)
- ➡ Bed & Bike (p361)
- ➡ Landhuis Jan Thiel (p364)
- ➡ Avila Beach Hotel (p362)

Why Go?

With its delightful Dutch-colonial architecture, thriving art and culinary scenes and excellent history museums, go-go Curaçao feels like a little piece of Europe at the edge of the Caribbean. A little piece of Europe, that is, with glorious hidden beaches, wondrous caves, amazing snorkeling and diving, and a wild, undeveloped windward coast dotted with prickly cacti and whiptail blue lizards.

Curaçao also has a surging economy beyond tourism, which means that Willemstad has factories, humdrum neighborhoods and sometimes bad traffic. Catering to visitors is not the primary aim here, which lends the island more authenticity than its neighbors tend to offer. So if you're looking for a Caribbean destination that's busy setting its own pace – a place where the adventuring tends to be a bit more unbridled – Curaçao is right for you.

When to Go

Dec–Apr High season, when accommodations fill and prices are higher.

Jan & Feb Party time: Carnival is Curaçao's biggest celebration.

Sep–Dec Curaçao is below the hurricane belt, but the island does get some rain.

Curaçao Highlights

1. **Willemstad** (p359) Discovering the Dutch-colonial architecture and rich local culture in this busy port town.
2. **Snorkeling and diving** (p368) Going straight from the beach to the reef at onshore snorkel and dive sites such as those at the National Underwater Park.
3. **Christoffel National Park** (p366) Summiting the island's tallest mountain, then visiting the nearby Savonet Museum.
4. **Museum Kura Hulanda** (p359) Bearing witness to the terrible legacy of slavery.
5. **Grote Knip** (p366) Finding your place in the sand on the island's most scenic beach.
6. **Playa Portomari** (p365) Following two underwater snorkel trails to discover the beach's unique double reef.
7. **Shete Boka National Park** (p366) Feeling the power of nature on the windblown and wave-tossed east coast.

Willemstad

Gazing across Sint Annabaai at the colorful town houses lined up on the shore, you might think that you're in the Old Country. Until you remember that the sun is shining, it's 28°C (82°F), and you're on your way to the beach. Despite the flawless weather, Willemstad feels like a Dutch city, complete with waterways and street cafes.

Residents live in the hills surrounding Schottegat, the deep inland harbor. Much of the sprawling city is traffic clogged and rather mundane. But the crowded streets of Punda are packed with galleries and shops, while nearby Pietermaai is coming alive with restaurants, bars and clubs. Throughout the old town the architecture is rich, with stunning examples of 17th- and 18th-century fortifications, Dutch colonial planning and diverse building styles, all of which earned this city its Unesco-protected status.

Sights

★Landhuis Bloemhof ARTS CENTER
(737-5775; www.facebook.com/pg/Landhuis Bloemhof; Santa Rosaweg 6; US$2; 9am-2pm Tue-Sat or by appointment) As visitors wander the leafy grounds of this 1735 plantation home they encounter a range of things. An old car covered in mosaic tiles depicting sea creatures. Plants growing out of discarded toilets. A towering cathedral constructed of thorns. Essentially, this is the epicenter of the avant-garde in Curaçao, and for a small fee someone will guide you through the wonders, many of which tell important stories of the island and its history.

★Museum Kura Hulanda MUSEUM
(462-9537; www.kurahulanda.com; Klipstraat 9, Otrobanda; adult/child US$10/7; 9am-4:30pm Mon-Sat) Located in a 19th-century merchant's house and slave quarters, this excellent museum documents the brutal history of slavery in the New World, including the slave trade, the culture of enslaved people, and abolition. There's also a fantastic collection of art and artifacts from West Africa – including a cool sculpture garden – showcasing the significant African influences on Caribbean culture.

Gallery Alma Blou GALLERY
(462-8896; www.galleryalmablou.com; Frater Radulphusweg 4; 9:30am-5:30pm Tue-Fri, 10am-2pm Sat) FREE Housed in the 17th-century Landhuis Habaai plantation house, this cooperative gallery has the city's largest collection of works by Caribbean artists. The rotating exhibits usually feature one or two artists with local connections, but there's always a great variety of works on display, including whimsical sculptures in the courtyard and gardens. Located about 3km northwest of Otrobanda.

Curaçao Maritime Museum MUSEUM
(465-2327; www.curacaomaritime.com; Van den Brandhofstraat 7, Scharloo; adult/child US$7/3, harbor tours US$10/5; 9am-4pm Tue-Sat, harbor tours 2pm Wed & Sat) Engaging displays trace the island's history, including exhibits on the Dutch West India Co, the growth of Willemstad, the slave trade and more. A highlight is **Steam for Oil** (guided tour adult/child US$6.50/3, self-guided tour US$2.50/free; tour 1pm Wed & Sat), a working model of the oil refinery that has been a centerpiece of the island's economy throughout the 20th century. The museum also runs informative biweekly harbor tours. Combination tickets are available.

Jewish Cultural-Historical Museum MUSEUM
(461-1067; www.snoa.com; Hanchi Snoa 29, Punda; US$10; 9am-4:30pm Mon-Fri) The 1651 Mikvé Israel Emanuel Synagogue has the oldest continuously operating Jewish congregation in the western hemisphere. Its small but fascinating museum occupies two 18th-century buildings that once housed the rabbi's residence and bathhouse. The museum's centerpiece is the original *mikveh* (bath), discovered during renovation. Also on display is a Torah scroll that was brought to Curaçao by the first Jewish settlers.

Tours

Gone Caribe OUTDOORS
(660-2504; www.gonecaribe.com; tours US$65-120) Jessica and Joey, an enthusiastic local couple with lots of insider knowledge, lead groups of up to six guests to some of Curaçao's best natural attractions, including beaches, national parks, snorkel sites and caves, as well as authentic local eateries and hidden gems. Guests can design their own trips. Tours are offered in English, French, Spanish, Dutch or Papiamento.

Sleeping

The transformation of Pietermaai has produced a handful of lovely new hotels, most of

Willemstad

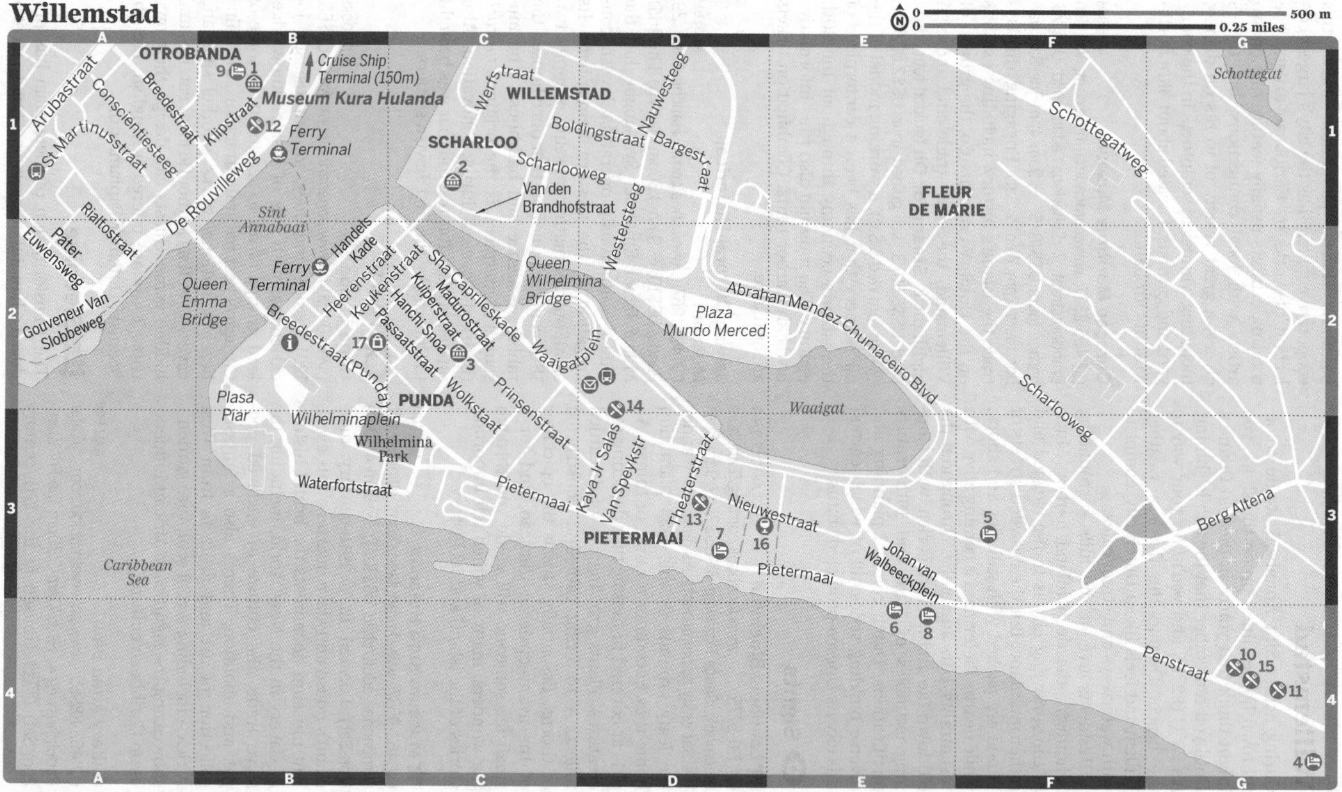

0 500 m
0 0.25 miles
OTROBANDA
Cruise Ship Terminal (150m)
Museum Kura Hulanda
WILLEMSTAD
SCHARLOO
FLEUR DE MARIE
PUNDA
PIETERMAAI
Arubastraat
Conscientiesteeg
Breedestraat
Klipstraat
St Martinusstraat
Ferry Terminal
De Rouvilleweg
Rialtostraat
Pater Euwensweg
Gouveneur Van Slobbeweg
Sint Annabaai
Queen Emma Bridge
Handels Kade
Heerenstraat
Keukenstraat
Kuiperstraat
Madurostraat
Hanchi Snoa
Passaatstraat
Sha Caprileskade
Breedestraat (Punda)
Wolkstaat
Prinsenstraat
Plasa Piar
Wilhelminaplein
Wilhelmina Park
Waterfortstraat
Werfstraat
Boldingstraat
Nauwesteeg
Bargestraat
Scharlooweg
Van den Brandhofstraat
Westersteeg
Queen Wilhelmina Bridge
Waaigatplein
Plaza Mundo Merced
Abrahan Mendez Chumaceiro Blvd
Waaigat
Kaya Jr Salas
Van Speykstr
Theaterstraat
Nieuwestraat
Pietermaai
Johan van Walbeeckplein
Schottegatweg
Schottegat
Berg Altena
Penstraat
Caribbean Sea
1 2 3 4 5 6 7 8 9 10 11 12 13 14 15 16 17
A B C D E F G

Willemstad

Top Sights

Sights

Sleeping

Eating

Drinking & Nightlife

Shopping

them occupying beautifully restored colonial-era buildings. If you want to see what these buildings looked like before, just look across the street or next door, where edifices are still crumbling and decrepit. In Punda and Otrobanda the accommodations options are quite dated though perhaps more affordable.

★Bed & Bike — HOSTEL $

(☎843-7373; www.bedandbikecuracao.com; Ansinghstraat 1; dm from US$32, r US$52-122; ❄📶) Willemstad's premier 'poshtel' (an upscale hostel, for the uninitiated) opened in 2017 in a formerly abandoned parliament building, and its central location in Pietermaai is a big draw. The restored interior is artsy and cheerful, fostering a convivial vibe, and the roof deck and communal kitchen are good spots to make friends. Every guest gets a complimentary bike!

★Scuba Lodge — HOTEL $$

(☎465-2575; www.scubalodge.com; Pietermaai 104, Petermaai; r from US$179, ste US$259-497; ❄📶🏊) Occupying a rainbow-colored row of colonial houses in Petermaai, this hotel exemplifies the district's exuberant blend of fashion and funk. Enormous rooms have luxe touches and mod design features. Service is superfriendly from the moment you walk in and receive a welcome drink. The on-site dive shop is also recommended.

Pietermaai Boutique Hotel — BOUTIQUE HOTEL $$

(☎465-0478; https://pietermaaiboutiquehotel.com; Pietermaai 51, Pietermaai; ste US$130; ❄📶🏊) An old colonial Pietermaai building has been beautifully restored, preserving historical details such as wooden shutters, narrow hallways, wooden floors and high ceilings, to create this lovely, atmospheric hotel. Rooms vary widely, but most have kitchenettes and a small seating area; some have open bathrooms. Accommodations surround a lush tropical garden with a plunge pool.

Sonesta Kura Hulanda Village — HISTORIC HOTEL $$

(☎434-7700; www.kurahulanda.com; Langestraat 8, Otrobanda; d/ste from US$134/220; P❄@📶🏊) *Kura Hulanda* is Papiamentu for 'Dutch courtyard,' which gives an idea of the atmosphere of this colonial village, where restored buildings cluster along cobblestone pathways, and shady courtyards are punctuated with sculptures. The rooms are uniquely decorated, featuring hand-carved furnishings and original art, along with plenty of modern amenities. The Museum Kura Hulanda is on the grounds.

Boutique Hotel BijBlaw — BOUTIQUE HOTEL $$

(☎650-0550; www.bijblauw.com; Pietermaai 82-84, Petermaai; r US$160-205, ste US$185-325; P❄📶🏊) The 13 rooms at this Pietermaai gem differ from each other in size and color, but they all feature clean, contemporary

DON'T MISS

CURAÇAO FESTIVALS

Carnival (⏱Jan & Feb) A packed schedule of fun begins right after New Year's Day.

Curaçao Pride (www.facebook.com/Curacaopride; ⏱Sep or Oct) The only Pride parade in the ABCs (Aruba, Bonaire and Curaçao) takes place in venues around Willemstad. Five days of events often include a Pride walk from Otrobanda to Wilhelmina Park, a big Friday-night bash at the Rainbow Lounge (p363), and numerous other dance and beach parties with live music and DJs.

lines, nature-inspired decor and lots of natural light. A lovely open-air restaurant and a cool 'concept store' with some rad fashions are on-site. It's all very hip.

Avila Beach Hotel BOUTIQUE HOTEL **$$$**
(☎461-4377; www.avilabeachhotel.com; Penstraat 130; r from US$245; P❄@📶🏊) The Avila Beach Hotel comprises the magnificently restored 18th-century home of a Dutch governor along with a couple of modern wings of luxurious accommodations and a charming adults-only tower with stunning sea views. The elegant grounds include two private beaches and a gorgeous infinity pool, along with an underwater coral nursery that's part of a restoration project.

Eating

The most innovative cooking is happening in the kitchens of Pietermaai and particularly near the intersection of Penstraat and Lombokstraat, which brims with new and inviting restaurants and bars. In Punda, keep your eyes open for humble backstreet eateries serving good traditional fare, but keep your wallet closed for most of the touristy places lining Sint Annabaai.

WORTH A TRIP

KLEIN CURAÇAO

Remember the one book/song/food/friend you would bring if you were going to be stuck on a desert island? That'll come in handy when you take a trip to this uninhabited island about 15 miles off the coast of Curaçao. Spend the day lounging on the sand, exploring the recently renovated lighthouse, frolicking in the waters and swimming with sea turtles (as well as reading that book, listening to the song, eating the food and hanging out with your BFF).

Find this paradise by signing up for an all-day or half-day tour with Mermaid Boat Trips (p364) or **Bounty Adventures** (☎767-9998; www.bountyadventures.com; Caracasbaaiweg; adult/child bus tour US$49/35, snorkeling US$75/38, Klein Curaçao trip US$108/54). Boats depart from the marina on Caracas Bay to make the 1½-hour trip to the island. The ride can be rough, so don't forget to take your Dramamine.

Old Market CARIBBEAN **$**
(Plasa Bieu; Sha Caprileskade, Punda; mains US$8-12; ⏲10:30am-3pm Mon-Sat) Folks of all stripes crowd into this vast, barn-like structure to snag seats at the picnic tables and feast on down-home Curaçao cooking. The specialty is local dishes such as goat stew, pumpkin pancakes, cactus stew and whole red snapper. It's tasty and absolutely authentic.

★**Rozendaels** CARIBBEAN **$$**
(☎461-8806; www.rozendaels.com; Penstraat 47, Pietermaai; meals US$15-25; ⏲5-10pm Sun-Fri; 🖉) Rozendaels will be a highlight of your trip. The secret-garden setting and the personable service are a good start, but the food is near perfection. It's a fantastic place to try local delicacies such as *keshi yena* (cheese and chicken casserole) and grilled *mahimahi*, but the varied menu features international fare as well.

★**Caña Bar & Kitchen** CARIBBEAN **$$**
(☎691-5429; www.canabk.com; Lombokstraat 4-6; share plates US$10-20; ⏲5pm-midnight Tue-Sat) With low-lit environs and provocative murals, Curaçao's first gastropub remains at the top of its game. Inventive tapas include the likes of passionfruit ceviche with sweet potato and red pepper, and they pair exceedingly well with the small, potent selection of rum-, pisco- and tequila-based cocktails. You can also build a highball with house-made sodas such as passionfruit-cucumber or grapefruit-basil.

Mundo Bizarro CUBAN **$$**
(☎461-6767; www.mundobizarrocuracao.com; Nieuwestraat 12, Pietermaai; mains breakfast $6-18, dinner US$16-29; ⏲8am-10pm, bar to midnight or 1am; 📶) The anchor of Pietermaai, this place evokes old Havana. The ground floor opens to the surrounding streets and alleys, and inside there's a faux look of urban decay, countered by the fine food. Upstairs is home to a bar with fab mojitos and live music on Tuesday (tango), Thursday (salsa) and Friday (varies).

Gouverneur de Rouville DUTCH **$$**
(☎462-5999; www.de-gouverneur.com; De Rouvilleweg 9, Otrobanda; mains lunch US$11-17, dinner US$19-28; ⏲10am-10:30pm, bar to midnight; 📶) The Dutch and Caribbean food served in this restored colonial building is good, but the views of Sint Annabaai are magic, especially when a huge freighter passes at night with a carnival of colored lights. Avoid the cute but viewless courtyard; the bar has a terrace.

Fishalicious SEAFOOD **$$$**
(461-8844; www.fishalicious.net; Penstraat 57; mains US$24-31; 6-10pm Mon-Sat) One of Willemstad's best seafood establishments since 2009, Fishalicious has taken the ambience to another level in its newer Dutch-colonial home on Penstraat. The covered but open-air dining room is pure elegance, with gorgeous tile work and oyster chandeliers. The menu focuses on North Sea fish dishes such as dover sole, cod and oysters, along with various tuna preparations.

Drinking & Nightlife

Miles Jazz Cafe BAR
(520-5200; www.facebook.com/milescuracao; Nieuwestraat 48, Pietermaai; 4pm-2am Mon-Thu, to 3am Fri & Sat, to midnight Sun) That's Miles as in Davis, one of the inspirations for this stylishly divey night spot in Pietermaai. This place is old school, as in jazz music from vinyl. There's live music on Saturday night, and one killer meatball sandwich.

Rainbow Lounge GAY & LESBIAN
(462-6111; www.facebook.com/rainbowloungecuracao; Floris Suite Hotel, Piscadera Bay; 6-11pm Fri late Sep-Mar) From the end of September through the end of March, Floris Suite Hotel bar is a Friday-evening gathering spot for gay and lesbian folks – and their friends – as well as anyone who wants to relax and drink in a welcoming, open atmosphere.

Shopping

Serena's Art Factory Store ARTS & CRAFTS
(738-0648; www.chichi-curacao.com; cnr Windstraat & Gomezplein, Punda; 10am-5pm Mon-Sat, to 9pm Thu) Serena Janet Israel is the creative mind (and hands) behind Chichi, the vibrantly painted, big-bosomed woman sculptures that decorate the island's courtyards and alleyways. Chichi comes in many sizes and designs, and you can pick your favorite – or opt for another colorful creation – at Serena's Art Factory Store.

Information

Punda Post Office (Waaigatplein 1, Punda; 7:30am-noon & 1:30-5pm Mon-Fri)

St Elisabeth Hospital (462-4900; www.sehos.cw; Breedestraat 193, Otrobanda; 24hr) A large and well-equipped medical facility a few blocks west of Sint Annabaai. Emergency care is available. At research time a new hospital, the Curaçao Medical Center, was nearly complete. That hospital will eventually replace St Elisabeth as the country's general hospital.

> **LOCAL KNOWLEDGE**
>
> ### LANDHUIS CHOBOLOBO
>
> Did you ever wonder why blue curaçao is blue? Find out at **Landhuis Chobolobo** (461-3526; www.chobolobo.com/en; Elias RA Moreno Blvd; guided tour incl 1/2 cocktails US$12/20; 8am-5pm Mon-Fri) FREE, where the liqueur is produced (in five colors, actually) from the peel of Valencia oranges. Walk yourself through an informative tour of the tipple's history and production process, then hit the gift shop to sample the goods. Landhuis Chobolobo is located on the eastern side of the Schottegat.

Tourist Information Kiosk (693-0253; www.curacao.com; Breedestraat, Punda; 9am-5pm Mon-Fri, to 4pm Sat) Has a wealth of information on museums, tours and shops. Located by Queen Emma Bridge.

Getting There & Away

Hato International Airport (p370) is on the outskirts of Willemstad, on the island's otherwise undeveloped northeastern coast. It's a 20-minute drive into town. Most hotels and resorts can help make arrangements for airport transfers (US$40 to US$50 to Willemstad). Otherwise, taxis and buses pick up at the plaza just outside the arrivals hall.

Public buses (NAf1.70 to NAf2.20) depart every two hours from Otrobanda Bus Station (p371) for the West End (stopping in Willibrordus en route) and from Punda Bus Station (p371) for the southeast (including Mambo Beach and Caracasbaai).

Cruise ships arrive at the terminal in Otrobanda or the Mega Cruise Ship Pier (p371).

Getting Around

When Queen Emma Bridge swings open to make way for oceangoing ships, two free public ferries shuttle passengers back and forth between Punda and Otrobanda.

For a taxi, contact the Dutch Caribbean Taxi Association (p371) or Taxi Max (p371).

Southeast of Willemstad

Southeast of Willemstad, much of the coast has been transformed into somebody's version of paradise. Artificial beaches Mambo and Jan Thiel are lined with resorts, shopping malls and private beach clubs. Artificial islands are surrounded by big ocean tanks, keeping captive the creatures of the sea. And beautiful people lounge on beach chairs, sip cocktails and stare out over the waves.

It's not all bad, of course. The beaches are lovely, with calm, refreshing water that's an eerily perfect shade of blue, and the clubs are fun, offering some of the island's best places to dine, drink, dance and shop.

Sights & Activities

Jan Thiel Beach BEACH
(☎747-0633; www.janthielbeach.com; Jan Thiel; US$3.50; ⏰8am-midnight) The beach at Jan Thiel was literally carved out of the coast – by humans. The whole thing is artificial, which explains why the swimming area is actually a saltwater infinity pool. The sand is brilliant white, the water is perfectly azure. Everything you might want is here: restaurants, bars, shopping, dive shop, beach tennis, gear rental. It's all lovely (fake, but lovely).

Mambo Beach BEACH
(Bapor Kibra; US$3.50; ⏰9am-late; 👪) By day this ribbon of white sand is a family-friendly beach with a full range of activities. By night it transforms into a beach club and disco branded 'Wet & Wild,' with DJs and dancing. The action gets frenetic after midnight from Thursday onward.

★Ocean Encounters DIVING
(☎461-8131; www.oceanencounters.com; Bapor Kibra; 2-tank dive US$109, Klein Curaçao dive trip US$150; ⏰8am-5pm) Curaçao's largest dive operation is one of its best, offering PADI (Professional Association of Diving Instructors) and SSI (Scuba Schools International) courses and the full gamut of snorkel and dive trips. It was the first shop to work with Coral Restoration Foundation Curaçao to grow and replant coral on the island. Certified divers can take a PADI course here on coral restoration and then help maintain the shop's nurseries.

Windsurfing Curaçao WINDSURFING
(☎524-4974; www.windsurfingcuracao.com; Caracasbaaiweg; rental per hour from US$20, lessons from US$49; ⏰10am-6pm) The island's top spot for windsurfing is the smooth and breezy Spaanse Water, a large inland bay. The experts at Windsurfing Curaçao are excellent teachers: the course is four lessons, but they promise you'll be surfing after the first one! If you already know your stuff, you can just rent equipment here.

Mermaid Boat Trips BOATING
(☎560-1530; www.mermaidboattrips.com; Caracasbaaiweg; adult/child US$109/54.50; ⏰departs 6:45am Tue-Fri & Sun) The *Mermaid* takes passengers to **Klein Curaçao** for a day of sunbathing, swimming and snorkeling. This is the only company with facilities on the island (eg picnic tables, shade umbrellas and restrooms). The price includes breakfast and lunch, snorkel gear and beach chairs. Scuba diving is also included, but divers must be experienced and licensed, with their own gear.

Sleeping & Eating

★Landhuis Jan Thiel HISTORIC HOTEL $$
(☎520-7368; http://landhuisjanthiel.com; r from US$135, ste US$160, cottages US$350; ❄📶🏊) On a breezy hilltop above Jan Thiel Beach, this historic plantation has served as a farm for salt, oranges, goats and cows since the 17th century. Three years ago new owners did a fabulous revamp and turned it into a boutique hotel, with highlights including incredible views, lovely walking trails and a relaxing pool.

★Pop's Place PUB FOOD $$
(Caracasbaai; sandwiches US$6, mains US$10-27; ⏰11am-9pm Wed-Mon, bar to 11pm) Here's a local favorite. Right on the beach at Caracas Bay, this brightly colored wooden shack serves crowd-pleasers such as goat stew, burgers and cold drinks.

Seaside Terrace SEAFOOD $$
(☎461-8361; Dr Martin Luther King Blvd, Marie Pompoen Beach; mains US$15-25; ⏰noon-10pm Tue-Sun) Here red snapper, mahi-mahi and other *fruits de mer* are pan-fried and served with a supertasty secret Creole sauce. The furniture doesn't match. The forks bend. And the service is endearingly gruff. Yet this place is an island institution, serving what many say is Curaçao's best seafood. Located just north of Mambo Beach.

Getting There & Away

You can take a bus (NAf1.70, hourly) from Punda Bus Station (p371) in Willemstad to Mambo Beach, Caracas Bay and Jan Thiel Beach (bus 6A).

Sint Willibrordus Area

Even before you get to the West End there are scores of beautiful beaches hidden in coves along this coastline. They are private

Around Willemstad

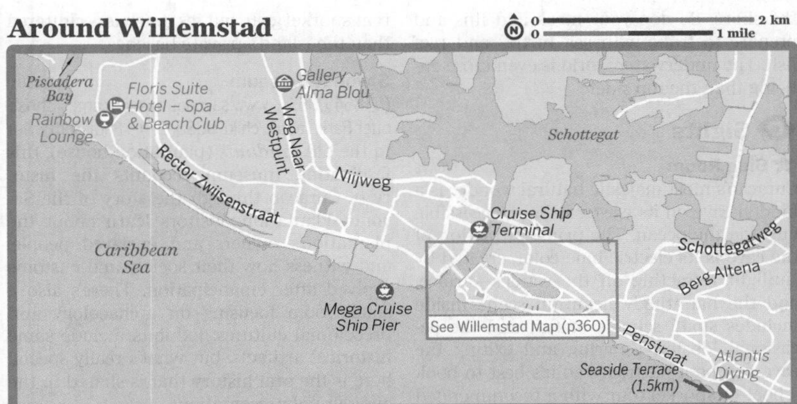

beaches, which means you'll pay to use them, but the trade-off is that the facilities are generally decent and they don't get quite as crowded on weekends.

The village of Sint Willibrordus isn't exactly a destination, but you'll surely find yourself stopping here, whether to snap pics of a photogenic flamingo or to get pampered at the island's best spa. While you're in town, don't miss the most famous landmark: the white, block-letter 'Williwood' sign on a wooded hillside.

Sights & Activities

Flamingo Sanctuary BIRD SANCTUARY
(Sint Willibrordrus) FREE Though the island is lacking in lawns, you may spot the occasional Caribbean flamingo. On rainy days the majestic pink birds congregate in the Saliña Sint Marie, the salt flats on the southern side of the road heading toward Playa Portomari. There are several places to pull off the road, but be sure to lock your car when you go to get a better look at the wading beauties (whose numbers can vary greatly, anywhere from none to dozens).

Cas Abao BEACH
(463-6367; www.casabaobeach.com; per car NAf10-12.50; 8am-6pm) This mid-coast beach (sometimes spelled Cas Abou) is an island favorite for its soft white sand, crystal-clear waters and surrounding scenery. It's a private beach with good facilities, including guarded parking lot, lockers, restaurant and massage hut. You can also rent snorkel gear, though you'll see more sea life further up the coast.

★ **Playa Portomari** SNORKELING
(www.playaportomari.com; adult/child US$3/free; 9:30am-6:30pm) There's a lot to love about Playa Portomari, including the white coral sand and the clear waters sheltering a unique double reef – excellent for snorkelers and divers. The artificial 'reef balls' were constructed to encourage new coral growth. Facilities include a dive shop and a restaurant. A couple of pigs (Willie and Woodie) are known to hang out in the area.

Getting There & Away

The easiest way to explore the area around Sint Willibrordus is by private vehicle. In fact, the west-coast beaches are *only* accessible by car. Buses do go through Sint Willibrordus (NAf2.20), departing from Otrobanda Bus Station (p371) in Willemstad, but it's a small place and you'll be stuck there until the next bus trundles through, which could be two hours later.

West End

Welcome to the wild, wild west. Curaçao's West End – also called Banda'bou – is where you'll find the island's most stunning beaches, most striking natural landscapes and most spectacular sea life. Here, two national parks give access to the rugged windward coast, allowing adventurers to witness the ferocity and artistry of the surf on the rocky cliffs.

On the more sedate west coast, the same cliffs are punctuated by fishing villages, sandy beaches and a glorious cave, all perched aside tranquil turquoise waters. Dive and snorkel sites are almost too numerous to count – and most are accessible from the shore. So don your mask and fins and prepare to frolic with sea turtles and reef fish. The underwater world is even more enticing than the top side!

Sights

★Blue Room CAVE

Curaçao's most majestic natural wonder is a hidden cave on its western shore, accessible only via the ocean. The prime attraction of the cave is its electric-blue color, created by sunlight refracting off the water's surface, and the hauntingly beautiful scene inside includes small schools of fish and the occasional lobster. Entering and exiting the cave can be a bit tricky, so it's best to book a boat or snorkel tour with a recommended operator.

More adventurous types can boat or kayak from a nearby **water-sports shop** (Let's Go Watersports; ☎864-0438; http://therealcaptaingoodlife.com; Playa Santa Cruz; boat trip per person US$22, double kayak per 3hr US$70; ⏱90min boat tours 1pm & 3pm), or hike to the spot and then plunge into the water from the top of the cave (ask for exact directions from a local). When the tide is low, it's possible to enter the cave without going underwater. As the tide rises, the only way to enter is to free dive, which can be frightening. Also note that those who hike and jump need considerable arm strength to climb back up the rocks.

★Christoffel National Park PARK

(☎864-0363; www.christoffelpark.org; Weg Naar Westpunt; adult/child US$15/5; ⏱6am-3pm, last entry 1:30pm) This 1800-hectare preserve is formed from three old plantations, including the Savonet Plantation, which is now the excellent Savonet Museum; combination ticket available. The park has two driving routes and eight hiking trails, which provide a variety of perspectives on the island's landscape, flora and fauna. It takes two to three hours to hike to the summit of **Christoffel Mountain** (375m), the island's highest point. To summit, you'll need to begin by 10am. Bring lots of water.

Grote Knip BEACH

(Kenepa Grande) This West End beach is a stunner. In fact, you've probably seen it on the cover of a Curaçao tourist brochure: a perfect crescent of brilliant white sand, framed by azure waters and verdant hills. There are a few snack shacks and places to rent snorkel gear, but it's much less cluttered than the island's private beaches.

Savonet Museum MUSEUM

(☎864-0363; www.savonetmuseum.org; Christoffel Park; adult/child US$3/2; ⏱8am-3pm) Set in the old *landhuis* (plantation house), this fascinating museum recounts the history of Curaçao through the story of the Savonet Plantation. Visitors learn about the plantation's owners and enslaved people, and witness how their society and customs evolved after emancipation. There's also a small room focusing on archaeology and precolonial cultures. Exhibits include some historical artifacts, but what's really special here is the oral history that is shared in the audiovisual presentations.

Shete Boka National Park PARK

(☎864-4444; www.carmabi.org; Weg Naar Westpunt; adult/child US$10/free; ⏱9am-5pm) Shete Boka means 'seven inlets' – the park is named for a series of picturesque coves carved out of the limestone along this 10km stretch of coastline. Park your car near **Boka Tabla**, where the powerful surf thunders into a cave in the cliffs. It's impressive from the bluff above, and even more so from inside the cave. From here you can walk or drive north along the coast to the other smaller inlets, which are sea-turtle nesting grounds.

Heading south from Boka Tabla, a second road leads to **Boka Pistol**, a very narrow inlet that produces a stunning – and startling – explosion when the waves roll in. You can also reach Boka Pistol by car, or follow a circular hiking trail, which takes about an hour.

Activities

Playa Forti SWIMMING

(Westpunt) There's really only one reason to stop at Playa Forti, but it's a good one: behind the restaurant, the sheer cliff walls and deep water create perfect conditions for some epic cliff jumping. It's about a 12m drop into crystal-clear coolness, where you might just find yourself swimming with sea turtles.

Playa Grandi SNORKELING

This isn't the prettiest beach on the island – or the cleanest – but it's a top-notch snorkel and dive site. You're almost guaranteed to spot sea turtles swimming in the bay. (Look, but don't touch, chase or otherwise harass these gentle creatures.)

Go West Diving DIVING
(☎864-0102; www.gowestdiving.com; Playa Kalki, Westpunt; unlimited air tanks per day/equipment rental per day US$33/45, 2-tank boat dive US$97; ⏰8am-5pm) The top dive shop on the West End, Go West offers a few things that other shops don't, such as boat dives (including to Klein Curaçao) and snorkel trips. It's also next to an excellent shore-diving site, Alice in Wonderland, which is a destination in itself. All divers do a 'welcome dive' to test equipment and weights (and competence, presumably).

Sleeping & Eating

Rancho El Sobrino APARTMENT $
(☎888-8822; www.ranchoelsobrino.com; Weg Naar Westpunt; r from US$75;) The price is right at this rustic resort south of Playa Forti, which features simple rooms decorated with mismatched furniture and quirky artwork. A couple of Wara-Wara birds, aka caracaras (rescues, by the way), keep guests company. There are a recommended **restaurant** and dive shop on-site. The weekly cleaning service may not be sufficient for some.

Kura Hulanda Lodge RESORT $$$
(☎839-3600; www.kurahulanda.com; Playa Kalki 1, Westpunt; r US$290-310, ste US$340-390;) Once you settle into this boutique resort overlooking **Playa Kalki** you may never want to leave. Tasteful lodgings surround tropical gardens, along with two pools and a private beach. The **restaurant** is recommended, especially for its amazing sunset views. Kayaks and stand-up paddle (SUP) boards are available, plus there's a dive shop on-site and a reef just offshore.

★ **Jaanchie's** CURAÇAOAN $$
(☎864-0126; Weg Naar Westpunt; set lunch US$20; ⏰noon-8pm) Jaanchie himself often visits the tables in his restaurant near Playa Grandi, chatting to customers and explaining the menu. And it does require some explanation, as it usually features island delicacies such as iguana soup and goat stew. Guests sit in the festive open-air dining room and watch colorful birds flocking to the nearby feeders.

Restaurant Playa Forti CARIBBEAN $$
(☎868-1551; Playa Forti; mains US$10-23; ⏰11am-8pm;) This restaurant is best known as the island's cliff-diving spot. But before you take the plunge, it's actually worth grabbing a margarita and some fresh seafood, not to mention enjoying the sweeping ocean view. The tablecloths are colorful and the servers sometimes sit down to take your order; it's all very charming.

Getting There & Away

Buses (NAf2.20) go to the West End (including Playa Lagún, Knip and Westpunt), departing from the Otrobanda Bus Station (p371) in Willemstad every two hours or so. Take the Banda'bou bus (via Barber) to reach Shete Boka or Christoffel.

You'll obviously have much more flexibility and freedom if you rent a vehicle. Aside from dive trips, there's a dearth of organized tours to this side of the island.

UNDERSTAND CURAÇAO

History

Caquetío History

The earliest inhabitants of Curaçao were the Caquetío peoples, a branch of the Arawaks who inhabited the island as early as 2500 BC. Archaeological evidence of these peoples include the petroglyphs at Hato Caves and some artifacts on display at the Savonet Museum. After the arrival of the Spanish in 1499, most of the indigenous population were killed by disease or sent to work elsewhere in the empire.

Dutch West India Co

The Dutch West India Co arrived in 1634, and so did commerce, agriculture and slavery. The island was divided into plantations for small-scale agriculture. Nowadays, many of the old *landhuis* (plantation houses) have been restored. The most vivid history of plantation life is on display at the Savonet Museum, formerly the Landhuis Savonet.

Half the enslaved people destined for the Caribbean passed through the markets of Curaçao. The Museum Kura Hulanda examines this horrible institution in depth, while Museo Tula remembers a tragic slave revolt.

Emancipation & Modernization

The collapse of the Dutch West India Co in 1792 and the end of slavery in 1863 sent Curaçao into economic decline. Small-scale farming (aloe and oranges) provided a meager living for most.

In the early 20th century, a refinery was built to process Venezuelan oil. This development jump-started the economy and the island flourished once again. You can see a working model of the refinery at the Maritime Museum's Steam for Oil exhibit.

Relative affluence and Dutch political stability have made Curaçao a regional center for commerce and banking. Tourism provides additional income, as does the growing expat population. In 2010, with the dissolution of the Netherlands Antilles, Curaçao became an independent entity within the Netherlands.

People & Culture

Historians do not believe that there are descendants of the original Caquetío inhabitants still living on the island. But the population of Curaçao is a rich mix of peoples. The majority have Afro-Caribbean roots (as they are descended from the enslaved people who worked the plantations), but there is a sizable Dutch minority, as well as Latinos, Southeast Asians and other Europeans. Some 73% of the population is Roman Catholic, a faith usually practiced with a healthy dose of Santería. Many other religions are represented, and there is a significant and long-standing Jewish presence.

Landscape & Environment

Curaçao is a mix of lush areas near the coasts and more arid regions inland. (The contrast is on full display at Christoffel National Park.) Human development has meant that land-based wildlife is limited, though birdlife is rich. The National Underwater Park protects a 20km stretch of coastline along the island's southern tip, but the reef is rich with marine life all along the west coast, where there are dozens of dive and snorkel sites.

The main environmental threats in Curaçao are water pollution from industry and overfishing, which damages and destroys coral reefs. Programs are in place to grow and replant coral, but whether they will have a long-term impact is still unclear. A growing traffic problem (along with exhaust-spewing diesels) means that getting stuck in a traffic jam is an unpleasant possibility.

SURVIVAL GUIDE

Directory A–Z

ACCESSIBLE TRAVEL

Curaçao has made strides in catering to travelers with disabilities, and it's getting better. Many resorts and rental units offer accessible rooms and zero-entry swimming pools, including the Avila Beach Hotel. Many restaurants and casinos around the island are also wheelchair accessible. Wheelchair-accessible sights include the Maritime Museum, the Savonet Museum, Landhuis Chobolobo, Gallery Alma Blou and Jan Thiel Beach.

Some other companies catering specifically to travelers with disabilities:

➡ **Dushi Taxi** (p371) Natasja Gibbs caters to cruise-ship passengers, offering tours and transportation in a wheelchair-accessible van.

➡ **Joseph Cares** (☎511-4888; www.josephcares.com; Rooseveltweg 505d) Specializes in taking care of travelers with special needs; in particular, it provides tours, transportation and other services for travelers with disabilities. It offers tours of some of the island's most remote spots, as well as airport transfers and rental of medical equipment.

ACCOMMODATIONS

Curaçao offers a wide variety of accommodations. There are resorts and rental units up and down the coast, giving easy beach access, but Willemstad also has interesting urban hotels. Although there aren't many budget options, prices are lower the further inland you go. Camping is uncommon.

High-season prices run mid-December to mid-April. A 7% sales tax applies to hotel rooms; some resorts may add a service charge of 12% or higher.

ACTIVITIES

Curaçao is an excellent destination for diving and snorkeling, not least because so many sites are located onshore. Dive shops do offer guided shore dives, but you and your dive buddy can just as easily go on your own (though the shops are still useful for recommendations and air). There are dive shops at almost every beach; good ones include Ocean Encounters (p364), **Atlantis Diving** (☎666-8293; www.atlantisdiving.com; Drielstraat 6; 2-tank dive from US$97, Klein

Curaçao dive day trip from US$125; ⏰8:30am-5:30pm Mon-Fri, to 4:30pm Sat & Sun), Go West Diving (p367) and Scuba Lodge (p361).

The main areas are along the west coast, from St Michiel out to Westpunt, and from Mambo Beach south to the tip. The latter coast and reefs have been protected as part of the National Underwater Park.

CHILDREN

Curaçao is an ideal destination for families, as there are sights and activities for kids of all ages. Many resorts, shopping malls and other facilities cater especially to families.

All of the beaches are along the tranquil west coast, which means they are protected from the strongest surf, making them ideal for kids to frolic, swim and build sand castles. Private beaches such as Mambo Beach (p364) and Jan Thiel Beach (p364) offer some kid-friendly activities, including an island of inflatable toys for children to play on. Also, kids as young as five can learn to snorkel, especially in calm, comfortable waters such as these. Playa Grandi (p366) is a surefire hit, with practically guaranteed sightings of sea turtles.

When they tire of sun and sand, take your kids to admire the power of the wind and waves at Shete Boka National Park (p366). The Museum Kura Hulanda (p359) and the Savonet Museum (p366) don't have a lot of flash, but they're both interesting and educational for older children.

Some resorts are adults-only, but most are family-friendly. Swimming pools are often designed with kids in mind. Most larger resorts offer kids' clubs, game rooms and other kinds of programming to keep little ones busy. Family-style rooms and suites are common, as are kitchenettes.

Many private developments are designed to suit families, so you'll find that facilities are up to snuff in resorts, shopping malls and the like. Public facilities are a different story: restrooms are few and far between, and practically nonexistent on public beaches. Changing tables are not common. Willemstad is an old city with narrow streets and some hills. Sidewalks are not always present, making it dangerous to walk with children or push a stroller.

ELECTRICITY

The supply is 110V to 130V and 220V, 50Hz. Generally, power plugs and sockets are of types A, B and F, and vary depending on your hotel. Bring an adapter just in case.

EMERGENCY NUMBERS

Ambulance	☎912
Fire & police	☎911
Hyperbaric chamber	☎910

SLEEPING PRICE RANGES

The following price ranges refer to the cost of a double room with private bathroom, not including taxes.

$ less than US$80

$$ US$80–200

$$$ more than US$200

FOOD

Curaçao has a surprisingly sophisticated dining scene – if you know where to look, that is: in the streets and alleyways of Pietermaai in Willemstad. The main tourist beaches are also packed with restaurants and bars. In the remote West End, the choices are mostly limited to resort restaurants and snack shacks on the beach.

HEALTH

St Elisabeth Hospital (p363) is a large and well-equipped medical facility in Willemstad. Emergency care is available.

Tap water in Curaçao is safe to drink.

INTERNET ACCESS

All hotels and resorts provide a wireless internet connection for their guests, and many offer computers in case you don't have your own.

LEGAL MATTERS

Unlike in the Netherlands proper, all drugs are illegal in Curaçao. Violating these laws can lead to arrest and imprisonment. As always, if you get arrested, your embassy can help you notify your family and contact an attorney, but it cannot do much else.

LGBT+ TRAVELERS

'We live and let live!' claims gay travel website Pink Curaçao (www.pinkcuracao.com), and the fact that the website exists pretty much proves the point. While gay and lesbian tourists will likely receive a warm welcome on the island, the LGBT scene is rather limited outside of the **Floris Suite Hotel** (☎462-6111; www.florissuitehotel.com; John F Kennedy Blvd, Piscadera Bay; ste US$129-349; ❄@🛜🏊). It's sometimes called a 'straight-friendly hotel,' and

EATING PRICE RANGES

The following price ranges refer to the cost of a main course.

$ less than US$10

$$ US$10–25

$$$ more than US$25

PRACTICALITIES

Magazines The *Curaçao Traveler* is a free full-color magazine complete with reviews, maps and more.

Newspapers The *Curaçao Chronicle* (www.curacaochronicle.com) is the island's weekly English-language newspaper, covering local and international news and events.

Smoking Prohibited in all public places. Most hotels and resorts are smoke-free, though some may offer a designated smoking area.

Television Local channels generally broadcast in Dutch and/or Papiamento.

Weights & measures The metric system is used.

its bar – the Rainbow Lounge (p363) – hosts a weekly LGBT happy hour from September to March. The island's five-day Curaçao Pride (p361) celebration happens in late September or early October.

MONEY

Although the island's official currency is the Netherlands Antillean guilder (NAf), prices are often quoted in US dollars and you can pay for just about everything in US currency. You might get change back in guilders.

ATMs are widely available, dispensing US dollars and Netherlands Antillean guilders. Credit cards are accepted at most hotels and restaurants.

Exchange Rates

Aruba	Afl1	NAf1.04
Australia	A$1	NAf1.32
Canada	C$1	NAf1.39
Euro zone	€1	NAf2.09
Japan	¥100	NAf1.68
New Zealand	NZ$1	NAf1.24
UK	£1	NAf2.42
US	US$1	NAf1.87

Tipping

Bars and restaurants For good service, tip 15% to 20% (sometimes included in the bill).
Resorts Bills usually include a 12% service charge.
Taxis A 10% tip is usual.
Tour guides Tip US$10 for a half-day outing.

PUBLIC HOLIDAYS

New Year's Day January 1
Carnival Monday Monday before Ash Wednesday
Good Friday Friday before Easter
Easter Monday Monday after Easter
King's Birthday April 27
Labour Day May 1
Ascension Day Sixth Thursday after Easter
Flag Day July 2
Curaçao Day October 10
Christmas December 25
Boxing Day December 26

TELEPHONE

Curaçao's country code is 599; the area code is 9.

To call out from Curaçao to any country with a country code of 1, just dial 1 and the local number. To reach other countries, dial the international access code (00), plus the country code, plus the number.

To dial Curaçao from another country, dial the country's international access code, plus Curaçao's country code (599), plus the area code (9), plus the local number. Within Curaçao there is no need to dial any code.

Cell Phones

GSM cell (mobile) phones are compatible with local SIM cards. The main operator is Digicel (www.digicelcuracao.com).

TIME

Curaçao runs to Atlantic Standard Time (AST), which is four hours behind Greenwich Mean Time. Daylight-saving time is not observed.

Getting There & Away

You can reach Curaçao by air or sea (on a cruise ship). Plans for ferries from Curaçao to neighboring islands perpetually sink before they can be launched, but flights to Aruba and Bonaire are frequent and short on various regional airlines.

Flights, cars and tours can be booked online at lonelyplanet.com/bookings.

AIR

Hato International Airport (CUR; ☎839-1000; www.curacao-airport.com; Plasa Margaret Abraham; ⏰6am-10pm), 10km from Willemstad on the northern side of the island, receives many international flights on airlines including Avianca, Air Canada, Air Century, American Airlines, Aruba Airlines, Copa Airlines, Condor, Fly Always, JetBlue, KLM, Sky High, SLM, Tui, Winair, West Jet, Wingo and Easy Air.

The most popular regional carrier is **Divi Divi Air** (☎839-1515; www.flydivi.com; Hato International Airport; ⏰9am-5pm Mon-Fri, to

DEPARTURE TAX

The departure tax varies according to your destination.

International	US$42
Aruba	US$30
Bonaire	US$15
Transfer	US$10

Most of the larger international airlines include the departure tax in the price of the ticket. If you're flying on a smaller regional airline, you will need to pay the tax at the designated window before going through security.

4pm Sat, to 3pm Sun), with about a dozen daily flights between Curaçao and Bonaire as well as charters to Aruba. The airplanes are tiny, so they book out well in advance.

SEA

Curaçao is part of cruise-ship itineraries that cover the southern Caribbean, often on longer 10-day and two-week trips.

Many cruise ships call in Curaçao. The really big ones dock at the Mega Cruise Ship Pier, which is just outside the capital's natural harbor. Smaller ships dock at the Cruise Ship Terminal in the harbor.

Despite their proximity to each other, there are no ferries running between the ABC islands (Aruba, Bonaire and Curaçao).

Getting Around

BICYCLE

For a Dutch island, Curaçao is surprisingly lacking in bike lanes and other cycling facilities. Traffic can be perilous in Willemstad, but once you get out of the city there's some pleasant cycling on country and coastal roads. Bicycles are available for rental at many resorts.

If you can get your hands on a mountain bike, there are some fantastic trails in Christoffel National Park (p366) and at Playa Portomari (p365).

BUS

There's a public bus network on Curaçao, with buses to the West End departing from **Otrobanda Bus Station** (Sebastopolstraat, Otrobanda) and buses to the southeast departing from **Punda Bus Station** (Waaigatplein, Punda), both in Willemstad. Most routes run buses every one or two hours.

CAR & MOTORCYCLE

Driving is on the right-hand side, seat belts are required and motorcyclists must wear helmets.

All the major international rental firms have affiliates at the airport, but there are many reliable local outfits, such as **Prins Car Rental** (☎888-6895; www.prinscarrental.com; Jan Noorduynweg 36; ⏰8am-noon & 1:30-5pm). Note that off-site agencies (the local ones) charge an additional $20 fee for airport transfers.

TAXI

Taxis wait at the airport and large hotels. Most now have meters. For a taxi, call **DCTA** (☎868-5319) or **Taxi Max** (☎697-6302). **Dushi Taxi** (☎516-8863; www.dushitaxi.weebly.com) offers tours and transportation in a wheelchair-accessible van.

Dominica

☎767 / POP 55,000

Includes ➡

Best Places to Eat

- ➡ Poz Restaurant & Bar (p387)
- ➡ C&D Beach Bar & Grill (p384)
- ➡ Keepin' It Real (p384)
- ➡ Old Stone Grill & Bar (p376)
- ➡ Riverside Cafe (p381)

Best Places to Stay

- ➡ Secret Bay (p384)
- ➡ Jacoway Inn (p386)
- ➡ Pagua Bay House (p387)
- ➡ Citrus Creek Plantation (p381)
- ➡ Wanderlust (p386)

Why Go?

Whether you arrive in Dominica by sea or by air, your likely first impression will be one of awe at the sheer dramatic majesty of the place, one with which few islands in the Caribbean can compete. Nicknamed 'the nature island,' Dominica (locals stress the third syllable) lures independent travelers and eco-adventurers with its boiling lake, rainforest-shrouded volcanoes, sulfurous hot springs, superb diving and the Caribbean's first long-distance hiking trail.

An English-speaking island wedged between francophone Guadeloupe and Martinique, Dominica is also on a different path to its neighbors in development terms, with no big cruise terminal nor an airport that can take even medium-haul flights. This means the island's traditional character has been far better preserved than elsewhere in the Lesser Antilles.

Hurricane Maria wreaked absolute havoc on Dominica in 2017, from which the island is still painfully – but determinedly – recovering.

When to Go

Feb–Jun The island's driest months are its most popular, but short bursts of rainfall are possible.

Nov–Jan Shoulder season is a good time to visit, when all businesses are open but prices are lower.

Jul–Oct Many businesses close in the rainy season. Hurricane season peaks in August and September. October sees Roseau's World Creole Music Festival.

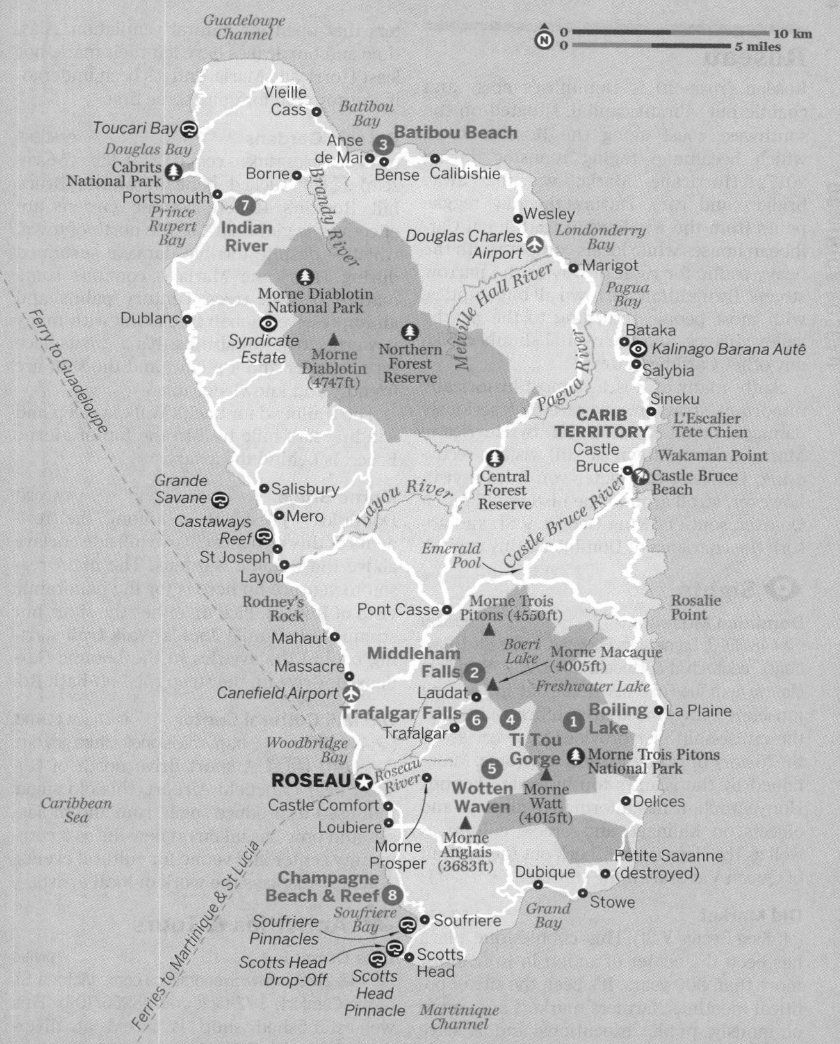

Dominica Highlights

1. **Boiling Lake** (p380) Trekking to a remote lake filled with boiling water.
2. **Middleham Falls** (p380) Hiking through breathtaking rainforest to this 200ft-high waterfall and pool.
3. **Batibou Beach** (p385) Sunbathing at Dominica's most spectacular beach.
4. **Ti Tou Gorge** (p380) Swimming through a narrow canyon to a gushing waterfall.
5. **Wotten Waven** (p378) Relaxing in hot sulfur springs amid stunning scenery in this verdant village.
6. **Trafalgar Falls** (p378) Taking a stroll to these easily accessible twin waterfalls and having a dip in the pools below.
7. **Indian River** (p383) Gliding through jungle down this placid west-coast river.
8. **Champagne Beach & Reef** (p382) Being tickled by the volcanic bubbles of Dominica's star underwater attraction.

Roseau

Roseau (*rose*-oh) is Dominica's noisy and chaotic but vibrant capital, situated on the southwest coast along the Roseau River, which became a raging monster during 2017's Hurricane Maria, washing away bridges and cars. During the day reggae pours from the windows of traditional Caribbean houses while locals compete with the heavy traffic for right of way in the narrow streets. By nightfall the town all but empties, with most people returning to the nearby valley villages, and the capital slumbers like any other Caribbean town.

Sadly, many of Roseau's most historically important structures were either seriously damaged or totally destroyed by Hurricane Maria, and the town is still visibly recovering. Don't let that deter you from a visit, however; stroll around the historical French Quarter, south of King George V St, and absorb the charisma of Dominica's tiny capital.

Sights

Dominica Museum MUSEUM
(☎448-8923; Dame Mary Eugenia Charles Blvd (Bayfront); adult/child & student EC$3/2; ⊙8am-5pm Mon, to 4pm Tue-Fri) This small but interesting museum above the tourist office right near the cruise-ship pier provides an overview of the history of Dominica and its people. Maintained by the island's top historian, Lennox Honychurch, it has informative displays and objects on Kalinago and Creole culture as well as the slave trade. Check out the portrait of Queen Victoria on the staircase.

Old Market SQUARE
(off King George V St) This cobblestone plaza has been the center of action in Roseau for more than 300 years. It's been the site of political meetings, farmers markets and, more ominously, public executions and a slave market. Nowadays it's got craft and souvenir stalls that get plenty of attention from cruise-ship passengers when the big ships are in port.

Roseau Cathedral CHURCH
(☎448-2766; www.dioceseofroseau.org/our-lady-of-fairhaven; Virgin Lane; ⊙closed for renovation) Gothic meets Caribbean at this landmark cathedral which evolved from a simple wooden hut to the majestic 1916 volcanic-stone pile you see today. The upper windows are stained glass, but much like a typical Creole home, the lower windows are wooden shutters that open for natural ventilation. Alas, time and hurricanes have left their mark, not least Hurricane Maria, and it's been undergoing restoration for quite some time.

Botanic Gardens GARDENS
(www.dominicagardens.com; Valley Rd; ⊙6am-7pm) FREE Tucked beneath Morne Bruce hill, Roseau's 40-acre botanic gardens are effectively a giant park to the north of town, which – despite terrible damage sustained during Hurricane Maria – contains some mature banyan trees, century palms and an impressive baobab tree along with many flowering tropical shrubs. It's a great place for a wander and a picnic, and the staff are friendly and knowledgeable.

The trailhead for 'Jack's Walk,' a steep and winding half-mile trail to the top of Morne Bruce, is behind the aviary.

Morne Bruce VIEWPOINT
Dominica's president is among the residents of this rather exclusive hillside enclave above the Botanic Gardens. The main reason to venture up here is for the panoramic vista of Roseau. Pick up either the short but strenuous half-mile **Jack's Walk trail** starting behind the aviaries in the Botanic Gardens, or drive up the steep road off Bath Rd.

Old Mill Cultural Center CULTURAL CENTRE
(☎449-1804; http://divisionofculture.gov.dm; Canefield) FREE A short drive north of Roseau, near Canefield Airport, this old sugar mill used to produce sugar, rum and molasses, and now has taken on new life as a community center and venue for cultural events. A gallery displays the work of local artists.

Activities & Tours

Dive Dominica DIVING
(☎448-2188; www.divedominica.com; Victoria St, Castle Comfort; 1-/2-tank dive US$66/109) This well-established shop is based at divergeared Ocean's Edge Lodge (p376) south of Roseau and enjoys a reef right on-site and easy access to Soufriere-Scotts Head Marine Reserve (p382). All diving needs to be reserved in advance, and afternoon dives only go out with a minimum of eight divers. Also offers whale-watching on Sundays in the season for US$69 per person.

Ken's Hinterland Adventure Tours TOURS
(KHATTS; ☎448-1660; www.khattstours.com; Fort Young Hotel, Victoria St; hikes US$40-85, 4-person minimum) This pro outfit based at the Fort Young Hotel (p376) offers a large selection

Roseau

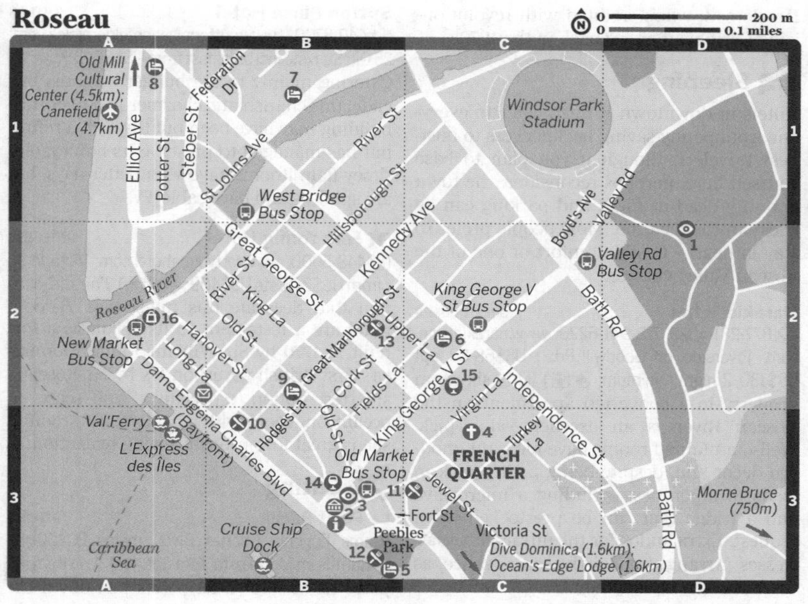

Roseau

Sights
1 Botanic Gardens ... D2
2 Dominica Museum ... B3
3 Old Market ... B3
4 Roseau Cathedral ... C3

Activities, Courses & Tours
Ken's Hinterland Adventure Tours ... (see 5)

Sleeping
5 Fort Young Hotel ... B3
6 Ma Bass Guest House ... C2
7 Narakiel's Inn ... B1
8 Potter's Place ... A1
9 Sutton Place Hotel ... B2

Eating
10 Le Petit Paris ... B3
11 Old Stone Grill & Bar ... C3
12 Palisades ... B3
13 Pearl's Cuisine ... B2

Drinking & Nightlife
14 Ruins Rock Cafe ... B3
15 Symes Zee ... C2
Warner's Bar ... (see 5)

Shopping
16 New Market ... A2

of standard as well as unusual tours, including hikes to Boiling Lake (US$60), a day trip to the Kalinago Territory (US$75) and birdwatching in the Syndicate rainforest (US$65). All activities require a minimum of four bookings; enquire with the office to see what tours are going ahead.

Festivals & Events

★**World Creole Music Festival** MUSIC
(Windsor Park Sports Stadium; late Oct) For three days, Roseau gets swept up in the head-rushing, feet-stomping beats of zouk, *compa*, soca, *bouyon,* afro beat, calypso and reggae during this famous annual festival. The rum-fueled party kicks off in the daytime, with bands, food and exuberant dancing and singing taking over the streets of downtown Roseau before ticket-holders head on down to Windsor Park Stadium.

Created in 1997, it's the region's only festival pulsating exclusively to a French-Caribbean beat. Its lineup usually includes such international hotshots as Kassav, Wyclef Jean, Third World and Tito Puente Jr alongside local luminaries including Gordon

Henderson, who's credited with revolutionizing Caribbean music back in the 1970s.

Sleeping

Hotels in downtown Roseau cater to everyone from penny-saving backpackers to business travelers, though if you plan to base yourself here, perhaps reconsider: the town is pretty dead at night and parking can be tricky in the daytime. Most people prefer to stay in nearby Castle Comfort or one of the Roseau Valley villages.

Narakiel's Inn GUESTHOUSE **$**
(☎877-281-4529, 718-941-6220; www.narakielsinn.com; Riverside, off Goodwill Rd; r US$68-88, apt US$130, 2-night minimum; ❄📶) This six-room property in a converted apartment on the Roseau River is an excellent-value pick. Well-maintained rooms have pleasant, modern decor and, despite being petite, pack in loads of amenities, including a microwave and a fridge that can be prestocked upon request. Extra kudos for the ultracomfy mattresses. Arrange your arrival in advance, as there is often nobody home.

Ma Bass Guest House GUESTHOUSE **$**
(☎448-2999; 44 Fields Lane; s/d from US$44/66; ❄📶) The friendly owner, Theresa Emanuel (better known as Ma Bass), offers true hospitality that's like staying with your auntie. Her guesthouse, on a quiet side street in the heart of Roseau, has 10 low-frills but clean well-kept rooms with old-school furnishings. Most have private bathroom and air-con. It's unsigned from the street: look for a red gate and go upstairs.

★ **Potter's Place** GUESTHOUSE **$$**
(☎440-1925; www.pottersplacedominica.com; 37 Goodwill Rd; r incl breakfast US$80-120; ❄📶) This immaculate, brand-new guesthouse just a couple of blocks from the Roseau River is terrific value, with eight gleaming, spacious and contemporary rooms, each of which comes with a fridge and TV. The welcome is warm and despite the roadside location, it's actually a quiet spot.

Ocean's Edge Lodge HOTEL **$$**
(☎616-7077; Loubiere Rd, Castle Comfort; r US$100-140; P❄📶) Under new management since Hurricane Maria, the former Castle Comfort Lodge enjoys a prime seafront location and has 15 simple but good-sized comfortable rooms dressed in bold colors, some with sea views. The alfresco restaurant-bar is perfect for post-dive chilling.

Sutton Place Hotel HOTEL **$$**
(☎449-8700; www.suttonplacehoteldominica.com; 25 Old St; r/ste incl breakfast from US$96/127; ❄📶) Catering mainly to the budget business brigade, this charismatic charmer in a historical building may have been put through a refurb but has managed to preserve its homey, old-timey flair. Rooms have seen better days, but are spotless and have cable TV.

★ **Fort Young Hotel** HOTEL **$$$**
(☎448-5000; www.fortyounghotel.com; Victoria St; r from US$248, ste US$409; ❄📶🏊) The old cannon that decorate this full-service 71-room hotel are a testament to its origin as a fort built in 1770 by Sir William Young, Dominica's first British governor. It's by far Roseau's smartest option, especially if you score an oceanfront room with a balcony. The rooftop spa is great for post-sightseeing relaxation.

Eating

Le Petit Paris FRENCH **$**
(Dame Eugenia Charles Blvd; mains EC$20-40; ⊙8am-5pm Mon-Fri, to 3pm Sat; 📶) An obvious place to wait for a ferry (it's just down the road from Roseau's passenger terminal), this friendly whitewashed French-run cafe serves good coffee, fresh pastries and is just about the best breakfast spot in town. Later in the day the menu runs to good pizzas, burgers and salads.

★ **Old Stone Grill & Bar** CARIBBEAN **$$**
(☎440-7549; Castle St; mains EC$40-60; ⊙3:30-10:30pm Mon-Thu, 3-11:30pm Fri & Sat; 📶) Leonard Lewis' locally adored bistro is in an open-fronted stone building that doubles as an art gallery. The extensive menu truly shines when it comes to the fresh fish paired with a choice of sides: try the fried dolphin (actually just the local term for *mahimahi*) and the *dasheen* (taro root) croquettes, or just have one of its superb burgers.

★ **Pearl's Cuisine** CARIBBEAN **$$**
(☎448-8707; Great Marlborough St; mains EC$25-50; ⊙9am-3pm Mon-Sat) This 25-year-old Roseau institution may keep changing location, but its much-loved Creole food stays the same. It's one of the best places for old-school staples such as bullfoot soup, chicken callaloo or stewed agouti (a rodent). It gets busiest on Saturdays when all dishes cost just EC$25. Leave room for the soursop ice cream.

Palisades CARIBBEAN $$$

(☎255-7604; Fort Young Hotel, Victoria St; buffet lunch EC$60, mains EC$60-125; ⊙7am-2:30pm daily, 6:30-10pm Wed-Sat;) The restaurant of the Fort Young Hotel is a smart and open-decked affair where the great and the good of Roseau (well, its business community, anyway) come for the buffet lunch or smarter à la carte dinner menu.

Drinking & Nightlife

Central Roseau has a bunch of dive bars (and we're not talking about the sport here) that are busy with tourists in the daytime and hard-scrabble locals at night, especially on Friday and Saturday. There's a score of simple places to go for a drink along the narrow beach south of town.

Ruins Rock Cafe PUB

(☎440-5483; cnr King George V & Hanover Sts; ⊙9am-6pm Mon-Sat;) This rustic, colorful beer-hall-sized pub in an actual ruin lures punters with cold Carib and cocktails and the *muy macho* with bizarre bush rums (infused with snake, centipedes or grasshoppers). There's a permanent cold mist sprayed on revelers as they drink, a great touch on hot cruise-ship days.

Warner's Bar BAR

(☎448-5000; www.fortyounghotel.com; Fort Young Hotel, Victoria St; ⊙11am-11pm) This genteel bar at the Fort Young Hotel is a popular spot to ring in the weekend during Friday's 'Cocktails and Conversations' event with live music. It has sweeping views over the water and is at its most atmospheric at sunset. Locals also head in for Monday night's 'Manager's Rum Punch' party and Wednesday's 'Unwine' wine evening.

Symes Zee BAR

(☎448-2494; Symes Zee Hotel, 34 King George V St; ⊙noon-11pm) Right in the heart of Roseau, this local bar gets especially hopping when there's live jazz on Thursdays.

Shopping

★**New Market** MARKET

(River Bank; ⊙8am-4pm Mon-Sat) As much a place for locals to gather and chat with friends as a source of fresh produce, this bustling riverfront market is busiest on Saturday mornings. It's a great spot to pick up the local vibe, try a bowl of goat water (stew) or put together a picnic.

The market spills over onto Dame Eugenia Charles Blvd (Bayfront) where the focus is on freshly caught fish and seafood.

Information

First Caribbean International Bank (☎255-7900; Old St, opposite Hodges Lane; ⊙8am-2pm Mon-Thu, to 5pm Fri) Has an ATM.

Main Post Office (☎266-5209; Dame Eugenia Charles Blvd; ⊙8am-5pm Mon, to 4pm Tue-Fri) Newly rebuilt since Hurricane Maria.

Princess Margaret Hospital (☎448-2231; Federation Dr) The main hospital and trauma facility on Dominica.

Tourist Office (☎448-2045; www.dominica.dm; cnr Dame Eugenia Charles Blvd & King George V St; ⊙8am-5pm Mon, to 4pm Tue-Fri) In a stately building also housing the Dominica Museum, the tourist office also opens on weekends if a cruise ship is in port. It offers plenty of information about the island.

Getting There & Away

BOAT

All ferry services leave from the ferry terminal on Dame Eugenia Charles Blvd (Bayfront Rd).

L'Express des Îles (p394) Regular scheduled ferry service between Roseau, Guadeloupe, Martinique and St Lucia. Buy tickets online.

Val'Ferry (p394) Offers ferry services between Roseau, Portsmouth, Pointe-à-Pitre, Marie-Galante, Martinique and St Lucia. Buy tickets online.

BUS

All of Dominica's bus routes originate in Roseau, but there is no central bus station. Instead, stops serving different destinations are scattered around the downtown grid. Buses run from Monday to Saturday between 6am and 7pm and come in the form of minivans with license plates starting with 'H' or 'HA.' The main bus stops:

King George V St (cnr King George V & Independence Sts) & **Valley Rd** Buses east to Trafalgar, Wotten Waven, Morne Prosper and Laudat.

New Market bus stop (River Bank) Buses to west-coast villages and Portsmouth, to Calibishie and Vielle Case, and to Kalinago Territory and east-coast villages.

Old Market bus stop (Old St) Buses south as far as Soufriere and Scotts Head.

West Bridge bus stop (cnr River Bank & Great George St) Buses to Canefield, Massacre, Mahaut and St Joseph.

Getting Around

The narrow maze of the downtown area is best explored on foot. Destinations further afield can be reached by bus or taxi.

Flag down a taxi on the street or pick one up at a taxi rank. Many drivers will offer you taxis as you walk around. Agree a price before you get in.

Roseau Valley

East of Roseau, the Roseau Valley is a ribbon of rural villages giving access to some of Dominica's most dramatic terrain and top wilderness sites. The village of Trafalgar is famous for its twin waterfalls, while Wotten Waven's hot sulfur springs are said to have medicinal benefits. In the north, Laudat is the gateway to the Unesco-protected Morne Trois Pitons National Park, a stunning landscape of lakes, fumaroles, volcanoes, hot springs and dense forest.

Trafalgar Falls

The village of Trafalgar is spread out among fabulously dramatic scenery in the verdant Roseau Valley. Most people come here to see the twin waterfalls of the same name, which surge out either side of a sheer rock face and down into dozens of small pools that vary in size with the rainfall, before joining the raging Roseau River. Their easy access puts them on the must-see list of just about every Dominica visitor, so expect crowds if there's a cruise ship in port, unless you're visiting in the low season or early or late in the day.

Sights

Trafalgar Falls WATERFALL
(Pailotte Rd, Trafalgar village; site pass US$5) Just beyond the visitor center here you'll find a viewing platform with full-on views of the two side-by-side falls: the 125ft 'Father' fall and 75ft 'Mother' fall. Following the narrow rocky trail beyond the platform means negotiating slippery boulders, so wear sturdy shoes and watch your step. You can cool off in the swimming hole below Mother fall. If you want to hike to the hot springs below Father fall, a guide is recommended.

Sleeping & Eating

Cocoa Cottage INN $$
(276-2920; www.cocoacottages.com; Paillotte Rd, Roseau Valley; d US$85-120;) This serene charmer has six cottages dotted around verdant grounds complete with organic garden. Made from local wood, lava stone, bamboo and other natural materials, each cottage reflects the artistic vision and gentle spirit of Iris, the owner. Less of a guesthouse and more of a commune setup, this is an ideal place to reconnect with nature.

River Rock Cafe & Bar CARIBBEAN $
(225-0815; Paillotte Rd; sandwiches EC$15, mains EC$25-50; 8am-8pm;) The welcome isn't particularly warm, but you can't really argue with the setting of this airy cafe overlooking the surging Roseau River. It serves sandwiches as well as big platters of filling Creole fare featuring chicken, goat, beef or fish alongside a pile of provisions. Order a cold Kubuli and relax at a verandah table with a valley view.

Stairs lead down to the water, in case you feel like plunging in.

Getting There & Away

Buses leaving from Roseau's King George V St (p377) and Valley Rd (p377) bus stops make the trip to Trafalgar Falls village in about 30 minutes. The falls themselves are about a mile further north – you might be able to persuade the driver to take you straight there by offering a little extra money.

Wotten Waven

The tiny, steep village of Wotten Waven has a stunning natural setting and is well known for its natural hot sulfur springs that are said to have medicinal qualities and help cure everything from rheumatism to foot fungus. After a hard day on the trail, taking off those boots and soothing sore muscles in the naturally muddy water is a delight. Enterprising villagers have created several spas where relaxation-seekers can wallow in open-air pools surrounded by lovely gardens. All stay open after sunset, allowing you to chill under the stars, Kubuli in hand while being serenaded by tree frogs.

The water looks 'dirty' but is actually naturally orange. Clean water is piped into the pools so that there's circulation, though you'll want to rinse your swimwear after bathing.

Activities

'Taking the waters' in Wotten Waven's spas is the thing to do. The Waitukubuli National Trail also passes through the village.

Ti Kwen Glo Cho SPA
(295-4432; adult/child US$10/5; 9am-11pm) *Ti kwen glo cho* is Creole for 'little corner of water,' a fitting name for this charming spa surrounded by tropical gardens at the top of the village. Hot sulfurous water bubbles up

from below and is cooled down with fresh water from a waterfall before gushing into two communal stone pools from bamboo pipes.

If you prefer privacy, fill up one of the three personal freestanding bath tubs. The reception doubles as a bar and also sells home-cooked food.

Tia's Sulphur Spa SPA
(225-4823; tiacottages@hotmail.com; open/private pool US$5/10; 9am-11pm Mon-Sat, 4-11pm Sun) Right in the village and set amid beautiful tropical gardens, Tia's has three open-air pools and two private ones inside bamboo huts. There's a restaurant-bar upstairs as well as a pleasant guesthouse offering one- and two-bed tree-house-like structures.

Sleeping

Tia's Bamboo Cottages GUESTHOUSE $
(225-4823; tiacottages@hotmail.com; d/q US$65/80;) As well as its much-loved sulfur pools, Tia's also offers a number of newly rebuilt tree-house-style accommodations, which are clean and comfortable. Rooms have either one or two double beds in them, are naturally ventilated and include small terraces.

Le Petit Paradis GUESTHOUSE $
(440-4352; www.lepetitparadisdominica.com; dm/d/apt US$20/45/66;) Popular with Waitukubuli National Trail hikers, this rambling inn set in flowering gardens is

OFF THE BEATEN TRACK

HIKE THE WAITUKUBULI NATIONAL TRAIL

Completed in 2011, the Caribbean's first **long-distance hiking trail** (WNT; www.waitukubulitrail.com; per day/15 days US$12/40) links Scotts Head in the far southwest with Cabrits National Park in the northwest, hitting all the key beauty spots along the way, including Boiling Lake and Emerald Pool. Its 115 miles are divided into 14 segments of various lengths and difficulty but each one is designed to be completed in one day. Accommodations are available close to the trailheads. The website has maps, addresses, guide referrals and other details.

Segments

- Segment 1: Scotts Head to Soufriere Estate
- Segment 2: Soufriere Estate to Bellevue Chopin
- Segment 3: Bellevue Chopin to Wotten Waven
- Segment 4: Wotten Waven to Pont Casse
- Segment 5: Pont Casse to Castle Bruce
- Segment 6: Castle Bruce to Hatten Garden (Pagua Bay)
- Segment 7: Hatten Garden (Pagua Bay) to First Camp Heights
- Segment 8: First Camp Heights to Petite Macoucherie Heights
- Segment 9: Petite Macoucherie Heights to Colihaut Heights
- Segment 10: Colihaut Heights to Syndicate
- Segment 11: Syndicate to Borne
- Segment 12: Borne to Penville
- Segment 13: Penville to Capuchin
- Segment 14: Capuchin to Cabrits

Passes & Fees

A day pass for one segment is US$12, a 15-day pass to hike all 14 segments costs US$40. Passes are sold at or near the trailheads, including Rubis Filling Station in Portsmouth, the Sea Breeze Inn in Castle Bruce, Kalinago Barana Aute, the Waitukubuli National Trail Management Unit in Pont Casse, Ken's Hinterland Adventure Tours in Roseau and Rodney's Wellness Retreat in Soufriere. Passes are also sold at Courtesy Car Rental at Douglas–Charles Airport and at the Forever Young Classic Souvenir Shop on Dame Mary Eugenia Charles Blvd in Roseau.

presided over by the big-hearted Joan and her charming family. While three rooms were lost in Hurricane Maria, today you can choose between doubles or twins with valley views; a rather cramped apartment; or superb-value dorm-style rooms offering a hammock and a bed to sleep in.

With advance notice, Joan will cook delicious meals (US$7 to US$20) served in the open dining room. Don't miss her famous 'Bullet' rum punch.

Getting There & Away

Buses to Wotten Waven make the trip from the King George V St (p377) and Valley Rd (p377) bus stops in Roseau in about 20 minutes.

Morne Trois Pitons National Park

One of Dominica's absolute highlights, Morne Trois Pitons National Park is an evocative landscape of lakes, fumaroles, volcanoes, waterfalls, hot springs and dense forest. It comprises five vegetation zones, mainly secondary rainforest but reaching up to cloud forest at the highest elevations. It is, in a word, breathtaking.

Established in 1975, the national park stretches across 17,000 acres surrounding the eponymous 4672ft-high three-peaked dormant volcano. Other volcanoes within the park are Morne Micotrin, Morne Watt and Morne Anglais. A Unesco World Heritage site since 1997, the park contains some of Dominica's signature sights – including the preeminent **Boiling Lake** (site pass US$5) – and should not be missed by any nature lover.

Sights & Activities

★Middleham Falls WATERFALL

(site pass US$5) The trail to one of Dominica's highest waterfalls (200ft) traverses thick rainforest with towering trees and ferns. Although well built and not terribly long, the trail gets slippery and requires rock clambering and fording several creeks, as well as long uphill slogs. Bring a swimsuit to cool off in the pool, which is easily one of Dominica's most beautiful sights. Allow about two to three hours round-trip. The main trailhead is just off the Laudat Rd.

Freshwater Lake LAKE

(near Laudat; site pass US$5) Shimmering shades of blue and green, Freshwater is the largest of Dominica's four lakes and the source of the Roseau River. It is easily reached via a paved road that veers uphill just before Laudat and delivers sweeping views of the valley, Morne Anglais and the sea.

At the T-junction, turn right for the lake parking lot and pick up the easy 2.5-mile trail around the lake to the right of the visitor center, past a hydroelectric station. The montane forest vegetation at this elevation (2500ft) is very different from the rainforest; trees are short and thin, and shrubs, ferns and herbs blanket the forest floor. Birders should keep an eye out for the mountain whistler, hummingbirds and egrets. Bring a sweater or light jacket; it gets chilly up here.

Ti Tou Gorge GORGE

(near Laudat) The short swim from a swimming hole through a narrow gorge to a powerful waterfall is charmingly spooky; it's dark down there with steep vine-clad lava walls no more than 5ft or 7ft apart. It's an ethereal and unusual place, but can get crowded. If there's a cruise ship in port, come early or late in the day for relative serenity.

The name, by the way, is Creole for 'small throat.' Don't swim the gorge after heavy rains when dangerous flash flooding may occur. Scenes from *Pirates of the Caribbean* were filmed here.

Emerald Pool NATURAL POOL

(http://tourism.gov.dm/news-and-media/brochures/76-emerald-pool; Imperial Rd, near Pont Cassé; US$5) This lovely swimming hole is fed by a 40ft waterfall and hemmed in by sumptuous foliage which gives it its distinctive green tinge. It's one of Dominica's more accessible – and hence, popular – natural wonders, and while the water can be on the cool side, on cruise-ship days it can be rammed with bus tours.

A path winds through dense rainforest and past two viewpoints, one looking out over the rainforest canopy to Morne Laurent and another treating you to panoramic views of the Atlantic coast. There's a visitor center with toilets and a snack bar.

Boeri Lake Trail HIKING

(near Laudat; site pass US$5) At 2800ft, moody Boeri Lake is Dominica's highest lake and fills a volcanic crater wedged between Morne Trois Pitons and Morne Macaque. For the trailhead, take the road to Freshwater Lake just before Laudat and turn left at the T-junction. The 1.25-mile-long rocky and sometimes slippery trail to the lake goes past streams and hot and cold springs.

En route, you'll enjoy sweeping views of the mountains, Freshwater Lake and the Atlantic Ocean from the ridge – weather permitting. The water is cold, so a dip will be quite refreshing indeed. Keep an eye out for scurrying *zandoli* (tree lizards), hummingbirds and butterflies.

Morne Trois Pitons Trail HIKING
(Imperial Rd, Pont Cassé; site pass US$5) At 4672ft, this dormant volcano is the highest elevation within the eponymous national park. The hike to the top is challenging, as it cuts through patches of razor grass and requires scrambling over steep rocks. You'll need not only good lungs and thighs but a solid sense of balance. Budget about six hours and consider hiring a guide.

Tours

Extreme Dominica ADVENTURE SPORTS
(285-9136, 245-4328; www.extremedominica.com; Paillotte Rd; canyoning tour US$160) This pro outfit runs exhilarating half-day expeditions that have you rappelling down waterfalls, jumping from pool to pool and floating in crystal-clear swimming holes at the bottom of deep canyon walls. It also offers guided hikes to Boiling Lake, and a turtle-watching tour (April to July only). Rates include pick-up, all gear and a training session.

No experience is necessary and there's no need to be superfit.

Sleeping & Eating

★ **Citrus Creek Plantation** BOUTIQUE HOTEL $$
(617-1234; www.citruscreekplantation.com; La Plaine; r incl breakfast from US$150; P 📶) Largely cut off from the rest of Dominica on its remote southeastern coast, gorgeous Citrus Creek offers total seclusion in a lovely setting on the banks of a river surrounded by thick forest. The six luxuriously appointed accommodations are built in wood and stone to differing specifications, each enjoying complete privacy, direct river access and breakfast served in the room.

Riverside Cafe CARIBBEAN $$
(La Plaine; mains EC$40-60; 10am-5pm Tue-Sun, dinner by reservation; 📶) This delightful restaurant at Citrus Creek Plantation warmly welcomes nonguests throughout the day, but only opens in the evening when there are reservations. It serves up a regularly changing menu of dishes such as chicken coconut curry, *mahimahi* steaks, and stewed pork on its lovely verandah overlooking the river.

Getting There & Away

Buses to Laudat leave from the King George V St and Valley Rd bus stops in Roseau and take around 40 minutes. A taxi from Roseau to Laudat costs EC$80.

Soufriere & Southwest Coast

It's sleepy down south in Dominica, but don't miss this part of the island, home to some superb snorkeling, natural mountain hot springs and the impressive geographic oddity of Scotts Head, which juts suddenly out of the sea where the Caribbean and the Atlantic meet. This unusual rocky isthmus has gorgeous views back to southern Dominica's dramatic coastline. The twin towns of Soufriere and Scotts Head were devastated by Hurricane Maria in 2017, and the damage is still readily apparent today. There are big plans to redevelop the region, with the construction of a much-needed new sea wall in Scotts Head and large-scale investment to lure visitors back.

Sights

Soufriere Sulfur Springs HOT SPRINGS
(Soufriere; 24hr) These naturally heated mineralized waters drain from two streams into several small pools in the hills above Soufriere. To find this place, walk past Soufriere Guesthouse (p382), turn left when the road splits and look for a small covered pavilion. From here follow your ears to find the streams.

Scotts Head Point HISTORIC SITE
(US$2) A narrow isthmus separating the fierce Atlantic and the calm Caribbean leads to Scotts Head, the rocky headland named for an 18th-century British lieutenant governor. A short hike leads up to a smattering of ruins, the remnants of the fort he erected in defense of Soufriere Bay. There's great snorkeling off the pebbly beach, and a bar that rents gear and serves cold drinks.

The point also marks the beginning of the Waitukubuli National Trail (p379).

Scotts Head VILLAGE
On Dominica's southernmost tip, the fishing village of Scotts Head has a gem of a setting along the gently curving shoreline of Soufriere

Bay. While it got very badly damaged by Hurricane Maria, colorful characters still hang out on the porches of pastel-painted houses, and locals seem surprised to see outsiders visiting this remote corner of the island.

Grand Bay BAY

This sweeping bay is on Dominica's south coast. Turn inland at Loubiere onto a wide and largely pothole-free curving road skirting the base of Morne Anglais and crossing a few rivers before reaching the coast.

Activities

★Champagne Beach & Reef SNORKELING

(Point Michel; marine reserve fee US$2) One of Dominica's most popular underwater playgrounds has you snorkeling amid volcanic bubbles emerging from vents beneath the sea floor and rising up as drops of liquid crystal, making it feel like you're swimming in a giant glass of champagne. Best of all, you can snorkel right off the (rocky) beach. Technicolor fish and coral abound.

A shop rents gear for US$19 and a small restaurant serves upscale local fare.

★Bubble Beach Spa & Bar HOT SPRINGS

(Soufriere; by donation) A hot bath in the Caribbean Sea? That's what you get on Bubble Beach where warm sulfurous water percolates right up from below the ocean floor. Enterprising local Dale Mitchell has created a lovely little retreat with a stone-walled hot pool for soaking, a sandy beach with loungers (US$5), and a small bar with cold beers and homemade bush rum.

Soufriere-Scotts Head Marine Reserve DIVING

(☎616-0404; Soufriere & Scotts Head; fee EC$5) The sweeping bay stretching from Soufriere to Scotts Head is a vast volcanic crater of unknown depth and a haven for divers and snorkelers with nearly 30 different sites. With its dramatic drop-offs, walls, pinnacles, coral reefs and underwater fumaroles, it delivers Caribbean diving at its finest and most pristine. The Kalinago associate many legends with these mysterious waters.

Champagne Reef Dive & Snorkel DIVING

(☎440-5085; www.champagnereef.com; 2-tank dive US$89) Right at the famous Champagne Beach, this outfit rents snorkeling gear for US$19, including the US$2 marine reserve fee, and also organizes boat dives, dive courses and rainforest tours. If your underwater explorations have left you hungry or thirsty, there's cold beer and upscale local fare to restore energy.

Nature Island Dive DIVING

(☎245-6505; www.natureislanddive.com; Gallion Rd, Soufriere; 1-/2-tank dive incl all gear US$88/120) Within a 10-minute boat ride of spectacular dive sites, this friendly operator specializes in small groups ranging from two to eight divers. It picks up cruise-ship passengers from Roseau and brings them down to Soufriere. Kayaking and paddleboarding are also available.

Sleeping

★Soufriere Guesthouse GUESTHOUSE $

(☎275-7000, 275-5454; www.soufriereguesthouse.com; Brooklyn Ave; dm US$20, r US$45-55; 📶) The brainchild of free divers Wes and John, this brand-new guesthouse has hostel prices for its excellent en suite dorms and slightly higher rates for its four spacious, spotless private rooms. There's a fully equipped kitchen, large lounge and a long verandah littered with hammocks. The local hot springs are just a short stroll away.

Getting There & Away

Buses down the main highway as far as Scotts Head depart from the Old Market (p377) bus stop in Roseau.

Mero

About halfway up the coast, the long and grayish beach at Mero is the west coast's most popular. It's accessed via a narrow one-way road off the main road, where a few bars serve drinks and meals and rent beach chairs. The beach (once you get past the color) is lovely and the water is usually fairly calm, making it good for swimming.

There are some beautiful dive sites just a 10-minute boat ride offshore, including Coral Gardens, Rena's Reef and Whale Shark Reef. East Carib Dive runs trips and snorkeling tours.

Activities

East Carib Dive DIVING

(☎612-0028, 316-4212; www.dominicadiving.com; Salisbury; 1-/2-tank dives US$60/90) This outfit has run boat dives, night dives and snorkeling trips for more than 20 years. There's diving at Doudou Reef right in front of the dive center, and half a dozen other sites just a 10-minute boat ride away. Book ahead, as the owners are often absent. They also offer simple accommodations right on the beach.

Sleeping & Eating

Mango Island Lodges BOUTIQUE HOTEL $$
(☎617-7963; www.mangoislandlodges.com; St Joseph; r US$160-360;) This gorgeous spot enjoys soaring sea views from its hilltop perch and has thatched cabins and a breezy bar-restaurant serving meals for guests. Each room has its own decorative style, and while the cheaper rooms are on the small side, the priciest is huge indeed and comes complete with African masks. Booking direct gets you a free breakfast.

Tamarind Tree Hotel HOTEL $$
(☎616-5258; www.tamarindtreedominica.com; Salisbury; s US$104-134, d US$134-164, villas US$200; closed Sep–mid-Oct;) Gifted a new beach (to which an access path is planned for the near future) by Hurricane Maria, this clifftop property with magnificent sea views is run by a friendly Swiss-German couple and enjoys attractively landscaped grounds and a good restaurant. All rooms have fans and solar-heated water; the upper units feature air-con, while three two-bedroom villas come with kitchen.

★**InDee's Beach Bar & Restaurant** CARIBBEAN $$
(☎613-2521, 612-0876; Mero Beach; mains EC$20-50; 10am-9pm;) This locally adored spot on the beach is the best choice in Mero and serves delicious fish and seafood, plus all the beer, juice and coffee you could wish for. Call ahead to check it's open as it has been a bit whimsical about opening hours since Hurricane Maria.

Getting There & Away

Mero Beach sits about halfway between Portsmouth and Roseau. Driving takes about 30 to 40 minutes from either. If coming by bus, ask the driver to drop you at the turnoff to Mero Beach and walk five minutes into the village.

Portsmouth

Set on sweeping Prince Rupert Bay, backed by steep hills and fronted by a long black-sand beach, Portsmouth was founded by the British, who intended to create a new capital for the French island they'd taken control of in 1763. It never quite took off as a town: its swampy surroundings gave rise to mosquitoes and thus disease, ensuring Roseau's status as capital was never seriously threatened. Despite its gorgeous setting, Dominica's second-largest town still feels pretty rough around the edges.

Possie, as locals call it, sustained massive damage in 2017's Hurricane Maria, leading to the relocation of US medical school Ross University to Barbados after some 40 years in Dominica. The massive exodus of staff and students has had an extremely adverse effect on Portsmouth; many of its hotels and restaurants have never reopened. Despite this economic setback, the town is friendly, charismatic and delightful compared to chaotic Roseau.

Sights & Activities

★**Cabrits National Park** NATIONAL PARK
(Bay St; site pass US$5; 8am-6pm) The star attraction of this small national park on a forested headland a mile north of downtown Portsmouth is Fort Shirley, an impressively restored 18th-century British garrison, just a five-minute uphill walk from the park entrance. Views over Prince Rupert Bay are especially lovely in the late afternoon. Three longer trails crisscross the park, leading past the officers' quarters, the soldiers' barracks, the powder magazine and other vestiges from the past.

The visitor center has exhibits and a snack bar. The Waitukubuli Trail ends just past Fort Shirley.

★**Indian River Boat Ride** BOATING
(site fee US$5, boat ride per person EC$50) The 1½-hour return boat ride along this shady mangrove-lined river glides past buttressed bwa mang trees with a chance to spot egrets, crabs, iguanas, hummingbirds and more. Trips include a walk through a plantation and a stop at 'Cobra's Bush Bar' for juice, snacks and signature rum drink 'The Dynamite.' Rowers wait by the bridge at the river mouth.

JC Ocean Adventures DIVING
(☎295-0757, 449-6957; www.jcoceanadventures.com; Cabrits National Park Rd; 2-tank boat dive US$85) JC are Jorge and Cindy, the owners of this dive center within Cabrits National Park, just past the entrance booth. Their operation includes boat, shore and night dives, as well as PADI (Professional Association of Diving Instructors) certification courses. Equipment rental available.

Sleeping

Most of Portsmouth's hotels and guesthouses closed after Hurricane Maria and only a few have reopened, though the town is slowly getting back to normal. Two large new resorts next to the Cabrits National Park were being completed at the time of writing, the first of their kind in Dominica.

★Toucari Cottages RENTAL HOUSE $$
(☎315-6560; www.toucaricottages.com; Toucari; cottages from US$115, 3-night minimum; 📶) These three cottages built above the beautifully set village of Toucari, just north of Portsmouth, are some of the best private accommodations on the island. Each house has a large terrace overlooking the sea, plus smart furnishings and every comfort taken care of by the British owners. You'll need a car to stay here – it's a significant distance into town.

★Secret Bay LUXURY HOTEL $$$
(☎445-4444; www.secretbay.dm; Ross Blvd; r from US$800, minimum 3-night stay; P❄📶≈) 🍃 Dominica's most exclusive hotel is the aptly named Secret Bay, ensconced in jungle on a rocky outcrop between two lovely, tranquil sandy bays, both of which can only be accessed through the property. There are just six lavish villas here (though a further 28 are planned) and each is delightfully furnished and has its own plunge pool.

The entire place exudes thoughtful luxury, with its superb Zing Zing restaurant, which caters for hotel guests only and prepares bespoke locally sourced meals that reinterpret pre-colonial Dominican cuisine for the palate of the international traveler. The Gommier spa pampers the guests, and water sports are laid on at the beach. For true seclusion you can take a boat trip around the outcrop and settle into the hotel's second beach, where you're guaranteed to be totally alone.

Hotel The Champs HOTEL $$$
(☎616-3001; www.thechampsdm.com; Blanca Heights, Picard; r incl breakfast from US$270; ❄📶≈) This comfortable family-run hotel clings to a steep hill above Picard, meaning superb views are guaranteed. There are two rooms at garden level and three larger ones upstairs, all with fridge, TV and a porch with lounge chairs. The restaurant serves dinner for guests nightly, and is well known locally for its wood-fired pizza served on Friday night.

Note that the road leading up to the hotel is very steep; it takes about 10 to 15 minutes on foot, which makes having your own wheels ideal.

Picard Beach Cottages RESORT $$$
(☎445-5131; www.picardbeachcottages.dm; Picard; cottages US$240-288; P❄📶) In a garden setting on an old coconut plantation right by a narrow black-sand beach, this cluster of 18 wooden cottages set amid lovely gardens offers atmospheric accommodations with basic kitchens, dark-wood furnishings and mosquito nets. Each unit has its own private porch, and offers one of the few chances in the entire country to be right on the beach.

Reception also runs the next door PBH hotel, which is far less charming and atmospheric; be sure you're getting a room at Picard Beach Cottages.

Eating

★Keepin' It Real CARIBBEAN $$
(☎225-7657; Toucari; mains EC$40-80; ⊙noon-10pm; 📶) Local legend Derrick, whose restaurant is famous across Dominica for its superb lobster, has had to rebuild it twice in the past few years, first following Hurricane Maria and then following a fire in 2019. The restaurant's third incarnation stands on Toucari's pretty little bay, and makes for a perfect lunch or dinner spot. Double-check opening hours before coming.

Coco Mango Cafe MIDDLE EASTERN $$
(Moo Cow Trail, Picard; mains EC$25-40; ⊙5-9pm Fri-Wed; 📶🖉) In a tranquil garden overlooking a gurgling stream, Coco Mango is a most unexpected find: an alfresco Syrian-run cafe offering plates of delicious hummus, baba ghanoush, lavash and falafel. It's also a pleasant – if quiet – place to come for a drink.

Purple Turtle Beach Club Bar & Restaurant CARIBBEAN $$
(☎445-5296; Bay St, Lagoon; mains EC$20-40; ⊙10:30am-10pm, bar till late; 📶) This Portsmouth institution sits on the main beach right in the sand and is a favorite end-of-day drinking and eating spot for locals and boaters. Its menu features all the expected Caribbean favorites, from Creole chicken to barbecued ribs. It becomes an exceptionally loud bar after dark, particularly on Wednesdays, when it hosts its famous reggae dance party.

★C&D Beach Bar & Grill CARIBBEAN $$$
(☎316-6776, 315-6291; Picard; mains EC$50-75; ⊙noon-10pm Wed-Sun; 📶) Portsmouth's most interesting menu can be found at Candy and David's charming restaurant right on

WORTH A TRIP

MORNE DIABLOTIN NATIONAL PARK

Established to protect the habitat of the national bird, the Sisserou parrot, and its pretty red-necked cousin, the Jaco parrot, this national park covers some 8242 acres. It's named for Dominica's tallest peak (4747ft), which dominates the area. There is no public bus service to the park. You will need your own wheels or hire a driver.

Closed at the time of writing due to hurricane damage, the **Morne Diablotin Trail** (near Dublanc; site fee US$5) takes you from the rainforest to the cloud forest. It may only be 1.25 miles long, but it's all steeply uphill and involves clambering over rocks, roots and trees. Check locally to see if the trail has reopened.

Allow at least two to 2½ hours each way, including stops to look for endemic Sisserou and Jaco parrots. Prepare to get muddy and bring a jacket as it gets chilly at the top. The trailhead is on the road to the Syndicate Nature Trail, which veers off the village of Dublanc. Look for the sign.

The Syndicate Nature Trial (p391) is an easy 1-mile loop trail through the rainforest on the western slopes of Morne Diablotin. It's beloved by birders for the good chance of spotting the Sisserou and Jaco parrots. The best spotting time is in the early morning and late afternoon. Also watch for hummingbirds and several dozen other feathered species.

To get to the reserve, turn onto the signposted road just north of the village of Dublanc and continue to Syndicate Estate, about 4.5 miles inland.

the beach, where music and lighting are at just the right level, service is friendly and the chalkboard menu includes dishes such as panko-crusted pork chop with sweet-chili tomato sauce, and garlic mussels simmered in Kubuli beer. Do not miss the Hurricane shrimp appetizer!

Information

National Bank of Dominica (☎255-2300; Michael Douglas Blvd) Has an ATM accepting foreign bank cards.

Police (Bay St)

Getting There & Away

Buses (cnr Bay St & Granby St) to Roseau's New Market (p377) bus stop (EC$9, one hour) leave from the south end of Bay St on the waterfront. For Calibishie (EC$5, 20 minutes) and the Douglas–Charles Airport (EC$10, 50 minutes), buses leave from the **Benjamin's Park bus stop** (Granby St) on Granby St.

Val'Ferry (p394) now connects Portsmouth directly with Pointe-à-Pitre in Guadeloupe.

Northeastern Coast

The narrow road cutting to the east coast from Portsmouth across Dominica's remote and sparsely populated north is a stunning drive past massive ferns, towering palms, wild heliconias and thick banana groves. Budget about two hours for the extremely curvy drive, and save plenty of time for beach exploration. Numerous scenes from *Pirates of the Caribbean* were filmed in this area.

Calibishie

Calibishie is the main village on Dominica's stunning northern coast and boasts a dramatic mosaic of steep cliffs, red rocks and rivers gushing down from rainforest-covered mountains as its backdrop. The coast cradles some of Dominica's best beaches, which enjoy a raw, untouched mystique helped by the total absence of big hotels and resorts. It's little wonder that many scenes from *Pirates of Caribbean* were filmed around here.

Although still sleepy and slow-paced, Calibishie has seen its tourism infrastructure grow in recent years, and while Hurricane Maria forced many businesses to close, the locals now have tourism in their blood; this is where you'll find some of Dominica's best guesthouses.

Sights

If you plan to snorkel, it's best to have your own gear; the closest rental outlets are in Portsmouth.

★**Batibou Beach** BEACH

(admission US$5) Easily Dominica's best beach, this gorgeously wild coconut-palm-fringed crescent has good swimming and snorkeling, and there's an (often unmanned) beach bar serving drinks. It sits at the end of a 0.6-mile dirt road that's only accessible by 4WD or on foot. The surrounding land is privately owned, and you may need to pay US$5 entry. Often there is nobody at the entrance and the barrier is locked, so leave your car and walk down to the beach.

Number One Beach BEACH

This moody black-sand beach is fringed by coconut palms, sea grape and white mangrove. The currents are too strong for swimming but it's a nice spot for a picnic or a stroll. It's about a 15-minute walk from the road – look for the sign.

During nesting season (April to June), various turtle species come ashore to lay their eggs.

Point Baptiste Beach BEACH

This beautiful quiet beach at the foot of a massive rock face has reddish sand, shallow waters and lots of shady coconut palms. You can snorkel right off the beach. Access is through the Pointe Baptiste estate.

Pointe Baptiste Estate Chocolate Factory FACTORY

(www.pointebaptiste.com/chocolaterie.html; Pointe Baptiste Estate) FREE Meet Alan Napier, whose grandparents came from Scotland to found the Pointe Baptiste Estate, and who took it upon himself to start making Dominica's first homegrown chocolate. It's still very much a cottage-industry affair. Come by for an interesting short tour of the process, and buy a few bars of the 60% to 100% dark chocolate as a delicious souvenir.

Sleeping

A number of properties flank the main highway, although the nicest overlook the rugged shore or are tucked into the hills above town. All are small and privately run, often by jovial (and sometimes eccentric) expats.

> **JACK SPARROW WAS HERE**
>
> With its wild coast, thick jungle and hidden coves, Dominica has always been a popular haunt of pirates between pillages, so it was only natural that Hollywood came calling when location scouting for the *Pirates of the Caribbean* films. In 2005, hundreds of cast and crew, led by Johnny, Orlando and Keira, invaded the island to shoot scenes for films two and three in locations such as Batibou Beach, Ti Tou Gorge, Soufriere and Indian River.

★Jacoway Inn B&B $

(☎445-8872; www.jacowayinn.com; John Baptist Ridge Rd; apt/cottages incl breakfast US$95/110; P 📶) Carol Ann's delightful guesthouse offers you the choice of two superb-value apartments (each with its own small kitchen and large terrace) and her 110-year-old wooden cottage, easily one of Dominica's most atmospheric sleeping options. Carol Ann herself is a delight: gourmet cook, bonne vivante and dog adopter who dotes on her guests and prepares sublime garden breakfasts.

It's a short, well-signed walk uphill from the main road.

Veranda View B&B B&B $

(☎445-8900, 613-9493; www.verandaviewdominica.com; Main Rd; apt incl breakfast US$75-85; 📶) This stylishly decorated B&B with three studio apartments sits right above the sand and has great beachfront vistas. Dutch Owner Hermien is a consummate host and excellent cook who will happily whip up a tasty lunch or dinner for you upon request. Apartments come with kitchenettes.

★Wanderlust BOUTIQUE HOTEL $$

(☎295-0890; www.wanderlustcaribbean.com; Hodges Bay; apt US$175-295, 4-night minimum, room only; P ❄ 📶) Hosts Tom and Sharie offer a unique all-inclusive boutique experience at Wanderlust, where guests stay in one of five stylish, spacious, fully equipped apartments overlooking the ocean, and spend their days doing different tailor-made tours and activities with their passionate hosts. Whether it's hiking, diving, biking or fishing, Tom and Sharie know Dominica backwards and can arrange it all.

It's also possible just to come and stay without purchasing the activities packages – the apartments are luxuriously appointed and overlook Hodges Bay with its wild and dramatic beach. Best of all is the rooftop bar, which is perfect for a sundowner.

Calibishie Gardens CABIN $$

(☎265-7915, 612-5176; landofpoz@gmail.com; off Main Rd; cabin incl breakfast US$125; 📶 📺) At this charming place hand-built by congenial Canadian expat Troy (aka Poz), you sleep in wooden cabins perched atop stone pillars – they're like eco-conscious Smurf houses. Interiors are rustic in style but first-rate in comfort (cable TV, fridge, mosquito net). Enjoy jungle views from your private porch, and Poz Restaurant & Bar, the best restaurant in northern Dominica, downstairs.

Pointe Baptiste Guesthouse VILLA **$$$**
(225-5378; www.pointebaptiste.com; Pointe Baptiste Estate; villas US$350, chocolate cottage US$75;) Previous guests at this magnificent wooden villa on the estate of the Napier family have included Mick Jagger and Princess Margaret, and it's not hard to see why; the view from the vast veranda is incredible, while the rest of the charmingly old-fashioned place oozes history. It sleeps up to eight people, though beds are on the small side.

The gorgeous garden gives access to two sandy beaches. Proprietor Alan Napier operates a small chocolate factory on the estate grounds, above which you'll find the gorgeously appointed chocolate cottage, a breezy cabin that sleeps up to three.

Eating

Sadly, Calibishie's swiftly growing number of eating options was badly impacted by Hurricane Maria; the food scene is still recovering. There's very little decent food to be had here, with the terrific exception of Poz Restaurant & Bar, one of the island's most enjoyable spots for a meal.

★**Poz Restaurant & Bar** INTERNATIONAL **$$**
(612-5176; off Main Rd; mains EC$40-60; 4-10pm Mon-Sat, 2-10pm Sun;) 'Poz' is really Troy from Toronto, a dreamer whose magical restaurant and bar has quickly evolved into a community hangout for expats, visitors and villagers. From bacon-wrapped plantain to oxtail stew, and lobster in garlic butter to curried goat, the tastes are superb and totally authentic. The poolside dining area built entirely from local wood is a cozy delight.

Oenophiles rejoice – Poz is planning a new wine bar next door, a first for Dominica.

Coral Reef Restaurant CARIBBEAN **$$**
(Seafront; mains EC$20-50; 8am-11pm;) This relaxed seafront restaurant is one of the very few currently open in Calibishie. It serves rather small portions of simple fare from an oral menu at its alfresco tables overlooking a small stretch of golden sand. The selection on offer in the evening is better, when additional dishes such as mussels and ribs are available.

Information

Tourist Office (445-8344; www.calibishiecoast.com; Seafront; 9am-5pm Mon-Fri) Friendly staff welcome travelers to the north of Dominica, offering good info on the many places to stay in the region. There's a selection of local handicrafts for sale.

Getting There & Away

Buses linking Douglas–Charles Airport and Portsmouth can be stopped anywhere along the main highway. Change buses in Portsmouth to get down to Roseau.

Marigot & Pagua Bay

Marigot encompasses Douglas–Charles Airport and several neighborhoods strung along the highway. Aside from the gas station (the only one for miles), there's little to make you want to stop. Instead, push on to gorgeous Pagua Bay, which has a rocky beach suitable for bodysurfing.

Sleeping & Eating

Hibiscus Valley Inn GUESTHOUSE **$$**
(445-8195; www.hibiscusvalley.com; Hatton Garden, Marigot; r US$69-145;) This convivial rainforest lodge 15 minutes from Douglas–Charles Airport has both 'nature bungalows' down by the Pagua River with shared facilities and a veranda for lounging in a hammock, as well as smarter hotel-standard rooms with air-con, TV and fridge. Meals and an extensive tour program are also available.

★**Pagua Bay House** BOUTIQUE HOTEL **$$$**
(612-6068; www.paguabayhouse.com; Dr Nicholas Liverpool Hwy, Pagua Bay; r US$288, ste with/without pool US$504/408, 3-night minimum;) This sophisticated boutique hotel could easily grace the pages of *Architectural Digest*. The six luxe *cabañas* and suites mix industrial stylings with dark-wood refinement and come with walnut platform beds, Frette linens and brushed-concrete bathrooms with walk-in showers. The hotel's equally stylish open-air restaurant has a delightful small pool and views across the road to the water.

★**Pagua Bar & Grill** INTERNATIONAL **$$**
(612-6068; www.paguabayhouse.com; Dr Nicholas Liverpool Hwy, Pagua Bay; mains lunch EC$15-45, dinner EC$40-65; 8am-8:30pm;) Part of Pagua Bay House, this open-air restaurant has breathtaking views of the pounding surf, an urban hip look and delicious contemporary cuisine with Caribbean accents. A popular lunch spot and famous for its fish

tacos and ceviche, it makes for an ideal stop en route to the airport.

Getting There & Away

There is bus service from Portsmouth along the north coastal road, while buses from Roseau come across the center of the island on an excellent new road. Any transport serving the airport will be able to drop you in the area.

Kalinago Territory

Dominica is the only island in the Eastern Caribbean that's still home to pre-Columbian indigenous people, the Kalinago. Their ancestors are believed to have migrated north from South America around AD 1200.

About 3000 of them live in the 3700-acre Kalinago Territory, an 8-mile-long coastal stretch south of Bataka on the east coast. Formed by the British in 1903, the communally owned territory is a remote and mountainous area where bananas, breadfruit trees and wild heliconia grow along the roadside.

The Kalinago – also known as the Island Carib or simply Carib – are a proud people who cherish their heritage and maintain their customs, traditions and crafts.

Sights

★Kalinago Barana Autê CULTURAL CENTRE
(☎445-7979; www.kalinagobaranaaute.com; Old Coast Rd, Salybia; site pass & tour US$10; ⊙10am-5pm Tue-Sun mid-Oct–mid-Apr, Tue & Fri-Sun mid-Apr–mid-Oct) This re-created traditional village on the Crayfish River near the Isukulati Falls is a good spot to get an overview of Kalinago history and culture. The 30- to 45-minute tour leads to various huts where locals demonstrate the crafts of basket-weaving, canoe-making and cassava-baking. An architectural highlight is the huge *Karbet* (men's house) where dances and cultural presentations take place. En route you get to enjoy awesome views of the falls and the crashing waves.

Touna Kalinago Heritage Village CULTURAL CENTRE
(☎285-1830; www.kalinagoterritory.com/attractions/touna-kalinago-heritage-village; Concord; ⊙tours by arrangement;) Created by former Kalinago chief Irvince Auguiste, this living village on the Pagua River was created to introduce visitors to the way of life of Dominica's indigenous people. On guided 90-minute tours, you'll visit a traditional herbalist and the homes of basket-weavers and craftspeople. Visits include a stop at Auguiste's own home. The project encourages active exchange between visitors and locals to break down cultural barriers. With advance notice, it's also possible to stay overnight (from US$30 per person).

Sleeping

Kalinago Territory Home Stay Programme HOMESTAY $
(www.kalinagoterritory.com/home-stays; per person US$30-50) The manager of the Kalinago Barana Autê heritage village can organize homestays with local Kalinago families so you can get a deeper understanding of the traditional ways and contemporary issues of Dominica's indigenous people. Stay either in modern homes or traditional thatched or wooden huts. Meals can be provided as well (breakfast/lunch/dinner US$10/15/10). Booking is via the website.

Sea Breeze Inn HOTEL $
(☎225-6287; www.seabreezedominica.com; beachfront, Castle Bruce; r US$50-60; P) Fallen on rather hard times since Hurricane Maria, Sea Breeze Inn has now reopened and is building a new story. Sea views from the eight simple existing accommodations are excellent, however, and the attached restaurant serves home-cooked local food from morning to night.

Domcan's Guest House APARTMENT $
(☎615-9107; dvwoodley2013@gmail.com; Castle Bruce; r US$40; P) A great pit stop for Waitukubuli (p379) hikers (it's on segment 5), this guesthouse has you sleeping in very basic but serviceable rooms or slightly bigger apartments with kitchenette, sitting area and balcony. There are some dramatic sea views.

The name, by the way, is short for Dominican and Canadian, which are the homelands of owners Harry and Grace.

Eating

Islet View Restaurant & Bar CARIBBEAN $
(☎265-6220, 276-9581; New Rd, Castle Bruce; mains EC$20-40; ⊙8am-4pm;) Enjoy breathtaking views of Castle Bruce Bay from this simple roadside shack, which was comprehensively distributed across the hillside during Hurricane Maria and has since been painstakingly reassembled. Ice-cold ginger beer comes in coconuts, the legendary bush-rum selection includes quirkily named

flavors such as Theresa May, and the fried plantain and spicy dip starter is nothing short of heavenly.

Daniel's Cassava Bakery BAKERY $

(☎617-5058; Main Hwy, Salybia; ⏰8am-4pm Tue-Sun) A staple of the Kalinago diet, cassava bread is traditionally made just from ground manioc, but local baker Daniel Frederick adds a bit of coconut or ginger to some of his creations for sweetness. He also sells the plain version hot from the oven (EC$5 per piece) from his simple shack, which is also something of a local hangout.

ℹ Getting There & Away

Buses to Castle Bruce and other points in the Kalinago Territory leave from the New Market (p377) bus stop in Roseau.

UNDERSTAND DOMINICA

History

Thanks to its abundance of fresh water, Dominica has long been popular with settlers. The first European to see the island was Columbus in 1493, and it was for centuries engaged in a tug of war between British and French colonizers and the indigenous Kalinago. Dominica achieved independence from Britain in 1978 and is a member of the Commonwealth.

Colonization

Dominica was the last of the Caribbean islands to be colonized by Europeans due chiefly to the fierce resistance of the Kalinago, the indigenous people whose ancestors are believed to have migrated here from South America around AD 1200. They called the island Waitukubuli, which means 'Tall is her body.' Christopher Columbus, with less poetic flair, named the island after the day of the week on which he spotted it – a Sunday ('Domenica' in Italian) – on November 3, 1493.

Daunted by the Kalinago and discouraged by the absence of gold, the Spanish took little interest in Dominica. France laid claim to the island in 1635 and wrestled with the British over it through the 18th century.

In 1805 the French burned much of Roseau to the ground and from then on the island remained firmly in the possession of the British, who established sugar plantations on Dominica's more accessible slopes, and planned a new capital at Portsmouth, which never took off due to the mosquitoes and disease that persisted there.

Independence

In 1967 Dominica gained autonomy in internal affairs as a West Indies Associated State and became an independent republic within the Commonwealth on November 3, 1978 (the 485th anniversary of Columbus' sighting of the island).

The initial year of independence was a turbulent one. In June 1979 the island's first prime minister, Patrick John, was forced to resign after a series of corrupt schemes surfaced, including one clandestine land deal to transfer 15% of the island to US developers. In August 1979 Hurricane David, packing winds of 150mph, struck the island with devastating force. Forty-two people were killed and 75% of the islanders' homes were destroyed or severely damaged.

In July 1980 Dame Mary Eugenia Charles was elected prime minister, the first woman in the Caribbean to hold the office. She survived two unsuccessful coup attempts right after her inauguration and subsequently managed to stay in office for 15 years.

Dominica in the 21st Century

After the sudden death of popular prime minister Roosevelt Douglas ('Rosie') in 2000, after only eight months in office, his successor Pierre Charles also died on the job, four years later. In 2004 31-year-old Roosevelt Skerrit stepped into the breach, and has gone on to become Dominica's longest-serving prime minister. A popular choice with young people, Skerrit was reelected in 2009, 2014 and 2019.

On a geopolitical level Skerrit severed long-standing diplomatic relations with Taiwan in favor of ties with mainland China in exchange for US$100 million in aid. He has also steered Dominica toward sustainable tourism, although this is somewhat at odds with his recent decision to support the construction of a brand-new international airport on the island which would allow Dominica to take direct long-haul flights. This is an exceptionally divisive issue locally, as many Dominicans fear the construction of such an airport would change the country irreparably. On the other hand, a new airport would lead to massive growth in the tourism sector and would create a large number of new jobs and thus serve as a massive injection into the local economy.

Dominica's most significant recent event occurred on September 18 2017, when it took a direct hit from Category 5 Hurricane Maria, which devastated the island and its economy, killing 65 people. Dominica is still recovering from the storm, and while the tourism industry has rebounded surprisingly quickly, the island's economy will take years to get back on track.

People & Culture

Dominica draws on a mix of cultures: French place names feature as often as English; African foods and customs mingle with European traditions as part of the island's Creole culture; and the indigenous Kalinago (also known as Caribs) still carve dugouts (canoes), build houses on stilts and weave distinctive basketwork. Rastafarian influences are also strong here.

About a third of Dominica's population live in and around Roseau. Some 87% are of African descent and about 3000 are Kalinago. With a 61% Roman Catholic population and religious observance commonplace, conservative values are strong and family holds an important place in Dominican society.

JEAN RHYS

Dominica's most celebrated author, Jean Rhys, was born in Roseau in 1890. Although she moved to England at age 16 and made only one brief return visit to Dominica, much of her work draws upon her childhood experiences in the West Indies. Rhys touches lightly upon her life in Dominica in *Voyage in the Dark* (1934) and in her autobiography, *Smile Please* (1979). Her most famous work, *Wide Sargasso Sea* (1966), a novel set mostly in Jamaica and an unnamed Dominica, was made into a film in 1993. Other important writers associated with Dominica include Phyllis Shand Allfrey and Elma Napier. The latter's memoir *Black and White Sands* (published posthumously in 2009) tells the remarkable story of her love affair with the island, where she moved and built a house in Calibishie in the 1930s.

Much has been made of the fact that Dominica has three times the number of centenarians than more developed nations. The most famous was Ma Pampo who died in 2003 reputedly at 128 years of age. There are currently more than 30 centenarians, and they are greatly respected and celebrated, with their deaths being publicly mourned across the island. Dominica's government contributes to their care with free cooking gas and a monthly cash stipend.

Landscape & Wildlife

Dominica is an island of rainforest-clad mountains and soaring volcanic peaks that provide ample habitat for hundreds of bird and animal species. What few beaches there are have been very lightly developed, mainly as the volcanic origin of the island means that there are very few stretches of golden sand. For the most part, the nature here is untouched, save for the scores of rusted cars that dot the roadsides like so many memorials to dangerous driving and hurricane season.

The Land

Dominica is 29 miles long and 16 miles wide and embraces the highest mountains in the Eastern Caribbean; the loftiest peak, Morne Diablotin, is 4747ft high. The mountains, which act as a magnet for rain, serve as a water source for the island's purported 365 rivers. En route to the coast, many of the rivers cascade over steep cliffs, giving the island an abundance of waterfalls. Three hydroelectric plants on the Roseau River produce 27.4% of the electricity supply.

The most abundant tree on the island is the gommier, a huge gum tree used by the Kalinago to make dugouts.

Wildlife

Whales and dolphins patrol the deep waters off Dominica's sheltered west coast. Sperm whales, which grow to a length of 70ft, breed in the waters around here and are the most commonly sighted cetacean, although chances of seeing pilot and humpback whales as well as bottlenose dolphins are also pretty good. The main season is November to March.

For near-shore divers, the marine life tends to be of the smaller variety – seahorses included – but there are spotted eagle rays, barracuda, sharks and sea turtles as well.

More than 160 bird species have been sighted on Dominica, giving it some of the most diverse birdlife in the Eastern Caribbean. Of these, 59 species nest on the island, including two endemic and endangered parrot species: Dominica's national bird, the Sisserou parrot, and the smaller Jaco parrot.

The island has small tree frogs, many lizards, 13 bat species, 55 butterfly species, boa constrictors that grow nearly 10ft in length and four other types of snake (none poisonous).

Dominica also used to have an abundance of large frogs known as 'mountain chicken,' which live only here and on Montserrat. It is now critically endangered because of a virulent fungus.

Environmental Issues

In 2017 Dominica was again named among the top 10 Developing World's Best Ethical Destinations by *Ethical Traveler*, a San Francisco-based all-volunteer, nonprofit organization affiliated with the Earth Island Institute. The decision was based on the country's record of environmental protection, social welfare and human rights. Contributing to the distinction was that, since 2008, Dominica has not allowed the Japanese to engage in commercial whaling in its waters. It was also lauded for its pilot project to reduce energy consumption in business sectors, to its commitment to get all its energy from renewable sources and even to start supplying its neighbors with renewable energy.

Nevertheless, environmentalists are worried about the impact of the growing number of cruise ships that dock here to refill water supplies and dump waste, as well as about the physical impact caused by 300,000 passengers per year.

SURVIVAL GUIDE

Directory A–Z

ACCESSIBLE TRAVEL

Dominica is harder than most countries for disabled travelers to navigate. Uneven, broken or nonexistent sidewalks and high curbs make wheelchair travel challenging. Some of the bigger hotels in Roseau and Portsmouth may be able to accommodate disabled travelers.

ACCOMMODATIONS

Dominica has no big resorts, though its first two were nearing completion just north of Portsmouth at the time of writing. Most accommodations are in cottages, boutique inns and remote hideaways. In most cases, listed room rates do not include the 10% value-added tax (VAT).

ACTIVITIES

Trail maps published by Dominica's Forestry Division are available for a small fee at the forestry office in Roseau's Botanic Gardens (p374). The division can also refer you to guides who are experts in the flora and fauna of the island. Certified guides are also recommended for some of the hikes, most notably the one to Boiling Lake. The tourist office (p377) can also make referrals.

CHILDREN

Dominica can be a great destination for family travel, if you don't pack too much into the day and calibrate your nature adventures to your children's interests and abilities. Some of the trails may be too long or challenging for younger kids, but even easy ones such as Emerald Pool (p380) and the **Syndicate Nature Trail** (site fee US$5) have their rewards. Riding a boat on the Indian River (p383), swimming on the west-coast beaches, splashing around sulfur springs and snorkeling at Champagne Reef (p382) are all kid-suitable water-based activities.

Diapers (nappies) and baby foods are available in the larger supermarkets in Roseau and Portsmouth.

ELECTRICITY

Power outlets are 220/240V, 50/60 cycles; Dominica uses three-pin British sockets, although increasingly accommodations are using international ones or provide adapters. Some accommodations have dual 220/110 voltage.

EMBASSIES & CONSULATES

There are a very few diplomatic missions in Roseau. The US, UK, Canada and New Zealand cover Dominica from their embassy in Bridgetown, Barbados. Australians should contact their embassy in Trinidad & Tobago should they require assistance.

SLEEPING PRICE RANGES

The following price ranges refer to a double with bathroom during high season (December to April). Unless otherwise stated, breakfast is not included.

$ less than US$100

$$ US$100–200

$$$ more than US$200

EATING PRICE RANGES

The following price ranges refer to a main course. Listed menu prices may or may not include 15% value-added tax (VAT) and a service charge of 10% or 15% – check ahead to avoid any surprises.

$ less than US$10

$$ US$10–20

$$$ more than US$20

EMERGENCY NUMBERS

Ambulance, fire & police	☎999

FOOD

Dining out in Dominica is a very casual affair, and sadly you're unlikely to have any particularly memorable meals on the island. Menus are usually fish or seafood served with a selection of 'provisions' (various local root vegetables). Lunch is the main meal of the day and many restaurants close around 3pm. Indeed, since Hurricane Maria it can be a challenge to find places open for dinner: always call ahead.

ECOTOURISM SITES PASSES

Dominica's ecotourism sites are its biggest attraction. In order to help maintain them, a fee of US$5 per site is levied on all foreign visitors for the following dozen sites:

Boeri Lake, Boiling Lake, Indian River, Morne Trois Pitons, Middleham Falls, Freshwater Lake, Morne Diablotin Trail, Cabrits National Park, Emerald Pool, Trafalgar Falls, Soufriere Sulphur Springs and the Syndicate Forest.

A weekly pass for unlimited entry to all 12 costs US$12, making it exceptionally good value.

Passes are available at site entrances, from nearby vendors or from the national parks office inside the Botanic Gardens (p374) in Roseau.

In addition, there is a US$2 user fee per entry to the Soufriere-Scotts Head Marine Reserve, which includes Champagne Beach & Reef.

For more information, contact the **Forestry, Wildlife and Parks Division** (☎266-3817; forestry@cwdom.dm).

Essential Food & Drink

➡ **Callaloo** A creamy thick soup or stew blending a variety of vegetables – eg *dasheen* (aka taro root), spinach, kale, onions, carrots, eggplant, garlic, okra – with coconut milk and sometimes crab or ham.

➡ **Oxtail stew** This much-loved local stew heaves with spices in its signature thick sauce and can be tried most famously at Poz Restaurant & Bar (p387) in Calibishie.

➡ **Sea moss** Nonalcoholic beverage made from seaweed mixed with sugar and spices and sometimes with evaporated milk. It's sold in supermarkets and at snackettes.

➡ **Kubuli** Dominica uses the island's natural springwater for its homegrown beer label; you'll see red-and-white signs all over the island with Kubuli's concise slogan – 'The Beer We Drink.'

➡ **Macoucherie** Rum connoisseurs crave this local concoction. Don't be fooled by the plastic bottles or cheap-looking label; it's a gem.

HEALTH

The standard of the medical care and equipment on Dominica are likely not as high, modern or comprehensive as you may be used to. Sophisticated diagnostic tests such as CT and MRI scans, anything but minor surgeries, and other treatments must be performed outside Dominica. Make sure your insurance policy covers medical transport and emergency repatriation.

Dominica's main facility, Princess Margaret Hospital (p377), has a hyperbaric chamber and a small intensive-care unit.

INTERNET ACCESS

Dominica has been rebuilding its online infrastructure since Hurricane Maria took the entire country offline for months in 2017. In building a new system virtually from scratch the country now has excellent bandwidth, although some of the more remote parts of the island were still not connected at the time of writing; double-check with your accommodations before you book if wi-fi access is important. Many bars, cafes and restaurants offer free wi-fi to their customers.

LEGAL MATTERS

Dominica's legal system is based on English common law. If you find yourself in trouble, you have the right to legal representation and are eligible for public legal aid if you can't afford to pay for private services. Foreign nationals should receive the same legal protections as nationals.

LGBT+ TRAVELERS

Same-sex sexual activity is still on the books as being illegal for both men and women and is theoretically punishable by up to 10 years in prison. The law is not enforced, but it's still worth remembering that Dominica is a socially conservative and deeply religious country. To avoid offense or confrontation, discretion is advised.

MONEY

Unless prices rates are posted in US dollars, as is usual with accommodations, it usually works out better to use EC dollars. If you pay in US dollars you will normally get change in EC dollars.

Most businesses now accept credit cards, but you shouldn't rely on that.

Exchange Rates

Australia	A$1	EC$1.94
Canada	C$1	EC$2.03
Euro zone	€1	EC$3.05
Japan	¥100	EC$2.41
New Zealand	NZ$1	EC$1.81
UK	UK£	EC$3.52
US	US$	EC$2.71

For current exchange rates, see www.xe.com.

Taxes & Refunds

Value-added tax (VAT) of 15% is levied on most goods and services. It drops to 10% on hotel rooms. Visitors are not eligible to reclaim VAT paid during their trip to Dominica.

Tipping

Hotels A tip of US$0.50 to US$1 per bag is standard; gratuity for cleaning staff is at your discretion.

Restaurants If the service charge is not automatically included in the bill, tip 10% to 15%; if it is, it's up to you to leave a small additional tip.

Taxi Tip 10% to 15% of the fare.

OPENING HOURS

Local businesses, including most restaurants and bars, close Sundays. The following are guidelines only; hours are erratic and may vary by the day, season or proprietor's mood. Call ahead for restaurants you plan to visit in the evening; since Hurricane Maria, hours are unreliable.

Banks 8am to 2pm Monday to Thursday, to 5pm Friday.

Bars noon to 11pm.

Businesses 8am to 4pm Monday to Friday, lunch break 1pm to 2pm.

Restaurants Breakfast 7:30am to 10am; lunch noon to 2:30pm; dinner 6pm to 9:30pm.

Shops 8am to 4pm Monday to Friday, to 1pm Sat (often lunch break 1pm to 2pm).

PUBLIC HOLIDAYS

New Year's Day January 1

Carnival Monday & Tuesday Two days preceding Ash Wednesday (the beginning of Lent, 46 days before Easter)

Good Friday/Easter Monday March/April

Labour Day First Monday in May

Pentecost/Whit Monday Forty days after Easter

Emancipation Day (August Monday) First Monday in August

Independence Day November 3

Community Service Day November 4

Christmas/Boxing Day December 25/26

TELEPHONE

- Dominica's country code is 767; there are no local codes.
- To call from North America, dial 1-767 + the seven-digit local number. From elsewhere, dial your country's international access code + 767 + the local number.
- To call abroad from Dominica, dial 011 + country code + area code + local number.
- For directory information dial 118.

Cell Phones

The local cell-phone networks are Digicel (www.digicelgroup.com/dm) and Flow (https://discov erflow.co/dominica). You'll need to get to their offices in Roseau or Portsmouth to buy a SIM card (EC$20). There are no kiosks at the airport.

- Coverage is generally very good along the coast of the island, though you'll often lose connectivity in the interior.
- Data and calls are both cheap; combined packages cost around EC$20 per week.

PRACTICALITIES

Newspapers The weekly *Chronicle*, published every Friday, has been the national newspaper since 1909.

Radio DBS 88.1FM (contemporary music), Kairi 93.1FM (local news and music).

Smoking There is no official smoking ban anywhere on the island, but most hotels and restaurants prohibit guests from smoking indoors. The use of marijuana, though officially illegal, is widespread.

Weights & measures The imperial system is used.

TIME

Clocks in Dominica are set to Eastern Caribbean Time (Atlantic Time), which is four hours behind GMT. The island does not observe daylight savings time.

TOURIST INFORMATION

Dominica (www.dominica.dm) Official tourist-office website.

VOLUNTEERING

Look for Dominica-based listings on the volunteer work exchange platforms HelpX (www.helpx.net) or Workaway (www.workaway.info). A popular option is to help locals run off-grid lodges, which may involve building, gardening, cooking, web work and other chores. There are also community-based programs focused on improving the lives of local children through arts projects.

Founded by former Peace Corps volunteers, Ready, Willing, Enable! (www.rwenable.org) needs volunteers to provide training and resources to children with disabilities, as well as their communities and families.

Getting There & Away

There are regular ferries from Dominica to Guadeloupe, Martinique and St Lucia, as well as regular scheduled flights to Antigua, Barbados, Guadeloupe, St-Martin/Sint Maarten, Martinique and Puerto Rico.

AIR

Douglas–Charles Airport (DOM; ☎445-7109; Marigot) Most flights arrive at this small airport, previously known as Melville Hall Airport. It's near Marigot on the northeast side of the island and about a 90-minute drive from Roseau. **LIAT** (☎toll-free within Caribbean Region 888-844-5428; www.liat.com; Douglas-Charles Airport), Winair, Hummingbird Air, Air Sunshine, Air Antilles and Seabourne Airlines provide service within the region.

Canefield Airport (DCF; Edward Olivier LeBlanc Hwy) This tiny airport is on the west coast near Massacre just north of Roseau. Winair flies to St-Martin/Sint Maarten from here but other flights are mostly private or charters.

There are no direct flights between North America or Europe and Dominica. You need to connect in Antigua, Barbados, St-Martin/Sint Maarten, Puerto Rico, Guadeloupe or Martinique.

> **DEPARTURE TAX**
>
> Departure tax for non-nationals is EC$59 (US$22) payable in cash at the airport or port. Some tickets already include this, so be sure to check.

SEA

Cruise Ship

Cruise ships dock in central **Roseau** (Dame Eugenia Charles Blvd); at Woodbridge Bay north of Roseau; and at Cabrits, north of Portsmouth. Downtown Roseau and popular places such as Champagne Reef and Trafalgar Falls get very busy when giant vessels are in port. Independent travelers wishing to avoid the crowds might want to check the cruise-ship schedule (eg at www.cruisetimetables.com/cruises-to-roseau-dominica.html) to plan their itinerary accordingly.

Ferry

Val'Ferry (☎255-1125; www.valferry.fr; Roseau ferry terminal, Dame Eugenia Charles Blvd) and **L'Express des Îles** (☎in Guadeloupe +590-590-91-95-20; www.express-des-iles.com; Roseau ferry terminal, Dame Eugenia Charles Blvd; one way adult/child under 2yr €79/49) both connect Dominica several times weekly with Martinique and Guadeloupe. Val'Ferry stops in both Portsmouth and Roseau, while L'Express des Îles only stops at Roseau but also connects to Castries in St Lucia. Prices vary enormously depending on the route, type of ticket and conditions, but can be bought online. Sample prices include Fort de France (Martinique) to Roseau for €49 one way and Portsmouth to Pointe-à-Pitre (Guadeloupe) for €52.

Getting Around

BUS

Government-licensed private minivans with number plates starting with 'H' serve communities on an erratic schedule along the main roads. All routes originate at various stops in downtown Roseau.

Buses can be flagged down anywhere along the route – just stick out your arm. Unless they're full, they will stop. Service runs from 6am to 7pm Monday to Saturday.

Fares are set by the government and cost EC$1.75 to EC$11.

CAR & MOTORCYCLE

Driving is by far the most convenient way to explore Dominica, although it can be quite stressful because of the terrain, poor road conditions and local driving practices – drive defensively and don't hurry.

Drivers need a local license issued by a car-rental agency. It costs US$12 or EC$30 and is valid for one month. Officially, you must be aged between 25 and 65 and have at least two years of driving experience, although this varies from company to company.

Car Rental

Several international agencies plus a few reputable local ones have offices in a separate building right outside the airport terminal. Because of poor road conditions, it's well worth investing in a high-clearance vehicle, preferably a (small) 4WD, especially if you're going to be exploring the mountains. Some agencies have offices in Roseau.

Before signing anything, carefully check the car for damage and take photographs of anything you find in addition to having the agent record it on the rental agreement. Make sure that the tires are in good condition.

Daily rates start at US$25 per day for sedans and US$50 for 4WDs, plus 15% VAT; many of the local agencies give discounts for rentals longer than two days. All companies offer free pickups and drop-offs, unlimited mileage and cell-phone rentals.

Courtesy Car Rental (☎448-7763; www.dominicacarrentals.com; Douglas-Charles Airport; ⏲per day from US$57)

Island Car Rentals (☎255-6844; www.islandcar.dm; Douglas-Charles Airport; per day from US$39; ⏲7am-7pm)

Road Runner Car Rental (☎275-5337; www.roadrunnercarrental.com; Douglas-Charles Airport; per day from US$49)

Valley Car Rental (☎275-1310; www.valleyrentacar.com; Douglas-Charles Airport; per day from US$39)

Road Conditions

Hurricane Maria did a lot of damage to the roads but conditions are improving slowly and bridges being rebuilt across the island. Still, driving in Dominica is not for the faint of heart. Roads are narrow and curving, have no dividing lines and are often hemmed in by deep, axle-killing rain gutters: take those corners slowly – this can do huge damage to your car.

Other dangers: potholes big enough to swallow small goats, blindingly blind corners, visitors not accustomed to driving on the left and locals getting impatient with them.

As a result, actual driving times are much greater than distances would suggest, especially when driving between the coasts through the vertiginous center. The smoothest driving is on the coastal road between Portsmouth and Roseau. The road from Portsmouth to the airport has been improved but is still narrow and winding, so the going is slow. Road conditions are worst in the Kalinago Territory and in the storm-battered southeast.

Road Rules

Driving is on the left. Honk the horn often around the blind corners. Always keep an eye out for potholes and the deep rain ditches to the side of the road. Take extra care at night as roads are not lit and you'll need to use your high beam to navigate. Of course, other drivers do the same but many don't bother dimming their lights for oncoming traffic.

To local drivers, speed limits seem to be more of a suggestion than a rule. If you're driving slowly and causing a backup, pull over to the side of the road whenever it's safe to let traffic pass.

Outside of Roseau, gas stations are few and far between. You'll find some in larger towns, including Canefield, Portsmouth and Marigot. Some take credit cards, many do not.

HITCHING

Hitching is never entirely safe, and we don't recommend it. Travelers who hitch should understand that they are taking a small but potentially serious risk.

However, locals of either sex and of all ages hitchhike here, and picking up hitchhikers, especially if there is only one of them and two or more of you, is a great way to meet locals and pick up good insider tips. Solo women travelers, though, should be extra careful.

TAXI

Taxis on Dominica have number plates beginning with 'H' or 'HA'. There are no meters and no standard fares, so use your negotiating skills and make sure you understand if the quoted fare is in US dollars or EC dollars. To order a cab, call 440-0944, 440-8126 or 276-2228.

Airport transfers from Douglas–Charles Airport are regulated by the government. The following quoted fares are per person in a shared taxi:

Calibishie or Kalinago Territory	US$17
Castle Comfort	US$28
Roseau or Portsmouth	US$30
Scotts Head	US$32

1

Dominica's Boiling Lake Hike

Probably Dominica's single most impressive hike, this stunner can be completed by anyone with a normal level of physical fitness.

Tackling the Trail

The well-marked **trailhead** (site pass US$5) begins at Ti Tou Gorge, and takes you steadily uphill through the rainforest to the first ridge, before descending to a river you'll have to cross. From here you'll walk up the spine of a ridge with superb views of the various peaks nearby, and you'll be able to see distant steam rising from the boiling lake. Once along the top of the ridge, a fairly challenging (and often very muddy) descent takes you into the sulfurous Valley of Desolation. There are some ropes to help you over trickier and slipperier parts. One of the highlights of the hike, the Valley of Desolation is where curious springs bubble boiling water, steam rises from volcanic pools and sulfurous waters have bleached the rocks and given the entire place the feel of another planet. Very little grows down here – hence its name – but it's a fascinating place to explore.

Keeping to the right as you cross the bottom of the valley, you'll then enter a wooded section on either side of a warm stream. There are several points where you can bathe in warm water here, including one under a waterfall. At the end of the valley, you veer to the left and then cross the stream coming down the hillside before walking to the right around the ridge to the viewpoint over the boiling lake itself. The views over the water are spectacular, although you may

1. Valley of Desolation
2. Natural hot pool near the boiling lake
3. Hiking pathway

need to wait for some time for the steam over the lake to clear.

Safety on the Trail

It's highly recommended to do the trip with a guide, as the second part of the route through the Valley of Desolation is far from obvious, and as an active volcanic plain there are potential dangers if you don't know where you're going – some geological formations are hollow, and can collapse if you're unlucky. Private guides usually charge around US$100 per person, with a minimum of two people, but it's possible to do it for less through an agency. Recommended private guides include Nigel George (☎767-285-3179) and Nahgie (☎767-245-4328).

If you insist on doing the trek without a guide, take it slowly. Guides report nearly always having to help trekkers without guides find their way out of the valley during a typical trip.

Need to Know

The entire trip takes about five hours return, but you can easily spend the whole day on it with plenty of time for photos, gazing at the lake itself and bathing in various streams and pools. A swim in the freezing waters of Ti Tou Gorge is the best way to end the walk. Bring a packed lunch, water bottle, waterproofs, sunscreen and good walking shoes.

Dominican Republic

☎809 / POP 10,299,000

Includes ➡

Best Places to Eat

- ➡ Passion by Martín Berasategui (p412)
- ➡ Pat'e Palo (p405)
- ➡ La Terrasse (p417)
- ➡ Casa Bonita (p426)

Best Places to Stay

- ➡ Casas del XVI (p404)
- ➡ Mahona Boutique Hotel (p416)
- ➡ Casa El Paraíso (p419)
- ➡ Eco del Mar (p426)
- ➡ Ki-Ra (p414)

Why Go?

The Dominican Republic is defined by its hundreds of kilometers of coastline – some with picturesque white-sand beaches shaded by rows of palm trees, other parts lined dramatically with rocky cliffs. The sea is the common denominator across remote fishing villages, sun-soaked and indulgent tourist playgrounds, charming small towns and the capital Santo Domingo – the Caribbean's largest and the site of so many New World firsts.

Beyond the capital, much of the DR is distinctly rural. Further inland are vistas reminiscent of the European Alps: four of the Caribbean's five highest peaks rise above the fertile lowlands surrounding Santiago. Remote deserts extend through the southwest, giving the DR a complexity not found on other islands. The country's past is writ large in the diversity of its people, and in the beautifully restored monasteries and cobblestone streets where conquistadors once roamed.

When to Go

Dec–Feb Peak tourist season, with higher prices and crowded beaches.

Feb Great weather, and you can enjoy Carnival and the whales in Samaná.

Nov You'll miss the whales, but catch baseball season.

Dominican Republic Highlights

1 Zona Colonial (p400) Taking a walk through history in Santo Domingo.

2 Bahía de Las Águilas (p425) Journeying to the country's most far-flung and beautiful beach.

3 Bávaro and Punta Cana (p409) Basking on idyllic beaches of soft, white sand or swimming in the aquamarine waters.

4 Península de Samaná (p414) Watching 30-ton humpbacks breaching on a whale-watching trip.

5 Cabarete (p420) Kitesurfing the year-round off-shore breezes.

6 Las Galeras (p418) Relaxing into a sleepy fishing village in this remote paradise.

7 Las Terrenas (p415) Mellowing in this cosmopolitan beachfront town.

8 Jarabacoa (p423) Rafting the turbulent Río Yaque del Norte.

SANTO DOMINGO

POP 3.2 MILLION

Santo Domingo, or 'La Capital' as it's typically called, is a collage of cultures and neighborhoods. It's where the sounds of life – domino pieces slapped on tables, backfiring mufflers and horns from chaotic traffic, merengue blasting from corner stores – are most intense. At the heart of the city is the Zona Colonial, where you'll find one of the oldest churches and the oldest surviving European fortress, among other New World firsts. Amid the cobblestone streets it would be easy to forget Santo Domingo is in the Caribbean. But this is an intensely urban city, home not only to colonial-era architecture, but also to hot clubs, vibrant cultural institutions and elegant restaurants. Santo Domingo somehow manages to embody the contradictions central to the Dominican experience: a living museum, a metropolis crossed with a seaside resort, and a business, political and media center with a laidback, affable spirit.

Sights & Activities

Zona Colonial

For those fascinated by the origin of the so-called New World – a dramatic and complicated story of the first encounter between the native people of the Americas and Europeans – the Zona Colonial, listed as a Unesco World Heritage site, is a great place to explore. It is 11 square blocks, a mix of cobblestone and pavement on the west bank of the Río Ozama, where the deep river meets the Caribbean Sea. Calle El Conde, the main commercial artery, is lined with *casas de cambio* (money changers), cafes, restaurants, shoe, clothing and jewelry stores, and vendors hawking cheap souvenirs.

★Catedral Primada de América CHURCH
(Nuestra Señora de la Anunciación; 809-682-3848; Parque Colón; adult/child RD$70/free; 9am-4:30pm Mon-Sat) The first stone of this cathedral, the oldest standing in the Western hemisphere, was set in 1514 by Diego Columbus, son of the great explorer (the ashes of father and son supposedly once resided in the chapel's crypt). Construction, however, didn't begin until the arrival of the first bishop, Alejandro Geraldini, in 1521. From then until 1540, numerous architects worked on the church and adjoining buildings, which is why the vault is Gothic, the arches Romanesque and the ornamentation baroque.

It's anyone's guess what the planned bell tower would have looked like: a shortage of funds curtailed construction, and the steeple, which undoubtedly would have offered a commanding view of the city, was never built.

The cathedral's current interior is a far cry from the original – thanks to Drake and his crew of pirates, who used the basilica as their headquarters during their 1586 assault on the city. They stole everything of value that they could carry away and extensively vandalized the church before departing.

Among the cathedral's more impressive features are its awesome vaulted ceiling and its 14 interior chapels. Bare shoulders and legs are prohibited, but shawls are provided for those who need to cover up.

Although Santo Domingo residents like to say their cathedral was the first in the Western hemisphere, in fact one was built in Mexico City between 1524 and 1532; it stood for four decades, until it was knocked down in 1573 and replaced by the imposing Catedral Metropolitano.

Tickets, purchased at the entrance in the southeastern corner of the site, include an audioguide available in a variety of languages (RD$50 without audioguide). Daily mass is at 5pm Monday to Saturday and noon and 5pm Sundays.

★Museo Alcázar de Colón MUSEUM
(Museum Citadel of Columbus; 809-682-4750; Plaza España; adult/child RD$100/20; 9am-5pm Tue-Sat, to 4pm Sun) Designed in the Gothic-Mudéjar transitional style, this was the early-16th-century residence of Columbus' son, Diego, and his wife, Doña María de Toledo. The magnificent edifice underwent three historically authentic restorations in 1957, 1971 and 1992, and the building itself, along with the household pieces on display (said to have belonged to the Columbus family), are worth a look.

★Museo Memorial de la Resistencia Dominicana MUSEUM
(809-688-4440; www.museodelaresistencia.com; Arzobispo Nouel 210; adult/child under 12yr RD$150/50; 9:30am-6pm Tue-Sun) For those interested in the details of one of the darkest periods of Dominican history, this austere memorial honors Dominicans who fought against the brutal regime of dictator Rafael Trujillo. 'El Chivo' (the goat) ruled with an iron fist from 1930 until 1961, touting his

own greatness and wiping out some 50,000 political dissenters. The museum features torture-center replicas and 160,000 photographs, films and other objects belonging to resistance fighters. Admission includes an audio guide (English or Spanish).

Museo de las Casas Reales MUSEUM
(Museum of the Royal Houses; ☎809-682-4202; Las Damas; adult/child under 7yr RD$100/free; ⏰9am-5pm Tue-Sat, to 4pm Sun) Built in the Renaissance style during the 16th century, this building was the longtime seat of Spanish authority for the Caribbean region, housing the governor's office and the powerful Audiencia Real (Royal Court). It showcases colonial-period objects, including treasures recovered from sunken Spanish galleons. Rooms have been restored according to their original style, with Taíno artifacts and period furnishings displayed.

Fortaleza Ozama HISTORIC SITE
(☎809-686-0222; Las Damas; adult/child RD$70/10; ⏰9am-5pm Tue-Sun) This is the New World's oldest colonial military edifice. The site, at the meeting of the Río Ozama and Caribbean, was selected by Fray Nicolás de Ovando and construction began in 1502. Over the centuries the fort served as a military garrison and prison, flying the flags of Spain, England, France, Haiti, Gran Colombia, the US and the DR. Public tours began in the 1970s. Multilingual guides at the entrance charge around US$3.50 per person for a 20-minute tour.

Amber World Museum MUSEUM
(☎809-686-5700; www.amberworldmuseum.com; Arzibispo Merino 452; RD$50; ⏰8am-6pm) This museum features an impressive collection of amber samples from around the world and excellent exhibits explaining (in Spanish and English) amber's prehistoric origins, its use throughout the ages, Dominican mining processes, and its present-day value to the science and art worlds. It also has a shop selling jewelry made from amber, larimar and more ordinary stones.

Las Damas HISTORIC SITE
(Ladies' Street; Calle de las Damas) Running north–south in front of Fortaleza Ozama is the first paved street in the Americas. Laid in 1502, the street acquired its name from the wife of Diego Columbus and her lady friends, who made a habit of strolling the road every afternoon, weather permitting.

Other Neighborhoods

Los Tres Ojos CAVE
(Three Eyes; Parque Mirador del Este; RD$200; ⏰8am-5pm) Consisting of three humid caverns with dark blue lagoons connected by stalactite-filled passages, this site is lovely if you show up early to beat the crowds. Upon entrance, a long stairway takes visitors down a narrow tunnel in the rock, and a cement path at the bottom leads through the caves. At the third *ojo,* a small boat can be hired for RD$20 to visit a fourth *ojo,* which is actually a gorgeous lake beneath open sky, filled with fish.

Faro a Colón MONUMENT
(Columbus Lighthouse; ☎809-592-1492, ext 251; Parque Mirador del Este; RD$100; ⏰9am-5pm Tue-Sun) Resembling a cross between a Soviet-era apartment block and a Las Vegas–style ancient Mayan ruin, this massive monument is worth visiting for its controversial history. Located on the east side of the Río Ozama, the Faro's cement flanks stand 10 stories high, forming the shape of a cross. At the intersection of the cross' arms is a tomb, guarded by white-uniformed soldiers and purportedly containing Columbus' remains. Spain and Italy dispute that, however, both saying *they* have the Admiral's bones.

Tours

Interesting and informative walking tours of the Zona Colonial are offered daily by official guides – look for men dressed in khakis and light-blue dress shirts, and ask to see their state-tourism license. Many hang out in and around Parque Colón, but you will likely encounter them near major attractions, also. Be sure to agree upon a fee before setting out.

Tours cover the most important buildings in the zone and can be tailored to your specific interests. Walks typically last 2½ hours and cost between US$20 and US$30 depending on the language that the tour is given in (ie Spanish and English are less expensive).

Trikke TOUR
(☎809-221-8097; www.trikke.do; Padre Billini 54; US$35; ⏰9am-6pm Mon-Sat, from 10am Sun) A one-hour tour that rents motor scooters that resemble a cross between a Segway and a tricycle. City tours (US$35) and a popular bar-hopping night tour (US$45) are also available. Group tours depart at 10am and 4:30pm each day, and all tours include a guide, water and riding lessons.

Zona Colonial

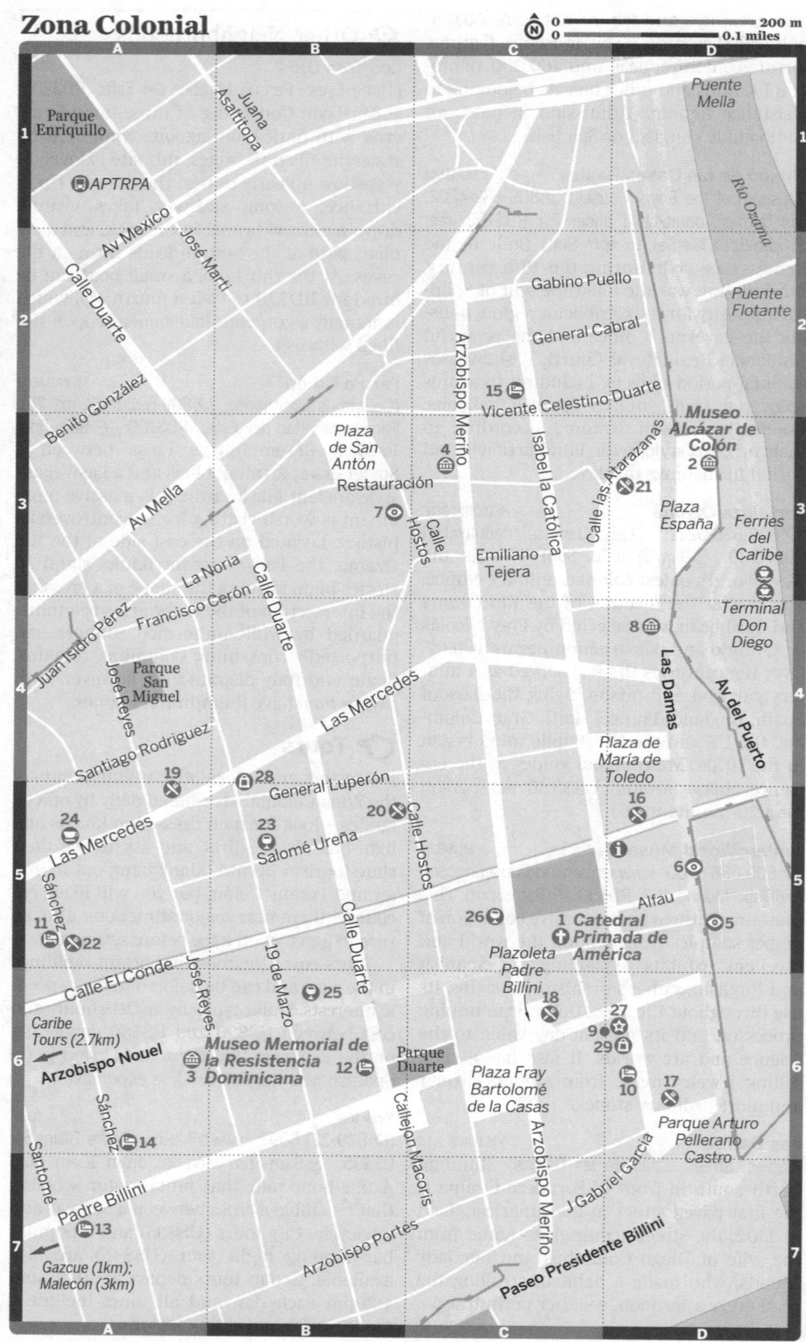

Zona Colonial

Top Sights
1 Catedral Primada de América C5
2 Museo Alcázar de Colón D3
3 Museo Memorial de la Resistencia Dominicana.................... A6

Sights
4 Amber World Museum C3
5 Fortaleza Ozama............................... D5
6 Las Damas... D5
7 Monasterio de San Francisco B3
8 Museo de las Casas Reales.................. D4

Activities, Courses & Tours
9 Trikke C6

Sleeping
10 Casa Naemie D6
11 Casa Sanchez A5
12 El Beatério Guest House B6
13 Hostal Suite Colonial A7
14 Hotel Villa Colonial............................. A6
15 Island Life Backpacker's Hostel... C2

Eating
16 Buche Perico...................................... D5
17 La Cocinia de Cheska.......................... D6
18 Lulú Tasting Bar C6
19 Maison Kreyol Restaurant.................... A5
20 Mesón D'Bari B5
21 Pat'e Palo D3
22 Sicily's Empanadas A5

Drinking & Nightlife
23 La Alpargatería B5
24 Mamey Librería Café........................... A5
25 Mercado Colón B6
26 Rooftop Tasting Terrace....................... C5

Entertainment
Cinema Boreal ....(see 24)
27 Colonial Gate 4D Cinema..................... D6
Monastery Sundays ....(see 7)

Shopping
Cava Billini......................................(see 18)
28 Desireé Cepeda Artesanía Interiorismo B4
29 Galería Bolós....................................... D6

Festival & Events

Carnival CARNIVAL
(Carnaval; Feb) Celebrated throughout the country every Sunday in February, culminating in a blowout in Santo Domingo during the last weekend of February or first weekend of March. Av George Washington (the Malecón) becomes an enormous party scene day and night. Central to the celebration are the competitions of floats, and costumes and masks representing traditional Carnival characters.

Merengue Festival MUSIC
(late Jul-early Aug) The largest in the country, this two-week celebration of merengue, *bachata* (guitar music based on bolero rhythms), salsa, Caribbean rhythms, reggaeton and reggae is held yearly. Most of the activity is on the Malecón, but there are related events across the city.

Sleeping

Zona Colonial

★Island Life Backpacker's Hostel HOSTEL $
(809-333-9374; www.islandlifebackpackershostel.com; Isabel La Católica 356; dm/d/tr incl breakfast from RD$695/1620/1760;) The expat owner of this Zona Colonial oasis traveled the world for years observing what backpackers like. Then he found a derelict colonial abode from the 1600s and transformed it into the best hostel in Santo Domingo. From the comfy dorm beds and courtyard hammocks to the superchill bar and dipping pool, this is a true travelers' paradise.

Hostal Suite Colonial HOTEL $
(809-685-1082; www.suitecolonial.net; Padre Billini 362; r incl breakfast US$45;) A solid budget choice with an exterior that blends in with the facades of the neighboring colonial-era buildings. However, once past an attractive high-ceilinged lounge area, some of the charm fades. Heavy couches and linoleum-floored hallways lead to rooms with aged basic furnishings and some haphazard choices. Breakfast is served in a small backyard patio.

Casa Sanchez BOUTIQUE HOTEL $$
(809-682 -7321; www.casasanchezhotel.com; Sanchez 260; incl breakfast d US$85-109, apt US$144;) One of the better and most affordable choices for a stay in a colonial-era building, just a block north of Calle El Conde. Each of the uniquely designed rooms has splashes of color and style and tile flooring, and the service is highly personalized. A lovely pool occupies most of the inner courtyard and there's a rooftop with a hot tub and views.

Casa Naemie HOTEL **$$**
(☎809-689-2215; www.casa-naemie-do.book.direct; Isabel la Católica 11; s/d incl breakfast RD$2200/3000; ❄📶) This charming oasis only a few blocks from the oldest cathedral in the Americas feels like a European pension. Surrounding a narrow central courtyard are three floors of cozy, clean rooms with large modern bathrooms. An elegant lobby with a vaulted entranceway and brick flooring does double duty in the morning when the excellent breakfast is served.

★**Casas del XVI** BOUTIQUE HOTEL **$$$**
(☎809-688-4061; www.casasdelxvi.net; Billini 252; r incl breakfast from US$320; P❄📶🏊) If these walls could talk, they'd tell this city's story. But this is no dusty museum. A stay in one of these six impeccably restored colonial-era homes means toggling between the 16th and 21st centuries. Imagine archways, terracotta floors and courtyards evocative of a medieval monastery crossed with Sub Zero refrigerators, iPhones to contact your personal assistant and heated plunge pools.

★**Hotel Villa Colonial** HOTEL **$$$**
(☎809-221-1049; www.villacolonial.net/en; Sánchez 157; s/d incl breakfast US$85/110; 📶🏊) The French owner has created an idyllic oasis, an exceptionally sophisticated combination of European elegance with a colonial-era facade and an art-deco design. The rooms lining the narrow garden and pool area all have high ceilings and four-poster beds, as well as flat-screen TVs and bathrooms with ceramic-tile floors.

El Beaterío Guest House GUESTHOUSE **$$$**
(☎809-687-8957; www.elbeaterio.fr; Duarte 8; s/d incl breakfast US$90/110; ❄📶) Get thee to this nunnery – if you're looking for austere elegance. Each of the 11 large rooms is sparsely furnished, but the wood-beamed ceilings and stone floors are truly special; the tile-floored bathrooms are modern and well maintained. It's easy to imagine the former function of this 16th-century building, with its heavy stone facade, and dark, vaulted front room.

Malecón

Catalonia Santo Domingo HOTEL **$$$**
(☎809-685-0000; www.cataloniahotels.com; Av George Washington 500, Malecón; r from US$166; P❄@📶🏊) Among the nicest of the luxury hotels on the Malecón, Catalonia Santo Domingo is part of a huge complex including a casino and movie theater. The highest of the high-rises, it's a long elevator ride from the atrium to the 21st floor at the top. Rooms have better views than nearby competitors, and a bar and restaurant feature stunning ocean views.

Downtown

JW Marriott Santo Domingo HOTEL **$$$**
(☎809-807-1717; www.marriott.com/hotels/travel/sdqjw-jw-marriott-hotel-santo-domingo; Blue Mall, Av Winston Churchill 93; r US$180-280; P❄@📶🏊) Housed within the upper floors of downtown's chic Blue Mall, the JW Marriott Santo Domingo is stylish and modern, with a snazzy cocktail bar, a relaxing infinity pool and a Peruvian restaurant with Asian flair. Rooms are pristine and state-of-the-art, with an option for an LED mirror TV in the bathroom. Amenities also include a 24-hour gym and cinema.

Eating

Unsurprisingly, Santo Domingo is the culinary capital of the country. It offers the full range of Dominican cuisine, from *pastelitos* (pastries with meat, vegetable or seafood fillings) sold from the back of street vendors' carts to extravagantly prepared meals in picturesque colonial-era buildings. The Zona Colonial has some of the best restaurants and is most convenient for the majority of travelers.

Zona Colonial

Sicily's Empanadas EMPANADAS **$**
(Sanchez; empanadas RD$50; ⏱4pm-midnight; 📶) Good, cheap meals to take on-the-go are rare in the Zona Colonial. This is one of the best with a selection of more than a dozen varieties of empanadas, including broccoli and cheese and potato and pork. It's a large, basic space with picnic tables inside and two on the street.

La Cocina de Cheska TAPAS **$**
(Arzobispo Portes; tapas RD$60-225; ⏱4pm-midnight Mon-Sat, from 2pm Sun) You might stick out at this locals-only spot with tables on the Parque Arturo Pellerano Castro, a charming cobblestone plaza at the southeastern tip of the Zona Colonial. Not to worry. This chef-run Spanish tapas place is all smiles. Chow down on complimentary peanuts with a glass of house wine while you wait.

Maison Kreyol Restaurant HAITIAN **$$**
(809-221-0459; www.maisonkreyol.com; Las Mercedes 321; mains RD$325-600) The simple, bare bones dining room belies the quality of the cooking here in delicious dishes such as grilled spicy goat, a whole snapper and okra fritters. Wash it all down with a bottle of Prestige, a Haitian beer, and fruit-juice flavors not often served in Dominican restaurants.

★ **Pat'e Palo** SPANISH **$$$**
(809-519-9687; Las Atarazanas 25; mains RD$650-1400; noon-1am) The most happening and deservedly longest-surviving of Plaza España's restaurant row, Pat'e Palo is for anyone tired of the same old bland pasta and chicken. Large, both physically and in terms of its selection, the menu includes creatively designed dishes such as Angus beef carpaccio in truffle oil and mushrooms and Chilean sea bass in a chili-and-black-bean stew.

Buche Perico DOMINICAN **$$$**
(809-475-6451; www.bucheperico.com; El Conde 53; mains RD$670-1300; noon-11pm Mon-Fri, to midnight Sat & Sun;) One of the city's more spectacular dining rooms, with light streaming through the greenhouse-like ceiling several stories above and a flowering vine-covered vertical garden, not to mention a waterfall! The quality of the service and food is no less impressive: dishes such as seared raw tuna, goat risotto, sweet plantain ravioli and the 40oz (1kg) Tomahawk steak (RD$3800) will satisfy several hungry eaters.

Lulú Tasting Bar TAPAS **$$$**
(809-687-8360; www.lulu.do; cnr Arzobispo Meriño & Padre Billini; tapas RD$500-1000, Sun brunch RD$1920; 6pm-3am Mon-Sat, from 11am Sun) Class it up at Lulú, a stylish Zona Colonial tapas bar that lures a fabulous after-work crowd looking to unwind over cigars and cocktails and nibble on small plates of octopus carpaccio and sautéed Peruvian-style lamb. Best not to go famished as the price to fill up is steep, but the atmosphere, with its towering arches, grand courtyards and charming koi pond, is unmatched in the city.

Downtown

Barra Payán SANDWICHES **$**
(Av Tiradentes 16; sandwiches RD$110-240; 7am-1am Sun-Thu, to 4am Fri & Sat) Capitaleños have been lining up for this fast-food joint's signature delicious pork sandwich (as well as burgers) before and after late nights out since the 1950s. Wash it down with one of its freshly made juices. There are several other outlets, including the original (corner of Av 30 de Marzo and Juan Bosco). This one is your safest bet at night.

Mesón D' Bari DOMINICAN **$$**
(809-692-0670; Sánchez, near cnr Cambiazo, Naco; mains RD$460-780; noon-11pm) The new and fashionable outpost of one of the Zona Colonial's most popular **places** (809-687-4091; cnr Hostos & Salomé Ureña; mains RD$425-800; noon-midnight) for traditional Dominican fare such as crab-meat empanadas, stewed conch and spicy goat meat. This Mesón d'Bari carries on the original's culinary legacy, but in a sunlit dining room with colorful stenciled drawings of lush tropical themes – all dreamed up by a well-known Dominican designer.

Trattoria Angiolino ITALIAN **$$$**
(809-563-3282; Henriquez Ureña 45, Piatini; mains RD$650-2000; noon-midnight;) Small and casually sophisticated, this old-school family-owned trattoria serves up delicious and large portions of pasta including pappardelle ragout, pasta osso buco and hefty steaks, many, such as the 3lb (1.4kg) sirloin, good for two or three people. The vibe feels more formal and upscale at dinnertime, but no matter when, the checkered tablecloths, uniformed waiters and brick walls create a cozy atmosphere.

Drinking & Nightlife

★ **Rooftop Tasting Terrace** BAR
(Sugarcane, La Casa del Ron; Arzopispo Meriño 204; 10am-6pm Tue, to 1am Wed & Thu, to 3am Fri & Sat, 2pm-1am Sun;) The dissidence, though pleasurable, couldn't be more extreme here, sipping rum-based cocktails on an astroturfed 3rd floor directly across the street from the oldest still-standing cathedral in the Western hemisphere. Cocktails are strong and pricier than elsewhere (from RD$300), but worth it, especially if you grab one of the rum barrel tables overlooking the street; small tapas such as ceviche are around RD$350.

★ **Mamey Librería Café** CAFE
(809-688-9111; www.mamey.co; Las Mercedes 315; 4pm-midnight Wed-Fri, from 10am Sat & Sun;) This fashionable cafe, art gallery, bookstore and **cinema** (www.cinemaboreal.com; Mercedes 315, Mamey Librería Cafe; RD$250) is housed within the charming former abode of Emilio Rodríguez Demorizi, one of the

Dominican Republic's first historians. Featuring stone courtyards, a fountain with a flowering trinitaria and vertical gardens, the space is ideal for relaxing with a book or grabbing a drink with friends. The small menu includes empanadas, salads, quiche and hummus and falafel.

★La Alpargatería COCKTAIL BAR
(☎809-221-3158; Salomé Ureña 59; margaritas RD$185; ⊙10am-midnight Tue-Sun; 📶) At the entrance, guests step into a shoe shop where artisans craft espadrilles. Continuing to the back, though, the store opens into a trendy cafe with comfy seating within intimate nooks and a leafy courtyard. The German beers and craft cocktails are standout here, especially the ginger-lemon margarita.

Mercado Colón BEER GARDEN
(☎809-685-1103; Arzobispo Nouel 105; ⊙noon-1am Tue-Sun; 📶) This collection of artisanal food and alcohol vendors is housed under one Zona Colonial roof, with communal courtyard seating. It's a good place to drink a craft beer and snack on fresh sushi, piping-hot pizza and a variety of tapas (RD$280 to RD$400), all assembled with local ingredients and innovative flavor combinations.

Cultura Cervecera CRAFT BEER
(www.facebook.com/ccervecerard; Rafael Augusto Sánchez 96b; draft beer from RD$210; ⊙4pm-midnight Mon-Thu, to 2am Fri & Sat, from 3pm Sun; 📶) A place of refuge for hopheads both Dominican and foreign, this is one of the city's best bets to escape the Presidente stranglehold on beer geeks. There are nearly 150 craft beers by the bottle along with six taps, often dedicated to local brews. It's 9km west of Zona Colonial and there's plenty of pub grub (mains RD$245 to RD$425) to wash down the IPAs!

☆ Entertainment

★Colonial Gate 4D Cinema CINEMA
(☎809-682-4829; www.thecolonialgate.com; Padre Billini 52; adult/child RD$400/350; ⊙9am-9pm Tue-Sun) Tucked away in the deep southeastern corner of the Zona Colonial, this hidden treasure is the country's first '4D' movie theater. The first three dimensions are what you'd expect, but the fourth brings in the elements – mist, fog, wind, heat, smells, motion seats and bubbles. Admission includes three short films and headsets that translate them into nine languages.

Estadio Quisqueya SPECTATOR SPORT
(☎809-616-1224; www.facebook.com/estadioquisqueya; Av Tiradentes 3456; tickets RD$250-1000; ⊙games 5pm Sun, 8pm Tue, Wed, Fri & Sat) One of the best places to experience Dominican baseball is at the home field of two of the DR's six professional teams, Licey and Escogido. You can get tickets to most games by arriving shortly before the first innings; games between the hometown rivals or Licey and Aguilas sell out more quickly.

Monastery Sundays MUSIC
(Monasterio de San Francisco, Hostos; ⊙6-10pm Sun) FREE Every Sunday night, the 16th-century ruins of the **Monasterio de San Francisco** (Hostos) come to life for a raging dance party. Beloved band Grupo Bonyé plays a mix of salsa, *bachata* (popular guitar music based on bolero rhythms), merengue and Caribbean rhythms, and hundreds of locals and tourists gather to drink and dance. The City Council has declared the event part of Santo Domingo's 'artistic patrimony.'

Shopping

More than anywhere else in the country, shopping in Santo Domingo runs the gamut from cheap tourist kitsch to high-end quality collectibles. The easiest – and best – neighborhood to shop in is the Zona Colonial, where you'll find rows of shops offering locally made products at decent prices.

Desireé Cepeda Artesanía Interiorismo ARTS & CRAFTS
(☎809-616-2278; Las Mercedes 206; ⊙10am-8pm Tue-Sun) Every nook and cranny of this charmingly idiosyncratic artisan crafts store displays the aesthetic vision of its passionately committed creator, including wooden figurines, straw bags, religious icons, ceramic vases and floral arrangements. There's also a charming little **cafe** where espresso drinks, sangria and small plates are served.

Galería Bolós ART
(☎809-686-5073; www.galeriabolos.blogspot.com; Isabel la Católica 15; ⊙7:30am-7pm) Manuel Bolós has never seen a piece of wood he didn't like. The energetic young artist builds stylish furniture from recycled wood he collects around the Zona Colonial and beyond, and he displays it here in his gallery alongside avant-garde art he sources across the DR and Haiti. Look for the 1.8m seahorse

composed entirely of recycled household goods.

Cava Billini WINE

(cnr Padre Billini & Arzobispo Meriño; ⌚noon-1am Mon-Sat, from 11am Sun) The only high-end wine shop in the Zona Colonial. It offers free tastings on Tuesdays (6pm to 8pm) and is a popular stop for those looking to enjoy a bottle at Lulú Tasting Bar (p405), which is under the same ownership, next door. Bottles run from RD$500, and a bottle of the priciest wine, Opus 1, is RD$2100.

Information

MEDICAL SERVICES

Centro de Obsetetricía y Ginecología (☎809-221-7100; www.cog.com.do; cnr Av Independencia & José Joaquín Pérez; ⌚24hr) Equipped to handle all emergencies.

Clínica Abreu (☎809-688-4411; www.clinicaabreu.com.do; Arzobispo Portes 853; ⌚24hr) One of the city's best hospitals.

Farmacia San Judas (☎809-685-8165; cnr Av Independencia & Pichardo; ⌚24hr) Pharmacy that offers free delivery.

Farmax (☎809-333-4444; cnr Av Independencia & Dr Delgado; ⌚24hr) Pharmacy that offers free delivery.

Hospital Padre Billini (☎809-333-5656; www.hdpb.gob.do; cnr Santomé & Arzobispo Nouel; ⌚24hr) A public hospital in the Zona Colonial. Service is free but expect long waits.

MONEY

There are several major banks with ATMs in the Zona Colonial. Gazcue also has a number of banks and others are scattered throughout the city, especially around major thoroughfares such as Av 27 de Febrero and Av Abraham Lincoln. Large hotels, particularly those on the Malecón, all have at least one ATM.

You can find *casas de cambio* (money changers) on Calle El Conde.

TOURIST INFORMATION

Colonial Zone (www.colonialzone-dr.com) A detailed site with information and reviews on everything – historical sites, hotels, restaurants, bars – as well as discussions on Dominican history, superstitions and more.

Ministry of Tourism (☎809-221-4660; www.mitur.gob.do; cnr Luperón & Germosén; ⌚8am-5pm Mon-Fri)

Tourist office (El Conde; ⌚9am-7pm Mon-Sat) Located beside Parque Colón, this little kiosk has a handful of brochures and maps for Santo Domingo and elsewhere in the country, as well as a half-dozen ones with a variety of Zona Colonial walking tours.

TRAVEL AGENCIES

Colonial Tour & Travel (☎809-688-5285; www.colonialtours.com.do; Arzobispo Meriño 209; ⌚8:30am-6pm Mon-Sat) This long-running professional outfit is good for booking flights, hotel rooms, and any and all excursions, from mountain biking to rafting to whale-watching. English, Italian and French spoken.

Explora Eco Tours (☎809-567-1852; www.exploraecotour.com; Gustavo A Mejia Ricart 43, Naco; ⌚9am-6pm Mon-Fri, to 2pm Sat) Specializes in organizing customized tours, from a single day to a week, of national parks, nature preserves and rural communities. Website announces regularly scheduled trips open to general public.

Tody Tours (☎809-686-0882; www.todytours.com; per day US$250) Former Peace Corps volunteer who specializes in tropical birding tours all over the country.

Getting There & Away

AIR

Santo Domingo has two airports: the main one, used by most international flights, Aeropuerto Internacional Las Américas (p434), is 26km east of Zona Colonial.

Aeropuerto Internacional La Isabela Dr Joaquin Balaguer (p433), around 20km north of the Zona Colonial, handles domestic carriers, charter flights and air-taxi companies.

BOAT

The DR's only international ferry service, run by Ferries del Caribe (p434) connects Santo Domingo with San Juan, Puerto Rico. The ticket office and boarding area are in the **Puerto Don Diego** (Av del Puerto, Zona Colonial), opposite Fortaleza Ozama. The ferry departs Santo Domingo at 7pm on Sunday, Tuesday and Thursday, before returning from San Juan at 7pm Monday, Wednesday and Friday. The trip from Santo Domingo takes 12 hours (eight hours in the other direction; difference is because of prevailing currents) and costs passengers US$180 round-trip.

BUS

The country's two main bus companies – **Caribe Tours** (☎809-221-4422; www.caribetours.com.do; cnr Avs 27 de Febrero & Leopoldo Navarro) and **Metro** (☎809-227-0101; www.metroserviciosturisticos.com; Francisco Prats Ramírez) – have individual depots west of the Zona Colonial. Caribe Tours has the most departures, and covers more of the smaller towns than Metro does. In any case, all but a few destinations are less than four hours from Santo Domingo.

It's a good idea to call ahead to confirm the schedule and always arrive at least 30 minutes before the stated departure time. Both bus lines publish brochures (available at all terminals) with up-to-date schedules and fares, plus the address and telephone number of their terminals throughout the country.

Expreso Bávaro Punta Cana (☎809-682-9670; www.expresobavaro.com; Juan Sánchez Ramirez 31) has a direct service between the Gazcue neighborhood (just off Av Máximo Gómez) in the capital and Bávaro. Departure times in both directions are 7am, 9am, 11am, 1pm, 3pm and 4pm (RD$400, three hours). Drivers are flexible and let passengers off at other stops in the city.

Another option is **APTRPA** (☎809-686-0637; www.aptpra.com; Ravelo), located amid the chaos of Parque Enriquillo, which services Higuey (RD$250), Bávaro and Punta Cana; there are six daily departures (on the hour) from 7am to 4pm for the latter two (RD$400).

CAR

Numerous international and domestic car-rental companies have more than one office in Santo Domingo proper and at Aeropuerto Internacional Las Américas, including **Avis** (☎809-535-7191; Av George Washington 517; ⏰7am-7pm), **Dollar** (☎809-221-7168; Av George Washington 365, Hotel Sheraton; ⏰7am-6pm), **Europcar** (☎809-688-2121; Av Independencia 354; ⏰7am-10pm) and **Hertz** (☎809-784-8753; Av George Washington 367, Renaissance Hotel; ⏰8am-5pm Mon-Fri, to noon Sat). All are open daily roughly from 7am to 6pm in Santo Domingo (sometimes later) and from 7am to 11:30pm at the airport (they're located in a small building just across the driveway from the terminal exit).

TAXI

Long-distance taxi service can be comfortable, if expensive. Sample fares from Apolo Taxi are La Romana (US$135), Samaná (US$190) and Punta Cana (US$200).

ℹ Getting Around

TO/FROM THE AIRPORT

There are no buses that connect directly to either of Santo Domingo's airports.

Aeropuerto Internacional Las Américas (p434) A taxi into the city costs US$40 to US$50, an Uber is around US$20.

Aeropuerto Internacional La Isabela Dr Joaquín Balaguer (p433) The fare from La Isabela is more reasonable at US$15.

BUS

The cost of a bus ride from one end of the city to the other is around RD$25 (6:30am to 9:30pm). Most stops are marked with a sign and the word *parada* (stop). The routes tend to follow major thoroughfares – in the Zona Colonial, Parque Independencia is where Av Bolivar (the main westbound avenue) begins and Av Independencia (the main eastbound avenue) ends. If you're trying to get across town, just look at a map and note the major intersections along the way and plan your transfers accordingly.

CAR

Driving in Santo Domingo can challenge the nerves and test the skills of the most battle-hardened driver. Heavy traffic, aggressive drivers (especially motorbikes), taxis and buses, and little attention to, or enforcement of, rules means it's a free-for-all. Many of the city's major avenues are gridlocked during rush hour and you're better off walking.

METRO

Santo Domingo's commuter train system (www.metrosantodomingo.com) was inaugurated in 2009. Line 1 from La Feria (Centro de los Héroes) near the Malecón to the far northern suburb of Villa Mella is a 14.5km route with 16 stations running primarily north–south above and below ground along Av Máximo Gómez. Line 2 runs east–west for 10.3km (entirely underground) along Av John F Kennedy, Expreso V Centenario and Av Padre Castellanos. The master plan calls for six lines.

Each ride costs RD$20 or a 24-hour pass costs RD$80; however, it's best to purchase a card at one of the ticket booths for RD$60, which can then be refilled when needed. Place the card on top of the turnstile to enter the station (6am to 10:30pm).

PÚBLICO

Even more numerous than buses are the *públicos* – mostly beaten-up minivans and private cars that follow the same main routes but stop wherever someone flags them down. They are supposed to have *público* on their license plates, but drivers will beep and wave at you long before you can make out the writing. Any sort of hand waving will get the driver to stop, though the preferred gesture is to hold out your arm and point down at the curb in front of you. The fare is RD$25 – pay when you get in. Be prepared for a tight squeeze.

TAXI

Taxis in Santo Domingo don't have meters, so you should always agree on the price before climbing in. The standard fare is around RD$250 from one side of the city to another; rates tend to be higher in the evening (RD$180 to the Caribe Tours or Metro bus station). Within the Zona Colonial it should be even cheaper. Taxi drivers don't typically cruise the streets looking for rides; they park at various major points and wait for customers to come to them. In the Zona Colonial, Parque Colón and Parque Duarte are the best spots.

You can also call for a taxi or ask the receptionist at your hotel to do so. Service is usually quick, the fare should be the same, and you don't have to lug your bags anywhere. Many of the top hotels have taxis waiting at the ready outside, but expect to pay significantly more for those. Reputable taxi agencies with 24-hour dispatches include **Apolo Taxi** (809-537-0000) and **Aero Taxi** (809-686-1212).

Taxis to the airport are cheaper than when arriving, around RD$1000 to RD$1300.

PUNTA CANA & THE SOUTHEAST

A Caribbean workhorse of sun and sand, the southeast is synonymous with go-big-or-go-home tourism and carries the weight of the Dominican Republic's most dramatic beaches and turquoise seas on its deeply tanned shoulders. Sprawling resort developments, some like city-states unto themselves, line much of the beachfront from Punta Cana to Uvero Alto, offering families, couples and the young and restless alike a hassle-free Caribbean holiday in some of the most idyllic environs in the region. But there is life beyond Punta Cana. Less-crowded beach towns such as Bayahibe and Juan Dolio offer only slightly less dramatic seascapes but sands that go unshared with the masses. Getaways like Playa Limón, beyond the sugar plantations and inland mountains to the north, showcase a different and worthwhile side of the southeast if you can tear yourself away from the buffets long enough to take the rewarding journeys required to make their acquaintance.

Bávaro & Punta Cana

It wouldn't be out of line to equate the eastern coast of the Dominican Republic as a sort of sea and sun Disneyland – after all, it is here where the all-inclusive resorts snatch up broad swaths of cinematic beaches faster than the real-estate agents can get the sun-soaked sands on the market. The beaches along the coastline from Punta Cana to Uvero Alto rival those anywhere else in the Caribbean, both in terms of their soft, white texture and their warm aquamarine waters. Despite a lack of restraint on development, especially in the geographically central area of Bávaro, the resorts and beaches here still manage to offer an idyllic Caribbean seascape for a seemingly endless crowd of sun-seekers.

But it's not all buffet lines and bottomless Cuba Libres. Independent travelers can enjoy the sun and fun, too – even if it is slightly more challenging than flopping down on a resort beach-lounger for a week.

Sights & Activities

Ojos Indígenas Ecological Park & Reserve NATURE RESERVE

(829-470-1368; www.puntacana.org; adult/child US$25/10, with guided tour US$50/30; 8:30am-5pm) Though development may eventually cover every inch of the Dominican coastline, for now there are still large areas of pristine coastal plains and mangrove forests. About 500m south of (and part of) the Puntacana Resort & Club (p412), this ecological park covers over 6 sq km of protected coastal and inland habitat and is home to some 100 bird species (27 of which are indigenous species native only to the DR), 160 insect species and 500 plant species.

Punta Espada Cap Cana Golf Club GOLF

(809-469-7767; www.capcana.com; Punta Cana) Cap Cana has one Jack Nicklaus Signature golf course, Punta Espada Golf Club, open for play since 2006 and consistently ranked one of the top courses in the Caribbean and in the world's top 100. Nonguest greens fees from May to October are US$235, from November to May they're US$295.

Hispaniola Aquatic Adventures BOATING

(800-282-5784; www.catamarantourpuntacana.com; from US$99) Runs highly popular party-boat catamaran tours for up to 25 people (or privately), taking in snorkeling at Cabeza de Toro as well a seafood lunch and lesser-known beaches and swimming holes. Prices include transportation and alcohol. It doesn't allow middleman sales and a portion of the price goes to a children's charity and an animal charity in the DR.

Beaches

Ten or so beaches fall under the Punta Cana umbrella, stretching across more than 50km of coastline. Public access is protected by the law, so you can stroll from less-exclusive parts such as **Playa El Cortecito/Los Corales**, the former of which tends to be crowded with vendors, to nicer spots in front of resorts – but without the proper color wrist bracelet you won't be able to get a towel or chair.

ORIENTATION

Punta Cana, shorthand for the region as a whole, is actually somewhat of a misnomer. Punta Cana actually refers to the area just east and south of the airport. The majority of resorts are scattered around the beaches of Bávaro, a town established to house resort workers and really nothing more than a series of small, spread-out commercial plazas. Within Bávaro, El Cortecito is a short, grungy strip of shops along a 'town beach,' and Los Corales is a nicer, more independently minded beach enclave just southeast of El Cortecito. Punta Cana (Grey-Haired Point), the easternmost tip of the country and where the airport is located, has some of the more luxurious resorts and Caribbean-hugging golf courses. More and more, Playa Uvero Alto, the northernmost beach in the area, is being colonized by large all-inclusives like those further south.

North of El Cortecito is **Playa Arena Gorda**, lined with all-inclusive resorts and their guests on banana boats, parasailing or just soaking in the sun. A further 9km north of here is the best accessible surf beach, **Playa del Macao**, a gorgeous stretch of sand best reached by car. It's also a stop-off for a slew of ATV (all-terrain vehicle) tours that tear up and down the beach every day – there's less noise at the far northern end of the beach. The golden sands of **Playa Uvero Alto**, the area's northernmost beach, are 10km further north.

In the other direction, south of Bávaro and El Cortecito, is **Playa Cabo Engaño**, an isolated beach that you'll need a vehicle, preferably a 4WD, to reach. And then there's the furthest southern beach, the gorgeous, snaking stunner **Playa Juanillo**, whose sands are cleaned daily by Cap Cana staff – just maybe the fairest of them all!

Tours

Runners Adventures TOURS
(☎888-280-5842; www.runnersadventures.com; Av Barcelo; US$80-180; ⏰7am-7pm) A well-established outfitter offering a range of adventure and cultural tours, the most popular of which takes in a squirrel-monkey reserve and the longest zip line in the Caribbean. Also offers popular trips in 4WD 'buggies', city tours to Santo Domingo, and a full day that includes horseback riding, a sugarcane plantation, a cigar factory, beach and buffet lunch.

RH Tours & Excursions TOURS
(☎809-543-3470; www.rhtours.com; El Cortecito; ⏰9am-2pm Mon-Sat) If you're looking to explore the region, this German-owned tour operator offers a number of decent day trips for tourists. Popular excursions include exploring Parque Nacional Los Haitises (US$138), boat trips to Isla Saona (US$99 to US$115) and tours of Santo Domingo's Zona Colonial (US$89). All full-day trips include lunch and drinks. English, German and Spanish are spoken.

Sleeping

★**Macao Beach Hostel** HOSTEL $
(☎829-913-6267; www.macaobeachhostel.com; El Macao; camping s/d without tent US$10/15, with tent US$15/20, dm US$18, r without bathroom US$33, all incl breakfast; P 📶) A warm and friendly Colombian-Mexican couple have cultivated a rural Dominican village experience at this hostel spread among several colorful traditional Caribbean clapboard shacks. Despite being a mere 10-minute walk from Macao Beach, it feels worlds away, with cows and horses grazing in pastures across the road (where unfortunately a resort development is being built), and chickens, cats, dogs and a community donkey roaming freely.

★**Hard Rock Hotel Punta Cana** RESORT $$$
(☎809-731-0099; www.hardrockhotelpuntacana.com; Playa del Macao; all-inclusive d from US$592; P ❄ @ 📶 ≋) Imagine Las Vegas with a Caribbean sea. This den of decadence and cool sits atop Punta Cana's list of bold and beautiful resorts. The lobby feels like a rock-and-roll hall of fame, with memorabilia galore, including Madonna's sequined-covered limo. It caters to a diverse hipster crowd.

The casino here is the DR's largest (as is the spa) and there are 13 pools (seven oceanfront), 10 restaurants and 17 bars, so you're never far from the party on the sprawling grounds. But why not party in your room? They feature family-sized Jacuzzis at the foot of the beds. Nonguests can visit the casino, the happening Oro nightclub and Epik, one of the resort's trendier restaurants (mains US$22 to US$55). Other bells and whistles include the 18-hole Hard Rock Golf Club at Cana Bay and an app from which guests can pretty much do anything.

Bávaro & Punta Cana

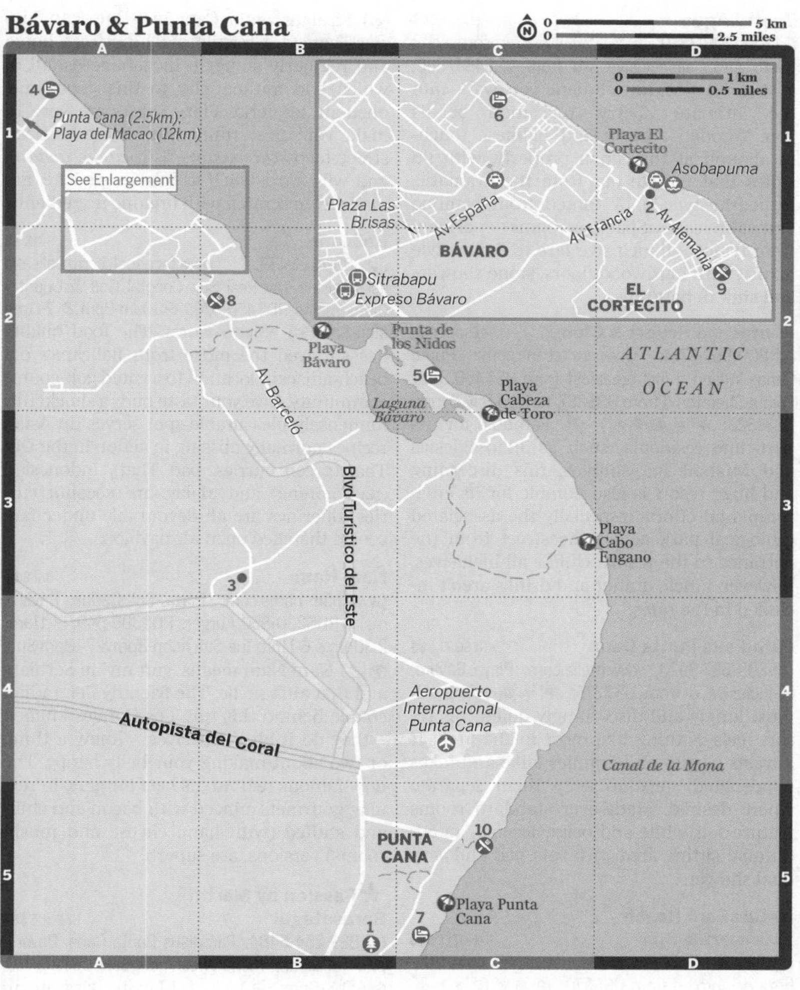

Bávaro & Punta Cana

Sights

1 Ojos Indígenas Ecological Park & Reserve B5

Activities, Courses & Tours

2 RH Tours & Excursions D1
3 Runners Adventures B3

Sleeping

4 Hard Rock Hotel Punta Cana A1
5 NaturaPark Beach Ecoresort & Spa C2
6 Paradisus Punta Cana C1
7 Puntacana Resort & Club C5

Eating

8 Balicana B2
9 Ñam Ñam D2
Passion by Martín Berasategui .... (see 6)
10 Restaurante Playa Blanca C5
Wacamole .... (see 9)

Zoetry Agua RESORT $$$
(☎888-496-3879; www.zoetryresorts.com; Uvero Alto; all-inclusive s/d from US$454/568; P@📶🏊) The moment you walk into the intimate Zoetry, relaxation befalls you. Wooden accents and Balinese touches abound at this small property, with 96 suites that radiate out from the dramatic, cathedral-style lobby forged from bamboo and palm leaves. Spacious rooms deport you from typical all-inclusive fare to Asian-style luxury, with hardwood floors, stone showers and sink-in bathtubs.

Puntacana Resort & Club RESORT $$$
(☎809-959-2714; www.puntacana.com; Punta Cana; Westin d incl breakfast from US$460, Four Points Sheraton d from US$267, Tortuga Bay d from US$1323; P❄@📶🏊) Famous for its part-time residents, such as Julio Iglesias and Mikhail Baryshnikov, this discerning and huge resort is also notable for its environmental efforts, especially the associated ecological park across the street from the entrance to the resort. Unlike all-inclusives, however, lunch, dinner and drinks aren't included in the rates.

Paradisus Punta Cana RESORT $$$
(☎809-687-9923; www.melia.com; Playa Bávaro; all-inclusive d from US$275; P❄@📶🏊) Almost jungly and discerningly quiet, this resort feels nothing like most in the area. It attracts singles and families alike and takes appreciated steps to keep them separate where desired. Made-over standard rooms feature soft white and beige accents, an additional sitting area with sofa bed and sexy dual showers.

NaturaPark Beach Ecoresort & Spa HOTEL $$$
(☎809-221-2626; www.blaunaturapark.com; Cabeza de Toro; d from US$270; P❄@📶🏊) NaturaPark has a narrow beach outside the village of Cabeza de Toro, halfway between Bávaro and Punta Cana. From the Lincoln Logs–style recycled coconut-wood lobby furniture to the beautiful free-growing mangroves on the property, it's all got a sustainable emphasis and the 524-room resort has won awards for reducing its environmental impact.

Eating

Wacamole MEXICAN $$
(www.facebook.com/wacamolepc; Av Alemania, Los Corales; mains RD$250-500; ⏲noon-midnight; 📶) Straight outta Cancún – Mexican hipsters lugged a tortilla machine from home and regularly smuggle in habaneros, all of which add authenticity to this good-time, open-air taqueria. Fiery salsas are sure to make your nose run, while classic Mexican street tacos (*al pastor*, fish, *carne asada*), and wild cards such as lobster ceviche, are made from scratch with organic ingredients.

Balicana FUSION $$
(☎809-707-3433; www.facebook.com/balicanaasiancuisine; Av Real Sur, Cocotal Golf & Country Club; mains RD$450-670; ⏲10am-3pm & 7-11pm Mon-Sat; 📶) Not to worry. The food quality has survived the move from Balicana's old beach-adjacent location to a gated golf-course community. Give your taste buds a shock: this immensely pleasurable spot serves up Asian recipes normally missing in action in the DR. Thai (green curries, pad Thai), Indonesian (nasi goreng) and Malaysian (coconut curries) offerings are all devourable under fan-cooled thatched open-air pavilions.

Ñam Ñam CAFE $$
(www.nam-nams.com; Plaza Sol Caribe, Bávaro; mains RD$230-550, burgers RD$399-549; ⏲11am-2:30pm & 6-11pm Tue-Sat, noon-3pm & 7-10pm Sun; 📶🖉) Ñam Ñam means 'yummy' in Serbian, and that ain't no lie. The friendly Belgradian couple behind this tiny Los Corales kitchen – they do it all themselves – know a thing or two about making your belly happy. The now-famous real Angus beef burgers, in regular, gourmet (minced with bacon and chili) and stuffed (with ham, cheese and mushrooms) versions, are superb.

★**Passion by Martín Berasategui** BASQUE $$$
(☎829-284-6484; Paradisus Punta Cana, Bávaro; prix-fixe tasting menu guest/nonguest US$80/110; ⏲6:30-10pm; 📶) Chef Martín Berasategui hails from San Sebastián in Spanish Basque country – not a bad place to eat for those who might not know – and he packed a few recipes in his gastro-luggage on his way to overseeing what is considered the best fine-dining experience in the Dominican Republic, at the Paradisus Punta Cana.

★**Restaurante Playa Blanca** FUSION $$$
(Puntacana Resort, Punta Cana; mains US$14-24; ⏲11am-10:30pm; 📶) Flanked by an army of palms, this stylish and atmospheric open-air restaurant is within the Puntacana Resort complex but open to the public and worth the trip (nonguests will have to show ID).

The beach here (Playa Blanca) is spectacular, and you can eat on the sand for lunch. The Dominican comfort menu is highlighted by some wild cards such as Dominican goat lasagna (US$16).

Little John SEAFOOD $$$
(809-469-7727; Cap Cana, Playa Juanillo; mains US$11-30; 11am-9pm;) With its photogenic, colored-up VW van and pleasant open-air, whitewashed setting on Playa Juanillo, Little John is the best spot to kick back with a wealth of properly mixed creative cocktails (RD$300 to RD$750) and a well-rounded, seafood-heavy menu on one of Punta Cana's prettiest beaches.

Information

EMERGENCY

The main **Cestur** (Cuerpo Especializado de Seguridad Turística, Tourism Police; 809-754-3082; www.cestur.gob.do; Av Estados Unidos, Bávaro; 24hr) station is in Friusa, next to the bus terminal in Bávaro, with additional stations at the Punta Cana airport, Cabeza de Toro and Uvero Alto.

MONEY

There is always an ATM around until you need one, in which case they are always far away, despite nearly every Dominican bank having a branch in Punta Cana! Most resorts have their own, of course. Otherwise, the closest ATMs to the scene around Los Corales are the **BanReserves and Banco Popular ATMs** (Av Alemania) at Palma Real Shopping Village, 2.2km southwest.

Banco Popular (Av España, btwn Plaza Brisas de Bávaro & Plaza Estrella) Has an ATM.

Scotiabank Has ATMs at Puntacana Village and Plaza Brisas de Bávaro.

MEDICAL SERVICES

All-inclusive hotels have small on-site clinics and medical staff who can provide first aid and basic care. Head to one of several good private hospitals in the area for more serious issues.

Centro Médico Punta Cana (809-552-1506; www.centromedicopuntacana.com; Av España 1, Bávaro) Name notwithstanding, this is the largest private hospital in Bávaro, with multilingual staff, 24-hour emergency room and in-house pharmacy.

Farmacia Estrella (809-552-0344; Plaza Estrella, Bávaro; 8am-midnight) Bávaro pharmacy offering delivery.

Hospitén Bávaro (809-686-1414; www.hospiten.com/en/hospitals-and-centers/hospiten-bavaro; Carretera Higüey-Punta Cana) English-, French- and German-speaking doctors and a 24-hour emergency room. The hospital is located on the old Hwy 106 to Punta Cana, 500m from Cruce de Verón.

International Medical Center (829-946-3991; Plaza Brisas de Bávaro; 24hr) The newest and one of the best of the area's private hospitals with multilingual doctors and 24-hour emergency care.

Pharmacana (809-959-0025; Puntacana Village, Punta Cana; 24hr) A good 24-hour pharmacy at Puntacana Village.

Getting There & Away

AIR

Several massive thatched-roof huts make up the terminals – Terminal A (Departures and Arrivals) and the larger and newer Terminal B – of the Aeropuerto Internacional Punta Cana (p434), located on the road to Punta Cana about 9km east of the turnoff to Bávaro. The arrival process, including immigration, baggage claim and customs, moves briskly.

Commercial airlines serving the Punta Cana airport year-round include the following: Aerolineas Argentinas, Aeromexico, Air Canada, Frontier, JetBlue, LATAM, Southwest, Spirit, Sunwing and United (from Terminal A); Air Berlin, Air France, American Airlines, Avianca, British Airways, Copa, Delta Airlines, Edelweiss/Swiss and GOL (from Terminal B). There are additional airlines and flights (including many charters), especially in high season.

Rental-car agencies at Aeropuerto Internacional Punta Cana, including **AmeriRent** (809-687-0505; www.amerirent.net), **Avis** (809-959-0534; www.avis.com.do; 8am-9pm), **Budget** (809-959-1005; www.budget.com; 8am-10pm), **Europcar** (809-686-2861; www.europcar.com; 8am-6pm), **National/Alamo** (809-959-0434; www.nationalcar.com.do), **Payless** (809-959-0287; www.paylesscar.com), **Thrifty** (809-466-2046; www.thrifty.com) and **Hertz** (809-959-0705; www.hertz.com; 8am-10pm), are a short walk across the loop driveway at Terminal A (Arrivals) and are generally open from 9am to 10pm. If arriving at Terminal B, arrange for the rental-car company to send a shuttle van to pick you up – it's much too long a walk if you have bags. Touts and taxis will no doubt quote exorbitant prices to take you there.

Resort minivans transport the majority of tourists to nearby resorts, but taxis are plentiful – look for the Siutratural guys in pink shirts. Fares between the airport and area resorts and hotels range between US$30 and US$80 depending on the destination.

BUS

The wonderfully smooth 70km Autopista del Coral toll road from La Romana to Punta Cana

WORTH A TRIP

BEST OF THE REST

Bayahibe, 22km east of La Romana, was originally founded by fishermen from Puerto Rico in the 19th century. Today it's a tranquil beach village caught in a schizophrenic power play. In the morning it's the proverbial tourist gateway, when busloads of tourists from resorts further east hop into boats bound for Isla Saona. Once this morning rush hour is over it turns back into a sleepy village. There's another buzz of activity when the resort tourists return, and then after sunset another transformation. What sets Bayahibe apart is that it manages to maintain its character despite the continued encroachment of big tourism (and the arrival of paved roads, which canvas the entire village).

A short drive from Bayahibe is Dominicus Americanus, an upscale Potemkin village centered on a terrific public beach with **Las Palmas** (829-850-2665; Playa Dominicus; prix-fixe from US$40; 10am-11pm Mon-Fri), a made-to-order fresh-lobster madhouse offering a meal to remember for crustacean lovers. Call ahead and make a reservation so they know to send a fisherman out to catch the right amount of lobsters, which will then be quickly thrown on the grill right in the middle of diners.

About halfway between Bayahibe and La Romana to the east is **Ki-Ra** (809-757-8661; www.ki-ra.com; Boca Chavón; tent US$80-106, r incl breakfast US$143-158; P), a serene, holistic retreat named for the Taíno expression 'birthplace of the earth spirit.' The three rooms and seven oceanfront tents, all designed in pastel hues, make for a dreamy escape for all comers. It's 6km down a passable dirt road from the main highway, just on the other side of the Rio Chavón from the marina for the Casa de Campo megaresort.

Nearly 90km north from Punta Cana, not far from beautiful Playa Limón where several high end resorts are being built, is **Montaña Redonda** (809-481-0712; www.montanaredondaparadise.com; RD$100; 8am-6pm), a dramatic mountaintop viewpoint – Dominicanos flock here on weekends to take photos swinging in sky-high swing sets, hammocks and teeter-totters, or flying on broomsticks. The 360-degree mountain and sea views are jaw-dropping, among the DR's most cinematic. Transport from the parking lot is RD$700, but you can group together and pay RD$100 each. The bumpy, steep ride up is as wild as a roller coaster (some folks walk the 2.1km).

Another 60km up the coast, the road dead-ends in the bayside town of Sabana de la Mar, the jumping-off point for **Parque Nacional Los Haitises** (caves RD$100; 7am-8pm). Its name means 'land of the mountains,' and this 1375-sq-km park at the southwestern end of the Bahía de Samaná indeed contains scores of lush hills, jutting some 30m to 50m from the water and coastal wetlands. The knolls were formed one to two million years ago, when tectonic drift buckled the thick limestone shelf that had formed underwater. The only place to stay in the area is the quirky and rustic **Paraíso Caño Hondo** (829-259-8549; www.paraisocanohondo.com; s/d/tr incl breakfast RD$2040/3212/4437; P), one of the more special places to stay anywhere in the DR, and the antithesis of the all-inclusives for which the country is famous. Coming upon Paraíso Caño Hondo so far out of the way after a long and rough road feels like an epiphany.

means it's only a two hour or so drive in your own vehicle from Santo Domingo.

The bus terminal is located on Av Estados Unidos in Friusa, near the main intersection in Bávaro, almost 2km inland from El Cortecito.

Expreso Bávaro (809-552-1678; www.expresobavaro.com; Cruce de Friusa) has direct 1st-class services between Bávaro and the capital (RD$400, three hours), with a stop in La Romana. Departure times in both directions are 7am, 9am, 11am, 1pm, 3pm and 4pm.

From the same terminal, **Sitrabapu** (809-552-0771; Av Estados Unidos), more or less the same company, has departures to La Romana (RD$225, 1¼ hours) at 6am, 8:20am, 10:50am, 1:20pm, 3:50pm and 6:20pm; and to Higüey (RD$120 to RD$130, one hour, every 20 minutes, 3am to 10:30pm). To all other destinations, head for Higüey and transfer there. You can also get to/from Santo Domingo this way, but it's much much slower than the direct bus.

Getting Around

BUS

Local buses start at the main bus terminal, passing all the outdoor malls on the way to El

Cortecito, then turn down the coastal road past the large hotels to Cruce de Cocoloco, where they turn around and return the same way. Buses have the local drivers' union acronyms – Sitrabapu or Traumapabu – printed in front and cost around RD$40, depending on distance. They generally pass every 30 minutes between 5am and 8pm, but can sometimes take up to an hour.

MOTOCONCHOS

Motoconchos congregate around Plaza Punta Cana in Bávaro and along the beach road in El Cortecito, and you can generally find one or two parked in front of the entrance to most resorts. Fares run around RD$100 to RD$200 within the El Cortecito/Bávaro area.

TAXI

There are numerous taxis in the area – look for stands at El Cortecito, Plaza Bávaro and at the entrance of most all-inclusive places. You can also call a cab – try Siutratural, in **Bávaro** (☎809-552-0617; www.taxibavaropuntacana.com.do) and **El Cortecito** (☎809-552-0617; El Cortecito), or **Taxi Turístico Berón** (☎809-466-1133; www.taxituristicoberon.com). Fares vary depending on distance, but some examples include US$10 (pretty much the minimum charge on a short trip within Bávaro), US$35 to the airport and US$40 to Playa Blanca. **Asobapuma** (☎829-638-5525; El Cortecito) water taxis can also be found on El Cortecito beach and cost between US$10 and US$20 per ride.

PENÍNSULA DE SAMANÁ

This sliver of land is the antithesis of the Dominican-Caribbean dream in the southeast, where resorts rule and patches of sand come at a first-class premium. Far more laid-back and, in certain senses, more cosmopolitan, Samaná offers a European vibe as strong as espresso; it's where escape is the operative word, and where French and Italian are at least as useful as Spanish. The majority of visitors base themselves in sophisticated and lively Las Terrenas, with sleepy Las Galeras – situated with several of the country's best and most secluded beaches within reach – a popular alternative. But distances are relatively short, so days can be spent exploring the peninsula's other natural attractions, including waterfalls, underwater geography and North Atlantic humpback whales doing their migratory song and dance from mid-January to mid-March.

Las Terrenas

POP 13,869

Once a rustic fishing village, Las Terrenas is now a cosmopolitan town and seems as much French (approaching a colony) and Italian as Dominican. The balancing act between locals and expats has produced a lively mix of styles and a social scene more vibrant than that anywhere else on the peninsula. Walking in either direction along the beach road leads to a beachfront scattered with hotels, tall palm trees and calm, aquamarine waters.

Las Terrenas is well suited to independent travelers and a good place to hook up with fellow nomads.

Sights

Playa Cosón BEACH

The sand at Playa Cosón, 8km west along the main highway from Playa Bonita, is tan rather than white, and the water greenish rather than blue, but it's a good place to lose yourself for the day, with some excellent surf-sprayed restaurants to enjoy. Two small rivers run through the thick palm-tree forest and into the ocean; the easternmost is said to contain agricultural runoff. A taxi to the beach is US$40 round-trip, a *motoconcho* (motorcycle taxi) RD$300.

Cascada El Limón WATERFALL

Tucked away in surprisingly rough landscape, surrounded by peaks covered in lush greenery, is the 52m-high El Limón waterfall. A beautiful swimming hole at the bottom can be a perfect spot to wash off the sweat and mud from the trip here, though it's often too deep and cold for a dip. The departure point is the small town of El Limón, only half an hour from Las Terrenas.

Activities

Las Terrenas has reasonably good diving and snorkeling and at least three shops in town to take you out.

Dive Academy DIVING

(☎829-906-9618; www.tdlasterrenas.com; 2nd fl, Beach Garden Plaza, Libertad; ⌚9am-6pm) This English-run National Association of Underwater Instructors (NAUI) outfitter, a Las Galeras transplant, also offers snorkeling trips to Cayo Levantado.

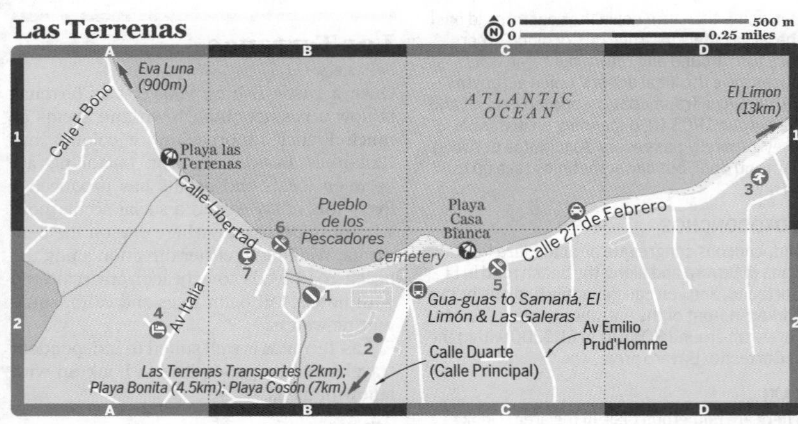

Las Terrenas

Activities, Courses & Tours
1 Dive Academy B2
2 Flora Tours B2
3 LT'Kite D1

Sleeping
4 Mahona Boutique Hotel A2

Eating
5 El Lugar C2
6 La Terrasse B2

Drinking & Nightlife
7 El Mosquito Art Bar B2

LT'Kite WATER SPORTS
(☎809-801-5671; www.lasterrenas-kitesurf.com; Calle 27 de Febrero; ⊙10am-6pm) Recommended kitesurfing school run by a friendly Frenchman who speaks Spanish and English as well. It rents surfboards (per day US$30) and kitesurfing equipment (per day US$70) and provides lessons and International Kiteboarding Organization (IKO) certifications for the latter. Six hours of kitesurfing lessons (really the minimum needed to have a sporting chance of making it work) cost US$300.

Tours

Flora Tours ECOTOUR
(☎829-923-2792; www.flora-tours.net; Principal 278; ⊙8:30am-12:30pm & 3:30-6:30pm Mon-Sat) This French-run agency takes top honors in town for ecosensitive tours to Parque Nacional Los Haitises and hard-to-access beaches, as well as more tranquil catamaran trips, culturally sensitive quad-bike tours to remote villages, mountain-bike excursions of varying levels and kayak tours through the mangroves at Playa Cosón.

Sleeping

★ **Mahona Boutique Hotel** BOUTIQUE HOTEL $$
(☎809-651-3078; www.mahona-lasterrenas.com; Calle Italia 1; r incl breakfast US$85; P) Perfectly coiffed and manicured, much like the warm and stylish French couple behind this small collection of whitewashed bungalows surrounding a small pool, Mahona does everything right, especially the fabulous multicourse breakfast served up in a sunny space. The rooms themselves have a bit of a Balinese flavor and each has a small terrace.

★ **Peninsula House** GUESTHOUSE $$$
(☎809-962-7447; www.thepeninsulahouse.com; Playa Cosón; r incl breakfast US$715-880; P@) One of the Caribbean's more exquisite accommodations, this Victorian B&B with a French-chateau aesthetic perched high on a hill overlooking Playa Cosón is without doubt one of the DR's top choices for exclusivity and service. Rooms are decorated with tasteful antiques, romantic four-poster beds and deep bathtubs. The average stay here is five nights, but you'll want to move in permanently.

★El Mosquito Boutique Hotel HOTEL $$$
(☎809-240-6161; www.mosquitoboutiquehotel.com; Playa Bonita; d/tr/q US$100/128/152; P❄📶) Establishing itself as Playa Bonita's coolest spot thanks to its buzzy bar-restaurant and its on-site surf school, the rooms at this renovated family-run place are also no slouch. Spacious and pleasantly furnished, they're just right for the French-colonial whitewashed exterior. Service is excellent and many guests end up just chilling on the property.

Costa las Ballenas VILLA $$$
(☎829-756-2253; www.hotelcostalasballenas.com; Playa Bonita; d incl breakfast US$115-190; P❄📶🏊) Serene and private, with a handful of large thatch-roofed villas surrounding an outdoor pool, this immaculately manicured property makes for a wonderful laid-back upscale retreat. The rooms are full of charm, with king-sized beds, a plant or two, tasteful artwork and high ceilings.

Eva Luna VILLA $$$
(☎809-978-5611; www.villa-evaluna.com; Marico, Playa Las Ballenas; villas incl breakfast from US$150; P❄@🏊) A paragon of understated luxury, these five Mexican-style villas come with fully equipped kitchens, gorgeously painted living rooms, and terraces where a delicious gourmet breakfast is served. The bedrooms are a bit cramped, but the serenity and exquisite decor more than make up for it.

Eating & Drinking

★La Terrasse FRENCH $$
(☎809-240-6730; Pueblo de los Pescadores; mains RD$380-730; ⏰11:30am-2:30pm & 6:30-11pm; 📶) The Dominican chef at this sophisticated French bistro deserves a few Michelin stars for his *steak au poivre* (pepper steak; RD$550), one of the most perfect meals in the entire DR – you'll be genuflecting at his kitchen's door after it graces your lips.

El Lugar STEAK $$
(☎849-248-2580; Calle 27 de Febrero; burgers RD$340-750, steaks RD$600-2000; ⏰noon-midnight, closed Tue; 📶) Hands-on Belgian owner Bruno found a Las Terrenas niche: fulfilling carnivorous desires with juicy, rich burgers (go for the one with Reblochon cheese) and wood-fired steaks (both national and imported black Angus), lobster and fish, all served in a trendy, high-table atmosphere that lures the town's bold and beautiful for the complete package – ambience, service and excellent eats.

The Beach INTERNATIONAL $$$
(☎809-847-3288; www.thepeninsulahouse.com; Playa Cosón; mains RD$600-1200; ⏰noon-3pm Tue-Sun; 📶) The beach-club component of the Peninsula House hotel – open to nonguests as well – is a wonderful little plantation-style bungalow on a private lawn steps from Playa Cosón. A long-standing Dominican husband-and-wife chef team serves up a variety of eclectic gourmet dishes (fresh shrimp tacos, grilled lobster, BBQ pork ribs) from an often-changing menu scribbled on ceramic plates.

★El Mosquito Art Bar COCKTAIL BAR
(Pueblo de los Pescadores; cocktails RD$250-400; ⏰5pm-2am; 📶) The hottest bar in Las Terrenas by a landslide, this open-air lounge is a good-time juxtaposition of rustic lounge furniture, fairy-light-lit trees, exposed brick and local art that caters to a who's who of expats and tourists.

Information

BanReservas (www.banreservas.com; Duarte 254; ⏰8am-5pm Mon-Fri, 9am-1pm Sat) Tellers can provide cash advances of at least RD$20,000 on many types of international credit cards.

Clínica Especializada Internacional (☎809-240-6701; www.ceiterrenas.com; Villa de Las Flores, Fabio Abreu; ⏰24hr) An excellent private hospital run by Cuban doctors.

Colonial Tours & Travel (☎809-240-6822; www.colonialtours.com; El Paseo; ⏰9am-1pm & 3-7pm Mon-Fri, to noon Sat) The town's main full-service travel agency; helpful for bus info as well.

Fort Knox (El Paseo; ⏰8:30am-1pm & 4-7:15pm Mon-Sat) Reliable and centrally located money exchange.

Super Farmacia del Paseo (El Paseo, Paseo de la Costanera; ⏰9am-7pm Mon-Sat, to 1pm Sun) Well-stocked pharmacy.

Getting There & Away

AIR

International flights arrive at Aeropuerto Internacional El Catey (p434), located 8km west of Sánchez and a 35-minute taxi ride (US$70) to Las Terrenas. Air Canada, Westjet and Air Transat, among others, serve Canadian destinations; XL Airways goes to Paris. There's also a handful of charter flights.

DON'T MISS

WHALE-WATCHING

For sheer awe-inspiring, 'the natural world is an amazing thing' impact, seeing whales up close is hard to beat, and Samaná town – officially Santa Barbara de Samaná – is considered to be one of the world's top 10 whale-watching destinations. Around 60,000 people travel here every year between January 15 and March 25 to see the majestic acrobatics of these massive creatures. February is peak season for humpback whales, but try to avoid the weekend of February 27 – the DR's Independence Day – as the associated Carnival makes it the busiest weekend of the winter and Samaná is packed.

Most of the whale-watching companies have a morning and an afternoon trip. There's little difference in terms of your likelihood of seeing whales, and although the water may be slightly rougher in the afternoon, it also tends to be less busy, with fewer boats out. The 38 vessels with legal permits belong to eight companies (two of them foreign owned – Canadian and Spanish) and the five 'rotating' permits are split between 20 Dominican-owned independent operators.

Whale Samaná (809-538-2494; www.whalesamana.com; cnr Mella & Av la Marina; adult/5-10yr/under 5yr US$59/30/free; 8am-1pm & 3-6pm Jan-Mar, from 9am Mon-Fri Apr-Dec), Samaná's most recommended whale-watching outfit, is owned and operated by Canadian marine-mammal specialist Kim Beddall, the first person to recognize the scientific and economic importance of Samaná's whales way back in 1985. The company uses a large two-deck boat with capacity for 60 people.

BUS

For Santo Domingo, **Las Terrenas Transportes** (809-240-5302; Duarte) operates direct coaches via the main highway (RD$400, 2½ hours, 5am, 7am, 9am, 2pm and 3:30pm), Puerto Plata (RD$400, 3½ hours, 6am), Santiago (RD$400, three hours, 6am and 12:30pm) and Nagua (RD$150, 1¼ hours, 7am and 2pm). Buses leave from the Esso gas station on the outskirts of town, 2.5km south of the sea; tickets can only be purchased here half an hour before departure.

Guaguas (local buses) leave from in front of Casa Linda at the corner of Calle Principal and the coastal road eight times daily to to Samaná (RD$100, 1¼ hours, 7:15am to 5pm), as well as for El Limón (RD$50, 35 minutes, every 15 minutes from 7:15am to 7pm), 14km away, and Las Galeras (RD$250, two hours, 9am & 2:45pm).

CAR

Las Terrenas is easily accessible by road. A portion of the US$150-million Blvd Turístico del Atlántico connects Las Terrenas with the airport (p434), 24km to the west, avoiding the need to transit through Sánchez. The toll charges, relative to kilometers, are high (RD$528), and it hasn't exactly been embraced by locals, but it's a beautiful drive all the same.

TAXI

The local **taxi consortium** (809-240-6339) offers rides for one to six passengers to just about anywhere. Some sample one-way fares are Playa Cosón (US$25), El Limón (US$25), Samaná (US$70), Las Galeras (US$100), Santo Domingo (US$180) and Punta Cana (US$400).

Las Galeras

POP 6305

The road to this small fishing community 28km northeast of Samaná ends at the beach. So does everything else, metaphorically speaking. One of the great pleasures of a stay here is losing all perspective on the world beyond – even the beautiful and isolated outlying beaches seem far away. By all means succumb to the temptation to do nothing more than lie around your bungalow or while the day away at a restaurant. But – if you summon the will to resist – Las Galeras offers a variety of land- and water-based activities.

The town's laid-back charms have not gone unnoticed, drawing a cosmopolitan mix of European and North Americans who have set up shop here, helping gear Las Galeras to independent travelers.

There's one main intersection in town (about 50m before the highway dead-ends at the beach) and most hotels, restaurants and services are walking distance from there.

Beaches

Playa Rincón BEACH

Pitch-perfect Playa Rincón, with soft, nearly white sand and multihued water good for swimming, stretches an uninterrupted 3km – enough for every day-tripper to claim their own piece of real estate. There's a small stream at the far western end, which is great for a quick freshwater dip at the end of your visit, and a backdrop of thick palm forest. Several restaurants serve seafood dishes and rent beach chairs, making this a great place to spend the entire day.

Playa Frontón BEACH

Playa Frontón boasts some of the area's best snorkeling. Apparently it's also popular with drug smugglers and Dominicans braving the Mona Passage on their way to Puerto Rico. Trails lead to the beach, but it's easy to get lost, so hire a local guide – contact Karin at **La Hacienda** (829-939-8285; www.lahaciendahostel.com – or, preferably, come by boat: **Asoldega** (Asociación de Lancheros de Las Galeras) charges about RD$3000 to Playa Frontón (RD$1000 per person with four or more).

Playa Madama BEACH

Playa Madama is a small beach framed by high bluffs at the edge of the country; keep in mind there's not much sunlight here in the afternoon.

Asoldega charges around RD$2500 to Playa Madama (RD$800 per person with four or more people).

Activities

Las Galeras Divers DIVING

(809-538-0220; www.las-galeras-divers.com; Plaza Lusitania; 8am-6pm) Las Galeras Divers is a well-respected, French-run dive shop at the main intersection. One-/two-tank dives including all equipment cost US$55/85 (US$10 less if you have your own gear). Discounted dive packages are offered. Various PADI-certification courses can also be arranged.

Sleeping

★Sol Azul BUNGALOW $$

(829-882-8790; www.elsolazul.com; s/d incl breakfast from RD$2000/2500; P) A warm and friendly Swiss couple (and their adorable dogs) runs these four earthy, natural-hued and spacious bungalows, set around a perfectly manicured garden and pleasant pool area just 50m from the town's main intersection. Two of the bungalows feature mezzanine levels, and the breakfast buffet gets high marks – especially for the oranges and avocados straight from Sol Azul's own trees.

Chalet Tropical CHALET $$

(809-901-0738; www.chalettropical.com; Calle por La Playita; s/d/tr US$75/80/85, without bathroom US$65/70/75, chalets from US$165; P) An Italian stylist is the big personality behind these rustic-chic A-frames, some broken into rooms, others open plan and all with creatively fashioned plunge pools. They boast a striking range of colors and unique interior details such as stone showers, coconut and bamboo wood accents, and all manner of creative combinations. Several offered on a per-room basis with shared common areas.

Casa Dorado B&B $$

(829-577-6777; www.casadoradodr.com; r incl breakfast US$75-90; P) This beautiful house, 1km from both the main intersection and Playita beach, features Mexican-influenced interiors styled by the American owner. Four rooms are available; the largest and most expensive comes with a hot tub.

Todo Blanco BOUTIQUE HOTEL $$

(809-538-0201; www.hoteltodoblanco.com; r with/without air-con US$100/90; P) Living up to its 'All White' name, this whitewashed, well-established inn sits atop a small hillock a short walk from the end of the main drag. Rooms are large and airy, with high ceilings, private terraces overlooking the sea, pastel headboards and new air-con, while the multilevel grounds are nicely appointed with gardens and a gazebo.

★Casa El Paraíso B&B $$$

(809-975-1641; www.facebook.com/CasaElParaisoRD; La Guázuma; r incl breakfast US$150-190; P) Santo Domingo veterinarians Nora and José, a gourmet Italian chef named Mirko and a gaggle of Italian greyhounds are your hosts at this extraordinary six-room B&B that practically tumbles out of the jungle into the sea below. Room 5 (nicknamed 'Africa') is completely open on two sides, framing jungle, mountain and sea as you've never seen.

El Monte Azul B&B $$$

(849-249-3640; www.restaurantsamana-monteazul.com; Loma del Monte Azul; r incl breakfast US$128; P) This boutique B&B attached to the stunning restaurant (p420) of the same name offers three modern rooms in the home of the Laotian-French owner-designer, Vanina, and her husband, Pierre, a French fisherman and the chef at the restaurant. Small and tastefully – if minimally – designed with turquoise and muted-gray tones, it offers sky-high R & R with views that awe.

Eating

★El Monte Azul SEAFOOD **$$**
(☎849-249-3640; vsafan.fcc@gmail.com; mains RD$650-790; ⏲11am-2:30pm, closed Tue; 📶) Clinging spectacularly to the edge of a cliff, El Monte Azul offers postcard-perfect views and a good-value menu split between French-leaning meat and seafood and a variety of Thai noodle dishes – the highlight of which is an excellent lionfish in a creamy white-wine, lemon and green-onion sauce. Go at sunset, when a kaleidoscopic flurry of hues melts into the sea.

Restaurante Il Pirata da Manuela ITALIAN **$$**
(☎809-935-2765; Calle a la Playita; mains RD$650; ⏲5:30-11pm) Locals, Italians even, claim the homemade gnocchi and other pastas made by the owner-chef, originally from Torino, are the best on the peninsula. Certainly, the tastiest and most authentic in Las Galeras. The ice cream, also made in-house, is pretty special too.

Head down the road to Playita, but continue past the turnoff; the last 200m of the road are pretty rough.

★El Cabito SEAFOOD **$$$**
(☎809-820-2263; mains RD850; 📶) Don't turn around. Sure, the rough road might take out the axel on an ordinary car. And the paved and messy parking area doesn't inspire confidence. And service can be lackluster. But the journey is worth it. Enjoy heaping plates of fresh seafood perched over a commanding cliffside with hawks soaring overhead and whales in the distance. Or come for a sundowner; just don't come in bad weather.

Information

There's a BanReservas (www.banreservas.com; Principal) one block north of the Malecón and another at Grand Paradise Samaná resort.

Cestur (Tourist Police; ☎849-754-2987; Principal; ⏲24hr)

Getting There & Away

The paved road coming from Samaná winds along the coast and through lovely, often forested countryside before reaching the outskirts of Las Galeras.

Guaguas head to Samaná (RD$100, 1½ hours, every 20 minutes from 6:30am to 6pm) from the beach end of Calle Principal, and they also pick up passengers as they cruise very slowly out of town. There are two daily trips to Las Terrenas (RD$250, two hours, 9am and 2pm) and three daily Asotrapusa buses to Santo Domingo (RD$400, four hours, 5:15am, 1pm and 3pm); both the music and air-con are on full blast.

Taxis (☎809-481-8526) are available at a stand just in front of the main town beach (as well as a more expensive stand near the beach at Grand Paradise Samaná resort). Sample one-way fares are US$100 to Las Terrenas, US$45 to Samaná, US$75 to Aeropuerto Catey, US$100 to Las Terrenas and US$220 to Santo Domingo. You may be able to negotiate cheaper fares, especially to Samaná.

Renting a car is an excellent way to explore the peninsula on your own. Prices are generally around RD$2700 per day with insurance; **RP Rent-a-Car** (☎809-538-0249; jreyes.jdrv@gmail.com; Principal; ⏲8am-5pm Mon-Fri, to 3pm Sat) is one option.

NORTH COAST

On the Dominican Republic's north coast, you'll find world-class beaches, water sports galore and out-of-the-way locales evocative of timeless rural life. This long coastal corridor stretching from the Haitian border in the west to Río San Juan in the east has enclaves of condo-dwelling expat communities that have endowed some towns with a whiff of international flavor. There are forested hills, dry desert scrublands, and jungly nature preserves with tumbling waterfalls. There are sleepy little towns with laundry drying on clotheslines, old folks holding court at sidewalk bars and mile after mile of sandy beaches. There's also the genteel, urban vibe of Puerto Plata, whose classic Caribbean architecture – Victorian-era buildings painted in bright pastels – belies its past as a regional capital. Independent travelers will find accommodations of all stripes and several good places to base themselves for further exploration, especially Cabarete, where you can kitesurf, surf or just plain bodysurf.

Cabarete

POP 14,600

This one-time fishing and farming hamlet is now the adventure-sports capital of the country, booming with condos and new development. You'll find a friendly, slightly raucous beach town, with great independent accommodations, and a beach dining experience second to none (not to mention the best winds and waves on the island). Cabarete is an ideal spot to base yourself for exploring the area – you're within two hours' drive of the best that the coast has to offer, and if you want to go surfing, or windsurfing, or kitesurfing, heck, you don't even need to leave town. You'll hear a babble of five or six languages as you walk Cabarete's single street, where the majority of the hotels, restaurants and shops are located.

Beaches

Cabarete's beaches are its main attractions, and not just for sun and sand. They're each home to a different water sport, and are great places to watch beginner and advanced athletes alike.

Kite Beach BEACH
Two kilometers west of town. A sight to behold on windy days, when scores of kiters of all skill levels negotiate huge sails and 30m lines amid the waves and traffic. On those days there's no swimming here, as you're liable to get run over.

Playa Encuentro BEACH
Four kilometers west of town. The place to go for surfing, though top windsurfers and kitesurfers sometimes come to take advantage of the larger waves. The beach itself is a long, narrow stretch of sand backed by lush tropical vegetation; strong tides and rocky shallows make swimming here difficult. To find the beach, look for the fading yellow archway and sign that says 'Coconut Palms Resort.' Definitely not safe to walk around here at night.

Playa Cabarete BEACH
Main beach in front of town. Ideal for watching windsurfing, though the very best windsurfers are well offshore at the reef line. Look for them performing huge high-speed jumps and even end-over-end flips. It can get a little leery here for solo women.

Activities

Kele Surf School SURFING
(☎809 445 0197; www.kelesurf.com; Playa Encuentro; group lesson per hour US$40, board rental per day $US20; ⏲7am-4pm) Owned by an inspiring young woman who grew up in Encuentro and works as a fashion model, Kele Surf School is hands down the best choice for aspiring female surfers. Her equipment is top quality and her prices are competitive.

Northern Coast Diving DIVING
(☎800-222-4545; www.northerncoastdiving.com) Well-respected Sosúa-based dive shop with a representative in Iguana Mama. Organizes excursions from Laguna Dudu in the east to Monte Cristi in the west.

Cabarete Surf Camp SURFING
(☎829-548-6655; www.cabaretesurfcamp.com; Calle B1, Pro Cab) One of the most popular camps in Cabarete, with fantastic accommodations and instructors. Also offers kitesurfing lessons.

Tours

★**Iguana Mama** OUTDOORS
(☎809-654-2325, 809-571-0908; www.iguanamama.com; Principal) This professional and family-run adventure-sports tour operator is in a class of its own. Its specialties are mountain biking (from US$50) – from easy to insanely difficult – and canyoning. Trips to Damajagua (US$89) go to the uppermost waterfall, and Iguana Mama pioneered a canyoning tour to Ciguapa Falls, which only this operator offers. The highest jump is over 10m.

Sleeping

★**Surf Break Cabarete** B&B $
(☎829-921-4080; www.surfbreakcabarete.com; Playa Encuentro; s/d incl breakfast from US$30/45; P❄📶🏊) The best-value stay in Playa Encuentro offers both surf and yoga packages, along with a range of serene, palapa-topped accommodations in two lush complexes. The pool area and yoga studio are superbly tranquil, and the owner is friendly and helpful. This is the hotel of choice for women traveling alone (and anybody else, really).

Cabarete Surf Camp HOSTEL $
(☎829-548-6655; www.cabaretesurfcamp.com; Calle B1, Pro Cab; s/d/apt incl breakfast & dinner from US$22/33/75; P❄📶🏊) On the edge of a lagoon a five-minute walk inland, this lushly landscaped property has small, colorful and rustic backpacker-style cabins; larger, modern rooms with kitchenettes in a two-story building; and two colonial-style, all-wood rooms with louvered windows in a 'tower' above the kitchen and dining area.

★**Natura Cabañas** RESORT $$$
(☎809-571-1507; www.naturacabana.com; r incl breakfast US$256; P@🏊) Owned and designed by a husband-and-wife team, this collection of marvelously designed, Thai-inspired thatched-roof bungalows about halfway between Cabarete and Sosúa is the epitome of rustic chic. Everything is constructed from natural materials – mahogany, bamboo and stone – and a gravel path leads

to a secluded beach. Two open-air restaurants serve delicious, health-conscious smoothies and meals (RD$500 to RD$1100).

Eating

Dining out on Cabarete's beach is the quintessential Caribbean experience – fairy lights hanging from palm trees, a gentle ocean breeze and excellent food (even if it does cost the same as you'd pay back home). Many of the bars on the beach serve good food as well, but note that many close up for part of October.

Wilson's at La Boca BARBECUE $
(809-610-1158; mains RD$300; 9:45am-6:45pm) This is a little BBQ shack on the Yasica River in Islabon, around 8km southeast of town on the way to Sabaneta de Yasica. The eponymous Wilson, who speaks perfect English, serves up wood-fired fish, chicken and lobster.

Vagamundo Coffee & Waffles CAFE $
(www.vagamundocoffee.com; Principal; waffles RD$100-250; 7am-4pm; P) Just outside of town, this third-wave coffee shop offers all the latest in coffee. Its aesthetic, with mason jars, pallet furniture, lanterns and a 2000s nostalgia soundtrack, feels like the love child of Brooklyn and Coachella went on spring break to the Caribbean. That said, the coffee and food are familiar and delicious.

La Casita de Papi SEAFOOD $$$
(809-986-3750; mains RD$890; noon-11pm Tue-Sun;) An institution in Cabarete, this homey beachfront restaurant does a great garlic shrimp paella dish as well as lobster and grilled fish, under twinkling fairy lights strung between palm trees. It's one of the best places on the beach.

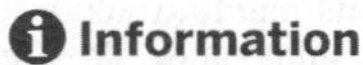

Information

There's a **Banco León** (Principal; 9am-5pm Mon-Fri, to 1pm Sat), **Banco Popular** (Principal; 9am-4:30pm Mon-Fri, to 1pm Sat) and **Scotiabank** (Principal; 9am-5pm Mon-Fri, to 1pm Sat) on Calle Principal.

Cestur (Tourist Police; 809-571-0713, 809-754-3036; Principal) At the eastern entrance to town.

Lavandería Janko (Principal; per kg RD$30; 9am-6pm Mon-Sat) Same day laundry service on the eastern end of town, opposite Janet's Supermarket.

Servi-Med (809-571-0964; Principal; 24hr) English, German and Spanish are spoken, and travel medical insurance and credit cards accepted.

Getting There & Around

BUS

None of the main bus companies offer services to Cabarete – the closest depots are in Sosúa. They zip through town without stopping on their

WORTH A TRIP

TWENTY-SEVEN WATERFALLS

Travelers routinely describe the tour of the **waterfalls** (829-639-2492; www.27charcos.com; Damajagua; highest waterfall RD$700, organized tour US$80-100) at Damajagua as 'the coolest thing I did in the DR.' We agree. Guides lead you up, via a path, stairs, over a new suspension bridge, swimming through pools and climbing through the waterfalls. To get down you jump – as much as 8m – into the sparkling pools below.

It's mandatory to go with a guide, but there's no minimum group size, so you can go solo if you wish. You can go up to the seventh, 12th or 27th waterfall, though most 'jeep safari' package tours only go to the seventh. You should be in good shape and over the age of 12. Foreigners pay RD$700 to the highest waterfall and less to reach the lower ones (US$1 of every entrance fee goes to a community development fund). Tour companies in Puerto Plata, Sosúa and Cabarete organize trips here for between US$80 and US$100. The falls are open from 8:30am to 3pm, but go early before the crowds arrive. A visitors center and restaurant are near the entrance.

To get to the falls, go south from Imbert on the highway for 3.3km (and cross two bridges) until you see a sign on your left with pictures of a waterfall. From there it's about 1km down to the visitors center. Alternatively, take a **Javilla Tours** (809-970-2412; cnr Camino Real & Av Colón; buses every 15min 5am-7:30pm) *guagua* (local bus) from Puerto Plata and ask to get off at the entrance. The big Texaco station at Imbert serves as a crossroads for the entire area. There is a frequent *guagua* service to Santiago (RD$100, one hour) and Puerto Plata (RD$50, 30 minutes).

way to Nagua before turning south to Santo Domingo.

A large, white bus with air-con on its way from Puerto Plata to Samaná stops at the gas station just east of town every day at 1:30pm. From Cabarete, the three-hour trip costs RD$275.

CAR

If you want to rent a car, you can do so at the airport or in town. A good option is **Easy Rider** (☎809-571-9798; www.easyrider-cabarete.com; ⏰8am-7pm), where prices are reasonable and full insurance coverage is provided (you will not be held responsible for damaged windows, tires or anything else). If you're in town and prefer to rent at the airport, you can take a *guagua* to the airport road (just past Sosúa), walk 500m to the terminal and shop around at the numerous car-rental agencies there.

It's around a 2½-hour drive in your own vehicle from Cabarete to Samaná.

GUAGUA

Heaps of *guaguas* ply the coastal road, including east to the hamlet of Sabaneta de Yasica (RD$40) and Río San Juan (RD$100, one hour) and west to Sosúa (RD$35, 20 minutes) and Puerto Plata (RD$110, 45 minutes). Hail them anywhere along Cabarete's main drag.

A *guagua* to Santo Domingo is RD$300, but you're better off catching a bus in Sosúa.

MOTOCONCHO

Transportation in town is dominated by *motoconchos* (motorcycle taxis), who will attempt to charge you two to three times the price you'd pay for a similar ride in Puerto Plata. Don't be surprised if you can't haggle them down. A ride out to Kite Beach should cost RD$75 and Playa Encuentro RD$130.

TAXI

The motorcycle-shy can call a **taxi** (☎809-571-0767; www.taxisosuacabarete.com), which will cost RD$600 to Encuentro, US$45 to Aeropuerto Internacional Gregorío Luperón 18km west, and US$35 to Puerto Plata. For the Santiago airport it's around US$100, and for Santo Domingo its US$200. There's also a taxi stand in the middle of town.

CENTRAL HIGHLANDS

Even die-hard beach fanatics will eventually overdose on sun and sand. When you do, the cool, mountainous playground of the Central Highlands is the place to come: where else can you sit at dusk, huddled in a sweater, and watch the mist descend into the valley as the sun sets behind the mountains? Popular retreats, roaring rivers, soaring peaks and the only white-water rafting in the Caribbean beckon. Down below in the plains of the Valle del Cibao is where merengue spontaneously erupted onto the musical landscape, and where you'll find some of the best Carnival celebrations in the country. Economic life in the Central Highlands revolves around Santiago, the Dominican Republic's second-largest city and the capital of a vast tobacco- and sugarcane-growing region. So, obviously, a visit here requires sipping rum and puffing a local cigar.

Jarabacoa

POP 69,855 / ELEV 529M

Nestled in the low foothills of the Cordillera Central, Jarabacoa maintains an under-the-radar allure as the as the 'City of Eternal Spring.' Nighttime temperatures call for light sweaters, a roiling river winds past forested slopes that climb into the clouds, and there are alpine landscapes around every bend in the road. This is the place to base yourself if you want to get into the mountains, via raft, bike, horse or on foot. At weekends, locals head 4km north of town to the Balneario la Confluencia, where the Río Yaque and Río Jimenoa meet, to swim and picnic. In the evenings, join them to share stories of adrenaline-pumping exploits over beers near the town's Parque Central. But you won't have to rough it: thousands of well-to-do Dominicans from Santo Domingo and Santiago have built summer homes here, which has upped the quotient of good restaurants and hotels in the area.

Activities & Tours

Rancho Baiguate ADVENTURE SPORTS
(☎809-574-6890; www.ranchobaiguate.com; Carretera a Constanza) Rancho Baiguate is recommended for safety and reliability. Activities offered range from rafting (US$50) to canyoning at Salto de Baiguate (US$50) to mountain biking (from US$25); it also offers waterfall tours (from US$18) and trips to Pico Duarte (three-day trip from US$255 per person).

Sleeping

★**Jarabacoa Mountain Hostel** HOSTEL $
(☎809-574-6117; dm/s/d/q from US$18/30/37/51; P❄📶) About 15 minutes' walk from town, this 'hostel' is actually a modern, two-story

WORTH A TRIP

PLAYA GRANDE & PLAYA PRECIOSA

Just 8km east of Río San Juan is Playa Grande, one of the most beautiful beaches in the DR. The long, broad, tawny beach has aquamarine water on one side and a thick fringe of palm trees on the other, with stark white cliffs jutting out into the ocean in the distance. A surf school here offers lessons.

Facilities at the eastern end of the beach include a little 'village' of pastel-colored clapboard shacks selling freshly caught seafood such as lobsters, prawns and grilled snapper served with rice and plantains, and piña coladas made with real pineapple and coconut juice. These amenities and the newly paved access road have diminished the previously remote and wild feel of the area. Vendors rent beach chairs (per day RD$200), umbrellas (per day RD$200), snorkel equipment (per day RD$500), bodyboards (per hour RD$200) and surfboards (per hour RD$500). If seeking solitude, walk west along the beach, away from the entrance.

Only 25m down a path leaving from just in front of Playa Grande's bathrooms is another spectacular stretch of sand called Playa Preciosa. The waves are enormous, and tend to attract surfers at dawn.

A word about safety: these beaches have heavy surf and a deceptively strong undertow. Riptides – powerful currents flowing out to sea – form occasionally, and people have drowned here.

If you take a *guagua* (local bus) from town, drivers will let you off just before the security gate marking the entrance to the beaches. You can also hire a *motoconcho* (motorcycle taxi; RD$150) or a taxi (RD$300) to take you directly there.

home, with a state-of-the-art, fully equipped kitchen and a variety of plush rooms, the best of which offer a balcony and hot tub. The extremely knowledgeable owners help guests plan their trips and provide complimentary coffee, laundry machines and bicycles.

Sonido del Yaque CABIN $

(Cabanas Cazuelas de Dona Esperanza; 809-727-7413; www.sonidodelyaque.com; Los Calabazos; r from RD$950) This community-tourism project consists of six wood and concrete cabins, each with bunks and a porch, set amid lush jungle above the roaring Río Yaque del Norte. There's electricity, hot showers and mosquito nets. Meals are available with notice. It's not signposted; coming from Jarabacoa, look for a tiny shop at the right-hand side of the road.

Hotel Gran Jimenoa HOTEL $$

(809-574-6304; www.granjimenoahotel.com; Av La Confluencia; s/d/tr incl breakfast from US$51/64/78; P ❄ @ ☕ ≋) Set several kilometers north of town right by the roaring Río Jimenoa, this is the Cordillera Central's most upscale hotel. It's neither on the beach nor an all-inclusive hotel, but you could easily spend a restful week here exploring the extensive grounds, which include a footbridge to a bar on the far riverbank.

Villa Celeste Estate B&B $$$

(829-766-3524; Los Pinos; r incl breakfast from US$99; P ❄ ☕ ≋) About 14km north of Jarabacoa, this divine eight-room guesthouse is tucked away in a private gated community designed, rather oddly, to mimic the Swiss Alps. The well-constructed, multilevel home features contemporary furnishings, colonial details and a classy rooftop gazebo that looks over the backyard swimming pool and the surrounding greenery, which can also be viewed from the rooms' terraces.

Eating

★La Baita ITALIAN $$

(809-365-8778, 829-451-0379; marco.brand@hotmail.it; Av La Confluencia 74; mains from RD$450; 11am-2pm & 5-11pm Mon & Wed-Fri, 11am-11pm Sat & Sun) This little Italian place north of town nails it with homemade pastas, wood-fired pizzas and imported meats and cheeses. The affable owner-chef helps guests select the perfect glass of Italian wine to go with any main dish, be it traditional pasta with sauce or fresh Caribbean fish.

Aroma de la Montaña INTERNATIONAL $$$

(829-452-6879; www.aromadelamontana.com; mains RD$600-1500; 8am-midnight; P ❄ ☕) Sweeping, practically aerial views of the Jarabacoa countryside are available from the terrace of this mountaintop restaurant, which holds the distinction of being the only rotating restaurant in the Caribbean. Lunchtime has a family atmosphere, but there's a romantic candlelit vibe in the evening (despite techno remixes of Justin Bieber). The menu includes steakhouse and Dominican favorites.

Information

Banco Popular (☎809-544-5555; Av La Confluencia; ⏲9am-5pm Mon-Fri, to 1pm Sat) In Plaza La Confluencia.

Cestur (Tourist Police; ☎809-754-3068, 809-754-3072; Miguel M Castillo) Behind the Caribe Tours terminal.

Clínica Dr Terrero (☎829-460-1691; Av Independencia 2A)

Getting There & Away

BUS

Públicos to Constanza (RD$150, 40 minutes, about 9am, 11:30am and 1:30pm) leave from diagonally opposite the Shell petrol station (at the corner of Duverge and Calle El Carmen). *Publicos* to La Ciénaga (RD$150, 1½ hours, about every two hours) leave from Calle Odulio Jiménez near Calle 16 de Agosto. The road is 42km long, of which the first 33km is mostly paved. (Returning can be a challenge, especially if you're coming back from an afternoon hike. Organize a taxi to collect you, or take your chances with hailing a ride on the road.)

Guaguas provide frequent services to La Vega (RD$90, 30 minutes, every 10 to 30 minutes, 6am to 6pm) leaving from the **terminal** (cnr Av Independencia & José Duran). Express *guaguas* to La Vega, with no stops on the way, leave from the same terminal but cost RD$100.

Caribe Tours (☎809-574-4796; www.caribetours.com.do; Leopoldo Jiménez) offers the only 1st-class bus service to/from Jarabacoa. It has four daily departures to Santo Domingo (RD$350, 2½ hours, 7am, 10am, 1:30pm and 4:30pm), which stop in La Vega (RD$100, 45 minutes).

CAR

The asphalt road to Constanza has made this scenic drive a breeze as far as your car's shock absorbers are concerned; dozens of switchbacks, however, will test your driving skills. Once you hit El Río, the remaining 19km passes through a lush valley.

TAXI

A cab to La Vega costs around RD$1000.

THE SOUTHWEST & PENÍNSULA DE PEDERNALES

Talk about criminally undervisited. Few travelers make it to the southwest of the Dominican Republic: it's fairly remote, and its highlights take some effort to uncover – but that's exactly the reason to visit. Heading west from Santo Domingo takes you not only in the opposite direction to the eastern beach resorts but also to a different DR – one whose landscape isn't defined by tourism but by scenes of everyday life. You can explore the cloud forests of the mountains with their soundtrack of birdsong, or the cactus-studded desert that stretches all the way to the Haitian border. Then there's the stunning coastline of the Península de Pedernales, which offers miles of empty sands and clear turquoise sea. If you make it to the Bahía de Las Águilas, a deserted 10km stretch of postcard-perfect beach, you'll feel as though you've hit the travel jackpot.

Península de Pedernales

The Península de Pedernales contains some outstanding natural attractions: the sublime beach at Bahía de Las Águilas, supersalty Laguna Oviedo, Parque Nacional Jaragua, the cloud forest of Cachóte and world-class birdwatching in the Parque Nacional Sierra de Bahoruco. Despite all this, tourism in this part of the country is surprisingly low.

The peninsula was originally a separate island, but tectonic movement pushed it north and upward into Hispaniola, closing the sea channel that once ran from Port-au-Prince to Barahona and creating many of the unique geographical features you see today.

The southwest is the best place on the island to go birdwatching, as you can see nearly all Hispaniola's endemic species here. At last count, there were roughly 310 known species of bird in the DR and 32 endemic bird species on the island. Half of these are migratory, making winter the best time to spot them.

Bahía de Las Águilas

Bahía de Las Águilas is the kind of beach that fantasies are made of. This pristine utopia is located in the extremely remote southwestern corner of the DR, but those who make it here are rewarded with 10km of nearly deserted shore, forming a gentle arc between two prominent capes. It's reachable mainly by boat from Playa Las Cuevas, a tiny and remote fishing community and the nearest settlement – the ride weaves in and out of rocky outcrops and past gorgeous cliffs with cacti clinging to their craggy edges and sea-diving pelicans nearby. Paradise found.

The gorgeously located **Rancho Tipico** (☎809-753-8058; cuevasdelasaguilas@hotmail.com; Playa Las Cuevas; mains RD$350-750; ⊙8am-7pm) restaurant in Playa Las Cuevas offers boat tours of the bay, including stunningly perfect beaches. Prices range from RD$2200 per boat for groups of one to five to RD$325 per person for 16 to 20 people. The owner rents snorkeling kits for RD$600.

You can also negotiate with the guides and boatmen who gather around the national-park ranger station just off the parking lot in Las Cuevas and mill about the small pier a few meters past Rancho Tipico. Snorkeling gear is included in their prices, but they don't always have it, so bring your own if you can. If you arrive here solo, the best option is to form a group to share the boat ride – easier at weekends, when it's busy.

With all choices you'll also need to pay the national-park entrance fee (RD$100) at the ranger station.

Ecotour Barahona (☎809-856-2260, 849-856-2260; www.ecotourbarahona.com; Apt 306, Carretera Enriquillo 8, Paraíso; ⊙9am-6pm) runs a day trip here (US$99). It organizes all the logistics, picks you up and drops you off at your hotel, supplies lunch, and can show you where the best coral is for snorkeling.

Fancy glamping in paradise? **Eco del Mar** (☎829-576-7740, 809-906-8170; www.ecodelmar.com.do; Playa Las Cuevas; per person incl breakfast RD$900-1500), has professional- style camping tents, strewn about the sands of Playa Las Cuevas. There's an excellent restaurant (mains RD$350 to RD$1150), but the real coup here is the stylish beach bar in the round.

To get to the beach, take the paved (and signposted) road to Cabo Rojo, about 12km east of Pedernales. You'll reach the port of Cabo Rojo after 6km.

South of Barahona

Once you pass Barahona's southernmost military checkpoint on the highway heading towards Pedernales, things begin to feel a bit more wild: the road hugs the peninsula on the right and there's a sea on the left that veers from pure turquoise to cobalt. Some of the best hotels and resorts in the southwest can be found here. Eventually the adjoining seaside villages of Bahoruco and La Ciénaga emerge: two typical small communities in the heart of larimar-mineral country, with curious locals and gravelly beaches used for mooring boats rather than swimming. From there things take a dramatic turn as the highway crests at one of the most beautiful landscapes in the southwest. An impossible swirl of cerulean sea commands your attention as the road rolls into tiny, aptly named Paraíso, and Los Patos beyond, home to yet another heavenly beach.

On Playa San Rafael, beach-bum-turned entrepreneur Raylin Romero's **San Rafael Surf School y Eco Tours** (☎829-729-8239; www.sanrafaelsurfschool.com; Playa San Rafael; ⊙9am-4pm Mon-Fri, 8am-5pm Sat & Sun) runs surf lessons, beach camping trips and hikes to Taíno caves and nearby larimar mine. **Casa Bonita** (☎809-476-5059; www.casabonitadr.com; Carretera Barahona-Paraíso Km 17; r incl breakfast from US$250, villas US$540; P ❄ @ ≈), one of the country's most spectacularly situated hotels, is set on a hill with stunning Caribbean and mountain views and features 16 newer rooms, all stunningly furnished and with private plunge pools.

UNDERSTAND THE DOMINICAN REPUBLIC

The Dominican Republic Today

The Dominican Republic has enjoyed an economic heyday of late, with tourism booming and free-trade zones flourishing, but stubborn problems have lingered, namely corrupt politicians and trouble with Haiti. Add to that some pretty bad weather and you can bet that average Dominicans, who are no strangers to hardship, approach the present with a healthy dose of skepticism.

In 2015 GDP was growing at 7%, the fastest rate of any country in Latin America, thanks to healthy tourism, construction and mining industries. Inflation was relatively low, and around US$1 billion was coming in via remittances from more than a million Dominicans living abroad. Although sugar, coffee and tobacco had for decades been the country's largest employers, the service sector overtook agriculture both in the number of jobs it provided and the revenue it brought in. In 2016 more than six million tourists are estimated to have visited the DR, which generated more than US$6.5 billion in revenue.

Unfortunately, corruption has remained a problem in the Dominican Republic, at all levels of government and within the private sector. The most recent example of this is the Odebrecht scandal.

Trouble with Haiti also persists, and in September 2013, the Dominican Constitutional Court ruled that 'people born in the Dominican Republic to undocumented parents' weren't automatically afforded citizenship themselves. The decision, which applied to anyone born after 1929, was condemned by many as a racist ruling that targets Dominicans of Haitian descent. In response to this, the government created a 'regularization process' in 2015 that allowed people to apply for residency.

In late 2016, just after Hurricane Matthew swung through and decimated southern Haiti, heavy rains fell for more than two weeks on the DR's north coast, causing widespread damage to the country's agriculture and infrastructure and forcing the president to declare a national emergency.

History

First Arrivals

Before Christopher Columbus arrived, the indigenous Taínos (meaning 'Friendly People') lived on the island now known as Hispaniola. Taínos gave the world sweet potatoes, peanuts, guava, pineapple and tobacco – even the word 'tobacco' is Taíno in origin. Yet the Taínos themselves were wiped out by Spanish diseases and slavery. Of the 400,000 Taínos who lived on Hispaniola at the time of European arrival, fewer than 1000 were still alive 30 years later. None exist today.

Independence & Occupation

Two colonies grew on Hispaniola, one Spanish and the other French. Both brought thousands of African slaves to work the land. In 1804, after a 70-year struggle, the French colony gained independence. Haiti, the Taíno name for the island, was the first majority-black republic in the New World. In 1821 colonists in Santo Domingo declared their independence from Spain. Haiti, which had long aspired to unify the island, promptly invaded its neighbor and occupied it for more than two decades. But Dominicans never accepted Haitian rule and on February 27, 1844, Juan Pablo Duarte – considered the father of the country – led a bloodless coup and reclaimed Dominican autonomy. The country resubmitted to Spanish rule shortly thereafter but became independent for good in 1864. The young country endured one disreputable *caudillo* (military leader) after the other. In 1916 US President Woodrow Wilson sent the marines to the Dominican Republic, ostensibly to quell a coup attempt, but they ended up occupying the country for eight years. Though imperialistic, this occupation succeeded in stabilizing the DR.

The Rise of Caudillo

Rafael Leonidas Trujillo, the then chief of the Dominican national police, maneuvered his way into the presidency in February 1930 and dominated the country until his assassination in 1961. He implemented a brutal system of repression, killing and imprisoning political opponents. Trujillo was also known to be deeply racist and xenophobic. In October 1937, after hearing reports that Haitian peasants were crossing into the DR, perhaps to steal cattle, he ordered the execution of all Haitians along the border and in a matter of days some 20,000 were killed. Trujillo never openly admitted a massacre had taken place, but in 1938, under international pressure, he and Haitian president Sténio Vicente agreed the DR would pay US$750,000 (US$50 per person) as reparation. During these years Trujillo and his wife established monopolies and by 1934 he was the richest man on the island. Many Dominicans remember Trujillo's rule with a certain amount of fondness and nostalgia, in part because he did develop the economy. Factories were opened, a number of grandiose infrastructure and public-works projects were carried out, bridges and highways were built and peasants were given state land to cultivate.

Caudillo Redux

Joaquín Balaguer was president at the time of Trujillo's assassination. Civil unrest and another US occupation followed Trujillo's death, but Balaguer eventually regained the presidency, to which he clung fiercely for the next 12 years. And like his mentor, Balaguer remained a major political force long after he gave up official control. In 1986 he became president again, despite frail health and blindness. Repressive economic policies sent the peso tumbling. Dominicans whose savings had evaporated protested and were met with violence from the national police. Many fled to the US. By the end of 1990, 12% of the Dominican population – 900,000 people – had moved to New York.

After the 1990 and 1994 elections, widely accepted as being rigged by Balaguer, the military had grown weary of Balaguer's rule. He agreed to cut his last term short, hold elections and, most importantly, not run as a candidate. But it wouldn't be his last campaign – he would run once more at the age of 92, winning 23% of the vote in the 2000 presidential election. Thousands would mourn his death two years later, even though he had prolonged the Trujillo-style dictatorship for decades. His most lasting legacy may be the Faro a Colón, an enormously expensive monument to the discovery of the Americas that drained Santo Domingo of electricity whenever the lighthouse was turned on.

Breaking with the Past

The Dominican people signaled their desire for change in electing Leonel Fernández, a 42-year-old lawyer who grew up in New York City, as president in 1996; he edged out three-time candidate José Francisco Peña Gómez in a runoff. Still, the speed of his initial moves shocked the nation. Fernández forcibly retired two dozen generals, encouraged his defense minister to submit to questioning by the civilian attorney general and fired the defense minister for insubordination – all in a single week. In the four years of his first presidential term, he presided over strong economic growth and privatization, and lowered inflation and high rates of unemployment and illiteracy – accusations of endemic corruption, however, remained pervasive.

Hipólito Mejía, a former tobacco farmer, succeeded Fernández in 2000 and immediately cut spending and increased fuel prices, not exactly the platform he ran on. The faltering US economy and September 11 attacks ate into Dominican exports, as well as cash remittances and foreign tourism. Corruption scandals involving the civil service, unchecked spending, electricity shortages and several bank failures, which cost the government in the form of huge bailouts for depositors, all spelled doom for Mejía's re-election chances.

More of the Same

Familiar faces reappear again and again in Dominican politics and Fernández returned to the national stage by handily defeating Mejía in the 2004 presidential elections. In May 2008, with the US and world economies faltering and continued conflict with Haiti, Fernández was re-elected to yet another presidential term. He avoided a runoff despite mounting questions about the logic of spending US$700 million on Santo Domingo's subway system, rising gas prices, the fact that the DR still had one of the highest rates of income inequality in Latin America and the government's less-than-stellar response to the devastation wrought by Tropical Storm Noel in late October 2007.

Though considered competent and by some even forward-thinking, Fernández was also a typical politician beholden to special interests. The more cynical observers long claimed that the Fernández administration was allied with corrupt business and government officials, and they were proven correct long after Fernández left office, when the Odebrecht scandal unraveled in 2016. During Fernandez' term, a Brazilian construction company caught bribing DR officials with US$92 million – which in turn allowed the company to collect US$163 million in profit, according to US Justice Department documents – had nine projects going on in the country.

People & Culture

History is alive and well in the DR. With a past filled with strong-arm dictators and corrupt politicians, the average Dominican approaches the present with a healthy skepticism – why should things change now? What is extraordinary to the traveler is that despite this there's a general equanimity, or at the very least an ability to look on the bright side of things. It's not a cliché to say that Dominicans are willing to hope for the best and expect the worst – with a fortitude and patience that isn't common.

In general, it's an accepting and welcoming culture, though Dominicans' negative attitudes toward Haitian immigration has not subsided. 'If the country could just solve the "Haiti problem" things would work out' is not an unusual sentiment to hear. Almost a quarter of Dominicans live in Santo Domingo, which is without question the country's political, economic and social center. But a large percentage of Dominicans still live by agriculture (or by fishing, along the coast).

Dominican families are large and very close-knit. Children are expected to stay close to home and help care for their parents as they grow older. That so many young Dominicans go to the US creates a unique stress in their families – it's no surprise that Dominicans living abroad send so much money home. The DR is a Catholic country, though not to the degree practiced in other Latin American countries – the churches are well maintained but often empty – and Dominicans have a liberal attitude toward premarital and recreational sex. This does not extend to homosexuality, though, which is still fairly taboo.

Baseball

Not just the USA's game, *beísbol* is an integral part of the Dominican social and cultural landscape. Dominican ballplayers who have made the major league are the most revered figures in the country, and over 400 have done so, including stars like David Ortiz, Albert Pujols, Robinson Canó and Sammy Sosa. In 2018, 84 players on the opening day rosters came from the DR (10 more than Venezuela), and pitchers Juan Marichal and Pedro Martinez and, in 2018, right fielder Vladimir Guerrero have all been inducted into the Hall of Fame.

The Dominican professional baseball league's season runs from October to January, and is known as the Liga de Invierno (Winter League). The winner of the DR league competes in the Caribbean World Series against other Latin American countries. The country has six professional teams. Because the US and Dominican seasons don't overlap, many Dominican players in the US major leagues and quite a few non-Dominicans play in the winter league in the DR as well.

Needless to say, the quality of play is high, but even if you're not a fan of the sport, it's worth checking out a game or two. It's always a fun afternoon or evening. Fans are decked out in their respective team's colors waving pennants and flags, as rabidly partisan as the Yankees–Red Sox rivalry, and dancers perform to loud merengue beats on top of the dugouts between innings. Games usually don't start on time and the stands aren't filled until several innings have passed. The best place to take in a game is Estadio Quisqueya (p406) in Santo Domingo. For tickets, head to the stadium with time to spare before the start of play (as early as possible for big games).

Music & Dance

Life in the Dominican Republic seems to move to a constant, infectious rhythm, and music has always been an important part of the country's heritage. Despite, or perhaps in part because of, the country's tumultuous history of bitter divisions, revolutions and dictatorial rule, the DR has made significant contributions to the musical world, giving rise to some of Latin music's most popular and influential styles.

Merengue is the national dance music of the Dominican Republic. From the minute you arrive until the minute you leave, merengue will be coming at you full volume: in restaurants, public buses, taxis, at the beach or simply walking down the street. Rhythmically driven and heavy on the downbeat, merengue follows a common 2-4 or 4-4 beat pattern and Domnicans dance to it with passion and flair. But what sets merengue apart from other musical forms is the presence of traditional signature instruments and how they work within the two- or four-beat structure. Merengue is typically played with a two-headed drum called a tambora, a guitar, an accordion-like instrument known as a melodeon, and a *güira* – a metal instrument that looks a little like a cheese grater and is scraped using a metal or plastic rod.

Whereas merengue might be viewed as an urban sound, *bachata* is definitely the nation's 'country' music, of love and broken hearts in the hinterlands. Born in the poorest of Dominican neighborhoods, *bachata* emerged in the mid-20th century, after Trujillo's death, as a slow, romantic style played on the Spanish guitar. The term initially referred to informal, sometimes rowdy backyard parties in rural areas, finally emerging in Santo Domingo shanties.

The term '*bachata*' was meant as a slight by the urban elite, a reference to the music's supposed lack of sophistication. Often called 'songs of bitterness,' *bachata* tunes were no different from most romantic ballad forms, such as the Cuban bolero, but were perceived as low class, and didn't have the same political or social support as merengue. In fact, *bachata* was not even regarded as a style per se until the 1960s – and even then it was not widely known outside the Dominican Republic.

Salsa, like *bachata*, is heard throughout the Caribbean, and is very popular in the DR. Before they called it salsa, many musicians in New York City had already explored the possibilities of blending Cuban rhythms with jazz. In the 1950s, the Latin big-band era found favor with dancers and listeners alike, and in the mid-1960s, Dominican flutist, composer and producer Johnny Pacheco founded the Fania label, which was exclusively dedicated to recording 'tropical Latin' music.

With Cuba cut off from the US politically as well as culturally, it was no longer appropriate to use the term 'Afro-Cuban'. The word 'salsa' (literally 'sauce') emerged as a clever marketing tool, reflecting not only the music but the entire atmosphere, and was the perfect appellation for a genre of music resulting from a mixture of styles: Cuban-based rhythms played by Puerto Ricans, Dominicans, Africans and African Americans.

Landscape & Wildlife

If wealth were measured by landscape, the DR would be among the richest countries in the Americas. Sharing the island of Hispaniola, the second-largest island in the Caribbean (after Cuba), it's a dynamic country of high mountains, fertile valleys and watered plains, and an amazing diversity of ecosystems.

The island's geography owes more to the Central American mainland than its mostly flat neighboring islands. The one thing that Hispaniola has in spades is an abundance of mountains. Primary among mountain ranges is the Cordillera Central that runs from Santo Domingo into Haiti, where it becomes the Massif du Nord, fully encompassing a third of the island's landmass. The Cordillera Central is home to Pico Duarte, the Caribbean's highest mountain (at 3087m), which is so big it causes a rain shadow that makes much of southwest DR very arid. Other ranges include the Cordillera Septentrional, rising dramatically from the coast near Cabarete, and the Cordillera Orientale, along the southern shoreline of Bahía de Samaná.

Between the ranges lies a series of lush and fertile valleys. Coffee, rice, bananas and tobacco all thrive here, as well as in the plains around Santo Domingo. In comparison, sections of southwest DR are semidesert and studded with cacti. The rich landscape is matched by an equally rich biodiversity with more than 5600 species of plants and close to 500 vertebrate species on the island, many of these endemic.

More than 300 species of bird have been recorded in the DR, including more than two dozen found nowhere else in the world. Abundant, colorful species include the white-tailed tropicbird, magnificent frigatebird, roseate spoonbill and greater flamingo, plus unique endemic species such as the Hispaniolan lizard-cuckoo, ashy-faced owl and Hispaniolan emerald hummingbird.

SURVIVAL GUIDE

Directory A–Z

ACCESSIBLE TRAVEL

Few Latin American countries are well suited for travelers with disabilities, and the Dominican Republic is no different. On the other hand, all-inclusive resorts can be ideal for travelers with mobility impairments, as rooms, meals and daytime and nighttime activities are all within close proximity, and there are plenty of staff members to help you navigate around the property. Some resorts have a few wheelchair-friendly rooms, with larger doors and handles in the bathroom. And, it should be said, Dominicans tend to be extremely helpful and accommodating people. Travelers with disabilities should expect some curious stares, but also quick and friendly help from perfect strangers and passersby.

Two associations in Santo Domingo that provide information and assistance to travelers with disabilities are the **Asociación Dominicana de Rehabilitación** (809-689-7151; www.adr.org.do) and the **Fundación Dominicana de Ciegos** (809-684-6253; cnr Av Expreso V Centenario & Tunti Cáceres; 7am-3:30pm Mon-Fri).

ACCOMMODATIONS

Compared to other destinations in the Caribbean, lodging in the Dominican Republic is relatively affordable. That said, there are limited options for independent travelers wishing to make decisions on the fly and for whom cost is a concern.

ELECTRICITY

Power plugs and sockets are of type A and B (110V, 60 Hz).

EMERGENCY NUMBERS

Emergency	911
Fire	112

EMBASSIES & CONSULATES

All of the following are located in Santo Domingo.

Canadian Embassy (809-262-3100; Av Winston Churchill 1099)

French Consulate (809-695-4300; Calle Las Damas 42)

German Embassy (809-542-8950; Núñez de Cáceres 11)

Haitian Embassy (809-686-7115; Calle Juan Sánchez Ramírez 33)

Netherlands Embassy (809-262-0320; Nuñez de Cáceres 11)

UK Embassy (809-472-7111; Av 27 de Febrero 233)

US Embassy (809-567-7775; Av República de Colombia 57

FOOD

Some visitors to the Dominican Republic never experience a meal outside of their all-inclusive resort, which can seem like a bargain. For travelers hoping to eat out on their own, food can be surprisingly expensive. Of course, prices tend to be much higher in heavily touristed areas, such as the Zona Colonial in Santo Domingo (comparable to US and European prices), and cheaper in small towns and isolated areas. However, outside of informal food stands and cafeteria-style eateries, a meal without drinks at most restaurants will cost a minimum of RD$450 (US$9), after the 18% ITBIS tax and 10% service charge have been added on. Many restaurants have a range of options, from inexpensive pizza and pasta dishes to pricey lobster meals.

Essential Food

La Bandera The most typical Dominican meal consists of white rice, *habichuela* (red beans), stewed meat, salad and fried green plantains, and is usually accompanied by a fresh fruit juice. It's good, cheap, easy to prepare and nutritionally balanced. Red beans are sometimes swapped for small *moros* (black beans), *gandules* (small green beans) or *lentejas* (lentils).

Guineos (bananas) A staple of Dominican cuisine and served in a variety of ways, including boiled, stewed and candied, but most commonly boiled and mashed, like mashed potatoes. Prepared the same way, but with plantains, the dish is called *mangú*; with pork rinds mixed in it is called *mofongo*. Both are filling and can be served for breakfast, lunch or dinner, either as a side dish or as the main dish.

Seafood Most commonly a fish fillet, usually *mero* (grouper) or *chillo* (red snapper), served in one of four ways: *al ajillo* (with garlic), *al coco* (in coconut sauce), *al criolla* (with a mild tomato sauce) or *a la diabla* (with a spicy tomato sauce). Other seafood such as *cangrejo* (crab), *calamar* (squid), *camarones* (shrimp), *pulp* (octopus), *langosta* (lobster) and *lambí* (conch) are similarly prepared or *al vinagre* (in vinegar sauce), a variation on ceviche.

Chivo Goat meat is popular and presented in many ways. Two of the best are *pierna de chivo asada con ron y cilantro* (roast leg of goat with rum and cilantro) and *chivo guisado en salsa de tomate* (goat stewed in tomato sauce). It's a specialty of the northwest: the highway between Santiago and Monte Cristi is lined with restaurants serving *chivo*.

Locrio This Dominican version of paella comes in a number of different variations and is also known as *arroz con pollo* (chicken with rice). The dish features caramelized chicken and vegetables atop fluffy flavored rice sometimes colored with achiote.

HEALTH

From a medical standpoint, the DR is generally safe as long as you're reasonably careful about what you eat and drink. As always, though, you should purchase travel or health insurance that covers you abroad. Typhoid and hepatitis A and B vaccinations should be considered, along with a prescription for a malaria prophylaxis such as Atovaquone-proguanil, chloroquine, doxycycline or mefloquine.

INTERNET ACCESS

Wi-fi access is widespread in cafes and restaurants, as well as at midrange and top-end hotels and resorts throughout the country. Travelers with laptops won't have far to go before finding some place with a signal. However, some

SLEEPING PRICE RANGES

The following price ranges refer to a double room with bathroom in high season (December to March and July to August). Prices are in the currency quoted on the ground – either RD$ or US$. Unless otherwise indicated the room tax of 28% is included.

$ less than RD$2335 (US$50)

$$ RD$2335–4670 (US$50–100)

$$$ more than RD$4670 (US$100)

EATING PRICE RANGES

The following price ranges refer to the average cost of a main course including tax.

$ Less than RD$230 (US$5)

$$ RD$230–700 (US$5–15)

$$$ More than RD$700 (US$15)

all-inclusives, as opposed to most midrange and even budget hotels, charge daily fees (around US$15 and up) for access. And some hotels that advertise the service free for guests only have a signal in public spaces like the lobby and limited access in guest rooms.

You can also buy a mobile internet device from Altice or Claro for around US$55.

The number of internet cafes is dwindling; most charge RD$35 to RD$70 per hour. Many of these cafes also operate as call centers. Most internet cafes have Spanish language keyboards – the '@' key is usually accessed by pressing 'alt', '6' and '4'.

LGBT+ TRAVELERS

In general, the Dominican Republic is quite open about heterosexual sex and sexuality, but still fairly closed-minded about homosexuality. Prejudice against the LGBT community is fairly widespread, though there has been some progress, in part attributable to Wally Brewster, the vocal and openly gay US ambassador to the DR under the Obama administration.

Gay and lesbian travelers will find the most open community in Santo Domingo, but even its gay clubs are relatively discreet. Santiago, Puerto Plata, Bávaro and Punta Cana also have gay venues, catering as much to foreigners as to locals. Everywhere else, open displays of affection between men are fairly taboo, between women less so. Same-sex couples shouldn't have trouble getting a hotel room.

MONEY

The Dominican monetary unit is the peso, indicated by the symbol RD$ (or sometimes just R$). Many tourist-related businesses, including most midrange and top-end hotels, list prices in US dollars, but accept pesos at the going exchange rate.

ATMs & Credit Cards

ATMs can be found throughout the DR. Credit and debit cards are widely accepted in cities and tourism-related businesses.

Exchange Rates

Australia	A$1	RD$35
Canada	C$1	RD$37
Europe	€1	RD$57
Haiti	HTG3	RD$2
Japan	¥100	RD$46
New Zealand	NZ$1	RD$33
UK	UK£1	RD$66
US	US$1	RD$50

For current exchange rates, see www.xe.com.

Money Changers

Money changers will approach you in a number of tourist centers. They are unlikely to be aggressive. You will get equally favorable rates, however, and a much securer transaction, at an ATM, a bank or a *cambio* (exchange office).

Tipping

A shock to many first-timers, most restaurants add a whopping 28% (ITBIS of 18% and an automatic 10% service charge) to every bill. Menus often don't indicate whether prices include the tax and tip.

Hotels A 10% service charge is often automatically included; however, a US$1 to US$2 per night gratuity left for cleaning staff is worth considering.

Restaurants Generally not expected since 10% is automatically added to the total. If especially impressed, you can add whatever else you feel is deserved.

Taxis Typically, you can round up or give a little extra change.

Tours You should tip tour guides, some of whom earn no other salary.

OPENING HOURS

Opening hours vary throughout the year. Hours generally decrease in the shoulder and low seasons.

Banks 8:30am to 5pm Monday to Friday, 9am to 1pm Saturday.

Bars 8pm to late, to 2am in Santo Domingo.

Government offices 7:30am to 4pm Monday to Friday, officially; in practice more like 9am to 2:30pm.

Restaurants 8am to 10pm Monday to Saturday (some close between lunch and dinner); to 11pm or later in large cities and tourist areas.

Supermarkets 8am to 10pm Monday to Saturday.

Shops 9am to 7:30pm Monday to Saturday; some open half-day Sunday.

PUBLIC HOLIDAYS

New Years Day January 1
Epiphany (Three Kings Day) January 6
Lady of Altagracia January 21
Juan Pablo Duarte Day January 26
Independence Day February 27
Good Friday Friday before Easter
Easter Sunday March/April
Labor Day May 1
Corpus Christi May 31
Restoration Day August 16
Our Lady of Mercedes Day September 24
Constitution Day November 6
Christmas Day December 25

SAFE TRAVEL

The Dominican Republic is not a particularly dangerous place to visit, but tourists should be aware of the following:

- Avoid talking on or looking at cellphones in public (thieves are known to snatch them).
- Don't drive at night, since obstacles like potholes, hard-to-spot speed bumps and other hazards are difficult to discern on unlit roads.
- Consider taking a cab when returning home late from bars, and bypass the beach on nighttime strolls.
- Be aware of and avoid riptides when swimming.
- Car theft is not unheard of, so don't leave valuables inside your car.
- Tensions along the Haitian border flare up occasionally: check the situation before crossing.
- Use purified water for drinking, brushing teeth and hand washing.
- Avoid drinking alcohol from minibar liquor dispensers.

TELEPHONE

For all calls within the DR (even local ones), you must dial 1 + 809 or 829 or 849. There are no regional codes. Toll-free numbers have 200 or 809 for their prefix (not the area code).

The easiest way to make a phone call in the DR is to pay per minute (average rates per minute: to the US US$0.20; to Europe US$0.50; to Haiti US$0.50) at a Codetel Centro de Comunicaciones (Codetel) call center or an internet cafe that operates as a dual call center.

Calling from a hotel is always the most expensive option.

Cell Phones

Local SIM cards can be used or phones can be set for roaming.

VISAS

The vast majority of tourists entering the Dominican Republic arrive by air. Independent travelers typically arrive at the main international airport outside of Santo Domingo, Aeropuerto Internacional Las Américas. Passing through immigration is a relatively simple process, especially now that tourist cards aren't required. You're allowed up to 30 days on a tourist visa. The procedure is the same if you arrive at one of the other airports such as Puerto Plata or Punta Cana; the latter is easily the busiest airport in the country in terms of tourist arrivals.

WOMEN TRAVELERS

Women traveling without men in the Dominican Republic should expect to receive some attention, usually in the form of hissing (to get your attention), stares and comments like *'Hola, preciosa'* (Hello, beautiful). Although it may be unwanted, it's more often a nuisance than anything else. Ignoring the comments is one possible line of defense. Unwanted physical touching, even assault, is of course rarer, but not unheard of, and there have been reports of foreign women travelers being the victim of attacks.

Women travelers should take the same precautions they would in other countries and follow their instincts about certain men or situations they encounter. Young, athletic Dominican men who 'target' foreign women, especially in beach resort areas like Punta Cana, are referred to as 'sanky-pankys'. Their MO is subtly transactional, usually involving 'promises' of affection in exchange for meals, drinks, gifts and cash from generally older North American and European women.

Getting There & Away

There are a variety of ways to get to and from the Dominican Republic, including flights into international airports, overland crossings, international cruiseships and ferries. Flights, cars and tours can be booked online at lonelyplanet.com/bookings.

AIR

There are nine so-called international airports, though at least three are used only for domestic flights. For information on most, check out www.aerodom.com. Perhaps the cheapest route between North America and the DR is Spirit Airlines' Fort Lauderdale to Santiago (around US$195 round trip).

Aeropuerto Internacional Arroyo Barril (DAB; ☎809-794-8807) West of Samaná, a small airstrip used mostly during whale-watching season (January to March).

Aeropuerto Internacional del Cibao (☎809-233-8000; www.aeropuertocibao.com.do) Santiago's airport is the third largest in the country, and offers frequent international air service to major destinations, including thrice-weekly flights to San Juan, Puerto Rico, on Seaborne Airlines. There's a good selection of rent-a-car agencies at the airport, too.

Aeropuerto Internacional Gregorío Luperón, Puerto Plata (POP; ☎809-291-0000) Most convenient airport for north-coast destinations including the beach resorts around Puerto Plata, Sosúa and Cabarete.

Aeropuerto Internacional La Isabela Dr Joaquín Balaguer (JBQ, Higüero; ☎809-826-4019) Located just north of Santo Domingo proper. It handles mostly domestic flights, plus Cuba, Haiti and a few other Caribbean destinations.

Aeropuerto Internacional La Romana (☎809-813-9000; www.romanaairport.com; Casa de Campo) Near La Romana and Casa de Campo; handles primarily charter flights from the US, Canada, Italy and Germany; also, regular Jet Blue and Spirit Airline flights from Miami, NYC and San Juan, Puerto Rico.

Aeropuerto Internacional Las Américas (SDQ; José Francisco Peña Gómez; ☎809-947-2225) The country's main international airport is located 20km east of Santo Domingo. It's generally cheaper to fly here than any other airport besides Santiago's.

Aeropuerto Internacional María Montez (BRX; ☎809-524-4144) Located 5km from Barahona in the southwest; charters only.

Aeropuerto Internacional Punta Cana (☎809-959-2376; www.puntacanainternationalairport.com; Carretera Higüey-Punta Cana Km 45) Serves Bávaro and Punta Cana, and is the busiest airport in the country. Prinair, a Puerto Rican airline, now offers twice-weekly half-hour flights between Aguadilla's Rafael Hernández International Airport and Punta Cana.

Aeropuerto Internacional Samaná El Catey (AZS; Presidente Juan Bosch; ☎809-338-0150) Located around 40km west of Samaná; Península de Samaná's main air gateway; Canadian airlines predominate.

LAND

These are the four points where you can cross between Haiti and the DR. Note that in recent years, tensions at the borders have sometimes been high due to shifting and confusing policies in the DR that have led to an increase in deportations of people of Haitian descent.

Jimaní–Malpasse The busiest and most organized crossing is in the south on the road that links Santo Domingo and Port-au-Prince. Disputes here can sometimes create tension along the border.

Dajabón–Ouanaminthe Busy northern crossing on the road between Santiago and Cap-Haïtien (a six-hour drive); try to avoid crossing on market days (Monday and Friday) because of the enormous crush of people and the risk of theft.

Pedernales–Ainse-a-Pietres In the far south; there's a small bridge for foot and motorcycle traffic; cars have to drive over a paved road through a generally shallow river. Migrant camps are set up on the Haitian side of this border for those who have been deported and have nowhere else to go. Be sure to have onward transport organized or else your wait can be a long one.

Comendador (aka Elías Piña)–Belladère Certainly the dodgiest crossing, but also the least busy. On the Haiti side, the immigration building is several hundred meters from the actual border. Transportation further into Haiti is difficult to access.

SEA

International cruise ships on Caribbean tours commonly stop at ports in Santo Domingo; at an anchoring spot off Catalina Island, part of Casa de Campo near La Romana; Cayo Levantado in the Península de Samaná; and at Amber Cove near Puerto Plata. Taino Bay, another large port project, including a waterpark and a 'Taíno-themed village,' is being built near Fort San Felipe in downtown Puerto Plata.

Yachts and sailboats can also anchor at marinas at Cap Cana (in the Punta Cana area in the southeast); the Bannister Yacht Club (just outside Samaná); and the small Puerto Blanco marina in Luperón on the north coast.

Caribbean Fantasy, run by **Ferries del Caribe** (☎San Juan, Puerto Rico 787-622-4800, Santiago 809-583-4440, Santo Domingo 809-688-4400; www.ferriesdelcaribe.com), offers a passenger- (one way US$100) and car-ferry (US$250) service between Santo Domingo and Puerto Rico (San Juan). The trip takes about 12 hours and departs three times weekly.

Getting Around

The DR is a fairly small country, so in theory at least it's easy to drive or take public transportation from one side of the country to the other. In practice, however, the inadequate road network will behoove some with limited time and a sufficient budget to consider flying.

Car Most convenient option if seeking freedom of movement, especially if interested in exploring rural and mountain regions.

Bus Three major companies, Caribe Tours, Expreso Bávaro and Metro, provide comfortable, frequent service along a network of major cities and towns.

Guaguas Basically small buses or minivans; ubiquitous, least expensive and least comfortable, but often the only available public transport.

Air Useful if short on time, though the most expensive option and sometimes unreliable depending on the time of year.

Grenada

473 / POP 111,219

Includes ➡

Best Places to Eat

- BB's Crabback (p439)
- Coconut Beach (p441)
- Andy's Soup House (p441)
- Bogles Round House (p451)
- Green Roof Inn (p450)
- Slipway (p452)

Best Places to Stay

- La Luna (p442)
- Calabash Hotel (p443)
- Almost Paradise (p446)
- La Sagesse Manor House (p444)
- Green Roof Inn (p449)
- Silver Sands (p440)

Why Go?

It's not called the Spice Island for nothing – you really can smell the nutmeg in the air on Grenada. And it could be called the Fruit Island for the luscious bounty growing in the gorgeous green hills. Then again, it could be called the Beach Island for the plethora of idyllic sandy strands. We could go on…

While the country's number-one attraction might be up for debate, what is not in doubt is that it's one of the most enchanting nations in the Caribbean: three islands that ooze authenticity and feel barely affected by mass package tourism.

Boasting a charming hilly capital and lovely waterfront, wide public beaches and a lush interior that's perfect for exploration, Grenada Island has enough to keep visitors enthralled. But it would be unwise to leave without getting to know the country's smaller islands, home to classic Caribbean communities that redefine tranquility.

When to Go

Nov–Apr Dry season, and Grenada's most popular time. Carriacou Carnival (February/March) is one of the best parties in the region.

May Dry weather but fewer crowds and generally lower prices.

Jun–Oct Rainy season, with heavy showers most days. September is the rainiest month and, with August, most prone to hurricanes.

GRENADA ISLAND

The island of Grenada is an almond-shaped, beach-rimmed gem of a place with 75 miles of coastline surrounding a lush interior filled with verdant tropical rainforest. It's a supremely relaxed place – there are no functioning traffic lights on the island – with great scenery, fantastic food and some of the friendliest residents in the Caribbean.

The vast majority of the population reside in colorful seaside villages and towns which are safe, friendly and great to explore. There are gorgeous beaches all over the island but especially in the southwest where the island's pride and joy, Grand Anse, is a favorite recreational spot for visitors and locals alike.

St George's

St George's is one of the most picturesque towns in the Caribbean. It's a fabulous place to explore on foot, from handsome old buildings to the Carenage harbor. Interesting shops and cafes dot the narrow and busy streets.

Sights

★Underwater Sculpture Park DIVE SITE
(Molinière Bay) An underwater gallery beneath the sea, just north of St George's in Molinière Bay. The project was founded by British artist Jason de Caires Taylor and there are now more than 80 pieces in more than a dozen main works all slowly becoming encrusted with coral growth. Fish and sponges have also colonized the area, forging a fascinating mix of culture with nature. The park is accessible to both snorkelers and divers, and all the dive shops organize visits.

The life-size sculptures include a man at a desk and a circle of children clasping hands, originally intended as a message of unity but since adopted as a memorial for Africans that died during the slave trade.

★Fort Frederick FORT
(Richmond Heights; EC$5; 8am-5pm) Constructed by the French in 1779, Fort Frederick was soon used – paradoxically – by the British in defense against the French, although it never fired a cannon in anger. It's the island's best-preserved fort, and offers striking panoramic views. There are a couple of short tunnels at the base – bring a torch as there is no lighting down there. The fort is atop Richmond Hill, 1¼ miles east of St George's on the road to St Paul's.

Fort George FORT
(Church St; EC$5; 7am-5pm Mon-Fri, to noon Sat) Grenada's oldest fort was established by the French in 1705 and it's the centerpiece of the St George's skyline. You can climb to the top to see the cannons and bird's-eye views. Just outside the main fort area is a series of dark defensive tunnels to explore.

A plaque in the parade ground marks the spot where revolutionary leader Maurice Bishop was executed, which set in motion events that led to the US invasion in 1983. At weekends it's possible to gain access through the police base around the back.

Grenada National Museum MUSEUM
(440-3725; cnr Young & Monckton Sts; adult/child EC$5/2.50; 9am-4:30pm Mon-Fri, 10am-1:30pm Sat) Staffed by enthusiastic members, this museum has displays that are a little haphazard. It is mostly dedicated to the original indigenous inhabitants of the island, the colonial period and slavery – there's precious little about Maurice Bishop's revolution. That said, with a history as colorful as that of Grenada, there's plenty here and it can easily absorb an hour.

St George's Anglican Church CHURCH
(Church St) Erected in 1825, St George's is topped by a squat four-sided clock tower that serves as the town's timepiece, and which didn't cease to work when the building was heavily damaged in the 2004 hurricane. Repairs to the structure are now complete, with the church boasting a wonderfully crafted new wooden ceiling and gallery.

St George's Market Square MARKET
(Halifax St; 8am-3pm Mon-Sat) Busiest on Friday and Saturday mornings, this is the largest market in Grenada, with stalls heaped with fresh island produce. It's a colorful sight that is worth checking out even if you're not buying.

Carenage HARBOR
A scenic inlet, the Carenage is a great place for a stroll along the water's edge, taking in the colorful fishing boats and the bustle of supplies being loaded for other islands. At the north end, some of the sturdy Georgian buildings have been restored.

Activities

Savvy Sailing SNORKELING
(www.sailingsavvy.com; Port Louis Marina; tours per person US$45-100) Offers snorkeling trips on a traditional wooden sailboat made on Pet-

it Martinique – a tranquil and atmospheric way to see Grenada's offshore wonders. Also has sunset cruises and two-day sailing trips to the Grenadines. It's mostly private charter so you'll need to get your own group together.

Sleeping

Deyna's City Inn GUESTHOUSE **$$**
(☎435-7007; cityinn@spiceisle.com; Melville St; r US$108-120; ❄@) Right in the town center, this welcoming little place has a range of

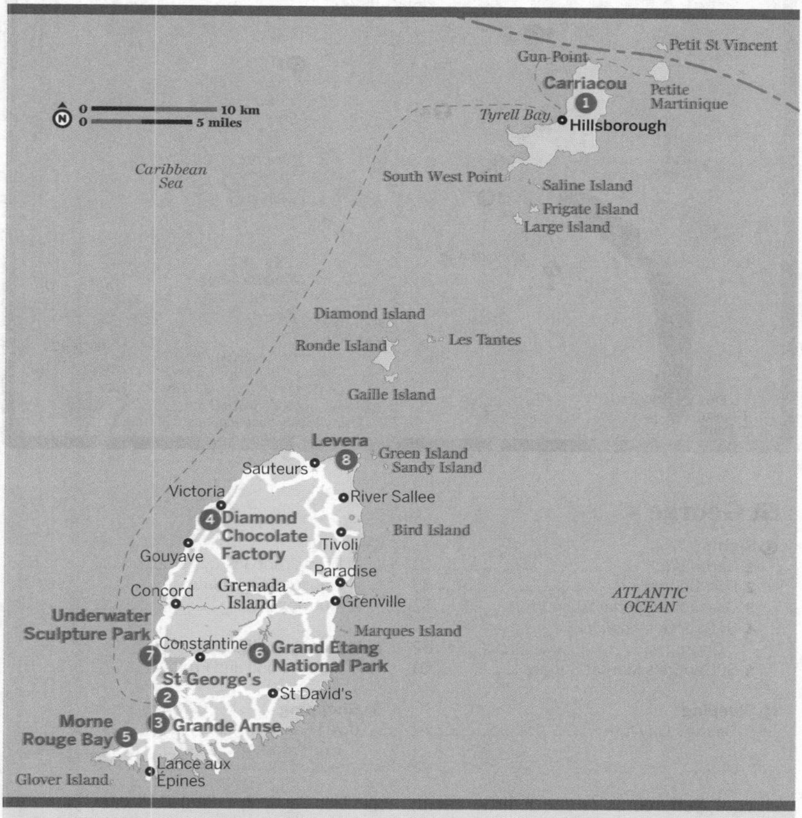

Grenada Highlights

❶ **Carriacou** (p448) Enjoying peace, quiet and beautiful beaches on this friendly island.

❷ **St George's** (p436) Exploring one of the Caribbean's prettiest capitals and taking in the panoramic views from its imposing forts.

❸ **Grand Anse** (p440) Mixing it up with the locals at Grenada's favorite recreational space.

❹ **Diamond Chocolate Factory** (p446) Following the chocolate process from bean to bar at this locally owned cooperative.

❺ **Morne Rouge Bay** (p442) Sinking your toes into the soft white sand and superblue water.

❻ **Grand Etang National Park** (p444) Hiking the trails and checking out the volcanic lake surrounded by rainforest.

❼ **Underwater Sculpture Park** (p436) Swimming among unforgettably surreal coral-encrusted sculptures in shallow waters a short boat ride from the capital.

❽ **Levera** (p447) Reveling in the isolation of the ultimate deserted beach with only sea turtles for company.

St George's

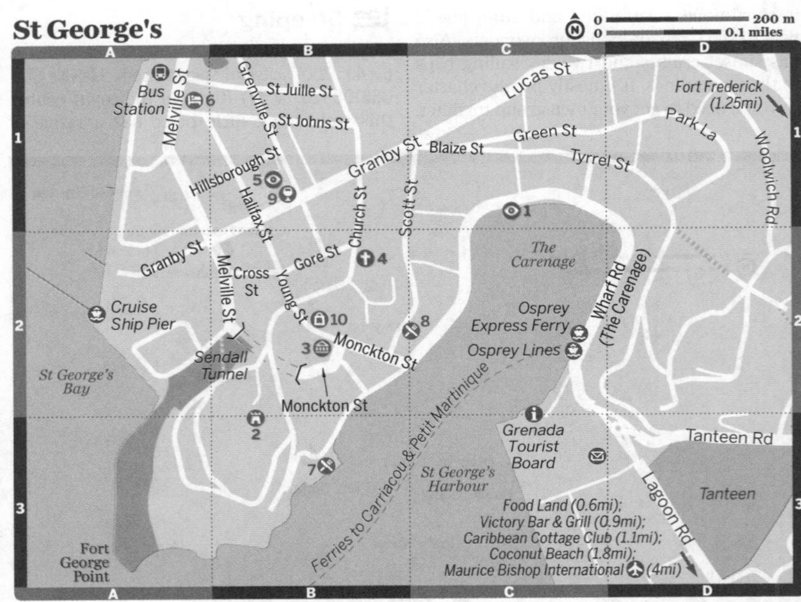

St George's

Sights
1 Carenage C1
2 Fort George B3
3 Grenada National Museum B2
4 St George's Anglican Church B2
5 St George's Market Square B1

Sleeping
6 Deyna's City Inn A1

Eating
7 BB's Crabback B3
House of Chocolate .... (see 3)
8 Nutmeg C2

Drinking & Nightlife
9 Native Food and Fruits B1

Shopping
10 Art Fabrik B2
Craft market .... (see 5)

well-equipped rooms (some a little small) with cable TV and bright, modern decor. Friendly staff, great local food from the restaurant downstairs, and a very convenient location for city sightseeing and transport around the island complete the offer. There are lots of stairs, however, and no lifts.

Eating & Drinking

During the day you'll find plenty of good cheap eats in the downtown area. For a nice sit-down meal, check out the restaurants at the Carenage.

House of Chocolate CAFE $
(☎440-2310; www.houseofchocolategnd.com; Young St; items EC$3-10, drinks EC$8-16; ⏰10am-6pm Mon-Sat, to 2pm Sun) Part cafe, part museum, part gift shop, this welcoming place is dedicated to all things cocoa. You can sample chocolate in both its liquid and solid forms, and buy bars from different local producers to take home. There are also delicious cakes and brownies.

Patrick's Local Homestyle Cooking CARIBBEAN $
(Lagoon Rd; mains from EC$25, menu EC$60; ⏰11am-10pm Mon-Fri, 6-10pm Sat & Sun; ✎) Set on the porch and in the covered front patio of a converted home on Lagoon Rd, this friendly and low-key restaurant is a fine place to try some local specialities. In addition to goat curry and seafood dishes, it also

GRENADA ISLAND TOURS

Mandoo Tours (☎440-1428; www.grenadatours.com) Offers full- and half-day tours of the island, which can be tailored for historical or photographic interests. Quality vehicles with air-conditioning.

Tropical Adventures (☎457-7592; www.tagrenada.com) An excellent locally run tour company specializing in nature hikes and birdwatching in the interior of the island. It's very popular – book in advance.

Sunsation (☎444-1594; www.grenadasunsation.com) One of the larger companies, with well-organized island tours, hiking and sailing.

Henry's Safari Tours (☎444-5313; www.henrysafari.com) Various treks into the interior are offered by this company, which specializes in hiking tours. Lunch and drinks are included. Try the five-hour tour that includes a hike to the Seven Sisters Falls (p445).

Grenada Seafaris (☎405-7800; www.grenadaseafaris.com) Powerboat coastal tours, with stops for snorkeling – including the Underwater Sculpture Park (p436) – and informed commentary on local fauna and flora.

Adventure Tours Grenada (☎444-5337; www.adventuregrenada.com; rental per day US$20, tours per hour US$15) A reputable operator that runs jeep tours around the island as well as river-tubing adventures. Also rents out mountain bikes (delivered to your hotel) and offers guided bike tours.

offers a changing 'tapas' menu with more than a dozen small plates of local dishes.

★BB's Crabback CARIBBEAN $$
(☎435-7058; www.bbscrabbackrestaurant.com; Carenage; mains EC$58-79; ⏰9am-10pm Mon-Sat) The namesake waterfront restaurant of celebrity chef and local bon vivant Brian Benjamin is on the water at the end of the Carenage. Local faves like callaloo soup (a rich stew) and fresh seafood are popular, as is the signature goat curry. Fussier appetites can order pancakes and everyone loves the chocolate dessert.

Victory Bar & Grill INTERNATIONAL $$
(☎435-7263; Port Louis Marina; light meals EC$20-39, mains EC$40-97; ⏰7am-11pm; 👪) Located in the upmarket Port Louis marina, with tables overlooking boats and the occasional megayacht. It's busy with happy yachties eating fresh salads, burgers and seafood brochettes. The atmosphere is fun, and the food is great.

Nutmeg CARIBBEAN $$
(Carenage; light meals EC$15-25, mains EC$45-80; ⏰11am-9pm Mon-Sat) Get above the bustle of the waterfront at this popular open-air balcony restaurant. Have a roti or traditional meaty main. Book ahead for a table by the windows.

Native Food and Fruits JUICE BAR
(Granby St; juices EC$9-12; ⏰9am-6pm Mon-Sat) On one side of the market plaza, this great local smoothie bar knocks out refreshing fruit-based beverages, as well as more filling shakes, that are full of flavor. Try the sea moss or order the oats, peanut and Guinness version and you'll happily skip a meal.

Shopping

Art Fabrik ARTS & CRAFTS
(☎440-0568; Young St; ⏰9am-4pm Mon-Fri, to 1pm Sat) A small shop filled with beautiful batik creations made right on Grenada. Ask to see the dyeing process. Also has a small gallery out back featuring paintings by a number of local artists.

Craft market GIFTS & SOUVENIRS
(⏰8am-6pm) Next to the market square, this craft market sells a broad collection of souvenirs including, of course, everything connected to spices.

Information

Grenada Tourist Board (☎440-2279; www.grenadagrenadines.com; ⏰8am-4pm Mon-Fri) Helpful tourism office at the southern end of the Carenage.

Main Post Office (☎440-2526; Lagoon Rd; ⏰8am-4pm Mon-Fri)

Scotiabank (☎440-3274; cnr Halifax & Granby Sts; ⏰8am-3pm Mon-Thu, to 5pm Fri) Has a 24-hour ATM.

St George's General Hospital (☎440-2051; Fort George Point) The island's main medical facility is up on the hillside in front of the fort.

Getting There & Around

St George's is best explored on foot – lose the rental ASAP as streets in the center are narrow and congested and driving is a huge headache.

Buses depart from St George's **central terminal** (Melville St) to destinations all over the island. A taxi to Grand Anse costs about EC$45.

BOAT

Osprey Express Ferry (☎440-8126; www.ospreylines.com; Carenage) has boats to Carriacou departing from the Carenage in front of the tourism office. You can buy tickets on board, but when it's busy consider buying in advance from the office across the water in the Huggins building.

Cruise liners dock at the purpose-built pier attached to the Esplanade Mall in the center of town.

Grand Anse

Running alongside the famous beach of the same name, Grand Anse is more a collection of hotels, restaurants and services than a real town. The beach here is one of the island's best and is justifiably popular.

To escape crowds, look for the small access road that spurs off the Grand Anse Rd toward the southern reaches of the bay; it leads to a small parking area and uncrowded sands.

Sights & Activities

Grand Anse BEACH

Grenada's main resort area is a lovely long sweep of white sand fronted by turquoise water and backed by hills. It has the highest concentration of big hotels, bars, eateries and water sports on the island but its essence has not been totally lost to development. Unlike some beaches in the Caribbean, it gets a good mix of visitors and locals, who come here to swim, exercise and play sports. It remains the essential Grenadian experience for many.

Camerhogne Park PARK

A well-maintained green space running from the Spiceland Mall down to the white sands of Grand Anse. If you're visiting for the day, it's a good place to base yourself – here you'll find change rooms (EC$1), loungers for rent, plenty of shade and snack bars.

Mocha Spoke CYCLING

(☎534-6243; www.mochaspoke.com; Le Marquis Complex; ⌚7:30am-7pm) This popular cafe is not just a great place to stop for quality coffee and baked goods; it also rents bicycles and runs cycling tours around the capital and to waterfalls.

Dive Grenada DIVING

(☎444-1092; www.divegrenada.com; Mount Cinnamon Resort; 1-/2-tank dives US$75/130; ⌚8am-4pm) A highly rated and professionally run dive shop based in the Grand Anse area. Also offers snorkeling trips to the Underwater Sculpture Park for US$55.

Sleeping

With the highest concentration of accommodations on the island, Grand Anse has everything from big resorts right on the sand to budget cottages up on the hillside.

Caribbean Cottage Club HOTEL **$**

(☎414-4097; www.grenadacottages.com; Greystone Rd; cottages US$60-70; ❄) Located on a breezy hillside just off the road between Grand Anse and the marina, this chilled little place has a handful of comfortable wooden cottages with small kitchens and sea views. Some rooms have air-con in the bedrooms although it's not always icy-cold. The staff is extremely helpful.

★**Silver Sands** LUXURY HOTEL **$$$**

(☎533-8888; www.silversandsgrenada.com; Grand Anse Main Rd; r/villas from US$1000/8000; ❄📶🏊) Raising the bar significantly in luxury on Grenada, this flash new hotel has cut no corners. Its centerpiece is a spectacular 100m infinity pool that runs the length of the property from the reception down to Grand Anse. Rooms are sleek and modern, with bathrooms bigger than many entire hotel rooms, and feature both state-of-the-art technology and quality original artworks.

Coyaba Beach Resort RESORT **$$$**

(☎444-4129; www.coyaba.com; Grand Anse Beach; r US$432; ❄@📶🏊) Set upon a great stretch of beach, the 80 rooms here exude relaxed luxury. The beachfront grounds are beautifully landscaped and there's also a spa. Throw in good service and it's an excellent choice.

Radisson Grenada Beach Resort HOTEL **$$$**

(☎444-4371; www.radisson.com; Grande Anse Main Rd; r from US$300; ❄@📶🏊) 🍃 Don't let the big exterior put you off; this enormous complex has a fairly intimate feel. The rooms are nothing special, but the facilities are impressive – the riverlike pool is a hit with little

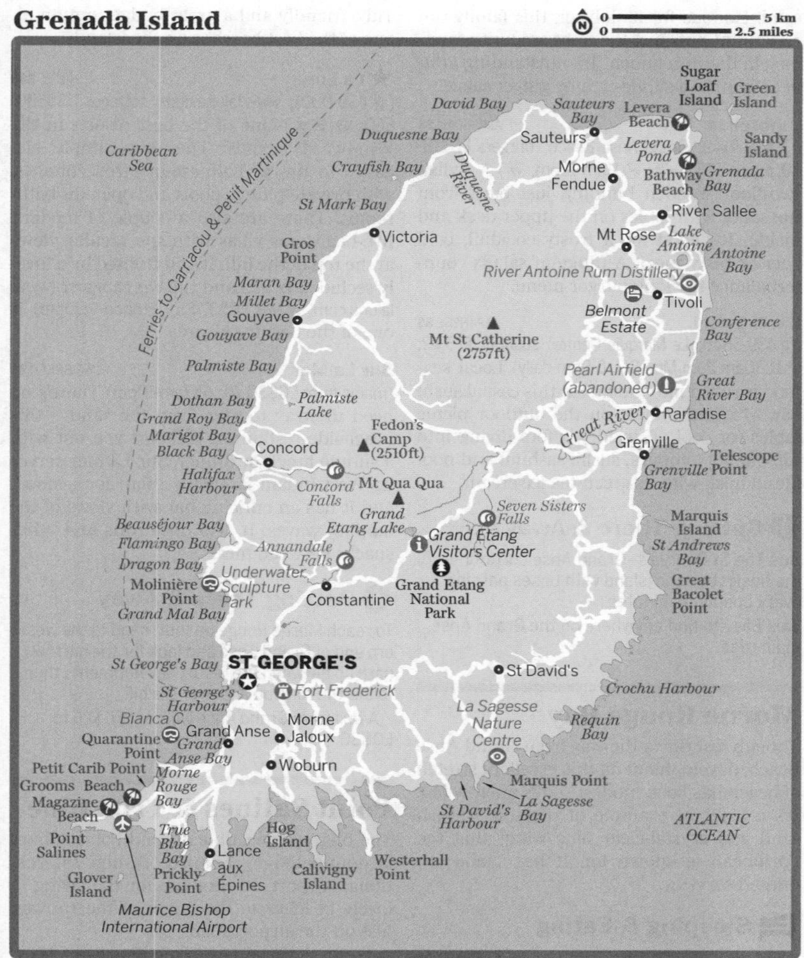

ones. The staff is friendly and there seems to be every amenity you'd need on-site.

Eating

★Andy's Soup House CARIBBEAN $

(☎406-1600; Grand Anse Valley Rd, Woodlands; soups EC$15, mains EC$15-25; ⏰7am-10pm) This humble roadside diner is our favorite place on the whole island for fantastic local eats. It serves a variety of traditional dishes and snacks including great rotis, but the main reason to come here is for the 'waters' (soups). There are usually at least five different varieties on offer; pick any, they're all delicious.

Jam Down JAMAICAN $

(Grand Anse Valley Rd, Mount Tout; chicken EC$10-15; ⏰noon-9pm Mon-Sat) It's worth making the trip slightly off the beaten path to this humble roadside wooden shack. It sells just one thing – outrageously tasty jerk chicken cooked the original Jamaican way. Come early, as they sell out fast. It's about half a mile up the hill from the intersection.

★Coconut Beach SEAFOOD $$

(☎444-4644; Grand Anse Beach; mains EC$45-98; ⏰noon-10pm Wed-Mon) French- and Creole-accented seafood is served up inside this old beachfront house, or at tables right on the sand. Famous for its lobster, this family-run restaurant puts just the right amount of nutmeg in the rum punch. Try outstanding *lambi* (conch) in a subtle creamy ginger sauce.

Umbrellas AMERICAN **$$**
(☎ 439-9149; Grand Anse Beach; burgers EC$18-40, mains EC$30-75; ⊙ 11am-10pm;) A stylish two-floor wooden building just back from the sand, with tables on the upper deck and inside. It's good for a frosty cocktail, cold beer or tasty meal. A range of salads counterbalance the long burger menu.

Carib Sushi JAPANESE **$$**
(☎ 439-5640; Le Marquis Centre; sushi EC$23-82; ⊙ 11:30am-2pm Mon-Sat, 6-9pm daily) Local seafood is rolled into the mix at this casual sushi bar. Mix and mingle on the outdoor picnic tables (or cool off inside) before diving into top-quality tempura, sushi, sashimi and noodles. Finish with its green-tea ice cream.

Getting There & Away

Bus The St George's–Grand Anse corridor is the busiest on the island with buses passing every couple of minutes.

Taxi Easy to find anywhere on the Grand Anse main road.

Morne Rouge Bay

Though just down the way from Grand Anse Beach, development on this excellent stretch of beach has been modest so it's uncrowded. It's a brilliant example of the soft whitish sand and crystal-clear blue water that the Caribbean is known for. It has shade but limited services.

Sleeping & Eating

Kalinago HOTEL **$$**
(☎ 444-5255; www.kalinagobeachresort.com; s/d US$200/220;) This cheerful resort has spacious and bright rooms with nice wooden furnishings overlooking the water (and just steps from the beach). There's also a pleasant oceanside pool with a swim-up bar and a restaurant on-site.

Gem Holiday Beach Resort HOTEL **$$**
(☎ 444-4224; www.gembeachresort.com; s/d from US$113/136, with sea view US$154/165;) Just up from the beach, this place is a real gem. The rooms are nothing too fancy, and perhaps a bit dated, but have all the basics you'd need including a small kitchen. Tidy, friendly and a great budget option on one of the best beaches on the island.

★**La Luna** HOTEL **$$$**
(☎ 439-0001; www.laluna.com; cottages US$580-860;) One of the best resorts in the Windward Islands. There's a simple elegance to the 16 Balinese-inspired cottages, with private plunge pools and open-air bathrooms. There are also a couple of modern five-bedrooms villas with spectacular views at the top of the hill. It's all fronted by a lovely secluded beach and the **restaurant** (www.laluna.com; mains EC$37-85; ⊙ noon-9:30pm) is one of the best in the area.

Sur La Mer CARIBBEAN **$$**
(mains from EC$30-70; ⊙ 7am-10pm) There's no need to stray too far from the sand – this beachside restaurant will sort you out with a simple lunch or dinner. Sur La Mer serves up West Indian fare with a flair for seafood, and it has an enticing bar with views of the lapping waves. It also does rotis and other snacks between meals.

Getting There & Away

To reach Morne Rouge on foot, head to the western end of Grand Anse and look for the narrow path up between the resort developments then follow the road up and over the hill.

A taxi from Grand Anse will cost EC$25 to EC$30.

Point Salines & True Blue

The filigreed coastline around Point Salines is dominated by Maurice Bishop International Airport. It's notable for the string of lovely beaches to the north of the runway, just off the airport road.

South of the airport, True Blue is a relaxed corner of the island with some nice top-end hotels, good eateries and yacht marinas.

Crowning the peninsula enclosing True Blue Bay, St George's Medical School (St George's University; SGU) is a sprawling campus inhabited almost exclusively by young Americans seeking offshore medical degrees (notoriously, President Ronald Reagan said he was defending these students when he ordered the American invasion in 1983).

Sights & Activities

Magazine Beach BEACH
The final port of call for travelers getting a last-minute dose of sea and sand before hop-

ping on a plane, Magazine Beach has been nicknamed by locals 'the Caribbean's prettiest departure lounge.' Its white sands and invigorating waters are bordered by a picturesque tumble of boulders at its southern end. It boasts fine snorkeling right from the shore.

Grooms Beach BEACH
(Parc a Beouf) A lovely secluded bay with a swath of soft powdery sand and warm blue waters that are good for snorkeling.

Aquanauts Grenada DIVING
(☎444-1126; www.aquanautsgrenada.com; True Blue Bay Resort) The dive-shop juggernaut on the island. It has it all, from the boats to the gear to an army of staff. Expect to pay around US$85 for a one-tank dive including gear rental and US$132 for two tanks. Open-water courses cost US$490. There's also a **branch** (☎444-1126; www.aquanautsgrenada.com; Grand Anse Beach; 1-/2-tank dives incl rental US$85/132; ⊙8am-5pm) at the Spice Island Resort on Grand Anse. Has a good online booking platform.

Sleeping

★Maca Bana HOTEL $$$
(☎439-5355; www.macabana.com; Point Salines; villas US$660-1020;) Maca Bana has gorgeous villas spreading down a hillside, with fabulous views down the coast to St George's and every possible detail attended to, from smartphone docks and flat-screen TVs to espresso machines and spacious wooden decks with private hot tubs. Solar panels provide all the power and everything is done with sustainability in mind.

True Blue Bay Resort & Marina HOTEL $$$
(☎443-8783; www.truebluebay.com; True Blue; r US$330-443;) Built at the edge of a yacht-filled bay, this family-owned resort is an island favorite, with rows of blue wooden huts springing up like mushrooms from the hill. It has grown considerably and there is a wide variety of accommodations available. All are elegantly furnished and feature artistic touches, but our favorites are the luxurious tower rooms with great 360-degree views.

Eating & Drinking

The area just outside the SGU campus gates is awash with food vans serving up comfort food to homesick Americans – think wings, gyros and tacos. You can also get good gringo-style coffees here.

Dodgy Dock INTERNATIONAL $$
(☎443-8783; True Blue Bay Resort; mains EC$26-99; ⊙7am-10pm) A waterside bar-restaurant on an inviting open-air deck, this place is good for a bite to eat or drink at any time and gets lively in the evenings although service is often inattentive. The menu has a bit of everything but it's dominated by Caribbean and Mexican flavors. Also does pizza.

Aquarium INTERNATIONAL $$$
(☎444-1410; www.aquarium-grenada.com; Point Salines; lunch EC$25-105, dinner EC$46-139; ⊙10am-10pm Tue-Sun;) Built right on the sands of Magazine Beach beneath some massive boulders, this ever-popular place has burgers and salads among the many options for lunch, plus some more sophisticated choices at dinner, with plenty of seafood and a wealth of choices for meat lovers. The Sunday barbecue with live music is always oversubscribed – book ahead.

Mocha Spoke CAFE
(☎533-2470; www.mochaspoke.com; True Blue Dr) A hip cafe just outside the university that serves a variety of caffeinated beverages to sleepless students. It has another branch (p440) in the Marquis complex near Grand Anse that runs cycle tours.

Getting There & Away

Bus The St George's–Grand Anse bus runs to Calliste, near the airport, which is a 10- to 15-minute walk from the attractions of Point Saline to the north and True Blue to the south.
Taxi From Grand Anse to Point Salines or True Blue taxis cost around EC$40.

Lance aux Épines

Lance aux Épines (*lance*-a-peen) is a peninsula that forms the southernmost point of Grenada. It's home to a pretty beach and a marina.

Activities

ScubaTech DIVING
(☎439-4346; www.scubatech-grenada.com; Calabash Hotel; 1-/2-tank dives US$110/150) A small and well-run outfit offering the full gamut of snorkeling and diving trips.

Sleeping & Eating

★Calabash Hotel HOTEL $$$
(☎444-4334; www.calabashgrenada.com; r incl breakfast US$925-1425;) Easily the

area's nicest place to bed down for the night. The beautifully manicured grounds sit hand in hand with a standard of service that is second to none. Lovely touches include having breakfast delivered to your room, and the sweeping lawns and swaying palms on the beach make the setting ripe for relaxation.

Lance aux Épines Cottages HOTEL **$$$**
(☎444-4565; www.laecottages.com; apt/cottages US$260/320; ❄@☎) Beautiful beach views are enjoyed here by 11 attractive rooms, which come complete with kitchens and large living areas. It's a peaceful and friendly place that is well set up for families. Extras abound including free kayaks. Rates drop outside peak periods.

Spice Affair INDIAN **$$$**
(☎444-4424; www.spiceaffair.gd; Lance aux Épines Main Rd; mains EC$30-99; ⏲11am-10pm) An upmarket eatery, even for posh Lance aux Épines, this Indian place combines authentic cuisine with stylish ambience. Pull up a comfy suede chair on the ample porch or in the striking air-con dining room and tuck into great curries with all the extras. It's a bit pricey but the quality and service are excellent.

West Indies Beer Company CRAFT BEER
(☎232-2337; www.westindiesbeer.com; Lance aux Épines Main Rd; ⏲1pm-1am Mon-Thu, to 2am Fri & Sat, 4pm-1am Sun) Good craft beer has a home in the Windward Islands. This neat local brewery started out as the house brewery at the True Blue Bay Resort and then expanded into its own smart premises with a lively beer garden which is the island's hottest nightspot. It produces a good variety of real ales and ciders which ensure a seriously fun atmosphere.

Good-value typical drinking food, including pizzas, burgers and wings are available.

Getting There & Away

Lance aux Épines is a 10-minute taxi ride from Grand Anse. There is no public transport onto the peninsula.

La Sagesse Bay

La Sagesse Bay is a lovely palm-lined crescent with protected swimming, backed by a wall of jungle hiding saltwater ponds that are home to egrets and herons. It has a secluded vibe and feels a world away from the more developed coves on the west of the island.

Sights

La Sagesse Nature Centre NATURE RESERVE
(☎444-6458; packages incl lunch & transport US$55; ⏲8am-5pm) The former estate of the late Lord Brownlow, cousin to Queen Elizabeth II, this nature center occupies the entire length of La Sagesse Bay. Unfortunately, the trails through the property are in poor condition and hikes are no longer available. Packages are available including transfers to and from your hotel, a meal and access to the beach facilities.

The on-site restaurant (mains EC$34 to EC$85) serves good Caribbean meals in a lovely waterside setting.

Sleeping

La Sagesse Manor House INN **$$$**
(☎444-6458; www.lasagesse.com; r US$185-210; ☎) At La Sagesse Nature Centre, Lord Brownlow's beachside former manor house, built in 1968, has been turned into a small inn. The stylish rooms in the new block are simple and alluring, with screened windows, while those in the old manor house and the more secluded cottage have ocean views and verandas.

Getting There & Away

La Sagesse is about a 25-minute drive from St George's on the Eastern Main Rd. The entrance is opposite an old abandoned rum distillery. Buses bound for the province of St David can also drop you here (EC$5).

Grand Etang National Park

Two and a half miles northeast of Constantine, after the road winds steeply up to an elevation of 1900ft, you enter Grand Etang National Park, a natural wonderland of misty landscapes centered around a lovely lake. At the **Grand Etang Visitor Center** (☎440-6160; EC$5; ⏲8am-4pm) you can pay your admission, learn a little about the park and get a refreshment.

Within the park you'll find four of Grenada's tallest peaks, the highest of which, bizarrely enough, is the only one without a name.

St George's–Grenville buses will drop you at the park visitor center or at the access point to the Seven Sisters falls – let the driver know in advance where you want to get off.

Activities

There are many hiking trails within the park, varying in duration and difficulty. Some are well maintained while others are overgrown and require the use of a guide. Most trails begin at or close to the visitor center and the helpful staff can arrange guides.

Hiking trails in the park include the following:

Concord Falls For serious adventurers only, this hike involves branching off towards the end of the Mt Qua Qua trek and continuing on to the Concord Falls. It is a five-hour trip one way and the trail is overgrown and even nonexistent in some parts – check on conditions before heading out. It's imperative to take a guide. From the falls it's another 1.5 miles on to the village of Concord, from where you can pick up bus transport.

Grand Etang Shoreline This 1½-hour loop walk around Grand Etang Lake is gentle but it's very muddy. Bring adequate footwear.

Morne La Baye This easy 15-minute walk starts behind the visitor center and takes in native vegetation.

Mt Qua Qua This is a moderately difficult three-hour round-trip hike that leads to the top of a ridge, offering some of the best views of the rainforest.

Seven Sisters Falls This two-hour hike passes seven waterfalls in the rainforest beginning at the highest cascade. It is a challenging trek but is considered one of the best hikes in Grenada. It requires a large jump down into the water between the 5th and 6th waterfall. Alternatively it's possible to visit the two lowest cascades on an easier 30-minute hike from the trailhead 1.25 miles north of the visitor center – you will be asked to pay EC$5 admission to the private property at the trailhead. Guides are available by the admission booth and work for tips.

Gouyave

Gouyave, roughly halfway up the west coast from St George's, is an attractive fishing village. It is well worth spending a couple of hours just walking around, having a drink and taking in the ambience.

Sights

★Nutmeg Processing Cooperative FACTORY
(☎444-8337; EC$2.70; ⏲8am-3:30pm Mon-Fri) On Gouyave's main road, you can literally smell one of the most important aspects of Grenada's heritage: nutmeg. This large nutmeg processing station is a vast, drafty old facility where workers sort the fragrant and tasty pods. Tours leave constantly and are a bargain.

Concord Falls WATERFALL
There are a couple of scenic waterfalls along the Concord River. The lowest, a picturesque 100ft cascade, can be viewed by driving to the end of Concord Mountain Rd, a side road leading 1.5 miles inland from the village of Concord. The half-mile trail to the upper falls begins at the end of the road and is a fun 45-minute hike through the forest. These falls are on private property and the owner charges a small fee to visit them.

Sleeping & Eating

Rumboat Retreat GUESTHOUSE $$
(☎437-1726; www.rumboatretreat.com; Mount Nesbit; r US$99; ❄📶) One of the few quality places to stay on this part of the island, Rumboat is a tranquil converted hillside home with just four rooms, two of which have sea views. It's run by enthusiastic young owners who run a variety of activities, including chocolate workshops and rum tastings onsite and adventurous nature hikes in the surrounding bush.

Gouyave Fish Fry CARIBBEAN $
(mains from EC$20; ⏲7-10pm Fri) Gouyave is Grenada's fishing capital, a fact that is celebrated in style with the festive Friday Fish Fry. Local vendors grill and fry fresh fish right off the boat, and serve it up with local sides. It's as much a party as a dining experience, with most locals sticking around for a few drinks well after their meal is done.

Getting There & Away

Buses run between St George's and Victoria along the Western Main Rd stop in Gouyave in both directions.

Sauteurs

On the northern tip of the island, the town of Sauteurs (whose French name translates as 'Jumpers') is best known for its grim history. In 1651 local Carib families elected to throw themselves off the 130ft-high cliffs that line the coast rather than surrender to the advancing French army.

Modern Sauteurs is a pretty little town with colorful houses and a magnificent **Anglican church**. Just to the northwest of town there is an inviting long beach backed by coconut palms that offers views over to the Grenadine islands. It's got a village vibe, especially in the late afternoon when locals come down to relax.

Sights

Mount Richmond Petroglyph ARCHAEOLOGICAL SITE
(by donation) Located a couple of miles south of Sauters, this large riverside stone is covered with carvings and is among the most important indigenous relics on the island. There is a small community-run interpretation center next to the road on the riverbank where they'll lend binoculars to get a closer look at the images. It's quite a steep scramble down to the rock itself, but if you really want to get up close, some kids next door act as guides.

Staff here work on a voluntary basis so tips are appreciated.

Leaper's Hill MONUMENT
(10am-6pm) It is from this cliff face that indigenous Carib families are said to have leapt in order to avoid advancing French forces. The small museum is no longer in operation but you can still visit the lookout point and imagine the macabre events. To get here, either walk through the Catholic cemetery behind the church or take the slightly rougher path down the right-hand side beside the school. The security guards on-site will give explanations on request.

> **WORTH A TRIP**
>
> **DIAMOND CHOCOLATE FACTORY**
>
> The **Diamond Chocolate Factory** (Jouvay Chocolate; 437-1839; www.jouvaychocolate.com; Diamond Estates, Victoria, St Marks; 8am-4pm Mon-Fri, 9am-5pm Sat & Sun), housed in a former distillery built by French monks, produces the Jouvay brand of chocolate that you'll see on sale around the country. The company is owned as a cooperative by local cocoa growers. Call ahead to book a tour of the buildings and chocolate-making machinery followed by a chance to taste the various products.

Sleeping & Eating

The best accommodations are outside town to the west, on the jungle-backed hillsides that slope down to the water.

★**Almost Paradise** HOTEL $$
(442-0608; www.almost-paradise-grenada.com; cottages US$129;) The hillside cottages at this tranquil little guesthouse are simple and bright with netted beds, kitchenette and hammocks on the balcony. But what really seals the deal are the fantastic views over to the Grenadine islands. The owners are seriously committed to ecology and the restaurant serves a range of excellent Mediterranean-influenced food and delicious cocktails.

Petite Anse HOTEL $$$
(442-5252; www.petiteanse.com; r US$297-358;) By far the most upmarket of the two places to stay in this stretch, Petite Anse also has more in the way of facilities, including a slip of beach. Rooms are beautifully decorated, with four-poster beds and private decks or patios. The restaurant has everything from salads and pasta to seafood.

Armadillo EUROPEAN $$
(417-5250; www.armadillo-grenada.com; Prospect Rd; mains EC$65-90;) Inside the guesthouse of the same name, this little restaurant serves some of the best meals on the north of the island. The gourmet menu changes according to what is fresh locally. There are only eight spots on the communal dining table so reserve in advance. Upstairs there are three tranquil guest rooms (US$125 to US$165) with sea views.

Getting There & Away

Grenville There are two bus routes from Sauteurs to Grenville. One passes by Rose Hill close to Lake Antoine and the other goes through Hermitage near Belmont Estate.

St George's Buses link Sauteurs with the capital via the Western Main Rd.

Eastern Grenada

Sparsely populated Eastern Grenada is often overlooked by visitors but is well worth shuffling your itinerary for, especially if you want to get close to some rugged nature. As you drive from village to village you'll encounter working cocoa plantations, traditional rum distilleries, remote beaches and hidden lagoons teeming with birdlife.

Be advised that apart from Bathway, the beaches in this area are mostly dangerous and not suitable for swimming.

Sights & Activities

★ Levera Beach BEACH

Backed by low, eroding sea cliffs, Levera Beach is a wild, beautiful sweep of sand that gets few visitors. Just offshore is the high, pointed Sugar Loaf Island, while the Grenadine islands dot the horizon to the north.

The road north from Bathway to Levera is unpaved, but it's fairly solid and shouldn't pose a problem to most vehicles. Walking it will take about 30 minutes. It's a very remote place; there's security during the day but avoid coming up here after dark.

The beach, the mangrove swamp and the nearby pond have been incorporated into Grenada's national-park system, and are an important waterfowl habitat and sea-turtle nesting site. Levera is off-limits in the evenings from April to August to protect nesting turtles although it's possible to visit on an authorised tour.

River Antoine Rum Distillery DISTILLERY

(☎442-7109; Tivoli; tours EC$5; ⏲8am-4pm Mon-Fri) River Antoine has produced rum since 1785 and still produces in the traditional way. Tours here cover all aspects of the smoky, pungent production process, from the crushing of cane to fermentation and distillation. Of course there are tastings and you can buy bottles to go.

Pearl Airfield MONUMENT

Once the island's main airport, this airfield just north of Grenville was taken over by marines during the US invasion, leaving two Cuban planes stranded beside the runway. Now it's a peculiarly peaceful scene with goats nibbling away at green pastures beneath the mangled wings. You can climb inside the Russian-built Antonov jet, but bring sturdy footwear as there are loose bits of metal with sharp edges.

Bathway Beach BEACH

From River Sallee, a road leads to Bathway Beach, a lovely long stretch of coral sands. A rock shelf parallels the shoreline, creating a very long sheltered pool that's great for swimming. There are usually lifeguards here from 9am to 6pm, and there are a couple of stands and small cafes selling drinks and meals.

GRAND ETANG ROAD

Overhung with rainforest and snaking uphill in a series of switchback turns, the Grand Etang Rd shoots right up the island's spine. The mountainous center of the island is often awash with misty clouds, and looks like a lost primordial world, its tangle of rainforest brimming with life – including monkeys that often get a bit too friendly.

Grenada's verdant splendor is on full display here; look for cassava, nutmeg, star fruit, cinnamon, clove, hibiscus, passion fruit, pineapple, avocado, mango, banana, coconut and much more.

An idyllic waterfall with a 30ft drop, **Annandale Falls** (EC$5; ⏲8am-4pm) is surrounded by a grotto of lush vegetation and has a large pool where you can take a refreshing swim. It's a two-minute walk from the visitor center. It gets crowded when cruise ships are in port.

Belmont Estate FARM

(☎442-9524; www.belmontestate.net; Belmont; tours adult/child EC$13/5; ⏲8am-4pm, closed Sat) Cocoa is Grenada's main crop and it's celebrated at this 300-year-old working organic plantation. Among the other crops here: cinnamon, cloves, bay leaf, ginger and nutmeg. Guided tours explain cocoa production, and you can walk the landscaped gardens and have a tasty lunch (EC$62.50). The estate is about 2 miles northwest of Tivoli.

Specto WILDLIFE WATCHING

(☎442-2721, 442-1748; specto.grenada@gmail.com; Bathway Beach) A community-based ecotourism organization that runs tours to watch enormous leatherback turtles coming ashore to lay eggs on and around Levera in the northeast of the island. The tour begins at the Bathway Beach interpretation center and participants are encouraged to come in their own vehicles.

Shopping

Grenada Chocolate Company CHOCOLATE

(☎442-0050; Hermitage; ⏲7am-4pm Mon-Fri) You can buy this farmer-owned company's great organic chocolate bars all over the island but it's worth visiting this little showroom in a hillside community to taste all the different varieties, as well as to tuck into brownies, cakes and individual gourmet chocolates. The chocolate is produced in a nearby facility around which you can take a tour.

Getting There & Away

While local buses will get you to most villages on this side of the island, many attractions are off the main road. It's best to hire a vehicle or negotiate with a taxi to fully explore the area.

Local buses from Grenville to Sauteurs run on two routes: 9A goes through River Sallee passing Lake Antoine and the turnoff to Bathway, while 9B goes inland via Belmont Estate.

CARRIACOU

The fact that most people don't realize that there are in fact *three* islands in the nation of Grenada is a fitting introduction to Carriacou (*carry*-a-cou). You won't find cruise ships, big resorts or souvenir shops – this is Caribbean life the way it was 50 years ago: quiet, friendly and relaxed.

Festivals & Events

Carriacou Carnival CULTURAL
(Feb/Mar) A vibrant event featuring fun street parades, live bands and the quirky 'Shakespeare Mas' – like a rap battle but with men dressed in bright garb reciting verses from the Bard of Avon. Get ready to be covered in paint and party. It takes place over two weeks after the beginning of Lent.

Carriacou Maroon & String Band Festival MUSIC
(www.carriacoumaroon.com; Apr) Bands from a number of islands come to Carriacou for this traditional music festival that takes place over three days at the end of April. A delicious sideshow is the preparation of traditional smoked foods.

Carriacou Regatta SAILING
(Aug) Being a proud boat-building island, Carriacou takes its regatta very seriously. The four-day festival takes place in the first week of August and attracts participants from all over the Caribbean and beyond.

Getting There & Away

To check on flights between Grenada Island and Carriacou, contact **SVG Air Grenada** (444-3549; www.svgair.com).

Most boat services from the island now run from the new Tyrell Bay Port, a 10-minute drive south of town.

Osprey Lines (www.ospreylines.com; Patterson St; 8am-3:30pm) runs a fast boat service from Grenada Island to Carriacou (adult EC$80, child EC$10 to EC$50, two hours) at 9am, returning from Hillsborough at 3:30pm, although it often departs a little late. On Sundays it leaves Grenada at 8am sharp.

A slower cargo boat (EC$50, four hours) leaves Carriacou around 6am for Grenada on Monday, Wednesday and Friday returning around 6pm – but the savings do not really justify the longer ride and inconvenient schedule.

Getting Around

Minivans serve as local buses and depart from the terminal behind Ade's Dream hotel, stopping to pick up passengers pretty much anywhere along its set route. The number 10 bus heads southwest while the number 11 heads up north. It costs EC$3.50 per ride. Less useful for visitors, the number 12 bus heads to the southeast.

Buses run during the day only, with last departures around 7pm, and on Sunday there's no service.

Carriacou is small and you can get most places on public transportation. However, if you want wheels, there are a few places to rent vehicles, with rates typically around US$50 to US$55 per day. **Wayne's Jeep Rental** (443-6120; Main Rd; vehicles EC$140-150), in Hillsborough just up from Ade's Dream hotel, has good prices. There is a gas station on Patterson St in Hillsborough.

Hillsborough

Carriacou's gentle pace is reflected in the sedate nature of its largest town, Hillsborough. There are a couple of streets lined with a mixture of modern blocks and classic Caribbean wooden structures. Go for a wander, appreciating glimpses of the turquoise waters at breaks in the buildings.

Sights

Beausejour Bay BEACH
(Silver Bay) Hillsborough's beach isn't the island's best, but it's pretty nonetheless. Fishing boats pull in along the Esplanade, where there are a couple of shady gazebos, and there's some nice shell collecting beyond this toward the northern headland. South of Hillsborough, it's a wilder affair, with crashing waves and pelicans roosting on the spines of long-gone piers.

Sandy Island
ISLAND

Sandy Island, off the west side of Hillsborough Bay, is a favorite daytime destination for snorkelers and sailors. It's a tiny postcard-perfect reef island of glistening sands surrounded by turquoise waters. Water taxis run from Hillsborough (US$10 per passenger round trip, 15 minutes). Be clear about when you want to be picked up – as the island takes only a couple of minutes to walk around, and has little shade, a whole afternoon can tick by very slowly.

Activities & Tours

Deefer Diving
DIVING

(☎443-7882; www.deeferdiving.com; Main St; 2-tank dives from US$105; ⊙8am-5pm Mon-Sat) A top local dive shop that runs trips to 33 dive sites around Carriacou. Professional Association of Diving Instructor (PADI) open-water courses are available for US$550. Also runs snorkeling trips. Nondiving friends can accompany divers on the boat for free to go snorkeling.

SUP Carriacou Grenada
WATER SPORTS

(☎404-2653; www.supcarriacougrenada.com; Airport Rd; rental per hour/day EC$50/150) Rents stand-up paddle (SUP) boards and offers classes in the calm waters around Carriacou. It's located next to the airport.

Isle of Reefs Tours
OUTDOORS

(☎404-0415; www.carriacoutours.com; Paradise Beach) A supremely well-run operation offering hiking tours on the island as well as turtle-watching tours and boating trips in the surrounding waters, including to the Tobago Cays (US$150 per visitor). Also runs a popular barbecue on Paradise Beach beneath some shady trees, with fresh conch, lobster, and fish on the grill. Meals include a round-trip water taxi to Sandy Island.

Sleeping

Hillsborough is a convenient base from which to explore the island – restaurants and transport are at your doorstep and nothing is far away. There's a decent budget hotel and several midrange options in the town proper which while not big on atmosphere make for convenient bases. Further afield on the northern outskirts there are a couple of charming guesthouses.

Rosa Guesthouse
GUESTHOUSE $

(☎443-7672; Main St; r US$70, 2-bed apt US$120) A bright and friendly family-run guesthouse in the center of town with six spotless and well-equipped apartments on the 2nd floor right across the road from the water. Rooms have functional kitchens and spacious modern bathrooms. Try to get the front two-bedroom apartment with full sea views.

LOCAL KNOWLEDGE

TRAVEL TO ST VINCENT

It's possible to travel from Carriacou to Union Island in St Vincent; from here, boats depart for other islands in the Grenadines and up to Kingstown. A water taxi from Hillsborough to Union Island will cost US$90 to US$100. It can be a rough and fairly wet crossing.

For a more economical trip, ask around town for Troy of the **Lady JJ** (☎in St Vincent 1-784-432-5728; gellizeau troy@gmail.com; adult/child EC$60/25), a working boat which runs a couple of times a week – usually Monday and Thursday – across to Union Island. Fares are EC$60 per passenger.

The fastest way to get to Union Island is with a direct flight from Carriacou with SVG Air but these are infrequent – call to check on schedules.

Green Roof Inn
HOTEL $

(☎443-6399; www.greenroofinn.com; s/d from US$75/95; 📶🚭) Half a mile up the road from Hillsborough, this is a quiet and beautiful place to stay. The simple rooms have mosquito-netted beds, and some have fab sea views. Rates include a fine buffet breakfast at the attached restaurant (p450).

Ade's Dream
GUESTHOUSE $

(☎443-7317; www.adesdream.com; Main St; r US$33-60; ❄📶) Popular with interisland travelers, those on a budget and people wanting to be right among the action, Ade's is in the dead center of town, above a bustling grocery/hardware/liquor/everything-else store. There are basic rooms with shared facilities and self-contained units with kitchens, and it's often booked to the hilt when the rest of the island is a ghost town.

Mermaid Hotel
HOTEL $$

(☎443-8286; www.mermaidhotelcarriacou.com; Main St; r US$107-165; ❄📶) This modern two-story hotel right by the water is the most comfortable place to crash in town. Bright and spacious rooms with modern bathrooms surround an internal courtyard.

Go for one of the two front rooms with sea views. Walk-ins can often get a good discount when things are slow.

Eating

Laurena II CARIBBEAN $

(Main St; mains EC$25; 8am-9pm;) Overlooking the Esplanade, this is often the liveliest spot in town. The Jamaican chef cooks up piles of jerk, fried or barbecued chicken, curried *lambi* (conch) or oxtail, served up with rice, peas and salad to queues of hungry locals. The bar is also a nice option for a rum, beer or local juice.

★ **Green Roof Inn** FUSION $$

(443-6399; www.greenroofinn.com; mains from EC$69; 5-9pm Tue-Sun;) The most sophisticated option in the Hillsborough area, with tables on a veranda overlooking the sea and fine meals to match the view. The menu changes according to what's fresh and available: it may feature fresh fish, steak or lobster if you're lucky, but it's all beautifully presented. Be sure to reserve a spot as the tiny dining area fills fast.

Kayak Kafe & Juice Bar CAFE $$

(Main St; breakfast EC$12-33, mains EC$33-45; 7:30am-3pm) On a diminutive deck overlooking the water near the dock, this cafe is a great place for a tasty breakfast. Also serves fresh juices and smoothies, burgers, wraps and fish mains.

Callaloo CARIBBEAN $$

(Mermaid Restaurant; 443-8286; Main St; lunch EC$14-35, mains EC$40-45; noon-9pm) Pull up a chair and enjoy Caribbean plates on the spacious wooden deck right over the sands at this popular place attached to the Mermaid Hotel (p449). The menu is not extensive but the flavors are pretty good and it's often open when not much else is around town. Make sure to bring repellent in the evenings or the mosquitoes may spoil your meal.

La Playa BAR

(Beausejour Bay; 10am-6pm) Right at the north end of Beausejour Bay, this great little beach bar serves up cocktails and light meals, including burgers and panini, in a cute pastel-colored wooden house right on the water. The beach right in front is apt for swimming and there are picnic tables under the trees. On Monday it does good-value lobster for EC$65.

Information

Hillsborough Immigration and Customs (443-8399; 8am-4pm Mon-Fri) Get your stamps here when leaving by boat for Union Island or elsewhere in St Vincent and the Grenadines.

Hillsborough Tourist Office (443-7948; Main St; 8am-noon & 1-4pm Mon-Fri) Helpful; located across from the pier.

Princess Royal Hospital (443-7400) In Belair, outside of Hillsborough.

Republic Bank (443-7289; Main St; 8am-2pm Mon-Thu, to 4pm Fri) Has a 24-hour ATM.

Getting There & Away

The *Osprey* ferry from St George's no longer docks in the heart of town so if arriving by boat you'll need to take a bus or taxi from the port at Tyrell Bay.

Water taxis will take you from Hillsborough to anywhere on Carriacou and beyond including Sandy Island (EC$27 round trip), Anse la Roche (EC$200 round trip), White Island (EC$200 round trip), Petit Martinique (EC$250 round trip) and Petit St Vincent (EC$250 round trip).

North of Hillsborough

The northern part of Carriacou is a delightful place to explore, with good scenery and tiny villages.

The first is cute little **Bogles**. Continuing on, the road traverses the crest of **Belvedere Hill**, providing sweeping views of the tiny islands of Petit St Vincent and Petit Martinique. Nearby are the remains of a couple of old sugar mills – one is close to the road.

From here, the route northeast (called the High Rd) leads down to **Windward**, a charming small village where, if you're lucky, some of the friendly locals will be out building a traditional Carriacou sloop. Just north of Windward is a wetland that is a good spot for birdwatching.

Sights

Anse la Roche BEACH

Getting here is a bit of a mission, but Anse la Roche is an idyllic stretch of soft sand backed by bush and flanked by headlands. Protected by cliffs, this secluded beauty – an important nesting spot for sea turtles – is a private paradise. You'll usually have it to yourself, although you may emerge from the jungle to find some yachties hanging around.

From Bogles, take a left at the wooden hut-like Boggles Bulletin Board where the main road bends. Follow that road, which quickly turns to dirt, for 25 minutes on foot veering right where the power lines veer left, until you see a small sign pointing to the narrow path. Follow that path down through the forest for 15 minutes. It's steep and a bit hard to follow at times but just keep heading down and towards the sound of the waves.

Alternatively you can just drop in with a water taxi from Hillsborough (US$75 round trip).

Sleeping & Eating

Bayaleau Point GUESTHOUSE **$$**

(443-7984; www.carriacoucottages.com; Windward; cottages US$110-185;) A great choice if you're after some peace and quiet, these well-maintained colorful wooden cottages are basic but neat and have everything you need including balconies, hammocks, kitchenettes and mosquito-netted beds. There's also a nice wooden deck area with views over to Union Island.

Meals are available as are excursions on the owner's boat. If you want to explore the island from here you may want to rent a vehicle.

★ **Bogles Round House** EUROPEAN **$$**

(443-7841; Bogles; mains from EC$52-85; noon-2:30pm & 6-9pm Mon-Sat) It's a round house and it's run by award-winning chef Roxanne Russell. The food – European dishes infused with Caribbean flavors – is inventive and up there with the best on the island. Three cute air-conditioned cottages with little porches (US$110 to US$120 including breakfast) are scattered around the grounds and there's a small private beach.

Call ahead to reserve a table or just pop in anytime for some homemade ice cream.

Getting There & Away

The northern part of the island is walkable if you're energetic and not in a hurry. It's worth taking the number of a local taxi to pick you up just in case.

The number 11 bus runs up past Bogles and through the center of the island to Windward. It's fairly frequent early morning and in the evening but in between it can become somewhat irregular.

South of Hillsborough

The biggest reason to venture to this part of the island is the aptly named Paradise Beach, a superb stretch of sand bordered by palms and sea-grape trees. Further on, **Tyrrel Bay** is a deep, protected bay. It's a popular anchorage for visiting yachts and there are a couple of cafes.

Sights & Activities

Paradise Beach BEACH

Carriacou's premier stretch of sand, Paradise Beach lives up to the name with a long stretch of white sand backed by palms and sea grape trees that fronts calm turquoise waters with views of Sandy Island just across the channel. It's delightful and usually never busy.

White Island ISLAND

White Island makes for a nice day trip, with a good, sandy beach and a pristine reef for snorkeling. It's about a mile off the southern tip of Carriacou. Water taxis run from Tyrrel Bay (about US$55 round trip, 30 minutes).

Lumbadive DIVING

(443-8566; www.lumbadive.com; Tyrrel Bay; 8:30am-5pm Mon-Sat) A great little dive shop in Tyrrel Bay with friendly and professional staff that offers two-tank dives for US$120 including equipment and six-dive packages for US$330. Also arranges accommodations in local apartments (US$55 to US$85).

Sleeping

There are a couple of accommodations options on Paradise Beach. Around Tyrrel Bay there are often houses to rent; ask in the dive shops or restaurants.

Beachside bars on Paradise Beach serve tasty local meals, and Tyrrel Bay has a couple of great casual restaurants.

Sunset Beach Paradise Inn HOTEL **$**

(443-8409; sunset.beach.paradise@gmail.com; Paradise Beach; r US$90-100;) Charming sand-side living, right on Paradise Beach. Eight rooms open onto a porch overlooking a grassy courtyard and are only steps from the sea; larger ones have kitchenettes. There's a great little restaurant and bar (mains from EC$25), tucked under a tree even closer to the waves, that serves up a good meal.

OFF THE BEATEN TRACK

HIKING FROM BOGLES TO WINDWARD

A good hike will take you from Bogles to Windward or vice versa via the High North Park, with possible detours to see Anse la Roche (p450) and the wetlands at Petit Carenage. It is partially shaded for most of the way and in some points affords good views of neighboring islands.

Heading out from Bogles, take the left road at the sign to the High North Park. This will quickly turn into a dirt road – it's a vehicle track but traffic is rare and you probably won't see any at all. Veer right where the power lines end; the road then continues along the hillside passing through bushland. After about a 30-minute hike, you'll reach the turnoff to Anse la Roche. Keep an eye out for iguanas and manicous (a local opossum) along the way.

The road then continues on through more bush and down an incline to the small collection of houses that marks the beginning of Petit Carenage, from where it's paved down to Windward. Turn down towards the water just after Petit Carenage to access the lagoon, a good spot for birdwatching.

From Bogles to Windward without detours will take around an hour and a half depending on your pace. Be sure to bring water and a hat, as there are no shops along the way.

Hard Wood Bar & Snacket CARIBBEAN $

(Paradise Beach; mains EC$20-25; ⏲9am-10pm) Near the center of Paradise Beach, this green, yellow and red shack dishes out cold beers and meals of fresh fish, oozing with local flavor. It's a serene, quintessentially Caribbean setting: locals, lifers, expats and the odd traveler pony up to the bar and settle in for a cold one on a hot day.

Slipway BURGERS $$

(☎443-6500; Tyrrel Bay; mains lunch EC$25-32, dinner EC$50-80; ⏲11:30am-2pm & 6-9pm) A chilled little open-air place, right by the water at the end of the bay. It's famed for its top-quality burgers and fish sandwiches but also serves more hearty seafood plates in the evening. As an added bonus it serves West Indies Beer Company ales, too, both in bottles and on tap.

Shopping

Fidel Productions GIFTS & SOUVENIRS

(☎404-8866; Paradise Beach; ⏲9am-4:30pm Mon-Sat) This charming little shop, built into an old shipping container, is a creative cave of niceties featuring locally made T-shirts, original artworks, jewelry, ceramics and some great photographs. Everything is well made and reasonably priced.

Getting There & Away

The local number 10 bus will drop you right at Paradise Beach. If you're heading to Tyrrel Bay it will drop you at the turnoff, from where it's a 10-minute walk down to the dive shops and restaurants or you can pay the driver a little extra to go all the way.

PETIT MARTINIQUE

They don't call it Petit for nothing – this little island is a scant 1 mile in diameter. It's an ideal spot to get away from everything.

With a steep volcanic core rising a stout 740ft at its center, there is little room on the island for much else. The solitary road runs up the west coast, but it is rarely used – locals prefer to walk. Nothing is very far and what's the hurry? The population subsists on the fruits of the sea, either as fishers or boat-taxi operators.

With barely a thousand inhabitants, most of whom are related to each other, this is a place to find peace, quiet – and little else.

Sights

Mang Beach BEACH

The best beach on the island for swimming – there's a reef here that forms a little pool of tranquil water.

Sleeping & Eating

Melodies GUESTHOUSE $

(☎443-9052; s/d US$32/45; 📶) Cheap and cheerful, Melodies has neat and simple rooms, some with balconies facing the impossibly blue ocean; it is worth the couple of extra dollars for an ocean-view room. Guests have access to a shared kitchen upstairs.

Millenium GUESTHOUSE $

(☎533-5847, 443-9243; s/d with air-con US$50/60, s with fan US$30; ❄📶) If you want air-con, this is pretty much your only option. It's a friendly place with decent rooms, but the downside is it's on the back road away from the water.

Palm Beach CARIBBEAN **$$**

(☎443-9103; lunch EC$25-35, dinner EC$33-55; ⏲8am-10pm; 📶) Boasting the biggest menu on the island, Palm Beach serves up delicious plates of conch, fish and lobster alongside burgers and chicken in a waterside setting. Vegetarian dishes are available on request. It also runs a basic guesthouse with two simple rooms overlooking the bay (US$52 to US$67), which include cable TV and a kitchenette.

ℹ Getting There & Away

The Osprey (p448) company ferries passengers between Hillsborough, on Carriacou, and Petit Martinique (one way EC$20) daily, except on weekends when there is no service. It leaves Carriacou from the pier in Hillsborough around noon and comes back from Petit Martinique around 2:30pm.

Another service leaves Carriacou at 3pm and returns at 7:15am the next morning.

An alternative way to get over is to take the mail boat (one way/round trip EC$20/35) from the small town of Windward, directly across from Petit Martinique on Carriacou. It takes school children from Petit Martinique over early in the morning and hangs around until the afternoon heading back around 3pm. On Wednesday and Friday it makes three round trips which makes day trips to Petit Martinique possible. Ask for Jason in Windward or at the tourism office.

A water taxi from Hillsborough to Petit Martinique costs around EC$250. From Windward you should be able to negotiate a much cheaper price with local boat owners.

UNDERSTAND GRENADA

History

Colonial Competition

In 1498 Christopher Columbus became the first European to sight the island of Grenada, during his third voyage to the New World. It wasn't until 1609, however, that English tobacco planters attempted to settle; within a year, most were killed by Caribs, who had first established communities on Grenada in around 1100, having displaced the more peaceful Arawaks, the island's first inhabitants. Some 40 years later, the French 'purchased' the island from the Caribs for a few hatchets, some glass beads and two bottles of brandy. But not all Caribs were pleased with the land deal and skirmishes continued until French troops chased the last of them to Sauteurs Bay at the northern end of the island. Rather than submitting to the colonists, the remaining Caribs – men, women and children – jumped to their deaths from the cliffs.

French planters established crops that provided indigo, tobacco, coffee, cocoa and sugar, and imported thousands of enslaved Africans to tend to the fields. Grenada remained under French control until 1762, when Britain first recaptured the island. Over the next two decades, colonial control of the land shifted back and forth between Britain and France – until 1783, when the French ceded Grenada to the British under the Treaty of Paris.

Animosity between the new British colonists and the remaining French settlers persisted after the Treaty of Paris. In 1795 a group of French Catholics, encouraged by the French Revolution and supported by comrades in Martinique, armed themselves for rebellion. Led by Julien Fedon, an African-French planter from Grenada's central mountains, they attacked the British at Grenville, capturing and executing the British governor and other hostages. Fedon's guerrillas controlled much of the island for more than a year, but were finally overcome by the British navy. Fedon was never captured. It's likely he escaped to Martinique, or drowned attempting to get there, though it's sometimes said that he lived out his days hiding in Grenada's mountainous jungles.

In 1877 Grenada became a Crown colony, and in 1967 it converted to an associated state within the British Commonwealth. Grenada, Carriacou and Petit Martinique adopted a constitution in 1973 and gained collective independence on February 7, 1974.

Independence

One-time trade unionist Eric Gairy rose to prominence after organizing a successful labor strike in 1950, and was a leading voice in Grenada's independence and labor movements. He established ties with the British government and monarchy, and was groomed to become the island's first prime

A PHOENIX RISES

On September 7, 2004, Hurricane Ivan made landfall on Grenada. The first major storm to hit the island in 50 years, Ivan struck with huge force, leaving a wave of destruction that saw 90% of buildings damaged or destroyed, towns decimated and staple crops like nutmeg obliterated.

The following months and years were a dark chapter for this small Caribbean nation, whose economy was left in ruins. Nonetheless, new crops were sown (with fast-growing cocoa replacing nutmeg as the nation's main agricultural export), and homes, shops and offices rebuilt, with Caribbean neighbors lending support to help repair the damage. But within this period of rebirth, instead of simply rebuilding what was once there, opportunity was found.

Hotels, schools, churches and restaurants have been rebuilt bigger and better, incorporating sustainable practices and larger floor plans. Structures that were long overdue to be upgraded were leveled and the new buildings are a massive improvement to what was once there. Today, the only real evidence of Ivan's path is the odd roofless building – and a certain wariness among locals come hurricane season.

minister when Britain relinquished some of its Caribbean colonies. After independence, Gairy's Grenada United Labour Party (GULP) swept to power.

Gairy made early political missteps, such as using his first opportunity to speak in front of the UN to plead for more research into UFOs and the Bermuda Triangle. There were rumors of corruption, of ties with General Augusto Pinochet of Chile and of the use of a group called the Mongoose Gang to intimidate and eliminate adversaries. Power went to Gairy's head and this former labor leader was soon referring to his political opposition as 'sweaty men in the streets.'

Revolutions, Coups & Invasions

Before dawn on March 13, 1979, while Gairy was overseas, a band of armed rebels supported by the opposition New Jewel Movement (NJM) party led a bloodless coup. Maurice Bishop, a young, charismatic, London-trained lawyer and head of the NJM, became prime minister of the new People's Revolutionary Government (PRG) regime.

As the head of a communist movement in the backyard of the US, Bishop tried to walk a very fine line. He had ties with Cuba and the USSR, but attempted to preserve private enterprise in Grenada. A schism developed between Bishop and hard-liners in the government who felt that he was incompetent and was stonewalling the advance of true communism. The ministers voted that Bishop should share power with the hard-line mastermind (and Bishop's childhood friend) Bernard Coard. Bishop refused and was placed under house arrest. While Coard had the support of the majority of the government and the military, Bishop had support of the vast majority of the public.

On October 19, 1983, thousands of supporters spontaneously freed Bishop from house arrest and marched with him and other sympathetic government ministers to Fort George. The army was unmoved by the display and Bishop, his pregnant girlfriend (Minister of Education Jacqueline Creft) and several of his followers were taken prisoner and executed by a firing squad in the courtyard. To this day, it is unclear if the order came directly from Coard – although most believe that it did.

Meanwhile, America became ever more nervous of another potentially destabilizing communist nation in the Caribbean, and six days later 12,000 US marines (along with soldiers from half a dozen Caribbean countries) were on Grenadian shores. US President Ronald Reagan cited the risk to the safety of students at the US-run St George's University as a justification for the invasion; 70 Cubans, 42 Americans and 170 Grenadians were killed in the fighting that ensued. Most of the US forces withdrew in December 1983, although a joint Caribbean force and 300 US support troops remained on the island for two more years. The US sunk millions of dollars into establishing a new court system to try Coard and 16 of his closest collaborators.

Fourteen people, including Coard, were sentenced to death for the murder of Bishop. His death sentence was repealed in 2007 by

Britain's Privy Council, and he was released from prison in September 2009.

The New Era

After the US invasion, elections were reinstituted in December 1985, and Herbert Blaize, with his New National Party, won handily. Many PRG members reinvented themselves politically and found jobs in the new administration. From 1989 to 1995 different political parties jockeyed for control and a few short-term leaders came and went, but all within the democratic process.

In 1995 Dr Keith Mitchell became prime minister, and remained in power for 13 years. Though he had some success building the tourism economy, his government was plagued by accusations of corruption and financial misdealing, and was sharply criticized for a weak initial response to the devastation of 2004's Hurricane Ivan. The 2008 election saw the center-left National Democratic Congress (NDC) take over the reins under Tillman Thomas but his rule was short lived with Mitchell's New National Party (NNP) bouncing back to win elections in a clean sweep in 2013 with the NNP leader now firmly entrenched once again.

People & Culture

Grenadian culture is an eclectic mix of British, French, African and East and West Indian influences. A growing number of expats from the UK, Canada and the Arabian peninsula, and to a lesser extent, the US are making Grenada home, bringing with them new attitudes and ways of life, while wider Caribbean influences also hold sway: as well as local calypso and soca, you'll hear Jamaican dancehall music blaring from speeding buses and nightclub dance floors.

Almost 60% of all Grenadians are Roman Catholic. There are also Anglicans, Seventh Day Adventists, Methodists, Christian Scientists, Presbyterians, Baptists, Baha'is and an increasing number of Jehovah's Witnesses. Because of the pervasive influence of Christian ideals, Sunday is a pretty quiet day around the islands, when many shops and services close. There is also a sizable and growing Muslim population on Grenada island.

The largely religious population makes for a fairly conservative culture, though once you scratch beneath the squeaky-clean veneer, you can see a population that enjoys having a few drinks and kicking up its heels, especially during the annual Carnival.

Education is on the rise and the population is quite learned. Political awareness is high, thanks in part to Grenada's brush with international infamy in the '80s. The shake-up of Hurricane Ivan in 2004 forced a deep cultural reexamination, something that many feel has led to a more mature and forward-thinking nation.

Grenadians themselves are friendly and welcoming. They are proud of their tiny nation and take care of it – there is less rubbish in the ditches and a sense of civic responsibility is palpable.

Though football is making inroads, cricket is followed with near fanaticism here, and remains the unofficial national sport.

Landscape & Wildlife

The Land

Grenada Island, Carriacou and Petit Martinique comprise a total land area of 133 sq miles. Grenada Island, at 121 sq miles, measures 12 miles wide by 21 miles long. The island is volcanic, though part of the northern end is coral limestone. Grenada's rainy interior is rugged, thickly forested and dissected by valleys and streams. The island rises to 2757ft at Mt St Catherine in the northern interior. Grenada's indented southern coastline has jutting peninsulas, deep bays and small nearshore islands.

Carriacou, at just under 5 sq miles, is the largest of the Grenadine islands that lie between Grenada and St Vincent. Many of the others are uninhabited pinnacles or sandbars in the ocean.

Wildlife

Grenada island has a wide range of distinct ecosystems. The lush rainforests that cover the hilly interior are home to armadillo, opossum and mongoose. Mona monkeys were introduced from Africa during the 17th or 18th century but numbers are in decline and their long-term future on the island is in doubt.

The island also supports a rich array of birdlife, both migratory and resident. The interior of the island is home to tiny hummingbirds; osprey and endangered hook-billed kites cruise the thermals; and pelicans, brown boobies and frigate birds patrol the coasts.

Smaller Carriacou and Petit Martinique are much drier and have few fresh-water resources resulting in a less diverse array of wildlife.

In the ocean, sea turtles cruise the grassy shoals and come ashore to nest and lay their eggs. Despite protected status, they are still sometimes slaughtered for their meat and shells; be sure to avoid buying anything made from turtle shell, or eating turtle meat.

Many different types of reef fish populate the surrounding waters. Snorkelers and divers have the pleasure of swimming among barracuda, butterfly fish and the odd nurse shark, as well as browsing forests of brightly colored hard and soft corals.

SURVIVAL GUIDE

Directory A–Z

ACCESSIBLE TRAVEL

- Grenada is a difficult place to get around for travelers with disabilities and many hotels have yet to prioritize accessibility.
- Getting around poses particular problems. Minivan buses are crowded and hard to access as a result of seats being crammed in, and many taxis are vans that are high off the ground.
- There are many places with no sidewalks and those that do exist are often damaged or uneven.
- While there are few dedicated resources for travelers with disabilities, Grenadians are helpful and will usually be willing to lend a hand in any situation.

ACCOMMODATIONS

Most of Grenada's accommodations are in the Grand Anse area, with big beach hotels and smaller guesthouses found just a short drive from the capital.

Though not on the beach, St George's itself makes a lively base with easy access to excellent places to eat and drink.

SLEEPING PRICE RANGES

The following price ranges refer to a double room with bathroom.

$ less than US$100

$$ US$100–250

$$$ more than US$250

On Carriacou accommodations are cheaper than on the main island and range from budget guesthouses in Hillsborough to breezy guesthouses and waterside cottages. There are a string of accommodations in Hillsborough, the capital, and around Paradise Beach, often the liveliest places to be on this superquiet island. There are great options further afield, though they can feel a bit isolated.

Petit Martinique is so small that you'll be sure to mix with the locals – they'll be your neighbors.

ACTIVITIES

Grenada has some first-class diving both on reefs and among the many wrecks that can be found in its waters. Many dive sites are found around the southwest of the island offshore from St George's, Grand Anse and Point Salines.

The Grenada Marine Protected Area covers a large area just north of St George's that includes many of the best reefs on the island.

The following are among the top dive sites:

MV Bianca C Referred to by locals as the *Titanic* of the Caribbean, this enormous cruiser is an awesome high-adrenaline swim-through for advanced divers.

Underwater Sculpture Park (p436) Located in the Grenada Marine Reserve, this underwater gallery is popular with fish as well as divers and snorkelers.

MV Shakem A sunken cement freighter remains for the most part intact – intriguing underwater industrial scenery.

Veronica L An easy shallow wreck dive right by the entrance to St George's – makes a good night dive.

Flamingo Bay In the northern part of the marine reserve, this all-level reef has an amazing variety of coral, sponges and fish. Also a top snorkeling spot.

Dragon Bay Sand channels between volcanic rocks provide a fantastic backdrop at this reef, which has many beautiful sponges and diverse marine life including angelfish, morays and octopuses.

CHILDREN

- Grenada has many calm, gently shelving beaches perfectly suited to children, such as La Sagesse, Lance aux Épines and Morne Rouge; in Carriacou; Paradise Beach is a good bet, too.
- Keep your eye on small children around the roads in St George's as the traffic can be on the wild side; and bear in mind that some of the forts are without sufficient railings or barriers.
- With the exception of major urban areas, sidewalks are absent on many parts of the island and where they are found they don't always have ramps. Avoid walking the Sendall Tunnel with young travelers.

➡ Getting around by public transport with children can be a challenge; vans rarely have seatbelts and are often busy meaning groups will be split among the remaining seats.

➡ Traveling in water taxis can be rough and not always suitable for young travelers; generally the bigger the boat the smoother the ride.

➡ Many hotels don't have TVs, and internet speeds can be too slow to stream so it's worth downloading content before departure.

ELECTRICITY

The electrical current is 220V, 50 cycles. British-style three-pin plugs are most common, but you'll sometimes see US-style two-pin plugs.

EMBASSIES & CONSULATES

US Embassy (☎444-1173; usemb_gd@caribsurf.com; Point Dr)

EMERGENCY NUMBERS

Ambulance, fire, police	☎911

FOOD

You'll find a full range of restaurants on the island of Grenada, from roadside shacks selling fantastic local dishes to formal waterside dining around St George's and Grand Anse.

On Carriacou things are a bit more low key, but there are still plenty of places to dine and the influence of travelers and yachties is evident in the presence of many international flavors. Petit Martinique has just a handful of simple restaurants.

Essential Food & Drink

Roti A tasty flat bread wrapped around curried meat and vegetables.

Oil down Beef and salt pork stewed with coconut milk.

Salt fish and bake Seasoned salt fish with onion and veg, and a side of baked or fried bread.

Lambi The local name for conch.

Carib beer Brewed in Grenada and always served ice cold.

Jack Iron rum Ice sinks in this lethal local belly wash.

HEALTH

➡ There is a public hospital (p439) in St George's and another on the hill above Hillsborough (p450) on Carriacou.

➡ Small private clinics can be found around St George's and the Grand Anse area but they are not well equipped for serious emergencies.

INTERNET ACCESS

➡ There is still the odd internet cafe in St George's and in Hillsborough in Carriacou, but in smaller towns they are becoming hard to find as locals get internet at home or on their phones. Rates run around EC$10 per hour.

EATING PRICE RANGES

The following price ranges relate to the cost of a main meal:

$ less than EC$35

$$ EC$35–70

$$$ more than EC$70

➡ Almost all hotels and many restaurants provide wi-fi for their patrons. Most yacht marinas have wi-fi setups for those docking there.

LGBT+ TRAVELERS

Attitudes to same-sex couples in Grenada (and the Caribbean generally) are not modern or tolerant. Gay and lesbian couples should be discreet in public to avoid hassles.

MONEY

➡ The official currency is the Eastern Caribbean dollar (EC$). There are 24-hour ATMs dispensing EC$ all over Grenada and in Hillsborough, Carriacou.

➡ Major credit cards are accepted by most hotels, top-end restaurants, dive shops and car-rental agencies. Most hotels, shops and restaurants accept US dollars at close to the official rate, but it's worth changing to Eastern Caribbean dollars for smaller transactions.

➡ Accommodations are usually priced in US dollars, as are tours and meals in more upmarket hotels; otherwise, EC$ is used.

➡ Be clear about whether prices are being quoted in Eastern Caribbean or US dollars, particularly with taxi drivers.

Exchange Rates

The Eastern Caribbean dollar is pegged to the US dollar at a rate of 2.70 to 1.

Australia	A$	EC$1.94
Barbados	B$1	EC$1.36
Canada	C$1	EC$2.03
Euro zone	€1	EC$3.05
Japan	¥100	EC$2.41
New Zealand	NZ$1	EC$1.81
UK	UK£1	EC$3.52
US	US$1	EC$2.70

Tipping

Hotels Tips of around EC$5 for porters carrying bags are the norm; gratuities for housekeeping are at guest discretion.

Restaurants A 10% service charge is added to many restaurant bills. If no service charge is added at restaurants, a 10% tip is generally expected.

PRACTICALITIES

Magazines *Lime & Dine* is a glossy magazine with general information on the island and listings of restaurants and entertainment.

Radio & TV Grenada has three main local TV stations and around a dozen radio stations.

Smoking Not particularly common in Grenada. You'll still find some bars that permit smoking but almost all hotels and resort rooms and most restaurants are now completely smoke free.

Weights & measures Grenada uses the imperial system for the most part.

Taxis Fares are generally fixed and tips are not usually expected.

PUBLIC HOLIDAYS

In addition to those observed throughout the region, Grenada has the following public holidays:

Independence Day February 7

Labor Day May 1

Corpus Christi Ninth Thursday after Easter

Emancipation Days First Monday & Tuesday in August

Thanksgiving Day October 25

TELEPHONE

Grenada's country code is 473. When calling from within Grenada, you only need to dial the seven-digit local phone number.

Cell Phones

Local SIM cards are available from Flow (www.discoverflow.co) and **Digicel** (☎415-7900; www.digicelgroup.com/gd; cnr Melville & Granby Sts; ⊙8am-5pm Mon-Fri, to noon Sat) outlets throughout Grenada and Carriacou and will work with unlocked GSM handsets.

TIME

Grenada, along with the rest of the Windward Islands, is on Atlantic Time (GMT/UTC minus four hours).

Getting There & Away

AIR

Grenada has direct air links to the US and UK as well as Barbados, St Vincent and Trinidad and Tobago.

Airports & Airlines

Maurice Bishop International Airport (GND; ☎444-4555; www.mbiagrenada.com) is large and has full services. It has flights from North America and the UK as well as regional Caribbean destinations.

Lauriston airport in Carriacou is a very modest affair with just one international flight – the irregular short hop over to Union Island in St Vincent.

American Airlines (www.aa.com; Maurice Bishop International Airport) Regular flights between Grenada and Miami.

Caribbean Airlines (www.caribbean-airlines.com; Maurice Bishop International Airport) Direct flights linking Grenada with Port of Spain.

LIAT (www.liat.com; Maurice Bishop International Airport) Links Grenada with many other regional destinations. Even if you book a direct flight, you may be sent through other islands.

SVG Air Grenada (☎444-3549; www.grenadaflights.com) Runs flights from Grenada to Union Island in St Vincent and the Grenadines.

SEA

Boat

There is a small mail boat that runs between Carriacou and Union Island (EC$60, one hour) in St Vincent and the Grenadines a couple of times a week.

Commercial ships that haul goods back and forth between Grenada, Carriacou, Petit Martinique and Union Island may sometimes accept foot passengers but it's not a regular possibility.

Cruise Ship

Grenada is a port of call for numerous cruise ships. They dock at the purpose-built pier (p440) just north of the harbor in St George's, Grenada Island. If more than two ships are in port, the old dock on the Carenage is also sometimes used; it's a short walk from the center of town.

Water Taxi

Water taxis between Union Island and Carriacou cost around US$100; it's a bumpy (and often wet) 40-minute ride. Boats can be chartered in Hillsborough or Windward in Carriacou, and Clifton in Union Island.

Yacht

Immigration (open 8am to 3:45pm Monday to Friday) can be cleared on Grenada Island at the following places:

Grenada Marine (☎443-1065; ⊙8am-noon Tue & Thu) St David.

Grenada Yacht Club (☎440-3270; Port Louis Marina) St George's.

La Phare Bleu Marina (☎444-2400; ⊙8am-4pm Mon-Fri, 9am-2pm Sat & Sun) Calivigny.

Prickly Bay Marina (☎444-4509; Prickly Bay Marina; ⊙8am-4pm Mon-Fri, 9am-2pm Sat & Sun) Prickly Bay.

On Carriacou, clearance can be made in Hillsborough (p450).

The most frequented anchorages are Prickly Bay, Mt Hartman Bay, Hog Island and True Blue Bay along the southwest side of Grenada; and Tyrrel Bay in Carriacou.

Getting Around

AIR

SVG Air Grenada has flights between Grenada and Carriacou.

BICYCLE

- Cycling is not big in Grenada, and good equipment is hard to come by, but it is slowly gaining popularity. Many roads are poorly lit and drivers are not used to encountering cyclists, so extra care is needed when getting around.
- It's possible to ride a full 62-mile circuit around the island, although the road is steep and winding in parts so endurance is necessary.
- The road between Grande Anse and the airport is wide and flat and has little traffic, making it a popular place for local cyclists and a good place to meet riding partners.
- Mocha Spoke (p443) in True Blue rents out cycles and also offers guided tours.

BOAT

The **Osprey** (440-8126; www.ospreylines.com) runs a large, fast boat connecting Grenada and Carriacou in less than two hours (one way EC$80) and a smaller vessel linking Carriacou to Petit Martinique (EC$20, 30 minutes) twice daily.

Reservations are rarely required, except on holidays. Tickets from Grenada are purchased on board, and from Carriacou at the office on Patterson St, Hillsborough. The Osprey arrives and departs at the east side of the Carenage in Grenada.

On Carriacou the Grenada services arrive and depart from Tyrrel Bay while Petit Martinique boats run from the Hillsborough pier in the middle of town. If travelling direct from Grenada to Petit Martinique you'll need to take a taxi between ports.

Yacht

Horizon Yacht Charters (439-1000; www.horizonyachtcharters.com; True Blue Bay Marina) is one of Grenada's largest yacht charter operators. You can arrange to have a crewed yacht, where all you have to do is sit back and enjoy the ride; or, if you have sailing experience and are traveling with suitable crew, you can get a 'bareboat' charter where you get sole charge of the vessel.

BUS

- Buses are a great way to get around Grenada and Carriacou. Privately operated minivans run a series of set, numbered routes crisscrossing the islands, and are inexpensive and fun – though they often reach madcap speeds, with drivers maniacally tooting their horn at friends and potential passengers as they go.
- Although main destinations are posted on the front of the bus, alongside the route number, you may need to ask the conductor or driver in order to find the best bus to get to smaller places outside St George's and Hillsborough.
- There are stops along all the major routes, and you can also flag down a bus pretty much anywhere. When you're ready to get off, tap on the roof; if that doesn't work, shout 'bus stop please driver.'

CAR & MOTORCYCLE

Main roads on Grenada are fairly good. Some major firms have agencies here but most rental companies are locally based. You can arrange for pickup at the airport and ferry dock.

Grenada's larger towns, including Grenville, Gouyave and Victoria, have gas stations. On Carriacou there's just one gas station, in Hillsborough.

Driver's License

To drive a vehicle you need to purchase a Grenadian driver's license (EC$60), which all car-rental companies can issue on the government's behalf.

Road Rules

- Driving is technically on the left-hand side of the road, but you can expect buses in particular to be going full bore wherever the hell they want to, with full-beam lights on permanently after dark.
- The roads are very narrow and curvy, and local drivers attack them with great speed. For safety, slow down when approaching blind curves and use your horn liberally.
- There are few road signs in Grenada, so a road map or app and a measure of caution are useful when driving.

TAXI

- You'll find plenty of taxis on Grenada and Carriacou.
- Fares to most destinations are preset.
- Taxis don't tend to circulate but rather wait at dedicated ranks.
- It's worth picking up a couple of cards with numbers for pickups.

Guadeloupe

590 / POP 395,700

Includes ➡

Best Places to Eat

➡ La Touna (p474)
➡ Le Mabouya dans La Bouteille (p469)
➡ La Playa (p482)
➡ Couleurs du Monde (p478)

Best Places to Stay

➡ Tendacayou Ecolodge & Spa (p472)
➡ La Toubana Hôtel & Spa (p466)
➡ Auberge Les Petits Saints (p478)
➡ Hostellerie des Châteaux (p468)
➡ Gwada'Camp (p463)

Why Go?

An archipelago of over a dozen sun-kissed islands, Guadeloupe is a varied place to holiday, with everything from deserted beaches to jungle-wreathed mountains. The country's two main islands look like the wings of a butterfly and are joined together by just a couple of bridges and a mangrove swamp. Grande-Terre, the eastern of the two islands, has a string of beach towns that offer visitors world-class stretches of sand to laze on and plenty of activities. Mountainous Basse-Terre, the western island, is home to thick, lush Parc National de la Guadeloupe, replete with waterfalls and topped by the spectacular La Soufrière volcano.

As well as the 'mainland' of Guadeloupe, small offshore islands – Les Saintes, Marie-Galante and La Désirade – give visitors a taste of Guadeloupe's yesteryear. These are some of the most evocative and untouched destinations in the French Antilles and shouldn't be missed.

When to Go

Dec-May High season, with warm dry weather. Christmas accommodation books up early

Jan-May Drier months are the bet time for for diving and snorkeling

Jul-Nov Rainy season, with average humidity reaching 85%. French holidays in Jul-Aug raise prices and demand.

GRANDE-TERRE

Grande-Terre – which despite its name (meaning 'big land') is far smaller than Basse-Terre – is the most visited island of Guadeloupe. Its south coast, with reef-protected waters and golden-sand beaches, is the country's main resort area.

By comparison, the eastern side of the island is barely touched by tourism: it's largely open to the Atlantic's waves, and instead of beaches has crashing surf off much of its

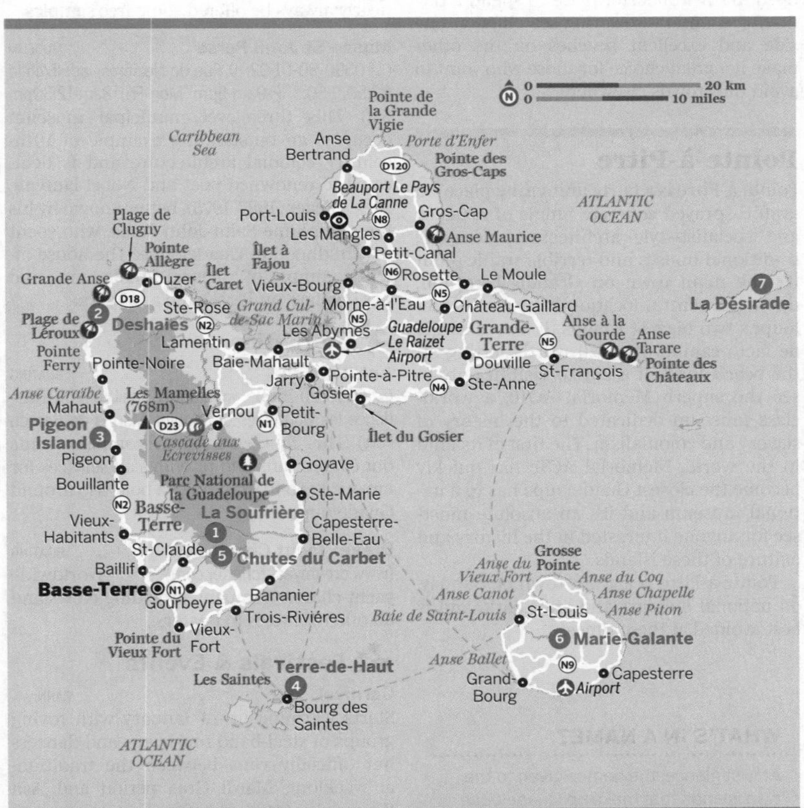

Guadeloupe Highlights

1. **La Soufrière** (p475) Hiking through the rainforest to the misty summit of this brooding active volcano.
2. **Deshaies** (p471) Nourishing your inner gourmet and encountering boaties from around the world in this charming fishing village.
3. **Pigeon Island** (p473) Exploring Jacques Cousteau's underwater reserve in a snorkel mask or with the aqualung he invented.
4. **Terre-de-Haut** (p477) Discovering the gorgeous beaches of this mountainous island full of low-key sophistication and Caribbean history.
5. **Chutes du Carbet** (p475) Hiking through the rainforest on well-marked trails to see this wonderful double waterfall.
6. **Marie-Galante** (p481) Finding your own slice of beach heaven on the unspoiled sands of this much-overlooked island.
7. **La Désirade** (p483) Escaping the mainland's crowds for the day on the beaches of this little slice of paradise.

rocky coastline. It is popular with surfers, however, who converge on the town of Le Moule.

Northern Grande-Terre is one of the most scenically impressive parts of Guadeloupe, but its tourism industry is very undeveloped. It's a wonderful place to spend a day driving around – towering sea cliffs on one side and excellent beaches on the other make it a great choice for those who want to avoid the crowds elsewhere.

Pointe-à-Pitre

Pointe-à-Pitre is a fairly uninviting place – a graffiti-sprayed concrete jungle of art-deco and socialist-style architecture, decaying traditional houses and terrible traffic – but it's the main town on Grande-Terre and, due to its central location between Guadeloupe's two biggest islands, it serves as the de facto capital. It's well worth getting off the beach for half a day to visit, if only to see the superb Mémorial ACTe, a world-class museum dedicated to the history of slavery and colonialism. The first of its kind in the world, Mémorial ACTe has quickly become the closest Guadeloupe has to a national museum and it's an absolute must-see for anyone interested in the history and culture of these islands.

Pointe-à-Pitre is a ghost town on Sunday, on national holidays and after dark, and is best avoided at these times.

WHAT'S IN A NAME?

At first glance, the names given to the twin islands that make up Guadeloupe proper are perplexing. The eastern island, which is smaller and flatter, is named Grande-Terre, which means 'big land,' while the larger, more mountainous western island is named Basse-Terre, meaning 'flat land.'

The names were not meant to describe the terrain, however, but the winds that blow over them. The trade winds, which come from the northeast, blow *grande* (big) over the flat plains of Grande-Terre but are stopped by the mountains to the west, ending up *basse* (flat) on Basse-Terre.

Sights

Marché de la Darse MARKET
(Inner Harbor; 6am-2pm Mon-Sat) This popular market on the seafront in front of Place de la Victoire is Pointe-à-Pitre's main fruit-and-vegetable market. It's full of characters and you'll nearly always be offered some free samples.

Musée St-John Perse MUSEUM
(0590-90-01-92; 9 Rue de Nozières; adult/child €2.50/1.50; 9am-5pm Mon-Fri, 8am-12:30pm Sat) This three-level municipal museum occupies an outstanding example of 19th-century colonial architecture and is dedicated to renowned poet and Nobel laureate Alexis Leger (1887–1975), better known by his nom de plume Saint-John Perse, who spent his childhood in Guadeloupe. The house offers a glimpse of a period Creole home and has displays on Perse's life and work.

Activities

Antilles Sail BOATING
(0590-90-16-81; www.antilles-sail.com; 1 Résidence les Boutiques du Moulin, Marina de Bas du Fort) This long-established company rents out catamarans and provides all services for anyone keen to undertake a boat trip around Guadeloupe.

Dream Yacht Charter BOATING
(www.dreamyachtcharter.com) Worldwide yacht-charter company providing crews and all other services to boaters.

Festivals & Events

Carnival CARNIVAL
Starts warming up in January with roving groups of steel-band musicians and dancers but officially runs between the traditional weeklong Mardi Gras period and Ash Wednesday (46 days before Easter).

Fête des Cuisinières CULTURAL
(Festival of Women Cooks; early Aug) During this colorful event women in Creole dress, carrying baskets of traditional foods, parade through the streets to the **cathedral** (Rue de l'Eglise), where they are blessed by the bishop.

Sleeping

Avoid spending the night in Pointe-à-Pitre if possible, as its hotels are lackluster. Normally the only reason to stay here is if you're catching a flight or ferry early the next morning.

Pointe-à-Pitre

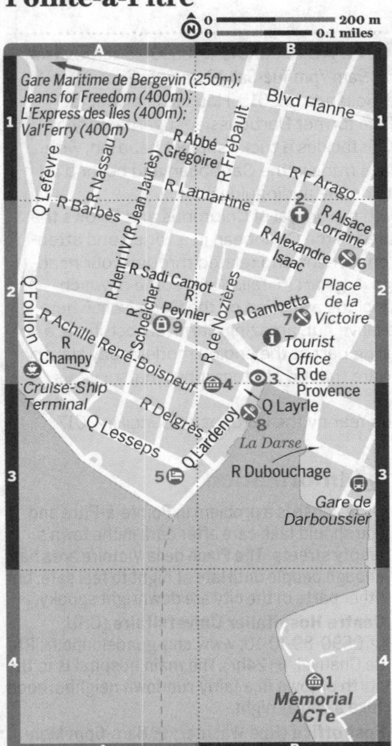

Pointe-à-Pitre

Top Sights
1 Mémorial ACTe B4

Sights
2 Cathédrale de St-Pierre et St-Paul B2
3 Marché de la Darse B2
4 Musée St-John Perse B3

Sleeping
5 Hôtel Saint-John Perse A3

Eating
6 Bella Vita B2
7 Café de France B2
8 Le Yacht Club B3

Shopping
9 Marché Couvert A2

Hôtel Saint-John Perse HOTEL $$
(☎0590-82-51-57; www.saint-john-perse.com; Quai Lesseps; s/d €75/90; ❄📶) This option is totally unexciting, but it's perfectly located between the harbor and the Gare Maritime (p464) and extremely convenient if you're catching an early-morning boat. It has 44 fairly cramped rooms with shared balconies. There's also free luggage storage for guests who want to travel light to the outlying islands.

★**Gwada'Camp** ACCOMMODATION SERVICES $$
(☎0690-26-61-23; www.gwadacamp.fr; 24bd Marina Bas du Fort; per week €550-720) This company run by a French couple rents out refurbished campervans by the week. They're nothing luxurious, but it's a shabby-chic way of seeing the island while saving on accommodation costs. Vans come with double beds, equipped kitchens and a full guide to campervanning in Guadeloupe. A €2000 deposit is required.

★**La Case En Mer** B&B $$$
(☎0590-26-45-13; www.im-caraibes.com/les-ilets; Îlet Boissard; d incl breakfast €150; ❄📶) In search of an escape? This lovely B&B on a quiet islet a free two-minute boat ride from Pointe-à-Pitre offers guests the chance to unplug in two cocoon-like rooms set amid beautifully landscaped gardens, with the bonus of a Jacuzzi. Dinner costs €25, and the affable owners speak good English. Three-night minimum.

Eating

Pointe-à-Pitre is certainly not a place for foodies – in fact, chain fast food might never seem this inviting! The bulk of the population seems to spontaneously vanish from the city at dusk; thereafter they're all usually to be found at the Marina de Bas du Fort (p488), 3km west. Here a number of decent restaurants surround a harbor full of yachts.

Café de France BAKERY $
(Place de la Victoire; pastries from €1.50, sandwiches from €5; ⏲6am-3pm Mon-Sat; 📶) This friendly bakery has a street terrace where you can observe the colorful goings-on of Place de la Victoire. Opening early and serving decent coffee, croissants and other freshly made pastries, it mainly serves as a breakfast spot for those who've stayed the night in Pointe-à-Pitre. It also does good made-to-order sandwiches.

Bella Vita PIZZA $
(Place de la Victoire; mains €8-17; ⏲9am-10:30pm Mon-Sat; 📶) With its ancient booths and Formica tables, this old-timer looks as though it used to be a sandwich shop. However, the people who work here are warm and welcoming,

DON'T MISS

MÉMORIAL ACTE

Top billing in the French Antilles goes to **Mémorial ACTe** (MACTe; ☎0590-25-16-00; www.memorial-acte.fr; Rue Raspail; adult/child €15/5; ⊙9am-7pm Tue-Sat, 10am-6pm Sun; P), a huge museum of slavery opened by President Hollande in 2015. Housed in a spectacular silver-latticework structure on the site of the former Darboussier sugar factory on Pointe-à-Pitre's long-neglected waterfront, ACTe tackles a tricky subject head-on, with various sections dedicated to stages of the slave trade in the Caribbean and beyond in chronological order. Allow at least two hours to do the audioguide justice.

The story starts right from the beginning with the arrival of Columbus and follows the development of slavery and the culture it created in the Caribbean in a varied and attention-grabbing way. The narrative is displayed on screens and related through your headset, but it's also very effectively evoked through large art installations, some of which have been exhibited at the Louvre. Highlights include a section on the Code Noir, where you can see real iron shackles, a mock-up of a slave hut, amazing Carnival costumes, a colourful display on Rastafarianism, and a chilling part at the end on modern-day slavery and people trafficking around the world. Be aware that no photography whatsoever is allowed in the museum, not even on phones.

ACTe was declared European Museum of the Year by the European Council in 2017.

and it's one of the few reliable places to eat in Pointe-à-Pitre after dark. As well as the good pizzas, there are salads, burgers, grilled meat and sandwiches on the menu.

Chez Dolmare SEAFOOD **$$**
(☎0590-91-21-32; Port de Pêche de Lauricisque; mains €11-15; ⊙noon-3pm Mon-Sat) You'll find the best seafood in town here, and it's no wonder – this unpretentious place is located at the small fishing harbor of Lauricisque, northwest of Pointe-à-Pitre's center. The menu is limited to a couple of daily specials, but they're well prepared and relatively good value. Service can be both indifferent and slow, however, so plan accordingly.

Le Yacht Club FRENCH **$$$**
(☎0690-74-57-11; Quai Lardenoy; mains €20-30; ⊙noon-3pm Mon-Wed & Sun, noon-3pm & 7-10pm Thu-Sat; 🛜) Waterside Le Yacht Club is by far the smartest place to eat in the center of town. It serves up refined French cooking from a daily changing menu in a pleasant semi-open-air dining room with fashionable decor. There's a popular barbecue at Sunday lunchtime.

Shopping

Marché Couvert ARTS & CRAFTS
(cnr Rues Peynier & Schoelcher; ⊙6am-4pm Mon-Sat) Pointe-à-Pitre's cast-iron Victorian market is a fairly good place to buy island handicrafts, including straw dolls, straw hats and African-style woodcarvings. It's also a good spot to pick up locally grown coffee and Creole spice blends.

Information

Drug abuse is a problem in Pointe-à-Pitre and you should take care after dark in the town's empty streets. The Place de la Victoire area has enough people until late at night to feel safe, but other parts of the city are downright spooky.

Centre Hospitalier Universitaire (CHU; ☎0590-89-10-10; www.chu-guadeloupe.fr; Rte de Chauvel; ⊙24hr) The main hospital is in the north of town in a fairly rundown neighborhood. Take a cab at night.

Post office (Rue Wachter; ⊙8am-6pm Mon-Fri, to noon Sat)

Tourist office (☎0590-82-09-30; www.lesilesdeguadeloupe.com; Place de la Victoire; ⊙7am-4pm Mon, Tue & Thu, to 12:30pm Wed & Fri) The main tourist office for all of Guadeloupe may be located in the town fewest tourists visit, but it's worth dropping by for the friendly English-speaking staff and the piles of info.

Getting There & Away

BOAT

Pointe-à-Pitre has ferries that connect internationally to Dominica, Martinique and St Lucia. The following companies operate ferries to Les Saintes (Bourg des Saintes) and Marie-Galante (Grand-Bourg), departing from the **Gare Maritime de Bergevin** (Blvd de l'Amitié des Peuples de la Caraïbe), an easy walk from the city center.

Jeans for Freedom (p488)

L'Express des Îles (☎0825-35-90-00; www.express-des-iles.com; Gare Maritime de Bergevin)

Val'Ferry (☎0590-91-45-15; www.valferry.fr; Gare Maritime de Bergevin)

The town also has a **port** (Quai Lesseps) and a cruise-ship terminal (p488).

BUS

In the unlikely event that you need to take a bus elsewhere on Guadeloupe, there are two (rather dilapidated) bus stations in Pointe-à-Pitre, one – **Gare de Darboussier** (Rue Dubouchage) – serving Grande-Terre, and another – **Gare Routière de Bergevin** (Blvd de l'Amitié des Peuples de la Caraïbe) – serving Basse-Terre. Buses to most destinations leave at least hourly, though they stop after dark and only a few services run on Sunday.

The bus from Pointe-à-Pitre to Gosier runs every 15 minutes, costs €1.80 (pay the driver) and takes about 15 minutes. If you're going to the Bas du Fort marina (p488), take this bus and get off just past the university (€1, 10 minutes).

Getting Around

It's perfectly feasible to get around Pointe-à-Pitre on foot, as it's a small town with a compact center.

You can call for a taxi by dialing **Radio Taxis** (☎0590-82-00-00) or **Taxi Leader** (☎0590-82-26-26) in the Pointe-à-Pitre area.

Gosier

Just 8km from Pointe-à-Pitre, Gosier is the biggest tourist spot in Guadeloupe – if you've booked a package holiday on the island, this may be where you end up. Half Caribbean, half high-rise resort, it's clear what brings the crowds to this spot: the beaches, especially the main Datcha beach below the town centre. The coast is given focus by pretty little Îlet du Gosier, a popular boat- or kayak-trip destination.

Sights & Activities

Datcha Beach BEACH

Possibly Guadeloupe's best beach, Datcha is a dreamy strip of cream-hued sand, backed by shade-giving trees and fronted by calm, reef-protected sea. The scene is given focus by the delightful Îlet du Gosier and the moody mountains of Basse-Terre across the water. Beach cafes and bars cater to beachgoers as they watch the numerous yachts that use the bay as safe anchor.

Kaya'Kool KAYAKING

(☎0690-16-51-64; www.kayakool.fr; Datcha Beach; half/full day €20/25; ⏲10am-5pm Tue-Sun) Run by French siblings, this small place rents out kayaks for trips to Îlet du Gosier, 15 to 20 minutes' paddle away. It also offers a package that includes a full day's kayak hire and a meal at the islet's beach restaurant (€39).

Sleeping

Gosier has the highest concentration of hotels in Guadeloupe, and it's precisely for this reason that most travelers will prefer to stay elsewhere on Grande-Terre in search of tranquility and privacy. Hotels are generally rather smart in Gosier, though competition is fierce and there are often bargains to be had.

Hôtel Les Bananiers HOTEL $$

(☎0590-84-10-91; www.les-bananiers.com; Rue des Phares et Basils, Perinet; d/studios incl breakfast €82/95; P❄📶🏊) It's a 1km walk to the town beach from this pretty little complex, but if you don't fancy that there's a small pool around which the four rooms and four studios with kitchenettes are arranged, surrounded by a charming garden. The welcome is very warm and breakfast on the terrace is lovely. A good find, but book ahead year-round.

Auberge de la Vieille Tour RESORT $$$

(☎0590-84-23-23; www.auberge-vieille-tour.fr; Montauban; d from €150; ❄📶🏊) This 103-room establishment incorporates an 18th-century windmill in the lobby and has a stunning location with its own beach. Some rooms sport '90s decor and could do with an update. The hotel restaurant is probably the best on this side of the island.

Eating

The Marina de Bas du Fort (p488), between Pointe-à-Pitre and Gosier, has excellent facilities and a large number of restaurants, bars and cafes.

★**Casa Datcha** INTERNATIONAL $

(☎0690-92-00-76; www.casadatcha.com; Datcha Beach; mains €6-16.50; ⏲11am-8pm) The town's coolest address, Casa Datcha has an enviable location on the sand, an inventive menu with everything from gorgeous salads to superb club sandwiches, and surely the best juice bar on the island, where you can design your own fresh drink to cool off with. There are lots of places to laze around, all set to a Caribbean soundtrack.

Affirmatif INTERNATIONAL $$

(☎0590-89-45-73; 20 Blvd du Général de Gaulle; mains €14-23; ⏲6:30-10pm; 📶) With a blood-red facade and a welcoming, cosy interior, this place multitasks between Creole-French combos and standard international fare such as pizza, pasta and Belgian mussels. The best bet is to stick to the local *acras* (fried fish, seafood or vegetable fritters in tempura), catch of the day, meat in Colombo seasoning and long cocktail list.

Le Bord de Mer CREOLE $$
(☎0590-84-25-23; Blvd Amédée Clara, Chemin de la Plage; mains €16.50-22.50; ⏲9:30am-11pm Mon-Sat, to 5:30pm Sun) This friendly Creole place opens directly onto the sea, and so almost any table has a cracking view toward Îlet du Gosier. The French and Creole fare leans heavily on fish and seafood, but there's also a selection of grilled meats and fresh salads.

★**Restaurant de l'Auberge** FRENCH $$$
(☎0590-84-23-23; Montauban; mains €20-30; ⏲noon-3pm & 6-11pm; 📶) The restaurant in Auberge de la Vieille Tour serves traditional French and Creole cuisine in an understatedly elegant setting and is one of the best fine-dining experiences on the island. It's a good idea to reserve a table if you're not staying at the hotel.

Getting There & Away

There are regular buses between Gosier and Pointe-à-Pitre (€2, 15 minutes). Simply pick up any bus heading west along Gosier's Blvd Charles de Gaulle.

Ste-Anne

The bustling town of Ste-Anne sees a lot of tourists but retains plenty of local character. While the main road between Pointe-à-Pitre and St-François runs through the middle of town, bringing a constant flow of traffic, Ste-Anne has an attractive seaside promenade, a lively beach market selling local produce and a superb white-sand beach stretching along the eastern side. The beach, which offers good swimming and is shaded by sea-grape trees, is particularly popular with islanders, who come here to surf, kayak and paddleboard. But for a less busy vibe, you can always head a short distance west to Plage de la Caravelle – for many, the best beach on Grand-Terre.

Sights & Activities

★**Plage de la Caravelle** BEACH
This headland of white sand about 2km west of Ste-Anne's center is one of Guadeloupe's very finest beaches – it's the Caribbean you probably came to see. Its main tenant is the Club Med resort (undergoing a complete rebuild at the time of writing), but the entire beach is public: anyone is free to walk right in to enjoy the warm, shallow, reef-protected lagoon, the shade of the palm trees and the resident iguanas. There are basic food stalls nearby.

Excursion Guadeloupe CRUISE
(☎0590-74-80-57; www.excursionguadeloupe.com; Plage de la Caravelle) Offers excellent, highly recommended day trips to Petite-Terre, boat tours of southern Grande-Terre and local mangrove ecosystems, and snorkeling trips to various reefs. The team also runs tours of Grande-Terre's interior by 4WD and quad bike. The office is on Plage de la Caravelle, in front of Club Med.

Sleeping

Casa Boubou COTTAGE $$
(☎0590-85-10-13; www.casaboubou.fr; Durivage; d from €75; P❄📶🏊) A good deal for chill-seekers, the 10 cottages here are comfortable, practical (most have kitchens) and clean. They're closely packed but buffered by lush gardens. Guests enjoy free use of snorkeling equipment, and there's a tiny pool. The nearest beach, Plage de la Caravelle, is a 1km walk away. Three-night minimum stay.

★**La Toubana Hôtel & Spa** LUXURY HOTEL $$$
(☎0590-88-25-78; www.toubana.com; Fonds Thézan; d incl breakfast from €280; ❄📶🏊) About 2km west of central Ste-Anne, La Toubana is pure magic. Poised on a quiet coastal cliff, it has stunning views of the sea, Marie-Galante and Les Saintes. The 32 bungalows and 12 suites are stylishly decorated, and there's a small private cove down the hill, two excellent on-site restaurants (including the recommended Grand Bleu) and a superb infinity pool.

Le Relais du Moulin HOTEL $$$
(☎0590-88-48-48; www.relaisdumoulin.com; Le Helleux; ⏲r from €190; P❄📶🏊) This impressive, recently renovated place, topped by its namesake windmill dating from 1843, has 70 bungalows spread among attractive tropical gardens. Bungalows are available as standards or suites, and there's a fantastic pool area, tennis courts, a spa and an on-site Italian restaurant. It's a 500m walk to the nearest beach.

Eating

Food Truck Strip FOOD TRUCK $
(Rue de la Plage; mains up to €10; ⊙11:30am-3pm) At least six food trucks set up on a scrap of land near Le Kontiki restaurant and offer local food and drink. Place your order and bag a plastic garden chair under the awnings – but get here early, as these places are packed out for lunch.

Le Kontiki CREOLE $$
(☎0590-23-55-42; Rue de la Plage; mains €6-23; ⊙7am-7pm; 📶) The superfluous South Seas theme may leave you cold, but the fantastic location at the western end of Ste-Anne beach and the satisfying menu – encompassing fish and meat grills, salads, omelets, pancakes and sandwiches – make this place worth seeking out. The food's inexpensive and snacky, and there's a long drinks list. The place also stays open longer than others here.

Le Grand Bleu FUSION $$$
(☎0590-88-25-57; www.toubana.com; La Toubana Hôtel & Spa, Fonds Thézan; mains €22-35; ⊙1:30-2pm & 7:30-10pm; 📶) The sublime poolside dining at this superb hotel restaurant is a real treat. Expect an elegant lineup of dishes and fabulous desserts, and a romantic, memorable evening. Pick out a table on the breezy veranda and savor the swoony ocean views. Wednesday night features a lavish Creole buffet.

Koté Sud CREOLE $$$
(☎0590-88-17-31; Rte de Rotabas; mains €21-25, menus €32-42; ⊙7-11pm; ❄) This sophisticated, long-standing post-beach restaurant is outside Ste-Anne on the road to Plage de la Caravelle. This is the place to come for the most impressive local cuisine: the menu is a blend of Creole favorites and traditional European dishes done to perfection.

Shopping

Géograines ARTS & CRAFTS
(☎0590-88-38-74; Durivage; ⊙9am-noon & 2-6pm Tue-Sat) This quirky place, clearly signposted off the main road, specializes in items made of seeds – and they all look good. There are seed wall hangings and even a coffee table where black and white seeds are arranged to make a chess board under glass. The shop only shows the work of Guadeloupean artisans that is produced using local materials.

Village Artisanal GIFTS & SOUVENIRS
(Blvd Georges Mandel; ⊙9am-7pm) Between La Caravelle and the town beach, this market has 15 stalls selling a wide choice of souvenirs, from hammocks to rum, soap to beachwear. There's a decent and surprisingly cheap cafe at the front and conveniences behind. On Blvd Georges Mandel (the N4).

Information

Office de Tourisme (☎0596-21-23-83; Ave Frantz Fanon; ⊙7:30am-12:30pm & 2-5pm Mon, Tue & Thu, 7:30am-1pm Wed & Fri) Hidden behind the Village Artisanal, this helpful office has English-speaking staff and can assist with local information, hotel bookings and excursions.

Getting There & Away

Ste-Anne is easy to reach by bus, as it's on the main road between Gosier (€2.50, 30 minutes) and St-François (€2.50, 30 minutes). Pick up buses at any of the stops along the main road through town.

St-François

St-François is a Jekyll and Hyde of a resort. Appealingly, its hotels are slightly higher end than those on most of the island, some of its restaurants are outstanding, the marina is the playground of yacht owners and the town has Guadeloupe's only golf course. On the flip side, though, the town center is a scruffy tangle of streets with lots of derelict buildings – it's an eerie place on weekends and after dark. However, most visitors never make it into town proper, stopping west of St-François at the Plage des Raisins Clairs, the area's best beach.

Another reason you might end up here is to take a ferry to Guadeloupe's smaller islands – there are services to all of them from here.

Just beyond St-François is windswept Pointe des Châteaux. This gorgeous peninsula boasts limestone cliffs pounded by crashing waves, some wonderful beaches and views of La Désirade island.

Sights

Pointe des Châteaux VIEWPOINT
This long peninsula right at the eastern tip of Grande-Terre is a beautiful stretch of landscape. With some good beaches on both sides, it's popular with locals, who head here to escape the crowds in St-François. It's also enormously popular with cyclists, who love the scenic flat road. The culmination of the peninsula is a cliff, topped with a giant cross,

that looks towards La Désirade island and offers spectacular ocean views.

Plage des Raisins Clairs BEACH

(P) The real reason to head to St-François, Plage des Raisins Clairs on the western outskirts of the town is a popular sandy beach where it's safe to swim. There's a gradual slope, no drop-off, a long stretch of relatively shallow water and plenty of shade. Several food trucks and other eateries can be found just back from the sand.

Activities & Tours

Noa Plongée DIVING

(☎0590-89-57-78; www.noaplongee.fr; Marina St-François) At the marina (p488), this small and friendly outfit takes divers to nearby sites twice a day, including ones off La Désirade and Petite-Terre.

Paradoxe Croisières BOATING

(☎0590-88-41-73; www.paradoxe-croisieres.com; Marina de St-François) Runs day trips on the *Paradoxe II* catamaran to the island of Petite-Terre for a spot of iguana-watching, beach-lounging, lunch and snorkeling. Boats leave at 8am and return at 5:15pm; trips cost €90/70 per adult/child under 12. Other catamaran day trips run to Marie-Galante (Thursday only; €105/95 per adult/child under 12) and include a bus tour and lunch.

Surf Action SURFING

(☎0690-31-88-28; www.surfantilles.com; Base Nautique de St-François) The place to come for surfing, windsurfing or stand-up paddleboarding. Surf Action has been one of the best-known surfing outfits in Guadeloupe for years.

Sleeping

Sunset Surf Camp GUESTHOUSE $

(☎0690-41-66-69; www.sunsetsurfcamp.com; Rte Touristique Seze; s €40-70, d €75; P) One of the few budget places to stay in St-François, this friendly guesthouse within easy reach of fantastic Raisins Clairs beach has comfortable rooms (though no air-con), a festive atmosphere, a thick tropical garden *and* charming owners. As well as surfing courses, the owners arrange kitesurfing, paddleboarding, diving and hiking. Free bikes are provided to all guests.

★**La Maison Calebasse** B&B $$

(☎0690-34-07-77; www.lamaisoncalebasse.com; Ste-Madeleine; d €110-150; P) This gleaming and stylish villa is nestled amid sugarcane fields about 2.5km north of St-François. Brigitte, your affable host, has decorated the place with great flair. Choose one of the gîtes (small cottages; rented by the week) or an exceptionally bright room with a handsome bathroom. This is one of Guadeloupe's very best hideaways.

★**Hostellerie des Châteaux** HOTEL $$

(☎0590-85-54-08; www.hostellerie-des-chateaux.com; Pointe des Châteaux; d €110-130) Set on a spacious lawn inland from the road to Pointe des Châteaux (p467), this idyllic hideout has just four rooms and four bungalows, making for total privacy in sublime surroundings. The on-site restaurant is open to the public and has great views, while superb beaches are just a short walk away. The pool is the cherry on the cake.

Hôtel Amaudo HOTEL $$

(☎0590-88-87-00; www.amaudo.fr; Anse à la Barque; d €100-205) This special little place is in the hamlet of Anse à la Barque, a short distance west of St-François. It's a beautiful spot, with communal areas attractively done in a colonial style and all 10 rooms enjoying fantastic sea views and private outdoor areas. There's no beach, but there's a fabulous infinity pool.

La Métisse HOTEL $$

(☎0590-88-70-00; www.hotel-lametisse.com; 66 Les Hauts de St-François; d €110-150) Tucked away in a complex of hotels high above St-François, this pretty place sports a pool in the abstracted shape of Guadeloupe and seven beautifully refitted rooms that combine Creole notes with minimalism. The town is just 1km from here, but it's a long walk to the nearest beach.

Eating & Drinking

St-François has a better range of restaurants than other places on the island.

Colmano INTERNATIONAL $$

(☎0590-53-98-59; Rue de la République, Port de Pêche; mains €18-24; ⊙9am-3pm & 6-10pm Tue-Sat, 9am-3pm Mon & Sun) Small, welcoming restaurant at the harbour serving a mix of Creole and international favourites in a simple dining room and on a tiny terrace out front. The pasta and seafood combos are the thing to go for here – few leave disappointed.

Le Restaurant du Lagon CREOLE $$

(☎0590-23-47-52; Rte du Lagon; mains €12-20; ⊙noon-3pm) At this jetty restaurant, south of the marina that shelters a big lagoon, the setting is ideal for a plate of freshly caught fish, and there's a gently buzzing ambience. It's also a great place to grab a juice or a ti-punch (strong cocktail of rum, lime and cane syrup) and drink in the view.

★ **Le Mabouya dans La Bouteille** FUSION $$$
(☎0590-21-31-14; www.lemabouya.fr; 17 Salines Est; mains €23-35; ⊙7-11pm Wed-Mon;) This outstanding restaurant in the heart of St-François boasts a notably more sophisticated menu than its nearby competitors, with standouts such as duck breast with tamarind and ginger, yam mousse and sweet pumpkin. The improvised space is gorgeous, with bottle openers used as wall decorations, a fabulous wine cellar, mood lighting and jazz in the background.

Le Métis Café SEAFOOD $$$
(☎0690-53-81-50; www.le-metis-cafe.com; Salines Est; mains €16-31; ⊙6-11pm Tue-Sun;) Hugely popular, this happening and convivial painted-timber restaurant serves up superb food and drinks and enjoys a buzz you'll find in few other Guadeloupe eateries. Its brochettes are just as giant as advertised – come hungry! There's usually great live music on Thursday and Friday. Reservations are always a good idea.

Information

Office de Tourisme (☎0590-68-66-81; www.destination-stfrancois.com; Ave de l'Europe; ⊙8am-5pm Mon-Fri, 9am-3pm Sat & Sun mid-Nov–mid-Apr, shorter hours & closed Sun rest of year) This large, modern tourist office with some English-speaking staff has up-to-date information on all ferry services from St-François.

Getting There & Away

BUS

St-François is well connected by bus to towns along the south coast of Grande-Terre, including Pointe-à-Pitre (€4.50, 55 minutes), Gosier (€3, 45 minutes) and Ste-Anne (€2.50, 30 minutes). Buses run at least hourly during the day from the town's Gare Routière at the ferry port.

BOAT

The **Achipel 1** (☎0690-49-49-33; Gare Maritime de St-François) connects St-François to La Désirade twice a day in both directions (45 minutes). **Comatrile** (☎0590-22-26-31; www.comatrile.com; Gare Maritime de St-François) runs the *Iguana Beach*, which connects St-François to Les Saintes each morning, stopping at St-Louis (Marie-Galante) on the way. It returns from Les Saintes via Marie-Galante each afternoon. Check the website for exact timings and prices, as these vary enormously.

Both services depart from St-François' Gare Maritime, where ticket offices open shortly before departures.

Le Moule

The town of Le Moule may have served as an early French capital of Guadeloupe, but it was an important Native American settlement in precolonial times, too, with some two millennia of history to its name (incidentally, its name is said to derive from the Creole word for pier, and has nothing to do with mussels). That said, unless you're a surfer or a pre-Columbian history enthusiast, Le Moule is unlikely to be on your itinerary.

Those passing through will enjoy the wide town square with its historic buildings, including a prettily painted town hall and a neoclassical Catholic church. Along the river are the discernible waterfront ruins of an old customs building and a fortress dating to the original French settlement. Parc Oüatibi-tibi, on the seafront, is an important Native American archaeological site, but the results of excavations are now nearly all in the town's museum.

Sights

Edgar Clerc Archaeological Museum MUSEUM
(Rte de la Rosette; ⊙9am-5pm Mon-Fri) FREE This relatively small but informative museum has a fascinating display of archaeological finds made on Guadeloupe and elsewhere in the Caribbean. Much of the Carib pottery, jewelry and tools made of shells and stone come from Le Moule itself, some discovered by Martinique archaeologist Edgar Clerc in the 1960s and '70s. He was also the museum's first curator. Highlights of the two rooms include a map of the Caribbean featuring all the islands' pre-Columbian names and a mock-up of an Amerindian village.

There are English explanations throughout. The museum is about 1km north on La Rosette road (D123), on the western outskirts of Le Moule.

Damoiseau Distillery DISTILLERY
(☎0590-23-78-23; www.damoiseaurhum.com; Bellevue; ⊙self-guided tours 8am-2pm Mon-Sat, gift shop 8am-5:30pm Mon-Sat; P) FREE For

those who don't speak French but know how distilleries work, this is a nice chance to wander around at will. It's particularly active during the cane harvest (February to June). The gift shop has a good selection of rums made on the premises and offers free tastings. It's well signposted about 3km west of Le Moule.

Sleeping & Eating

The tourist office can provide a list of vacation rentals, including gîtes and apartments in the area. Apart from that there are almost no accommodation options in Le Moule. Most visitors prefer to stay on Grande-Terre's south coast.

Le Spot CAFE $$
(0590-85-66-02; Blvd Maritime; mains €16-26; noon-10pm Tue-Sun;) There are incredible views into the churning waters below from this open-air bar and restaurant on Le Moule's seafront. It's the perfect place to watch surfers frolicking in the waves while you enjoy a fancier-than-usual assortment of fish and seafood dishes.

Information

Office de Tourisme (0590-23-89-03; Blvd Maritime; 9am-1pm & 2-5pm Mon-Fri) Has lots of maps and free booklets (in French). It can also provide a list of vacation rentals, including gîtes and apartments in the area.

Getting There & Away

There are hourly buses between Le Moule and both Pointe-à-Pitre (€3, 40 minutes) and St-François (€2, 20 minutes).

Northern Grande-Terre

Largely agricultural, Northern Grande-Terre offers chunks of semiwilderness, occasional spectacular scenery and a smattering of delightful beaches. Tourists largely skip the area as attractions are thin on the ground and there are very few places to stay. This makes a day's drive through the north all the more intriguing, as away from the natural beauty the towns have a Caribbean charm that's all but gone in other parts of Guadeloupe.

Sights

Anse Bertrand BEACH
This beach in the small town of the same name has golden sand and is backed by palm trees. It's rarely too crowded and is one of the loveliest beaches in Northern Grande-Terre.

Pointe de la Grande Vigie VIEWPOINT
The island's northernmost point, Pointe de la Grande Vigie offers scenic views from its high sea cliffs. A rocky path – walkable in flip-flops but better in trail shoes – makes a windy loop through scrubland from the parking lot to the cliffs and back, and has some fantastic views. On a clear day you can see Antigua to the north and Montserrat to the northwest, each about 75km away.

Anse Laborde BEACH
Make a beeline for this oft-overlooked white-sand beach about 1.5km north of Anse Bertrand. Strong riptides make it quite dangerous for swimming, but the peace you find sitting under a tree here may be as good as it gets in Northern Grande-Terre. A rightly popular beach restaurant, Au Coin des Bons Amis, provides Caribbean sustenance just steps from the sand.

Anse du Souffleur BEACH
(Port-Louis) This long, gently arching beach in northwestern Grande-Terre has soft, pale sand, lapis-lazuli waters and fabulous views of mountainous Basse-Terre in the distance. Despite being very popular at weekends, it remains gently developed, with just a couple of simple restaurants – and instead of hotels at one end there's a large cemetery!

Porte d'Enfer NATURAL FEATURE
(D122) 'Hell's Gate' is actually a long, narrow lagoon that could be mistaken for a river. Its banks are a nice place for a picnic lunch on a drive around the north, though swimming and snorkeling are not advised as the water can be murky. Some say the rather dramatic name comes from the water crashing at the mouth of the lagoon; others say it's from the sulfuric pong of rotting seaweed that sometimes builds up here.

Sleeping & Eating

Domaine de la Grande Vigie VILLA $$
(0590-22-14-74; www.domainedelagrandevigie.com; Pointe de la Grande Vigie, Anse Bertrand; d €85-113;) Your money goes far with these well-equipped, spacious and well-spaced-out bungalows scattered amid a garden overflowing with blossoming tropical vegetation, plus there are magnificent ocean views from the decked swimming pool. While you're nowhere near the beach, each villa includes a hire car for the duration of

your stay, so it's easy to reach Anse Bertrand and other nearby beaches.

Au Coin des Bons Amis CREOLE $
(Anse Laborde; mains €8-13; ⏲10am-4pm) Right on Anse Laborde beach, this place raises the bar for beach-shack cuisine. You'll be surprised that such good eats can come from such an unprepossessing place. Excellent grilled freshwater prawns and tasty catch-of-the-day grilled fish are some of the specialties on offer. It's just a pity it closes so early.

Chez Coco CREOLE $$
(☎0690-75-34-84; Porte d'Enfer; mains €12-18; ⏲noon-4pm; P) Dining under the trees on the beach right on the lagoon at Porte d'Enfer is the main draw at this charming shack. The menu abounds in local flavor and includes everything from grilled fish to skewered conch. Coconut sorbet for dessert is a must, and don't forget to try one of the many specialty rums or excellent cocktails.

Note that Chez Coco is only open when there are likely to be lots of people on the beach.

ℹ Getting There & Away

Although the odd shared taxi runs to towns in Northern Grande-Terre, you need a car to get the most out of this remote area.

BASSE-TERRE ISLAND

Basse-Terre is Guadeloupe's trump card. Despite its name meaning 'low land,' it rather confusingly boasts soaring peaks, including the active La Soufrière volcano, and is by far the more dramatic of Guadeloupe's two main islands. Indeed the entire center of Basse-Terre is covered in thick rainforest and makes up the impressive Parc National de la Guadeloupe.

But this magnificent scenery is not at the expense of good beaches, and you'll find some wonderful stretches of sand on Basse-Terre as well as one of the best dive sites in the Caribbean around Pigeon Island. The northwestern corner of Basse-Terre is the most scenic. Starting from the western side of Route de la Traversée, most of the west coast is rocky and many of the drives snake along the tops of towering sea cliffs, with tantalizing glimpses of the azure bays below. Whatever you do in Guadeloupe, do not miss Basse-Terre.

ℹ Getting There & Around

Most travellers to Guadeloupe rent a car at the airport for their entire stay and you'll certainly need one to reach many parts of the national park and out-of-the-way beaches.

It's perfectly possible to reach Basse-Terre by bus, however: from Pointe-à-Pitre's Gare Routière de Bergevin (p465) there are regular buses to all towns on the island. Sample prices and travel times include Deshaies (€2.40, 40 minutes), Plage de Malendure (€3.70, 50 minutes) and Trois-Rivières (€4.20, one hour). All buses go at least hourly during daylight hours, though they stop after dark and generally don't run on Sunday.

Trois-Rivières also has numerous daily boats to Les Saintes. Prices and timings vary enormously due to season, demand and current offers, but you can check details on the website of one of the following operators:

- **CTM Deher** (p489)
- **Navette Beatrix** (p489)
- **Val'Ferry** (☎0590-94-97-09, 0590-91-45-15; www.valferry.fr; Allée des Espadons; ⏲7am-7pm)

Deshaies

Framed by green hills, charmingly sleepy Deshaies has just the right balance of traditional fishing village and good eating and drinking options to keep visitors coming here year-round. It may not have a beach of its own, but a short drive away is arguably the best stretch of grains on Guadeloupe for swimming and sunbathing: Grande Anse. Thanks to its sheltered bay, the village is a popular stop with yachties and sailors, and has a slightly cosmopolitan air despite its diminutive size.

Sights

★Grande Anse BEACH
This superb golden-sand beach with no hotel development in sight is just 2km north of Deshaies. This is one of Basse-Terre's longest and prettiest stretches of sand. The place is no secret, though, and you won't be alone, but it's easy to escape the crowds by walking down the bay. However, with children you should head to the middle of the beach, where the waves are least powerful. Restaurants and cafes cluster around the parking lot.

Jardin Botanique de Deshaies GARDENS
(☎0590-28-51-37; www.jardin-botanique.com; Villers; adult/child €15.90/10.90; ⏲9am-5.30pm; P 👪) Away from the beach, Deshaies' top

attraction is its botanical garden, which also has some interesting animal life to keep the kids entertained. Among the well-organised displays of amazing tropical flora (with signage in French only), vending machines issue small amounts of feed (€0.50) that children can sprinkle onto fish and hold out to free-flying parrots. Iguanas wander the grounds, and at the end you can stroke a goat. There's also a playground and a snack bar.

Plage de Clugny BEACH

Between Grande Anse and Ste-Rose, at the northern tip of Basse-Terre, this dazzling stretch of golden sand is lapped by jade waters that just beg to be swum in. The beach has views toward a dramatic islet in the bay and, beyond, to Montserrat when visibility is good. Bar one little terrace snack bar at the far end of the beach, Plage de Clugny is totally undeveloped. Kids in particular love it for its shallow water and thrilling wave action.

Sleeping

While there are few sleeping options in Deshaies itself, there's a great number of charming guesthouses and hotels in the surrounding hilly countryside, and nearly all of them come with superb views.

★**Le Rayon Vert** HOTEL $$

(☎0590-28-43-23; www.hotels-deshaies.com; La Coque Ferry; s/d from €119-148;) Situated in Ferry, south of Deshaies, this sunset-friendly seducer is a great place to enjoy a small-scale resort complete with an infinity pool that boasts stunning sea views. The 22 rooms are generously proportioned and functional, with sleek design elements. It's well worth paying for the higher-category rooms with extra space.

Caraïb'Bay Hotel HOTEL $$

(☎0590-28-54-43; www.caraibbayhotel.com; Allée du Coeur; s/d/tr incl breakfast €160/190/240;) Set in gorgeous tropical gardens just a few minutes' (uphill) walk from Grande Anse, one of Guadeloupe's best beaches, this very pleasant, family-friendly hotel has comfortable and brightly painted duplexes and villas scattered through its grounds. All the accommodations are clean, and while the decor can sometimes be a little uninspiring, the place exudes a welcoming atmosphere.

Ali Naïs GUESTHOUSE $$

(☎0690-42-07-01; www.gite-cabane-ali-nais.com; Allée Capado, Bas Vent; d/cabanas/ste €109/140/140;) Well north of Deshaies, this adults-only guesthouse is run by the warm and welcoming Valérie, who has created three gorgeous rooms (well, a room, a *cabana* and a suite) and a pool on the grounds of her own mountainside home, all with great views toward the sea.

Langley Resort Fort Royal RESORT $$

(☎0590-68-76-70; www.fortroyal.eu; Petit Bas Vent; d incl breakfast €105-235;) This sprawling resort enjoys almost exclusive access to two fabulous stretches of beach either side of it, and also has a large pool, a full water-sports center, tennis courts, a restaurant overlooking the beach and a kids' club. The cheaper rooms occupy a soulless monolith but enjoy divine sea views; the more appealing bungalows cling to a lush hillside.

★**Tendacayou Ecolodge & Spa** BOUTIQUE HOTEL $$$

(☎0590-28-42-72; www.tendacayou.com; Matouba, Hauts de Deshaies; d incl breakfast €195-454;) This incredible hideaway in the mountains above Deshaies is run with flair by a French architect and his wife, and it may well be the most memorable and unique accommodation in Guadeloupe. The 11 spacious duplexes include three full-on villas and one multilevel wooden treehouse. All are wonderfully designed and set in fabulous tropical grounds.

Eating

Mahina SEAFOOD $$

(☎0590-88-95-38; Blvd des Poissonnières; mains €14-28, pizza €10-13; ⏲noon-2:30pm & 7-10pm Wed-

WORTH A TRIP

BEAUPORT LE PAYS DE LA CANNE

Since it ceased operations, the former sugar factory **Beauport le Pays de la Canne** (☎0590-48-96-30; www.beauport-guadeloupe.com; Port-Louis; adult/child €15/10; ⏲9am-5pm Tue-Sun; P) has been converted into a learning center about the local region and the history of slavery and sugar growing in the Caribbean. You can take a 50-minute train ride through the old sugar plantation, and there are some excellent exhibits to see in and around the surviving buildings that make up the large complex.

Sun;) Overlooking the bay and boasting a great terrace as well as a 2nd-floor dining room with good views, this simple-looking place churns out far more sophisticated food than you might expect. As well as the usual seafood offerings, there's a daily changing tapas menu and in the evening excellent pizzas, made in a wood-fired oven to a reggae beat.

L'Amer FRENCH CARIBBEAN **$$**
(0590-28-50-43; Blvd des Poissonnières; mains €18-25; 8am-11pm Mon-Sat;) Ignore the lobster tank at the entrance to this conspicuously orange building, which is actually a refined Deshaies institution. The interesting menu takes in seafood and swordfish, and combines French tradition with attention to local flavors. Downstairs has a simple vibe during the day, when you can eat a good sandwich on the sunny terrace; evenings upstairs are more formal.

La Savane FRENCH **$$**
(0590-91-39-58; Blvd des Poissonnières; mains €17.50-23; 7-10pm Thu-Sat, Mon & Tue, noon-3pm & 7-10pm Sun;) Look past the naff African-animal theme to find high-quality cuisine and a divine location right on the seafront, with a terrace from which to drink it all in. The menu blends classic French such as veal kidneys in mustard sauce and Creole dishes such as shrimps in coconut milk and red curry. Wonderful desserts round out the offerings.

Le Coin des Pêcheurs CREOLE **$$**
(0590-28-47-75; Rue de la Vague Bleue; mains €15-29; 5:30-7:30pm Mon & Wed-Fri, 11:30am-7:30pm Sat & Sun;) This colorful one-story beach restaurant has a great position overlooking the bay. Many alfrescoholics would go back to this breezy veranda by the sea for the location alone, but the well-priced Creole-eclectic fare is delightful, too.

Les Hibiscus CREOLE **$$**
(0590-28-22-50; Grande Anse; mains €10-17; from 11am) This ramshackle but welcoming open-air eatery overlooking the beach serves classic Creole fare done properly. It's arguably the pick of the extensive bunch at Grande Anse. There's often live music at weekends, frequently to the annoyance of those tanning themselves nearby.

★ Le Poisson Rouge INTERNATIONAL **$$$**
(0590-28-42-72; www.tendacayou.com; Tendacayou Ecolodge & Spa, Matouba, Hauts de Deshaies; mains €25-35; noon-3pm & 6-11pm Wed-Sun;) This elegant restaurant within Tendacayou Ecolodge & Spa is an atmospheric place for destination dining. Mains such as tuna tataki in granadilla sauce are delicious and beautifully presented, and you could lose yourself in the homemade *moelleux au chocolat* (chocolate cake) that arrives at the end of the meal.

> **BASSE-TERRE TOWN**
>
> The capital of both Basse-Terre island and Guadeloupe as a whole is the very unremarkable town of Basse-Terre. It has nothing to detain visitors.

Getting There & Away

There are at least hourly direct buses to Deshaies (€2, 40 minutes) from Pointe-à-Pitre's Gare Routière de Bergevin, and connections to other towns in Basse-Terre from Deshaies.

Plage de Malendure & Pigeon Island

This long stretch of overlapping beachside towns and villages is an ideal destination for divers and snorkelers, who come to explore the superb Réserve Cousteau around little Pigeon Island and relax on Plage de Malendure's dark sand. Backed by steep hills, the coast is pure pleasure to drive along. Plage de Malendure is not the finest beach in the area, but it's one of the best in Guadeloupe for activities, and competition between myriad diving and kayaking companies keeps prices reasonable.

Sights & Activities

★ Réserve Cousteau NATURE RESERVE
Jacques Cousteau brought Pigeon Island to international attention by declaring it to be one of the world's top dive areas, and the waters surrounding the island are now protected as an underwater park. The majority of the dive sites around Pigeon Island are very scenic, with big schools of fish and coral reefs shallow enough for good snorkeling. It's only a 10- to 15-minute boat ride to the dive sites; myriad operators run trips from Malendure Beach.

Nautilus WILDLIFE WATCHING
(0590-98-89-08; www.lesnautilus.com; Plage de Malendure; adult/child €25/13; 9am-4pm;) This glass-bottom boat is an easy way to see the wildlife teeming around Pigeon

Island – it's ideal for people with limited mobility or families with young children. The view from the windows below water level is stupendous, with fish often nosing right up to onlookers. There's a 30-minute snorkeling halt and a free drink for all.

★Gwada Pagaie KAYAKING
(0590-10-20-29, 0690-93-91-71; www.gwadapagaie.com; Plage de Malendure) Fancy seeing Réserve Cousteau from a different perspective? With a kayak you can reach Pigeon Island at your own pace. This outfit rents two- and four-seaters for €25/35 per half/full day. Life jackets and waterproof containers are provided; bring a picnic. Note that children under 12 have to be able to swim at least 25m without a flotation aid.

PPK-Plaisir Plongée Karukera DIVING
(0590-98-82-43; www.ppk-plongee-guadeloupe.com; Plage de Malendure) This efficiently run dive shop (introductory/single dive €45/40) gets good reviews. It also fits snorkeling in during its dive outings (€15), organises night dives and runs courses.

Centre de Plongée des Îlets DIVING
(0590-41-09-61; www.plongee-guadeloupe.fr; Plage de Malendure) Diving here starts at an incredibly good-value €38 for divers with their own equipment. An introductory dive costs €47. With two boats, this operation tends to have larger groups and offers all kinds of instruction for beginners.

Les Heures Saines DIVING
(0590-98-86-63; www.heures-saines.gp; Le Rocher de Malendure, Bouillante) This extremely versatile operation is based under Le Rocher de Malendure restaurant. In addition to the standard dive courses and outings, it can organize hikes, canyoning and dolphin-watching trips.

Canopée HIKING
(0590-26-95-59; www.canopeeguadeloupe.com; Plage de Malendure) The area's best canyoning and hiking operation runs a huge number of trips into the nearby mountains, from half-day walks (€35) to more challenging canyoning adventures (from €55).

Sleeping & Eating

There are several accommodations inland from Plage de Malendure, but most are private setups such as gîtes or studios, and there are almost no hotels here. One excellent option, though, is Le Jardin Tropical, a perfect base if you plan to spend a few days doing various activities.

Le Jardin Tropical HOTEL $$
(0590-98-77-23; www.guadeloupehebergement.fr; Rue de Poirier, Bouillante; d from €80; P❄📶≋) Le Jardin Tropical stands out for its welcoming owners, a pool that feels nearly private, and a super location on a greenery-shrouded hillside with views of the sea and Pigeon Island. The bungalow rooms are sparkling clean, simply furnished and good value, and all have patios and kitchens. Dinner can be waiting for you post-dive by arrangement.

★La Touna SEAFOOD $$
(0590-98-70-10; www.la-touna.com; Bouillante; mains €16-25; 10am-2pm & 6-10pm Tue-Sat, 10am-2:30pm Sun; 📶) This fantastic and riotously popular seafront restaurant just south of Plage de Malendure has an enticing and innovative menu and is the best place to eat along this part of the coast. The tasty Creole food with a French twist focuses on fresh seafood, while the terrace has pretty views of Pigeon Island.

Chez Loulouse CREOLE $$
(590-98-70-34; Plage de Malendure; mains €14-23; 11am-9pm; 📶) They've been serving salt-encrusted divers at this beach restaurant since 1969 and it's still the best place to eat amid the kiosks and dripping diving gear on Plage de Malendure. Local grilled fish, lobster in secret sauce and a long drinks card set the tone on the menu, and the sea's so close that you can take a dip while waiting.

Le Rocher de Malendure INTERNATIONAL $$$
(0590-98-70-84; Bouillante; mains €16-34; noon-9:30pm) This sprawling complex is actually built on the eponymous rock just south of Plage de Malendure and has incredible views on all sides. The restaurant offers everything from beef fillet to the fresh lobsters it keeps in a small pool (if that's your thing). Pricey desserts.

Getting There & Away

Hourly buses between Pointe-à-Pitre and Basse-Terre town pass through Plage de Malendure (€3.50, 50 minutes) and Bouillante (€3.50, 55 minutes), and will drop you at one of several stops along the main road through both towns. Similarly priced, hourly buses between Pointe-à-Pitre and Vieux-Habitants also stop in both places.

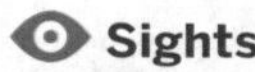

Ste-Rose

Ste-Rose was once a simple seaside village, primarily involved with fishing and agriculture. While sugarcane is still an important crop in the area, Ste-Rose also sees a bit of tourist traffic, not least because it's the main launching pad for boat excursions to Grand Cul-de-Sac Marin, a marine park dotted with idyllic islets ringed by sandy beaches, mangrove swamps and healthy reefs. Otherwise there's little to keep you here among the fish guts, begging frigates and piles of fishing net.

Sights

★Grand Cul-de-Sac Marin NATURE RESERVE
This Unesco Biosphere Reserve just off the coast of Basse-Terre makes for an enjoyable day trip. A chain of coral islets sitting atop a 25km-long coral wall, the reserve supports unique ecosystems, including mangrove forest, rich birdlife and reefs bursting with tropical fish. There are also some gorgeous white-sand beaches where you'll never have to worry about overcrowding. Book a boat trip through one of the many agencies in Ste-Rose.

DON'T MISS

PARC NATIONAL DE LA GUADELOUPE

Guadeloupe's only national park, **Parc National de la Guadeloupe** (☎0590-41-55-55; www.guadeloupe-parcnational.fr; Montéran) is an absolute stunner, covering much of the interior of Basse-Terre and including such sights as the Chutes du Carbet waterfall and La Soufrière, the active volcano that soars over the island. There's a large number of well-signed and well-maintained hiking paths and the Maison de la Forêt information centre, which is conveniently located in the middle of the park on the Route de la Traversée.

Unless it's overcast, the drive up to the **Chutes du Carbet** lookout gives a view of two magnificent waterfalls plunging down a sheer mountain face. From the lookout you can see the two highest waterfalls from the upper parking lot, where a signboard marks the trailhead to the falls' base. The well-trodden walk to the second-highest waterfall (110m) takes 20 minutes; it's about a two-hour hike to the highest waterfall (115m).

Note that at the time of writing the trails were off-limits due to landslides caused by renewed activity at La Soufrière volcano at the beginning of 2019.

Active volcano **La Soufrière** (1467m) looms above Basse-Terre's southern half. For an adventurous 1¾-hour hike to the sulfurous, moonscape-like summit, a well-beaten trail starts where the road to the volcano ends at a parking lot. The trail travels along a gravel bed and continues steeply up the mountain through a cover of low shrubs and thick ferns. You'll have a close-up view of steaming La Soufrière as well as some fine vistas of the island. Start early in the morning.

There are a couple of ways to get to La Soufrière. The most direct route is to follow the N3 from Basse-Terre town in the direction of St-Claude. From St-Claude, signs point to La Soufrière, 6km northeast on the D11.

Note that at the time of writing the trails around La Soufrière were officially out of bounds due to the volcano's renewed activity in early 2019.

Cascade aux Ecrevisses (Rte de la Traversée; P) is an idyllic jungle waterfall dropping from a Basse-Terre mountainside into a small riverside pool where you can swim. It's a wonderful and therefore popular spot and can get a bit crowded at weekends, mainly as it's right on main road through the Parc National de la Guadeloupe. On the other side of the road is a large, uncrowded picnic area, also by the river, with shaded benches and barbecue pits.

The **Maison de la Forêt** (⏲9am-4:30pm Mon-Sat, to 12:30pm Sun Nov-Apr, Jul & Aug, 9:30am-4:30pm Mon-Fri May, Jun, Sep & Oct) is a useful and well-run information center for anyone keen to explore the Parc National de la Guadeloupe. It includes a staffed exhibit center with French-signed displays and English-language pamphlets, plus maps of the geographical features of the park. It's located along the Route de la Traversée, aka D23, the main road through the park.

Several hikes begin and end at the center, including an easy 20-minute taster through the jungle nearby.

WORTH A TRIP

ZOO DE GUADELOUPE

One of Guadeloupe's must-sees, the excellent **Zoo de Guadeloupe** (0590-98-83-52; www.zoodeguadeloupe.com; D23; adult/child €15.50/9; 9am-6pm; P), high in the mountains of Basse-Terre, combines animal enclosures with a jungle adventure. Follow the prescribed route along a boardwalk through lush vegetation to visit toucans, anacondas, iguanas, tortoises, monkeys and parrots. The visit ends at a long canopy walk high above the jungle floor. A highlight for children is feeding the racoons near the entrance. There's lots of educational info in English, so allow two to three hours to do the place justice.

Musée du Rhum MUSEUM
(Rum Museum; 0590-28-70-04; www.rhum-reimonenq-musee.com; Bellevue; adult/child €6/4; 9am-5pm Mon-Sat) Those who want to understand how the ambrosia called rum starts in the sugarcane fields and ends on their palate should head to this museum, which has thorough explanations in English. It's at the site of the Reimonenq Distillery, about 500m inland from the N2 in the village of Bellevue, just southeast of Ste-Rose. Exhibits include an old distillery, cane-extraction gears and a vapor machine dating from 1707.

Activities & Tours

Tam Tam KAYAKING
(0690-75-70-02; www.guadeloupe-kayak.com; Port de Pêche; half day adult/child €35/15) For those who prefer to explore the reefs and islands under their own steam and in the most ecofriendly way, this agency will lend you a kayak and a map for a half- or full-day tour.

BleuBlancVert BOATING
(0690-63-82-43; www.bleublancvert.com; Port de Pêche; half day adult/child €35/15) This well-regarded operator runs half-day lagoon and mangrove tours on a motorized raft. Your guide will impart environmental and geological knowledge, and you'll have the opportunity to snorkel along the barrier reef. Small groups only (four people maximum).

Eating

Le Poulpe SEAFOOD $$
(0590-28-74-21; Blvd St-Charles; mains €12-25; noon-3pm Mon-Sat) This small, open, terraced place is a local institution and locals tell you it is the place to go for the best Creole take on seafood dishes. Do not miss its excellent *fricassée de chatroux* (octopus stew). Hours can be erratic.

Chez Clara CREOLE $$
(0590-28-72-99; Blvd St-Charles, Bord de Mer; mains €16-29; lunch Thu-Tue, dinner Mon, Tue & Thu-Sat; ) Across the road from Ste-Rose's small fishing harbor, this casually gracious place has sea views and serves up classics such as tuna tartare, veal cutlet and lamb steak. Don't come here in a hurry – this is the classic place for a relaxed lunch.

Getting There & Away

Ste-Rose is on the main road between Pointe-à-Pitre and Deshaies. Half-hourly buses between Pointe-à-Pitre and Deshaies drop off here (€2.50, 40 minutes); there are various stops along the main road skirting the town.

Trois-Rivières

POP 8700

Despite its wonderful natural position – scattered across a series of steep, verdant hillsides that tumble dramatically into the Caribbean Sea, with the glorious silhouettes of Les Saintes in the distance – Trois-Rivières is rarely visited for its own attractions but because it has the shortest and most regular ferry connections to Terre-de-Haut in Les Saintes. Few people stop here for long, but there are basic facilities, and the town is perfectly pleasant if you need to kill time before your boat leaves.

Getting There & Away

There are hourly buses to Trois-Rivières from Pointe-à-Pitre (€4, one hour). Buses wind their way along the main road through the town and end their journey at the port.

Trois-Rivières is the main point of departure for Les Saintes: regular daily ferries connect Trois-Rivières to Bourg des Saintes (on Terre-de-Haut). Prices vary enormously and the journey takes around 30 minutes. Services are run by CTM Deher (p489), Val'Ferry (p471) and Navette Beatrix (p489).

LES SAINTES

These tiny islands 10km south of Basse-Terre are many people's Guadeloupean highlight, as they allow visitors to enjoy a slice of the old Caribbean, far from the development and urban sprawl that have afflicted the mainland. As mountainous charmers with great beaches, Les Saintes may not exactly be a secret – many Basse-Terre day-trippers venture here – but they're still probably Guadeloupe's least explored corner, and easily one of its most beautiful regions. As well as splendid beaches, there's first-class diving and some wonderful restaurants.

Terre-de-Haut is where most people go, though some also drop by next-door Terre-de-Bas, the chain's only other inhabited island. Don't miss this charming part of Guadeloupe.

Terre-de-Haut

Lying 10km off Guadeloupe, unhurried Terre-de-Haut is the largest of the eight small islands that make up Les Saintes and feels like a slice of southern France transported to the Caribbean. English is widely spoken thanks to a big international sailing scene, and it's definitely the most cosmopolitan of Guadeloupe's outlying islands. Divers love its waters for their good visibility and healthy reefs.

Since Terre-de-Haut was too hilly and dry for sugar plantations, slavery never took hold here. Consequently, older islanders can trace their roots to the early seafaring Norman and Breton colonists, and many locals have light skin and blond or red hair.

Home to most of the island's residents, Bourg des Saintes is a picturesque village with a decidedly Norman accent. Its narrow streets are lined with whitewashed red-roofed houses with shuttered windows and yards of flowering hibiscus.

Sights

Fort Napoléon FORT

(adult/child €5/2.50; 9am-12:30pm) Built in 1867 on the site of an earlier fort destroyed by the British in 1809, this installation sitting over 100m above sea level affords a splendid view of Bourg des Saintes and the surrounding islands. Walk through on your own or join a tour (in French). The naval museum inside is only of interest to dedicated historians – the 1782 battle of Les Saintes is documented in exacting detail. The fort is a sticky 1.5km walk uphill from Bourg des Saintes.

★ Baie de Pompierre BEACH

The horseshoe-shaped Baie de Pompierre is perhaps Terre-de-Haut's loveliest beach: a reef-protected golden strand with a splendid setting. There are even tame goats that mosey onto the sand and lie down next to sunbathers, as well as a small island to swim out to. Pompierre is an easy (though steep) 1.6km walk northeast of Bourg des Saintes. There are showers and bathrooms on the beach and plenty of wooden picnic tables.

Anse Rodrigue BEACH

South of Grande Anse and about 2km from town is Anse Rodrigue, a nice beach on a protected cove that usually has good swimming conditions.

Anse à Cointe BEACH

Two kilometers southwest of Bourg des Saintes is Anse à Cointe, a good beach for combining swimming and snorkeling. The snorkeling is best on the north side.

Pain de Sucre MOUNTAIN

(Anse à Cointe) The Pain de Sucre (Sugarloaf) is an imposing 53m-high basalt peninsula. You'll find good snorkeling and a sandy beach here.

Anse Crawen BEACH

The oddly named Anse Crawen is a secluded, clothing-optional beach just a couple of minutes' walk down a dirt path that starts at the southwestern end of the Terre-de-Haut coastal road.

Le Chameau VIEWPOINT

A winding cement road leads to the summit of Le Chameau, which at 309m is Terre-de-Haut's highest point. From Bourg des Saintes it's a moderately difficult hour-long walk to

DON'T MISS

MAISON DE CACAO

One of Basse-Terre's most enjoyable attractions, the **Maison du Cacao** (0590-98-25-23; www.maisonducacao.fr; Rte de Grande Plaine, Pointe-Noire; adult/child €8/4; 9am-5pm Mon-Sat; P) is for anyone who loves their chocolate. Presentations in English take place at 10am, noon and 3pm, but arrive around 20 minutes earlier to explore the garden packed with different types of cocoa trees. You're then invited to attend a lecture and demonstration on cocoa and chocolate that takes you from raw cocoa seeds to finished product via much tasting (and spitting out if there are kids!).

the top. Note that you're not allowed to use scooters to get up here, so prepare to hike!

Activities

Pisquettes Diving DIVING
(0590-99-88-80; Bourg des Saintes) A professional and highly recommended dive shop that offers the full range of scuba activities. Introductory dives cost €56, single dives €51. Dive packages and certification courses are also available.

La Dive Bouteille DIVING
(0590-99-54-25, 0690-49-80-91; www.dive-bouteille.com; Plage de la Colline, Bourg des Saintes) A reputable outfit at the southwestern end of the bay, La Dive Bouteille charges €120 for a two-tank outing and €79 for an introductory dive.

Sleeping

★ Auberge Les Petits Saints BOUTIQUE HOTEL $$
(0590-99-50-99; www.petitssaints.com; Rue de la Savane, Bourg des Saintes; d €131-166;) Occupying a former mayor's residence, this opulent villa guesthouse has quite an exquisite location and interesting rooms furnished in antique style. Each room is different, but terraces with sea views and big canopy beds are standard, and it manages to have a refined feel without being stuffy. The decked swimming pool has fabulous views over the bay.

LoBleu Hôtel HOTEL $$
(0590-92-40-00, 0690-63-80-36; www.lobleuhotel.com; Rue Benoît Cassin, Bourg des Saintes; r €99-200;) LoBleu is a real heartbreaker. Slap-bang on the beach, it could hardly have a more enviable setting. Unfortunately, only two rooms (out of 10) have direct sea views. They're all cheerful, with mural paintings, a small balcony and plenty of natural light. Kayaks are available for rent. Good English is spoken.

Kanaoa HOTEL $$
(0590-99-51-36; www.hotelkanaoa.com; Rue de Coquelet, Anse Mire, Bourg des Saintes; s/d from €80/115, bungalows from €175;) At the far northern end of Bourg des Saintes, this two-star hotel sits on the beach and has a private pier and restaurant. Its rooms have rather cheesy tropical decor, so you won't be overwhelmed by its style, but a number of rooms have gorgeous sea views. As well as the standard rooms, there are four duplex bungalows with kitchenettes.

Eating

For such a small place, Terre-de-Haut has some superb restaurants. Most are in and around Bourg des Saintes, the only real town, though there are a few casual beach places elsewhere.

★ Couleurs du Monde SEAFOOD $$
(0590-92-70-98; Le Mouillage, Bourg des Saintes; mains €14-22; noon-3pm & 7-10pm Mon-Wed, Fri & Sat, noon-3pm Sun;) This seafront place definitely lives up to its name, with a luminously painted interior and polychrome tables that give directly onto the bay. The menu is first-rate and includes daily changing tapas. The house specialty is tuna tataki with ginger – few leave disappointed.

Le Salako Chez Z'amour CREOLE $$
(0590-92-03-96; mains €10-15; noon-3pm Mon-Sat) This popular joint is worth visiting for its good, wholesome Creole staples, fish dishes, salads and sandwiches. Try the traditional Saintoise dessert *tourment d'amour* (love's torment), a cake-like concoction with melted chocolate in the middle. Nab a seat if it's not too busy; otherwise, take your order to go and enjoy it on nearby Plage de Pompierre.

Ti Bo Doudou CREOLE $$$
(0590-98-56-67; 58 Rue Benoît Cassin; menus €23-25; noon-3pm & 7-10pm Tue-Sat, noon-3pm Sun) Occupying a beautifully restored Creole hut that opens onto the beach, this is a much-loved local institution. There's great fresh food served in interesting Creole and Western combinations, with several appetizers and hot dishes of the day on offer. Dishes are presented gourmet style, with much stacking and drizzling.

Le 480 INTERNATIONAL $$$
(0590-99-50-99; Rue de la Savane, Bourg des Saintes; mains €18-30; 7-11pm Tue-Sat, noon-3pm Sun;) Top billing on Terre-de-Haut goes to this lovely restaurant within Auberge Les Petits Saints. Its menu is short and simple, but you're unlikely to find better cooking anywhere else. Another draw is the setting, with an open-air terrace shaded by a massive 200-year-old, intricately carved wooden wall. Reservations are essential for Sunday lunch.

Information

Office de Tourisme (0590-94-30-61; www.lessaintes.fr; Rue Jean Calot; 8am-noon & 2-5pm Mon-Sat, 8am-noon Sun) This helpful and English-speaking office just in front of

Terre-de-Haut & Terre-de-Bas

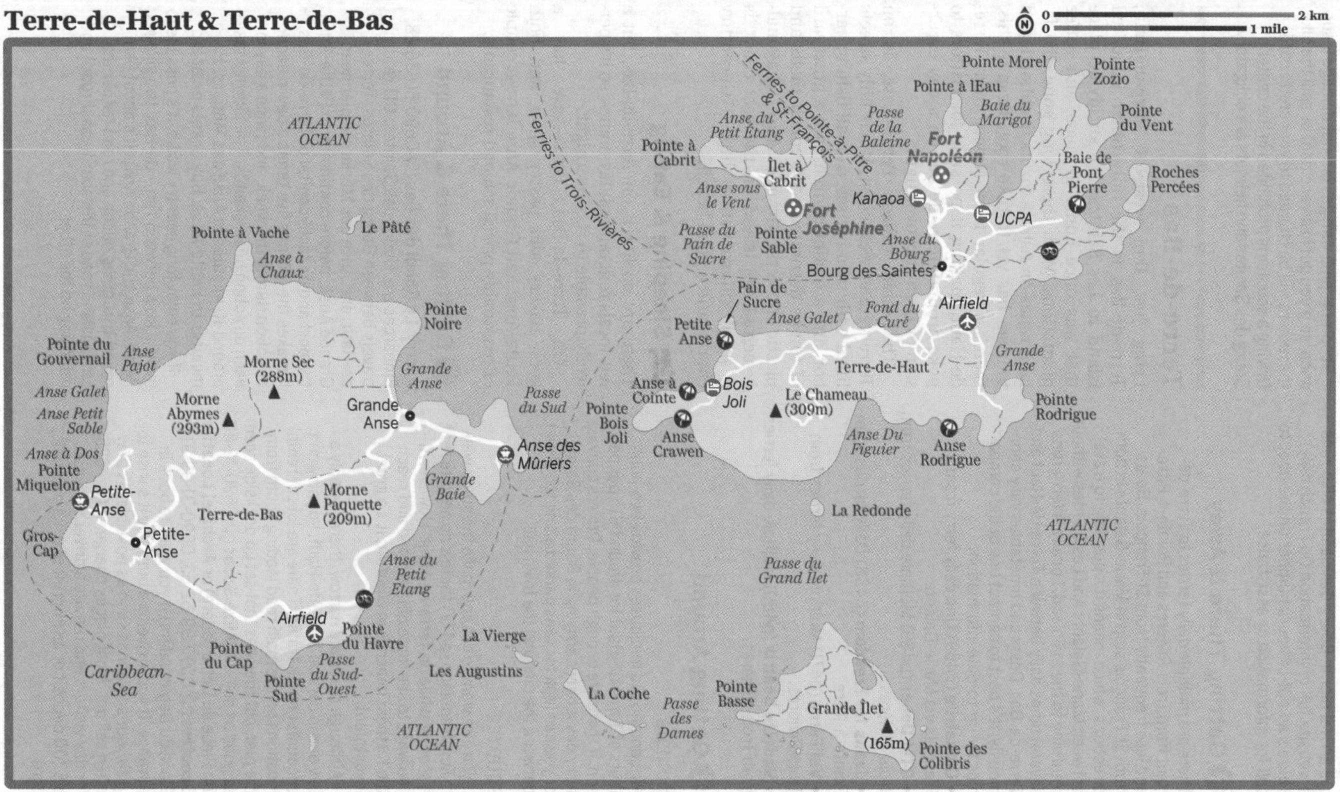

the arrival pier in Bourg des Saintes also runs a website full of information (in French only). There's an out-of-hours number on the door to call for information or assistance.

Getting There & Away

There are multiple daily ferries to Terre-de-Haut from Trois-Rivières and Pointe-à-Pitre, and less frequently from St-François. Boats from St-François stop in Marie-Galante in both directions, which means it's possible to travel between Marie-Galante and Les Saintes without returning to the mainland. Locally, a ferry runs several times daily between Terre-de-Haut and Terre-de-Bas. Costs and timetables vary enormously; it's best to contact one of the companies for up-to-date information:

- **Comatrile** (p469) One daily ferry from St-François via Marie-Galante.
- **CTM Deher** (p489) Multiple daily ferries from Trois-Rivières.
- **Jeans for Freedom** (p488) Daily ferries from Pointe-à-Pitre.
- **Val'Ferry** (p471) Multiple daily ferries from Trois-Rivières.
- **Vedette Beatrix** (p489) Multiple daily ferries from Trois-Rivières.

Getting Around

MINIBUS

Air-conditioned minibuses provide two-hour tours of Terre-de-Haut for around €15 per person, if there are enough people. Drivers canvass ferry passengers arriving in Bourg des Saintes, or you can look for vans parked along the street between the pier and the town hall.

SCOOTER

If you just want to eat and make the steep walk to Fort Napoléon (p477) there's no need to rent a scooter while on Terre-de-Haut. However, if you want to see more of the island and reach the furthest beaches in comfort, it's a great investment.

Although roads are narrow, there are only a few dozen cars on Terre-de-Haut, so you won't encounter much traffic. There are lots of rental locations on the main road leading south from the pier, but the ones that set up dockside seem as good as any. Try **Alizé Scoot** (☎0690-72-80-74; Place du Débarcadère) or **Archipel Location Scooters** (☎0590-99-52-63, 0690-31-99-91; Place du Débarcadère) if you want to book in advance. If you arrive on a busy day it's wise to grab your scooter as soon as possible, as they often sell out. Most places charge €20 to €25 for day visitors and require a driver's license, a €200 deposit or an imprint of a major credit card.

Scooters come with gas but not damage insurance, so if you get in an accident or spill the bike, the repairs will be charged to your credit card. Driving a scooter is prohibited in the center of Bourg des Saintes and helmets are obligatory.

Terre-de-Bas

Lying just 1km west of Terre-de-Haut, Terre-de-Bas is the only other inhabited island in Les Saintes. It's an idyllic place that was once home to sugar and coffee plantations. With these long gone, the island relies on fishing for its livelihood, and tourism has yet to take root. Despite this, there's a regular ferry service from Terre-de-Haut, making it possible for visitors to poke around Terre-de-Bas on a day excursion or even stay overnight.

The main village, Petite-Anse, is on Terre-de-Bas' west coast. It has hilly streets lined with trim houses, a small fishing harbor, and a quaint church with a graveyard of tombs decorated with conch shells and plastic flowers. Grande Anse, diagonally across the island on the east coast, is a small village with a little 17th-century church and a good beach.

Sleeping & Eating

There are no hotels on Terre-de-Bas, but a few locals rent out holiday homes, so it's perfectly possible to stay overnight.

On Terre-de-Bas, Petite-Anse has a good bakery and pastry shop, and both Petite-Anse and Grande Anse have a couple of reasonably priced seafood restaurants.

Getting There & Around

A ferry, **Le Soleil des Îles** (☎0690-50-36-28; Embarcadère, Bourg des Saintes; €11 return), travels between Bourg des Saintes, Terre-de-Haut, and Anse des Mûriers, a pier near Grande Anse, before continuing to Petite-Anse, the port and de facto capital of Terre-de-Bas. It makes the journey five times a day in each direction during the week, and twice a day in each direction on weekends. The journey takes around 10 minutes to Anse des Mûriers, 15 minutes to Petite-Anse. Buy tickets on board.

If you enjoy long country walks, it's possible to make a loop between Terre-de-Bas' two villages, Petite-Anse and Grande Anse. It's about 9km round-trip, going out on one road (either the cross-island road or the south-coast road) and returning on the other.

MARIE-GALANTE

Marie-Galante is a delightfully undeveloped island beloved by those who enjoy life's quieter pleasures and particularly by beach bums who want to escape the crowds. Compared with the archipelago's other islands, Marie-Galante is relatively flat, its dual limestone plateaus rising only 150m, but even if it doesn't enjoy a dramatic landscape, it has knockout beaches, some fascinating old buildings, and top-notch eating and sleeping options. Plan at least two full days here to do the island justice.

There are three settlements: Grand-Bourg is the commercial and administrative center, while the other two villages, Capesterre on the southeastern coast and St-Louis on the northern coast, are both dreamily laid-back fishing ports with good beaches nearby. However, as the island can be crossed in half an hour and nearly everyone hires a car, it makes little difference where you decide to base yourself.

Sights

Rum distilleries are Marie-Galante's main sights, and you have three to choose from. Idyllic beaches include Plage de la Feuillère and Plage de Petite Anse, just west of Capesterre, as well as Plage de Vieux Fort and Plage de l'Anse Canot, which both lie north of St-Louis.

Domaine de Bellevue DISTILLERY
(0590-97-29-58; www.habitation-bellevue.com; Section Bellevue, Capesterre; 9am-1pm) This remotely located rum distillery has a historic setting and a wonderful old windmill. The modern operation uses totally sustainable and nonpolluting methods to produce its rums and is a local leader in responsible rum production. Self-guided visits are free.

Distillerie Poisson DISTILLERY
(0590-97-03-79; Habitation Edouard, Rameau, Grand-Bourg; 8am-3pm Mon-Sat, 9am-1pm Sun) Midway between St-Louis and Grand-Bourg, this famous distillery bottles the island's best-known rum under the Père Labat label. There's also a good restaurant on the premises and plenty of chances to buy souvenir samples.

Distillerie Bielle DISTILLERY
(0590-97-93-62; Section Bielle, Grand-Bourg; 9:30am-1pm Mon-Sat, 10am-2pm Sun) Between Grand-Bourg and Capesterre, this historic distillery offers free self-guided tours of its age-old operation and a fully stocked gift shop selling the rum it produces.

Festivals & Events

★ **Terre de Blues** MUSIC
(www.terredeblues.com; early Jun) By far the biggest event of the year on Marie-Galante is this popular jazz and blues festival. Over four days dozens of acts from France, the Caribbean and beyond take to stages at various restaurants, bars and the Habitation Murat.

Sleeping

Marie-Galante has some superb accommodation options, although you'll find yourself with much more choice if you stay longer than a night or two – many of the best guesthouses do not accept visitors for less than two or three nights.

Le Soleil Levant HOTEL $
(0590-97-31-55; www.hotel-marie-galante.com; 42 Rue de la Marine, Capesterre; d €55-80;) Perched high above the center of Capesterre, this hotel offers stunning views over the coast. Rooms are practical and unexciting, but you'll be too busy lounging by the pool and drinking up the view to mind. There's an on-site restaurant, though it isn't always open when it should be.

★ **Coco Beach Resort** GUESTHOUSE $$
(0590-97-10-46, 0690-49-86-66; www.cocobeachmariegalante.com; Grand-Bourg; s/d/ste €89/99/129;) Probably too small to call itself a resort, this gorgeous place will appeal to anyone who would never dream of staying at a big, impersonal hotel complex. There are just eight rooms, all facing the sea and overlooking a gorgeous little beach with views towards Dominica. The welcome is warm and the whole place feels like a shared house.

Au Village de Ménard BUNGALOW $$
(0590-97-09-45; www.villagedemenard.com; Section Vieux Fort, St-Louis; d €78-96, tr €130;) With its cluster of 11 comfortable, attractive bungalows and villas, Au Village de Ménard is the perfect spot to relax after a long day's adventures. It boasts an enviable position on a cliff next to an old mill overlooking the bay, a great poolside restaurant and a nicely laid-out tropical garden.

Village de Canada COTTAGE $$
(0590-97-86-11, 0690-50-55-50; www.villagedecanada.com; Section Canada, Grand-Bourg; d €70-99;) This Creole-style venture

consists of eight cottages and an apartment set in a flowery plot. The casual atmosphere and quiet location make this the kind of place where you quickly lose track of the days. The cottages are nothing special but are well kitted out. There's a good pool, too. Minimum stay of two nights in high season.

Le Touloulou HOTEL **$$**
(☎0690-48-76-77, 0590-97-32-63; Plage de Petite Anse; d/q €100/200; ❄📶) Le Touloulou has two major advantages: it's set right on the beach and it has a wonderful restaurant. It's otherwise a fairly basic setup, but all five bungalows have porches overlooking the beach, and the family rooms have small kitchenettes. There's a pool and friendly management.

L'Oasis GUESTHOUSE **$$**
(☎0690-50-87-38, 0590-97-59-55; http://oasismariegalante.monsite-orange.fr; 7 Rue Sony Rupaire, Grand-Bourg; r €80-120; ❄📶) Each one of the three apartments here has something special to recommend it – a small tropical garden, a Jacuzzi or a terrace with views to Dominica. It's located in the center of the village, 1km from the seafront, toward the Grande-Savane area. There are discounts for staying longer than one night.

Eating

Le Footy CREOLE **$$**
(☎0690-39-80-17; Blvd de la Marine, Grand-Bourg; mains €11-20; ⊙noon-3pm Mon-Thu, noon-3pm & 7-11pm Fri & Sat) Owned by a former soccer player, this place has a great sea-view terrace and a reputation for the best pork chops on the island. It has live music in the club area in back most Friday and Saturday nights. Make a right from Grand-Bourg's ferry dock on the pier and head down the main road for a few minutes.

L'Ornata BRASSERIE **$$**
(☎0590-97-54-16; 1 Place Félix Eboué, Grand-Bourg; mains €10-20; ⊙8am-10pm; 📶) A great-value option in a pleasant old Creole house right across from the ferry dock, L'Ornata features all the Creole classics as well as moderately priced *plats du jour* (specials) and snack options, best enjoyed on the breezy terrace. Takeaway is available, and it's a decent place to head for drinks in the cool evening breeze.

Chez Henri GRILL **$$**
(☎0590-97-04-57; www.chezhenri.net; 8 Ave des Caraïbes, St-Louis; mains €13-22; ⊙noon-3pm & 7-11pm Mon-Sat; 📶) This is an unexpected gem for such a tiny backwater: a lively jazz bar and a great beachside restaurant perfect for whiling away Caribbean evenings. Local art is on display, handmade local crafts are for sale, the live music is good and the simple Creole food is delicious.

★ **La Playa** INTERNATIONAL **$$$**
(☎0690-51-84-77, 0590-93-66-10; Rte du Littoral, Capesterre; mains €20-35; ⊙from 7pm; 📶) Possibly the best place to eat on Marie-Galante, this well-respected restaurant occupies a cute house across the road from Petite Anse beach. The menu strays a touch from the familiar Creole path: fish tartare, skewered beef, the very exotic lobster in mango sauce, crab in coconut sauce and paella are some of the highlights, as is the impeccable service.

Sun 7 Beach SEAFOOD **$$$**
(☎0590-97-87-58; Grand-Bourg; mains €17-35; ⊙noon-9pm Mon-Fri; 📶) This charming beach restaurant with serious culinary credentials is run by a young, friendly team trying to enliven the gastronomic offerings on the island. It's just a timber shack, but it's been painted in bright colors and is an alluring and fun place for a meal, serving up the likes of *magret de canard* (duck fillet) cooked with honey and cumin.

Information

Office du Tourisme (☎0590-97-56-51; www.ot-mariegalante.com; Rue du Fort, Grand-Bourg; ⊙9am-noon & 1-4pm Mon-Fri, 8am-noon Sat & Sun mid-Dec–mid-Apr, shorter hours & closed Sat & Sun rest of year) Handily located just a block from Grand-Bourg's harbor. Can provide information on local rental houses, gîtes and guesthouses. Its website has a comprehensive English-language section.

Getting There & Away

Air Caraïbes (p488) has daily flights to Marie-Galante from Pointe-à-Pitre. The airport is midway between Grand-Bourg and Capesterre, 5km from either.

There are daily ferry connections between Pointe-à-Pitre and Grand-Bourg (one hour), while St-Louis has daily connections to both St-François (45 minutes) and Les Saintes (45 minutes). Prices vary enormously and depend on deals and the current level of competition on each route. Companies running these routes:

Comatrile (p469) Runs services to Les Saintes and St-François from St-Louis.

Express des Îles (p489) Runs services to Pointe-à-Pitre from Grand-Bourg.

Val'Ferry (p464) Runs services to Pointe-à-Pitre from Grand-Bourg.

The interisland crossing to Marie-Galante can be a bit rough, so if you're not used to bouncy seas it's best to travel on a light stomach and sit in the middle of the boat. One saving grace is that the boats leaving from Pointe-à-Pitre are very big (and more stable) and quite comfortable.

St-Louis is the island's main anchorage for yachters.

Getting Around

BUS

During the day, except for Sunday, infrequent minibuses make runs between Grand-Bourg, Capesterre and St-Louis (€1 flat fare, approximately 15 minutes between each village). It's not a very convenient way to get around Marie-Galante, however, and it's far easier to hire a car or scooter to explore properly. Find the bus stops on the main road through each village.

CAR

You really need your own transport to get the most out of Marie-Galante. Car and scooter hire are inexpensive and readily available at both ports of entry to the island, Grand-Bourg and St-Louis. Cars generally start at €25 per day, scooters at €15 to €20. Be sure to inspect your vehicle closely, as standards may not be as high as you're used to.

Auto Moto Location (0590-97-19-42; Ave des Caraïbes, St-Louis)

Hertz (0590-97-59-80; www.hertz.com; Rue du Fort, Grand-Bourg)

Toto Location (0590-97-59-16, 0690-65-64-99; www.toto-location.com; Grand-Bourg)

MINIBUS

Minibus tour drivers are usually waiting for arriving ferry passengers at both ferry ports, Grand-Bourg and St-Louis. A four-hour guided tour that makes a nearly complete circle around Marie-Galante costs about €15. Stops on the tour usually include a distillery, the Ste-Marie Hospital parking lot (which has the best view on the island), a shop where people make manioc flour, and an abandoned sugar plantation.

The buses will sometimes leave you on the town beach in St-Louis for a few hours and pick you up in time to make whichever boat back you plan to take. Some tour guides don't speak much standard French, or English, so be sure to converse a bit beforehand to make sure they can explain sights clearly in your language.

LA DÉSIRADE

With its soaring central mountain, thick vegetation and palm-strewn beaches, tiny La Désirade is the quintessential Caribbean island of popular fantasy. Its unusual name comes from the fact that it was the first sight of land caught by Columbus on his second voyage in 1493 – thus 'the desired' landfall that his crew were hoping for. Indeed, it's hard to imagine them being disappointed, and today La Désirade retains much of its natural charm. From from one side at least, it looks pretty much as it did in Columbus' time, albeit now with a couple of prominent wind farms.

Just 11km long and 2km wide, La Désirade makes a wonderful day trip from Grande-Terre. Even the best beaches are nearly deserted, and there are some excellent restaurants where you can enjoy a long lunch.

Sleeping

La Désirade has just a handful of hotels and a few private rentals.

★ **Hôtel Oasis** HOTEL **$$**

(0590-20-02-12; www.oasisladesirade.com; Rue de la Dési, Beauséjour; s/d €49/98;) Located within walking distance of the ferry dock and Fifi Beach, this brightly painted, two-level Creole-style house could not be a better deal, with six compact but tidy rooms and modern, stylish decor. The welcome is warm, and the hotel runs its own restaurant nearby.

Oualiri Beach Hotel HOTEL **$$**

(0590-20-20-08; Beauséjour; s/d €75/90;) The simple and rather small rooms here would be totally unremarkable were they not directly on the beach. Yes, it's a petite and rather rocky cove, and management is a little too relaxed for the hotel to really live up to its potential, but if being on the beach is what you want, this is your place.

Eating

The name of the game here is seafood, of course, and La Désirade specializes in lobster, conch and octopus, which are on the menu in practically every restaurant. Places to eat are concentrated around Beauséjour, the main settlement, and can also be found on several of the more picturesque beaches.

★ **La Roulotte** CREOLE **$$**

(0590-20-02-33; Plage du Souffleur; mains €16-25; noon-3pm) Despite its appearance, this is no mere shack on gorgeous Souffleur beach but a La Désirade institution that's been around for almost two decades. Jean-Edouard does everything alone here, so order and then enjoy a leisurely swim before lunch. You won't find better grilled fish, conch stew, octopus curry, lobster or fried chicken on the island.

Rose-Ita SEAFOOD $$

(☎0690-71-98-26; mains €6-35; ⏰10am-4pm Fri-Wed, dinner Fri-Mon; 📶) This pink, breezy sea-view restaurant sits on a bluff overlooking the small fishing beach below. The menu is wider than at most other local places, so you could go for the splash-out *assiette de langouste* (lobster platter; €35), or a far simpler burger or croque monsieur (ham-and-cheese toastie; €6).

La Payotte CREOLE $$

(☎0590-20-01-29; Beauséjour; mains €13-21; ⏰9am-3pm daily, plus 6:30-11pm Fri & Sat) Right on La Désirade's Grande Anse beach, La Payotte serves a tasty variety of Creole dishes as well as a small breakfast menu on its charming beachside terrace. Don't miss the stir-fried chicken with cashews or the grilled lobster.

ℹ Getting There & Around

There are two crossings per day on the Achipel 1 between St-François and La Désirade (45 minutes). Buy tickets shortly before departure at St-François' Gare Maritime. The ferry leaves St-François at 8am, returning at 3:45pm. It leaves La Désirade at 7am, returning at 5pm. Outside high season there are no boats on Tuesday.

Scooter rental (€20 to €25 per day) is available at La Désirade's ferry dock. Cars can be rented for €40 per day. There's no public transport.

UNDERSTAND GUADELOUPE

History

Caribs in Karukera

When sighted by Columbus on November 14, 1493, Guadeloupe was inhabited by Caribs, who called it Karukera (Island of Beautiful Waters). The Spanish made two attempts to colonize Guadeloupe in the early 1500s but were repelled both times by fierce Carib resistance. Finally, in 1604, they abandoned their claim to the island.

Three decades later, French colonists sponsored by the Compagnie des Îles d'Amérique, an association of French entrepreneurs, set sail to establish the first European settlement on Guadeloupe. On June 28, 1635, the party, led by Charles Liénard de l'Olive and Jean Duplessis d'Ossonville, landed on the southeastern shore of Basse-Terre and claimed Guadeloupe for France. They drove the Caribs off the island, planted crops and within a decade had built the first sugar mill. By the time France officially annexed the island in 1674, a slavery-based plantation system was well established.

France vs Britain in Guadeloupe

The English invaded Guadeloupe several times and colonized it from 1759 to 1763. During this time they developed Pointe-à-Pitre into a major harbor, opened profitable English and North American markets to Guadeloupean sugar, and allowed the planters to import cheap American lumber and food. Many French colonists actually grew wealthier during the British occupation, and the economy expanded rapidly. In 1763 the occupation ended with the signing of the Treaty of Paris, which relinquished French claims in Canada in exchange for the return of Guadeloupe.

Amid the chaos of the French Revolution, the British invaded Guadeloupe again in 1794. In response, the French sent a contingent of soldiers led by Victor Hugues, a black nationalist. Hugues freed and armed Guadeloupean enslaved people. On the day the British withdrew from Guadeloupe, Hugues went on a rampage and killed 300 royalists, many of them plantation owners. It marked the start of a reign of terror. In all, Hugues was responsible for the deaths of more than 1000 colonists, and as a consequence of his attacks on US ships the USA declared war on France.

In 1802 Napoléon Bonaparte, anxious to get the situation under control, sent General Antoine Richepanse to Guadeloupe. Richepanse put down the uprising, restored the prerevolutionary government and reinstituted slavery.

Guadeloupe was the most prosperous island in the French West Indies, and the British continued to covet it, invading and occupying the island for most of the period between 1810 and 1816. The Treaty of Vienna restored the island to France, which has maintained sovereignty over it continuously since 1816.

Modern Guadeloupe

Slavery was abolished in 1848, following a campaign led by French politician Victor Schoelcher. In the years that followed, planters brought laborers from Pondicherry, a French colony in India, to work in the cane fields. Since 1871 Guadeloupe has had representation in the French parliament, and since 1946 it has been an overseas department of France.

Guadeloupe's economy is heavily dependent upon subsidies from the French government and upon its economic ties with mainland France, which absorbs the majority of Guadeloupe's exports and provides 75% of its imports. Agriculture remains a cornerstone of the economy. The leading export crop is bananas, the bulk of which grow along the southern flanks of La Soufrière.

People & Culture

Guadeloupean culture draws from a pool of French, African, East Indian and West Indian influences. The mix is visible in the architecture, which ranges from French colonial buildings to traditional Creole homes; in the food, which merges influences from all the cultures into a unique Creole cuisine; and in the widely spoken Creole language, the local dialect that is a heavily accented and very colloquial form of French. Guadeloupe is also one place in the Caribbean where you're likely to see women wearing traditional Creole dress, especially at festivals and cultural events.

The total population of Guadeloupe is about 400,000, with a third of the population aged under 20. About three quarters of the population is of mixed ethnicity, a combination of African, European and East Indian descent. There's also a sizable population of white islanders who trace their ancestry to the early French settlers, as well as a number of far more recently arrived French from the mainland.

The predominant religion is Roman Catholicism. There are also Methodist, Seventh Day Adventist, Jehovah's Witness and evangelical denominations, and a significant Hindu community.

The island is fertile ground for the literary imagination. Guadeloupe's most renowned native son is Saint-John Perse, the pseudonym of Alexis Leger, who was born in Guadeloupe in 1887. Perse won the Nobel Prize for literature in 1960 for the evocative imagery of his poetry. One of his many noted works is *Anabase* (1925), which was translated into English by TS Eliot.

The leading contemporary novelist in the French West Indies is Guadeloupe native Maryse Condé. Many of her bestselling novels have been translated into English. The epic *Tree of Life* (1992) centers on a Guadeloupean family, their roots and the identity of Guadeloupean society itself. *Crossing the Mangrove* (1995) is a perfect beach read. Set in Rivière au Sel near the Rivière Salée, it unravels the life and untimely death of a controversial villager.

Landscape & Wildlife

Beaches line nearly every shore in Guadeloupe, which explains the island's appeal to generations of French holidaymakers. Outside of the mountainous Parc National de la Guadeloupe (p475), the interior is made for the most part of gently rolling fields of sugarcane. The beaches, hiking trails and picnic areas are almost always completely litter free.

Underwater life includes sea horses, lobsters, lots of parrotfish, and crabs. Divers may occasionally spot a ray or barracuda, but for the most part the waters support large schools of smaller fish.

Birds found on Guadeloupe include various members of the heron family, pelicans, hummingbirds and the endangered Guadeloupe wren. A common sighting is the bright yellow-bellied banana quit, a small nectar-feeding bird that's a frequent visitor at open-air restaurants, where it raids unattended sugar bowls.

You'll probably see drawings of raccoons on park brochures and in Guadeloupean advertising; it is the official symbol of Parc National de la Guadeloupe and its main habitat is in the forests of Basse-Terre, but visitors are unlikely to see it in person.

Guadeloupe has mongooses aplenty, introduced long ago in a futile attempt to control rats in the sugarcane fields. Agoutis (short-haired, short-eared rabbitlike rodents that look a bit like guinea pigs) are found on La Désirade. There are iguanas on Les Saintes and La Désirade. All of these animals are commonly seen by visitors.

SURVIVAL GUIDE

Directory A–Z

ACCESSIBLE TRAVEL

By comparison with other Caribbean Islands, Guadeloupe makes good provision for travelers with disabilities. Many hotels have wheelchair-accessible rooms, and many public places have toilets for patrons with disabilities.

ACCOMMODATIONS

Most hotels in Guadeloupe are midsize and midrange, and prices are fairly reasonable by the standards of the region. You'll also find private *chambres d'hôte* (rooms for rent in private homes) or villas and gîtes (cottages) to rent, but they must generally be booked by the week. Guadeloupe has no backpacker hostels and provides poorly for the needs of travellers on a tight budget.

CHILDREN

Because of all the French families that come here, hotels and activities are pretty child-friendly on the whole. Many hotels have play areas, activities just for kids and a special children's menu. All restaurants will allow children to dine, and they'll often have a simple and good-value *menu enfant* (children's set meal).

Particularly child-friendly sights on the island include the Jardin Botanique de Deshaies (p471) and the Zoo de Guadeloupe (p476). Kids will also enjoy the Nautilus (p473) glass-bottom-boat trip around Pigeon Island.

Practically all hotels will provide cots, and some hotels provide babysitting services. European brands of baby formula, foods and diapers can be bought at pharmacies.

ELECTRICITY

Power is 220V, 50Hz; plugs are European style, with two round pins.

> **SLEEPING PRICE RANGES**
>
> The following price ranges refer to the cost of a double room in high season (December to April and July to August).
>
> **€** less than €80
>
> **€€** €80–150
>
> **€€€** more than €150

EMERGENCY NUMBERS

Ambulance	☎15
Fire	☎18
Police	☎17

FOOD

Guadeloupe has some fantastic eating, from the catch of the day at beachside grills to gastronomic multicourse feasts. Seafood-lovers will be particularly happy, with fresh lobster, conch, octopus and shrimp to enjoy. While there's limited choice if you don't want Creole or French food, pizza is ubiquitous.

Self-catering is a double-edged sword: wonderful local produce is readily available, but Guadeloupe's supermarkets are expensive, with almost all items imported from France.

Essential Food & Drink

- **Acras** A universally popular hors d'oeuvre in Guadeloupe, *acras* are fried fish, seafood or vegetable fritters in tempura. *Acras de morue* (cod) and *crevettes* (shrimp) are the most common and are both delicious.
- **Ti-punch** Short for *petit punch*, this ubiquitous and strong cocktail is the normal *apéro* (aperitif) in Guadeloupe: it's a mix of rum, lime and cane syrup, but mainly rum.
- **Crabes farcis** Stuffed crabs are a typical local dish. Normally they're stuffed with a spicy mixture of crabmeat, garlic, shallots and parsley that is then cooked in the shell.
- **Blaff** This is the local term for white fish marinated in lime juice, garlic and peppers and then poached. It's a favorite dish in many of Guadeloupe's restaurants.

HEALTH

Medical care in Guadeloupe is equivalent to that in mainland France: very good. The biggest hospital is the Centre Hospitalier Universitaire (p464) in Pointe-à-Pitre, though there are smaller hospitals in almost every region. There are plenty of pharmacies everywhere; look for the green cross, often flashing in neon. EU citizens can get health-care costs refunded through their European Health Cards. When paying for medical care, nationals of other countries should keep all receipts to reclaim money from their health-insurance providers.

INTERNET ACCESS

Wi-fi is generally very good across Guadeloupe and available in almost all hotels and restaurants and at the airport. No hotel would now consider making guests pay for the service as an extra.

LGBT+ TRAVELERS

Guadeloupe usually earns OK marks from gay travel organizations, as gay and lesbian rights are protected under French law. However, attitudes on the ground tend to be far less tolerant and prejudice against gay people is not unusual, although it's not nearly as extreme as on some Caribbean islands. Gay couples usually do not publicly express affection or advertise their sexual orientation, although hoteliers don't seem to mind if same-sex couples share a bed. There is little or no gay scene here – most introductions happen via the internet.

LEGAL MATTERS

French law governs legal matters in Guadeloupe, and there is a presumption of innocence as well as the right to a lawyer. Most travelers will have no interaction with the police at all.

MONEY

ATMs are common, but not all accept all cards. Hotels, larger restaurants and car-rental agencies accept Visa and MasterCard, but American Express is not widely accepted.

Exchange Rates

Australia	A$1	€0.62
Canada	C$1	€0.65
Japan	¥100	€0.82
New Zealand	NZ$1	€0.58
South Africa	ZAR100	€6.13
Switzerland	CHF1	€0.89
UK	UK£1	€1.12
US	US$1	€0.89

For current exchange rates, see www.xe.com.

Taxes & Refunds

If you do not live in France, it is possible to claim back VAT on certain purchases at the airport when leaving Guadeloupe. This isn't possible if you're flying from Guadeloupe to France.

Tipping

Tipping is not common or expected in Guadeloupe.

PUBLIC HOLIDAYS

New Year's Day January 1
Easter Monday March/April
Labor Day May 1
Victory Day May 8
Ascension Thursday 40th day after Easter
Slavery Abolition Day May 27
Bastille Day July 14
Schoelcher Day July 21
Assumption Day August 15
All Saints' Day November 1
Armistice Day November 11
Christmas Day December 25

EATING PRICE RANGES

The following price ranges reflect the cost of a main course.

€ less than €12

€€ €12–20

€€€ more than €20

TELEPHONE

The country code for Guadeloupe is 590. Confusingly, all local landline numbers also begin with 0590: these numbers are separate, however, and therefore must be dialed twice when calling from abroad. Cell-phone numbers begin with 0690.

To call Guadeloupe from abroad, dial your country's international access code, followed by the country code (590) and the local number (dropping the initial zero). When calling from within the French West Indies, simply dial the local 10-digit number.

Cell Phones

European mobile phones should work as they do at home. SIM cards are widely available. Coverage is generally pretty good, but far from total. Calls and data are expensive by regional standards: 1GB costs around €20.

TIME

Guadeloupe is on Eastern Caribbean Time (GMT/UTC minus four hours). Daylight-saving time is not used.

Getting There & Away

AIR

Guadeloupe's only international airport is **Guadeloupe Pôle Caraïbes Airport** (☎0590-21-14-98; www.guadeloupe.aeroport.fr; Les Abymes), which is north of Pointe-à-Pitre, 6km from the city center.

Airline offices at Guadeloupe Pôle Caraïbes Airport:

Air Canada (☎0590-21-12-77; www.aircanada.com) Flights from Montreal.

Air Caraïbes (☎0820-83-58-35; www.aircaraibes.com) Flights from Paris.

Air France (www.airfrance.com) Flights from Paris, Cayenne (French Guiana), Miami (USA) and Port-au-Prince (Haiti).

American Airlines (www.aa.com) Flights from San Juan (Puerto Rico) and Miami.

Corsair (www.corsair.fr) Flights from Paris.

There are direct regional services to Antigua, Barbados, Dominica, Fort-de-France, Port-au-Prince, St-Barthélemy, St-Martin/Sint Maarten, Santo Domingo, St Lucia, and Trinidad and

Tobago. Regional airlines serving Guadeloupe include **Air Caraïbes** (☎0820-83-58-35; www.aircaraibes.com; Guadeloupe Pôle Caraïbes Airport), **Air Antilles Express** (www.airantilles.com; Guadeloupe Pôle Caraïbes Airport), **LIAT** (☎0590-21-13-93; www.liat.com; Guadeloupe Pôle Caraïbes Airport; ⊙3hr before flights) and **Winair** (www.fly-winair.sx; Guadeloupe Pôle Caraïbes Airport).

SEA

There are excellent connections to nearby Caribbean islands from Guadeloupe, as well as the possibility to charter your own yacht or catamaran to make the trip.

Cruise Ship

Cruise ships don't always call at Pointe-à-Pitre, as neither the port area nor the city itself is particularly attractive. However, when ships do arrive, they normally dock at the cruise-ship terminal, just a short walk from the center of town. Most passengers take a tour to somewhere else on the island.

Ferry

There are plenty of connections between Guadeloupe and neighboring islands, particularly Martinique, although if your destination is Martinique, bear in mind that it's nearly always cheaper – and certainly faster – to fly.

L'Express des Îles (p464) and **Jeans for Freedom** (☎0590-68-53-09; www.jeansforfreedom.com; Gare Maritime de Bergevin; ⊙7am-7pm) run ferries between Guadeloupe and its neighboring islands of Dominica, Martinique and St Lucia. The two companies are always offering special deals and promotions, and competition is fierce. In general it pays to book ahead as far as possible.

Departure days and times for these services change frequently and, due to weather conditions, often bear no relation to the printed schedule. The only way to be sure is to call the ferry companies on the day of travel.

Yacht

Popular with yachties and sailors, Guadeloupe has three marinas:

Marina de Bas du Fort (☎0590-93-66-20; www.marinaguadeloupe.com) Between Pointe-à-Pitre and Gosier.

Marina de Rivière-Sens (☎0590-86-79-43; www.marina-rivieresens.com) On the southern outskirts of the town of Basse-Terre.

Marina de St-François (☎0590-88-47-28) In the center of St-François, Grande-Terre.

Customs and immigration offices are located in Pointe-à-Pitre, Basse-Terre and Deshaies.

The yacht-charter companies Antilles Sail (p462) and Dream Yacht Charter (p462) are based at Marina de Bas du Fort.

PRACTICALITIES

Newspapers & magazines *France-Antilles* (www.martinique.franceantilles.fr) is the main daily newspaper for the French West Indies. French newspapers and magazines are commonly found everywhere; print editions in English are far rarer.

Radio Tune in to Réseau Outre-Mer 1ère (www.la1ere.fr).

Smoking France has a comprehensive smoking ban that is also observed in Guadeloupe. Smoking in all enclosed public spaces is against the law, though due to the number of outdoor places in Guadeloupe, there are still many situations in which there might be smoking around you. Smoking is not widespread among locals; the biggest culprits are normally tourists from France.

TV Catch up on local TV on Guadeloupe 1ère.

Weights & measures Guadeloupe uses the metric system and the 24-hour clock.

Getting Around

For travelers visiting more than one place in Guadeloupe, a rental car is almost a necessity. The main tourist spots on the southern coast of Grande-Terre are navigable without one, but for the most part a vehicle comes in handy and rental prices are very low. Most visitors pick up a car at the airport and keep it throughout their stay, although as transporting cars to the outlying islands is expensive, most people hire scooters or cars on each island rather than taking one with them.

AIR

Air Caraïbes has almost daily flights between Pointe-à-Pitre and Marie-Galante. These are the only scheduled domestic flights in Guadeloupe at present.

BICYCLE

The flat roads of Grande-Terre are very popular with cyclists, particularly the stretch between St-François and Pointe des Châteaux. Bicycles are an adventurous and fun way to get around the islands of Terre-de-Haut, La Désirade and Marie-Galante. Rentals start at €10 per day.

BOAT

Ferries are the principal way to get between the various islands of Guadeloupe. Multiple operators run services between Grande-Terre and Terre-de-Haut, Marie-Galante and La Désirade. There are also ferries from Trois-Rivières on Basse-Terre to Terre-de-Haut in Les Saintes. Prices tend to be similar across companies, though things change frequently: most companies have promotions or discounted fares and seem to be in a constant price war with each other. Shop around for the best deal, and always confirm sailing times by phone as schedules change regularly.

CTM Deher (☎0590-92-06-39; www.ctmdeher.com; Allée des Espadons; ⊙7am-7pm)

Jeans for Freedom

L'Express des Îles (☎0590-91-95-20; www.express-des-iles.com; Gare Maritime de Bergevin; ⊙7am-7pm)

Val'Ferry (p464)

Navette Beatrix (☎0590-25-08-06; www.facebook.com/navettebeatrix; Rue de la Dissidence; ⊙7am–7pm)

BUS

Guadeloupe has a good public bus system that operates from about 5:30am to 6:30pm on weekdays, with fairly frequent service on main routes. The Saturday-afternoon service is much lighter, and there are almost no buses on Sunday.

Many routes start and end in Pointe-à-Pitre and destinations are written on the buses. Bus stops have blue signs picturing a bus; in less developed areas you can wave buses down along their routes. Pay the driver when you board.

CAR & MOTORCYCLE

In Guadeloupe, drive on the right. Traffic regulations and road signs are identical to those in mainland France. Exits and intersections are clearly marked, and speed limits are posted.

Car Rental

Multiple car-rental companies have offices at the airport (p487) and in major resort areas. Some agents will let you rent a car near your hotel and drop it off free of charge at the airport, which can save you a hefty taxi fare.

Advertised rates usually have little to do with the real price if you book ahead through international rental companies. Cars can be had for less than €10 per day if you reserve ahead and keep the car for at least a week. Local companies should possibly be avoided, as vehicle standards can vary wildly and cars are generally more expensive.

Road Conditions

Roads are excellent by Caribbean standards and almost invariably hard surfaced, although secondary and mountain roads are often narrow.

Around Pointe-à-Pitre there are multilane highways with cars zipping along at 110km/h. Outside the Pointe-à-Pitre area, most highways have a single lane in each direction and an 80km/h speed limit.

HITCHHIKING

Hitchhiking is common on Guadeloupe, especially in areas with poor bus connections, in the evenings and on Sunday. The proper stance is to hold out an open palm at a slightly downward angle. All the usual safety precautions apply.

TAXI

Taxis are plentiful but expensive in Guadeloupe. There are taxi stands at the airport in Pointe-à-Pitre, and you can call one almost anywhere on Grande-Terre, Basse-Terre and Marie-Galante. Fares are 40% higher from 9pm to 7am, as well as all day on Sunday and holidays.

WESTEND61/GETTY IMAGES ©

1. Iguana, Bonaire **2.** Flamingos, Bonaire **3.** Dolphins, Bahamas
4. Hummingbird, Cuba

WALTER NIEDERBAUER/500PX ©

Wildlife

Iguanas & Other Land Animals

Except for large iguana populations and tree rats on certain islands, land animals have largely been hunted to extinction. Responsibility is shared between humans and other introduced species including the mongoose, raccoons, cats, dogs and donkeys. Trinidad, home to 100 types of mammal, is the exception to the rule.

Birds

Hundreds of bird species, both endemic and migratory, frequent scores of islands. Look for iconic pink flamingos on the Bahamas and Bonaire. Rainforests on islands such as Dominica and St Vincent are home to all manner of colorful native birds. Parrots in a profusion of colors are found on almost any island with forests, while hummingbirds and banana quits are always around, searching for something sweet. Common Caribbean water birds include brown pelicans, white cattle egrets and herons.

Ocean Dwellers

If you're anxious to behold the Caribbean's richest fauna, you're going to get wet. One of the world's most complex ecosystems is coral, a diminutive animal that lives in giant colonies that form over millennia. Fish pecking away at nutritious tidbits or hiding out in the reef include the iridescent Creole wrasse, groupers, kingfish, sergeant majors and angel fish. Hang – or float – around and you might see inflatable porcupine fish, barracudas, nurse sharks, octopus, moray eels and manta rays.

Other species you may see include pilot, sperm, blue and humpback whales, famous for their acrobatic breaching from January to March. Spinner, spotted and bottlenose dolphins, and loggerhead, green, hawksbill and leatherback turtles are common sights for divers. Manatees or sea cows, herbivorous marine mammals so ugly they're cute, are found in waters around Cuba, the Dominican Republic, Jamaica and Puerto Rico.

Haiti

509 / POP 10.98 MILLION

Includes ➡

Best Places to Eat

- Papaye (p496)
- Lakou Lakay (p502)
- Manje Lokal (p503)
- Sesanet (p499)
- Lolo's (p500)

Best Places to Stay

- Inn at Villa Bambou (p494)
- Hostellerie du Roi Christophe (p500)
- Chato Relaxo (p501)
- Port Morgan (p504)
- Cormier Plage Resort (p501)

Why Go?

Every country is unique, but Haiti is first among them. Here, modern wonders include the Caribbean's finest art scene, incubated by its most unmanageable city. Deforested mountaintops abut the region's most biodiverse cloud forest. Carnival finds young and old paying raucous homage to Haitian saints, in Haitian Kreyòl, birthed during Haiti's revolution. The violence, victories and uncountable victims of Haiti's history make other countries' origin myths seem like fairy tales.

Haitians' ownership over their story allows them to preternaturally rebound from setbacks with a shrug and a '*pa gwen pwoblem*' – 'no problem.' You'd do well to adopt this Haitian attitude of joyful resilience in the face of hardship: travel here means embracing rough edges that have been sanded down in easier places. But the challenges make those travel highs – a perfect Labadie beach, lewd papier-mâché in Jacmel, a lucky roulette spin in Cap-Haïtien's town square – all the better.

When to Go

Nov–Mar The hottest driest days. Don't miss the country-wide Fet Gédé Vodou festival in November and February's Carnival in Port-au-Prince and Jacmel.

Apr–Jun Quite a bit of rain in the south, and in Port-au-Prince.

Aug–Oct Hurricane season; travel is feasible if there are no big storms.

Haiti Highlights

1. **Jacmel Carnival** (p503) Joining the country's theatrical street party, celebrating Vodou, sexand revolution.
2. **Citadelle Laferrière** (p501) Sighting the mountaintop fortress, a proud symbol of the world's first black republic.
3. **Croix-des-Bouquets** (p497) Finding bargains in Haiti's finest art, and supporting a local artisan community.
4. **Vodou ceremony** (p498) Plugging into Haiti's subconscious by attending a Vodou ceremony outside Gonaïves.
5. **Île-à-Vache** (p504) Kicking back on this sliver of paradise and feasting on fresh lobster.
6. **Cap-Haïtien** (p499) Settling into the Haitian rhythm in this town of crumbling architecture and raucous nightlife.

PORT-AU-PRINCE

Let's admit the obvious: Port-au-Prince doesn't have the image of somewhere you'd visit for fun. A true city of the developing world, just a couple of hours by air from Miami, the city was preceded by a reputation for impoverished chaos even before the 2010 earthquake shook it to its foundations. Years later the recovery is still slow going, the gulf between rich and poor is as wide as ever, and the streets remain cluttered with trash and rubble.

And yet the city continues to be one of the most vibrant and exciting in the Caribbean. Like a bottle of local *klerin* liquor, Port-au-Prince takes the raw energy of Haiti and distills it into one buzzing shot, and witnessing the self-sufficient spirit of its people might be the most life-affirming experience you have on your travels. It's a chaotic, exhilarating, compelling place, and it may well capture your soul.

Sights

Musée du Panthéon National MUSEUM
(Mupanah; ☎3417-4435; Champs de Mars; US$5; ⏲8am-4pm Mon-Thu, to 5pm Fri, 10am-4pm Sat, noon-5pm Sun) This modern, mostly subterranean history museum, set below gardens, hosts a permanent exhibition chronicling Haiti's history, from the Taínos and slavery to independence and the modern era. Fascinating exhibits include exquisite Taíno pottery; the rusting anchor of Columbus' flagship, the *Santa María;* a copy of the fearsome Code Noir that governed the running of the plantations; the silver pistol with which revolutionary leader Christophe took his own life; Emperor Faustin's ostentatious crown; and 'Papa Doc' Duvalier's trademark black hat and cane.

★**Grand Rue Artists** ARTS CENTER
(www.atis-rezistans.com; 622 Grand Rue; ⏲8am-8pm) While most of Haiti's artists are represented in the rarefied air of Pétionville's galleries, a collective of sculptors and installation artists produces spectacular work in an unlikely setting, squeezed into the cinder-block houses among mechanics and body workshops on Grand Rue. In this Caribbean junkyard gone cyberpunk, the artists turn scrap and found objects into startling Vodou sculpture, exploring a heady mix of spirit, sex and politics, all grounded in the preoccupations of daily Haitian life.

Marché de Fer MARKET
(Grand Rue; ⏲7am-5pm) Several of Haiti's cities have iron markets, but Port-au-Prince's is the original and the best. Constructed in 1889, the exuberant red-metal structure looks like something out of *Arabian Nights*. Although it burnt down after the earthquake, it was magnificently and speedily restored, reopening on the one-year anniversary. It's rich in food, art and Vodou paraphernalia.

Tours

Tour Haiti TOURS
(☎2812-2223, 2813-2223; www.tourhaiti.net; 38 Rue Darguin, Pétionville; ⏲8am-4pm Mon-Fri, to 1pm Sat) A reputable tour agency that does custom trips all over Haiti.

Voyages Lumière TOURS
(☎3607-1321; www.voyageslumiere.com/haiti) Long-standing and reputable tour agency owned by Englishwoman Jacqui Labrom, who has spent decades in Haiti and arranges excellent cultural, historic and adventure trips all over the country.

Festivals & Events

Fet Gédé CULTURAL
On the first and second days of November, Fet Gédé takes over Grand Cimetière de Port-au-Prince; celebrations are also held in other cemeteries and temples nationwide. They all honor the Gédé, the Vodou trickster spirits of the dead.

Sleeping

Port-au-Prince

Hôtel Oloffson HOTEL $$
(☎3810-4000; www.hoteloloffson.com; 60 Ave Christophe; d/ste from US$100/200; P❄@🛜🏊) If Haiti has an iconic hotel, it's the Oloffson. Immortalized as Hotel Trianon in Graham Greene's *The Comedians,* the elegant gingerbread building is one of the city's loveliest, further tricked out with paintings and Vodou flags. There's a very sociable bar for your rum punches, and every Thursday the house band RAM plays up a storm until the small hours.

Sadly, the Oloffson isn't beyond trading on its name, and the rooms, fixtures and service don't quite live up to the tariff. Still, it remains a lively scene.

★**Inn at Villa Bambou** BOUTIQUE HOTEL $$$
(☎3702-1151; www.villabambouhaiti.com; 1 Rue Marfranc, Pacot; d incl half board from US$250;

) A 1920s house rebuilt since the earthquake, this is a truly gorgeous boutique hotel. There are half a dozen rooms, each named for a herb and beautifully decorated. The quality of the food is a particular selling point, along with the leafy garden – and if there's a guesthouse offering better views of Port-au-Prince, we'd like to know about it.

Karibe Hôtel HOTEL **$$$**
(2812-7000; www.karibehotel.com; Juvenat 7, Juvenat; d from US$159;) One of the fanciest big hotels in Haiti, this hotel-cum-conference-center is where you'll find the plummiest businessfolk, international consultants and even presidents putting their bills on expenses (Bill Clinton and 'Baby Doc' Duvalier have been guests). Rooms and service are impeccable, and the posh rooftop bar gets packed on Friday nights.

Marriott Port-au-Prince HOTEL **$$$**
(2814-2800; www.marriott.com; 147 Ave Jean-Paul II, Turgeau; d US$149;) When the Marriott opened in 2014, it set a new bar (and price point) for hotels in its class. The ceilings are a bit higher, the counter tops glisten whiter, and the staff is a touch more professional. When well-heeled residents grow weary of daily struggles in Haiti, they make for the Marriott and its potent rum sours.

Pétionville

La Lorraine BOUTIQUE HOTEL **$$**
(2816-8300; www.lalorrainehaiti.net; 36 Rue Clerveaux; d/ste incl breakfast US$110/130;) This restored 1950s home-turned-boutique-hotel is Pétionville's quirky little gem. Apart from the high-arching door frames, each room is uniquely arranged with contemporary furnishings and fine Haitian art, with some rooms featuring balconies and hammocks and others containing mini gardens. The owner's meticulous attention to detail is apparent at every turn, but service can be oddly gruff.

El Rancho BOUTIQUE HOTEL **$$$**
(2815-1000, in USA 212-219-7607; www.nh-hotels.com; 5 Rue Jose Martin; d from US$154;) In 2013 the Spanish hotel Chain NH took the reins at this upscale Pétionville hotel and casino, revamping the elegant, fountain-lined entryway and the 72 modern rooms surrounding an alfresco restaurant and pool. The outdoor area is stunning, and often hosts nightlife events with performers including the likes of Sweet Micky, the famous *compâs* singer and former president.

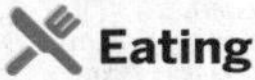

Eating

Port-au-Prince

★ **Les Jardins du Mupanah** CARIBBEAN **$$**
(2811-6764; lesjardinsdumupanah@gmail.com; Rue Oswald Durand, Champs de Mars; sandwiches US$8, mains US$13; 11am-4pm Mon-Sat) With floor-to-ceiling windows looking out over leafy gardens, Mupanah's cafe and restaurant offers one of the most elegant lunching experiences in the city. Artsy white imitation trees adorn the dining area, and well-dressed waitstaff provide top-notch service. The Caribbean-themed menu includes such items as Creole shrimp and a tropical chopped salad with grilled lobster and green papaya.

Pétionville

Pâtisserie Marie Beliard BAKERY **$**
(2813-1516, 2813-1515; www.patisseriemariebeliard.com; cnr Rues Faubert & Lambert; pastries US$1-5; 6am-6:30pm Mon-Sat, to 1pm Sun) Hands down the best bakery in Pétionville, this bright French cafe has a homey vibe, with inlaid brick and twee wallpaper. The *pain au chocolat* and other pastries are flaky perfection; this is also the place to get your *petits gâteaux á la française*.

Quartier Latin INTERNATIONAL **$$**
(3445-3325; 10 Place Boyer; mains US$15-22; 11am-midnight) An established mainstay, Quartier Latin throws French, Italian, Asian and Spanish dishes into the mix with satisfying results. The real draw is the rambling old building and garden, first a house, then a school, and now the playground of NGO types and diplomats. There's live jazz music on Friday and Saturday nights, too.

Café 36 INTERNATIONAL **$$**
(2233-3636; La Lorraine Hotel, 36 Rue Clerveaux; tapas US$8-10, mains US$12-18; 6am-10pm;) Attached to the boutique hotel La Lorraine, this classy restaurant, event space and art gallery is the kind of place you end up heading back to time and again. For the food, sure, but also the rum punches and trivia nights and attached Lakou Lakay boutique. The menu offers small bites (like the delicious Levantine-Hispaniolan *kibby*) along with salads and sandwiches.

Port-au-Prince

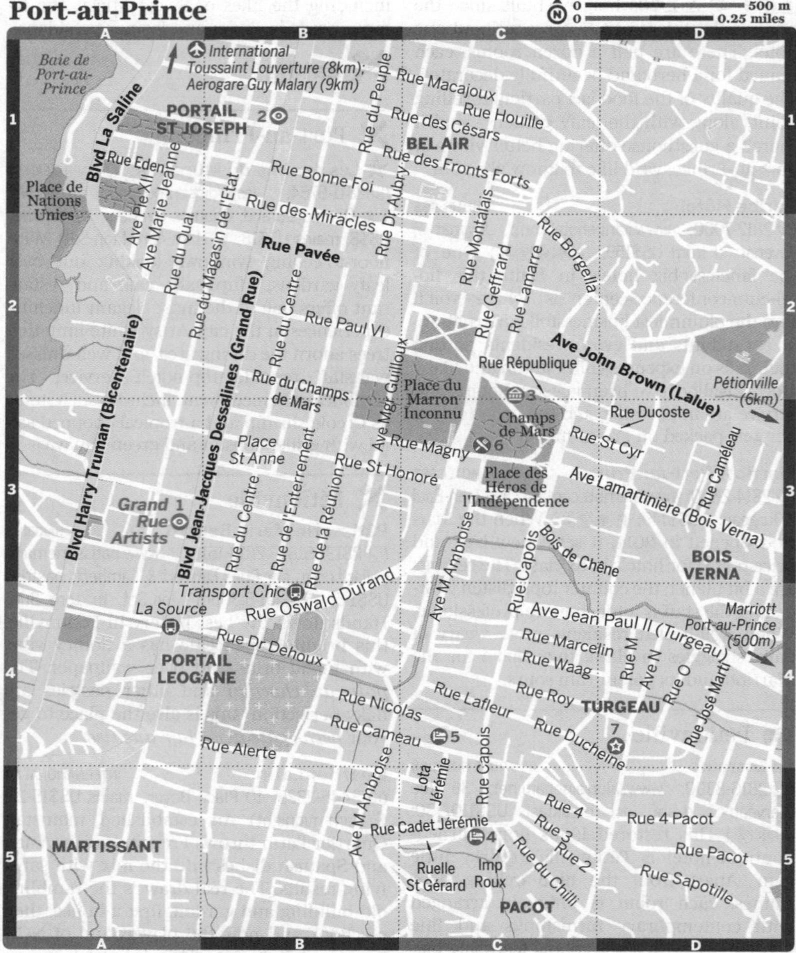

Papaye FUSION $$$

(☎4656-2482; 48 Rue Métellus; mains US$18-28; ⏲noon-2:30pm & 7-11pm Tue-Fri, 1-11pm Sat) 'Caribbean fusion' aren't words you expect to see written in a Haitian restaurant review, but Papaye carries off the idea with considerable aplomb, taking Creole dishes and jamming them up against Asian, European and other culinary influences. Somehow it works, producing one of Haiti's classiest restaurants. Weekend nights here are for the see-and-be-seen set, with a price tag to match.

☆ Entertainment

★Hôtel Oloffson LIVE MUSIC

(☎3810-4000; 60 Ave Christophe) On Thursday nights, from about 11pm, crowds gather here to dance until the small hours to the Vodou rock and roots music of RAM – the hotel band. A potent blend of African rhythms, *rara* horns, guitar and keyboards, the shows have an irresistible atmosphere. At the center of everything is band leader (and Oloffson owner) Richard Morse.

Port-au-Prince

Top Sights
1 Grand Rue Artists A3

Sights
2 Marché de Fer B1
3 Musée du Panthéon National C2

Sleeping
4 Hôtel Oloffson C5
5 Inn at Villa Bambou C4

Eating
6 Les Jardins du Mupanah C3

Entertainment
Hôtel Oloffson .... (see 4)
7 Yanvalou D4

Yanvalou LIVE MUSIC
(☎4329-1347; yanvaloubar@gmail.com; Ave N, Pacot; ⏰9am-11:30pm Tue-Sun) Thursday nights in Haiti's capital are synonymous with Yanvalou. At around 9pm, the artsy cafe and bar begins to swell with the city's in-crowd, be they UN workers, embassy types or local business owners. Some sip rum cocktails in the courtyard while others socialize by the bar. Eventually a Vodou folklore band shows up and everybody dances like crazy.

Information

Hôpital Bernard Mevs (☎3771-8247; 2 Rue Solidarite; ⏰24hr) A reputable hospital with a trauma center, run in partnership with Project Medishare.

Hôpital du Canapé Vert (☎3767-8191, 2245-0984; 83 Rte de Canapé Vert, Canapé Vert; ⏰24hr) Excellent doctors and emergency service, recommended by foreign residents.

Police station (☎2257-2222, 2222-1117, emergency 114; Rue Légitime, Port-au-Prince; ⏰24hr)

ATMs are widespread. To beat bank queues and maximize safety, head to supermarkets to change money; most have dedicated counters and security guards.

Scotiabank (cnr Rues Geffrard & Louverture, Pétionville; ⏰9am-4:30pm Mon-Fri)

Unibank (118 Rue Capois, downtown Port-au-Prince; ⏰8am-4:30pm Mon-Fri)

Getting There & Away

AIR

International flights depart from Aéroport International Toussaint Louverture (p511) and domestic flights from Aérogare Guy Malary (p511); the two are adjacent on the northern outskirts of Port-au-Prince.

It takes around 30 to 45 minutes to reach the city center from the airports, depending on the time of day. Airport taxis are run by the Association des Chauffeurs Guides d'Haïti. Fares should be between US$25 and US$40.

BUS

Port-au-Prince has no central bus station; instead, there is a series of mildly anarchic departure points according to the destination. Most buses and taptaps (local buses or minibuses) leave when full – exceptions are for Cap-Haïtien, Les Cayes and Jérémie, which you can buy seats for in advance.

From the area around Sylvio Cator Stadium you can catch **Transport Chic** (☎3107-5423; Rue Oswald Durand, Port-au-Prince) buses for Les Cayes (HTG400, five hours) and La Source buses for Jacmel (HTG225, four hours). For taptaps to Cap-Haïtien (HTG1000, seven hours) go to **Estasyon O'Cap** (Grand Rue, Port-au-Prince).

For Santo Domingo in the DR, **Caribe Tours** (☎3785-1946; cnr Rues Clerveaux & Gabart, Pétionville), **Metro Bus** (☎2949-4545; www.metroserviciosturisticos.com; 69 Ave Pan Américaine, Pétionville) and **Capital Coach Line** (☎2813-1880; Blvd 15 Octobre, Tabarre) all have daily departures at around 8am, arriving in Santo Domingo nine hours later, with tickets costing around US$50, usually including border taxes.

Getting Around

Moto-taxis are useful for weaving through traffic jams, but certainly not the safest form of transport. They cost around HTG50 for short trips; haggle for longer distances.

Port-au-Prince's taptaps run along set routes and are a very cheap way of getting around. The usual fare is HTG10 per trip. Routes are painted on the side of the cab doors. All stop on request.

Nick's Taxis (☎3401-1021; 31 Ave Pan Américaine, Pétionville) To travel between Port-au-Prince and Pétionville, hire the services of this radio-taxi firm, especially useful if you're out late. The cost comes out to around HTG1300 between downtown and Pétionville.

AROUND PORT-AU-PRINCE

Croix-des-Bouquets

Almost sucked in by Port-au-Prince's inexorable urban sprawl, Croix-des-Bouquets is home to one of Haiti's most vibrant art scenes. Its Noialles district is home to the *boss fé* (ironworkers), who hammer out incredible decorative art from flattened oil drums and vehicle bodies.

Steel drums are the most common material for the art. They're cut in half and flattened, the designs chalked and then cut out with chisels. Once free, the edges are smoothed and relief work beaten out. The smallest pieces are the size of a book; the most gloriously elaborate can stand over 2m. Popular designs include the Tree of Life, the Vodou *lwa* La Siren (the mermaid), birds, fish, musicians and angels.

Buses from Port-au-Prince (US$1, 30 minutes) depart from the junction of Rue des Fronts Forts and Rue du Centre. Taptaps from Port-au-Prince (HTG20, 30 minutes) leave from Carrefour Fleuriot in Tabarre, on Blvd 15 Octobre. For Croix-des-Bouquets, get out at the police post, where the road splits left to Hinche and right to the DR. Take the right-hand road, then turn right at Notre Dame Depot. For Noailles, turn right at the Seventh Day Adventist Church, and follow the sound of hammered metal: the artist village is signed.

Côte des Arcadins

From Port-au-Prince, Rte National 1 stretches north along the coast before turning inland toward Gonaïves and Cap-Haïtien. The area is named for the Arcadins, a trio of sand cays surrounded by coral reefs in the channel between the mainland and Île de la Gonâve.

Beach hotels are the order of the day along the Côte des Arcadins, including the **Royal Decameron Indigo Beach Resort & Spa** (2815-0111, in USA 855-308-0375; www.decameron.com; Km 78, Rte National 1; all-inclusive d from US$99; P ❄ @ ≋), a bright and breezy hotel on a gorgeous white-sand beach with dazzling turquoise water, and cocktails flowing freely from four bars and three tasty restaurants. The **Moulin sur Mer** (2813-1042, 3701-1918; www.moulinsurmer.com; Km 77, Rte National 1; d incl breakfast from US$115; P ❄ @ ≋) is a large and charming complex with a nice selection of rooms, including 'gingerbreadized' rooms near the beach and more Spanish-hacienda style ones further back. The excellent **Musée Colonial Ogier-Fombrum** (3701-1918; Km 77, Rte National 1; US$5; 10am-6pm; P) is a short (complimentary) golf-buggy ride away.

Diving is a popular activity in these parts, and can be arranged by **Pegasus** (3411-4775; haitidivingpegasus@yahoo.com; Kaliko Beach Club, Km 61, Rte National 1; 8am-5pm) or **Marina Blue Dive & Excursion Center** (2811-4043; www.marinabluehaiti.com; Moulin sur Mer, Km 77, Rte National 1; open water certification US$275, dives from US$65; 8am-5pm).

Hotels offer private transport to and from the area.

LOCAL KNOWLEDGE

SOUVENANCE & SOUKRI

People from all over Haiti congregate near Gonaïves to take part in Souvenance and Soukri, the country's two biggest Vodou festivals.

Souvenance begins on Good Friday, and continues for a week, to the constant sound of *rara* music. Prayers are offered to sacred tamarind trees, initiates bathe in a sacred pond and bulls are sacrificed for the Vodou spirits.

Soukri is a ritual dedicated to the Kongo *lwa*. The service is divided into two branches: 'the father of all Kongo' takes place on January 6, and the second, larger ceremony, 'the mother of all Kongo,' occurs on August 14. The rituals last two weeks each, a true test of endurance. Many of the celebrations are similar to those in Souvenance.

Route de Kenscoff

The main road from Pétionville's Pl Saint-Pierre winds steeply uphill toward the cool of the mountains. After just a few kilometers you're in a rich agricultural area, with steep terraced fields clinging to the sides of the mountains, and the congestion of the city replaced by fresh breezes.

The crisp air of Kenscoff makes it a popular weekend destination for city dwellers – at 1980m above sea level, it's often referred to as the Switzerland of the Caribbean (there are even a few funky Caribbean–Alpine architectural hybrids). With sweeping views everywhere you look and the brooding cloud-capped backdrop of Massif de la Selle behind you, it's tailor-made for day walks. Coffee and vegetables are grown in great quantities here, which are sold at Kenscoff's local market (along with toiletries, kitchen hardware and some arty tat).

Fort Jacques was erected during the burst of fort-building following independence in 1804. It was built by Alexandre Pétion and named after Jean-Jacques Dessalines, and though it is well preserved, the structure was slightly damaged in the 2010 earthquake. The ruined **Fort Alexandre** is a short walk away. Overlooking Port-au-Prince, they both offer breathtaking views. The forts are a 3km walk or moto ride from the main road – take the sharp uphill road opposite Fermathe's covered market.

Just off the Route de Kenscoff, **L'Observatoire de Boutilliers** (☎3454-0118; Boutilliers; mains HTG1000-1800; ⏲10am-10pm) is a romantic mountaintop restaurant offering the best possible view of Port-au-Prince and beyond. The food is pricey (but decent, with all the typical Haitian favorites, including goat, port and conch, as well as burgers and wings) and service can be slow, but just remember: the point is the glorious view.

Getting There & Away

Taptaps leave Pétionville throughout the day from the corner of Rue Gregoire and Villate, departing when full (HTG50, 30 minutes) and passing through Fermathe. Change at Kenscoff for Furcy.

Furcy

In the tiny village of Furcy, pine trees abound and a whiff of fresh cilantro is on the breeze. There are stellar views of the Massif de la Selle, and locals rent out horses (around US$5 per hour) to take visitors to a waterfall above the village (it's 1½ hours on foot). If you plan to stay overnight, don't forget some warm clothes – temperatures drop once the sun starts to dip, making for a cozy change from steamy Port-au-Prince.

Sleeping

★O-zone the Village HOSTEL $
(☎2811-5170, 4806-6929; www.facebook.com/pg/ozonethevillage; Pl Furcy; d from US$65, tree house US$125, all incl breakfast; P 📶) Unique in Haiti, this inspired mountain stay is encircled by pine trees and constructed with recycled materials – discarded wire-holders as walkways, old tires as art, reclaimed wood and bottles as walls. There's a rugged feel to the place, and it features a rustic tree house guests enter via a hanging bridge. It's romantic, in a steampunk kind of way.

★Sesanet GUESTHOUSE $$$
(Madame Hélène's; ☎3443-0443; s/d incl half board US$125/150; P) With just three rooms, this charming, secluded guesthouse is usually full – and for good reason. The owner, Madame Hélène, has filled the place with exquisite art and homey touches, and her fusion meals (French and Middle Eastern; dinner US$35) are something truly special. Specialties here include tabbouleh, guinea fowl and rabbit, all prepared with whatever is fresh at the market.

Getting There & Away

To arrive in Furcy, rent a 4WD or hop on a moto-taxi from Kenscoff (HTG100, 45 minutes) up the mountain. Make a left at Kenscoff Commissariat, then right after the fast-food places and continue uphill. Those continuing on to Parc National la Visite will eventually reach the entrance, from where you can hike over the mountains to Seguin.

NORTHERN HAITI

If you're interested in how Haiti came to be as it is today, head north. From Columbus' first landfall on Hispaniola to the key events of the revolution, it all happened here.

Start at Cap-Haïtien, Haiti's second city. Once one of the richest colonial ports in the world, it's the ideal jumping-off point to visit the world-class Citadelle Laferrière, the largest fortress in the Americas, perched high on a mountain, and the ruined palace of Sans Souci sitting below. There are plenty of smaller forts along the coast, while Île de la Tortue evokes an age when pirates ruled this coastline.

The crashing Atlantic waves give the north some spectacular coastline and great beaches. Cormier Plage and Plage Labadie, a stone's throw from Cap-Haïtien, are home to some exciting new tourist ventures. They are ideal places to unwind from the chaos of Haiti's cities.

Cap-Haïtien

Haiti's second city feels a world away from the throng and hustle of Port-au-Prince. During the French colonial era it was the richest city in the Caribbean, and even if that grandeur has long since faded, the city still maintains a relaxed atmosphere (relative to Port-au-Prince at least), and the old port architecture of high shop fronts and balconies makes it a pleasant place to wander. Most people refer to the city as 'Cap,' or

'O'Kap' in the high-lilting local Kreyòl accent of its residents.

There isn't much to do in Cap-Haïtien beyond enjoy the atmosphere, but it's an ideal place to base yourself to enjoy the nearby attractions.

Sights

Place d'Armes SQUARE

(cnr Rues 18 & H) Cap's pretty main square, bordered on the southern side by the Notre-Dame cathedral on Rue 18, has a dark past. François Mackandal, leader of a pre-revolutionary guerrilla slave war, was burned at the stake here in 1758. Subsequent revolutionary Vincent Ogé was broken on the wheel here in 1791. But nowadays things seem extremely relaxed, at least during the daytime: benches clustered around a small statue of Jean-Jacques Dessalines are invariably occupied by students and other friendly chillers.

Sleeping

★**Habitation des Lauriers** HOTEL $$

(☎3836-0885; www.habitationdeslauriers.com; cnr Rues 13 & Q; dm US$25, s/d with fan US$50/60, with air-con US$80/110; P@🛜🏊) The best-value option in Cap-Haïtien offers striking views of the city from its mountaintop perch on the western outskirts, along with top-notch service, delicious home-cooked meals, and charming accommodations for every budget. A diverse mix of guests socialize on the veranda of the historic main house and around the dipping pool, surrounded by lush gardens, hummingbirds and butterflies.

★**Hostellerie du Roi Christophe** HOTEL $$$

(☎3687-8915; hotroi24b@hotmail.com; cnr Rues 24 & B; s/d US$126/150; P❄🛜🏊) Cap-Haïtien's oldest and most charming hotel, this French colonial building has something of a haunted Spanish hacienda about it. There's an elegant, leafy central courtyard with plenty of rocking chairs and wooden busts of Haitian revolutionary leaders, a terrace restaurant, and a peaceful pool surrounded by flowering plants. The rooms are large, with period furniture and art, and many have balconies.

Le Picolet HOTEL $$$

(☎2810-1111; Blvd de Mer; s/d US$130/150; P❄🛜) A popular hotel with an elegant vibe and comfy rooms centered on a small, verdant courtyard. Walls throughout are adorned with colorful Haitian art. The restaurant is very good, with a refreshing sea breeze. It's a great place to sample catch of the day; be sure to ask for a free Haitian *dous* (a kind of fudge) after dinner.

Eating

★**Lolo's** ITALIAN $$

(☎3778-9635; Rue A; mains from US$12; ⏲2-11pm Mon-Sat) Lolo Silvera has ratcheted up the food scene in Cap with this delightful spot. The walls of the outdoor patio are lined with seashells, driftwood and Haitian paintings, and tables are set up under strings of lights. The food is the best in town: order the fresh pasta or the risotto *djon-djon* (Haitian black mushrooms).

Kokiyaj INTERNATIONAL $$

(☎3227-4821; Blvd de Mer; mains US$8-15; ⏲8am-10pm) A self-styled sports restaurant above a supermarket sounds unimpressive, but Kokiyaj is actually a cut above. As well as Creole classics there are some good continental and American mains, pleasant service and a well-stocked bar.

Lakay CREOLE $$

(☎3188-6881; info@lakayhaiti.com; Blvd de Mer; mains US$8-19; ⏲11:30am-2am Tue-Sat, from 6pm Sun) One of the busiest restaurants in Cap-Haïtien, and it's not hard to see why. There are tables facing the seafront where you can enjoy a drink, otherwise step inside to eat under bamboo thatch and load up on generous plates of Creole food or pizza. The atmosphere is lively, and at weekends there are often bands (US$4 admission applies).

Information

Hôpital Justinien (☎2262-0512, 3356-2004; cnr Rues 17 & Q; ⏲24hr) Cap-Haïtien's main hospital.

Sogebank (cnr Rues 11 & A) Has an ATM open during banking hours.

Getting There & Away

AIR

Hugo Chávez International Airport (p511) is 3.5km east of the city (US$7/1.50 by taxi/moto-taxi). **Sunrise Airways** (Hostellerie du Roi Christophe, cnr Rues 24 & B), with offices conveniently located in the lobby of the Roi Christophe, has three daily flights to Port-au-Prince (8am, 10am and 4:15pm, US$100, 30 minutes).

BUS

Caribe Tours (cnr Rues 29 & A) runs a direct coach service to Santiago (US$52, four hours)

WORTH A TRIP

BEACHES NEAR CAP-HAÏTIEN

A new road leads west from Cap-Haïtien, winding along the northwest coast of the cape toward some of the loveliest coastal scenery in the country, where green hills tumble straight into the Atlantic, broken up by crescents of golden sand.

The road hits the north coast of the cape near **Cormier Plage Resort** (3702-0210; www.cormierhaiti.com; Rte de Labadie; d incl breakfast from US$106; P ❄ @), the picture of a Caribbean beach and resort, where white breakers roll in to shore and rum punches are the order of the day. Further around the point is **Plage Labadie** (also called Coco Plage), a walled-off peninsula leased by Royal Caribbean Lines for its cruise-ship guests, who arrive five times a week.

From Plage Labadie, *bateaux-taxis* (water taxis) ferry passengers to their guesthouses, beaches further west (Kadras Bay is particularly gorgeous) and to the uninhabited island of **Île-à-Rat,** (Amiga Island) one of the country's most beautiful places to spend a day sunning, snorkeling, and feasting on freshly caught seafood.

Chato Relaxo (www.chatorelaxo.com; 1 Rue Belly Beach; apt incl breakfast weekdays/weekends US$130/145;) is run by the Mangs family, who have lived in Labadie since the 1970s. Their love for the area is clearly apparent in the cliffside bungalow, constructed from repurposed building material from colonial-era forts. The balcony offers 180-degree views, and Dillon Mangs can organize boats to Île-à-Rat, Kadras and other idyllic spots. Dinners of Haitian specialties can be arranged for US$30 per person.

The bungalow sleeps up to three, and is deservedly popular: book well in advance.

and Santo Domingo (US$60, nine hours) in the DR.

Sans-Souci Tours (4855-7071; Rte National 1) has routes between Cap-Haïtien and Port-au-Prince (HTG1000, seven hours).

For Cormier Plage and Plage Labadie, taptaps leave from the corner of Rues 21 and Q in Cap-Haïtien (HTG25, 30 and 40 minutes respectively). For the Citadelle, taptaps to Milot (HTG20, one hour) leave from Stasyon Pon near the main bridge.

The Citadelle & Sans Souci

The awe-inspiring mountain fortress of Citadelle Laferrière is a short distance from Cap-Haïtien on the edge of the small town of Milot. Built to repel the French, it's a monument to the vision of self-appointed king Henry Christophe, who oversaw its construction. A visit here is an essential part of any trip to Haiti, and actually takes in two sites – the Unesco World Heritage–listed fortress itself and the palace of Sans Souci.

The ticket office is at the far end of Milot, next to the huge dome of **Église Immaculée Conception de Milot**, facing the ruins of Sans Souci. There are many guides and horse wranglers here. One that comes recommended is Maurice Etienne, who also runs the Lakou Lakay (p502) cultural center. A reasonable fee for a good guide is US$20 to US$30, plus the hire of a horse; Etienne charges US$50 for a tour of both sites.

Sights

★Citadelle Laferrière FORTRESS

(Citadelle Henri; Sans Souci & Citadelle US$10; 7am-4pm) Haitians call the Citadelle the eighth wonder of the world and, having slogged to the 900m summit of Pic Laferrière (or ridden horseback for US$15), you'll likely agree. This battleship-like fortress gives commanding views in every direction. Completed in 1820, it employed 20,000 people and held supplies to sustain the royal family and a garrison of 5000 troops for a year. With 4m-thick walls up to 40m high, the fortress was impenetrable, although its cannon were never fired in combat.

Inside the ramparts the fort has a series of drawbridges and blind corners to fox attackers. These lead through a gallery containing the first of several cannon batteries. The Citadelle contains over 160 cannon, mostly captured in battle from the English, the Spanish and the French. Throughout the fort are huge piles of cannonballs – once 50,000 in total – though many have been stolen.

At the heart of the fort is the central courtyard, with its officers' quarters. Christophe himself was buried here after his suicide – his grave is under a huge boulder that forms part of the mountain. On the level above is the whitewashed tomb of his brother-in-law, Prince Noel.

It's possible to spend a couple of hours exploring the site, which constantly reveals hidden passages, halls and new views from its ramparts. Sheer drops protect the Citadelle from every angle except its rear, where you can look south to Site des Ramiers, a huddle of four small forts protecting its exposed flank. It's possible to walk out to the Ramiers sites, which are crumbling and in the slow process of being overtaken by the humid forest, but you'll need to be comfortable scrambling.

Sans Souci HISTORIC SITE
(Sans Souci & Citadelle US$10; ⏲7am-4pm) Built as a rival to Versailles in France, Henry Christophe's palace of Sans Souci has lain abandoned since it was ruined in the 1842 earthquake. The years of neglect have left an elegantly crumbling edifice. Finished in 1813, Sans Souci was more than just a palace; it was designed to be the administrative capital of Christophe's kingdom, housing a hospital, a school and a printing press, as well as an army barracks.

Eating

Lakou Lakay CREOLE $$
(☎3614-2485, 3483-7810; Milot; meals US$10-20) This cultural community center is a long-standing institution. Run by guide Maurice Etienne and his family, the center welcomes visitors with traditional dancing, folk songs and drumming, along with a huge Creole feast (reservations required). They're constructing a swimming pool and community rooms. Simple rooms for visitors (US$50 per person) are available if you want to overnight.

Getting There & Away

Taptaps from Cap-Haïtien (HTG20, one hour) drop you a short walk from Sans Souci. Don't plan to return too late, as transport dries up by late afternoon. Taxis, arranged by your hotel, cost around US$50.

SOUTHERN HAITI

Haiti's south is about taking it easy. After hairy traffic out of Port-au-Prince, the urban hustle is replaced by a relaxed air as you head toward a more familiar Caribbean.

Jacmel

Sheltered by a beautiful 3km-wide bay, the old port of Jacmel is one of the most fascinating and picturesque towns in Haiti, and host to one of its best Carnivals.

Part of Jacmel's charm lies in its old town center, full of mansions and merchants' warehouses with a late-Victorian grace peeking out from behind the rusty wrought-iron balconies and peeling facades. Although some of Jacmel's historic buildings were damaged in the 2010 earthquake, the town has received a facelift in recent years, including the installation of innumerable urban mosaics, the most impressive of which are displayed along the kilometer-long beachfront boardwalk, Promenade du Bord de Mer, which buzzes with activity day and night.

The town is also the undisputed handicrafts capital of Haiti, with dozens of workshops producing hand-painted souvenirs, from wall decorations to elaborate papier-mâché masks produced for the Carnival festivities.

Sights

★Bassin Bleu WATERFALL
(HTG100; ⏲dawn-dusk) Tucked into the mountains 12km northwest of Jacmel, Bassin Bleu is a series of three cobalt-blue pools linked by waterfalls that make up one of the prettiest swimming holes in Haiti. Experience Jacmel will take you to a hamlet close to the pools via moto-taxi, then a local guide will escort you down an uneven path (at one point you'll rappel down a rock face) to the gorgeous pools, where kids often jump from high rocks.

Cayes Jacmel VILLAGE
From the small fishing village of Cayes Jacmel, about 14km east of Jacmel, the beach spreads a further 3km to **Plage Ti Mouillage**, a gorgeous white-sand beach fringed with coconut palms, plus a bar for drinks and seafood. Cayes Jacmel is known for making the vertiginous rocking chairs seen throughout Haiti.

Tours

Experience Jacmel ADVENTURE
(☎3722-5757; www.facebook.com/ExpJacmel; Promenade du Bord de Mer; ⏲8am-1pm) The most reputable tour company in the south, Experience Jacmel offers city tours, Carnival-focused art excursions, journeys to

Bassin Bleu, and even a Vodou night tour involving an encounter with a Vodou priest. Local owner Markensy is as nice and helpful as they come, and incredibly knowledgeable about the town.

Sleeping & Eating

★Hôtel Florita HOTEL $$

(☎3785-5154; www.hotelflorita.com; 29 Rue du Commerce; s/d US$80/100; ❄@) Damaged in the earthquake but rebuilt, this converted mansion from 1888 oozes charm. There are polished floorboards and period furniture, while rooms are whitewashed and airy, with mosquito nets and balconies. Service is sometimes inexplicably slow, but the bar serves great drinks, is frequented by modern-day characters straight out of Tennessee Williams and is chock-full of fabulous art.

Unfortunately, we hear that security is sometimes lacking, so plan accordingly if your heart is really set on this gorgeous, one-of-a-kind spot.

★Cyvadier Plage Hôtel HOTEL $$

(☎3844-8264; www.hotelcyvadier.com; Rte de Cyvadier; s/d with fan US$60/73, with air-con US$80/95; P❄@≋) Off the main highway, this is the furthest of the beach hotels from the center of Jacmel, but also one of the best. Good rooms in a cluster of buildings face the terrace restaurant, helmed by the Swiss-trained chef-owner Jean Christophe, and out to the private cove of Cyvadier Plage (nonresidents welcome).

Colin's Hotel HOTEL $$

(☎3704-4877, 2818-8686; www.colinshotel.com; 13 Rue St-Anne; s/d incl breakfast US$88/99; P❄≋) Just off the beach boardwalk, the oversized rooms at this colorful hotel surround a large courtyard and pool area full of NGO types tapping away on Apple devices. The downstairs restaurant is very good and stands out for its friendly, efficient service, and the sea views from just about anywhere in the hotel are fantastic.

★Manje Lokal CREOLE $

(Jacmel Beach; mains US$4-6; ⏲noon-midnight) Right off the boardwalk behind a concrete wall with an opening at the center, this is a collection of half-a-dozen shacks (with accompanying sound systems), each serving up plenty of beer and cheap food. Fish, chicken and plantains are all filling staples, and the party here sometimes goes late into the night. For food, Chantal's section is where it's at.

Cafe Koze CAFE $

(☎4147-5000; www.facebook.com/pg/cafekoze; Rue du Commerce; mains HTG200, lobster roll HTG300; ⏲noon-9pm Tue-Sun; 📶) When the wait at the Florita becomes unbearable, those in the know head next door to the more efficient Cafe Koze, an espresso bar

DON'T MISS

JACMEL CARNIVAL

Jacmel's **Carnival** (⏲Feb) celebrations are famous across Haiti, and every year thousands of partygoers descend on the city to take part in this fantastic spectacle. Jacmel turns into one giant gothic, surrealist theater for the event: it's a world away from the sequins and sparkle of Carnival in Rio de Janeiro.

The Carnival season starts its buildup in late January, with events every Sunday leading up to the giant celebrations and procession on the Sunday of the week before Shrove Tuesday (it's held a week earlier than other Carnivals so it doesn't clash with Port-au-Prince's party).

The streets swell and everywhere you look are strange figures in fantastical papier-mâché masks – the signature image of Jacmel Carnival. You can see the masks being made and on display in the ateliers year-round. Jungle animals jostle with mythical birds, giant fruit and *lwa* (Vodou spirits). Mixed in with the procession are celebrants dressed as Arawaks and colonists, and horned figures covered in molasses and soot, who tease revelers with their sticky grab. St Michael and his angels ritually fight the devil, while gangs of monsters – caricaturing military misrule – growl scarily at the crowds. There's even a donkey dressed up in peasant clothes and sneakers (an old Carnival favorite).

Music is everywhere, from bands on organized floats to *rara* (one of the most popular forms of Haitian music) bands on foot. It's an enormous party. The procession kicks off roughly around noon, with celebrations continuing late into the night.

WORTH A TRIP

SURFING IN HAITI

About 30 minutes east of Jacmel, just down the street from Cayes Jacmel, the sleepy fishing village of Kabic has a picturesque azure beach that offers decent waves for surfers. The friendly locals, known as Kabiquois, make guests feel welcome and are one of the main reasons so many return time and again.

Moto-taxis from Jacmel run around HTG100 in the daytime and HTG150 at night, and taptaps (HTG25) travel up and down the beachfront road from sunrise until 8pm.

Founded by a nonprofit in 2011 and staffed with locals who learned to surf on discarded planks of wood, **Surf Haiti** (☎4906-2119, 3159-9414, 4286-9277; www.surfhaiti.org; Kabic Beach; lessons US$15, board rental half-/full day HTG500/1000; ⌚dawn-dusk) is Haiti's first and only surf school. More advanced instruction is available by prior arrangement. Rooms are available at the charming guesthouse, complete with a river-fed swimming pool, up the hill from the beach for US$45/55 per single/double.

and lounge with great pizza, tapas and a delicious lobster pressed sandwich situation. On weekends there is live music.

Information

Banque Nationale de Crédit (Grand Rue; ⌚8:30am-4pm Mon-Fri)

Hôpital St Michel (☎2288-2151; Rue St-Philippe; ⌚24hr) For emergencies, but not great.

Getting There & Away

La Source (☎4300-9525; 16 Av de la Liberté, near Maré Geffard) buses (HTG225, at least four hours) and taptaps (HTG200, five hours) to Port-au-Prince leave from the Bassin Caïman station 2km out of town.

The Southwest

Les Cayes

You'd be hard-pressed to find a sense of urgency in Haiti's fourth-largest city. More popularly known as Aux Cayes, Les Cayes is an old rum port sheltered by a series of reefs that has sent many ships to their graves (its first recorded victim was one of Columbus' ships on his final voyage to Hispaniola). Pirates were another threat, notably from nearby Île-à-Vache. Today Les Cayes has little to offer the visitor, although it's a good transit hub for other destinations in the south.

Le Cayenne Hôtel (☎3105-3959; lacayenneht@yahoo.fr; Rue Capitale; s/d incl breakfast from HTG4750/6150; P❄@🏊) is the closest thing Les Cayes gets to a beach hotel: the sea is on the other side of Le Cayenne's boundary wall. There's nothing wrong here – rooms are standard, and there's plenty of space and a pool – but nothing spectacular either.

Bistro Gourmand (☎2270-5718; 41 Rue Geffrard; mains HTG400; ⌚8am-11pm) is an indoor-outdoor bar. It's a hit with the NGO crowd that passes through Les Cayes on the way to jobs further along the southern peninsula. Salads and pizzas are big sellers, and the bar gets busy in the evenings. Great rum sours.

Getting There & Away

Transport Chic (☎3630-2576; 227 Ave des Quatre Chemins) have luxury air-conditioned minibuses running daily to Port-au-Prince (US$8, four hours).

Voyageur (☎3633-2361; voyageurbus@gmail.com; Meridien Hotel, Rte National 2) and Taptaps to Port Salut (HTG200, 45 minutes) leave from Carrefour des Quatre Chemins.

Île-à-Vache

The so-called 'Cow Island,' Île-à-Vache lies about 15km south of Les Cayes. In the 16th century it was a base for the Welsh pirate Henry Morgan as he terrorized the Spanish Main. Three centuries later Abraham Lincoln tried to relocate emancipated American slaves here, but it was a short-lived and ill-provisioned experiment.

The island today is scattered with rural houses, plantations, mangroves, the odd Arawak burial ground and some great beaches.

Sleeping

★**Port Morgan** RESORT $$$
(☎3923-0000; www.port-morgan.com; Cayes Coq; s/d incl full board from US$115/205; P❄@🏊)
One day in the 1970s, a young Frenchman named Didier sailed into Port Morgan on a

family holiday. He never left, luckily for the blissed-out tourists at the Port Morgan. Didier's resort, comprising bright-and-breezy gingerbread chalets with lovely views of the yachts in the harbor, is the most restful place on the island.

Abaka Bay Resort RESORT **$$$**
(☎3721-3691; www.abakabay.com; Anse Dufour; s/d incl full board US$135/220; ❄@) This hotel has one of the most fabulous beaches in the Caribbean, a smooth white curve of a bay, met by lush foliage and a series of pleasant bungalows and villas. The atmosphere is laid-back, but a dearth of tourists means that staff can be a little too relaxed. Private transport to and from the island costs an additional US$50 per boat.

ℹ Getting There & Away

All three hotels on Île-à-Vache offer transfers from the Les Cayes wharf from US$50 to US$60 per trip (which can be split among groups). Otherwise, *bateaux-taxis* (water taxis) leave from the wharf several times daily (US$2, 30 minutes) for the village of Madame Bernard. Depending on fuel prices, the trip can take much longer (captains will drive slower to conserve fuel). You'll want to wear sunscreen and a hat.

Port Salut

A lovely road leads west from Les Cayes to the spectacular beaches of Port Salut. This area was hit hard by Hurricane Matthew in 2016; it's much recovered now but destroyed buildings are still being cleaned up, and some palms on the beach are eerily missing their tops. There's not much action here, but if you're after some quiet days along the beach Port Salut may be just the ticket.

The one-street town is strung for several kilometers along the coast, and still offers wide swaths of palm-fringed white sand with barely a person on it, and the gorgeously warm Caribbean to splash around in. The largest cave in Haiti, **Grotte Marie Jeanne** (☎3702-3941, 3638-2292; HTG100; ⏲8am-4pm), is about 45 minutes up the coast in Port-à-Piment, and worth a visit if you're in the area.

Sleeping & Eating

★**Sunset Cove Beach Hotel** HOTEL **$$**
(☎3664-0404, 4912-4211; www.sunsetcovebeachhotel.com; d from US$88) Clustered around a tiny, sandy cove are these large, multiroom bungalows with a charming whiff of gingerbread about them, as well as a **top-notch restaurant** (☎3797-0978, 3664-0404; Rte Départmentale 205; mains HTG200; ⏲hours vary) and bar. The manager's friendly professionalism imbues the place with a sense of security and calm; this is one of the best places to stay in southern Haiti.

Chez Kaliko SEAFOOD **$$**
(☎3878-9601; Port Salut beach; mains US$12; ⏲hours vary) Joe, the owner of this beachfront shack in Port Salut, doesn't know his business' opening hours, and doesn't seem aware of time in general. But if you've got several hours to spare and are a fan of fresh octopus, conch and grilled fish, this is the best place to get it.

ℹ Getting There & Away

Taptaps to Les Cayes (HTG150, 45 minutes) leave throughout the day.

UNDERSTAND HAITI

History

From Taínos to Revolution to the French

Hispaniola's earliest inhabitants were called the Taínos, and by the time Christopher Columbus landed on the island in 1492, they numbered some 400,000. However, within 30 years of Columbus' landing, the Taínos were gone, wiped out by disease and abuse.

The Spanish neglected their colony of Santo Domingo, and through the 17th century it became a haven for pirates and, later, ambitious French colonists. The French turned St-Domingue over to sugar production on a huge scale. By the end of the 18th century it was the richest colony in the world, with 40,000 colonists lording it over half a million black slaves. Following the French Revolution in 1789, free offspring of colonists and female slaves demanded equal rights, while the slaves themselves launched a huge rebellion. Led by the inspiring slave leader Toussaint Louverture, the slaves freed themselves by arms and forced France to abolish slavery.

The World's First Black Republic

After 13 years of struggle (and the death of Toussaint Louverture) and the final defeat of the French on the battlefield on January 1, 1804, at Gonaïves, the revolutionary leader Jean-Jacques Dessalines proclaimed independence for St-Domingue and restored its Taíno name, Haiti, meaning 'Mountainous Land.'

Unfortunately, independent Haiti soon slipped into disorder. Dessalines was murdered by those who saw him as a despot and in the aftermath the country was split by civil war. The north became a kingdom under Henry Christophe, and it wasn't until his death in 1820 that the country was reunited.

in 1825 President Boyer paid a crippling indemnity to France in return for diplomatic recognition. The debt took the rest of the century to pay off and turned Haiti into the first third-world debtor nation. Of the 22 heads of state between 1843 and 1915, only one served his full term in office; the others were assassinated or forced into exile.

In 1915, after President Vilbrun Guillaume Sam was killed by a mob, the US sent in the marines, with the stated aim of stabilizing the country.

During its nearly 20-year occupation of the country, the US replaced the Haitian constitution and built up the country's infrastructure by instituting the hated corvée, labor gangs of conscripted peasants.

The occupation brought predictable resistance, in which thousands of Haitians were killed. The US occupied Haiti until in 1934.

The Duvaliers & Aristide

Change came in 1956 with the election of François 'Papa Doc' Duvalier, whose support came from the burgeoning black middle class and the politically isolated rural poor.

Duvalier consolidated his power by creating a notorious militia called the Tontons Macoutes, named for the Haitian folk figure who carries off small children in his bag at night.

'Papa Doc' died on April 21, 1971, and was succeeded by his son Jean-Claude 'Baby Doc' Duvalier. Periodic bouts of repression continued until major civil unrest forced Baby Doc to flee to France in February 1986.

Control changed hands between junta leaders until finally the Supreme Court ordered elections for December 1990. A young priest named Father Jean-Bertrand Aristide, standing as a surprise last-minute candidate with the slogan 'Lavalas' (Flood), won a landslide victory.

Aristide promised radical reforms to aid the poor, but after just seven months he was pushed out of office in a military coup. An alliance of rich, mixed-race families and army generals staged a bloody coup. He returned in 1994 with the help of the US military, but at the cost of implementing an economic restructuring plan that eviscerated his original ideas for reform.

After a period in opposition, Aristide returned to the presidential palace after the 2001 elections, but again his rule proved short. The opposition refused to accept the result and the country again looked chaos in the face. Aristide fled Haiti in 2004, claiming he was effectively kidnapped by US agents and bundled out of Port-au-Prince; the US denies this but maintains that his overthrow was necessary to return stability to Haiti. Either way, a UN peacekeeping mission (Minustah) was sent to the country.

HAITI – UNREST?

In October 2017, a Haitian Senate report detailed how US$2 billion in funds deriving from the country's participation in Petrocaribe, a Venezuelan-subsidized oil-purchasing program, had been embezzled or otherwise mishandled by government officials. The funds had been intended to boost the Haitian economy and make life easier for the millions who live below the poverty line. The report helped spark mass protests against corruption, with calls for President Moïse – one of the alleged beneficiaries – to resign. Simultaneously, the government found itself unable to pay for fuel imports, leading to pervasive blackouts and the gourde to crash in value.

The protests, which continue as we went to press, have led to the US and UK issuing travel advisories for Haiti, and some international organizations evacuating their staff. With no immediate resolution to the crisis, and Haitian politics being played out on the street once more, seek up-to-date travel and security advice before planning any travel to Haiti.

HAITI'S EARTHQUAKE

At 4:53pm on January 12, 2010, Haiti was shaken to its core when shock waves from a fault line 13km below the earth's surface caused a 7.0-magnitude earthquake on the outskirts of Port-au-Prince. Haitians dubbed the earthquake Godou-Godou, named for the sound it made as the buildings collapsed. It's thought that 230,000 people were killed, 300,000 injured and 2.3 million people displaced, while over 180,000 buildings were either damaged or destroyed. Striking at the heart of the nation, Godou-Godou is one of the largest natural disasters on record.

The earthquake prompted an enormous humanitarian response, with billions of dollars in international assistance flooding into Haiti, and tens of thousands of NGO workers and soldiers arriving to assist. But much of that 'help' was misguided and even counterproductive, undermining Haiti's potential to help itself. The Interim Haiti Recovery Commission (IHRC) set up to coordinate billions of dollars in reconstruction aid and led by Bill Clinton frequently delivered disorganized development experiments and unfinished projects.

Haiti already had more aid organizations per capita than any other nation, and has been disparagingly referred to as the 'Republic of NGOs.' The high media visibility of the Haitian earthquake, and the difficulties faced in the response effort, prompted continuing debate on the limits of aid in a disaster situation.

Natural & Political Disasters

Under new president René Préval, Minustah launched a controversial but largely successful military campaign to uproot Port-au-Prince's gangs, bringing a modicum of normality to the streets of the capital, until violent demonstrations in 2008 again shook the government, this time in the name of rocketing food prices. The same year, Hurricane Hanna devastated Gonaïves.

The new decade started out with natural disasters. The unprecedented and tragic 7.0-magnitude earthquake of 2010 crippled Port-au-Prince, taking the lives of 230,000 people, injuring another 300,000 and displacing some 2.3 million. The large-scale destruction was met with an enormous, but often misguided, humanitarian response, with billions of dollars in international aid being misspent or wasted. Hurricane Matthew took its own billion-dollar toll on the people and economies of the country's south, right in the middle of the already contentious transfer of power from president and *compás* legend 'Sweet Micky' Martelly to his hand-picked successor Jovenel Moïse. Violent protests and dubious accusations of voter fraud delayed the election for more than a year, until Moïse was finally declared the winner in 2017.

People & Culture

Vodou

It's hard to think of a more maligned and misunderstood religion than Vodou. Even its name sparks an instantly negative word-association game of voodoo dolls, zombies and black magic – less a religion than a mass of superstitions. The truth is somewhat distant from the hype.

Vodou is a sophisticated belief system with roots in Haiti's African past and the slave rebellion that brought the country to independence in 1804. Central to Haiti's national identity, these roots have also led to the demonization of Vodou in the West. For three centuries, enslaved people were shipped to Haiti from the Dahomey and Kongo kingdoms in West and Central Africa. As well as their labor, the slaves brought with them their traditional religions; Vodou is a synthesis of these, mixed with residual Taíno rituals and colonial Catholic iconography.

It wasn't until 1991 that Vodou was finally recognized as a national religion alongside Christianity.

Music

One of the most popular Haitian music is *rara*. During Carnival, Port-au-Prince and

Jacmel fill with *rara* bands moving through the streets on floats. Cuban *son* has influenced the troubadour bands that entertain in restaurants and hotels, singing and gently strumming guitars. Merengue, the Dominican big-band sound, has always been played enthusiastically on dance floors, and in the 1950s evolved into *compás* direct (or just *compas* for short), with its slightly more African beat.

Racines (roots) music grew out of the Vodou-jazz movement of the late 1970s and was propelled by Vodou rhythms overlaid with electric guitars, keyboards and vocals. The most notable racines bands are Boukman Eksperyans, Boukan Ginen and RAM.

Haitian popular music and politics seem destined to be intertwined: in the 2010 presidential election, musician Wyclef Jean was only disqualified from running for office on a technicality, while *compás* singer Michel 'Sweet Micky' Martelly went on to win the vote for high office.

SURVIVAL GUIDE

Directory A–Z

ACCESSIBLE TRAVEL

Haiti is going to be hard going for travelers with disabilities or mobility issues. Crowded and broken streets, anarchic traffic and the absence of wheelchair-accessible buildings all pose serious problems. Traveling with an able-bodied companion can help immensely in overcoming these obstacles. At the very least, hiring a vehicle and a guide will make moving around a great deal easier. Travelers with disabilities shouldn't be surprised at stares from Haitians, but they'll often also receive offers of assistance where needed.

For more information, consider contacting Mobility International USA (www.miusa.org), which offers general travel advice for travelers with physical disabilities.

SLEEPING PRICE RANGES

The following price ranges refer to a double room with bathroom; breakfast is usually included, along with a ceiling fan. Air-conditioning is often included in midrange and top-end properties.

$ less than US$70

$$ US$70–130

$$$ more than US$130

ACCOMMODATIONS

Most levels of accommodations are available in Haiti, from super-basic guesthouses to top-end hotels and beach resorts. Port-au-Prince naturally has the widest choice, along with Cap-Haïtien and Jacmel. Budget accommodations are extremely limited though, due to a huge population of NGO workers (with expense accounts) throughout the country.

ELECTRICITY

Power plugs and sockets are type A and B (110V, 60 Hz).

EMBASSIES & CONSULATES

All of the embassies and consulates are in Port-au-Prince or Pétionville. Australia, New Zealand and Ireland do not have diplomatic representation in Haiti; British citizens can seek assistance at the UK Embassy in Santo Domingo.

Brazilian Embassy (☎2256-0900; ppinto@mr.gov.br; 168 Rue Darguin, Pétionville)

Canadian Embassy (☎2812-9000; www.port-au-prince.gc.ca; Rte de Delmas btwn Delmas 71 & 75, Port-au-Prince; ⏰7am-3:30pm Mon-Thu, to 12:30pm Fri)

Cuban Embassy (☎2256-3504; www.cubadiplomatica.cu/haiti; 3 Rue Marion, Pétionville; ⏰8am-12:30pm Mon-Fri)

Dominican Embassy (☎2813-0887; embadomhaiti@gmail.com; 121 Ave Pan Américaine, Pétionville)

French Embassy (☎2999-9000; www.ambafrance-ht.org; 51 Rue Capois, Port-au-Prince)

Mexican Embassy (☎2229-1040; embmxhai@yahoo.com; 2 Musseau, cnr Delmas 60, Port-au-Prince)

US Embassy (☎2229-8000; http://haiti.usembassy.gov; 41 Rte de Tabarre, Tabarre; ⏰7am-3:30pm Mon-Fri)

Venezuelan Embassy (☎3443-4127; embavenezhaiti@hainet.net; 2 Blvd Harry Truman, Port-au-Prince)

EMERGENCY NUMBERS

Fire	☎115
Police	☎114

FOOD

In Haiti you can spend just a few gourdes on *fritay* (fried street food) or dine in posh Pétionville for US$30 a dish. The most typical eatery is a bar-resto (a bar-restaurant, less formal than a proper restaurant), with a plateful of goat or chicken with plantains, salad and a beer, all for US$5. Vegetables aren't common, but there's plenty of fresh fruit. Excellent seafood is abundant along the coast.

HEALTH

Travel in Haiti is generally safe as long as you're reasonably careful about what you eat and drink. The most common travel-related illnesses, such as dysentery and hepatitis, are acquired by consumption of contaminated food and water. There is a small but significant malaria risk in certain parts of the country, and you should check before travel as to required prophylaxis. Following the 2010 earthquake, Haiti suffered a widespread cholera outbreak.

Medical services are limited and care can be substandard in Haiti. Expect to pay cash for services, and consider being evacuated to another country should you sustain a serious injury.

INSURANCE

Travel insurance that includes health coverage is highly recommended. Policies vary widely, but it's essential to have as much medical coverage as possible (including emergency evacuation cover). Medical services insist on payment on the spot, so collect all the paperwork you can when being treated so you can claim later. Some policies ask you to call them (they'll usually call you back) so that an assessment of your problem can be made.

INTERNET ACCESS

Getting online isn't a problem in any decently sized Haitian town, and internet cafes open and close frequently. Broadband connections are increasingly standard, along with webcams and USB connections for uploading digital photos. Prices cost around HTG100 (about US$1) per hour. The more expensive the joint, the better the electricity supply is likely to be. If you're bringing a laptop, wi-fi access is widespread.

LEGAL MATTERS

Drugs are illegal in Haiti, and you will be jailed for possession. If you are involved in a car accident, the law requires you to stop your car and call the police as soon as possible. In general, Haitian law presumes innocence until guilt is proven, and it's unlikely that you'll actually be arrested unless there are supportable charges against you. Always try to contact your embassy without delay, and keep its contact details on you. If the problem is an imaginary one, being extremely patient may eventually see the issue disappear.

MONEY

ATMs

ATMs are common in Port-au-Prince, Pétionville and Cap-Haïtien. In the rest of the country you may find one or two in larger towns, which may or may not be working. They're the simplest way to manage your money on the road, although you'll need to make sure you have plenty of cash when heading out into the countryside. Most ATMs are directly on the street, with some in secure booths and even under armed guard. Always be aware of your surroundings when using an ATM and pocketing a wad of cash – use machines in large grocery stores that staff security guards when possible.

Credit Cards

Most midrange and all top-end hotels (and many Port-au-Prince restaurants) will happily let you flash the plastic. Visa, MasterCard and (to a slightly lesser extent) American Express will all do nicely. With an accompanying passport, cash advances on credit cards can be made in the larger banks.

Exchange Rates

Australia	A$1	HTG64
Canada	C$1	HTG71
Dominican Republic	RD$1	HTG1.85
Euro zone	€1	HTG105
Japan	¥100	HTG88
New Zealand	NZ$1	HTG62
UK	UK£1	HTG114
US	US$1	HTG94

For current exchange rates, see www.xe.com.

Tipping

Hotels It's considerate to give maids and porters a little extra at your discretion; all gratuities will be happily accepted.

Restaurants A 10% tax and 5% service charge are included in restaurant bills. Anything more for great service is up to you.

Taxis A bit extra for a good driver is considerate, but remember that drivers generally will have factored a tip into their quoted rate.

> **EATING PRICE RANGES**
>
> Prices are based on the average cost of a main dish and include tax.
>
> **$** less than US$10
>
> **$$** US$10–20
>
> **$$$** more than US$20

OPENING HOURSE

Many restaurants and most businesses close on Sunday.

Banks 8:30am to 1pm Monday to Friday; some major branches also open 2pm to 5pm.

Bars & Clubs 5pm to late.

Offices 7am to 4pm Monday to Friday; many close earlier Friday; government offices close for an hour at noon.

Restaurants 7am to 9pm.

Shops 7am to 4pm Monday to Saturday; some close earlier Friday and Saturday.

PHOTOGRAPHY

Taking photos of airports and police buildings is forbidden, and it's a good idea to obtain permission first before snapping a policeman or a UN soldier. Haitians are well aware of their country's poverty, and often dislike being photographed in work or dirty clothes. Always ask permission.

PUBLIC HOLIDAYS

Government offices and most businesses will be closed on the following days:

Independence Day January 1

Ancestors' Day January 2

Carnival February (three days before Ash Wednesday)

Good Friday March/April

Agriculture and Labor Day May 1

Flag and University Day May 18

Ascencion Day Thirty-nine days after Easter

Corpus Christi May/June

Anniversary of the death of Jean-Jacques Dessaline October 17

Anniversary of the death of Toussaint Louverture November 1

All Soul's Day November 2

Anniversary of the Battle of Vertières November 18

Christmas Day December 25

SAFE TRAVEL

Many governments advise against nonessential travel to Haiti, and certainly caution is advised.

➡ Large-scale gang and kidnapping problems have generally abated, but keep your ear to the ground for protests around election time, which can get violent and should be avoided.

➡ To avoid street crime, use hotel safes for anything you're not willing to lose. Hide your money in pockets, and avoid taking out smartphones on the street. It's not a good idea to walk anywhere after dark, even in a group of men and women.

PRACTICALITIES

Smoking Smoking is allowed in public places in Haiti.

Weights & measures Haiti uses the metric system, although gasoline is sold in gallons.

➡ Common annoyances include a poor electricity supply, snarling traffic, begging, and getting stared at or called *blanc*, which is a generic word for a foreigner.

TELEPHONE

Landlines Connections can sometimes be patchy. Most businesses list several numbers on their cards and many people carry two cell phones on different networks.

Cell (mobile) Phones Haiti uses the GSM system. The main operators are Digicel and Natcom. Coverage is generally good. The providers have international roaming agreements with many foreign networks, but it can be cheaper to buy a local handset on arrival in Haiti for about US$20, or a SIM card for about US$5. SIM cards are available from guys on the street in red Digicel or Natcom vests. Take a copy of your passport to the dealer for identification.

Costs Within Haiti calls cost around US$0.10 per minute, and to call overseas around US$0.90 per minute. Top-up scratch cards are available from shops and ubiquitous street vendors.

Codes Haiti's country code is 509. There are no area codes. To make an international call, first dial 00.

Calling The quickest option is to find a phone 'stand' – usually a youth on the street with a cell phone that looks like a regular desk phone, who will time your call and charge accordingly.

WOMEN TRAVELERS

A woman traveling alone in Haiti is subject to a great deal of attention. This can take the form of the same staring and catcalling you might experience in many other places, ranging from the laughable to the lewd. A more alarming possibility is somebody following you; if this happens, duck into the nearest shop or hotel and ask for help. Ultimately, how you process the attention will depend on a variety of personal factors. Remember that ignoring someone will usually cause them to lose interest, while responding in any way will probably make it worse. Unless you are very familiar with an area and know some of your neighbors enough to ask for help, it would be unwise to walk anywhere alone after dark.

Getting There & Away

Most travelers enter Haiti by air through Port-au-Prince, with the most common flight routes all being from the US – Miami, Fort Lauderdale and New York. The international airport at Cap-Haïtien also handles a small number of incoming flights.

By land, there are several border crossings with the Dominican Republic, and direct bus services link Port-au-Prince with Santo Domingo, and Cap-Haïtien with Santiago. There are no international boat services to Haiti.

Flights and tours can be booked online at www.lonelyplanet.com/bookings.

AIR

Haiti has two international airports: **Aéroport International Toussaint Louverture** (☎4865-6436) in Port-au-Prince and **Hugo Chávez International Airport** (☎4478-5057, 2262-8539) in Cap-Haïtien. Numerous international carriers offer services to Haiti, including Sunrise Airways, JetBlue Airways, American Airlines, Spirit Airlines, Air France, Air Antilles, Insel Air, InterCaribbean Airways, Delta, Copa, Aeromexico, IBC and Avianca.

LAND

The Haitian–Dominican border has three official crossing points. Most useful to travelers is the Malpasse–Jimaní crossing between Port-au-Prince and Santo Domingo, followed by the northern Ouanaminthe–Dajabón crossing on the road between Cap-Haïtien and Santiago. A third, and little-used, crossing is from Belladère to Comendador (aka Elías Piña).

There are direct coach services linking the two capitals, and also Cap-Haïtien to Santiago. Entering the DR you must pay US$10 for a tourist card. The situation with fees entering and leaving Haiti by land is fluid – officials regularly ask for US$10 to stamp you in or out.

Haitian borders can be slightly chaotic if you're traveling independently.

ℹ Getting Around

AIR

Domestic flights operate from **Aérogare Guy Malary** (☎2250-1127), near the international terminal in Port-au-Prince. The two airlines that operate there are **Sunrise Airways** (☎2811-2222, 2816-0616; www.sunriseairways.net; Aérogare Guy Malary) and **Mission Aviation Fellowship** (MAF; ☎2941-9209, 3791-9209; www.maf.org; Aérogare Guy Malary; ⏰7am-4pm Mon-Sat).

Haiti's small size means that flights are short (no flight is longer than 40 minutes), saving many sticky hours on bad roads. The planes are small, typically carrying 16 passengers or fewer. One-way tickets usually cost around US$100.

Flights are understandably popular. Book well in advance.

BUS

Getting around Haiti by bus and minibus isn't always comfortable, but it's the cheapest way to travel within the country, and services run to most places you'll want to get to. Sturdy beasts, buses have the advantage of taking you to places that you'd usually need a 4WD to reach.

CAR & MOTORCYCLE

Although having your own wheels is a convenient way of seeing Haiti, be aware that you need nerves of steel, a sense of humor and a strategy if you are stopped at a roadblock. Terrible roads, a lack of road signs and the perils of wayward pedestrians and oncoming traffic are all part of the mix, as well as potentially dangerous people eyeing up you and your vehicle. Unless you're extremely familiar with the roads and the political situation of both where you're going and the places in between, it's probably best to leave the driving to a professional.

MOTO-TAXI

The quickest and easiest way to get around any town is to hop on the back of a moto-taxi (motorcycle taxi), often just referred to as a 'moto'. A trip will rarely cost more than about US$0.75, although rates can climb steeply if you want to travel any serious distance. Motos in Port-au-Prince are more expensive than elsewhere.

TAPTAP & CAMIONETTE

Smaller vehicles than buses ply the roads carrying passengers. A taptap is a converted pick-up, often brightly decorated, with bench seats in the back. Fares are slightly cheaper than a bus. The same rules for buses apply to taptaps, which leave from the same *estasyon:* they go when full, the comfy seats next to the driver are more pricey, and you can hail one and get off where you like.

Taptaps are better suited for short trips, and in many areas are likely to be the only feasible way of getting around.

TAXI

Port-au-Prince and Cap-Haïtien operate collective taxis called *publiques* for getting around town. You might find them hard to spot initially, as they look like any other battered car, but look for the red ribbon hanging from the front mirror and license plates starting with 'T' for transport.

Jamaica

☎876 / POP 2.84 MILLION

Includes ➡

Best Places to Eat

- ➡ Little Ochie (p540)
- ➡ Wilkes Seafood (p527)
- ➡ Mi Hungry (p519)
- ➡ Stush in the Bush (p524)
- ➡ Usain Bolt's Tracks & Records (p534)

Best Places to Stay

- ➡ Jake's Hotel (p542)
- ➡ Rockhouse (p538)
- ➡ Neita's Nest (p518)
- ➡ Polkerris B&B (p533)
- ➡ Germaican Hostel (p526)

Why Go?

Jamaica is one of those countries that everyone thinks they know before they arrive, such is the power of its cultural branding. Who hasn't listened to a Bob Marley song, or gasped at the lightning feet of Usain Bolt?

The island is more than just a parade of clichés about dreadlocked Rastas and hot-heeled athletes though. Long white beaches are twinned with steep green mountains; relaxed resorts are contrasted against adrenaline-charged ghettoes, the sophistication of the capital Kingston and the charm of fishing villages. Sweet reggae and slack dancehall vie with gospel and the sound of a country mixing up its very African roots with the opportunities of some 21st-century hustle – all in one of the most beautiful islands in the Caribbean. Jamaica has a complicated national soundtrack, but one that's impossible not to groove along to.

When to Go

Dec–Mar High seasons: warm sunny days and little rainfall (except in Port Antonio and the northeast), with sometimes chilly nights, especially in the mountains.

Jun–Nov Low season: sporadic heavy rainfall across Jamaica, including the possibility of hurricanes from August to October.

Jul & Aug Midsummer: many of Jamaica's best festivals happen at this time.

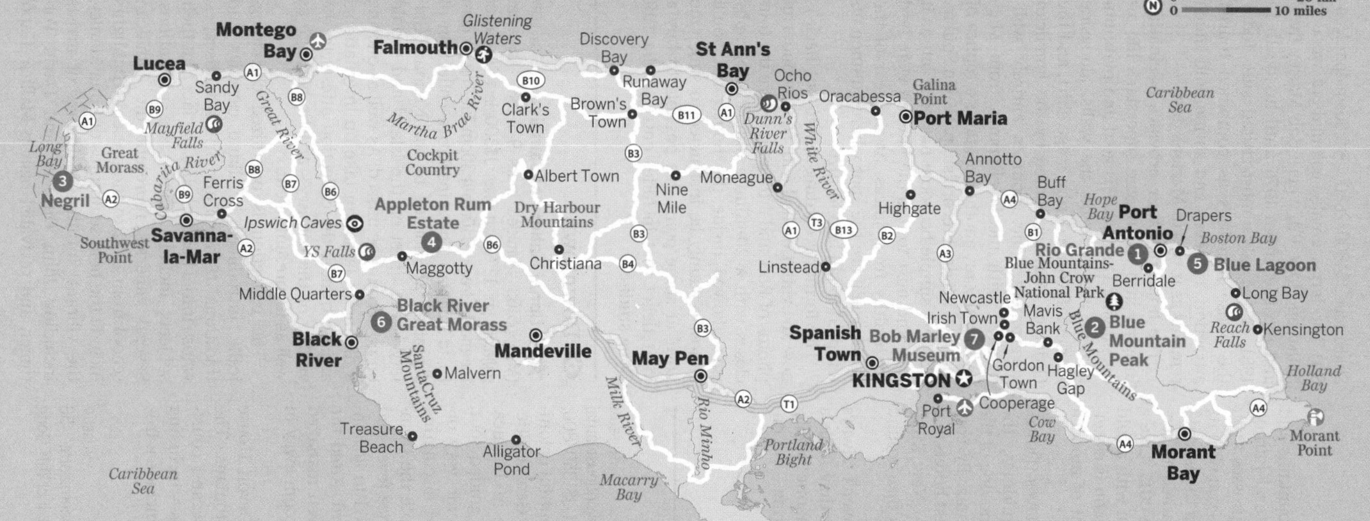

Jamaica Highlights

1 **Rio Grande** (p529) Drifting on a raft down the Rio Grande past former banana plantations.

2 **Blue Mountain Peak** (p521) Setting out before dawn to experience the greatest high in Jamaica.

3 **Negril** (p537) Exploring Jamaica's underwater topography with some of the island's best scuba outfits.

4 **Appleton Rum Estate** (p542) Sampling blends at the island's largest rum distillery.

5 **Blue Lagoon** (p528) Diving through the famous Blue Hole.

6 **Black River Great Morass** (p543) Croc-spotting in the mangroves.

7 **Bob Marley Museum** (p514) Delving into the life of Jamaica's revered contemporary hero at his former home and studio.

KINGSTON

POP 669,800

Tucked in between the Blue Mountains and the world's seventh-largest natural harbor, Kingston simultaneously impresses you with its setting and overwhelms you with its sprawl, noise and hustle. This is the island's cultural and economic heart, named a Creative City of Music by Unesco in 2015. Like a plate of spicy jerk washed down with a cold Red Stripe beer, a visit to Kingston is essential to taste the rich excitement of modern Jamaica.

Kingston is a city of two halves. Downtown is home to historic buildings, the courts, banks, street markets and one of the Caribbean's greatest art museums. By contrast, Uptown holds the city's best hotels and restaurants, largely confined to New Kingston, with its cluster of tall buildings around Emancipation Park.

Uptown and Downtown haven't always mixed well, but taken together they form a compelling and sometimes chaotic whole. Kingston is certainly never boring – we encourage you to jump right in.

Sights

Uptown

★Devon House MUSEUM

(Map p515; ☎929-6602; www.devonhousejamaica.com; 26 Hope Rd; adult/child J$1350/800; ⏰9:30am-5pm Mon-Sat) This beautiful colonial house was built in 1881 by George Stiebel, the first black millionaire in Jamaica. Antique lovers will enjoy the guided tour, highlights of which include some very ornate porcelain chandeliers and fascinating paintings and photographs. Note the trompe l'oeil of palms in the entrance foyer and the roundabout chairs, designed to accommodate a man wearing a sword. Amid the grand surroundings, Stiebel even managed to discreetly tuck a gambling room away in the attic.

The tree-shaded lawns of Devon House are very popular with Kingstonians. The popular former carriage house and courtyard are home to several shops – including Devon House I-Scream (tours include a free scoop).

★Bob Marley Museum MUSEUM

(☎927-9152; www.bobmarleymuseum.com; 56 Hope Rd; adult/child J$3000/1440, incl Tuff Gong Studio tour J$4800/2880; ⏰9:30am-4pm Mon-Sat) The large, creaky, colonial-era wooden house on Hope Rd, where Bob Marley lived and recorded from 1975 until his death in 1981, is the city's most-visited site. Today the house functions as combined tourist attraction, museum and shrine, and much remains as it was in Marley's day.

The hour-long tour provides fascinating insights into the reggae superstar's life after moving Uptown. His gold and platinum records are there on the walls, alongside Marley's favorite denim stage shirt, and the Order of Merit presented by the Jamaican government. One room is entirely wallpapered with media clippings from Marley's final tour; another contains a replica of Marley's original record shop, Wail'n Soul'm. Marley's simple bedroom has been left as it was, and next to it is the kitchen were he'd fix healthy fresh juices. At the rear of the house you'll see the spot where gunmen attempted to kill him in 1976.

The former recording studio out back is now an exhibition hall with some wonderful photos of Bob, and a theater, where the tour closes with a 20-minute film. Photography isn't allowed inside the house, but you'll almost certainly be instructed to sing 'One Love' at some point. It's possible to buy a joint ticket that includes entry to the Tuff Gong studios.

Downtown

★National Gallery of Jamaica GALLERY

(Map p516; ☎guided tours 922-1561; www.natgalja.org.jm; 12 Ocean Blvd; J$500, last Sunday of the month free; ⏰10am-4:30pm Tue-Thu, to 4pm Fri, to 3pm Sat) The superlative collection of Jamaican art housed by the National Gallery is the finest on the island and should on no account be missed. As well as offering a distinctly Jamaican take on international artistic trends, the collection attests to the vitality of the country's artistic heritage as well as its present talent.

The collection is organized chronologically, introduced by Taíno carvings and traditional 18th-century British landscapes, whose initial beauty belies the fact that their subjects include many slave plantations. Several galleries represent the Jamaican school from 1922 to the present. Highlights include the bold sculptures of Edna Manley, the vibrant 'intuitive' paintings of artists including John Dunkley and David Pottinger, and revivalist bishop Mallica 'Kapo'

Uptown Kingston

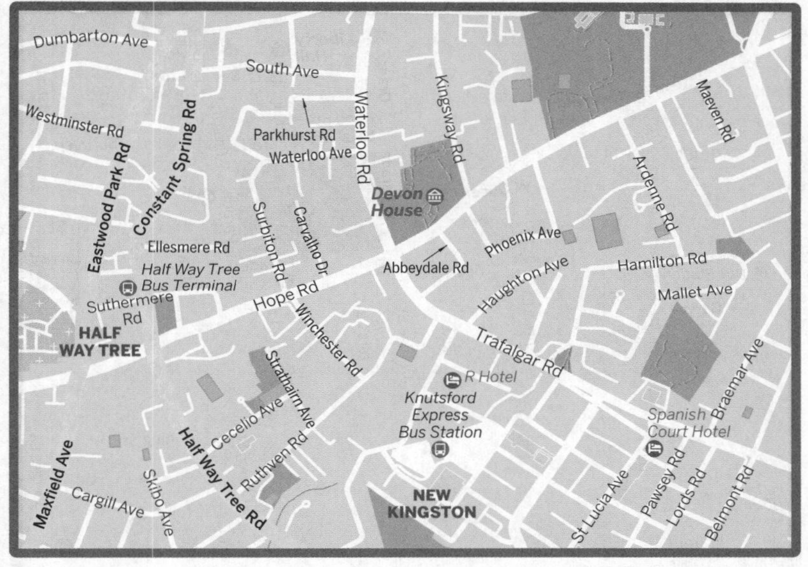

Reynolds. Other displays chart the course of Jamaican art up to the present, including abstract religious works by Carl Abrahams, Colin Garland's surrealist Caribbean fantasias, ethereal assemblages by David Boxer, and the work of realist Barrington Watson.

Temporary exhibition spaces frequently offer up the best of contemporary Jamaican art, as seen during the superb biennial temporary exhibition that takes place on alternate (even-numbered) years between mid-December and March.

★Liberty Hall MUSEUM
(Map p516; ☎948-8639; www.libertyhall-ioj.org.jm; 76 King St; J$600; ⏰9am-5pm Mon-Fri) At the end of a tree-lined courtyard, decorated with cheerful mosaics and a mural depicting Marcus Garvey, stands Liberty Hall, the headquarters of Garvey's UNIA (Universal Negro Improvement Association) in the 1930s. The building now contains an excellent multimedia museum about the man and his work, which allows the visitor to appreciate Garvey's impact as a founder of pan-Africanism.

Parade SQUARE
(William Grant Park; Map p516) William Grant Park, more commonly known as 'Parade,' is the bustling heart of Downtown, and originally hosted a fortress erected in 1694 with guns pointing toward the harbor. The fort was replaced in 1870 by Victoria Park, renamed a century later to honor Black Nationalist and labor leader Sir William Grant. The north and south entrances are watched over by cousins and political rivals **Norman Manley** and **Alexander Bustamante** respectively. A large fountain stands at its center.

At North Parade, the distinguished **Ward Theatre** (Map p516; www.wardtheatrefoundation.com; North Parade), built in 1911, once hosted the annual Boxing Day pantomime – a riotous, irreverent social satire. Sadly, the building has fallen into disrepair over the years, although there are plans to restore it. For now, you can admire the cracked sky-blue facade with white trim.

The gleaming white edifice facing the park's southeast corner is **Kingston Parish Church**, which replaced an older church destroyed in the 1907 earthquake. Note the tomb dating to 1699, the year the original was built. The tomb of Admiral Benbow, commander of the Royal Navy in the West Indies at the turn of the 18th century, is near the high altar, while plaques commemorate soldiers of the colonial West Indian regiments.

Downtown Kingston

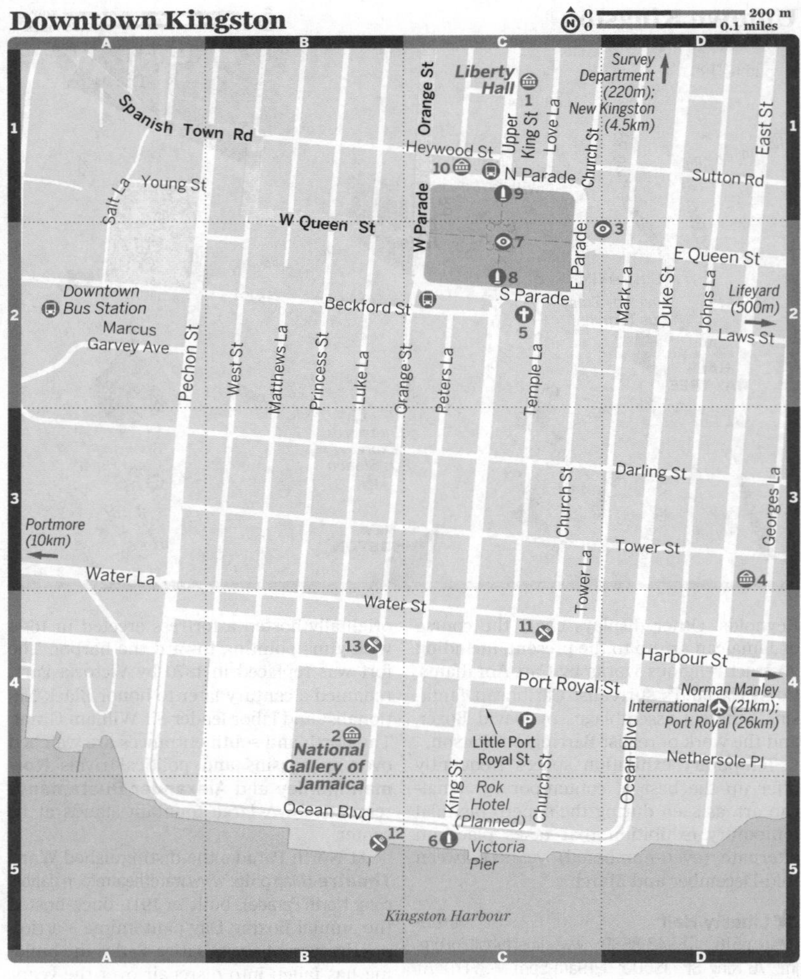

Downtown Kingston

Top Sights

1 Liberty Hall C1
2 National Gallery of Jamaica B4

Sights

3 Coke Memorial Hall D2
4 Institute of Jamaica D3
5 Kingston Parish Church C2
6 Negro Aroused Statue C5
7 Parade C2
8 Statue of Alexander Bustamante C2
9 Statue of Norman Manley C1
10 Ward Theatre C1

Eating

11 F&B Downtown C4
12 Gloria's Seafood City B5
13 Moby Dick B4

DON'T MISS

LIFE YARD

An innovative art and permaculture scheme, **Life Yard** (Paint Jamaica; ☎401-5276, 351-8604; www.lifeyard.org; Fleet St; donation requested, full day tours including lunch US$90) is regenerating an area of Downtown Kingston once beset with gang problems. The program is centered on an urban farming project, and its Rastafari organizers have also worked with the community and visiting artists to cover the whole street with beautiful and uplifting murals. It's not just pretty pictures though – youth projects include breakfast and homework clubs, workshops, educational support and media training, so the community can tell its own stories.

There's a cafe selling vegan food (8am to 6pm), with much of the produce coming from the permaculture garden. Several of the residents are registered tour guides – contact them in advance to set up a full-day's tour. It's essential to introduce yourself when you arrive – this is a residential area, so don't just snap photos of the walls without asking permission (it is readily given). Inquiries from long-term volunteers with transferable skills are welcomed.

The crenelated redbrick building facing East Parade is the 1840 **Coke Memorial Hall**, named after the founder of the Methodist churches in the Caribbean, Thomas Coke.

South Parade, packed with street vendor stalls and the blast of reggae, is known as 'Ben Dung Plaza' because passersby have to bend down to buy from hawkers whose goods are displayed on the ground. King St leads from here to the waterfront, and to a replica of Edna Manley's **Negro Aroused statue**, depicting a crouched black man breaking free from bondage; the original is in the National Gallery of Jamaica.

Trench Town Culture Yard CULTURAL CENTER
(☎803-1509; www.ttcultureyard.com; 6-8 Lower First St; tours J$1000; ⏲6am-6pm) Trench Town, which began life as a much-prized housing project erected by the British in the 1930s, is widely credited as the birthplace of ska, rocksteady and reggae. It has been immortalized in numerous reggae songs, not least Bob Marley's 'No Woman No Cry,' the poignant anthem penned by Marley's mentor, Vincent 'Tata' Ford, which was written here.

The yard's museum is stocked with Wailers memorabilia, along with the rusted-out carcass of a VW bus that belonged to the Wailers in the 1960s, and the small bedroom that was Bob and Rita Marley's home before superstardom. Tours include a visit to the house and yard, parts of the surrounding neighborhood and its series of splendid murals.

Also on-site is the **Trench Town Development Association**, responsible for transforming the home into a community-based heritage site, and dedicated to promoting social justice and self-reliance.

Institute of Jamaica MUSEUM
(JCDT; Map p516; ☎922-0620; www.instituteofjamaica.org.jm; 10-16 East St; adult/child J$600/400; ⏲8:30am-5pm Mon-Thu, 8:30am-4pm Fri) The Institute of Jamaica is the nation's small-scale equivalent of the British Museum or Smithsonian, housed in three separate buildings – the National Museum, the Jamaica Music Museum and the Natural History Museum. The institute hosts permanent and visiting exhibitions.

The **National Museum** holds an eclectic array of exhibits, from Taíno carvings and colonial samplers, to a model Air Jamaica plane and a particularly fine bust of the famed nurse Mary Seacole.

The small but informative **Music Museum** traces the history and development of Jamaica's music, from traditional instruments to drum machines and keyboards used by artists like Sly & Robbie and Augustus Pablo.

The **Natural History Museum's** small collection of preserved specimens on display is of perhaps least interest to casual visitors, but it does most of its important work in community outreach and environmental education.

Tuff Gong Recording Studios CULTURAL CENTER
(☎923-9380; www.tuffgong.com; 220 Marcus Garvey Dr; adult/child J$3000/1440, incl Bob Marley

Museum J$4800/2880) Tuff Gong is one of the Caribbean's largest and most influential studios. It was Bob Marley's favorite place to record and is now run by his son Ziggy. Visitors are taken on a one-hour 'Making of the Music' tour with the entire music production process explained from rehearsal room through mixing desk to vinyl pressing, centered (of course) around Bob Marley.

Activities

★Kingston Creative Art Walk
WALKING

(www.kingstoncreative.org; ⌚last Sunday of the month) FREE Vibrant arts initiative highlighting the best of Jamaican culture centered on Downtown Kingston. On the last Sunday of every month, there's a walking tour starting at William Grant Park (Parade), each with a different theme, from art to music and theater to fashion. Tours coincide with the free entry day at the National Gallery of Jamaica. There are also monthly meetups held at F&B Downtown, with talks and networking related to Kingston's title as a Unesco Creative City.

Tours

Jamaica Cultural Enterprises
CULTURAL

(☎540-8570, 374-6370; www.jaculture.com; Kingston tours half-/full day US$65/90) Highly recommended cultural tours in and around Kingston, including to the Blue Mountains. Excellent themed tours include history, food, music and art – either as a group or tailor-made. Every Thursday they offer a free Kingston walking tour, starting at 9am at Emancipation Park (museum entrance fees not included).

★Irie Moto-Tours
ADVENTURE

(☎773-8811; www.iriemototours.com; 37 Shortwood Rd; 1-/3-/5-day tour from US$250/1200/2250) Kyle and Allan are serious about dirt-bike riding and they are happy to introduce experienced bikers to Jamaica's varied terrain. A day ride on a KTM 250XC, Honda CRF250L or Kawasaki KLR650 takes in Blue Mountain trails. Longer, tailor-made trips take in beaches, country roads, cane fields and river crossings; the riders' experience is taken into account.

Festivals & Events

Carnival
CARNIVAL

(www.carnivalinjamaica.com; ⌚Mar/Apr) Jamaica has been putting a lot of effort in recent years into promoting its relatively new Carnival. It's a week of brightly costumed revelers taking to the streets, with parades, all-night parties, and live reggae, calypso and particularly soca. Also known as Bacchanal, events take place in Montego Bay and Ocho Rios as well as Kingston.

Sleeping

★Dancehall Hostel
HOSTEL $

(☎827-6761; www.dancehallhostel.com; 321 Molynes Rd/11 Embers Way; dm US$20, r US$50-55, r without bathroom US$32-45; ❄📶) Popular hillside hostel with two well-sized dorms sleeping six and eight, plus a handful of simple doubles, some of which have air-con. Music is the big deal here – guests come to take daily dancehall dance classes (private lessons available), and there are also regular DJ nights and a small recording studio. Self-caterers can use the kitchen, or chill at the bar and then flop in the Jacuzzi.

★R Hotel
HOTEL $$

(Map p515; ☎968-6222; www.rhotelja.com; 2 Renfrew Rd, Kingston 10; incl breakfast r US$164-228, apt US$338; P❄🏊) This is a new concept for Kingston, an 'extended stay' hotel where even the simplest rooms have their own kitchenette and washing machine. Rooms are spacious and everything is finished to a very high standard. There's a gym and a small rooftop pool (and bar), as well as a basement art gallery – the cheery colors here offset the deadening gray inexplicably used in all the common areas.

The rooftop restaurant is a new iteration of Kingston's celebrated Redbones Jazz & Blues Bar.

★Neita's Nest
B&B $$

(☎469-3005; www.neitasnest.com; Stony Hill, Bridgemount; s/d US$130/170; 📶) A truly delightful art-filled B&B tucked up high in Stony Hill, with great views from the terrace of Kingston and the mountains. Cozy rooms, huge delicious breakfasts and a gracious host who welcomes you into the family make this feel like a perfect retreat away from the city.

Spanish Court Hotel BOUTIQUE HOTEL $$$
(Map p515; ☎926-0000; www.spanishcourtho tel.com; 1 St Lucia Ave; r US$179-209, ste US$245-319; P❄@🛜🏊) A long-standing favorite with Jamaica's business elite, this hotel is big enough to offer everything you need but small enough to remain intimate. Thoroughly modern and cheery rooms have Jamaican-designed furniture. Relaxation options include the rooftop pool, a gym and spa. The cafe serves food throughout the day, while the restaurant has beautifully presented international and Jamaican dishes.

Eating

Uptown

★Mi Hungry VEGETARIAN $
(Market Place, 67 Constant Spring Rd; half/whole pizza J$600/1150, salads J$550-700; ⏲8:30am-11pm Mon-Sat, noon-10pm Sun) Mi Hungry serves up 'sun cooked' I-tal (natural) food that you wouldn't believe. The 'pleaza' comes with a base of seeds and grains, topped with sun-dried tomatoes and crunchy veg (we recommend ackee with a few chilies) and is delicious in a way that the words 'raw vegan pizza' can't convey – you'll definitely want to come back for more.

The nyam burgers with ackee and plantain are equally hearty, and there's a fabulous array of fresh juices on offer. Made with love.

Triple T's JAMAICAN $
(Annette Cres, off Upper Waterloo Rd; mains around J$1500; ⏲7am-9pm Mon-Fri, 8am-9pm Sat, 8:30am-9pm Sun) An open-sided garden restaurant with trees growing through the dining room and funky art hanging everywhere, Triple T's is a great relaxed place for generous servings of traditional Jamaican dishes, both delicious and well presented. The daily specials are always worth going for. There's a bar and a host of fresh juices if you want to linger for a drink.

Kitchen service can sometimes be a bit relaxed – if you're in a rush, ask what's ready to go and you'll be eating in a trice. If you have trouble finding it, look for it opposite the giant Megamart supermarket.

Fromage FRENCH $$
(☎622-9856; 8 Hillcrest Ave; salads J$2000, mains J$1800-3600; ⏲8am-10pm Mon-Sat, to 4pm Sun) Charming French-international-style restaurant, decorated in cool urban black and grays. Lunch is about sandwiches, burgers and pasta (the crab 'burger' is tasty), while dinner is about meat – well-cooked steak, stuffed chicken and rich sauces. There's an extensive wine menu. Take a packet of the delicious cookies home to enjoy for later.

★Pallet INTERNATIONAL $$
(☎576-0603; North Ave; mains from J$1800, sides J$450; ⏲11am-midnight Mon-Fri, 6pm-1am Sat) A low-key restaurant, open air and rustic enough to make you think it's made from real shipping pallets. The menu is anything but haphazard though – think yam-and-cheese-stuffed chicken roulade, mango sticky ribs, or grilled citrus lamb. A relatively new addition to the Kingston restaurant scene, but one that's quickly making a name for itself.

Come on Thursdays, when there is excellent live music – the house band welcomes drop-in players, and there are regular impromptu concerts from top musicians.

Downtown

F&B Downtown CAFE $
(Swiss Stores; Map p516; 107 Harbour St; mains from J$800; ⏲8am-4:30pm Mon-Fri; ❄🛜) Easily taking the prize for the most unexpected mash-up, this fancy Downtown watch store also has a great relaxed restaurant serving pasta, pepperpot soup, sandwiches, roti wraps and a glass of wine inside a welcome bubble of air-con. Formerly known as Swiss Stores, it is an essential Downtown lunch and meeting spot.

★Moby Dick JAMAICAN $$
(Map p516; 3 Orange St; mains J$1200-2000; ⏲9am-7pm Mon-Sat) Don't let the plastic tablecloths fool you: this unassuming hangout has been popular with besuited lawyers and judges for nearly a century. The curried goat (J$1200) is outstanding, served with roti, rice and salad and washed down with one of the excellent fresh fruit juices. Be prepared for lunchtime queues.

★Gloria's Seafood City SEAFOOD $$
(Map p516; ☎619-7905; Victoria Pier, Ocean Blvd; mains J$200-2400; ⏲11am-11pm Sun-Thu, 11am-midnight Fri & Sat) The new Victoria Pier development on the waterfront is part of the reinvigoration of Downtown, and Gloria's is at the heart of it. Sit on the deck looking over the sea with a plate of roast, grilled or stewed seafood.

WORTH A TRIP

PORT ROYAL

A dilapidated, ramshackle sprawl of tropical lassitude, Port Royal is replete with important historical buildings collapsing into dust. Today's fishing hamlet was once the pirate capital of the Caribbean. Later it was the hub of British naval power in the West Indies, but the remains give little hint of the town's former glory. The English settled the isolated cay in 1656, called it 'Cagway' or 'the Point' and built Fort Cromwell (renamed Fort Charles after the Restoration in 1660). The town boomed, but a massive earthquake in 1692 put an end to Port Royal's ascension, and survivors crossed the harbor to settle in what would become Kingston.

Port Royal's highlight is historic **Fort Charles** (967-8438; adult/child J$1000/500; 9am-5pm), where Horatio Nelson was once stationed. **Gloria's** (5 Queen St; fish J$1300, lobster J$1750; 10:30am-11pm Mon-Thu & Sun, to 1am Fri & Sat) is a famous seafood restaurant, much beloved of Kingstonians.

The zingy curry shrimp particularly set our taste buds on fire, but even with just a beer or juice and maybe a side of fries, it's a tremendous place to watch the sun on the sea, and the pelicans lazily flying by.

Drinking & Nightlife

★ Dub Club CLUB

(www.facebook.com/officialkingstondubclub; Skyline Dr, Jack's Hill; J$1000; 8pm-2am Sun) Dub Club is the house party that's become a major Kingston brand. And what a house! Set high on Jack's Hill, it looks down over the lights of the city, twinkling in the night. The huge sound system treats you to the deepest dub and rootsiest reggae, with the selector standing at a pair of decks under a huge mango tree.

There's a laid-back bar and I-tal food, and the doors open from 8pm, so you can treat it as a fine early drinking spot, though things don't get going until way after 10pm. Every reggae artist and DJ worth their salt rotates through the Dub Club at some time – if there's a cooler night out in Kingston, we'd like to know about it.

Tracks & Records SPORTS BAR

(906-3903; www.facebook.com/UBTracks; Market Place, 67 Constant Spring Rd; 11:30am-11:30pm) Music meets athletics at this punning sports bar owned by Usain Bolt. The atmosphere is lively, with plenty of drinks and good bar meals, and there's always a match on the screens to watch. Make sure you snap your selfie at the entrance next to Usain's world record scoreboard.

Information

Uptown, there are half a dozen banks along Knutsford Blvd and around Half Way Tree. Most banks have foreign-exchange counters as well as 24-hour ATMs. There are also ATMs along Hope Rd, particularly by the shopping malls. Always use an ATM inside a booth with a lockable door.

Andrews Memorial Hospital (926-7401; www.andrewsmemorialhospital.com; 27 Hope Rd)

Downtown Police Station (922-9321; 11 East Queen St)

Half Way Tree Police Station (142 Maxfield Ave, Half Way Tree)

Scotiabank ATM (cnr King & Tower Sts)

University Hospital (927-1620; www.uhwi.gov.jm; University of the West Indies campus, Mona)

Getting There & Around

AIR

Norman Manley International Airport (KIN; 924-8452; www.nmia.aero), 19km southeast of central New Kingston, handles international flights. There's a tourist information desk in the arrivals hall, and a money-exchange bureau before customs. As you exit, there's a bank, car-rental booths and a booking station for official taxis.

Outside, you'll find phone shops to buy local SIM cards. Bus 98 operates between the arrivals hall and Parade, Downtown (J$100, 35 minutes, every 30 minutes).

A taxi between the international airport and New Kingston costs about US$35. There's a **Caribbean Airlines** (924-8331; www.caribbean-airlines.com; 128 Old Hope Rd, Kingston) office in town.

BUS

Buses, minibuses and route taxis run between Kingston and every point on the island. They arrive and depart primarily from Downtown **long-distance bus terminal** (Map p516; Beckford St). Buses depart when full and are often packed beyond capacity; there are fewer departures on Sunday.

Comfortable **Knutsford Express** (☎971-1822; www.knutsfordexpress.com) buses run from their own terminal (p553) in New Kingston to the following destinations:

Destination	Cost (J$)	Duration (hr)	Frequency (daily)
Falmouth	2800	3	9
Mandeville	2150	2	4
Montego Bay	3250	4	9
Negril	3400	5	2
Ocho Rios	2150	1½	7
Port Antonio (via Ocho Rios)	2450	4	2
Savannah-la-Mar	2950	4	4

Be at the bus station no later than 15 minutes before departure to register your ticket.

Minibuses to Port Antonio (J$450, two hours) arrive and depart from outside **Half Way Tree Bus Terminal** (Map p515).

If you're traveling to Kingston, find out where you will be dropped before boarding a bus.

PUBLIC TRANSPORTATION

Buses, minibuses and route taxis arrive and depart from North Parade (Map p516) and South Parade (Map p516) in Downtown; Half Way Tree bus station in Uptown; Cross Roads, between Uptown and Downtown; and **Papine** (Main St), at the eastern edge of town off Old Hope Rd.

Jamaica Urban Transport Co Ltd (JUTC; www.jutc.com; city fares J$100) operates a fleet of yellow Mercedes-Benz and Volvo buses. Most are air-conditioned. JUTC buses stop only at official stops.

Minibuses and route taxis (look for their red license plates) ply all the popular routes (J$100), stopping on request.

BLUE MOUNTAINS

The Blue Mountains are a hiker's dream, and 30 recognized trails lace the hills. Many are overgrown due to lack of funding and ecological protection programs, but others remain the mainstay of communication for locals.

The most popular route is the steep, well-maintained trail to 'The Peak,' which in Jamaica always means Blue Mountain Peak.

These trails (called 'tracks' locally) are rarely marked. Get up-to-date information on trail conditions from the main ranger station at Holywell. If a trail is difficult to follow, turn back. Mountain rescue is slow and you could be lost for days. When asking for directions from locals, remember that 'jus a likkle way' may in fact be a few hours of hiking.

Whether you're hiking with or without a guide, the following tips are useful:

- Wear sturdy hiking shoes.
- Bring snacks, plenty of water and a flashlight (torch).
- Let people know where you're headed.
- Buy the 1:50,000 or 1:12,500 Ordnance Survey topographic map series, available

DON'T MISS

HIKING BLUE MOUNTAIN PEAK

Highest of the highlights, Blue Mountain Peak reaches 2256m above sea level, and no visit to the area should omit a predawn hike to its summit for a sunrise view. Most hikers set off from Penlyne Castle around 2am to reach Blue Mountain Peak for sunrise. Fortified with breakfast, you set out single file in the pitch black along the 12km round-trip trail (you'll need a flashlight and a spare set of batteries, just in case). The first part of the trail – a series of steep scree-covered switchbacks named Jacob's Ladder – is the toughest. Midway, at Portland Gap (4km above Abbey Green), there's a ranger station where you pay the US$5 park fee. You should arrive at the peak around 5:30am, while it is still dark.

Never hike without a guide at night. Numerous spur trails lead off the main trails and it is easy to get lost. Although hiking boots or tough walking shoes are best, sneakers will suffice, though your feet will likely get wet. At the top, temperatures can approach freezing before sunrise, so wear plenty of layers. Rain gear is also essential, as the weather can change rapidly.

from the **Survey Department** (☎750-5263; www.nla.gov.jm; 23½ Charles St, Kingston).

Guides can be hired at the guesthouses in Hagley Gap and Penlyne Castle, or through most local accommodations for US$40 to US$50 for a group of up to five people, while guided hikes in the Blue Mountains are also offered:

Forres Park Guest House & Farm

Jamaica Conservation & Development Trust (☎960-2848; www.jcdt.org.jm; 29 Dumbarton Ave, Kingston 10; ⌚8:30am-4:30pm Mon-Fri) Manages trails in the national park and can recommend hiking guides.

Sleeping

★Jah B's Guest House GUESTHOUSE $
(☎377-5206; www.jahbcoffee.com; Whitfield Hall, Hagley Gap; dm US$20, r with/without bathroom US$50/40, breakfast US$8; P) This friendly place, run by a family of Bobo Rastas and particularly popular with shoestring travelers, has a basic but cozy guesthouse with bunks and simple rooms. I-tal meals are prepared amid a cloud of ganja smoke and a nonstop volley of friendly banter, and served with homegrown Blue Mountain coffee. Hot showers are available on request.

Guides are available for hiking up Blue Mountain Peak, as well as to the family coffee plantation at Radnor.

Forres Park Guest House & Farm GUESTHOUSE $$
(☎927-8275; www.forrespark.com; cabins US$75, r US$90-220; P) This guesthouse/resort is a top choice for birdwatchers. All rooms have balconies and the plushest sports a whirlpool tub. Excellent meals are cooked on request and are available to nonguests. You can enjoy on-site spa treatments after tackling the steep, rewarding hiking trails in Forres Park. Excellent tours and guided hikes are offered.

Getting There & Away

BUS

Buses 60 and 68 run hourly from Half Way Tree in Kingston up Hope Rd to Papine (J$100, 20 minutes), from where you connect to the Blue Mountains by minibus or route taxi. There is no regular service across the mountains to Buff Bay.

CAR

From Kingston, Hope Rd leads to Papine, from where Gordon Town Rd (B1) leads into the mountains. Papine is your last opportunity to fill up with gas, so make sure you have a full tank. The B1 continues across the mountains all the way to Buff Bay – during the rainy season take advice on this road in case of landslips.

THE NORTH COAST

Ocho Rios

POP 17,000

Until the 1980s, Ocho Rios was little more than a fishing village with a couple of hotels on a blissfully wide bay. That all changed when it was developed as a tourist hub. Forty years later, it's one of the most popular destinations in the country, with thousands arriving by cruise ship.

All this can give 'Ochi' a slightly 'packaged' feel, but the town has a relaxed vibe when there's no ship in dock, and even the hassle from would-be guides and souvenir sellers is pretty low key.

Tourism has endowed the town with a good eating and nightlife scene. Throw in some of Jamaica's best waterfalls on its doorstep, and Ocho Rios makes an excellent base for exploring the north coast.

Sights

★Blue Hole WATERFALL
(Thatch Hill; US$15; ⌚8am-5pm) High on the White River, the heavenly Blue Hole is a vision of what Dunn's River Falls was 20 years ago, and is an undisputed highlight of the north coast. You make your way up a series of magical falls and blue pools surrounded by forest, with ample opportunity to swim, dive and swing off ropes into the water. Guides accompany you through the cascades on a well-marked trail (with steps and ropes where necessary for safety).

The tiny cave climb under one of the falls is safe but isn't for claustrophobes. The guides are excellent, know the best places to take photos of you (and show off their diving skills), and are attentive to both kids and more senior visitors who might be uncertain on some of the climbs. Vendors sell jelly shoes at the entrance, and life jackets are also available for those who want to enjoy the falls but aren't strong swimmers. There are refreshment stands at the entrance to the falls. Take nothing you aren't happy to get wet.

Dunn's River Falls WATERFALL
(☎974-2857; www.dunnsriverfalls.net; adult/child US$25/17; ⏲8:30am-4pm) These famous falls, 3km west of town, are Jamaica's top-grossing tourist attraction. Great throngs of people at peak hours can sometimes make it seem more like a theme park than a natural wonder, but this doesn't make the climb up the falls any less exhilarating. You clamber up great tiers of limestone that step down 180m in a series of beautiful cascades and pools. The water is refreshingly cool, with everything shaded by tall rainforest.

Guides can help with the climb (tip expected), but aren't strictly necessary; although the current is strong in places, the ascent is easily achieved by most able-bodied people. Swimwear is essential. There are changing rooms, and you can rent lockers (J$500) and buy jelly shoes from vendors.

The park also includes food stalls and a restaurant, a kids' playground, and a hard-selling craft market.

Try to visit when the cruise ships aren't in dock, and ideally when the gates open in the morning (note that when cruise ships are in Ocho Rios, the falls open at 7am). Route taxis from Ocho Rios to St Ann's Bay can drop you at the entrance.

Mahogany Beach BEACH
(P) FREE The small and charming Mahogany Beach is particularly popular with locals; it comes to life on weekends with loud music, smells of jerk cooking and impromptu football matches. There is plenty of parking plus showers, and a small shop selling beach goods. The beach is about 1km east of the town center – it's quickest to jump in a taxi to get here.

Activities

Garfield Diving Station DIVING
(☎395-7023; www.garfielddiving.com; Turtle Beach) Ocho Rios' longest-running water-sports operator with more than 30 years' experience. Dive packages include one-tank dives (US$60), PADI certification courses (US$480) and wreck dives. Other activities offered include snorkeling excursions (US$40), glass-bottom-boat rides (US$35) and Jet Ski rental (prices on request). Boat charter is available for deep-sea fishing (half-day for up to four people US$700).

Sleeping

Rooms RESORT $
(☎467-8737; www.roomsresorts.com; Main St; r US$90-135; P❄@≋) This family-friendly resort has all the trappings of an all-inclusive, without being one. Rooms are spacious and fresh, and all face either the sea or the pool. Breakfast is included, and after a day of water sports (not included) you can eat at the Hummingbird restaurant or have a drink at the beach grill bar.

★Te Moana Cottages COTTAGE $$
(☎974-2870; info@harmonyhall.com; cottages US$135; P❄) With its small clifftop garden overhanging a reef, this exquisite property with two delightful cottages is an intimate alternative to the resort experience. Both cottages have fully equipped kitchens and separate living areas, plus verandas with hammocks, and are generously decorated with art collected from across the Caribbean. Steps lead down through lawns to a coral cove good for snorkeling.

★Jamaica Inn HOTEL $$$
(☎974-2514; www.jamaicainn.com; r US$349-560, cottages from US$610; P⊖❄📶≋) Jamaica Inn has been hosting guests since way before cruise ships ever thought of stopping at Ocho Rios – Churchill stayed here in the 1950s. Tucked into a private cove, this subtly luxurious hotel has delightful airy rooms, water-sports facilities, a superb restaurant and extra pampering in its own spa.

The bar and cocktail terrace have a refined air, no doubt reinforced by the shirt-and-trousers-for-men evening dress code. There's a minimum three-night stay; half- and full-board are available.

Blue House B&B $$$
(☎994-1367; www.thebluehousejamaica.com; White River Bay; r US$180-360; P❄@📶≋) This B&B near White River offers luxurious bedrooms in cool blue hues – a real home away from home with a welcoming, well-traveled host. The separate two-bedroom Cozy Cottage provides even greater seclusion, hidden behind its curtain of flowers. The resident chef cooks up lavish

DON'T MISS

STUSH IN THE BUSH

Stush in the Bush (562-9760; www.stushinthebush.com; Bamboo; meals US$70-95;) is an organic farm-to-table Rasta dining experience, and home to some of the best food you'll eat in your entire trip to Jamaica. Your experience here starts with a walking tour of the farm, learning about what you'll eat, and then proceeds to a gorgeous rustic cabin with tremendous views for your meal.

There are two options, the gourmet pizza (US$70) and the full spread (US$95), of four and six courses respectively, with sides of delicious salads, crunchy plantain chips with zingy dips, rich soups and lively juices. It's vegan-friendly too – even the chocolate cake. Advance booking essential.

three-course dinners that are worth every penny (US$40, nonguests by advance reservation only).

Eating

Ocho Rios Jerk Centre JERK $
(974-2549; 16 Da Costa Dr; mains J$550-1000; 11am-midnight) The liveliest jerk joint in town serves excellent jerk pork and chicken in quarter-pound servings and up, along with heaps of sides. There are daily specials, the best being *escoveich* fish (Wednesdays, J$1290) and curry goat (Friday to Sunday, J$1350). Grab a Red Stripe or rum and watch sports on the big-screen TV while you're waiting for your food. DJs play on Friday nights.

Mongoose Restaurant & Lounge JAMAICAN $
(Main St; mains J$900-2500; 9am-1am) Lively restaurant and bar that quickly serves up big plates of hearty food. If you want Jamaican, go for the stew; otherwise you can get really good burgers, grilled fish, pizzas and the like. It's pretty quiet during the day unless there's a cruise ship in town, when it absolutely heaves. Evenings are more relaxed, and there's live reggae on Saturdays.

★ **Whalers** SEAFOOD $$
(seafood dishes J$1500-3000; 9am-11pm) This long-standing Ochi favorite has finally reopened after the redevelopment of Fisherman's Beach, and the good news is that it was worth the wait. Sit inside the cool interior or enjoy the balcony view over the beach while enjoying big plates of seafood in all its Jamaican variations – *escoveich*, curried, grilled or served up in brown stew.

Those with a hankering for garlic will be satisfied with the buttery-rich shrimp and lobster.

★ **Miss T's Kitchen** JAMAICAN $$
(795-0099; www.misstskitchen.com; Main St; mains J$1800-2800; 11:30am-1pm Mon-Sat, 11:30am-9pm Sun) The high tin roof and brightly painted wood of this popular restaurant are palate refreshers for the big plates of Jamaican classics, with good vegetarian options served up quickly by friendly, efficient staff. If you want drinks more sophisticated than a simple Red Stripe, take a glass or two on the veranda of the 'wine yaad' overlooking the garden.

Drinking & Nightlife

John Crow's Tavern SPORTS BAR
(10 Main St; 10am-1am) The big TV above the bar screens the latest football games and the outdoor terrace is perfect for a beer, a burger and a spot of people-watching on the main street. The beer is icy and there's an excellent selection of rum. Come on Sunday nights, when there is live reggae from around 8pm.

Shopping

★ **Kaya Herb House** GANJA
(627-9333; www.kayaherbhouse.com; Drax Hall, next door to Scotchies; 9am-10pm Mon-Thu, 9am-11pm Fri & Sat) When super-stylish Kaya opened its doors in 2018, it became the first legal marijuana dispensary in the Caribbean. Equal parts clinic and hipster boutique, to enter you'll need ID (over-18s only) and you must complete a self-certified medical certificate. Inside, ganja buds and liquid for e-cigarettes are offered from a list of 30 medical strains.

Knowledgeable staff can talk you through the extensive wine-list-style menu, according to THC and CBD content, as well your own medical needs. There is a smoking room and dab bar, and Skype consultations are available for medical conditions. Kaya also has a thatched bar and cafe, with great coffee, pizzas and zingy fruit juices. It runs its own ganja plantations, and farm tours are planned for the future. All purchases must be made in cash, but there is an on-site ATM.

Information

There are numerous banks along Main St. All have foreign-exchange facilities and ATMs.

Police Station (974-2533; Da Costa Dr) Ocho Rios police are used to dealing with tourist matters.

The nearest hospital is in **St Ann's Bay** (972-2272), which has an emergency room.

Complete Care Medical Centre (974-3357; 16 Rennie Rd)

Ocho Rios Pharmacy (974-9182; Main St, Ocean Village Plaza; Mon-Sat 9am-6pm)

Tourist Information (974-7705; Main St, Shop 3, Ocean Village Plaza; 9am-5pm Mon-Thu, to 4pm Fri) Represents the Jamaica Tourist Board, with helpful, knowledgeable staff.

Getting There & Away

CAR

If you have your own vehicle and are driving between Ocho Rios and Kingston, note that the fast toll highway costs around J$1000.

BUS

Buses, minibuses and route taxis arrive at and depart from Ocho Rios' **Transportation Center** (Evelyn St). During daylight hours there are frequent departures – fewer on Sundays – for Kingston (via the old A3 through the mountains, rather than the toll highway) and destinations along the north coast. There is no set schedule: they depart when full. Sample destinations:

Discovery Bay J$180, 30 minutes
Kingston J$400, 2½ hours
Montego Bay J$500, two hours
Port Maria J$200, 50 minutes
Runaway Bay J$150, 30 minutes
St Ann's Bay J$150, 15 minutes

Knutsford Express (www.knutsfordexpress.com; Island Village) has scheduled departures on comfortable air-con coaches to Kingston and Montego Bay from its depot at Island Village. Arrive 15 minutes prior to departure to register your ticket. Sample fares include Kingston (J$2150, 90 minutes), Montego Bay (J$2150, two hours), Negril (J$3000, four hours) and Port Antonio (J$2150, two hours).

Around Ocho Rios

The resorts of Ocho Rios quickly give way to isolated villas and fishing villages as the highway winds its way in both directions along the coast.

Several notable foreign visitors have left their marks near Ocho Rios. Author Noël Coward made his home at Firefly, with its spectacular view down on the coastline. While colonial occupants of Seville Great House are overlooked, their house has been remodeled into a fantastic museum of Jamaica's history of plantation slavery.

★Firefly HISTORIC BUILDING

(994-0920, 997-7201; J$1000; 9am-5pm Mon-Thu & Sat) Set amid wide lawns high atop a hill 5km east of Oracabessa and 5km west of Port Maria, Firefly was the home of Sir Noël Coward, the English playwright, songwriter, actor and wit, who was preceded at this site by the notorious pirate Sir Henry Morgan. When he died in 1973, Coward left the estate to his partner Graham Payn, who donated it to the nation.

Your guide will lead you to Coward's art studio, where he was schooled in oil painting by Winston Churchill. The studio displays Coward's original paintings and photographs of himself and a coterie of famous friends. The drawing room, with the table still laid, was used to entertain such guests as the Queen Mother, Sophia Loren and Audrey Hepburn. The upper lounge features a glassless window that offers one of the most stunning coastal vistas in all Jamaica. The view takes in Port Maria Bay and the coastline further west. Contrary to popular opinion, Coward didn't write his famous song 'A Room with a View' here (it was written in Hawaii in 1928).

Coward lies buried beneath a plain white marble slab on the wide lawns where he entertained many illustrious stars of the stage and screen. A dance floor nearby covers his old pool – the house is now used as an exclusive venue for society weddings.

★Seville Great House HISTORIC SITE

(J$500; 9am-4pm Sat & Sun) This historical park overlooking the sea, less than 1km west of present-day St Ann's, marks the site of the first Spanish capital on the island – Sevilla la Nueva – and one of the first Spanish settlements in the Americas. It houses a fascinating great house, plantation remains and reconstructions of Taíno houses and African houses for the enslaved, along with their kitchen gardens.

When the English captured Jamaica from the Spanish, the land on which Sevilla la Nueva had been built was granted to an army officer, who developed a sugar estate here. The great house was originally built in 1745; on the lawn in front of the house there is a touching memorial to the enslaved Africans whose remains were discovered on the site and reburied here in 1997.

The restored house contains a truly excellent museum depicting the history of the site from Taíno times through the era of slavery and the colonial period. The everyday lives of the Jamaican Africans forced to work here are reconstructed with particular sensitivity; their experiences stand in stark contrast to the grandeur of the intricate stone architectural carvings from the Spanish period and the dainty bone china teacups of the British.

Traces of the original Spanish buildings, including a church and the castle-house of the first Spanish governor, are visible, along with the ruins of the English sugar mills and the overseer's house. This was also the site of the Taíno village of Maima; the inhabitants were forced to work as serfs under the Spanish *encomienda* (forced labor) system, and quickly died from a combination of disease, overwork and suicide.

Port Antonio

POP 15,000

Port Antonio, tucked into the endlessly lush hills of Portland, is a world away from the cruise-ship strips and resorts that lie along the opposite end of Jamaica's northern coast. It's a compact tangle of markets, Georgian and Victorian architecture, and laid-back bars. There's not a Margaritaville in sight – and scanty formal 'attractions' – but we wouldn't have it any other way. As a gateway to Portland, its laid-back attitude makes it a perfect destination for travelers seeking to get away from it all.

Sights

Port Antonio's heart is the Town Sq, at the corner of West St and Harbour St. It's centered on a clock tower and backed by a handsome redbrick **Georgian courthouse** from 1895; the building is surrounded by a veranda supported by Scottish iron columns and topped by a handsome cupola, and is now a branch of National Commercial Bank. About 50m down West St is the junction of William St, where the smaller Port Antonio Sq has a **cenotaph** honoring Jamaicans who gave their lives in the two world wars.

On the west side of Port Antonio Sq is **Musgrave Market** (West St; ⏲Mon-Sat), decked out in yellows and blues, a quintessential chaotic developing-world market supported by thick limestone columns. Following William St south to Harbour St, you can turn left to peek inside **Christ Church**, a redbrick Anglican building constructed in neo-Romanesque style around 1840 (much of the structure dates from 1903).

On the north side of the Town Sq is the marvelously baroque facade of the **Royal Mall**, a three-story complex painted a striking red. It is now a covered shopping parade decorated and designed in a plethora of styles, including Tudor and Renaissance.

Folly RUINS

This rather appropriately named two-story, 60-room mansion on the peninsula east of East Harbour was built entirely of concrete in pseudo-Grecian style in 1903 by Olivia Tiffany Mitchell, heiress to the Tiffany fortune. It was only lived in for 35 years before being abandoned and given to the government in lieu of unpaid taxes, after which it fell into disrepair.

The story that it was abandoned due to the use of seawater in the concrete, causing the iron reinforcing rods to rust and the roof to collapse in 1936, is apocryphal, if more exciting than the story of unpaid taxes. The shell of the structure remains, held aloft by limestone columns, and makes a perfectly peculiar locale for a picnic. The orange candy-striped **Folly Point Lighthouse**, built in 1888, overlooks Monkey Island – so named for the primates once kept there by Mitchell's son-in-law Hiram Bingham, who rediscovered Machu Picchu in 1911.

It's a great place to explore, but we'd advise against solo exploration, especially for women, as there have been reports of muggings here.

Sleeping

★**Germaican Hostel** HOSTEL $

(☎866-2222; www.germaican-hostel.com; incl breakfast dm US$22, d US$62, cottages US$80; 📶) This superb hilltop German-run hostel outside Port Antonio has astounding views over the coast. The dorm is spacious and the doubles are well presented, plus there's a cottage looking out to sea. The kitchen is well set up (buffet breakfast is included) but the real gem is the veranda with views, and the peace of getting away from it all.

It's some distance from town, but the managers will pick you up and do a transfer run into Port Antonio a couple of times a day (a route taxi from Port Antonio to Stony Hill will take you most of the way).

Finjam Cottage GUESTHOUSE $
(☎293-2265; r US$45, with sea view & balcony US$55; 📶) On the highest point of Titchfield Hill, Finjam is a homely and laid-back place, with simple rooms, a pleasant veranda to chill out on, use of the kitchen and a great location close to town. The name comes from the Finnish-Jamaican hosts.

DeMontevin Lodge GUESTHOUSE $
(☎993-2604; www.facebook.com/Demontevin Lodge; 21 Fort George St; d US$70-100, without bathroom US$45) This venerable Victorian guesthouse – built in 1881 – has a homey ambience that blends modern kitsch and antiques reminiscent of granny's parlor, or some tropical Sherlock Holmes story. The simple bedrooms (six with private bathrooms) and some of the sheets are certainly timeworn, but everything's as clean as a whistle.

Eating

★Italian Job ITALIAN $
(29 Harbour St; pasta J$1200-3000, pizza from J$1100, mains J$1350-3500; ⏰noon-10pm Tue-Sat) This is a jolly, Italian-run, checked-tablecloth sort of a place, with great pasta, pizza and salads, plus crepes for dessert. Keep an eye on the specials board too, as the chef puts a great twist on local offerings; beware the potent lobster cooked in ganja-infused butter. The wine is pretty good, too.

Yosch Café INTERNATIONAL $
(Craft Village; sandwiches from J$450, mains J$800-1700; ⏰9am-9pm Sun-Thu, to 10pm Fri & Sat) This cafe on the edge of the craft village complex is all decking, driftwood and bamboo, open to the sea breeze and looking back onto Titchfield and the bay. The breakfasts and sandwiches are winners, as is the seafood if you come here for dinner, but be prepared that service from the kitchen operates very much on island time.

Piggy's Jerk JERK $
(jerk chicken J$500, half-chicken J$900, soup J$150; ⏰10am-9pm Mon-Sat) A very simple jerk shack offering tasty chicken with *festival* (deep-fried dumplings), hearty soup and cold drinks (and despite the name, no jerk pork). It's takeout only – eat on the seafront, or grab a half-chicken for a picnic elsewhere. Great value.

★Wilkes Seafood SEAFOOD $$
(☎378-5970; Allen Ave; salads J$500-1000, catch of the day J$3000, mains J$2600-3800; ⏰10:30am-9:30pm Mon-Sat, 8am-9:30pm Sun) This place looks like a thoroughly unassuming beach bar from the front, but is a delightful small restaurant inside, overlooking the sea and with a semi-open kitchen that lets the cooking aromas make you hungry. Nothing you order will disappoint, though we found the coconut curried fish to be a particular winner. Dining here is a real Jamaican highlight.

Reservations aren't a bad idea here. On Sundays, visit early for filling Jamaican, continental and full English breakfasts.

Information

Two useful banks with ATM facilities:

National Commercial Bank (☎993-9822; 5 West St)

Police Station (☎993-2527, 993-2546)

Port Antonio Hospital (☎993-2646; Nuttall Rd; ⏰24hr) Above the town on Naylor's Hill, south of West Harbour.

Scotiabank (☎993-2523; 3 Harbour St)

Getting There & Away

There's a **transportation center** (Gideon Ave) that extends along the waterfront, with minibuses leaving regularly for Kingston (to Half Way Tree bus station; J$450, two hours) via Buff Bay and Annotto Bay (where you change for Ocho Rios). Route taxis depart constantly for Fairy Hill (J$100, 10 minutes), Boston Bay (J$150, 20 minutes) and Manchioneal (J$250, 40 minutes).

Knutsford Express (Errol Flynn Marina) has air-conditioned coaches to countrywide destinations. Sample departures include twice a day to Ocho Rios (J$2150, two hours) and four times a day to Kingston (J$2050 to J$2400, via either Junction or Ochi).

Around Port Antonio

The road east of Port Antonio has some of the prettiest landscapes in Jamaica, with gorgeous beaches and lush green hills.

Reach Falls, a particularly beautiful waterfall in a country that abounds in them, is a highlight.

Route taxis run throughout the day along this stretch of road between Port Antonio and Boston Bay. You'll never have to wait for long to flag someone down, and you'll pay J$150 for the full trip, or J$100 to J$120 for a segment of it.

Port Antonio to Fairy Hill

The A4 meanders east of Port Antonio through thick forest, jagged-tooth bays, pocket coves and the coastal villages of Drapers, Frenchman's Cove and Fairy Hill. This is where most visitors to Port Antonio, and indeed to Portland, will find accommodations and explore the nearby Blue Lagoon, the luxuriant sands of Winnifred Beach and Frenchman's Cove, as well as the Rio Grande Valley and Reach Falls.

Sights

★Blue Lagoon LAGOON

The waters that launched Brooke Shields' movie career are by any measure one of the most beautiful spots in Jamaica. The 55m-deep 'Blue Hole' (as it is known locally) opens to the sea through a narrow funnel, but is fed by freshwater springs that come in at a depth of about 40m. As a result, the water changes color through every shade of jade and emerald during the day, thanks to cold fresh water that blankets the warm mass of seawater lurking below.

You can swim at the entrance to the lagoon, or take a boat (US$30) on a short ride past some glitzy seafront villas to nearby Cocktail Beach (where parts of the Tom Cruise movie *Cocktail* were filmed) and rustic Monkey Island.

Note that if it's been raining heavily, runoff water from the hills turns the lagoon a disappointing murky green.

★Winnifred Beach BEACH

Perched on a cliff 13km east of Port Antonio is the little hamlet of Fairy Hill. Follow the road steeply downhill and you'll reach Winnifred Beach, yet another totally gorgeous strip that puts a lot of the sand in more famous places to shame. It's the only truly public beach on this stretch of the coast, and has a great vibe, with food and drink stands, weekend sound systems and Jamaicans from all walks of life.

If you drive, please make a donation for parking – the beach relies on public funds for its upkeep.

★Frenchman's Cove BEACH

(J$1000; ⏲9am-5pm) This beautiful little cove just east of Drapers boasts a small but perfect white-sand beach, where the water is fed by a freshwater river that spits directly into the ocean. The area is owned by the Frenchman's Cove resort. There's a snack bar serving jerk chicken and fish, alfresco showers, bathrooms, a secure parking lot and the option of taking boat tours (US$20) to the Blue Lagoon.

Sleeping & Eating

Drapers San Guest House GUESTHOUSE $

(☎993-7118; www.draperssan.com; A4, Drapers; r US$65-85; 📶) Run by an Italian expat, activist and font of local knowledge, this cozy little house comprises two cottages with five doubles and one single room (two share a bathroom), all with fans, louvered windows and hot water. It's all very welcoming and family-oriented, and there's a comfy lounge and communal kitchen.

Breakfast is available, but make sure you also enjoy dinner (on request) – the Italian owner claims local chef TJ cooks better pasta than her!

★Hotel Mocking Bird Hill HOTEL $$$

(☎993-7267; www.hotelmockingbirdhill.com; Mocking Bird Hill Rd; r US$245-295; 📶❄) 🌿 The Mocking Bird is one of the most vigorous proponents of ecotourism in Portland and supporter of local environmental causes. The property is a lovely house at the end of a winding dirt road; airy rooms are lovingly appointed with well-chosen fabrics and art, ocean views and private balconies. The **Mille Fleurs** (lunch mains US$10-16, dinner mains US$26-48; ⏲noon-2pm & 7-9pm; 🌱) restaurant serves delicious locally sourced slow food.

Trails through the hillside gardens are fabulous for birdwatching – well-trained local guides are available for birding further afield.

Woody's JAMAICAN $

(A4, Drapers; burgers J$350-500; ⏲noon-8pm) This truly brilliant spot – with an outdoor patio and an indoor counter that doubles as a local meeting place – prepares tremendous hot dogs and burgers, grilled cheese and Jamaican dinners to order. There's a great veggie plantain burger, and sublime homemade ginger beer. Service is anything but rushed, but the charming hosts always make this a worthy pit stop.

Boston Bay

Boston Bay is a lick of a town with a cute pocket-size beach shelving into turquoise waters. High surf rolls into the bay, making it a popular place to catch some waves.

Boston is equally famous for its highly spiced jerk. Today, jerk has a worldwide fan base and is pretty much synonymous with Jamaican cuisine, but until the 1950s it was virtually unknown outside this area. The practice of marinating meat with jerk seasoning was first developed centuries ago not far from here by Maroons (escaped slaves), and the modest shacks at Boston Bay were among the first to invite attention – well worth making a detour for.

Sights & Activities

Boston Bay Beach BEACH
(Boston Bay; J$200) Boston Bay's beach sits in a small pretty cove, and while its golden sand is draw enough, the shape of the bay and prevailing weather make it a perfect surf spot. There are showers, changing rooms, a lifeguard and a small restaurant.

Boston Bay Surfing SURFING
(board hire US$20, 1hr surf lessons with board US$20) The cove at Boston Bay is a perfect place to learn to surf, or to hire a board for the day and hit the waves yourself. The instructors here will have you standing up on the board in no time – or at least enjoy the splash as you topple into the water.

Sleeping & Eating

★**Great Huts** RESORT $$
(353-3388; www.greathuts.com; Boston Beach Lane; camping tent US$42, huts d from US$88, tree houses from US$198, African Annexe for 8 people US$1500;) A green 'ecovillage' meets sculpture park overlooking Boston Bay; this is a distinctive and imaginative collection of African-style huts and tree houses with open verandas, bamboo-walled bedrooms and alfresco showers. There's a private beach, a walking trail along the cliff, yoga, an Afro-centric library and a restaurant-bar with live music on Saturday. If only all resorts in Jamaica felt this 'inclusive.'

Near the entrance to Boston Bay beach on the main road you'll see half a dozen smoky jerk pits on the roadside. Vendors vie for your custom, but they're all equally good, serving up hot and sweet jerk (from J$500) with *festival*, plantain and breadfruit, washed down with a cold drink. They'll also sell jars of locally made jerk sauce (J$800) to take home – a great souvenir.

Rio Grande Valley

Errol Flynn supposedly initiated rafting on the Rio Grande during the 1940s, and moonlight raft trips were considered the ultimate activity among the fashionable.

Today, paying passengers make the 13km journey of two to three hours (depending

DON'T MISS

REACH FALLS

Even in a country that abounds in waterfalls, **Reach Falls** (adult/child US$15/8; 8:30am-4:30pm Wed-Sun) stands out as one of the most beautiful places in Jamaica. The white rushing cascades are surrounded by a bowl of virgin rainforest; the water tumbles over limestone tiers from one hollowed, jade-colored pool into the next. It's possible to walk, wade and swim your way up to the edge of the falls, by an unmarked jungle path some way below the main entrance.

Once you enter the falls, guides will offer their services – crucial if you want to climb to the upper pools, which we highly recommend (there's a little underwater tunnel a bit up the falls; plunging through is a treat). The Mandingo Cave, the crown jewel of the falls, can be accessed at the top of the cascades, but you need to bring climbing shoes and be prepared for a long climb.

Excellent local guides Leonard Welsh (849-6598) and Kenton Davy (438-3507) can take you and point out plants and wildlife along the way if you choose to hike to the falls.

The turnoff to Reach Falls is well signed about 2km north of Manchioneal. Any Port Antonio–Manchioneal route taxi can drop you; it's a further 3km uphill to the falls.

on water level) from Grant's Level (Rafter's Village), about 2km south of Berrydale, to Rafter's Rest at St Margaret's Bay. When the moon is full, unforgettable nighttime trips are sometimes offered. These are less regimented; your guide will be happy to pull over on a moon-drenched riverbank so that you can canoodle with your sweetie or just open the ice chests to release the beer.

If you're rafting during the day, ask your 'captain' to stop for lunch at **Belinda's** (Rio Grande; mains from J$400), a riverside restaurant that belies its rustic appearance by serving fantastic lunches.

Reserve at **Rio Grande Experience** (☎993-5778; per raft US$65) or at Rafter's Village at Grant's Level if you don't have reservations. This is a one-way trip, so if you're driving you need to hire a driver to bring your car from Berrydale to St Margaret's Bay, or get Rio Grande Experience to arrange transport for J$2000.

A route taxi from Port Antonio to Grant's Level costs J$200; they depart from the corner of Bridge St and Summers Town Rd. Licensed taxis cost about US$20 round trip.

MONTEGO BAY & NORTHWEST COAST

Montego Bay

Montego Bay has two distinct faces: there's the smooth tourist countenance that grins contentedly from the pages of a thousand glossy Caribbean brochures; and there's MoBay proper, a pretty gritty city, second only to Kingston in terms of status and chaos. Most of the big all-inclusive resorts are located well outside the urban core in the fancy suburb of Ironshore. Stay in the city, however, and you're faced with an entirely different proposition – a riot of cacophonous car horns and bustling humanity that offers an unscripted and uncensored slice of Jamaican life, warts and all.

The Hip Strip (aka Gloucester Ave), with its midrange hotels and ubiquitous souvenir shops flogging Bob Marley T-shirts, acts as a kind of decompression chamber between MoBay's two halves. You won't find many hipsters here, but in among the hustlers and smoky jerk restaurants there's a detectable Jamaican rhythm to the action on the street.

Sights

Doctor's Cave Beach BEACH
(☎952-2566; www.doctorscavebathingclub.com; Gloucester Ave; adult/child US$6/3; ⏲8:30am-5:30pm) It may sound like a rocky hole inhabited by lab-coated troglodytes, but this is actually Montego Bay's most famous beach and the one with the most facilities. A pretty arc of sugary sand fronts a deep-blue gem studded with floating dive platforms and speckled with tourists sighing happily. Er, *lots* of tourists – and a fair few Jamaicans as well. The upside is an admission charge keeps out the beach hustlers, though it doesn't ensure that the beach is kept spotless.

Founded as a bathing club in 1906, Doctor's Cave earned its name when English chiropractor Sir Herbert Barker claimed the waters here had healing properties. People flocked to Montego Bay, kick-starting a tourism evolution that would culminate in the appearance of *Homo Margaritavillus* decades later. There are lots of facilities on hand, including a restaurant, a grill bar, an internet cafe and water sports, and lots of things to rent (beach chairs, towels, snorkeling gear).

★**National Museum West** MUSEUM
(☎940-6402; www.museums-ioj.org.jm; Sam Sharpe Sq, Montego Bay Cultural Centre; J$500; ⏲9am-5pm Tue-Sun) This well-curated, revamped museum, peppered with period objects, takes you through the history of western Jamaica, from the Cohaba ceremonies of the indigenous Taínos and the arrival of the Spanish, followed by the English, to the trans-Atlantic slave trade, the advent of king sugar, Maroon rebellions, emancipation and the development of 20th-century Montego Bay as a tourist destination. A separate room introduces you to the rise of Rastafarianism, the alleged divinity of Haile Selassie and the back-to-Africa movement.

Montego Bay Marine Park & Bogue Lagoon NATURE RESERVE
(☎952-5619; www.mbmpt.org) The waters of Montego Bay are gorgeous to behold both above and below the surface, but they have long been compromised by the effects of

fishing, water sports and pollution. With the creation in 1991 of the Montego Bay Marine Park, environmental regulations at last began to be strictly enforced to protect the area's coral reefs, flora and fauna, and shoreline mangroves.

The park extends from the eastern end of the airport westward (almost 10km) to the Great River, encompassing the mangroves of Bogue Lagoon and the fishing waters around Airport Point.

You can hire canoes or set out with a guide to spot herons, egrets, pelicans and waterfowl; swimming and crawling below are barracudas, tarpon, snapper, crabs and lobsters. Request a guide two days in advance; there's no charge but donations are gladly accepted.

Sam Sharpe Square SQUARE
This bustling, cobbled square is named for Samuel Sharpe (1801–32), national hero and leader of the 1831 Christmas Rebellion; it is also where he was hanged in its aftermath. At the square's northwest corner is the **National Heroes' Monument**. Nearby is the **Cage**, a tiny brick building built in 1806 as a lockup for vagrants and other miscreants.

Activities

Watery activities – sunset boat cruises, diving, snorkeling and fishing – are very popular in MoBay. Many travelers also use MoBay as the jumping-off spot for day tours along the north coast and the western half of Jamaica.

Rafters' Village RAFTING
(☎940-6398; www.jamaicarafting.com; per raft 1-2 people US$70) Contact for trips along the Martha Brae, near Falmouth on the northwest coast, within easy day-tripping distance of Montego Bay and Ironshore. Hotel pickups available.

★**Dressel Divers** DIVING
(☎in USA 321-392-2338; www.dresseldivers.com; off A1, Iberostar Rose Hall Resort; 1-/2-tank dive US$60/100) Acclaimed international diving outfit with a scuba center in Iberostar Rose Hall Resort, 20km east of MoBay. Nonhotel guests are welcome on trips. Patient diving instructors, PADI courses and snorkeling trips on offer. For customized dive-package prices, use the online form on the website.

Dreamer Catamaran Cruises BOATING
(☎979-0102; www.dreamercatamarans.com; Doctor's Cave Beach Club; cruise incl transfer adult/under 12yr US$88/40; ⊙cruises 10am-1pm & 3-6pm Mon-Sat) This outfit offers a catamaran adventure on three swift boats specially designed for partying, with an open bar and a snorkeling stop in the marine park. Choose between sail and snorkel, sunset cruise, or sail to Negril. Cruises depart from Doctor's Cave Beach Club. A bus will pick you up at your hotel.

Festivals & Events

★**Reggae Sumfest** MUSIC
(www.reggaesumfest.com; ⊙mid-Jul) The largest reggae festival in Jamaica typically includes more than 50 world-class reggae and dancehall artists. Held in July at the Catherine Hall Entertainment Center, it starts with a beach party on Walter Fletcher Beach, followed by a week of nonstop partying. Past performers have included Luciano, Beenie Man, Gregory Isaacs, Damien 'Jr Gong' Marley and Alicia Keys.

Sleeping

★**Mobay Kotch** HOSTEL $
(☎820-9883; www.mobaykotch.com; 16 Church St; dm/s/d from US$22/45/65; ❄📶) Montego Bay's best hostel resides inside the 1765 Town House, its handsome redbrick frontage buried under a cascade of bougainvillea and laburnum. High ceilings and splashes of contemporary art and lots of comfy common spaces create a homey atmosphere that encourages mingling among guests. Backpackers end up lingering here, using MoBay as a base for day trips further afield.

Originally, this was the home of a wealthy merchant. It has since served as a church manse and later as a town house for the mistress of the Earl of Hereford, Governor of Jamaica. In the years that followed, it was used as a hotel, a warehouse, a Masonic lodge, a lawyer's office and a synagogue.

Ridgeway Guest House GUESTHOUSE $
(☎952-2709; www.ridgewayguesthouse.com; 34 Queens Dr; s/d US$60/70, without air-con US$45/55; ❄📶) The rooms here surround a pretty garden and are as good a deal as any you'll find in MoBay. They're comparable to midrange digs: cozy beds, tiled floors, nice furnishings, all kept quite clean and presentable. The cheapest ones are fan

Montego Bay

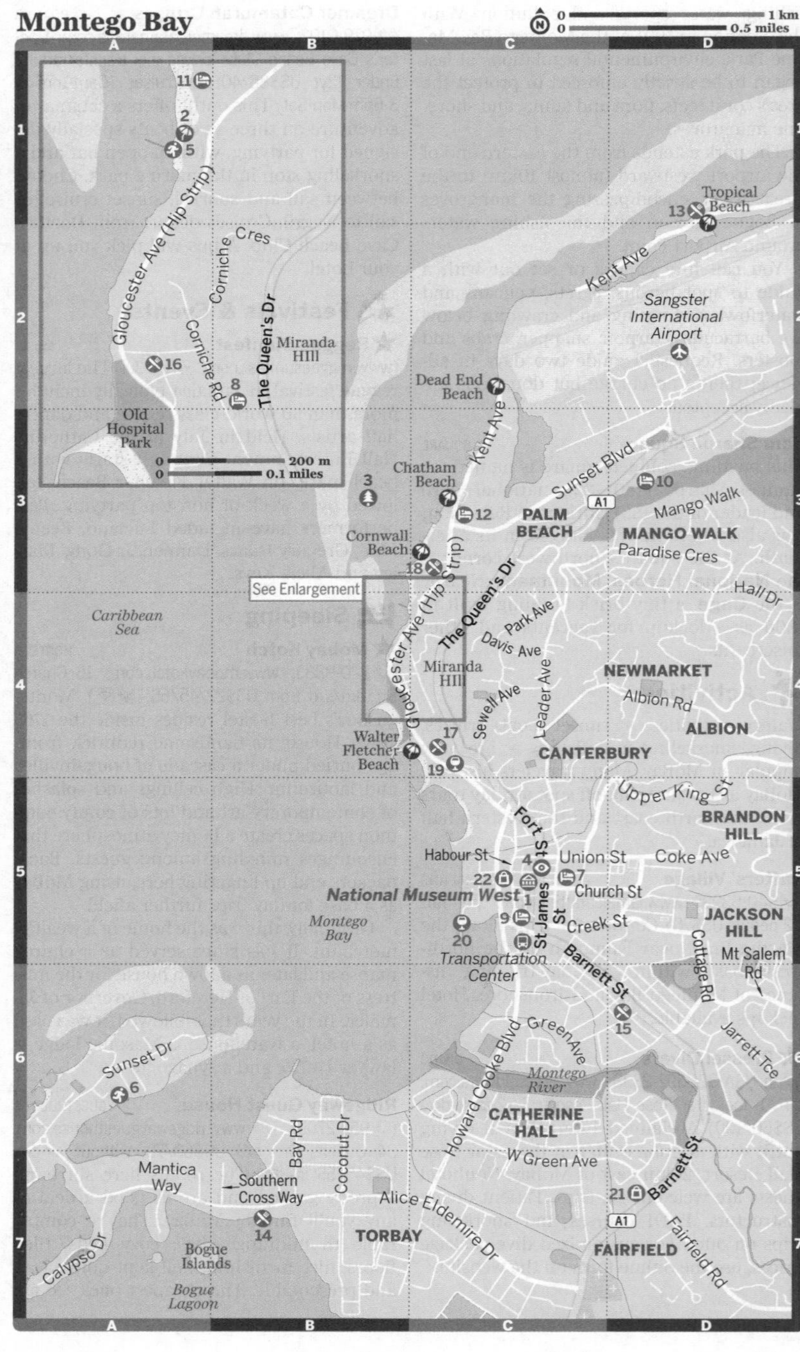
0 1 km
0 0.5 miles
See Enlargement
Caribbean Sea
Tropical Beach
Kent Ave
Sangster International Airport
Dead End Beach
Chatham Beach
Cornwall Beach
Walter Fletcher Beach
Sunset Blvd
A1
PALM BEACH
MANGO WALK
Mango Walk
Paradise Cres
Hall Dr
Gloucester Ave (Hip Strip)
The Queen's Dr
Park Ave
Davis Ave
Miranda Hill
Sewell Ave
Leader Ave
NEWMARKET
Albion Rd
ALBION
CANTERBURY
Upper King St
BRANDON HILL
Fort St
Habour St
Union St
Coke Ave
National Museum West
Church St
St James St
Creek St
JACKSON HILL
Montego Bay
Transportation Center
Barnett St
Cottage Rd
Mt Salem Rd
Jarrett Tce
Green Ave
Howard Cooke Blvd
Montego River
Sunset Dr
CATHERINE HALL
W Green Ave
Bay Rd
Coconut Dr
Mantica Way
Southern Cross Way
Alice Eldemire Dr
TORBAY
FAIRFIELD
Fairfield Rd
Calypso Dr
Bogue Islands
Bogue Lagoon
Corniche Cres
Corniche Rd
Old Hospital Park
0 200 m
0 0.1 miles

Montego Bay

Top Sights
1 National Museum West C5

Sights
Cage ..... (see 4)
2 Doctor's Cave Beach A1
3 Montego Bay Marine Park & Bogue Lagoon B3
National Heroes' Monument ..... (see 4)
4 Sam Sharpe Square C5

Activities, Courses & Tours
5 Dreamer Catamaran Cruises A1
6 Montego Bay Yacht Club A6

Sleeping
7 Mobay Kotch C5
8 Polkerris B&B B2
9 Reggae Hostel C5
10 Ridgeway Guest House D3
11 S Hotel Jamaica A1
12 Toby's Resort C3

Eating
13 Evelyn's On The Beach D1
14 Houseboat Grill B7
15 Millennium Victory D6
Nyam 'n' Jam ..... (see 22)
16 Pelican Grill A2
17 Pork Pit C4
18 Usain Bolt's Tracks & Records C3

Drinking & Nightlife
19 MoBay Proper C4
20 Pier One C5

Shopping
21 Gallery of West Indian Art D7
22 Harbour Street Craft Market C5

cooled. Located away from the beaches near the airport, but a free shuttle gets you to the sea and sand.

★ Waterfield Retreat VILLA $$
(☎597-8962; www.waterfieldretreat.com; Spring Gardens, Clarridge Hall; r from US$174; ❄📶🏊) On a hilltop a 10-minute drive south of Montego Bay, this villa is the ultimate in romantic seclusion. There are unparalleled views of the city and the sea from the terrace, you can pick fruit and veg from the garden for the chef to cook for you, and the bathroom comes with a deep soaking tub. Romance your sweetie here.

★ Polkerris B&B B&B $$
(☎877-7784; www.montegobayinn.com; 31 Corniche Rd; r incl breakfast US$204-255; P❄📶🏊) The best B&B in Montego Bay? No question. Hanging above the Hip Strip, Polkerris, run by a British expat and his Jamaican wife, is sublime in every detail. There's the trickling waterfall, the swimming pool, the view-embellished veranda, the stupendous breakfast and – most importantly – the one-of-the-family style of service that reminds you that you're in the real Jamaica.

Toby's Resort HOTEL $$
(☎952-4370; www.tobyresorts.com; cnr Gloucester Ave & Sunset Blvd; s/d/tr from US$120/140/160; P❄📶🏊) Located just off the 'top' of the Hip Strip, Toby's provides an admirable local vibe with amenities geared towards international travelers. Staff make Toby's feel like a gracious guesthouse, but with the benefits of large grounds, comfy rooms, a big pool and a smaller pool, and a good bar and restaurant serving a mix of Jamaican and international dishes.

★ S Hotel Jamaica RESORT $$$
(☎979-0000; www.shoteljamaica.com; Gloucester Ave; r from US$259; P❄📶🏊) This terrific new hotel is a winner. The entrance leads you into a splendid, airy atrium that looks out on the vast pool and Doctor's Cave Beach beyond. Staff welcome you like a long-lost friend and there's an impressive inventory of perks, including a suspended plunge pool and an excellent restaurant. Splurge on an ocean-view room; cheapest rooms are nothing special.

Eating

★ Pork Pit JERK $
(☎952-1046; 27 Gloucester Ave; mains J$600-900; ⏰11am-11pm; 📶) At this glorified food shack on the Hip Strip, your meal is cooked over a traditional jerk pit fashioned from pimento wood sticks laid over smoking hot coals. The delicious aroma wafting down Gloucester Ave provides a perfect advert for the Pork Pit's obligatory jerk pork (and chicken). Eat it under the 300-year-old cotton tree out back.

★ Millennium Victory VEGAN $
(☎887-5545; www.millenniumvictory.weebly.com; 65 Barnett St; mains J$600-1000; ⏰8:30am-6pm Mon-Sat, 8:30am-3pm Sun; 🌿) Cheap and cheerful I-tal food shack, decorated in Rasta

colors and serving creative dishes such as *escoveich* tofu (tofu in a spicy, vinegary sauce), ackee stew and gungo pea stew. Great fruit juices, too.

Evelyn's On The Beach SEAFOOD $
(☎952-3280; Kent Ave, Whitehouse; mains J$650-1200; ⏲9am-9pm Mon-Sat, 10am-6pm Sun) Fantastic choice: a true local's spot, this rustic seafood shack (near Sandals Montego Bay) is also patronized by some very in-the-know tourists. Come here for the likes of brown stew fish with rice, and even filled rotis.

Nyam 'n' Jam JAMAICAN $
(☎952-1922; 17 Harbour St; mains J$600-1100; ⏲8am-11pm) On the cusp of the craft market, you can retreat to check out this truly authentic Jamaican dining experience. Settle down for snapper with a spicy sauce; jerk or brown stew chicken; curried goat; or oxtail with rice and peas.

★Usain Bolt's Tracks & Records INTERNATIONAL $$
(☎971-0000; www.tracksandrecords.com; 7 Gloucester Ave; mains J$1200-1950; ⏲12:30pm-midnight; ❄) Usain Bolt is not a subtle man. A vast statue of him stands sentinel by the entrance, striking his famous pose, while TV screens inside replay his sporting victories. That said, the food is terrific – from the pepper shrimp and janga soup to the jerk platters, delicate seafood curries and killer milkshakes. Bolt wins gold, again.

Pelican Grill JAMAICAN $$
(☎952-3171; Gloucester Ave; mains J$1355-4175; ⏲7am-11pm; ❄📶) Both upper-crust Jamaicans and tourists are beckoned by Pelican Grill's air-con chill and superlative goat curry and oxtail, consumed while sitting on leather banquettes. Opened the same year Jamaica gained independence (1962) and armed with the same chef since the early 1980s, this seminal Hip Strip restaurant has fully earned its right to be called a MoBay institution.

★Houseboat Grill JAMAICAN $$$
(☎979-8845; www.thehouseboatgrill.com; Southern Cross Blvd; mains J$1945-5195; ⏲4-11pm Tue-Sun) Moored in Bogue Lagoon at Montego Bay Freeport, this converted houseboat is still among the best restaurants in the city. The changing menu offers eclectic Caribbean fusion cuisine: mussels in a fiery red curry, Moroccan-style lamb kofta or Cajun-style shrimp. You can dine inside or reclusively out on the moondeck. Reservations strongly recommended.

Drinking & Nightlife

★Pier One CLUB
(☎952-2452; www.pieronejamaica.com; Howard Cooke Blvd; ⏲11am-11pm Mon, Tue, Thu & Sat, to 2am Wed, to 4am Fri) If you're into big nightclubs, Pier One is the place to go in Montego Bay. It attracts a largely local crowd, dressed to impress and dancing as if their lives depend on it. The music is bass-heavy, the dance floor is crowded (especially on Wednesdays and during Pier Pressure Fridays) and the locals can teach you the latest dancehall moves.

MoBay Proper BAR
(☎940-1233; www.facebook.com/mobaypropersportsbar; Fort St; ⏲11:30am-1am) Proper is often packed with locals and expats returned to the motherland. It's a friendly, occasionally raucous spot and probably the easiest bar for tourists to access off the Hip Strip. Beneath a 'chandelier' of Heineken bottles, the pool table generates considerable heat, while dominoes are the rage with an older crowd out on the patio.

Shopping

★Gallery of West Indian Art ART
(☎952-4547; 11 Fairfield Rd; ⏲10am-5pm Mon-Fri) In the suburb of Catherine Hall, this is the best-quality gallery in town. It sells genuinely original arts and crafts from around the Caribbean including Cuban, Haitian and Jamaican canvases, hand-painted wooden animals, masks and handmade jewelry. Most of the work here is for sale. Find it on Facebook and call ahead.

Harbour Street Craft Market GIFTS & SOUVENIRS
(Harbour St; ⏲7am-7pm) The largest selection of typical Jamaican souvenirs in MoBay – coconut-palm baskets, woven hats, Rasta-themed wood carvings and Haitian art rip-offs – is found at this market, which extends for three blocks between Barnett and Market Sts. Clothing in Rasta colors is mass-produced in China.

Information

Banks on Sam Sharpe Sq and in the Baywest Shopping Center all have 24-hour ATMs. Flanking the Doctor's Cave Beach Club are ATMs operated by National Commercial Bank and **Scotiabank** (Gloucester Ave).

Cornwall Regional Hospital (☎emergency 275-1119; www.cornwallregionalhospital.com; Mt Salem Rd; ⊙24hr) Has a 24-hour emergency ward.

Fairview Medical (☎979-8589; www.fairviewmedicalcentre.com; Alice Eldermire Dr; ⊙7am-7pm Mon-Fri, 9am-5pm Sat, 10am-3pm Sun) Private clinic offering dental and medical emergency services.

Police stations Barnett St (☎952-2333; 14 Barnett St; ⊙24hr); Church St (☎952-5310; 29 Church St; ⊙24hr)

Police Tourism Liaison Unit (☎952-1540; Summit Police Station, Sunset Blvd; ⊙8am-8pm)

Getting There & Away

AIR

The majority of international visitors arrive at **Donald Sangster International Airport** (MBJ; ☎952-3124; www.mbjairport.com; A1), 3km north of Montego Bay. There's a Jamaica Tourist Board (JTB) information booth in the arrivals hall and a 24-hour money-exchange bureau immediately beyond immigration. There is also a transportation information counter plus desks representing tour companies, hotels and rental cars immediately as you exit customs, as well as a booth for taxis.

You'll find taxis waiting outside the arrivals lounge at the airport. A tourist taxi to Gloucester Ave costs US$15 to US$20. Alternatively, you can catch a minibus or route taxi from the gas station at the entrance to the airport (J$100).

BUS

Public buses other than **Knutsford Express** (☎971-1822; www.knutsfordexpress.com; Market St; ⊙4am-9:30pm), minibuses and route taxis arrive and depart from the **transportation center** (Barnett St) at the south end of St James St. Destinations are written on the bus/van/taxi and people will direct you to the correct vehicle if you ask around.

Minibuses (ie vans) and shared taxis run directly to Ocho Rios (J$500, two hours; onward transfers to Port Antonio and Kingston), Lucea (J$225, one to 1½ hours; onward transfers to Negril), Negril (J$350, 1½ hours), Kingston (J$650, five hours), some inland villages and also Ironshore and Rose Hall (J$150, 30 minutes).

Montego Bay Metro Line bus service links MoBay with the suburbs and outlying villages, such as Anchovy and Grange Hill.

You can almost always find a route taxi early in the morning or around 4pm to 5pm (ie commuting hours); there will likely be a wait at other times of the day, and long-distance taxi service slacks off after sunset. It's always easier to get a ride to towns on the coast compared to towns in the interior.

CAR

Car-rental companies:

Avis (☎952-0762; www.avis.com.jm; Sangster International Airport; ⊙8am-10pm)

Hertz (☎979-0438; www.hertz.com; Sangster International Airport; ⊙8am-10pm)

Island Car Rentals (☎952-7225; www.islandcarrentals.com; Sangster International Airport; ⊙8am-10pm)

Getting Around

Route taxis ply set routes and charge set fares for set distances and are the cheapest way to get around Montego Bay.

The usual cost for a route is about J$100, perhaps double that if heading to the outer suburbs.

Rose Hall to Greenwood

East of Montego Bay is Jamaica's most famous (and allegedly haunted) mansion, Rose Hall, while Greenwood, with its own great house, is further east again. Several restaurants are clustered around Half Moon Village, en route to Rose Hall from Montego Bay.

Sights

★Rose Hall Great House — HOUSE

(☎toll-free 888-767-3425; www.rosehall.com; off A1; adult/child under 12yr US$25/10; ⊙9am-5:15pm & 6:30-9pm) This splendid 1770s mansion is the most famous great house in Jamaica. John Palmer, a wealthy plantation owner, and his wife, Rose (after whom the house was named), hosted some of the most elaborate social gatherings on the island. Much of the attraction is the legend of Annie Palmer, alleged to have murdered three husbands, whose ghost is said to haunt the house. Rose Hall is 3km east of Ironshore. Entry is by entertaining tour only.

Beyond the Palladian portico the house is a bastion of historical style, with a magnificent mahogany staircase and doors, and silk wall fabric that is a reproduction of the original designed for Marie Antoinette during the reign of Louis XVI. Unfortunately, because the house was cleaned out by looters back in the 19th century, almost all of the period furnishings were brought in from elsewhere, and quite a few are from the wrong century. With that said, the exquisite imported antique furnishings are the genuine article, and many are the work of past leading English master carpenters.

Slaves destroyed the house in the Christmas Rebellion of 1831 and it was left in ruins for more than a century. In 1966 the three-story building was restored to its haughty grandeur.

Tours take in the rooms, including Annie Palmer's bedroom upstairs (which has been decorated in crimson silk brocades because, y'know, red is the color of blood), the secret passage through which she was visited by her slave lover, her tomb, and the cellar with period objects and an English-style pub.

Day tours focus on the sumptuous furnishings, while evening tours are theatrical and fun, with staff leaping at you from dark corners, ideal for those with a stout disposition.

★Greenwood Great House HOUSE

(☎953-1077; www.greenwoodgreathouse.com; off A1; adult/child US$20/10; ⊙9am-6pm) This marvelous estate, sitting high on a hill, is not as famous as Jamaica's most famous great house, but offers a far more intimate and interesting experience. Unique among local plantation houses, Greenwood survived unscathed during the slave rebellion of Christmas 1831. Most of the furnishings are authentic, and some of the rare objects are truly remarkable. Greenwood is 11km east of Ironshore and around 10km west of Falmouth, off the A1; turn inland and follow the pitted road uphill.

Construction of the two-story, stone-and-timber structure was begun in 1780 by the Honorable Richard Barrett, whose family arrived in Jamaica in the 1660s and amassed a fortune from its sugar plantations. (Barrett was a cousin of the famous English poet Elizabeth Barrett Browning.) In an unusual move for his times, Barrett educated his slaves.

The original library is still intact, as are oil paintings, a 1626 map of Africa and plentiful antiques, including a mantrap used for catching runaway slaves (one of the few direct references we found in any Jamaican historical home to the foundations of the plantation labor market, ie slavery). Among the highlights is the rare collection of musical instruments, including an exquisitely inlaid piano made for Edward VII by Thomas Broadwood (who also made pianos for Beethoven). You'll also see one of three working barrel organs in the world and two polyphones, one of which the guide is happy to bring to life. The resident ghost is decidedly low-key and you can drink in the view of the entire coast from the upstairs veranda.

Falmouth

Built on riches amassed from sugar and slavery, and advanced enough by the early 19th century to have running water before even New York City, Falmouth feels like a time warp. Little altered architecturally since the 1840s, when slave emancipation dramatically reversed its fortunes, the town retains one of the finest ensembles of Tropical-Georgian buildings in the Caribbean.

For anyone with an interest in Jamaican history and architecture, Falmouth is an essential stopover. It is a bustling, proper Jamaican town, where old ladies in their Sunday best congregate outside the limestone-bricked, English-style church and market traders ply roasted yam and sugarcane under the pretty gingerbread verandas of commerce-packed Harbour Lane. This quintessential Jamaican-ness is under threat, as the produce market has been banished from the town center and there are some attempts to turn the latter into a sanitized version of Jamaican life for cruise-ship passengers.

Sights

Water Square SQUARE

The best place to orient yourself is Water Sq, at the east end of Duke St. Named for an old circular stone reservoir dating from 1798, the square (actually a triangle) has a fountain that replaced a system powered by water wheels that gave Falmouth running water before New York City. In the evening, the square really comes to life, with people limin' under the coconut trees, blaring reggae and delicious smells wafting from stalls.

Many of the wooden shop fronts in this area are attractively disheveled relics. In the 18th century, the shops were staffed by Jewish merchants; now the shop owners tend to be Jamaican Chinese.

William Knibb Baptist Memorial Church CHURCH

(cnr King & George Sts; ⊙hours vary) On July 31, 1838, slaves gathered outside this church for an all-night vigil, awaiting midnight and then the dawn of full freedom (to quote the emancipist Reverend Knibb: 'The monster is dead'), when slave shackles, a whip and an iron collar were symbolically buried in a coffin nearby. Behind the church you can find Knibb's grave. A plaque inside the church displays the internment of these tools of slavery; to get in, ask at the Leaf of Life Hardware store on King St.

Glistening Waters LAGOON
(Luminous Lagoon; www.glisteningwaters.com; 30min boat trip per adult/under 12yr/family US$25/12/50; ⊙tours from 6:45pm) Glistening Waters, also known as 'Luminous Lagoon,' actually lives up to the hype. Located in an estuary near Rock, 1.6km east of Falmouth, the water here boasts a singular charm – it glows an eerie green when disturbed. The green glow is due to the presence of microorganisms that produce photochemical reactions when stirred; the concentrations are so thick that fish swimming by look like green torpedoes and when you swim, sparks run down your body.

Swimming through the luminous lagoon is semihallucinogenic, especially on starry nights, when it's hard to tell where the water ends and the sky begins. The experience is made all the more surreal thanks to the mixing of salt- and freshwater from the sea and the Martha Brae River; the freshwater 'floats' on the saltwater, so you not only swim through green clouds of phosphorescence, but alternating bands of cold and warm.

You have to take a boat out to reach the bioluminescent spots. Half-hour boat trips are offered from Glistening Waters Marina and two other locations next to it; the three boat companies are comparable. Any hotel from Ocho Rios to Montego Bay should be able to organize a trip out here.

There's a decent restaurant by the marina.

Tours

★ **Falmouth Heritage Walks** HISTORY
(☎407-2245, Marina 878-7277; www.facebook.com/FalmouthHeritageWalks; ⊙cruise ship days & by reservation) This excellent outfit consists of a knowledgeable guide offering three ways of exploring history-rich Falmouth. The Heritage Walking Tour (adult/child US$30/15) is an interesting two-hour look at Falmouth's handsome Tropical-Georgian architecture. The Food Tour (adult/child US$55/25) combines snippets of culture with tastings of street food, while the Jewish Tour (adult/child US$17/12) visits Falmouth's Jewish cemetery with gravestones etched in Hebrew.

Walks usually take place on the days a cruise ship is in port, though it's possible to book tours on non-cruise-ship days (minimum two people). Marina is one of Jamaica's top Jewish history experts.

Getting There & Away

Buses, minibuses and route taxis arrive and depart on opposite sides of Water Sq for Martha Brae (J$140, 15 to 20 minutes), Montego Bay (J$220, 45 minutes), Albert Town (1½ hours, J$250) and Ocho Rios (J$370, 80 minutes). The **Knutsford Express** (☎971-1822; www.knutsfordexpress.com; Glistening Waters) stops in Glistening Waters 2km east of Falmouth.

NEGRIL & WEST COAST

If you thought the north and east coasts of Jamaica were relaxed, head west to a land of long beaches and crimson sunsets where the pleasure-seeking resort of Negril shimmers like an independent republic of guilt-free sloth. Aside from producing sugarcane and surreptitiously growing Jamaica's best ganja, western Jamaica's raison d'être is almost exclusively touristic; elongated Negril and its hotel developments stretch for more than 16km along the entire western coast. In the quiet bucolic hinterland, little pockets of local life can still be glimpsed in places such as Lucea, a pretty coastal enclave bypassed by tourist traffic, wild and wet Mayfield Falls, and diminutive Little Bay, a nonresort that still feels like Negril, circa 1969. Few come to the west with a to-do list, electing instead to enjoy life in the true spirit of the hippies who founded Negril. Join them on a sun lounger and relax, *mon*.

Negril

POP 9890

Stuck out on Jamaica's western tip and graced with its finest and longest natural beach, Negril was first colonized by hippies in the early 1970s. Unsurprisingly, 40 years of development has left its mark – not all of it good: Negril is renowned for its hustlers. But it's not all hassle. A strong local business community, fueled by a desire to safeguard Negril's precious ecology, has kept the area from becoming a full-on circus. Consequently, Negril remains a laidback place of impromptu reggae concerts and psychedelic sunsets.

Sights & Activities

★Seven Mile Beach BEACH

(Negril Beach, Long Beach) Seven Mile Beach was initially touted on tourism posters as 'seven miles of nothing but you and the sea.' True, sunbathers still lie half submerged in the gentle surf, and the sweet smell of ganja smoke continues to perfume the breeze, but otherwise the beach has changed a great deal. Today it's lined with restaurants, bars and nightspots, and every conceivable water sport is on offer. It is still beautiful to behold, but if you're looking for solitude, look elsewhere.

It's worth noting that Seven Mile Beach is actually only 4 miles (6.5km) long.

★Negril Adventure Diver DIVING

(☎487-0002; www.negriladventurediver.com; Norman Manley Blvd, Hidden Paradise Beach; 1-/2-tank dives US$60/115; ⊙8am-4pm) This diving outfit gets particularly high marks for the patience and friendliness of its diving instructors. Particularly good for beginners, though it gets rave reviews for its PADI certification courses, too.

★Dream Team Divers DIVING

(☎957-0054; www.dreamteamdiversjamaica.com; One Love Dr, Coral Seas Cliff; 1-/2-tank dives US$60/110) Highly recommended, professional diving outfit. A full range of PADI courses on offer, as well as discovery scuba dives (US$90).

Festivals & Events

Rastafari Rootzfest CULTURAL

(www.rastafarirootzfest.com; ⊙Dec) Held for three days in December in Negril, this festival celebrates the Rastafarian lifestyle, from music and art to I-tal cuisine, ganja cultivation and religious beliefs.

Sleeping

Long Bay

Negril Yoga Centre RESORT $

(☎957-4397; www.facebook.com/negrilyogacentre.jamaica; Norman Manley Blvd; r US$58-99; ❄📶) A hearkening back to hippie days of yore, these rustic yet atmospheric rooms and cottages surround an open-air, wood-floored, thatched yoga center set in a garden. Options range from a two-story, Thai-style wooden cabin to an adobe farmer's cottage; all are modestly furnished. Naturally, yoga classes are offered (US$10 for guests and US$20 for visitors).

Rondel Village RESORT $$

(☎957-4413; www.rondelvillage.com; Norman Manley Blvd; r US$155-255, villas US$310-560; ❄📶🏊) 🍃 Rondel is a charmer. Rooms encased in beautiful white chalets are set off with sharp purple accents and are surrounded by snaking swimming pools and verdant foliage. Eschewing big-resort ambitions, it is the epitome of Negrilian calm – relaxed, hassle-free and filled with all the ingredients for a week enjoyed doing absolutely nothing. Service is exemplary.

West End

★Judy House Cottages & Rooms HOSTEL $

(☎957-0671, 424-5481; www.judyhousenegril.com; Westland Mountain Rd; dm/s/d US$15/22/54, cottages US$65-72; 📶) This lush tropical garden on a hill above the West End guards two tiny, self-contained cottages with kitchen, plus three singles and two dorms, all with shared bathroom and kitchen access, aimed at backpackers. English owner Sue is a mine of candid info, the honesty bar and the friendly discourse are refreshing, and the hammocks in the garden are…*zzzzzz*.

★Rockhouse HOTEL $$

(☎957-4373; www.rockhousehotel.com; One Love Dr; r/villa from US$180/395; ❄📶🏊) One of the West End's most beautiful and well-run hotels, with luxury thatched rondavels (African huts) built of pine and stone, plus studio apartments that dramatically cling to the cliffside above a small cove. Decor is basic yet romantic, with net-draped four-poster beds and strong Caribbean colors. Catwalks lead over the rocks to an open-sided dining pavilion overhanging the ocean.

Catcha Falling Star HOTEL $$

(☎957-0390; www.catchajamaica.com; One Love Dr; cottages incl breakfast from US$135, ste US$350; P📶) In inimitable West End style, these pleasant fan-cooled cottages – including several with two bedrooms – sit on the cliffs. Each is named for an astrological sign and the rooms do have the genuine variety of the zodiac; some peek into gardens abloom with tropical flowers, while others lip out on to the blue-on-blue vista of ocean. Breakfast is delivered to your veranda.

Westender Inn GUESTHOUSE **$$**
(800-223-3876; www.westenderinn.com; West End Rd; cottage US$115, r/ste from US$159/259;) About as far south as you can get in the West End without leaving Negril, the Westender Inn lets you play out your fantasy of romantic seclusion, with swimming spots just off the rocks and a range of lodgings – from simple garden cottages to wood-paneled, individually decorated suites.

Eating

Long Bay

Cosmo's SEAFOOD **$**
(957-4784; www.facebook.com/cosmoseafood; Norman Manley Blvd; mains J$700-1400; 9am-10pm;) A tatty hippie outpost that sits like an island of good taste amid an ocean of insipid all-inclusive buffets. Cosmo's, in Negril-speak, is a synonym for 'fantastic seafood.' Eschew fine dining for burying your toes in the sand at a beachside picnic table – the plates of melt-in-your-mouth lobster, grilled fish and curried conch are deliciously spicy.

Canoe Beach Bar JAMAICAN **$**
(878-5893; www.facebook.com/CanoeBeachBar; One Love Dr; mains J$650-1500; 7am-10pm) Simple wooden shack. Right on the water. Live steel-drum performances. Fresh fish plucked from the nearby ocean. Thoroughly reasonable prices. Big portions of Jamaican favorites. Gently lapping waves. Red Stripe sunsets. What more do you want?

West End

★**Just Natural** VEGAN **$**
(957-0235; www.facebook.com/JustNaturalNegril; Hilton Ave; mains J$600-1700; 8am-8pm Mon-Fri, to 9pm Sat & Sun;) Quintessentially Jamaican, Just Natural is a jumble of tables, trees and foliage at the southern end of the West End strip that serves up a formidable breakfast of fruit, porridge, smoothies and eggs. It's quite incredible what delicacies emerge from the wooden shack of a kitchen. Top of the morning!

Pimentoz Jerk JERK **$**
(957-4556; www.islandluxbeachparkja.com; Norman Manley Blvd, Island Lux Beach Park; quarter pork/sausage/chicken J$800/850/750; noon-10pm) Yes, this place caters to escapees from nearby all-inclusives, but we love it anyway. There's a real depth of flavor to the jerk sausage, the pork and chicken are a satisfying hit of smoky flesh and spice, the homemade hot sauce rocks, and the cornucopia of sides includes sweet potato and breadfruit. Sea views and thatched bar ambience to boot.

★**Rockhouse Restaurant & Bar** FUSION **$$$**
(957-4373; www.rockhousehotel.com/eat; One Love Dr; mains US$15-35; 7:30am-10pm;) With the terrace subtly lit at night, this relaxed cliffside spot leads the pack when it comes to nouvelle Jamaican cuisine in the western parishes. Savor dishes such as jerk-spiced calamari, seafood simmered in rundown sauce and blackened *mahimahi* with mango chutney. At the very least, stop by for a Rockwell – a sinful original cocktail.

Drinking & Nightlife

★**Drifters Bar** BAR
(826-2116; www.facebook.com/DriftersBarNegril; Norman Manley Blvd; 11am-10pm) Swing by this beach bar run by former Drifters singer Luddy for the terrific reggae and soul jam on Friday afternoons, or live tunes on Sunday – or enter a friendly vocal contest with locals during karaoke Wednesdays. There's a decent jerk pit here, too.

★**Rick's Cafe** BAR
(957-0380; www.rickscafejamaica.com; One Love Dr; noon-9:30pm;) You'll be joining the touristy throng at this ever-popular West End institution, but why not? Just for one evening. The drinks menu features empty-your-wallet cocktails and pricey Red Stripes (skip the food): you're paying for the ambience, pool access and the live band. Watch local divers try to outdo each other from the 10m-tall cliffs, or jump yourself.

Sir D's BAR
(521-0260; One Love Dr; 4-10pm) If all you want is to watch the greatest show on earth – Negril's fiery sunset – with a Red Stripe in your hand, then this friendly little place that clings to the clifftop fits the bill perfectly.

Entertainment

Negril's reggae concerts are legendary, with live performances every night in peak season. Several venues offer regular weekly jams, so they all get a piece of the action. You will also find sound-system jams where the DJs play shatteringly loud music – usually dancehall – on giant speakers. Most bars start the night playing reggae oldies and bust out the dancehall later.

OFF THE BEATEN TRACK

LITTLE OCHIE, ALLIGATOR POND

Little Ochie (☎852-6430; Alligator Pond; mains per lb J$880-2365; ⏲9am-close) is a culinary phenomenon that, despite a cult following, refuses to sell out. Set on a slice of black-sand beach, it uses the same charcoal-blackened kitchen and scribbled chalkboard menu it has for eons. The secret? Fish and seafood straight out of the sea, served steamed, jerked, curried, or grilled in boats on stilts under thatched awnings.

You make your choice from what the fishers have just brought in, pay by weight and then elect how you want it cooked. The jerk is always a good bet, though it can be *hot*. Grilled lobster and jerk parrotfish and snapper also have a dedicated following. And 'dedicated' is the word. Little Ochie is one of Jamaica's few bona fide destination restaurants and has established itself as the No 1 attraction in Alligator Pond. Jamaicans drive from Kingston just to eat here; when you find yourself happily covered in scales from the fish you've just eaten, like something out of Lord of the Flies, you'll know why.

Minibuses and route taxis operate between Alligator Pond and the Beckford St transportation center in Kingston (J$650). Coming from Treasure Beach (J$430), you have to change in Pedro Cross and Southfield. It's possible to hire a taxi in Treasure Beach to take you to and from Alligator Pond for around US$45 round trip.

★ **Bourbon Beach** LIVE MUSIC
(☎957-4432; www.facebook.com/BourbonBeachJamaica; Norman Manley Blvd; entry varies; ⏲from 8pm Mon, Thu & Sat) The best spot for live reggae on Seven Mile Beach, Bourbon Beach has hosted such greats as John Holt and Gregory Isaacs; younger talent appears on Thursdays. Saturday is dancehall night. The lively bar is open daily and the jerk is excellent, too.

Alfred's Ocean Palace LIVE MUSIC
(☎957-4669; www.alfreds.com; Norman Manley Blvd; US$5; ⏲Tue, Fri & Sun) This Negril institution is one of the oldest beach bars. The Live Reggae Beach Parties feature local and occasional international acts, beginning around 10pm and continuing deep into the night.

ℹ Information

For any major medical issues, head to the private hospitals in Montego Bay.

National Commercial Bank (NCB; One Love Dr; ⏲24hr)

Negril Health Centre (☎957-4926; Sheffield Rd; ⏲8:30am-5pm Mon-Fri)

Police Station (☎957-4268; Sheffield Rd)

Scotiabank (☎957-4236; Negril Sq; ⏲9am-5pm Mon-Sat)

DANGERS & ANNOYANCES

While Negril is generally a safe destination, visitors are likely to encounter touristy Jamaica at its most blatant: the hard sell, the hustling, restaurants ignoring environmental regulations and serving endangered seafood, short-changing and prostitution.

ℹ Getting There & Away

From the **transportation center** (Sheffield Rd), dozens of minibuses and route taxis run between Negril and Montego Bay. The 1½-hour journey costs between J$350 and J$500. Minibuses and route taxis also leave for Negril from Sangster International Airport in Montego Bay (the price is negotiable, but expect to pay about US$15).

The handy and comfortable **Knutsford Express** (☎971-1822; www.knutsfordexpress.com; Norman Manley Blvd; ⏲6:15am-8pm) runs from Times Square Plaza to destinations across the country.

ℹ Getting Around

Negril stretches along more than 16km of shoreline, and it can be a withering walk.

Route taxis cruise the length of Seven Mile Beach and One Love Dr all the time. The fare between any two points was J$130 at research time during the day; in the evenings, it can be up to J$200 per hop.

SOUTH COAST & CENTRAL HIGHLANDS

Treasure Beach

Welcome to a unique part of Jamaica that gets all the facets of the quintessential Caribbean experience exactly right. Winding country lanes, a dearth of hustlers, a local population of poets and artists, deserted beaches, no gimmicky resorts, and – above all – a proud, foresighted local community that promotes sustainability and harbors a bonhomous but mellow culture.

Beaches

Several fishing beaches beckon within easy walking distance of the major accommodations. Ask about best swimming spots, as there can be strong undertows.

Fishermen's Beach BEACH
(Frenchman's Bay) This is the most centrally located beach, running east from the Treasure Beach Hotel as far as Jack Sprat Beach. It is watched over by a landmark buttonwood tree that has long attracted the attention of poets, painters and wood-carvers who ply their wares. It's a good place for sunning and swimming, and a popular spot for watching the sunset.

Great Bay Beach BEACH
(Great Bay) All the way at the eastern 'bottom' of Treasure Beach; this is its least developed portion, where the main business remains a Fisher's Co-op building. There are a couple of beachside shacks serving beer and cooking up fresh seafood. Swimming is possible.

Jack Sprat Beach BEACH
(Frenchman's Cove) At the western edge of Jake's Hotel, brightly painted wooden fishing boats are pulled up on the sand, and there is invariably a fisher or two on hand tending the nets. Good for swimming, as it's somewhat sheltered.

Calabash Bay Beach BEACH
(Calabash Bay) The long, narrow arc of Calabash Bay Beach has a few beach shacks plying rum and – if you're lucky – some basic potluck cuisine (fish, mainly). Swimming is possible but can be choppy.

Tours

★ **Treasure Beach Walking Tour** WALKING
(☎572-8835; per person US$15; ⏲7-8:30am Wed & Fri or by appointment) Local historian Lilleth Lynch takes you on an engaging stroll around Treasure Beach. She's grown up here, and can tell stories about residents past and present, waxing lyrical about a humble fishing village turned hip yet still offbeat retreat for bohos, artists and celebrities alike. Tours depart from the turnoff for the Sports Park. Book ahead.

Mr Nice Guy BOATING
(☎433-0252; bebesutherland@yahoo.com) The Mr Nice Guy in question is Bernard 'BeBe' Sutherland, a fisherman who's active in the protection of Treasure Beach's critically endangered hawksbill turtles. This experienced boat captain runs trips to Black River and Pelican Bar, as well as fishing outings.

Festivals & Events

Calabash International Literary Festival LITERATURE
(☎965-3000; www.calabashfestival.org; ⏲late May/early Jun) An acclaimed biannual literary festival at Jake's Hotel, drawing literary voices both domestically and internationally. Held in even-numbered years.

Sleeping

Welcoming Vibes GUESTHOUSE $
(☎538-8779; www.facebook.com/WelcomingVibes; Church St; r US$44; 📶) The open-air terrace of this rambling house on the hill drinks in the full expanse of Frenchman's Bay and amazing sunsets, while the common area fills with the aromatic smoke of di 'erb. The four spacious, en-suite, bug-netted rooms are airy and cool, and friendly owner Paul is happy to shoot the breeze. Cleanliness and maintenance could improve, though.

★ **Lashings Boutique Hotel** BOUTIQUE HOTEL $
(☎550-1610; www.lashings.co.uk; Old Wharf Rd; r US$85; ❄📶🏊) With a killer view of the coastline from its lofty location, Lashings comprises a clutch of sleek, contemporary rooms with hanging lanterns and quirky posters. Whether you're soaking in the view from the infinity pool or mixing it up with British politicians at the bar, it's hard not to appreciate the wallet-friendly luxury.

★ **Shi Shed! Africa Village** GUESTHOUSE $$
(☎342-9200; Old Wharf Rd, Calabash Bay; r US$95; 📶) Decorated with original artwork by owner/artist/musician/writer/diva Sharon Martini, these three rooms were all individually designed and executed by the indomitable woman herself. Fan-cooled and rustic, with curved adobe walls, they are among the most memorable digs in Treasure Beach, and you may find yourself lingering longer than anticipated. Two-night minimum.

★ **77 West** BOUTIQUE HOTEL $$
(☎469-4828; www.77west.net; Billy's Bay; r US$130; P❄📶🏊) Run by knowledgeable local Annabelle and her partner, this delightful boutique

hotel comprises five breezy cottages, all with excellent beds and sea views. The terrace with pool overlooks the waves, as does the breezy restaurant that serves the likes of stuffed crab backs and curried fish. The owners can arrange excellent walking tours of Treasure Beach and Pelican Bar outings.

★ Jake's Hotel BOUTIQUE HOTEL **$$$**
(965-3000, in the USA 800-688-7678; www.jakeshotel.com; Calabash Bay; r US$115-395;) If you haven't been to Jake's, you haven't really been to Treasure Beach. This romance-drenched boutique hotel is the nexus of pretty much everything in the area – cooking courses, yoga classes and mosaic workshops all happen here. Individually crafted rooms and secluded seafront villas with private sundecks and open to the sea breeze are big on style and atmosphere.

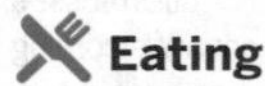

Eating

Gee Whiz VEGAN **$**
(573-5988; www.facebook.com/Geewizvegierest; Main Rd; mains J$520-900; 11:30am-7pm Tue-Sun;) Run by delightful Rasta Delroy, this simple restaurant is a great stop for vegan dishes, such as curried chickpeas and garlic cauliflower, all served with a mountain of rice and beans and freshly pressed fruit juices. I-tal, mon!

★ Jack Sprat PIZZA **$$**
(965-3583; www.jakeshotel.com/grown-locally/jack-sprat-restaurant; Calabash Bay; mains J$790-2650; 10am-11pm) Seafood and pizza aren't obvious bedfellows until you wander into Jack Sprat's, where it puts fresh lobster on its thick Italian-style pies. Flavor is enhanced by the dreamy location (seafront, candlelit tables under twinkle-lit trees) and bohemian interior (a mix of retro reggae and movie posters). The pizza is the best in Jamaica and the homemade crab cakes are ace.

★ Strikie-T JAMAICAN **$$**
(869-8516; Billy's Bay; mains J$1200-2000; 3-10pm Mon-Sat Nov-Apr) A seasonal affair run by the energetic, ever-friendly Chris 'Strikie' Bennett, who has worked as a professional chef in the US and at Jake's. This understated food shack in Billy's Bay, festooned with fairy lights, is anchored by secret recipes and a hand-built jerk smoker. The food is great: Jamaican favorites, from jerk to lobster, home-cooked and mouth watering.

Drinking & Nightlife

★ Pelican Bar BAR
(10:30am-sunset) A thatched hut on stilts, built on a submerged sandbar 1km out to sea after owner Floyd saw it in a dream, is still Jamaica's – and perhaps the planet's – most enjoyable spot for a drink. You can carve your name into the floorboards, play a game

WORTH A TRIP

APPLETON RUM ESTATE

You can smell the sweetness of molasses wafting from the **Appleton Rum Estate** (963-9215; www.appletonestate.com; B6; factory tour & rum tasting US$30; 9am-3:30pm Mon-Sat, closed public holidays) well before you reach it, 1km northeast of Maggotty. The largest and oldest distillery in Jamaica has been blending rums since 1749. After complimentary rum cocktails and a short video, the sleek tour explains how molasses is extracted from sugarcane, then fermented, distilled and aged to produce the Caribbean's own rocket fuel, which you can sample at the end of the tour.

Three varieties are available for sampling: the Signature Blend, aged for at least four years; the six-year-old Reserve Blend; and the 12-year-old Rare Blend. The limited batch of 50-year-old rum celebrating 50 years of Jamaica's independence from 2012 has been sold out, but if you're around in 2062, perhaps you'll be lucky enough to taste the limited edition Nine Prime Ministers rum, being aged in time to mark Jamaica's 100-year anniversary as an independent country. You also get a small complimentary bottle at the end of the tasting!

This tour is well priced and well executed, with humor and a dose of audience participation. At the end of the tour you can opt for a heaped plate of tasty jerk chicken or pork with rice and beans and all the trimmings at the on-site Black River Lounge. Most tour companies in Jamaica can get you to and from the Appleton estate (the 'from' part is pretty fun after three varieties of rum). Otherwise, it's easiest to get here from Maggotty; taxis will take you there and back for around J$600.

DON'T MISS

YS FALLS

The series of seven cascades known as **YS Falls** (997-6360; www.ysfalls.com; B6; adult/child US$19/10; 9:30am-5pm Tue-Sun, last entry 3:30pm, closed public holidays), hemmed in by limestone cliffs and surrounded by lush jungle, are among the most beautiful in Jamaica. The cascades fall 36m from top to bottom, separated by cool pools perfect for swimming. Lifeguards assist you with the rope swing above one of the pools and a stone staircase follows the cascades to the main waterfall. There are no lockers, so watch your stuff.

Take a tour or drive the 5.5km paved road from Middle Quarters. The more adventurous can fly, screeching, over the falls along a canopy zip line for US$50/35 per adult/child under 12 years. A tractor-drawn jitney takes all visitors to the cascades, where you'll find picnic grounds, changing rooms, a tree house and a shallow pool fed with river water.

Almost every tour operator in Jamaica (and many hotels) offers trips to YS Falls, but if you want to get here ahead of the crowds, drive yourself (or charter your own taxi) and arrive right when the grounds open.

The YS Falls entrance is just north of the junction of the B6 toward Maggotty. From the A2 (a much smoother road if you're driving), the turnoff is 1.5km east of Middle Quarters; from here you'll head 5.5km north to the falls.

The waters of YS (why-ess) take their name from the original landowners, ranchers John Yates and Richard Scott.

of dominoes, or just chill with a Red Stripe while wading in the shallows.

Getting there is half the fun: hire a local boat captain in Treasure Beach (around US$40) or Parottee (around US$20), who will call ahead to arrange things if you want to eat. This is essential for those who want to take a meal out here (mains are US$10 to US$20), which is novel but frankly not necessary – you'll get better food on land. It's best to come here for a cold Red Stripe (or rum, if such is your fancy). The bar's fame has spread far and wide, and the clientele is a mix of enchanted travelers and repeat-business fishers who while away the hours exchanging pleasantries with the owner.

Information

There are no banks serving international travelers here, but there is a 24-hour ATM in the Kingfisher Plaza in Calabash Bay.

For information online, a good starting point is www.treasurebeach.net.

The **Treasure Beach Foundation (Breds)** (Breds; 965-3000; www.breds.org; Kingfisher Plaza; 9am-5pm) is dedicated to fostering heritage pride, sports, health and education among the community, and represents a partnership between the Treasure Beach community, expats and stakeholders (Jamaican and foreign) in the local tourism industry (Breds is short for Brethren). This little place also acts as the unofficial tourist office.

Work includes restoring decrepit housing, sponsorship of both a soccer team and a basketball team, the introduction of computer labs at local schools and education for the children of fishers lost at sea.

Getting There & Away

Route taxis run several times daily to/from Black River (J$250 to J$350); from Mandeville, you'll need to get a route taxi to Junction or Santa Cruz and another taxi to Treasure Beach (J$220).

A private taxi will run around US$40 from Black River. Most hotels and villas arrange transfers from Montego Bay or Kingston for US$140.

Black River

The capital of St Elizabeth, Black River is a busy little place that was the most prosperous port in Jamaica in the late 19th century. The namesake river is a slow-moving slick of moldering tannins patrolled by crocodiles and boats full of curious tourists. Most visitors opt to stay in nearby Treasure Beach, but Black River makes a good jumping-off point for visiting attractions like YS Falls and the Appleton Rum Estate, and there's a charm to its historic core that's well worth exploring. The town's Georgian buildings attest to its 19th-century prosperity, when Black River exported sugarcane and local logwood from which Prussian blue dye was extracted for textiles.

Locals proudly point out the Waterloo Guest House, which in 1893 became the first house in Jamaica to have electricity installed.

Tours

J Charles Swaby's Black River Safari BOATING
(962-0220, 965-2513; tour US$20; tours 9am, 11am, 12:30pm, 2pm & 3:30pm) Longest-established operator of croc safari tours offering five daily departures from the east side of the river.

St Elizabeth Safari BOATING
(965-2374; tour US$20; tours 9am, 11am, 2pm & 3:30pm) Tours of Great Morass on large watercraft depart from behind the Hendricks Building.

Way Back When Heritage Tours WALKING
(530-6902; www.real-jamaica-vacations.com/way-back-when.html; per person US$30) Local historian Allison Morris runs engaging walking tours, departing from the parish church and lasting around 1½ hours. She talks you through the history of Black River, shows you local monuments and historic buildings, and brings prominent local figures to life, including her own ancestors. She typically runs tours on Thursdays and Fridays, and also during school holidays; call ahead.

Eating

★ **Cloggy's on the Beach** SEAFOOD $$
(634-2424; 22 Crane Rd; mains J$800-2500; noon-10pm) This beachside joint is your best culinary bet in Black River; it's an all-round pleaser with a relaxed vibe, breezy beachfront terrace and mellow reggae grooving from the oversized speakers. Try a cup of conch soup for a revelation, and follow that up with some gorgeous curried lobster or jerk parrotfish. It occasionally throws well-attended beach sound-system parties, too.

Getting There & Away

Black River is a nexus for route taxis that shoot off in all directions. Along High St there are taxis that depart for Treasure Beach (J$250). Minibuses go to Montego Bay (J$250 to J$300) and Sav-la-Mar (J$220) from the **transportation center** (Brigade St) behind the market.

UNDERSTAND JAMAICA

Jamaica Today

Jamaica sells itself as a destination where you're rarely troubled by anything more pressing than where your next rum cocktail is coming from, but the country is a far more interesting, exciting and complicated place than that. In recent years the economy has stabilized greatly, with the government's debt-to-GDP ratio finally falling below 100%. Tourism remains the most important hard currency earner, but the state of emergency in some parts of the country (including Montego Bay) in response to violent crime hasn't helped perceptions.

The country has been eyeing up changing social (and legal) attitudes to marijuana, with efforts to build up a medical ganja industry, including dispensaries that have become popular with visitors. Even more successful, however, remains its world-beating music scene, with recent triumphs like the return of reggae hero Buju Banton complemented by the rise of bright young stars like Koffee.

History

Columbus & the Arawaks

Christopher Columbus landed on Jamaica in 1494. At the time there were perhaps 10,000 peaceful Arawaks, who had settled Jamaica around AD 700. Spanish settlers arrived from 1510 and quickly introduced two things that would profoundly shape the island's future: sugarcane production and slavery. By the end of the 16th century the Arawak population had been entirely wiped out, worn down by hard labor, ill-treatment and European diseases.

Arrival of the English

In 1654 an ill-equipped and badly organized English contingent sailed to the Caribbean. After failing to take Hispaniola, they turned to weakly defended Jamaica. Despite the ongoing efforts of Spanish loyalists and the guerilla-style campaigns of runaway enslaved Africans (*cimarrones* – 'wild ones' – or Maroons), England took control of the island.

Slave Colony

New slaves kept on arriving; bloody insurrections kept occurring. The last and largest was the 1831 Christmas Rebellion, inspired by Sam Sharpe, an educated slave who incited passive resistance. The rebellion turned violent as up to 20,000 slaves razed plantations and murdered planters. When the slaves were tricked into laying down arms with a false promise of abolition – and 400 were hanged and hundreds more whipped – there was a wave of revulsion in England, causing the British parliament to finally abolish slavery.

The transition from a slave to wage-labor economy caused chaos, with most of the formerly enslaved rejecting the starvation wages offered on the estates and choosing to fend for themselves.

Road to Independence

A banana-led economic recovery was halted by the Great Depression of the 1930s, and then kick-started again by WWII, when the Caribbean islands supplied food and raw materials to Britain. Adult suffrage for all Jamaicans was introduced in 1944, and virtual autonomy from Britain was granted in 1947. Jamaica seceded from the short-lived West Indies Federation in 1962 after a referendum called for the island's full independence.

Postindependence politics have been dominated by the legacy of two cousins: Alexander Bustamante, who formed the first trade union in the Caribbean just prior to WWII and later formed the Jamaican Labor Party (JLP); and Norman Manley, whose People's National Party (PNP) was the first political party on the island when it was convened in 1938. Manley's son, Michael, led the PNP toward democratic socialism in the mid-1970s, causing capital flight at a time when Jamaica could ill afford it. Bitterly opposed factions engaged in open urban warfare preceding the 1976 election, but the PNP won the election by a wide margin and Manley continued with his socialist agenda.

Power Struggles

The US government was hostile to the path Jamaica was taking and when Manley began to develop close ties with Cuba, the CIA purportedly planned to topple the government. Businesses pulled out, the economy went into sharp decline and the country lived virtually under siege. Almost 700 people were killed in the lead-up to the 1980 elections, which were won by the JLP's Edward Seaga. Seaga restored Jamaica's economic fortunes somewhat, severed ties with Cuba and courted Ronald Reagan's USA. Seaga was ousted in 1989 and replaced by Manley, who took a short, second crack at the prime ministerial office. He retired in 1992, handing the reins to his deputy, Percival James Patterson, Jamaica's first black prime minister.

Present & Future

In 2007 Bruce Golding of the JLP was elected prime minister, ending 18 years of PNP rule. Three years later the USA called for the extradition of Christopher 'Dudus' Coke, the don of Tivoli Gardens ghetto and one of the most powerful men in Jamaica. The demand for extradition was originally refused by Golding, who claimed that the evidence against Dudus was gathered illegally, but after American pressure the police moved against Dudus in a bloody battle that left 67 dead. Dudus himself was apprehended at a roadblock, disguised as a woman and en route to the US embassy to negotiate his surrender.

Jamaica's current prime minister is Andrew Holness of the JLP. Most Jamaicans will tell you the greatest issues facing the country are crime and the brain drain to the USA, Canada and the UK. Illiteracy is also a major concern, as are threats to the environment through deforestation and overdevelopment. In the meantime the Jamaican people face the future with resolve and a measure of good humor – they've endured worse in the past.

People & Culture

Religion

Jamaica professes to have the greatest number of churches per square kilometer in the world. Although most foreigners associate the island with Rastafari, more than 80% of Jamaicans identify themselves as Christian and the Church remains a powerful political lobby group in the country.

Literature

The current star on Jamaica's literary scene is undoubtedly Marlon James, author of *A Brief History of Seven Killings* and *The Book of Night Women*, but other hot names to look out for include Kei Miller (*The Last Warner Woman, August Town*), Olive Senior (*Dancing Lessons*) and Garfield Ellis (*For Nothing at All*). Nicole Dennis-Benn's debut novel *Here Comes the Sun* announced the arrival of another great Jamaican writer in 2016.

The novels of Anthony Winkler are celebrated for the wry eye they cast over Jamaican life, most notably in *The Lunatic*, *The Duppy* and *The Family Mansion*.

Music

Modern Jamaican music starts with the acoustic folk music of mento. In the early 1960s, this blended with calypso, jazz and R&B to form ska, the country's first popular music form. This evolved, via the intermediate step of rocksteady, into the bass-heavy reggae of the 1970s, the genre that ultimately swept all before it. Dancehall, a faster and more clubby sound than its predecessors, followed thereafter, and continues to dominate the contemporary music scene today. For all that these styles are distinct, they constantly blend and feed off each other – this syncretism is the true magic of Jamaican music.

REGGAE

In his song 'Trench Town,' Bob Marley asked if anything good could ever come from Jamaica's ghettoes. In doing so, he challenged the class-based assumptions of Jamaican society, with the minority elite ruling over the disenfranchised masses. Of course, the answer came in the message of pride and spiritual redemption contained in the music itself, as reggae left the yard to conquer the world, in the process turning Bob Marley into a true global icon.

Bob Marley's band, The Wailers, sprang from the ska and rocksteady era of the 1960s. Producers Lee 'Scratch' Perry, Clement 'Sir Coxsone' Dodd and King Tubby played a key role in evolving the more spacious new reggae sound, while the resurgence of Rastafarianism that followed Haile Selassie's 1966 visit to Jamaica inspired the music's soul. Through his signing of The Wailers, the Jamaican-born founder of Island Records, Chris Blackwell, helped introduce reggae to an international audience.

Reggae is more than just Marley. His original bandmates Peter Tosh and Bunny Wailer both became major stars, joining a pantheon that runs from Desmond Dekker and Dennis Brown to Burning Spear and Gregory Isaacs. While dancehall has since taken over as Jamaica's most popular domestic music, in recent years there has been something of a roots reggae revival, with artists such as Chronixx, Proteje and Jah9 bringing back some rasta consciousness to rejuvenate the genre for the new century.

RASTAFARI

Dreadlocked Rastas are as synonymous with Jamaica as reggae. Developed in the 1930s, the Rastafari creed evolved as an expression of poor, black Jamaicans seeking fulfillment, boosted by Marcus Garvey's 'back to Africa' zeal.

Central to Rastafari is the concept that the Africans are one of the displaced 12 Tribes of Israel. Jamaica is Babylon, and their lot is in exile in a land that cannot be reformed. The crowning of Ras Tafari (Haile Selassie) as emperor of Abyssinia in 1930 fulfilled the prophecy of an African king and redeemer who would lead them from exile to the promised land of Zion, the black race's spiritual home.

Ganja smoking is a sacrament for many (if not all) Rastas, allowing them to gain wisdom and inner divinity through the ability to 'reason' more clearly. The parsing of Bible verses is an essential tradition, helping to see through the corrupting influences of Babylon. The growing of dreadlocks is an allegory for the mane of the Lion of Judah.

Despite its militant consciousness, the religion preaches love and nonviolence, and adherents live by strict biblical codes advocating a way of life in harmony with Old Testament traditions. Some Rastas are teetotalers who shun tobacco and keep to a strict diet of vegan I-tal food, prepared without salt; others, like the 12 Tribes Rastafari, eat meat and drink beer.

DANCEHALL

The modern sound of Jamaica is definitely dancehall: rapid-fire chanting over bass-heavy beats. It's simplistic to just call dancehall Jamaican rap, because the formation of the beats, their structure and the nuances of the lyrics all have deep roots in Jamaica's musical past.

The new sound sprang up at the close of the 1970s, with DJs such as Yellowman, Lone Ranger and Josey Wales, who grabbed the mic and powered the high-energy rhythms through the advent of faster, more digital beats. This was a period of turmoil in Jamaica, and the music reacted by moving away from political consciousness towards a more hedonistic vibe. The scene centered on the sound systems and 'sound clashes' between DJs, dueling with custom records to win the crowd's favor and boost their reputation.

By the 1990s the success of artists such as Shabba Ranks turned dancehall global, but stars including Buju Banton, Beenie Man, Bounty Killer and Sizzla continue to be criticized for lyrics celebrating violence and homophobia. This came to a peak in 2014 with the conviction for murder of 'World Boss' Vybz Kartel, dancehall's biggest and most innovative star. Curiously, his prison sentence has barely slowed his music release schedule. Criticism of dancehall's more outlandish facets is a staple of the Jamaican press, but for all this, dancehall remains in rude health – Sean Paul and Konshens have long ascended into international stardom, while acts such as Cham and Tommy Lee ride the riddims at home.

Sports

If anyone can wrest away Bob Marley's mantle as the world's most recognizable Jamaican, it's the ultra-charismatic Usain Bolt, currently the fastest man on the planet and 'triple-triple' Olympic gold winner, winning gold in the 100m, 200m and 400m relay at the Beijing, London and Rio games. He's part of Jamaica's astonishing home-grown crop of athletics champions, along with Shelly-Ann Fraser-Pryce and Elaine Thompson (both Olympic 100m and 200m gold medal holders).

Jamaica is cricket mad, and cricketers like fast bowler Courtney Walsh and batsman Chris Gayle are revered. Jamaica plays nationally as part of the West Indies team, who were quarter-finalists in the 2011 and 2015 World Cups, and champions in the 2012 and 2016 World Twenty20. Jamaican cricket's home is Sabina Park in Kingston, which hosts national and international test matches as well as the Caribbean Premier League (CPL), of which the Jamaican Tallawahs are the 2016 champions.

Landscape & Wildlife

The Land

At 10,991 sq km (roughly equal to the US state of Connecticut, or half the size of Wales), Jamaica is the largest of the English-speaking Caribbean islands. It is one of the Greater Antilles, which make up the westernmost Caribbean islands, and is a near neighbor to Cuba and Haiti.

'Mainland' Jamaica is rimmed by a narrow coastal plain, except for the southern broad flatlands. Mountains form the island's spine, rising gradually from the west and culminating in the Blue Mountains in the east, which are capped by Blue Mountain Peak at 2256m. The island is cut by about 120 rivers, many of which are bone dry for much of the year but spring to life after heavy rains, causing great flooding and damage to roads. Coastal mangroves, wetland preserves and montane cloud forests form small specialized ecosystems that contain a wide variety of the island's wildlife. Offshore, small islands called cays offer further habitats for marine life.

Wildlife

The island has more than 255 bird species. Stilt-legged, snowy-white cattle egrets are ubiquitous, as are 'John crows' (turkey vultures), which are the subject of several folk songs and proverbs. Jamaica's national bird is the 'doctor bird' or red-billed streamertail – an indigenous hummingbird with shimmering emerald feathers, a velvety black crown with purple crest, a long bill and curved tail feathers.

Coral reefs lie along the north shore, where the reef is almost continuous and much of it is within a few hundred meters of shore. Over 700 species of fish zip in and out of the exquisite reefs and swarm through the coral canyons. Last but not least, three species of endangered marine turtles – the green, hawksbill and loggerhead – lay eggs on Jamaica's beaches.

DANEFROMSPAIN/GETTY IMAGES ©

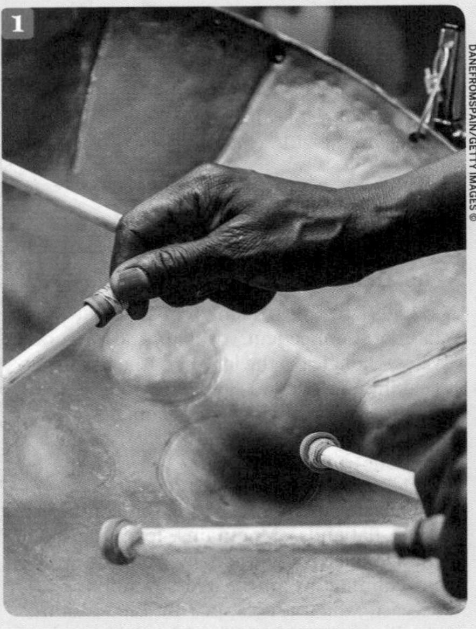

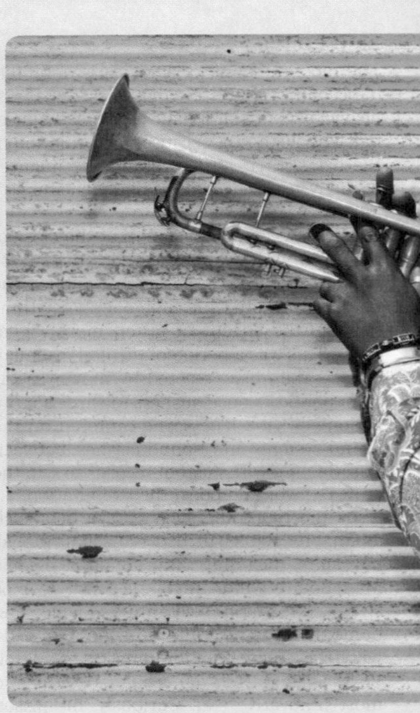

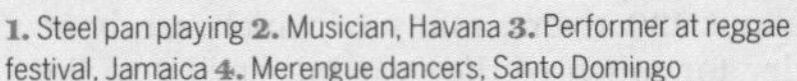

1. Steel pan playing **2.** Musician, Havana **3.** Performer at reggae festival, Jamaica **4.** Merengue dancers, Santo Domingo

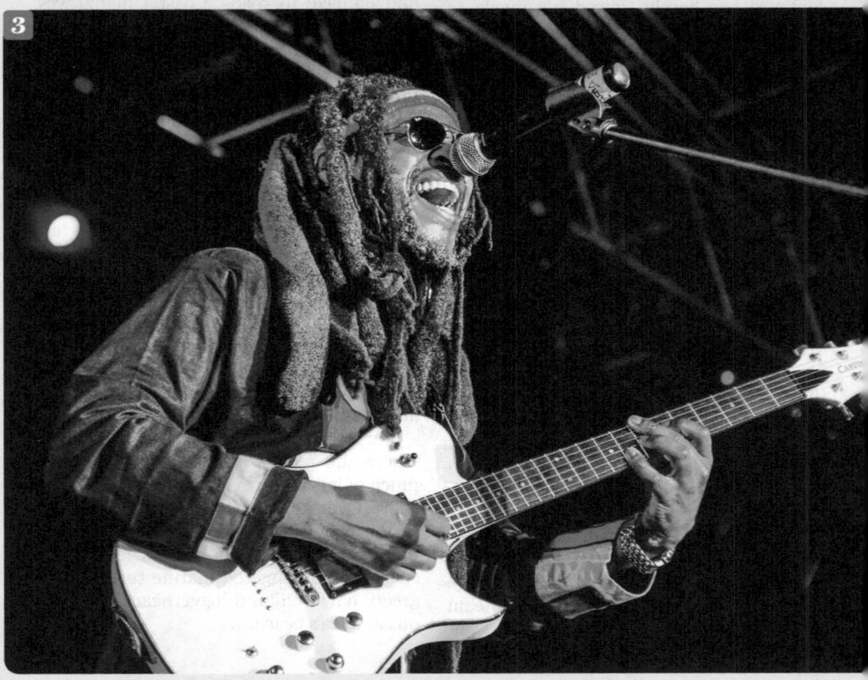

BIM/GETTY IMAGES ©

Sounds of the Caribbean

From the brassy swagger of a salsa band to the lolling gait of reggae, the music of the Caribbean draws influences from both plantation fields and colonial parlors, and is as elemental to the islands as the sound of crashing surf.

Steel Pan & Calypso

Hammered from oil barrels, the ringing drums of steel-pan bands are a testament to the adaptive ingenuity of Caribbean musicians. The drums play buoyant calypso, often punched up with braggadocio lyrics or laced with social commentary.

Reggae

Born in the late '60s, reggae is the musical descendant of uniquely Jamaican genres ska and rocksteady. With a languid offbeat shuffle and an ambassador in Bob Marley, it's a cornerstone of island culture.

Cuban Music

Though every destination has its own musical language, no place speaks as fluently as Cuba, where music seems to pour out of every alleyway.

Salsa

Like trade winds circling Puerto Rico, the Dominican Republic, Cuba and Nueva York, salsa's hip-grinding groove is a prized multi-island export. The sound has roots in African rhythms and indigenous islander instruments.

Merengue

The blistering rhythms of this Dominican genre of music are inseparable from the highly stylized, passionate dance bearing the same name.

SURVIVAL GUIDE

Directory A–Z

ACCESSIBLE TRAVEL

Very few allowances have been made in Jamaica for travelers with disabilities, although larger hotels and all-inclusives (especially those owned by international brands) tend to be more accessible, with ramps and elevators.

ACCOMMODATIONS

If you're traveling on a shoestring, head to simple guesthouses or hostels. In the midrange category there's a wide range of choice in appealing small hotels, many with splendid gardens, sea views or both. If traveling with your family or a group, consider one of the hundreds of villas available to rent across the island. And if you've decided to splurge, Jamaica's luxury hotels rank among the finest in the world.

Low season (summer) is usually mid-April to early December; the high season (winter) is the remainder of the year, when hotel prices increase by 40% or more. All-inclusive packages are usually based on three-day minimum stays.

ELECTRICITY

Power plugs and sockets are of type A and B (110V, 50 Hz).

EMBASSIES & CONSULATES

If your country isn't represented in this list, check 'Embassies & High Commissions' in the Yellow Pages of the Greater Kingston telephone directory.

Canadian High Commission (926-1500; www.canadainternational.gc.ca/jamaica-jamaique; 3 West Kings House Rd, Waterloo Rd entrance; 8am-noon & 1-4:30pm Mon-Thu, 8am-noon Fri)

Dutch Consulate (754-1248; netherlandsinjam@gmail.com; 58 Hope Rd; 9am-noon Mon-Fri)

French Embassy (619-7812; www.ambafrance-jm-bm.org; 13 Hillcrest Ave, Kingston 6; 9am-noon Mon-Fri)

German Embassy (926-6728; www.kingston.diplo.de; 10 Waterloo Rd, Kingston 10)

Japanese Embassy (929-7534; www.jamaica.eab-japan.go.jp; 6th Floor, NCB Towers, North Tower, 2 Oxford Rd, Kingston 5; 9am-5pm Mon-Fri)

UK High Commission (936-0700; www.gov.uk/world/jamaica; 28 Trafalgar Rd, Kingston; 9am-4pm Mon-Thu, 9am-1pm Fri)

US Embassy (702-6000, after hours 702-6055; https://jm.usembassy.gov/; 142 Old Hope Rd, Kingston; 7:15am-4pm Mon-Fri)

SLEEPING PRICE RANGES

Unless otherwise stated, the following price ranges refer to a double room in high season with European Plan (room only with bathroom), with the compulsory 6.25% to 15% GCT included in the price.

$ less than US$90

$$ US$90–200

$$$ more than US$200

EMERGENCY & IMPORTANT NUMBERS

Ambulance	110
Directory assistance	114
International operator	113
Police	119
Tourism board	929-9200

FOOD

Jamaican cuisine has the weight and heft of a peasant's diet, with heavy starches and the colorful flavor you associate with the crossroads of the Caribbean. The Taínos introduced callaloo, cassava, corn, sweet potatoes and tropical fruits; the Spanish tossed in *escoveich* (a variation on ceviche); the Africans added yams, rice, stews and smoked meat; Indians contributed their curries and rotis; and the English wrapped it all up in a meat pie.

HEALTH

Acceptable health care is available in most major cities and larger towns throughout Jamaica, but may be hard to locate in rural areas. To find a good local doctor, your best bet is to ask the management of the hotel where you are staying or contact your embassy in Kingston or Montego Bay. Note that many doctors and hospitals expect payment on the spot, regardless of whether you have travel health insurance, and even at the island's best hospitals in Kingston you may encounter nonfunctioning MRI scanners and similar.

Many pharmacies are well supplied, but important medications may not be consistently available. Be sure to bring along adequate supplies of all prescription drugs.

INTERNET ACCESS

- Wi-fi is available in Jamaican hotels, but internet access is still restricted in rural areas. Data services are available throughout the country, although 3G reception can be patchy.
- Most town libraries offer internet access (US$1 for 30 minutes), and there's usually at least one commercial entity where you can get online.

LEGAL MATTERS

➡ Jamaica's drug and drink-driving laws are strictly enforced.

➡ Don't expect leniency just because you're a foreigner. Jamaican jails are distinctly unpleasant.

➡ Ganja has been decriminalized and possession of up to 2oz attracts a fine rather than arrest.

➡ If arrested, insist on your right to call your embassy in Kingston to request assistance.

LGBT+ TRAVELERS

There is a gay scene in Kingston, but it is an underground affair as Jamaica is a largely homophobic society. Sexual acts between men are prohibited by law and punishable by up to 10 years in prison. Many reggae dancehall lyrics by big-name stars could be classified as antigay hate speech. Gay-bashing incidents are almost never prosecuted, with law enforcement, in most cases, looking the other way.

Nonetheless, you shouldn't be put off from visiting the island. In the more heavily touristed areas you'll find more tolerant attitudes and hotels that welcome gay travelers, including all-inclusives. Publicly, though, discretion is important and open displays of affection should be avoided.

Useful websites:

Gay Jamaica Watch (www.gayjamaicawatch.blogspot.com)

J-FLAG (www.jflag.org)

Quality of Citizenship Jamaica (www.qcjm.org)

MONEY

➡ The unit of currency is the Jamaican dollar, the 'jay,' which uses the same symbol as the US dollar ($). Jamaican currency is issued in bank notes of J$50, J$100, J$500, J$1000 and (rarely) J$5000. Prices for hotels and valuable items are usually quoted in US dollars, which are widely accepted.

EATING PRICE RANGES

The following price ranges are based on the cost of an average meal at a Jamaican restaurant. Watch out for menus adding 16.5% government tax and a further 10% service charge to the bill.

$ Less than J$1900

$$ J$1900–3200

$$$ More than J$3200

➡ Commercial banks have branches throughout the island. Those in major towns maintain a foreign-exchange booth.

➡ Most towns have 24-hour ATMs linked to international networks such as Cirrus or Plus. In more remote areas, look for ATMs at gas stations. In tourist areas, some ATMs also dispense US dollars.

➡ Traveler's checks are little used and attract fees for cashing.

➡ Major credit cards are accepted throughout the island, although local groceries and the like may not be able to process them, even in Kingston.

Exchange Rates

Australia	A$1	J$91
Canada	C$1	J$101
Euro zone	€1	J$149
Japan	¥100	J$127
New Zealand	NZ$1	J$87
UK	UK£1	J$163
US	US$1	J$135

For current exchange rates see www.xe.com.

Tipping

Hotels A 10% tip is normal in hotels and restaurants.

GANJA

The Jamaican parliament decriminalized possession of ganja in 2015, and possession of up to 2oz (56g) is now treatable in the same manner as a parking offense, garnering a fine of up to J$500 (around US$3) but no criminal record. Smoking in private residences is no longer an offense. A number of licensed medical marijuana dispensaries have opened, for which a prescription is required.

While some travelers are keen to seek it out, even those wanting to avoid it are unlikely to get through their trip without at least a whiff of secondhand smoke. You'll undoubtedly be approached by people offering to sell you ganja, whether a 'nudge wink' hustler, or a vendor at a dancehall street party openly selling it alongside candies and rum. If you want to smoke, we still recommend doing so discreetly, at your hotel. Some local strains are particularly strong, and tourists have reported suffering harmful side effects from ganja, especially from ganja cakes and cookies.

Resorts Some all-inclusive resorts have a strictly enforced no-tipping policy.
Restaurants Check your bill carefully – some restaurants automatically add a 10% to 15% service charge.
Taxis Outside Kingston, tourist taxi drivers often ask for tips but it is not necessary; JUTA (Jamaica Union of Travelers Association) route taxis do not expect tips.

OPENING HOURS

The following are standard hours for Jamaica; exceptions are noted in reviews. Note that the country virtually shuts down on Sunday.
Banks 9:30am–4pm Monday to Friday
Bars Usually from noon until the last customer stumbles out
Businesses 8:30am–4:30pm Monday to Friday
Restaurants Breakfast dawn–11am; lunch noon–2pm; dinner 5:30pm–11pm
Shops 8am or 9am–5pm Monday to Friday, to noon or 5pm Saturday, late-night shopping to 9pm Thursday and Friday

PUBLIC HOLIDAYS

New Year's Day January 1
Ash Wednesday, **Good Friday** & **Easter Monday**
Labor Day May 23
Emancipation Day August 1
Independence Day First Monday in August
National Heroes Day Third Monday in October
Christmas Day December 25
Boxing Day December 26

PRACTICALITIES

Newspapers The *Jamaica Gleaner* (www.jamaica-gleaner.com) is the high-standard newspaper. Its rival is the *Jamaica Observer*, followed by the gossipy tabloid *Jamaica Star*.

Radio Of the 43 radio stations, Irie FM (105.1FM; www.iriefm.net) is the most popular.

Smoking Banned in public places (including bars and restaurants).

TV There are nine channels; most hotels have satellite TV with US channels.

Weights & measures Metric and imperial measurements are both used. Distances are measured in meters and kilometers, and gas in liters, but coffee (and ganja) is most often sold by the pound.

SAFE TRAVEL

Organized crime is present in Jamaica but rarely affects visitors. In cities such as Kingston and Montego Bay, commonsense precautions apply.

- Take a taxi back to your accommodations if you're out at night in Kingston, MoBay or any large town.
- If hustlers are trying to sell you something you don't want, be polite but firm.
- Be equally polite but firm when turning down unwanted sexual advances.
- Be aware that while ganja is decriminalized, other drugs are not.
- Watch your wallet in crowded places.
- Carry as little cash as you need when away from your hotel and don't flash your valuables.

TELEPHONE

Jamaica's country code is 876. To call Jamaica from the US, dial 1-876 + the seven-digit local number. From elsewhere, dial your country's international dialing code, then 876 and the local number.

For calls within the same parish in Jamaica, just dial the local number. Between parishes, dial 1 + the local number. We have included only the seven-digit local number in Jamaica listings.

Cell phones

You can bring your own cell (mobile) phone into Jamaica (GSM or CDMA). Some networks in the US and in Europe include Jamaica in their roaming packages; otherwise, beware of hefty roaming charges and buy a local SIM card.

If your phone is unlocked, buy a local SIM card from one of the two local cell-phone operators, Digicel (www.digiceljamaica.com) or Flow (www.discoverflow/jamaica), or you can buy a cheap handset. You'll need to bring ID to buy either. SIM cards are free – ask for the best current offers, usually from around J$500 for calls plus data. Prepaid top-up cards are sold in denominations from J$50 to J$1000, and you'll find them at many gas stations and grocery stores.

Getting There & Away

AIR

There are daily direct flights to Jamaica's two international airports from major cities in Europe and North America, as well as a number of Caribbean destinations.

Jamaica has two international airports, Norman Manley International Airport (p520) in Kingston and Donald Sangster International Airport (p535) in Montego Bay.

Useful regional airlines:
Caribbean Airlines (876-744-2225; www.caribbean-airlines.com)
Cayman Airways (www.caymanairways.com)

COPA Airlines (www.copaair.com)

Fly Jamaica (☎876-656-9832; www.fly-jamaica.com)

SEA

Jamaica is a popular destination on the cruise roster, mainly for passenger liners but also for private yachts.

For maps and charts of the Caribbean, contact **Bluewater Books & Charts** (☎800-942-2583; www.bluewaterweb.com). The **National Oceanic & Atmospheric Administration** (☎888-990-6622; www.nauticalcharts.noaa.gov) sells US government charts.

Many yachties make the trip to Jamaica from North America. Upon arrival in Jamaica, you *must* clear customs and immigration at Montego Bay, Kingston, Ocho Rios or Port Antonio. In addition, you'll need to clear customs at *each* port of call. The main ports for yachts:

- **Errol Flynn Marina** (☎993-3209, 715-6044; www.errolflynnmarina.com; Port Antonio, GPS N 18.168889°, W -76.450556°)
- **Montego Bay Yacht Club** (☎979-8038; www.mobayyachtclub.com; Montego Bay Freeport, GPS N 18.462452°, W -77.943267°; ⏲10am-10pm)
- **Royal Jamaican Yacht Club** (☎924-8685; www.rjyc.org.jm; Palisadoes Park, Kingston; GPS: N 17.940939°, W -76.764939°)

Getting Around

BICYCLE

Mountain bikes and 'beach cruisers' (bikes with fat tires, suitable for riding on sand) can be rented at most major resorts (US$10 to US$30 per day). Road conditions can be poor when off the main highways, and Jamaican drivers are not considerate of cyclists. For serious touring, bring your own mountain or multipurpose bike.

CAR & MOTORCYCLE

To drive in Jamaica, you must have a valid International Driver's License (IDL) or a current license for your home country or state, valid for at least six months, and be at least 21 years of age.

Car Rental

Most major international car-rental companies operate in Jamaica, including **Avis** (www.avis.com.jm) and **Hertz** (www.hertz.com).

Local car-hire firms can be a lot cheaper than the international brands. Recommended firms:

Beaumont Car Rentals (☎876-926-0311; www.beaumontcarrentalja.com)

Island Car Rentals (☎876-929-5875; www.islandcarrentals.com)

Fuel & Spare Parts

Many gas stations close at 7pm or so. In rural areas, stations are usually closed on Sunday. At the time of writing, gasoline/diesel cost about J$120/112 per liter.

Road Conditions

Jamaica's roads run from modern multilane highways to barely passable tracks.

Jamaica's best road is the new highway between Kingston and Ocho Rios, which has dramatically cut transit times to the north coast. It's a toll road – cars pay around J$1000.

You can expect any road with the designation 'A' to be in fairly good condition. 'B' roads are generally much more narrow and often badly potholed, but still passable in the average rental car. Minor roads, particularly those in the Blue Mountains and Cockpit Country, can be hellish. If you plan to drive off the major routes, it's essential to have a stalwart 4WD.

Laid-back Jamaica has some of the world's rudest and most dangerously aggressive drivers. Use extreme caution and drive defensively.

Road Rules

- Always drive on the left.
- Jamaica has a compulsory seat-belt law.
- Speed limits range from 50km/h to 80km/h and vary from place to place across the island.
- Carry ID and all relevant car-rental paperwork at all times, since police may pull you over.

PUBLIC TRANSPORTATION

An extensive transportation network links virtually every village and comprises several options that range from standard public buses to private taxis, with minibuses and plentiful route taxis in between that have become more prolific and reach most places.

There is usually no set timetable – buses leave when the driver considers them full – and passengers are crammed in with little regard for comfort. Taxis and buses tend to fill quickly early in the morning (before 8am) and around 5pm as people depart for work or home. There are fewer public transport options on Sunday.

Public buses, minibuses and route taxis depart from and arrive at each town's transportation station, which is usually near the main market. Locals can direct you to the appropriate vehicle, which should have its destination marked above the front window (for buses) or on its side.

Bus

Knutsford Express (Map p515; ☎971-1822; www.knutsfordexpress.com; 18 Dominica Dr, New Kingston Shopping Center parking lot) operates big comfortable, air-conditioned coaches and covers most destinations. Sample fares/times are Kingston–Ocho Rios (J$2150, two hours) and Kingston–Montego Bay (J$3250, four hours). Online booking is available, along with student, senior and child fares.

Minibus

Private minibuses, also known as 'coasters,' have traditionally been the workhorses of Jamaica's regional public transportation system. All major towns and virtually every village in the country are served.

Licensed minibuses display red license plates with the initials PPV (public passenger vehicle) or have a JUTA (Jamaica Union of Travelers Association) insignia. JUTA buses are exclusively for tourists. Public coasters don't run to set timetables, but depart their point of origin when they're full. They're often overflowing, and most drivers seem to have a death wish.

Route Taxi

Communal route taxis are the most universal mode of public transportation, reaching every part of the country. They run on set routes, picking up as many people as they can along the way. They're very convenient and are a cheap way of getting around the island and to remoter villages. Simply pick them up at their terminal in town (they go when full), or flag them down on the road and tell the driver where you want to get off. If you get in an empty taxi – particularly at the taxi station – be clear if you just want to pay the regular fare instead of a charter.

Most route taxis are white station wagons marked by their red license plates. They should have 'Route Taxi' marked on the front door, and they are not to be confused with similar licensed taxis, which charge more. Avoid any taxi that lacks the red license plate.

Martinique

☎596 / POP 390,000

Includes ➡

Best Places to Eat

- La Table de Mamy Nounou (p574)
- New Cap (p563)
- 1643 (p571)
- Le Guérin (p571)
- Cocoa Beach Cafe (p574)

Best Places to Stay

- Domaine Saint Aubin (p570)
- L'Anse Bleue (p563)
- La Maison Rousse (p571)
- Hotel Bakoua (p562)
- Hotel Simon (p556)

Why Go?

Volcanic in origin, Martinique is a mountainous stunner crowned by the still-smoldering Mont Pelée, the volcano that famously wiped out the former capital of St-Pierre in 1902. Offering a striking diversity of landscapes and atmospheres, Martinique is a cosmopolitan and sophisticated island that boasts world-class beaches, top-notch hiking, great culinary experiences, an enormous array of activities and some colorful cultural life.

While it suffers from overcrowding and urban sprawl in some places, particularly in and around the busy capital, Fort-de-France, life – and travel – becomes more sedate as one heads north or south through some of the island's alluring scenery. The rainforested, mountainous north is the most spectacular, but the south has its fair share of natural wonders, including lovely bays and miles of gorgeous beaches. Add to this a dash of Gallic joie de vivre and you'll understand why so many people love Martinique.

When to Go

Dec–Apr Dry season, and Martinique's busiest time, with crowds of French holidaymakers and peak hotel costs.

May–Nov Rainy season, with heavy showers most days. September is the rainiest month and, with August, most prone to hurricanes.

Oct–May The best months for diving.

FORT-DE-FRANCE

Even if you've come to Martinique for the beaches, you'll be very glad to spend a day in vibrant Fort-de-France, the island's capital and by far the biggest city in the French West Indies. A popular destination for cruise ships, international yachties and French tourists, the bustling center has everything from tranquil parks and a tiny beach to colorful local markets and worthwhile restaurants, its lively streets contrasting starkly with the rest of often sleepy Martinique.

The obvious attraction is Fort St-Louis, from which the city takes it name. The capital is also a superb shopping destination and the best place to source local souvenirs.

Sights

★Fort St-Louis FORT

(☎0596-75-41-44; adult/child €8/4; ⏰9am-4pm Tue-Sat, tour in English at noon; 🚸) The hulking fortress that gave the city its name lies on the far side of La Savane and dates from 1640, although most of what stands today is the result of subsequent additions. It's easily the top sight in town, and guided tours are informative and fun. Buy tickets at the **tourist information kiosk** (⏰8am-5pm Mon-Sat) in La Savane.

Bibliothèque Schoelcher NOTABLE BUILDING

(☎0596-55-68-30; 1 Rue de la Liberté; ⏰1-5pm Mon, 8:30am-5:30pm Tue-Thu, to 5pm Fri, to noon Sat) FREE Fort-de-France's most visible landmark, the Bibliothèque Schoelcher is an elaborate, colorful building with a Byzantine dome and an interesting ornate interior. The library was built in Paris and displayed at the 1889 World Exposition. It was then dismantled, shipped in pieces to Fort-de-France and reassembled in its current location. It's the work of Pierre-Henri Picq (1833–1911), who also designed Fort-de-France's **cathedral** (Rue Schoelcher; ⏰dawn-dusk) and **covered market** (Rue Blénac; ⏰6am-6pm Mon-Sat).

Note that this is a working library where students come to write essays. No photography is permitted inside the building.

La Savane PARK

This rectangular park at the heart of Fort-de-France was created when a mangrove swamp was drained after the city became the capital. As well as a hallowed central lawn that nobody walks on, there are all sorts of spaces to sit and relax. A long strip of cafes, restaurants and bars along the western side serves as the city's main evening entertainment area. The park hosts everything from school sports days to rock concerts.

Plage La Française BEACH

This tiny but clean beach in front of the Fort St-Louis is a popular place to cool off right in the middle of Fort-de-France. Nearby is a playground popular with kids from the yachts moored in the bay and the many iguanas who call the area home.

TOUR COMPANIES

Star Voyage (www.starvoyage.com; Port de Plaisance, Marin) Based in Marin, this operator has over 30 years' experience offering chartered yachts to an international clientele.

Sparkling Charter (☎0596-74-81-68; www.sparkling-charter.com; Porte de Plaisance, Marin) A well-established and reputable company offering yachts for charter, with or without a skipper.

Tour Cycliste de la Martinique (www.cyclismemartinique.com; ⏰mid-Jul) You don't have to drive on Martinique's roads for long to see how popular cycling is here. This weeklong bicycle race is the highlight of the season, a kind of mini Tour de France.

Festivals & Events

Mardi Gras Carnival CARNIVAL

(⏰Feb/Mar) Booming, colorful festivities during the five-day period leading up to Ash Wednesday.

Sleeping

★L'Impératrice HOTEL $$

(☎0596-63-06-82; www.limperatricehotel.fr; 15 Rue de la Liberté; r from €90; ❄📶) Central and with a perfectly preserved art deco facade, the grand old Impératrice is a local landmark almost as well known for its atmospheric downstairs cafe as for its upstairs hotel. The 23 rooms are excellent, with laminate floors, dark-wood furniture, sparkling bathrooms and all modern comforts. Ask for a room on the upper floors – room 53 has the best views.

★Hotel Simon BUSINESS HOTEL $$

(☎0596-50-22-22; www.hotel-simon.com; 1 Ave Loulou Boilaville; r from €135; ❄📶) This impressive hotel next to Pointe Simon cruise-ship

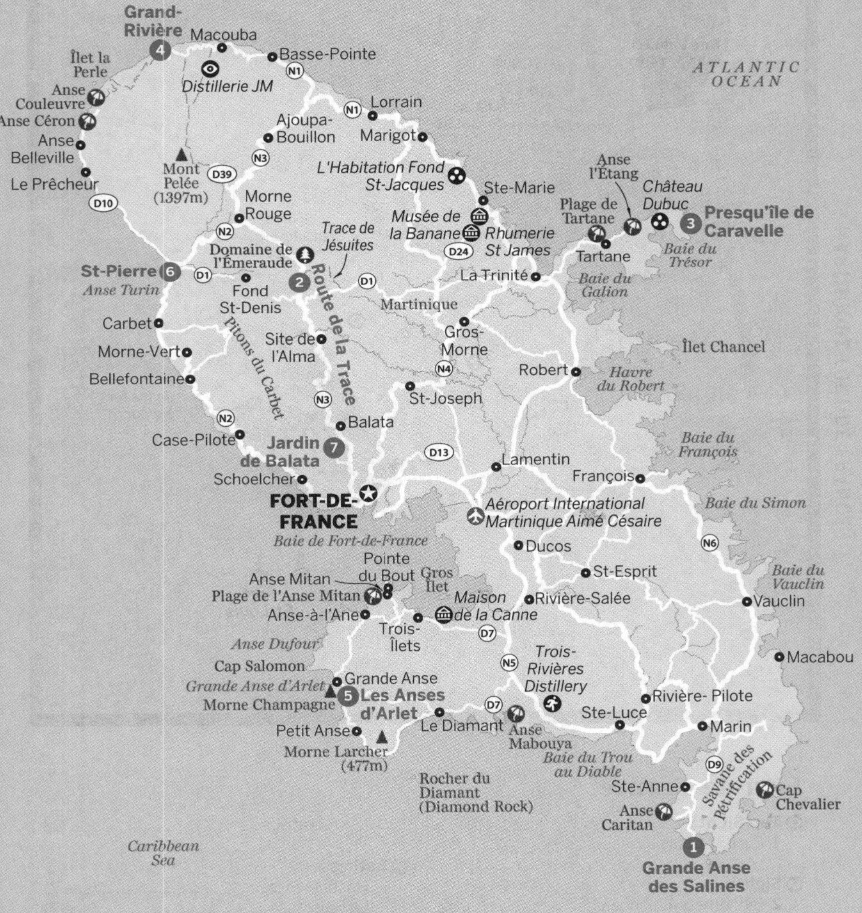

Martinique Highlights

1 Grande Anse des Salines (p567) Swimming and sunning yourself at one of the most beautiful beaches in the French Antilles.

2 Route de la Trace (p569) Driving this superb scenic road through the island's center, stopping for a walk in the foothills of Mont Pelée.

3 Presqu'île de Caravelle (p572) Delighting in the sun and sand by day and the gourmet flavors by night.

4 Grand-Rivière (p572) Hiking a dramatic 20km trail along Martinique's pristine and dramatic northern coast.

5 Les Anses d'Arlet (p563) Enjoying a beach day at any of these gorgeous coves in southwestern Martinique.

6 St-Pierre (p566) Witnessing the devastation of Mont Pelée firsthand, as the volcano broods in the distance.

7 Jardin de Balata (p559) Exploring the amazing variety of local plants at this excellent botanical garden.

Fort-de-France

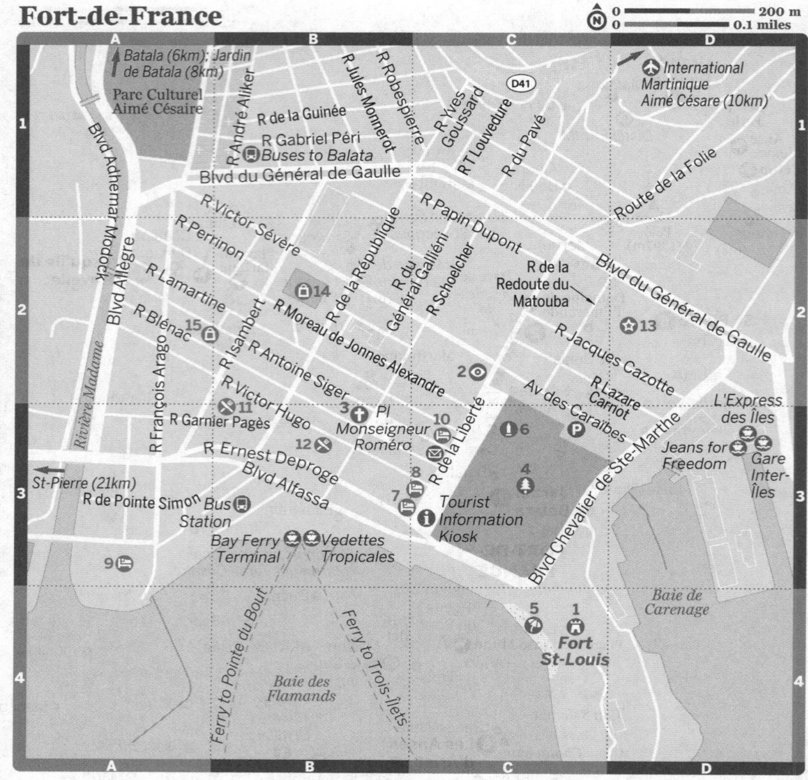

Fort-de-France

Top Sights
1 Fort St-Louis C4

Sights
2 Bibliothèque Schoelcher C2
3 Cathédrale St-Louis B3
4 La Savane C3
5 Plage La Française C4
6 Statue of Empress Josephine C3

Sleeping
7 Bayfront Hotel B3
8 Fort Savane C3
9 Hotel Simon A3
10 L'Impératrice C3

Eating
Hasta la Pizza .... (see 7)
La Baie .... (see 7)
11 Le Vieux Foyal B3
12 Le Yellow B3

Entertainment
13 Tropiques Atrium D2

Shopping
14 Cour Perrinon B2
15 Grand Marché A2

terminal (p560) opened in 2016 and overnight raised the bar in the Fort-de-France hotel market. The gorgeous, spacious rooms boast espresso machines and flat-screen TVs, and are crisply appointed and furnished with an appreciation for minimalist aesthetics. Public areas are similarly impressive, making this a cool oasis away from the city.

Fort Savane BUSINESS HOTEL $$
(☎0596-80-75-75; www.fortsavane.fr; 5 Rue de la Liberté; r/studios/ste €120/140/190; ❄📶) Once

you're buzzed into the building by rather indifferent staff, you'll discover an excellent-value place to stay with a great location and rather stylish rooms. All come with espresso makers and minimalist furnishings; studios also have kitchens, and suites have kitchens and lounges.

Bayfront Hotel HOTEL **$$**
(☎0596-55-55-55; bayfronthotel.mq@gmail.com; 3 Rue de la Liberté; r €90; ❄📶) Fort-de-France's most central hotel is located above a small cafe and boasts useful touches such as kitchens in most rooms. The 12 rooms are clean and comfortable, even if devoid of flair, and some have nice views over the sea and La Savane (p556).

Eating

★**Le Vieux Foyal** CREOLE **$$**
(☎0596-77-05-49; 22 Rue Garnier Pagès; mains €14-20; ⏲10am-3pm & 7-10pm Mon-Sat; ❄) Brimming with good cheer, this restaurant in a street running parallel to the seafront is that easy-to-miss 'secret spot' that local gourmands like to recommend. Everything is fresh and tasty – unfussy market cuisine at its best. The plant-filled rear patio is a haven of peace. Live dinnertime jazz on Thursday cranks the hip atmosphere up a notch.

Hasta la Pizza PIZZA **$$**
(Rue de la Liberté; pizza €7-25; ⏲9am-10:30pm Mon-Sat, 4-11pm Sun; 📶) This friendly pizzeria has a prime seafront location and always seems to be busy with people crowding around its roadside tables and waiting for takeout. The delicious pizza is cooked in a wood-fired oven. Crepes and pastries are also available.

Le Yellow FRENCH **$$**
(☎0596-75-03-59; www.the-yellow.fr; 51 Rue Victor Hugo; mains €12-24; ⏲noon-2:30pm & 7-11pm Mon-Fri, 7-11pm Sat; ❄🖉) Charm, warmth and conviviality rarely seen elsewhere in Fort-de-France are the main draws at this 1st-floor restaurant, where a small but delightful and regularly changing menu of French-Creole and Spanish specialties will have you coming back for more. Reservations are normally essential.

La Baie CREOLE **$$**
(☎0596-42-20-38; Rue de la Liberté; mains €15-24; ⏲10:30am-3pm & 6-10:30pm Mon-Sat; ❄📶) This friendly place, whose owner hails from Brittany, has an intimate 1st-floor dining room with sea and park views. The menu stretches from seafood and fish to delicious galettes (savory crepes made with buckwheat flour), and is enticing day or night. Book ahead for the evening.

WORTH A TRIP

JARDIN DE BALATA

Just 10km north of Fort-de-France, the **Jardin de Balata** (☎0596-64-48-73; www.jardindebalata.fr; Rte de la Trace; adult/child €14/8; ⏲9am-6pm, last entry 4:30pm; P 👪), a mature botanical garden in a rainforest setting, is one of Martinique's top attractions and will please anyone with even a passing interest in the island's plant life. The hour-long walk around the garden is clearly marked, and a tree walk and fish ponds will keep kids interested. Otherwise (unless you encounter a cruise tour), this is a tranquil place of rattling bamboo, hummingbirds, dramatic views down to the sea and rustling tropical leaves.

There's a good gift shop and restaurant as well as ample free parking. To get here by public transportation from Fort-de-France, take a suburban bus (€1.50, 20 minutes) from Rue André Aliker.

Entertainment

★**Tropiques Atrium** PERFORMING ARTS
(☎0596-70-79-29; www.tropiques-atrium.fr; 6 Rue Jacques Cazotte; ⏲ticket office 9am-7pm Tue-Fri, to 1pm Sat; 📶) This superb cultural center runs an interesting program of indie films and documentaries, and hosts theatrical and musical shows in its state-of-the-art auditoriums. There's a pleasant cafe-bar-restaurant here, too, and it's definitely the best place in town to pick up info on cultural and artistic events. Check the website for the program.

Shopping

Downtown Fort-de-France is crammed with shops, with the main boutique area lying along Rue Victor Hugo, particularly between Rue de la République and Rue de la Liberté. The markets are also worth checking out, even if you don't want to buy anything. **Cour Perrinon mall** (www.cour-perrinon.com; Rue Perrinon; ⏲8am-7pm Mon-Sat) has a concentration of high-street shops, plus air-con, parking and a large Carrefour supermarket.

DON'T MISS

SEEING RED

The **statue of Empress Josephine** (La Savane) holding a locket with a portrait of Napoleon in it stands in La Savane. In the 1990s the head was lopped off and red paint was splashed over the body, and the statue remains as it was after the attack. Josephine is not highly regarded by islanders, who believe that she was directly responsible for convincing Napoleon to reintroduce slavery in the French West Indies so that her family plantation in Trois-Îlets would not suffer.

Information

Banks with ATMs are easy to find in the center, while money can be changed at **Change Caraïbes** (4 Rue Ernest Deproge; ⌚8am-5:30pm Mon-Fri, to 12:30pm Sat).

CHU de Martinique (Centre Hospitalier Universitaire de Martinique; ☎0596-55-20-00; www.chu-martinique.fr; Ave Zobda Quitman)

Main Post Office (cnr Rues Antoine Siger & de la Liberté; ⌚7am-5pm Mon-Fri, 7:30am-noon Sat)

Pharmacie Glaudon (cnr Rues de la Liberté & Antoine Siger; ⌚7:30am-6pm Mon-Fri, to noon Sat)

Police Station (Rue Victor Sévère; ⌚24hr)

Getting There & Away

Theoretically Aéroport International Martinique Aimé Césaire (p579) is just a 15-minute drive from Fort-de-France, but the permanent traffic jam on the motorway means that the journey often takes much longer. Taxis are readily available at the airport (about €25 to Fort-de-France), but a much better option is to take the brand-new **TCSP road train** (www.tcsptoutsavoir.com; ⌚5:30am-8pm; €1.45), which runs right into the city center.

BOAT

Vedettes Tropicales (☎0596-63-06-46; www.vedettestropicales.com; Blvd Alfassa; ⌚6am-11pm) runs multiple daily shuttles between the Bay Ferry Terminal on Fort-de-France's seafront and the resort towns of Trois-Îlets, Pointe du Bout, Anse Mitan and Anse à l'Ane. See the website for exact schedules, as they change according to season. All trips take 20 to 30 minutes.

Cruise ships dock at **Pointe Simon** (Rue des Caraïbes) or Quai des Tourelles.

Jeans for Freedom (☎590-68-53-09; www.jeansforfreedom.com; Ferry Terminal, Rue Bouillé) and **L'Express des Îles** (www.express-des-iles.com; Ferry Terminal, Rue Bouillé) run ferries to Dominica, St Lucia and Guadeloupe from Fort-de-France's **Gare Inter-Îles** (Rue Bouillé; ⌚6am-11pm).

BUS

The busy main **bus station** (Blvd Alfassa) is on the seafront, with *taxis collectifs* (privately run minivans) fanning out to every town on the island. These often battered vehicles, usually without air-con, depart when full, but they should only be used as a last resort. There are very few services after 5pm and none on Sunday. Pay the driver.

For buses to Jardin de Balata (€1.70, 20 minutes), head to **Rue André Aliker** (Rue André Aliker) south of the Parc Floral in Fort-de-France; buses leave every 30 minutes during the day, Monday to Saturday.

SOUTHERN MARTINIQUE

Martinique's south has the island's best beaches by far and is definitely the center of gravity for tourism. If you're looking for a straightforward sun-and-sand holiday, head to Ste-Anne. If you have your own transportation, consider basing yourself in Diamant or Ste-Luce, both of which have several good beaches within easy driving distance and some great eating options nearby.

The largest concentration of places to stay is in the greater Trois-Îlets area, which encompasses the busy resort town of Pointe du Bout. While there are some lovely stretches of beach and plenty of activities on offer here, this is also as touristy as Martinique gets. A far more charming and less heavily trafficked alternative are the gorgeous coves and tranquil villages of Les Anses d'Arlet, which remain pleasingly undeveloped and have a calm, local feel even in high season.

Trois-Îlets

Directly across the bay from Fort-de-France is the commune of Trois-Îlets, which includes several distinct small towns and villages. First is Trois-Îlets itself, a historic settlement that retains quite a bit of charm and is well known as the birthplace of Marie Josèphe Rose Tascher de la Pagerie, later

Empress Josephine of France through her marriage to Napoleon Bonaparte. Her childhood plantation home is now an interesting museum.

Also here is Pointe du Bout, Martinique's most developed resort, home to the island's most-frequented yachting marina and some of its largest hotels. There are good beaches here, but you'll be sharing them with some serious crowds. Overall, it's a popular place for a beach holiday, and a great base for families. If you're looking for a more Caribbean vibe, head elsewhere.

Sights

Anse Mitan BEACH

The main beach in Trois-Îlets is a gorgeous stretch of white sand that shelves gradually into a turquoise sea. The views are of Fort-de-France and the shuttle boats racing to get sunseekers across the bay – it drops them off at a jetty on the beach. A few eateries back the beach and there are more in the streets behind. Anse Mitan attracts holidaying families.

Musée de la Pagerie MUSEUM

(☎0596-68-38-34; Quartier Pagerie; adult/child €5/2; 9am-4:30pm Tue-Fri, 9:30am-12:30pm Sat, 9:30am-2:30pm Sun; P) This former sugar estate was the birthplace of Marie Josèphe Rose Tascher de la Pagerie, the future Empress Josephine of France. A picturesque stone building, once the family kitchen, has been turned into a museum containing Josephine's childhood bed and other memorabilia. Other buildings contain such things as the Bonaparte family tree, old sugarcane equipment and love letters to Josephine from Napoleon.

Multilingual guides relate anecdotal tidbits about Josephine's life, such as the doctoring of the marriage certificate to make Josephine, six years Napoleon's elder, appear to be the same age as her spouse.

You can poke around in the ruins of the old mill directly opposite the museum for free.

Maison de la Canne MUSEUM

(Sugarcane Museum; ☎0596-68-32-04; Rte de Trois-Îlets; adult/child €4/1; 8:30am-5:30pm Tue-Thu, to 5pm Fri & Sat, 9am-5pm Sun; P) This slightly aging museum occupies the site of a sugar refinery and rum distillery, and tells the sad story of the slave trade and the sugar business. Inside the main building are period photos and items such as the Code Noir, which outlined appropriate conduct between enslaved people and refinery/plantation owners. There's also a mock-up of a slave hut and a scale model of the Anse Latouche refinery at its zenith. Rusting bits of machinery litter the grounds.

Activities

Dauphins Martinique WILDLIFE WATCHING

(☎0696-02-02-22; www.dauphin-martinique.com; Marina de la Pointe du Bout; half-day tours adult/child €55/35;) This reputable outfit runs environmentally aware small-group dolphin-watching trips with minimal impact on the animals. Trips include a swimming/snorkeling stop.

Schéhérazade BOATING

(☎0696-39-45-55; Marina de la Pointe du Bout; half-day tours adult/child €50/30) This company runs boat tours to the superb Rocher du Diamant (p562), allowing you to swim on the reef, see a cave of bats and just get up close to this amazing but hard-to-reach place. It also runs dolphin-watching trips that come highly recommended. Tours include snacks and drinks.

Espace Plongée DIVING

(☎0596-66-01-79; www.epm972.fr; Marina de la Pointe du Bout) This outfit offers morning and afternoon dives every day and, if enough people want to go, night dives. It's located right beside the water in the marina. English is spoken. Introductory dives cost €60, standard ones €55.

Attitude Plongée DIVING

(☎0596-72-59-28; www.attitudeplongee.com; Marina de la Pointe du Bout) Right in the heart of Pointe du Bout, this outfit charges €65 for an introductory dive, €50 for a single dive

Sleeping & Eating

Most of Trois-Îlets' hotels and resorts are concentrated in and around the Pointe du Bout and tend to be rather closely packed together. While they offer decent value and have plenty of facilities, they may not appeal to independent travelers.

Le Panoramic Hotel HOTEL $$

(☎0596-68-78-48; www.lepanoramic.fr; Anse à l'Ane; d from €100;) This hillside hotel in Anse à l'Ane, a few kilometers west of Trois-Îlets, has an impressive location with views over the bay and a gorgeous tropical-garden setting. The 36 fully equipped rooms are brightly furnished; be sure to ask for a room with a sea view. The beach nearby is where most guests decamp to during the day.

Hotel Bakoua RESORT **$$**
(☎0596-66-02-02; www.hotel-bakoua.fr; Pointe du Bout; d incl breakfast from €131; ❄📶🏊) Perched on a hillside, this four-star resort has 132 units of varying size and shape. They're comfortably furnished (the best are right on the beach) and have a minimalist, contemporary vibe. Guests have access to a small artificial beach that comes complete with water-sports equipment as well as Martinique's best infinity pool, offering gobsmacking sea views.

Le Ti Taurus CREOLE **$$**
(☎0596-76-33-39; Anse Mitan; mains €13.50-23; ⏰noon-10pm; 📶) Right on the beach by the jetty for ferries from Fort-de-France, this is one of the best restaurants in town, with a blue-and-white beach-shack vibe, an English-speaking staff, fresh seafood including lobster, and a long cocktail card. Be sure to book, especially on Sunday, as this place is madly popular.

La Mandoline FRENCH **$$$**
(☎0596-69-48-38; www.poterie-village.fr; Le Village de la Poterie, Rte de Trois-Îlets; mains €23-29; ⏰noon-2:30pm Tue-Thu, noon-2:30pm & 7:30-10pm Fri & Sat; 📶) The best place to eat at the **La Poterie** (☎0596-68-24-64; www.poterie-village.fr; Rte des Trois Ilets; ⏰10am-6pm Mon-Sat, to 1pm Sun) complex of shops and restaurants is gourmet-style La Mandoline. Sit outside surrounded by greenery or in the historic building's cozy dining room, sample the famous piña colada, and peruse the menu of refined, traditional French cooking.

Information

Otitour (L'Office du Tourisme de Trois-Îlets; ☎0596-68-47-63; Rue du Chacha; ⏰8am-1pm & 2-5pm Mon-Fri, 9am-1pm Sat)

Getting There & Away

Trois-Îlets is served by regular ferries (€5, 20 minutes) from Fort-de-France, which makes getting to this part of Martinique a cinch. Ferries are run by Vedettes Tropicales (p560) and also serve Pointe du Bout (€5, 20 minutes), Anse Mitan (€2.50, 25 minutes) and Anse à l'Ane (€2.50, 30 minutes).

Le Diamant

Le Diamant, both a town and a commune, is one of the most scenic destinations in southern Martinique, although there's no real center as things are scattered along about 2km of sandy, wave-tossed shore and in the hills immediately behind. Though lacking the lively vibe of other places in southern Martinique, it's a tranquil base for exploring the western horn of the island. It's also an obvious launching pad for the superb dive sites around Rocher du Diamant, while the haunting Mémorial Cap 110 in Anse Cafard acknowledges Martinique's brutal colonial history.

Sights

Mémorial Cap 110 MEMORIAL
(Slave Memorial; Anse Cafard; ⏰24hr) This haunting memorial on a grassy headland overlooking the sea is made up of 15 formless Easter Island–esque figures in stone, heads hung in mourning. It commemorates the scores of enslaved people who lost their lives in a shipwreck off the coast here in April 1830, and more generally, the tens of thousands of enslaved Africans who were taken to Martinique as part of the transatlantic slave trade.

The memorial is off the D37.

Rocher du Diamant NATURAL FEATURE
(Diamond Rock) This extraordinary-looking 176m-high pointed volcanic islet, just under a mile offshore from Le Diamant, is a very popular dive site, with interesting cave formations but tricky water conditions. Various companies also run boat excursions that take in the islet – don't miss your chance to get close to this natural wonder.

Plage du Diamant BEACH
This beautiful stretch of white sand extends for 2km to the west of Le Diamant. Swimming is not recommended, as the waves can be very strong, but it's a picture-perfect place for sunbathing, beachcombing, picnicking in the shade of the trees or simply enjoying the view of the nearby Rocher du Diamant.

Activities

Antilles Sub Diamond Rock DIVING
(0696-82-14-35; www.plongeemartinique.fr; Port de Pêche Départemental de la Taupinière) Capably managed by a French couple, this outfit is known for friendly service and small groups. It offers introductory dives (€50), three-dive packages (€126), certification courses and snorkeling trips.

Sleeping & Eating

Le Diamant has a few independently run guesthouses that are far more enticing than the many larger resorts along the coast.

★ **L'Anse Bleue** BUNGALOW $$
(0596-76-21-91; www.hotel-anse-bleue.com; La Dizac; d €70-95;) This place is very simple but somehow manages to get things just right, with 25 delightful one- or two-room bungalows spread across spacious grounds, a decent-size pool, a superb restaurant, friendly management and a peaceful location. It all adds up to make this one of the best hotels in Martinique's south. The beach is a short walk away.

Rêve Bleu GUESTHOUSE $$
(Ecrin Bleu; 0596-76-41-92; Rte des Anses d'Arlet; d from €80;) A good choice for families, this great-value guesthouse on a hillside overlooking Le Diamant has spacious, bright and well-maintained rooms, each with a large terrace that includes a kitchenette. It's a bit of a hike into town, though, so it's worth having your own car.

New Cap INTERNATIONAL $$
(0596-76-12-99; Anse Cafard; mains €17-24; noon-10pm Wed-Mon;) This beachside restaurant wins the popular vote, though for newcomers it can be difficult to find. Choose from its 'legendary salads,' tapas, burgers, and daily fish and seafood specials chalked up on the blackboard. It's in Anse Cafard, 3km west of Le Diamant, accessed from the D37 via the delightfully named Allée de la Bonne Humeur.

Note that the beach here is a scrappy affair.

La Paillotte Bleue FRENCH $$
(0596-58-33-21; La Dizac; mains €16-23; 7:30-10pm;) The poolside dining at this superb dinner-only restaurant is a real treat. Located within the L'Anse Bleue compound, La Paillotte Bleue serves up classic French dishes with a dash of Caribbean influence, such as sautéed octopus cooked with aromatic herbs or curried chicken. There's a good wine list and service is excellent.

Chez Lucie CREOLE $$$
(0596-525-107; 64 Rue Justin Roc; mains €18-28; 11am-3pm & 6:45-10pm Mon & Wed-Sat, 11am-3pm Sun) Chez Lucie is possibly the best place on the coast to watch the sea as you dine, especially on rougher days. The broad menu offers all sorts of tempting goodies, such as *blaff* (white fish marinated in lime juice, garlic and peppers, then poached) and dorado steak, or you could just plump for the catch of the day.

There are few places on earth where the waves crash this close to your table.

Getting There & Away

Shared taxis run from Fort-de-France's bus station (€5, 45 minutes). There's no service after dark or on Sunday. Car is a much better way to enjoy the area.

Les Anses d'Arlet

Les Anses d'Arlet is without doubt the most charming corner of southern Martinique, retaining as it does an undiscovered feel, some gorgeous scenery and wonderful beaches. The commune of Les Anses d'Arlet contains a string of villages, each named descriptively after its respective *anse* (cove): Grande Anse, Anse Noire, Anse Dufour and – confusingly – Anse d'Arlet Bourg, the administrative center of Les Anses d'Arlet. The villages are connected by an often steep and winding coastal road that offers superb glimpses down to the waves below.

Anse d'Arlet Bourg is crowned by an 18th-century Roman Catholic church whose doors open almost directly onto the beach, the entire scene framed by steep, verdant hills. The next-door village of Grande Anse is set along a beachfront road lined with brightly painted boats and a string of restaurants, while lovely Anse Dufour and Anse Noire remain almost untouched by tourism.

Sights

★ **Plage Anse d'Arlet** BEACH
(Anse d'Arlet Bourg) This gorgeous stretch of dark-golden sand in front of Anse d'Arlet Bourg is backed by the village's 18th-century church and is one of the loveliest places to swim in Martinique. The beach is bookended

by restaurants and bars, and it's rarely difficult to find your own spot beneath the various trees that back the beach.

If you've perused the holiday brochures before you came to the island, you're sure to have seen the shot of the church and beach from the end of the pier – one of Martinique's most photogenic vistas and a perfect selfie spot. Come on the weekend to see weddings spilling onto the square in front to a Creole beat.

It's very popular with holidaying families.

Anse Dufour BEACH

Approximately halfway between Anse Mitan and Grande Anse, a secondary road peels off the D7 and plunges (literally) straight to Anse Dufour 2km below. You're sure to be smitten by the mellow tranquility of this fishing hamlet, which has a golden-sand beach and a handful of Creole restaurants, though it's well known to local day-trippers, who come here in droves on weekends.

Anse Noire BEACH

If you're after an intimate, secluded strip of sand, head to lovely Anse Noire, which is reached by taking the side road to Anse Dufour and continuing around the hillside. This tiny, dreamlike cove lapped by jade waters offers a small patch of black sand studded with palm trees. Swimming and snorkeling are excellent here.

Activities

L'Arlésienne BOATING

(☎0696-82-54-41; http://baladesdelarlesienne.free.fr; Ave Robert Deloy, Grande Anse; half/full-day tour €30/55) This operator runs an interesting tour that takes in the bays and coves between Grande Anse and Le Diamant. It's an ideal way to gain an overview of the coast's delights, and there's a swimming stop in a lovely little cove. Trips to northern Martinique can also be arranged.

Kazd'o Kayaks de l'Anse Noire KAYAKING

(☎0696-34-86-36; Anse Noire; 1hr €7, half/full day €14/22) This beachfront operation rents out kayaks, which are a great way to explore the nearby bays at a gentle pace.

Alpha Plongée DIVING

(☎0696-81-93-42, 0596-48-30-34; www.alpha-plongee.com; 138 Ave Robert Deloy, Grande Anse) This low-key diving venture specializes in small groups and offers aquatic adventures with an intimate feel. Single-dive trips cost €48, while introductory dives are €55. Certification courses and dive packages are available. It also runs *randonnée palmée* (guided snorkeling tours; €25) and rents snorkeling gear (€10 per day).

Plongée Passion DIVING

(☎0596-68-71-78; www.plongeepassion.com; 1 Allée des Raisiniers, Grande Anse) On the beach, this friendly and well-known dive outfit offers morning and afternoon outings daily. A single dive, including equipment, costs €45.

Sleeping

By some incredible stroke of luck, Les Anses d'Arlet is still rather undeveloped, but this means there's hardly any provision for people who want to base themselves here. (This, of course, also accounts for the area's continued charm, as nearly everyone who comes here is a day-tripper.) Grande Anse and Anse d'Arlet Bourg both have small guesthouses.

Résidence Madinakay HOTEL $

(☎0596-68-70-76; 3 Allée des Arlésiens, Anse d'Arlet Bourg; d €60; ❄📶) Right in the thick of things and just across the road from Anse d'Arlet Bourg's beach, this tiny hotel is excellent value for money given its prime location. The eight studios are fairly functional and not particularly exciting, but they're clean and equipped with all necessary comforts.

Résidences Colombier VILLA $$

(☎0696-80-51-52, 0596-68-63-38; Rue Général de Gaulle, Anse d'Arlet Bourg; d from €80; ❄📶) The kindly host here offers a number of apartments and gîtes (cottages) in the heart of Anse d'Arlet Bourg for families and couples, normally for rent by the week. Accommodations are regularly maintained and very comfortable, and are just moments from one of the best beaches (p563) on Martinique. Particularly popular with French families.

Eating

There are plentiful eating possibilities along the region's coast, particularly in Grande Anse, which has a seafront full of wonderful little restaurants, some right on the beach. Seafood is – of course – the name of the game here, and you're spoiled for choice about where to eat it.

★Bidjoul CREOLE $$

(Ave Robert Deloy, Grande Anse; mains €10-20, pizzas €11-14; ⏰10am-10pm; 📶) This charming wooden house on the beach has a very reasonably priced menu and serves up all the Creole favorites, as well as pizza. The multicolored tables are set on the sand, meaning you can easily have a dip while you're waiting for your meal!

★Ti Payot CREOLE $$
(☎0596-69-07-38; http://plongeepassion.com/ti-payot; 1 Allée des Raisiniers, Grande Anse; mains €13-16; ⊙8am-7pm; 📶) Owned and operated by Plongée Passion, this is a great beachside place to relax after a dive. Amid the dripping wetsuits, kids in snorkels and blackboard menus, you can enjoy the catch of the day, vegetarian dishes and lots of seafood-fruit combos in a laid-back atmosphere.

Le P'ti Bateau SEAFOOD $$
(☎0596-53-17-35; 108 Ave Robert Deloy, Grande Anse; mains around €20; 📶) This popular beachside place has almost all its seats on the beach near the jetty, while inside are great seafood offerings that include a set menu for kids and a rather more extravagant lobster menu (€50). In between you'll find local favorites such as conch fricassee or fish tartare, to be enjoyed to a jolly Gallic-Creole soundtrack.

Au Dessous du Volcan CREOLE $$
(☎0596-68-69-52; 79 Rue des Pêcheurs, Petite Anse; mains €15.50-22.50; ⊙noon-3pm & 7-10pm Fri-Wed; 📶) At the southern end of Petite Anse, this is arguably the village's best place to eat, serving very high-quality Creole food in a beautiful tropical garden. The shrimp flambéed in rum is the signature dish, and the restaurant also specializes in local desserts such as flambéed banana or mojito sorbet with white rum.

Valy et Le Pêcheur CREOLE $$
(☎0696-93-60-87; Anse d'Arlet Bourg; mains €10-20; ⊙noon-3pm Wed-Mon) This beachside kiosk sporting aging plastic chairs is run by a dynamic crew that serves excellent local specialties, among them pork ribs, conch fricassee and braised chicken. Servings are large. It's definitely the pick of the beach shacks in Anse d'Arlet Bourg.

Ti Sable INTERNATIONAL $$$
(☎0596-68-62-44; www.tisablemartinique.com; 35 Allée des Raisiniers, Grande Anse; mains €18-26; ⊙9am-6pm Mon-Thu, 9am-6pm & 7-10pm Fri-Sun; 📶👪) Head to this large, shady complex at the northern end of Grande Anse's beach for a lovely waterside-eating experience. The fish dishes, exotic salads and barbecued meats are top quality and the setting is magical. There's a kids' menu for €12 and cocktails for around €7. Sunday (the best day) brings a buffet lunch and live music in the evening.

ℹ Getting There & Away

Shared-taxi minivans connect Les Anses d'Arlet with Fort-de-France (€4, 50 minutes), passing through Le Diamant and Petite Anse beforehand. However, to get the most out of the area you'll need a hire car.

Ste-Luce

Busy Ste-Luce isn't really worth visiting in itself, but the stretch of hotels along the coast in the suburbs of Gros Raisin and Trois-Rivières keeps visitors coming, as does the historic Trois-Rivières Distillery, Martinique's most famous rum producer. The hotels are far enough from the main road for you to avoid feeling as though you're staying on a freeway, but they're close enough to make this a great base for exploring the southern half of the island. The lovely beaches at Ste-Anne and Les Anses d'Arlet are within easy reach for enjoyable day trips.

Sights & Activities

Trois-Rivières Distillery DISTILLERY
(☎0596-62-51-78; www.plantationtroisrivieres.com; Quartier Trois-Rivières; guided tour €3; ⊙9am-5:30pm Nov-May, closed Sun Jun-Oct) Martinique's oldest and best-known rum producer actually provides the worst visitor experience of all the island's distilleries. Unless you join a guided tour (10am, 11am, noon, 2pm, 3pm and 4pm) there's virtually nothing to see here, though the factory shop is a glitzy, well-stocked affair. There's no self-guided tour, and the plant is scrappy and surprisingly small. However, this is a great place to buy Martinique's most famous rum at the source.

The distillery is hard to find: most satnavs put it just off the highway, but you have to leave at the next exit and double back on yourself. Signs to the place are misleading.

Kawan Plongée DIVING
(☎0696-76-58-69; http://sainteluce.kawanplongee.com; Blvd Kennedy) Éric, Cécile and their team welcome you to this friendly place in the middle of Ste-Luce. Introductory dives cost €55, while a standard dive is €45. Numerous packages and courses are available.

Sleeping

Much of the accommodations in and around Ste-Luce are made up of rather unexciting mass-market resorts, but there are a few gems.

★Ti' Paradis B&B $$
(☎0696-76-09-76, 0596-62-78-20; www.ti-paradis-martinique.com; 69 Anse Gros Raisin; d incl breakfast €130-150;) Somewhere between a boutique hotel and B&B, Ti' Paradis harbors seven immaculate rooms, furnished in muted earth tones, with sparkling bathrooms and superb sea views. Laze on the shady terrace, lounge by the pool or step down to Gros Raisin beach just below. Evening meals are available by arrangement. Two-night minimum.

Le Verger de Ste-Luce BUNGALOW $$
(☎0596-62-20-72; www.facebook.com/VergerdeSainteLuce; d/q €85/115;) For a warm welcome, look no further than this charming place. Bungalows surround a small pool with sun chairs and there's a stand-alone Jacuzzi – and the friendly owner loves to practice her English. The simple bungalows each have their own porch with kitchenette, while a good amount of greenery keeps the small place feeling private.

Hotel Le Panoramique HOTEL $$
(☎0596-62-31-32; www.hotel-le-panoramique.com; Trois-Rivières; d from €75;) Just a little north of Le Verger de Ste-Luce, some way out of town, this place is handy for beach access. Five of the 15 rooms have kitchenettes, not to mention the best views, though they also suffer from having a road right below them. There's a bar and restaurant on the property.

Hotel Corail Résidence HOTEL $$
(☎0596-62-11-01; www.hotelcorail.com; Anse Mabouya; d from €110;) This is definitely one of the best spots to base yourself in Ste-Luce. It's supremely laid-back, and all 25 rooms have kitchenettes and little porches with amazing bay views. There's a great pool area and a top-notch restaurant. It's also just a short stroll to Anse Mabouya, the best beach in town.

Eating

★Le Mabouya FRENCH CARIBBEAN $$$
(www.hotelcorail.com/le-restaurant-le-mabouya; Hôtel Corail Résidence, Anse Mabouya; mains €15-28; ⏲7-10pm Mon, Tue & Fri, noon-2:30pm & 7-10pm Sat & Sun;) This superb restaurant at Hôtel Corail Résidence is one worth splurging on, with a fantastic and inventive French-Creole menu. Try a signature dish such as lobster ravioli, scallops with risotto or just the life-affirming crème brûlée. Reservations are a good idea.

La Pura Vida FRENCH CARIBBEAN $$$
(☎0596-53-89-35; http://restaurantpuravida.fr; Gros Raisin; mains €20-26; ⏲noon-2pm & 7-10pm Tue-Sun;) Combining French traditional cooking and local ingredients, La Pura Vida is a stand-out on Ste-Luce's dining scene. Its premises alone are a breath of fresh air: an expansive terrace with attractive wooden tables and lounging sofas. Choose your lobster from the tank (€7 per 100g) or order the excellent conch stew. This is also a great place for a cocktail.

The kids' menu is €12, but desserts are possibly the island's priciest at a hefty €13.

Case Coco FRENCH $$$
(☎0596-62-32-26; 58 Rue Schoelcher; mains €19-25; ⏲6:30-10pm Tue, noon-3pm & 6:30-10pm Wed-Sun;) In a carefully restored Creole house, this atmospheric establishment provides a winning combination of innovative French fare and tropical style, plus warmth and intimacy – not to mention an enviable position along the seafront promenade. Order the rum-flambé pork fillet if it's on the menu. Not a bad place for a romantic dinner or a day-ending cocktail.

Getting There & Away

Shared-taxi minivans run between Fort-de-France and Ste-Luce throughout the day (€4.50, one hour).

Ste-Anne

The southernmost town on Martinique, Ste-Anne has an attractive seaside setting with wooden houses, a lovely central square with a brightly painted stone church on one side, and several good restaurants. Despite the large number of people who flock here on weekends and during high season, Ste-Anne remains a casual, low-key place and never feels swamped by visitors.

But the main reason people head here is for Martinique's most celebrated beach: Grande Anse des Salines, at the undeveloped southern tip of the island. If you don't have your own wheels, the town beach with abundant near-shore reef formations is good for snorkeling.

A 15-minute drive to the northeast – and just 6km east as the crow flies – lies another world along the Atlantic-battered east coast. Here, around impressive Cap Chevalier, you'll find some great isolated beaches.

Sights

★Grande Anse des Salines BEACH

A perfect arc of white sand, Grande Anse des Salines is the Caribbean you came to see. Palm trees lean over the ribbon of beach that shelves ever so gently into a classic turquoise sea. It's located about 5km south of Ste-Anne along the D9 and there are hundreds of parking spaces just back from the sand. Snack bars and artisan sorbet sellers provide sustenance in the shade, but otherwise it's wonderfully undeveloped – a slice of fabulously raw nature.

Pointe Marin BEACH

Ste-Anne's most popular swimming beach is the long, lovely strand that stretches along the peninsula 800m north of the town center. It's backed by restaurants and bars, and though it can be quite crowded, the beach is long enough that you'll be able to find a quiet spot on most occasions.

Anse Michel BEACH

The steady winds that buffet this part of the coast, together with the reef-sheltered lagoon, provide the perfect conditions for kitesurfing and windsurfing. This *anse* also offers excellent sunbathing and swimming.

Activities

★Taxi Cap BOATING

(☎0596-76-93-10, 0696-45-44-60; www.taxi-cap.com; Cap Chevalier; full-day excursion adult/child €38/15) The best way to discover the lagoon, the nearby islets and the mangrove ecosystems around Ste-Anne is by joining a boat excursion. The widely advertised Taxi Cap runs an array of these, and the return crossing to Îlet Chevalier costs as little as €4. The classic full-day excursion includes lunch and a host of activities.

Alize Fun-Lagon Evasion WATER SPORTS

(☎0696-91-71-06; www.alizefunkitemartinique.com; Anse Michel, Cap Chevalier) To brush up on your windsurfing or kitesurfing skills, or try a first lesson (from €95), contact this small outfit right on the beach. It also rents kayaks (€16 per hour) and can arrange guided kayak tours to nearby islets.

Natiyabel OUTDOORS

(☎0696-36-63-01; http://plongee-martinique.fr; Bourg) This well-run center organizes a variety of dive trips and certification. Introductory/single dives cost €55/48. Snorkeling is €16. Kayaks are available for rent (€16 per half day).

Sleeping

Salines Studio HOTEL $

(☎0596-76-90-92, 0596-76-82-81; salinestudios@hotmail.fr; 7 Rue Jean-Marie Tjibaou; d €70-80; ❄📶) Dependable, low-key and quiet, Salines Studio resembles a typical motel and best suits budget travelers looking for kitchenette studios. It's in the center of the village, so it has easy access to local services and transport.

★Airstream Paradise CARAVAN PARK $$

(☎0596-58-45-19; www.airstreamparadise.fr; Pointe Marin; caravans from €130; ❄📶) Right on Pointe Marin beach, this park has a collection of revamped Airstream luxury trailers, each of which can accommodate two to four people. Each Airstream includes an outdoor Jacuzzi, an espresso machine, a grill and a flat-screen TV. Management is proactive and friendly, and it's a great spot for kids. There's also an American-style snack bar.

Eating & Drinking

★Les Tamariniers CREOLE $$

(☎0596-76-75-62; 30 Rue Abbé Saffache; mains €13-23, menus from €20; ⏲11am-2:30pm & 6-9:30pm, closed Wed & lunch Sun; ❄) Arguably the best place to eat in town, this friendly restaurant next to the church has a varied menu of Creole food and French specialties. Be sure to sample the rum-flambé shrimp, and if you're really going to town, order the full seafood grill (€93 for two people).

La Cour Créole CREOLE $$

(☎0596-62-59-18; 15 Rue Jean-Marie Tjibaou; mains €6-20; ⏲11am-9pm Tue-Sun; ❄📶) As central as it gets, this multitasking place can do everything, from lunchtime sandwiches and ice cream to an evening gourmet-style Creole tasting menu. Take a seat in the air-conditioned dining room or out on the terrace and choose from the wide-ranging options, which include vegetarian dishes.

Otantik CREOLE $$

(☎0696-08-40-26; Rue Frantz Fanon; mains €12-19; ⊙10am-10pm Wed-Sun;) This clifftop shack a short walk from the center is built around a tree and has dazzling sea views. Seasonal ingredients are paired with the catch of the day to create a small, great-value and wonderfully tasty daily menu. There's a hippieish air, and vegetarians are well provided for.

Basilic Beach SEAFOOD $$

(☎0696-32-67-92; Pointe Marin; mains €14-23; ⊙noon-3pm Tue-Sun) Consisting of a wooden shack and sand-floored tent overlooking the water between Ste-Anne and Pointe Marin beach (p567), this place serves the perfect seaside lunch. The food is typical of Martinique: *acras* (deep-fried balls of dough filled with fish or shrimp), tuna tartare, catch of the day and conch are all on the menu, as is a superb basil mojito.

La Dunette BAR

(☎0596-76-73-90; www.ladunette.com; Rue Jean-Marie Tjibaou; ⊙noon-11pm;) In the center of town, this hotel restaurant is one of the best spots to grab a drink. The location alone – a wooden deck and a pontoon overlooking the water – guarantees memorable sunset cocktails. There's live music on weekends.

Information

Tourist Office (☎0596-76-73-45; www.sainteanne-martinique.fr; Ave Frantz Fanon; ⊙8:30am-3:30pm Mon-Fri) In the north of town near Marin beach (p567), this office hands out maps of Ste-Anne and can help with car or hotel arrangements.

Getting There & Away

Buses run between Fort-de-France and Ste-Anne roughly every hour during daylight hours (€4.50, one hour 15 minutes). There are also half-hourly local buses running along the coast to Ste-Luce (€2.50, 45 minutes). Ste-Anne's one-bus **Gare Routière** (Rue Abbé Saffache) is in the center of town.

NORTHERN MARTINIQUE

The far north of Martinique is a side of the island that few beach tourists see. Rugged, windswept and mountainous, it contains much of the island's most impressive scenery and best hiking opportunities, including its trump card: massive Mont Pelée, the active volcano that has profoundly shaped Martinique's geology and history.

Unlike the south, this is not a region known for its beaches, though there are a few terrific ones here if you know where to look. With fantastically scenic landscapes such as the Presqu'île de Caravelle and Grand-Rivière, not to mention the historic charm of St-Pierre, it's easy to see why northern Martinique is for Caribbean connoisseurs.

St-Pierre

St-Pierre is undoubtedly one of Martinique's loveliest towns, tucked between a mountainside covered in steamy rainforest and a tranquil azure bay. Replete with disheveled charm, it's full of colonial-era buildings and boasts an attractive dark-gray sand beach and the perfect location for superb sunsets.

It's hard to believe amid all this tranquility that St-Pierre was once Martinique's capital and at one point perhaps the most cosmopolitan city in the entire Caribbean. That all ended abruptly on May 8, 1902, when Mont Pelée erupted and wiped out the town (and some 30,000 of its inhabitants) in just 10 minutes, leaving just three survivors. Unsurprisingly, St-Pierre has never recovered from the catastrophe. The capital was moved to Fort-de-France and St-Pierre became the offbeat seaside town you see today. Whether you come for its tragic history or its laid-back present, St-Pierre is an authentic Caribbean treat.

Sights

Zoo de Martinique ZOO

(Habitation Latouche; ☎0596-52-76-08; www.zoodemartinique.com; Anse Latouche; adult/child €16.50/9; ⊙9am-6pm;) One of northern Martinique's biggest attractions, this zoo-botanical garden–historical site almost gives you three for the price of one. Amid the ruins of a sugar mill that was destroyed in the 1902 eruption of Mont Pelée, enclosures and cages house monkeys, parrots, butterflies, jaguars, flamingos and cougars. The whole scene is given color by myriad tropical plants, and there's information throughout on the mill's history and demise. If you're in the area it's unmissable.

WORTH A TRIP

ROUTE DE LA TRACE

The Route de la Trace (known more prosaically on maps as the N3) winds up into the mountains north of Fort-de-France. It's a beautiful drive through a lush rainforest of tall tree ferns, anthurium-covered hillsides and thick clumps of roadside bamboo. The road passes along the eastern flanks of the volcanic mountain peaks of the Pitons du Carbet. Several well-marked hiking trails lead from the Route de la Trace into the rainforest and up to the peaks.

The road follows a route cut by the Jesuits in the 17th century: the Trace de Jésuites. Islanders like to say that the Jesuits' fondness for rum accounts for the twisting nature of the road.

Less than a 10-minute drive north of Fort-de-France, in the village of Balata, is **Sacré-Coeur de Balata**, a scaled-down replica of the Sacré-Coeur basilica in Paris. This domed church, in the Roman-Byzantine style, has a stunning hilltop setting – the Pitons du Carbet rise up as a backdrop, and there's a view across Fort-de-France to Pointe du Bout below.

On the western side of the N3, 10 minutes' drive north of the Balata church, is one of the island's best non-beach attractions: the **Jardin de Balata** (p559), a mature botanical garden in a rainforest setting. After the garden, the N3 winds into the mountains and reaches an elevation of 600m before dropping to the Alma River, which runs through a lush gorge. Make sure you have a picnic to enjoy on the boulders before tackling a couple of short trails into the rainforest.

Beyond the gorge the Route de la Trace passes banana plantations and flower nurseries before reaching a T-junction at **Morne Rouge**, which was partly destroyed by a Mont Pelée eruption in August 1902, several months after the eruption that wiped out St-Pierre. At 450m, it has the highest elevation of any town on Martinique, and it enjoys some impressive mountain scenery.

About 2km north of the T-junction, a road (D39) signposted to Aileron leads 3km up the slopes of **Mont Pelée**, from where there's a rugged trail (four hours round trip) up the volcano's south face to the summit.

Distillerie Depaz DISTILLERY

(0596-78-13-14; www.depaz.fr; Plantation de la Montagne Pelée; 10am-5pm Mon-Fri, 9am-4pm Sat; P) FREE Learn how rum is made at this interesting operation perched on a hillside amid sugarcane fields on St-Pierre's northern outskirts. Self-guided tours, with signs in English, are on offer. In the tasting room you can sample the products, including *rhum vieux* (vintage rum), the Mercedes of Martinique rums, which truly rivals cognac. There's an on-site restaurant.

Domaine de l'Émeraude NATURE RESERVE

(0596-52-33-49; www.pnr-martinique.com/visiter/domaine-demeraude; adult/child €6/3; 9am-4pm; P) This wonderful natural reserve has been curated with exhibits and labeling to allow visitors to get the most out of its many trails, making it a slice of wild nature with great learning possibilities. Give yourself plenty of time to do the three walks through the forest, ranging from 1km to 5km, where you'll see all manner of indigenous plants, flowers and trees.

Theater Ruins RUINS

(Rue Bouillé) St-Pierre's most impressive ruins are those of the town's 18th-century theater. While most of it was destroyed in the 1902 eruption of Mont Pelée, enough remains to give a sense of the building's former grandeur. It once seated 800 and hosted theater troupes from mainland France. On the ruins' northeastern side you can peer down into the tiny, thick-walled jail cell that housed Louis-Auguste Cyparis, one of the town's three survivors.

Look out for the 1917 sculptural work that Madeleine Jouvray – a pupil of Rodin's – created to depict the suffering of the town.

Another area rich in ruins is the **Quartier du Figuier**, also along Rue Bouillé.

Centre de Découverte des Sciences de la Terre MUSEUM

(0596-52-82-42; www.cdst.e-monsite.com; Rte du Prêcheur; adult/child €5/3; 9am-5pm Tue-Sun Sep-Jun, 10am-6pm Tue-Sun Jul & Aug; P) Just 1.5km north of town, the earth-science museum looks like a big white box set atop some columns. It hosts a permanent exhibit on Mont Pelée and volcanoes in general, most of which is in French. An almost hour-long film, *Volcans des Antilles,* is shown in the large cinema and recounts Pelée's eruption and the dire consequences. It's subtitled in English and shown at 9:30am, 11:30am, 2pm and 4pm (10:30am, 12:30pm, 3pm and 5pm in July and August).

Kids may grow weary of the film, but the interactive experiment room will soon rekindle their interest.

Musée Volcanologique et Historique MUSEUM
(Musée Frank A Perret; 0596-78-15-16; Rue Victor Hugo; 9am-5pm Mon-Sat; P) FREE This small but very interesting museum, founded in 1932 by American adventurer and volcanologist Frank Perret, gives a glimpse of the devastating 1902 eruption of Mont Pelée. On display are items plucked from the rubble and photos of the town before and immediately after the eruption.

Activities

Hiking

The island's most famous natural attraction, Mont Pelée is a must-do for walkers, with strenuous trails leading up its northern and southern flanks. The shortest and steepest is up the southern flank, beginning at Réfuge de L'Aileron in Morne Rouge (it's signposted), and takes about four hours round trip. Ask at the tourist office for a map. Early morning is the best time to climb the volcano, as there's a better chance of clear views.

> **WORTH A TRIP**
>
> **DOMAINE SAINT AUBIN**
>
> Completely bucking the trend in northern Martinique, the **Domaine Saint Aubin** (0596-69-34-77; www.ledomainesaintaubin.com; Petite Rivière Salée, La Trinité; d/tr from €185/220;) is an atmospheric boutique hotel housed in a dreamy former plantation house, surrounded by acres of forested land. The comfortable, well-maintained rooms are decorated with antique furniture. The owners, whose family have lived in Martinique since 1715, take very good care of their guests. There's a restaurant and a sumptuous breakfast.

Diving

Centre de Plongée à Papa D'Lo DIVING
(0696-50-13-68; www.apapadlo.net; Rue Bouillé) This small dive outfit with modern equipment specializes in wreck diving and has good premises right on the seafront. Individual dives start at €37, introductory ones at €60.

Tropicasub DIVING
(0696-24-24-30; www.tropicasub.com; Anse Latouche; Tue-Sun) One of the most experienced dive operators in the area, Tropicasub is in St-Pierre's southern outskirts. Introductory dives go for €55, while single dives cost €50. Certification courses and dive packages are also available.

Festivals & Events

Mai de St-Pierre CULTURAL
(May 8) The island commemorates the May 8, 1902, eruption of Mont Pelée with live jazz performances and a candlelight procession through the town from the cathedral along the seafront.

Sleeping

St-Pierre has just one hotel and not many private rentals – which shows just how little touristed this lovely destination is – but there are several other hotels and guesthouses in the vicinity. In nearly all cases you'll need a car if you plan to stay anywhere but the town center.

Hôtel de l'Anse HOTEL $
(0696-38-91-70, 0596-78-30-82; www.hoteldelanse.com; Anse Latouche; d from €50, bungalows €65-90; P) In a charming cove on the road between Carbet and St-Pierre, this well-priced abode occupies an atmospheric converted chapel that offers nine impeccably simple and airy rooms. The upstairs rooms are a tad smaller than those downstairs and supremely basic, though they're a good deal. Behind the main hotel are three cozy bungalows in a tropical garden.

Le Fromager CHALET $
(0596-78-19-07; Quartier St-James; d €40; P) This popular hilltop restaurant has four superb-value timber studios, each with its own balcony and mind-blowing sea views. At these prices it's no wonder they're usually booked up – reserve ahead.

★La Maison Rousse GUESTHOUSE $$
(☎0596-55-85-49; www.maisonrousse.com; Quartier Fonds Mascret, Fonds St-Denis; r €110-140, ste €210-220; ❄📶) This gorgeous retreat amid thick jungle in the heights of Fonds St-Denis is one of Martinique's most exquisite escapes. The simple, brightly painted rooms sleep up to four and surround a small pool with dizzying views down to the river below. The best rooms are the gorgeous and spacious suites with their own private terraces.

The excellent restaurant is a great place for a long lunch and is open to nonguests – though note that the trails through the private reserve around the house are open only to hotel residents.

Hôtel Villa Saint-Pierre HOTEL $$
(☎0596-78-68-45; www.hotel-villastpierre.fr; Rue Bouillé; d €137-147, tr €182; P❄📶) The only hotel in town is a good one, right on the waterfront with a small beach just meters from the front door. The nine comfortable rooms of recent vintage, complete with locally made wooden furniture, have an almost boutique feel, and the welcome is friendly. Rooms with a sea view are inundated with natural light and well worth the extra €10.

Eating

There are some excellent restaurants in and around St-Pierre, though outside high season it can be an effort to find one that's open. Evenings are particularly tough, with only a few places staying open year-round. Wonderful seafood is available, and Le Guérin on the seafront at lunchtime is the best spot to eat it.

★Le Fromager CREOLE $$
(☎0596-78-19-07; Quartier St-James; mains €10-15; ⏰noon-3pm Tue-Sun; P) What's not to love at this superb-value lunch-only place with incredible sea views from the mountainside overlooking St-Pierre? The welcome is warm and the Creole cooking is both wonderful and authentic. On Sunday there's a buffet (€25 per person) with Creole dancing – it's very popular and a local cultural highlight, so reservations are essential.

★Le Guérin CREOLE $$
(☎0596-78-18-07; covered market, Rue Bouillé; mains €10-15, menu €15; ⏰lunch Mon-Sat; 👪) Upstairs within the old market, this is the most popular lunch spot in town – no contest. There can be a wait during the rush, but with some of the best *acras* and *boudin créole* (blood sausage) on Martinique, the extra time is worth it. There's also a kids' menu.

Chez Marie-Claire CREOLE $$
(☎0596-69-48-21; covered market, Rue Bouillé; mains €12-18, menus €14-17; ⏰noon-2:30pm Mon-Sat; 👪) Upstairs on a metallic mezzanine overlooking the covered market, Chez Marie-Claire is about as unfussy and informal as dining gets on this French island, but that doesn't make its Creole dishes (such as stewed beef, freshwater crayfish and conch) any less delicious. The various *menus* (set meals) are a steal and there's a good children's menu.

Le Tamaya FRENCH CARIBBEAN $$
(☎0596-78-29-09; 85 Rue Gabriel Péri; mains €13-19.50, lunch menu €15; ⏰noon-2pm & 6:30-9pm Thu-Tue, 6:30-9pm Wed; ❄📶) This simple little restaurant near the imposing Maison de la Bourse on the seafront road is a reliable choice. It prepares delectable French-inspired dishes with a tropical twist – one of the more unusual items is grouper in vanilla sauce. The lunchtime *menu* is great value and children are also catered for.

Resto Beach Grill SEAFOOD $$
(☎0596-78-34-02; Carbet; mains €16-29; ⏰11:30am-2pm Tue-Sun, 7-10pm Fri & Sat; 📶) This hugely popular sand-floor and plastic-chair place on Carbet's beach (about 4km south of St-Pierre) is very professionally run, with attentive staff members and an excellent menu of seafood and meat dishes. The salads are huge and the fish is fresh and delicious.

★1643 FRENCH $$$
(☎0596-78-17-81; www.restaurant1643.com; Anse Latouche; mains €22-29; ⏰noon-2pm & 7-9pm Tue-Sat, noon-2:30pm Sun; 📶) The best place in St-Pierre for an extravagant gastronomic experience, this delightful restaurant is in the same historic property as the Hotel de l'Anse, though it's separately run. The name refers to the year in which the Habitation Anse Latouche was founded. The house specialty is *magret de canard* (duck fillet) with foie gras. Need we say more?

Information

Tourist Office (Rue Victor Hugo; ⏰8am-4pm Mon-Fri) This proudly francophone office offers guided tours of St-Pierre in French and English at 9:30am and 2:30pm Monday to Friday (hours can vary). The office was about to move at the time of research, though the staff didn't know where.

Getting There & Away

There are regular buses between St-Pierre and Fort-de-France (€5, 45 minutes) throughout the day, though these end around 4pm and don't run on Sunday. Buses leave from the tiny bus station on Rue Bouillé near the Hôtel Villa Saint-Pierre (p571) but pick up passengers at any stop along the main road.

The most central place to park is around the old Maison de la Bourse (Exchange) on the seafront.

Grand-Rivière

Set at Martinique's northernmost point, in a gorgeous position beneath coastal cliffs covered in jungle, Grand-Rivière is an isolated and unspoiled fishing village full of pastel cottages. Mont Pelée forms a rugged backdrop to the south, and there's a fine view of black-sand beaches on either side, plus – in good conditions – neighboring Dominica to the north. This is Martinique at its wildest and most remote.

The main road dead-ends at the sea, where there's a tiny fish market and rows of brightly colored fishing boats in the small harbor. There's little to do here except lie on the beach, but it's the starting point for a delightfully scenic hike along the northwestern side of Mont Pelée all the way to Le Prêcheur, and it's also a very worthwhile day trip for a good lunch and some dramatic scenery.

Sights & Activities

Plage de Sinaï BEACH

West of the harbor, this palm-and-cliff-backed beach has sand blacker than the darkest of chocolate that shelves gently into the warm sea.

Au Fil des Anses BOATING

(☎0696-44-50-66, 0696-38-90-68; www.aufildesanses.com; trips from €29) Run by the friendly Omer, this well-organized operation offers good-value boat excursions that take you to various scenic spots along the wild coast between Grand-Rivière and Le Prêcheur for swimming, snorkeling and trying your hand at fishing. It can also pick you up from Le Prêcheur or Grand-Rivière at the end of a hike for €15.

Sleeping & Eating

Tante Arlette GUESTHOUSE $

(☎0596-55-75-75; www.tantearlette.com; 3 Rue Lucy de Fossarieu; r from €70;) The only hotel option in Grand-Rivière, Tante Arlette offers a smart but slightly overpriced set of 10 rooms upstairs from her popular restaurant. The superior rooms at the back are a big step up from the poky standards at the front. There's a Jacuzzi for guest use.

Le Floup Floup CREOLE $

(☎0696-81-38-49; 2 Chemin Rural de Malakoff; mains €7-12; lunch & dinner) If Tante Arlette is too expensive or you just want a quick lunch near the beach, this basic but superb snack bar serves excellent Creole chicken and seafood, as well as the best homemade coconut ice cream you'll taste in Martinique.

Tante Arlette CREOLE $$

(☎0596-55-75-75; www.tantearlette.com; 3 Rue Lucy de Fossarieu; mains €14-45; noon-3:30pm Tue-Sun, dinner for hotel guests only;) This long-standing favorite is the best place in northern Martinique to try authentic Creole food. The house specialty is the seafood grill (€45), which includes half a lobster, conch and shrimp, or – for the same price – a stew of the same creatures.

Getting There & Away

A bus from Fort-de-France (€11.20, 80 minutes) leaves a few times a day. It's often quicker to take a bus to the town of Basse-Pointe (€10.50, one hour) and try to get on a minibus (€1.50, 20 minutes) from there to Grand-Rivière. Be prepared to wait in Basse-Pointe, however, and make the journey in the morning if you want to avoid spending the night in Grand-Rivière.

Presqu'île de Caravelle

The attractive Presqu'île de Caravelle is a little-visited peninsula with some gorgeous stretches of beach and a wild, untamed feel. A gently twisting road with spectacular views runs through sugarcane fields to the charming main village of Tartane and on to Baie du Galion. On the northern side of the peninsula are a couple of protected beaches, including some spots favored by surfers. With several superb restaurants, a very atmospheric colonial ruin and some excellent walking, it's surprising that there's not as much tourism here as in other parts of the island. Most people visit on a day trip by hire car.

Sights

★ Anse l'Etang BEACH

(P) This palm-fringed beach with coarse golden sand and lots of shade is one of Martinique's most appealing strands. It's not altogether suitable for swimming, though, because the waters are rough, with lots of wave action. It's popular with surfing children.

Plage des Surfeurs BEACH

(Anse Dufour) This is where most surfers in Martinique are heading, a fantastic spot with great waves crashing onto a golden shore. There's nothing here other than lots of other surfers, but several surf schools are located in the houses directly behind the beach, and some instructors even hang out on the sand looking for customers.

Plage de La Brèche BEACH

(P) On the eastern outskirts of Tartane, this crescent of sand edged by manchineel trees is a stunning beach to sun yourself on, the view out to sea entirely blocked by landmasses. The sand is brown-gray, and there are picnic tables and a beach restaurant.

Anse de Tartane BEACH

(Tartane) Fronting the village of Tartane, this long strand of soft beige sand has lots of fishing shacks, a fish market and colorful *gommier* (gum-tree) boats. It can get crowded with locals at weekends but is a great place to swim, with calm waters and an island the intrepid can swim out to.

Château Dubuc RUINS

(☎0596-58-09-00; adult/child €5/2.50; ⏱9am-4:30pm) The ruins of this 17th-century estate are set almost at the end of the peninsula and are a haunting and atmospheric sight. The story goes that the master of the estate used a lantern to lure ships into wrecking themselves off the coast and then gathered the loot. Now the place is a superbly run attraction, and your entry fee includes an excellent audio tour that really brings it to life. Allow plenty of time here, as it's an enormous site.

Several hiking trails start from here, including a 3km walk to a historic lighthouse, from where there are great views.

To get here from Tartane you'll need your own wheels (the road is unpaved, but you don't need a 4WD). Due to the lack of shade, this is not a place you'll want to bring the kids.

Activities

Surf Up SURFING

(☎0596-77-73-60; www.martinique-surf.com; 19 Rue de Surf, Plage des Surfeurs) Offering surfing and paddleboarding courses, this enthusiastically run place just by Plage des Surfeurs is good value. English is spoken.

Ecole de Surf Bliss SURFING

(☎0596-58-00-96; www.surf-martinique.com; Rue de Surf, Plage des Surfeurs; group lessons per hour €35) This professional outfit offers group or private surfing lessons for people of all ages and experience levels on the nearby beach; it also rents surfboards and bodyboards. Group lessons begin at 10:30am, 2pm and 3:30pm. English is spoken.

Sleeping

Hôtel Résidence Océane HOTEL $$

(☎0596-58-73-73; www.residenceoceane.com; Rte du Château Dubuc, Anse l'Etang; d €99-125; ❄📶🏊) The Océane ticks all the right boxes. It's small enough to be low-key and relaxed but big enough to have a bit of buzz – the surfer crowd likes to stay here. Best of all, it's blessed with stunning ocean views, and the nearest beach – Plage des Surfeurs – is within easy walking distance. Some rooms have terraces with kitchenettes.

Hotel Restaurant Caravelle HOTEL $$

(☎0596-58-07-32; www.hotel-la-caravelle-martinique.com; Rte du Château Dubuc; s/d from €76/89; ❄📶) This small, friendly, family-run hotel is a great choice. There's a hibiscus-covered terrace with glorious views of the Atlantic, and the public areas are all beautifully furnished and well looked after. Rooms are very pleasant and come in several sizes, including studios that have well-equipped kitchenettes and a spacious front porch with great views. There's an excellent on-site restaurant. Some English is spoken.

Hotel Le Manguier HOTEL $$

(☎0596-58-48-95; www.hotel-martinique-le-manguier.com; Tartane; d with garden/sea view €84/98; ❄📶🏊) A great-value port of call. This charming collection of whitewashed units is perched high above the center of Tartane. The simple yet rather sleek rooms have small outdoor hot-plate kitchens, redone bathrooms and great balconies, many of which face the Atlantic Ocean. There's a small pool, and breakfast is served with a sea view.

Eating

The eating options in Tartane are plentiful, both along the seafront and just off the beaches.

Ti Carbet CREOLE $

(☎0696-27-17-01; Tartane; mains €10-12; ⊙noon-5pm) This little local treasure overlooks the attractive Plage de la Brèche on the eastern outskirts of Tartane. It concocts good, fresh food at competitive prices, especially given the enviable location. You won't get much variety, but tasty staples usually include grilled fish, octopus stew and curried chicken.

★Cocoa Beach Cafe INTERNATIONAL $$

(☎0596-38-31-03; Anse l'Etang; mains €14-23; ⊙noon-11pm;) Jérémie and his cooks offer a wonderfully eclectic Asian-Créole fusion menu to a young crowd right on the gorgeous beach at Anse l'Etang. Dishes include Balinese-style chicken, Tahitian-style raw fish, *bò bun* of beef and a superb *mi cuit de thon teriyaki* (semicooked tuna teriyaki). Vegetarian and gluten-free versions of some dishes can be ordered, and service is friendly and efficient.

In the evenings this turns into a great beach hangout with a long cocktail card and a cool sea breeze. Hours can vary.

Fond de la Mer CREOLE $$

(☎596-58-26-85; Tartane; mains €8-25; ⊙noon-3pm & 7-10pm) Under new management, this reliably open restaurant set high above the cars and loudspeakers of Tartane's seafront plates up well-crafted helpings of *blaff*, fish broth, conch fricassee and *touffé de requin* (stewed shark). The views are as good as the service is courteous.

Le Phare FRENCH $$

(☎0596-58-08-48; Anse Bonneville; mains €15-25, menus €16-20; ⊙noon-10pm Tue-Sat;) Don't be fooled by the disheveled frontage: Le Phare has a terrific hilltop setting next to the end of the road that leads to Château Dubuc and is famous for the incredible views of Anse Bonneville and the sea from its deck; you may never have tuna tartare or a kangaroo fillet with a view to rival this one.

L'Escapade CREOLE $$

(☎0596-58-43-08; Tartane; mains €15-20, lunch menu €17; ⊙10am-3pm & 7-10pm Mon, Tue, Thu & Fri) It doesn't get much simpler than this, but that's why you should head to the western end of the main strip in Tartane and this informal, family-run eatery serving up simple yet well-executed Creole dishes such as conch stew or spicy goat stew. It sure packs them in at lunchtime and is a real slice of local life.

★La Table de Mamy Nounou FRENCH $$$

(☎0596-58-07-32; Hôtel Restaurant Caravelle, Rte du Château Dubuc; mains €9-29; ⊙noon-2pm & 7-9pm Wed-Mon;) This lauded restaurant at the Hôtel Restaurant Caravelle is a winner, thanks to its sophisticated mains, wonderful homemade desserts and breezy veranda with lovely sea views. Standout dishes might include *grenadin de porcelet* (larded fillet of suckling pig) and lamb with aromatic herbs. The flambéed-banana dessert is a treat. There are different lunch and dinner menus.

Le Ratelot FRENCH $$$

(☎0596-63-26-11; www.restaurant-leratelot.fr; Anse l'Etang; mains €17-30; ⊙noon-9pm Mon, Tue, Fri & Sat, to 4pm Wed, to 4:30pm Sun;) Right under the palm trees on the most attractive beach (p573) in Tartane, this respected restaurant turns out superb dishes that include beefsteak, duck breast in a variety of sauces, and marlin with gorgonzola cheese. There's dining on the terrace and, from virtually all points, a superb view of the beach.

Information

Office de Tourisme (☎0596-38-07-01; Tartane; ⊙1-4:30pm Mon, 8:30am-1pm & 2-4:30pm Tue-Thu, 8:30am-noon Sat & Sun, closed Wed, Fri & public holidays) This helpful local tourist office is housed in an inconspicuous gated building next to the Oasis Beach restaurant on Tartane's seafront.

Getting There & Away

The gateway to Presqu'île de Caravelle is the town of La Trinité, which has direct hourly buses to and from Fort-de-France (€4.50, 45 minutes) that stop at its small bus station in the town center. Here you'll need to transfer to the local *navette* (shuttle bus) to Tartane (€1.20, 15 minutes, every 30 minutes). Buses run into the center of Tartane and stop along the seafront.

UNDERSTAND MARTINIQUE

History

When Christopher Columbus first sighted Martinique it was inhabited by Caribs, who called the island Madinina, meaning 'island of flowers.' In 1635 the first party of French settlers, led by Pierre Belain d'Esnambuc, landed on the northwestern side of the island. There they built a small fort and established a settlement that would become the capital city, St-Pierre. The next year, on October 31, 1636, Louis XIII signed a decree authorizing the use of enslaved Africans in the French West Indies.

The settlers quickly went about colonizing the land with the help of slave labor; by 1640 they had extended their grip south to Fort-de-France, where they constructed a fort on the rise above the harbor. As forests were cleared to make room for sugar plantations, conflicts with the Caribs escalated into warfare, and in 1660 those Caribs who had survived the fighting were finally forced off the island.

The British also took a keen interest in Martinique, invading and holding the island for most of the period from 1794 to 1815. The island prospered under British occupation; the planters simply sold their sugar in British markets rather than French ones. Perhaps more importantly, the occupation allowed Martinique to avoid the turmoil of the French Revolution. By the time the British returned the island to France in 1815, the Napoleonic Wars had ended and the French empire was again entering a period of stability.

Not long after the French administration was re-established on Martinique the golden era of sugarcane began to wane, as glutted markets and the introduction of sugar beets on mainland France eroded prices. With their wealth diminished, the aristocratic plantation owners lost much of their political influence, and the abolitionist movement, led by Victor Schoelcher, gained momentum.

It was Schoelcher, the French cabinet minister responsible for overseas possessions, who convinced the provisional government to sign the 1848 Emancipation Proclamation, which brought an end to slavery in the French West Indies. Widely reviled by the white aristocracy of the time, Schoelcher is now regarded as one of Martinique's heroes.

In 1946 Martinique went from being a colony to an overseas *département* of France, with a status similar to those of metropolitan *départements*. In 1974 it became a one-*département* region of France.

People & Culture

The earliest colonists on Martinique were from Normandy, Brittany, Paris and other parts of France; shortly afterward, enslaved Africans were brought to the island. Later, smaller numbers of immigrants came from India, Syria and Lebanon. These days, Martinique is home to thousands of immigrants, some of them here illegally, from poorer

THE ERUPTION OF MONT PELÉE

At the end of the 19th century, St-Pierre – then the capital of Martinique – was a flourishing port city. Mont Pelée, the island's highest peak at 1397m, was just a scenic backdrop.

In spring 1902, sulfurous steam vents on the mountain began emitting gases and a crater lake started to fill with boiling water. Authorities dismissed it all as the normal cycle of the volcano, which had experienced harmless periods of activity in the past.

But at 8am on Sunday May 8, 1902, Mont Pelée exploded in a glowing burst of suffocating, superheated gas and burning ash. The force of the explosion was 40 times that of the later nuclear blast over Hiroshima. St-Pierre was laid waste in minutes.

Of the city's 30,000 inhabitants, there were just three survivors. One of them, a prisoner named Louis-Auguste Cyparis, escaped with only minor burns – ironically, he owed his life to having been locked in a tomblike solitary-confinement cell at the local jail. He went on to tour the world with Barnum & Bailey's Circus as part of its 'Greatest Show on Earth.'

Mont Pelée continued to smolder for months, but by 1904 people had begun to resettle the town, building among the crumbled ruins.

Caribbean countries such as Dominica, St Lucia and Haiti. Martinique's population today hovers around 400,000; more than a quarter live in the Fort-de-France area.

The majority of residents are of mixed ethnic origin. The Black Pride movement known as *négritude* emerged as a philosophical and literary movement in the 1930s, largely through the writings of Martinique native Aimé Césaire, a *négritude* poet who was eventually elected mayor of Fort-de-France. The movement advanced black social and cultural values and re-established bonds with African traditions, which had been suppressed by French colonialism.

The beguine, an Afro-French style of dance music with a bolero rhythm, originated in Martinique in the 1930s. Zouk is a more contemporary French West Indian creation, drawing on the beguine and other French-Caribbean folk forms. Retaining the electronic influences of its 1980s origins with its Carnival-like rhythm and hot dance beat, zouk has become as popular in Europe as it is in the French Caribbean.

Landscape & Wildlife

At 1080 sq km, Martinique is the second-largest island in the French West Indies. Roughly 65km long and 20km wide, it has a terrain punctuated by hills, plateaus and mountains.

The highest point is the 1397m-high Mont Pelée, an active volcano at the northern end of the island. The island's center is dominated by the Pitons du Carbet, a scenic mountain range reaching 1207m. Martinique's irregular coastline is cut by deep bays and coves, while the mountainous rainforest in the interior feeds numerous rivers.

The Land

The Carib name for Martinique was Madinina, meaning 'island of flowers,' and it's not difficult to see why. Martinique has lots of colorful flowering plants, with the vegetation varying with altitude and rainfall. Rainforests cover the slopes of the mountains in the northern interior, luxuriant with tree ferns, bamboo groves, climbing vines and hardwood trees such as mahogany, rosewood, locust and *gommier* (gum tree).

The drier southern part of the island has brushy savanna vegetation such as cacti, frangipani trees, balsam, logwood and acacia shrubs. Common landscape plantings include splashy bougainvillea, the ubiquitous red hibiscus and yellow-flowered allamanda trees. To truly appreciate the range and magnificence of the island's varied flora, head to the unbeatable Jardin de Balata on the mountainous Route de la Trace and see the many flowers that gave Martinique its name.

Wildlife

Martinique is home to anole lizards, manicous (opossums), mongooses and venomous fer-de-lance snakes. The mongoose, which was introduced from India in the late 19th century, preys on eggs and has been responsible for the demise of many bird species. Some native birds, such as parrots, are no longer found on the island at all, while others have significantly declined in numbers. Endangered birds include the Martinique trembler, white-breasted trembler and white-breasted thrasher.

The underwater life tends to be of the smaller variety: lots of schools of tiny fish that swim by in a cloud of silver or red. There's a decent number of lobsters hiding under rocks, and occasionally a ray will glide by.

SURVIVAL GUIDE

Directory A–Z

ACCESSIBLE TRAVEL

By comparison with other Caribbean Islands, Martinique makes good provision for travelers with disabilities. Many hotels have wheelchair-accessible rooms, and many public places have disabled toilets.

ACCOMMODATIONS

Hotels on Martinique aren't particularly charming or cheap, and many guesthouses are run in a semiprofessional manner, meaning that the owners have other jobs. You can expect receptions to be unstaffed, so it's a good idea to make arrangements in advance. On the plus side, hotels here are generally small by Caribbean standards and large resorts are rare.

CHILDREN

Children will be welcome on vacation in Martinique. Many hotels are family oriented and the island is a very safe place overall. Practically all hotels will provide cots, and some hotels provide babysitting services.

All restaurants welcome children, and they'll often have a simple and good-value *menu enfant* (children's set meal) to offer them. Kids will love the island's artisan ice cream, especially coconut sorbet available on every beach.

European brands of baby formula, foods and diapers can be bought at pharmacies.

Top activities to look out for if you're traveling with kids include the impressive Zoo de Martinique (p568) near St-Pierre and Dauphins Martinique (p561) for marine wildlife spotting. Particularly child-friendly beaches are Plage Anse d'Arlet (p563) and Grande Anse des Salines (p567), both in the south.

ELECTRICITY

Power runs on 220V, 50Hz. Plugs have two round prongs; a plug adapter is essential for non-European chargers and other electrical equipment.

EMERGENCY NUMBERS

Ambulance	☎15
Fire	☎18
Police	☎17

FOOD

Martinique is a treat for lovers of good food. The French influence has placed food and drink at the center of life and led to a preponderance of competitive and inventive restaurants, and the fish and seafood are of superb quality. Almost every town has an outstanding restaurant, and it's also hard to go wrong at any beach shack. Prices are high, though, even in beach shacks and pop-up cafes.

Essential Food & Drink

➡ **Acras** A universally popular snack in Martinique, *acras* are fish, seafood or vegetable tempura. *Acras de morue* (cod) and *crevettes* (shrimp) are the most common and are both delicious.

➡ **Ti-punch** Short for *petit punch*, this ubiquitous and strong cocktail is the normal *apéro* (aperitif) in Martinique. It's a mix of rum, lime and cane syrup – but mainly rum.

➡ **Crabes farcis** Stuffed crabs are a common local dish. Normally they're stuffed with a spicy mixture of crabmeat, garlic, shallots and parsley, and cooked in their shells.

➡ **Blaff** This is the local term for white fish marinated in lime juice, garlic and peppers, then poached. While it's popular across the Caribbean, its true home is Martinique.

HEALTH

Medical care is similar to that in mainland France, and so is excellent by the standards of the region. The biggest hospital is the CHU de Martinique (p560) in Fort-de-France, though there are smaller hospitals in almost every region. There are plenty of pharmacies throughout the island; look for the green cross, often flashing in neon.

EU citizens can get health-care costs refunded through their European Health Insurance Cards. When paying for medical care, nationals of other countries should keep all receipts to reclaim money from their health-insurance providers.

INTERNET ACCESS

Wireless (often called WLAN locally) is ubiquitous in Martinique, and can be found for free at nearly all hotels and guesthouses, as well as in most cafes and restaurants. Fort-de-France has free wi-fi zones in the city center, but they're slightly hit and miss.

LEGAL MATTERS

French law governs legal matters in Martinique. There is a presumption of innocence as well as the right to a lawyer. Most travelers will have no interaction with the police at all.

LGBT+ TRAVELERS

Gay rights are legally protected in Martinique, as it is part of France. However, homophobia is still prevalent and there is little or no gay scene on the island. Gay and lesbian travelers have nothing to worry about, though, and same-sex couples booking a double room will cause no problems.

MONEY

Hotels, larger restaurants and car-rental agencies accept Visa and MasterCard, but American

SLEEPING PRICE RANGES

The following rates refer to a double room in high season (December to April and July to August).

€ less than €80

€€ €80–150

€€€ more than €150

EATING PRICE RANGES

The following price ranges are for the cost of a main course, though note that pricier seafood comes in at over €30 a plate. Also watch out for very steeply priced desserts.

€ less than €12

€€ €12–20

€€€ more than €20

Express isn't widely accepted. ATMs are common, but not all accept all cards.

Exchange Rates

Australia	A$1	€0.62
Canada	C$1	€0.65
Japan	¥100	€0.82
New Zealand	NZ$1	€0.58
South Africa	ZAR100	€6.13
UK	UK£1	€1.12
US	US$1	€0.89

For current exchange rates, see www.xe.com.

Taxes & Refunds

If you do not live in France, it is possible to claim back VAT on certain purchased items at the airport when you leave Martinique. This isn't possible if you're flying from Martinique to France.

Tipping

Tipping is not normally expected in Martinique, though it's polite to round up your bill to the nearest euro, and to give a tip for any exceptional service.

OPENING HOURS

Banks 9am to 4pm Monday to Friday.
Bars 9pm to midnight.
Restaurants 11:30am to 10pm Monday to Saturday (some closed between lunch and dinner).
Shops 9am to 7pm Monday to Saturday.
Supermarkets 8am to 8pm Monday to Saturday, 9am to 1pm Sunday.

PRACTICALITIES

Newspapers & magazines *France-Antilles* (www.martinique.franceantilles.fr) is the main daily newspaper for the French West Indies. French newspapers and magazines are commonly found everywhere; print editions in English are fairly rare.

Radio Tune in to Réseau Outre-Mer 1ère (www.la1ere.fr).

Smoking Banned in all enclosed public spaces, though due to the number of outdoor places in Martinique, there are still many situations in which there might be smoking around you.

TV Catch up on local TV on networks RFO 1 and RFO 2.

Weights & measures Martinique uses the metric system and the 24-hour clock.

PUBLIC HOLIDAYS

New Year's Day January 1
Easter Sunday Late March/early April
Ascension Thursday Fortieth day after Easter
Pentecost Monday Eighth Monday after Easter
Labor Day May 1
Victory Day May 8
Slavery Abolition Day May 22
Bastille Day July 14
Schoelcher Day July 21
Assumption Day August 15
All Saints' Day November 1
Armistice Day November 11
Christmas Day December 25

SAFE TRAVEL

Martinique is generally a very safe island and the vast majority of visits pass without incident.

- As with anywhere in France, occasional strikes can bring services to a screeching halt.
- It's not advisable to wander around the largely empty backstreets of Fort-de-France after dark.
- Drivers on Martinique can be erratic and often aggressive – drive defensively and stay away from drivers acting oddly.
- Mosquitoes can carry Zika virus and dengue fever – use fans, nets and mozzie spray.

TELEPHONE

The country code for Martinique is 596. Confusingly, all local numbers begin with 0596 as well. These numbers are separate, however, and therefore must be dialed twice when calling from abroad. Local mobile numbers begin with 0696.

When calling from within the French Antilles, simply dial the local 10-digit number. From elsewhere, dial your country's international access code, followed by the 596 country code and the local number (omit the first zero).

Cell Phones

Coverage generally pretty good; SIM cards widely available. Calls and data relatively expensive: around €20 for 1GB. Local providers, with offices in most larger towns: SFR, Orange and Digicel. European cell (mobile) phones should work as they do at home.

TIME

Martinique runs to Eastern Caribbean Time (GMT/UTC minus four hours). Daylight saving is not observed.

TOURIST INFORMATION

The Martinique Promotion Bureau site (www.martinique.org) is a good source of information, in English and several other languages. Many towns have at least one small tourist office where the staff will speak English and can usually give you free maps and some useful local advice. Pamphlets, mainly in French but with enough pictures and maps to convey the gist, are available at airports and many hotels.

Getting There & Away

AIR

The island's only airport is **Aéroport International Martinique Aimé Césaire** (FDF; www.martinique.aeroport.fr; Lamentin; 📶), near the town of Lamentin in the southeast of Martinique, a short distance from Fort-de-France.

A number of airlines serve Martinique:

Air Canada (www.aircanada.com; Aéroport International Martinique Aimé Césaire) From Montréal.

Air France (www.airfrance.com; Aéroport International Martinique Aimé Césaire) From Paris.

American Airlines (www.aa.com; Aéroport International Martinique Aimé Césaire) From San Juan (Puerto Rico) and Miami.

Corsair (www.corsair.com; Aéroport International Martinique Aimé Césaire) From Paris.

There are direct regional services to Dominica, Guadeloupe, Port-au-Prince (Haiti), Havana (Cuba), San Juan, St-Barthélemy, St Lucia, St-Martin/Sint Maarten and Santo Domingo (Dominican Republic).

Regional airlines serving Martinique include **Air Caraïbes** (www.aircaraibes.com; Aéroport International Martinique Aimé Césaire), **Air Antilles Express** (www.airantilles.com; Aéroport International Martinique Aimé Césaire) and **LIAT** (www.liat.com; Aéroport International Martinique Aimé Césaire).

SEA

Ferry

L'Express des Îles (p560) operates large, modern catamarans between Fort-de-France and Pointe-à-Pitre (Guadeloupe; three hours), with a stop in Roseau (Dominica; 1½ hours). In the other direction there are departures from Fort-de-France to Castries (St Lucia; 80 minutes). There are three to five weekly crossings in both directions.

Jeans for Freedom (p560) operates services between Fort-de-France and Pointe-à-Pitre. There are one to three weekly services depending on the season.

There are discounts of 50% for children aged under two, 10% for students and for passengers aged under 12, and 5% for passengers younger than 26 or older than 60. Departure days and times change frequently and, due to weather conditions, often bear no relation to the printed schedule. The only way to be sure is to call the ferry company or check with a local travel agent.

Yacht

The main port of entry is in Fort-de-France, but yachts may also clear at St-Pierre or Marin, both of which have marinas.

Yachting and sailing are very popular in Martinique and numerous charter companies operate on the island, including Sparkling Charter (p556), based at the **Marina du Marin** (www.marina-martinique.fr), and Star Voyage (p556), based at the **Marina de la Pointe du Bout** (Marina des Trois-Îlets; ☎0596-66-07-74; www.marina3ilets.com).

Getting Around

Most visitors hire a car for their time here, as hire rates are low and the road network is good, though traffic jams around Fort-de-France can slow things down considerably.

BICYCLE

Martinique is decidedly hilly, but it's perfectly possible to hire a bike here. Drivers generally respect cyclists, but it's important to use lights at night and high-visibility clothing in the rain.

BOAT

A regular *vedette* (ferry) between Martinique's main resort areas and Fort-de-France provides a nice alternative to dealing with heavy bus and car traffic; it also allows you to avoid the hassles of city parking and is considerably quicker.

BUS

Although there are some larger public buses serving the urban area around Fort-de France, most buses elsewhere in Martinique are minivans marked 'TC' (for *taxis collectifs*) on top. Destinations are marked on the vans, sometimes on the side doors and sometimes on a small sign stuck in the front window. However, this mode of transport is not really recommended for visitors as services are erratic and vehicles often decrepit.

The new TCSP (p560) road train looks like a tram but is in fact a very long, bendy bus. It's a godsend for those traveling between the airport and central Fort-de-France as it has a dedicated lane on the motorway so doesn't get stuck in jams. It's also good for reaching the large, out-of-town shopping areas between the city and the airport.

CAR & MOTORCYCLE

Renting a car is the most reliable form of transportation in Martinique. Car rental is a breeze, rates are low and the road network is excellent.

Car Rental

There are numerous international and local car-rental agencies at Martinique's airport (p579). (You cannot walk to their offices – free shuttle buses take you between the terminal and the car-hire village.) You'll find the best rates on the company websites; local firms are generally cheaper than international agencies. You must be at least 21 years of age to rent a car, and some companies add a surcharge for drivers under 25.

Local companies:

Carib Rentacar (☎0596-42-16-15; www.rentacar-caraibes.com; Aéroport International Martinique Aimé Césaire; ⏰8am-6pm)

Pop's Car (☎0596-42-16-84; www.popscar.com; Aéroport International Martinique Aimé Césaire; ⏰8am-6pm)

Road Conditions

Roads in Martinique are excellent by Caribbean standards, and there are multilane freeways (along with rush-hour traffic) in the Fort-de-France area. Drivers can be quite badly behaved in Martinique, so drive defensively.

Road Rules

Drive on the right. Traffic regulations and road signs are the same as those in Europe, speed limits are posted, and exits and intersections are clearly marked.

HITCHHIKING

With only a threadbare, semi-official public-transportation system, hitchhiking is very common on Martinique. You will often see locals thumbing a ride at bus stops, having given up on a shared taxi ever arriving. The odd tourist can also be seen waving down cars, especially in the evenings and on Sunday, when no shared taxis run.

Hitchhiking is never entirely safe, and we don't recommend it. Travelers who hitch should understand that they are taking a small but potentially serious risk.

TAXI

Taxis are fairly pricey in Martinique. A 40% surcharge is added to all fares between 8pm and 6am, and all day on Sunday and holidays.

Montserrat

☎664 / POP 5000

Includes ➡

Best Places to Eat

➡ Pont's Beach View (p585)

➡ People's Place (p585)

➡ Olveston House Restaurant (p585)

Best Places to Stay

➡ Gingerbread Hill (p584)

➡ Olveston House (p585)

➡ Essence Guesthouse (p584)

Why Go?

Montserrat is one of the Caribbean's most dramatic islands, not only in terms of its soaring peaks and rainforest-covered hillsides, but also due to the cataclysmic eruptions of the Soufrière Hills Volcano that took place in the late 1990s. Hundreds of successive eruptions devastated the tiny island, leading to the abandonment of the capital Plymouth and the removal of the entire population from the island's lower two-thirds, the repercussions of which are still felt today.

Two decades later, this modern-day Pompeii is slowly recovering. The population is growing, and sand-mining and geothermal energy provide new sources of income. Tourists are returning too, a trickle to be sure and mostly for volcano-related day trips, but those who stay are drawn by the slow rhythm of life, friendly locals, fabulous hiking and birdwatching, and the blessedly tranquil ambience of the old Caribbean, where gated communities and cruise ships are yet to arrive.

When to Go

➡ **Mar** Paint the island even greener during St Patrick's week.

➡ **Jul–Nov** Hurricane season; storms can disrupt transport to and from the island. The Volcano Half Marathon is in November.

➡ **Dec** Montserrat Festival, the local version of Carnival, runs from Christmas to New Year.

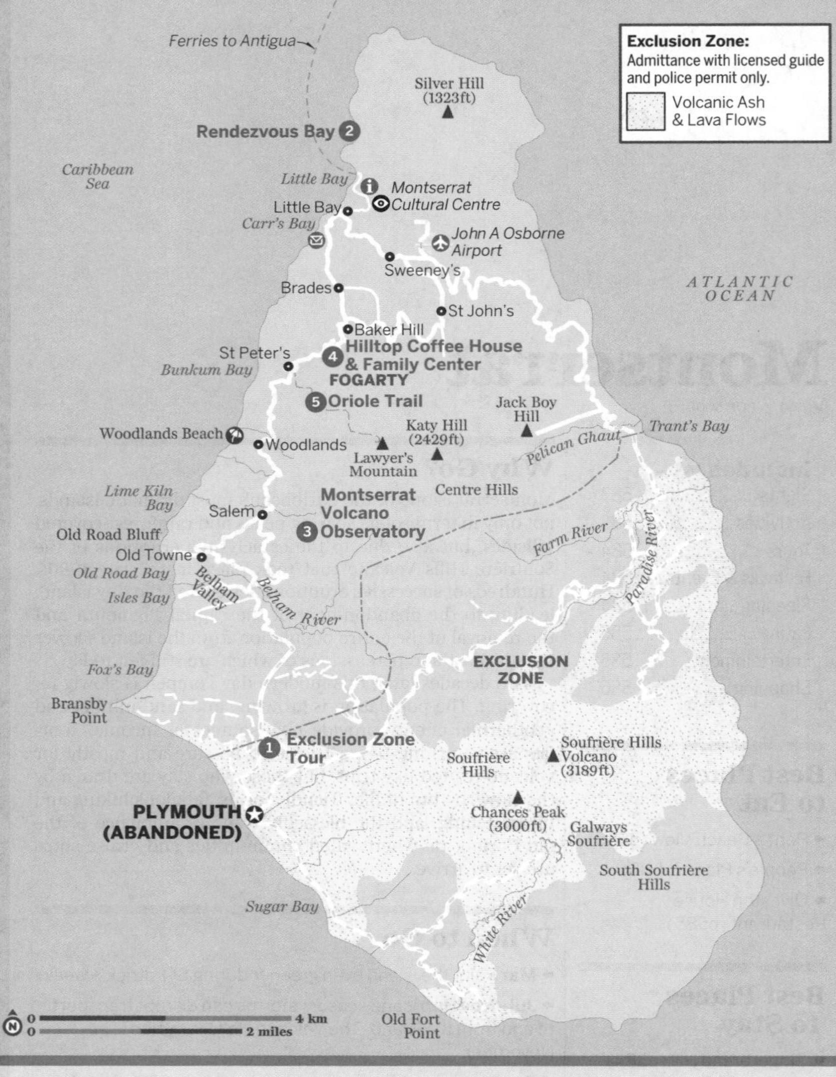

Montserrat Highlights

1 **Exclusion Zone Tour** (p584) Witnessing the destruction wreaked on the buried city of Plymouth and seeing the way nature is reclaiming the abandoned capital.

2 **Rendezvous Bay** (p583) Kayaking or hiking to and then swimming and snorkeling at Montserrat's only white-sand beach.

3 **Montserrat Volcano Observatory** (p583) Enjoying panoramic views of the Exclusion Zone and unraveling the mysteries of the Soufrière Hills Volcano.

4 **Hilltop Coffee House & Family Center** (p583) Stopping by this nonprofit cafe for unique art and memorabilia, plus a volcano video and fresh juices.

5 **Oriole Trail** (p584) Plunging on through the rainforest on this moderate 1.3-mile hike that's perfect for birders and nature lovers.

Sights

★Hilltop Coffee House & Family Center
MUSEUM

(www.gingerbreadhill.com; Cedar Dr, St Peter's; ⌚8am-1pm Mon-Sat) A must-see on any Montserrat visit, this nonprofit cafe founded by filmmaker David Lea and his wife Clover does multi-duty as museum, art gallery, community center and de facto tourist office. Have a juice or cuppa on the veranda, then time travel through Montserrat milestones by watching David's acclaimed documentary on the Soufrière Hills Volcano eruption; paying tribute to soca star Arrow; and marveling at memorabilia rescued from the buried city and George Martin's AIR Studios.

All proceeds go to community projects.

★Rendezvous Bay
BEACH

Montserrat's only white sandy beach is a lovely (though totally facility-free) crescent perfect for swimming, snorkeling and diving. It can only be accessed via a steep 0.7-mile trail from Little Bay. Alternatively, get there by kayak, a far more pleasant adventure. Rentals are available in Little Bay.

If you're hiking, budget about 20 minutes, including a stop at the top of the trail to enjoy great views.

Jack Boy Hill
VIEWPOINT

After about a 3-mile drive south along the east coast (from where the main road reaches the coast), the badly battered road turns into the hills and leads to this well-maintained viewpoint with fixed binoculars and picnic tables. You can see where the island has increased in size due to volcanic activity, as well as the remains of the old airport.

Montserrat Volcano Observatory
MUSEUM

(MVO; ☎664-491-5647; www.mvo.ms; Flemmings; adult/child EC$10/free; ⌚10am-4pm Mon-Fri) Scientists at the MVO keep track of the volcano's every belch and hiccup. At the interpretation center, an 18-minute documentary by local filmmaker David Lea includes riveting live footage of the eruptions and insight into the physical and social upheaval they caused. The terrace offers sweeping views of the volcano. The observatory is often included on tours of the Exclusion Zone.

Woodlands Beach
BEACH

(Woodlands) About halfway down the western coast, this easily accessible dark-sand beach is often footprint-free but has little shade. A covered clifftop picnic area provides benches, showers, toilets and barbecues. Good snorkeling can be had by the cliffs on the south end.

Isles Bay
BEACH

(Garibaldi Hill) This small beach at the mouth of the Belham River is great for swimming and is home to a popular beach barn and restaurant. It gets busy with locals on weekends.

National Museum of Montserrat
MUSEUM

(☎664-491-3086; www.montserratnationaltrust.ms; Little Bay; adult/child under 12yr EC$5/free; ⌚10am-2pm Mon-Fri) This modest little museum presents exhibits on aspects of island culture and history from Amerindian times to the present, including photos and dioramas illustrating pre-eruption Plymouth and a flamboyant stage costume worn by soca superstar Arrow. Opening times can vary.

Belham Valley
RIVER

Now buried under mud and volcanic debris, Belham Valley used to be home to an 18-hole golf course, a bridge and a three-story building. After heavy rain, the area is sometimes closed because of mud flows coming down the mountain.

Runaway Ghaut
SPRING

Ghauts (pronounced 'guts') are steep ravines that send rainwater rushing down from the mountains into the sea. The most famous on the island is Runaway Ghaut, on the side of the road just north of Salem, named after a famous confrontation between the English and French from which the latter apparently ran away. According to legend, those who drink from it will return to Montserrat again.

Activities

Scriber's Adventures & Tours
HIKING

(☎664-492-2943; www.scribersadventures.com) For close encounters with Montserrat's unique flora and fauna, sign up for a hiking tour with James 'Scriber' Daly, who seems to know every bird, bat, turtle or lizard by name and has a knack for spotting the national bird, the elusive Montserrat oriole. Outings run from 90 minutes to three hours and can be tailored to your fitness level.

Montserrat Island Dive Centre
DIVING

(☎664-496-4995; www.islanddivecentre.com; Saint Julian Dr, Woodlands; 2-tank boat dive US$110) This new outfit offers inexpensive shore dives (from US$40) as well as boat dives and an interesting drive-and-dive program, which combines tours of the island and spectacular viewpoints with some excellent shore dives.

Oriole Trail HIKING
(St Peter's) This moderate 1.3-mile trail cuts through the rainforest to the top of Lawyer's Mountain, from where you'll have bird's-eye views of the island. It can easily be done without a guide, although having someone to explain the flora and fauna along the way can deepen your experience. The trailhead is up from the Hilltop Coffee House (ask for directions here).

Scuba Montserrat DIVING
(☎664-491-7807, 664-496-7807; www.scubamontserrat.com; Little Bay; 2-tank dive US$90-100; ⊙office 8am-5pm) Aside from diving trips, this experienced dive shop also runs snorkeling trips to Rendezvous Bay, and the Volcano Boat Tour to the shores off the buried city of Plymouth. Snorkeling gear and kayak rentals are also available, as are beers and coffee in its clubhouse-style premises right on the beach at Little Bay.

Caribbean Helicopters Limited SCENIC FLIGHTS
(☎268-460-5900; www.flychl.com; per person US$285) Caribbean Helicopters operates 50-minute flyovers of Soufrière Hills Volcano and the Exclusion Zone from Antigua's VC Bird International Airport and the helipad near the cruise-ship terminal in St John's.

Tours

★Montserrat Island Tours TOURS
(☎606-658-0077, 664-491-2124; www.montserratislandtours.com; tours per person US$50-100; ⊙office 8am-5pm Mon-Fri) These island tours are run with passion and dedication by charismatic local Sun Lea, who acquaints visitors with Montserrat's unique features and tells personal stories from his childhood here. The most fascinating tours enter the buried city of Plymouth (dependent on seismic and weather conditions; subject to a permit fee of US$100 per group), a truly unique and haunting experience.

Aqua Montserrat TOURS
(☎664-392-9255; www.aquamontserrat.com; Little Bay; tours US$30-150; ⊙Tue & Sat) Founded by Veta Wade, a young and energetic Montserratian returnee from the UK, this outfit takes visitors on customized adventure tours that show off the island's secret nooks and crannies above and below the water. Aqua also rents kayaks and snorkeling equipment. Advanced booking for tours is important.

Veta is also the creator of Fish N Fins, a year-round program teaching local kids how to swim and snorkel.

Festivals & Events

St Patrick's Day Parade PARADE
(Salem; ⊙Mar 17) The Irish were some of Montserrat's first colonists. The island is one of the few places in the world where St Patrick's Day is an official holiday, although its local popularity is linked to a failed slave rebellion that was planned for the holiday in 1768. Join islanders for a weeklong party centered on the village of Salem.

This has in recent years grown to become Montserrat's biggest annual event, with extra flights and ferries laid on to bring thousands of revelers to the island.

Sleeping

★Gingerbread Hill GUESTHOUSE $
(☎664-491-5812; www.gingerbreadhill.com; St Peter's; d US$60-140; P❄️📶🌊) Created by David and Clover Lea, American hippie transplants and devoted Montserrat champions, this charismatic hilltop refuge consists of four artistically decorated self-catering units with spacious verandas and sublime ocean views surrounded by gorgeous gardens. The crown jewel is the Heavenly Suite with a rooftop terrace and views for miles. The Sweet & Simple room downstairs is Montserrat's best budget pick.

Erindell Villa GUESTHOUSE $
(☎664-491-3655; www.erindellvilla.com; Gros Michael Dr, Woodlands; r incl breakfast US$80; P📶🌊) This friendly guesthouse near the rainforest offers two fan-cooled rooms that are comfortable and good value. There are plenty of freebies, including snorkeling gear and a snack basket for all guests, as well as plenty of local contacts thanks to hosts Shirley and Lou who make visitors feel like part of the community.

Essence Guesthouse GUESTHOUSE $$
(☎664-393-7973; www.essence.ms; Old Towne Bluff Dr, Old Towne; r US$90-115; P📶🌊) Run with a personal touch by Belgian couple Annie and Eric, this charismatic and stylishly decorated place has views out over Belham Valley and the volcano from roomy apartments with full kitchen and private patio or balcony. Reservations are necessary as the owners are not always home.

Tropical Mansion Suites HOTEL $$
(☎664-491-8767; www.tropicalmansion.com; Main Rd, Sweeny's; r from US$107; P❄📶🏊) About the only real hotel on Montserrat, Tropical Mansion is popular with business travelers, but is also a perfectly good choice for independent tourists not looking for the guesthouse experience. Views from its hilltop perch are superb, and with spacious modern rooms plus a restaurant serving all three meals, this is a good option for a comfortable stay.

Olveston House GUESTHOUSE $$$
(☎664-491-3942; www.olvestonhouse.com; Loblolly Lane, Salem; r from US$129; P❄📶🏊) The former winter home of the late Sir George Martin is now an utterly delightful inn run by the affable trio of Margaret, Sarah and Carol. There are six charming rooms (three with air-con, three with access to the wraparound porch), and lots of memorabilia and photographs of famous musicians. The hugely popular attached restaurant opens for dinner each night.

Eating

Nostalgia CARIBBEAN $
(☎664-496-9925; Main Island Rd; dishes EC$10-30; ⏰8am-4pm Mon-Fri, to 7pm Sat) This canary-yellow food truck parked by the side of the road just before Carr's Bay is a local favorite for bulging sandwiches; it also does burgers and fried or grilled chicken or fish. It's a handy lunch stop, but as service tends to be slow the clued-in call ahead for their order and avoid the lunchtime rush.

People's Place CARIBBEAN $
(☎664-752-8491; Main Island Rd, St Peter's; meals EC$25; ⏰10am-7pm Mon-Sat) John's blue hilltop shack enjoys a cult following among islanders, especially on Friday and Saturday nights when everybody gathers for beers and a chat. The Caribbean fare is simple, ample and delicious, and served with a big smile. You can't go wrong with the roti, but if it's Friday, try goat water; this spicy stew is the national dish.

★**Olveston House Restaurant** BRITISH $$
(☎664-491-5210; www.olvestonhouse.com; Loblolly Lane, Salem; mains EC$25-50; ⏰7:30am-9pm; P📶) At this all-day restaurant in the home of the late Sir George Martin you get to tuck into Caribbean-infused British favorites such as pork tenderloin or beef lasagna, all with a view of the tropical garden. Friday pub nights are great for eavesdropping on gossiping islanders, as are the barbecue feasts that draw capacity crowds every other Wednesday. Reservations advisable.

Pont's Beach View CARIBBEAN $$
(☎664-496-7788; Little Bay; mains EC$25-50; ⏰10am-4pm Tue-Sun, dinner 6-9pm by reservation; 📶) John Ponteen is a man with a big heart who serves big platters of top Caribbean food – from catch of the day to succulent baby back ribs and spicy Creole chicken. Sit at handcrafted mahogany tables in a garden pergola festooned with detritus washed up by the sea, or grab a table on the breezy octagonal deck overlooking Little Bay.

Isles Bay Beach Bar CARIBBEAN $$
(Isles Bay Beach; dishes EC$30-90; ⏰noon-10pm Thu-Sun; 📶) This gorgeously appointed beach hangout sits right on Isles Bay at the mouth of the Belham River and gets busy with locals on weekends. Take a seat on the breezy veranda decked out with fairy lights and tuck into seafood, burgers, chicken, salads and pizza. The Guinness brownie with ice cream is superb.

Time Out Bar & Restaurant CARIBBEAN $$
(☎664-491-9046; Look Out Circle, Little Bay; mains EC$15-55; ⏰noon-11pm Mon-Sat; 📶) Part of an ever-growing complex of bars and restaurants on the beach, this contemporary grill serves big platters of seafood, barbecued ribs, pork and wings. It's a popular spot, and one of the few places open late.

Soca Cabana CARIBBEAN $$
(☎664-493-1820; www.socacabana.com; beachfront, Little Bay; mains EC$40-65; ⏰10am-6pm Sun-Thu, to 2am Fri & Sat; 📶) Dance in the sand at this chilled beach bar, which gets packed for Saturday-night karaoke. The rest of the time it serves simple meals such as burgers, rotis and sandwiches, as well as a changing daily special. The wooden bar was rescued from Sir George Martin's AIR recording studio.

The owners also put on the wildly successful annual Montserrat Idol singing contest.

Entertainment

Montserrat Cultural Centre CONCERT VENUE
(☎664-491-4242; www.themontserratculturalcentre.ms; Robert Griffith Dr, Little Bay) FREE This stately performance hall was donated by the late Beatles producer Sir George Martin in 2006 and hosts a wide variety of events, from concerts to funerals. A 'Wall of Fame' features bronze handprints of famous musicians who made recordings at Martin's

Montserrat-based AIR Studios during the 1970s and '80s, including Elton John and Paul McCartney.

Shopping

National Trust Gift Shop GIFTS & SOUVENIRS
(664-491-3086; http://montserratnationaltrust.ms; Olveston; 8:30am–4:30pm Mon-Fri) The well-stocked gift shop inside the National Trust building in Olveston has a good selection of Montserrat-themed gifts, including T-shirts, rum, postcards and locally produced handicrafts.

EasiLiving GIFTS & SOUVENIRS
(664-392-3274; www.easiliving.net; Top Hill, St Peter's; 10am-5pm Mon-Fri, 9am-2pm Sat) This well-stocked boutique sells handicrafts and other locally made products, including brightly hued clothing, paintings by Montserratian artists and various island souvenirs.

Last Chance Souvenir Shop GIFTS & SOUVENIRS
(John A Osborne Airport; 8am-5pm) A handy spot to pick up some last-minute souvenirs, including quality crafts. Also has an outlet in Little Bay.

UNDERSTAND MONTSERRAT

People & Culture

Montserrat's small population is tightly knit and nearly everyone knows everyone. More than 90% of the population is of African descent, although less than half the population was born on Montserrat, with many emigrating here from other islands in the Caribbean. The flag bears Montserrat's coat of arms, which depicts a woman clutching a harp and hugging a cross. The harp refers to the long history of Irish immigration to Montserrat, which can most obviously be seen during the island's riotous weeklong St Patrick's Day festivities, which see the number of people on the island double.

Quite predictably for a British Overseas Territory, cricket is huge and when the national team practices on the pitch near Little Bay, few cars pass without pausing for a critical look. Passion for the national football (soccer) team is also rife, while basketball is growing in popularity, with a huge, if rather ugly, set of indoor basketball courts in a tent-like structure in Little Bay.

Landscape & Wildlife

Volcanic eruptions destroyed about 60% of Montserrat's forest ecosystem, leaving the Centre Hills as the main refuge for flora and wildlife. Laced with hiking trails, they harbor numerous species, including the endemic Montserrat oriole; the practically extinct 'mountain chicken' (actually a huge frog); and a shy lizard called Montserrat galliwasp. The island is also home to three species of sea turtle, as well as a snake and a tarantula found in the wild nowhere else on earth. The Montserrat National Trust arranges turtle-watching treks during nesting time in August and September.

VOLCANIC APOCALYPSE

Montserrat has seen more than its fair share of nature's destructiveness but never more so than in 1995–97 when the Soufrière Hills Volcano (now 3180ft) ended its 400 years of dormancy. A series of ash falls, pyroclastic flows and mud flows destroyed the capital Plymouth, plus smaller settlements, farmland and forests. Around 11,000 residents were evacuated and either resettled in the north or emigrated to the UK. Eruptions continued until the last major one in 2010, but since then Soufrière has, by and large, been peaceful.

An increasing number of those displaced by the volcano are returning to the island as new houses are built. Many say that they never felt at home in Britain and miss their lives on the island. Still, the population remains at less than half its pre-eruption total and the economy is still trying to recover.

Two-thirds of the island is still an Exclusion Zone, with life now focused in Brades and the planned new capital of Little Bay in the north. But nature is slowly reclaiming the destroyed areas. You can take in the spectacle from safe viewing points that include the Montserrat Volcano Observatory, on boat trips and helicopter flyovers. With a guide and police permit, it's even possible to visit Plymouth for a firsthand look at the destruction wrought by nature, a chilling, moving and fascinating experience that should not be missed.

SURVIVAL GUIDE

Directory A–Z

ACCESSIBLE TRAVEL

Not much is done on Montserrat to aid mobility-impaired and other disabled travelers. Access to buildings and transportation is very difficult, sidewalks (where they exist) are steep and uneven, curbs often high and ramps rare.

ACCOMMODATIONS

Montserrat does not have any resorts or large hotels. If you're spending just a night or two, it's best to stay in a small guesthouse run by locals who will be happy to help you maximize your time on the island. If you're staying longer, consider renting a self-catering apartment or villa.

CHILDREN

Montserrat is very laid-back and part of its charm is that there just isn't that much to do. Consider taking older kids to the Montserrat Volcano Observatory (p583) and on hikes, go on a boat ride out to Plymouth or rent a kayak. The four beaches are small but offer good swimming and snorkeling (bring equipment to save on rental costs).

ELECTRICITY

Most places have dual 220/110 voltage; North American two-pin sockets are prevalent but three-pins are around too, so bring an adapter.

EMERGENCY NUMBERS

Fire	☎911
Police	☎999

FOOD

It's fair to say that nobody comes to Montserrat for the food, but it's still possible to eat perfectly well here, with fresh fish and seafood nearly always the best choice. Self-caterers can pick up supplies at a handful of small supermarkets, although selection is extremely limited and prices can be high.

Essential Food & Drink

➡ **Goat water** Montserrat's national dish is far more loved than its dubious-sounding name would suggest. 'Got some?' is a frequent conversation starter and refers to the spicy clove-scented broth accented with floating chunks of goat meat. It's eaten hot with a crusty bread roll.

➡ **Fruit juices** Exotic fruits grow in abundance on Montserrat and make delicious fresh juices. Depending on the season, you'll find mango, guava and papaya as well as the more unusual West Indian cherry, five fingers (star fruit) and soursop, which tastes a little like a creamy strawberry with hints of pineapple and coconut.

SLEEPING PRICE RANGES

The following price ranges refer to a double with bathroom during peak season (December to April). Unless otherwise stated, breakfast is not included.

$ less than US$80

$$ US$80–120

$$$ more than US$120

HEALTH

Only basic medical care is available on Montserrat; the best option is **Glendon Hospital** (☎664-491-2802; Look Out Circle). The nearest full-service hospital is in Antigua; the nearest hyperbaric chamber is in Guadeloupe.

INTERNET ACCESS

Hotels, restaurants and cafes generally provide free wi-fi for their guests. If you'd like to get a local SIM card, go to Digicel (p588) in Brades.

LEGAL MATTERS

Montserrat's legal system is based on British common law. In case of legal difficulties, you have the right to legal representation and are eligible for legal aid if you can't afford to pay for private services.

If you are arrested, local police must notify your nearest embassy or consulate of your predicament.

LGBT+ TRAVELERS

Homosexuality is legal under Montserrat law, but most people are quite conservative and public displays of affection between same-sex couples are not advisable. There's no problem for same-sex couples sharing a hotel room.

MONEY

Some shops, hotels and restaurants accept credit cards, but never rely on that. Note that US dollars must be in pristine condition to be accepted.

EATING PRICE RANGES

The following price ranges refer to a main course. Most places add a 10% service charge.

$ less than EC$25

$$ EC$25–50

$$$ more than EC$50

There is currently just one **ATM** (Brades Rd, Brades) on Montserrat that accepts foreign cards. The shiny Bank of Montserrat in Brades only accepts local cards.

Exchange Rates

Australia	A$1	EC$1.94
Canada	C$1	EC$2.03
Euro zone	€1	EC$3.05
Japan	¥100	EC$2.41
New Zealand	NZ$1	EC$1.81
UK	UK£1	EC$3.52
US	US$1	EC$2.71

For current exchange rates, see www.xe.com.

Taxes & Refunds

Hotels add 10% accommodation tax (7% at guesthouses) to the final bill. There is no sales tax or value-added tax (VAT).

Tipping

Restaurants If the service charge is not automatically included in the bill, tip 10%.

Taxi Tips are not generally expected.

OPENING HOURS

Local businesses, including most restaurants and bars, are closed on Sundays, although some minimarts may open for a few hours in the morning and afternoon. In most cases, the following are guidelines only.

Banks 8am to 2pm Monday to Thursday, to 3pm Friday.

Bars noon to 11pm or midnight.

Businesses 8am to 4pm Monday to Friday.

Restaurants breakfast 7:30am to 10am, lunch noon to 2:30pm, dinner 6pm to 9:30pm.

Shops 9am to 5pm Monday to Saturday, some close at noon on Wednesday, grocery stores later and on Sunday.

PRACTICALITIES

Newspapers The weekly *Montserrat Reporter* (www.themontserratreporter.com) is the main newspaper.

Radio Catch local news, tunes and eruption alerts on ZJB Radio, 91.9FM.

Smoking There is no smoking ban in force on Montserrat, but many establishments forbid it.

Weights & measures The imperial system is used.

PUBLIC HOLIDAYS

In addition to holidays observed throughout the region, Montserrat celebrates the following public holidays:

New Year's Day January 1

St Patrick's Day March 17

Good Friday/Easter Monday March or April

Labor Day May 1

Pentecost/Whit Monday Forty days after Easter

Queen's Birthday First, second or third weekend in June

Emancipation Day First Monday in August

Christmas Day December 25

Boxing Day December 26

SAFE TRAVEL

The Soufrière Hills Volcano has been active since 1995, but there's been no major volcanic activity since February 2010. Still, about two-thirds of Montserrat is still vulnerable. The former capital of Plymouth and the entire south belong to the so-called 'Exclusion Zone.' Visits here are subject to current threat levels and only possible with a licensed tour guide, who needs to obtain prior authorization from police. Note that there's a US$100 fee per entry in addition to any tour charges.

On occasion, southern winds blow ash and volcanic gases across the entire island, which can lead to flight cancellations. The situation is constantly monitored by Montserrat Volcano Observatory staff. Sirens warning of impending volcanic activity are tested every weekday at noon. If they go off at other times, immediately seek local advice, or turn your radio to 88.3 FM or 95.5 FM and follow instructions.

TELEPHONE

- Montserrat's country code is 664.
- To call from North America, dial 1 + 664 + local number. From elsewhere, dial your country's international access code + 1 + 664 + local number.
- To call abroad from Montserrat, dial 011 + country code + area code + local number.

Cell Phones

You can buy local SIM cards from **Digicel** (Brades Rd, Brades; ⏲8am-5pm Mon-Sat) in Brades giving you local calls and data packs that will also work in Antigua, St Kitts and Dominica.

TIME

Clocks in Montserrat are set to Eastern Caribbean Time (Atlantic Time), which is four hours behind GMT. The island does not observe daylight saving time.

TOURIST INFORMATION

Tourist office (☎664-491-4703; www.visitmontserrat.com; 2nd fl, Montserrat Bldg Society Bldg, Brades; ⊗8:30am-4:30pm Mon-Fri)

VOLUNTEERING

Coral Cay Conservation (www.coralcay.org) This UK-based nongovernmental environmental organization needs volunteers for its scientific surveys to collect data from tropical forest and coral reefs and to run community education programs about conservation skills and sustainability.

Turtle Conservation Montserrat (http://ccoleby2001.wixsite.com/turtlesmontserrat) Volunteers working with local turtle conservationist John Jeffers help monitor the annual arrival of leatherback, loggerhead, hawksbill and green turtles, which come to nest in Montserrat, and assist with the release of hatchlings at the beach.

 Getting There & Away

AIR

Tiny **John A Osborne Airport** (MNI; near Gerald's village) is served several times daily by eight-passenger aircraft from Antigua operated by **Fly Montserrat** (☎664-491-3434; www.flymontserrat.com; John A Osborne Airport) and **SVG Air** (☎in Antigua 268-562-7183, in Montserrat 664-491-4200; www.flysvgair.com; John A Osborne Airport). Larger aircraft cannot land on the tiny airstrip, so nearly all visitors arrive via Antigua. High winds, heavy rain or volcanic ash may delay service for hours or even days in extreme cases.

SEA

The **Jaden Sun** (☎in Antigua 268-778-9786, in Montserrat 664-496-9912; round trip adult/child 2-12yr EC$300/150) runs between St John's in Antigua and **Little Bay Ferry Terminal** (Little Bay) on Montserrat in 90 minutes for EC$300 round trip. Service typically runs five times a week in both directions, normally with an early-morning departure from Montserrat and an evening return from Antigua. Call or check www.visitmontserrat.com/sea for the latest schedule. Bad weather will suspend service.

Getting Around

If you're staying on Montserrat, your host will arrange for a pick-up from the airport or the ferry dock. If you're just here for the day, it's best to prearrange for a guided tour. See the tourist office website for details.

 DEPARTURE TAX

The combined departure and security tax for stays longer than 24 hours is EC$55 or US$21 – cash only.

BUS

Minibuses ply the main road from Monday to Saturday between 7am and 5pm. There is no schedule and no official stops, so just hail one as it passes. The flat fare is EC$3. For an additional EC$2 fee, buses will travel off route to where you need to go.

CAR

Hiring a car on Montserrat requires obtaining a local driver's license (EC$50) at the airport, ferry port or the police station in Brades. Arrange a car through your accommodation or contact any of the agencies listed on www.visitmontserrat.com/get-around.

Driving is on the left. The speed limit is 20mph because of the curvy roads and steep terrain. Use your horn at hairpin curves. There are no traffic lights.

HITCHHIKING

Naturally, there are some inherent risks in accepting a ride from strangers but on Montserrat this is actually a common way to get around the island. It's customary to waggle your forefinger rather than stick out your thumb.

Hitching is never entirely safe, and we don't recommend it. Travelers who hitch should understand that they are taking a small but potentially serious risk.

TAXI

Taxis sometimes wait at the ferry terminal and the airport, but cannot always be relied upon, so it's best to order one in advance through your guesthouse or hotel. See www.visitmontserrat.com/taxi-tours-operator for a list. Cars are not metered, so agree on the fare in local currency before setting off.

All drivers double as guides and charge about US$25 per hour for all passengers.

Puerto Rico

787 / POP 3.2 MILLION

Includes ➜

Best Places to Eat

➜ Raya (p600)

➜ Chateau Rose at the Horned Dorset Primavera (p616)

➜ Vianda (p601)

➜ Kioskos de Luquillo (p606)

Best Places to Stay

➜ Hacienda Tamarindo (p610)

➜ Rainforest Inn (p605)

➜ Villa Flamenco (p608)

Why Go?

Golden sands, swashbuckling history and wildly diverse terrain make the sun-drenched backyard of the United States a place fittingly hyped as the 'Island of Enchantment.' It's the Caribbean's only island where you can catch a wave before breakfast, hike a rainforest after lunch and race to the beat of a high-gloss, cosmopolitan city after dark. Between bling-rich casinos and chirping frogs, Puerto Rico is also a land of dynamic contrasts, where the breezy lifestyle of the Caribbean sits alongside the hustle of contemporary American culture.

A quick visit for Puerto Rico's beaches, historic forts and thumping nightclubs will quicken the visitor's pulse, but the island's singular essence reveals itself to those who go deeper, exploring the misty crags of the mountainous interior and pastel facades of the island's remote corners.

When to Go

Feb Carnival is one of the most colorful times to find yourself in a Puerto Rican city.

May The best time to hike the El Yunque National Forest, avoiding the winter rush and the wet summer.

Dec The surfing season reaches its peak in mid-winter.

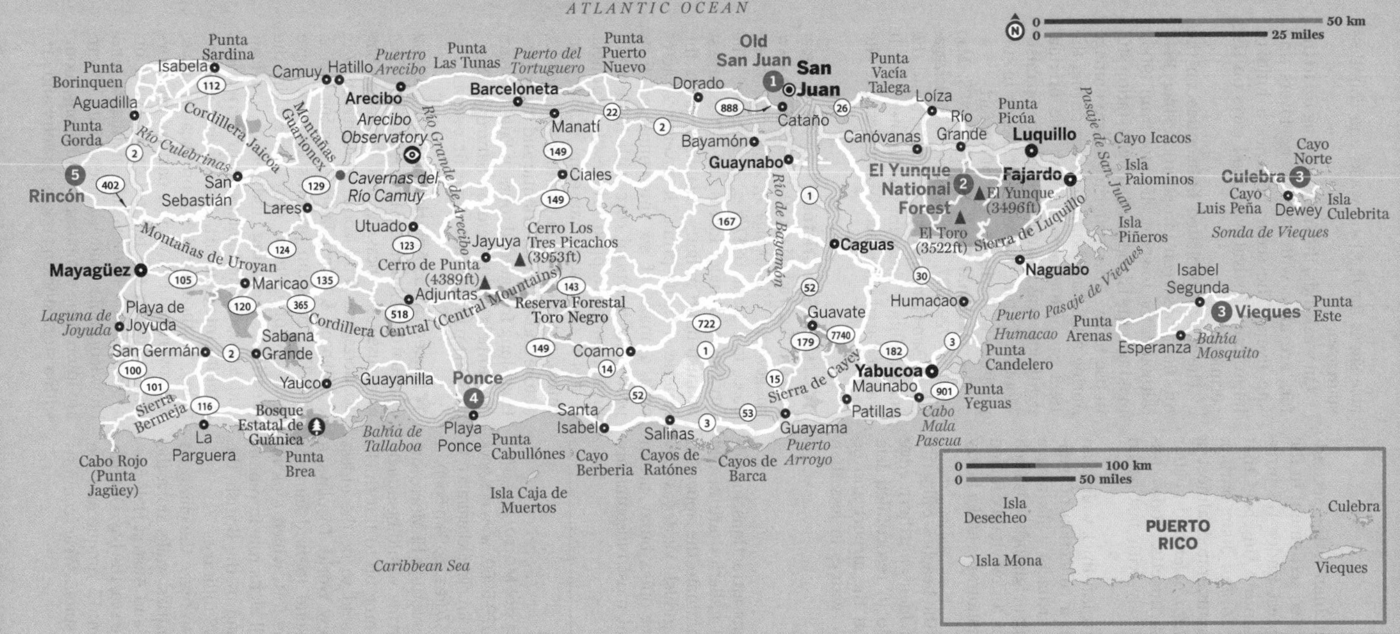

Puerto Rico Highlights

1. **Old San Juan** (p592) Being seduced by the charm and beauty of the old town while wandering the blue cobblestone streets.

2. **El Yunque National Forest** (p605) Hiking on lush rainforest trails with views of the ocean beyond.

3. **Culebra and Vieques** (p606) Reveling in some of the best beaches in the Caribbean plus kayaking in bioluminescent waters.

4. **Museo de Arte de Ponce** (p612) Falling in love with Flaming June in the cultural hot spot of Ponce.

5. **Rincón** (p615) Surfing beside beach bums and vacationing businesspeople on legendary breaks.

SAN JUAN

Founded in 1521, San Juan is the second-oldest European-founded settlement in the Americas and the oldest under US jurisdiction. Shoehorned onto a tiny islet that guards the entrance to San Juan harbor, the old town was inaugurated almost a century before the *Mayflower* laid anchor in present-day Massachusetts. Today antiquity blends seamlessly with fast-paced modernity.

Beyond its timeworn 15ft-thick walls, San Juan is far more than a collection of well-polished colonial-era artifacts – it's also a mosaic of ever-evolving neighborhoods such as Santurce, which has a raw vitality fueled by street art, superb restaurants and a buzzy bar scene.

And then there are the beaches. Silky ribbons of sand line San Juan's northern edge from swanky Condado to resort-filled Isla Verde. You can land at the airport and be splashing in the azure waters in less than an hour.

Sights

Most of San Juan's major attractions, including museums and art galleries, are in Old San Juan. Beaches dominate the appeal of Condado, Ocean Park and Isla Verde (as they should), while Santurce offers buzzy, urban delights. Be aware that most museums are closed on Mondays.

Old San Juan

★Castillo San Felipe del Morro — FORT

(El Morro; Map p594; ☎729-6960; www.nps.gov/saju; 501 Norzagaray; adult/child incl entrance to Castillo San Cristóbal US$7/free; ⏲9am-6pm) A star of Old San Juan, brooding El Morro sits atop a headland, deterring would-be attackers. The 140ft walls (some up to 15ft thick) date to 1539 and it's said to be the oldest Spanish fort in the New World. Displays, a short video and weekend tours document the construction of the fort, which took almost 200 years, as well as its role in rebuffing attacks on the island by the British, the Dutch and, later, the US military.

At a minimum, try to make the climb up the ramparts to the sentries' walks along the Santa Barbara Bastion and Austria Half-Bastion for the views of the sea, the bay, Old San Juan, modern San Juan, El Yunque and the island's mountainous spine. Wear comfortable shoes for the long walks and countless staircases.

On weekends, the fields leading up to the fort are alive with picnickers, lovers and kite flyers. The scene becomes a kind of impromptu festival with food carts on the perimeter.

The gray, castellated **lighthouse** on the 6th floor has been in operation since 1846 (although the tower itself dates from 1906), making it the island's oldest light station still in use today. After suffering severe damage during a US navy bombardment during the 1898 Spanish–American War, the original lighthouse was rebuilt with unique Spanish-Moorish features, a style that blends in surprisingly well with the rest of the fort.

The **National Park Service** (NPS; Map p594; ☎729-6777; www.nps.gov; 501 Norzagaray; ⏲9am-6pm) maintains this fort and the small military museum on the premises. It was declared a Unesco World Heritage site in 1983.

★Castillo San Cristóbal — FORT

(San Cristóbal Fort; Map p594; ☎729-6777; www.nps.gov/saju; 501 Norzagaray; adult/child incl entrance to El Morro US$7/free; ⏲9am-6pm) The city's second major fort is one of the largest Spanish-built military installations in the Americas. In its prime, it covered 27 acres with a maze of six interconnected forts protecting a central core with 150ft walls, moats, booby-trapped bridges and tunnels. It has a fascinating museum, military archives, a reproduction of military barracks, a store and stunning Atlantic and city views. Hour-long free guided tours in English roam the tunnels at 10:30am on Saturdays (Sundays in Spanish); first-come, first-served.

★Museo de las Américas — MUSEUM

(Museum of the Americas; Map p594; ☎724-5052; www.museolasamericas.org; cnr Cuartel de Ballajá, Norzagaray & del Morro; adult/child US$7/5; ⏲9am-noon & 1-4pm Tue-Fri, noon-5pm Sat & Sun) This museum presents an impressive overview of cultural development in the Americas, including indigenous, African and European influences. Four permanent exhibits integrate art, history and anthropology in thoughtful and provocative ways; the coverage of slavery is particularly moving, including the re-creation of travel on a slave ship. Audiovisual highlights and knowledgeable guides enrich visits. There are interesting temporary exhibitions, along with a store stocking books, jewelry and art.

Cuartel de Ballajá NOTABLE BUILDING
(Museo de las Américas; Map p594; ☎721-3737; www.ballaja.com; cnr Norzagaray & del Morro; ⏰9am-noon & 1-4pm Tue-Sat, noon-5pm Sun) FREE Built in 1854 as a military barracks, the *cuartel* is an impressive three-story edifice with large gates on two ends, a series of arches and a large central courtyard. It was the last building constructed by the Spaniards in the New World. Facilities once included officers' quarters, warehouses, kitchens, dining rooms, prison cells and stables; today it's home to several administrative offices, a dance studio, a music school, several cafes and the first-rate Museo de las Américas.

Museo de San Juan MUSEUM
(Map p594; ☎480-3555; www.sanjuanciudadpatria.com/servicios/arte-cultura-e-innovacion/museo-de-san-juan; 150 Norzagaray; by donation; ⏰9am-noon & 1-4pm Tue-Sat, noon-5pm Sun) Set in a former marketplace, this small museum offers the definitive take on the city's 500-year history. A permanent exhibit showcases well-laid-out pictorial testimonies from the Caparra ruins to modern-day neighborhoods. There's also a 120-seat theater and two temporary exhibition spaces that feature work from contemporary Latin American artists. Every Saturday morning a small **farmers market** (Map p594; snacks from US$2; ⏰8am-1pm Sat;) is held in the pretty courtyard.

Catedral de San Juan Bautista CHURCH
(San Juan Bautista Cathedral; Map p594; ☎722-0861; 153 del Cristo; ⏰8am-4pm) FREE While San Juan's cathedral is smaller and less flamboyant than many Spanish churches, it retains a simple elegance. The first church on this site was founded in 1521 and destroyed by a hurricane eight years later. They began constructing its replacement in 1540 and it slowly evolved into today's neoclassical-inspired monument. Look out for the marble tomb of Ponce de León and the mummified body of religious martyr St Pio.

Plaza de Colón SQUARE
(Columbus Plaza; Map p594; cnr San Francisco & Tetuán) Tracing its roots back more than a century to the 400-year anniversary of Columbus' first expedition, Plaza de Colón is dominated by its towering statue of Columbus atop a pillar. Ringed with tall trees and outdoor cafes, the plaza sees a lot of action. At this end of Old San Juan, the city wall was torn down in 1897 and the plaza stands on the site of one of the city's original gated entries, Puerta Santiago.

La Fortaleza HISTORIC SITE
(El Palacio de Santa Catalina; Map p594; ☎ext 2211 721-7000; Recinto; suggested donation US$3; ⏰tours 9am-3:30pm Mon-Fri) Guarded iron gates mark the imposing La Fortaleza. Dating from 1533, it's the oldest executive mansion in continuous use in the western hemisphere. The original fortress for the young colony, La Fortaleza eventually yielded its military preeminence to the city's newer and larger forts and was remodeled and expanded to domicile island governors for more than three centuries. There are free, 30-minute guided tours between 8:15am and 3:30pm. They include the mansion's Moorish gardens, the dungeon and the chapel.

Miramar & Santurce

★**Museo de Arte de Puerto Rico** MUSEUM
(MAPR; Map p598; ☎977-6277; www.mapr.org; 299 Av de Diego, Santurce; adult/concession US$6/3, after 2pm Wed free; ⏰10am-8pm Wed, to 5pm Thu-Sat, from 11am Sun; T5, T21) San Juan boasts one of the largest and most celebrated art museums in the Caribbean. Housed in a splendid neoclassical building that was once the city's Municipal Hospital, MAPR holds 18 exhibition halls spread over an area of 130,000 sq ft. The artistic collection includes paintings, sculptures, posters and carvings from the 17th century to the present, chronicling such renowned Puerto Rican artists as José Campeche, Francisco Oller, Nick Quijano and Rafael Ferrer.

MADMi MUSEUM
(Museum of Art & Design Miramar; Map p598; ☎995-7063; www.madmi.org; 607 Cuevillas, Miramar; adult/concession US$5/3; ⏰10am-5pm Mon-Sat) This new addition to the city's buzzy art scene is set in a restored Miramar landmark, a striking pink building dating to 1913. Engaging, interactive exhibitions focus on design and the decorative and visual arts, from modernism to the present, with text in Spanish and English. It also hosts talks, workshops and courses; guided tours on request.

Beaches

★**Balneario El Escambrón** BEACH
(Map p598; off Av Muñoz Rivera, Puerta de Tierra; parking US$5; ⏰parking 8:30am-5pm; D53, T3, T5, T21) This sheltered arc's raked sand,

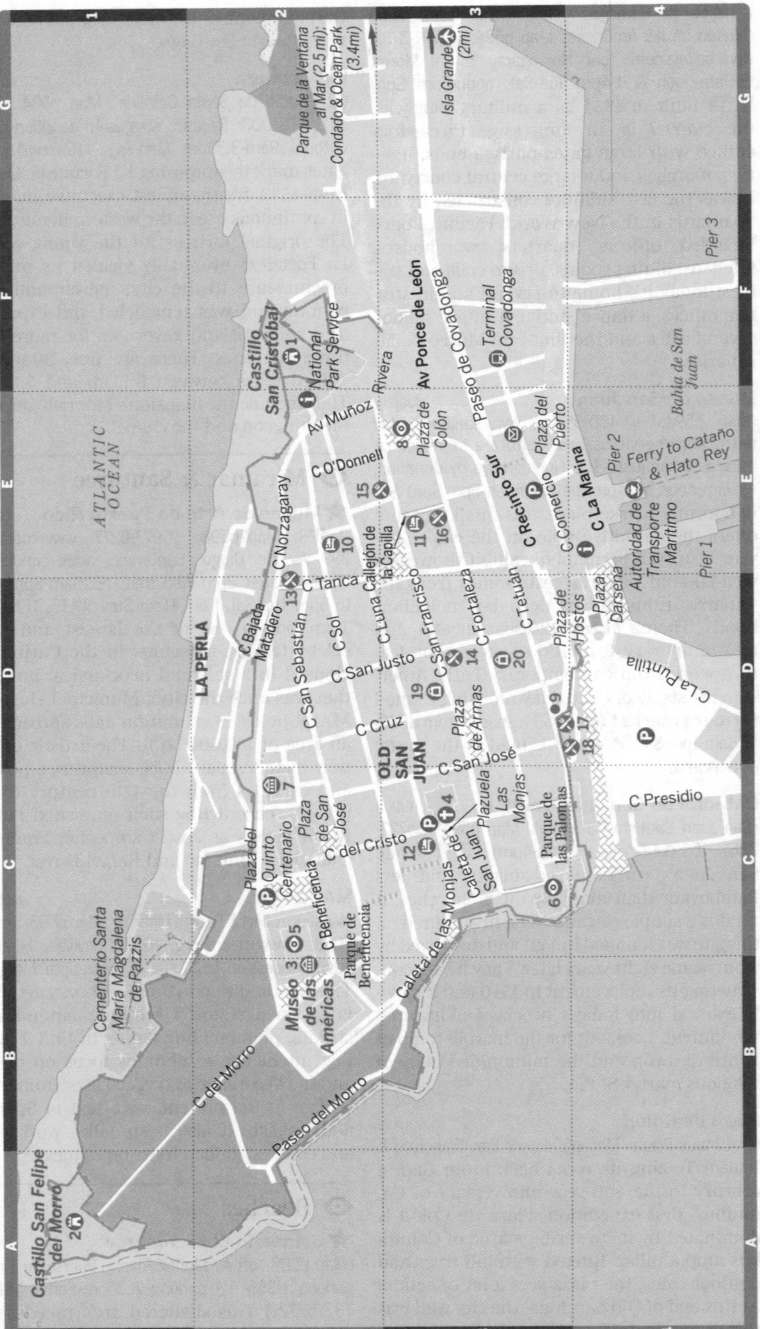

Old San Juan

0 500 m
0 0.25 miles
Castillo San Felipe del Morro
2
Cementerio Santa María Magdalena de Pazzis
ATLANTIC OCEAN
LA PERLA
C del Morro
Paseo del Morro
Plaza del Quinto Centenario
7
Museo de las Américas
3
5
C Beneficencia
Plaza de San José
Parque de Beneficencia
C Bajada Matadero
C Norzagaray
13
C San Sebastián
C Sol
10
C Tanca
15
C O'Donnell
Av Muñoz Rivera
Castillo San Cristóbal
1
National Park Service
Parque de la Ventana al Mar (2.5 mi); Condado & Ocean Park (3.4mi)
C del Cristo
OLD SAN JUAN
C Cruz
C San Justo
C Luna
Callejón de la Capilla
8
Plaza de Colón
Av Ponce de León
Isla Grande (2mi)
12
4
Caleta de las Monjas
Caleta de San Juan
Plazuela Las Monjas
C San José
19
C San Francisco
11
16
Plaza de Armas
14
C Fortaleza
Paseo de Covadonga
Terminal Covadonga
20
C Tetuán
C Recinto Sur
6
Parque de las Palomas
9
18
17
Plaza de Hostos
C Comercio
Plaza del Puerto
C La Marina
Plaza Darsena
Pier 2
Autoridad de Transporte Marítimo
Ferry to Cataño & Hato Rey
C Presidio
C La Puntilla
Pier 1
Bahía de San Juan
Pier 3

Old San Juan

Top Sights
1 Castillo San Cristóbal ... F2
2 Castillo San Felipe del Morro ... A1
3 Museo de las Américas ... B2

Sights
4 Catedral de San Juan Bautista ... C3
5 Cuartel de Ballajá ... C2
6 La Fortaleza ... C3
7 Museo de San Juan ... C2
8 Plaza de Colón ... E3

Activities, Courses & Tours
9 Para la Naturaleza ... D3

Sleeping
10 Casa Sol ... E2
11 Da'House ... E3
12 Hotel El Convento ... C3

Eating
13 Antojitos del Callejón ... D2
14 Chocobar Cortés ... D3
15 La Madre ... E3
16 Marmalade ... E3
Mercado Agrícola Natural Viejo San Juan ... (see 7)
17 Señor Paleta ... D3
18 Verde Mesa ... D4

Shopping
19 Concalma ... D3
20 Puerto Rican Art & Crafts ... D3

decent surf breaks, plenty of local action and a 17th-century Spanish fort shimmering in the distance are the hallmarks of what's considered San Juan's finest beach, with Blue Flag status and only a stone's throw from the old city and the busy tourist strip of Condado. Best of all, it's often uncrowded.

★Playa Ocean Park BEACH
(Map p598; off McLeary, Ocean Park) Protected by offshore reefs and caressed by cooling seasonal trade winds, this wide sweep of diamond-dust sand is a favorite of locals. But this residential 'hood's namesake beach is open to all – just pick a road through the low-rise gated community and follow it to the water.

★Playa Isla Verde BEACH
(off Av Isla Verde, Isla Verde) With countless tanned bodies lounging or flexing their biceps around the volleyball net, this urban beach basks in its reputation as the Copacabana of Puerto Rico. Serenity seekers may prefer to head west to Ocean Park but despite the crowds, this broad, mile-long swath of sand lying between Punta Las Marías and Piñones is an undeniable beauty, especially at sunset. Jet Skis, flyboards, beach chairs and umbrellas are all available to rent; banana boats and parasailing are on offer too.

Playa Condado BEACH
(Map p598; off Av Ashford, Condado) Hemmed in by hotel towers and punctuated by rocky outcrops, Condado's narrow beaches are busier than Ocean Park's and less exclusive than Isla Verde's. Expect boisterous games of volleyball and plenty of crashing Atlantic surf. Families congregate around the big hotels, while gay men like the beach at the end of Calle Vendig. **Parque La Ventana al Mar** (Map p598; Av Ashford, Condado) has lovely waterfront views.

Activities

The glittering azure waters are an obvious draw for outdoor fun in San Juan. Beaches that open to the Atlantic are great for kitesurfing and surfing, while the reefs draw snorkelers and divers. The city's glassy lagoons and waterways are perfect for kayaking and paddleboarding. On land you can get out and about in the nearby green hills and mangrove forests.

Scuba Dogs DIVING, SNORKELING
(Map p598; ☎977-0000; www.scubadogs.net; Parque Nacional del Tercer Milenio, Puerta de Tierra; snorkeling/dives from US$55/75; ⏲8am-4pm) This large, long-running outfit has been a tireless supporter of the offshore coral wonderland that is **Escambrón Marine Park** (Map p598; off Av Muñoz Rivera, Puerta de Tierra; 🚌D53, T3, T5, T21). The Dogs offers a host of shore- and boat-dive trips, plus training and snorkeling.

Acampa Camping & Travel Store OUTDOORS
(☎706-0695; www.acampapr.com; 517 Av Andalucía, Hato Rey; ⏲11am-5pm Mon-Sat) One of the best places on the island to buy or rent tropical-weather camping equipment and outdoor gear from the likes of Patagonia and Osprey. Sister company **Acampa Nature Adventures** (☎706-0695; www.acampapr.com; 517 Av Andalucía, Hato Rey; 3-night tour US$649; ⏲tours May-Nov) organizes exclusive tours to Mona Island aka 'the Galápagos of the Caribbean.'

Pine Grove Surf Club WATER SPORTS
(☎361-5531; www.pinegrovesurfclub.com; 6985 Horizonte, Carolina; tours/surfing lessons from US$45/55; ⏲7am-5pm) Owned and run by the friendly Nogales brothers and based on Playa Isla Verde, this operation offers fun surf lessons on Pine Grove beach, paddleboarding tours in the lagoons of Piñones and snorkeling excursions off the gorgeous Balneario El Escambrón (p593).

15 Knots Kiteboarding School KITESURFING
(☎215-5667; www.15knots.com; Puerto Interior, Carolina; full gear rental per 24hr US$200, private lessons US$250, 2-student lessons US$149; ⏲10am-6pm) The often-gusty conditions around San Juan make the waters prime kitesurfing territory. This recommended outfit offers rentals and two-, three- and four-hour lessons.

Tours

★**Para la Naturaleza** ECOTOUR
(Map p594; ☎722-5834; www.paralanaturaleza.org; Casa de Ramón Power y Giralt, 155 Tetuán, Old San Juan; ⏲9am-5:30pm Tue-Fri, check website for tour schedule) This nonprofit aims to integrate society into the conservation of natural ecosystems, with the goal that 33% of Puerto Rico's landmass is protected by 2033. Besides organizing volunteer and educational events, it manages more than 60 natural areas throughout the island. Tours are led by knowledgeable and enthusiastic guides and its San Juan HQ hosts small but fascinating exhibitions.

★**Aqua Fitness** WATER SPORTS
(Map p598; ☎903-2141; www.aquafitnesspr.com; 1022 Av Ashford, Condado; rentals per 2hr from US$25, paddleboard yoga per 1hr class US$25, tours per person from US$30; ⏲8am-6pm Mon-Fri, to 7pm Sat & Sun) This small outfit rents out paddleboards and kayaks just a half-block from Laguna del Condado. For newbies, a free briefing is given before you're let loose on the water. It also offers paddleboard-yoga classes and tours of the lagoon.

Excursiones Eco TOURS
(☎565-0089; www.excursioneseco.com; walking/boat tours from US$15/45) This community-oriented tour company offers boat tours through the city's lagoons and excursions into economically under-served neighborhoods. Tours include historical background, flora and fauna details, and information about the struggles faced by the residents. Approximately 85% of all proceeds go directly to the guides themselves. Uber is the best way to get to the tour starting points.

Festivals & Events

★**Festival Casals** MUSIC
(☎723-5005; www.facebook.com/festivalpablocasals; Centro de Bellas Artes Luis A Ferré, 22 Av Ponce de León, Santurce; tickets US$15-75; ⏲late Feb-early Mar) Since 1956 renowned soloists and orchestras have come from all over the world to join the Puerto Rico Symphony Orchestra in performing virtuoso concerts night after night, primarily at the Centro de Bellas Artes Luis A Ferré (p602). The performances usually stretch over two to three weeks from late February into March.

★**Fiestas de la Calle San Sebastián** CULTURAL
(SanSe, Fiestas de la Calle; San Sebastián, Old San Juan; ⏲mid-Jan) For a full week around the third weekend of January, Old San Juan's Calle San Sebastián is jam-packed with processions, food stalls and people partying. During the day, it's folk art and crafts; at night, it's raucous revelry. All to a rhythmic soundtrack of *bomba, plena* and salsa.

Festival de Cine Internacional de San Juan FILM
(San Juan International Film Festival; ☎946-9730; www.festivalcinesanjuan.com; Caribbean Cinemas Fine Arts Miramar, 654 Av Ponce de León, Miramar; tickets from US$7.75; ⏲Oct) Screens new films over one week in October, with an emphasis on Caribbean cinema. Given the number of Puerto Ricans/Nuyoricans making good on the big screen – Lin-Manuel Miranda, Rosario Dawson, Benicio del Toro – this event has been pulling in bigger luminaries each year.

Sleeping

Old San Juan

★**Casa Sol** B&B $$
(Map p594; ☎725-4470; www.casasolbnb.com; 316 Sol; r US$170-230; ❄📶) This charming, ecofriendly B&B is set in a beautifully restored 18th-century house in the heart of the old town. Rooms are spacious and thoughtfully decorated with antique furnishings and folk art. The sunflower-yellow courtyard doubles as a dining space where the delicious homemade breakfast is served. The amiable owners live on-site and are generous with their local knowledge.

Da'House HOTEL $$

(Map p594; ☎977-1180; www.dahousehotelpr.com; 312 San Francisco, Old San Juan; r US$110-140; ❄@📶) This boho hotel is one of Old San Juan's best bargains, with boutique-style rooms kitted out with chic furnishings and eye-catching contemporary art, with each room dedicated to a different local artist. At the time of research, a cafe-bar was set to open on the ground floor.

Hotel El Convento HISTORIC HOTEL $$$

(Map p594; ☎723-9020; www.elconvento.com; 100 del Cristo, Old San Juan; r US$270-400, ste US$660-1440; P❄@📶≋) In a prime spot in Old San Juan, El Convento is a historic monument-turned-luxe boutique hotel. Built in 1651 as the New World's first Carmelite convent, the 67 rooms and five suites channel Spanish-colonial style, with tiled floors and mahogany furniture. Service is polished, from the reception to the alfresco patio restaurant.

Condado

Casa Condado Hotel HOTEL $$

(Map p598; ☎200-8482; www.casacondadohotel.com; 60 Av Condado; r US$95-130; ❄📶) Casa Condado is a small hotel about two blocks from the beach. Rooms are spread out over three floors; there's no elevator so prepare to exercise a little. Units are modern and minimalist with wood floors and large windows, and it boasts a ground-floor restaurant. A solid option for the rate.

★**O:live Boutique Hotel** BOUTIQUE HOTEL $$$

(Map p598; ☎705-9994; www.oliveboutiquehotel.com; 55 Aguadilla; r incl breakfast US$200-430; ❄📶) At this luxe, Mediterranean-inspired boutique, each of the 15 rooms is unique, showcasing *talavera* tiled floors, heavy wooden doors and eclectic objet d'art – some even have alfresco patio with Jacuzzi and plush seating areas. The restaurant continues the Med theme, while the rooftop lounge-bar has creative cocktails and killer views over Condado; the perfect place for a nightcap and breakfast.

★**Condado Vanderbilt Hotel** LUXURY HOTEL $$$

(Map p598; ☎721-5500; www.condadovanderbilt.com; 1055 Av Ashford; r/ste from US$270/435; P❄@📶≋) One of the city's most opulent hotels when it opened in 1919, this iconic grande dame overlooking the Atlantic has been lavishly restored and expanded. Its 323 rooms, including 90 in the original building, are spacious and elegant, many with breathtaking ocean views. Its luxe amenities include a beach club, spa, casino and several gourmet restaurants.

Ocean Park

★**Dreamcatcher** B&B $$

(Map p598; ☎455-8259; www.dreamcatcherpr.com; 2009 España; r US$89-385; ❄📶) This boho-chic B&B artfully mixes up retro and contemporary furniture, modern art and vintage knick-knacks, indoor and outdoor space. There are quiet nooks and plant-filled patios for relaxing and communal kitchens for socializing. It serves some of the best vegetarian breakfasts in town and there's a farm-to-table communal dinner every Friday. The beach is just a block away.

Numero Uno Beach House GUESTHOUSE $$

(Map p598; ☎726-5010; www.numero1guesthouse.com; 1 Santa Ana; r from US$129; ❄📶≋) A whitewashed 1940s beachfront house has been turned into a chic boutique. Minimalist rooms come with stylish design details, smart TV and ceiling fan. There's a pool, a feet-in-the-sand bistro and if you want to take on the waves lapping the sand just feet from your window, the owners run a kiteboarding school.

Isla Verde

Boriquen Beach Inn HOTEL $

(☎866-728-8400, 728-8400; www.borinquenbeachinn.com; 5451 Av Isla Verde; r US$80-130; P❄📶) This old-school inn is one of the best budget deals on the beach. Rooms may be dated but they're spotlessly clean with good beds, strong air-con and decent bathrooms. There's a spacious kitchen for guest use and free parking on-site. Streetside rooms can get noisy but you're just a pebble's throw from the beach and five minutes from the airport.

★**El San Juan Hotel, Curio Collection by Hilton** RESORT $$$

(☎791-1000, 888-579-2632; www.elsanjuanhotel.com; 6063 Av Isla Verde; r from US$269; P❄@📶≋) Fresh from a US$65 million makeover, this storied grande dame's lobby (p602) is all gleaming Italian-marble floors, hand-carved mahogany ceilings and showstopping chandeliers. Rooms are lighter and brighter, and there's a state-of-the-art fitness center and

Condado & Ocean Park

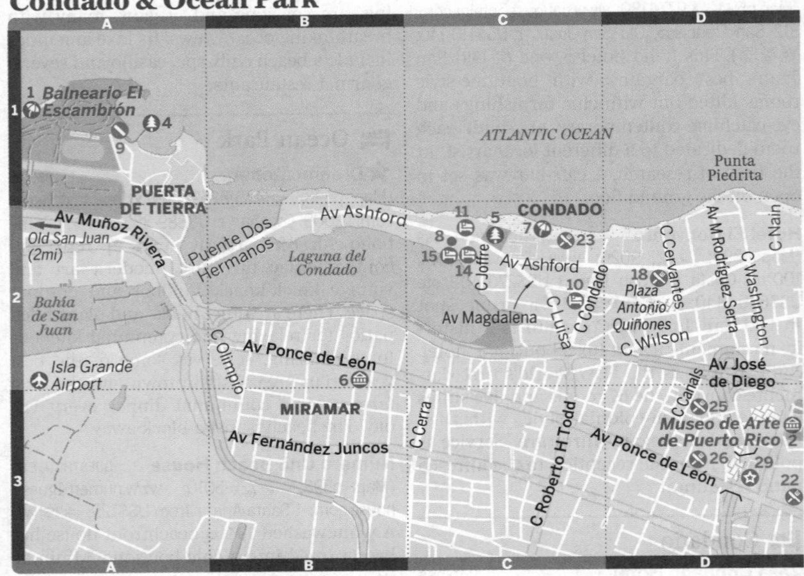

Condado & Ocean Park

Top Sights

1 Balneario El Escambrón A1
2 Museo de Arte de Puerto Rico D3
3 Playa Ocean Park E2

Sights

4 Escambrón Marine Park A1
5 La Ventana al Mar C2
6 MADMi B2
7 Playa Condado C2

Activities, Courses & Tours

8 Aqua Fitness C2
9 Scuba Dogs A1

Sleeping

10 Casa Condado Hotel C2
11 Condado Vanderbilt Hotel C2
12 Dreamcatcher F2
13 Numero Uno Beach House F1
14 O:live Boutique Hotel C2
15 O:LV Fifty Five C2

Eating

1919 Restaurant .... (see 11)
16 Acapulco Taqueria Mexicana F2
17 Berlingeri Cocina Artesanal F2
18 Freshmart D2
19 Kamoli E2
20 La Casita Blanca F3
21 Loiza 2050 .... F2
22 Lote 23 .... D3
23 Oceano C2
Pernileria Los Próceres .... (see 22)
Raya .... (see 15)
24 Round Eye Ramen E2
25 Santaella D3
26 Vianda D3
27 Volando Bajito F2

Drinking & Nightlife

28 Cafe Comunión E3
VC Lounge .... (see 11)

Entertainment

29 Centro de Bellas Artes Luis A Ferré D3

pampering spa. Dine on gourmet local fare at Caña (p600), then dance the night away at **Brava** (☎389-0002; www.elsanjuanhotel.com/entertainment/brava; cover US$20-30, hotel guests free; ⏰10pm-late Thu-Sat). Beyond the organically shaped pools lies Isla Verde beach.

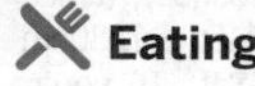

Eating

Old San Juan

★Antojitos del Callejón PUERTO RICAN $
(Map p594; ☎721-6227; 281 San Sebastián; meals US$3-8; ⏲8am-10pm) This hole-in-the-wall is a local favorite known for its delicious *criollo* dishes and *antojos* (fried finger foods). Plastic tables are set up in front, in an empty lot carpeted in Astroturf, with a view of ocean just beyond. Service is efficient and friendly, the Medalla beer ice cold and the salsa gets the joint jumping at weekends.

★Señor Paleta ICE CREAM $
(Map p594; ☎724-2337; www.facebook.com/srpaletapr; 153 Tetúan; paletas US$3.50-5; ⏲10:30am-10pm) This hole-in-the-wall institution sells artisanal *paletas* (popsicles) made from fresh fruit, nuts and other tasty treats. Flavors range from coconut, passionfruit and *guanabana* (soursop) to cheesecake, amaretto and chocolate. Watch the sidewalk queue grow longer as the city starts to sizzle, but it's worth the wait. It accepts credit cards for orders US$5 and over.

Chocobar Cortés AMERICAN $
(Map p594; ☎722-0499; www.chocobarcortes.com; 210 San Francisco; mains US$10-22; ⏲8am-8pm) A chocoholic's delight, this family-run company squeezes chocolate into – almost – every dish. Fancy a chocolate grilled cheese or *churrasco* with a chocolate chimichurri sauce? All are possible (and delicious) at the Chocobar, along with an array of more traditional choccie treats. Upstairs, the Fundación Cortés' small gallery champions local artists.

La Madre MEXICAN $$
(Map p594; ☎647-5392; 351 San Francisco; mains US$15-25; ⏲noon-11pm Mon-Wed, to midnight Thu, to 2am Fri, from 10am Sat, to 11pm Sun; ❄) Gourmet Mexican cuisine is the theme at this cool and cozy restaurant-lounge. Start with delectable coconut margaritas or opt for fruity alternatives like tamarind or *acerola* (cherry). The food boasts creative twists – the fish tacos never disappoint, neither does the fried brownie.

★Verde Mesa CARIBBEAN $$$
(Map p594; ☎390-4662; www.verdemesa.com; 107 Tetuán; mains US$15-32, prix-fixe 3-course lunch US$26; ⏲noon-3pm & 5-10pm Tue-Sun; ❄✍) Tucked down a historic old-town street, this little gem of a restaurant is lauded for its creative menu, with great options for vegetarians and vegans. Verde Mesa's fresh and flavorful dishes are made with ingredients from local organic farms, like their scallops in corn velouté. Antiques and mood lighting create a romantic ambience. And don't miss the crème brûlée.

Marmalade FUSION $$$
(Map p594; ☎724-3969; www.marmaladepr.com; 317 Fortaleza; mains US$18-45, tasting menu US$75-95; ⏲5-10pm Mon-Sat; ❄✍) The personal vision of James Beard Award–winning chef Peter Schintler, Marmalade was one of the first restaurants to bring real foodie recognition to Old San Juan. The interior is stylishly minimal, while the menu takes full advantage of top-notch local produce – yellowtail, pork belly, avocados – to create delicious food art. The wine list is equally impressive.

Condado

Freshmart MARKET $
(Map p598; ☎999-7800; www.freshmartpr.com; 1310 Av Ashford; snacks US$2-9; ⏲7am-9pm, deli to 8pm; P❄✍♿; 🚌D53, T21) Freshmart is Puerto Rico's take on Whole Foods. A market dedicated to organic food and products, it also has a mezzanine-level cafeteria with a great selection of vegetarian, vegan

and gluten-free dishes. Carnivores are also catered for. Sandwiches, salads, pizzas and more are prepared fresh every day.

★ Raya CARIBBEAN $$

(Map p598; ☎705-0820; www.olvhotel.com/restaurants; 55 Barranquitas; mains US$14-38; ⏲5:30-10pm Tue-Thu, to midnight Fri & Sat; P ❄ 📶) This sleek, art-deco-style restaurant from Mario Pagán, one of Puerto Rico's top chefs, puts the focus on Caribbean-Asian fusion. Scattered with edible flowers, the tuna poke is sensational. The lobster lollipops and miso sea bass aren't bad either. A sommelier will talk you through the wine, sake and cocktail list. On the ground floor of **O:LV Fifty Five** (Map p598; ☎705-8421; www.olvhotel.com; 55 Barranquitas).

Oceano SEAFOOD $$

(Map p598; ☎724-6300; www.oceanopr.com; 2 Vendig; mains US$25-35; ⏲5-10pm Mon-Thu, 2-4pm & 5-10pm Fri & Sat, 11am-10pm Sun) In a one-of-a-kind oceanfront mansion with a terrace smack bang in front of Condado Beach, this cool and contemporary restaurant-bar serves up just-caught seafood – ginger coconut shrimp, ahi-tuna tartare, red snapper – and perennial favorites like surf 'n' turf. The Nolita, a refreshing mix of gin, cucumber and pineapple juice, makes the perfect sundowner. It does a good brunch too.

1919 Restaurant PUERTO RICAN $$$

(Map p598; ☎721-5500; www.condadovanderbilt.com/condado-1919-restaurant; Condado Vanderbilt Hotel, 1055 Av Ashford; mains US$45-55; ⏲6-10pm Tue-Thu, to 11pm Fri & Sat; P ❄ 📶) Juan José Cuevas is the Puerto Rican, Michelin-starred executive chef at the Condado Vanderbilt fine-dining flagship restaurant. He champions local farmers and spent months sourcing the island's finest ingredients for dishes such as tuna-*hiramasa* crudo with local radish, lobster and salami risotto and his specialty *cochinillo,* or pig cheek. Pricey but the elegant surroundings are perfect for a special occasion.

Ocean Park

★ Berlingeri Cocina Artesanal VEGETARIAN $

(Map p598; ☎527-3224; www.berlingeri.com; 1958 McLeary; mains US$8-13; ⏲11am-3pm Mon-Fri; P ❄ 🌱 👪) One of the best vegetarian and vegan restaurants in the city is tucked away at the back of an Ocean Park car park. Once you've found it, choose from a short list of flavorful and creative dishes, such as the chickpea Thai burger, tofu Cuban sandwich and bean lasagna. Homemade ice creams, cookies and fresh juices complete the appetizing menu.

Isla Verde

Caña by Juliana Gonzalez PUERTO RICAN $$

(☎791-1000; www.elsanjuanhotel.com/restaurants/cana; El San Juan Hotel, 6063 Av Isla Verde; mains US$9-29; ⏲7am-2pm & 5-11pm Mon-Fri; P ❄) This relaxed restaurant celebrates the island's produce and dishes while giving them a gourmet twist. The Puerto Rican chef's farm-to-fork dinner menu is divided into sea (slow-cooked octopus, crispy snapper salad), mountain (*mofongo* and pork belly) and orchard (pickled root vegetables, crisp salads). Mixing up traditional tiles, family photos and contemporary furniture, it has a sweeping terrace and rum bar.

There's a popular weekend brunch too.

Santurce

★ Round Eye Ramen ASIAN $

(Map p598; ☎305-316-7768; www.roundeyeramen-pr.com; 105 Pomarrosa; mains US$15; ⏲11:30am-3pm Mon-Fri, 6-11pm Mon & Wed-Sat) If you're craving authentic ramen, this long, skinny resto is the place. It serves steaming bowls of flavorful broth and homemade noodles topped with pork belly (veggie options too), sublime gyoza and lunchtime bento boxes. Pair it with a craft cocktail and round off with a sinful Chocolatissimo. No reservations but it's worth the wait. Just off Calle Loíza.

★ Acapulco Taqueria Mexicana MEXICAN $

(Map p598; ☎727-5568; 2021 Loíza; meals US$8-14; ⏲11:30am-10pm Tue-Sat, 10am-9pm Sun; 🌱) The best street tacos in town. Acapulco is a purist – no cheese, lettuce or hard shell, but the real deal: a pair of stacked corn tortillas, sizzling meat, cilantro, onion and lime. Look for the *trompo* (a vertical skewer of slow-cooked pork topped with pineapple), the heart of the classic taco *al pastor.* Down it with a Negra Modelo. Perfection.

Lote 23 FOOD TRUCKS $

(Map p598; www.facebook.com/lote23pr; 1552 Av Ponce de León; ⏲7:30am-10pm Sun-Tue, to midnight Thu-Sat; 🌱) An abandoned lot has been turned into a gourmet food park where you can feast alfresco on everything from fried chicken at Hen House, to slow-roasted Puerto Rican pork at Pernileria Los Próceres and

Peruvian *anticuchos* at Panka. Wash it down with cocktails from Caneca or coffee from Cafe Regina. Sunday-morning yoga will burn off the calories.

Pernileria Los Próceres PUERTO RICAN $
(Map p598; www.facebook.com/pernilerialosproceres; Lote 23, 1552 Av Juan Ponce de León; mains US$12-20; ⏲8am-10pm Tue & Wed, to midnight Thu-Sat, to 10pm Sun) The focus of this food truck in Lote 23 is firmly on pork, especially *pernil*, filling Puerto Rican pork-shoulder sandwiches with homemade mayo, lettuce and tomato in a brioche bun. But it also branches out in other small plates, perhaps ramen and salt-cod sandwiches. Enjoy it with a local craft beer.

Volando Bajito FUSION $
(Map p598; ☎939-338-0182; www.facebook.com/volandobajitoloiza; 101 Ismael Rivera, cnr Loíza; mains US$7-16; ⏲5-10pm Mon, Thu & Fri, from noon Sat & Sun) Chicken rules the roost at this quirky resto, where locals come for a taste of Puerto Rican and Korean fusion. Choose drumsticks or wings, add a sauce – perhaps Puerto Rican beer, sweet mojo or Korean spicy soy garlic – and choose a few tasty sides; try the truffle fries or their campanelle pasta smothered in three cheeses.

Kamoli CAFE $
(Map p598; ☎721-4326; 1706 Loíza; dishes US$6-16; ⏲7:30am-11pm Mon-Wed, to 9:30pm Thu & Fri, 8:30am-10pm Sat & Sun; ❄✎) This boho cafe's eclectic menu can take you through the day, starting with coffee, banana pancakes and the breakfast salad (sunny-side-up eggs on a bed of greens). Plus a monster list of freshly prepared energizing, wellness and detox concoctions, as well as a full bar. Upstairs there's a small terrace and pop-ups from local clothes and jewelry designers.

La Casita Blanca PUERTO RICAN $
(Map p598; ☎726-5501; 351 Tapia; mains US$10-15; ⏲11:30am-4pm Mon-Wed, to 5pm Thu & Sun, to 9pm Fri & Sat) Down-home cooking has been the order of the day at this low-key cafe for decades. Locals, including chefs, come from far and wide to kick back at the simple tables and feast on food like their grandmother used to make. Expect quintessential dishes like stuffed avocado, fish stew and coconut *arepas* (pancakes).

★**Vianda** PUERTO RICAN $$
(Map p598; ☎939-475-1578; www.viandapr.com; 1413 Av Ponce de León; mains from US$19; ⏲5:30-10pm Wed, Thu & Sun, to 11pm Fri & Sat) This fine-dining, farm-to-fork restaurant from husband-and-wife team Francis Guzmán and Amelia Dill has quickly become a key fixture on the city's vibrant foodie scene. Stylish and contemporary, its super-seasonal menu reinvents Puerto Rican staples, such as the zucchini tostada topped with homemade ricotta and arugula pesto, and short-rib *encebollado*. The same goes for the standout cocktails and mocktails.

Loiza 2050 ITALIAN $$
(Map p598; ☎726-7141; www.facebook.com/pg/loiza2050; 2050 Loíza; mains US$13-19; ⏲5-10pm Thu-Sat, from 4:30pm Sun; ❄♿) This tiny, family-owned pizza place has been serving exceptional pies for more than 20 years. And its more recent inventions – such as coconut-crusted pizza topped with smoked salmon, brie and caramelized onions – have made it the go-to pizza joint for a new generation.

★**Santaella** PUERTO RICAN $$$
(Map p598; ☎725-1611; www.santaellapr.com; 219 Canals; mains from US$19; ⏲11:30am-10:30pm Tue & Wed, to 11:30pm Thu, to midnight Fri, from 6pm Sat; ❄✎) Puerto Rican chef José Santaella's namesake restaurant is one of San Juan's best. It buzzes with excitement, thanks to the tropical vibe, the craft cocktails and the standout contemporary Puerto Rican cuisine. Flavors sing in dishes such as red snapper with herb chimichurri and *tostones* (fried plantain). Book in advance.

Drinking & Nightlife

★**VC Lounge** COCKTAIL BAR
(Map p598; ☎721-5500; www.condadovanderbilt.com; 1055 Av Ashford, Condado Vanderbilt Hotel, Condado; ⏲11am-11pm Sun-Tue, to midnight Wed & Thu, to 2am Fri & Sat) Condado's most historic hotel has a suitably opulent lobby bar. The master mixologists craft classic and one-of-a-kind cocktails, partnered with some first-class bar nibbles and more substantial snacks. Enjoy the breezy, ocean-view terrace or the luxe lounge with a live piano soundtrack. Happy hour from 5pm to 7pm daily.

★**Cafe Comunión** COFFEE
(Map p598; www.facebook.com/cafecomunion; 1616 Av Ponce de León, Santurce; ⏲7am-6pm Mon-Sat, 9am-3pm Sun; 📶🐾) Set up by award-winning Puerto Rican barista Abner Roldan, this contemporary cafe wouldn't look out

of place in New York or London. Supporting the island's farmers, as well as showcasing beans from the likes of Colombia and Ethiopia, it goes without saying that the coffee's first-rate; so are the locally baked chocolate-chip cookies. Popular with digital nomads.

★El San Juan Hotel Lobby Bars COCKTAIL BAR
(☎791-1000; www.elsanjuanhotel.com; 6063 Av Isla Verde, Isla Verde; ⏲8pm-2am) This iconic hotel's three lobby bars are undeniably the most glamorous in town, with acres of gleaming marble and lashings of art deco elegance. Choose from the circular wine bar, the gold-hued rum bar and the dazzling chandelier bar, which sits under the world's third-largest chandelier, sparkling with 7000 crystals. Live Latin bands get the crowds dancing at weekends.

☆ Entertainment

Centro de Bellas Artes Luis A Ferré THEATER
(Bellas Artes; Map p598; ☎724-4747; www.cba.gobierno.pr; 22½ Av Ponce de León, Santurce; ⏲box office 10am-6pm Mon-Fri, hours vary Sat & Sun; 🚌T3, T5) Built in 1981, this center has more than 1900 seats in the festival hall, about 750 in the drama hall and 200 in the experimental theater. It hosts international stars and the annual Festival Casals (p596), while the Puerto Rican Symphony Orchestra's weekly winter performances are held in the complex's newer 1300-seat Pablo Casals Symphony Hall.

Shopping

★Concalma FASHION & ACCESSORIES
(Map p594; ☎238-8585; www.shopconcalma.com; 207 Francisco, Old San Juan; ⏲10am-6pm Mon & Wed-Sat, to 4pm Sun) This standout store from designer Matilsha Marxuach stocks locally made fair-trade products as well as promoting up-and-coming Puerto Rican designers. Expect stylish cloth bags and totes, one-of-a-kind jewelry pieces and quirky, cutting-edge clothes.

★Puerto Rican Art & Crafts ARTS & CRAFTS
(Map p594; ☎725-5596; www.puertoricanart-crafts.com; 204 Fortaleza, Old San Juan; ⏲10am-6pm Mon-Sat, noon-5pm Sun) A cavernous shop specializing in Puerto Rican folk art, paintings and jewelry. Items come from artisan workshops from across the island. The prices are on the high end, but so is the quality.

ℹ Information

MEDICAL SERVICES

Ashford Presbyterian Community Hospital (El Presby; ☎721-2160; www.presbypr.com; 1451 Av Ashford, Condado; ⏲24hr; 🚌T21) El Presby is the best-equipped and most convenient hospital for most travelers.

MONEY

Banks and ATMs are found in most neighborhoods, including Condado, Santurce, Ocean Park and Isla Verde. **Banco Popular** (www.popular.com; 206 Tetuán, Old San Juan; ⏲8am-4pm Mon-Fri) is one of the most popular.

POST

Ocean Park Post Office (Map p598; ☎727-2452; www.usps.com; 1959 Loíza, Santurce; ⏲8am-4:30pm Mon-Fri, to noon Sat)

Old San Juan Post Office (Map p594; ☎724-2098; www.usps.com; 100 Paseo de Colón, Old San Juan; ⏲8am-4pm Mon-Fri, to noon Sat)

TOURIST INFORMATION

Puerto Rico Tourism Company Distributes information in English and Spanish at two venues in San Juan: the **Luis Muñoz Marín International Airport** (PRTC; ☎791-1014; www.seepuertorico.com; Terminal C, Luis Muñoz Marín International Airport; ⏲9am-7pm) and near the cruise-ship terminal in **Old San Juan** (PRTC; Map p594; ☎722-1709; www.seepuertorico.com; Edificio Ochoa, 500 Tanca, Old San Juan; ⏲9am-5:30pm).

ℹ Getting There & Away

AIR

International flights arrive at and depart from San Juan's busy **Luis Muñoz Marín International Airport** (SJU, LMM Airport; ☎289-7240; www.aeropuertosju.com; off Hwy 26, Isla Verde; ⏲24hr), which is about 8 miles east of Old San Juan. There are daily direct flights from the US mainland, including Miami, Atlanta, Dallas, New York City and Philadelphia. Domestic destinations from San Juan include Vieques, Ponce, Aguadilla and Mayagüez. Several airlines serve Luis Muñoz including United, Delta, JetBlue and **Seaborne Airlines** (☎946-7800, 866-359-8784; www.seaborneairlines.com; Luis Muñoz Marín International Airport).

Private aircraft, charter services and many of the commuter flights serving the islands of Culebra and Vieques arrive at and depart from San Juan's smaller **Isla Grande Airport** (SIG, Fernando Luis Ribas Dominicci Airport; Map p598; ☎729-8715; www.prpa.gobierno.pr;

Lindbergh, Isla Grande, Miramar), on the Bahía de San Juan. Airlines include **Vieques Air Link** (☎741-8331, 888-901-9247; www.viequesair-link.com; ⏰call center 7:30am-5pm Mon-Fri, from 8am Sat), **Air Flamenco** (☎724-6464; www.airflamenco.net) and **Cape Air** (☎1-800-227-3247; www.capeair.com).

BOAT

Around 25 cruise lines call on San Juan, with many cruisers starting and ending their voyages here. It's the second-largest port for cruise ships in the western hemisphere, serving nearly two million passengers each year. Most ships dock at the piers along Calle La Marina near the Customs House, just a short walk from the cobblestoned streets of Old San Juan; others dock at the Pan American Pier on nearby Isla Grande. Popular cruise lines serving San Juan include Royal Caribbean and Viking Ocean Cruises.

PÚBLICO

While there's no island-wide bus system, *públicos* (public vans, also known as *guaguas*) offer a limited alternative, providing an inexpensive though often time-consuming link between San Juan and other major towns such as Fajardo, Ponce or Mayagüez.

In San Juan, *público* centers include LMM international airport and the **Río Piedras Público Terminal** (Terminal de Carros Públicos de Río Piedras; ☎294-2412; cnr Arzuaga & Vallejo, Río Piedras). Vans leave once they're full and make frequent stops, dropping off and picking up passengers along the way. Service runs Monday through Saturday. Cash only.

Getting Around

TO/FROM THE AIRPORT

Fixed-price taxis from Luis Muñoz Marín International Airport cost from US$10 to Isla Verde, US$14 to Condado and Ocean Park, and US$21 to Old San Juan, plus luggage fees etc. You'll find taxis outside baggage claim areas, where taxi touts hustle passengers into cabs in a remarkably efficient way. Rates are visibly posted. Recent rule changes mean that Uber is now allowed to pick up from the airport, making this an attractive transportation alternative.

The bus is the cheapest option into town at US$0.75 a ride. Look for the 'Parada' sign outside the departures concourse at Terminals A and D. The D53 and T5 buses serve Old San Juan. The D53 via Isla Verde, Ocean Park and Condado; the latter via Isla Verde and Santurce.

PUBLIC TRANSPORTATION

Bus

AMA Metrobus (Autoridad Metropolitana de Autobuses, Metropolitan Bus Authority; ☎294-0500; fare US$0.75, exact change only; ⏰most routes 5am-8pm Mon-Sat) operates San Juan's public buses and the main hub is **Terminal Covadonga** (Old San Juan Bus Terminal; Map p594; ☎294-0500; cnr Paseo de Covadonga & Juan Antonio Corretjer, Old San Juan; ⏰most routes 6am-10pm, reduced service Sun). The buses are clean and air-conditioned, but the system itself is not easy for visitors. Route maps and information are hard to find and few bus stops have any indication of what buses stop there. Service can also be erratic, with wait times between 30 and 60 minutes. Your best bet is to ask around, especially at bus stops, where veteran riders will offer advice.

Routes taken most often by visitors (bus numbers are followed by associated route descriptions:

T3 Old San Juan, Puerta de Tierra, Av Ponce de León (Miramar/Santurce), Sagrado Corazón (Tren Urbano station)

T5 Old San Juan, Puerta de Tierra, Av Ponce de León (Miramar/Santurce), Isla Verde (via Loíza), Luis Muñoz Marín International Airport

T9 Old San Juan, Puerta de Tierra, Convention Center, Av Fernández Juncos (Miramar/Santurce), Sagrado Corazón (Tren Urbano station), Río Piedras

T21 Old San Juan, Puerta de Tierra, Av Ashford (Condado), Av Ponce de León (Santurce), Sagrado Corazón (Tren Urbano station)

C35 Convention Center, Av Ponce de León (Miramar/Santurce), Sagrado Corazón (Tren Urbano station), Av Fernández Juncos (Miramar/Santurce)

D45 Sagrado Corazón (Tren Urbano station), Isla Verde, Piñones, Loíza

D53 Old San Juan, Puerta de Tierra, Condado, Ocean Park (via McLeary), Isla Verde, Luis Muñoz Marín International Airport

Train

Tren Urbano (Urban Train; ☎294-0500; fare US$1.50; ⏰5:30am-11:30pm) connects Bayamón with downtown San Juan as far as Sagrado Corazón on the southern side of Santurce. Modern trains run every eight to 16 minutes, serving 16 stations. The line, which mixes elevated and underground tracks, is useful for visitors traveling to destinations such as the **Mercado de Río Piedras** (Río Piedras Market Square; ☎250-1818; Paseo de Diego, Río Piedras; ⏰9am-6pm Mon-Sat; Ⓜ Río Piedras), UPR's **Botanical Garden** (University of Puerto Rico Botanical Garden; www.upr.edu/jardin-botanico; off Hwy 1, Río Piedras; ⏰6am-6pm Mon-Fri; Ⓜ Río Piedras) and the **Museo de Arte Francisco Oller.** (☎785-6010; www.facebook.com/museooller; Plaza de Bayamón, 13 Degetau, Bayamón; ⏰8:30am-4pm Tue-Sat; Ⓜ Bayamón)

TAXI

Taxi fares are set in the main tourism zones. From Old San Juan, trips to Condado, Ocean Park or Isla Grande Airport cost US$12, and US$19 to Isla Verde and Luis Muñoz Marín International Airport. Journeys within Old San Juan cost US$7.

Outside the major tourist areas, cab drivers are supposed to use meters, but that rarely happens. Insist on it, or establish a price from the start. Here's the math: meter rates are US$1.75 initially and US$1.90 per mile or part thereof, though the minimum fare is US$3. You'll also pay a US$2 gas surcharge per trip plus US$1 for each piece of luggage. There's a US$1 reservation charge; add a US$1 surcharge between 10pm and 6am. And if there are more than five passengers, US$2 per person is added.

Taxis line up at the eastern end of Calle Fortaleza in Old San Juan; in other places you will likely need to call one. Try **Metro Taxi** (☎725-2870; ⏲24hr) or **Rochdale Radio Taxi** (☎721-1900; www.taxiprrochdale.com; ⏲24hr).

AROUND SAN JUAN

You can be three-quarters of the way across the island and still be within an hour or two's drive of San Juan (traffic permitting). Day trips from the capital can thus take you almost anywhere in the commonwealth. If you're keen to probe deeper, it's worthwhile traveling more slowly and making overnight stops.

Sights

★Birth of the New World Statue — STATUE

(Estatua de Cristóbal Colón; Km 9.5, Hwy 681) Undeniably Puerto Rico's biggest, most bizarre attraction, the 362ft likeness of Christopher Columbus (Cristóbal Colón) navigating toward the Americas is the work of Russian sculptor Zurab Tsereteli. Still not entirely completed in 2019, it's become Arecibo's top attraction since it first appeared on the skyline in 2012.

The statue, the tallest in North America and Puerto Rico's highest structure, stands astride a green rise overlooking an alluring expanse of beaches and mangroves: a wild area that may one day become the TerraVista Park, a future adventure complex in which the statue will take center stage. Development was halted by Hurricane Maria in September 2017.

You can ascend to a viewing gallery about halfway up and imagine the crowds-to-be descending on this peaceful place.

The irony surrounding the statue is as much a talking point as the structure itself. First, that it should be raised within sight of an important ceremonial site for the Taíno, whose culture was decimated following the explorer's arrival on these shores; and second, that it should be raised at all with construction costs of millions of dollars on a heavily debt-saddled island. Many are also concerned about the statue's environmental impact in an ecologically sensitive area.

Love it or hate it, the statue exhibits some splendid workmanship and has launched a revival of this entire stretch of coast.

★Observatorio de Arecibo — NOTABLE BUILDING

(☎878-2612; www.naic.edu; Hwy 625; adult/child US$12/8; ⏲10am-3pm Jun & Jul, 10am-3pm Wed-Sun rest of the year) Puerto Ricans reverently refer to it as 'El Radar'; to everyone else it is simply the largest radio telescope in the world. Resembling a spaceship grounded in the middle of karst country, the Arecibo Observatory looks like something out of a James Bond movie – probably because it is (007 aficionados will recognize the saucer-shaped dish and craning antennae from the 1995 film *GoldenEye*).

The 20-acre dish, operated in conjunction with SRI International, is set in a sinkhole among clusters of haystack-shaped *mogotes* (limestone monoliths), like Earth's ear into outer space. Supported by 50-story cables weighing more than 600 tons, the telescope is involved in the SETI (Search for Extraterrestrial Intelligence) program and used by on-site scientists to prove the existence of pulsars and quasars, the so-called 'music of the stars.' Past work has included the observation of the planet Mercury, the first asteroid image and the discovery of the first extra-solar planets.

Top scientists from around the world perform ongoing research at Arecibo, but an informative visitors center with interpretative displays and an explanatory film provide the public with a fascinating glimpse of how the facility works. There's also a well-positioned viewing platform offering you the archetypal 007 vista.

To get to the observatory, follow Hwys 635 and 625 off Hwy 129. It's only 9 miles south of the town of Arecibo as the crow flies.

EL YUNQUE & EAST COAST

The east coast is Puerto Rico in microcosm; a tantalizing taste of almost everything the island has to offer squeezed into an area you can drive across in a couple of hours. Verdant rainforest teems with vociferous wildlife and jungle waterfalls at El Yunque National Forest, the island's tropical gem. Down at sea level, beach lovers bask on the icing-sugar sand of Playa Luquillo.

Unvarnished Fajardo is the island's uncrowned water-sports capital, where adventurers kayak, dive, snorkel and fish, and yachters park their sailboats. And golfers and those craving a one-stop holiday will find delight in the highest concentration of large, upscale resorts outside San Juan.

Cutting through the region like a thin, green ribbon is the Northeast Ecological Corridor, a slender tract of undeveloped and endangered pristine land featuring one of Puerto Rico's stunning bioluminescent bays at Las Cabezas de San Juan Reserva Natural.

El Yunque

Sights

★El Yunque National Forest NATURE RESERVE
(☎888-1880; www.fs.usda.gov/elyunque; Km 4, Hwy 191, Northern entrance; ⏰7:30am-6pm; P) The US National Forest System's only rainforest, El Yunque is one of Puerto Rico's highlights. Access the lush forest along 25 miles or so of trails, passing waterfalls and crisscrossing rivers on route – there's a northern entrance near Luquillo and a southern entrance near Naguabo, both off Hwy 191. The **El Portal Visitors Center** (adult/child US$4/free; ⏰9am-5pm) was closed for renovation at time of research, due to reopen 2021. In the meantime, El Portalito is the place to get information before setting out to explore.

The northern side is more visited and has lots of well-marked trails and parking areas; the southern side is wilder and less developed, making for beautiful off-the-beaten-track experiences. Note: Hwy 191 does not cut through the forest – mudslides closed the middle section of the road years ago. Unless on foot, visitors must take Hwy 3 (which becomes Hwy 53) to access both sides of El Yunque.

Sleeping & Eating

Palmer, the colorful strip where Hwy 191 heads south from Hwy 3 toward El Yunque, has some good eating options. Inside the park, there are a few cheap-and-cheerful roadside stands and the visitors center will have a cafe when it reopens in 2021.

★Casa Flamboyant B&B $$$
(☎559-9800; www.casaflamboyantpr.com; Km 8, Hwy 191, Naguabo; r incl breakfast US$180-299; P) Tucked in to the mountains with panoramic views over El Yunque, adults-only Casa Flamboyant makes the most of its spectacular setting. Three well-appointed rooms (two with private terrace), a cozy living room and an infinity pool are as stylish as Puerto Rico's rainforest gets. Trails lead through the gorgeous gardens to waterfalls and swimming holes, without another soul in sight.

★Rainforest Inn B&B $$$
(☎378-6190; www.rainforestinn.com; Hwy 186, off Km 22.1, Naguabo; r incl breakfast US$175-230; P) In a gated community on the borders of El Yunque, three villas come with stunning forest views and romantic touches such as a hanging bed or twin tubs. Gourmet breakfasts include fruits and herbs plucked from the gorgeous tropical garden. The eco-conscious owners will help plan your hiking adventures, starting with their own private trail leading to a waterfall pool.

★Lluvia Deli Bar CAFE $
(☎657-5186; www.lluviapr.com; 52 Principal, Palmer, Rio Grande; mains US$5-12; ⏰7am-3pm Mon-Thu, to 6pm Fri-Sun;) This stylish contemporary cafe dishes up a range of creative meals, from excellent breakfasts – don't miss the guava pancakes – to lunchtime outsized sandwiches, salads, flatbread pizza and more. The orange juice is freshly squeezed and the coffee brewed from premium Puerto Rican beans.

Information

El Portalito Visitors Center (www.fs.usda.gov/elyunque; 54 Principal, Palmer; ⏰10am-4pm) Aspiring rainforest explorers should make this temporary visitors center their first stop. You can pick up free basic maps and information on the status of the trails and forest ecology. Also check out the ongoing hurricane recovery effort. Striking photographs show the scale of devastation after two Category 5 hurricanes blew through in 2017.

Getting There & Away

Since there's no public transportation to El Yunque, you will need to get here with private vehicle or on a guided tour from San Juan or Fajardo.

Driving from San Juan, there will be signs directing you from Hwy 3 to Hwy 191. Turn south at Palmer and follow the signs to El Yunque National Forest.

Luquillo

POP 20,068

Dubbed *La Capital del Sol,* Luquillo may sit in the green shadow of El Yunque but its spectacular crescent of powder-fine sand lapped by translucent water is considered one of the island's finest *balnearios* (public beaches).

The town traces its history to an early Spanish settlement in 1797 and its name to a valorous *cacique* (Taíno chief), Loquillo, who made a brave standoff against early colonizers here in 1513.

Today, laid-back Luquillo is colonized by *sanjuaneros* (people from San Juan) at weekends. It's the perfect place to take up surfing, laze on a palm-shaded beach and indulge in a *chinchorro* – a Puerto Rican–style bar crawl – along its 60-strong line of famed beachfront food stalls.

Beaches

★Playa Luquillo BEACH
(Balneario La Monserrate; parking US$5.50; 8:30am-6pm Apr-Aug, to 5pm Wed-Sun Sep-Mar; P) Along with its must-visit *kioskos,* Luquillo is synonymous with its fabulous – and hugely popular – beach. Set on a calm, northwest-facing bay and protected from the easterly trade winds, this arc of powder-soft sand is shaded by coco palms. And its raft of facilities and gentle slope into crystal-clear water make it perfect for families. Don't expect to have it to yourself, especially on weekends and holidays; just order a piña colada, enjoy the salsa rhythms and soak up the atmosphere.

Sleeping & Eating

★St Regis Bahia Beach Resort RESORT $$$
(809-8000; www.stregisbahiabeach.com; Km 4.2, Rte 187, Rio Grande; from US$735; P) Set on an expanse of icing-sugar sand and surrounded by tropical greenery, this sophisticated resort's rooms and suites are spacious, bright and contemporary. Lounge by two pools, get pampered at the spa, take a nature tour and feast on Greek-inspired or gourmet Puerto Rican cuisine. It's ecoconscious too, conserving 65% of its land and working to protect endangered wildlife.

★Kioskos de Luquillo PUERTO RICAN $
(Luquillo Kiosks; Playa Luquillo, off Hwy 3; dishes US$3-20; hours vary, generally noon-10pm; P) Luquillo's 60 beachfront food stalls line the western edge of Hwy 3, serving up delicious dishes at budget-friendly prices. Choose from sit-down restaurants to rustic beach bars selling everything from *comida criolla* (Creole food) to top-notch burgers and Peruvian ceviche – La Parilla (#2) and Terruño (#20) come recommended. Wash it down with a Medalla beer; many stalls have full cocktail menus.

Getting There & Away

Hwy 3 leads directly to Rte 193 (aka Calle Fernandez Garcia), which is the main artery of Luquillo.

Públicos run from the Río Piedras terminal (p603) in San Juan to Luquillo's central plaza (US$7) from Monday to Saturday. Trips take from 2½ to 3½ hours, depending on the traffic. If you're going to the beach, make sure you disembark next to the food kiosks, a mile or so before Luquillo town.

CULEBRA & VIEQUES

Culebra

Long feted for its diamond-dust beaches and world-class diving reefs, sleepy Culebra is probably more famous for what it *hasn't* got than for what it actually possesses. There are no big hotels here, no golf courses, no casinos, no fast-food chains, no rush-hour traffic and, best of all, no stress. Situated 17 miles off mainland Puerto Rico, but inhabiting an entirely different planet culturally speaking, the island's slow pace can sometimes take a bit of getting used to. It's home to rat-race dropouts, earnest idealists, solitude seekers, myriad eccentrics and anyone else who's forsaken the hassle and hustle of modern life. It's also home to a range of gorgeous natural areas, bays, snorkeling sites, hiking trails and all manner of fine beaches. Embrace the local vibe and explore one of Puerto Rico's most gorgeous destinations.

Sights

★Culebra National Wildlife Refuge WILDLIFE RESERVE
(☎457-0082; www.fws.gov/caribbean/refuges/culebra) More than 20% of Culebra is part of a spectacular national wildlife refuge, which was signed into law more than 100 years ago. Most of it lies along the coastline, including more than 20 cays. Home to three different ecosystems, the refuge is a habitat for endangered sea turtles and the largest seabird nesting grounds in the Caribbean. For visitors, it's a place for hiking, birdwatching and secluded beaches. The US Fish & Wildlife Service (p608) office has maps and information.

★Playa Carlos Rosario BEACH
(off Hwy 251) This remote thin, white-sand beach has one of the best snorkeling areas in Puerto Rico thanks to a barrier reef that almost encloses the beach's waters; you can snorkel on either side of it by swimming through the boat channel – look for the floating white marker – at the right-hand side of the beach. But be warned: water taxis and local powerboats cruise this channel, and swimmers have been hit.

★Playa Flamenco BEACH
(end of Hwy 251) Stretching for a mile around a sheltered, horseshoe-shaped bay, Playa Flamenco is not only one of Culebra's best beaches, it also makes a regular appearance on the world's best beaches lists. Backed by low scrub and trees rather than lofty palms, Flamenco gets very crowded on weekends and holidays, especially with day-trippers from San Juan, so plan a weekday visit. Alone among Culebra's beaches, it has a full range of amenities.

★Isla Culebrita ISLAND
If you need a reason to hire a water taxi, Isla Culebrita is it. This small island, just east of Playa Zoni, is part of the national wildlife refuge. With its six beaches, tide pools, reefs and nesting areas for seabirds, Isla Culebrita has changed little in the past 500 years. The north beaches, especially the long crescent of **Playa Tortuga**, are popular nesting grounds for green sea turtles – you might even see them swimming near the reefs just offshore.

★Playa Zoni BEACH
(off Hwy 250) Head to the eastern end of the island and you'll eventually run out of road at Playa Zoni. Many locals think this is a better beach than Flamenco and it's hard to argue. It's not quite as wide and curving, but it certainly is stunning in its own right with soft sand, turquoise waters and idyllic views of Cayo Norte, Isla Culebrita and even St Thomas on the horizon. Do as the locals do and bring a picnic cooler.

Activities

★Culebra Snorkeling & Dive Center DIVING, SNORKELING
(☎435-3662; www.culebrasnorkelingcenter.com; Pedro Márquez, Dewey; ⏲8:30am-5pm Mon-Sat, to 1pm Sun) This friendly shop offers excellent snorkeling excursions around the island where you're sure to see turtles, stingrays and all sorts of tropical fish. If DIY is more your thing, staffers will share snorkeling maps and tips, and point you in the right direction. High-end snorkel gear, kayaks, underwater cameras and even rash guards are available for rent too.

Kayaking Puerto Rico KAYAKING, SNORKELING
(☎245-4545; www.kayakingpuertorico.com; from Culebra/Ceiba US$59/79; ⏲8am-9pm) If you're already on this island you can start this Fajardo outfit's Culebra Island Aquafari from **Playa Tamarindo** (off Hwy 251), combining kayaking and snorkeling in the rich waters of the Luis Peña Channel Natural Reserve, ending with some time on Playa Flamenco. If you're coming from the mainland, the tour departs from Ceiba's ferry terminal at 8:15am.

Sleeping & Eating

For a small island, there are plenty of choices when it comes to eating. Seafood figures prominently, much of it sourced from the fishing boats bobbing the bay. Not surprisingly, most of Culebra's restaurants are in the tiny town of Dewey. Beyond town, keep your eyes out for food trucks, which offer cheap, tasty eats perfect for beach picnics.

Culebra International Hostel HOSTEL $
(☎732-547-8831; www.culebrahostel.com; Fulladoza, Dewey; dm/r per person US$30/85; ❄📶) Once an auto-parts shop, this rambling hostel offers two spacious dorms (including one female-only) with good bunk beds and air-con. There's a simple kitchen and lots of outdoor seating, mostly in a wild garden of potted plants (over 350 at last count). Expat manager Tommy often cooks dinner for guests, served family-style.

★Villa Flamenco Beach APARTMENT **$$**
(383-0985; www.villaflamencobeach.com; Playa Flamenco, off Hwy 251; studio/apt US$135/180;) Gentle waves lull you to sleep and you wake up to one of the best beaches on the planet just outside your window: this six-unit home-away-from-home is an absolute winner. There are self-catering kitchen facilities and inviting hammocks, and friendly owners Violetta and Juan are on-hand to offer island advice. Closed from the beginning of October to mid-November.

★Blac Flamingo Coffee CAFE **$**
(682-220-7892; 10 Jesús M Ortiz, Barriada Clark; dishes US$6-9; 6:30am-2pm Wed-Mon) For the best caffeine fix on Culebra, head to this cool, industrial-chic cafe a 10-minute walk north of Dewey, where there's everything from cappuccino to cold brew and Chemex. Then linger over breakfast or brunch – smooth avocado on crunchy toast, and the sweet-and-savory combination of scrambled eggs with French toast topped with fresh fruit garner rave reviews.

Zaco's Tacos MEXICAN **$**
(www.zacostacos.com; 21 Pedro Márquez, Dewey; mains US$6-9; noon-9pm Mon-Fri, hours can vary;) This hip restaurant dishes up ultrafresh Mexican fare plus a smattering of super salads. Tasty tacos include *carnitas* (pork shoulder braised in chilies and papaya juice), beef and shrimp, or if you're extra hungry, order a monster burrito with all the trimmings. Enjoy your meal in the clapboard dining room or on the shady alfresco patio at the back.

Vibra Verde CAFE **$**
(www.facebook.com/vibraverdeculebra; Pedro Márquez, Dewey; mains US$6-12; 8:30am-2pm Thu-Sat & Mon, to 1pm Sun;) The menu of this great little place is bursting with healthy, organic, gluten-free and delicious fare. Opt for the organic açaí bowl, the bumper breakfast sandwich, or the quinoa salad bowl. Wash it down with strong Puerto Rican coffee or the ginger and mint limeade.

Information

The vast majority of the island's services are in the town of Dewey.

MEDICAL SERVICES

Hospital de Culebra (742-3511; Calle Font, Dewey; 24hr) Culebra's hospital has a 24-hour emergency room. The island also keeps a plane on emergency standby at the airport for medical transportation to the main island.

MONEY

Banco Popular (742-3572; www.popular.com; 9 Pedro Márquez, Dewey; 8am-3:30pm Mon-Fri) The only full-service bank in Culebra. It has a 24-hour ATM.

POST

Post Office (742-3862; www.usps.com; 26 Pedro Márquez, Dewey; 9am-4pm Mon-Fri, to noon Sat) Super-efficient, well cooled and right in the center of town.

TOURIST INFORMATION

Tourist Information Office (742-1033; Pedro Márquez, Dewey; 8am-5pm Mon-Fri;) Island-wide information can be found at this tourist information counter, a block from the ferry terminal. Wi-fi is free and extends to the shady plaza right outside its doors.

US Fish & Wildlife Service (457-0082; www.fws.gov/caribbean/refuges/culebra; Hwy 250, off Km 4.2; 8am-4pm Mon-Fri) This government agency is responsible for managing the Culebra National Wildlife Refuge (p607).

Getting There & Away

AIR

Culebra's **Benjamín Rivera Noriega Airport** (CPX; 742-0022; Hwy 251) is a tiny affair with a snack bar, a couple of car-rental booths and check-in counters. There's frequent service from San Juan, Ceiba and, handily for island-hoppers, Vieques. Airlines serving the airport include **Vieques Air Link** (888-901-9247; www.viequesairlink.com; Hwy 251, Aeropuerto Benjamín Rivera Noriega), **Air Flamenco** (724-1818; www.airflamenco.com; Hwy 251, Benjamín Rivera Noriega Airport) and **Cape Air** (800-227-3247; www.capeair.com; Hwy 251, Benjamín Rivera Noriega Airport), along with charter companies **M&N Aviation** (630-2662; www.mnaviation.com; Hwy 251, Aeropuerto Benjamín Rivera Noriega) and **Taxi Aereo** (718-8869; www.taxiaereopr.travel; one way Ceiba/Isla Grande to Vieques & Culebra for 6 passengers US$360/895; 7am-6pm).

BOAT

The most popular – and cheapest – way to Culebra from the mainland is on the **Autoridad de Transporte Marítimo** (Autoridad de Transporte Marítimo (ATM); 494-0934; www.porferry.com; Pedro Márquez, Dewey; one way adult/child US$2.25/1; office open before sailings) ferry service from Ceiba. The service is reasonably reliable, but delays often occur.

Buy your ticket and check times at www.porferry.com and get to the ferry terminal at least an hour early. Schedules vary but there are usually at least five round trips a day; journey times are 45 minutes.

Getting Around

Arriving by ferry, you can easily walk to any point in Dewey proper. Elsewhere you'll want your own transportation; a golf cart is a good option.

BOAT

Water taxis provide round-trip service to Culebra's nearby cays, including Isla Culebrita, Cayo Norte and Cayo Luis Peña. Fares start at around US$40 per person, depending on the destination. Try **Cayo Norte Water Taxi** (376-9988; Isla Culebrita per person US$65) or **H2O Water Taxi** (685-5815; amarog1281@hotmail.com; per person US$40-50).

CAR & GOLF CART

Mainland rental companies forbid you to bring cars to Culebra on the ferry. Locally, rental agencies push 4WDs hard but there's no reason for these on Culebra's well-maintained paved roads. Golf carts make good alternatives.

Carlos Jeep Rental (742-3514; www.carlosjeeprental.com; Hwy 250; 24hr golf-cart rental from US$50, Jeep Wrangler from US$90; 5:30am-9pm) A short walk from the airport; free pickup and drop-off.

Jerry's Jeep Rental (742-0526; www.jerrysjeeprental.com; 139 Escudero Airport Rd; golf cart/SUV/Jeep from US$70/72/83; 8am-5pm Sat-Thu, 7am-7pm Fri) Across from the airport, rents golf carts, Jeep Wranglers and SUVs. Offers courtesy pickup and drop-off.

PÚBLICO

Públicos have one route on the island, from the ferry terminal to Playa Flamenco (per person around US$4). As long as there's room, passengers can flag them down anywhere along the route. The fare remains the same, regardless where you get on.

TAXI

There's taxi service on the island, mostly *público* drivers supplementing their income, so you'll likely be picked up in a van. Fares run from US$5 to US$20, depending on where you're headed on the island.

Raul Transportation (358-4816) Raul and Frida provide reliable door-to-door service in two vans each with capacity for 17 people.

Xavier Transportation Services (463-0475) Xavier is a reliable taxi driver.

Vieques

Measuring just 21 miles long by 5 miles wide, Vieques is renowned for its gorgeous beaches, semiwild horses and sparkling bioluminescent bay. It's substantially larger than Culebra and while it's still a world away from the bright lights of the mainland, the larger population here means more accommodations, swankier restaurants and generally more buzz.

Sights & Activities

★ **Bahía Mosquito** MARINE RESERVE

(Bioluminescent Bay; off Hwy 997) Locals claim that this magnificent bay, a designated wildlife preserve about 2 miles east of Esperanza, has the highest concentration of phosphorescent dinoflagellates not only in Puerto Rico, but in the world. A trip through the lagoon – take a tour – is nothing short of psychedelic, with the movement of your kayak, paddle, electric boat, even fish, whipping up fluorescent-blue sparkles below the surface. Reservations for tours are essential in high season; the best time to go is at new moon.

Vieques National Wildlife Refuge NATURE RESERVE

(741-2138; www.fws.gov/caribbean/refuges/vieques; Km 3.2, Hwy 997; 7am-6:30pm Oct-Feb, to 7:30pm Mar-Sep; P) Lying within these protected confines are the best reasons to visit Vieques. This 18,000-acre refuge occupies the land formerly used by the US military. The 3100-acre western segment was used mainly as a storage area during the military occupation and is very quiet. The 14,700-acre eastern segment, which includes a former live firing range (still off-limits), has the island's best beaches along its southern shore. Both sections have beaches that are considered among the most beautiful in Puerto Rico.

★ **Aqua Sunset Tours** KAYAKING

(939-208-6147; www.aquasunsettours.com; tours from US$55) Touring Vieques' Bio Bay in a crystal-clear canoe makes an already magical experience extra-special. Knowledgeable and fun guides will explain all about the dinoflagellates that are making the water sparkle; they even point out the glittering constellations. This outfit offers daytime kayaking tours too, and snorkeling trips with full-face masks.

★ **Vieques Paddleboarding** OUTDOORS

(366-5202; www.viequespaddleboarding.com; tours US$60-125) This outfit leads informative and fun paddleboarding trips along Vieques' coast, including its mangroves, with entertaining guides happy to share their knowledge of the island's history, flora and fauna. Just paddleboard, or paddleboard and snorkel; you can even hike and snorkel. All skill levels and ages welcome, including young children who can join as ride-alongs with an adult.

Beaches

★Playa Caracas BEACH

(Red Beach; Vieques National Wildlife Refuge, Hwy 997, off Km 3.2, Southern Shore) Calm and clear, this beach is reached on a paved road and has gazebos with picnic tables to shade bathers from the sun; there's excellent snorkeling – lots of healthy sea fans and underwater life – off the eastern side of the beach. Walking west, Playuela is a lesser-known cove with less shade, meaning you'll find few people here and you can enjoy the view back to lovely Playa Caracas.

★Playa La Chiva BEACH

(Blue Beach; Vieques National Wildlife Refuge, Hwy 997, off Km 3.2, Southern Shore; ⏲6am-6:30pm Oct-Mar, to 7:30pm Apr-Sep) FREE A favorite with locals, this gorgeous *playa* at the eastern end of the main road is long and open with occasionally rough surf. It's easy to find your own large patch of sand and you can find shade in the shrubs. There's good snorkeling toward the eastern side of the beach, just off a small island.

★Sun Bay BEACH

(Balneario Sun Bay; ☎741-8198; Parque Nacional Sun Bay, off Hwy 997; parking US$4; ⏲8am-4:30pm Wed-Sun; P) Part of Puerto Rico's national park system, this half-moon-shaped bay, less than a half-mile east of Esperanza, is the island's *balneario*, with all the amenities you could hope for, including lifeguards and a cafe serving *criollo* treats. Measuring a mile in length, it rarely appears busy – even with 100 people sunning and playing on it, it will still seem almost deserted. The surf is gentle.

Head to the eastern end for shady parking places amid the palms and few other sunbathers. For even more solitude, keep heading east on the beach road to **Playas Media Luna & Navio** (Parque Nacional Sun Bay, off Hwy 997; Mon & Tue free, Wed-Sun US$4; ⏲8:30am-5pm Mon-Thu, to 6pm Fri-Sun). In the evening, kayak companies often begin their tours in the parking lot, taking Sun Bay's dirt roads to access Bahía Mosquito.

★Playa La Plata BEACH

(Silver Beach; Vieques National Wildlife Refuge, Hwy 997, off Km 3.2, Southern Shore; ⏲6am-6:30pm Oct-Mar, to 7:30pm Apr-Sep) This secluded beach is as far east as you can go at present, spread across a mushroom-shaped bay with icing-sugar sand and a calm sea that shimmers with a thousand different shades of blue. The snorkeling is good toward the western side of the beach. The road here is very rough; only a 4WD will get you close without walking.

Playa Escondida BEACH

(Vieques National Wildlife Refuge, Hwy 997, off Km 3.2, Southern Shore; ⏲6am-6:30pm Oct-Mar, to 7:30pm Apr-Sep) This deliciously deserted stretch of sand has absolutely no facilities – just jaw-dropping beauty. It faces Bahía Ensenada Honda, which is good for kayaking. The road here is very rough and is 4WD-only, especially after storms.

Sleeping

★Finca Victoria GUESTHOUSE $$

(☎741-0495; www.lafinca.com; Km 2.2, Hwy 995; r US$110-160, houses from US$175; P) Perched on a breezy hilltop, this rustic-luxe retreat is an antidote to city living. Choose from spacious suites, a cool casa, tree houses on stilts and the singular tiny home. There's a pool, hammocks, an open-fronted communal space and daily yoga. Ingredients for the vegan breakfasts, massage oils and scrubs are all plucked from the organic garden.

★Casa de Amistad GUESTHOUSE $$

(☎247-1017; www.casadeamistad.com; 27 Benitez Castaño, Isabel Segunda; r from US$108; P) Everything a great guesthouse should be: welcoming, comfortable, well located and well priced. Nine mid-century-meets-Caribbean rooms come with air-con, modern bathroom and TV; some have balcony or patio. The lounge-library, guest kitchen, pool and rooftop deck make meeting fellow travelers easy. The ferry is a five-minute walk and there are great restaurants close by. Beach gear is available free of charge too.

Hacienda Tamarindo GUESTHOUSE $$

(☎741-8525; www.haciendatamarindo.com; Km 4.5, Hwy 997; r from US$175, ste US$214, 2-bedroom villa US$309; P) Perched on a hilltop, this gorgeous 17-room guesthouse mixes a relaxed island vibe with lashings of style. Rooms come with tropical wood furnishings, wrought-iron balcony, colorful textiles and original art. The manicured gardens, where to-order breakfasts are served alfresco, have hammocks and a pool.

★Malecón House BOUTIQUE HOTEL **$$$**
(939-239-7113, 930-4455; www.maleconhouse.com; 105 Flamboyan, Esperanza; r US$180-310, ste US$325, incl breakfast;) At the western end of the *malecón*, travertine floors, luxe fabrics and uncluttered modern rooms make this 13-room upscale boutique a stylish choice. Three rooms have sea-facing balconies, there's a small lounge-library, the lush garden – perfect for iguana spotting – boasts a pool, while the rooftop is perfect for morning pastries. Friendly staff complete the picture.

★Hix Island House APARTMENT **$$$**
(741-2302; www.hixislandhouse.com; Km 1.5, Hwy 995; Rectangular Gallery from US$115, other lofts from US$135;) This hilltop ecoretreat takes its design cue from the elements, with 18 loft-style rooms spread over four stark yet beautiful concrete casas. At off-the-grid Casa Solaris, the sun powers the electricity and heats the water, and you can shower under the sun or stars. And no need for air-con: the open-fronted lofts allow the outside in. No kids under 14.

Eating

Esperanza Food Trucks FOOD TRUCK **$**
(Flamboyan, Esperanza; meals US$3-8; hours vary) Every weekend, food trucks set up shop at the parking lot facing **El Blok** (741-6020; www.elblok.com; 158 Flamboyan, Esperanza; r from US$140;) at the eastern end of town. You'll find cheap, delicious eats including *criollo*, tacos and, of course, *fritangas* (fried food) – it wouldn't be street food if there weren't a few artery-blocking goodies. Enjoy your meal on the beach.

Buen Provecho MARKET **$**
(529-7316; 123 Muñoz Rivera, Isabel Segunda; meals US$8-10; 8am-5pm Mon-Sat;) This small market has a good selection of gourmet goodies, artisanal bread, Angus-beef steaks and cheeses. Toward the back, there's a small sit-down cafe serving smoothies, breakfast dishes, high-end sandwiches and hearty salads, as well as a full bar. Takeout available.

★Coqui Fire Cafe MEXICAN **$$**
(741-0401; 421 Quiñones, Isabel Segunda; mains US$12-25; 5-9pm Mon-Fri) This cafe lights up Isabel Segunda's foodie scene with delicious Mexican dishes served with flair. Try the *carnitas* (pork shoulder braised in chilies and papaya juice) or the blackened shrimp with coconut *mole*. The signature margarita is a hit, prepared with a dash of heat; its homemade sauces make great souvenirs. Reservations recommended.

★El Quenepo SEAFOOD **$$$**
(741-1215; www.elquenepovieques.com; 148 Flamboyan, Esperanza; mains US$26-34; 5:30-10pm Mon-Sat) Upscale El Quenepo has a lovely interior and an equally delectable menu. The food is catch-of-the-day fresh – a family of seven brothers supplies the seafood – and the decor is contemporary. Specialties include whole Caribbean lobsters, *mofongo* made with mashed breadfruit grown in the backyard, and delicately pan-seared scallops with coconut crème fraîche and caviar. Be sure to book ahead.

Information

MEDIA

Vieques Insider (www.viequesinsider.com) is a good resource on everything Vieques.

MONEY

Isabel Segunda has several ATMs, as do Esperanza's two grocery stores.

Banco Popular (741-2071; www.bancopopular.com; 115 Muñoz Rivera, Isabel Segunda; 8am-3:30pm Mon-Fri) Fully operating bank with ATM.

Cooperativa de Ahorro y Crédito Roosevelt Roads (863-3045; www.cooprr.com; 112 Muñoz Rivera, Isabel Segunda; 8:15am-4:30pm Mon-Fri, to noon Sat) This credit union has an ATM.

POST

Post Office (741-3891; www.usps.com; 97 Muñoz Rivera, Isabel Segunda; 8am-4:30pm Mon-Fri, to noon Sat) The island's only post office.

TOURIST INFORMATION

Good websites for directories of island businesses, services and accommodations include www.enchanted-isle.com and www.viequesisland.com.

Puerto Rico Tourism Company (PRTC; www.seepuertorico.com; Vieques Airport; 9am-4pm Mon-Fri) A small stand at the airport gives out information, brochures and maps. Hours vary.

US Fish & Wildlife Service (741-2138; www.fws.gov/southeast/maps/vi.html; Km 3.2, Hwy 997; 8am-noon & 1-3pm Mon-Fri) Manages several refuges, including those at Cabo Rojo, Culebra and Vieques. The emphasis is on preserving places where wildlife breed, migrate or simply live. On Vieques, it maintains a visitor center in the eastern side of the wildlife refuge (p609), which was closed for reconstruction at the time of research.

Getting There & Away

AIR

Vieques' tiny **Antonio Rivera Rodríguez Airport** (VQS; ☎729-8715; Km 2.6, Hwy 200; 📶) has frequent flights from San Juan, Ceiba and, handily for island-hoppers, Culebra with Vieques Air Link (p608) and **Cape Air** (☎741-7734, 866-227-3247; www.flycapeair.com; Antonio Rivera Rodríguez Airport). Charter flights can be arranged through **M&N Aviation** (☎630-2662; www.mnaviation.com; Antonio Rivera Rodríguez Airport) and **Taxi Aereo** (☎718-8869; www.taxiaereopr.travel; one way Ceiba/Isla Grande to Vieques & Culebra for 6 passengers US$360/895; ⏲7am-6pm).

Check bag size and weight limits before flying. Note that San Juan's Luis Muñoz Marín International Airport (p602) has restrictions on liquid size, while flying from Isla Grande airport means more flexible baggage allowances.

Públicos greet most flights and will take you anywhere you want to go on the island.

BOAT

By far the cheapest way to get between Vieques and the mainland is by ferry or *lancha* (45 minutes) from Ceiba. Plan to arrive at Vieques **ferry terminal** (Autoridad de Transporte Marítimo; ATM; www.porferry.com; German Rieckehoff, Isabel Segunda; adult/child US$2/1; ⏲ticket office open before sailings) at least an hour in advance. Schedules vary but there are normally five passenger ferries a day; go to www.porferry.com to check times and buy tickets, or buy them at the terminal.

Getting Around

CAR & SCOOTER

Transport is essential for exploring Vieques, as the island is large and most of the best beaches are off the main routes. Expect to pay about US$55 to US$85 a day for a small car or 4WD. The latter are useful if you want to get to the outer beaches in the wildlife refuge. There's no need for a large SUV unless you're traveling in a group.

PÚBLICO

Públicos typically greet both ferries and airplanes – they read '*Vieques y Sus Barrios*' (Vieques and its Neighborhoods) on the windshields. These vans cover the entire island, but don't be in a hurry to get where you're going. The trip between Isabel Segunda and Esperanza costs US$3, with *públicos* running reasonably regularly from 7am to 11pm. Sometimes there's an additional US$0.50 charge per bag.

TAXI

A fare of US$10 to US$20 should get you anywhere on the island. Try **741 Taxi** (☎741-8294; www.741taxi.com; ⏲24hr), as they have the most vehicles and are often the most responsive. Your accommodations will usually have their go-to drivers; **Edna Robles** (☎630-4673) and **Nate** (☎364-5911) come recommended.

SOUTHERN & WESTERN PUERTO RICO

Ponce

Ponce es Ponce (Ponce is Ponce) is a simple yet telling Puerto Rican saying: the explanation given as to why the nation's haughty second city does things, well, uniquely – and in defiance of the capital. Native son and author Abelardo Díaz Alfaro went further, calling Ponce a *baluarte irreductible de puertorriqueñidad* – a bastion of the irreducible essence of Puerto Rico. Strolling around the sparkling fountains and narrow, architecturally ornamented streets of the historical center certainly evokes Puerto Rico's stately past. That past may be better than Puerto Rico's present, which is more than evident in the congested traffic, economic stagnation and cookie-cutter urban sprawl that surrounds the center, but stay central and your experience will be a pleasant one.

Sights

★**Museo de Arte de Ponce** GALLERY
(MAP; ☎848-0505; www.museoarteponce.org; 2325 Av Las Américas; adult/concession US$6/3; ⏲10am-5pm Wed-Sat & Mon, noon-5pm Sun, tours 11am & 2pm) *Brush Strokes in Flight*, a bold primary-colored totem by American pop artist Roy Lichtenstein, announces the smartly remodeled MAP, where an expertly presented collection ranks among the best in the Caribbean. It is itself worth the trip from San Juan. A US$30-million renovation celebrated the museum's 50th anniversary and the smart curation – some 850 paintings, 800 sculptures and 500 prints presented in provocative historical and thematic juxtapositions – represents five centuries of Western art.

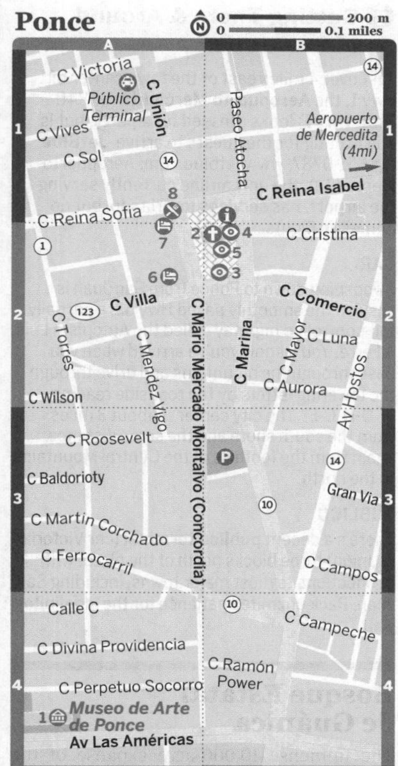

Ponce

Top Sights
1 Museo de Arte de Ponce A4

Sights
2 Catedral Nuestra Señora de Guadalupe B2
3 Fuente de los Leones B2
4 Parque de Bombas B2
5 Plaza Las Delicias B2

Sleeping
6 Hotel Bélgica A2
7 Ponce Plaza Hotel & Casino A2

Eating
8 Lola A1

Plaza Las Delicias SQUARE

Within this elegant square you'll discover Ponce's heart as well as two of the city's landmark buildings, **Parque de Bombas** (☎840-1045; Plaza Las Delicias; ⏲9am-5pm) FREE and Catedral Nuestra Señora de Guadalupe. The **Fuente de los Leones** (Fountain of the Lions), a photogenic fountain rescued from the 1939 World's Fair in New York, is the square's most captivating attraction. The smell of *panaderías* (bakeries) follows churchgoers across the square each morning, while children squeal around the majestic fountain under the midday heat, and lovers stroll under its lights at night.

Catedral Nuestra Señora de Guadalupe CATHEDRAL

(Our Lady of Guadalupe Cathedral; Plaza Las Delicias; ⏲7am-7pm) The twin bell towers of this striking cathedral and local landmark cast an impression of noble piety over Ponce's Plaza Las Delicias. The cathedral appeared on the city's skyline in 1931, on a site where colonists erected their first chapel in the 1660s, which (along with subsequent structures) succumbed to earthquakes and fires. Its stained-glass windows and interior are impressive. Several services a day take place here.

Centro Ceremonial Indígena de Tibes ARCHAEOLOGICAL SITE

(Tibes Indian Ceremonial Center; ☎840-5685; Km 2.2, Hwy 503; adult/child US$3/2; ⏲9am-3pm Tue-Sun) The ancient ceremonial center of Tibes is one of the Caribbean's most important archaeological sites, due largely to evidence found here of pre-Taíno civilizations, such as the Igneris. Though Tibes lacks the dramatic scale of sites such as Mexico's Uxmal, it is a quiet spot, ideal for imagining the people who once dwelled here (brought alive by enthusiastic staff and an excellent interpretation center), and is a highly recommended way to spend an afternoon away from the beach.

Festivals & Events

Carnaval CARNIVAL

(⏲Feb/Mar) Ponce's Carnaval is a time of serious partying. Events kick off on the Wednesday before Ash Wednesday with a masked ball, followed by parades, a formal *danza* competition and the coronation of the Carnaval queen and child queen. The party ends with the ceremonial burial of a sardine and the onset of Lent.

Sleeping & Eating

★**Hotel Bélgica** HOTEL $$

(☎844-3255; www.hotelbelgica.com; 122 Villa; r from US$90; ❄📶) Just off the southwest corner of Plaza Las Delicias, this traveler favorite has a creaking colonial-era ambience, with 15ft ceilings, parquet floors and wrought-iron balconies. The hallways are a bit of a maze and dimly lit, but the place is charming, with delightful antique-style furniture in many of the 20 rooms.

Ponce Plaza Hotel & Casino HOTEL **$$**
(☎813-5050; www.ponceplazahotelandcasino.com; cnr Reina Isabel & Unión; d from US$110; P❄📶🏊) Standing grandly over a corner of the plaza, this 69-room, lemon-yellow colonial-era building is one of Ponce's most engaging places to unpack. The historical building, location and clutch of amenities, plus a mix of classic colonial and modern rooms, keep it among the top options in the city center.

★**Lola** INTERNATIONAL **$$$**
(☎813-5033; www.lolacuisine.com; cnr Reina Isabel & Unión; mains US$19-36; ⏲11:30am-10pm; ❄📶) With its traditional yet modern and crisp interior design, gourmet-style plates of interesting twists on local and Mediterranean dishes, impeccable service and central location, Lola is one of the best places for a special dinner in town. The fish dishes come in for particularly high praise, and it does some excellently mixed cocktails for post-prandial relaxation.

Information

MEDICAL SERVICES

Hospital Manuel Comunitario Dr Pila (☎848-5600; 2435 Blvd Luis A Ferré; ⏲24hr) Hospital with a 24-hour emergency room.

Walgreens (☎812-5978; Km 225, Hwy 2; ⏲7am-11pm) The only pharmacy that can accommodate a late-night need for aloe.

MONEY

Banks line the perimeter of Plaza Las Delicias: finding a cash machine is no problem.

TOURIST INFORMATION

Puerto Rico Tourism Company (PRTC; ☎290-2911; www.visitponce.com; Parque de Bombas, Plaza Las Delicias; ⏲9am-5:30pm) You can't miss the big red-and-black structure in the middle of Parque de Bombas, where friendly English-speaking members of the tourist office are ready with brochures, answers and suggestions.

Getting There & Around

AIR

Just over 4 miles east of the town center off Hwy 1, the **Aeropuerto Mercedita** (☎840-3151; Hwy 1) looks dressed for a party, but is still waiting for the guests to arrive. **JetBlue** (☎651-0787; www.jetblue.com; Aeropuerto Mercedita), the only airline currently serving the airport, has services to Orlando, but no domestic flights.

CAR

Swooshing down to Ponce from San Juan is easy on the smoothly paved Hwy 52, a partially toll-controlled highway called the Autopista Luis A Ferré. You'll know you've arrived when you pass through the mountains and drive through the towering letters by the roadside reading 'P-O-N-C-E.' The city center is about 3 miles from the south shore and the same distance again from the foothills of the Central Mountains to the north.

PÚBLICO

There's a decent **público terminal** (cnr Victoria & Unión) three blocks north of the plaza, with connections to most major towns, including San Juan. Pack unlimited patience for the indefinite wait.

Bosque Estatal de Guánica

The immense 10,000-acre expanse of the Guánica Biosphere Reserve is one of the island's great natural treasures. Located in two wonderfully untrammeled sections just east and west of Guánica, this remote desert forest is among the world's best examples of subtropical dry forest vegetation, containing extraordinary flora and fauna as a result. In the larger, more tourist-friendly eastern portion, numerous trails intersect this astonishing ecosystem, lending themselves well to mountain biking, birdwatching and hiking.

Scientists estimate that only 1% of the earth's original spread of dry forests of this kind remain, and the fact that there is such a vast acreage here renders this a rare sanctuary.

More than 700 varieties of plants, many near extinction, thrive in the reserve. Some of the unusual species here include the squat melon cactus with its brilliant pink flowers that attract hummingbirds. Another plant, with the unseemly name of the Spanish dildo cactus, grows into huge treelike shapes near the coast and attracts bullfinches and bats. Of the fauna, nine of Puerto Rico's 14 endemic bird species can be found here, including the Puerto Rican woodpecker, the Puerto Rican emerald hummingbird and – the ultimate prize for birdwatchers – the exceedingly rare 'prehistoric' Puerto Rican nightjar, of which there are estimated to be as few as 1500.

When out hiking or biking, the 30-odd miles of trails hammer you with contrasts at every turn, alternating between arid, rocky, scrub-covered highlands and almost 12 miles of remote, wholly untouched coast.

Several trails sally forth from the Bosque Estatal de Guánica's ranger station and are of varying lengths and difficulty. Camino Ballena perhaps best demonstrates the contrasting topography of the reserve, while the most exhilarating route of all is the reserve's coastal hike, the Vereda Meseta. Most of the trails here are wide and at least a little metaled, making for great mountain biking as well. Nothing technical, but superb scenery and deserted routes.

There are two main routes into the eastern section of the reserve: Hwy 334 climbs from Guánica to the reserve's ranger station and the nexus of the majority of the trails, while Hwy 333 traverses the eastern reserve's coast to Bahía de la Ballena and further hikes.

Information

Ranger Station (821-5706; 7am-4pm) A solitary ranger is usually in evidence at this small center next to the main parking area at the end of Hwy 334 in the eastern portion of the Bosque Estatal de Guánica.

Getting There & Away

If you're driving to Guánica from either direction along the expressway, Hwy 2, turn off on Hwy 116, from where it's 4 miles south. You can get between Guánica and La Parguera via a 12.5-mile drive on the coast road, Hwy 324, or the slightly more circuitous but swifter Hwy 116.

The Bosque Estatal de Guánica can be reached from Guánica via two main routes. To get to the eastern section of the reserve and the ranger station, follow Hwy 116 northeast from Guánica towards Hwy 2 and then turn right onto the narrow Hwy 334 to wind up to the reserve entrance. The southern extent of the eastern section of the forest – including the ferry to Gilligan's Island and Guánica's plushest accommodations possibilities – is also accessible by Hwy 333, to the southeast of Guánica.

Rincón

You'll know you've arrived in Rincón – 'the corner' – when you pass the sun-grizzled *gringos* cruising west in their rusty 1972 Volkswagen Beetle with surfboards piled on the roof. Shoehorned in the island's most remote corner, Rincón is Puerto Rico at its most unguarded, a place where the sunsets shimmer scarlet and you're more likely to be called 'dude' than 'sir.' This is the island's surfing capital and one of the premier places to catch a wave in the Caribbean.

For numerous Californian dreamers this is where the short-lived Summer of Love ended up. Arriving for the World Surfing Championships in 1968, many never went home. Rincón became a haven for draft-dodgers, alternative lifestylers, back-to-the-landers and people more interested in riding the perfect wave than with bagging US$100,000 a year and living in the 'burbs.

Activities

Rincón Surf School SURFING
(823-0610; www.rinconsurfschool.com; 3hr group lessons US$95) Rincón Surf School often runs lessons at Sandy Beach and is a good option for beginning adults. Also on offer are surf-and-yoga combo packages and lessons specifically for women.

Tres Palmas SURFING
This is the big kahuna of the Rincón surf spots, with massive breaks of up to 25ft.

Sleeping & Eating

Rincón Surf Hostel HOSTEL $
(678-744-8556; Km 0.5, Hwy 413; dm/s/d US$25/70/80;) This hostel is a particularly tempting option for surfers and beachgoers, one block back from the beach on the northwestern side of Rincón. Clean dorms and small private rooms, a communal kitchen and a little takeaway coffee shack out front make this a good stopover for those on a budget.

★**Tres Sirenas** B&B $$$
(823-0558; www.tressirenas.com; 26 Sea Beach Dr; d US$195-300;) A stone's throw

from two of the bigger, more luxurious hotels, Rincón's best B&B is certainly one of Puerto Rico's finest. True indulgence beckons at this tranquil end-of-street detached house, from the freshly brewed coffee in your room to the lovingly prepared breakfasts served to all guests on their private terraces (with views out to the glimmering ocean).

★ **Horned Dorset Primavera** RESORT $$$
(823-4030; www.horneddorset.net; Km 0.3, Hwy 429; ste from US$299; P) Undoubtedly the best small resort in Puerto Rico, this place rightly claims to offer the 'epitome of privacy, elegance and service.' There are 30 suites in private villas furnished with hand-carved antiques and with their own private plunge pools (in case you get bored of the communal infinity pool, which overlooks the setting sun).

★ **La Copa Llena** INTERNATIONAL $$
(823-0896; www.attheblackeagle.com; Black Eagle Marina; mains US$17-36; 5pm-late Wed-Sun; P) Is your glass half empty or half full? It's hard not to look on the bright side of life at La Copa Llena (the full cup). Down by the Black Eagle Marina, this is one of the best restaurants in Rincón, for the elegantly understated interior and huge sea-fronting patio but mostly for the innovative food.

Chateau Rose at the Horned Dorset Primavera FUSION $$$
(823-4030; www.chateauroserincon.com; Km 0.3, Hwy 429; 3-course dinner US$65-110; 7-9:30pm Wed-Mon) Elegant, exclusive and a million miles from the surf scene, the Chateau Rose restaurant at the Horned Dorset Primavera is among Puerto Rico's best fine-dining options – fitting for a hotel that's one of Puerto Rico's most admired. Climb the sweeping staircase to the black-and-white-tiled dining room with billowing lined drapes and an atmosphere right out of a Caribbean culinary dream.

Information

MEDICAL SERVICES

In Rincón town, this **health center** (823-5500, 823-5555; www.costasalud.com; Muñoz Rivera 28, cnr Calle A; clinic 8am-4pm Mon-Fri, emergencies 7am-11pm Mon-Fri) is a block south of Plaza de Recreo.

POST

The **post office** (Hwy 115; 8am-3:45pm Mon-Fri, to noon Sat) is 650yd north of the Plaza de Recreo on Hwy 115.

TOURIST INFORMATION

The **tourist office** (823-5024; www.rincon.org; Sunset Bldg, Cambija; 8am-4:30pm Mon-Fri) is in the Sunset Building adjacent to Rincón's public beach.

Getting There & Away

The easiest way to approach the town by road is via Hwy 115, which intersects Hwy 2 both at the northern end of the Rincón peninsula near Aguadilla and the southern end, not far north of the Mayagüez airport. As Hwy 115 sweeps into town, it becomes Calle Muñoz Rivera.

Getting Around

Rincón – despite its mantle as an 'alternative' beach haven – has little provision for nonmotorized transport. The spread-out community with minimal public transport has few sidewalks and almost no facilities for bicycles.

The only reliable way to get around the area is by rented car, taxi, irregular *públicos* or – if you're energetic and careful – walking.

UNDERSTAND PUERTO RICO

History

Taíno Roots

Indigenous peoples are thought to have arrived – via a raft from Florida – around the 1st century AD, quickly followed by groups from the Lesser Antilles. The Taínos created a sophisticated trading system on the island they named Borinquen and became the reigning culture, although they were constantly fighting off Carib invaders.

Colonization of the Taíno

All that changed forever in 1508, when Juan Ponce de León came back to the island he had glimpsed from one of Christopher Columbus' ships. Driven by a desire for gold, Spanish conquistadores enslaved, murdered, starved and raped natives with impunity. Virtually wiped out by war, smallpox and whooping cough, a few remaining Taínos took to the mountains. Soon Dutch and French traders became frequent visitors, dropping off human cargo from West Africa. By 1530 West African slaves – including members of the Mandingo and Yoruba tribes – numbered about half the population of 3000 in Puerto Rico.

And so it went for several generations. The Spanish–American War of 1898 finally pried Puerto Rico out from under the yoke of the Spanish empire, but it established the small island as a commonwealth of the United States – Borinquen was liberated from Spain, but not quite free.

From Spanish Colony to American Commonwealth

Operation Bootstrap poured money into the island and set up highways, post offices, supermarkets and a few military posts. Puerto Ricans have accepted the US economic and military presence on their island, with varying degrees of anger, indifference and satisfaction, for more than 100 years now – and the strong *independentista* movement that wanted to cut all ties with the US in the 1950s has mostly receded into the background. The biggest question for Puerto Ricans – a passionately political people who muster at least a 90% voter turnout on election days – is whether to keep the status quo or become, officially, the United States' 51st state.

Headline News

In September 2017 Puerto Rico was hit by two major hurricanes. Passing to the north of the island, Irma did most damage on the outlying islands of Culebra and Vieques, as well as in the mountainous areas and along the north coast. But on September 20, Category 4 Hurricane Maria made landfall at Yabucoa with winds of 155mph and continued to move slowly across Puerto Rico, causing billions of dollars worth of damage, taking thousands of lives and wiping out an entire season's crops and Puerto Rico's electricity grid.

In July 2019 another storm passed over Puerto Rico, but this time it was a political one. A transcript of a group chat on the Telegram app came to light in which Governor Ricardo Rosselló made misogynistic and homophobic comments as well as jokes about hurricane victims. Rosselló resigned after huge protests in San Juan.

People & Culture

Most Puerto Ricans live a lifestyle that weaves together two primary elements: the commercial and material values of the United States and the social and traditional values of their 'enchanted' island. Because of the strong connection to the mainland United States, Puerto Ricans have espoused many of the same social values as their cousins in New York. Even so, the Puerto Rican flags that fly from the fire escapes of NYC leave no doubt that many Puerto Ricans will never fully lose themselves to mainstream American culture.

Modern practicalities of the island's political and cultural position have meant that, for three or four generations now, many Puerto Ricans have grown up bouncing between mainland US cities and their native soil. Even those who stay put assimilate by proxy: young people in a wealthy San Juan suburb may wander the mall past American chain stores and chat about Hollywood blockbusters; obversely, their counterparts living in the uniformly Puerto Rican neighborhoods of New York or Chicago may have a day-to-day existence that more closely resembles Latin America. This makes the full scope of their bilingual and multicultural existence difficult to comprehend for outsiders. Many Puerto Ricans are just as comfortable striding down New York's Fifth Ave for a little shopping during the week as they are visiting the *friquitines* (roadside kiosks) with their families at Playa Luquillo on the weekend.

The Arts

Abundant creative energy hangs in the air over Puerto Rico (maybe it has something to do with the Bermuda Triangle) and its effects can be seen in the island's tremendous output of artistic achievement. Puerto Rico has produced renowned poets, novelists, playwrights, orators, historians, journalists, painters, composers and sculptors. The island's two most influential artists are considered to be rococo painter José Campeche and impressionist Francisco Oller. As well as being a groundbreaking politician, Puerto Rican Governor Luís Moñez Marín was also an eloquent poet. In the world of entertainment Rita Morena is the only Puerto Rican to have won an Oscar, a Grammy, a Tony and an Emmy, while the island's hottest film talent is actor Benicio del Toro, star of Steven Soderbergh's 2008 two-part biopic of Che

Guevara. While it's known for world-class art in many mediums, music and dance are especially synonymous with the island.

Landscape & Wildlife

The Land

It's the astonishing beaches that captivate most minds when planning a first visit to Puerto Rico. But as seasoned aficionados know, the sand and surf intimate only a part of the full, rich picture of the topography. Shores also yield internationally crucial swaths of mangrove reserve, and behind the beachside hotels the mythical, densely forested contours of the Central Mountains stretch invitingly upwards. The island rears a number of crops: bananas, coffee, yams and citrons are of great importance.

Wildlife

Seeking out the wildlife of Puerto Rico can be very rewarding. The island's jungle-clad mountains and surreal variety of terrain – including some of the wettest and driest forests in the subtropical climate – have a bit of everything (albeit no huge beasts or flocks of colorful birds). The island's most famous creature is the humble common coquí. The nocturnal serenade of this small endemic frog is the poignant soundtrack of the island, an ever-present reminder of Puerto Rico's precious natural environment.

SURVIVAL GUIDE

Directory A–Z

ACCESSIBLE TRAVEL

Travel to and around Puerto Rico is becoming easier for people with disabilities as the country is subject to the Americans with Disabilities Act (ADA). Public buildings are now required to be wheelchair-accessible and to have appropriate restroom facilities. Similarly, public transportation services must be made accessible to all, and telephone companies are required to provide relay operators for the hearing impaired.

> **SLEEPING PRICE RANGES**
>
> The following price ranges refer to a double room with bathroom in high season. Unless otherwise stated, a tax of 9% to 15% is included in the price.
>
> **$** less than US$90
>
> **$$** US$90–200
>
> **$$$** more than US$200

ACCOMMODATIONS

Puerto Rico has a wide range of accommodations. Book ahead in high season.

Hotels Available island-wide in price ranges from US$60 to US$400+ nightly, with a good selection under US$200.

B&Bs A relatively new midrange option; owners live on or near the premises and breakfast is included.

Guesthouses Ranging from family-run places with a few rooms to larger motel-like stays; many can also be apartments under another name.

Resorts World-class properties line San Juan's beachfront and other coastal areas. There are few all-inclusive resorts.

Camping Possible on Culebra and in a handful of nature parks; must be booked well ahead.

ELECTRICITY

As per the US, power plugs and sockets are of type A and B (120V, 60 Hz).

EMBASSIES & CONSULATES

Most nations' principal diplomatic representation is in Washington, DC, which means many countries do not maintain consulates in Puerto Rico. Consulates in Puerto Rico tend to be the honorary kind that have very limited services – if any – for travelers. The following consulates in San Juan may be of use:

Dominican Republic Consulate (☎977-0399; www.domrep.org; 1607 Av Ponce de León, Suite 101, Santurce; ⌚9am-2pm Mon-Fri)

French Consulate (☎767-2428; www.consulfrance-miami.org; 270 Av Luis Muñoz Rivera, Suite 301, Hato Rey; ⌚phone inquiries 9am-noon Mon, Wed & Fri, in-person by appointment only; Ⓜ Roosevelt)

Netherlands Consulate (☎774-2222; www.the-netherlands.org; 2 Carretera #2, Guaynabo; ⌚by appointment only)

Spanish Consulate (☎758-6090; www.exteriores.gob.es; Mercantil Plaza, 2 Av Ponce de León, Hato Rey; ⌚8:30am-1:30pm Mon-Fri)

EMERGENCY & IMPORTANT NUMBERS

Directory assistance	☎411
Emergency	☎911
International access code	☎011

FOOD

Puerto Rico's traditional cuisine hauls in influences from North America, its Caribbean neighbors, Africa and Spain, and is spliced together by the succulent dominance of *lechón* (pork) in as many forms as you could shake some barbecue tongs at. A network of experimental chefs is striving island-wide to spice up the food scene with their own bold influences, which run from European to Middle Eastern.

HEALTH

If you have a medical emergency or a need for health care in Puerto Rico, the array of pharmacies and hospitals is good compared to most other places in the Caribbean. For medical emergencies, dial 911.

INTERNET ACCESS

Wi-fi is common in places to stay, cafes and many public places and squares.

In Lonely Planet products, the wi-fi symbol means that wi-fi is available throughout the property unless otherwise noted, while the internet symbol means there are public internet terminals available.

LGBT+ TRAVELERS

Puerto Rico is probably the most gay-friendly island in the Caribbean. San Juan has a well-developed gay scene, especially in the Condado district and Santurce. Vieques and Culebra are popular destinations for an international mix of gay and lesbian expatriates and travelers. Rincón and Ponce, whilst some way behind in specifically gay venues, are gay-friendly destinations.

MONEY

➡ Major bank offices in San Juan and Ponce will exchange foreign currencies. There are also exchange desks at San Juan's Luis Muñoz Marin International Airport and major resorts (which offer terrible rates).

➡ ATMs are easily found in all but the smallest towns and villages. Before departure make sure your debit card can be used outside your home country/continent.

Exchange Rates

Australia	A$1	$0.68
Canada	C$1	$0.75
Euro zone	€1	$1.10
Japan	¥100	$0.92
New Zealand	NZ$1	$0.63
UK	UK£1	$1.24

For current exchange rates see www.xe.com.

Tipping

Generally, tip in Puerto Rico as you would on the US mainland. Service charges may have been included in your bill at touristy restaurants, even for groups smaller than six. Remember to check.

Bars US$1 per drink.

Luggage attendants US$1 to US$2 per bag.

Restaurants 15% of the bill. Tip servers with cash even when paying by credit card; this precludes management taking a cut.

Taxis 15% of the fare.

OPENING HOURS

Hours can vary from those posted and they change sporadically, so check before setting off.

Banks 8am–4pm Monday to Friday, 9:30am–noon Saturday

Bars 2pm–2am, often later in San Juan

Government offices 8:30am–4:30pm Monday to Friday

Museums 9:30am–5pm, often closed Monday and Tuesday

Post offices 8am–4pm Monday to Friday, 8am–1pm Saturday

Restaurants 11am–10pm, later in San Juan

Shops 9am–6pm Monday to Saturday, 11am–5pm Sunday, later in malls

PUBLIC HOLIDAYS

In addition to holidays observed in the region, Puerto Rico also celebrates the following public holidays:

Three Kings Day (Feast of the Epiphany) January 6

Eugenio María de Hostos' Birthday January 10

Martin Luther King Jr Day Third Monday in January

Emancipation Day March 22

Palm Sunday Sunday before Easter

Easter A Sunday in late March/April

José de Diego Day April 18

Memorial Day Last Monday in May

Luis Muñoz Rivera's Birthday July 18

José Celso Barbosa's Birthday July 27

Labor Day First Monday in September

Columbus Day Second Monday in October

Thanksgiving Fourth Thursday in November

EATING PRICE RANGES

The following price ranges refer to a standard one- or two-course meal. Tipping is extra.

$ less than US$18

$$ US$18–30

$$$ more than US$30

PRACTICALITIES

Newspapers Some main newspapers have good websites. El Nuevo Dia (www.elnuevodia.com) is Puerto Rico's leading news publication and has one of the island's most popular websites. It also has an English section.

Smoking Banned in most public places, including hotel rooms and restaurants.

TV & radio American TV is broadcast across the island. Radio is mostly in Spanish. Places to stay will have the full complement of US cable/satellite channels.

Weights & measures Puerto Rico follows the American imperial system with two major exceptions: all distances on road signs are in kilometers (confusing sometimes in hire cars that use miles) and gas is pumped in liters not gallons.

TELEPHONE

Puerto Rico's area code is +787. To call locally, just dial the local seven-digit telephone number. To call the island from the US, dial 1 + 787 + the seven-digit number. From elsewhere, dial your country's international access code followed by 787 + the seven-digit number.

All major US cell-phone carriers provide service in Puerto Rico without any extra charges.

TIME

Puerto Rico is on Atlantic Standard Time (GMT/UTC minus four hours). Clocks in this time zone read an hour later than the Eastern Standard Time zone, which encompasses such US cities as New York and Miami. There is no Daylight Saving Time observed on the island.

TOURIST INFORMATION

Puerto Rico Tourism Company is the Commonwealth's official tourist bureau. It has a fair range of general-interest materials and a decent website, See Puerto Rico (www.discoverpuertorico.com). Privately produced tourist magazines and brochures are abundant.

Welcome to Puerto Rico (http://welcome.topuertorico.org) is part encyclopedia, part travel guide, and is an excellent online resource on the island of Puerto Rico.

VISAS

You only need a visa to enter Puerto Rico if you need a visa to enter the US, since the commonwealth follows the United States' immigration laws. For many countries, an Esta (Electronic System for Transport authorization, https://esta.cbp.dhs.gov/esta) must nevertheless be applied for.

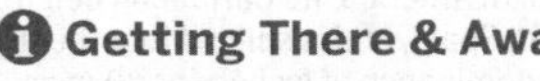

Getting There & Away

ENTERING PUERTO RICO

US nationals need proof of citizenship (such as a driver's license with photo ID or birth certificate) to enter Puerto Rico, but be aware that if traveling to another country in the Caribbean (other than the US Virgin Islands, which, like Puerto Rico, is a US territory), you require a valid passport in order to reenter the US. Visitors from other countries must have a valid passport to enter Puerto Rico.

AIR

There are a few airports on the island that service international flights.

Luis Muñoz Marín International Airport (p602) San Juan's main airport; this is where almost all flights arrive or depart.

Rafael Hernández Airport (http://aguadilla.airport-authority.com; Av Engineer Orlando Alárcon) Aguadilla's airport receives a few international flights, with several airlines flying to New York, Newark and Orlando from here. Other mainland US destinations are served too, with specific routes changing frequently. A few other Caribbean destinations such as Santo Domingo, St Lucia and Aruba are also served.

Small planes fly to the British Virgin Islands from Isla Grande Airport (p602), Benjamín Rivera Noriega Airport (Culebra Airport) and Antonio Rivera Rodríguez Airport (Vieques Airport).

Most major destinations in mainland US are served by airlines including American Airlines, JetBlue, United, Delta, Spirit, LATAM, Air Canada, Emirates and Avianca. Other direct international routes of interest include Madrid (Iberia), Frankfurt (Condor) plus St Thomas in the US Virgin Islands and Santo Domingo in the Dominican Republic (Seaborne Airlines).

SEA

San Juan is the second-largest port for cruise ships in the western hemisphere (after Miami). More than one million cruise-ship passengers pass through the ports in Old San Juan annually, and all the major cruise-ship lines operate cruises from here.

Following substantial investment, Ponce's **Port of the Americas** (Muelle de Ponce) also now has cruise-ships calling.

Getting Around

AIR

Because Puerto Rico is such a small island, its domestic air transportation system is basic. Cape Air (p603) and **JetBlue** (☎1-800-538-

2583; www.jetblue.com; Luis Muñoz Marín International Airport) connect San Juan with Mayagüez on the mainland several times daily; airlines serving the offshore islands of Culebra and Vieques from San Juan include **Vieques Air Link** (☎741-8331; www.viequesairlink.com) and Air Flamenco (p603).

BOAT

The **Autoridad de Transporte Marítimo** (ATM; ☎497-7740; www.porferry.com; Roosevelt Roads, Ceiba; adult/child to Culebra US$2.25/1, to Vieques US$2/1) offers daily service to Vieques and Culebra on *lanchas* (passenger boats) and *ferries* (cargo boats). Service runs three to four times daily.

CAR

Despite the occasional hazards of operating a car in Puerto Rico, driving is currently the most convenient way to see the island; public transport is about as poor as it gets, and cycling is deemed too dangerous.

Puerto Rico has the same basic rules of the road as the US: traffic proceeds along the right side of the road and moves counterclockwise around traffic circles.

Car rental rates run US$30 to US$60 per day. A valid driver's license issued from your country of residence is all that's needed to rent. Major international car-rental companies as well as local firms operate on the island. Most prohibit taking rentals from the mainland to Culebra and Vieques.

PÚBLICO

Públicos are essentially public minibuses that run prescribed routes during daylight hours, typically Monday to Saturday. Traveling via *público* offers an inexpensive local experience, but requires a lot of patience and time. Some *públicos* make relatively long hauls between places such as San Juan and Ponce or Mayagüez, but most make much shorter trips, providing a link within and between communities.

Saba

☎599 / POP 1915

Best Places to Eat

- ➡ Island Flavor (p630)
- ➡ Chez Bubba (p627)
- ➡ Queen's Gardens Restaurant (p630)
- ➡ Brigadoon (p628)

Best Places to Stay

- ➡ Queen's Gardens Resort (p630)
- ➡ Selera Dunia (p626)
- ➡ Juliana's (p626)

Why Go?

Imagine a place without crime, traffic or Starbucks. What sounds like earthly paradise is the island of Saba, a tiny speck in the ocean and perhaps the Caribbean's best-kept secret. Aptly nicknamed the 'Unspoiled Queen', this forest-draped volcano pokes out from the sea just 45km from bustling St-Martin/Sint Maarten. The landing on the world's shortest commercial runway may quicken your pulse, but moments later you'll be enveloped by a sense of calm.

Saba moves to its own rhythm, a beat not driven by reggae or soca but by birds chirping on its many glorious hiking trails. There are no powdery beaches, but many living treasures below the waterline that make Saba a darling with divers. Plunge into the crystalline sea for close-ups of rays, sharks, turtles and luminous tropical fish.

Saba is an easy day trip from St-Martin/Sint Maarten, but its unique aquatic and terrestrial features reward longer exploration.

When to Go

Jul Saba erupts in island-wide merriment during its colorful Carnival at the end of the month.

Jul–Sep Temperatures stay pleasant on Saba as other islands swelter.

Oct The Sea & Learn festival hosts a range of ecological activities.

Windwardside

Teeming with gingerbread-trimmed Saban cottages that seem like oversized dollhouses, the quaint hilltop hamlet of Windwardside is Saba's commercial heart. Key stops include a dive shop (p625), the tourist office (p629) and the Trail Shop (p629), which dispenses a wealth of advice on hiking. The 'suburb' of Booby Hill is an exceptionally steep 600m trek southeast.

Windwardside has a couple of small, intriguing museums and a clutch of art galleries and craft shops. Up at Booby Hill, you

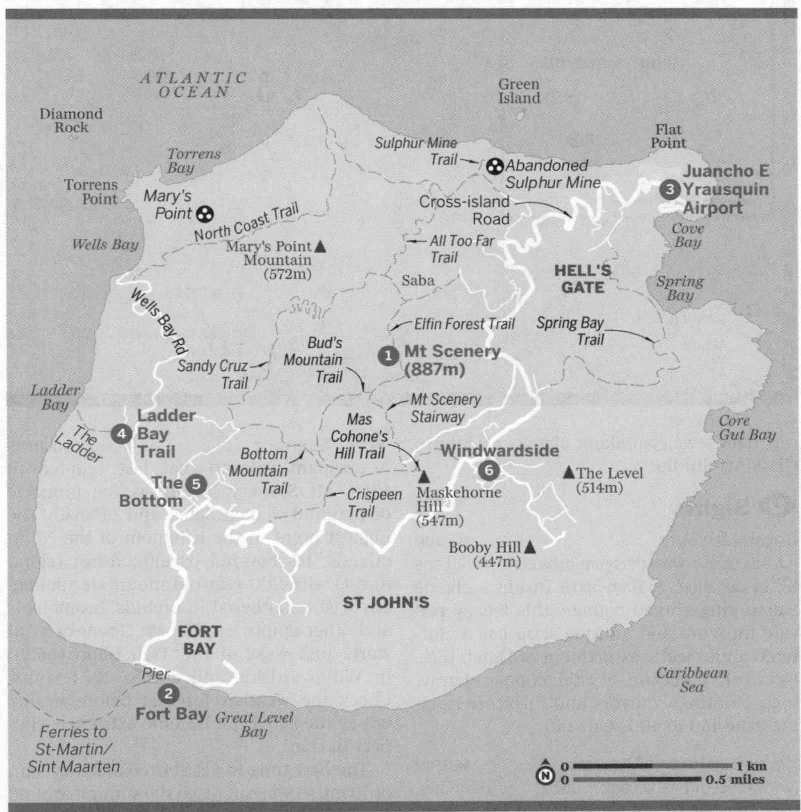

Saba Highlights

1 Mt Scenery (p624) Hiking to the summit of Saba's soaring volcano while taking in dizzying views of the sea far below.

2 Diving (p632) Scuba diving among submerged pinnacles teeming with nurse sharks and large colorful fish on a trip from Fort Bay.

3 Juancho E Yrausquin Airport (p635) Landing on the world's smallest commercial runway alongside sheer, steep cliffs at Flat Point.

4 Ladder Bay Trail (p629) Tackling the hundreds of steps hewn into the rock where supplies and even visiting royalty were hauled up.

5 Island Flavor (p630) Dining on fruit, veggies and herbs from the owners' gardens at this tree-shaded restaurant in The Bottom.

6 Harry L Johnson Museum (p624) Learning about the island's pioneering history in a traditional Windwardside gingerbread-trimmed cottage.

Windwardside & Around

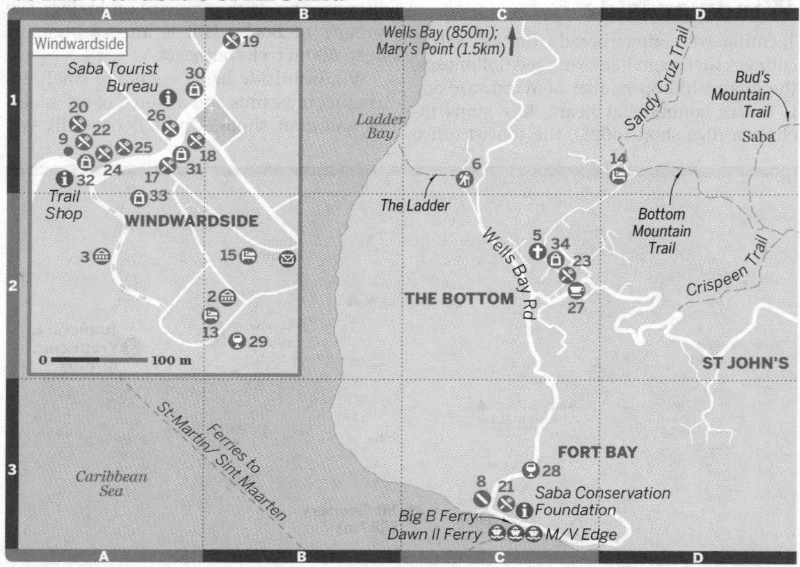

can take jewelry-making classes at Jobean Glass Art Studio.

Sights

Dutch Museum MUSEUM

(☎416-6030; www.museum-saba.com; Park Lane 12; by donation; ⏰11am-5pm) Inside a classic Saban gingerbread cottage, this teensy private museum and antique shop has a cluttered and eclectic assortment of Dutch tiles, lacework, porcelain, crystal, copper engravings, paintings, mirrors and furniture ranging from 150 to 400 years old.

Harry L Johnson Museum MUSEUM

(www.museum-saba.com; US$2; ⏰10am-3pm Wed, Thu, Sat & Sun) Surrounded by a flowering garden, this pint-sized museum in a quaint 1840-built sea-captain's cottage is crammed with an eclectic collection. Highlights include vintage photographs of Dutch royalty, a 100-year-old organ harmonium and a dining table set with 19th-century Wedgwood china. A museum guide brings the stories behind the objects to life. Outside, look for the large cistern used to gather water and, above it, the family cemetery.

Also note the original kitchen with its carved stone hearth.

★Mt Scenery MOUNTAIN

A dormant volcano that last erupted in 1640, Mt Scenery (887m) is the pinnacle of pyramid-shaped Saba, and officially the highest point in the Kingdom of the Netherlands. It's covered by elfin forest (cloud forest) with 200-year-old mountain mahogany trees smothered in orchids, bromeliads and other epiphytes. The **Mt Scenery Trail** starts just west of the Trail Shop (p629) in Windwardside and climbs 1064 stairs. Check the weather forecast before setting out as the steps can become extremely slippery in rain.

The best time to get started is about 9am or 10am, so you can reach the summit around noon, the least cloudy part of the day.

Another trail leading to the Mt Scenery summit is the new **Elfin Forest Trail**, which starts in Upper Hell's Gate.

Jobean Glass Art Studio ART STUDIO

(☎416-2490; www.jobean-glass.com; Booby Hill Rd; half-/full-day glass workshop US$95/150; ⏰studio 10am-5pm Mon-Sat, to 3pm Sun, classes by arrangement) Local artist Jobean works out of her colorful studio up on Booby Hill. During a half-day glass workshop, you're set up with a torch and an unlimited supply of thin glass shafts that you melt down into swirling balls or cylinders, before making beads of all

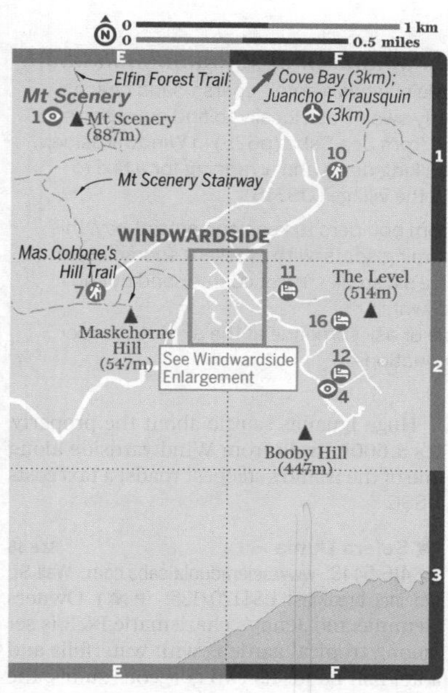

shapes and sizes while incorporating gold foil and quirky objects.

Your creations are yours to keep; otherwise just drop by and browse the shop. Some of Jobean's more unusual designs include plates made from Heineken bottles and wine bottles and a huge array of animals large and small.

Activities & Tours

★Sea Saba DIVING

(☎416-2246; www.seasaba.com; Lambee's Pl, Main St; 1-/2-tank dives from US$65/131, night dives US$85; ⏲8am-5pm) Passionate about marine education and keeping Saba pristine, PADI-affiliated Sea Saba runs a range of small-group dive trips and various courses including a one-day Discover Scuba for US$125 and open-water courses from US$350, gear included. Snorkelers can tag along on the afternoon dive (US$39, including gear).

Snorkeling gear by itself rents for US$15, dive equipment for US$20.

Saba Archaeological Center OUTDOORS

(SABARC; www.facebook.com/pg/sabarchaeology; tours per person US$50; ⏲on request) This NGO runs historical tours of Windwardside and The Bottom and guided hikes to archaeological sites, including Mary's Point (p630). Find out how The Bottom got its name or why there are so many private graveyards on the island.

Mas Cohone's Hill Trail HIKING

(Maskehorne Hill) If you're short on time or stamina but still want a great view, hit this shortie. It has you standing atop 547m-high Mas Cohone's Hill and staring out over

Windwardside & Around

Top Sights

1 Mt Scenery E1

Sights

2 Dutch Museum B2
3 Harry L Johnson Museum A2
4 Jobean Glass Art Studio F2
5 Sacred Heart Church C2

Activities, Courses & Tours

6 Ladder Bay Trail C1
7 Mas Cohone's Hill Trail E2
8 Saba Divers C3
9 Saba Freediving School A1
Sea Saba .... (see 22)
10 Spring Bay Trail F1

Sleeping

11 Cottage Club F2
12 El Momo Cottages F2
13 Juliana's B2
14 Queen's Gardens Resort & Spa D1
15 Scout's Place B2
16 Selera Dunia F2

Eating

17 Big Rock Market A1
18 Bizzy B Bakery A1
19 Brigadoon B1
20 Chez Bubba A1
21 Deep End Bar & Grill C3
22 Different Tastes A1
23 Island Flavor C2
24 Long Haul Grill A1
My Store .... (see 23)
Queen's Gardens Restaurant & Ocean Bar .... (see 14)
25 Saba Snack A1
26 Swingin' Doors A1
Tropics Cafe .... (see 13)

Drinking & Nightlife

27 Bottom Bean Cafe C2
28 Think About It Bar C3
29 Tipsy Goat Bar B2

Shopping

30 Five Square Art Gallery A1
31 Jewel Cottage A1
32 Kakona A1
33 Marie de Saba A2
34 Saba Artisan Foundation C2

SNORKELING SPOTS IN SABA

Wells Bay Backed by sheer cliffs, this rocky little bay has a small, coarse-sand beach that comes and goes depending on the northerly swell – ask locally to find out when's best to visit. There's great snorkeling; rent gear from Sea Saba (p625) in Windwardside. It's about 2.5km from The Bottom. Consider walking down and arranging for a taxi to save yourself the thigh-burning climb back into the village (US$16).

Cove Bay Behind a breakwater constructed from boulders to keep currents at bay, this little cove is one of the island's two ocean swimming spots, with excellent snorkeling in calm weather. It's sunniest in the morning; there's a small strip of coarse sand but no amenities. From the airport, it's a 150m walk downhill.

Make pickup arrangements with your cabbie or ask someone at the airport to order you a taxi for the trip back up to your accommodations.

Windwardside and the sea in about 20 minutes from the trailhead at the end of Mountain Rd (turn left).

Courses

Saba Freediving School WATER SPORTS
(416-9213; www.sabafreediving.com; Main St; half-/2-/3-day course US$150/220/345; by appointment) Saba's clear waters are a superb place to try the increasingly popular sport of free diving. Affiliated with both PADI and AIDA (the International Association for the Development of Apnea), instructor Luis Fonseca teaches techniques for holding your breath and the mental and physical disciplines needed to reach depths normally only achievable with scuba equipment.

No more than four people per class. Must be 18 or over.

Sleeping

There are four hotels in and around Windwardside, all of which have their own unique flavor, as well as a dozen or so holiday cottages. Reserve well ahead as places book out quickly, particularly in December and January.

El Momo Cottages GUESTHOUSE $
(416-2265; www.elmomocottages.com; Booby Hill; s/d with bathroom US$80/95, with kitchenette US$100/115;) A near-vertical flight of 69 stone steps leads from the road to reception for these small, rustic cottages with outdoor bathroom; some with kitchenette. Tucked into a rugged hillside smothered in tropical foliage, they have breathtaking views, especially from the aptly named 'Cottage in the Sky.' There's an honesty bar and breakfast (US$8.50) but no restaurant. Wi-fi can be patchy.

Huge iguanas scuttle about the property. It's a 600m walk from Windwardside along one of the island's steepest roads; a taxi costs US$6.

★ **Selera Dunia** B&B $$
(416-5443; www.seleradunia-saba.com; Wall St; s/d incl breakfast US$120/135;) Owners Hemmie and Jenny's charismatic B&B is set among tropical gardens with waterfalls and a koi-fish pond. Its two gorgeous suites, the stately Dutch and exotic Iban rooms, have extra-long king-size beds and epic Mt Scenery and Windwardside views from small balconies. Homemade breakfasts are delivered to your room. It's a steep 700m walk or US$6 taxi ride from town.

Jenny is also a fashion designer with a small atelier and boutique on the premises.

Cottage Club COTTAGE $$
(416-2386; www.cottage-club.com; cottage US$150;) In a central yet peaceful location with spectacular views of Mt Scenery (p624) towering above, these 10 spacious, gingerbread-trimmed cottages come with full kitchen and private balcony. The garden-framed swimming pool overlooks the sea and airport far below. Optional breakfast (US$11.50) is served in the lounge next to reception, which is also the only place to get reliable wi-fi.

A laundry service is available (per load US$15). Iguanas and goats occasionally roam the lush grounds.

Juliana's HOTEL $$
(416-2269; www.julianashotelsaba.com; Park Lane 7f; s/d/ste incl breakfast from US$155/180/215, cottages US$250;) Juliana's has charmingly captured Saba's laissez-faire vibe for over 30 years. Each unit has different features, perhaps a ham-

mock, a private balcony, a colorful mural, a four-poster bed, a lily pond or a mango tree (feel tree to pick the ripe fruit). Not all rooms have air-con but the suites and off-site cottages come with full kitchen.

A popular cafe-bar, Tropics, overlooks the pool.

Scout's Place HOTEL $$
(☎416-2740; www.scoutsplace.com; d US$135-165, cottage from US$226; ❄📶🏊) Furnishings may not be of the latest vintage but all rooms have fridge and kettle, and even 'standard' rooms come with those million-dollar views of hills and sea. Go for a 'cottage room' if you want your own balcony (C2 has the largest, sunniest deck). The detached two-bedroom Pirate Cottage has a kitchen, lounge area and terrace.

Eating

Windwardside is home to most of the island's dining options, from a fabulous bakery to a couple of fine-dining establishments. Book ahead for dinner as many restaurants only cook enough food for guests with reservations and/or have a limited number of tables.

If you're self-catering, you can stock up at Saba's largest (albeit still small) market, Big Rock Market.

★**Different Tastes** INTERNATIONAL $
(☎416-5577; www.facebook.com/sabalifeplus; Lambee's Pl, Main St, Chez Bubba; mains US$10; ⌚noon-3pm Tue) If you're on the island on a Tuesday, make lunch reservations at Chez Bubba, a fine-dining bistro that on that day is taken over by the nonprofit Different Taste initiative. It trains locals with special challenges to prepare and serve simple but delicious food such as lobster bisque, pesto pasta or pork sate. Also available for takeaway or delivery.

Bizzy B Bakery BAKERY $
(☎416-2900; www.facebook.com/sababakery; Breadline Plaza, Main St; dishes US$3-9.50; ⌚7am-4pm Mon-Fri, to 3pm Sat; 📶) A tantalizing aroma of coffee and freshly baked bread wafts out of Bizzy B, Saba's best bakery, which also makes delicious croissants, pastries and cookies to take away or eat in the flower-filled courtyard out front. If you're hitting the trail, drop by to pick up generously stuffed sandwiches or paninis.

Big Rock Market SUPERMARKET $
(☎416-2280; Main St; ⌚8am-7pm Mon-Sat) Windwardside's largest grocery store stocks frozen meat, fresh veggies, some pharmacy items and two dozen varieties of rum, including the local Saba Spice.

Saba Snack INTERNATIONAL $
(Main St; mains US$9-22, lobster US$35; ⌚8am-7:30pm Wed-Mon) This little kitchen opens to a covered terrace and serves Mexican and international fare – burritos, quesadillas, chicken fajitas, burgers, Creole-spiced grouper, coconut shrimp, lasagna – to eat on-site or take away. Quality can be hit and miss.

Long Haul Grill INTERNATIONAL $$
(☎416-2013; www.facebook.com/pg/longhaulgrillsaba; Main St; mains US$12-28; ⌚4-10pm Tue-Sun) In the early evening, Long Haul's big covered terrace fills with chatty locals along with carb-craving divers and hikers hungry for oven-baked sandwiches, two-fisted burgers or hand-tossed pizzas named after Saban locales like Hell's Gate and Ladder Bay. It doubles as a good-time bar with beer, wine and cocktails along with sports screenings and occasional live music.

Swingin' Doors BARBECUE $$
(☎416-2506; Main St; chicken & ribs/steak US$16/21; ⌚6-8pm Tue, Fri & Sun) Bookings are a must for this wildly popular, smoke-filled barbecue venue when the saloon-style wooden doors swing open for finger-lickin' chicken and ribs (Friday) or steak (Sunday), as only enough food is ordered to cater for reservations. Sides include salads, roast potatoes, rice and beans; the well-stocked bar has US and South American wines and Caribbean beers.

★**Chez Bubba** FRENCH $$$
(☎416-2539; www.chezbubbabistro.com; Lambee's Pl, Main St; mains US$25-35; ⌚5:30-10pm Wed-Mon) Pronounced 'boo-ba' and named for the owner's late dog, this darling bistro has a small but choice menu starring seafood risotto, beef carpaccio and grilled steak. Oenophiles will swoon at the 2500 bottles stored in the elegant wine room – most are available by the glass.

Save room for spectacular desserts. We liked molten chocolate lava cake with homemade rum-and-raisin ice cream or piña colada pudding.

SABA FESTIVALS & EVENTS

Saba Hell's Gate Triathlon (www.facebook.com/sabatriathlon) An 800m open-water swim from Fort Bay, 7km bicycle race (with a 600m elevation gain) and a 7km run on mountain trails (with a 350m elevation gain) ending in Windwardside make up Saba's arduous triathlon, held on a Saturday in mid- to late January. It attracts about 50 international participants every year.

Saba Carnival Also known as the Saba Summer Festival, the island's Carnival takes place over the last week of July and includes a Carnival queen contest, a calypso king competition, a costumed parade around The Bottom and a grand-finale fireworks display.

Sea & Learn (☎416-2246; www.seaandlearn.org) Throughout October, all of Saba becomes a learning center as naturalists and scientists shine the spotlight on various topics, from fish communication to invasive terrestrial species, in nightly presentations. Additionally, enthusiasts are welcome to take part in field and research projects or to help with nature surveys. Check the website for upcoming activities.

Saba Lobster Fest (www.lobsterfestsaba.com) Over the first weekend in November, several of the island's restaurants have lunch and dinner specials starring the local delicacy, Saba Bank spiny lobster, caught on the Saba Bank offshore.

Saba Rainbow Festival (www.facebook.com/sabarainbowfestival; all-access ticket US$75) For one long weekend in November, Saba painted the island pink with the inaugural edition of the Caribbean's first festival celebrating LGTBI+ diversity, featuring music, art, workshops and nature outings. Check the website for upcoming dates.

Saba Days (www.facebook.com/annualsabaday) Held in the first week in December, this island-wide festival built around Saba Day, the national holiday, features sporting events, steel bands, dance competitions and barbecues.

On Tuesdays, the space is taken over by the Different Tastes social dining initiative at lunchtime.

★Brigadoon INTERNATIONAL $$$
(☎416-2380; Main St; mains US$20-38; ⏲dinner 6-11pm) Housed in a romantic cottage with a wood-beamed ceiling, stone floors and antique red trim, Brigadoon is one of Saba's best restaurants. The menu blends Caribbean, French and Asian touches (Thai shrimp, teriyaki *mahimahi*), and usually includes a couple of meat-free mains. Don't skip the homemade desserts, including a ridiculously rich chocolate mousse.

Movie nights also occasionally take place.

Tropics Cafe INTERNATIONAL $$$
(☎416-2469; www.sabatropicscafe.com; breakfast US$7-11, lunch & dinner US$20-55; ⏲7-10am, 11am-3pm & 6:30pm-close Tue-Sun; 📶) Original artwork and pillows by local artist Heleen Cornet decorate this cheerful dining room overlooking the swimming pool of Juliana's (p626) hotel. From chocolate-chip pancakes for breakfast to red-curry coconut shrimp for lunch and lobster straight from the tank for dinner, meals here will leave a lasting impression.

Drinking & Nightlife

Windwardside has the island's only real drinking scene, with several bars, some of which double as restaurants. For an outstanding wine selection, head to Chez Bubba. Tipsy Goat Bar has a daily happy hour.

Tipsy Goat Bar BAR
(☎416-2469; www.sabatropicscafe.com; Tropics Cafe; ⏲11am-late; 📶) Part of Tropics Cafe, this lively bar is a fun post-dive or hike hangout. Happy hour (4pm to 6pm) brings two-for-one beers and is best on Fridays. On Wednesdays, pick up inspiration for your next Saba hike during a screening of a nature film narrated by its director Tom van't Hof, a cofounder of Saba Conservation Foundation (p631).

Shopping

Marie de Saba JEWELRY
(☎416-5222; https://mariedesaba.business.site; Museum St; ⏲10am-4pm) Hailing from France, Marie Petit is a self-taught artist who collects

and grows seeds on Saba to turn them into unique jewelry – bracelets to elaborate necklaces – in her studio/boutique in an adorable Saban cottage. Drop by for a browse or to chit-chat about her technique and the types of natural beads she uses.

Five Square Art Gallery ARTS & CRAFTS
(☎416-2509; www.fivesquareart.com; Main St; ⊙9am-6pm Mon-Sat) Paintings, sketches, drawings, prints, silk screening, cards, carvings, sculptures and other unique works by artists from Saba and around the Caribbean are all for sale at this gallery in Windwardside's village center. Look out for watercolors by Dutch-born local artist Heleen Cornet, who painted the famous mural inside the Sacred Heart Church in The Bottom.

If no staff is around, check in at the attached gift shop Everyt'ings.

Kakona ARTS & CRAFTS
(www.kakonasaba.com; Lambie's Pl, Main St; ⊙8am-5pm) This superb gift shop showcases the work of Saban artists and craftspeople in a cute cottage. Many items are made from local plants and natural products (such as Saba Spice shampoo), and there's also unique jewelry made from seeds, volcanic sand or lionfish fins along with hand-forged knives.

A separate room is dedicated to Saba lace masterpieces; watch them being created by the Saba Lace Ladies on Thursday afternoons.

Jewel Cottage JEWELRY
(☎416-6150; www.thejewelcottage.com; Main St; ⊙10am-6pm Mon-Sat) Drop by the adorable gingerbread-trimmed traditional cottage of jeweler Mark Johnson to browse unique pieces including necklaces, bracelets and earrings for men and women. Designs inspired by Saba's extraordinary flora and fauna incorporate dazzling gems set in gold and silver.

Information

Post Office (☎416-2221; ⊙9am-1pm Mon-Fri)

RBC Bank Has a 24-hour ATM.

Saba Tourist Bureau (☎416-2231; www.sabatourism.com; Main St; ⊙8am-5pm Mon-Thu, to 4:30pm Fri) Superfriendly and helpful staff has maps and brochures, and can arrange island tours and diving trips.

Trail Shop (☎416-2630; www.sabapark.org; Main St; ⊙noon-4pm Mon, 10am-2:30pm Tue & Thu, to 4pm Wed & Fri, to 2pm Sun, varies seasonally) If you plan on hitting the trails, make this your first stop for maps, nature books and the latest on trail conditions. Guides, including head ranger James Johnson (aka Crocodile James), lead two-hour guided hiking treks (US$50 including transport) that will open your eyes to Saba's extraordinary eco-diversity.

Getting There & Away

From Windwardside, a taxi to the airport costs US$13; to The Bottom it's US$10 and to Fort Bay it's US$15.

Morgan Car Rental (p635) rents cars from US$55 per day.

The Bottom

Although home to Saba's administrative and government buildings, the island's tiny capital is at no risk of being staid on account of the approximately 250 students studying at the Saba University School of Medicine, located in the village. There isn't a lot on offer for tourists, but it's a pretty spot for a quick wander and a number of hiking trails start or end here.

Sights

Sacred Heart Church CHURCH
(⊙sunrise-sunset) Locals refer to this charming 1935-built stone Catholic church as 'Saba's Sistine Chapel' thanks to Dutch-born local artist Heleen Cornet's colorful and stunningly detailed altar mural, which infuses biblical scenes with a Saban rainforest twist.

You can browse and buy Cornet's works at the Five Square Art Gallery in Windwardside.

Activities

Ladder Bay Trail HIKING
(off Wells Bay Rd) Until the mid-20th century, before Fort Bay was enlarged as a port, everything – from supplies to the Queen – was hauled up to The Bottom via the Ladder, more than 800 steps hard-carved into the rock on the island's west coast. Panoramic views aside, there's not much here now other than an abandoned customs house halfway along the 800m-long route.

Budget about 90 minutes for the round trip.

Snorkeling is possible in the bay when the weather's calm.

OFF THE BEATEN TRACK

MARY'S POINT

The far-flung village of Mary's Point was once a 45-minute walk from even the next village. In 1934 the Dutch government decided to move every single villager and house to an area behind Windwardside known as the 'Promised Land,' thus lessening the isolation of being so far from any other signs of civilization. You can see the ruins of Mary's Point while hiking on the **North Coast Trail** (Lower Hell's Gate Trailhead; guide required, check with the Trail Shop).

Sleeping

★Queen's Gardens Resort & Spa BOUTIQUE HOTEL $$$
(☎416-3494; www.queensaba.com; Troy Hill Dr; ste incl breakfast from US$284; P❄☎≋) With regal views, the hillside 'Queen' has indeed welcomed Dutch royalty. Its 12 spacious suites are filled with elegant Caribbean furnishings; most have private Jacuzzi. Plenty of mindful touches include the in-room 'gym in a basket', yoga classes on a sky deck and plastic-saving 'hydration stations'. There's an excellent restaurant/bar and the island's only spa with massages and beauty treatments.

The on-site Frangipani Spa has its own line of Caribbean beauty products and includes a Finnish sauna and Turkish steam bath. It's a supersteep 700m walk from The Bottom.

Eating

My Store SUPERMARKET $
(☎416-3263; Flamboyant St; ⌚8am-6pm Mon-Sat) The largest supermarket in The Bottom, My Store has a good selection of fruit and veggies, and imported goods including wine and plenty of frozen ready meals. Note the small gallery of historical photographs.

★Island Flavor INTERNATIONAL $$
(☎416-3643; Captain Matthew Levenstone St; breakfast US$7-13, mains US$13-28; ⌚7:30am-7pm Wed-Mon; ☎) The best dining spot on Saba, this wonderful place's outdoor tables sit beneath shady coconut palms and a Moringa tree. Fruit, herbs and veggies come from the owners' gardens (including one attached to the restaurant), while seafood is straight off the boats. Freshly pressed juices, smoothies, herbal teas and Illy coffee are served alongside beer, wine and cocktails. Cash only.

Queen's Gardens Restaurant & Ocean Bar INTERNATIONAL $$$
(www.queensaba.com; Troy Hill Rd; mains US$25-45; ⌚7-10am & noon-2pm daily, 7-10pm Tue-Sun; P) Sit under the old mango trees or in the warm glow of the elegant dining room to sample refined, beautifully plated dishes of local, organic products from land and sea. A perennial hit is the truffle pasta tossed in a big wheel of Parmesan cheese. For the ultimate romantic dinner, book the Bird's Nest high up in a mango tree.

The bar has an impressive selection of 75 gin varieties for the ultimate gin tonic. It's open from 9am until the restaurant closes.

Drinking & Nightlife

Bottom Bean Cafe COFFEE
(☎416-3385; www.bottombeancafe.com; ⌚7am-3pm Mon-Fri, 10am-2pm Sat) This is Saba's only coffeehouse and it's a gem. Pop by for a cuppa or a fresh juice on the tree-shaded terrace or fuel up for the day with a pastry, breakfast wrap or bagel with lox. Lunch might bring wraps, sandwiches, tacos and salads.

It's a favorite with students from the nearby medical school.

Shopping

Saba Artisan Foundation ARTS & CRAFTS
(☎416-3260; ⌚8:30am-4pm Mon-Fri) A small guild of locals produces an eclectic assortment of Saba-specific arts, crafts and souvenirs, including intricate Saba lace as well as hats, T-shirts, bags and hand-screened linens (tablecloths, tea towels and curtains), sewn on-site. Homemade jams and potent liqueurs including Saba Spice rum, guava rum, guavaberry rum and ginger rum (free tastings available) are also on the shelves.

Information

AM Edwards Medical Center (☎416-3288; www.sabahealthcare.org; Paris Hill Rd; ⌚24hr) Has a 24-hour emergency room but only treats uncomplicated fractures, trauma and emergency patients. Severe trauma is stabilized and emergency transport to St-Martin/Sint Maarten is arranged.

WIB Bank (⌚24hr) 24-hour ATM.

Getting There & Away

A taxi to Windwardside costs US$10, to Fort Bay US$8 and to the airport US$20.

Fort Bay

Saba's working port, Fort Bay, serves ferries and yachts as well as fishing vessels and dive boats.

Activities

Saba Divers DIVING

(☎416-2526; www.sabadivers.com; single-tank dive US$60, night dive US$85, 90min snorkeling trip US$39; ⊙by appointment) PADI-affiliated Saba Divers heads out to 30 different locations such as Third Encounter and Twilight Zone at the Pinnacles, which rise from the ocean floor up to 30m with black-tip reef sharks, turtles and Nassau groupers; and Hot Springs, where you can experience underwater volcanic activity. There's one guide per four divers. Full equipment rental is US$20.

Eating & Drinking

Deep End Bar & Grill SEAFOOD $$

(☎416-0596; mains US$15-25; ⊙11am-4pm Wed & Thu, to 6pm Fri & Sun;) Panoramic glass windows look out over Fort Bay's port from Deep End's light-filled dining room. Fresh-as-it-gets seafood comes straight off the boats docking out front; the restaurant also cooks hearty breakfasts along with burgers, sandwiches, salads and pastas.

Think About It Bar BAR

(☎416-5034; ⊙9pm-4am Fri & Sat) On weekends, check out the vibes at Byron's funky outdoor bar where strong drinks, DJs and gregarious locals keep the party buzzing until the wee hours.

Information

Saba Conservation Foundation (☎416-3295; www.sabapark.org; ⊙8am-4pm Mon-Fri) Established in 1987, this nonprofit management organization is in charge of keeping Saba in pristine condition, both on land and in the surrounding ocean, and has information about hiking trails and the Saba Marine Park.

Getting There & Away

Saba's three ferries, Dawn II (p635), M/V Edge (p635) and Big B (p635), serve St-Martin/Sint Maarten. Taxis meet arriving ferries; a fare to Windwardside costs US$15.

UNDERSTAND SABA

History

Saba was intermittently inhabited by the Arawaks and Caribs before Columbus sailed past the island in 1493 on his second voyage to the Americas. Although English pirates and French adventurers briefly inhabited the island, it wasn't until 1640 that the Dutch set up a permanent settlement, the remains of which are still scattered around the island.

Saba changed hands a dozen times or so over the next 200 years, resulting in mostly Irish and English settlers, but Dutch ownership. Life on Saba was difficult at best. Many of the men made their living from the sea, as fishermen or as pirates such as Hiram Beakes (who coined the phrase 'dead men tell no tales'), leaving so many women on the island that it became known as 'The Island of Women.'

Because the steep topography of the island precluded large-scale plantations, colonial-era slavery was quite limited on Saba.

The close-knit community beat seemingly impossible conditions and thrived in this little outpost. Tourism found Saba when the airport opened in 1963, but it wasn't until 1970 that Saba got uninterrupted electricity. The pier was built in 1972.

Along with Aruba, Bonaire, Curaçao, Sint Eustatius and Dutch Sint Maarten, Saba became part of the Netherlands Antilles in 1954, a constituent country of the Netherlands. After its dissolution in 2010, Saba, Sint Eustatius and Bonaire became 'special municipalities' of the Netherlands, which effectively strengthened the bond between these islands and the mainland. As 'overseas countries and territories' they now share similar rights to those living in the Netherlands and have a more closely linked government system. On January 1, 2011, Saba adopted the US dollar as its currency.

In 2019 Saba's solar park by the airport started operating. It creates enough energy to meet daytime demand.

People & Culture

Barely 2000 people make their home in Saba's three villages, but after a few days it feels as though you know half of them. Everyone says hello and seems genuinely happy to see you. Most locals are descendants of English, Irish, Scottish, Dutch and Scandinavian settlers, along with those from other Caribbean islands and the descendants of African slaves.

Saba has developed its own style of architecture: enchanting white-timber cottages with red roofs and gingerbread trim. Walking around, you'll occasionally see small family graveyards in gardens next to private homes. It's a tradition copied by early Europeans from indigenous people they encountered when landing on Saba. Today, people are buried in public or church cemeteries.

Artists and artisans have long been inspired by the island's natural beauty and Saba has a small but vibrant handicraft scene. Saba's most famous traditional craft is lace making, a skill that was brought to the island in the 1870s by a woman who'd been sent to live in a Venezuelan convent. Older women in the community still weave the lace in their spare time, although as they die, the art is slowly dying out with them.

Landscape & Wildlife

Saba's topography encompasses seven different ecozones that provide a home to more than 700 plant species, including orchids, bromeliads, mountain fuchsia, mahogany, elephant and sea-grape trees, wild plantains, massive ferns and other flora. Across the island, you'll see Saba's national flower, the yellow-petaled, dark-centered black-eyed Susan; petals can also be white or orange.

You'll also encounter about 100 bird species such as the red-billed tropic and Audubon's shearwater along with endemic reptiles such as Saba green iguanas (also known as black dragons), the anoles lizard and the (harmless) red-bellied racer snake.

SURVIVAL GUIDE

Directory A–Z

ACCESSIBLE TRAVEL

Wheelchair users and travelers with limited mobility may have a problematic time on Saba, as the island is extremely steep and riddled with stairs.

Accommodations and restaurant bathrooms invariably aren't wheelchair-friendly.

ACCOMMODATIONS

Most accommodations are midrange and reasonably priced considering there are few options on the island (advance reservations are strongly recommended). Not many rooms have air-conditioning, but thanks to the elevation and constant breezes ceiling fans are usually sufficient.

Hotels add a 6% government room tax; a 10% to 15% service charge is usually at the discretion of the visitor. Each guest must also pay a US$2 per day conservation fee.

ACTIVITIES

Diving & Snorkeling

Saba's beauty extends to 26 diverse diving sites, including pinnacles, sheer walls, caves and spires. Evidence of the island's volcanic activity can be felt at sites such as Hot Springs and nearby Ladder Labyrinth, with yellow-tinged geothermally heated sand that's hot to touch even at depths of 16m. Dazzling multicolored corals, sponges and marine life from barracudas to turtles, seahorses and black-tipped reef sharks abound.

Since 1987 the area has been protected as the Saba Marine Park by nonprofit Saba Conservation Foundation (p631). All divers must go through a dive operator and pay a US$3 fee per dive. Saba has two diving outfits, Sea Saba (p625) in Windwardside, and Saba Divers (p631) by the port in Fort Bay. Both are PADI five-star centers and offer several boat dives daily and the gamut of courses and certifications.

For snorkelers, Wells Bay and the caves and tunnels at adjacent Torrens Point are ideal for spotting goatfish, parrotfish, blue tangs and even the occasional angelfish. Ladder Bay (p629) is also good, but it's a 30-minute hike down to the shore from the road and double that back up. The most accessible area is Cove Bay, near the airport, which is idyllic when conditions are calm. Sea Saba (p625) rents snorkeling gear.

Hiking

Saba is a hiker's dream destination with many century-old trails once used by the earliest settlers to get from village to village or to access their farms on the mountain slopes. Before setting out, drop by the Trail Shop (p629) for maps, nature books and the latest on trail conditions. When you're hiking, dress in layers, wear sturdy walking shoes and bring water. Some hikers might appreciate a walking stick (available for free at the Trail Shop) to navigate steep and slippery sections.

New routes are being created all the time. Currently, some 17 marked trails cut across seven ecosystems, including coastal meadows, rainforests and elfin forests (cloud forests).

After Mt Scenery (p624), the most popular hikes are the moderately strenuous **Sulphur**

Mine Trail (Lower Hell's Gate Trailhead), which offers views of the airport landing strip; the thigh-burning **Spring Bay Trail** (Kelbey's Ridge Trail) from the airport to Windwardside; and the long but easy **Sandy Cruz Trail** (Upper Hell's Gate Trailhead) from Upper Hell's Gate to The Bottom. A nice short hike for families and offering great views is the Mas Cohone's Hill Trail (p625) from Windwardside.

Established in 2019, the new Elfin Forest Trail (p624) branches off from the Sandy Cruz Trail and provides an alternative route to the summit of Mt Scenery.

The one trail you shouldn't attempt without a guide is the North Coast Trail (p630) from Lower Hell's Gate to Wells Bay, which passes the village ruins of Mary's Point (p630). All the others are accessible to reasonably fit hikers, although they're much more fun in the company of a ranger such as Crocodile James.

The best hiking guide with detailed descriptions of trails and the flora and fauna you'll encounter is *Hiking on Saba* (US$15) by Tom van't Hof, a cofounder of the Saba Conservation Foundation (p631).

CHILDREN

Saba's steep hills and streets are difficult for parents to navigate with prams/buggies, although much of Windwardside, The Bottom and Fort Bay are reasonably flat. Activities for children are also extremely limited, although older kids may enjoy hiking, snorkeling or a Discover Scuba course such as those offered by Sea Saba (p625).

Cribs (cots) and high chairs are rare. Supermarkets sell baby-care items such as diapers (nappies).

ELECTRICITY

Saba's electric current is 110V, 60 cycles. North American–style plugs are used.

EMERGENCY NUMBERS

Ambulance, fire, police ☎911

FOOD

Except for a smattering of gems, Saba's few eating options are nothing to write home about. Most restaurants are concentrated in Windwardside, with fewer in The Bottom and one at Fort Bay along with a bar.

Even self-caterers may struggle as the supply ship only comes once a week (Wednesday mornings); there are small supermarkets in Windwardside (p627) and The Bottom (p630).

The Saba Lobster Fest (p628) takes place in early November.

HEALTH

Health care on Saba is quite good for minor ailments and injuries. For anything more serious, you'll need to visit the hospital in St-Martin/Sint Maarten.

AM Edwards Medical Center (p630) In The Bottom.

Saba Marine Park Hyperbaric Chamber (☎416-6301, emergency 416-3288; www.facebook.com/sabahyperbaric; ⏰24hr) Opposite the pier at Fort Bay.

Saba Wellness Pharmacy (☎416-3400; www.sabawellnesspharmacy.com; ⏰9am-5pm Mon-Fri, 10am-noon Sat) The island's only pharmacy is located in The Bottom.

INTERNET ACCESS

Hotels and many restaurants and cafes on Saba have wi-fi, although the signal can be patchy at times depending on the weather. Hotels will generally print documents such as boarding passes.

LEGAL MATTERS

Drugs of all kinds are prohibited; being caught with any in your possession will result in prosecution.

Saba is very environmentally conscious, and importation and exportation of wildlife such as lizards is illegal.

LGBT+ TRAVELERS

Although there is no LGBT 'scene' on Saba, islanders are very tolerant and welcoming of the community. Public displays of affection and booking a double room or vacation cottage do not pose any problems.

Saba was the first Caribbean island to legalize same-sex marriage in 2012; in November 2019 it hosted the inaugural Saba Rainbow Festival

SLEEPING PRICE RANGES

The following price ranges refer to a double room with private bathroom in high season (mid-December to mid-April).

$ less than US$100

$$ US$100–200

$$$ more than US$200

EATING PRICE RANGES

The following prices are for a main course.

$ less than US$15

$$ US$15–30

$$$ more than US$30

PRACTICALITIES

Smoking is at the discretion of individual establishments but is generally not allowed inside hotel rooms island-wide and some restaurants.

Weights & measures Saba uses the metric system.

(p628), the first in the region celebrating LGBTI+ diversity.

MONEY

Saba uses the US dollar. There are ATMs in Windwardside and The Bottom. Credit cards (including foreign cards) are accepted at most establishments.

RBC Bank (p629)
WIB Bank (p630)

Exchange Rates

Australia	A$1	US$0.67
Canada	C$1	US$0.75
Euro zone	€1	US$1.12
Japan	¥100	US$0.94
New Zealand	NZ$1	US$0.64
Switzerland	Sfr1	US$1.02
UK	UK£1	US$1.20

For current exchange rates, see www.xe.com.

Tipping

Hotels A 10% to 15% service charge may be added to your bill. Tips for cleaning staff are greatly appreciated.

Restaurants Service charges are included on restaurant bills, but it's customary to leave a little extra in cash for servers.

Taxi Tipping taxi drivers and guides is at visitors' discretion but 10% is ballpark.

OPENING HOURS

General business hours 9am to 5pm Monday to Saturday.

Restaurants breakfast 7am to 10am, lunch 11:30am to 2:30pm, dinner 6pm to 9pm.

Supermarkets 8am to 8pm Monday to Saturday.

DRINKING WATER

For now it's best to drink bottled water since the island's water supply comes from rain gathered on private rooftop cisterns or in giant communal cisterns and pumped up through pipelines.

PUBLIC HOLIDAYS

New Year's Day January 1
Good Friday March/April
Easter Sunday March/April
Easter Monday March/April
King's Day (Koningsdag) April 27
Labor Day May 1
Ascension Day Fortieth day after Easter
Pentecost Seventh Sunday after Easter
Carnival Monday July 31
Saba Day First Friday in December
Christmas Day December 25
Boxing Day December 26

TELEPHONE

- Saba's country code is 599.
- Local numbers are seven digits.
- There are no area codes on Saba.
- If you are calling locally, just dial the seven-digit number.
- To call the island from overseas, dial your country's international access code + 599 + the local number.

Cell Phones

Check with your home provider about roaming capabilities and costs. Chippie (UTS) and TelCell are the main local providers. ICS, which also operates Morgan Car Rental, sells SIM cards that can be used in an unlocked phone.

TIME

Saba is on Atlantic Time (GMT/UTC minus four hours). Daylight saving time is not observed.

TOURIST INFORMATION

Saba Tourist Bureau (p629)
Trail Shop (p629)

VOLUNTEERING

Volunteering opportunities such as maintaining hiking trails, monitoring reefs and marine life, and assisting staff at the Trail Shop (p629) are available through Saba Conservation Foundation (p631). Projects run for two to a maximum of three months.

Getting There & Away

Note that bad weather (heavy wind is worse than rain) may cancel air and sea travel to and from Saba – check ahead.

AIR

Flying into Saba is a hair-raising experience: its airport is home to the world's shortest commercial runway (400m), with flights coming in breathtakingly close to the sheer cliffs (fear not: Saba pilots must pass regular tests).

Saba's **Juancho E Yrausquin Airport** (SAB; ☎416-2222; Flat Point; wi-fi) is served by **Winair**

(☎416-2255; www.fly-winair.com), with daily direct flights to St-Martin/Sint Maarten's Princess Juliana International Airport (p728). Taxis meet flights.

The airport has a small bar but no ATM or other facilities.

SEA

Three ferry operators run boats between Fort Bay and Simpson Bay and Philipsburg in Sint Maarten. No cruise ships serve Saba.

Ferry

Dawn II (☎416-2299; www.sabaferrry.com; per adult/child one way US$55/35, return US$110/55) M/V Dawn II, the smoothest of Saba's ferries if you're prone to motion sickness, links Fort Bay with Philipsburg in about 90 minutes several times weekly on a seasonal schedule.

M/V Edge (☎Sint Maarten +1-721-544-2640; www.stmaarten-activities.com; adult/child one way US$55/28, return US$110/55, day trip US$80/40) This catamaran connects Fort Bay with the Pelican Marina at the Simpson Bay Resort in Sint Maarten up to three times weekly.

Big B Ferry (☎416-2299; www.sabaferry.com; adult/child return €100/60) Travels between Fort Bay and Bobby's Marina in Philipsburg in Dutch St-Martin.

Yacht

Contact the harbor master between 6am and 6pm on VHF channel 16 or the Saba National Marine Park office (☎416-3295) to arrange docking and customs and immigration clearance. See www.sabaport.com for additional details.

Getting Around

There is no bus service on Saba. Most travelers use taxis, walk or hitchhike. Cab fares are fixed and drivers meet arriving flights and ferries; otherwise, locals can call you a taxi. Renting a vehicle is not recommended for short stays.

DEPARTURE TAX

Departure tax is US$10 for both flights and ferries.

CAR & MOTORCYCLE

Saba's roads are narrow, steep and winding, with tight corners, and driving conditions are difficult. The island's sole **gas station** (☎416-3272; ⏲9am-5pm Mon-Sat) is in Fort Bay.

If you decide to drive, a driver's license from your home country will suffice. Driving is on the right-hand side of the road. Drivers tend to drive slowly, as there are many sharp turns and two-way streets that only fit one car at a time. The speed limit is 20km/h in the villages and 40km/h outside.

Morgan Car Rental (☎416-2881, 416-5893; www.icssaba.com; Breadline Plaza; per day US$65; ⏲9am-6pm Mon-Fri, 10am-3pm Sat) in Windwardside rents cars from US$65 per day.

HITCHHIKING

Hitching is never entirely safe, and we don't recommend it. Travelers who hitch should understand that they are taking a small but potentially serious risk. However, hitching on Saba is common and often necessary, and the island is one of the safest destinations in the region.

TAXI

Taxis operate on a fixed rate schedule. The fare between the airport and Windwardside is US$13; between Fort Bay and Windwardside it's US$15. Between The Bottom and Windwardside, a taxi costs US$10. Fares increase by 25% between 9pm and 6am, and there's a US$1 surcharge per piece of luggage. An island tour is available for US$50.

Your hotel, restaurant or any local for that matter can arrange a cab. A full list of drivers is posted on www.sabatourism.com, or try Donna (416-6266), Peddy (416-7062) or Garvis (416-6114).

THIERRY64/GETTY IMAGES ©

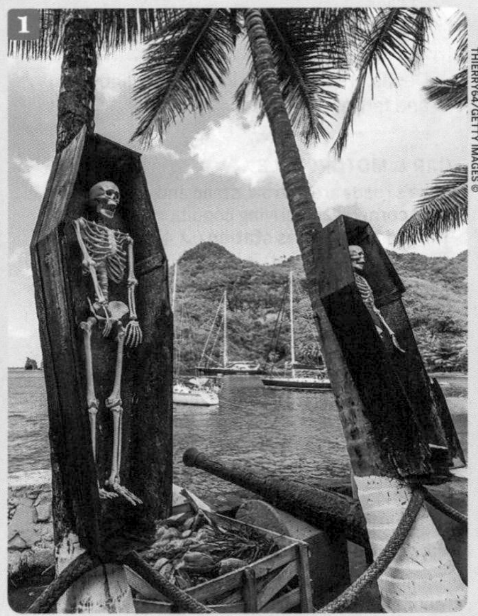

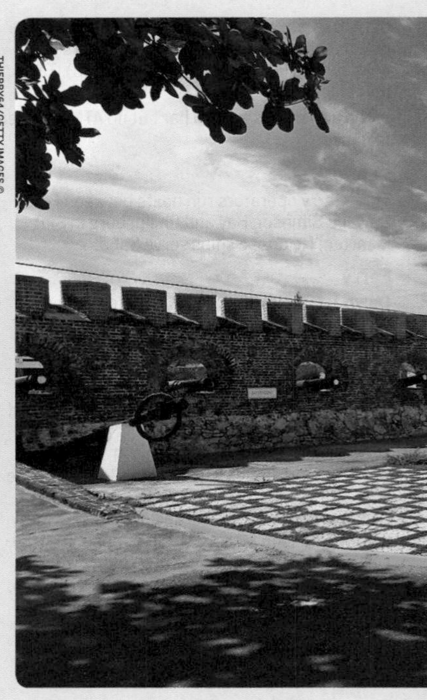

1. *Pirates* props, Wallilabou Bay, St Vincent **2.** Fort Charles, Port Royal, Jamaica **3.** Brimstone Hill Fortress, St Kitts **4.** Fort San Cristobal, San Juan, Puerto Rico

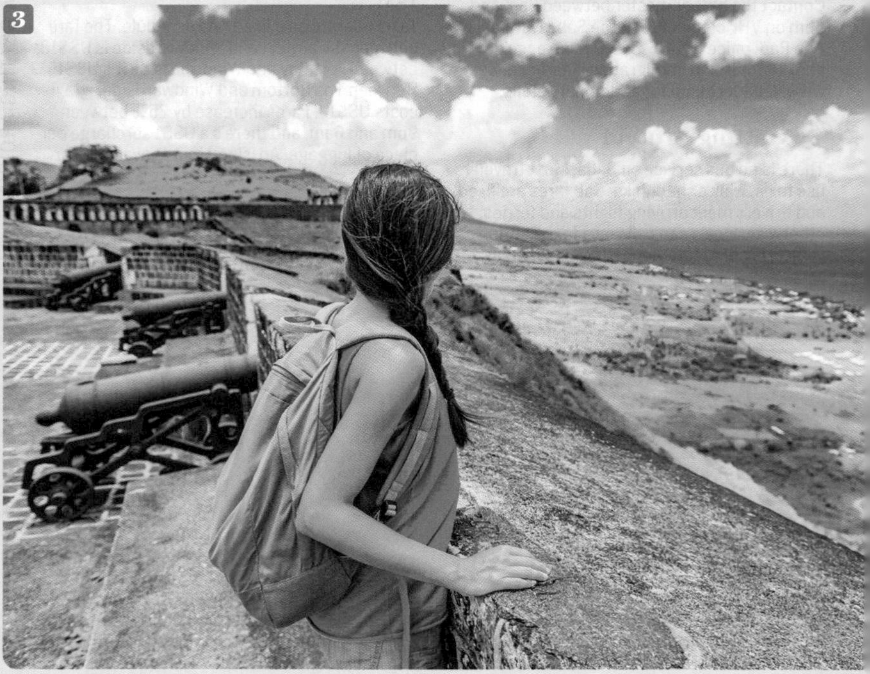

2

ROSTASEDLACEK/SHUTTERSTOCK ©

4

Pirates, Forts & Ruins

The Caribbean has a bounty of booty for pirate fans. Old forts and other crumbling ruins recall the days when sailing-ship dramas played out on the high seas.

Port Royal, Jamaica

A dilapidated, ramshackle place of tropical lassitude, today's funky fishing hamlet was once the pirate capital of the Caribbean. Later, it was the hub of British naval power in the West Indies. There are fascinating historic sites here, including old Fort Charles.

Old San Juan, Puerto Rico

Two Unesco World Heritage forts are a commanding presence in Old San Juan. Secrets and surprises wait around every ancient corner, all in the huge shadow of 16th-century El Morro (Castillo San Felipe del Morro) and Castillo San Cristóbal.

Brimstone Hill Fortress, St Kitts

More than 8000 French troops fought with 1000 British troops for a month in order to seize Brimstone Hill Fortress. This amazing Unesco World Heritage fort has views north, west and south across the Caribbean.

St Vincent

You can walk the very beaches and bay where much of the first *Pirates of the Caribbean* was filmed. Although the sets are fading away like old buccaneers, the small village and bay of Wallilabou is still recognizable.

Île-à-Vache, Haiti

About 15km off the coast of Les Cayes, Île-à-Vache was the hideout in 1668 of Captain Morgan, the Welsh pirate who looted every Spanish galleon he saw. Today it's home to some good resorts.

Sint Eustatius

☎ 599 / POP 3200

Includes ➡

Best Places to Eat

- ➡ Harbourclub Statia (p643)
- ➡ Old Gin House Restaurant (p643)
- ➡ Para Mira (p643)
- ➡ Boardwalk Cafe (p643)

Best Places to Stay

- ➡ Orange Bay Hotel (p641)
- ➡ Old Gin House (p641)
- ➡ Harbor View Apartments (p642)
- ➡ Statia Lodge (p645)

Why Go?

Tiny Sint Eustatius, commonly called Statia, is a rare throwback to the traditional Caribbean, a slow-paced, laid-back island with just a handful of nonflashy places to stay, eat and drink. A national park cradling a long-dormant volcano – the Quill – as well as numerous well-preserved colonial-era buildings in Oranjestad, the capital and sole town, are the main above-ground attractions. But the jewels of this castaway-style outpost lie under the sea: dazzling reefs, teeming marine life, rusting wrecks and vestiges of the 17th-century Lower Town, which is now largely submerged. It's truly a divers' paradise.

Incredibly, Statia was the world's busiest seaport for cargo transported between Europe and the American colonies in the late 18th century. In 1776 the island made world history when it became the first nation to recognize the newly independent USA. Later part of the since-dissolved Netherlands Antilles, Statia became a 'special municipality' of the Netherlands in 2010.

When to Go

Dec–Jan While neighboring islands swell with visitors, Statia stays remarkably calm.

Apr–May Savor the last of the dry season before the thundershowers plow through.

Jul Celebrate Carnival with locals amid live music and seafood feasts.

Oranjestad

The only town on Sint Eustatius, tiny Oranjestad evokes a bygone era with its colorfully painted wooden cottages, historic ruins (including its centerpiece Fort Oranje (p640)) and narrow, virtually traffic-free streets.

Oranjestad is split into the waterfront Lower Town (part of which now lies ruined underwater following hurricanes, with only four 17th-century buildings remaining) and the Upper Town, where most services are located, including the government headquarters.

Sint Eustatius Highlights

1. **Diving** (p640) Cavorting with reef sharks and sea turtles at shipwreck-turned-artificial-reef, the *Charles L Brown* wreck, in Statia's fabled national marine park.
2. **The Quill** (p644) Ascending Statia's dormant volcano before clambering down to the bottom of the crater to walk among giant elephant ears, ferns and silk cotton trees.
3. **Fort Oranje** (p640) Visiting the fort dominating the island's sole town, Oranjestad, with views radiating out to sea.
4. **Old Town Wall** (p640) Snorkeling among the sunken ruins off Lower Town Beach to spot rays, turtles and juvenile fish.
5. **Sint Eustatius Museum** (p640) Delving into local lore and history in an old planter's mansion and admiring such artifacts as a 2000-year-old skeleton.
6. **Friday Night Jam** (p643) Kicking back with islanders, expats and fellow visitors over beer, rum punch and dancing at the harborfront Boardwalk Cafe.

Sights

★Fort Oranje FORT

(Bay Path, Upper Town) Soak up history and sweeping views from this extensively restored fort, a mighty citadel complete with cannon, triple bastions and cobblestone parade grounds. The current stone structure was built by the British in 1703, replacing the original wooden fort the French erected in 1629. It's the best preserved of the 16 remaining defensive forts on the island and is where the first salute was fired in recognition of US independence on November 16, 1776, now commemorated as Statia Day.

Structures include barracks, the former governor's and commander's residence and a jail. Note the plaque commemorating the First Salute presented by US President Franklin Delanore Roosevelt.

★Sint Eustatius Museum MUSEUM

(☎318-2288; Emmaweg, Upper Town; adult/child US$5/3; ⏰9am-5pm Mon-Thu, to 3pm Fri, to noon Sat) Set inside an 18th-century mansion built by wealthy merchant Simon Doncker, this modest if eclectic museum chronicles island history with exhibits on colonial trade and slavery, Statia's Jewish community and the famous 'First Salute' to the US. Upstairs period rooms illustrate the lifestyle of rich colonialists like Doncker, while the basement zeroes in on the pre-Columbian era with artifacts including a skeleton with an enviable set of teeth.

Synagogue Ruins RUINS

(Synagogue Path, Upper Town) Tucked into an alleyway in Upper Town are the roofless ruins of the Honen Dalim synagogue, built in 1739 from yellow brick brought in from the Netherlands as ships' ballast. For nearly 100 years it was the center of Jewish life on Statia. Off to the side, note steps leading down to a *mikvah* (a cleansing bath for women). A plaque provides historical background.

Lower Town Beach BEACH

This tiny and narrow patch of oyster-gray sand is hardly your typical Caribbean beach. However, it's the only one on Statia where you can swim safely and explore the extraordinarily rich underwater world of the sunken 17th-century town. Built on sand behind a seawall, over time the town sank into the water as hurricanes wreaked destruction.

Dutch Reformed Church RUINS

(Kerkweg) FREE The sturdy tower and thick stone walls of the Dutch Reformed Church, built in 1755, remain perfectly intact, but the roof collapsed during a 1792 hurricane and the building has been open to the heavens ever since. The grounds are the resting place of many of the island's most prominent citizens of the past.

Activities

★Old Town Wall SNORKELING

(Lower Town) Statia is one of those rare places where even nondivers can easily sample the richness of the underwater world. Grab fins and a mask from Scubaqua or Golden Rock Dive Center and snorkel along the submerged 17th-century seawall, keeping an eye out for rays, turtles, angelfish and other tropical critters. There's also an old anchor just off Lower Town Beach.

★Scubaqua Dive Center DIVING

(☎319-5450; www.scubaqua.com; Oranjebaai, Lower Town; per dive US$52, gear per dive/day US$25/35; ⏰Oct-Aug) In a lovingly restored historical building, this dive center is owned and operated by an international team of passion-driven scuba pros who organize superb day and night boat dives in small groups of no more than six divers per guide. Many people stick around afterward to swap stories and make new friends over cold beers. Open-water certification courses are US$425.

Golden Rock Dive Center DIVING

(☎318-2964; www.goldenrockdive.com; Oranjebaai, Lower Town; 1-/2-tank dives incl gear US$60/110 plus marine-park fee per dive US$6; ⏰Oct-Aug) With their dive shop a victim of Hurricane Irma, this American-run professional diving outfitter is operating from a seafront container for now but still has two dive boats and loads of high-quality equipment. The team also offers four-hour coastal or offshore deep-sea fishing charters (per two people including rods, reels and bait US$350). Snorkeling gear rents for US$25 per day.

Secar VOLUNTEERING

(Sint Eustatius Center for Archaeological Research; ☎319-1631; http://secar.org; Road to English Quarter 42, Upper Town) Nongovernmental organization Secar is the island's sanctioned organization dedicated to unearthing and restoring relics from the past. Volunteers have the opportunity to work at one of the island's 600 documented archaeological sites.

Festivals & Events

Statia Carnival CULTURAL

(Jul) Music, beauty and calypso competitions, parades with themed floats and sizzling local food all feature at Statia's biggest festival, with events all over Oranjestad. Founded in 1964, it's held over 10 days in the second half of July, culminating on a Monday with the burning of a King Momo effigy (the symbolic spirit of festivals in many Latin American countries).

Statia Day CULTURAL

(Nov 16) Fort Oranje is the site of ceremonies on Statia Day, the national holiday, which commemorates the date in 1776 when Statia became the first foreign land to salute the US flag and recognize the country's independence. On this date in 2004, Statia adopted a new flag. Parties, barbecues and celebrations kick off all over the island from the preceding week.

Golden Rock Regatta SAILING

(www.facebook.com/goldenrockregatta; mid-Nov) This colorful sailing race is held between Statia and the nearby islands of St-Martin/Sint Maarten and St-Barthélemy over five days. It attracts both amateur and pro sailors and is accompanied by food, music and a street party on Statia.

Sleeping

★ **Orange Bay Hotel** HOTEL $$

(318-2010; Oranjebaai 211, Lower Town; d incl breakfast US$160-235;) This well-managed newcomer on the waterfront has eight sparkling modern rooms with touches of tropical flair from a big painting and accent pillows. Mod-cons include fast internet, quiet air-con and a big flat-screen TV. The extra expense for a unit with sea-facing balcony is well worth it; for extra privacy, book the rustic freestanding cabin with big fridge and microwave.

Papaya Inn INN $$

(318-0044; www.facebook.com/papayainn; William Plantz Rd; s/d incl breakfast US$115/130;) Juliette's little oasis of charm is a rambling villa near the airport where rooms pair homey flair, tiled floors and cooking facilities with distinctive assets. Room 1, for example, has a secluded patio, while room 4 comes with its own deck. The communal garden is nice for chilling and meeting fellow travelers. Rates include a big breakfast served alfresco.

★ **Old Gin House** HOTEL $$$

(318-2319; www.oldginhouse.com; Oranjebaai 1, Lower Town; d/ste incl breakfast from US$195/355;) Restored to its 17th-century glory, this stately cotton-seed ginning station makes a romantic spot to unwind. Most of the 20 traditionally furnished units are in a two-story complex overlooking the garden and pool behind the historic structure and come with mahogany sleigh beds, balcony, updated bathroom and small fridge. For extra romance, book an oceanfront room or suite.

STATIA DIVE SITES

Blair Lobsters, seahorses and schooling fish call this underwater coral reef home.

Blue Bead Hole One of the most photogenic sites, due to the friendly and prolific schools of colorful fish, Blue Bead is also one of the best spots for finding a coveted cobalt-colored bead.

Charles L Brown Cable-laying ship the *Charles L Brown*, measuring 100m long, was sunk in 2003 as an artificial reef for divers. The superstructure broke apart in Hurricane Irma and is now inhabited by schools of barracuda. Divers can explore the interior.

Chien Tong A 52m Taiwanese fishing vessel, the *Chien Tong* is home to multicolored fish and reef sharks and is best at night, when you'll see green and hawksbill turtles.

Gibraltar So named for the 14m-high, 16m-wide rock here, Gibraltar is covered in deep-water sea fans, and frequented by schools of sennet fish. Nurse sharks rest nearby.

Grand Canyon Like its US namesake, this awesome site is dwarfed by steep sides, which are covered in black coral. Eagle rays, sharks and jackknife fish are among the marine life here.

Lost Anchor Barracuda and rabbitfish live around two huge anchors on this offshore reef, along with queen angelfish.

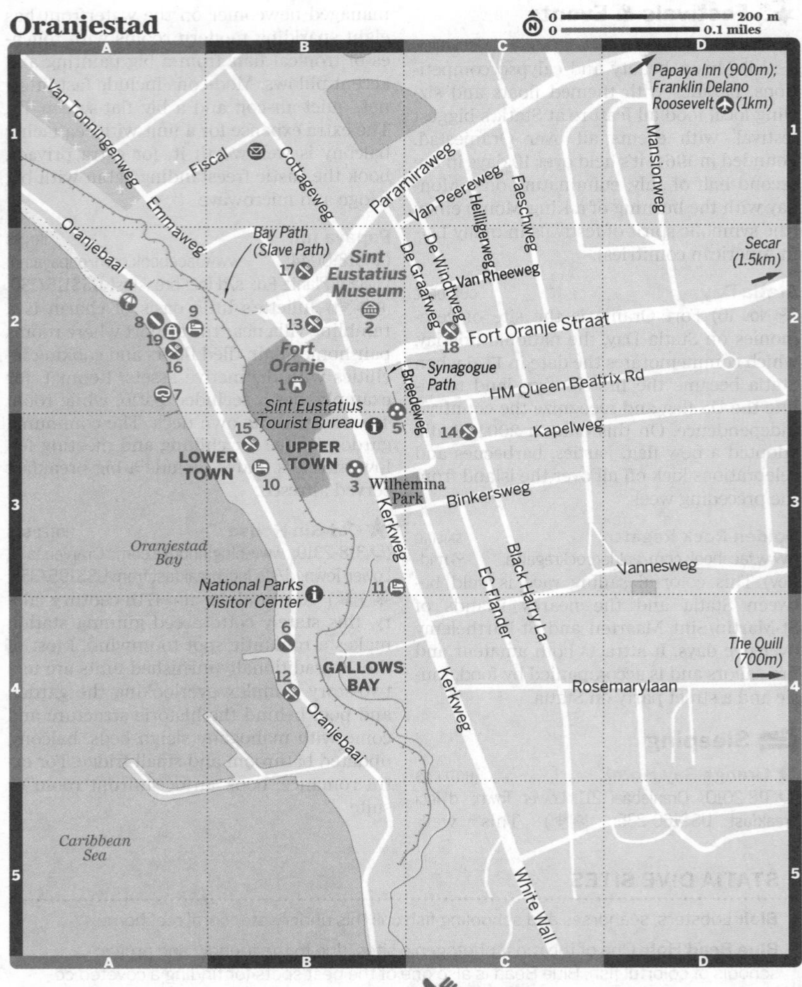

Statia Harborview Apartments APARTMENT $$$
(☎318-4159; www.statiaharborviewapartments.com; Kerkweg 8, Upper Town; apt US$250, per week US$1568; P ❄ 📶) Self-sufficient travelers will find it hard to beat this contemporary block of four light, bright one-bedroom apartments sleeping up to four people (living rooms have convertible sofa beds). Set behind a security gate with a shared garden and terrace with barbecue facilities, apartments come with full kitchen, washing machine and balcony with sweeping ocean views. Minimum stay is two nights.

Eating

Cool Corner CHINESE $
(☎318-3386; Emmaweg 3, Upper Town; mains US$10-22; ⏲noon-10pm, hours can vary; 📶) An island favorite, Cool Corner hides an incongruously woodsy ski-hut-lodge look behind a weathered exterior. The menu is as long and confusing as Confucius and hopscotches from *char siu* (barbecued pork), *kung pao* (hot garlic chicken) and salt-and-pepper shrimp to such meatless options as spicy sesame-garlic tofu and scallion pancakes. Portions are huge, and takeaway is available.

Oranjestad

Para Mira CAFE $

(☎318-4612; 1 Paramiraweg, Upper Town; dishes US$2-6.50; ⏰8am-2pm Mon-Sat, hours vary; 📶✍) An adorable yellow-green-trimmed wooden cottage houses this traditional Dutch lunchroom. Dutch *frikandel* (meat patties) and *kroket* (croquettes) are served alongside ham-and-Gouda sandwiches on the porch or in the garden under big umbrellas. Takeaway available. Also a nice stop for coffee or a fresh juice.

Super Burger BURGERS $

(☎318-2412; Fort Oranje Straat, cnr De Graaftweg, Upper Town; burgers US$5.20-10.50, dishes US$4.50-8.50; ⏰8am-3pm & 6-9pm) In his screaming yellow outdoor cafe, owner Skell offers more than three dozen burger choices, spanning beef, turkey, chicken, fish and veggie varieties, along with sandwiches and other fast-food classics. Wash them down with shakes or finish with an ice-cream sundae. On Friday nights, half the town comes out to party until the wee hours.

★**Harbourclub Statia** INTERNATIONAL $$

(☎318-2010; www.orangebayhotel.com; Oranjebaai 21, Lower Town; mains US$5-32; ⏰7am-10pm; 📶) This covered veranda across from the waterfront is a casual and welcoming port of call. Grab a cold drink from the fridge before ordering at the counter decorated with salvaged corrugated metal. The menu covers all the bases, no matter if you're a salad-grazer, have a passion for pizza or want to try local bites like curried-goat stew.

Boardwalk Cafe INTERNATIONAL $$

(☎318-0800; www.facebook.com/statiaboardwalk; Statia Harbor, Lower Town; mains US$15-28; ⏰10am-10pm Mon-Thu, to 12:30am Fri Oct-Jul; 📶) Werner from Austria livens up Lower Town with this easygoing cafe serving booze and a small, rotating menu of local delicacies, from taco salad and grouper piccata to key lime pie. Order at the food truck and eat under the white tents with harbor views. Best night is Friday, when happy hour and DJs fuel merriment and dancing until midnight.

Franky's BARBECUE $$

(☎318-0166; Black Harry Lane; mains US$12-28; ⏰10am-10pm Tue-Sun) Franky's does good business with his barbecue, where chicken, fish and ribs are fire-tickled to perfection on the smoky grill and dished up with deep-fried johnnycakes, coleslaw and other sides.

Old Gin House Restaurant INTERNATIONAL $$$

(☎318-2319; www.oldginhouse.com; Oranjebaai, Lower Town; mains lunch US$14-29, dinner US$22-38, bar snacks US$7-15; ⏰7-10am & 4-9pm Thu-Mon; 📶) Statia's best hotel (p641) is also home to its most refined restaurant with a grand waterfront deck with views of Saba. Dinner is a classy affair with possible menu stops including lobster soup, baked goat cheese, Creole red snapper and Old Dutch-style apple pie. Also a nice spot for sunset drinks and bar bites like fried calamari or bruschetta.

Shopping

Mazinga on the Bay GIFTS & SOUVENIRS

(☎318-3345; www.mazingaonthebay.com; Oranjebaai, Lower Town; ⏰1-6pm Wed-Sun; 📶) Inside one of the four remaining 17th-century Lower Town buildings, Mazinga is named for the highest point on Statia, located on the crater rim of the Quill volcano. It stocks local crafts and jewelry, books, Statia-themed T-shirts, sun hats, beach gear and rum, as well as Dutch cheeses, cookies and chocolates.

Information

National Parks Visitor Center (Stenapa; ☎318-2884; www.statiapark.org; Gallows Bay, Lower Town; ⏰7am-5pm Mon-Fri) This nonprofit organization was started in 1998 to protect Statia's ample natural resources. It manages the Statia National Marine Park, Quill National Park and Miriam C Schmidt Botanical Gardens. Stop by the office to pick up free maps and brochures, and for advice about exploring Statia above and below the waterline. Stenapa also has opportunities for volunteering (p649) around the island.

Post Office (☎318-2678; Fiscal Rd, Upper Town; ⏰7:30am-4pm Mon-Fri)

Queen Beatrix Medical Centre (☎318-2211, emergency 912; www.sehcf.org; HM Queen Beatrix Rd, Upper Town) Has quite a good reputation considering the island's remoteness and minuscule population. There are always two doctors on call 24 hours a day.

Sint Eustatius Tourist Bureau (☎318-2433; www.statia-tourism.com; Godet House, Kerkweg 9, Upper Town; ⏰8am-noon & 1-5pm Mon-Thu, to 4:30pm Fri) Has maps, brochures and helpful staff. The airport tourist information desk (p649) is staffed for arriving flights.

Getting There & Away

A taxi between the airport (p649) and Oranjestad costs US$8 to US$10.

Around Sint Eustatius

Sights & Activities

★The Quill — HIKING

(www.statiapark.org; Rosemary Lane; trail pass US$10) Statia's looming dormant volcano, the Quill (derived from the Dutch word *kuil,* meaning pit or hole) soars 601m high. The 1.6km trail to the crater rim is the most popular on the island and starts at the top of Rosemary Lane in Oranjestad. Walk or get a taxi to near the trailhead (about US$10 from the airport, US$8 from town).

Pay hiker fees in advance at the tourist office, St Eustatius National Parks Foundation (Stenapa) or the dive shops in Lower Town.

The Quill was designated a national park in 1998. The volcano last erupted in AD 400. There's a viewpoint down into the junglelike crater, which lies 273m above sea level, but for the full experience you need to continue on the **Crater Trail** to the bottom. Ropes and stairs help you on the very steep and slippery descent. Once down, a fairly even path weaves through a dense canopy of ferns, elephant ears, silk cotton trees and other vegetation, ethereally illuminated by streaks of sunlight. Even though the entire trail is only 600m long, allow at least 90 minutes for the experience.

For a walk along the crater rim, experienced hikers can follow all or parts of the often rough and challenging 2km **Mazinga Trail**, which leads to the highest point on Statia and delivers great views over the island and St Kitts.

Throughout the national park, keep an eye out for hermit crabs, lizards and such endemic species as the Lesser Antillean iguana, the (nonpoisonous) red-bellied racer snake and the bridled quail.

Fort de Windt — RUINS

(Whitewall Rd) Pose with two patina-covered cannon while enjoying sweeping views of St Kitts from this clifftop fort 5km southeast of Lower Town at the foot of the Quill volcano. The stone structure was completed in 1756 and monitored shipping routes to St Kitts until it was abandoned in 1815. From January to April keep an eye out for migrating whales.

Miriam C Schmidt Botanical Gardens — GARDENS

(☎318-2884; www.statiapark.org; ⏰dawn-dusk) On the lower eastern slopes of the Quill, these botanical gardens have suffered from hurricane damage, drought and roaming animals, and are in the process of being restored. Since the road leading to the grounds is often impassable even with a 4WD, it's best to approach on foot. The Bird Trail, a 300m side trail off the Around the Mountain Trail, provides access.

Boven National Park — HIKING

(trail pass US$10) The northern section of Statia is protected as Boven National Park. It's crisscrossed by several trails, including the scenic Butterfly Trail with views of the Quill and Zeelandia Bay. A shorter walk leads to the beach at Venus Bay (no swimming). The trailhead is at the end of paved Zeelandia Rd, about 1.5km north of the airport.

The park gets little rainfall and has vegetation dominated by grassland and acacia thorn scrub.

Around the Mountain Trail — HIKING

(www.statiapark.org; Rosemary Lane; ⏰trail fee $US10) This 4.5km moderately strenuous looop trail branches off the Quill Trail – the turnoff for the southern route is after about 800m, for the northern route it's at 1.2km. The more interesting southern section climbs high above the White Wall escarpment with excellent views of St Kitts and the Fort de Windt ruins. After about 1.5km, the 300m **Bird Trail** leads out to what's left of the Miriam C Schmidt Botanical Gardens. The northern part of the loop is narrow and less traveled.

Zeelandia Bay BEACH

Some 3km north of the airport, Zeelandia Bay takes its name from Statia's first Dutch settlers, who hailed from Zeeland province in the Netherlands. Swimming is prohibited because of dangerous currents and undertows, but the sandy beach is a tranquil strip for walks.

Sleeping

Statia Lodge BUNGALOW $$

(☎318-4089; www.statialodge.com; White Wall Rd; s/d US$110/125; ⊙Oct-Aug; P📶🏊) Statia Lodge's 10 red-roofed wooden bungalows with outdoor kitchen are nicely spaced out across a windswept bluff some 2.3km east of Lower Town. Knock back a cold beer on your private terrace or gaze out to the Quill or St Kitts from the bar by the L-shaped freshwater pool.

UNDERSTAND SINT EUSTATIUS

History

Statia has a rich and fascinating history that lives on in the island's extraordinary collection of ruins and restored buildings.

The first settlers are believed to have been the Saladoid people, who migrated from the Orinoco River valley in today's Venezuela around AD 300 but had already moved on by the time Columbus sailed past Statia in 1493. The first European settlers were the French, who established a wooden fort in 1629. Just a few year later, in 1636, the Dutch West Indies Company established another fort in the southern part of the island. Dutch settlers soon outnumbered the French. Over the next couple of centuries, Statia changed hands at least 22 times among the Dutch, French, British and Spanish before becoming permanently Dutch in 1816.

Statia was a primary link between Europe and the Atlantic world for much of the later 18th century. While the English and French levied duty after duty on their islands, the Dutch made Statia a free port in 1756 and trade became the island's economic mainstay. Every year, thousands of ships used Oranjestad as their main stopping point between Europe and the American colonies, making it the busiest trading port in the world at one point and earning it the nickname 'Golden Rock'.

By 1770 some 600 stone warehouses lined the bay in today's Lower Town, while merchants built their private residences – and an astonishing number of churches – around the fort in the Upper Town. At its peak, Statia was home to no fewer than 10,000 full-time residents, both European colonists and African slaves.

On November 16, 1776, Statia made world history when it became the first nation to officially recognize the newly founded US with a gun salute fired from Fort Oranje.

The British were none too pleased and, in 1781, attacked Statia and auctioned off the warehoused goods. They also deported the male Jewish population, who returned in the 1790s when first the Dutch and then the French gained control of Statia. It was taxes imposed by the French in 1795, though, that started the island's downward spiral, eventually driving merchants away to nearby islands and leading to a significant population decline for the next 150 years.

In 1954 Statia became part of the Netherlands Antilles, together with Aruba, Bonaire, Curaçao, Saba and Sint Maarten. On Statia Day, November 16, 2004, the island adopted a new flag, but in 2005 it voted to remain part of the Netherlands Antilles. However, other members voted to disband the island nation group, effectually leaving Statia the sole member. In October 2010 the Netherlands Antilles was officially dissolved and Statia – along with Saba and Bonaire (Aruba had seceded in 1986) – became a 'special municipality' of the Netherlands. Statians now share similar rights to those living in the Netherlands. On January 1, 2011, Statia adopted the US dollar as its currency.

Since 1982 Statia's largest source of income is from oil transhipment, with some 60 circular storage tanks dotting the hills north of Oranjestad. The largest employer is the government, with tourism playing only a supporting role.

Statia itself, though, is a model in renewable energy as its vast solar park supplies 100% of the island's energy between 9am and 7:30pm, thereby reducing its carbon footprint by 4.5 million kg per year.

People & Culture

Most islanders are descendants of African slaves brought over to work in the warehouses in Lower Town and on the long-vanished plantations. The culture is a mix of African and Dutch heritages along with other expats. The population expanded in the mid-1990s, with a surge in immigrants from the Dominican Republic and Aruba in particular. Following the dissolution of the Netherlands Antilles, it declined by 13% between 2011 and 2016 due to a lack of employment opportunities.

Landscape & Wildlife

The Land

About 5km long and 7km wide, Statia gets its conical silhouette from the Quill, an extinct volcano in the southern part of the island that last erupted around AD 400. It tops out at 601m at Mazinga, the highest point on the rim. The Boven area in the north, past the oil storage terminal facility, consists of five dry hills, the largest being Boven Hill. Together the two areas form the Quill/Boven National Park, created in 1997 to protect the island's biodiversity.

Statia's central plain contains the airport and the town of Oranjestad. Otherwise, cliffs drop straight to the sea along much of the shoreline, resulting in precious few beaches, with only Lower Town Beach suitable for swimming and snorkeling.

The Dutch Caribbean Nature Alliance (www.dcnanature.org) has a wealth of information about the island's flora and fauna. On Statia, drop by the office of the National Parks Visitor Center (Stenapa) in Lower Town Oranjestad.

Flora & Fauna

Most of the northern end of the island is dry with scrubby vegetation, although oleander, bougainvillea, hibiscus and flamboyant flowers add a splash of color here and there. The greatest variety of flora is inside the Quill National Park, which collects enough cloud cover for its crater to harbor an evergreen seasonal forest (which is closely related to a rainforest), with ferns, elephant ears, bromeliads, bananas, and tall kapok and silk cotton trees that are many centuries old. The island also has over two dozen varieties of orchid; new species are still being discovered.

At certain locations across the island, including the Miriam C Schmidt Botanical Gardens, look out for the fuchsia-pink flowers of a creeping vine called Statia morning glory, which is unique to the island. Once thought to be extinct, it's now the rarest and most endangered plant in the Kingdom of the Netherlands.

With some 75 resident and migratory bird species, Statia is a birders' paradise, especially in and around the Quill. White-tailed tropic and purple-throated carib birds nest on the cliffs along the beach north of Lower Town, in Oranjestad. There are also nonpoisonous red-bellied racer snakes, which are only found on Statia and Saba, as well as the rare Lesser Antillean iguana, lizards, tree frogs, fruit-eating bats, land crabs and leatherback, hawksbill and green turtles, which nest on the beach in Zeelandia Bay. Invertebrates such as monarch butterflies also call Statia home, along with the *glyphyalus quillensis* land snail, discovered in 2015 and named for the Quill, where it lives. Most other terrestrial animal life is limited to introduced free-roaming goats, chickens, cows and donkeys.

The Sint Eustatius National Marine Park encircles the island's entire coastline, where coral reefs shelter sharks, manta rays, turtles and seahorses alongside hundreds of colorful fish species, including schools of cuttlefish and local spiny lobster.

SURVIVAL GUIDE

Directory A–Z

ACCESSIBLE TRAVEL

Statia's rugged terrain and poor infrastructure are problematic for travelers with disabilities and limited mobility.

ACCOMMODATIONS

With only a handful of properties on the entire island, accommodations on Statia are quite limited and booking ahead is a good idea. The nicest digs are on the waterfront in Lower Town.

Unlike other Caribbean islands, prices don't fluctuate with the seasons.

ACTIVITIES

The nonprofit Sint Eustatius National Parks Foundation (Stenapa) was established in 1998 to protect Statia's ample natural resources. It manages the Quill (p644) and Boven National Park (p644), the Statia National Marine Park and the Miriam C Schmidt Botanical Gardens (p644). The office (p644), situated in a traditional timber building in Lower Town, has detailed information, books and maps about diving, hiking, birding and other outdoor pursuits.

Diving & Snorkeling

Among aficionados, Statia's 36 dive sites are regarded as some of the best in the Caribbean. Protected as the Sint Eustatius National Marine Park since 1996, the waters are rich with coral reefs, drop-offs, canyons and wrecks inhabited by a host of underwater creatures from ethereal seahorses to giant octopuses, plus stingrays, barracudas, coral, lobster and tropical fish. Also submerged in the clear waters is plenty of colonial detritus, including anchors and cannon. Whales come through between January and April. The submerged 18th-century ruins off the beach in Lower Town (p640) offer fascinating snorkeling.

Diving is only allowed through the two local dive shops, Scubaqua Dive Center (p640) and Golden Rock Dive Center (p640), both in Lower Town. Each operates all manner of day and night dives as well as PADI certification courses. Divers must purchase a dive tag for US$6 per dive or US$30 per year to help maintain the pristine conditions. There's a recompression chamber at Queen Beatrix Medical Centre (p644).

Hiking

Along with diving, exploring the island's pristine nature on foot is a hugely popular pastime on Statia. Some 17 trails crisscross the untouched nature of the Quill (p644) and Boven (p644) national parks. The most popular trail is the 1.6km trek to the crater rim of the lushly forested Quill volcano. From here you can continue down into the crater and along the crater rim. The trailhead is at the end of Rosemary Lane in Oranjestad.

Boven National Park in the north is much dryer and consists of grassland, cacti and acacia bushes. A fun three-hour hike follows the Butterfly Trail, which crosses three ridges and takes you past an old sugar mill and remnants of a fort. It also delivers great views of Zeelandia Bay (p645) and the Quill. If you have just an hour or two, steer toward secluded Venus Bay to watch pelicans nosedive into the rolling waves. The trailhead is at the end of paved Zeelandia Rd, about 1.5km north of the airport.

Before setting out, drop by the National Parks Visitor Center (p644) in Lower Town to obtain a trail pass for US$10 (valid for one year, free for children under eight) and pick up information, maps, brochures and books. Passes are also sold by the tourist office (p644), Golden Rock Dive Center (p640), Scubaqua Dive Center (p640) and the Old Gin House Hotel (p641). All proceeds go toward trail maintenance. There's no one on the trail to check if you actually have a pass, but the funds are badly needed and you'll definitely earn karma points by getting one.

Be sure to wear good hiking shoes and bring plenty of water. It's always a good idea to have a hiking buddy, especially on the more challenging trails. If you're a solo hiker, consider getting a guide (ask at the visitor center).

CHILDREN

Children are warmly welcomed on Statia. However, facilities catering specifically to them, such as high chairs or baby-changing areas, are minimal, so parents need to be self-sufficient. Footpaths are narrow or nonexistent, so they're not ideal for prams/buggies. Baby-care products such as nappies/diapers are sold in the island's small supermarkets.

ELECTRICITY

Statia's electric current is 110V, 60 cycles; North American–style sockets are common.

EMERGENCY NUMBERS

Ambulance	913
Fire	912
Police	911

SLEEPING PRICE RANGES

The following price ranges refer to a double room with bathroom.

$ less than US$100

$$ US$100–200

$$$ more than US$200

EATING PRICE RANGES

The following price ranges are for a main course.

$ less than US$15

$$ US$15–US$25

$$$ more than US$25

PRACTICALITIES

Smoking Banned inside hotel rooms and enclosed spaces such as restaurants. Outdoor areas, including dining areas, however, are generally not smoke-free.

Weights & measures The metric system is used.

FOOD

Oranjestad is home to almost all of Statia's limited dining options. Locally caught seafood is a delicacy, while goat with rice and peas is the national dish.

The island's few small supermarkets have the best selection on Tuesday and Wednesday after the supply boat arrives. By the weekend, the selection of fresh food has usually dwindled significantly.

Monthly food festival **Statia Taste of the Cultures** (☎318-2433; Mike van Putten Youth Center; ⊙6-9pm last Thu of the month) brings out the entire community.

HEALTH

Oranjestad's Queen Beatrix Medical Centre (p644) has quite a good reputation considering the island's remoteness and minuscule population. There are always two doctors on call 24 hours a day.

INTERNET ACCESS

Wi-fi is available across the island at many restaurants and most accommodations. Communal-use computers no longer exist, so you'll need your own device.

LGBT+ TRAVELERS

Statia is not overly tolerant, so public displays of affection are not advised. Since 2012, same-sex marriage has been legal on the island but it's strongly opposed by many locals.

MONEY

Currency is the US dollar. ATMs are in Oranjestad and at the airport. Credit cards are not widely accepted.

ATMs are located in Oranjestad and at the airport, but they sometimes run out of cash, especially on the weekend. It's best to bring some cash with you.

Exchange Rates

Australia	A$1	US$0.67
Canada	C$1	US$0.75
Euro zone	€1	US$1.12
Japan	¥100	US$0.94
New Zealand	NZ$1	US$0.64
Switzerland	Sfr1	US$1.02
UK	UK£1	US$1.20

For current exchange rates, see www.xe.com.

Taxes & Refunds

Statia is duty-free.

Tipping

Tipping is not necessary or expected.

OPENING HOURS

Expect lengthy lunch-break closings and variable hours of operation, especially on weekends.

Grocery stores 8am to 8pm Monday to Saturday, 9am to 2pm Sunday.

Restaurants Breakfast 7am to 10am, lunch 11:30am to 2:30pm, dinner 6pm to 10pm.

Shops 8am to 5:30pm Monday to Friday.

PUBLIC HOLIDAYS

New Year's Day January 1
Good Friday March/April
Easter Sunday March/April
Easter Monday March/April
King's Day (Koningsdag) April 27
Labor Day May 1
Ascension Thursday Fortieth day after Easter
Emancipation Day July 1
Statia Day November 16
Kingdom Day December 15
Christmas Day December 25
Boxing Day December 26

TELEPHONE

Statia's country code is 599. To call the island from overseas, dial your country's international access code + 599 + the local number.

Cell Phones

Check with your home provider about roaming capabilities and costs. The local provider is St Eustatius Telephone company. The post office sells SIM cards that can be used in an unlocked phone.

TIME

Statia is on Atlantic Time (GMT/UTC minus four hours). Daylight saving time is not observed.

ℹ DRINKING WATER

Statia's water comes from a variety of sources including rainfall collection and runoff; it's best to drink bottled water or to boil water from other sources first.

TOURIST INFORMATION

Sint Eustatius Tourist Bureau (p644) has a few brochures and a free but basic island map. At the airport, staff also operate a **tourist information desk** (www.statia-tourism.com; FD Roosevelt Airport; ⏲ hours vary) for incoming flights.

VOLUNTEERING

Statia is a good stop for educational volunteering trips. Stenapa (p644) connects long- and short-term volunteers with opportunities like tagging sea turtles on Zeelandia beach (p645), trail building or maintaining, staffing the office, cataloguing Statian flora and restoring the Miriam C Schmidt Botanical Gardens.

The nongovernmental Sint Eustatius Center for Archaeological Research (Secar) is the island's sanctioned organization dedicated to unearthing and restoring relics from the past. Volunteers have the opportunity to work at one of the island's 600 documented archaeological sites.

Getting There & Away

AIR

Franklin Delano Roosevelt Airport (EUX; ☎316-2887; Max T Pandt Blvd) is Statia's only airport. It's tiny and currently only accommodates **Winair** (☎318-2381; www.fly-winair.com) puddle jumpers from Saba and St-Martin/Sint Maarten. From the latter you can connect to other islands and intercontinental flights.

Facilities are minimal; there's an ATM outside, but no car-hire desks. A tourist information desk is staffed for arriving flights.

SEA

No cruise ships alight here. A ferry service to/from Saba was expected to start in late 2019; check with Statia's tourist office for updates.

Yachts need to radio the Marine Park, part of the St Eustatius National Parks Foundation (Stenapa), at VHF channel 17/16, as there are many protected spots around the island and there is only anchorage for 12 yachts at a time. There's a US$20 harbor fee, plus marine park fees (per day/week US$10/30).

DEPARTURE TAX

Departure tax is US$15, payable only in cash.

Getting Around

Statia has no buses, but Oranjestad itself is small enough to explore on foot. Taxis or rental cars take you further afield.

CAR & MOTORCYCLE

Driving is on the right side of the road. Road conditions are spotty outside of Oranjestad and the road to the Miriam C Schmidt Botanical Gardens is often impassable. Watch out for roaming goats, cows and chickens all over the island, even in town. Also keep an eye out for surprise one-way streets – they tend to appear out of nowhere and the locals can get very upset if you're heading the wrong way.

Car Rental

Little Statia has a ridiculous number of car-rental agencies, although none of the big international agencies are based here. Expect to pay around US$40 to US$60 per day for a car or 4WD. Cash is preferred but credit cards are sometimes accepted.

Rental companies don't have offices or desks at the airport, but meet customers at the airport for pickup and drop-off. If you haven't prebooked, the tourist information desk at the airport can usually arrange a rental at short notice.

ARC Car Rental (☎318-2595)
Brown's Car Rental (☎318-2266; bcr_nv@yahoo.com)
Island Essence (☎318-0585; info.islandessence@gmail.com)
Rainbow Car Rental (☎318-2811)
Reddy Car Rental (☎318-5564; reddycarrental@gmail.com)
Rivers Car Rental (☎318-2309)

HITCHHIKING

Hitching is never entirely safe, and we don't recommend it. Travelers who hitch should understand that they are taking a small but potentially serious risk. While the usual safety precautions apply, hitching on Statia is generally safer than many other destinations in the region.

TAXI

The island's handful of taxis are independently run. The tourist information desk at the airport will call you one. Elsewhere ask a local, hotel or restaurant to phone for you. Prices average US$8 to US$15 per person per trip, plus an extra US$1 if you're carrying luggage, and an additional US$2 after sunset.

St-Barthélemy

☎590 / POP 9035

Includes ➡

Best Places to Eat

- Bonito (p653)
- Le Grain de Sel (p659)
- Le Toiny Beach Club (p658)
- Le Tamarin (p659)
- La Petite Colombe (p657)
- Maya's To Go (p656)

Best Places to Stay

- Hôtel Le Toiny (p658)
- Le Sereno (p658)
- Salines Garden Cottages (p659)
- Fleur de Lune (p659)
- Eden Rock (p656)

Why Go?

In the treasure-packed Caribbean, St-Barthélemy (or, as it's locally known, St-Barth) is a multifaceted jewel. This exquisite island blends French sophistication with an undulating tropical landscape of isolated stretches of sun-soaked and silky sands, windswept cliffs, scrubby green hills, flowering gardens filled with bougainvillea, hibiscus and fragrant frangipanis, and turquoise bays dotted with yachts.

With such a dreamlike setting, St-Barth is, unsurprisingly, a destination of choice for the rich, famous and beautiful for its laid-back tempo, luxurious small-scale hotels, designer-label boutiques and outstanding restaurants. But although St-Barth is undeniably an expensive destination, all beaches are accessible, public and free, and activities from surfing, windsurfing and kitesurfing to sailing, diving and snorkeling are all possible here. If you visit outside high season, you can score fantastic accommodations deals.

When to Go

Dec &Jan Share the island with Academy Award winners and tycoons.

Feb–Apr Low-season prices kick in by April, late in the *carème* (dry season).

Jul & Aug *Hivernage* (hurricane season) officially runs from June 1 to November 30; grab bargains before the rains hit.

St-Barthélemy Highlights

1. **Plage de Saline** (p659) Unfolding your towel on a perfect stretch of sand.
2. **Plage de Colombier** (p655) Following scenic walking trails to St-Barth's most secluded beach.
3. **Le Toiny Beach Club** (p658) Enjoying a toes-in-sand lobster lunch shaded by palm trees and sea grapes.
4. **Grand Cul-de-Sac** (p658) Swimming, snorkeling or kayaking with sea turtles in a calm, lagoon-like bay.
5. **St Bartholomew's Anglican Church** (p652) Hearing renowned local choir La Chorale de Bons Choeurs at this Gustavia church built in 1855.
6. **Le Ti St Barth** (p659) Catching a cabaret (and plenty of celebrities) amid a sumptuous jumble of wrought-iron chandeliers and velvet drapes at this Pointe Milou club.

Gustavia

Back in the 1950s, St-Barthélemy's capital was a windswept fishing village. Change came in the 1960s, when wealthy visitors including the Rockefeller and Rothschild families jetted in, followed by superyachts carrying Hollywood stars and influential Europeans in the 1970s. Today this port town is nothing short of majestic. Although relatively small when compared to other capitals in the Caribbean, Gustavia has a string of high-end boutiques, upmarket restaurants and a handful of historical sights.

Sights

Shell Beach BEACH
(Rue des Normands) In case you're tired of getting powdery-white sand everywhere, take the five-minute saunter from the harbor to this midsize beach awash with tiny crunched seashells. Although the water gets deep quickly, it's generally calm, making it ideal for swimmers and snorkelers (bring your own gear). Daredevils can jump off nearby cliffs and casual-fancy Shellona Beach restaurant provides sustenance.

St Bartholomew's Anglican Church CHURCH
(☎0690-54-17-99; www.stbartholomewsanglicanchurch.com; Rue Samuel Fahlberg; ⏰8:30am-6pm) Completed in 1855 from French bricks and limestone, local stone and Sint Eustatius volcanic black rock, white-painted St Bartholomew's has an open-sided design with original pine pews and louvered shutters that let in celestial rays of light. Sunday services (9am to 10am) are held in English; it also hosts concerts in April and November by renowned local choir La Chorale de Bons Choeurs, which regularly rehearses here.

Fort Gustave RUINS
(Rue August Nyman, La Pointe; ⏰24hr) FREE Built in 1787 by the Swedish as one of three forts to protect the harbor, this site today has the remains of a vaguely bottle-shaped lighthouse along with vestiges of a stone guardhouse, cisterns and four cannon, including two on loan from a Swedish maritime museum. The main reason to make the trek up here though is for the panoramic view of Gustavia and the harbor. A plaque points out local sights and landmarks.

Wall House Museum MUSEUM
(Musée Territorial; ☎0590-29-71-55; Rue de Pitea, La Pointe; ⏰8:30am-1pm & 2:30-5pm Mon-Fri, 9am-1pm Sat; 🐾) FREE An imposing stone building from the Swedish period at the tip of the peninsula houses a modest collection of oil lamps, period furniture, farming tools, fishing boats and other relics of yesteryear that sadly reveals little of importance about St-Barth's history. Upstairs is the historical library and in the courtyard you'll find the remains of a brick-made bread oven.

Le P'tit Collectionneur MUSEUM
(☎0590-27-67-77; Rue des Marins, La Pointe; €2; ⏰10am-noon & 4-6pm Mon-Sat) A diverse array of objects ranging from oil lamps, old nautical equipment and model ships to 18th-century British smoking pipes and the island's first phonograph tell the story of St-Barth's colorful history at this small but absorbing museum.

Activities & Tours

★ **Birdy Dive Center – St-Barth Plongée** DIVING
(☎0690-41-96-66; www.stbarthplongee.com; Quai de la Collectivité; 1-/2-tank dive €95/170; ⏰8am-8pm Nov-Aug) This five-star PADI dive center offers dive trips to some 22 sites including wrecks, canyons, caves and reefs (some just a few minutes from the harbor) that feel personalized due to a 10-person maximum. Introductory dives cost €115; snorkeling trips lasting two to four hours start from €80.

Jicky Marine Service BOATING
(☎0590-27-70-34; www.jickymarine.com; 26 Rue Jeanne d'Arc; boat hire per half-/full day from €390/490) This full-service center offers boat charters with and without crew with boats fitting between eight and 12 passengers. It also operates various trips on a set weekly schedule, including sunset champagne cruises (€124), half-day catamaran cruises (€188) and Jet Ski tours (from €100) as well as customized fishing charters.

Big Blue DIVING
(☎0690-35-86-35; www.stbarthbigblue.fr; Rue Jeanne d'Arc; 1-/2-tank dives from €70/100; ⏰8:30am-5pm Mon-Fri, to noon Sat Nov-Aug) Quality dive center Big Blue runs trips to sites including Pain de Sucre, where gray reef sharks swim alongside barracudas, rays and turtles.

Festivals & Events

Carnival CARNIVAL
(⏰late Feb/early Mar) Held for five days before Lent, St-Barth's carnival celebrations include a pageant, children's costume party, a paja-

ma parade and street dancing. It all ends on Ash Wednesday with the burning of an effigy of Vaval, the king of Carnival, at Shell Beach.

Festival of St Barthélemy CULTURAL
(Aug 24) August 24, the feast day of the island's patron saint and namesake, St Barthélemy, is celebrated with dance performances, a public ball, boat races and other competitions. Most events take place in Gustavia where festivities culminate with fireworks in the harbor.

Sleeping

★ Sunset Hotel HOTEL $
(0590-27-77-21; www.st-barths.com/sunset-hotel; Rue de la République; s/d/tr from €130/150/200;) Sunset across from the ferry terminal (p663) is an excellent budget pick. Its 10 rooms are simple but clean and come with fridges; pricier ones have stunning harbor and sunset views but also street noise. Breakfast (€8) is served on the panoramic terrace. Two caveats: it's on the 3rd floor, with no lift/elevator, and wi-fi is in public areas only.

Eating

★ Le Petit Deauville ICE CREAM $
(0590-52-37-67; 15 Rue de la République; ice cream per 1/2/3 scoops €3/5/7; 11am-12:30pm & 3:30-6pm Mon-Sat;) The sublime, all-natural, fruit-based sorbets (such as pineapple, mango, guava and passion fruit) and rich, creamy ice creams (including roast chestnut, pistachio, chocolate and crème brûlée) handmade at this tiny takeout shop by *maître glacier* (master ice-cream maker) Yann Colin star on the menus of some of St-Barth's finest restaurants.

Fish Market MARKET $
(Rue de la République; 6:30am-noon Mon-Sat, hours can vary) If you have your own kitchen, head to the covered, open-sided fish market to pick up the day's catch, all freshly unloaded off the fishing boats. Arrive early: the market closes once all is sold. It's also closed when weather conditions prevent the boats from heading out.

La Crêperie de St Barth CAFE $
(0590-27-84-07; www.creperiestbarth.com; Rue du Roi Oscar II; crepes savory €4.50-22.50, sweet €4.50-11; 9am-10pm Mon-Sat, from 4pm Sun) Wholly no-frills and unpretentious, this Gustavia stalwart (since 1986) is a dependable any-time-of-day standby for breakfast, burgers, salads and sandwiches but the main reason to swing by are the freshly made sweet and savory crepes.

Black Ginger THAI $$
(0590-29-21-03; www.blackgingersbh.com; Rue Samuel Fahlberg; mains €27-33; 6:30-10pm Wed-Mon) Filled with glossy timber furniture and lush plants and lit by oversized lamps, this split-level space is a seductive spot for spicy Thai flavors. Menu standouts include *mahi-mahi* with black pepper, roasted Thai duck and the signature Black Ginger seafood salad.

L'Isoletta ITALIAN $$
(0590-52-02-02; www.lisolettastbarth.com; Rue du Roi Oscar II; dishes €14-18, pizza half-/1m from €25/45; noon-11pm Tue-Sat, from 6pm Sun;) The casual sibling of fine-dining establishment L'Isola (p654) has a chic terrace with outsized wooden furniture strewn with cushions. Pizzas (by the half-meter or meter, served on wooden planks) are the mainstay, along with homemade focaccia, crisp salads and lasagna. All are made with imported Italian ingredients, with meals accompanied by Italian wines.

Le Repaire FRENCH $$
(0590-27-72-48; Rue de la République; mains €14-32; 7am-midnight;) In a prime spot on Gustavia's waterfront opposite the ferry terminal, this locally loved, reasonably priced brasserie serves solid French mains (steak tartare with raw egg, duck breast with honey and spices...) along with pub staples like salads and burgers and a 30-strong cocktail list. Breakfast, from 7am, is the earliest option in town.

Eddy's Ghetto FUSION $$
(0590-27-54-17; www.eddysghetto.com; 12 Rue Samuel Fahlberg; mains €21-32; 7pm-midnight Mon-Sat Nov-late Aug) Tucked behind a timber gate (look for the iguana motif on the stone pavement out front), this ironically named hideaway filled with tropical plants and wooden furniture is a perennial local favorite. The menu blends French, Caribbean and Asian influences in dishes like shrimp with curry and coconut or rack of lamb with Indian spices. Don't miss Eddy's homemade rum.

★ Bonito LATIN AMERICAN $$$
(0590-27-96-96; www.bonitosbh.com; Rue Lubin Brin; mains €42-72; 6:30-10:30pm, closed Sep-Oct & Sun Apr-Aug) One of St-Barth's most buzzed-about restaurants, Bonito cooks up a tantalizing blend of seafood-centric Latin

American and French cuisine. A culinary journey might start with lobster ceviche, fold in grilled-beef tataki and peak with sautéed scallops, all served in a vibe of calm poshness underlined by mellifluous sounds. Exquisite cocktails make this a nice sunset spot to boot.

L'Isola ITALIAN **$$$**
(☎0590-51-00-05; Rue du Roi Oscar II; mains €34-58; ⊙6-11:30pm Tue-Sun Nov-Aug; ❄) So authentically Italian, you half expect to espy the Coliseum around the corner. This elegant restaurant will put tongue and tummy into a state of contentment from the antipasti to the *dolci* (dessert) courses. For mains, choose from handmade pasta, creamy risotto and classic mains like breaded Milanese pork cutlets.

Drinking & Nightlife

★**Le Select** BAR
(☎0590-27-86-87; cnr Rue de la France & Rue du Général de Gaulle; ⊙10am-11pm or later Mon-Sat) Plastered in a pirate's chest of photos, T-shirts and other detritus collected during many a drunken night since 1949, Le Select is your quintessential salt-of-the-earth watering hole with cheap cold beers and strong rum punches. A tiny kitchen overlooking the beer garden serves lunchtime burgers (€8 to €16) in keeping with its anthem: Jimmy Buffet's famous song 'Cheeseburger in Paradise'.

Rhum Room BAR
(www.rhumroom.com; Rue du Général de Gaulle; ⊙8pm-2am Mon-Sat) The Rhum Room is an extraordinary shrine to spirits with a mind-boggling lineup of around 650 rums from Anguilla to Venezuela, some of them aged as much as 30 years. If you're not a connoisseur ask the congenial rummelier to make a recommendation or go for a rum tasting and ferret out your favorite.

WORTH A TRIP

PLAGE DE GOUVERNEUR

Cradled by high cliffs and untouched nature, **Plage de Gouverneur** (Governor's Beach; Anse de Gouverneur) is a gorgeous, broad, secluded sandy beach fringing a U-shaped bay. It's splendid for sunbathing and for picnics. The lack of visitors – even in high season – means beachgoers often sunbathe au naturel. It's at the end of a steep road – watch for turtle crossings!

Baz Bar BAR
(☎0590-29-74-09; www.bazbar.com; Rue Samuel Fahlberg; ⊙11:30am-2pm & 6-11pm Oct-Jul) Many a band has whipped patrons into a dancing and clapping frenzy at Baz Bar, a wood-shingled harborside hangout in business since 1999. When there's no live music, it's still the go-to place for sushi and tapas or, if you've partied too much the night before, a Hangover smoothie.

Shopping

★**Les Petits Carreaux** ARTS & CRAFTS
(Passage de la Crémaillère, off Rue du Roi Oscar II; ⊙10am-1pm & 4-7pm Mon-Sat; 📶) Artist Véronique Vandernoot's iconic hand-painted ceramic tiles appear at the entrance to every beach on the island, with bright Caribbean colors vividly evoking each location. You can watch Véronique paint and buy her tiles here at her studio-shop, along with other items incorporating her designs, such as coffee mugs, coasters, place mats, jewelry, postcards, bags, books and clothing.

Information

BNP Paribas (☎0590-27-63-70; Rue du Bord de Mer; ⊙7:45am-noon & 1:35-4pm Mon & Tue, 7:45am-12:30pm Wed, 7:30am-11:30pm Thu & Fri, 8:30am-1pm Sat) Has an ATM.

Hôpital De Bruyn (☎0590-27-60-35, emergency 0590-51-19-00; Rue du Père Irenée de Bruyn; ⊙24hr) This 20-bed hospital has a doctor in attendance around the clock, but for more serious matters visit the St Maarten Medical Center (p714) in Philipsburg.

Post Office (☎0590-27-62-00; Rue Samuel Fahlberg; ⊙8am-3pm Mon, Tue, Thu & Fri, to noon Wed & Sat; 📶)

Tourist Office (☎0590-27-87-27; www.saintbarth-tourisme.com; Rue Samuel Fahlberg; ⊙8:30am-5pm Mon-Fri, to noon Sat) St-Barth's tourist office can help with accommodations bookings, restaurant recommendations, island tours and activities. It also has a map and a smattering of free brochures.

Getting There & Away

Gustavia is 1.5km southwest of the airport. The ferry terminal is right in town.

Flamands

Set below steep cliffs, this small settlement stretches to St-Barth's longest and widest beach, Plage des Flamands. Badly hit by Hurricane Irma, there's still quite a bit of noisy and dusty restoration and new construction throughout the village.

Sights

★Plage de Colombier BEACH

(Anse de Colombier) This is the tropical paradise you've daydreamed about: a dazzling, secluded white-sand carpet lapped by turquoise waters and backed by undulating hills. The bay is ideal for swimming and snorkeling around the coral reef on the northeast side of the beach, but can only be reached by boat or on foot.

A scenic trail begins past the Auberge de la La Petite Anse, just beyond Flamands (750m, around 20 minutes); another leads downhill from the viewpoint at road's end in Colombier (600m, about 20 minutes downhill).

There are no facilities, so bring whatever you need. Note that parking is limited to about 10 cars at the Colombier trailhead, while there's space for at least 20 at La Petite Anse. The only other way to get here is by private boat.

Plage des Flamands BEACH

(Anse des Flamands) The widest beach on the island, Flamands' clear waters seduce beach-goers and surfers when the swell's up. Most of its shadeless sweep is backed by private houses along with a couple of hotels toward the eastern end with bars, sun loungers and umbrellas for paying customers. While much of the village is still undergoing major post-Irma reconstruction, many of the laneways leading to the beach remain closed. For now, the main access is at the western end.

Sleeping

Auberge de la Petite Anse BUNGALOW $

(0590-27-64-89; www.auberge-petite-anse.com; Anse des Flamands; cottages s/d/tr €150/200/220; P ❄ 🛜) As the snaking road starts to peter out at the far end of Flamands, the 16 apartments spread over eight semidetached bungalows with terraces overlooking the cerulean waters come into view. If you fancy a dip, the nearest beach is a 200m walk east. Two-night minimum stay.

Auberge de Terre-Neuve COTTAGE $

(0590-27-75-32; www.aubergedeterreneuve.com; Rte de Flamands; r €150-180; P ❄ 🛜) On the way down into Flamands, this cluster of cottages is a great affordable option if you don't mind not being right on the beach (it's a 650m walk down a *steep* hill). The apricot-colored cabins have basic but comfy furniture, sparkling white tiles, kitchenettes and spacious furnished terraces. Rates include a rental car.

Cheval Blanc RESORT $$$

(0590-27-61-81; www.chevalblanc.com; Anse des Flamands; d/ste incl breakfast from €1125/3500; ⊙mid-Oct–Aug; P ❄ 🛜 ≋) If you're searching for a cocoon-like sanctum where daily stresses melt away, the White Horse is it. This glamourous pit stop has 61 units dotted around the tropical gardens or overlooking the white sand of St-Barth's longest beach; many have private Jacuzzis or pools. Its divine spa includes treatments in a garden pavilion.

Eating

Chez Rolande CARIBBEAN $

(0690 84-08-12, 0590-27-51-42; Main Rd; mains €21-25; ⊙noon-3pm & 7-10pm Tue-Sat, noon-3pm Sun Nov-Aug; 🛜 👪) Don't be fooled by the mix-and-match garden furniture strewn below two flamboyant trees: in her citrus-yellow cottage with azure trim and red roof, the affable Rolande whips up some of the island's best traditional Creole fare with passion and smiles. Lunch brings *bokits* (Guadeloupian fried sandwiches) while mains range from aromatic goat stew to conch fricassee.

La Langouste SEAFOOD $$$

(0590-27-63-61; www.flamandsbeachhotel.com; Hôtel Baie des Anges; mains €20-55; ⊙noon-2:30pm & 7-9:30pm Oct-Aug; ❄ 🛜) A Flamands icon, La Langouste is famous for its live tank filled with crustaceans, which are grilled and served with a trio of sauces – a feast best enjoyed at a white tablecloth–covered table on the veranda overlooking the hotel pool. Other menu highlights include Pastis-flambéed sea bass, and an outstanding lobster bisque. The wine list is tops.

St-Jean

After Gustavia, spread-out St-Jean is St-Barth's second-busiest settlement, teeming with upscale shops, restaurants and hotels. Its lively beach scallops out on either side of the bluff-top landmark Eden Rock (p656), St-Barth's first and premier hotel. The western end of the beach is near the end of the airport runway and a great spot to watch the hair-raising takeoffs and landings.

Activities

Hookipa Surf Shop St Barth WATER SPORTS
(☎0590-27-71-31; www.facebook.com/pg/hookipa.stbart; Rte de Saline; snorkeling gear/bodyboard/surfboard/longboard rental per day €7/9/24/40; ⊙9am-7pm Mon-Sat, 10am-12:30pm Sun) A one-stop shop for renting water-sports equipment, Hookipa can also let you in on the island's surfing hot spots, including where conditions are best on the day, and put you in touch with local instructors. It also sells boards, wax, sunscreen, clothing, footwear and water-sports accessories.

Carib Waterplay WATER SPORTS
(☎0690-61-80-81; www.caribwaterplay.com; Baie de St-Jean; ⊙9am-5pm) This small outfit on the beach rents out the gamut of sea toys, including kayaks (single/double €20/30), stand-up paddle boards (SUPs; €25), bodyboards (€10) and snorkeling gear (€10). You can also set sail on catamarans (from €50) and windsurf (€30). Rates are per hour with discounts for longer rentals. Also offers surfing, SUP and sailing lessons.

Sleeping

Hotel Le Village St Barth HOTEL $$
(☎0590-27-61-39; www.levillagestbarth.com; Colline de St-Jean; d incl breakfast €285-590, cottage €340-690;) Comfort, charm and atmosphere: this place has the lot. Accommodations vary from standard hotel rooms to traditional cottages with mahogany furniture, kitchenette and wraparound patio. A real hit is the dazzling infinity pool, with stunning ocean views. It's a 250m walk uphill from the beach.

★**Eden Rock** LUXURY HOTEL $$$
(☎0590-29-79-99; www.oetkercollection.com/hotels/eden-rock-st-barth; Baie de St-Jean; r incl breakfast from €1500;) Spilling onto St-Jean's powder-white beach from a craggy bluff, this legendary luxury hotel has bedded the moneyed and famous since the 1950s and just underwent a complete post-Irma-drubbing revamp. As befits such a posh spot, even the most 'basic' of the 37 seaview suites and villas dazzle with style and mod-cons, including Nespresso machines and Ligne St Barth toiletries.

Pearl Beach Hotel HOTEL $$$
(☎0590-52-81-20; www.pearlbeachstbarth.com; Plage de St-Jean; r from €620) Tropical gardens, tiled rooms with four-poster beds, sublime views of the sea and a prime location on St-Barth's most action-packed beach are among the assets of this newcomer. The pool is open around the clock in case you feel like combating jet lag with a 2am swim. The location below the airport runway should appeal to plane-spotters.

Eating

Maya's To Go DELI $
(☎0590-29-83-70; www.mayastogo.com; Les Galeries du Commerce; dishes €6.50-14; ⊙7am-7pm Tue-Sun;) A casual cousin of famous fine-dining restaurant **Maya's** (☎0590-27-75-73; www.mayas-stbarth.com; Plage de Public, Public; mains €34-56; ⊙7-11pm Mon-Sat), this sleek deli in the mall opposite the airport is handy for picking up gourmet beach-picnic supplies: savory quiches, fat sandwiches, salads and delectable pastries. The actual menu depends on whatever is fresh and in season.

Come early for maximum selection and sip your first coffee of the day among gossiping locals on the breezy terrace.

Kiki-é Mo DELI $
(☎0590-27-90-65; www.kikiemo.com; breakfast €9-15, sandwiches €7-16, mains €15; ⊙7am-7:30pm;) In the heart of St-Jean, this laid-back deli uses market-fresh ingredients in its French and American breakfasts, outstanding sandwiches (on baguettes, ciabatta, focaccia or multigrain toast) and vitamin-packed salads. For the modular main courses you pick the main ingredient (tuna, chicken, veggies etc) and then choose its preparation (burger, tacos, bowls or on a plate). Takeaway available.

Zion St-Barth INTERNATIONAL $$
(☎0590-27-63-62; www.zion-sbh.com; Centre Vaval; mains €25-31; ⊙noon-2pm Mon-Fri & 7-10pm Mon-Sat;) This gorgeous new spot juxtaposes tropical laissez-faire with urban sophistication both in its looks and on the plate. Dishes pair local choice meats and fish with a potpourri of international ingredients like zaatar, rapini, smoked ricotta or black cardamom. Kudos for the eco-conscious design – note the recycled-paper lamps, vertical plant garden and coconut timber furniture.

Sand Bar INTERNATIONAL $$$
(☎0590-29-81-64; www.edenrockhotel.com; Baie de St-Jean, Eden Rock; mains €30-70, pizzas €26-45; ⊙7am-10pm) The elegant beach bar at celebrity-filled Eden Rock hotel serves food

and drinks all day long in a colonial-style setting. Signature dishes include truffle pizza, caramelized foie gras and crème brûlée.

Drinking & Nightlife

Le Papillon Ivre WINE BAR

(☎0690-73-25-30; www.facebook.com/pg/lepapillonivresbh; Centre Commercial Les Amandiers; ⊙6:30pm-1am Tue-Sat; 📶) St-Barth's first traditional wine bar looks like it was plucked from a hip Parisian backstreet and set down here. A timber bookcase-style cabinet of prime bottles lines an entire wall, with many of them bottled by small estates throughout France. The vibe is casual and many wines are available by the glass.

Nikki Beach BAR

(☎0590-27-64-64; https://saint-barth.nikkibeach.com; Plage de St-Jean; ⊙10:30am-7pm Nov-Aug; 📶) Completely rebuilt after Hurricane Irma, this vaunted beach club is back with a vengeance as well as an outdoor dining area, a sushi bar and a rotisserie. Its barefoot-chic parties are legendary, especially on Sundays when the buff and bronzed flirt and mingle while guzzling champagne and tucking into luscious morsels. Other days are more chill.

Lil'Rock Beach BAR

(☎0690-40-56-62; www.facebook.com/lilrockbeach; Baie de St-Jean; ⊙noon-6pm Wed-Mon; 📶) For a sweet time of counting the shades of the sea, plant yourself at a wooden table in the sand in this artily ramshackle beach joint and mellow out over cocktails, champagne or a bottle of rosé.

Shopping

Kiwi St Tropez CLOTHING

(☎0590-27-57-08; La Villa Creole; ⊙10am-12:30pm & 3-6:30pm Mon-Sat) There's one place on St-Barth where you'll want to be looking good, and that's the beach. If it's time for a new swimsuit, Kiwi can get you kitted out. The stylish store packs a huge assortment of mix-and-match bikini tops and bottoms along with hats, bags, sandals, shades and other covetable items into its compact frame.

Lorient

The site of St-Barth's first French settlement, in 1648, Lorient fans out from its family-friendly white-sand surf beach. Charming historic stone structures here include a small Caribbean-style convent and one of the island's three Catholic churches. In 2017 famous French crooner Johnny Hallyday (the 'French Elvis') was buried in its cemetery.

Sights

Plage de Lorient BEACH

(Anse de Lorient) With calm waters at its eastern end and gentle surf at the western end, this coral-reef-cradled curve of golden sand is one of St-Barth's most family-friendly beaches. The reef is ideal for snorkeling amid friendly barracuda, sea turtles and rays. The nearest place to rent surfboards and snorkeling gear is Hookipa in St-Jean.

Sleeping & Eating

Hotel Les Mouettes BUNGALOW $$

(☎0590-27-77-91; www.lesmouetteshotel.com; Plage de Lorient; bungalow €165-260; ⊙reception 9am-noon & 2:30-6pm Sun-Fri, 9am-noon & 3-6pm Sat; P❄📶) Opening onto Lorient's sands, this small, family-owned seven-unit compound has you sleeping in well-kept bungalows dressed in soft whites and pastels. Sea-facing terraces come with outdoor kitchenettes cleverly concealed by motorized roll-up blinds (a supermarket is steps away).

★ **La Petite Colombe** BAKERY $

(☎0590-29-74-30; www.facebook.com/pg/petitecolombestbarth; sandwiches €5.50-8; ⊙5:30am-1:30pm Mon-Fri, to 1pm Sat & Sun; 📶) To kick off your day with scrumptious croissants or pains au chocolat, make a beeline to this breezy bakery that also does mouthwatering pastries, homemade ice cream and coffee to go. Its generously stuffed baguette sandwiches are great for beach picnics but often sell out by 11am.

JoJo Burger BURGERS $

(☎0590-27-50-33; burgers €10-29, sandwiches €6-14; ⊙10am-10:30pm) Huge burgers at this open-sided shack next to the eponymous supermarket range from the 'old school' (beef, bacon, cheddar and mustard) to the 'Tex-Mex' (steak, avocado, beans and cheese) to the 'JoJo' (steak, shallots, eggs, bacon). Choose from regular beef or black Angus patties by premium purveyor Pat La Frieda.

Burritos, salads and panini sandwiches are also served. There are a handful of tables; otherwise take your order to the beach.

La Boulangerie Choisy BAKERY $

(☎0590-27-96-96; Centre Oasis; dishes €1.20-6.40, breakfast €6.90; ⊙5:30am-1pm) Choisy's tantalizing pastries and cakes line up for inspection in huge glass vitrines, from shell-shaped Madeleines and flaky mille-feuilles to clafoutis (cherry flan). Savory options include quiches and freshly baked breads. Take away or stay for light breakfast on the large, shaded terrace.

Grand Cul-de-Sac & Pointe Milou

Arcing across a large horseshoe-shaped bay, Grand Cul-de-Sac's reef-protected sandy beach is one of the island's top spots for water sports including windsurfing, kitesurfing and snorkeling. You can wade out far into the shallow lagoon-like waters that teem with sea turtles and are ideal for families with small children. Advanced water rats can catch some great wave action beyond the reef.

To its northwest is the steep, predominantly residential settlement of Pointe Milou.

Sights & Activities

Plage de Grand Cul-de-Sac BEACH

Count the shades of blue and turquoise while chilling on the gleaming sands of this dreamy lagoon, where you can wade through knee- or thigh-deep water pretty much all the way to a protective reef (snorkeling spot!), making it an ideal spot for families with small children. Sea-turtle sightings are pretty much guaranteed on the cove's western end in front of the Sereno hotel.

Ouanalao Dive DIVING

(☎0690-63-74-34; www.ouanalaodive.com; Grand Cul-de-Sac; 2-tank/introductory dive €150/95, instruction from €230; ⏲8am-6pm, closed early–mid-Sep) This professional outfit runs three dives daily (9am, 11am and 2:30pm) as well as night dives on request. There are special rates for multiday diving. It also rents out snorkeling gear (per day €20), SUPs (per hour €25), glass-bottomed canoes and pedal boats (per hour €25). Two-hour snorkel trips to a nearby island cost €65 including gear.

Sleeping

Le Sereno LUXURY HOTEL $$$

(☎0590-29-83-00; www.lesereno.com; Grand Cul-de-Sac; bungalow incl breakfast from €1150; P❄📶🏊) Back in business after getting wiped out by Hurricane Irma, this luxe contender was rebuilt using sustainable wood and stone and is a class act. Good-sized units have breezy design and energy-saving high-tech touches. Relax by the pool, swim with turtles in the bay, paddle around in a kayak or enjoy a gourmet meal in the stunning alfresco restaurant.

For a special treat, work out the kinks in the petite spa run by a certified osteopath.

Hotel Les Ondines Sur La Plage BOUTIQUE HOTEL $$$

(☎0590-27-69-64; www.st-barths.com/hotel-les-ondines; Grand Cul-de-Sac; incl breakfast d €400, 1-/2-bedroom €785/1485; ⏲closed Jun & Sep–mid-Oct; P❄📶🏊) Keep an eye out for sea turtles popping up for air from the terrace of your spacious suite at this hypercasual beachfront charmer. You'll sleep safely in units featuring hurricane-proof concrete-frame beds, full kitchen and sitting area. Hang out – cold Carib beer in hand – by the palm-fringed pool or hit the calm sea with a free kayak or SUP.

Hôtel Christopher HOTEL $$$

(☎0590-27-63-63; www.hotelchristopher.com; Pointe Milou; d incl breakfast €450-1200; ⏲mid-Oct–late Aug; P❄📶🏊) One of the swankiest options on the island, the Christopher has 42 streamlined rooms and suites with sea views, a small spa and two restaurants: the casual Mango and fine-dining Christo. It sits on a rocky shore without a beach, but the vast free-form pool – complete with

> WORTH A TRIP
>
> **ANSE DE TOINY**
>
> Draped across a sea-facing hillside on St-Barth's eastern Côte Sauvage (Wild Coast), **Hôtel Le Toiny** (☎0590-27-88-88, in USA 800-680-0832; www.letoiny.com; Anse de Toiny; ste incl breakfast from €1980; P❄📶🏊) has 22 villas flaunting massive and ultraprivate suites, with flower-flanked private pools and terraces with gorgeous bay views. Furnishings are sumptuous and oversized, kitchenettes cleverly concealed in armoires. A shuttle service runs 400m to the **beach club** (☎0590-29-77-47; mains €26-45; ⏲11am-5pm) for lunch and lounging (beware of strong currents).
>
> Its gourmet restaurant, **Le Toiny**, (☎0590-29-77-47; dinner €38-54; ⏲7-10pm) is superb. Room rates drop by 50% in low season.

palm-studded 'island' and timber-decked poolside bar – is a fair trade.

Eating & Drinking

Le Sereno Restaurant MEDITERRANEAN $$$
(☎0590-29-83-00; www.serenohotels.com; Hotel Sereno, Grand Cul-de-Sac; mains €29-53; ⏰7:30am-10:30pm; P📶) If the stylish alfresco dining room with saturated views of the jade-hued bay doesn't make you swoon, then surely head-chef Alex Simone's cuisine inspired by his homeland of Italy and neighboring countries will. The homemade pasta is a dependable palate-pleaser but his talent truly shines with such dishes as the salt-encrusted fish and the *mahimahi* ceviche.

Christo Lounge Restaurant INTERNATIONAL $$$
(☎0590-27-63-63; www.hotelchristopher.com; Hôtel Christopher, Pointe Milou; mains €35-70; ⏰7-10pm; P❄📶) Chef Nicolas Tissier has a near-fanatical dedication to quality, using only sustainably grown meat, fish and produce and listing ingredients' provenance right on the menu. Tuck into milk lamb from the Pyrenees, local lobster ravioli or Salet Farm chicken in an uncluttered dining room overlooking pool and sea.

Le Ti St Barth CLUB
(☎0590-27-97-71; www.letistbarth.com; Pointe Milou; mains €39-128; ⏰7pm-2am or later Tue-Sat) Moulin Rouge meets Cirque du Soleil in this supper-club cabaret where the chic and inhibition-free frolic in a sensuous fantasy setting. Reservations are best (and essential for groups), but one or two might be able to squeeze into the Pirate-themed bar – even if this puts you a bit away from the action. Come early for pre-show happy-hour drinks and tapas.

Anse de Grande Saline

Behind its staggeringly beautiful, dune-fringed beach, this remote, rugged area spreads out around St-Barth's largest salt pond and towering mountains. Amid the cacti and scrub, look out for wildlife including iguanas and land tortoises.

Sights

★Plage de Saline BEACH
(P) Secluded Plage de Saline is the most photogenic and serene of all St-Barth's beaches. Bookended by rocky hillside, this sweep of golden sand is ideal for working on your tan and frolicking in the crashing surf, but be aware that there's neither shade nor facilities. From the car park, it's a 200m walk through the scrub and over the dunes. Like many of St-Barth's more remote beaches, it's a favorite spot with nudists.

Sleeping & Eating

Fleur de Lune APARTMENT $$
(☎0690-56-59-59, 0590-27-70-57; www.st-barth-fleurdelune.com; Grande Saline; d/bungalow & afternoon drinks from €250/480; P❄📶🏊) Situated 900m from Plage de Saline, this is a rambling boho-chic cocoon. Each of the rooms and bungalows has its own character, handpicked designer furniture and unique features like an outdoor shower, a private deck with Jacuzzi or an outdoor living room. Meet other guests in the outdoor lounge overlooking the minuscule pool with a free aperitif.

Salines Garden Cottages COTTAGE $$
(☎0690-41-94-29; www.salinesgarden.com; Grande Saline; d incl breakfast €200-250; P❄📶🏊) Inland on the Grande Saline's parched terrain, five semidetached cottages – each styled after one of owners Laurence and Jean-Phillipe's favorite surf spots around the world: Essaouira, Pavones, Padang Padang, Cap Ferret and Waikiki – huddle around a small plunge pool shaded by pandanus trees. Some units have kitchenettes. It's a short walk from three excellent restaurants.

★Le Grain de Sel FRENCH CARIBBEAN $$
(☎0590-52-46-05; Grande Saline; mains €16-27; ⏰noon-3pm & 5-10:30pm Tue-Sun Oct-Aug; 👪) After a swim on divine Saline beach, drag your sandy feet to this equally stunning restaurant built into the rocky hill behind desert shrubs. The menu elevates native cuisine to gourmet status with cod-stuffed christophine (local root vegetable), creamy conch fricassee and shrimp flambéed in aged rum. Despite the heavenly grub, the ambience is refreshingly down-to-earth.

★Le Tamarin FRENCH $$$
(☎0590-29-27-74; www.tamarinstbarth.com; Rte du Grande Saline; mains €32-46; ⏰5:30pm-1am Tue-Sun; P) Getting our vote for St-Barth's most romantic restaurant, Le Tamarin is an enchanted garden retreat that lulls you into a sense of luxurious calm. Sitting on the terrace below the namesake 200-year-old

tamarind tree, you'll feast on such inspired dishes as baked cod with puffed dark rice or wild-shrimp ravioli with octopus that are born of both passion and technique.

UNDERSTAND ST-BARTHÉLEMY

History

Due to its inhospitable landscape and lack of fresh water, St-Barth never had a big Arawak or Carib presence.

When Christopher Columbus sighted the island on his second voyage in 1493, he named it after his older brother Bartolomeo. The first Europeans who attempted to settle the island, in 1648, were French colonists. They were soon killed by Caribs. Norman Huguenots gave it another try in 1659 and prospered, not due to farming (which was near impossible) or fishing, but by setting up a way station for French pirates plundering Spanish galleons.

In 1784 the French king Louis XVI gave St-Barth to the Swedish king Gustaf III in exchange for trading rights in Göteborg. There are still many reminders of Swedish rule on the island – such as the name Gustavia, St-Barth's continuing duty-free status, and several buildings and forts. However, Sweden sold St-Barth back to France in 1878 after declining trade, increasing disease and a destructive fire affected the island.

Throughout the 19th and early 20th centuries, St-Barth wasn't much more than a quaint French backwater, and life was tough for residents. Without the lush vegetation typical of the Caribbean, farming was difficult. Many former slaves emigrated to surrounding islands to find work, leaving St-Barth one of the only islands in the region without a substantial African population.

In 1946 St-Barth, as a member of Guadeloupe, was part of an overseas *région* and *département*. By the 1950s tourists slowly started arriving at the tiny airport on small planes and private jets. The rugged island suddenly found new natural resources: beaches, sunsets, quiet. Quick-thinking islanders created laws limiting mass tourism to guard their hard-earned lifestyle; as a result, you won't see casinos, high-rise hotels or fast-food chains, but you will pay for the unspoiled atmosphere.

An overwhelming 90% of St-Barth's population voted in a referendum for more fiscal and political independence from France and Guadeloupe in 2003, which was achieved in 2007. After separation, the island became an 'overseas collectivity', which meant that the island gained a municipal council rather than having a single island-wide mayor. Despite the separation, the island has remained part of the EU, but retains its duty-free port status.

As with other Caribbean islands, several hurricanes did major damage to St-Barth, most notably humongous Hurricane Irma that roared through in 2017. But the island got on its feet remarkably quickly and has roared back with nary a trace of calamity still visible.

People & Culture

Most residents of St-Barth fall into one of three categories: descendants of the pioneers from Normandy who have called St-Barth home for more than 300 years; mainland French setting up expensive shops and restaurants; or foreigners looking for a more relaxed lifestyle. As tourism blossomed, the first group of residents largely traded in their fishing careers for tourism-related jobs, so virtually everyone is working in hospitality of some sort.

Despite the island's location, the general atmosphere is much more that of a quiet seaside province in France than a jammin' Caribbean colony.

For hundreds of years, St-Barth's residents were too busy toiling in near-impossible conditions to create much art, thus the traditional handicrafts were largely utilitarian, such as hats and baskets woven from the leaves of latanier palms.

Today there's a smattering of art galleries and workshops around the island devoted to exhibiting local paintings, photography and sculpture. For more information about visiting artists' studios, stop by the tourist office.

Landscape & Wildlife

St-Barth's total land area is a mere 24 sq km, although its elongated shape and hilly terrain make it seem larger. The island lies 25km southeast of St-Martin/Sint Maarten.

St-Barth has numerous dry and rocky offshore islets. The largest, Île Fourchue, is a half-sunken volcanic crater whose large bay is a popular yacht anchorage and a destination for divers and snorkelers.

St-Barth's arid climate sustains dryland flora, such as cacti and bougainvillea. Local fauna includes the red-footed land tortoise, the Lesser Antillean iguana, the Anguilla Bank anole lizard and the endangered Anguilla Bank racer snake (all snakes on St-Barth are harmless, though they can bite). From April to August, sea turtles lay eggs along the beaches on the northwest side of the island. The islets off St-Barth support seabird colonies, including those of frigate birds.

Considering the island's minuscule size, St-Barth has an impressive 16 beaches. Those looking for 'in-town' beaches will find that St-Jean, Flamands and Lorient all have beautiful sandy strands while Gustavia's Shell Beach consists of, well, crushed shells. The most famous secluded beaches – Colombier, Saline and Gouverneur – are picture-perfect powdery expanses of sand and gently lapping warm waves.

The St-Barth Natural Marine Reserve encompasses five zones where activities such as fishing, diving and boating are restricted or forbidden. Three cover outlying islands like Île Fourchue and Île Fregate but also Baie de Colombier in the northwest and Baie de Grand Cul-de-Sac in the northeast.

Environmental initiatives on land include the introduction of a color-coded recycling system, but when it comes to renewable energies, including solar, St-Barth for now lags behind neighboring islands.

SURVIVAL GUIDE

Directory A–Z

ACCESSIBLE TRAVEL

St-Barth's steep terrain makes things difficult for travelers with disabilities or limited mobility but the low-rise architecture means many properties are accessible. Numerous hotels offer wheelchair-friendly rooms with rails and barrier-free showers, and there is also a range of wheelchair-accessible villas. Not all restaurant bathrooms are equipped for wheelchair users, however – confirm when you book.

ACCOMMODATIONS

St-Barth's largest hotel has only 67 rooms and the second biggest barely half that number. Others are small, typically with fewer than a dozen rooms. Private villas are dotted across the island with most controlled by Wimco Villas (www.wimco.com); check Airbnb for other options.

In high season, everything books up fast (especially Christmas and New Year's, when prices are at a premium). Room rates drop between late April and November.

ACTIVITIES

Although St-Barth is celebrated for its leisurely pursuits, swimming, snorkeling, surfing, windsurfing, kitesurfing, scuba diving, fishing, kayaking, hiking and horseback riding are all possible here, with operators located across the island.

To dive on your own, you must pay a fee of €2 per dive and register with the **St-Barth Natural Marine Reserve** (☎0590-27-88-18; www.reservenaturellestbarth.com; Quai de la République; ⏰8:30am-12:30pm Mon-Sat).

ELECTRICITY

The current used is 220V (50/60 cycles); wall plugs are Western European style. Many hotels offer American-style shaver adapters.

EMERGENCY NUMBERS

Ambulance/Fire	☎18
Police (Gustavia)	☎0590-27-66-66

FOOD

St-Barth has a sophisticated dining scene, with boulangeries (bakeries) turning out fabulous breads and exquisite pastries, casual beachside restaurants offering great-value prix-fixe *menus* (set meals) and fine-dining restaurants run by celebrated chefs.

For self-caterers, supermarkets including **Marché U** (☎0590-27-68-16; www.magasins-u.com/marcheu-saintbarthelemy; ⏰8am-8pm Mon-Sat, 9am-1pm Sun; P ❄), opposite the airport, and **U Express Oasis** (☎0590-29-72-46; Centre Commercial de Oasis; ⏰9am-9pm Mon-Sat, 9am-1pm & 4-8pm Sun; P ❄), in Lorient, stock quality products.

HEALTH

Medical facilities in Gustavia include the small hospital, Hôpital De Bruyn (p654), and eight local doctors. There are two pharmacies on the island: one in **Gustavia** (☎0590-27-61-82; www.facebook.com/pharmagustavia971; Rue de la République; ⏰8am-7:30pm Mon-Fri, 8am-7pm

SLEEPING PRICE RANGES

The following price ranges refer to a double room with bathroom in high season (mid-December to mid-April).

€ less than €200

€€ €200–400

€€€ more than €400

EATING PRICE RANGES

The following price ranges refer to a main dish.

€ less than €20

€€ €20–40

€€€ more than €40

Sat, 9am-noon & 4-7pm Sun) and one in **St-Jean** (☎0590-27-66-61; La Savane Commercial Center; ⊙8am-8pm Mon-Sat, 9am-1pm & 3:30-7pm Sun & public holidays).

INTERNET ACCESS

Free wi-fi is available at most cafes and bars, and at virtually all hotels. Reception is good, overall.

LGBT+ TRAVELERS

In 2013 France (and thus St-Barth) became the 13th country in the world to allow same-sex marriage. Even beforehand, it's long been said that St-Barth is the most gay-popular spot on Earth without a gay bar, which pretty much sums up the nature of the island's gay tourism today. Locals and other travelers are very laid-back and it's not uncommon to see gay couples holding hands at the beach or having a romantic dinner, although there's no major nightlife scene.

MONEY

Currency used is the euro. ATMs are easy to find in Gustavia and in St-Jean. Credit cards are accepted widely.

Exchange Rates

Australia	A$1	€0.60
Canada	C$1	€0.67
Japan	¥100	€0.84
New Zealand	NZ$1	€0.57
Switzerland	Sfr1	€0.92
UK	UK£1	€1.16
US	US$	€0.89

For current exchange rates, see www.xe.com.

Tipping

Hotels Bills usually include a service charge, but it's nice to leave a small tip for the cleaning staff.

Restaurants Service charge is included but most people tip an extra 10%. If paying by credit card, advise the server before you get your check or leave cash (preferred).

Taxis Tip about 10% of the fare.

PUBLIC HOLIDAYS

New Year's Day January 1

Good Friday March or April

Easter Monday March or April

Labor Day May 1

Victory Day May 8

Ascension Day Fortieth day after Easter

Pentecost Monday Seventh Monday after Easter

Bastille Day July 14

Assumption Day August 15

Slavery Abolition Day October 9

All Saints' Day (Toussaints) November 1

Armistice Day November 11

Christmas Day December 25

Boxing Day December 26

TELEPHONE

➡ St-Barth's country code is +590.

➡ Be aware that the island's landline numbers then begin with 0590 (mobile phones start with 0690).

➡ If you're calling from abroad, dial your country's international access code, then St-Barth's country code, then drop the initial '0' of the local 10-digit number. For example, calling from North America, dial 011 + 590 + 590-12-34-56.

Cell Phones

Check with your home provider about roaming capabilities and costs. Orange is the main local provider, followed by Digicel. Shops including **St-Barth Electronique** (☎0590-27-50-50; www.stbarthelectronique.com; Galeries du Commerce; ⊙9am-12:30pm & 3-6:30pm Mon-Sat), opposite the airport, sell SIM cards that can be used in an unlocked phone.

TIME

St-Barth is on Atlantic time (GMT/UTC minus four hours). Daylight saving time is not observed.

ℹ Getting There & Away

AIR

Only teeny-tiny puddle jumpers and private jets can land on St-Barth, and only during daylight hours. The majority of flights are to/from St-Martin/Sint Maarten's two airports but there are also less frequent and seasonal flights to/from regional destinations including Anguilla, Antigua, Nevis, St Thomas and Puerto Rico.

St-Barth's only airport, **Gustaf III** (Aéroport de St-Barthélemy; SBH; ☎0590-27-65-41; 📶), has the second-shortest commercial runway in the world (the shortest is on Saba). Airlines serving St-Barthélemy include **Air Antilles Express** (☎0590-29-62-79; www.airantilles.com), **St-Barth Commuter** (☎0590-27-54-54; www.stbarthcommuter.com), **Tradewind Aviation** (☎in USA 203-267-3305; www.flytradewind.

com) and **Winair** (☎ in Sint Maarten 721-545-4237; www.fly-winair.sx).

SEA

Cruise Ship

No cruise ships dock at St-Barth, but a few anchor offshore and launch tenders to Gustavia's ferry terminal.

Ferry

The ferry service between St-Barthélemy and St-Martin/Sint Maarten often hits choppy water so prepare if you're prone to suffer from motion sickness.

Voyager (☎ 0590-87-10-68; www.voy12.com; Rue de la Republique; one way/return/same-day return from €63/87/70; 📶)

Edge Ferry (☎ Sint Maarten 721-544-2640; www.stmaarten-activities.com; one way/return/same-day return US$55/110/80)

Great Bay Express (☎ in Philipsburg +1-721-520-5015; www.greatbayferry.com; Rue de la Republique; one way/return from €55/95)

Gustavia Ferry Terminal

Yacht

If you're arriving by yacht, you must contact the **port office** (☎ 0590-27-66-97; www.portdegustavia.fr; Rue du Bord de Mer; ⏲ 7am-6pm) on VHF channel 12 two hours prior to arrival. Upon arrival, proceed to the port office with all passenger and crew passports and your vessel's registration details.

ℹ Getting Around

There is no bus system on St-Barth. Taxis are pricey, so strongly consider renting a car.

CAR & MOTORCYCLE

Driving is on the right-hand side, and the speed limit is 45km/h, unless otherwise posted. Keep an eye out for land tortoises, which have right of way on roads.

Car Rental

All major car-rental companies have desks at the airport. Peak-season prices start at around €70 per day, dropping to around €35 during low season.

Car-rental companies include the following.

Barth'Loc (☎ 0590-27-52-81; www.barthloc.com; Rue de la France; scooter/car/quad-bike rental per day from €35/60/75; ⏲ 8am-6:30pm Mon-Sat, 8am-12:30pm & 4-6pm Sun) Also rents scooters and ATV quad bikes.

Budget (☎ 0590-27-66-30; www.budget.com; car rental per day from €46; ⏲ 8am-6:30pm)

Europcar/Turbé Car Rental (☎ 0590-27-71-42; www.turbe-car-rental.com; car rental per day from €40; ⏲ 7:45am-6pm)

Gumbs Rental (☎ 0690-67-33-83; www.gumbs-car-rental.com; car rental per day from €55; ⏲ by appointment)

Soleil Caraibes (☎ 0590-27-67-18; www.soleilcaraibes.com; car rental per day from €30; ⏲ 8am-6pm)

Fuel

There are only two gas stations on the island, one opposite the airport in St-Jean (7:30am to noon and 2pm to 7pm Monday to Saturday) and one in Lorient (7:30am to 5pm Sunday to Wednesday and Friday, to 2pm Thursday to Saturday). After hours you can pay by credit card as long as it has an embedded chip and you know your PIN.

TAXI

Taxi fares range from pricey to outrageous, even for short distances. There are no set fares, so prices are all over the board. At minimum, it costs between €15 and €45 from Gustavia to the airport, and between €30 and €60 from Gustavia to Anse de Toiny on the east cost. All prices then increase by about 50% between 8pm and 6am and all day on Sunday.

To book a taxi in Gustavia, call 0590-27-66-31; at the airport, call 0590-27-75-81. There are taxi stands at the airport and the ferry terminal in Gustavia. You can also contact drivers directly – a list of drivers and their phone numbers is available at the tourist office and online at www.saintbarth.net/taxi.

PRACTICALITIES

Smoking Under French law, smoking is banned in all enclosed public spaces including hotel rooms, restaurants, cafes and bars. Smoking is still permitted in outdoor areas, however, such as terraces, so you may still encounter smoke.

Weights & measures The metric system and 24-hour clock are used.

St Kitts & Nevis

☎869 / POP 57,000

Includes ➡

Best Places to Eat

- ➡ Bananas Restaurant (p679)
- ➡ Gin Trap Bar & Restaurant (p678)
- ➡ Golden Rock Inn (p679)
- ➡ Sprat Net Bar & Grill (p674)
- ➡ El Fredo's (p668)

Best Places to Stay

- ➡ Golden Rock Inn (p679)
- ➡ Belle Mont Farm (p674)
- ➡ Hermitage Plantation Inn (p679)
- ➡ Montpelier Plantation Inn & Beach (p679)

Why Go?

This warm and welcoming two-island nation combines some lovely beaches with impressive mountains, activities on land and water, and a rich history. The local culture is mellow, friendly and infused with a pulsing soca beat, and revolves around limin' (hanging out, drinking and talking).

But if the pair offer much that's similar, they differ in the details. St Kitts is larger and more commercial, from bustling Basseterre and its huge Port Zante cruise terminal to the party strip and resorts of Frigate Bay. Across the Narrows, tranquil Nevis is a neater package, anchored by a single volcanic mountain buttressed by a handful of wonderful beaches and tiny colonial capital, Charlestown. Nature walks take you to the verdant upper reaches of the peak, while the island's history takes in British admiral Horatio Nelson, US founding father Alexander Hamilton and several well-preserved sugar plantations, now luxurious hotels.

When to Go

Dec–Apr High season: late November and early December are the best times to visit, with temperatures a little lower and less rain from February onward.

Apr–Jun Shoulder season: April and May are dry, and accommodations are cheaper. The St Kitts Music Festival is in June.

Jul–Nov Low season: this is the hurricane season; sights, attractions and restaurants open fewer days and shorter hours and hotels sometimes close for a couple of months.

ST KITTS

St Kitts is the more developed and busy of the two islands making up this nation. Its capital, Basseterre, is a bustling place with a large cruise-ship port that heaves with visitors during the season. Elsewhere, the Unesco-recognized Brimstone Hill Fortress National Park ranks among the Caribbean's prime historical sights, while in the south, the island's glorious beaches invite rum-fueled tanning sessions, long seafood lunches and plenty of water sports.

Sugar drove the local economy for centuries but since the last plant closed in 2005, St Kitts has put most of its eggs into the tourist basket, especially that of the cruise-ship

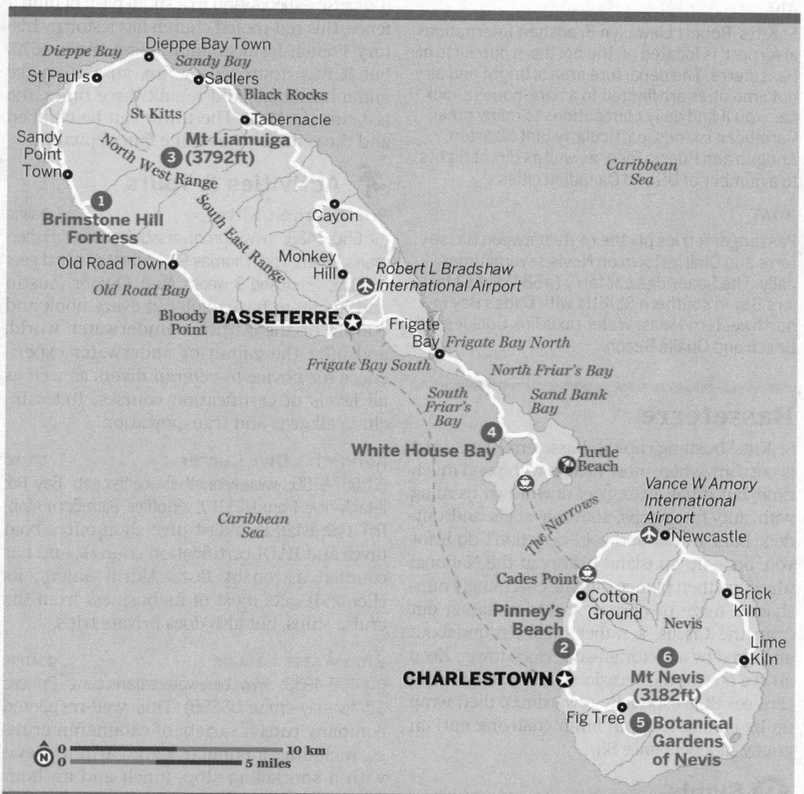

St Kitts & Nevis Highlights

1 Brimstone Hill Fortress (p673) Marveling at British colonial might at this superbly preserved hilltop citadel with extraordinary views out to sea.

2 Pinney's Beach (p676) Giving in to slothdom during a long day at this wide, long stretch of sand on Nevis' west coast.

3 Mt Liamuiga (p673) Staring into the crater of a volcano after a thigh-burning trek.

4 White House Bay (p671) Enjoying a swim and a snorkel followed by sunset drinks at chic Salt Plage beach bar.

5 Botanical Gardens of Nevis (p678) Calming down amid a symphony of flowers, trees, exotic statues and water-lily ponds.

6 Mt Nevis (p677) Clambering up the perfect cone of Nevis' namesake volcano for extraordinary island views.

industry. More recently, the island has also begun to tap into the luxury travel market with new resorts, ritzy villas, a superyacht marina and Tom Fazio–designed golf course. Far from the undiscovered Caribbean it may be, but St Kitts is alluringly relaxed and enjoyable.

Getting There & Away

AIR

St Kitts' Robert Llewellyn Bradshaw International Airport is located on the northern outskirts of Basseterre. The departure area is bright and airy but amenities are limited to a bare-bones snack bar. You'll find daily connections to many other Caribbean islands, particularly Sint Maarten, Antigua and Puerto Rico, as well as direct flights to a number of US and Canadian cities.

BOAT

Passenger ferries ply the route between Basseterre and Charlestown on Nevis several times daily. The Seabridge car ferry (p684) links Majors Bay in southern St Kitts with Cades Bay in northwestern Nevis. Water taxis link Cockleshell Beach and Oualie Beach.

Basseterre

St Kitts' bustling capital, Basseterre (bass-*tear*) is not somewhere most visitors will spend much time, but it has a compact downtown teeming with duty-free shops, souvenir stalls and outdoor bars. If that and cold beer don't do it for you, bone up on island history at the National Museum, then plunge into the charmingly ramshackle maze of narrow streets radiating out from the Circus, a rather quaint roundabout anchored by a Victorian-style clock tower. Keep an eye out for the occasional architectural gem (Princes St is especially rewarding), then wrap up by joining locals in limin' (hanging out) on grassy Independence Sq.

Sights

National Museum MUSEUM

(466-2744; Bay Rd; adult/under 12yr US$7/free; 8am-4pm Mon-Fri, to 2pm Sat) This modest museum is a good place to start your explorations of St Kitts. Displays deal with colonial history, the rise of the sugar industry, the road to independence, and local lifestyle and traditions. It's housed in the 1894 Old Treasury Building, a stately pile built from hand-cut volcanic limestone.

Independence Square SQUARE

Locals 'lime' and exchange gossip at this grassy park anchored by a circular fountain crowned by three topless nymphs. Once called Pall Mall Sq, its dark past as a venue for 18th-century slave auctions is not readily apparent, and the entire place has a curiously genteel air, with its red phone boxes, 18th-century Georgian buildings and **cathedral**.

St George's Anglican Church CHURCH

(Cayon St; hours vary) In a small park behind a fence, this red-roofed church has a stormy history. French Jesuits built the first one in 1670, but it was destroyed by fire, an earthquake and a hurricane, and rebuilt three times, the last time in 1869. The tower can be climbed and the cemetery has some fancy epitaphs.

Activities & Tours

Pro Divers St Kitts DIVING

(660-3483; www.prodiversstkitts.com; Fisherman's Wharf, Fort Thomas Rd; 2-tank dive incl gear US$115; closed 3 weeks Aug) Owner Austin and his team have explored every nook and cranny of the Kittitian underwater world, and offer the gamut of underwater experiences for novice to veteran divers as well as all levels of certification courses. Rates include all gear and transportation.

Kenneth's Dive Center DIVING

(667-9186; www.kennethdivecenter.net; Bay Rd; 2-tank dive from US$110; office 8am-5pm Mon-Fri) The island's oldest dive shop offers boat dives and PADI certification courses, and has counted astronaut Buzz Aldrin among its clients. It gets most of its business from the cruise ships, but also does private trips.

Blue Water Safaris BOATING

(466-4933; www.bluewatersafaris.com; Princes St; full-day cruise US$95) This well-respected company runs a variety of catamaran cruises, including a popular all-day trip to Nevis with a snorkeling stop, lunch and an hour on Pinney's Beach (p676). Departures are tied to the cruise-ship schedule but private charters are also available.

Leeward Islands Charters BOATING

(465-7474; www.leewardislandschartersstkitts.com; Unit C8, The Sands Complex, Bay Rd) This class act offers a range of options, including a full-day St Kitts tour including snorkeling, drinks and beach barbecue (US$95), a three-hour Sail and Snorkel trip for US$50 (Nevis departures US$66), and two-hour sunset cruises for US$50. Boats leave from Port Zante Marina on St Kitts or the Four Seasons pier on Nevis.

Basseterre

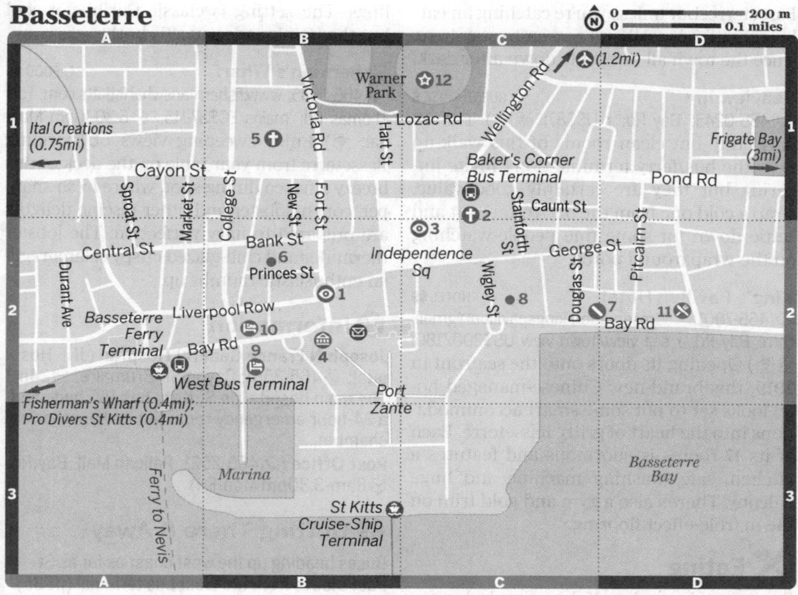

Basseterre

Sights
1 Circus B2
2 Immaculate Conception Cathedral C1
3 Independence Square C2
4 National Museum B2
5 St George's Anglican Church B1

Activities, Courses & Tours
6 Blue Water Safaris B2
7 Kenneth's Dive Center C2
8 Leeward Islands Charters C2

Sleeping
9 King's Pavilion Hotel B2
10 Seaview Inn B2

Eating
11 El Fredo's D2

Entertainment
12 Warner Park C1

Greg's Safaris ADVENTURE
(☎465-4121, 662-6002; www.gregsafaris.com) Greg Pereira leads various island tours including a popular half-day 4WD tour into the forest with stops at a viewpoint and a beach as well as a lunch of local fruit and pastries (US$65 per person). Other options include a four-hour rainforest tour, with plenty of chances to see wildlife and to swim in a freshwater spring (US$75).

Festivals & Events

Carnival CARNIVAL
(Basseterre) Also known as Sugar Mas, Carnival is the biggest yearly event on St Kitts. It starts in mid-November but kicks into high gear for two weeks on 26 December with dance and music competitions, beauty pageants, costumed parades and steel-pan music enlivening streets and venues throughout town.

St Kitts Music Festival MUSIC
(www.stkittsmusicfestival.com; Warner Park, Basseterre; ⏲late Jun) This three-day festival brings top-name Caribbean performers from all musical genres – calypso to soca, reggae to salsa, jazz to gospel – to Basseterre's **Warner Park** (☎466-2007; btwn Victoria Rd, Lozac Rd & Park Range). Recent lineups have included Smokey Robinson and 50 Cent.

Sleeping

There are a few simple guesthouses and one rather fancy new hotel in downtown

Basseterre, but unless you're catching an early ferry there's really no reason to stay here, since the town all but shuts down after dark.

Seaview Inn GUESTHOUSE $

(465-0243; Bay Rd; r US$87;) The 10 dark, tiny but clean rooms of this walk-up near the bus/ferry terminal don't invite lingering but they are certainly good value. Grab a cold one from the bar/restaurant and settle down for some fine people-watching on the wraparound porch.

King's Pavilion Hotel HOTEL $$

(466-7001; reservation.kingspavilion@gmail.com; Bay Rd; r sea view/town view US$200/180;) Opening its doors onto the seafront in 2019, this brand-new Chinese-managed hotel looks set to put some smart accommodations into the heart of gritty Basseterre. Each of its 17 rooms is enormous and features a kitchen, safe, washing machine and huge balcony. There's also a gym and gold trim on the marble-effect flooring.

Eating

Basseterre has a handful of simple but rewarding restaurants. In Frigate Bay, the restaurant row along Zenway Blvd has some international fare, while along the coast the platters of grilled fresh fish cooked up at simple beach bars should not be missed. If you're exploring the northern part of the island, food options are more or less limited to roadside bars and snackettes.

Ital Creations VEGETARIAN $

(661-1029; Bypass Rd; sandwiches & wraps EC$15-25; 8am-4pm Mon-Sat;) This meat-free food stand based on an organic farm by the airport is rather hidden. To get here look for the blue 'yoga' sign and walk up the stairs into the trees, where you can order sandwiches, wraps, salads, smoothies and other invigorating drinks. Take a seat under the mango tree and watch the planes coming in to land.

★ **El Fredo's** CARIBBEAN $$

(466-8871; www.facebook.com/ElFredosRestaurantandBar; cnr Bay & Sandown Rds; mains EC$30-50; 11am-4pm Tue-Sat) Equally popular with locals and cruise-ship escapees wanting to sample Kittitian cooking, El Fredo's is a busy lunchtime hot spot. Try its creole snapper, garlic shrimp, oxtail soup or goat stew, all paired with a potpourri of provisions (starchy sides), including delicious dumplings. The setting is classic Caribbean cool but the homemade sauce is hot!

Fisherman's Wharf SEAFOOD $$

(466-5535; www.fishermanswharfstkitts.com; Fort Thomas Rd; mains EC$37-115; 6:30-10pm Mon-Sat;) Enjoy sweeping views of sparkling Basseterre from your table on the deck of this breezy alfresco dining spot, where fresh snapper, conch, lobster and other piscine delights are prepared to juicy perfection. The lobster thermidor and chili-glazed crispy calamari get an enthusiastic thumbs up.

Information

Joseph N France General Hospital (JNF Hospital; 465-2551; Cayon St, Brumaire; 24hr) The main hospital on St Kitts has 156 beds and a 24-hour emergency room but no hyperbaric chamber.

Post Office (465-2521; Pelican Mall, Bay Rd; 8am-3:30pm Mon-Fri)

Getting There & Away

Buses heading up the west coast as far as St Paul's leave from the West bus terminal (p685) next to the ferry terminal, while buses heading east as far Saddlers leave from Baker's Corner bus terminal (p685).

Frigate Bay

Frigate Bay, some 3 miles southeast of Basseterre, is an isthmus dividing the calm Caribbean side and the surf-lashed Atlantic side, which is dominated by the hulking Marriott Resort. The road leading to the resort – Zenway Blvd – is restaurant row, but the area's key draw is 'the Strip,' a row of funky beach bars along Frigate Bay South. Swimming is good on both sides, although the Caribbean waters are far calmer.

Sights

Frigate Bay South BEACH

In season, the party never stops along the Strip, a beach-shack-backed golden sweep of sand with mellow, kid-friendly waves, and bars that keep the party going long after dark.

Sleeping

Frigate Bay has the greatest concentration of lodging options on St Kitts, ranging from large condo communities to full-service beach resorts such as the Marriott. There's little on offer that's particularly budget-oriented, however.

Timothy Beach Resort HOTEL $$
(☎465-8597; www.timothybeach.com; Frigate Bay South; r from US$215,1-/2-bedroom ste US$340/525; P ❄ 📶 ≋) This low-key pad is right on a fine beach and snorkeling reef, and is within stumbling distance of the Strip's row of raucous bars. Rooms are distributed across several two-story buildings and, though not of the latest vintage, they're large and comfortable enough. Request an ocean-facing room on the upper floor.

St Kitts Marriott Resort RESORT $$$
(☎466-1200; www.marriott.com; Frigate Bay Rd; r from US$295; P ❄ 📶 ≋) This hulking resort on a wide sandy beach within strolling distance of Frigate Bay's 'restaurant row' is like a small village unto itself with multiple pools, restaurants and bars, a gym, a spa, a nightclub, duty-free shops and even a casino. It's the perfect choice for those who need all the comforts of home in a blue-sky locale.

Eating & Drinking

★**Mill St Kitts** CAFE $
(www.facebook.com/millstkitts; Zenway Blvd; sandwiches EC$25-40; ⏲7am-3:30pm; 📶) One of the few places in St Kitts that feels even remotely hip, this industrial-style cafe inside a converted container ensemble makes for a great breakfast or lunch stop. Sip excellent coffee surrounded by corrugated walls plastered in sheets from old editions of *Pravda* (the owner hails from Russia) or just pick up a pastry or sandwich to go.

Cathy's Ocean View Bar & Grill CARIBBEAN $$
(☎665-0561; the Strip, Frigate Bay South; mains US$17-25; ⏲6-11pm Wed-Mon; 📶) With its plastic covered tables, it might not look like much inside, but Cathy's serves superb ribs, grilled meats and fish dishes. Grab a table in the sand for more breeze and the chance to be serenaded by the disco music of the nearby bars.

Patsy's Beach Bar & Grill CARIBBEAN $$
(☎664-3185; the Strip, Frigate Bay South; burgers EC$10-20, mains EC$25-80; ⏲11am-10pm or later; 📶) Beach gourmets flock to Patsy's for finger-lickin' barbecued ribs and mouthwatering shrimp pasta served in her cheerfully painted outpost toward the northern end of the Strip. Take-out is available as well, though with a view like this, why would you leave?

Rock Lobster MEDITERRANEAN $$$
(☎466-1092; www.rocklobsterstkitts.com; Zenway Blvd; mains US$26-60, tapas US$11-17; ⏲5-10pm Thu-Tue; 📶) This relaxed open-sided patio and bar is a fixture on Frigate Bay North, and it gets very busy on the weekend. Aside from the locally caught namesake crustacean, top choices include the mixed seafood pasta and the blackened mahimahi.

Mr X's Shiggidy Shack Bar & Grill BAR
(☎762-3983; the Strip, Frigate Bay South; ⏲4pm-midnight Mon-Fri, 8am-midnight Sat & Sun; 📶) Lanterns on battered picnic tables on the sand put you in instant party mood at this high-energy joint popular with expats and tourists. On bonfire night (Thursday), bands hook up to the generator and jam, while on Saturdays it gets full for karaoke night. Burgers and fresh fish help keep brains balanced (mains EC$40 to EC$120).

Southeast Peninsula

St Kitts ends with a flourish at this wild and hilly peninsula ringed by sublime sandy beaches. There are no villages down here and, until recently, no residential development to speak of. That all changed with the construction of Christophe Harbour, centered on a superyacht marina and including luxurious villas, a members-only beach club and a Tom Fazio–designed golf course. The opening of the luxurious Park Hyatt next to Cockleshell Beach has also put this remote stretch on the map.

Heading south on the main road, which runs for 8 miles from Frigate Bay, you cross over steep St Timothy's Hill (which offers stunning views) before shooting downhill via a new tunnel through the mountainside. The road itself – called Kennedy A Simmons Hwy after the islands' first prime minister – has also been completely resurfaced, making this area a breeze to reach.

Sights

★**Cockleshell Beach** BEACH
Enjoy great views of Nevis across the Narrows on what is arguably St Kitts' best beach. This crescent of white powdery sand with calm, shallow waters and several bars, restaurants and water-sports outfits can get seriously crowded when the cruise ships visit, so it's best to go early, late or not at all when the big boys are in port.

South Friar's Bay BEACH
There are excellent tanning and snorkeling possibilities along this long sandy beach backed by palm trees and sea grapes, and bookended by two restaurants: the snazzy

St Kitts & Nevis

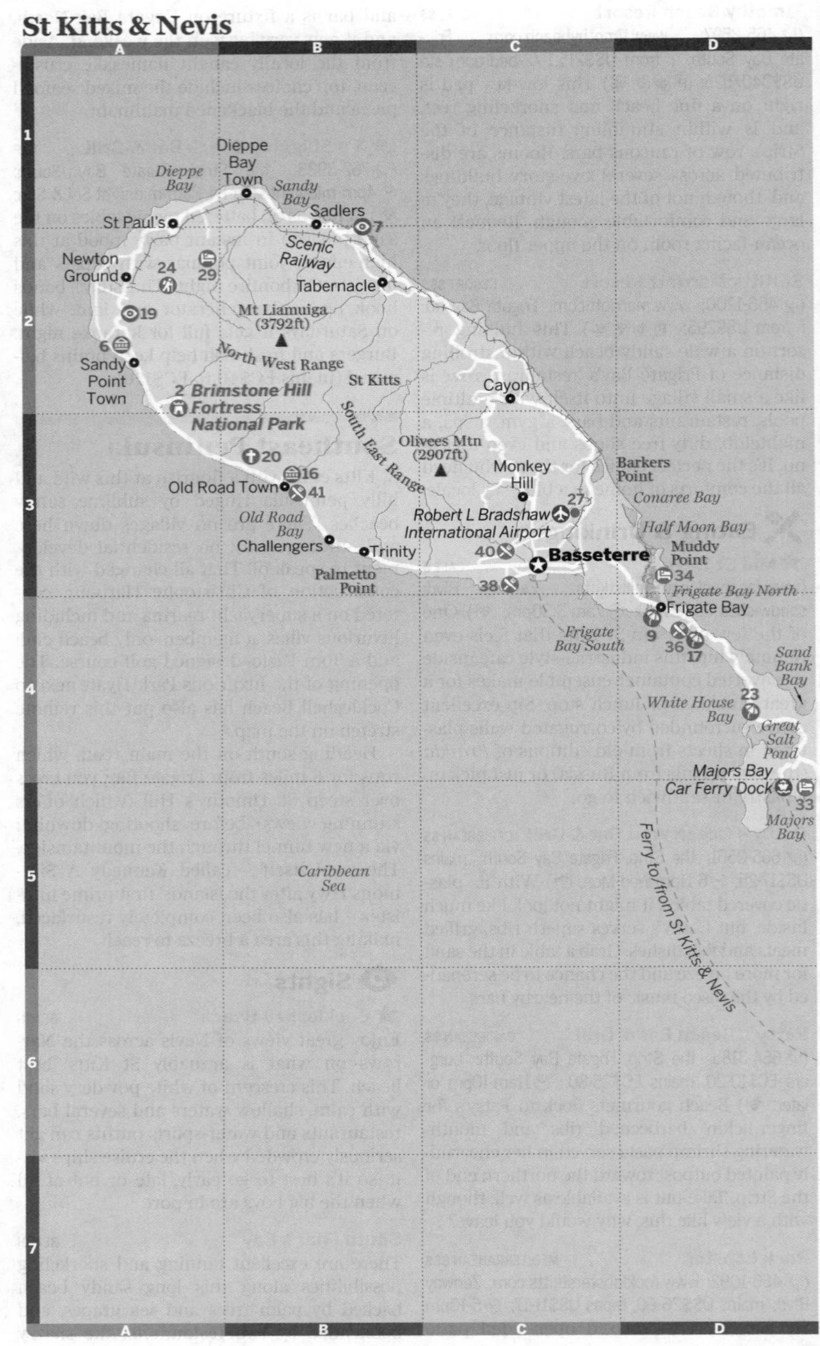

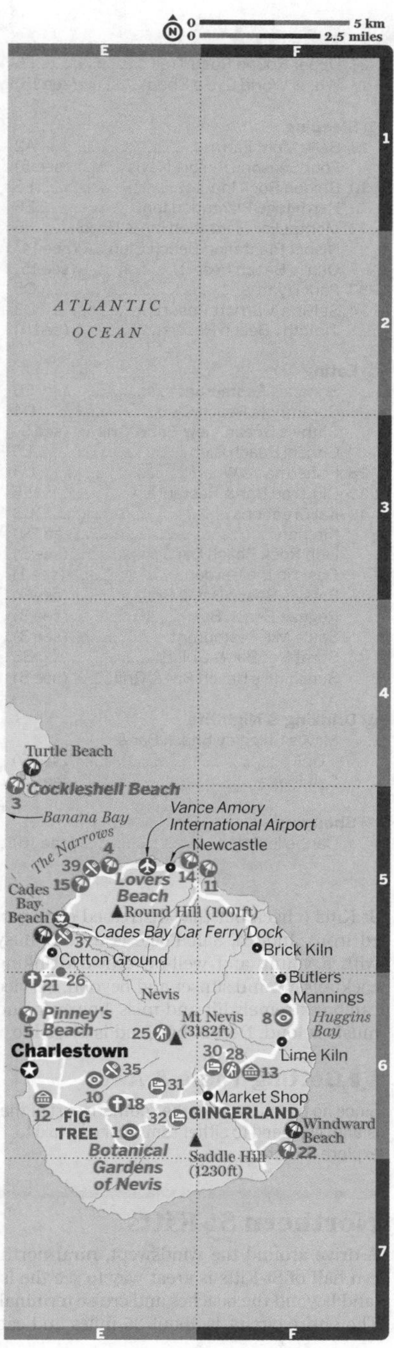

Carambola Beach Club (☎465-9090; www.carambolabeachclub.com; South Friar's Bay; mains lunch US$14-22, dinner US$25-44; ⊙6-9pm Mon-Sat, 9am-9pm on cruise-ship days; 📶) and the far more down-to-earth Shipwreck Bar & Grill. Both get very busy on cruise-ship days; crowd-evaders should stroll over to one of the locally owned bars set up in between the two.

White House Bay BEACH

The beach itself ain't much, but there's some pretty good snorkeling here thanks to offshore reefs and a couple of sunken wrecks. These days, though, the reason most people visit is for sublime sunset drinks at the chic Salt Plage (p672) beach bar.

Sleeping & Eating

Aside from the Park Hyatt in Banana Bay, the only places to stay in the south are private villas or luxury apartments.

★Park Hyatt RESORT $$$

(☎468-1234; https://stkitts.park.hyatt.com/en/hotel/home.html; Banana Bay; d from US$495; P ❄ 📶 🏊) This low-key but glamorous and contemporary resort sits on crescent-shaped Banana Bay. It has 126 rooms designed to feel effortlessly elegant; it's perfect for a luxurious retreat. The social hub is the 'Great House' with restaurants, fitness facilities and shops. The resort's highlights are superb service, a great beach and sumptuous views across the Narrows toward Nevis.

Reggae Beach Bar CARIBBEAN $$

(☎762-5050; www.reggaebeachbar.com; Cockleshell Beach; mains EC$30-90; ⊙10am-6pm Sat-Thu, to 10pm Fri; 📶) A rough-and-ready crowd fuels up on Caribs and seafood at this castaway bar on picturesque Cockleshell Beach. Sleep it off on an umbrella-shaded beach chair (US$10 per day), get a massage or snorkel with tropical fish hiding out in the protected reef. Best night: Fridays for the lobster-fest (reservations recommended).

Lion Rock Beach Bar CARIBBEAN $$

(☎663-8711; www.facebook.com/lionrockbeachbar; Cockleshell Beach; mains EC$20-50; ⊙10am-5pm) A white-haired Rasta named Lion presides over this charmingly shabby beach shack, which serves cheap cold beer and the signature 'Lion Punch' alongside big lunches of ribs and chicken. Staff also rent out the cheapest beach chairs on Cockleshell Beach (US$10 per day for two loungers and an umbrella).

St Kitts & Nevis

Top Sights
1 Botanical Gardens of Nevis E6
2 Brimstone Hill Fortress National Park A2
3 Cockleshell Beach E4
4 Lovers Beach E5
5 Pinney's Beach E6

Sights
6 Amazing Grace Experience A2
7 Black Rocks B2
8 Eden Brown Estate F6
9 Frigate Bay South D4
10 Hamilton Estate Ruins E6
11 Herbert's Beach F5
12 Horatio Nelson Museum E6
13 Nevisian Heritage Village F6
14 Nisbet Beach E5
15 Oualie Beach E5
16 Romney Manor B3
17 South Friar's Bay D4
18 St John's Fig Tree Church E6
19 St Kitts Eco-Park A2
20 St Thomas Anglican Church B3
21 St Thomas' Lowland Church E6
22 White Bay Beach F6
23 White House Bay D4
Wingfield Estate St Kitts .... (see 16)

Activities, Courses & Tours
Bath Hot Spring .... (see 12)
Four Seasons Golf Course .... (see 5)
Golden Rock Nature Trail .... (see 28)
24 Mt Liamuiga Volcano Hike A2
25 Mt Nevis E6
26 Nevis Equestrian Centre E5
Pro Divers St Kitts .... (see 38)
Scuba Safaris .... (see 15)
Sky Safari Tours .... (see 16)
27 St Kitts Scenic Railway C3
28 Upper Round Road Trail F6
Wheel World Cycle Shop .... (see 15)

Sleeping
29 Belle Mont Farm A2
Four Seasons Resort Nevis .... (see 5)
30 Golden Rock Inn F6
31 Hermitage Plantation Inn E6
32 Montpelier Plantation Inn & Beach E6
Nisbet Plantation Beach Club .... (see 14)
Oualie Beach Resort .... (see 15)
33 Park Hyatt D5
34 St Kitts Marriott Resort D3
Timothy Beach Resort .... (see 9)

Eating
35 Bananas Restaurant E6
36 Carambola Beach Club D4
Cathy's Ocean View Bar & Grill .... (see 9)
37 Chrishi Beach Club E5
38 Fisherman's Wharf C3
39 Gin Trap Bar & Restaurant E5
40 Ital Creations C3
Kitchen .... (see 29)
Lion Rock Beach Bar .... (see 3)
Oasis in the Garden .... (see 1)
Patsy's Beach Bar & Grill .... (see 9)
Reggae Beach Bar .... (see 3)
Spice Mill Restaurant .... (see 3)
41 Sprat Net Bar & Grill B3
Sunshine's Beach Bar & Grill .... (see 5)

Drinking & Nightlife
Mr X's Shiggidy Shack Bar & Grill .... (see 9)
Salt Plage .... (see 23)

Shopping
Caribelle Batik .... (see 16)

Spice Mill Restaurant CARIBBEAN $$$
(☎762-2160; www.spicemillrestaurant.com; Cockleshell Beach; mains lunch US$10-20, dinner US$28-48; ⊙beach bar 10am-sunset, restaurant noon-4pm daily, 5:30-9:30pm Fri-Wed; 📶) With its shingle roof, crayfish-trap lamps and dugout-canoe bar, Spice Mill gives the rustic beach shack a contemporary and luxurious makeover. While its lunch menu aimed at the cruise crowd is nothing extraordinary, come dinnertime its local produce and fresh seafood are transformed with delicious homemade rubs and hot sauces.

Salt Plage BAR
(☎466-7221; www.facebook.com/SaltPlage; White House Bay; ⊙4-10pm; 📶) This nattily designed beach bar right on tranquil White House Bay is about as cool as things get in St Kitts (check out that distressed corrugated iron). Indeed, Salt Plage is usually busy with a young and well-off crowd drinking cocktails around sunset and beyond. Service can be extremely hit-and-miss, however, and music is loud. Decent bar food is available.

Getting There & Away

Since no buses travel to the southern part of the island, you need to either rent a car or a taxi to explore this area.

Northern St Kitts

A drive around the windswept, rural northern half of St Kitts is great way to see the island beyond the beaches and cruise terminal. The entire circuit is about 35 miles and can easily fill a day, especially with an extended stop at the landmark Brimstone Hill Fortress, a leisurely lunch at a plantation hotel, a spot of zip-lining and a visit to one of the area's quirky museums. Here sheep graze on meadows of grass, and old sugarcane fields run up the hills with spectacular views towards Mt Liamuiga, the soaring 3792ft dormant volcano that dominates the interior.

Sights

★ Brimstone Hill Fortress National Park — FORT

(465-2609; www.brimstonehillfortress.org; adult/child US$10/5, audio guide US$10; 9:30am-5:30pm) Even if you're not a fan of military installations, this massive hilltop compound with its citadels, bastions, barracks and ramparts will likely leave a lasting impression. The British began construction of what was then a state-of-the-art fortress in 1690 and, using slave labor, kept refining it for about a century. In 1999 it became a Unesco World Heritage site.

Start your visit by watching the 10-minute video on the history of the island and the construction of the fortress, then wander up to polygonal Fort George to stand on the gun deck, take in the views and imagine the cannon firing all the way out to sea. One floor below are exhibits on the construction of the fortress, life at the fort, slavery, punishment and other topics, along with a recreated barrack room where six soldiers slept side by side in hammocks. For a more in-depth experience, pick up an audio guide at the ticket gate. The fortress sits at the end of a steep 0.75-mile-long road – don't try to walk it; take a taxi or drive.

Wingfield Estate St Kitts — HISTORIC SITE

(Old Road Town; 24hr) FREE Wingfield is one of the island's oldest sugar estates, founded in 1625 and in operation until all cane processing was centralized in Basseterre in the 1920s. Today it's a picturesque ruin with a partly restored mill, smoke stack, aqueduct, lime kiln and other structures, evoking the lives of slaves who once toiled to produce sugar, molasses and rum on these grounds. There's decent signage to explain what you're looking at.

Romney Manor — HISTORIC BUILDING

(465-6253; www.caribellebatikstkitts.com; Old Road Town; adult/child under 11yr EC$5/free; 8:30am-4pm Mon-Fri, also 9am-1pm Sat Nov-Apr) A favorite pit stop on island tours, the former residence of the owners of the Wingfield Estate sugar plantation has since 1964 been the home of the Caribelle Batik (p674) workshop and store. Horticulturists will be in floral heaven in the surrounding gardens (note the 350-year-old saman tree), which also hide an old bell tower that once regulated the working-day routine of slaves. Stand in the chilling viewing gallery, from where plantation owners kept an eye on the sugar works.

St Thomas Anglican Church — CHURCH

(Middle Island) The oldest Anglican church in the Caribbean was built in 1625, shortly after the arrival of British sea captain and colony founder Thomas Warner. He is buried beside his friend Samuel Jefferson, believed to be the great-great-great-grandfather of US President Thomas Jefferson. The current stone building dates to 1860, and the bell tower is currently undergoing a full restoration.

Amazing Grace Experience — MUSEUM

(465-1122; www.amazinggraceexperience.com; Main Island Rd, Sandy Point Town; US$5; 10am-4pm Mon-Fri, by appointment Sat) This small private museum tells the spiritual journey of John Newton, from British slave trader to abolitionist and writer of 'Amazing Grace,' through exhibits and a 12-minute video that is as saccharine as the hymn. Call ahead to confirm opening times.

Black Rocks — LANDMARK

(near Saddlers village) FREE Wind and water have chiseled black lava belched up eons ago by Mt Liamuiga into fanciful coastal rock formations. There are lovely views of the waves crashing onto the rocks from the parking lot where, on some days, souvenir and drinks vendors set up shop.

Activities & Tours

Mt Liamuiga Volcano Hike — HIKING

Getting to the crater rim of Mt Liamuiga, at 3792ft the country's highest volcanic peak, involves a lung-busting, thigh-burning 2.5-mile trek from the village of Newton Ground. The deep crater with its active fumaroles and seasonal lake is an incredible sight. The entire trip takes about 4½ to five hours return and is tough, tough, tough. Since the trail is not well marked and partly overgrown, it's easy to get disoriented, which is why a guide is recommended.

St Kitts Scenic Railway — RAIL

(465-7263; www.stkittsscenicrailway.com; Needsmust train station; adult/child from US$89/44.50;

Dec-Apr) This cheerfully painted historical train previously transported sugarcane from plantations to the Basseterre factory. Today, it takes tourists along 18 miles of the original tracks, followed by a 12-mile bus ride. The upper deck is great for sightseeing and the lower deck has air-con. The entire trip takes three hours; trains only run if a cruise ship is in port.

Sky Safari Tours ADVENTURE

(466-4259; www.skysafaristkitts.com; Wingfield Rd, Old Road Town; full tour adult/child US$89/65, half tour US$50/35; call for opening hours) Whoosh above the rainforest treetops at the historical Wingfield Estate (p673) at speeds of up to 50mph while suspended on cables. The longest of the five zip lines runs 1350ft and puts you 250ft above the ground. It's as close to flying as you can get without growing wings. Timings depend on cruise-ship activity.

Sleeping & Eating

Northern St Kitts has no beaches and is largely residential, with only a few rather exclusive places to stay.

You'll pass plenty of snackettes and roadside bars – especially between Basseterre and Sandy Point Town – but upscale eating options are limited to the Belle Mont Farm.

★Belle Mont Farm RESORT $$$

(465-7388; www.bellemontfarm.com; Kittitian Hill, St Paul's; villa from US$425; P ❄ 🛜 ≋) Hugging the foothills of Mt Liamuiga, this vast luxe boutique resort has sublime West Indian–style villas set within an organic, sustainable farm. Expect lots of unusual treats such as outdoor bathrooms with claw-foot tubs, private plunge pools, porches with views out to Saba and Sint Eustatius, and a restaurant that turns local and on-site produce into culinary miracles.

Sprat Net Bar & Grill CARIBBEAN $$

(465-7535; Old Rd, Middle Island; mains EC$40-125; 6-11pm Wed-Sun; 🛜) Join local families at this fuss-free waterfront institution for cheap beers and humongous platters of grilled fish and lobster served family-style on plastic plates amid nautical decor. Everything's caught by the owners that day and cooked up in the open kitchen. Best night: Wednesdays when a band whips everyone into a shimmying frenzy.

If you're self-catering, you can buy the catch of the day next door from around 4pm.

★Kitchen CARIBBEAN $$$

(465-7388; www.bellemontfarm.com/food/the-kitchen; Belle Mont Farm, Kittitian Hill, St Paul's; lunch small plates US$12-20, dinner mains from US$75; 7am-9pm; 🛜) The main restaurant at luxurious Belle Mont Farm flaunts decor that pays tribute to the island's sugar-centric past while offering a trendy farm-to-table concept that sees its kitchen sourcing 90% of its ingredients from the farm's own land or other local suppliers. The menu is constantly in flux, although the *dasheen* (taro root) risotto is a perennial palate pleaser.

Shopping

Caribelle Batik ARTS & CRAFTS

(465-6253; www.caribellebatikstkitts.com; Romney Manor, Old Road Town; 8:30am-4pm Mon-Fri, also 9am-1pm Sat Nov-Apr) Set in a former plantation Great House tinged in shades of citrus, mint and tangerine, Caribelle Batik has churned out gorgeous batik products since 1974. Local ladies demonstrate and explain the process of creating the often-intricate designs that you can buy in the attached store. While you're here, take a spin around the surrounding gardens with their 350-year-old saman tree.

To visit, you'll need to pay to enter the gardens at Romney Manor (EC$5 per person).

Getting There & Away

The St Kitts Scenic Railway covers the northern loop but if you prefer independent travel, a car is the best way to go, either using your own rental or a taxi.

There is no bus service covering the entire route. Buses leaving from Basseterre's West bus terminal (p685) only go as far as St Paul's. Those traveling counterclockwise depart from Basseterre Baker's Corner bus terminal but only go as far as Saddlers. There are no buses at all between St Paul's and Saddlers.

NEVIS

There's nothing showy about Nevis, St Kitts' sweet and unhurried sister island, where blissfully uncrowded beaches fringe a forested interior that rises to the majestic, often cloud-shrouded Mt Nevis (3182ft). Sprinkled with rustic charm and infused with a keen historical awareness, Nevis is a very different place to its bigger, brasher neighbor, and while many visitors come here just for the day, those in the know try to stay longer.

The coastal lowlands support bougainvillea, hibiscus and other flowering bushes that attract numerous hummingbirds. It's this lush landscape that makes Nevis so popular with cyclists, hikers, birders and other nature and outdoor fans. History buffs, meanwhile, can snoop around the legacy of Horatio Nelson and Alexander Hamilton, while beach bums and foodies will have plenty of choice as to where to indulge themselves.

Getting There & Away

Vance Amory International Airport (p684), in Newcastle, is a small operation with an ATM. It gets regional flights only (Sint Maarten, Antigua and Anguilla) and is mainly used by private jets. Some air services are seasonal and only weekly.

Passenger ferries ply the Charlestown–Basseterre route several times daily. The Seabridge car ferry (p684) links Cades Bay on Nevis with Majors Bay on St Kitts, while water taxis go back and forth between Basseterre and Oualie Beach.

Charlestown

The ferry from St Kitts docks right in charismatic Charlestown, Nevis' toy-town-sized capital with narrow streets steeped in colonial history and lined with both brightly painted gingerbread Georgian and Victorian stone buildings. It's well worth strolling up and down the main street with its banks, businesses, tourist office, bars and restaurants. At night the town all but shuts down. The closest beach, lovely Pinney's, is about 1.5 miles north of here.

Sights & Activities

Museum of Nevis History MUSEUM
(Hamilton House; ☎469-5786; www.nevisheritage.org; Main St; adult/child US$5/2; ⏲8:30am-4pm Mon-Fri, 8:30am-noon Sat) American statesman Alexander Hamilton (1757–1804) was many things in his short life: soldier, lawyer, author of the *Federalist Papers,* US founding father, the country's first Secretary of the Treasury and, finally, the victim of a fatal duel with his political nemesis Aaron Burr. He was also born – scandalously, out of wedlock – in or near this restored 1840 stone building that today contains a modest museum chronicling his rags-to-riches career.

Horatio Nelson Museum MUSEUM
(☎469-0408; www.nevisheritage.org; Bath Village Rd; adult/child US$5/2; ⏲8:30am-4pm Mon-Fri, 10am-1pm Sat) This small museum trains its focus on Horatio Nelson, the British naval commander who married a local widow, Fanny Nisbet, in 1787 and met his demise leading the victorious British at the Battle of Trafalgar in 1805. An endearing collection of maps, paintings, documents, busts, vases and other memorabilia help tell his story.

Hamilton Estate Ruins HISTORIC SITE
(⏲24hr) FREE Enjoy views of Charlestown from this romantically ruined sugar estate, which is being reclaimed by the jungle. Wander among the foundations of the Great House, the windmill, the boiling house and the chimney. It's hard to find, so ask for directions at the tourist office or go with a guide.

Bath Hot Spring HOT SPRINGS
FREE Right on the banks of the Bath Stream, you can join locals taking the 107°F (42°C) hot mineral waters of a natural spring bubbling forth through layers of crushed stones through the bottom of five pools. It's said to have therapeutic qualities and to even cure arthritis and gout.

Festivals & Events

Culturama CULTURAL
(www.culturamanevis.com; ⏲late Jul-early Aug) FREE Since 1974, Nevisians have celebrated their heritage with a joyous program of street jams, calypso tents, fashion shows, boat rides, parades, parties, dance and various pageants – from Mr Cool to Ms Culture Swimsuit.

NEVIS BY ROAD & FOOT

As you drive the island ring road, look for the blue road markers pointing out locations on the **Nevis Heritage Trail** (www.nevisheritage.org), including churches, sugar estates, military installations and natural sites. For orientation, pick up a leaflet at the **tourist office** (☎469-7550; www.nevisisland.com; Main St, Charlestown; ⏲8am-4pm Mon-Fri) or the museums.

For a delightful and informative nature experience, hit the trail in the company of Nevis native and environmentalist Lynell Liburd through **Sunrise Tours** (☎669-1227; www.nevisnaturetours.com; per person US$25-40; ⏲by request), whose hiking menu ranges from a gentle village walk to the strenuous trek up Mt Nevis.

Sleeping & Eating

Aside from a few locally run and inexpensive guesthouses, Charlestown does not have any lodging options. Most people visit for the day from the beachside hotels or the plantation inns.

JP's Guest House GUESTHOUSE $
(☎469-0319; jpwalters@sisterisles.kn; Lower Prince William St; r US$72; ❄📶) Two minutes' walk from the ferry dock, this tidy upstairs place in a modern building has 10 rooms that are a tad twee but spotless. They're outfitted with air-con, cable TV and fridge. Guests can make use of the communal kettle and microwave.

★Wilma's Diner CARIBBEAN $
(☎663-8010; www.facebook.com/Wilmasdiner; Main St; mains EC$55; ⊙11am-3pm Mon-Sat; 📶) The gracious Wilma is a wizard in the kitchen and dishes out a daily changing menu of hearty local fare such as barbecue pork ribs, tannia fritters or stewed chicken in her quaint green-trimmed cottage. A more fanciful three-course dinner is available by reservation only (US$40 per person), for which you should call at least one day ahead.

Cafe des Arts CAFE $
(☎667-8768; www.facebook.com/thecafedesarts; Bayfront, Samuel Hunkins Blvd; mains EC$15-40; ⊙8am-2pm Mon-Fri, 6-10pm Tue, 8:30am-3pm Sat; 📶) Infused with charming boho flair and set in a little banana-tree-shaded park by the sea, this colorful outdoor cafe does brisk business with its cooked breakfasts and freshly made sandwiches, salads and quiches. Locals and clued-in visitors roll in on Tuesdays after 6pm for the ritual burger bonanza.

Drinking & Nightlife

Octagon Bar BAR
(☎469-0673; Samuel Hunkins Blvd; ⊙6am-11pm Mon-Thu, to 1am Fri & Sat) For a big dose of local color, belly up to this outdoor bar on the waterfront, order one of its cheap, simple lunches (dishes EC$8 to EC$18) or join a local in a game of pool.

Information

Plenty of banks with ATMs line up along Main St, though the only one doling out US dollars is the Scotiabank outside town.

Alexandra Hospital (☎469-5473; Government Rd) This 52-bed facility can handle minor emergencies, including some surgeries. Anything more serious must be dealt with in St Kitts.

Getting There & Away

The ferry from St Kitts drops anchor at the pier right in the heart of Charlestown. If you're arriving via the Seabridge car ferry (p684), you need to arrange for a taxi to pick you up. A taxi ride from the airport costs US$20. Minivan buses run along the western side of the island from Charlestown. For points north of town, board any bus for Newcastle at Delisle Walwyn Plaza. For points south, board any bus for Gingerland on Memorial Square. Pay the driver when you get onboard; prices vary between EC$2 and EC$3.50. To get to the eastern side of the island your only option is a taxi or car hire.

Northern Nevis

Nevis' west and north coasts are ringed with superb beaches, from long and lovely Pinney's and busy Oualie to romantic Lovers and white-sand Nisbet and Herbert's. The island's only five-star resort, the Four Seasons, is a major presence on Pinney's Beach, which is also home to a cluster of lively beach bars and restaurants. Further north, Cades Bay is the launchpad for the Seabridge car ferry to St Kitts. Some of Nevis' best dive sites are a short boat ride from here.

Sights

★Lovers Beach BEACH
(Main Island Rd) Curtained off by sea grapes, mile-long Lovers Beach charms with white sands and an untamed beauty. Its lack of facilities keeps it nearly deserted; currents and a steep drop make the water less suitable for kids or inexperienced swimmers. Between April and November, the beach is a turtle-nesting ground.

Park by the side of the road next to the sign saying 'Sea Haven Beach' and walk 500ft through the trees to the sea.

★Pinney's Beach BEACH
(Main Island Rd) This 3-mile-long stretch of golden-gray sand along the west coast has decent snorkeling right offshore. The northern end is punctuated by the massive Four Seasons Resort and several beach bars, but quiet patches abound. Sundays are busiest.

Herbert's Beach BEACH
(Camps) A quarter-mile dirt track spills out into this practically deserted Atlantic-side beach with white sand buttressed by clumps of sea grapes. Several reefs close to shore make it a popular spot with snorkelers provided the sea isn't too choppy. There are no

facilities and very little shade here, but you'll often be alone.

Nisbet Beach BEACH

(Main Island Rd) This Atlantic-facing beach near the airport is a divine palm-lined strip of soft white sand, but windy conditions can make the sea quite choppy. An upscale beach bar belonging to Nisbet Plantation Beach Club provides sustenance and facilities.

Access is via the resort – turn into the hotel driveway, then follow the dirt track on the right down to the beach.

Oualie Beach BEACH

(Main Island Rd) In the northwest, family-friendly Oualie has yellowish-gray sand, shallow calm waters and sunset views of St Kitts. The eponymous resort provides drinks and eats, beach chairs and water-based activities.

St Thomas' Lowland Church CHURCH

(Main Island Rd, Cotton Ground) About 3 miles north of Charlestown, Nevis' oldest church (1643) stares serenely out to sea from its hilltop perch. Goats keep the cemetery grounds trimmed. Take a walk around the moody cemetery where the oldest graves belong to some of the original settlers. The oldest is from 1649.

Activities & Tours

Mt Nevis HIKING

Nevis' highest peak (3182ft) is seemingly perpetually cloaked in clouds, a phenomenon that gave the island its name: *nieve* is Spanish for snow. Since the climb to the top is steep and strenuous, and the trail is not always marked, it should only be attempted by experienced hikers or with a guide. The round trip takes about four hours return.

Wheel World Cycle Shop CYCLING

(469-9682; www.facebook.com/pg/wheelworldcycleshop; Oualie Beach Resort, Main Island Rd; bike rentals per day from US$25; 8am-4pm Mon-Sat) From his base at the Oualie Beach Resort, Winston Crooke gets visitors in the saddle on guided tours. The most popular is the Island Discovery Tour (US$65), an easy two-hour spin along historical sugarcane trails with stops in small villages and at plantations. Hike-and-bike combination tours (US$85) are also available, as are normal bike rentals.

Scuba Safaris DIVING

(662-8047; www.divenevis.com; Oualie Beach Resort, Main Island Rd; 2-tank dive US$140) This five-star PADI outfit at the Oualie Beach Resort runs boat dives to coral reefs and wrecks around Nevis and St Kitts, and also offers certification courses, night diving and snorkel safaris.

Nevis Equestrian Centre HORSEBACK RIDING

(662-9118; www.nevishorseback.com; Cotton Ground; rides US$75; rides 10am, 2pm & 5pm) Saddle up and explore verdant and sandy scenery on a variety of rides, including the popular 90-minute Beach & Trail Ride (US$75), which also takes in a secluded beach, a lagoon and historical villages. Riding lessons are US$30 per hour.

Sleeping

Four Seasons Resort Nevis LUXURY HOTEL $$$

(469-1111; www.fourseasons.com/nevis; Pinney's Beach; r from US$470; P ❄ 🛜 ≋) This full-service luxury resort on the manicured grounds of a former sugar and coconut plantation has 196 rooms discreetly set in low-rise garden cottages along Pinney's Beach. The oversized rooms face either Mt Nevis or the ocean, are dressed in soothing natural tones and outfitted with all expected luxe amenities; it's an ideal place for a high-end vacation.

Wrap up a day on the beach in the tropical spa or hit balls on a tennis court or championship 18-hole **golf course** (469-1111; www.fourseasons.com/nevis/services_and_amenities/golf/course; Main Island Rd, Pinney's Beach; 9/18 holes US$165/230).

Oualie Beach Resort RESORT $$$

(469-9735; www.ouaiebeach.com; Oualie Beach; r from US$320; P ❄ 🛜) Tailor-made for families and sporty types, characterful Oualie has 32 breezy white rooms with four-poster beds and floral touches in gingerbread cottages on a calm, coconut-palm-studded beach. The restaurant serves island cuisine, while the bar gets hopping nightly with a mix of locals and guests. A top-rated dive shop and bike-tour outfit are also on-site.

Nisbet Plantation Beach Club RESORT $$$

(469-9325, in the US 800-724-2088; www.nisbetplantation.com; Nisbet Beach, Newcastle; d incl breakfast from US$245; P ❄ 🛜 ≋) This former plantation is where Nelson met and fell in love with Fanny Nisbet. It attracts traditionalists keen on afternoon tea and the 'no shorts after 6pm' policy. The 36 sun-yellow cottages exude casual glam and are less about luxury than comfort. They're set around the 'Avenue of Palms,' a long sweep of lawn flanked by soaring palms.

Eating

Sunshine's Beach Bar & Grill CARIBBEAN $$
(☎469-5817; www.sunshinesnevis.com; Pinney's Beach; mains lunch US$8-15, dinner US$15-30; ⏰11am-late; 📶) This legendary rum-and-reggae beach joint has been getting people in a party mood for decades. A cold Carib goes well with its 'secret sauce'-marinated grilled ribs and chicken, but the signature 'Killer Bee' rum punch demands your respect: its 'sting' has been documented by hundreds of photos decorating the walls.

★ **Gin Trap Bar & Restaurant** CARIBBEAN $$$
(☎469-8230; www.thegintrapnevis.com; Main Island Rd, Jones Bay; mains US$18-40; ⏰noon-2:30pm & 5-9pm; 📶) Sunset views out to St Kitts are positively dreamy at this worldly farm-to-table outpost with a kitchen showcasing the very best of Caribbean cooking with dishes such as conch chowder with coconut dumplings, island spiced scallops, and shrimp curry. Kick things off in the stylish bar with a jalapeño-laced Gin Trap cocktail before moving on to the louvered dining room.

Chrishi Beach Club INTERNATIONAL $$$
(☎469-5959; www.chrishibeachclub.net; Main Island Rd, Cades Bay; mains US$18-40; ⏰9am-10pm Tue-Sat, 9am-5pm Sun; 📶) A contemporary Caribbean vibe hangs over this Norwegian-owned white beachfront pavilion on a quiet stretch of sand close to the Seabridge car ferry. It's mostly a daytime venue but now also serves dinner in season. Sunday brunch gets busy. The burgers are great; we also like the Deep French Kiss (prosciutto and brie baguette with pesto and pear).

Getting There & Away

Northern Nevis is served by buses that run from Charlestown as far as Newcastle. If you want to go any further than that, you'll need to take a taxi or have your own wheels.

Southern Nevis

The circular island road traverses the lush southern part of Nevis between cloud-shrouded Mt Nevis and Saddle Hill, skirting crumbling sugar mills and plantation estates-turned-hotels. In the east, the population thins out and the sloping green flatlands – once sugarcane plantations – run down to the turbulent Atlantic. It's a desolate and dramatic landscape.

Sights

★ **Botanical Gardens of Nevis** GARDENS
(☎469-3509; www.botanicalgardennevis.com; St John Figtree; adult/child 6-12yr US$13/8; ⏰9am-4pm Mon-Sat, 10:30am–3pm Sun) It's easy to spend a couple of hours wandering around this enchanting symphony of orchids, palms, water-lily ponds, bamboo groves and other global flora interspersed with sculpture, pools, ponds and fountains. In the Rainforest Conservatory parrots patrol the huge tropical plants, waterfalls and Mayan-style sculpture, while in the Great House an excellent Thai restaurant serves lunch. Note that the gardens may close on occasion between mid-August and mid-October – call ahead.

Eden Brown Estate HISTORIC SITE
(btwn Mannings & Lime Kiln) FREE On the remote east coast, this ruined 18th-century sugar plantation has the dubious distinction of being Nevis' most haunted site. The grounds are open but badly overgrown and hard to find.

The year was 1822 and Miss Julia Huggins was all set to get married and move into the estate with her future husband when said husband and his best man killed each other in a duel. Heartbroken, Julia became a recluse and can allegedly still be heard roaming the grounds at night.

White Bay Beach BEACH
Wild and remote White Bay Beach has views across to Montserrat and is the only easily accessible stretch of sand on the south side of Nevis. Backed by morning glory and low scrubby trees, it has fine gray sand and is great for meditative walks and beachcombing. The Atlantic surf should be braved by experienced swimmers or bodysurfers only.

St John's Fig Tree Church CHURCH
(Main Island Rd, Church Ground) This 1680 stone church is famous for displaying – in a glass case in the back – a copy of the marriage record of Horatio Nelson and Fanny Nisbet. If you peek beneath the red carpet in the center aisle, you'll find a continuous row of tombstones of island notables who died in the 1700s.

Nevisian Heritage Village MUSEUM
(☎469-3366; Fothergills Estate, Gingerland; adult/child EC$4/2; ⏰9am-4pm Mon-Fri, by arrangement Sat) This open-air museum illustrates Nevisian social history, from Carib times to the present, through a collection of recreated traditional buildings furnished with

period relics. Exhibits include a Carib chief's thatched hut, slave houses and a blacksmith's shop.

Activities

Upper Round Road Trail HIKING

Built in the late 1600s, this trail once linked the sugar estates, cane fields and villages surrounding Mt Nevis. Today, it travels 9 miles from Golden Rock Inn in the east to Nisbet Plantation Beach Club in the north, past farms, orchards, gardens and rainforest.

Budget about five hours for the entire trek or walk a shorter section. Along the way, sample fresh fruit and observe monkeys and butterflies.

Golden Rock Nature Trail HIKING

(Gingerland) The Golden Rock Inn is the departure point for this easy-to-moderate rainforest hike along a ridgeline and down a gentle ravine past giant ferns and trees. Keep an eye out for troops of vervet monkeys. A free map is available at the inn's reception desk.

Sleeping & Eating

Three plantation estates – one arty, another traditional, the third contemporary – offer wonderful stays on the south of the island that beautifully connect you with Nevis' history and its sweet and unhurried character.

★ **Golden Rock Inn** INN $$$

(☎469-3346; www.goldenrocknevis.com; Gingerland; d incl breakfast from US$250; closed mid-Aug–mid-Oct; P) Fall asleep to a symphony of tree frogs and crickets at this intimate retreat that's perfect for unplugging from the daily grind in comfort while fully cocooned by nature. The 11 cool-classy cottages are tucked into a riotous tropical garden where vervet monkeys chase butterflies. Up above, a good-sized pool and a series of hiking trails beckon.

Hermitage Plantation Inn INN $$$

(☎469-3477; www.hermitagenevis.com; Hermitage Rd, St John Figtree; r incl breakfast US$180-400, cottage US$280-500; P) Country comfort and Caribbean flair combine at this cluster of candy-colored stone cottages set amid beautiful gardens on a former plantation and surrounding what is purportedly the Caribbean's oldest wooden house. Even if you're not staying, swing by to soak up the ambience and a nutmeg-dusted rum punch during its famous West Indian Pig Roast on Wednesdays.

Montpelier Plantation Inn & Beach LUXURY HOTEL $$$

(☎469-3462; www.montpeliernevis.com; St John Figtree; r/ste incl breakfast from US$565/1110; closed mid-Aug–early Oct; P) This blissful hideaway on the estate where Nelson wed Fanny consists of a Great House with a lavish art-, flower- and antique-filled parlor and gardens dotted with modern-colonial-chic bungalows. Despite vestiges from the past, such as the old sugar mill, the overall ambience is classy and contemporary. A private beach is a free 20-minute shuttle-bus ride away.

Eating

Oasis in the Garden THAI $$

(☎469-2875; Botanical Gardens of Nevis, St John Figtree; mains US$18-26; 10am-4pm Mon-Sat, & 6-10pm Fri;) Set on the upper floor of the Great House at the botanical gardens, this Thai restaurant enjoys sweeping views across the island down to the sea, plus gentle breezes and some excellent Thai dishes from a large and varied menu. Reservations for Friday dinner are advisable.

★ **Bananas Restaurant** INTERNATIONAL $$$

(☎469-1891; www.bananasnevis.com; Upper Hamilton Estate, Morning Star village; mains lunch US$18-30, dinner US$28-45; 11am-11pm Mon-Sat, 5-11pm Sun; P) A torchlit walkway leads to this enchanting garden hideaway hand-built by British transplant, former dancer Gillian Smith. Come for a cocktail and the exceptional sunsets upstairs before heading to the animated veranda downstairs and tucking into food inspired by Gillian's travels around the world. Local flavors such as conch gratin, curried goat, salt fish and tannia fritters stuff the menu.

Getting There & Away

Buses run from Charlestown as far as Gingerland, and most places aren't far off the main road. That said, your own car or a taxi is a much better option for exploring this area.

UNDERSTAND ST KITTS & NEVIS

History

Populated by three distinct ethnic groups since around 2900 BC, St Kitts and Nevis were first sighted by Europeans in 1493 during Columbus' second voyage to the New World. The islands were the two oldest British colonies in the Caribbean, established in 1623 and 1628, respectively, until they were united as one entity in the mid-20th century. Like many islands in the region, their growth was fueled by sugar and enslaved Africans who worked on the plantations. Even after St Kitts and Nevis became independent of Britain in 1983, sugar continued to drive the economy until 2005.

Pre-Columbian Period

First inhabited by the Siboney people around 2900 BC, the islands were later settled by the Arawaks in around AD 800, and then later by the Caribs, who arrived around 1300 and were still living on the islands when Columbus sighted them on his second voyage to the New World, in 1493. The island known today as St Kitts was called Liamuiga (Fertile Island) by the Caribs, but Columbus named it St Christopher after his patron saint, later shortened to 'St Kitts.'

Columbus used the Spanish word for 'snow,' *nieve,* to name Nevis, presumably because the clouds shrouding its mountain reminded him of a snowcapped peak. Caribs knew the island as Oualie (Land of Beautiful Waters).

Colonial Times

St Kitts was first colonized by the British under Sir Thomas Warner in 1623, only to be joined soon after by the French, a move the British only tolerated long enough to massacre the indigenous Caribs. In one day, 2000 Caribs were slaughtered, causing blood to run for days at the site still known as Bloody Point.

A century and a half of Franco-British battles culminated in 1782, when a force of 8000 French troops laid siege to the important British stronghold at Brimstone Hill on St Kitts. Although they won this battle, they lost the war and the 1783 Treaty of Paris brought the island firmly under British control.

Nevis had a colonial history similar to St Kitts. In 1628 Warner sent a party of about 100 colonists to establish a British settlement on the west coast of the island. Although the original settlement, near Cotton Ground, fell victim to an earthquake in 1680, Nevis eventually developed one of the most affluent sugar-plantation societies in the Eastern Caribbean. As on St Kitts, most of the island's wealth was built upon the labor of enslaved Africans who toiled in the island's sugarcane fields. Sugar continued to play a role in the local economies until the last plantation closed in 2005.

By the late 18th century, Nevis, buoyed by the attraction of its thermal baths, had become a major retreat for Britain's rich and famous.

Road to Independence

In 1816 the British linked St Kitts and Nevis with Anguilla and the Virgin Islands as a single colony. In 1958 these islands became part of the West Indies Federation, a grand but ultimately unsuccessful attempt to combine all of Britain's Caribbean colonies as a united political entity. When the federation dissolved in 1962, the British opted to lump St Kitts, Nevis and Anguilla together as a new state. Anguilla, fearful of domination by larger St Kitts, revolted against the occupying Royal St Kitts Police Force in 1967 and returned to Britain as an overseas territory.

In 1983 St Kitts and Nevis became a single nation within the British Commonwealth, with the stipulation that Nevis could secede at any time. In the 1990s a period of corruption on St Kitts and pro-independence on Nevis almost brought an end to the federation. A referendum held on Nevis in 1998, however, failed to produce a two-third majority needed to break away.

Looking Ahead

St Kitts has in recent years seen the construction of several big new residential and leisure developments on the island's previously uninhabited southeast peninsula, chief among them Christophe Harbour, a high-end residential area with villas, a private-member beach club, a superyacht marina and a Tom Fazio–designed golf course. The area is also home to a new Park Hyatt resort, the brand's first in the Caribbean. A new tunnel and resurfaced road have also been completed, making it a breeze to reach this once rather remote area of the island. Elsewhere on the island, the big news is the planned reopening of the famous Ottley Plantation, a controversial change of style for what was once one of St Kitt's most traditional hotels, now set to reopen as an ultraluxurious and contemporary resort.

Nevis, on the other hand, continues to look to its past as the island's greatest asset. The expanded Nevis Heritage Trail goes a long way toward education and heritage preservation, as do the island's three charming plantation hotels. Unlike its glitzier neighbor, there is no appetite on Nevis for significant development such as new resorts or the construction of a cruise terminal.

People & Culture

Although the population of St Kitts and Nevis is predominantly (90%) of African descent, culturally the islands draw upon a mix of European, African and West Indian traditions.

Rather than selling their soul and identity to mass tourism, both islands still exude unhurried Caribbean flair. Walk through a residential area on St Kitts on any given night and locals will be out in the streets, listening to reggae or calypso blaring out of homes and chatting with friends. On weekends, villagers on Nevis organize communal barbecues.

Kittitians are obsessed with cricket. Both international matches as well as those featuring the national Caribbean Premier League team, the St Kitts and Nevis Patriots, are played at Warner Stadium in Basseterre.

Landscape & Wildlife

Both islands have grassy coastal areas, a consequence of deforestation for sugar production. Forests tend to be vestiges of the large rainforests that once covered much of the islands, or they are second-growth.

Away from developed areas, the climate allows a huge array of beautiful plants to thrive, especially on Nevis. Flowers such as plumeria, hibiscus and chains-of-love are common along roadsides and in garden landscaping.

Nevis is fairly circular and the entire island benefits from runoff from Mt Nevis. St Kitts' shape resembles a tadpole. The main body is irrigated by water from the mountain ranges. However, this is of little value to the geographically isolated, arid southeast peninsula, which is covered with sparse, desert-like cacti and yucca.

Aside from the vervet monkey, a ubiquitous creature is the mongoose, imported from Jamaica by plantation owners to rid their sugarcane fields of snakes. Both islands provide plenty of avian life for birdwatchers.

As two small islands in a region with a hurricane season that unleashes increasingly extreme weather events, St Kitts and Nevis is particularly threatened by climate change and the government has committed the country to developing sustainable tourism. The islands boast four national parks, two marine parks and a bird sanctuary, and new hotel and housing developments have to go through stringent approval processes to ensure their environmental impact is limited.

SURVIVAL GUIDE

Directory A–Z

ACCESSIBLE TRAVEL

International resorts generally have good accommodations for people with disabilities. Otherwise, both of the islands are something of a challenge. Fortunately, almost everything of interest can be reached directly by car. The

WILD VERVET MONKEYS

You'll see them on the beach, the trail and the golf course – packs of wild vervet monkeys brought from Africa to St Kitts and Nevis by French settlers in the 17th century. Since then, they have flourished so well that they outnumber humans two to one. They may look cute and are even used in promoting the islands to tourists, but to local farmers they're a nightmare because of their ravenous appetite for fruit and vegetable crops.

In order to get the problem under control, a nonprofit company called Arnova Sustainable Future has partnered with the Department of Agriculture to set up feeding stations on the upper slopes to curb the incentive to come down from the mountain to forage for food at lower-lying farms. Other planned measures include a spay and neuter program as well as taste, smell and hearing aversions.

Meanwhile, the Kittitian monkey population is being further reduced by trapping and selling the animals to medical research and testing laboratories worldwide, despite vocal international campaigns against the practice. Two such facilities on St Kitts also use vervet monkeys in their research.

SLEEPING PRICE RANGES

The following prices ranges refer to a double room with bathroom. Unless otherwise stated, breakfast is not included in the price.

$ less than US$100

$$ US$100–250

$$$ more than US$250

must-see Brimstone Hill Fortress has both accessible and inaccessible areas.

ACCOMMODATIONS

There are large resorts on both islands, but most accommodations are still small- to medium-sized hotels, plantation inns, guesthouses and apartment rentals. The government-mandated hotel tax (10%) and a 10% service fee are usually not included in quoted rates; always check what's included when making a reservation.

CHILDREN

Children receive a warm welcome on St Kitts and Nevis. Many restaurants have kids' menus or are happy to cook up simple dishes. Larger resorts provide organized children's activities, kids' clubs and day-care or babysitting.

Most beaches are safe for children to play on and many of the beaches are calm enough for younger swimmers. Older kids enjoy water sports, zip-lining, historical fortresses, guided hikes and bike trips.

ELECTRICITY

220V, 60 cycles; North American–style two-pin sockets.

EMERGENCY NUMBERS

Ambulance	☎911
Fire	☎333
Police	☎911

FOOD

Eating in St Kitts and Nevis is more often than not a farm-to-table and sea-to-table experience, and a palate-rewarding endeavor at all budget levels. Even at roadside stands and humble snackettes you can often fill up for little. On Nevis, some of the best food is served at the restaurants of the plantation inns, though prices rise steeply there.

Essential Food & Drink

Stewed saltfish Official national dish; served with spicy plantains, coconut dumplings and seasoned breadfruit.

Pelau Also known as 'cook-up,' this dish is the Kittitian version of paella: a tasty but messy blend of rice, meat, saltfish, vegetables and pigeon peas.

Conch Served curried, marinated or soused (boiled).

Cane Spirit Rothschild More commonly known as CSR, this locally distilled libation is made from pure fermented cane juice and best enjoyed on the rocks mixed with grapefruit-flavored Ting soda, another local treasure.

Brinley Gold Rum This locally blended rum comes in such flavors as vanilla, coffee, mango, coconut and lime.

Tannia fritters These gorgeous root vegetable fritters are a much-loved accompaniment to any Kittitian meal.

EATING PRICE RANGES

The following price ranges refer to a main course.

$ less than US$10

$$ US$10–25

$$$ more than US$25

HEALTH

For minor illnesses, nearly all hotels will have a doctor on call or will be able to help you find assistance. Health care is expensive and the standard of the medical equipment and facilities locally is not particularly high, although a brand-new private hospital is currently under construction at Christophe Harbour on St Kitts. At present anything but minor surgeries and other simple treatments must be performed outside the islands. The CDA Technical Institute of the West Indies on Bay Rd in Basseterre operates two hyperbaric chambers.

Alexandra Hospital (p676) Nevis' small hospital can only handle minor surgeries and procedures.

Joseph N France General Hospital (p668) Main hospital on St Kitts with emergency room and trauma department.

INTERNET ACCESS

Nearly all hotels, restaurants, cafes, bars and even many businesses provide free wi-fi for their guests.

LEGAL MATTERS

St Kitts and Nevis' legal system is based on British common law. In case of legal difficulties, you have the right to legal representation and are eligible for legal aid if you can't afford to pay for private services. Foreign nationals should receive the same legal protections as local citizens.

Note that you can get fined for using foul language in public and that wearing camouflage clothing is illegal.

LGBT+ TRAVELERS

There is no real gay and lesbian scene on St Kitts and Nevis and, though rare, discrimination does occur. Avoid public displays of affection, especially outside the resorts. Officially, homosexual 'acts' between men (though not women) are on the books as being punishable with up to 10 years' imprisonment. However, the law is not enforced.

MONEY

St Kitts and Nevis use the Eastern Caribbean dollar (EC$), but US dollars are widely accepted. However, unless rates are posted in US dollars, as is the norm with accommodations, some restaurants and dive shops, it usually works out better to use EC dollars. If you pay in US dollars, you will normally get change in EC dollars.

There are several banks with ATMs on or near the Circus in Basseterre. In Charlestown, banks line Main St. There's also an ATM at both airports. All dispense Eastern Caribbean dollars, while some also offer US dollars.

Credit cards are widely accepted at hotels, restaurants and shops, although the smaller a business, the less likely it will take plastic.

Exchange Rates

Australia	A$1	EC$1.94
Canada	C$1	EC$2.03
Euro zone	€1	EC$3.05
Japan	¥100	EC$2.41
New Zealand	NZ$1	EC$1.81
UK	UK£1	EC$3.52
US	US$1	EC$2.71

For current exchange rates, see www.xe.com.

Tipping

Hotels US$0.50 to US$1 per bag is standard; gratuity for cleaning staff is at your discretion.

Restaurants If the service charge is not automatically added to the bill, tip 10% to 15%; if it is included, it's up to you to leave a little extra.

Taxi Tip 10% to 15% of the fare.

PUBLIC HOLIDAYS

New Year's Day January 1
Good Friday/Easter Monday March/April
Labor Day First Monday in May
Pentecost/Whit Monday Forty days after Easter
Emancipation Day First Monday in August
Culturama Day August 8
National Hero's Day September 16
Independence Day September 19
Christmas Day December 25
Boxing Day December 26

TELEPHONE

The country code for St Kitts and Nevis is 869. To call from North America, dial 1 + 869 + local number. From elsewhere, dial your country's international access code + 869 + local number.

To call abroad from St Kitts and Nevis, dial 011 + country code + area code + local number. If making a call within or between the islands, you only need to dial the seven-digit local number. For directory assistance, dial 411.

In hotels, local calls are often free but international calls are charged at exorbitant rates.

Cell Phones

The two cell (mobile) phone operators in St Kitts & Nevis are **Digicel** (www.digicelgroup.com/kn) and **Flow** (https://discoverflow.co/saint-kitts). Both have offices in Basseterre and Charlestown where you can buy good-value SIM cards and data/calling packages.

TIME

Clocks in St Kitts and Nevis are set to Atlantic Time, which is four hours behind GMT. The islands do not observe daylight saving time.

VOLUNTEERING

Nevis Turtle Group (www.nevisturtlegroup.org) Needs volunteers to collect information

PRACTICALITIES

Newspapers The main local newspaper is the weekly *St Kitts Nevis Observer.*

Radio For Caribbean sounds, turn to Sugar City 90.3FM, ZIZ 96FM and Winn 98.9FM.

Smoking St Kitts and Nevis do not have any antismoking legislation, but tobacco use is not common among locals and most hotels and resorts ban smoking indoors.

Weights & measures The imperial system is used.

DRINKING WATER

It's perfectly fine to drink the local tap water, though many locals filter it. However, the US-based Center for Disease Control (CDC) recommends bottled water, which is cheap and widely available.

about turtles nesting on beaches from June to October.

Getting There & Away

AIR

Robert L Bradshaw International Airport (SKB; ☎465-8121; Basseterre) is on the northeastern outskirts of Basseterre. It is served seasonally by Air Canada (Toronto), American Airlines (Miami, New York City, Charlotte), British Airways (London-Gatwick), Delta (Atlanta) and United Airlines (New York-Newark).

Regional carrier LIAT (www.liat.com; Robert L Bradshaw International Airport) provides year-round services to Antigua, Tortola, US Virgin Islands, St-Martin/Sint Maarten, St Croix and San Juan. Trans Anguilla Airways flies to Anguilla.

Nevis' diminutive **Vance Armory International Airport** (NEV; ☎469-9040; www.nevisports.com; Newcastle) is in Newcastle, on the island's northeastern edge, and is only served by such regional airlines as **Winair** (www.fly-winair.com; St-Martin/Sint Maarten), Air Sunshine (Anguilla, St Thomas, Virgin Gorda, Tortola, Dominica), Seaborne Airlines (San Juan) and Tradewind Aviation (St-Barths, San Juan).

SEA

Cruise Ship

Scores of cruise ships on Eastern Caribbean itineraries visit St Kitts. Sometimes two or three of these behemoths are docked at Basseterre's deepwater-harbor **cruise-ship terminal** (Port Zante). On those days, the beaches in the south or the St Kitts Scenic Railway get very busy. Independent travelers might want to check the cruise-ship schedule (eg at www.cruisetimetables.com/cruises-to-basseterre-st-kitts.html) to plan their itinerary accordingly.

Nevis lacks a dock that can handle the big ships, so visits are limited to passengers brought ashore by tender from small ships (usually under 300 passengers) anchored offshore, or those on day excursions from St Kitts.

Yacht

St Kitts and Nevis are right on the Eastern Caribbean yachting circuit, although their lack of natural harbors like those on Antigua keep the numbers of people mooring for any period of length low.

The two ports of entry are Basseterre and Charlestown. There's a customs office at Zante Marina in Basseterre, while the immigration office is at the adjacent cruise-ship terminal. Open since 2015, the ultraluxe Christophe Harbour marina is tailor-made for superyachts and has its own customs house.

Vessels headed for Nevis must contact the port authority in order to be assigned a mooring within 24 hours of arrival. Customs and immigration are near the ferry dock in Charlestown.

If moving between St Kitts and Nevis, no special clearance is required.

Getting Around

AIR

Winair offers daily scheduled flights between St Kitts and Nevis.

BOAT

St Kitts and Nevis are linked by passenger ferry between Basseterre and Charlestown, by car ferry between Majors Bay and Cades Bay, and by on-demand water taxis between Cockleshell Beach and Oualie Beach.

Car Ferry

The **Seabridge car ferry** (☎662-7002, 662-9565; car EC$100, passengers EC$20; ⏱7am-7pm) service links Majors Bay in the south of St Kitts with Cades Bay on Nevis' northwest coast in 30 minutes (EC$100 per car).

There are six scheduled departures in either direction from Monday to Saturday and three on Sunday. The first ferry leaves Cades Bay at 7am and Majors Bay at 8am; the last at 6pm and 7pm, respectively. The schedule often runs late and services may get cancelled because of bad weather. If demand is high, the captain sometimes runs an additional trip.

If you have a rental car, check with your rental company if you're allowed to take it across to the other island. Cars must be backed onto the ferry and parked with just a few inches between them. Ask one of the deckhands to help you, if necessary.

Passenger Ferry

Six passenger ferries shuttle between Basseterre (Bay Rd) and Charlestown. The trip takes about 45 minutes, costs EC$26/16 per adult/child and is both a pleasant and scenic way to travel. The main companies are **MV Mark Twain/Sea Hustler** (☎469-0403; adult/child EC$26/10) and **MV Caribe Breeze/Caribe Surf** (☎466-6734; fare EC$16-26).

The actual schedule varies day by day, but there's roughly one sailing per hour. Ask at your hotel, call 466-4636 or text 'Ferry' to 7568 to get the day's schedule on your cell phone.

Tickets are sold from about 30 minutes before sailings. It's a good idea to arrive early as some boats sell out.

Water Taxi

Using a water-taxi service between the islands can be a good way to go if you want to be independent. Boats run between Reggae Beach Bar (p671) on Cockleshell Beach, St Kitts, and Oualie Beach (p677) on Nevis. The cost for the 10-minute trip costs US$20 to US$30 per person, usually with a two-person minimum. Rides should be scheduled in advance, though it's often possible to just show up and arrange a crossing.

Local operators include the following:

Black Fin	663-3301
Perfect Life	663-3595
Sea Brat	662-9166

BUS

Government-licensed private minivans serve communities on an erratic schedule along the main roads. All have green license plates starting with 'H' or 'HA' and many are hilariously painted and festooned with names such as 'De Punisher' or 'Love Bug.'

Buses can be boarded at designated stops in Basseterre and Charlestown or flagged down anywhere along the route. Service is more frequent in the morning and in the afternoon, and all but stops around 7pm or 8pm. Sunday service is less frequent.

Fares cost EC$2.50 to EC$5 and are payable to the driver. Sometimes it's possible to pay a little extra to be dropped off at places off the main route.

St Kitts

There is no bus service south to Frigate Bay and beyond and in the far north between St Paul's and Ottley's.

Basseterre has two bus terminals:

West Bus Terminal (Bay Rd) Buses heading up the west coast as far as St Paul's.

Baker's Corner bus terminal (Cayon St) Buses heading east as far as Saddlers.

Nevis

From Charlestown, buses travel both clockwise and counterclockwise along the Main Island Rd. Buses leave when full, but they only go as far as Newcastle in the north and Gingerland in the south.

Memorial Square bus stop (p676) Destinations south of Charlestown.

Delisle Walwyn Plaza bus stop (p676) Destinations north of Charlestown.

CAR & MOTORCYCLE

A local driving permit, available from car-rental agencies, is required for driving on St Kitts and Nevis. It costs US$24 or EC$62.50 and is valid on both islands for three months.

Driving is on the left side of the road. The speed limit is posted in miles per hour and is generally 20mph in built-up areas and 40mph on highways.

There are no traffic lights on either island but traffic circles are common.

If you have an accident, call the police and don't move the vehicle.

Car Rental

Rental companies will usually meet you at the airport, ferry port or your hotel. Daily rates start at about US$45. You really won't need a 4WD for going anywhere – unless it's rainy season. Most of the major international firms have local affiliates.

Local St Kitts companies:

Avis (465-6507; www.avis.com; Bay Rd, Basseterre; 8am-5pm Mon-Fri, to noon Sat, 9-11am Sun)

Sunny Blue Scooter Rentals (664-8755; www.sunnybluerental.com; Pond Rd, Basseterre)

Local Nevis companies:

1st Choice Car Rental (469-1131; www.neviscarrental.com; Shaws Rd, Newcastle)

Nevis Car Rentals (469-9837; www.neviscarrentals.com; Shaws Rd, Newcastle; per day from US$45; 7am-7pm)

Strikers Car Rental (469-2654; www.strikerscarrentals.com; Hermitage Rd, St John's)

TAXI

Taxis on St Kitts and Nevis are usually minibuses with yellow license plates beginning with 'T' or 'TA.' Fares are regulated by the government, with one tariff applying to up to four passengers. However, it's best to confirm the price (and which currency is quoted) before riding away. Service between 10pm and 6am adds 50% extra.

Taxis meet scheduled flights on both islands. Taxi island tours on both islands cost around US$80. Those short on time can take a three-hour half-island tour for US$60.

ROBERTO MOIOLA/GETTY IMAGES ©

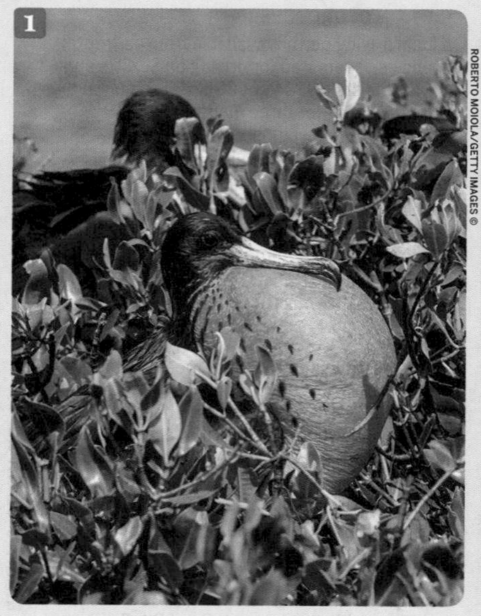

1. Frigate birds, Barbuda **2.** Mayreau, Grenadines **3.** Loblolly Beach, Anegada **4.** Scuba diving off Little Cayman

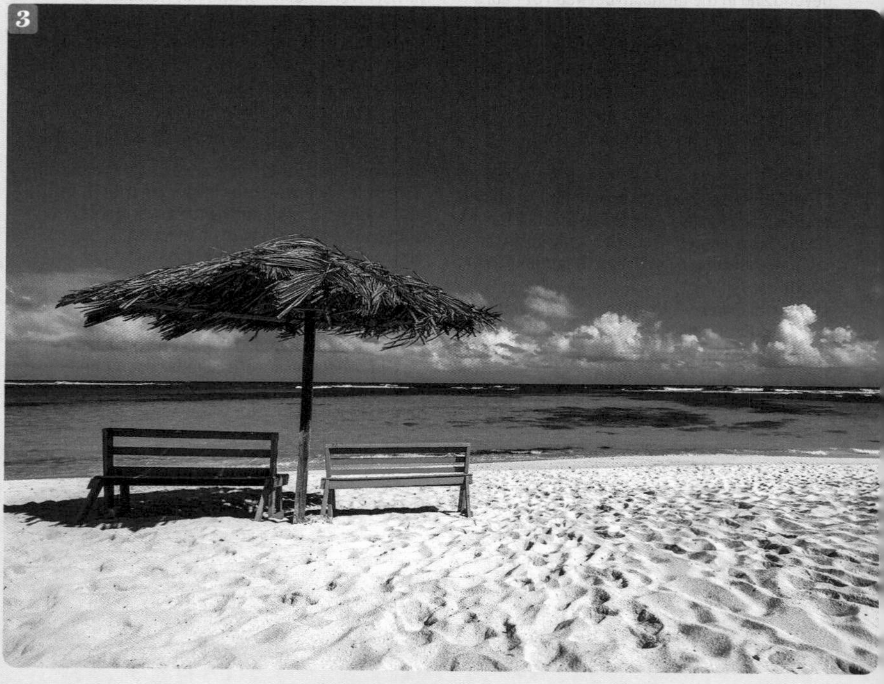

KENKISTLER/SHUTTERSTOCK ©

Hidden Caribbean

While more than 90% of the Caribbean's 7000 islands are minute and uninhabited, these are largely inaccessible to the average traveler. But there is a small club of islands well off the tourist track that are *almost* uninhabited, offering the adventurous traveler the kind of escape many dream about.

Little Cayman

Little Cayman has a population that barely cracks three figures – and that's the iguanas. Come here for some of the world's best wall diving.

Mayreau

A double crescent of perfect beaches awaits on Mayreau, an island near the southern end of the Grenadines. The killer diving at Tobago Cays is nearby and it's possible to rent a room in a home.

Anegada

The nicknames of Anegada say it all: 'Mysterious Virgin' and 'Ghost Cay.' Hang your hammock in this magical, remote bit of sand in the British Virgin Islands.

Barbuda

Frigate birds outnumber humans on Barbuda, an island that's happy to remain in the shadow of Antigua. Some beach cottages can only be reached by boat.

Petit Martinique

Grenada itself isn't exactly on the beaten path, and its island of Petit Martinique is almost unknown. The little beach here is just 10 minutes by foot from the guesthouses serving the island.

St Lucia

☎758 / POP 178,696

Includes ➡

Best Places to Eat

- ➡ Coal Pot (p691)
- ➡ Orlando's (p702)
- ➡ Boucan (p702)
- ➡ Elena's (p694)
- ➡ Spice of India (p695)
- ➡ Flavours of the Grill (p695)

Best Places to Stay

- ➡ East Winds Inn (p694)
- ➡ Boucan (p702)
- ➡ Cap Maison (p697)
- ➡ Balenbouche Estate (p703)
- ➡ Ladera (p702)
- ➡ Fond Doux Resort & Plantation (p701)

Why Go?

Blessed by nature, St Lucia has geographic and cultural riches enough to embarrass far bigger nations. Notwithstanding, it remains a down-to-earth place that wears its breathtaking beauty with nonchalance.

Noted for its oodles of small and luxurious resorts that drip color and flair, it is really two islands in one. Rodney Bay in the north offers lazy days and modern comforts amid a beautiful bay. In the south, Soufrière is at the heart of a gorgeous region of old plantations, hidden beaches and the geologic wonder of the impossibly photogenic Pitons.

Nature lovers can hike to jungle-clad waterfalls, climb extinct volcanic cones and zip through the forest canopy on land, or dive beneath the calm Caribbean to get up close to St Lucia's marine life. Foodies will be enamored with the island's delicious Creole cuisine.

When to Go

Nov–Apr High season: the driest months (February to April) are the most popular. Short periods of rainfall at this time.

May Shoulder season: this is a good time to visit, with dry weather and fewer crowds. Most businesses are open but prices are generally lower

Jun–Oct Rainy season: many businesses close; hurricane season peaks in August and September. October is Creole Heritage Month, with events all over the island.

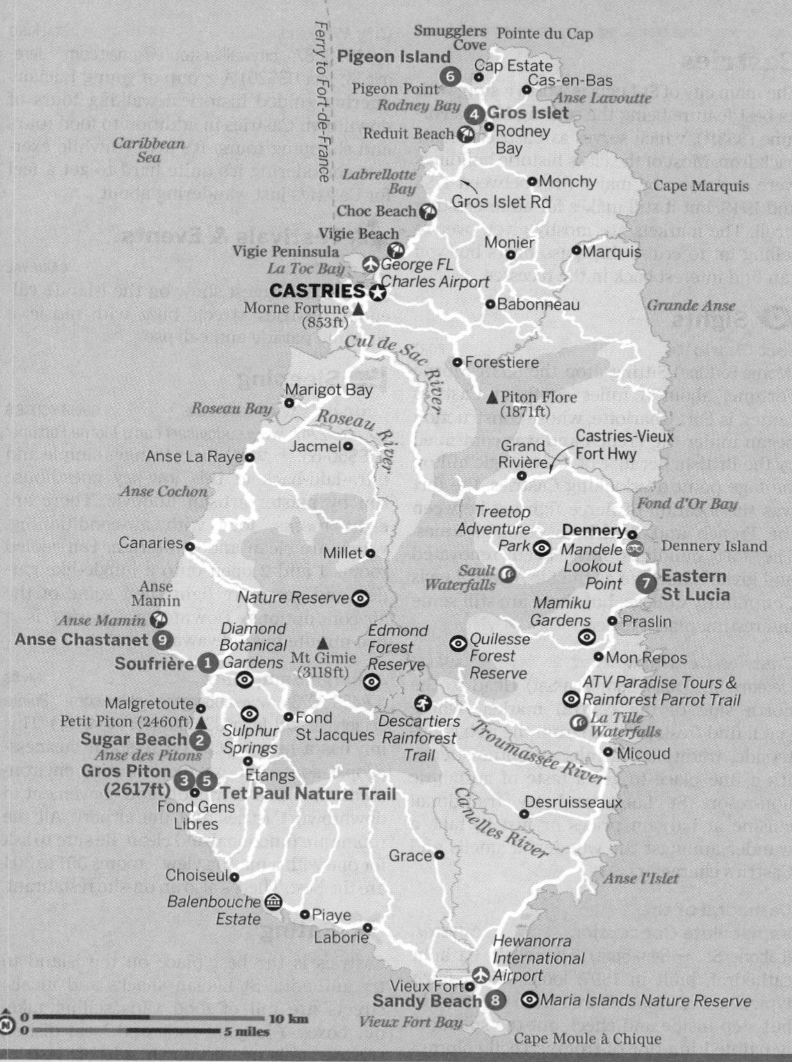

St Lucia Highlights

1. **Soufrière** (p699) Heritage hunting among the grand estates.
2. **Sugar Beach** (p699) Sipping a cocktail on one of the Caribbean's most dramatic stretches of sand.
3. **Gros Piton** (p701) Huffing up the steep trail for astounding views.
4. **Gros Islet** (p693) Dancing the night away at the famous Friday-night bash.
5. **Tet Paul Nature Trail** (p700) Enjoying a hike through some of the island's most gorgeous landscapes.
6. **Pigeon Island** (p696) Picnicking on the beach beneath wonderful ruins.
7. **Eastern St Lucia** (p697) Driving through the fishing villages to hidden waterfalls and lush gardens.
8. **Sandy Beach** (p704) Kiteboarding across the brilliant blue waters.
9. **Anse Chastanet** (p699) Snorkeling or diving in the fish-filled waters.

Castries

The main city of St Lucia is worth a stop, with its best feature being the soaring Morne Fortune (853ft), which serves as Castries' scenic backdrop. Most of the city's historic buildings were destroyed by major fires between 1785 and 1948, but it still makes for an interesting stroll. The markets are mostly given over to selling tat to cruise-ship passengers but you can find interest back in the recesses.

Sights

Fort Charlotte FORT

(Morne Fortune) Sitting atop the 853ft Morne Fortune, about 3 miles south of Castries center, is Fort Charlotte, whose construction began under the French and was continued by the British. Because of its strategic hilltop vantage point overlooking Castries, the fort was the location of fierce fighting between the French and British in colonial times. The fort buildings have been renovated and given a new life as the Sir Arthur Lewis Community College, but there are still some interesting places to see.

Castries Central Market MARKET

(Jeremie St; 6am-5pm Mon-Sat) Head to the north side of the central market, where you'll find fresh produce from the rich countryside, traditional drinks and other items. It's a fine place to get a taste of authentic non-resort St Lucia and try traditional cuisine at bargain prices or just to take a wander amongst the wonderful smells and Castries characters.

Cathedral of the Immaculate Conception CATHEDRAL

(Laborie St; 8am-5pm) The city's Catholic cathedral, built in 1897, looks like a fairly typical grand stone church from the outside, but step inside and check out the splendidly painted interior of trompe l'oeil columns and colorfully detailed biblical scenes. The island's patron saint, St Lucia, is portrayed directly above the altar. When children's choirs are practicing, it's magical.

Activities & Tours

Hackshaw's BOATING

(453-0553; www.hackshaws.com; Seraphine Rd, Vigie) Hackshaw's runs a variety of boat tours including whale- and dolphin-watching outings (from US$69) as well as deep-sea fishing trips (from US$95).

City Walkers WALKING

(451-8687; citywalkerstours@gmail.com; Jeremie St; tour US$20) A group of young Lucians offering guided historical walking tours of downtown Castries in addition to food tours and shopping tours. It's a worthwhile exercise considering it's quite hard to get a feel for Castries just wandering about.

Festivals & Events

Carnival CARNIVAL

(Jul) The biggest show on the island's calendar. Castries' streets buzz with music, a costume parade and calypso.

Sleeping

Eudovic's Guesthouse GUESTHOUSE $

(452-2747; www.eudovicart.com; Morne Fortune; r US$60-65;) Everything is simple and ultra-laid-back at this low-key guesthouse run by master artisan Eudovic. There are eight rooms, four with air-conditioning, which are clean and utilitarian. Fan-cooled rooms 1 and 2 open onto a jungle-like garden and get more light than some of the air-con options. Downtown Castries is a five-minute bus ride away.

Auberge Seraphine INN $$

(453-2073; www.aubergeseraphine.com; Pointe Seraphine; s/d from US$130/145;) This inn has a heavy focus on regional businesspeople, so it's not exactly a vacation environment, though it is friendly and convenient to downtown Castries and the airport. All the rooms are functional and clean. Be sure to ask for one with a marina view – rooms 301 to 304 are the best. There's also an on-site restaurant.

Eating

Castries is the best place on the island to try authentic St Lucian snacks and meals; streets are full of food vans selling takeout boxes. For good rotis and local dishes, try the stalls on the north side of Castries Central Market where you can get a plate with all the sides for around EC$15. After-dark options are limited to mostly take-out chains and cafes.

Livity VEGAN $

(722-3660; Jeremie St; juices EC$7-12, rotis EC$12, mains EC$20; 7am-6pm Mon-Thu, to 3pm Fri) Bright and with wonderful energy, this vegan restaurant, smoothie bar and bakery is one of the best of its kind in the Windward Islands and is worth a trip to Castries just to try. In addition to daily changing specials, it has inventive rotis filled with a choice of a dozen different types of legumes and vegetables, and excellent baked goods.

★**Pink Plantation House** CREOLE $$
(☎452-5422; Chef Harry Dr, Morne Fortune; mains EC$45-89; ⊙11:30am-3pm Mon-Fri, 6:30-9pm Fri, 11:30am-3pm Sat, 9am-3pm Sun) This art gallery housed in a splendid colonial mansion sitting on a lush property doubles as a fantastic restaurant that serves outstanding traditional Creole cuisine based on fresh island produce. The views from the veranda are to die for. The Sunday breakfast spread, at EC$65, is unmissable. Wonderful cocktails, too.

Coal Pot CARIBBEAN $$
(☎452-5566; Vigie Cove; mains EC$47-96; ⊙noon-3pm & 6:30-9pm Mon-Sat, 6:30-10pm Sun) Follow the road around the harbor to find this little hidden open-air gem. It's right on the water and far enough from town that the tranquility of the sea lulls you into a diner's dream. The cooking is modern French-Creole, with fresh produce and local spices combining in dishes bursting with flavor.

Shopping

★**Eudovic's Art Studio** ART
(☎452-2747; www.eudovicart.com; Morne Fortune; ⊙8am-4:30pm Mon-Fri, to 2pm Sat & Sun) Vincent Joseph Eudovic is a renowned master carver, and his studio at Morne Fortune is a magnificent art gallery. The craftsman is now in his seventies and doesn't work as much anymore but his son Jallim has followed in his father's footsteps and is very active. You can watch the carvers in action in the workshop.

Caribelle Batik ARTS & CRAFTS
(☎452-3785; Howelton Estate, Morne Fortune; ⊙8am-5pm Mon-Sat) Housed in an enticing Victorian Caribbean mansion nestled amid lush tropical gardens, this working batik studio is a feast for the eyes. All the batik items incorporate tropical motifs and are handmade downstairs. There is also a variety of items (purses, bags, jewelry) made by other artisans around the island. Make sure to visit the rear balcony for amazing views over town.

Information

Most banks have branches with ATMs in the center.

Tapion Hospital (☎459-2000; www.tapion-hospital.com; Tapion Rd, La Toc) St Lucia's best private medical facility.

Getting There & Away

BUS

Frustratingly, bus services in Castries don't depart from one central location but rather from dedicated stops spread around the city.

Buses for **Gros Islet** (Darling Rd) and Rodney Bay depart from the northern side of town, a block away from the market, while those to **Vieux Fort** (Lower Hospital Rd) and the south depart from the other side on Lower Hospital Rd.

Soufrière buses (Jeremie St) leave from the south side of the market, while **Morne Fortune** (St Louis St) services are found in the center of town.

TAXI

There are many taxi ranks within central Castries. The one on Bridge St is generally manned by friendly older gentlemen who charge fair prices right off the bat.

Always ask hotels and restaurants to call a cab on your behalf.

Castries Region

Going north past George FL Charles Airport along Gros Islet Rd from Vigie Peninsula, the oceanside highway snakes its way to Rodney Bay. This stretch is far busier and more built-up than any other area in St Lucia.

Heading south from Castries the old highway quickly begins to wind up into the hills, passing scenic La Toc.

Sights

Choc Beach BEACH
A promontory separates Vigie and Choc Bays. The southern section of this long swath of honey-colored sand is flanked by the highway (noise!) but if you walk to the north it gets much quieter.

Vigie Beach BEACH
This 2-mile beach runs parallel to the George FL Charles Airport runway. Vigie Beach is where you can find locals taking a quick dip on hot days. The color of the sand? Brown-gray.

La Toc Beach BEACH
South of Castries, this splendid golden-sand beach remains largely off the tourist radar, not least because it's a bit hard to find. Go in the direction of Morne Fortune, then head to

Castries

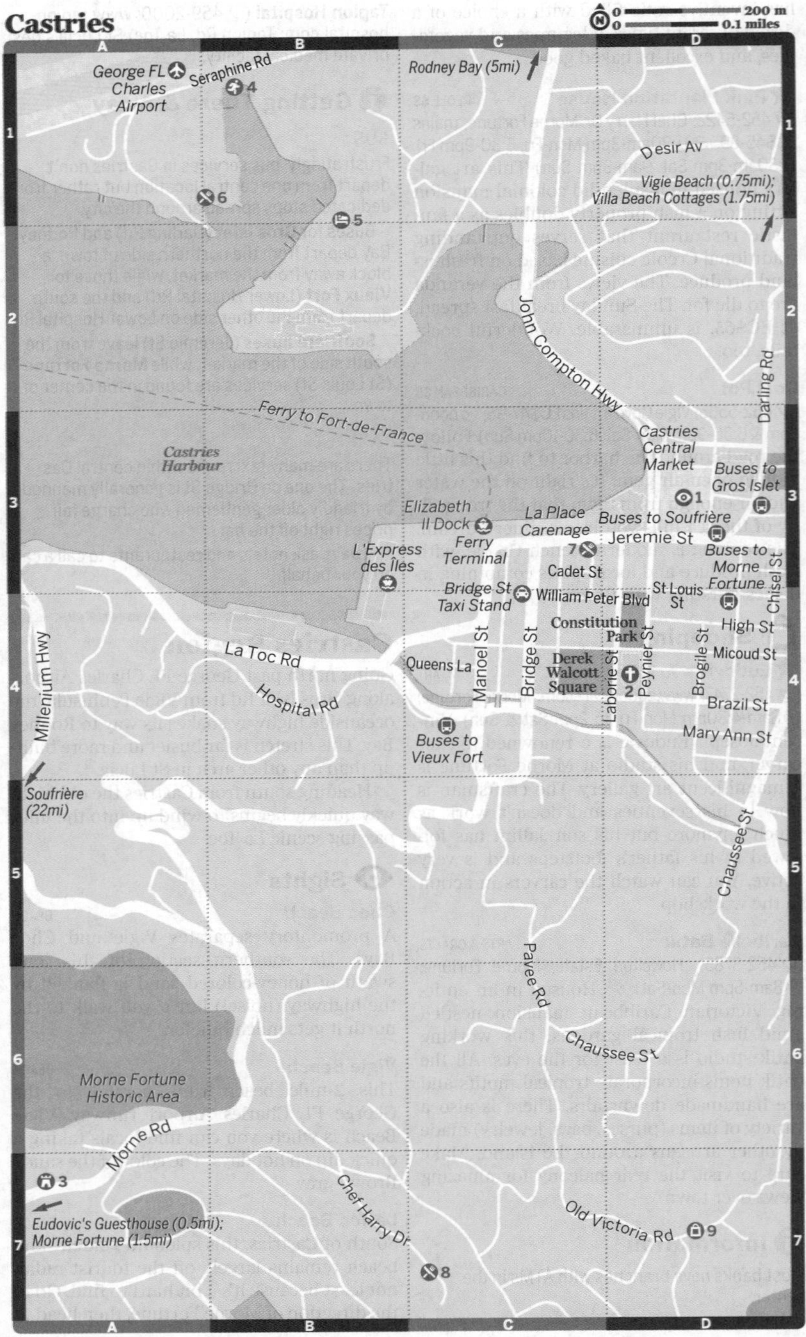

0 200 m
0 0.1 miles

A B C D

1 2 3 4 5 6 7

George FL Charles Airport
Seraphine Rd
4
6
5
Rodney Bay (5mi)
Desir Av
Vigie Beach (0.75mi); Villa Beach Cottages (1.75mi)
John Compton Hwy
Darling Rd
Ferry to Fort-de-France
Castries Harbour
Castries Central Market
Buses to Gros Islet
1
Elizabeth II Dock
Ferry Terminal
La Place Carenage
Buses to Soufrière
Jeremie St
L'Express des Îles
7
Cadet St
Buses to Morne Fortune
Chisel St
Bridge St Taxi Stand
William Peter Blvd
St Louis St
Constitution Park
High St
La Toc Rd
Queens La
Manoel St
Bridge St
Derek Walcott Square
Laborie St
2
Peynier St
Brogile St
Micoud St
Hospital Rd
Brazil St
Millenium Hwy
Buses to Vieux Fort
Mary Ann St
Soufrière (22mi)
Chaussee St
Pavee Rd
Chaussee St
Morne Fortune Historic Area
Morne Rd
3
Chef Harry Dr
Eudovic's Guesthouse (0.5mi); Morne Fortune (1.5mi)
Old Victoria Rd
9
8

Castries

Sights

Activities, Courses & Tours

Sleeping

Eating

Shopping

the lower gate of the Sandals Regency Golf Resort & Spa, where the guards will show you the path that leads down to the beach.

Sleeping

Villa Beach Cottages HOTEL $$$
(☎450-2884; www.villabeachcottages.com; Choc Bay; 1-bed villas US$285-340) Offering around a dozen spacious and elegantly furnished villas, this polished place on Choc Beach is more personal than some of the bigger resorts and offers outstanding value. All rooms have full kitchens, comfy living spaces and private balconies overlooking the sea. The only downside: it's right on the main road.

Getting There & Away

With Castries being the transport hub of the island, local buses pass through all areas surrounding the capital. Most attractions around Castries can also be reached by taxi for around EC$30 to EC$40.

Rodney Bay & Gros Islet

About 6 miles north of Castries, the vast horseshoe of Rodney Bay boasts the island's most diverse tourist facilities. Within the bay is a large, artificial lagoon and marina, flanked by Rodney Bay Village, a somewhat bland assemblage of bars, restaurants and shops.

Far more interesting is the fishing village of Gros Islet to the north. Here the historic streets are lined with rum shops and fishing shacks draped with drying nets.

Sights

Reduit Beach BEACH
(Rodney Bay) This long stretch of white sand is the most popular beach on the island. The sea ranges from turquoise to azure, the waves are benign and there are plenty of beach activities and cafes at hand. The central part of the beach gets mobbed, so head to the south end on the far side of the vast Rex Resorts. It's less crowded and has more shade.

Activities

Boating

Seeing St Lucia from the sea is a real treat. Several companies organize day sails and motorboat trips (from US$110) along the west coast from Rodney Bay. Sunset cruises are also hugely popular.

Endless Summer Cruises CRUISE
(☎450-8651; www.stluciaboattours.com; Rodney Bay Marina; cruises US$85-110) A popular operator with full-day sailing trips down to Soufrière as well as sunset cruises. Also offers catered charter trips.

Sea Spray Cruises BOATING
(www.seaspraycruises.com; Rodney Bay Marina; cruises US$66-195) A reliable operator offering a variety of boat cruises including complete day trips to Soufrière.

Diving & Snorkeling

There are several dive sites and snorkeling spots of note off the northwestern coast. You'll find dive operators in many of the larger resorts.

Eastern Caribbean Diving DIVING
(☎456-9581; www.easterncaribbeandivingstlucia.com; Windjammer Resort) Offers dive outings to Anse Cochon and Soufrière, as well as snorkeling trips. A two-tank dive costs from US$138 (gear included).

Scuba Steve's Diving DIVING
(☎450-9433; www.scubastevesdiving.com; Flamboyant Dr, Rodney Bay; 2-tank dives from US$85; 👪) Offers dives across the island and snorkel trips (US$60 to US$75). It's located inside the Harmony Suites hotel.

Tours

Rainforest Adventures ADVENTURE
(☎458-5151; www.rainforestadventure.com; Chassin; tours from US$50; ⊙9am-3pm Mon-Fri & Sun) Enjoy the rainforest from a Tarzan perspective? Just 30 minutes east of Rodney

Bay, Rainforest Adventures offers zip lines through the trees in the lush, protected Babonneau park (US$80). For the less adventurous, it offers a 1½-hour aerial 'tram' ride (US$80) over the canopy, plus birdwatching tours (US$60) and hikes (US$45).

Lucian Style WILDLIFE
(☎452-8300; www.lucianstyle.com; Reduit Beach Dr, Rodney Bay; tours US$50-165) This outfit offers Segway tours to Mt Pimard. They follow a dirt track leading to various lookouts and last two hours, including a 15-minute practice session. The guide gives insights into the local flora and fauna, and you'll stop at interesting historical relics. Tours usually leave at 2pm and 4pm from Rodney Bay. Also offers hikes and complete island tours.

Sleeping

Bay Guesthouse GUESTHOUSE $
(☎450-8956; www.bay-guesthouse.com; Bay St, Gros Islet; d from US$50, apt US$70-120;) Within easy walking distance of Gros Islet, this simple waterfront guesthouse is excellent value. While the former owners have left the island, meaning the ambience has lost some gloss, it's still a fantastic base from which to explore the area. Rooms range from compact to spacious; some offer kitchens and stunning views. The grounds have hammocks.

There's no sign – look for the pale blue building on the waterside.

La Terrasse GUESTHOUSE $$
(☎721-0389, 572-0389; Seagrape Ave, Rodney Bay Village; r US$100-150;) This small guesthouse is under new management but still feels remarkably homey. It has a tropical courtyard and dining deck, and there are four handsomely decorated rooms with modern fixtures. It's in a quiet street off the main avenue and a five-minute walk from the beach.

★**East Winds Inn** RESORT $$$
(☎452-8212; www.eastwinds.com; Labrellotte Bay, Gros Islet; s/d all-inclusive per night from US$1015/2010;) Understated yet beautiful, relaxed yet luxurious, this all-inclusive inn is one of St Lucia's most appealing beachside resorts. It has a mere 30 rooms spread over a garden- and bird-filled site ranging from spacious gingerbread cottages with private gardens to waterfront suites; all have high wooden ceilings and modern appliances. Service is superb, as is the food.

Ginger Lily Hotel HOTEL $$$
(☎458-0300; www.gingerlilyhotel.com; Reduit Beach Ave, Rodney Bay; r US$180-198;) An excellent alternative to the bigger resorts nearby, Ginger Lily Hotel is functional, intimate and blissfully quiet. Set in a peaceful garden, the 11 well-designed rooms have balconies and terraces with hammocks but no sea views. They are delightfully cool inside. Reduit Beach is just across the road.

Coco Palm HOTEL $$$
(☎456-2800; www.coco-resorts.com; Reduit Beach Ave, Rodney Bay Village; d US$176-258;) A harmonious blend of modern lines and Creole styling. Although the Coco Palm isn't on the beach, it has an inviting setting on a grassy terrace overlooking Rodney Bay Village. With varied accommodations, it's appropriate for singles, couples and families alike. Some rooms have private steps into the enormous pool, which is sure to be a hit with younger travelers.

Bay Gardens Beach Resort & Spa RESORT $$$
(☎457-8500; www.baygardensresorts.com; Reduit Beach Ave, Rodney Bay; d/ste US$357/590;) An excellent choice if you prefer a full-service resort, the BGBR has an idyllic beachfront location. Rooms are in three-story buildings designed with a neoclassical flair; many overlook the large cloverleaf pool or the beach and most have been decked out with bright new furnishings. The suites have functional kitchens, making them a great choice for families.

Eating

Elena's ICE CREAM $
(Baywalk Mall, Rodney Bay; EC$5-13) A smaller branch of Elena's Italian gelati shop conveniently located outside the Baywalk Mall in Rodney Bay. It's ice cream only here, but they also run a **casual restaurant** (☎572-2900; Rodney Bay Marina; ice cream EC$5-13, pizzas EC$19-55, mains EC$40-110; ⊙7am-11pm Mon-Sat, 8am-11pm Sun) a couple of doors down for meals.

Lucian Cuisine CARIBBEAN $
(☎519-2323; Rodney Bay; breakfasts EC$3-15, mains EC$15-20; ⊙7am-4pm Mon-Sat) At odds with the rest of Rodney Bay's pricey dining scene, this cute little spot offers fantastic-value traditional St Lucian cuisine. Grab one of the tables on the small wooden deck to the side and choose from a rotating choice of mains served with five or six different sides.

The plates are huge and the quality is top notch.

Gros Islet Fish Fry SEAFOOD $

(Duke's; Bay St, Gros Islet; meals EC$20-25; ⌚5-10pm Wed, Fri & Sat) A couple of open-air joints across from the water serve up excellent seafood grills a few nights a week at the Gros Islet Fish Fry. They are ultracasual: wait for a plate of barbecued fresh fish, get a few sides, then find a spot in the dark at a picnic table.

Cafe Ole CAFE $

(Rodney Bay Marina; mains EC$16-40; ⌚7am-10pm Mon-Sat, 8am-10pm Sun) This sprightly eatery sitting on a covered wooden deck overlooking the marina is the perfect venue for enjoying a drink, snack or a meal – and to people-watch. It serves some of the best coffee on the island (EC$5 to EC$11).

★ **Spice of India** INDIAN $$

(☎458-4253; www.spiceofindiastlucia.com; Baywalk Mall, Rodney Bay; mains EC$46-74; ⌚noon-4pm & 6-11pm Tue-Sun) You'd never guess it from the outside but this restaurant next to the mall complex at the beginning of the Rodney Bay strip consistently serves some of the best Indian food in the Caribbean. Everything is carefully prepared by veteran Indian chefs; the delectable curries are perfectly spiced and the lamb biryani is phenomenal. Book in advance.

Flavours of the Grill CARIBBEAN $$

(☎450-9722; Castries-Gros Islet Hwy, Bois d'Orange; mains EC$30-55; ⌚11:30am-10pm Mon-Sat) Having outgrown its humble beginnings in Gros islet, this popular eatery has moved to expansive new digs out on the Castries highway but still serves refined versions of Caribbean classics. The seafood is a highlight. There is a buffet at lunch while dinner is from the menu.

Amici ITALIAN $$$

(☎285-9290; Baywalk Mall, Rodney Bay; pizzas from EC$20, mains EC$35-180) Run by a team of expat chefs, upscale Amici serves gourmet Italian plates and great pizzas in the heart of the Rodney Bay strip. It's pricey but the menu is more sophisticated compared to other Italian places on the island and is well worth a splurge.

Big Chef STEAK $$$

(☎450-0210; www.bigchefsteakhouse.com; Reduit Beach Ave, Rodney Bay Village; mains EC$79-199; ⌚6-11pm) If you fancy splashing out on something other than lobster, step into this smart air-conditioned dining room and tuck into quality imported cuts at St Lucia's favorite steakhouse. You'll have to change out of the shorts and sandals but it's worth it for a top-quality meal.

Drinking & Nightlife

Rodney Bay is the most 'happening' area in St Lucia. Most restaurants feature a bar section, which on weekends can pull in a crowd. You can also check out the bars in the large hotels.

On Friday nights in Gros Islet the weekly jump-up gets going. Stalls sell fresh fish, grilled chicken and other delights. The music plays at full volume and there's dancing in the streets. Popular with locals and visitors alike, it's St Lucia's best party.

Felly Belly JUICE BAR

(Rodney Bay Mall; smoothies EC$14-18; ⌚7:30am-8pm Mon-Sat) Pop into this tiny place in the Rodney Bay Mall for great juices and smoothies. Take your pick from the two boards full of different mixes or make your own from scratch.

Boardwalk BAR

(Rodney Bay Marina; ⌚noon-midnight) A popular spot where you can cut loose over some sunset cocktails in pleasant surrounds and eavesdrop on the yachties' tall tales. It's at the marina, on the waterfront.

Shopping

Island Mix Art Emporium ARTS & CRAFTS

(☎584-7877; Seagrape Ave, Rodney Bay Village; ⌚10am-6pm Fri-Wed, to 8pm Thu) A bright waterside gallery featuring works by artists and craftspeople from across the island. There is a good cafe on-site serving lunch by the water. On Wednesday evenings they offer workshops with different artists while on Thursday evenings from 6pm to 8pm they prepare fish-and-chips (EC$25).

Getting There & Away

Both Rodney Bay and Gros Islet can be reached from Castries via the same regular public minivan service.

There are usually taxi drivers hanging out in front of the malls in Rodney Bay, and there is a taxi booth at the Rodney Bay Marina.

From the Reduit Beach area it's quicker and more fun to travel to Gros Islet via **water taxi** (☎518-8236; www.saluna-watersports.com; Reduit Beach). Boats also serve Rodney Bay Marina and Pigeon Island. Expect to pay around EC$40 return per passenger.

Pigeon Island

This former island was joined to the mainland in the 1970s when a sandy causeway was constructed; it's one of Rodney Bay's best sights.

Pigeon Island has a fascinating range of historic sites scattered across the peninsula. Its spicy history dates back to the 1550s, when St Lucia's first French settler, Jambe de Bois (Wooden Leg), used the island as a base for raiding passing Spanish ships. Two centuries later, British admiral George Rodney fortified Pigeon Island, using it to monitor the French fleet on Martinique.

Pigeon Island National Landmark (☎452-5005; www.slunatrust.org; adult/child EC$21/8; ⏲ticket booth 9am-5pm) is a fun place to explore, with paths winding around the remains of barracks, batteries and garrisons; the partially intact stone buildings create a ghost-town effect. The grounds are well endowed with lofty trees, manicured lawns and fine coastal views. Bring a picnic and make a day of it. Guided tours of the site can be arranged at the ticket office for EC$59 for groups of one to seven visitors.

Locals, yachties and frequent visitors know they'll get a delicious meal and a wonderful view of the bay at **Jambe De Bois** (☎450-8166; mains EC$37.50-47.50; ⏲9am-10pm Tue-Sun, to 5pm Mon). The menu is fairly small but varied, with local specialties lining up with Mediterranean plates.

Pick out a table on the breezy veranda for a romantic meal. On weekends there is great live music.

You can access the cafe even when the Pigeon Island main gate is closed – just tell security you're going for a meal.

Getting There & Away

Public buses do not run all the way to Pigeon Island but it's a short taxi ride from Rodney Bay or Gros Islet.

It's possible to walk all the way up the beach from Gros Islet to Pigeon Island. When you get to the channel at the luxurious Landings Hotel, ring the bell and a small boat will carry you across. Then make your way through the sea of sun loungers in front of Sandals – it's a public beach, don't mind the security guards.

The easiest way to get to Pigeon Island from Rodney Bay is via a water taxi from Reduit Beach, which costs around EC$40 return per passenger.

The Northern Tip

Outside bustling Rodney Bay life becomes more sedate as you head toward the island's northernmost reaches. On Cap Estate the hilly terrain is dotted with chichi villas, large estates and the island's main golf course. From there it's an easy drive downhill to secluded **Cas-en-Bas beach**. This is the wilder side of the island – the winds and surf here can be lively.

Sights

Smugglers Cove BEACH

Smugglers Cove is a secluded crescent of brown sugary sand. It's a small beach that is somewhat dominated by the loungers and cafe from the neighboring hotel but there's still usually room to throw down a towel.

Activities

Horseback Riding

There are a number of stables in the area offering trail rides as well as beach canters along Cas-en-Bas beach. Expect to pay around US$65 for two hours. Free pickup services can be arranged from most hotels in the Rodney Bay area. Children are welcome.

Holiday Riding Stables HORSEBACK RIDING

(www.holidayridingstablesstlucia.weebly.com; Cas-en-Bas; rides US$60) A flexible stables offering different riding trips along remote Cas-en-Bas beach, including time in the water with the horses.

Water Sports

Cas-en-Bas always has a stiff breeze, which makes it an excellent kitesurfing spot. There are a couple of kite places located here but they're not always open so reserve in advance.

Aquaholics KITESURFING

(☎726-0600; www.aquaholicsstlucia.com; Cas-en-Bas Beach; lessons per hour US$90) A recommended kitesurf school run by charismatic instructor Simon. He runs right alongside beginners on a Jet Ski to offer instant tips and training. Introductory classes are US$60 per hour and can be shared with a friend. Aquaholics also offers powerboat tours including water sports such as waterskiing and wakeboarding.

Kitesurfing St Lucia KITESURFING

(☎714-9589; www.kitesurfingstlucia.com; Cas-en-Bas Beach; lessons 1/2hr US$90/150, rental per hour from US$35; ⏲hours vary) Offers lessons with an instructor on a Jet Ski as well as two-hour discover kitesurfing introductions (US$120). Also rents out gear to experienced kiters.

Sleeping & Eating

★ Cap Maison BOUTIQUE HOTEL $$$
(☎ 457-8670; www.capmaison.com; Cap Estate; d incl breakfast US$459-1200; ❄📶🏊) Privacy, luxury and service are hallmarks of this sanctuary built on a seaside bluff. The elegant Moroccan-Caribbean architecture features suites that are elegantly furnished and decorated. Another draw is the superb Cliff at Cap restaurant (open to nonguests), which has a wonderful sea-view platform for cocktails and cigars. Downside: the nearest beach requires hiking down (and back up) 92 steps.

Marjorie's Beach Bar & Restaurant CARIBBEAN $$
(☎ 520-0001; Cas-en-Bas Beach; mains EC$40-65; ⏱ 8am-6pm) Feel the sand between your toes at this funky cafe on the sand. Enjoy tasty Creole dishes and wicked rum punch. The management also organizes guides for a two-hour nature hike (US$30 per visitor) in the area that visits Donkey Beach, Secret Beach and Cactus Valley.

Getting There & Away

There's no public transport in this corner of the island but there are unmarked pirate buses that run irregularly from Gros Islet up to Cap Estate. Wait at the bus stop on the highway on the north side of the entrance road to Gros Islet. They're usually beaten-up old white vans.

Eastern St Lucia

A 30-minute drive from Castries transports you to yet another world, along the Atlantic-battered east coast, where you can experience a St Lucia that's very laid-back and little visited.

While this coast lacks the beaches of the west, it makes up for it with lovely bays backed by spectacular cliffs, a rocky shoreline pounded by thundering surf, and a handful of picturesque fishing towns, including Dennery and Micoud.

Sights

La Tille Waterfalls WATERFALL
(☎ 489-6271; Vollet River, Micoud; EC$20; ⏱ 9am-6pm) Off the beaten track and rarely visited, La Tille is one of the better waterfalls on the island, with a high-volume cascade falling into a large pool surrounded by greenery. But a visit here is about more than just the falls; the Rasta guardians of the site constantly work on the flower-filled grounds and a relaxed, natural vibe abounds. There is a nature trail and rope swing, and vegetarian meals are offered.

Mamiku Gardens GARDENS
(☎ 455-3729; www.mamikugardens.com; EC$20; ⏱ 9am-5pm) A relaxing focal point for any eastern day trip, the Mamiku botanical gardens are located on the grounds of a former plantation and boast an extensive collection of tropical flora including some wonderful orchids. Upon arrival you'll be given a booklet to assist in identifying the 297 named species in the gardens. But it's not just about the plants, there are also historical ruins to explore, hiking trails and birdwatching tours.

Activities

Between March and August the long stretch of Grande Anse on the northeast coast is a favorite nesting ground for leatherback turtles. Visitors are allowed to check out the turtle rookeries at night and observe eggs being laid or hatching – a fantastic spectacle. Poachers are a continual problem here with many turtles being butchered for their meat and their eggs harvested. Sustainable tourism activities are an important component in protecting these animals. A licensed guide must accompany all visitors. Note that Grande Anse beach is only accessible by 4WD.

Des Cartiers Rainforest Trail HIKING
(☎ 715-0350; Anbre, Desruisseaux; EC$27; ⏱ 8am-3pm Mon-Fri) A 1-mile loop through stunning, rarely visited rainforest. If you're lucky you might spot the St Lucia parrot, but even if you don't it's a breathtaking hike. Admission includes the services of a guide. The trailhead is around 6 miles inland from the Dennery Hwy. It's possible to link this trail with the Edmund Rainforest Trail (p700) above Soufrière.

Sleeping

Fox Grove Inn HOTEL $$
(☎ 455-3800; www.foxgroveinn.com; Mon Repos; r incl breakfast US$105; ❄📶🏊) One of the few long-running hotels on this side of the island, the Fox Grove is set up on a hillside and has neat and tidy rooms with high

LOCAL KNOWLEDGE

DENNERY FISH FRY

The big culinary event on this side of the island is the Dennery fish fry, which takes place every Saturday from around 4pm onward. While similar fish festivals in Gros Islet and Anse La Raye are major parties, the Dennery edition is more focused on the food, with a wider variety of seafood on offer. It takes place at the collection of colorful wooden huts right by the waterside near the town fish market.

wooden ceilings and Atlantic views. The bar and restaurant downstairs (meals EC$38 to EC$90) is a popular lunch spot for day-trippers to the area.

Getting There & Away

The Castries–Vieux Fort Hwy runs through the heart of the region, and buses running between those towns will drop you anywhere along the route.

The northern reaches of the east side of the island are rugged and isolated. To reach many of the beaches here you'll need a good 4WD or be prepared to hike in.

Marigot Bay

Deep, sheltered Marigot Bay is an exquisite example of natural architecture. Sheltered by towering palms and the surrounding hills, the narrow inlet is said to have once hidden the entire British fleet from French pursuers. Yachts play the same trick these days – the bay is a popular place to drop anchor and hide away for a few nights while enjoying nearby beaches.

Sights & Activities

Millet Bird Sanctuary NATURE RESERVE

(☎519-0787; Millet; walking EC$27, birdwatching EC$81; ⊙8:30am-3pm Mon-Fri) This nature reserve lies about 6 miles inland from the west-coast highway, in Millet. Here's your chance to spot endemic species, including the St Lucia parrot and the St Lucia warbler. Book in advance and a knowledgeable forest ranger will take you on a tour. There's also a scenic 2-mile loop hiking trail that alternates between thick forests and wide-open hilltops.

Dive Fair Helen WATER SPORTS

(☎451-7716; www.divefairhelen.com; Marigot Beach Club; ⊙8:30am-4:30pm Mon-Fri, to 12:30pm Sat) Based at Marigot Beach Club, Dive Fair Helen charges US$126 for a two-tank dive, including equipment, and US$78 for a snorkeling excursion (US$56 for kids). It also offers kayaking tours along the coast and up a river (US$66) or further afield to Anse Cochon for lunch and snorkeling, returning by boat (US$140).

Sleeping

Marigot Bay has an excellent range of accommodations, both down by the waterside and up in the surrounding hills. Most are toward the upper end of the budget spectrum.

JJ's Paradise HOTEL $

(☎451-4761; www.jjsparadise.com; r US$60-130) The only budget digs on the bay, depending on which room you get, JJ's can actually be quite nice, with spacious wooden bungalows decked out with good mattresses, flat-screen TV and split-system air-con. It's on the innermost point of the bay – you'll need to walk up and over the hill or take a water taxi to reach the action.

Nature's Paradise B&B $$

(☎458-3550, 488-1112; www.stluciaparadise.com; r incl breakfast US$155-225;) Nature's Paradise is magical, if you don't mind the steep winding road between the bay and the B&B. Poised on a greenery-shrouded promontory, it offers cracking views of sea and bay. The two rooms in the main building are a tad small, while the two cottages nestled in a Garden of Eden are roomy and fully equipped.

Marigot Bay Resort and Marina HOTEL $$$

(☎458-5300; www.marigotbayresort.com; r from US$1146;) Occupying a nicely landscaped plot on the southern shores of the bay, this upmarket resort is the most comfortable place to stay in the area. The smartly finished rooms boast dark-wood features, clean lines, ample space and heaps of amenities. Service is courteous and professional.

Eating & Drinking

There are several great places to eat right on the bay. For very cheap eats hike back up the hill into Marigot Village where you'll find a bakery and some small shops.

Julietta's Restaurant & Bar CARIBBEAN $$
(☎ 458-3224; Marigot Bay Rd; mains EC$45-95; ⏰ 11am-10pm) Overlooking the bay from the top of the hill, Julietta's offers exceptional views. Enjoy fresh fish and other casual fare. Call ahead and they'll send a free shuttle to save the hike up the hill.

Chateau Mygo CREOLE $$
(☎ 451-4722; mains EC$40-125; ⏰ 8am-11pm) This unfussy little eatery could hardly be better situated: the dining deck is right on the waterfront with picnic tables looking out onto the bay. The food consists of simply prepared seafood and meat dishes served in generous portions; can be a bit hit and miss.

Roots Bar BAR
(LaBas Beach; ⏰ 7am-7pm) Under the coconut palms on LaBas Beach, this laid-back local bar serves good-value drinks with a classic reggae soundtrack. Also rents beach loungers. Opening hours are flexible to say the least.

Getting There & Away

There's no public transport all the way down to the bay, but Castries–Jacmel buses will drop you at Marigot Village, from where it's a 10-minute walk down the hill. If you offer the driver a tip it's usually possible to continue all the way to the port.

You'll find a taxi stand right outside the marina. A taxi to or from Castries costs around EC$60 to EC$80.

Soufrière & The Pitons

If one town were to be the heart and soul of St Lucia, it would have to be Soufrière. Its attractions include a slew of colonial-era edifices scattered amid brightly painted wooden storefronts and a bustling seafront.

The surrounding landscape is little short of breathtaking: the skyscraping towers of rock known as the Pitons stand guard over the town. Jutting from the sea, covered in vegetation and ending in a summit that looks otherworldly, these are St Lucia's iconic landmarks.

The area boasts beauty above and below the water as well as historic and natural sights aplenty.

Many visit only as a day trip from the north – don't join them! There are far too many attractions to pack into a couple of hours. Spend a couple of nights down here soaking up the ambience accompanied by the hum of the rainforest.

Sights

★ Sugar Beach BEACH
(Jalousie Beach) The most famous beach on the island, gorgeous Sugar Beach is spectacularly situated between the two Pitons, ensuring phenomenal views both from the sand and in the water. Like most in the area, it was originally a gray-sand beach – the soft white sands are imported from abroad. There are free basic public loungers at the far northern end; alternatively, when occupancy is low, you can rent one of the resort's more luxurious models.

Public access is through the Viceroy resort (p702) by paying for the expensive day pass (US$50), which is consumable at the restaurant. If you have a reservation at the **watersports center** (☎ 456-8000; 1-/2-tank dives US$85/110), a shuttle will be sent for you. Otherwise it's a long walk from the entrance gate; it feels even longer on the way back up. A stress-free way to visit is by boat as part of an island cruise.

Anse Chastanet BEACH
Stretched out in front of the resort of the same name, Anse Chastanet is a fine curving beach. The sheltered bay is protected by high cliffs. The snorkeling just offshore is some of the best on the island; hassle-free access is through the resort, which also offers day passes if you want to use the sun loungers and water-sports facilities.

Anse Mamin BEACH
Backed by lush rainforest, this dreamy secluded enclave of sand edges a gently curved cove that's about a 10-minute walk north of Anse Chastanet, or about 30 minutes from town. The resort also has sun loungers and a grill restaurant here but they are tastefully done and don't take away from the absolute tranquility.

Fond Doux Plantation PLANTATION
(☎ 459-7548; www.fonddouxresort.com; off Vieux Fort Rd; tours with snack/lunch US$25/40; ⏰ 11am-4pm) 🍃 At this bijou hideaway you can catch an informative one-hour walking tour that allows you to take in the plantation and a cocoa-processing plant. They also offer a new chocolate-making tour (guests/

nonguests US$30/40) where participants can watch and sample the house bar.

The hike up to the lookout with fine views of the Pitons is for hotel guests only.

Pitons Waterfall WATERFALL
(☎487-9564; EC$7.50; ⊙7am-5:45pm) In the mood for a dip in tepid waters? Make a beeline for this picturesque cascade surrounded by lush forest and fed by a mix of natural streams and underground thermal sulfur springs from Soufrière volcano. There are two small concrete pools fed by the main waterfall and another at the end of a side channel. You can shower under the flow but watch out for the slippery rocks.

Diamond Falls Botanical Gardens & Mineral Baths GARDENS
(☎459-7565; www.diamondstlucia.com; adult/child EC$17.50/8.75, baths from EC$15; ⊙10am-5pm Mon-Sat, to 3pm Sun) Wander amid tropical flowers and trees at this old estate. The mineral baths date from 1784, when they were built atop hot springs so that the troops of France's King Louis XVI could take advantage of their therapeutic effects. You can take a dip in small public pools among nature or in the less appealing enclosed private bathhouse. The gardens are 1 mile east of Soufrière town center.

Sulphur Springs NATURAL FEATURE
(☎459-7686; admission EC$22.50, thermal baths EC$25, combined ticket EC$37.50; ⊙tours 9am-5pm, hot springs 9am-11pm) Looking like something off the surface of the moon, the Sulphur Springs are saddled with the unfortunate tagline of being the world's only drive-in volcano. The reality is far from the garish description. There isn't a classic crater, or a cauldron of magma, to check out – but it's still an awe-inspiring place. Stinky pools of boiling mud are observed from platforms surrounded by vents releasing clouds of sulfur gas. Kids will love it.

There is a thermally heated river that has been dammed to form four small pools where visitors can relax in the mineral-rich waters and apply mud facials. Try to get the first pool – the water flows from one to the next so can be pretty dirty by the fourth. It's no longer permitted to remove mud from the site so the cottage industry of take-home volcano facials has shut down.

The springs are a couple of miles south of Soufrière, off the Vieux Fort Rd.

Gateway to Soufrière VIEWPOINT
Around a mile and a half up the road to Castries, this lookout at the side of the road affords fantastic views across the Soufrière valley to the Pitons.

Activities

Diving & Snorkeling

Action Adventure Divers DIVING
(☎485-1317, 459-5599; www.aadivers.net; Hummingbird Beach Resort, Anse Chastanet Rd; 1-/2-tank dives incl equipment US$65/120) A recommended outfit that offers a wide range of trips and usually keeps groups small.

Scuba St Lucia DIVING
(☎459-7755; www.scubastlucia.com; Anse Chastanet Resort; shore/boat dives incl equipment US$69/75) Well-organized and friendly Scuba St Lucia is right on the beach at Anse Chastanet and has a fleet of good boats. Offers night dives, too.

Hiking & Climbing

★ **Tet Paul Nature Trail** HIKING
(☎457-1122; tetpaul2016@gmail.com; off Vieux Fort Rd; tours adult/child EC$27/13.50; ⊙9am-5pm) Don't miss this community-run nature trail. During the 45-minute tour, a guide will show you an organic farm and take you to a lookout; the view of the Pitons jabbing the skyline is stunning, but even better are the insights into traditional local life. It's signposted, 3.1 miles south of Soufrière.

Edmund Rainforest Trail HIKING
(☎457-1427; EC$27; ⊙8am-3pm Mon-Fri) High in the mountains above Soufrière you'll find the trailhead for this challenging hike into the heart of the St Lucian rainforest. At the entrance there's a Ministry of Agriculture van where you pay the admission fee, but it's best to call in advance to make sure a guide will be around.

The main route passes up to the island divide to offer views down to the east side. A spur route off the main trail, the Enbas Saut trail, leads to waterfalls deep in the jungle.

If you choose the full route, it's possible to join up with the Des Cartiers trail (p697), which finishes at a trailhead above Micoud; the trail exit is in a remote area so you should organize transport to pick you up in advance.

The trails here are not well signed and guides are highly recommended. The Agriculture Department in Castries can point you in the right direction.

To get to the trailhead take the road up the Soufrière valley past the Toraille waterfalls, taking the left at the T-intersection.

Gros Piton Nature Trail Guides CLIMBING
(☎285-7431, 459-3965; www.soufrierefoundation.org; per visitor US$50) Official guides for climbs up Gros Piton work on a turn-based system out of this office at the trailhead. Turn up before 1pm to ensure a trip. While prices have soared, trail conditions remain rough in some parts.

Tours

★Jungle Biking CYCLING
(☎457-1400; www.bikestlucia.com; Anse Mamin; 2½hr trips US$60; ⏰8am-3:30pm Mon-Sat) This outfit, which is part of the Anse Chastanet Resort (p702; nonguests are welcome), offers mountain-biking tours along trails that meander through the remnants of an old plantation, just next to Anse Mamin beach. It's suitable for all fitness levels. Various stops are organized along the way, where the guide will give you the lowdown on flora, fauna and local history.

Mystic Man Tours BOATING
(☎459-7783; www.mysticmantours.com; Bridge St; ⏰8am-4pm Mon-Sat) Runs quality boat excursions in the area, from whale-watching and snorkeling trips to sunset cruises and deep-sea fishing outings. Also runs land-based ATV tours to a local beach and plantation.

Real St Lucia Tours TOURS
(☎486-1561; www.realsaintluciatours.com) Run by a group of enthusiastic young locals in Soufrière, this company offers tailor-made tours across the island.

Rabot Estate FOOD & DRINK
(☎459-7966; Vieux Fort Rd; tours US$28-61; ⏰Tree to Bean 9-10am Mon, Tue & Thu & 1-2pm Mon, Wed & Fri; Bean to Bar 10:30-11:30am Mon, Tue & Thu & 2:30-3:30pm Mon, Wed & Fri) The team at the Boucan hotel (p702) offer two interesting chocolate-themed tours on its plantation. The Tree to Bean Tour (US$28) explains everything about cocoa growing and processing while the Bean to Bar Experience (US$61) lets visitors make their own chocolate using beans from the estate. Call to make reservations.

Sleeping

Most resorts and larger hotels are fairly isolated, so a rental car is advised. Some hotels provide shuttle services to nearby beaches. There are a couple of small hotels and guesthouses in the center of town.

Church St Guesthouse GUESTHOUSE $
(r with/without kitchen US$71/67) The most pleasant option in the center of town, this friendly place has inviting rooms. It's worth paying the extra for one with a kitchen.

Downtown Hotel HOTEL $
(☎459-7185; Bridge St; r US$89; ❄📶) The Downtown doesn't exactly scream vacation (it's within a small shopping mall), but it's very central, convenient, well maintained and affordable. Aim for a room at the back for sea views and to avoid the road noise.

★Fond Doux Plantation & Resort RESORT $$$
(☎459-7545; www.fonddouxresort.com; off Vieux Fort Rd; cottages US$360-510; 📶🏊) 🌿 Hidden in the hills to the south of Soufrière,

DON'T MISS

CLIMBING THE PITONS

If you have time for only one trek during your stay, choose the Gros Piton (2617ft) climb. Starting from the hamlet of Fond Gens Libres, you walk mostly through a thick jungle. The final section is very steep, but the reward is a tremendous view of southern St Lucia and the densely forested mountains of the interior. Allow roughly four hours there and back. A guide is mandatory; contact Gros Piton Nature Trail Guides.

While climbing Petit Piton is discouraged by local authorities – some sections involve clambering on near-vertical slabs of rock – many experienced hikers and climbers do journey to the summit. Expect to take around three to four hours round trip. The smaller peak affords better views of the island's Caribbean beaches than Gros Piton does.

You can find guides (US$60 to US$70) at the Pitons Waterfall, which is just across from the entrance to the trail, or keep an eye out for the wooden signs advertising guide services on the road on the way in. It's best to begin early as it gets hot on the climb.

this 250-year-old working cocoa plantation (p699) is a great place to unwind. Fifteen tastefully refurbished cottages with private balconies are surrounded by tropical gardens. Some boast private plunge pools. There is also a fine split-level communal pool with great views, and guests are offered a free plantation tour.

Ladera RESORT **$$$**
(459-6618; www.ladera.com; off Vieux Fort Rd; ste incl breakfast US$1100-1700;) The location is one of the best in St Lucia: an 1100ft-high ridge with full-frame views of the Pitons and the ocean. The spacious rooms have a rich, naturalistic design and plunge pools; there's also a spa and a Piton-view yoga space is in the works. It's 2.5 miles south of town.

Viceroy Sugar Beach RESORT **$$$**
(456-8000; www.viceroyhotelsandresorts.com; Anse des Pitons; r from US$960;) Boasting the best location on the island, nestled in a coconut grove smack between the Pitons, this luxurious resort opens onto a perfect white-sand beach. Rooms have private plunge pools, hardwood floors and all the amenities you'd expect.

Boucan RESORT **$$$**
(Hotel Chocolat; 572-9600; www.thehotelchocolat.com; Rabot Estate; r incl breakfast US$661-977;) What sets this place apart is the design scheme; cocoa is the dominant theme, and it's no wonder – the resort is set in a cocoa plantation (p701) that makes its own chocolate. And all of it is every bit as decadent as fine chocolate – especially the wonderful Piton-view infinity pool. The hotel also prides itself on its engaged ethics.

Stonefield Estate Villa Resort RESORT **$$$**
(459-5648; www.stonefieldresort.com; off Vieux Fort Rd; 1-bed villas US$450-660;) This historic lime plantation estate sports a cache of well-proportioned gingerbread-style cottages with private plunge pools scattered amid a lush property, and glorious views over Petit Piton. Perks include an on-site restaurant, a spa and a pool. The property also has a superb petroglyph inscribed on a big basaltic boulder. It's on the southern outskirts of Soufrière.

Anse Chastanet Resort RESORT **$$$**
(459-7000; www.ansechastanet.com; Anse Chastanet; r from US$630;) The hillside-beachside location is supremely enjoyable. Whether you want to dive, snorkel, cycle, get pampered, experience fine dining or simply do nothing, this resort on its dreamy namesake beach has it all. Rooms down by the beach have air-con while those on the hill get the views.

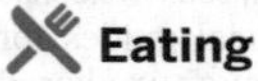

Eating

Fedo's CARIBBEAN **$**
(New Development; mains EC$12-50; 9am-5pm Mon-Sat) Hidden away on the eastern edges of town several blocks back from the waterfront, this no-nonsense diner serves up quality Creole dishes at reasonable prices. It's difficult to find; ask any local for directions.

Marie's Local Cuisine CARIBBEAN **$$**
(723-5466; Diamond Gardens Rd; meals EC$40; 11am-4pm) A welcoming restaurant next to the botanical gardens with a quality Creole lunch buffet. Good, hearty meals and a fair price.

Martha's Tables CARIBBEAN **$$**
(459-2770; off Vieux Fort Rd, Malgretoute; meals from EC$40; 11:30am-2pm Mon-Fri) Just up the hill from Malgretoute Beach, this home-style restaurant is in Martha's actual home. Each day she prepares a spread of excellent comfort food using local flavors. Grab a plastic chair and enjoy. Opening hours are irregular.

★Orlando's CARIBBEAN **$$$**
(459-5955; Cemetery Rd; 3-course meals US$55-60; noon-2pm & 6-9pm Wed-Sun) Chef Orlando Sachell made a name for himself basically inventing the concept of farm-to-table cuisine at some of St Lucia's best resorts. Now he has his own fine restaurant right in Soufrière. The menu changes constantly but the high level of service doesn't. Book in advance.

★Boucan Restaurant & Bar FUSION **$$$**
(459-7966; www.hotelchocolat.com/uk/boucan; Rabot Estate, Vieux Fort Rd; mains EC$51-123; 7am-10pm) Succulent cocoa-inspired cuisine in relaxed, contemporary surrounds. You'll find cocoa from the plantation in many plates over all three courses. The dessert menu alone is reason enough to come here; try the Rabot Marquise – house dark chocolate with cream marquise served atop a crunchy cocoa base. Reserve ahead as this is one of the island's high-profile spots.

Dasheene CARIBBEAN **$$$**
(459-6623; Ladera, off Vieux Fort Rd; dinner EC$96-128; 7am-11pm) This open-air place

in the Ladera resort serves Caribbean and European fare in magical surrounds, headlined by incomparable Pitons views. Reservations are mandatory.

Shopping

Zaka Masks ARTS & CRAFTS
(☎457-1504; www.zaka-art.com; Waterfront; ⏲9am-5pm Mon-Sat, to 1pm Sun) Walk into this quirky studio on the waterfront in Soufrière and you'll be welcomed by friendly Zaka, who creates lovely wooden masks that are painted in vivid colors. His works embellish a number of hotels on the island. They are irresistible and highly collectible, so bring plenty of cash (or a credit card) if you're thinking of buying.

Information

First Caribbean Bank (Church St; ⏲9am-2pm Mon-Thu, to 4pm Fri) Reliable ATM in town.

Getting There & Away

Regular buses connect Soufrière to Castries and the north of the island by a scenic winding mountain road (EC$8, 45 minutes). Take care if driving, as local vehicles often fly around the corners.

There's also a regular bus service connecting the town to Vieux Fort (EC$6, 30 minutes).

On Sundays the bus service is limited to non-existent – plan accordingly.

South Coast & Vieux Fort

St Lucia's expansive south coast is stunning, yet most travelers just see it from the window of a taxi after landing at the Hewanorra International Airport.

On the road from Vieux Fort to Soufrière, **Laborie** is a pretty little fishing village with a fine stretch of sand right in front of town. It's a very local, very laid-back place without the hassles of some more visited areas. The beach is narrow but is backed by coconut palms and slopes down to tranquil green waters.

A little further north, **Choiseul** is another traditional fishing village; it has an active handicraft industry.

Activities

★**Atlantic Shores Stables** HORSEBACK RIDING
(☎285-1090; atlanticshores758@gmail.com; St Helen Estate, Beanfield Rd; adult/child from US$65/55) Professionally run stables just south of Micoud offering a range of great rides along beaches and through the lush countryside in the south of the island. The horses are in great condition and the landscapes here are wild and inspiring.

Sleeping & Eating

Sunset Lane GUESTHOUSE $
(☎716-7146; www.sunsetbaylc.com; Flamboyant Ave, Laborie; r US$65-80) The modern air-con rooms at this neat place on a hillside at the southern end of the bay are comfortable enough, but the reason to stay here are the great decks with panoramic sea views. Perfect for reading or an evening drink.

★**Balenbouche Estate** HERITAGE HOTEL $$
(☎455-1244; www.balenbouche.com; Balenbouche; r US$130-170; 📶) 🍃 Between Choiseul and Laborie you'll find this tranquil 18th-century estate home with an eco-bent, comprising six simple yet delightful garden cottages. You'll feel like you've stepped back in time here. The cottages don't have air-conditioning but are designed to catch plenty of breeze and most feature inviting indoor-outdoor bathrooms. There is no pool, but there are two dark-colored sandy beaches nearby.

Mama Rose's CARIBBEAN $
(☎455-9084; Bay St; mains EC$25; ⏲10am-9pm) A local institution, this family-run affair offers a modern take on traditional Creole cuisine at its downtown bar/restaurant just back from the water. Meals are tasty and priced just right.

Salt Rush Cafe CAFE
(☎454-3686; Laborie; mains EC$25-30; ⏲10:30am-8pm) Sit at the breezy bar overlooking the water at this fantastic little cafe right on the sand at Laborie and enjoy great smoothies, local juices or a cold beer. The ultra-chilled-out owners also bake authentic banana, coconut and pumpkin bread, and serve light meals and more filling traditional plates.

Getting There & Away

There are buses from Vieux Fort that enter both Laborie and Choiseul, while the Vieux Fort–Soufrière bus will leave you close by on the highway.

Vieux Fort

St Lucia's second-largest town lies on a vast plain at the southern tip of the island, where the azure waters of the Caribbean blend with those of the rough Atlantic Ocean. The town is next to a lovely bay that is recognized as a prime destination for kitesurfing and windsurfing; it's also a lovely place for a walk.

The town itself won't leap to the top of your list of preferred destinations in St Lucia but the surrounding coastal area is very scenic. Plans are afoot for a mega tourism development on the shores of the bay, which would totally change the vibe in the area, but for now it remains wild and peaceful.

Sights & Activities

The combination of constant strong breezes, protected areas with calm water and a lack of obstacles make the bay of Anse des Sables and Sandy Beach a world-class destination for kitesurfers and windsurfers.

Sandy Beach BEACH
(Anse des Sables) At the southern tip of the island, Sandy Beach is a beautiful strand of white sand that looks out on the rugged Maria Islands. There's always a stiff breeze, making it a hot spot for kitesurfers. It's also suitable for swimming – on a calm day. It's never crowded.

Reef Kite & Surf KITESURFING
(☎454-3418; www.slucia.com/kitesurf; Sandy Beach, Anse des Sables; rentals per half-day from US$70) A one-hour 'taster session' is US$50; a three-hour course costs US$220 while a complete nine-hour course runs at US$625. It also rents kayaks (US$17 to US$25 per hour) and stand-up paddle (SUP) boards (US$20 per hour).

Sleeping & Eating

Accommodations in Vieux Fort are very limited. The best options are the B&Bs up on the hill near the lighthouse although they are somewhat isolated. There are some simple hotels in town but they mainly cater to regional business travelers and don't have much island atmosphere.

Charlery's Inn HOTEL $
(☎454-6448; www.charlerysinnslu.com; Laborie-Vieux Fort Hwy; r from US$65) Located in a building that looks like an office block right beside the bus stops, the rooms here are nothing special, but they're clean and will do the trick if you just need a place to crash close to the center. If there's no one in reception – there probably won't be – ask in the gas station across the road.

Reef Beach Huts GUESTHOUSE $
(☎454-3418; www.reefstlucia.com; Sandy Beach, Anse des Sables; s/d from US$60/72; ❄) There are four simple, renovated rooms in a wooden lodge out the back of the Reef Cafe. They don't have any views and suffer from road noise from the highway and the occasional party – but the location is a hit: you're just steps from the water. The air-con comes in handy.

Reef Cafe INTERNATIONAL $
(☎454-3418; Sandy Beach, Anse des Sables; mains EC$20-46, light meals EC$10-20; ⏲8am-10pm Tue-Sun, to 6pm Mon) Sit under the trees at tables with sea views and tuck into some of the best cuisine on the south of the island at this casual cafe. The Creole seafood dishes are delectable and there are also great rotis, pizzas and salads. Excellent value.

Island Breeze CARIBBEAN $$
(☎454-6754; Sandy Beach, Anse des Sables; mains EC$30-80; ⏲9am-10pm) Pull up a table at this attractive wooden restaurant right on the sand and enjoy quality Caribbean specialties with a view. The seafood plates are great, and the ribs and jerk dishes are also winners. It's also a fresh spot to get out of the sun and enjoy a drink.

Getting There & Away

Public minivans for Soufrière (EC$6, 50 minutes) leave when full from the intersection near the Sol gas station.

Buses for Castries (EC$8, one hour) depart from near the roundabout on the eastern edge of town and take the eastern road via Dennery.

UNDERSTAND ST LUCIA

History

Archaeological finds on the island indicate that St Lucia was settled by Arawaks between 1000 BC and 500 BC. Around AD 800 migrating Caribs conquered the Arawaks and established permanent settlements.

St Lucia was outside the routes taken by Columbus during his four visits to the New World and was probably first sighted by the Spanish during the early 1500s. Caribs successfully fended off two British attempts at colonization in the 1600s, only to be faced with French claims to the island a century down the road, when they established the island's first lasting European settlement,

Soufrière, in 1746 and went about developing plantations. St Lucia's colonial history was marred by warfare, however, as the British still maintained their claim to the island.

In 1778 the British successfully invaded St Lucia and established naval bases at Gros Islet and Pigeon Island, which they used as staging grounds for attacks on the French islands to the north. For the next few decades possession of St Lucia seesawed between the British and the French. In 1814 the Treaty of Paris finally ceded the island to the British, ending 150 years of conflict during which St Lucia changed flags 14 times.

Culturally the British were slow in replacing French customs, and it wasn't until 1842 that English nudged out French as St Lucia's official language. Other customs linger, and to this day many speak a French-based patois among themselves, attend Catholic services and live in villages with French names.

St Lucia gained internal autonomy in 1967 and then achieved full independence, as a member of the Commonwealth, on February 22, 1979. Politics has stabilized in recent times, with election results usually coming in the form of landslide victories for the opposing party. The downturn in the banana industry has meant that a diversification of industry is vital for economic prosperity. Tourism is now the main source of revenue.

In late 2010 the island was severely hit by a hurricane, which caused much damage in the Soufrière area. However, the area has now fully recovered and is once again one of the island's tourism hot spots.

People & Culture

St Lucians are generally laid-back, friendly people influenced by a mix of their English, French, African and Caribbean origins. For instance, if you walk into the Catholic cathedral in Castries, you'll find a building of French design, an interior richly painted in bright African-inspired colors, portraits of a Black Madonna and child, and church services delivered in English. About 85% of St Lucians are Roman Catholics.

The population is about 180,000, one-third of whom live in Castries. Approximately 85% are of pure African ancestry. Another 10% are a mixture of African, British, French and Indian ancestry, while about 4% are of pure Indian or European descent.

The predominantly African heritage can be seen in the strong family ties that St Lucians hold and the survival of many traditional customs and superstitions. Obeah (Vodou) is still held in equal measures of respect and fear in places like Anse La Raye. The local snakeman is visited by islanders for his medicinal powers. One such muscular remedy he uses involves massaging the thick fat of the boa constrictor on aching limbs.

There is an eclectic mix of cultural ideologies within St Lucia. But with the arrival of globalization, economic disparity has had a negative effect on the cultural identity of some young people. Violent crime, mostly drug-related, is on the rise.

Landscape & Wildlife

The Land

The striking landmass of St Lucia is one of its defining features. At only 27 miles long, the teardrop-shaped island packs a variety of topography into its 238 sq miles. Standing nearly as tall as they are long, the rolling hills and towering peaks of the interior make this green island an apparition of altitude rising from the sea.

Banana plantations dominate every flat section of land, and some not so flat. The Caribbean cash crop is a staple industry for St Lucia, although it now falls behind tourism in contributions to the national economy. Lush tropical jungle forms a rat's nest of gnarled rainforest, filling the interior of the island with thick bush.

In the north the island flattens out a little and the beaches get a bit wider – allowing infrastructure to get a foothold. In the south the land rises sharply and continues in folds of green hills that stretch right to

DEREK WALCOTT, NOBEL LAUREATE

In the art world St Lucia's most revered local export is the late writer Derek Walcott. The gifted poet and playwright won the Nobel Prize for literature in 1992. Strongly influenced by Tolstoy, Homer and Pushkin, his writing is literate, intense and sweeping. His 1990 epic poem *Omeros* is a shining example of his work. The ambitious project, retelling Homer's *Odyssey* in the modern-day Caribbean, was praised for its panache, scope and success.

BIRDING IN ST LUCIA

Twitchers are sure to get a buzz in St Lucia – there are a number of desirable new ticks for their list, including five endemic species: the St Lucia parrot, the St Lucia warbler, the St Lucia oriole, the St Lucia or Lesser Antillean peewee and the St Lucia black finch. The St Lucia parrot *(Amazona versicolor)*, locally called the Jacquot, is the national bird and appears on everything from T-shirts to St Lucian passports.

Good birdwatching spots include Millet Bird Sanctuary and the Des Cartiers Rainforest Trail.

the shoreline. It's in this portion of the island, near Soufrière, that St Lucia's iconic landmarks are found. The twin peaks of the Pitons, which are extinct volcano cones, rise 2600ft from the sea and dominate the horizon.

Wildlife

St Lucia's vegetation ranges from dry and scrubby areas of cacti and hibiscus to lush, jungly valleys with wild orchids, bromeliads, heliconias and lianas.

Under the British colonial administration much of St Lucia's rainforest was targeted for timber harvesting. In many ways the independent St Lucian government has proved a far more effective environmental force, and while only about 10% of the island remains covered in rainforest, most of that has now been set aside as a nature reserve. The largest indigenous trees in the rainforest are the *gommier*, a towering gum tree, and the *chatagnier*, a huge buttress-trunked tree.

Fauna includes endemic birds, bats, lizards, iguanas, tree frogs, introduced mongooses, rabbitlike agoutis and several snake species, including the fer-de-lance and the boa constrictor.

SURVIVAL GUIDE

Directory A–Z

ACCESSIBLE TRAVEL

- Most large resorts have some facilities for travelers with disabilities, but it is best to inquire before heading out.
- The area around Rodney Bay Village has good wide sidewalks and some ramps but the rest of the country is difficult for travelers with limited mobility.
- Public transport is not designed for travelers with disabilities, and getting in and out of minivans is likely to pose some difficulty.

ACCOMMODATIONS

St Lucia has a pretty wide range of accommodations options. In addition to swish hotels and all-inclusive resorts, which form the core of the market, it offers a range of more intimate ventures, including boutique inns and self-catering villas.

Most accommodations are concentrated in the area from the northeast down to Marigot Bay. If you prefer a quiet retreat, opt for the Soufrière area. Many hotels have an on-site restaurant.

CHILDREN

Although purpose-made kids' attractions are scarce, St Lucia is an eminently suitable destination for those traveling with children. With its abundance of beaches and opportunities for outdoor activities, including horseback riding, snorkeling, zip-lining and diving, there's plenty to do in a generally safe environment. Whale- and dolphin-watching excursions are also popular with families. A popular floating water park is anchored just off Reduit Beach in Rodney Bay.

There are some hotels that won't take children under a certain age, but a number of all-inclusive resorts cater specifically to families and have an impressive range of amenities for children. Most hotels also offer reduced rates for children staying in their parents' room.

Moving around the island with children can be a challenge outside of Rodney Bay and Castries as there are often no sidewalks on the roads and highways. Therefore it may be easier to take taxis even short distances. Public transport is often crowded and groups may have to sit in different parts of the van. It is rare to find taxis with seats for young children but rental-car companies can provide these on request.

ELECTRICITY

Electricity is 220V (50 cycles); three-pronged, chunky UK-style plugs.

EMBASSIES & CONSULATES

British High Commission (☎452-2485, 452-2484; www.facebook.com/ukinstlucia; 2nd fl, Francis Compton Bldg, John Compton Hwy, PO Box 227)

EMERGENCY NUMBERS

Emergency line	☎999

FOOD

Dining options on St Lucia are fantastically varied, with local French-Creole–inspired dishes jostling for space on menus alongside pan-Caribbean classics and quality international cuisine.

All over the island you'll find 'fish fry' events where local seafood is grilled outside on massive barbecues and eaten at communal picnic tables.

Rodney Bay Village and the nearby marina on the north side of the island are lined with modern, high-end international eateries.

Essential Food & Drink

Seafood Dorado (also known as mahimahi), kingfish, marlin, snapper, lobster, crab and shellfish feature high on the menu.

Meat dishes Chicken and pork dishes are the most commonly found, beef is less usual.

Local specialties Try callaloo soup, *lambi* (conch) and salt fish with green fig (seasoned salt cod and boiled green banana).

Piton The beer of St Lucia; crisp and sweet, it's perfectly light and refreshing.

St Lucian rum The island's sole distillery produces white rums, gold rums and flavored rums.

HEALTH

You'll find major public medical facilities in Castries and Vieux Fort, as well as smaller clinics around the island; however, the public system is for the most part slow and inefficient. There are good private clinics in the north of the island, the best of which is the Tapion Hospital (p691) just south of Castries.

INTERNET ACCESS

Internet cafes are not widespread, but most accommodations and many restaurants offer wi-fi. Connection speeds vary, but are generally fast enough.

LGBT+ TRAVELERS

As with most destinations in the region, St Lucia isn't all that friendly to those identifying as LGBT+. While problems aren't as serious as in some larger Caribbean nations, gay men should be especially aware that homosexuality is generally not accepted in St Lucian society.

MONEY

The Eastern Caribbean dollar (EC$) is the island's currency. Visa, American Express and MasterCard are widely accepted at hotels, car-rental agencies, shops and restaurants.

Prices for many tourist services, including accommodations, activities, excursions and car hire, are often quoted in US dollars and can be paid in US dollars. But you can also pay the equivalent in EC dollars or with a major credit card.

SLEEPING PRICE RANGES

Taxes, which include a 10% service charge and a 10% government tax, are included in our listed prices. Watch out, though, because most places will quote before-tax prices.

$ less than US$100

$$ US$100–250

$$$ more than US$250

Exchange Rates

The Eastern Caribbean dollar is pegged to the US dollar at a rate of 2.70 to 1.

Australia	A$1	EC$1.94
Barbados	B$1	EC$1.36
Canada	C$1	EC$2.03
Euro zone	€1	EC$3.05
Japan	¥100	EC$2.41
New Zealand	NZ$1	EC$1.81
UK	UK£1	EC$3.52
US	US$1	EC$2.70

For current exchange rates, see www.xe.com.

Tipping

Hotels At least EC$2 per bag for porters is recommended; gratuity for cleaning staff at your discretion.

Restaurants Most restaurants add a 10% service charge. If it's not included in the bill, tip 10% to 15%; if it is included, it's up to you to leave an additional tip.

Taxi Fares are usually fixed and tips are not usually expected; if service is excellent, a tip of 10% to 15% of the fare is appreciated.

PUBLIC HOLIDAYS

In addition to holidays observed throughout the region, St Lucia has the following public holidays:

New Year's Holiday January 2

Independence Day February 22

EATING PRICE RANGES

Eating places can be categorized according to the following price brackets, based on the cost of the cheapest main meal, inclusive of taxes.

$ less than EC$35

$$ EC$35–70

$$$ more than EC$70

PRACTICALITIES

Newspapers *The Voice* (www.thevoiceslu.com) is the island's main, triweekly newspaper.

Radio Tune into music, news and patois programs on Radio Caribbean International (101.1FM).

Smoking St Lucia does not yet have blanket regulations on smoking; it's mostly left up to individual businesses. In general, smoking is not permitted in enclosed spaces.

Weights & measures St Lucia has formally adopted the metric system but many places still use imperial measurements – especially in markets.

Labor Day May 1
Corpus Christi Ninth Thursday after Easter
Emancipation Day August 3
Thanksgiving Day October 5
National Day December 13

TELEPHONE

St Lucia's area code is 758. To call from abroad, dial your country's international access code plus 758 and the seven-digit local number.

Cell Phones

If you have a GSM phone that is unlocked, you can purchase a new SIM card for about EC$25 from any **Flow** (www.discoverflow.co/saint-lucia) or **Digicel** (www.digicelgroup.com/lc) branch. This gives you a local number to call from and access to prepaid data packets; much cheaper than global roaming.

TIME

St Lucia is on GMT/UTC-4, the same as its Windward Island neighbors.

Getting There & Away

AIR

St Lucia receives direct long-haul flights from the US, Canada and the UK; during peak season there are also direct flights to Germany. It also has regional connections to Antigua, Martinique, Trinidad and Tobago, Barbados and St Vincent.

St Lucia has two airports:

Hewanorra International Airport (UVF; www.slaspa.com) in Vieux Fort is at the remote southern tip of the island. It handles flights from North America, the UK and Europe plus a few regional flights.

George FL Charles Airport (SLU; www.slaspa.com; Nelson Mandela Dr, Vigie) is conveniently located in Castries but due to the short runway is only served by regional flights on prop planes from Liat (www.liat.com), Air Caraibes (www.aircaraibes.com) and Caribbean Airlines (www.caribbean-airlines.com).

SEA

Cruise Ship

Cruise ships dock in Castries, either at Pointe Seraphine or right in town at La Place Carenage. Smaller vessels sometimes call at Soufrière; they anchor offshore and bring passengers ashore via tenders.

Ferry

The fast-ferry service **L'Express des Îles** (☎456-5022; www.express-des-iles.com; Castries Dock, Castries) operates a daily 80-minute express catamaran between the **ferry terminal** (Manoel St) in Castries and Fort-de-France on Martinique. It also has continuing service to Dominica (four hours) and Guadeloupe (seven hours). Departure days and times change frequently; check in advance.

Yacht

Customs and immigration can be cleared at Rodney Bay, Castries, Marigot Bay, Soufrière or Vieux Fort. Most yachties pull in at Rodney Bay, where there is a full-service marina and a couple of marked customs slips opposite the customs office.

It's easy to clear customs and immigration at Marigot Bay, where you can anchor in the inner harbor and dinghy over to the customs office. Castries is a more congested scene, and yachts entering the harbor are required to go directly to the customs dock. If there's no room you should head for the anchorage spot east of the customs buoy. In Soufrière the customs office is right on the waterfront. At Vieux Fort you can anchor off the big ship dock, where customs is located.

Popular anchorages include Reduit Beach, the area southeast of Pigeon Island, Rodney Bay Marina, Marigot Bay, Anse Chastanet, Anse Cochon and Soufrière Bay.

Yacht charters are available in Marigot Bay and Rodney Bay.

Bateau Mygo (☎721-7007; www.bateaumygo.com)

DSL Yachting (☎452-8531; www.dsl-yachting.com; Rodney Bay Marina)

Moorings (☎451-4357; www.moorings.com; Rodney Bay Marina)

Getting Around

AIR

There is a 10-minute **domestic helicopter link** (☎453-6950; www.stluciahelicopters.com; Sunny Acres, Castries; per passenger US$175) between George FL Charles Airport, near Castries, and Hewanorra International Airport, near Vieux Fort, which is convenient if you're staying in the north and have a long-haul flight.

BOAT

Water taxis can be hired to travel to virtually anywhere on the west side of the island, with the most popular routes running between Rodney Bay in the north and Marigot Bay or Soufrière in the south.

BUS

Bus service is via privately owned minivans. They're a cheap way to get around. St Lucia's main road forms a big loop around the island, and buses stop at all towns along the way. They're frequent between main towns and generally run until around 7pm, except on the busy Castries–Gros Islet corridor where they run until after 10pm. With the exception of services in the north, very few run on Sunday.

In urban areas buses are only permitted to stop at designated bus stops. In rural areas, if there's no bus stop nearby, you can wave buses down anywhere on the route as long as there's space for the bus to pull over. When you want to get off, announce your intention by calling out 'stopping driver' well in advance of your stop.

Sample fares from Castries to Gros Islet or Marigot Bay are EC$2.50, and to Soufrière, EC$8. Route numbers and destinations are displayed on the buses.

CAR & MOTORCYCLE

Drivers are required to purchase a local driving permit (US$22), which is sold by the car-rental companies, although authorities have been known to accept international driver's licenses – ask your rental company.

- Drive on the left-hand side.
- Speed limits are generally 15mph in towns and 30mph on bigger roads.

Car Rental

- You can rent a car when you arrive in St Lucia, be it at the airport or in town.
- Most companies require the driver to be at least 25 years old and to have had a driver's license for at least three years.
- Some major rental firms have franchises here but you'll often find better prices with local outfits.
- The cheapest cars rent for about US$60 a day.
- Nearly all car-rental agencies offer unlimited mileage.
- If you're planning an extensive tour of the island, it's advisable to hire a 4WD, as many of the roads are steep and smaller ones can become little more than potholed mudslides after a bout of rain.

Avis (www.avis.com; George FL Charles Airport, Castries)

Courtesy Car Rentals (☎452-8140; www.courtesycarrentals.com)

H&B Car Rental (☎452-0872; Reduit Beach Ave, Rodney Bay Village; ⏲8am-6pm)

Sixt (www.sixt.com)

West Coast Jeeps (☎459-5457; www.westcoastjeeps.com)

Road Conditions

Main roads are generally good, while conditions on secondary roads vary greatly, with some sections being newly surfaced and others peppered with abyssal potholes. Make sure you have a workable jack and spare tire available. Many of the interior and southern roads are also very winding and narrow.

Gas stations are distributed around the island.

TAXI

Taxis in St Lucia are expensive, with cross-island trips reaching US$80 to US$90. They're available at the airports, the harbor, in front of major hotels and at taxi ranks in towns. They aren't metered but more or less adhere to standard fares, especially on short trips. On longer journeys prices are somewhat negotiable. Confirm the fare before getting in.

It's possible to prebook a private airport transfer with **St Lucia Airport Shuttle** (☎486-1561; www.saintluciaairportshuttle.com).

St-Martin & Sint Maarten

☎590 / POP ST-MARTIN 32,125; SINT MAARTEN 43,990

Includes ➡

Best Places to Eat

- Le Pressoir (p721)
- Lolos of Grand Case (p720)
- Kkô Beach Bar & Restaurant (p722)
- Les Délices Créoles (p717)
- Ocean Lounge Restaurant & Bar (p713)

Best Places to Stay

- Le Temps des Cerises (p719)
- L'Esplanade (p719)
- Les Balcons d'Oyster Pond (p723)
- Hotel Hevea (p719)

Why Go?

The world's smallest area of land divided into two nations, this half-French, half-Dutch island's fascinating cultural mix incorporates a rich African heritage and 120 different nationalities speaking 80-plus languages, giving rise to some of the finest cuisine in the Caribbean.

Spread out around the island are 37 white-sand beaches, from busy stretches lined with pumping bars to tranquil hidden bays and coves. Water sports from snorkeling and diving to Jet Skiing abound, along with land-based adventures like hiking and zip-lining.

Calamity struck in September 2017 when monster hurricane Irma unleashed eight hours of fury over St-Martin/Sint Maarten. Devastation was thorough and widespread with some 90% of all buildings damaged or destroyed. Although recovery is still ongoing, the island is well on its way back. A reliable indicator was the return of the cruise-ship industry with up to seven vessels docking at Philipsburg port at once.

When to Go

Feb & Mar The party's in full swing during the Heineken Regatta and Carnival festivities.

May & Jun Capitalize on reduced prices and quieter beachscapes before hurricane season roars up.

Nov–early Dec Stop by just before the massive crowds roll in for the holiday season.

St-Martin & Sint Maarten Highlights

❶ **Îlet Pinel** (p718) Boarding a boat for snorkeling and sunbathing on this tiny islet off St-Martin's northeast coast.

❷ **Loterie Farm** (p720) Flying through the treetops on a zip line or lounging in a *cabana* by this oasis-like plantation's spring-fed pool.

❸ **Restaurants of Grand Case** (p720) Enjoying a gourmet meal in a fancy restaurant or smoky *lolo* (barbecue shack).

❹ **Topper's Rhum** (p714) Bottling your own rum on a tour of Topper's distillery in Simpson Bay.

❺ **Maho Bay** (p717) Letting the landing planes whoosh over your head while enjoying the sun and a piña colada at Sunset Bar & Grill.

❻ **Flavors of St Martin** (p713) Setting off from the Amsterdam Cheese & Liquor Store in Philipsburg for an island-wide food tour.

SINT MAARTEN

Sint Maarten, the Dutch side of the island, has an urban feel with its lively mix of sprawling resorts, shopping malls, garish casinos and bustling beach bars. Its capital, Philipsburg, which has great duty-free shopping and a clutch of restored historic churches and public buildings, is also home to the cruise-ship dock. Traffic snarls to a crawl when as many as seven giant ships disgorge their human cargo by the tens of thousands. Still, the beaches are gorgeous and there are plenty of fun diversions in and out of the water.

Philipsburg

Philipsburg, the capital of St-Martin/Sint Maarten's Dutch side, sprawls out along a wide arcing bay that mostly functions as an outdoor shopping mall for cruise-goers. When the crowds are back on board, it's well worth strolling down Front St for a peek at the clutch of handsomely restored historic churches and other colonial-era vestiges tucked among the Calvin Klein and Tommy Hilfiger boutiques. Numerous cute alleyways link Front St with the beach and the Boardwalk, which is jammed with boisterous bars.

Sights

Sint Maarten Museum MUSEUM

(☎542-4917; www.museumsintmaarten.org; 7 Front St; by donation; ⏲10am-4pm Mon-Fri) Arawak pottery shards, plantation-era artifacts, period photos and a few items from HMS *Proselyte,* the frigate that sank off Fort Amsterdam in 1801, are among the displays at this island history museum, along with exhibits covering the devastating 1995 Hurricane Luis, the salt industry and slavery. The little shop downstairs sells an assortment of Caribbean arts and crafts.

> **CARNIVAL TWO WAYS**
>
> On the French side of the island, **Carnival** (www.sxm-carnival.com; ⏲Feb/Mar & Apr/May) celebrations are over three weeks preceding Ash Wednesday, while on the Dutch side, which has the larger Carnival, activities usually begin the second week after Easter and last for two weeks. Expect parades, calypso competitions, bands, dancing and plenty of good drinks and food.

Yoda Guy Movie Exhibit MUSEUM

(☎542-4009; www.netdwellers.com/mo/ygme/index.html; 19a Front St; US$12; ⏲10:30am-4pm Mon & Sat, 9:15am-5pm Tue-Fri, plus 10:30am-4pm Sun when cruise ships in port) This 1st-floor museum is the brainchild of make-up artist Nick Maley, whose role in creating Yoda of *Star Wars* fame garnered him the nickname 'That Yoda Guy'. It winds though a whirlwind of rotating movie memorabilia that may include Han Solo frozen in carbonite, celebrity lifecasts from Marlon Brando to Michael Jackson and a robotic Yoda puppet alongside photos, props, scripts, vintage posters, storyboards, and items from other films Maley has worked on including *Men in Black, Alien, Terminator* and *Hellraiser*.

The unexpectedness of encountering such a museum in Sint Maarten is summed up by the sign held by C-3PO on the staircase up to the museum, which reads: 'R2-D2 says "The probability of finding a *Star Wars* exhibit in the Caribbean is 125,316 to 1."' If Maley is around, he will autograph any gift-shop purchase over $20.

Activities & Tours

Sea Trek Helmet Diving WATER SPORTS

(☎520-2346; www.seatrekstmaarten.com; Bobby's Marina; per person US$95; ⏲by reservation) Experience dazzling marine life without being a certified scuba diver on a 'sea trek': a 30-minute guided walk along the sea floor at a depth of around 6m. A water taxi whisks you to Little Bay, where there are natural and artificial reefs including sunken helicopter cannon and a submarine.

You'll wear a full-head helmet hooked up to an air hose so you can breathe normally. The helmet lets you wear glasses and keeps your hair dry. Put on your swimsuit before arriving at the departure point, as there are no changing facilities. Kids must be aged eight or over. The entire experience takes about 2½ hours.

Dive Sint Maarten DIVING

(☎553-5363; www.divesintmaarten.com; Bobby's Marina; 2-tank dive US$99, snorkeling excursion US$55, snorkeling-gear rental per day US$15; ⏲8am-5pm) Professional outfit runs boat dives to wrecks and reefs to frolic with sharks, turtles, rays and lots of tropical fish. Also offers open-water certification and an introductory course for those wishing to give diving a try.

Random Wind BOATING
(☎587-5742; www.randomwind.com; Juancho Yrausquin Blvd, Chesterfields, Dock Maarten; day trip adult/child US$119/95) The 54ft luxe catamaran *Random Wind* has circumnavigated the globe twice and now runs day trips for up to 32 passengers to some of the quieter bays around the island. The signature Paradise Day Sail (10am to 3pm) includes snorkeling gear, a Tarzan swing, kayak, stand-up paddle board (SUP), lunch and an open bar. The dock is just off Chesterfields Restaurant, close to the cruise-ship terminal.

★ **Flavors of St Martin** FOOD & DRINK
(☎in Puerto Rico +939-397-3343; www.stmartinfoodtours.com; Juancho Yrausquin Blvd; adult/child US$130/100) A four-hour tour by air-conditioned bus is a tasty way to discover this multicultural island's French, Dutch and Caribbean flavors. Tours meet at the Amsterdam Cheese & Liquor Store (p714), starting with a cheese tasting, before heading off to sample such treats as sizzling barbecue, local rum, seafood and Sint Maarten–made gelato, learning about the island's history en route.

Arrive hungry as there will be 10 tastes in all.

Pelican Peak Zipline OUTDOORS
(☎542-1333; www.pelicanpeaksxm.com; Juancho Yrausquin Blvd, Dock Maarten; rides from US$50; ⏲9:30am-3:30pm Mon-Sat) Squarely aimed at cruise-ship travelers, this zip line is just steps from the pier. Show up at the office next to Chesterfields Restaurant, where you'll be strapped into a harness and transported to the top of Pelican Peak in an open truck. Enjoy the views before hurtling back down a steep 550m.

Sleeping

With its casinos and 'gentlemen's bars', Philipsburg is not the most wholesome place to spend the night, although there are a couple of beach-fronting hotels on Front St that don't rent rooms by the hour. Generally speaking, though, if you're keen to stay on the Dutch side, Maho and Simpson Bay are somewhat more appealing options.

Holland House Beach Hotel HOTEL $$
(☎542-2572; www.hhbh.com; 43 Front St; r from US$250; ❄📶) With rooms dressed primly in shades of white and rose, this is a great base for shopping and the beach. Spend a little more for a unit with a sea-facing balcony to keep on eye on the cruise ships while sipping a cold beer from your in-room fridge, or get social in its buzzing Ocean Lounge Restaurant & Bar.

Sea View Beach Hotel HOTEL $$
(☎542-2323; www.seaviewbeachhotel.com; 85c Front St; d/tr/q from US$134/154/174; ❄📶) The 42 spartan rooms above a tacky casino are small and not particularly inviting, but they're good value (for Sint Maarten) given their beachfront location and handy mod-cons, including a small fridge. Wi-fi works only in the lobby.

Eating & Drinking

Most cafes and restaurants here open only during the day as they cater to cruise-ship passengers. The Ocean Lounge Restaurant & Bar at the Holland House Hotel is a classy option.

Self-caterers should head to the well-stocked **Carrefour** (☎542-4400; www.cmsxm.net; 79 Bush Rd; ⏲8am-8pm Mon-Sat, 9am-6pm Sun) supermarket.

Greenhouse Restaurant & Bar INTERNATIONAL $$
(☎542-2941; www.thegreenhouserestaurant.com; Bobby's Marina; sandwiches US$12.50-19, mains US$25-36; ⏲11am-10pm; P📶) Deluged with cruise-ship passengers in the daytime, this Philipsburg landmark lures locals and overnight visitors with prime rib, steak or lobster specials on weeknights. The regular menu features a few local tastes like conch Creole and jerk chicken wraps, among the expected line-up of burgers, salads, pasta and sandwiches.

Happy hour (4:30pm to 7pm) brings two-for-one drinks and discounted appetizers.

★ **Ocean Lounge Restaurant & Bar** SEAFOOD $$$
(☎542-2572; www.hhbh.com; Boardwalk, Holland House Beach Hotel; mains US$20-35, seafood platter for 2 US$145; ⏲kitchen 7am-10pm, bar to midnight) With a breezy terrace opening onto the seafront, the restaurant and bar at Holland House Beach Hotel is a popular place for a sunset beverage or all-out meal of fish, seafood risotto or *mahimahi,* perhaps capped with a Dutch apple pie. The seafood platter comes with grilled lobster, tuna tataki, salmon tartare, fresh oysters, lobster salad and shrimp.

Blue Bitch Bar BAR
(☎542-1645; www.bluebitchbar.com; Boardwalk; ⏲11am-11pm) This boisterous beach bar is a

fun pit stop for booze-fueled afternoons but also has a full menu of crowd-pleasing burgers, pizza, pasta, steaks, ribs and sandwiches to help keep brains in balance. There's even a kids' menu but with shots named 'breast milk' the ambience is hardly wholesome.

The sign on the Boardwalk features a blue-painted dog, but Blue Bitch Bar is in fact named for the shiny local gravel that was originally used for making cement on the island.

Shopping

Guavaberry Emporium DRINKS
(542-2965; www.guavaberry.com; 8 Front St; per bottle $22; 9:30am-5:30pm Mon-Sat, plus 9am-5pm Sun when cruise ships in port;) In a sparkling red-and-white original Dutch West Indies house from the late 1700s, this store trades solely in the official liqueur of St-Martin/Sint Maarten. The original blend is made from rum, cane sugar and wild guavaberries from the island's interior, and has a bittersweet spiced flavor. Other releases feature almond, wild lime and mango. Ask for a free sample.

Amsterdam Cheese & Liquor Store FOOD & DRINKS
(581-5408; 26 Juancho Yrausquin Blvd; 8:30am-5:30pm Mon-Sat) Past a pair of giant red Dutch wooden shoes (selfie alert!) lies this Gouda nirvana, which does a roaring trade in everything from soft-textured Young Gouda to well-aged Old Amsterdam along with other Dutch goodies like *jenever* (gin), spicy *speculaas* cookies and blue-and-white delftware. Cheeses are vacuum-packed and keep for up to six weeks without refrigeration.

It's only a 10-minute walk from the cruise-ship terminal.

Information

Post Office (542-2289; 2 N Debrot St; 7:30am-5pm Mon-Sat)

Sint Maarten Tourist Bureau (549-0200; www.vacationstmaarten.com; 6 Juancho Yrausquin Blvd; 8am-5pm Mon-Fri) Limited tourist information.

St Maarten Medical Center (SMMC; 543-1111; www.smmc.sx; 30 Welgelegen Rd, Cay Hill) The island's main hospital is west of Philipsburg and has a 24-hour emergency room.

Getting There & Away

Philipsburg is home to the Port St Maarten (p728) cruise-ship terminal, where you'll find taxis and car-rental companies, as well as marinas with services to St-Barthélemy and Saba. Buses are infrequent, so a taxi or your own wheels are best.

Simpson Bay

Although close to the runway at Princess Juliana International Airport (p728), beautiful Simpson Bay has some of the most captivating crystal tidewater out of all the beaches on the island. Swimming and sunbathing aside, other pursuits here include boating, horseback riding and heading behind the scenes of a rum distillery. Welfare Rd is chockablock with cafes, bars and small markets.

Activities & Tours

Seaside Nature Park HORSEBACK RIDING
(544-5255; www.seasidenaturepark.com; 64 Cay Bay Rd; 8am-4pm;) Explore St-Martin on horseback on a one-hour trot through dry scrub and cacti of a former plantation to the beach where you ride your four-legged friend into the sea for a cool-down (US$65). The two-hour sunset rides also include a beachside bonfire and champagne (US$100, two-person minimum). Private one-hour riding lessons cost US$45.

The property also has a small farm where you can see and pet miniature horses, rabbits, turtles, peacocks, geese and ducks.

★ Topper's Rhum DISTILLERY
(520-2266; www.toppersrhumtours.com; Bay 3, 9 Well Rd; tour US$20; 9am-3pm, tours by reservation) Tours lasting 1½ hours take you behind the scenes of this distillery, where you learn the history of rum-making in the Caribbean and view the creation, blending and bottling processes, followed by a tasting session. Infusions include coconut; spice; banana, vanilla and cinnamon; mocha; and white chocolate and raspberry. You can bottle your own rum to take home.

It's also possible to just drop by and sample some rums without a tour. The distillery is off Union Rd at the rear of an industrial complex (on your left as you enter); look for the aqua sign.

Trisport OUTDOORS
(545-4384; www.trisportsxm.com; 148 Airport Rd; 10am-5pm Mon-Sat) This versatile outfit has a range of bike, kayak, snorkeling and hiking tours (from US$39), and also offers rentals of bikes (from US$20 per day), SUP

boards (US$19 per hour) and kayaks (single/double per hour US$15/19).

Rainforest Adventures OUTDOORS
(543-1135; www.rainforestadventuressxm.com; Rockland Estate; packages adult/child from US$99/85;) This outfit operates a cable car to the top of Sentry hill for 360-degree views over the island. You can return the same way, although adrenaline junkies won't turn down the chance of whooshing down the Flying Dutchman, the world's steepest zip line, which drops over 300m over its 850m length and lets you reach speeds over 80km/h.

Another way down is the less scary Sentry Hill zip line, followed by the Schooner Ride where you 'surf' downhill in an inner tube.

Aqua Mania Adventures BOATING
(544-2640; www.stmaarten-activities.com; Pelican Marina, Simpson Bay Resort) Aqua Mania has a host of tours, including half-day snorkeling trips (from US$45), sunset lagoon sailing trips (from US$40), and daylong catamaran trips (from US$120) to Anguilla's Shoal Bay and Prickly Pear Cays. It also operates the **Edge** (one way/round trip $55/110, day trip $80) high-speed ferry to/from St-Barthélemy and to/from Saba.

Festivals & Events

Heineken Regatta SAILING
(www.heinekenregatta.com; early Mar) This hugely popular, long-running annual event bills itself as 'serious fun' and features four days of top-level boat races around the island.

Sleeping

The southern end of Simpson Bay is home to several resorts and hotels (of varying quality). There are also a few hotels along Welfare Rd, the main thoroughfare. Just south of the airport you'll find a handful of hotels opening onto the beach.

Mary's Boon Beach Resort & Spa HOTEL $$
(545-7000; www.marysboon.com; 117 Simpson Bay Rd; studio from US$135, 1-/2-bedroom apt from US$225/275;) A stone's throw from the airport runway, this rambling plantation-style inn has been sitting pretty in a prime beach location since the early '70s but, despite post-Irma renovations, is feeling a bit dated. Still, it's a comfortable place to hang your hat and has room configurations for all needs and budgets, from no-view-basement rooms to beachfront units with kitchen.

Horny Toad Guesthouse GUESTHOUSE $$
(545-4323; www.thtgh.com; 2 Vlaun Dr; d US$240;) Completely rebuilt in 2018, this beachfront guesthouse still brims with character and conviviality. All eight apartment-style units sport full kitchens and a dining area facing the sea. Guests (called 'Toadies') gather nightly in a breezy pavilion to make friends over BYOB happy hour or to fire up the gas barbecues.

Eating

Carousel GELATO $
(544-3112; 60a Welfare Rd; gelato or ice cream per 1/2/3 scoops US$4/6/9; 2-10pm Tue-Thu, to 11pm Fri-Sun;) After you've deliberated over 30-plus ice-cream and gelato flavors, and peeked through the glass windows to watch them being made, head out the back to ride this gelateria's beautiful old-fashioned carousel (aka merry-go-round; per ride US$2), which was imported piece by piece from Italy. Gelato flavors with a native touch include soursop, tamarind, guavaberry and pineapple.

Top Carrot VEGETARIAN $
(544-3381; Welfare Rd, Simpson Bay Yacht Club; dishes US$8-16; 7am-5:30pm;) Boho hangout Top Carrot serves scrumptious plant-based fare in a chilled-out cushion-clad dining room adjoining a New Age shop selling crystals, candles etc. It makes its own Bulgarian yogurt, pastries such as quiches and cinnamon scrolls, and market-fresh salads, using primarily local organic ingredients. There's also a wide range of freshly squeezed juices, smoothies and herbal teas.

Around a tenth of its dishes have meat or fish.

Bamboo SUSHI $$
(544-2693; www.bamboo-sxm.com; Welfare Rd; maki & nigiri US$5-20, mains US$20-31; noon-10pm Mon-Thu, to 11pm Fri-Sun) Relocated from Maho Bay, Bamboo now serves its famous Maui Wowi and Kuta rolls in the Shops at Puerto del Sol mall but has also expanded its menu to include tiger-shrimp tacos, ceviche and a massive grilled rib eye. The food is as much eye-candy as the crowd, and there's a new cocktail lounge for postdinner flirting.

Karakter INTERNATIONAL $$
(523-9983; www.karakterstmaarten.com; 121 Simpson Bay Rd; mains US$10-34; 9am-10pm or later;) Next to the airport runway, this easygoing beach club serves breakfast

DON'T MISS

PLANE SPOTTING

At the end of the runway of Princess Juliana International Airport, the **Sunset Bar & Grill** (☎545-2084; www.sunsetsxm.com; 2 Beacon Hill Rd; ⊙7:30am-4am; 📶) is a rite of passage for plane-spotters: where else can you sip an ice-cold beer while jets take off right above you? A surfboard shows the daily flight schedule (it's usually busiest around midday) – rent a beach chair and umbrella for US$10 or take a dip in the pool.

Food is served both day and night. Mains (US$13 to US$20) include pizzas with names such as Turbulence, Layover and Nonstop, along with burgers and barbecued ribs, salads, chicken and fish.

(including fresh OJ and strong coffee), and gourmet salads, sandwiches and burgers at lunch. Dinner mains include faves like barbecued lobster and pork tenderloin as well as the 'Impossible' vegan burger and Bolognese. Live music nightly and on Sunday afternoon.

Getting There & Away

Simpson Bay is home to Princess Juliana International Airport (p728). All the major car-rental companies have offices along Airport Rd, a short drive from the terminal (free shuttles). Taxis are prevalent. Buses run to Philipsburg and Marigot but schedules are unpredictable.

The Anguilla ferry pier is about 300m from the airport terminal. Ferries bound for Saba and St-Barth leave from the Simpson Bay Resort.

ST-MARTIN

More relaxed and built up than its Dutch counterpart, the French half of the island is a charming mix of white-sand beaches, excellent restaurants and stretches of bucolic mountainside. Several areas, most notably Orient Beach, Anse Marcel and Oyster Pond, still bear the scars of Hurricane Irma but, by and large, recovery has been remarkable.

Marigot

The capital of French St-Martin, the port town of Marigot is dominated by a colonial-era stone fort high up on the hill. It was virtually leveled by Hurricane Luis in 1995, and hard-hit by subsequent hurricanes including Irma in 2017, but a few historic buildings with wrought-iron balconies and belle-epoque lampposts remain. Down by the ferry dock vendors set up a colorful market in the mornings, but other than that and perhaps a handful of boulangeries (bakeries) and a restaurant, there's little to hold your attention.

Sights

Fort Louis RUINS

(Rue du Fort Louis; ⊙24hr) FREE It's a short but steep climb up to what's left of this once mighty fort, completed in 1789 under St-Martin's then-governor Jean Sebastian de Durat to protect the settlement of Marigot and its harbor warehouses storing rum, salt, coffee and sugarcane from British and Dutch pirates. It's been abandoned for centuries but English and French interpretive panels detail its history and the view alone is worth the effort.

From here you can see Marigot, Simpson Bay, Baie Nettlé and, on a clear day, as far as Anguilla. The cannon on the grounds are replicas.

Musée de Saint Martin MUSEUM

(St-Martin Museum; www.museesaintmartin.e-monsite.com; 7 Rue Fichot; ⊙9am-1pm & 3-5pm Mon-Fri) FREE Clay figurines from 550 BC (the oldest discovered in the Antilles), Arawak-sculpted gemstones and shells and period photography are among the historical displays that bring the island's history to life at this small but absorbing museum, which spans the Arawak period (from 3250 BC) to European colonization and island fashion in the 1930s. Interpretative panels are in English and French.

Marigot Market MARKET

(Blvd de France; ⊙food 7am-3pm Wed & Sat, bric-a-brac & clothing 7am-3pm Mon, Tue, Thu & Fri) Although there are fewer vendors after Hurricane Irma, this colorful waterfront market is still worth a spin to browse for art, crafts and trinkets, pick up a bottle of local rum like the bark-infused Mauby or Shrub (infused with crushed orange peel) or simply sip freshly prepared coconut juice. Locals swing by for fresh meat on Saturdays and just-off-the-boat fish sold on Wednesdays and also on Saturdays.

Avoid coral and turtle-shell products, which are illegal, and clothing, which is mostly imported from China.

Sleeping & Eating

Since Marigot is practically a ghost town at night, there's little reason to stay here except, perhaps, to catch an early-morning flight or ferry. If you do stay, consider the freshly renovated Centr'Hotel.

Centr'Hotel HOTEL $
(0590-87-86-51; www.centrhotel.fr; 4 Rue du Général de Gaulle; r €75-110;) Emerging from a total post-Irma makeover in July 2019, this good-value budget pick is about 500m from the ferry terminal and has 38 simple but nicely furnished units. Of the four categories, all but the standard rooms have kitchenette while the duplex and suite come with a private terrace and sitting area.

★ **Les Délices Créoles** CREOLE $
(www.facebook.com/creoledelightssxm; 19 Rue de La République; breakfast €2-10, mains €10-14; 6:30am-3:30pm Mon-Sat) For a down-to-earth local experience, head to this bustling kitchen that often sells out long before the official closing time. Best drop by around noon for the best selection of the daily feast that might include spicy Creole shrimp, smoky grilled ribs, barbecued red snapper or goat curry. Also makes St-Martin's best johnnycakes.

Ô Plongeoir INTERNATIONAL $$
(0590-87-94-71; www.oplongeoir.com; Front de Mer; mains €13-23; 8am-11pm Mon-Sat Sep-Jul;) Settle into a pillowed bench at this languid place opposite the marina with the silhouette of Anguilla barely rising in the distance. Flank steak roll stuffed with goat cheese is the signature dish, but other tummy fillers like shrimp flambéed in pastis, tuna tartare and Creole-style *mahimahi* are just as tasty.

Also a good spot to ring in the evening with cocktails and tapas.

Information

Centre Hospitalier LC Fleming Saint Martin (St-Martin Medical Center; 0590-52-25-25, emergency 0590-52-26-29; www.chsaint-martin.org; Spring Concordia) Has a 24-hour emergency room.

Marigot Post Office (25 Rue de la Liberté; 7am-3pm Mon-Fri, 7:30am-12:30pm Sat)

Marigot Tourist Office (0590-87-57-21; www.st-martin.org; 10 Rue du Général de Gaulle; 9am-5pm Mon-Fri) Has a limited range of brochures and maps.

Getting There & Away

Public ferries (Gare Maritime de Marigot) to Anguilla depart from Marigot's ferry terminal at Fort Louis' marina, as do **Voyager** (0590-87-10-68; www.voy12.com; Gare Maritime de Marigot; one way/return/same-day return from €63/87/70) ferries to St-Barthélemy.

Buses connect Marigot with Philipsburg and Grand Case, but schedules are highly unpredictable so you're better off taking a taxi or traveling with your own wheels.

Terres Basses

Terres Basses (pronounced 'tair bass'), also known as the French Lowlands, is a sloping plateau connected to the rest of St-Martin/Sint Maarten by two thin strips of land. Originally a sugar plantation, the land was bought by an American developer in the 1950s and turned into an upscale gated residential area with private villas and estates but no shops or restaurants. For visitors, its main appeal are the three quiet and facility-free sandy beaches that are open to the public.

Sights

★ **Baie Longue** BEACH
(Long Bay) Baie Longue embraces two splendid miles of white sand and rocky outcrops, making it a prime spot for long strolls and meditative sunsets. The impossibly clear turquoise waters are exceptionally calm. It's 1.6km northwest of the French–Dutch border at Cupecoy; look for the entrance to the car park opposite the Grand Étang salt pond.

Baie Rouge BEACH
Named for the red-tinged color of the sand, Baie Rouge is a long, beautiful strand with good swimming. Although it's just 150m from the main road, it retains an inviting natural setting. For the best snorkeling,

WORTH A TRIP

BAIE NETTLE

Sandy Ground is the long, narrow, curving strip of land that connects Marigot with the prestigious gated community of Terres Basses. Sandy Ground's settlement is hardly appealing (and a no-go area after dark), but the beach at Baie Nettlé (Nettle Bay), with views of Marigot and across to Anguilla, is a beautiful white-sand flat stretch. Watch out for currents and submerged rocks if you're swimming.

swim to the eastern end of the beach toward the rocky outcrop. From the French-Dutch border at Cupecoy Bay, it's 3km northeast.

Baie aux Prunes BEACH

(Plum Bay) A gently curving bay with polished shell-like grains of golden sand, Baie aux Prunes is popular for swimming and snorkeling when it's calm, and for surfing when the swell's up. There are neither facilities nor shade but on a clear day you can spy Saba in the distance. A path leads down to the beach from Rue de la Falaise.

Sleeping

Belmond La Samanna RESORT $$$

(0590-87-64-00; www.belmond.com/la-samanna-st-martin; Baie Longue; d/ste from US$990/1765; Nov-Jul;) La Samanna is one of the most lavish – and expensive – places to stay on the island. Fronting a magnificent stretch of beach, this tropical hideaway has a state-of-the-art spa, two pools, two restaurants, and rooms, suites and villas with luxurious fittings such as mahogany and teak furniture, Italian marble, private plunge pools, rooftop sundecks and floor-to-ceiling windows with mesmerizing views.

Getting There & Away

Taxis or your own wheels are essential for visiting this area.

Friar's Bay

Friar's Bay is a postcard-worthy cove with a broad sandy beach, great sunsets and two legendary beach bars. Find this popular local swimming spot just past the residential neighborhood of St Louis; the road leading in is signposted.

If you're looking for an off-the-beaten-track beach, head to the northernmost point of Friar's Bay beach and look for the dirt path that twists for 450m over a bumpy headland with great views of Anguilla to perfectly deserted **Happy Bay**. This serene strip of powdery sand is completely bare (as are many of those who hang out here), so bring whatever you need to make you even more happy.

Pretty and protected, **Friar's Bay Beach** is a west-facing cove with two beach bars, chic **Friar's Bay Beach Café** (0690-49-16-87; Rue de Friar's Bay; mains €16-30; breakfast 9-11am, lunch noon-5pm, bar from 9am;) and funky **Kali's Beach Bar** (0690-49-06-81; Rue de Friar's Bay; mains €12-20; 10am-sunset, hours can vary;), which hosts famous full-moon parties. Both rent sun chairs and umbrellas. The beach is popular with locals and rarely deluged by cruise-ship passengers.

To get there, look for the turnoff on your left about 2km north of Marigot, just before the road makes a sharp right bend. The beach itself is about 1.2km from the road via the residential community of St Louis.

DON'T MISS

ÎLET PINEL

This petite offshore **islet** (Pinel Island; Grand Cul-de-Sac; ferry round trip €10; ferry 10am-5pm Dec-Apr, to 4pm May-Aug & Nov) is fab for a sun-soaked afternoon. Refreshingly undeveloped (it's part of the Reserve Naturelle Saint Martin or St-Martin Nature Reserve), Pinel's calm west-facing beach has excellent swimming and decent snorkeling. Rent gear from **Caribbean Paddling** (www.caribbeanpaddling.com; Embarcadero de Pinel, Cul-de-Sac; snorkeling-gear rental per day €10; 9:30am-5pm Dec-Apr, closed Fri May-Aug & Nov, closed Sep & Oct) by the ferry pier in French Cul-de-Sac, from where boats head to the island roughly every 30 minutes (five-minute trip, cash only). Casual **Yellow Beach** (0690-33-88-33; mains €12-18; 10am-5pm;) and more upscale **Karibuni** (0690-39-67-00; www.facebook.com/karibunipinel; mains €17-32; 10am-5pm) provide sustenance and sun loungers (€20 for two, including umbrella).

Tiny trails weave uphill from the beach into the shrub-covered backcountry and to two more beaches with rougher waters on the northern and eastern shore. Keep an eye out for iguanas.

If you want to make your own way over to Pinel Island, Caribbean Paddling also rents kayaks and stand-up paddleboards. Arriving under your own steam also gives you a chance to stop en route at uninhabited **Petite Clef** islet, which has the bay's best snorkeling. With a bit of luck you might spot sea turtles and rays.

Grand Case

The small beachside settlement of Grand Case has not been dubbed the 'Gourmet Capital of the Caribbean' for nothing. Each evening, a ritual of sorts takes place on Grand Case's beachfront road, Blvd de Grand Case, with restaurants placing their menus and chalkboard specials out front, and would-be diners strolling along the strip until they find somewhere that takes their fancy. Hurricane Irma whipped through town with a vengeance but most restaurants have reopened and more are soon coming online.

While dining is the premier attraction, there's also a decent beach for swimming and snorkeling, while other pursuits include skydiving and perfume making.

Activities

SXM Parachute SKYDIVING

(0690-77-15-41; www.sxmparachute.com; Rte de l'Espérance, Aéroport de Saint-Martin Grand Case; tandem jump €280; 9am-7pm early Nov-late Apr) For the most exhilarating aerial views of the island, head up into the skies aboard a Cessna 206G then hurl yourself out to free fall 3000m on a tandem skydive with an instructor. A video costs €95; photos are €50. Takeoff is from the airport on Grand Case.

Tijon ARTS & CRAFTS

(0690-22-74-70; www.tijon.com; 1 Rte de l'Espérance; 9:30am-5pm Mon-Fri, by appointment Sat & Sun) As well as shopping for perfumes, candles, soaps, jewelry and other covetables at this heady boutique, you can learn how to create your own fragrances from the 'organ of 300 oils' during a one-hour mix-and-match course (€95, no reservation needed). There's also a two- to three-hour workshop (€159) that teaches you the history of perfume and offers more advanced mixing.

Both include a gift bag worth up to €45. If your time's limited, there's also the 'fragrance in a flash' option where you choose up to four favorite oils, which staff will then blend and put in a pretty bottle (€69).

Sleeping

Grand Case has some of the most charming boutique places to stay on the island as well as a couple of budget options.

Hotel Hevea GUESTHOUSE $

(0690-29-36-71; www.hotelhevea.com; 163 Blvd de Grand Case; d €85-130, tr/q €143/150; reception 7:30am-noon & 4-7pm; P ❄) This rambling cottage is a perfect pick for people who prefer a personal vibe over the gamut of luxe mod-cons. Which is not to say that the nine, charmingly furnished rooms are not well equipped. Fridge and kettle are standard, and there's a communal area with microwave and dining table. SUPs, kayaks and beach towels are available for rent.

At the front of the property, its on-site cafe serves breakfast.

★Grand Case Beach Club RESORT $$$

(0590-87-51-87; www.grandcasebeachclub.com; 21 Rue de la Petite Plage; r €370-625; P ❄) On the quiet northeast end of the beach, this gently sprawling resort's low-rise red-roofed buildings have airy renovated rooms facing the sea. Its sparkling pool sits out on a promontory; there's also a water-sports center and snorkeling a few fin-strokes away, along with an on-site tennis court. Kids under 12 stay for free in their parents' room.

Bonus: if you book directly, you're welcomed with a free bottle of wine. Its cafe-restaurant, Sunset Café (p720), has the best ocean views around.

★L'Esplanade HOTEL $$$

(0590-87-06-55; www.lesplanade.com; Rte de l'Espérance; studios/lofts/ste US$425/485/525; P ❄) This romantic, impeccably run hillside hotel is an estate-like haven from the hustle of Grand Case, with a beautiful pool, swim-up bar, spa and free yoga classes. Its 24 sumptuous and spacious studios, lofts and suites have full kitchen and private ocean-view terrace, French linen and handcrafted Balinese furniture. A footpath leads to the beach and village.

There's a free shuttle to local restaurants. Cooked-to-order breakfasts can be arranged the previous evening.

★Le Temps des Cerises BOUTIQUE HOTEL $$$

(0590-51-36-27; www.ltc-hotel.com; 158 Blvd de Grand Case; d €290-340; ❄) 'Have a Good Karma' is the motto of this chic laid-back seaside property. Eight balconied doubles are decked out in airy neutral tones with natural materials including polished hardwood floors and vintage timber furniture; all have king-sized bed and minibar. Quirky design touches (garden gnomes, vintage bicycle, Chinese room numbers) abound. Rates include nonmotorized sea toys, sun loungers and umbrellas.

Its open-plan bar area and restaurant are popular with locals as well as visitors.

Le Petit Hotel BOUTIQUE HOTEL $$$
(☎0590-29-09-65; www.lepetithotel.com; 248 Blvd de Grande Case; studio/ste incl breakfast from US$475/635; P ❄ ☜) Behind a facade embellished with Moroccan tiles, the 10 rooms of this boutique jewel come with sea-facing balconies, Balinese furniture, Frette linen and modern kitchens. The suite sleeps up to four people. Top-floor balconies have full sun; lower ones are shaded.

Eating & Drinking

The island's best restaurants line up along Blvd de Grand Case, although for more local flavor, so to speak, an order of grilled chicken or snapper from one of the *lolos* (barbecue shacks) on the waterfront is a lot cheaper and just as yummy.

★Lolos BARBECUE $
(52 Blvd de Grand Case; mains €6-16; ⊙11am-11pm; ⓗ) The most famous of St-Martin's Creole *lolos* is a cluster of a half dozen or so open kitchens where ribs, cod fritters, lobster, chicken and stuffed crabs are fire-tickled to perfection on big grills. Sides such as coleslaw, potato salad, rice and beans, or fried plantains usually cost a couple of euros extra.

L'Ile Flottante BREAKFAST $
(☎0590-29-08-28; Blvd de Grand Case; dishes €3-7; ⊙6am-6pm Tue-Sun; ☜) This bougainvillea-cradled terrace with vinyl-covered tables is the earliest breakfast option in town and the cheapest to boot. Join the predominantly local crowd in fueling up for the day on croissants or cooked-to-order crepes and omelets.

Lunch brings sandwiches, salads and the *plat du jour* (daily dish). Little English is spoken but don't let that stop you.

Le Temps de Cerises FRENCH $$
(☎0590-51-36-27; www.ltc-hotel.com; 158 Blvd de Grand Case; mains €20-32; ⊙8am-10:30pm; ☜) With its rustic-elegant beach-villa vibe – complete with hanging chairs, overstuffed pillows on a wooden bench and a stilted terrace above the sand – this restaurant is almost too good-looking. Thankfully, there's also plenty of substance in the Mediterranean menu with Caribbean touches. The Saturday lobster beach barbecue is legendary (€58).

Rainbow Cafe INTERNATIONAL $$
(☎0690-88-84-44; 176 Blvd de Grand Case; mains €18-35; ⊙9am-10:30pm Tue-Sun; P ☜ ✎) Despite the name, it's actually crimson red that makes this grown-up day-to-night beach club a visual standout on Grand Case's sandy sliver. Not only is the facade bright red but so are the chairs and the umbrellas on the beach where you can sip and nibble all day long. Dinners are more elaborate and best enjoyed on the breezy veranda. Occasional live entertainment.

Sunset Café FRENCH $$
(☎0690-65-02-60; www.grandcasebeachclub.com; 21 Rue de la Petite Plage, Grand Case Beach Club; mains breakfast €8.50-22, crepes €6-15, lunch & dinner €15-30; ⊙8am-9:30pm; ☜) In an area that abounds with fabulous ocean views, Sunset Café at the Grand Case Beach Club

DON'T MISS

PIC PARADIS

The highest point on the island is 424m Pic Paradis. It offers fine vistas and good hiking opportunities, although it's hardly a 'paradise' thanks to communications towers. It is accessible by a rough maintenance road that doubles as a hiking trail. You can drive as far as the last house and then walk the final 1km to the top.

If you're driving, the road to Pic Paradis is 500m north of the 'L' in the road between Friar's Bay and Grand Case that splinters off to the inland community of Colombier. Take the road inland for 2km, turn left at the fork (signposted 'Sentier des Crêtes NE, Pic Paradis') and continue 500m further to the last house, where there's space to pull over and park.

Don't leave anything of value in your car as break-ins are common. Alternatively, leave your car at the bottom and walk up, for instance from **Loterie Farm** (☎0590-87-86-16; www.loteriefarm.com; 103 Rte de Pic Paradis, Rambaud; trail access €5, pool access & daybed €20, cabañitas €75, cabanas from €190, fly zone €40, fly zone extreme €60; ⊙9am-5pm; P ⓗ) 🍃, a private nature reserve featuring a high-ropes course, zip-lining, a couple of hikes, a gorgeous spring-fed swimming pool and a restaurant.

(p719), with a breezy terrace that juts out over the glittering water, takes first prize. Casual by day, it serves set breakfasts, daily blackboard specials, snacks, and sweet and savory crepes. At night, it morphs into a more elegant, candlelit affair.

Le Cottage FRENCH CARIBBEAN **$$**
(☎0690-62-26-86; www.lecottagesxm.com; 97 Blvd de Grand Case; mains €22-31, 3-course menu with wine €79, 4-course lobster menu €59; ⏰5:30-10pm Mon-Sat; 👪) The good-value lobster menu is clearly Le Cottage's best kitchen ambassador, but chef David Hanquer also orchestrates other local fish and meats into culinary symphonies with Caribbean aromas. For traditionalists, the menu also features foie gras, escargot (snails) and *fromage* (cheese). The wine list is outstanding, with many available by the glass.

Le Pressoir FRENCH **$$$**
(☎0590-87-76-62; www.lepressoirsxm.com; 32 Blvd de Grand Case; mains €34-45, 3-course menu €65; ⏰6-11pm Mon-Sat mid-Oct–mid-Sep; ❄) Named for the giant salt press outside and ensconced in a rare traditional Creole house from 1871, Le Pressoir stands for sophisticated dining with a relaxed undercurrent. Chef Alexis creates a rotating repertoire of gorgeous dishes that harness the best seasonal ingredients from land and sea, and imported jewels like caviar, foie gras and truffles.

★**Blue Martini** BAR
(☎0690-56-24-34; www.blue-martini.fr; 63 Blvd de Grand Case; ⏰5:30pm-midnight Mon-Sat; 📶) Casual and boisterous, the Blue Martini serves French Caribbean bites but is really more the perfect end-of-day destination for quick mood enhancers or dedicated drink-a-thons. The vibe kicks up a notch when bands fill the huge garden with beats from jazz to reggae.

Try the namesake cocktail, a cheerful blend of gin, pineapple syrup and lemon juice with a splash of blue curaçao for that ocean color.

Getting There & Away

Just inland is the smaller of St-Martin/Sint Maarten's two airports, Aéroport de Saint-Martin Grand Case (p728). There are taxi ranks and car-rental desks for companies. Buses stop by but schedules are erratic at best. A taxi or your own wheels are the way to go.

Anse Marcel

At the end of a steep and twisting road over a headland, Anse Marcel's breathtaking secluded bay is first glimpsed from high up before you gently descend to the coast. The village got torn to bits by Hurricane Irma and is still one giant construction site. Two luxury resorts and other commercial places were expected to come online in 2020. Until then, you have the ethereally beautiful sandy beach practically to yourself.

Sights

Petites Cayes BEACH
One of the island's top hidden beaches, Petites Cayes is accessible via the *Sentier des Froussards* (Froussards Trail), a narrow, steep and rocky trail that traverses St-Martin's last unspoilt forest. Wear close-toed shoes for the 2.5km trek to the beach that begins on the road leading into Anse Marcel (there should be a sign marked 'beach'). It's a bit of a challenge, but worth the effort if you like privacy and don't mind bringing all you need with you.

Surfers flock to Petites Cayes when the swell's up. From the beach, the trail continues east along the coast as far as Grandes Cayes for a total distance of about 4.5km.

Anse Marcel BEACH
Protected by two large headlands, this gorgeous and wide white-sand beach with clear sapphire waters is calm and popular with families. Snorkeling is particularly good (and safe) here, especially around the headlands. Enjoy views out to Anguilla from the sand or the posh Anse Marcel Beach restaurant. Caraïbes Watersports rents gear.

Activities

Caraïbes Watersports WATER SPORTS
(☎0690-88-81-02; www.caraibeswatersports.com; ⏰9am-5pm) Beachside shack Caraïbes Watersports has a nice range of water toys, including kayaks and SUPs (per hour €30), snorkeling gear (per half-day €20) and flyboards (per 30 minutes €120). Snorkelers should sign up for its 90-minute boat tour to top site Creole Rock (€55).

Eating

Anse Marcel Beach FRENCH CARIBBEAN **$$**
(☎0690-26-38-50; www.ansemarcelbeach.com; mains €20-26; ⏰noon-2:30pm Nov–mid-Aug; 🅿📶) The first restaurant to reopen in

devastated Anse Marcel, Anse Marcel Beach exudes Côte d'Azur–style elegance and opens up right onto the sultry sands. Dine on sophisticated salads and seafood served on linen-draped tables below the tented stone-tiled terrace, or retreat to a dining gazebo for extra privacy. Rent a pair of sun loungers and umbrella for €23.

Getting There & Away

No buses serve Anse Marcel, so you'll need to arrange a taxi or rental car (or watercraft to dock at the marina).

Orient Beach

Before Hurricane Irma, Orient Beach was St-Martin/Sint Maarten's most glamorous resort, famous for its bustling beach clubs and clothing-optional policy. Few places on the island bore Irma's brunt more than this little community. If the lashing by wind and water was not enough, a severe storm surge wiped out all beach bars and vegetation, and badly stressed the underwater world of the surrounding marine reserve. But even Orient Beach is rebounding nicely. Several beach bars have reopened along the 2km-long sandy beach (including a clothing-optional one at the southern end), the village square is again flanked by upscale restaurants, bakeries and shops line Ave des Plages, and kitesurfers bounce across the eternally beautifully sea. There's just no keeping a good thing down.

Activities

Wind Adventures WATER SPORTS

(0590-29-41-57; www.wind-adventures.com; 8am-6pm) Right on the sand, this water-sports center rents equipment for a wide range of activities, including windsurfing (two hours €50), kitesurfing (two hours from €100), SUP boarding (per hour €20), kayaking (two hours €22) and sailing (two hours €75). It also offers lessons and various tours from one-hour kayak trips to Green Bay to two-day catamaran cruises to St-Barths.

Sleeping & Eating

Most hotels and resorts are inland from the beach along with apartment and villa rentals. There are no budget options.

Hotel La Plantation RESORT $$$

(0590-29-58-00; www.la-plantation.com; Baie Orientale; studio/ste incl breakfast from €291/422; mid-Oct–Aug; P) A 450m walk from the beach, this plantation-style resort's spacious suites and studios are scattered across a landscaped slope along with a timber-decked swimming pool and two tennis courts. All units sleep six, and have patio and open kitchen. There's also an on-site cafe serving breakfast buffets, lunch and dinner, plus lobster on Monday evenings.

The village square has a clutch of gourmet restaurants, while the beach is lined with daytime beach bars that also serve food. More affordable options, including a bakery and a small supermarket, can be found along Ave des Plages and dotted around the residential areas away from the coast.

Le P'tit Bistro FRENCH $$

(0690-74-50-93; The Village; mains €15-38; 5:30-10:30pm Wed-Mon) The 'little bistro' is a throwback to traditional French fare with nary a dish that does not incorporate some sort of cheese – and that includes the fish soup! It's all quite delicious but if you're not the damn-the-calories (or arteries) kind of person, you can always order the daily catch.

Kkô Beach Bar & Restaurant INTERNATIONAL $$

(0590-87-43-26; www.kakaobeachsxm.com; Orient Bay Beach; mains €15-29; 10am-4pm Mon-Sat, to 5pm Sun;) The chicest of the resurrected beach clubs on Orient Bay, Kkô (pronounced 'kakao') delivers toes-in-sand bliss shaded by thatch-roofed beach beds and a thicket of cobalt-blue umbrellas. The kitchen is helmed by a Peruvian chef, which accounts for menu appearances of *tiradito de salmon* (sashimi-style salmon) and l*omo saltado* (sautéed beef), best paired with a pisco sour from the bar.

Coté Plages FRENCH $$

(0590-52-47-37; www.coteplages.com; The Village; tapas €8-19, mains €14-29, 2-/3-course menus €26/35; 6-10:30pm Mon-Sat;) The oldest restaurant in the Village trades in culinary gems that are both comforting and exciting. If picking your plate date from the live lobster tank is not your thing, go for the tuna tartare, dock-fresh fish filleted tableside or a dreamy-creamy roasted Camembert. Mussel nights, usually on Thursdays, are renowned island-wide.

Stachy's Hut BAR

(0690-57-41-30; www.facebook.com/stacheyshut; 69 Rue de Cul de Sac; hours vary) Ask any St-Martin resident about Stachy's Hut and their eyes start rolling as they recall – mistily – nights spent partying at this rollicking joint on the road to Pinel Island. Larger-than-life Stachy and his crew dole out strong potions, including homemade bush rum infused with, ahem, local herbs and, so we hear, possibly an iguana tail. Don't say you weren't warned! Best night: Friday for live reggae.

Some of the island's best bands get revelers swaying, drinking and flirting until the wee hours in this charmingly ramshackle bar put together with salvaged wood and corrugated metal, and decorated with original art and flotsam and jetsam from around the world. Weekdays are quieter and a good time to try the blackboard specials, usually Creole-style grilled fish and meats, created in the tiny kitchen.

Bikini Beach BAR

(0590-77-39-90; www.bikinisxm.com; Orient Bay Beach; 9am-9pm Mon-Thu, to 10pm Fri-Sun;) The post-Irma incarnation of this long-running beach bar exudes a relaxed yet elegant vibe. Savor tropical drinks and Caribbean-French bites like snapper baked in banana leaf (mains €16 to €26) on its stone deck hemmed in by young palm trees or kick back on a sun chair below a lime-green umbrella.

Kontiki BAR

(0690-66-24-25; www.facebook.com/kontikibeachsxm; Orient Bay Beach; 9am-6pm or later;) A maze of driftwood, booths and cushioned sun loungers with red umbrellas, this good-time venue serves local and European ice-cold beer alongside a small but stellar wine selection, freshly pressed juices and an extensive cocktail list. DJs spin at beach parties every Sunday.

For sustenance, the emphasis is on grilled fish and meat as well as a small selection of Asian dishes (mains €17 to €32).

Getting There & Away

Buses run infrequently from Marigot and Philipsburg but a taxi or your own wheels are more reliable options.

Oyster Pond

The Dutch–French border slices straight across Atlantic-facing Oyster Pond, which actually isn't a pond at all but a stunning sunken bay nestled between two jagged hills. Until Hurricane Irma wiped out its centerpiece, the landmark Captain Oliver's Marina, it was a major destination for yachties and boating people. Recovery has been slow but steady, exemplified by the re-opening of numerous hotels and restaurants and the return of a daily ferry to St-Barth.

Sleeping & Eating

Colombus Hotel HOTEL $

(0590-87-42-52; 29 Rue de l'Escale; studio from €103, 1-/2-bedroom apt from €140/171;) You'll sleep sweetly at this value-priced small hotel with studios and apartments equipped with microwave, fridge and coffee machine and set around a well-maintained pool. Terraces are big enough to do your yoga exercises. Rates include taxes and service charge.

★ **Les Balcons d'Oyster Pond** BUNGALOW $$

(0690-75-58-71; www.lesbalcons.com; 15 Ave du Lagon; bungalows €145-245;) Completely redone post-Irma, this charming collection of good-value bungalows sits on a hill amid tropical gardens, with sweeping views of the bay and sleepy marina below. Each bungalow has completely different decor but all have private terrace with gas grill and kitchen, and two cottages come with private plunge pool.

Oasis PIZZA $

(0690-76-64-27; www.oasissxm.com; Residence les Rochers; pizza US$10-16, mains US$17-29; 7:30-10:30am, noon-2pm & 6-10pm) Gently illuminated palm trees around the dining area bathe this popular restaurant on the French side in an ambience of calm. Its main ammo are the pizzas, thin-crust pies loaded with goodies, although the linguine with clams and the beef filet with foie gras and truffle oil are also tantalizing options. Also serves breakfast.

BZH INTERNATIONAL $$

(0690-10-16-01; www.facebook.com/bzhsxm; Ave du Lagon; dishes €5-17; 11am-2:30pm & 5:30-10pm Mon-Sat;) Locally renowned for its pizzas, such as the BZH (tomatoes, onion, minced beef and egg) or the Calabraise (bacon, egg and olives), Breton-turned-global BZH also serves creative salads, sweet crepes and savory galettes as well as burgers, pasta and beef tartare.

Pizzas can be delivered around Oyster Pond for orders over €20. BZH stands for 'Breizh' – 'Brittany' in Breton.

Quai Ouest FRENCH $$

(0690-73-76-01; www.captainolivershotel.com; Captain Oliver's Marina; mains €19-29; 6-10pm Mon-Sat) In a peaceful spot with a roofed deck with prime views of the marina, this little joint crawled its way back into existence post-Irma and now plies hungry patrons with French home-cooking like beef bourguignon, duck breast or lamb shank. Come early for a good table at sunset.

ℹ Getting There & Away

Infrequent buses pass through en route between Marigot and Philipsburg, but you're better off arranging a taxi or traveling with your own wheels. The daily **Voyager** (☎ 0590-87-10-68; www.voy12.com; Captain Oliver's Marina; one way/return/same-day return from €63/87/70) ferry whisks you to St-Barth in half an hour.

UNDERSTAND ST-MARTIN & SINT MAARTEN

History

For a thousand years, St-Martin/Sint Maarten was sparsely populated by the Arawaks and later the fiercer Caribs. They named the island Soualiga after the brackish salt ponds that made it difficult to settle.

Columbus sailed past on November 11, 1493, which happened to be the feast day of St Martin of Tours, after whom he named the island Isla de San Martin. But it was the Dutch who were the first to take advantage of the land, a nice stopping-off point between the Netherlands and their colonies in Brazil and New Amsterdam (New York City). After a few abortive attempts by the Spanish to regain the island, now found to be brimming with lucrative salt deposits, the French and Dutch ended up fighting for control of it.

As legend has it, the Dutch and the French decided to partition St-Martin/Sint Maarten from a march originating in Oyster Pond. The French walked northward, the Dutch south. While the French quenched their thirst with wine, the Dutch brought along *jenever* (Dutch gin). Halfway through, the Dutchmen stopped to sleep off the ill effects, effectively giving the French a greater piece of the pie.

St-Martin became a plantation island much like many of its neighbors. The end of slavery (1848 on the French side; 1863 on the Dutch side) brought an end to the plantation boom and by 1930 the population stood at just 2000 hardy souls. The island became duty-free in 1939. In 1943, during WWII, the US Navy built large runways on the island to use as a base in the Caribbean. The French capitalized by using the runways to fly in tourists; by the 1950s this had brought the population of St-Martin/Sint Maarten up to about 70,000 and made tourism the number-one industry on both sides of the island.

In the 1980s Aruba's secession from the Netherlands Antilles sparked movements on St-Martin/Sint Maarten toward greater independence from their parent entities. The Dutch were first in 2000, when they received a *'status aparte'* with the Netherlands. The French side followed in 2003, voting to secede from Guadeloupe to form their own separate overseas collectivity (Collectivité de Saint-Martin). In 2010 the Netherlands Antilles dissolved, propelling Sint Maarten toward independence when it officially became recognized as a 'constituent country' of the Kingdom of the Netherlands.

People & Culture

St-Martin/Sint Maarten is a melting pot of ethnicities like no other place in the Caribbean. The island culture has its roots largely in African, French and Dutch influences, though scores of more recent immigrants – including many from the Dominican Republic, Haiti and China – have added their own elements to this multicultural society. Today, the island claims 120 different nationalities speaking over 80 languages, although French dominates St-Martin and English dominates Sint Maarten.

St-Martin/Sint Maarten has adapted to tourism better than any other island nearby. You'll rarely meet someone who was actually born on the island. As the smallest area of land in the world divided into two nations, each side functions symbiotically while attracting tourists in very different ways. The French side embraces its European roots and puts an emphasis on good food and a relaxed lifestyle. Home to the cruise-ship port, the Dutch side is much more built up with solid hurricane-resistant concrete high-rises, and a constant hum of low-lying debauchery that accompanies the dozens of gentlemen's clubs, casinos and beach bars, although it also offers a huge range of watersports activities along its coast.

Landscape & Wildlife

The west side of the island is more water than land, dominated by the expansive Simpson Bay Lagoon, which is one of the largest landlocked bodies of water in the Caribbean and has moorings for a large array of boats. The island's interior is hilly, with the highest point, Pic Paradis, rising 424m from the center of French St-Martin.

Birdwatching is excellent here, with over 100 different species of bird recorded. Of them, some 60 migratory species include herons, egrets, stilts, pelicans and laughing gulls, which frequent the island's salt ponds. Frigate birds can be spotted along the coast, and hummingbirds and yellow-breasted banana quits in gardens. Dragonflies and butterflies are prevalent all over the island.

The only native mammals are bats, of which there are eight species. There are also mongooses, raccoons, iguanas, geckos, tortoises, sea turtles and several species of tree frog.

The waters on the entire Dutch side, from Cupecoy Bay to Oyster Pond, are protected by Sint Maarten Marine Park. Much of the French side is part of the protected Réserve Naturelle de St-Martin.

SURVIVAL GUIDE

Directory A–Z

ACCESSIBLE TRAVEL

Although St-Martin is rugged and quite mountainous, the massive amount of tourist development has made it relatively hassle-free for travelers with disabilities to experience the island. Towns and villages along the coast are mostly flat, and wheelchair ramps are quite prevalent in shops and restaurants in Philipsburg.

Many resorts have wheelchair-friendly rooms and bathrooms with rails and barrier-free showers. Not all restaurant bathrooms are equipped for wheelchair users, however – confirm when you book.

ACCOMMODATIONS

Hurricane Irma destroyed many properties, especially on the French side, but room inventory is slowly rebounding. It's best to book in advance, especially during high season (mid-December to mid-April).

Large resorts dominate Maho and Mullet Bay and Simpson Bay on the Dutch side. Properties on the French side are small and range from simple hotels to fancy villas. Grand Case has some charming boutique properties.

SLEEPING PRICE RANGES

The following price ranges refer to a double room with bathroom in high season.

$ less than US$150

$$ US$150–300

$$$ more than US$300

ACTIVITIES

St-Martin/Sint Maarten is a great destination for families and anyone up for an active vacation. Water sports are most popular, but there are plenty of outdoor pursuits on land too, including horseback riding, hiking, zip-lining and skydiving.

Cultural activities range from food tours to rum-distillery tours and perfume-making workshops.

Diving & Snorkeling

St-Martin/Sint Maarten has about 17 dive sites, mostly in the waters south and southeast of the island. The most popular wreck dive is at Proselyte Reef, south of Philipsburg, where, in 1802, the 42m, 32-gun British frigate HMS *Proselyte* sank in 15m of water.

Other prime dive sites include the Maze, where you can go cave diving and spot turtles, angelfish, sponges and corals; Turtle Reef, a deep dive of up to 18m with octopuses, eels, lobster and namesake turtles; and One Step Beyond, which has large schools of fish along with barracudas, morays, lobster and sharks.

For more information and links to local dive shops, see https://travel.padi.com/d/sint-maarten. Serious divers should consider a day trip to neighboring Sint Eustatius or Saba.

The best snorkeling is at Creole Rock between Grand Case and Anse Marcel on the French side. Decent snorkeling is around the shallow waters surrounding Îlet Pinel and Petite Clef, and at Tintamarre island with sheltered coves and geologic faults.

ELECTRICITY

French side: 220V, 60 cycles, European-style sockets. Dutch side: 110V, 60 cycles, North American–style sockets.

EMERGENCY NUMBERS

Ambulance (St-Martin)	15
Police (St-Martin)	17
Ambulance (Sint Maarten)	912
General emergency (Sint Maarten)	911
Police (Sint Maarten)	911

EATING PRICE RANGES

The following price ranges refer to a main course.

$ less than US$15

$$ US$15–30

$$$ more than US$30

FOOD

Grand Case, on the French side, is the island's gourmet epicenter. There are also some great hidden beach-bar restaurants and *lolos* (barbecues) scattered around the coastline. Many resorts have top restaurants. Cruise-ship port Philipsburg is home to mainly fast-food and casual cafes (of varying quality), although there are a couple of notable standouts.

The two best-stocked supermarkets are **Marché U** (☎0590-29-54-32; www.magasins-u.com; Rue de Hollande, Howell Center; ⊙8am-8pm Mon-Sat, to 12:45pm Sun) on the French side and Carrefour (p713) on the Dutch side.

HEALTH

The island has two small but well-equipped hospitals.

St Maarten Medical Center (p714) The island's main hospital is west of Philipsburg and has a 24-hour emergency room.

Centre Hospitalier LC Fleming Saint Martin (p717) In Marigot on the French side; has a 24-hour emergency room.

INTERNET ACCESS

Wi-fi is widely available across the island at hotels, cafes and bars, although it had not yet been restored at the airports at the time of writing.

LGBT+ TRAVELERS

While same-sex marriage is legally recognized on both sides of the island – and although the French side is generally more tolerant – some homophobia does exist, so it's best to avoid public displays of affection, especially outside the more touristy area. Booking a double room as a same-sex couple shouldn't pose any problems. For more detailed tips and insights, visit www.gaysintmaarten.com.

DRINKING WATER

Tap water on both sides of the island comes from desalination plants. It is generally safe to drink, though doesn't taste very appealing so many locals prefer to drink bottled water.

MONEY

The official currencies are the euro on the French side and the Netherlands Antillean guilder (called NAf) on the Dutch side. However, the latter are not in circulation and the US dollar is effectively the main currency. US dollars are also accepted in St-Martin.

If you're paying with cash, establishments on both sides sometimes accept one-for-one dollars to euros and vice versa. Depending on the current exchange rate, this may work against you.

As not all ATMs accept foreign cards, it's worth keeping cash on hand.

Credit cards (including foreign cards) are widely accepted.

Exchange Rates

Australia	A$1	US$0.67
Canada	C$1	US$0.75
Euro zone	€1	US$1.12
Japan	¥100	US$0.94
New Zealand	NZ$1	US$0.64
Switzerland	Sfr1	US$1.02
UK	UK£1	US$1.20

For current exchange rates, see www.xe.com.

Tipping

Hotels Many (but not all) hotels and restaurants include a 15% service charge, in which case no further tipping is necessary (otherwise, add 15% to the bill).

Restaurants Diners commonly leave a small amount for exceptional service.

Taxis About 10% to 15%.

OPENING HOURS

Some activities operators, hotels, bars and restaurants shut in September and/or October.

Restaurants both sides lunch 11:30am–2:30pm; dinner French side 7pm–10pm, Dutch side 5pm–10pm

Shops & supermarkets 8am–8pm Monday to Saturday, 9am–1pm Sunday

PUBLIC HOLIDAYS

New Year's Day January 1 (both sides)

Good Friday March/April (Dutch side)

Easter Sunday March/April (Dutch side)

Easter Monday March/April (both sides)

King's Day (Koningsdag) April 27 (Dutch side)

Labor Day May 1 (both sides)

Victory Day May 8 (French side)

Carnival Monday Monday before Ash Wednesday (both sides; unofficial)

Carnival Tuesday Tuesday before Ash Wednesday (both sides; unofficial)

Ash Wednesday February/March (both sides; unofficial)

Ascension Thursday Fortieth day after Easter (both sides)

Abolition Day May 27 (French side)

Whit Sunday Seventh Sunday after Easter (Dutch side)

Pentecost Monday Eighth Monday after Easter (French side)

Emancipation Day July 1 (Dutch side)

Bastille Day July 14 (French side)

Assumption Day August 15 (French side)

Constitution Day October 9 (Dutch side)

All Saints' Day (Toussaints) November 1 (French side)

Sint Maarten Day/Armistice Day November 11 (both sides)

Christmas Day December 25 (both sides)

Boxing Day December 26 (Dutch side)

SAFE TRAVEL

By and large, Sint Maarten and St-Martin are quite safe, although crimes of opportunity like pickpocketing and purse snatching do occur.

➡ No-go areas at night include Sandy Ground (2km southwest of Marigot), Quartier d'Orléans (3km south of Orient Beach) and Lower Prince's Quarter (the area immediately north of Philipsburg).

➡ The parking area atop Pic Paradis is notorious for break-ins, so avoid or don't leave anything of value in the car.

➡ The regionwide sargassum seaweed bloom, which first made landfall on St-Martin/Sint Maarten in 2011 and 2012, returned to east-facing beaches in 2019, including those at Orient Beach, Grand Cul-de-Sac and Dawn Beach. Depending on the amount, swimming in seaweed-infested waters may be unpleasant to impossible. If not removed, it releases a sulfurous odor that can cause respiratory problems.

Rental-car Safety

➡ Do not leave anything whatsoever in your car when you leave it parked, especially in isolated destinations and car parks (but it's not worth taking a chance anywhere or at anytime). Even if you don't mind that something minor was stolen, you might end up paying dearly to repair your smashed-in window.

➡ Before taking your rental car out of the lot, check the car doors – many have had the locks jimmied open at some point.

➡ Take photos or a video with your smartphone when you pick up the car to avoid rental-company scams claiming you caused pre-existing damage.

TELEPHONE

➡ St-Martin's country code is 590; Sint Maarten's is 1-721.

➡ St-Martin's 10-digit landline numbers begin with 0590, 10-digit mobile-phone numbers begin with 0690.

➡ Sint Maarten's local numbers are seven digits; landline numbers begin with 54, while mobile numbers begin with 55.

➡ Calls between the two sides are treated as international calls.

➡ The exit code for both sides of the island is 00.

➡ To call the Dutch side from the French side (landline or mobile), dial 00-1-721, then the seven-digit number.

➡ To dial the French side from the Dutch side, dial 00-590, then drop the '0' and dial the remaining nine digits.

Cell Phones

Check with your home provider about roaming capabilities and costs. Telem and UTS (Chippie) are the main providers on the Dutch side; Orange and Dauphin dominate on the French side. Post offices and supermarkets sell prepaid SIM cards that can be used in an unlocked phone.

TIME

St-Martin/Sint Maarten is on Atlantic Time (GMT/UTC minus four hours). Daylight saving is not observed.

VOLUNTEERING

➡ Check first with the French and/or Dutch representation in your home country to see whether volunteering affects your visa status.

➡ One popular volunteering option for both locals and visitors is the annual Heineken Regatta (p715).

➡ You could also try contacting the Nature Foundation St Maarten (www.naturefoundationsxm.org) to ask about monitoring wildlife such as sea turtles as well as various island rehabilitation projects.

➡ SXM Doet (www.doet.com) organizes numerous projects where you can participate as a volunteer, including beach cleanups or sanitizing toys at a day-care center.

PRACTICALITIES

Smoking On both sides of the island, smoking is banned in all enclosed public spaces including hotel rooms, restaurants, cafes and bars. It's permitted in outdoor areas, however, such as terraces, so you may still encounter smoke.

Weights & measures Both sides of the island use the metric system and 24-hour clock.

Getting There & Away

AIR

Princess Juliana International Airport (SXM; ☎546-7542; www.sxmairport.com; Airport Rd) (SXM), on the Dutch side, is where all intercontinental flights arrive and depart. Major airlines from North America include American, Delta, JetBlue, Spirit and United. Air France connects the island with Paris and KLM has flights from Amsterdam. SXM is also a major regional hub with flights to and from Anguilla, Antigua, Curaçao, Guadeloupe, Montserrat, Saba, Sint Eustatius, St-Barthélemy, St Kitts, St Thomas, Tortola and Trinidad. Regional airlines serving Sint Maarten include LIAT (www.liat.com), Winair (www.fly-winair.com), Air Antilles (www.airantilles.com) and St-Barth Commuter (www.stbarthcommuter.com).

Aéroport de Saint-Martin Grand Case (L'Espérance; SFG; ☎0590-27-11-00; www.saint-martin-airport.com; Rte de l'Espérance), on the French side, has prop planes serving Anguilla, St-Barthélemy, Guadeloupe and Martinique. It's served by Air Caraïbes (www.aircaraibes.com), Air Antilles and St-Barth Commuter.

SEA

Cruise Ship

St-Martin/Sint Maarten is a hugely popular cruise-ship destination. Sometimes up to seven giant ships dock in Philipsburg's **Port St Maarten** (☎542-8503; www.portstmaarten.com; Juancho Yrausquin Blvd), where passengers disembark directly onto land.

Ferry

Ferries depart from Marigot (French side) and Simpson Bay (Dutch side) for Anguilla; from Marigot, Philipsburg (Dutch side) and Oyster Pond (French side) for St-Barth; and from Philipsburg and Simpson Bay for Saba.

Yacht

There are marinas on the Dutch side at Great Bay (Philipsburg) and Simpson Bay Lagoon, on the border at Oyster Pond, and on the French side at Anse Marcel along with two in Marigot (Fort Louis and Port La Royale).

Those arriving by yacht must contact the immigration office in **Philipsburg** (☎542-2277; ⏲7am-5pm) or **Simpson Bay** (☎545-0031; ⏲8am-4pm, varies seasonally) on VHF channel 12 to arrange clearing immigration before docking at the island's marinas.

Three bridges open to allow boats to enter the coves at Simpson Bay. They are the Simpson Bay Bridge (a drawbridge) and the post-Irma Simpson Bay Causeway swing bridge on the Dutch side, and the Sandy Ground drawbridge on the French side (under repair, limited hours). For the latest opening times, consult www.portstmaarten.com.

> **DEPARTURE TAX**
>
> For flights, the departure tax is included in the ticket price.
>
> Departure tax for ferries depends on the destination, the operator and the place of departure. It can be as little as US$3 for the public ferry from Marigot to Anguilla to US$10 for trips to Saba or St-Barth. Some companies build the tax into their ticket price.

Getting Around

Although the island is divided into two separate land claims, there are no official border crossings (besides billboards and flags welcoming drivers to each side of the island). Traffic moves freely across both sides of the island as if it were one entity.

BICYCLE

To tackle the island's hilly terrain, Wind Adventures (p722) in Orient Beach, on the French side, has mountain bikes for €25 per day, while **Trisport** (☎0590-87-08-91; www.trisportsxm.com; Rue du Hollande; ⏲10am-5pm Mon-Sat) in Philipsburg, on the Dutch side, rents bikes for US$25 per day. Take care riding on the roads, as traffic is heavy and not considerate of cyclists.

BUS

- Buses are by far the cheapest method of transportation, but if you need to be somewhere fast, take a taxi, or better yet rent a car.
- Buses run daily from 5am to midnight but do not have a set schedule. Tickets cost between US$1 and US$2.
- Service mostly moves through Philipsburg, Mullet Bay, Simpson Bay, Marigot and Grand Case. When you need to get off, simply shout a friendly 'stop.'
- In Marigot and Philipsburg you have to stand at bus stops (called 'Bushalte' in Philipsburg).
- In rural areas you can flag down buses anywhere along the route.
- Buses have their final destination posted on the front shield, but most are bound for either Philipsburg or Marigot.

CAR & MOTORCYCLE

Drive on the right side of the road on both sides of the island. Your home driver's license is valid. Road signs and car odometers are in kilometers. The speed limit is 50km/h.

The amount of traffic on the island can shock visitors expecting a peaceful getaway. Traffic jams occur regularly. Factor in plenty of time to reach your destination.

Gas stations can be found on both sides of the island and most are open 24 hours. Many, especially those on the Dutch side, only take cash.

Car Rental

Until reconstruction of Princess Juliana International Airport is completed, all international and local car-rental agencies have offices along Airport Rd. Minivan shuttles with the company logo line up outside the terminal for the short ride. Some companies also have offices at Aéroport de Saint-Martin Grand Case.

In high season prices for a small car start at US$45/€45 per day. During low season they can start as low as US$28/€28.

Make sure you take a good look at your vehicle before leaving the lot, and take photos or a video with your smartphone to avoid being charged for alleged damage upon returning it. Comprehensive insurance is strongly recommended.

Rental companies include the following.

Auto Discount (☎0690-59-94-62; www.auto-discount.fr; Rte de L'Espérance, Aéroport de Saint-Martin Grand Case; per 3-day car rental from €100; ⌚8:30am-noon Mon-Sat & 2:30-6pm daily) At Aéroport de Saint-Martin Grand Case.

Avis (☎in Sint Maarten 545-2847; www.avis-sxm.com; 120 Airport Rd; ⌚7am-6pm) At both airports.

Budget (☎545-2316; www.sxmbudget.com; Airport Rd; ⌚7am-10:30pm) At Princess Juliana International Airport.

Coastal Car Rental (☎toll-free 866-978-8361; www.coastal.sx; Airport Rd; ⌚7:30am-6pm) At the cruise-ship terminal and Princess Juliana International Airport.

Hertz (☎in Sint Maarten 545-4541; www.hertz.sxmrentacar.com; ⌚6am-10pm) Has 12 locations around the island including both airports and the Port St Maarten cruise-ship terminal.

Johnny's Scooter Rental (☎587-0272; www.johnnysscooterrental.com; 26 Juancho Yrausquin Blvd; scooter/ATV rental per day US$65/99; ⌚8am-5:30pm) In Philipsburg.

Paradise Car Rental (☎545-3737; http://paradisecarrentalsxm.com; Airport Rd; ⌚7am-6pm) At Princess Juliana International Airport.

HITCHHIKING

You'll often see locals hitching, but tourists shouldn't follow suit. Petty theft and violent crime are common on the island and hitchhikers are easy targets.

TAXI

- To book a taxi, call 542-2359 (Sint Maarten) or 0590-87-56-54 (St-Martin).
- On the Dutch side, never get in a car that doesn't have a license plate reading 'TXI' indicating that it's a registered taxi.
- From Juliana airport it's US$8 to Maho, US$20 to Philipsburg, US$20 to Marigot, US$35 to Grand Case, US$35 to Orient Beach and US$45 to Anse Marcel. Drivers only take cash. It's best to have change as drivers aren't always willing or able to take larger notes.
- Rates increase by 25% from 10pm to midnight and by 50% between midnight and 6am; there's an additional US$5 charge per passenger for three or more people.
- Day or night, agree on a fare before hopping in a cab.

St Vincent & the Grenadines

784 / POP 109,991

Includes ➡

Best Places to Eat

- ➡ Sugar Reef Cafe (p742)
- ➡ Fig Tree (p739)
- ➡ Basil's Bar & Restaurant (p735)
- ➡ De Reef (p741)
- ➡ French Veranda (p735)

Best Places to Stay

- ➡ Cotton House (p742)
- ➡ Petit St Vincent Resort (p748)
- ➡ Palm Island Resort (p748)
- ➡ Bequia Plantation Hotel (p739)
- ➡ Firefly (p742)

Why Go?

Just the name St Vincent and the Grenadines (SVG) evokes visions of idyllic island life. Imagine an island chain in the heart of the Caribbean Sea, uncluttered by tourist exploitation, with white-sand beaches on deserted islands, sky-blue water gently lapping the shores and barely a soul around.

While it may sound like a playground for the rich and famous, you don't need your own yacht to enjoy SVG. In fact local ferries make exploring this archipelago nation independently fairly cost effective and with so many islands to choose from, there's sure to be one that perfectly meets your needs.

And while it's famed for its islands and beaches, the country offers more than just a relax in a hammock. There are volcanoes to climb, refreshing waterfalls to explore and great hiking throughout.

When to Go

Nov–Apr Dry Season, the best time to island hop, though some rainfall can be experienced at this time too.

May Shoulder season is a good time to visit, with fairly dry weather to enjoy and fewer crowds, and prices are generally lower.

Jun–Oct Rainy season sees many businesses close or reduce hours, but Vincy's party season is in full swing, led by the raucous Vincy Mas Carnival.

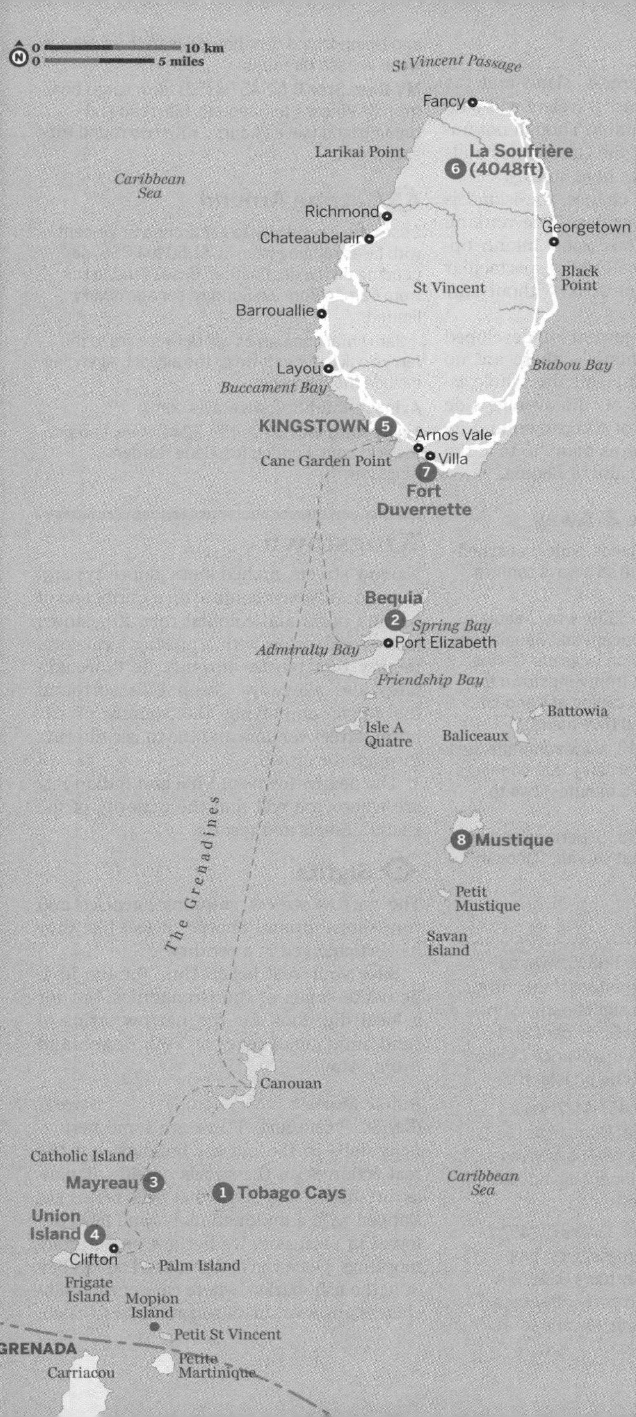

St Vincent & the Grenadines Highlights

1 **Tobago Cays** (p747) Visiting these five picture-perfect islands that are the essential SVG snorkeling experience.

2 **Bequia** (p738) Tossing away your return ticket upon settling into one of the region's best small islands.

3 **Mayreau** (p744) Chilling out on postcard-perfect Saltwhistle Bay before partying in local bars with new friends.

4 **Union Island** (p745) Taking a swim at one of the numerous empty beaches on this remote island outpost.

5 **Kingstown** (p732) Keeping it real on the cobblestone streets of SVG's biggest city and capital, a vibrant and decidedly nonupscale mélange.

6 **La Soufrière** (p737) Hiking to the top of this immense sulfur-spitting volcano.

7 **Fort Duvernette** (p732) Climbing the spiral staircase to the top of this rock fortress jutting out of the sea.

8 **Mustique** (p742) Kicking up your heels with rock stars at this impossibly beautiful and expensive island.

ST VINCENT

St Vincent is SVG's largest island and the hub through which most travelers will pass on their visit to the country. Though not uninspiring, the allure of the Grenadines pulls most visitors away from here quickly.

But if you give it a chance, the island is a fascinating place to explore. The verdant, rainforested interior has good hiking options and there are waterfalls, spectacular old forts and lush gardens without any crowds at all.

The island is somewhat undeveloped compared to its neighbors – there are no functioning traffic lights on the whole island. The beaches are on the average side and the frenetic pace of Kingstown and its unpolished edges inspires many to take the first boat down to the calm of Bequia.

Getting There & Away

Several ferries link the islands. Note that schedules can change on a whim so always confirm timings.

Bequia Express (457-3539; www.bequiaexpress.com) Links St Vincent and Bequia (one hour) several times daily on large car ferries. It also runs twice a week from Kingstown to the southern Grenadines calling at Canouan, Mayreau and Union Island (five hours).

MV Admiral (458-3348; www.admiralferries.com/schedule) A large car ferry that connects St Vincent and Bequia (75 minutes) two to three times daily.

MV Barracuda (455-9835; perrysshipping@vincysurf.com) Cargo boat serving Canouan and Union Island (five hours), with three trips a week in each direction.

MV Gem Star II (457-4157) Slow cargo boat from St Vincent to Canouan, Mayreau and Union Island (seven hours), with two round trips each week.

ISLAND TOURS

Baleine Tours (593-9398; www.baleinetours.com) A long-established outfit that takes visitors on sightseeing tours and boat trips around St Vincent and the Grenadines. Book in advance as the boat spends a lot of time off island.

Fantasea Tours (457-4477; www.fantaseatours.com; Villa) Runs trips to the Falls of Baleine as well as cruises up both sides of St Vincent island and through the Grenadines.

Sailor's Wilderness Tours (457-1274; www.sailorswildernesstours.com; Upper Middle St; full-day tours US$95) A popular local tour company offering a range of trips, including volcano tours and visits to waterfalls.

Getting Around

Buses are a good way to get around St Vincent, with fares ranging from EC$1.50 to EC$6, depending on the destination. Buses tend to run from 6am to 8pm; on Sunday, service is very limited.

Car-rental companies will deliver cars to the ferry dock in Kingstown or the airport. Agencies include the following:

Avis (456-6861; www.avis.com)

Lewis Auto World (456-2244; www.lewisautoworld.com; London Rd, Cane Garden, Kingstown)

Kingstown

Narrow streets, arched stone doorways and covered walkways conjure up a Caribbean of banana boats and colonial rule. Kingstown heaves and swells with a pulsing local community that bustles through its thoroughfares and alleyways. Steep hills surround the town, amplifying the sounds of car horns, street vendors and the music filtering through the crowd.

The nearby towns of Villa and Indian Bay are where you will find the majority of the island's hotels and resorts.

Sights

The narrow streets, shipping agencies and rum shops around Sharpe St feel like they haven't changed in a century.

Save your real beach time for the idyllic white sands of the Grenadines, but for a local dip, look for the narrow strips of sand amid small coves at **Villa Beach** and **Indian Bay**.

Public Market MARKET

(Bay St; 6am-3pm) There are some permanent stalls in the market building, but the real action is on the streets outside. Bananas in shapes and sizes that will never get slapped with a multinational-brand label are found in profusion. It's liveliest on Saturday mornings. Once you're done, head across Bay St to the fish market, where cleavers and machetes bang away in unison at the fresh catch.

★Fort Duvernette FORT

(Rock Fort; ☎451-2921; svgntrust@gmail.com; EC$5; ⊙8am-6pm) Perched atop a large volcanic rock offshore from Villa, this eerie fort was constructed to defend the town of Calliaqua and affords fantastic 360-degree views of the southern shoreline. There are 225 steps in the spiral staircase that has been carved into the rock; take care as it can be slippery, with small stones often covering the walkway – bring footwear. At the top, 200ft above sea level, you'll find two batteries of cannon and a picnic area.

Fort Duvernette is only accessible by boat. Ask for Nato in Indian Bay, who will take you over in his little rowboat for EC$27 per visitor. Alternatively, motorboat operators hang out at the Young Island dock and charge around EC$100 round trip.

There is an admission fee, but there's not always an official there to collect it.

St Mary's CHURCH

(North River Rd) Brooding St Mary's is the most eye-catching of Kingstown's churches and stands in dramatic contrast to the prim, whitewashed Anglican cathedral across the way. The castle-like complex blends Gothic

St Vincent

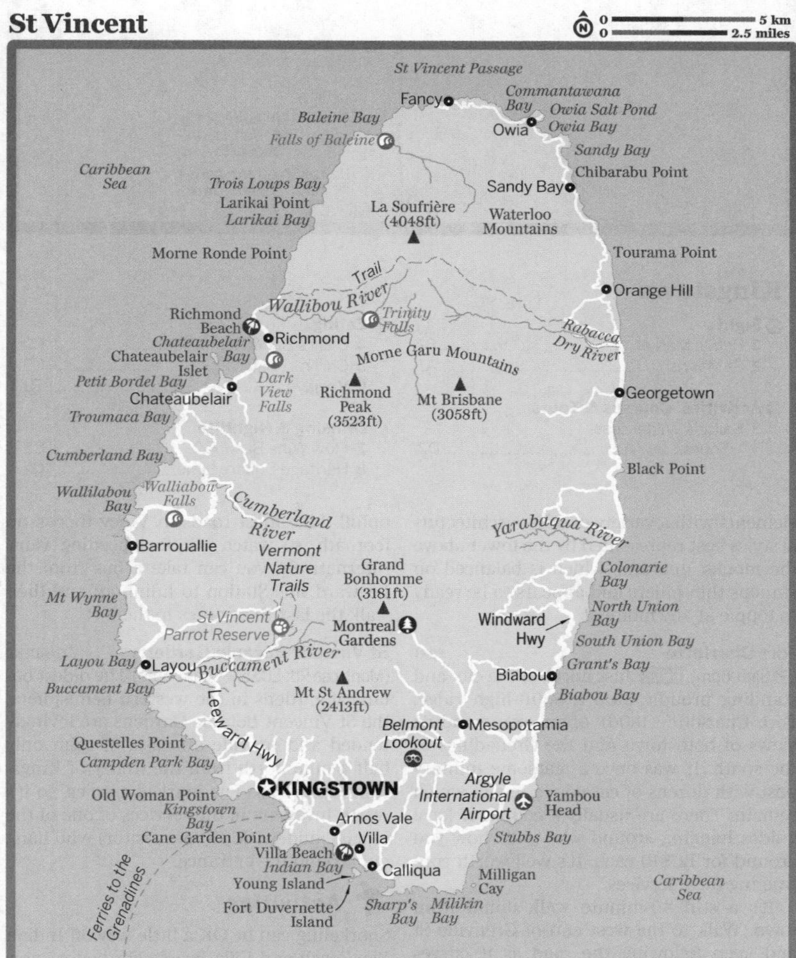

Kingstown

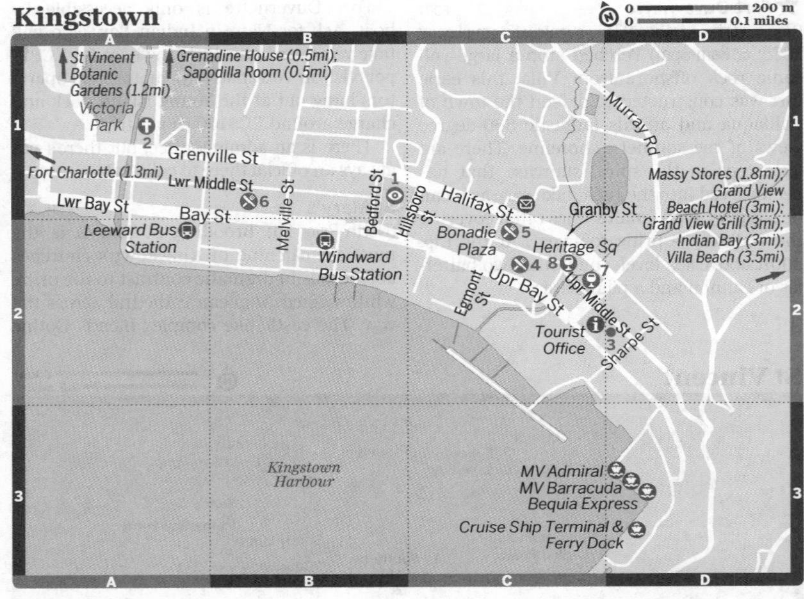

Kingstown

Sights
1 Public Market B1
2 St Mary's A1

Activities, Courses & Tours
3 Sailor's Wilderness Tours D2

Eating
4 Basil's Bar & Restaurant C2
5 Chill'n C2
6 Veejays B1

Drinking & Nightlife
7 Flow Wine Bar C2
8 Heritage Square Lime C2

elements with a variety of other architectural styles best represented by the tower above the monks' quarters, which is balanced on sinuous thin pillars and appears to be ready to topple at any moment.

Fort Charlotte FORT

(6am-6pm) FREE Just north of the city and standing proudly atop a 660ft-high ridge, Fort Charlotte (1806) offers commanding views of both town and the Grenadines to the south. It was once a fearsome military post with dozens of cannon, a few of which remain. There are usually a couple of local guides hanging around who will show you around for EC$10 each. It's well worth contracting their services.

It's a stiff 40-minute walk uphill from town. Walk to the west end of Grenville St and keep following the road as it curves uphill. Like most roads in Vincy there's no footpath, so watch out for speeding vans. Alternatively, you can take a bus from the Leeward Bus Station to Edinboro and then walk the last 10 minutes to the fort.

St Vincent Botanic Gardens GARDENS

(Montrose Rd; EC$5; 6am-6pm) The oldest botanical gardens in the western hemisphere, the St Vincent Botanic Gardens are lovingly tended and provide an oasis of calm only half a mile north from the frenzy of Kingstown. There are few marked species, so it's worth investing in the services of one of the official guides (EC$10 per visitor) who hang out around the entrance.

Activities

Snorkeling can be OK a little way off Indian Bay Beach and Villa Beach. For better snorkeling take a boat trip up the west coast to some secluded bays.

Indigo Dive DIVING
(☎ 493-9494; www.indigodive.com; Blue Lagoon Marina, Ratho Mill; 1-/2-tank dives US$70/130; ⏰ 8am-6pm) An intimate shop offering dives around St Vincent as well as Professional Association of Diving Instructors (PADI) dive courses.

Dive St Vincent DIVING
(☎ 457-4714; www.divestvincent.com; Young Island Dock, Villa Beach; 1-/2-tank dives US$75/130) Friendly dive shop offering boat dives, rentals and instruction, as well as snorkeling trips.

Festivals & Events

Vincy Mas CARNIVAL
(www.carnivalsvg.com; ⏰ end Jun & early Jul) *The* big yearly event in St Vincent. This enormous carnival culminates in a street party in Kingstown with steel-pan bands, dancers and drinks.

Sleeping

Downtown Kingstown empties out after dark. There are just a couple of midrange guesthouses in the downtown area and a couple of slightly more upmarket options in the hills behind town. The majority of visitors choose to stay in the beachside communities of Indian Bay and Villa where there are several modest resorts and guesthouses right by the water.

Skyblue Apartments APARTMENT $
(☎ 457-4394; skybluesvg@gmail.com; Indian Bay; r US$65-75; ❄@📶) Nestled in the suburban neighborhood of Indian Bay, this well-managed place offers some of the best value on the island. It's neat, tidy and just steps from the water. The tranquil rooms are indeed very blue and come with all the necessary fittings and a functional separate kitchen area. There's also a grassy area with tables outside.

Mariner's Hotel HOTEL $
(☎ 457-4000; www.marinershotel.com; Villa Beach; s/d/tr from US$85/95/175; 🏊) At the end of Villa Beach, this comfortable hotel has straightforward rooms with vaulted wooden ceilings available with both garden and sea views. The seaside pool with views of Young Island and Bequia is inviting. Skip the newer luxury rooms at the back – while they have a more modern design and facilities they don't have much of a view.

★ **Grenadine House** BOUTIQUE HOTEL $$
(☎ 458-1800; www.grenadinehouse.com; Kingstown Park; r US$150-230; ❄@🏊) Perched in the hills overlooking Kingstown like a fortress of whitewashed luxury, Grenadine House is away from the beach and near the genteel district of the botanical gardens. The property offers fantastic views of town and the Grenadines. White linen with thread counts to brag about, wicker headboards and fresh flowers complement the bedrooms. The food and drink options are excellent.

★ **Beachcombers Hotel** RESORT $$
(☎ 458-4283; www.beachcombershotel.com; Villa; s/d from US$85/115; @📶🏊) This is a real find on Villa's west side. Multicolored buildings dot the landscape in true Caribbean style. The entry-level rooms are fairly basic, but the midrange options have fine furnishings and are fantastic value. The best rooms have large verandas overlooking the harbor and islands. An elegant restaurant (mains EC$60 to EC$75) and sea-view pool seal the deal.

Grand View Beach Hotel RESORT $$
(☎ 458-4811; www.grandviewhotel.com; Villa Point; s/d from US$114/129; ❄@📶🏊) Sweeping views of the island-dotted waters and curvaceous shore at Villa Point are reason enough to stay at this modest hillside resort with a truthful name. The 19 rooms are split between cozy but charismatic in an old plantation house and larger rooms in a modern Spanish-style wing. The grounds are lovely and the beach is a short stroll away.

Young Island Resort RESORT $$$
(☎ 458-4826; www.youngisland.com; r from US$392; ❄@🏊) It's only 200m offshore from Villa, but the private, vaguely heart-shaped Young Island is a whole world away. The 29 units here include sexy villas, some with plunge pools, killer views and everything you need to forget about the little hotel ferry back to St Vincent.

Eating

Chill'n CARIBBEAN $
(☎ 456-1776; www.chillnsvg.com; Egmont St; mains EC$15-36; ⏰ 7am-8pm Mon-Thu, to 11pm Fri & Sat) An unpretentious restaurant with a social vibe that's a good place to get an affordable bite to eat or just hang out for some drinks. There's a daily local meal and a menu of Asian mains, plus pizzas, sandwiches and desserts. At night the music gets turned up

and it morphs into a fun bar popular with locals and expats alike.

★**Basil's Bar & Restaurant** INTERNATIONAL $$
(☎457-2713; Cobblestone Inn, Upper Bay St; mains EC$35-87; ⏰8am-late) If the food wasn't so good, you might think you'd entered a pirate's dungeon, given the moody lighting and stone walls. Food spans American and Caribbean favorites; the lunch buffet (EC$50) is great. It has Kingstown's classiest bar.

Veejays CARIBBEAN $$
(Bay St; buffet EC$12.50-22.50, rotis EC$11-30, mains EC$30-50; ⏰10am-9pm Mon-Thu & Sat, to midnight Fri) On the northern edge of Kingstown, buzzing Veejays has a popular lunch buffet featuring traditional Vincentian dishes. Eat inside the air-conditioned dining area downstairs, or on the open-air terrace at the top. There's also an extensive menu of other dishes; locals rate Veejays' rotis as the best on the island and they're even available in meat-free soy versions.

Sapodilla Room CARIBBEAN $$
(☎458-1800; www.grenadinehouse.com; Grenadine House; mains EC$43-65; ⏰7-10pm, terrace 7-10am & noon-3pm) The classic dining room of the Grenadine House hotel offers a small menu featuring locally sourced produce in dishes that combine Creole, Caribbean and American flavors. Start your night in the elegant Mayfair-style British pub. For casual fare outside with great views, try the terrace.

Young Island Resort FUSION $$$
(☎458-4826; www.youngisland.com; lunch mains EC$37-48, dinner EC$168; ⏰noon-2pm & 7-10pm) There are few places that can boast that its specialty is bread, but here at Young Island the proof is in the pumpernickel. Every meal comes with a barge full of fresh bread to accompany the equally fresh seafood and other dishes prepared with some of St Vincent's best bounty. Tables are set in beautiful gardens by the beach.

French Veranda FRENCH $$$
(☎453-1111; www.marinershotel.com; Mariner's Hotel, Villa; mains EC$50-105; ⏰noon-10pm) It's not all French – there's also curry, satay sauce and pizza on the menu – but there are escargots and it's all served on a lovely veranda with sweeping views in a mood of casual elegance. Portions can be a bit on the small side for the price.

Drinking & Nightlife

Impromptu bars rule the streets in the center of town as the Saturday market wanes in the afternoon. The area around Heritage Sq is Kingstown's number-one limin' (hanging out) spot.

Flow Wine Bar WINE BAR
(☎457-0809; James St; ⏰11am-10pm Mon-Thu, to midnight Fri, 6pm-midnight Sat) Fabulously chic for grubby downtown Kingstown, Flow is a dimly lit top-floor bar with sofas to spare, a chilled soundtrack and an extensive selection of wine by the glass and bottle. The food here is inventive and excellent value – try the jalapeño wontons. A place to put your Caribbean escape on hold just for a moment.

Heritage Square Lime BAR
(River Rd; ⏰6pm-midnight) Vincentians take street drinking to the next level at this outdoor party in the heart of Kingstown. Dozens of vendors hawk beers from coolers while sound systems on the backs of trucks belt out dancehall tunes. There are usually some hardcore drinkers around, but the main event is on Friday evenings when it seems like half the city turns up.

ℹ Information

General Post Office (☎456-1111; Halifax St; ⏰8:30am-3pm Mon-Fri, to 11:30am Sat)

Milton Cato Memorial Hospital (Kingstown General Hospital; ☎456-1185; Leeward Hwy; ⏰24hr) For serious illness or decompression sickness you will be sent to Barbados.

Tourist office (☎456-6222; www.discoversvg.com; NIS Bldg, Bay St; ⏰8am-noon & 1-4pm Mon-Fri) Government tourism office. It maintains a list of licensed guides throughout the country. There's another branch in the cruise-ship terminal and one in the airport.

ℹ Getting There & Away

BOAT

Services to the Grenadines depart from the ferry dock on the southern side of Kingstown Bay, while cruise ships dock at the adjacent purpose-built terminal. Both are walking distance from downtown Kingstown.

BUS

There are two bus stations in Kingstown, both of which are located on Bay St near the center of town.

Leeward Bus Station (Bay St) For buses to the western side of the island.

Windward Bus Station (Bay St) Buses to the east and south of the island.

Leeward Highway

The Leeward Hwy runs north of Kingstown along St Vincent's west coast for 25 very slow miles, ending at Richmond Beach. Offering some lovely scenery, the road climbs into the mountains as it leaves Kingstown, then winds through hillsides and back down to deeply cut coastal valleys that open to coconut plantations, fishing villages and bays lined with black-sand beaches.

Sights

Dark View Falls WATERFALL

(EC$5) Set among striking mountains covered with lush foliage, this double waterfall is the most beautiful on the island that you don't need a boat to get to. The turnoff is almost at the northern end of the Leeward Hwy, between Chateaubelair and Richmond; look for the small sign on the right after passing the hydroelectric plant. From the turn, it's about a 10-minute drive to the reception area.

Layou Petroglyph Park ARCHAEOLOGICAL SITE

(Layou; EC$2) Around half a mile off the main road, this lovely park is centered around a large rock perched on the side of a rushing stream that was carved by St Vincent's original indigenous inhabitants. The petroglyph itself, while interesting to look at, will not hold your attention for long, but the park is a lovely place to relax. Bring a picnic lunch to enjoy in one of the gazebos.

Wallilabou Falls WATERFALL

(531-1310; EC$5; 9am-6pm) An inviting waterfall that splits into two streams over three large boulders before filling a large swimming hole surrounded by trees and birdlife. Downstream, the river passes beneath a colonial-era dam that has been reclaimed by nature, with trees growing out from gaps in the stones.

Cumberland Bay BEACH

A lovely secluded bay framed by jungle-covered bluffs, Cumberland is a popular anchorage for more adventurous yachties. It's also a fine place for a swim. If you're looking for even more seclusion, head to the next bay, Troumaca Bottom, which is equally beautiful and rarely visited.

Activities

Richmond Vale Diving & Hiking OUTDOORS

(458-2255; www.richmondvalehiking.com; Richmond Vale, Chateaubelair; volcano hike US$75-85) Run out of the Richmond Vale Academy (an international school focused on environmental and social issues), this adventure shop is the only one of its kind in the island's north. It organizes treks to the summit of La Soufrière volcano, as well as along other nature trails. The attached dive shop offers both shore and boat dives.

Vermont Nature Trails HIKING

(EC$5; 9am-5pm) About 5 miles north of Kingstown along the Leeward Hwy, a sign points east to the Vermont Nature Trails, 3.5 miles inland, where you'll find the **Parrot Lookout Trail**. The 1.75-mile loop (two hours) passes through the southwestern tip of the St Vincent Parrot Reserve, a thick rainforest where, if you're lucky, you might spot the namesake bird in its natural habitat.

OFF THE BEATEN TRACK

HIKING LA SOUFRIÈRE VOLCANO

St Vincent's La Soufrière volcano dominates the northern part of the island and a hike to its summit is a highlight for adventurous travelers.

The crater is an otherworldly environment with shag-carpet-like moss growing on the ground and mounds of black rocks all around. There are also some active sulfur outlets.

There are two routes to the top. The easiest route, and the one that is officially promoted to visitors, begins from the windward side of the island, where a proper trail leads up from the car park to the summit. It's a moderate 2½-hour hike.

But if you're looking for real adventure, consider the leeward trail that begins near Chateaubelair at the end of the Leeward Hwy. It's a longer, more challenging hike, but you'll be rewarded with views of both the volcano and the sea all the way up, and there's more bush along the trail. It takes around four hours from the trailhead and a local guide is essential as the path is not clearly marked.

WORTH A TRIP

MESOPOTAMIA

Tucked away at the end of a rough road at the top of the valley above Mesopotamia – the SVG version – St Vincent's **Montreal Gardens** (EC$13; ⏲9am-4pm Mon-Fri) are in many ways superior to their more famous Kingstown counterparts. Surrounded by craggy mountains and rolling hills, the setting is spectacular and the gardens themselves are a deliciously lush and colorful affair awash with birdsong.

On the road to Mesopotamia there is the excellent **Belmont Lookout**, where you peer down into the impossibly green valley, known as the breadbasket of St Vincent. It's a lush landscape dotted with small farms and palm trees. On the other side of the road the view is equally impressive across to Bequia, Mustique and Garifuna Rock, which was the first prison of the Black Caribs before they were expelled to Honduras.

Getting There & Away

Buses run from Kingstown's Leeward Bus Station (p736) up to Chateaubelair, a short distance short of Richmond at the end of the highway. Many attractions are well off the main road, so to fully explore the area it's best to hire a vehicle.

BEQUIA

Bequia (beck-way) is the most perfect island in the whole Grenadines. Stunning beaches dotting the shoreline, accommodations to fit most budgets and a slow pace of life all help to create an environment that is unforgettable. There are fine restaurants, shops that retain their local integrity and enough golden sand and blue water to keep everybody blissful.

Getting There & Away

Ferry services link Bequia with St Vincent main island, with all services arriving and departing from the main dock in Port Elizabeth. There are no longer direct services from Bequia to the southern Grenadines; in order to head further south it's necessary to head to Kingstown and pick up a boat there.

Bequia Express (☎458-3472; www.bequiaexpress.com; Port Elizabeth) Most reliable car ferry running to St Vincent (one way/return EC$25, one hour) several times daily.

MV Admiral (☎458-3348; www.admiralferries.com/schedule; Port Elizabeth) Car ferry to St Vincent (one way/return EC$25/45, one hour), running several times daily. It's an older boat that spends a lot of time in the boatyard so call to check it's running.

Bequia's airport doesn't see many regular flights. SVG Air (p753) has one to two daily flights between Bequia and Barbados. It also runs an irregular service between Bequia and St Vincent, although by the time you mess around at both airports it's quicker to take the boat. Schedules change frequently so check the website before making plans. SVG Air Grenada (p458) offers occasional service between Bequia and Grenada.

Getting Around

Bikes are easily rented; cars cost about US$60 per day.

Local minibuses run on a set route from the dock to Paget Farm, near the airport, and cost EC$2 to EC$5. If you pay extra they will detour to Lower Bay or down to the water at Friendship Bay.

Private taxis (EC$15 to EC$50) can be minivans, SUVs or open-top pickups. Prices are fixed and can be obtained at the Bequia Tourism Association (p740). One reliable operator is **Gideon's Taxi and Rentals** (☎458-3760; www.bequiajeeprentals.com; Friendship Bay).

Port Elizabeth

The appealing small town of Port Elizabeth is little more than a line of shops rimming the beach of Admiralty Bay and backed by a natural amphitheater of green hills. The harbor is often packed with yachts from the world over.

Sights

★Princess Margaret Beach BEACH

Simply divine. Located just around the corner from Port Elizabeth, this is one of the loveliest stretches of sand on the island. It is backed by a wall of lush vegetation and the deep, calm waters are perfect for swimming.

To get here on foot from Port Elizabeth, follow the Belmont Walkway right to the end of Admiralty Bay and look for the steps leading to a dirt path up the bluff. From town it's a short journey, but not ideal for those who fear heights.

Alternatively, follow the vehicular access route, traveling on the main road south and turning down the signed narrow access road to the beach (about a five-minute, EC$25 taxi trip). Or arrive in style by getting a ride on one of the water taxis idling in the harbor.

Note that if there is a cruise ship in port the sands here can get very crowded.

Activities & Tours

★Friendship Rose BOATING
(☎457-3888; www.friendshiprose.com; Belmont Walkway; day trips from US$140) This 80ft vintage schooner is a beautiful example of classic boatbuilding and once served as a mail boat. Now it runs popular day trips to other Grenadines islands, either to Mustique or the Tobago Cays. Prices include breakfast, lunch and refreshments. Each paying adult can bring on a free junior traveler while children under 12 sail free.

Sail Grenadines BOATING
(☎457-3590; www.sailgrenadines.com; Belmont Rd) A comprehensive yacht charter outfit that offers bareboat, skippered and full-crewed charters for journeys throughout the Grenadines. Also offers tours including day trips to the Tobago Cays. It's located next to the Tradewinds yacht club.

Dive Bequia DIVING
(☎458-3504; www.divebequia.com; Belmont Walkway; 1-/2-tank dives US$75/130; ⏲8am-4:30pm) A highly rated dive shop with plenty of local experience. Also runs snorkeling trips. They generally dive at 9am, 11:30am and 2:30pm if there is demand.

Bushman Brent HIKING
(☎495-2524; per hour EC$50) Local character Bushman Brent knows the hills and trails of the Bequia like the back of his hand and offers guided hikes all over the island. He is good company and is very knowledgeable about local flora and fauna, especially plants used for traditional medicine.

Festivals & Events

Easter Regatta SAILING
(⏲Easter) Around Easter, this is SVG's main sailing event.

Bequia Music Fest MUSIC
(www.bequiamusicfestival.com; ⏲Jan) An international music event that includes acts on loan from the Mustique Blues Festival alongside artists across a range of genres from the Caribbean and beyond. Events are spread around hotels and bars all over the island.

Sleeping

Port Elizabeth has the biggest range of accommodations on the island. You'll find several hotels lining the Belmont Walkway, as well as some cheaper options up in the hills right behind town.

Gingerbread Hotel HOTEL $$
(☎458-3800; ginger@vincysurf.com; Belmont Walkway; r US$230-290; ❄📶) Like a set piece from a production of *Hansel and Gretel*, Gingerbread looks exactly as you'd expect, with ornate eaves nailed to a steep roof. The six spotless rooms are superbly designed by the architect owners and are spread over the lovely grounds. Rooms offer private balconies with comfy chairs overlooking the bay and large windows onto the back garden.

Village Apartments APARTMENT $$
(☎458-3883; www.villageapartments.bequia.net; Belmont; apt/2-bed cottage from US$90/135; ❄📶) Choose from a mix of studios, cottages and one- and two-bedroom units at this little compound a five-minute walk up the hill from town. With the glorious views, you'll easily know when your ship has come in. Units are simply decorated in white with wicker furniture. When it's busy there is a minimum stay of one week required.

Bequia Plantation Hotel HOTEL $$$
(☎534-8677; www.bequiaplantationhotel.com; r US$290, cottages US$375-520; ❄) Set on spacious grounds at the end of Admiralty Bay, this hotel feels removed from the downtown hustle but is just an effortless stroll from the action. There are six comfortable rooms upstairs in the main building, the best of which are the two with sea-view balconies, and bigger, more private stand-alone cottages spread among the coconut palms.

Eating

Green Boley CARIBBEAN $
(Belmont Walkway; rotis EC$10-18; ⏲9am-10pm) Adding a bit of local character to the Belmont Walkway, this simple green wooden bar sells cheap and delicious rotis; take your pick of chicken, conch or beef. There's also a full selection of drinks, including the famous Green Boley rum punch. Inside has all the atmosphere, but the picnic tables outside have the first-class views.

★Fig Tree CARIBBEAN $$
(☎457-3008; www.facebook.com/thefigtreerestaurantbequia; Belmont Walkway; dinner mains

EC$40-70; ⌚8am-10pm, closed Tue) A short stroll along the waterfront west of the docks, this open-air restaurant has views to match both the great food and hospitality of the owner, Cheryl Johnson. During the day its light meals with rotis are the main attraction, while in the evening full-flavored Creole dishes are offered. Book ahead for the Friday-night fish fry.

Mac's Pizzeria PIZZA **$$**
(☎458-3474; Belmont Walkway; pizzas EC$45-85; ⌚11am-10pm) Mac's is a fine choice for good food and great atmosphere. Delicious pizzas, burgers and seafood mains are served on the elevated deck or down under the tree in the yard overlooking the water. It's usually overflowing with happy diners swapping slices and telling stories. Make sure to leave some room for the Bequia lime pie.

Jack's INTERNATIONAL **$$**
(☎458-3809; www.jacksbeachbar.com; Princess Margaret Bay; mains EC$48-80; ⌚11am-11pm) With a privileged position right on Princess Margaret Bay, Jack's is a large, fairly smart open-air beach bar. Sit at wooden tables under the high canvas roof and choose from a menu of fried favorites alongside lobster and grilled fish. It's good drinking food rather than gourmet but it's a lively place to hang out.

Shopping

Mauvin's Model Boat Shop GIFTS & SOUVENIRS
(Front St; ⌚9am-5pm Mon-Sat) Carefully crafted model boats are made here under a breadfruit tree and sold in a tidy little gallery.

Bequia Bookshop BOOKS
(Front St; ⌚8:30am-4:30pm Mon-Fri, 9am-1pm Sat) The best bookstore in the region stocks everything from charts and survey maps to yachting books and flora and fauna guides. Browse West Indian, North American and European literature, and you'll even find some long-out-of-print tomes just waiting for a buyer.

Information

Bank of St Vincent & Grenadines (☎458-3700; ⌚8am-2pm Mon-Thu, to 4pm Fri) Bank with the only ATMs on the island. It is not totally reliable so bring backup funds. It's located in front of the hospital a couple of blocks back from the dock.

Bequia Customs & Immigration Office (☎457-3044; Port Elizabeth; ⌚8:30am-6pm Mon-Fri, 8:30am-noon & 3-6pm Sat, 9am-noon & 3-6pm Sun) Located across from the main dock.

Bequia District Hospital (☎458-3294; ⌚24hr) Refurbished hospital serving the Grenadines. Also has a walk-in clinic for minor health issues.

Bequia Tourism Association (☎458-3286; www.bequiatourism.com; ⌚9:30am-6pm) An excellent resource, located in the small building on the ferry dock and staffed by helpful locals. Offers currency exchange services too.

Post Office (Front St; ⌚9am-noon & 1-3pm Mon-Fri, 9-11:30am Sat) Opposite the ferry dock on Front St.

Getting There & Away

James F Mitchell Airport is near Paget Farm, at the southwest end of the island. The frequent ferries from Kingstown dock right in Port Elizabeth.

Many places are accessible on foot from Port Elizabeth.

Lower Bay

The tiny beachside community of Lower Bay has the best beach on the island: the stunningly clear waters of Admiralty Bay spread out in front like a turquoise fan from a base of golden sand. It's never crowded. Vendors rent out beach chairs and there are a couple of cute beachfront cafes.

Not quite as famous as the island's star Princess Margaret Beach, Lower Bay is an equally splendid stretch of sand that has a couple of places to get meals and a drink. Note: beware of manchineel trees here as they can cause a bad rash.

Sleeping & Eating

De Reef Apartments APARTMENT **$**
(☎458-3484; dereef@vincysurf.com; apt from US$100; ❄) Offering some of the best value on the island, these homely apartments are decked out with everything you'll need, including air-con in the bedrooms, and are set in a garden full of fruit trees just across the road from inviting Lower Bay. They all boast spacious terraces and are a great choice for peace and quiet.

Fernando's Hideaway CARIBBEAN **$$**
(☎458-3758; mains EC$50-55; ⌚7-10pm Mon-Sat) Set on a colorfully painted porch up a hilly side road in Lower Bay, this place is indeed hidden away but it's worth making the effort to find it to enjoy fantastic fresh seafood dishes. There's no fixed menu – it all

depends on what owner and chef Fernando catches that morning. Call ahead to find out what's cooking. Reservations essential.

De Reef CAFE $$
(☎458-3484; dereef@vincysurf.com; mains EC$38-75; ⊙8am-late) Right on the sand, this cafe serves up expertly grilled fish and lobster, conch curry and a variety of snacks throughout the day. The bar serves a flavorful rum punch and you can have yours on a lounger in the sand. Take a dip in the perfect surf and have another. Hugely popular on Sundays.

Getting There & Away

It's possible to walk from Port Elizabeth to Lower Bay via Princess Margaret Beach along the waterfront path.

Alternatively, the Paget Farm bus from Port Elizabeth will drop you at the Lower Bay junction, from where it's a 10-minute walk down the hill to the village. If you pay a little extra, the bus will take you all the way down.

A taxi from town costs around EC$30.

Friendship Bay

Located over the hill on the southeast coast of the island, the gentle curve of Friendship Bay is about 1.5 miles from Port Elizabeth.

A rarely crowded crescent of sand, the beach here is a top reason to make the short yet strenuous walk over the spine of the island (or wimp out on a short taxi or bus ride). A dense thicket of palms provides shade and that nicely clichéd tropical look.

Sleeping & Eating

Sugar Apple HOTEL $$
(☎475-3148; www.sugarapplebequia.com; r US$150-300;) Offering outstanding value, these bright and spacious apartments have separate kitchens with walls of windows that open out to reveal fine sea views. Spotless, spacious and with all the amenities, it's just a short walk from Friendship Bay. There are also a couple of cottages right down on the sand. Service is warm and public transportation runs right past the door.

★ **Bequia Beach Hotel** RESORT $$$
(☎458-1600; www.bequiabeach.com; r US$262-426;) A sprawling low-rise resort with a privileged location right on Friendship Bay that manages to balance style and elegance with an unpretentious atmosphere. Accommodations range from garden-view cottages to suites overlooking the water and villas with private pools. All are finished with top-quality furnishings.

Bagatelle SEAFOOD $$$
(Bequia Beach Hotel; dinner mains EC$70-84; ⊙8am-10pm) Located right on the water at Friendship Bay, this fine restaurant is popular with both visitors and locals for its high-quality fare. The constantly changing dinner menu has just a few options for mains, but you'll always find local fish dishes.

Getting There & Away

Friendship Bay is close enough to walk from Port Elizabeth, although you have to climb up and over a steep hill. Alternatively, the Paget Farm bus will drop you at the top of the hill overlooking the bay; if you pay a bit extra it will take you all the way down.

Spring Bay & Industry Bay

On a quiet island, this is the quiet end. It's a brief hop over the central spine from Port Elizabeth to Spring Bay and Industry Bay. Sugar plantations still operate here, and there are good views of the often-turbulent waters to the east.

This side of the island can be affected by sargassum seaweed arrivals – check the situation before booking accommodations.

Sights

Old Hegg Turtle Sanctuary WILDLIFE RESERVE
(Park Beach; EC$15; ⊙9am-5pm) At this 'sanctuary,' a well-known institution on Bequia, turtle eggs are hatched and transferred to small concrete pools, ostensibly to give them a better chance in the wild. While there's no reason to doubt the good intentions of the ecologically minded owner, it's unclear whether the hand-reared turtles have the skills necessary to survive on their own or find it back to their birthplace to breed.

Sleeping & Eating

Most of the accommodations in the area are high-end boutique hotels up on the hillside overlooking the water.

Sugar Reef BOUTIQUE HOTEL $$
(☎458-3400; www.sugarreefbequia.com; Industry Bay; r US$150-300;) An impeccable hotel with beautiful rooms spread over 65 acres; half are on the hillside in an imposing stone mansion and the others down by the cafe

fronting a palm-shaded beach. The seaside rooms are superb with whitewashed stone walls and double doors right onto the sands. There's no air-con but you won't need it with the constant sea breeze.

Firefly BOUTIQUE HOTEL **$$$**
(☎458-3414; www.fireflybequia.com; Spring Bay; r from US$250; ❄📶🏊) Just a 10-minute drive from Port Elizabeth and you're transported to tranquil luxury. The four rooms are tastefully decorated with minimalist flare, accented with views worthy of royalty. It's set in a working tropical-fruit plantation that dates from the 1700s; informative walking tours are available. There is also a two-bedroom cottage and fully equipped beachfront villas available for rent.

Spring House Hotel BOUTIQUE HOTEL **$$$**
(☎457-3707; www.springhousebequia.com; Spring Bay; r US$233-299; ❄📶🏊) Right at the top of the hill overlooking Spring Bay, this intimate hotel feels like your private retreat on a secluded island. The 10 rooms are elegant with hardwood floors, massive bathrooms and classic furnishings, and the only sound you'll hear is birdsong from the surrounding bush. A number of terraces, including one with a spa bath, offer fantastic sea views.

It's a bit of a hike to town or the water, but management offers a free shuttle and will even load the complimentary kayaks onto the truck if you fancy paddling from bay to bay.

★**Sugar Reef Cafe** CAFE **$$**
(☎458-3400; Industry Bay; mains EC$42-90; ⌚noon-9pm) Sit under fantastic driftwood chandeliers in the seaside dining room and tuck into superb gourmet delights at this wonderful cafe inside the Sugar Reef hotel (p741). Fresh fish features prominently on the small menu, but there are always a couple of veg options, too. It's also a great place for a drink, either at the bar or out by the water.

Getting There & Away

There's no public bus to Spring Bay or Industry Bay and it's quite a long hike. A taxi will cost EC$40 to EC$45.

MUSTIQUE

What can you say about Mustique other than 'Wow!'? First, take an island that offers stunning beaches and everything else you expect to find in paradise, then add to the mix accommodations that defy description or affordability. With prices that exclude all but the superrich, film stars and burnt-out musicians, this island is the exclusive playground of the uberaffluent.

The documentary *The Man Who Bought Mustique* (2000) tells the unlikely story of Lord Glenconner, the man who turned the island into a playground for the rich. Most visitors not staying in a fabulous retreat come on widely marketed day trips from Bequia. They join the local swells for drinks and more at Basil's, one of the Caribbean's great waterfront bars.

Sleeping

★**Cotton House** BOUTIQUE HOTEL **$$$**
(☎456-4777; www.cottonhouse.net; Endeavour Bay; r from US$865; ❄📶🏊) Centered around a beautifully renovated colonial-era cotton warehouse, the luxurious Cotton House is set on 13 acres of beautiful grounds. Accommodations are in a range of villas and cottages, including seafront rooms with plunge pools. It strikes a fine balance between relaxed atmosphere and great service and facilities.

It has the only spa on the island and runs down to Mustique's best beach, Endeavour Bay, which has a breezy open-air cafe, luxury loungers and waiter service. There is also a dive shop on-site which is open to hotel guests and visitors alike.

Mustique Company ACCOMMODATION SERVICES **$$$**
(☎448-8000; www.mustique-island.com; villas per week US$8000-85,000) Nothing is short of perfection at these properties, and every need is catered for by your villa staff. Most of the villas were built by the rich and famous according to their personal tastes, so there's a wide variety to choose from. Log onto the website to browse.

Drinking & Nightlife

★**Basil's** BAR
(☎488-8350; www.basilsbar.com; Britannia Bay; ⌚9am-late; 📶) Managed by the Mustique Company, famous Basil's has undergone a major overhaul – how you spend US$6 million renovating open-aired, thatched roof huts is hard to fathom – but remains one of the Caribbean's most iconic beach bars. Extending out into Britannia Bay, it's the place to eat, drink and meet up with others in Mustique and a must-stop for seemingly every passing sailboat.

Getting There & Away

Mustique's tiny airstrip receives regular scheduled flights from St Lucia's Hewanorra International Airport. There are also less regular scheduled services from Barbados, and charter flights from St Vincent and anywhere else you fancy, really.

You'll need a confirmed hotel or villa reservation in order to purchase flights; accommodations should be able to sort out tickets.

A smattering of day trips run to Mustique from St Vincent and Bequia. From the latter, the Friendship Rose (p739) sailing boat offers the classiest mode of transport. Otherwise you can charter a small boat for the day from Port Elizabeth on Bequia for around US$80 per passenger (minimum of US$300).

CANOUAN

Canouan (cahn-oo-ahn) is literally a divided island. A beautiful hook-shaped isle, it has some of the most brilliant waters and finest beaches in the entire Grenadines chain, but unfortunately for independent travelers more than half of the island is taken up by a massive resort. Despite this, the island remains worth a visit for its landscapes and marine environment; you'll find lovely beaches with good snorkeling not too far from the ferry dock.

Unless you have a yacht to sleep on, or manage to get a room at the one fine hotel right on the sand by town, Canouan is not the best choice as a base to explore the region. The tiny main town of Charlestown lacks the sense of community that you'll find in other neighboring islands. A large marina on the south of the island, catering to superyachts and their fly-in owners, further diminishes the slow island vibe.

If you're staying in Charlestown you have fine beaches facing both west and east just a very short walk away. Pick your favorite! If you're staying at the resort, you have your choice of some of the best and most secluded beaches in the Grenadines.

Sleeping

Canouan has very slim pickings for budget and midrange travelers. A couple of places around town rent out apartments, but these often fill up with visiting workers from the main island. Make sure to reserve something before you arrive.

DON'T MISS

CANOUAN'S BEST HIDDEN BEACH

Part of coming to St Vincent and the Grenadines is finding that perfect beach where you really feel like you've been stranded in paradise. On Canouan, if you're willing to take a bit of a hike, you can get to deserted **Twin Bay**, on the east side of the island, just south of the resort zone. Ask a local for directions, pack a lunch and get lost in paradise for the day.

Scooby's and Sea Lover's Apartments APARTMENT $
(Zico's Place; ☎532-5935; Charlestown; apt from US$78; 📶) Located on a hillside overlooking Charlestown, this pair of fully equipped apartments have fantastic views and are the best choice for budget travelers on pricey Canouan. The owner is particularly helpful and they are within walking distance of the wonderful sands of Twin Bay.

★**Mandarin Oriental Canouan** RESORT $$$
(Canouan Resort; ☎458-8000; www.mandarinoriental.com; Godahl Beach, Carenage Bay; ste from US$1300, villa US$4500-6000; ❄@📶🏊) Canouan's ultraluxurious megaresort on Godahl Beach was relaunched as the Mandarin Oriental Canouan in 2018 and remains the most upscale place to stay in the Grenadines. It's a fairly flashy affair with plenty of marble, mirrors and pink flourishes in the 26 suites and six huge three-floor Lagoon Villas, all of which have sea views. Services abound including an infinity pool and golf course.

Tamarind Beach Hotel & Yacht Club RESORT $$$
(☎458-8044; Charlestown; s/d/tr incl breakfast US$250/310/480; ❄@📶🏊) Giant thatched-roof buildings stand guard over the beach and invite you in for pure relaxation. Elegant rooms, accented with white walls and chocolate-colored hardwood, entice the visitor and make it hard to return to the daily grind. The beach is right out front of every room and suite and, as is typical for Canouan, it's a fine strip of sand.

Service is warm and professional throughout the resort. At time of research Tamarind had been taken over by an international boutique chain and is likely to be rebranded. Call ahead.

Eating

Pompeys CARIBBEAN $
(Airport Rd, Charlestown; mains EC$15-16; ⌚11am-2pm Mon-Fri) A favorite with local workers, Pompeys serves good home-style Caribbean plates in a tiny dining room or out on a little porch. Best-value meals on the island. Get there early or there'll be nothing left.

Mangrove CARIBBEAN $$
(☎482-0761; Charlestown; lunch mains EC$45-55, dinner mains EC$50-90; ⌚9am-2pm & 5-10pm) At the end of the bay, overlooking a wide stretch of sand, Mangrove is a fun open-air restaurant serving a small menu of local dishes and pasta. The portions are generous and it's a peaceful place to hang out and chill once the plates are cleared.

Sea Grape CARIBBEAN $$$
(Charlestown; pizzas EC$45-90, mains EC$60-100; ⌚8am-10pm) Right by the dock, this lounge-like restaurant serves up tasty Caribbean classics during the day and adds pizzas to the menu in the evening. A good spot for a drink while you wait for your boat. There's a separate light meal menu that offers options for those on a budget, including good fish-and-chips for EC$30.

Information

Bank of St Vincent & the Grenadines
(Charlestown; ⌚8am-2pm Mon-Thu, to 4pm Fri) The only ATM on the island. From the dock, walk up to the main road and turn left.

Getting There & Away

AIR

Canouan's well-equipped airport is the only one in the Grenadines that can receive jet aircraft, making it the preferred fly-in point for wealthy boat owners. You can get a charter flight here from pretty much anywhere in the region.

SVG Air (p753) has regular flights between St Vincent and Canouan (one way/return US$52/100, 20 minutes), leaving the main island at 10:15am and returning at 5:10pm. There is often an additional morning service leaving St Vincent at 8:15am and turning right back around to depart Canouan at 8:45am.

The company also offers two daily scheduled flights to/from Barbados (one way/return US$195/390, one hour) with departures from Canouan at 10:30am and 1:20pm, and from Barbados at 12:30pm and 4pm.

BOAT

Canouan has ferry links to St Vincent to the north and Union island to the south, with boats usually calling at least every other day if not more frequently.

Bequia Express (p732) Large boat running twice a week to and from St Vincent (EC$50), and to Mayreau (EC$30) and Union Island (EC$30).

MV Barracuda (☎455-9835; perrysshipping@vincysurf.com) Cargo boat; serves St Vincent (EC$50) and Union Island (EC$30), with three runs each way each week.

MV Gem Star II (☎457-4157) Slow cargo boat; serves St Vincent (EC$50), Mayreau (EC$30) and Union Island (EC$30), with two runs each way each week.

MAYREAU

Blessed with breathtaking beauty yet very little development, the compact palm-covered island of Mayreau is the authentic Grenadines' dream. With only a handful of vehicles, no airport and just a smattering of residents, it often feels like the fabled desert isle.

Mayreau is a fantastic destination for independent travelers wanting to enjoy some of the Grenadines' best beaches and get a good dose of culture at the same time. There are no resorts and while yachts and bigger ships do dock here, once the sun goes down you'll have the place to yourself.

The island is so small you can't help get to know the friendly locals, who are famed throughout the Grenadines for their hard-partying ways. With around a dozen bars for its 400-odd residents, it's fairly clear it's not just a myth. It's said that tiny Mayreau's weekly beer order is more than twice that of Union Island, its far bigger neighbor.

Sights

Mayreau's main beach near the dock is a lovely thick golden stretch of sand abutted by cliffs and with clear waters that are great for snorkeling. It has nice views across to Union Island's impressive peaks. When there's no wind, though, the sand flies can be vicious.

★Saltwhistle Bay BEACH
On the northern, uninhabited side of Mayreau you'll find Saltwhistle Bay, a double crescent of beautiful beaches split by a narrow palm-tree-fringed isthmus that seems to come right

out of central casting for tropical ideals. The turquoise water laps both sides of the sandy strip, in some places only a few feet away.

Yachts drop anchor in the bay and occasional day-trippers come ashore for a bit of lunch and a sandy frolic. A few rickety huts along the shore sell cold drinks and simple snacks as well as souvenirs to passing yachties. It's a very low-key scene.

It's a 20-minute walk from the ferry dock over the steep hill.

Sleeping & Eating

There are only three functioning hotels on the island, but it is also possible to rent a room or a house from locals, sometimes for a good nightly rate. Ask at Robert Righteous & De Youths restaurant.

There are also a couple of private rental villas in the area overlooking Twassante Bay on the east of the island.

Waterloo Guesthouse GUESTHOUSE $
(☎458-8561; apt US$100; ❄) Brand-new air-conditioned apartments decked out with full-sized kitchens and everything you need. Go for the upstairs one for better views. Ask for information at the **Combination Cafe** (☎458-8561; mains EC$50-65; ⌚7am-late). It's located a few hundred meters up the steep hill from the dock.

Dennis' Hideaway HOTEL $
(☎458-8594; www.dennis-hideaway.com; dm/s/d from US$20/70/92; ❄📶🏊) The eponymous Dennis seems to be related to half the island's residents, many of whom work here. Rooms are on a hill with views west to Union Island and beyond. There's also a very basic hostel-style room for those on a tight budget. The restaurant (mains EC$25 to EC$60) serves basic fare and fresh seafood – Dennis cooks a mean conch.

Salt Whistle Bay Resort HOTEL $$
(☎1-784-497-5352; www.saltwhistlebay.com; Saltwhistle Bay; tent/r US$100/170; 📶) With a prime location next to the sand of the best beach on the island, this small resort has simple duplex stone cottages dotted around beneath the coconut palms. It's a laid-back place that fits in well with the local scenery. The beachfront bar/restaurant serves good meals and is popular with the yachties anchored out front.

Robert Righteous & De Youths SEAFOOD $$
(☎458-8203; mains EC$55-70; ⌚6am-10pm) This place is overflowing with Rasta flavor and enough Bob photos to make you think you're in a college dorm room. With pork chops and strong drinks on the menu, it's hard to tell how authentic the Rastafarianism is – but no matter, the food is tasty and the vibe is, as you'd expect, chilled out. Go for the lobster.

Getting There & Away

Boats on the Union Island–Kingstown run sometimes bypass Mayreau so make sure to ask before boarding. If there is no direct boat running, grab a boat to Union Island and take a water taxi or the morning school boat (EC$20, 45 minutes) from the dive school dock.

Bequia Express (p732) Large boat running twice a week to and from St Vincent, Canouan and Union Island.

MV Gem Star II (☎457-4157) Slow cargo boat serves St Vincent, Canouan and Union Island, with two trips each way each week.

UNION ISLAND

Union Island feels like an outpost at the bottom of a country – and that's just what it is. Before the introduction of fast boats, its remote location enabled it to become a base for contraband (which historically propped up the economy here) from all over the Caribbean.

The small port town of **Clifton** has an unpretentious charm and a more local feel than some of the towns on the more-visited Grenadine islands. You can easily spend a day wandering its short main street and the surrounding hills. It's an important anchorage for yachts and a transport hub – there are boats to Carriacou in Grenada. It also has decent accommodations, services and just enough nightlife.

Sights

Union Island's first-class beaches are never crowded.

Big Sand BEACH
(Richmond Bay) One of the best beaches on the island, Big Sand on Richmond Bay is around half a mile north of Clifton. It has plenty of white sand and brilliant blue waters, with forest-covered mountains as a backdrop. It's an easy walk from town.

Chatham Bay BEACH
A favorite hangout among Union Island locals and a popular anchorage for yachties in the know, Chatham Bay is a lovely thin

crescent of white sand backed by steep, forest-covered hills on the western side of the island. The calm turquoise waters are perfect for snorkeling. On the edge you'll find a couple of simple bars and a restaurant.

You'll need a good 4WD vehicle to get here, or you can hike down (20 minutes) from the main road. A water taxi can drop you right on the sand.

Activities & Tour

Hike up into the hills behind Clifton, including **Fort Hill**, about 500ft up, for magnificent views of the surrounding islands.

The quiet fishing village of **Ashton**, some 1.5 miles away, makes a good walk.

Excursions to Tobago Cays are popular. They usually include a stop in Mayreau, lunch and refreshments, and cost around US$100 per person.

Grenadines Dive DIVING
(☎458-8138; www.grenadinesdive.com; Clifton; 1-/2-tank dive US$80/140) A friendly dive shop that organizes custom excursions to Tobago Cays and elsewhere in the Grenadines. It also arranges pickups from other islands, including Mayreau and Canouan. Mayreau Gardens is a popular drift dive on one of the longest reefs in the region. If you plan on checking out various dive spots, good-value six-dive packages are available for US$372.

JT Pro Center KITESURFING
(☎527-8363; www.kitesurfgrenadines.com; Clifton; private/group lessons US$195/265, 5-day course US$1275) Runs kitesurfing classes out on the 'Kite Beach' behind the airport. You can get information at the Snack Shack in the middle of Clifton. Also rents gear, organizes accommodations and has a popular beach bar right on the sand.

Happy Kite Grenadines KITESURFING
(☎430-8604; www.happykitegrenadines.com; Clifton; lessons per hour US$150-200, 3-day courses US$450-600) Offers kitesurfing lessons at Frigate Island just offshore from Ashton and also organizes kite tours. Booking office is inside the **Gypsea Cafe/Captain Gourmet deli** (Captain Gourmet; Front St, Clifton; ⏰7am-10pm Mon-Sat; 📶).

Scaramouche BOATING
(☎458-8418; scaramouche@vincysurf.com; tours from US$95) Union Island's very own movie star, the wooden sailboat *Scaramouche* was built on neighboring Carriacou and featured in the original *Pirates of the Caribbean* movie. Now visitors can sail to the Tobago Cays or cruise around the Grenadines on her deck. Tours include meals and drinks.

Sleeping

Kings Landing Hotel HOTEL **$**
(☎485-8823; www.kingslandingunionisland.com; Clifton; s/d from US$85/100; ❄📶🏊) A clean and functional two-story hotel at the south end of Clifton, set around a pool with a sea view. The 17 rooms are basic but clean and the hotel is well managed. A good spot for families wanting a bit of peace; kids like the pool.

Islanders Inn HOTEL **$**
(☎527-0944; www.theislandersinn.com; Belmont Bay, Zion; r US$90-130; ❄📶) This bright, small hotel offers a slice of tranquility within walking distance of the best stretches of sand on the island. Rooms are simple but spacious enough and have private balconies overlooking the water. It's around a 20-minute walk from town, but feels very remote. Wi-fi is available in the common areas and meals can be organized with advance notice.

TJ Plaza Guesthouse GUESTHOUSE **$**
(☎458-8930; www.tjplaza.weebly.com; Clifton; r US$37-56; ❄📶) The best bet for budget travelers, this family-run guesthouse has a variety of options, including budget rooms with fans on the 2nd floor and air-conditioned options with hot water downstairs. If there's no one around, ask at the two-story pink wooden building on Front St directly behind the guesthouse.

Bougainvilla Hotel HOTEL **$$**
(☎458-8678; www.grenadines-bougainvilla.com; Clifton; r from US$157; ❄📶) Not far from the main yacht dock, this French-accented hotel has lovely rooms divided among standard options, and apartments with kitchenettes and living space. Each has a nice warm palette of colors – there's plenty of marigold yellow, touches of art and classic furnishings. Service is good.

Anchorage Yacht Club Hotel HOTEL **$$**
(☎458-8221; www.aycunionisland.com/hotel.html; Clifton; r US$127-170; ❄📶) Right at the yacht docks and popular with visiting sailors and holidaymakers. There are rooms on the 1st floor and cottages in the adjacent yard; all offer a simple nautical vibe and views of the harbor. The vast terrace bar is popular with people transacting business of all kinds and yacht passengers desperate for dry land.

Eating

Yummy Stuff Bakery BAKERY $

(Front St, Clifton; items EC$2-18; ⏰6:30am-6pm) Out the back of the mall on the main street, this inviting little bakery is a great place for a cheap bite to eat. Sit in the patio and enjoy filling chicken rotis, banana bread, brownies and more.

The Local CARIBBEAN $$

(Front St, Clifton; light mains EC$10-35, mains EC$50; ⏰noon-10pm) A modern and welcoming spot on the 2nd floor overlooking Clifton's main road, the Local serves up quality burgers, wraps and fish plates. It's especially worthwhile at lunch when it offers affordable portions of typical local dishes. Try the salt fish with coconut dumplings.

Snack Shack CAFE $$

(Front St, Clifton; breakfast EC$15-30, light mains EC$25-40; ⏰8am-midnight) Pull up a chair at one of the tables outside this popular little cafe right in the center of town and watch the gentle pace of Clifton life as you enjoy great crepes, quesadillas and panini. Throw in good tunes, a decent cocktail list and a fun atmosphere and you'll see why it's so busy.

Sparrows Beach Club EUROPEAN $$$

(☎458-8195; sparrowsbeachclub@gmail.com; Big Sand, Richmond Bay; pizza EC$25-65, mains EC$62-130) Located right on the sands of the best beach on the island, Sparrows is as much a destination as a restaurant. You can order meals right to your lounger, or sit on the deck in the brightly painted restaurant. The food is a mixed bag; the high-end dishes are excellent, but the cheaper ones are banged out without much love.

A free shuttle is offered to diners; otherwise it's a 20-minute walk from town. There's a small hut on-site offering massages. If you want to just come and use the facilities (loungers, wi-fi, showers etc) it costs EC$35, including round-trip transport.

Drinking & Nightlife

Union's drinking and nightlife is the best in the southern Grenadines but mostly involves waterside beers when the sun is out and visiting small bars and staying on for drinks in restaurants in the evenings rather than raucous clubs. However, on weekends the main road often turns into one big street party.

WORTH A TRIP

TOBAGO CAYS

The **Tobago Cays Marine Park** (adult/child US$10/5) encompasses the five uninhabited islands of Tobago Cays – Petit Bateau, Petit Rameau, Jamesby, Baradal and Petit Tabac – as well as the populated island of Mayreau, and Catholic Island, Jondall and Mayreau Baleine to the north.

The five Tobago Cays sit above a large sand-bottomed lagoon protected by 2.5-mile-long Horseshoe Reef. The lagoon is an important habitat for sea turtles. Other dive and snorkel spots include Egg Reef and World's End Reef on the eastern side of the cays and Mayreau Gardens to the west.

Also within the boundaries of the reserve is the wreck of the *Purina,* a British gunboat, which lies just west of Mayreau.

Catholic Island is a designated seabird reserve, while there's a small mangrove forest on Petit Rameau.

There is a marked sea-turtle observation area for snorkelers around the beach of Baradal Cay, where boating activity is prohibited.

All scuba-diving activity must be accompanied by a registered local guide. Kitesurfing is only permitted in the designated area to the north of Petit Rameau.

Getting to Tobago Cays

You can get a day trip to the cays from any place in the Grenadines. Some good operators are found on Bequia and Union Island, while the cheapest place to visit from is Mayreau. Expect to pay from US$90 to US$200 for a full day out, depending where you set out from.

If you've got your own sails you can only anchor in the sand-bottomed areas around Baradal and the small strip in front of Petit Tabac; mooring fees are applied.

Many visitors begin their sundowner expedition on the spacious terrace at the Anchorage Yacht Club (p746).

Happy Island BAR
(24hr;) Located right in front of Clifton, in the bay, you'll find this one-bar island. There didn't used to be any land in this part of the bay, but local fishermen would throw conch shells in the shallows and eventually an island began to form. And what do you do with some free land? You put a bar on it!

Information

Bank of St Vincent & Grenadines (458-8347; Clifton; 8am-2pm Mon-Thu, to 4pm Fri) Turn right out of the dock to find the island's only ATM facility (24 hours), with two machines available.

Erika's Marine (485-8335; www.erikamarine.com; Clifton) A one-stop solution to your travel needs, it offers cash advances on credit cards when the ATM is out of service. Other services include internet access, a travel agency and laundry. It's located inside the Bougainvilla Hotel (p746).

Union Island Tourist Bureau (458-8494; Front St, Clifton; 9am-noon & 1-4pm Mon-Fri) The most friendly and efficient tourism office in the Grenadines, if not the Caribbean. Has details on boat departures as well as hotels, restaurants and tours to the Tobago Cays. If staff don't know the answer, they'll find it out.

Getting There & Away

AIR

Clifton's airport is an easy walk from any place in town. In addition to services to St Vincent, it receives regular scheduled flights from Barbados and sometimes St Lucia.

BOAT

There are regular boats heading north into the Grenadines and St Vincent.

Bequia Express (p732) Large boat running twice a week to and from St Vincent via Mayreau and Canouan.

MV Barracuda (455-9835; perrysshipping@vincysurf.com) A cargo boat that runs three times a week to Canouan and on to Kingstown.

MV Gem Star II (457-4157) Slow cargo boat making two trips a week to Mayreau, Canouan and Kingstown.

There is a daily school boat to Mayreau (EC$20 one way) leaving from the Grenadines Dive dock in Clifton at 6:30am and again at around 3:30pm when school is in session.

The commercial ships that haul goods back and forth between Grenada, Carriacou, Petit Martinique and Union Island sometimes accept foot passengers.

You can charter a small open boat to take you between Clifton and Carriacou for a negotiable US$130. It's a bumpy (and often wet) 40-minute ride for a maximum of four people.

PALM ISLAND

Once called Prune Island, the now more attractively titled Palm Island is just a 10-minute boat ride southeast of Union Island. It's a private island, but visitors can still come ashore at **Casuarina Beach**, which is a stopover on many day tours between Union Island and the Tobago Cays.

A water taxi to Palm Island from Union Island costs around US$20.

Palm Island Resort (458-8824; www.palmislandresortgrenadines.com; s/d from US$1049/1349;) is a delightful place to hole up for a week. The manicured tropical grounds are spotted with palms (obviously) and dotted with villas. The rooms are well fitted out, with an emphasis on luxury living and sea views. The large pool is a nice place for mixing with your fellow guests.

PETIT ST VINCENT

It's not called *petit* for nothing – this island is the smallest and southernmost in the Grenadines chain. Sequestered and exclusive, PSV has a formidable reputation as one of the best private islands in the world. That reputation isn't unwarranted – the beaches are just as spectacular as those on its neighboring islands, and having the place (almost) to yourself makes the price seem a bit more affordable.

Nonguests are able to visit a dedicated area of beach as well as the beach bar on day trips.

The **Petit St Vincent Resort** (in the US 1-954-963-7401; www.petitstvincent.com; cottages/villas US$1649/2240;) is a luxurious escape featuring 22 cottages and villas designed with comfort and privacy in mind. There are spacious sundecks only feet from the ocean, and living spaces that bristle with fine stonework and whitewashed luxury. The first-class facilities include a tree-top spa, two bar-restaurants, a 6000-bottle wine cellar and a dive shop.

Getting There & Away

Cargo ships from Kingstown sometimes continue on to PSV after docking at Union Island but it's by no means regular. A water taxi from Union costs around US$60.

UNDERSTAND ST VINCENT & THE GRENADINES

History

Siboneys, Arawaks & Caribs

St Vincent and the Grenadines is not as remote as it appears; it has been inhabited for some 7000 years. Originally it was sparsely populated by the hunter-gatherer Siboneys. Around 2000 years ago they were replaced by the Arawaks, who moved up from present-day Venezuela. The raiding Caribs eventually took over from the Arawaks, but held some of the islands for as little as 100 years before the arrival of the heavily armed Spanish. Fierce Carib resistance kept the Europeans out of St Vincent long after most other Caribbean islands had fallen to the colonists. This was in part because many Caribs from other islands fled to St Vincent (Hairoun, as they called it) after their home islands were conquered – it was the Caribs' last stand. On the island, Caribs intermarried with Africans who had escaped from slavery, and the new mixed generation split along ethnic lines as Black Caribs and Yellow Caribs.

Colonial Times

In 1783, after a century of competing claims between the British and French, the Treaty of Paris placed St Vincent under British control. Indigenous rebellions followed and British troops rounded up the insurgents, forcibly repatriating around 5000 Black Caribs to Roatán island, Honduras. With the native opposition gone, the planters capitalized on the fertile volcanic soil. However, prosperity didn't last long: two eruptions of La Soufrière, the abolition of slavery in 1834 and a few powerful hurricanes stood in the way of their colonial dreams. For the remainder of British rule the economy stagnated – plantations were eventually broken up and land was redistributed to small-scale farmers.

Modern St Vincent & the Grenadines

In 1969, in association with the British, St Vincent became a self-governing state. On October 27, 1979, it was cobbled together with the Grenadines as an independent member of the Commonwealth.

The nation remains rather poor. It is still dependent on banana exports, though crops have been badly hit by black sigatoka disease, which has severely depleted exports. Tourism, while important, still has a long way to go in terms of bringing in needed wealth. Crown lands continue to be sold off to foreign investors to generate funds and stimulate economic development, but the accompanying jobs boom has failed to materialize and many Vincentians have slipped well below the poverty line.

The long-serving prime minister, Ralph Gonsalves, began serving in 2001 and has been a polarizing figure throughout the country. In 2009 SVG was the first country in the British Caribbean to vote on replacing the Queen of the United Kingdom as the head of state. Gonsalves – a self-declared anticolonialist fighter – promoted the vote to ditch the monarch but lost the referendum.

He was reelected for the fourth time in 2015 in a result that was controversial among some Vincentians. In the last decade he has been busy forming alliances with Bolivia, Venezuela, Cuba and pretty much any country willing to send aid to SVG, such as Canada, Japan and China. He made headlines in early 2016 by calling on the Caribbean to investigate marijuana as a possible substitute for banana crops throughout the region.

While Gonsalves shows no sign of giving up power soon, opposition throughout the country continues to grow, especially in the Grenadines, where many locals feel he has prioritized development on the St Vincent mainland at the expense of the archipelago. They point to the loss of fast boat connections and poor infrastructure including the lack of drinking water on many islands as evidence of this neglect.

People & Culture

Pigeonholing Vincy culture is a tough task. With eight inhabited islands – nine if you include Young Island – in the chain, the cultural variance is as vast as the sea in which they sit. Locals tend to be conservative, quiet and a tough nut to crack for outsiders, but then again, wash ashore on some of the tiny islands and everybody has something to say to you.

To a certain degree there is a feeling of detachment from the outside world. But the isolation of the islands is fading fast, with easy access to pop culture and mass media.

Most locals find work in traditional industries such as fishing, agriculture or laboring. Tourism is also becoming important, but, outside Bequia and Canouan, it's still quite modest compared to neighboring islands such as Barbados or even Grenada.

Landscape & Wildlife

The Land

St Vincent is a high volcanic island, forming the northernmost point of the volcanic ridge that runs from Grenada in the south up through the Grenadine islands. It is markedly hilly and its rich volcanic soil is very productive – St Vincent is often called the 'garden of the Grenadines.' It has a rugged interior of tropical rainforest, and lowlands thick with coconut trees and banana estates. The valley region around Mesopotamia, east of Kingstown, has some of the best farmland and most luxuriant landscapes.

The island of St Vincent gobbles up 133 sq miles of the nation's 150 sq miles. The other 17 sq miles are spread across 32 islands and cays, just nine of which are populated. The largest of the islands are Bequia, Mustique, Canouan, Mayreau and Union Island. The larger Grenadine islands are hilly but relatively low-lying, and most have no source of freshwater other than rainfall. All are dotted with stunning white-sand beaches and abundant sea life.

Wildlife

The crystal-clear waters surrounding St Vincent and the Grenadines are abundant with sea life. Plentiful reefs are a flurry of fish activity, with turtles, moray eels, angelfish, barracuda, octopus, nurse sharks and countless other species calling the region home. Dolphins also frequent the area and are often seen surfing the bow waves of oceangoing vessels.

On land, the fauna becomes decidedly more sparse. The sun-drenched islands are home to a few interesting species, such as the St Vincent parrot, an endangered and strikingly beautiful bird that has multicolored plumage and is seen in the jungle interior of St Vincent. This rainforest also provides the home for manicou (opossum) and agouti (a rabbitlike rodent). Agouti roam freely on Young Island, where they are easy to spot.

Environmental Issues

The concepts of climate change and environmental responsibility are slowly creeping into the collective mindsets of Vincentians. The government has been very proactive in this regard, with SVG becoming one of the first countries in the region to ban the use of styrofoam under new laws passed in 2017.

SVG has also started a program to try to curb damage done to the sea by overfishing and irresponsible boating practices.

Hotel rooms across the country attract a US$3 climate resilience levy, which is used to investigate ways to mitigate impacts of climate change on the country.

Freshwater is also a major concern, with a combination of runoff, wells and desalination plants supplying the hydration for the islands. Demand outstrips supply when cruise ships roll up and refill their tanks and this continues to be a divisive issue for locals, depending on which side of the economic equation they sit.

In the southern Grenadines the situation is critical; there is no government water supply so each household is required to collect their own rainwater. Once that runs out, residents are forced to buy bottled water shipped in from the main island or desalinated water from one of the large resorts. It seems a little perverse that guests lounge in infinity pools while local residents don't have water with which to wash clothes.

SURVIVAL GUIDE

Directory A–Z

ACCESSIBLE TRAVEL

Travelers with disabilities, especially those in wheelchairs, will have difficulty traveling throughout SVG. There are rarely sidewalks, pathways are often sand, and ferries and other seagoing transportation are not designed with special needs in mind.

ACCOMMODATIONS

There's a wide range of accommodations options throughout SVG, with beds to suit most budgets. On most of the main islands you can find places that are decidedly casual. At other places, however (read: Mustique), you'll have to remortgage the house to spend the week, and you're expected to dress accordingly.

Hotels are generally quite personal, with only a few rooms for the relaxed staff to look after.

ACTIVITIES

The warm, clear waters of SVG draw divers from around the globe. They come to swim with a stunning array of sea life, from reef-hopping angelfish and grass-munching sea turtles to ocean predators such as nurse sharks. The reefs are pristine, with forests of soft and hard coral colored every hue of the rainbow. Wrecks, rays and the odd whale just add to the appeal. Spearfishing is prohibited.

Visibility is often unlimited and the warm water makes for comfortable diving. Great sites can be found at the very recreational depth of 60ft to 80ft and currents are minimal.

You can find good dive operators on all the main islands. The going rates for a one-tank dive start at around US$70. Great for novices looking to get their feet literally wet are 'resort courses,' which include a couple of hours of instruction and a shallow dive geared to first-timers; they average US$85.

Most dive shops run snorkeling trips parallel to dive excursions. The obvious destination here is beautiful Tobago Cays.

ELECTRICITY

The electric current is 220V to 240V (50 cycles). British-style three-pin plugs are used. Some resorts also have US-style outlets with 110V power.

EMERGENCY NUMBERS

Emergency ☎999

FOOD

Meals in SVG are almost always enjoyed with a fantastic sea view. In the popular tourist areas on the main island and in the Grenadines, you'll find restaurants serving all kinds of international cuisine, but almost all also have at least a couple of traditional dishes on the menu and they're well worth trying out.

Essential Food & Drink

As far as West Indian food goes, SVG is one of the better destinations for enjoying its unique flavors.

Fresh produce St Vincent produces top-quality and delicious fruit and vegetables.

Seafood Lobster, shrimp, conch and fish are all popular and readily available.

Callaloo A spinach-like vegetable used in soups and stews. Many vitamins!

Savory pumpkin soup More squash-like than the American Thanksgiving staple; often like a rich stew.

Saltfish Dried fish that has been cured; delicious when made into fish cakes.

Rotis Curried vegetables, potatoes and meat wrapped in a flour tortilla are a national passion.

Hairoun (high-rone) The light and tasty local lager.

HEALTH

St Vincent has both public hospitals and private clinics in the area around Kingstown. Being a small developing nation, the level of care is well below that of the US or Europe and the public facilities are often stretched way beyond capacity.

There are public hospitals and clinics throughout the islands, with each place (with the exception of Mayreau) having some form of medical center. Any serious problems, however, will require a trip to St Vincent, if not further.

INTERNET ACCESS

Internet access is widely available on all the larger islands in SVG. Wi-fi access is common at hotels and increasingly at bars and restaurants. Most towns will have some version of an internet cafe.

LGBT+ TRAVELERS

As with elsewhere in the Caribbean, the view about LGBT+ travelers is outdated, to say the

SLEEPING PRICE RANGES

Prices listed are for the high season (December to April/May). Rates do not include 10% VAT that is added to all hotel rooms, or the 10% service charge that is frequently tacked on to bills. Prices are in either EC$ or US$, depending on the hotel.

The following price ranges refer to a double room with bathroom.

$ less than US$100

$$ US$100–250

$$$ more than US$250

EATING PRICE RANGES

The following price ranges are based on the cost of a main course.

$ less than EC$35

$$ EC$35–70

$$$ more than EC$70

PRACTICALITIES

Newspapers The *Vincentian* is published weekly and is the oldest newspaper in the country. The *Caribbean Compass* is an excellent monthly magazine that covers marine news and travel issues.

Radio The main national radio station, NBCSVG, broadcasts at 107.5 and 90.7 on the FM Band. There are half a dozen other stations broadcast on the FM band out of Kingstown.

Smoking Smoking is fairly uncommon in St Vincent. It is still possible to smoke in some bars, but all hotel rooms and most restaurants are generally now smoke-free.

Weights & measures St Vincent uses the imperial system.

least. You won't find any gay-friendly events, resorts or cruises here. LGBT+ travelers should be cautious with public affection, but should otherwise be fine.

MONEY

The Eastern Caribbean dollar (EC$) is the local currency. Major credit cards are accepted at most hotels, car-rental agencies, dive shops and some of the larger restaurants.

Exchange Rates

The Eastern Caribbean dollar is pegged to the US dollar at a rate of 2.70 to 1.

Australia	A$	EC$1.94
Barbados	B$	EC$1.36
Canada	C$1	EC$2.03
Euro zone	€1	EC$3.05
Japan	¥100	EC$2.41
New Zealand	NZ$1	EC$1.81
UK	UK£1	EC$3.52
US	US$1	EC$2.70

For current exchange rates, see www.xe.com.

Tipping

Hotels A minimum of EC$2 per bag for porters is standard; gratuity for cleaning staff is at your discretion.

Restaurants Most restaurants add the service charge to the bill. If it's not automatically included, tip 10% to 15%; if it is included, it's up to you to leave a small additional tip.

Taxi Prices are generally fixed and tips are not expected but if service is excellent, tip 10% to 15% of the fare.

PUBLIC HOLIDAYS

In addition to those observed throughout the region, SVG has the following public holidays:

St Vincent & the Grenadines Day January 22

Labor Day First Monday in May

Caricom Day Second Monday in July

Carnival Tuesday Usually second Tuesday in July

Emancipation Day First Monday in August

Independence Day October 27

TELEPHONE

The country code is 1; the area code is 784. To call any other country with a country code of 1 (most of North America and the Caribbean), just dial 1 and the 10-digit number. For other countries, dial the international access code 011+country code+number.

Cell Phones

GSM cell (mobile) phones are compatible with local SIM cards. There is also 4G service. The main operators are Digicel (www.digicelgroup.com/vc) and Flow (www.discoverflow.co/saint-vincent).

TIME

St Vincent, along with the rest of the Windward Islands, is on UTC minus four hours.

TOURIST INFORMATION

The Department of Tourism St Vincent & the Grenadines (p736) has an office on St Vincent. Bequia has an excellent semiprivate tourist office, as does Union Island. Several free publications are also highly useful, including *Ins & Outs St Vincent & the Grenadines*.

Getting There & Away

AIR

St Vincent is the main air hub for SVG, with **Argyle International Airport** (www.svg-airport.com) near Yambou Head receiving direct flights from the US and Canada in addition to services to nearby islands such as Barbados, St Lucia and Grenada. The main islands in the Grenadines also have airports that have direct service to Barbados. Several airlines serving the Grenadines work together for ticketing through the **Grenadine Air Alliance** (☎458-4380; www.grenadine-air.com).

LIAT (www.liat.com) Connects St Vincent with Antigua, Barbados, Grenada, St Lucia and Trinidad.

Mustique Airlines (www.mustique.com) A charter company connecting St Vincent, Bequia, Canouan, Mustique and Union Island with Barbados. It works in tandem with SVG Air on some services.

SVG Air Connects St Vincent, Bequia, Canouan, Mustique and Union Island with Barbados and Grenada. Flights between St Lucia and the Grenadines are now on a charter basis only.

SEA

There is a twice-weekly small mail boat that runs between Union Island and Carriacou in Grenada. Commercial ships that haul goods between Grenada, Carriacou, Petit Martinique and Union Island sometimes accept foot passengers but it's not common.

You can charter a small open boat to take you from Clifton on Union Island to Carriacou in Grenada.

Getting Around

AIR

Flights within SVG are a quick and inexpensive way to shuttle around the country. There are airports on all the main Grenadine islands except Mayreau.

SVG Air (☎457-5124; www.flysvgair.com) Main national airline offering inter-Grenadine flights.

BOAT

Ferry

The main islands of SVG are well linked by boats. It's very important to confirm schedule details in advance as they change frequently.

Fishing Boat

You can usually find someone who will get you between islands in the Grenadines. Usually this will be on a small, open fishing boat with room for, at best, four people with minimal luggage. The rides can be quite exciting and should not be undertaken in rough seas. Places to stay on the islands always have reliable contacts.

Costs are negotiable – for an example, you should be able to get from Mayreau to Union Island for under EC$150.

Yacht

You just never know if you'll be able to hitch a ride somewhere. The Grenadines get a lot of traffic so there are opportunities. Hang out dockside in Union Island, or at bars popular with sailors on Bequia, and see what you can arrange.

BUS

Buses are a good way to get around St Vincent. It is possible to catch one on Bequia and Union Island, but these islands are so small that you'll rarely use them.

The buses themselves are usually minivans that are often jammed full. You can expect to get to know at least 20 fellow commuters as you are squeezed into every available space in the bus. There's usually a conductor on board who handles the cash and assigns the seats. When you get to your stop, either tap on the roof or try to get the attention of the conductor over the thumping music, and the bus will stop for you just about anywhere.

Fares vary by distance, ranging from EC$1.50 to EC$6, depending on the destination.

CAR & MOTORCYCLE

St Vincent is really the only island where you may wish to drive. It has enough roads to make exploration interesting and worthwhile. However, expect to drive slowly over its very narrow and winding roads – think 20mph as a good average.

Car Rental

Rentals typically cost from US$60 a day for a car and from US$70 for a 4WD.

There are car-rental agencies on St Vincent and Bequia, but most of the Grenadine islands have no car rentals at all.

Road Rules

Driving is on the left-hand side. To drive within SVG you must have a visitor license, which costs a whopping EC$100 and can be obtained at the central police station on Bay St in Kingstown, or at the airport. Travelers holding an international permit are exempt from this requirement but must register their permit with the local police before driving.

TAXI

Taxis are abundant on St Vincent and Bequia. Prices are usually set by authorities but even so, agree on a fare before departure.

BLACQBOOK/SHUTTERSTOCK ©

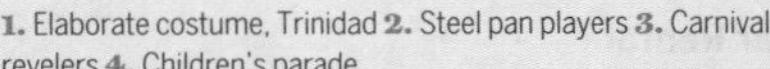

1. Elaborate costume, Trinidad **2.** Steel pan players **3.** Carnival revelers **4.** Children's parade

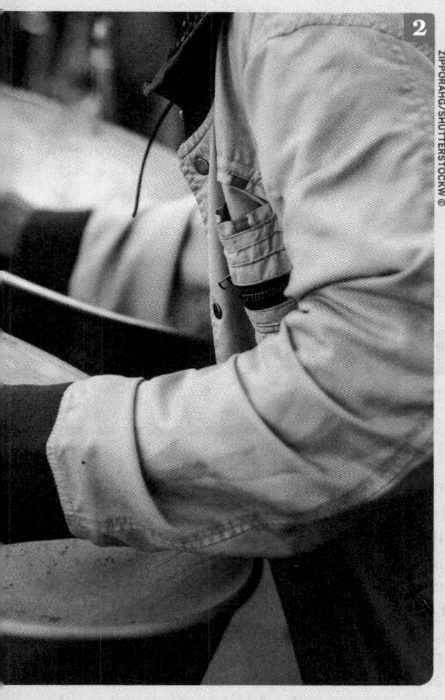

ZIPPORAHG/SHUTTERSTOCK ©

Carnival in Trinidad & Tobago

Truly awesome in its scale and spectacle, T&T's pre-Lenten carnival is an uncontainable explosion of creativity that completely overtakes the nation from its epicenter in Port of Spain.

The hype starts months before at lavish catwalk launches showcasing mas-band costumes, from teeny-weeny spangles to couture-style creations, and the anticipation builds to an ever greater intensity after New Year's Day as the main event approaches. Carnivalistas scrabble to secure tickets for the endlessly fabulous round of soca parties (aka fetes), the Queens Park Savannah rings out with the percussive roar of 300-strong steel-pan bands battling it out to win the Panorama competition, armies of costumed kids overtake Port of Spain at the children's parades, and the Woodbrook streets are stalked by old-mas gangs of fire-breathing blue devils, whip-cracking jab jabs and towering moko jumbie stilt-walkers.

Once the monolithic King and Queen costumes have been judged on the Savannah stage and the Soca Monarch crowned, the infectious excitement reaches fever pitch and the carnival opens with J'ouvert, a wonderful and wanton predawn street party where bands of revelers shimmy through the city under a coating of mud, paint, oil and liquid chocolate, only to return again a few hours later, scrubbed and party-ready, for the first of the main parades. The big day is the Tuesday parade, when the costume bands come out in force in a kaleidoscopic storm of feathers and sequins, glitter and glamour.

Carnival is all about participation – you can have a great time just watching from the sidelines, but hitting the road with a mas band will guarantee the party of a lifetime: just sign up online, and get in early for the pick of the costumes.

Trinidad & Tobago

868 / POP 1.3 MILLION

Includes ➡

Best Places to Eat

➡ Kariwak Village (p782)

➡ Fish Pot (p786)

➡ Freebird (p777)

➡ Seahorse Inn Restaurant & Bar (p786)

➡ Veni Mangé (p764)

Best Places to Stay

➡ Castara Retreats (p786)

➡ Plantation Beach Villas (p785)

➡ Top O'Tobago (p785)

➡ Mt Plaisir Estate (p774)

➡ Miller's Guesthouse (p784)

Why Go?

Trinidad and Tobago (T&T) are an exercise in beautiful contradiction. In Trinidad, pristine mangrove swamps and rainforested hills sit side by side with smoke-belching oil refineries and unpretty industrial estates. Tobago has everything you'd expect from a Caribbean island, with palm trees and white sand aplenty, yet it's relatively unchanged by the tourist industry. Combined, this twin-island republic offers unparalleled birdwatching; first-class diving; and luxuriant rainforests perfect for hiking and waterfall swimming. Then there's the electric nightlife and a fabulous Carnival, easily the biggest and best of the region's annual blowouts. And thanks to the legacy of T&T's melting-pot population, the cuisine is a foodie dream, from sensational curries to the freshest of fish.

But don't expect anyone to hold your hand here. The oil and gas industry leaves tourism low on the priority list, so it's up to you to take a deep breath, jump in and enjoy the mix.

When to Go

Nov–Apr Dry season, with clear skies and balmy nights. Crowds flock (and accommodations prices rise) for the pre-Lenten Carnival.

May A good chance of rain.

Jun–Nov Rainy season, with fewer visitors and cheaper rates; Grande Riviere prices are higher in the March to August turtle-nesting season.

TRINIDAD

Put the tourists of Trinidad in a room and you'll have an awkward party: on one side will be wallflower birdwatchers tangled in camera and binocular straps, and on the other – the side with the bar – you'll have the party-hound Carnival fans turning up the music and trying on their spangly costumes.

But here's the secret: there's much more to Trinidad than is seen through binoculars or beer goggles. The swamps and forests are a birdwatcher's dream, and Port of Spain's Carnival will blow your mind, but there are also verdant hiking and cycling trails, spectacular waterfalls and deserted bays of shocking beauty, alongside flamboyant Hindu temples and the decidedly oddball Pitch Lake.

As oil, gas and manufacturing have long been the country's bread and butter, Trinidad tends to treat tourists in a blasé manner. And to some visitors that's a boon. Genuine adventure awaits here if you choose to accept.

Tours

★ ARCTT Chocolate Tours WALKING
(☎ 493-4358; www.facebook.com/thenewruralltt; tours from TT$100) Fantastic walking tours focused on the re-indigenization of T&T's chocolate industry, with passionate and knowledgeable guides giving the lowdown on the history of cocoa and its influence on Port of Spain's (and Trinidad's) development. Routes vary: you might visit a market,

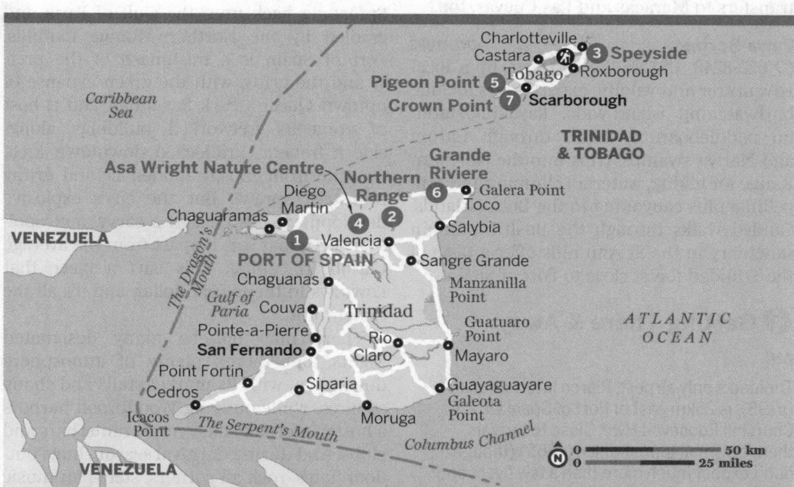

Trinidad & Tobago Highlights

1 Port of Spain (p758) Exploring the atmospheric downtown and city sights, sampling street food or fine-dining meals, visiting panyards and partying on Ariapita Ave or at the fabulous Carnival.

2 Northern Range (p772) Scouting the waterfalls, wildlife and ruggedly gorgeous Trinidad coastline.

3 Diving (p789) Submerging yourself among Speyside's spectacular underwater canyons and coral gardens.

4 Asa Wright Nature Centre (p773) Grabbing your binoculars to spy on Trinidad's prolific birdlife.

5 Pigeon Point (p780) Dipping your toes into whiter-than-white sand and turquoise waters at Tobago's most popular beach.

6 Grande Riviere (p772) Peeking at leatherback turtles laying eggs on this remote Trinidad beach (March to August) and holding your breath as the hatchlings make a bid for the sea (May to September).

7 Boat ride (p781) Following Tobago's Caribbean coastline from Crown Point to snorkel at hidden coves and eat fresh fish at a beach barbecue.

check out fascinating historical documents at National Archives or stop off at cacao hot spots such as Cocobel (p766) or the **Cocoa Pod** (326-1952; www.facebook.com/cocoapod chocolate; 23 Gordon St; 9am-4pm Mon-Fri).

Island Experiences TOURS
(621-0407, mobile 781-6235; www.islandexperiencestt.com; Normandie Hotel, 10 Nook Ave, St Ann's; tours US$45-95, beach shuttle US$30-40) Reliable outfit, with fun and knowledgeable multilingual guides leading island-wide tours covering all the main sights, plus 'ecocultural' trips, which visit lesser-known places from swimmable mud volcanoes to markets. There are also boat trips to remote Bocas islands beaches, sunset cruises, evening panyard trips, and liming tours seeking out the best places to party. Beach transfers to Maracas and Las Cuevas, too.

Paria Springs ADVENTURE
(620-8240; US$105-150;) Run by a local adventurer and wildlife expert, tours include birdwatching island-wide, kayaking/stand-up paddleboardng (SUP) through Caroni and Nariva swamps, trips into the Northern Range for hiking, waterfall climbing and rappelling, plus canyoning in the Bocas islands. Guided walks through the Bush Mountain sanctuary in the St Ann hills offer a taste of the Trinidad forest close to Port of Spain.

Getting There & Away

AIR

Trinidad's only airport, Piarco International (p798), is 25km east of Port of Spain via the Churchill Roosevelt Hwy. Close to arrivals, there's a small tourist office (p765) (though don't expect much more than a few flyers and brochures) and car-rental booths, while the central atrium holds ATMs, a device-charging station, several eateries and a currency-exchange office (6am to 10pm).

BOAT

Ferries operated by the Inter-Island Ferry Service (p767) run multiple times daily between Port of Spain on Trinidad and Scarborough on Tobago.

Getting Around

BUS

Trinidad's bus company, PTSC (p799), operates buses throughout the island; most are air-con and generally in good shape. Most routes originate from the **City Gate** (60 South Quay) terminal on South Quay in Port of Spain. Services aren't that frequent, but make a cheap way to get around if you're not in a rush. Check online (www.ptsc.co.tt) or at the **information/ticket booth** (623-2341; City Gate, 60 South Quay; 6am-8pm Mon-Fri) at City Gate for schedules.

CAR

A number of small, reliable car-rental companies operate on Trinidad. Prices start at about TT$200 a day, including insurance and unlimited mileage. **Econo-Car** (669-1119; www.econocarrentalstt.com; Piarco International Airport) and **Kalloo's** (669-5672; www.kalloos.com; Piarco International Airport) have booths at Piarco International Airport, as well as offices in Port of Spain.

Port of Spain

Spreading back from the Gulf of Paria and cradled by the Northern Range foothills, Port of Spain is a mishmash of the pretty and the gritty, with the green expanse of uptown Queen's Park Savannah and a host of gorgeous fretworked buildings alongside a frenetic, gridlocked downtown area, its waterfront mostly hidden behind grimy industrial sprawl. But the city's explosive development has created a savvy, metropolitan verve that sets it apart from the average Caribbean capital. This isn't a place that kowtows to the tourist dollar, and it's all the richer for it.

There may not be many designated 'sights,' but there's plenty of atmosphere downtown, with its market stalls and shady squares, while outlying Woodbrook harbors a host of eternally busy restaurants, bars and clubs. And during Carnival season, huge outdoor 'fetes' rock all corners, steel-pan music fills the air and the atmosphere is electric.

Sights

★Fort George FORT
(Fort George Rd, St James; 9am-6pm) Get a truly spectacular bird's-eye view of the Port of Spain cityscape and the Gulf of Paria from this colonial-era fort, with stone-built defensive walls pierced by a row of ancient cannon. There's a wooden signal station with a diorama of the fort and a board detailing its construction by Ashanti prince Kofi Nte in 1883. Benches and picnic tables dot the manicured lawns (bring your own refreshments), and there are telescopes to zoom in on the panorama below.

The road to the fort is steep and winding, and passes through some less than salubrious areas; don't attempt to walk it, and go in a group if possible. There's a security guard on duty during opening hours. Best time to come is the afternoon, when the heat dies down, but it's a wonderfully breezy spot throughout the day.

★Queen's Park Savannah PARK

Once part of a sugar plantation, formerly home to a racecourse and now the epicenter of the annual Carnival, this public park is encircled by a 3.7km perimeter road that locals call the world's largest roundabout. In the early evening when the scorching heat subsides, the grassy center is taken up with games of cricket or football, while joggers crowd the perimeter path and vendors sell cold coconut water.

★National Museum & Art Gallery MUSEUM

(623-0339; www.facebook.com/nationalmuseumandartgallerytt; 117 Frederick St, cnr Keate St; 10am-6pm Tue-Sat; P) FREE Housed in a classic colonial building, the rather dry historical exhibits range from the oil industry to Amerindian settlers, the colonial era and indentured Indians.

There are also geological and natural-history displays – check out the tarantulas and fearsome-looking giant centipede. The rotating collection of artwork on the top floor is the highlight, and gives an excellent introduction to the Trinbago art scene. And don't miss the classic T&T films screened on a loop in the audio-visual room.

★Botanical Gardens GARDENS

(622-1221; Circular Rd, St Ann's; 6am-6:30pm; P) FREE Resplendent with exotic trees and plants, and networked by paved paths, the Botanical Gardens date from 1818. Take a stroll or relax in one of the handsome wooden gazebos; at Christmas time, trees along the Savannah-facing walkway are lit up with thousands of colorful fairy lights.

A graceful mansion built in 1875, the adjacent **President's House** (Circular Rd, St Ann's) is undergoing major repairs and sits shrouded under a protective roof, its west wing having collapsed in early 2010.

Woodford Square PARK

(Frederick St) This grassy square with its central Eros and Aphrodite fountain and ornate bandstand is the symbolic center of downtown Port of Spain. Dr Eric Williams, Trinidad and Tobago's first prime minister, gave stirring speeches here, which eventually led to independence from Britain; the 1970s Black Power demonstrations also took place here. Known as the 'University of Woodford Square,' it remains a 'speakers corner' where people can express opinions via soapbox discussions; daily topics are posted on a blackboard.

Independence Square AREA

The hustle and bustle of downtown culminates along Independence Sq, two parallel streets that flank the central Brian Lara Promenade, named for Trinidad's cricketing hero.

The commanding 1836 **Roman Catholic Cathedral** (623-5232; www.moth erchurchtt.org; 31 Independence Sq) caps the promenade's eastern end; at its western end, past the high-rise blocks of the Nicholas and Central Bank towers, and a statue of Brian Lara, the square feeds onto the coastal highway, Wrightson Rd. A raised walkway over Wrightson Rd connects the promenade to the waterfront.

Sleeping

Port of Spain holds the bulk of Trinidad's accommodations, and as most of the country's better-known attractions are within an hour's drive, it's quite feasible to stay here and explore the whole island.

During Carnival season, most places offer packages for a set number of days, and raise rates to twice the regular room price.

★Gingerbread House GUESTHOUSE $

(627-8170; www.trinidadgingerbreadhouse.com; 8 Carlos St, Woodbrook; r US$70; @) Renovated by its architect owner, this beautiful fretworked 1920s house has bags of character, with a breezy veranda and a stylish outdoor space at the back with sundeck and a creatively tiled splash pool.

The high-ceilinged rooms in the main house are spacious and pleasantly decorated, and have fridge and TV, while the stylish annex rooms share a kitchenette. Book ahead.

Inna Citi Place GUESTHOUSE $

(622-0415; www.inna-citi-place.com; 15 Gaston Johnson St, Woodbrook; s/d incl breakfast US$45/65; @) Excellent little budget choice on a quiet residential street, offering

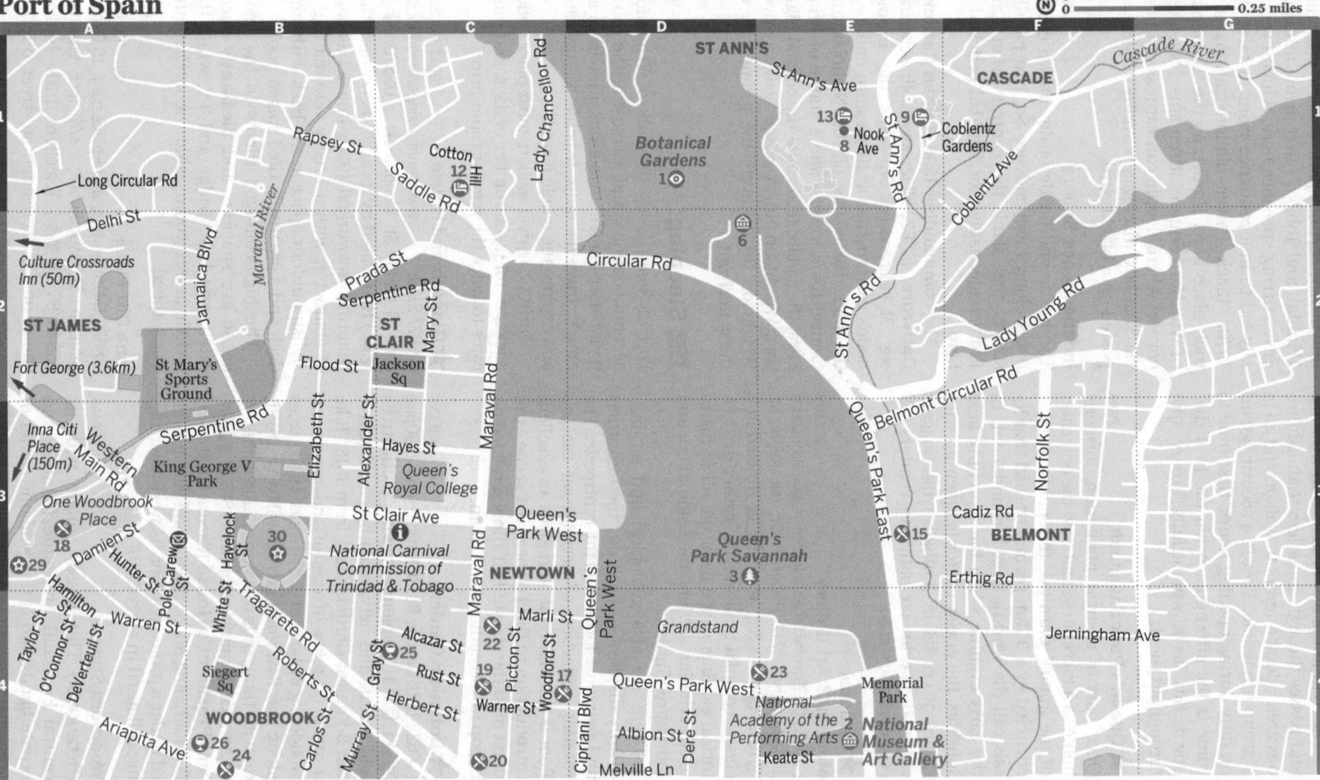
Port of Spain
0 500 m
0 0.25 miles
A
B
C
D
E
F
G
1
2
3
4
ST ANN'S
St Ann's Ave
CASCADE
Cascade River
13
9
Nook Ave
8
Coblentz Gardens
St Ann's Rd
Coblentz Ave
Botanical Gardens
1
6
Lady Chancellor Rd
Cotton Hill
12
Saddle Rd
Rapsey St
Long Circular Rd
Delhi St
Culture Crossroads Inn (50m)
Jamaica Blvd
Maraval River
Prada St
Serpentine Rd
Circular Rd
St Ann's Rd
Lady Young Rd
ST JAMES
ST CLAIR
Mary St
Jackson Sq
Flood St
Fort George (3.6km)
St Mary's Sports Ground
Belmont Circular Rd
Queen's Park East
Norfolk St
Serpentine Rd
Elizabeth St
Alexander St
Maraval Rd
Hayes St
Inna Citi Place (150m)
Western Main Rd
King George V Park
Queen's Royal College
One Woodbrook Place
St Clair Ave
Queen's Park West
Cadiz Rd
15
BELMONT
18
Damien St
Hunter St
Pole Carew St
Havelock St
30
National Carnival Commission of Trinidad & Tobago
Maraval Rd
NEWTOWN
Queen's Park Savannah
3
Erthig Rd
29
Hamilton St
Warren St
White St
Tragarete Rd
Marli St
Queen's Park West
Grandstand
Jerningham Ave
Taylor St
O'Connor St
DeVerteuil St
Siegert Sq
Roberts St
Gray St
25
Alcazar St
22
Picton St
Woodford St
23
Rust St
19
17
Queen's Park West
Memorial Park
Herbert St
Warner St
National Academy of the Performing Arts
2
National Museum & Art Gallery
WOODBROOK
Carlos St
Murray St
Cipriani Blvd
Albion St
Dere St
Ariapita Ave
26
24
20
Melville Ln
Keate St

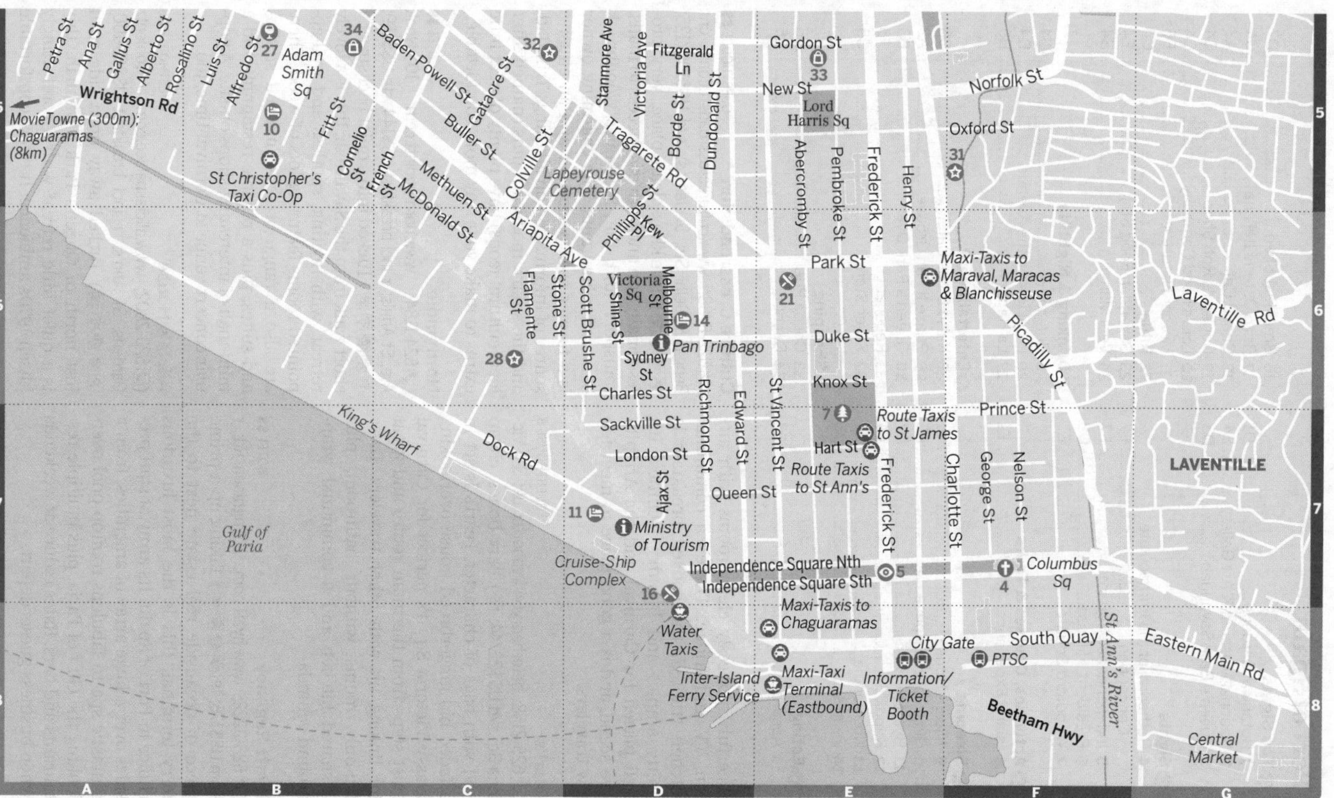

TRINIDAD & TOBAGO PORT OF SPAIN

Port of Spain

Top Sights
1 Botanical Gardens ... D1
2 National Museum & Art Gallery ... E4
3 Queen's Park Savannah ... D3

Sights
4 Cathedral of the Immaculate Conception ... F7
5 Independence Square ... E7
6 President's House ... D2
7 Woodford Square ... E7

Activities, Courses & Tours
8 Island Experiences ... E1

Sleeping
9 Alicia's House ... E1
10 Gingerbread House ... B5
11 Hyatt Regency ... D7
12 Kapok ... C1
13 Normandie ... E1
14 Pearl's ... D6

Eating
15 Apsara ... E3
16 Breakfast Shed ... D7
17 Buzo Osteria Italiana ... C4
18 Chaud Café ... A3
19 Dopson's Roti Shop ... C4
20 Lola's Food Company ... C4
21 Mother Nature's ... E6
22 Rituals ... C4
23 Savannah Food Stalls ... E4
24 Veni Mangé ... B4

Drinking & Nightlife
25 Bungalow ... C4
26 Frankie's on the Avenue ... B4
27 La Habana ... B5

Entertainment
28 Kaiso Blues Café ... C6
29 Phase II Pan Groove ... A3
30 Queen's Park Oval ... B3
31 Renegades ... F5
32 Silver Stars ... C5

Shopping
33 Cocoa Pod ... E5
34 Cocobel ... B5

cheerful, spotlessly clean rooms with air-con, TV and fridge. There's a communal kitchen (though the cooked breakfast is pretty ample) and laundry facilities. It's well placed for Carnival and the Ariapita Ave scene, and is a good place to meet fellow travelers.

Pearl's GUESTHOUSE **$**
(☎625-2158; peterhenry64@yahoo.co.uk; 3-4 Victoria Sq; s/d US$22/44; 📶) Bare bones, cheap and with bags of character, Pearl's is set in a faded old gingerbread house overlooking grassy Victoria Sq. It's perfect for Carnival (just steps from the main route) and great for linking up with other travelers. Basic fan-only rooms without bathroom, plus a shared kitchen and a communal wrap-around veranda.

Hyatt Regency HOTEL **$$**
(☎623-2222; www.hyatt.com; 1 Wrightson Rd; r from US$176; P ❄ @ 📶 🏊) Taking up a prime piece of oceanside real estate next to the ferry terminal, this is the most luxurious choice in Port of Spain. Its army of staff presides over a huge array of amenities, from a fantastic spa to fabulous rooftop pool overlooking the Gulf of Paria, plus multiple restaurants and bars. Rates reduce at weekends when business guests depart.

Culture Crossroads Inn GUESTHOUSE **$$**
(☎622-8788; www.culturecrossroadstt.com; cnr Bengal & Delhi Sts, St James; s/d US$100/125; P ❄ @ 📶) Sparkling-clean place, very professionally run and with easy access to malls, transport and the St James/Woodbrook bars and restaurants. The charming owner is a former soca performer and an effusive source of information on all things Trinidad, and the smart, modern rooms (named after local cultural icons) have plenty of neat little extras to make your stay more comfortable.

Normandie HOTEL **$$**
(☎624-1184; www.normandiett.com; 10 Nook Ave, St Ann's; r incl breakfast US$144, ste US$159; P ❄ @ 📶 🏊) Tucked into a quiet backstreet a short walk from the Savannah, this is a lovely retreat, with inviting, spotless and well-appointed rooms featuring lots of wood. There are also a range of self-contained studios and suites, plus a reliable restaurant and a mini-mall of interesting shops on-site. A popular concert venue at Carnival time, too.

Alicia's House GUESTHOUSE **$$**
(☎623-2802; www.aliciaspalace.com; 7 Coblentz Gardens, St Ann's; r incl breakfast US$65-100; P ❄ @ 📶 🏊) Tucked away on a side road just north of Queen's Park Savannah, this is a quiet little retreat with a comfortingly kitsch 1970s ambience. It offers comfortable

rooms with fridge, air-con, cable TV and wi-fi, plus nice communal areas, including sundeck and pool/hot tub. Meals are served in its restaurant.

★Kapok HOTEL $$$
(☎622-5765; www.kapokhotel.com; 16-18 Cotton Hill, St Clair; r/ste from US$180/259;) Not just a business hotel, the smart Kapok boasts an authentic Caribbean vibe. It's located toward the south end of Saddle Rd, within throwing distance from Queen's Park Savannah, and perfect for Carnival. Rooms and suites are decked out in cool modern style and it has a pool, two excellent restaurants and a useful self-service launderette.

Eating

Port of Spain has some truly excellent restaurants, serving everything from sushi to pizza, with a host of places cooking up some memorable Trinbago cuisine, too. Most are located in and around Woodbrook, but there are also plenty of options in neighboring St Clair and Newtown, as well as the terrace of the One Woodbrook Place complex in Woodbrook and MovieTowne's Fiesta Plaza.

★Lola's Food Company DINER $
(☎345-5439; www.facebook.com/lolasfoodcompany; 82 Tragarete Rd, Newtown; breakfast TT$25-75, mains TT$45-75; ⊙7am-3:30pm Mon-Thu, to 4:30pm Fri, 8am-4:30pm Sat;) Fabulous family-run place, with truly friendly servers and a fun, casual atmosphere. Breakfast runs from pancakes, eggs and waffles to *sada* roti and saltfish. For lunch, there's an excellent roasted beet salad, plus substantial burgers (including a fish one with herby remoulade) and memorably crispy fried chicken; the 'sandwich of the month' is always good, too.

★Dopson's Roti Shop INDIAN $
(☎628-6141; 28 Maraval Rd, Newtown; rotis from TT$30; ⊙6:45am-5pm Mon-Sat;) This tiny place is a favorite locals' spot – many Trinis claim it makes the best rotis in Port of Spain. Fillings are fresh, succulent and generous (try the curried duck). There are lots of veggie choices and fabulous traditional breakfasts such as *sada* roti with *choka* (eggplant or tomato, chargrilled till tender and laced with garlic).

★Breakfast Shed CARIBBEAN $
(Femmes du Chalet; Wrightson Rd; mains from TT$50; ⊙6:30am-4pm) Under an awning right on the water, this is the place to go for Trini tastes and great views over the Gulf, with stalls arranged around an open-air, picnic-benched eating area. The large servings of local fare include fish or chicken with macaroni pie, callaloo soup, stewed beans, plantain and rice. Breakfasts include saltfish *buljol* or smoked herring with fresh coconut bread.

Savannah Food Stalls STREET FOOD $
(Queen's Park West; gyros from TT$25, roti from TT$30; ⊙6pm to late) The paved section of the Savannah has taken off as a cool spot to enjoy some Trinbago street food. Hunkered under white tents, stalls sell everything from fresh fruit juices and smoothies to roti, *pholouri* (chickpea-flour doughballs with tamarind dipping sauce), bake and fish or corn soup, plus barbecued meats, Lebanese-style gyro wraps and Jamaican jerk chicken.

Mother Nature's VEGETARIAN $
(☎623-3300; cnr Park & St Vincent Sts; mains TT$25-50; ⊙6am-3pm Mon-Fri, from 7am Sat;) Whole-wheat roti? Yes, it exists here, as do dairy-free desserts (including a showcase of ice creams) and deliciously healthy vegetarian dishes from the local repertoire. The fresh-pressed or squeezed natural juices, from barbadine to sugar cane, are delectable; you can also build your own drink from the display of fresh fruit and veggies.

Rituals CAFE $
(66 Maraval Rd, cnr Marli St, Newtown; sandwiches from TT$25; ⊙6:30am-7pm;) This coffeehouse chain (one of many Port of Spain branches) serves smoothies, coffee drinks, paninis, hot-filled wraps, salads, bakery goods, bagel sandwiches and Jamaican patties. It's a cool stop for a quick breakfast or lunch. Tap into the free wi-fi and take refuge from the heat in the blasting air-con.

LOCAL KNOWLEDGE

STREET FOOD

Street food is a big deal in Port of Spain. Trini treats are available from dusk until late into the night along Western Main Rd in St James, the traditional street food hot spot. More easily accessible are Ariapita Ave in Woodbrook, where you'll find a string of stands selling gyro wraps; and the Savannah Food Court at the southeastern corner of the Queen's Park Savannah.

CARNIVAL

With roots in both West Africa and Europe, Carnival is the ultimate indulgence before the sober disciplines of Lent – and everyone's welcome to participate in this heavyweight of Caribbean festivals.

Background information is available from the **National Carnival Commission** (☎622-1670; www.ncctt.org; 11 St Clair Ave, St Clair), which posts an essential schedule of Carnival events on its website each year, and the **National Carnival Bands Association** (☎628-8650; www.ncbatt.com; 1 Picton St, Newtown). Trinidad Carnival Diary (www.trinidadcarnivaldiary.com) provides mas (carnival) band listings and reviews, and topical articles on all things Carnival: check out the Masquerader Corner section of the site, and its more active Facebook/Instagram pages. For fete reviews and the latest news, check out the Carnival section of LoopTT (www.looptt.com).

Mas Camps

Mas camps are workshops where carnival bands create their costumes and display them to prospective revelers. Costumes cost anything from TT$2000 for a basic outfit to TT$10,000 or more for a 'frontline' extravaganza; buying a costume allows you to parade along the Carnival route with the band on the main Monday and Tuesday festivities, and usually covers food and drinks as well. Costumes can be bought directly from mas camps or online, and they go very quickly. Latecomers can try their luck finding a costume from websites such as Carnival Junction (www.carnivaljunction.com) or Fineahban (www.fineahban.com). First-choice bands include **Tribe** (☎625-6800; www.carnivaltribe.com; 20 Rosalino St, Woodbrook) and its offshoot **Lost Tribe** (☎mobile 350-6219; www.losttribecarnival.com; 59 Alberto St, Woodbrook), **Fantasy** (☎mobile 221-4966; www.mycarnivalfantasy.com; 6 Alberto St, Woodbrook), **Bliss** (☎625-6800; www.blisscarnival.com; 18 Rosalino St, Woodbrook), **K2K Alliance** (☎637-1668; www.k2k-carnival.com; 22 Oleander Row, Victoria Gardens, Diego Martin), **Trini Revellers** (☎625-1881; www.trinirevellers.com; 35 Gallus St, Woodbrook), **Legacy** (☎622-7466; www.legacycarnival.com; 76 Roberts St, Woodbrook) and budget-friendly **Showtime** (☎681-6117; www.showtimecarnival.com; 51 French St, Woodbrook). For full band listings check the National Carnival Bands Association website.

Pre-Carnival Highlights

➡ Lavish pre-Carnival fetes start on January 1 and continue until Carnival.

➡ The Panorama semis and finals see steel-pan bands battle it out on the last two Saturdays before Carnival weekend; the semis are the big event, attended by huge crowds.

➡ There are cute Kiddie Mas parades on the final two Saturdays preceding Carnival.

➡ Don't miss fabulous traditional mas featuring blue devils, jab jabs, moko jumbies and all the classic characters of the T&T mas canon. There's an evening Individuals competition at Adam Smith Sq and a daytime parade from downtown Port of Spain to Woodford Sq; dates vary, so check the National Carnival Commission website for details.

★Veni Mangé CARIBBEAN **$$**
(☎624-4597; www.facebook.com/venimangett; 67a Ariapita Ave, Woodbrook; mains TT$120-140; ⏲11:30am-3pm Mon-Fri, 7-10:30pm Wed-Fri;) West Indian flavor, art and enthusiasm infuse this vibrant restaurant. Serving classic Caribbean cuisine cooked with love, it's one of the best spots for authentic Trini food in Port of Spain. Try the oxtail with dumplings, the grilled fresh fish with tamarind sauce or the excellent veggie options. From coconut ice cream to rum-laced trifle, the desserts are equally delicious.

Chaud Café FUSION **$$**
(☎628-9845; www.chaudkm.com; One Woodbrook Place, Damian St, Woodbrook; brunch dishes TT$60-230, small plates TT$60-150, mains TT$95-295; ⏲11am-11pm Mon-Thu, to midnight Fri & Sat, 10am-3pm Sun;) Part wine bar, part upscale bistro, overseen by local chef extraordinaire Khalid Mohammed, this is a lovely spot for lunch, perhaps seared salmon with lentils, kale and a tomato concasse, or seven-vegetable tagine. The pasta (including gluten free) is always delicious. Great for evening drinks, with good cocktails and

* Watch mesmerizingly huge costumes dance across the stage at the final of the King and Queen of the Bands competition, an evening event staged at Port of Spain's Queen's Park Savannah in the week before the main parade days – dates have shifted around, so check the schedule on the National Carnival Commission website.

* Expect pyrotechnics, elaborate stage decorations and a sea of huge flags waving in the crowd as the Caribbean's leading soca artists give it their all at the International Soca Monarch competition, an electric all-night show in the Savannah on the Friday before Carnival.

* Immerse yourself in the roots of Carnival at the Canboulay Riots re-enactment, staged at Piccadilly Greens in downtown Port of Spain from 4am on the last Friday before Carnival: stickfighting, blue devils and a recreation of the uprising that followed the prohibition of Carnival in 1881.

* Dimanche Gras, on the Sunday evening before Carnival at Queen's Park Savannah, sees the crowning of the Calypso Monarch, as well as pan bands and mas costumes.

J'ouvert

Trinidad's Carnival opens with J'ouvert ('joo-vay'), a no-holds-barred predawn street party where revelers have permission to indulge in their most hedonistic inclinations, as they welcome in the festivities by playing 'dirty mas.' From 4am, partygoers file into the streets, slather themselves and others in mud, paint, *abir* powder oil and even liquid chocolate, and gyrate through the streets while following trucks blasting soca or percussion bands known as 'rhythm sections,' beating out a hypnotic tempo. It's an anarchic scene, so you're best off signing up with an established band like **3Canal** (☎622-1001; www.3canal.com; Big Black Box, 33 Murray St, Woodbrook), **Red Ants** (☎625-6800; www.facebook.com/redantscarnival; 20 Rosalino St, Woodbrook), **Friends for the Road** (☎mobile 776-3387; www.friendsfortheroad.com) or **Chocolate City** (☎mobile 704-9999; www.chocolatecitymas.com; 16 Ariapita Ave, Woodbrook), which employ security and lay on drinks and music trucks as well as mud, paint and a basic costume for TT$500 to TT$650. You can register online for most bands, or visit their mas camp.

Playing Mas

On Carnival Monday and Tuesday, tens of thousands parade and dance in the Port of Spain streets with their mas bands, accompanied by soca trucks with DJs; steel bands also parade and attract a loyal local following. Carnival is all about participation, but if you don't join a band, you can take in the action streetside – though stewards rope off the areas for each band, and won't allow nonmasqueraders in. You can also watch from the judging points at Adam Smith Sq, South Quay and the main stage at the Queen's Park Savannah. Another good spot is the 'Socadrome,' an alternative stage in the Jean Pierre Complex on Wrightson Rd that's popular with the big-name bands.

wine, and tasty tapas-like small plates. Solid weekend brunch offerings, too.

Apsara INDIAN **$$**
(☎623-7659; www.apsaratt.com; 13 Queen's Park East; lunch set menu TT$150, takeaway TT$59, mains TT$125-280; ⏲11am-3pm daily, 6-11pm Mon-Sat; 📶🌱) Named after the dancers of the court of Indra, who could move freely between heaven and earth, Apsara is a stalwart Port of Spain restaurant, popular with a well-dressed business crowd. Specializing in North Indian cuisine, its curries and tandoori meats and fish will melt in your mouth, and there are plenty of vegetarian options. Pricey, but weekday lunch specials are good value.

★ **Buzo Osteria Italiana** ITALIAN **$$$**
(☎223-2896; www.buzorestaurant.com; 6 Warner St, Newtown; pizza & pasta TT$110-150, mains TT$160-320; ⏲11:30am-11pm Mon-Sat; 🌱👪) Set in a gorgeous old stone building, with a courtyard that's ideal for evening cocktails, this is one of Trinidad's best restaurants. The Italian chef cooks authentic antipasti and pasta (from crab-stuffed portobello mushrooms to pork *fagottini* with gorgonzola

and walnuts), plus superb mains such as squid-ink gnocchi with lobster and shrimp or Marsala chicken. Pizzas are equally sublime. Booking advisable.

Drinking & Nightlife

Port of Spain's drinking scene is concentrated along Woodbrook's Ariapita Ave, with a string of bars and clubs (and places that are somewhere between the two, with DJs and a dance floor). The nightlife scene is especially happening Thursday through Saturday, and places change quite quickly. Note that full-on clubs operate a strict dress code: no sneakers, hats or flip-flops.

★Frankie's on the Avenue BAR

(☎622-6609; www.facebook.com/frankiesontheave; 68a Ariapita Ave, cnr Alberto St, Woodbrook; ⊙7am-2am Mon-Thu, until 3am Fri & Sat, 3pm-2am Sun) First opened as an inexpensive lunch spot, Frankie's has morphed into one of Ariapita Ave's best-loved liming locations. You can still get local lunches (and breakfast too), but it's best after dark, when the friendly crowd spills out from the outdoor tables onto the pavement and the drinks flow. Football matches on a big screen in the air-con inside section, too.

Bungalow BAR

(☎610-2864; www.thebungalowtrinidad.com; 20 Rust St, Newtown; ⊙11:30am-3pm & 5pm-midnight Tue-Thu, 11:30am-3pm & 4pm-2am Fri, 5pm-2am Sat) Popular with a well-heeled, older crown, this is a lovely spot for a drink and a lot less frenetic than many Port of Spain bars, with lots of tables on an open-air veranda. Regular live music, great cocktails and excellent food, too, including a nice selection of tapas.

OFF THE BEATEN TRACK

NIGHTLIFE TOURS

If you'd like someone to guide you through the best of Port of Spain's nightlife scene, contact Island Experiences (p758) for an evening entertainment tour, which usually includes visits to a couple of panyards, a calypso show and a sampling of street-food stalls. Tours focused on clubbing or hitting the city's bars are also available. About two hours of fun, including transportation, starts at US$60 per person.

Book ahead for drinks or dinner and you get reserved secure parking.

La Habana BAR

(☎622-6609; 61 Ariapita Ave, Woodbrook; ⊙11am-2am Mon-Sat, 6pm-2am Sun) An ever-busy bar that's popular with the expanding Venezuelan community. Drinkers crowd onto the pavement outside come the weekend, and DJs spin Latin tunes as the crowd salsas the night away on the dance floor inside; the Wednesday Latin night is always busy. Regular drink deals and excellent margaritas.

☆ Entertainment

Kaiso Blues Café LIVE MUSIC

(☎477-2262; www.facebook.com/kaisobluescafe; 1d Wrightson Rd; entry TT$50-150, karaoke free; ⊙11am-11pm) In a new location behind the SWWTU Hall on Wrightson Rd, this is a great place to catch live music throughout the year – from calypso to blues, jazz, reggae and R&B, with performances by up-and-coming artists as well as stalwart acts. There are also DJ parties (often with a 'back in times' playlist), plus stand-up comedy, open-mic nights and karaoke.

Shopping

The central area of Port of Spain, especially around Independence Sq, Charlotte St and Frederick St, is filled with malls and arcades selling everything from spices to fabric by the yard. International shops cluster at the enormous **Falls at West Mall** (☎632-1239; www.thefallsatwestmalltt.com; Western Main Rd, Westmoorings; ⊙10am-7pm Mon-Thu, to 8pm Fri & Sat, noon-6pm Sun;), just west of town. For a quality selection of local crafts, clothes and books, head to the mini-mall at the Normandie (p762) hotel in St Ann's.

★Green Market MARKET

(☎221-9116; www.facebook.com/greenmarketsantacruz; Upper Saddle Rd, Santa Cruz; ⊙6am-1pm Sat, 7am-noon Sun;) Set in the verdant Santa Cruz Valley, this fabulous spot has an organic farmers market selling all kinds of sustainably grown tropical delights, as well as wonderful food offerings, from Venezuelan *arepas* (corn pancakes) to Creole treats, hot cocoa tea (hot chocolate) and pure fresh juices. Kick back on a bench under the trees and enjoy brunch alfresco.

★Cocobel CHOCOLATE

(☎622-1196; www.cocobelchocolate.com; 37 Fitt St, Woodbrook; gift boxes TT$60-380, bars TT$12-

PANYARDS

For much of the year, panyards are little more than vacant lots where steel bands store their instruments. Come Carnival season, they become lively rehearsal spaces, pulsating with energy and magnificent sound, with pan-lovers crowding in to buy drinks from the bar and take in the music. It's a window into one of the most important and sacred parts of Trinidad's urban landscape, with aficionados discussing every note and tempo change, and excitement building as the Panorama competition gets closer.

Steel bands start gearing up for Carnival as early as late September, and some rehearse and perform throughout the year. The best way to find out about practice and performance schedules is by asking around. You can also contact the steel-pan governing body, **Pan Trinbago** (☎623-4486; www.pantrinbago.co.tt; 37 Victoria Sq, cnr Duke & Melbourne Sts).

Some popular panyards that welcome visitors:

Phase II Pan Groove (☎627-0909; www.facebook.com/phasellpangroove; Hamilton St, Woodbrook)

Renegades (☎627-1543; www.facebook.com/bp.renegad; 138 Charlotte St)

Silver Stars (☎629-2241; www.facebook.com/silverstarssteel; 56 Tragarete Rd, Newtown)

80, barks TT$38; ⏱10am-6pm Mon-Fri, 11am-3pm Sat) Made from the finest Trinitario beans, Cocobel chocolates are available only in Trinidad and Tobago, but can stand up as some of the finest you'll taste anywhere in the world. Each of the individual bonbons are works of art, hand-decorated and incorporating local flavors such as Maracas sea salt, sorrel, cilantro-like *chadon beni* and guava. Beautifully packaged and a unique taste of Trinidad.

ℹ Information

DANGERS & ANNOYANCES

Port of Spain has a bad reputation for crime, with robberies and shootings (invariably drug-related) besetting low-income areas such as Laventille, which most travelers never venture into. Busy areas – downtown, Woodbrook, St Clair, Newtown and the Savannah – are safe during the day.

➡ Avoid walking at night around downtown Port of Spain and across the Savannah.

➡ Take a taxi back to your hotel at night rather than walk.

HEALTH

General Hospital (☎623-2951; 56-57 Charlotte St) A large full-service public hospital; conditions are basic.

St Clair Medical Centre (☎628-1451; www.medcorpltd.com; 18 Elizabeth St, St Clair) A private hospital preferred by expatriates.

MONEY

The major banks – RBTT, Republic Bank, Royal Bank and First Citizens – all have branches on Park St east of Frederick St, and on Independence Sq. There are also banks in West Mall, Long Circular Mall and on Ariapita Ave. All have 24-hour ATMs.

POST

TT Post has outlets all over town, selling stamps and offering courier services as well as international postal services; one of the most accessible is the **TT Post Office** (☎622-3364; www.ttpost.net; 177 Tragarate Rd, Woodbrook; ⏱8am-4pm Mon-Fri) on Tragarete Rd.

TOURIST INFORMATION

The Ministry of Tourism has an **airport office** (☎669-5196; www.gotrinidadandtobago.com; Piarco International Airport; ⏱8am-11pm) offering basic advice on accommodations and attractions etc, but no outlet in Port of Spain.

The National Carnival Commission (p764) can provide background information on Carnival, while Pan Trinbago give the gen on steel-pan happenings.

ℹ Getting There & Away

Ferries from Tobago run by the **Inter-Island Ferry Service** (☎625-3055; https://ttitferry.com; Wrightson Rd; one way adult/child TT$50/25) dock at the terminal on Wrightson Rd. **Water taxis** (☎624-3281, 800-4987; www.nidco.co.tt; Wrightson Rd; one way TT$15; ⏱Port of Spain to San Fernando 6:45am, 3:30pm, 4:30pm & 5:40pm Mon-Fri) to San Fernando also depart regularly from Monday to Friday. A taxi from Piarco International Airport (p798) will cost US$30 to Port of Spain, US$35 to Woodbrook.

Trinidad

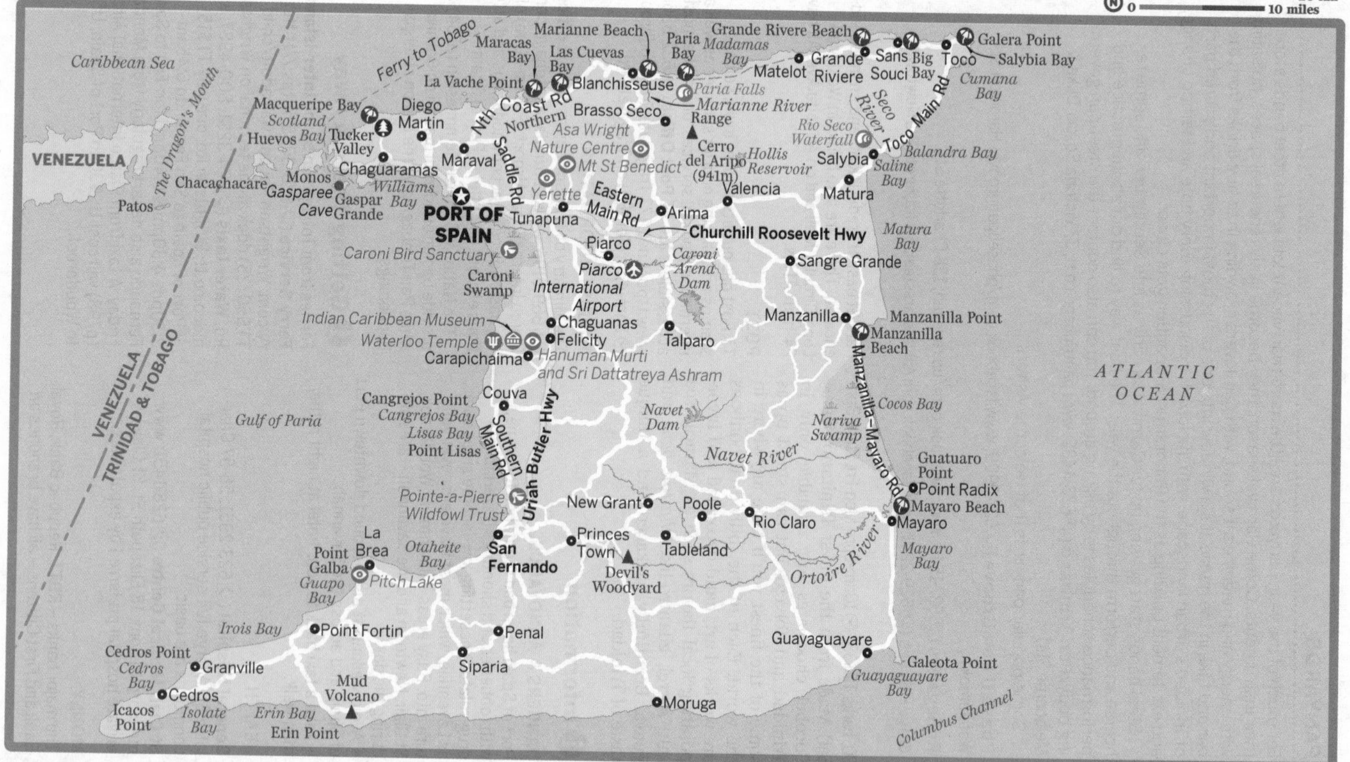
0 20 km
0 10 miles
Caribbean Sea
VENEZUELA
Patos
The Dragon's Mouth
Ferry to Tobago
VENEZUELA
TRINIDAD & TOBAGO
Chacachacare
Huevos
Monos
Gasparee Cave
Gaspar Grande
Macqueripe Bay
Scotland Bay
Tucker Valley
Chaguaramas
Williams Bay
Diego Martin
La Vache Point
Maracas Bay
Nth Coast Rd
Maraval
Saddle Rd
PORT OF SPAIN
Las Cuevas Bay
Marianne Beach
Blanchisseuse
Northern
Brasso Seco
Asa Wright Nature Centre
Mt St Benedict
Yerette
Tunapuna
Eastern Main Rd
Paria Bay
Paria Falls
Marianne River
Range
Cerro del Aripo (941m)
Hollis Reservoir
Arima
Valencia
Grande Rivere Beach
Madamas Bay
Matelot
Grande Riviere
Sans Souci
Big Bay
Toco
Galera Point
Salybia Bay
Cumana Bay
Seco River
Rio Seco Waterfall
Toco Main Rd
Balandra Bay
Salybia
Saline Bay
Matura
Churchill Roosevelt Hwy
Matura Bay
Caroni Bird Sanctuary
Piarco
Piarco International Airport
Caroni Arena Dam
Sangre Grande
Caroni Swamp
Indian Caribbean Museum
Waterloo Temple
Chaguanas
Felicity
Carapichaima
Hanuman Murti and Sri Dattatreya Ashram
Talparo
Manzanilla
Manzanilla Point
Manzanilla Beach
ATLANTIC OCEAN
Cangrejos Point
Cangrejos Bay
Lisas Bay
Point Lisas
Couva
Southern Main Rd
Uriah Butler Hwy
Gulf of Paria
Navet Dam
Nariva Swamp
Cocos Bay
Navet River
Manzanilla–Mayaro Rd
Guatuaro Point
Point Radix
Mayaro Beach
Mayaro
Pointe-a-Pierre Wildfowl Trust
New Grant
Poole
Rio Claro
Princes Town
Tableland
Devil's Woodyard
Ortoire River
Mayaro Bay
La Brea
Point Galba
Pitch Lake
Guapo Bay
Otaheite Bay
San Fernando
Irois Bay
Point Fortin
Penal
Siparia
Guayaguayare
Galeota Point
Guayaguayare Bay
Cedros Point
Cedros Bay
Granville
Cedros
Icacos Point
Isolate Bay
Mud Volcano
Erin Bay
Erin Point
Moruga
Columbus Channel

Getting Around

Port of Spain is a relatively small city; you could explore all of the downtown area on foot, though the heat might make you want to jump in a taxi to travel between downtown and Woodbrook, St Clair or Newtown. The downtown sights are detailed in a useful walking tour booklet, usually available at the Piarco Tourist Office (p765).

From downtown, you can take shared route taxis to **St Ann's** (Hart St, cnr Frederick St) or **St James** (Hart St, cnr Frederick St). Take maxi-taxis to **Chaguaramas** (cnr South Quay & St Vincent St), via Ariapita Ave in Woodbrook, and the north-coast towns of **Maraval, Maracas and Blanchisseuse** (cnr Charlotte & Park Sts). There are also maxis to destinations east along the highway from the **Maxi-Taxi Terminal** (cnr South Quay & Wrightson Rd). Private taxis wait at the large hotels, or you can call **St Christopher's Taxi Co-Op** (☎221-6981; www.scttservices.com; 23 Wrightson Rd).

Reliable local car-rental agencies include **Econo-Car** (☎622-8072; www.econocarrentals tt.com; 191-193 Western Main Rd, Cocorite) and **Kalloo's** (☎622-9073; www.kalloos.com; 31 French St, Woodbrook). Both Econo-Car (p758) and Kalloo's (p758) have branches at the airport.

Chaguaramas

Occupying Trinidad's northwest tip, the Chaguaramas (sha-guh-*ra*-mus) Peninsula was the site of a major US military installation during WWII, and was fully handed back to Trinidad only in the 1970s. Today the string of oceanside marinas draws in yachties taking advantage of dry-docking facilities or waiting out the weather – Trinidad lies safely south of the hurricane belt.

The area is a popular recreation spot, with a couple of beaches, a golf course and hiking in verdant Tucker Valley; there's also a couple of family-friendly mini theme parks along the waterfront. Chaguaramas is the launching point for tours to a chain of offshore islands, the **Bocas**. Popular options are Gaspar Grande, better known as **Gasparee**, where you can visit caves that drip with stalactites, or the most distant, 360-hectare **Chacachacare**, a former leper colony. Boat tours, hiking, swimming and historical excursions can be arranged with Island Experiences (p758) or the **Chaguaramas Development Authority** (☎225-4232; www.facebook.com/chaguaramasdevelopmentauthority; 1 Airways Rd; tours TT$40-140), which manages the peninsula.

Sights

Chaguaramas Military Museum MUSEUM
(☎722-8765; www.facebook.com/militarymuseumtt; Western Main Rd; adult/child TT$50/30; 9am-5pm Tue-Sat; P) Doing a sterling job in the face of limited budgets, this fascinating privately run museum celebrates the role of Caribbean soldiers in overseas warfare by way of battle re-creations, photographs and military hardware. There's also a decommissioned BWIA passenger jet slowly rusting in the ocean breeze.

Macqueripe Beach BEACH
(Tucker Valley, off Western Main Rd; parking TT$20; P) The main road through Tucker Valley ends at Macqueripe, formerly the swimming spot of American troops and now a pretty place to dive into cool green waters, with views over to the misty Venezuelan coastline and lovely landscaped gardens around the steep path down to the sand. A kiosk in the car park sells snacks and drinks.

Activities & Tours

Kayak Centre KAYAKING
(☎325-2627; www.facebook.com/kayakcentre.williamsbay; Williams Bay; per hour weekdays/weekends single kayaks TT$30/40, tandems TT$50/60, SUPs TT$30/40; 6am-6pm) Right on the waterfront as you enter Chaguaramas from Port of Spain, this cool little operation offers kayaking and SUP explorations of calm Williams Bay. Life jackets are available. Rates raise by TT$10 at weekends.

Zip-Itt Adventure ADVENTURE SPORTS
(☎303-7755; www.zipitt.net; Macqueripe Bay, Tucker Valley; zip line TT$200, 1hr bike rental TT$60; 10am-4pm Tue-Fri, to 4:30pm Sat & Sun) Nine zip lines of varying lengths, one of which swoops right over Macqueripe Bay, plus five canopy walks/net bridges. Tickets are sold at the cafeteria in the beach car park; wear covered shoes. Bike rental is also available.

Sleeping & Eating

Bight GUESTHOUSE **$$**
(☎634-4420; www.peakeyachts.com; Peake's Marina, 5 Western Main Rd; r US$85; P) Simple, tidy rooms right on the water make this the nicest midrange option in the area – sit on the porch and enjoy the views of pelicans diving and yachts bobbing.

CrewsInn HOTEL **$$$**
(☎607-4000; www.crewsinn.com; Western Main Rd, Point Gourde; d incl breakfast US$240;

WORTH A TRIP

MOUNT ST BENEDICT MONASTERY

A Benedictine monastery sits on 240 hectares on a hillside north of Tunapuna, 13km east of Port of Spain. Though not a major sight in itself, Mount St Benedict attracts people who want to stay or eat at its secluded guesthouse, birdwatch or walk in the surrounding forest. Unless you have a car, however, it's inconvenient to get to. The thickly wooded hills behind the monastery provide hiking opportunities and possible glimpses of hawks, owls and numerous colorful forest birds, and maybe a monkey, and the road up offers panoramic views of Trinidad's central plains.

Under the monastery, peaceful **Pax Guest House** (☎662-4084; www.paxguesthouse.com; Mt St Benedict, Tunapuna; s incl breakfast US$65-90, d US$95-120; P ❄) is a delightful place to come for a delicious local lunch (US$15; noon to 1:30pm) or afternoon tea (TT$50; 3pm to 5:30pm), with scones, pastries or Trinidadian sweetbread; book in advance. A favorite hike from here is the 30-minute trail to the fire tower, which offers eye-popping views and birding.

P ❄ @ 🏊) The most upmarket option in Chaguaramas, with a pool and resort-like trappings, CrewsInn has luxurious, smart modern rooms, all with patios and complete amenities. The hotel is within a marina complex with two restaurants.

U-Pick Vegetable Farm CAFE $
(☎271-2681; www.facebook.com/upicktt; Tucker Valley Rd; breakfast from TT$40, lunch mains TT$50-85; ⏰7am-2pm Tue-Sun; 👪) The restaurant of this fantastic pick-your-own farm is a great breakfast or lunch spot, from smoked salmon bagels to chicken and waffles or brioche French toast, plus more substantial offerings from omelets to fish sandwiches and specials such as herb-infused lamb. There are tables inside and in the outdoor recreation area amid the towering stands of bamboo.

★ **Sails** INTERNATIONAL $$
(☎634-1712; www.facebook.com/sailstrinidad; Sweet Water Marina, Western Main Rd; sandwiches & burgers from TT$56, mains TT$90-350, lunch special TT$50; ⏰11am-11pm daily, to midnight Fri; 👪) This popular hangout is one of the most appealing eating options in Chaguaramas, with seating overlooking the water and in the air-con interior. You can get bar snacks and grilled food here, as well as steaks, ribs and local dishes such as callaloo soup, and fresh fish or seafood with plentiful sides. Pasta dishes and vegetarian options, too.

Boqueron SEAFOOD $$$
(☎398-9067; www.boquerontrinidad.com; 256 Western Main Rd, Williams Bay; mains TT$145-450; ⏰4-9:30pm Tue & Wed, 11am-3pm & 4-10pm Thu & Fri, 4-10pm Sat, 10am-3pm & 4-10pm Sun) In a distinctive thatch-roofed building with an ocean-facing 1st-floor deck, Boqueron's setting is as much of a draw as its high-end seafood menu, from lobster thermidor, grilled with pico de gallo and tamarind chutney, or with pasta and a champagne sauce. There's also grouper *en papillote,* Peruvian-style tempura-battered fish and paella. Substantial salads and pasta dishes, too, including a vegetarian option.

ℹ Getting There & Away

Yellow band maxi-taxis (p769) run from Port of Spain into Chaguaramas, but you'll need a car or a private taxi at night.

Maracas Bay

Reached by a spectacular 45-minute coastal drive from the capital, Maracas Bay is Trinidad's most popular beach. The wide, white-sand shore, dotted with palm trees contrasting against the backdrop of verdant mountains, remains an irresistible lure for both locals and travelers. Despite the curving headland, the sand is often pounded by waves that serve up good bodysurfing. On weekends the beach can get pretty crowded, but during the week it can feel almost deserted.

The scene is somewhat marred by ongoing construction of new vendor huts and visitor facilities on the sand, but once beyond these, the beach itself remains glorious. On the inland side, a huge car park caters for visitors that flood in on weekends; changing facilities have been constructed, though persistent problems with sewerage means it may be open only intermittently.

Activities

Maracas Beach BEACH

(North Coast Rd; changing rooms TT$1, car park TT$30; lifeguards 10am-5pm) A glorious white-sand shore sprinkled with palm trees and backgrounded by the verdant Northern Range – though the rash of buildings for bake-and-shark concessions adds an unwelcome density of concrete. The wave-battered waters are often good for bodysurfing. During the week, the crowds thin out and it can feel almost deserted, but things get much busier at weekends, especially Sundays, when music blares and Trinis descend in droves to swim and lime.

Eating & Drinking

Huts on and opposite the beach sell Maracas' famed specialty, bake and shark: seasoned shark steaks, served in a fried bake bread, which you then slather with dressings (try the tamarind, hot pepper and *chadon beni*) and salad. Shark numbers are threatened in Trinidad so a more sustainable choice is bake and kingfish. You can also get fries, burgers, pies, hot dogs and other snacks, as well as beers and soft drinks.

Richard's CARIBBEAN $

(328-1676; Maracas Bay Beach; bake & shark TT$35, bake & kingfish TT$45; 8am-7pm;) Follow the crowds to Richard's, easily the most popular of the bake-and-shark outlets. The extensive fresh salad bar is kept well stocked, and the sauces are delicious.

Getting There & Away

Maracas is about 40 minutes' drive from Port of Spain. Maxi-taxis are irregular and not really a practical option; better to take a private taxi or hop in one of the beach shuttles organized by Island Experiences (p758), which cost US$30 to Maracas and US$40 to Las Cuevas.

Blanchisseuse

Winding north from Port of Spain, Saddle Rd becomes the North Coast Rd, climbing over the jungle-slathered mountains of the Northern Range and descending to the Caribbean coastline at Maracas Bay. The road narrows east of Maracas Bay, ending at the tiny village of Blanchisseuse (blan-she-*shuhze*), where the beautiful craggy coastline is dotted with plush holiday homes. The three beaches aren't the best for swimming, especially in the fall and winter, but the surfing can be pretty good. The village is also the starting point for some great hikes, from coastal treks to Paria Bay to freshwater swimming in the Marianne River.

Sleeping & Eating

Northern Sea View Villa GUESTHOUSE $

(759-9514; kayakeric@gmail.com; Paria Main Rd; s/d TT$150/300;) Just across from the main Marianne Beach, this simple guesthouse has a clean, basic fan-cooled apartment with full kitchen and a porch overlooking the garden. Great value. The friendly owner can organize meals, and hikes in the local area.

Second Spring GUESTHOUSE $$

(669-3909; www.secondspringtnt.com; Lamp Post191,Paria Main Rd;studios/cottages US$70/120) The best guesthouse in the area, with comfortable, endearing self-contained studios and cottages, decorated with local art and overlooking a rocky yet gorgeous section of coast, with lovely gardens and steps down to the sea.

Cocos Hut CARIBBEAN $$

(477-5881; Laguna Mar, Paria Main Rd; mains from TT$90; 7am-7pm) Right on the roadside, adjacent to a track down to the beach, the restaurant of **Laguna Mar** (628-3731, 477-5881; www.lagunamar.com; Mile 65.5, Paria Main Rd; r TT$550;) hotel is a small, cozy spot and usually the only place in town

WORTH A TRIP

LAS CUEVAS

Just east of Maracas Bay along the North Coast Rd, quieter and less commercial Las Cuevas is another beautiful bay. Its wide sweep of sand is overhung by cliffs and forest, and is lapped by clear blue waters that are calmer and cleaner than at Maracas. There's usually good surfing at its west end. Conditions are best at its center, where lifeguards patrol and you can rent beach loungers and umbrellas. The car park above the sand has changing rooms (TT$1; open 10am to 6pm). The cafe here is no longer in operation (though there are plans to open it up again); vendors sometimes sell drinks from coolers, but it's a good idea to bring your own refreshments. Take repellent, as the sandflies can be bad here.

where you can get a meal. It serves up decent fresh fish or chicken platters, as well as cold beers and rum drinks.

Getting There & Away

Maxi-taxis and route taxis are infrequent; you'll need a car to get here.

Brasso Seco

Plum in the middle of the lush rainforest that smothers the Northern Range, Brasso Seco is a quiet little village that once made its living from growing cocoa and other crops. Today, it has reinvented itself as a low-key base for nature lovers in search of hiking, birdwatching, cocoa-cultivation tours or just a bit of insight into the slow, slow pace of life in rural Trinidad.

Activities & Tours

Chocolate Tours

The cool hills around Brasso Seco are ideal for the cultivation of cocoa, and this once-waning industry has been revived by the Tourism Action Committee and its **Brasso Seco Chocolate Company** (493-4358; www.facebook.com/brassosecochocolates; Brasso Seco Community Centre, Brasso Seco Village; chocolate tours TT$100;), which has a community-run cocoa estate close to the village where you can do an excellent 'tree to bar' tour. This includes a walk through the cocoa trees of the Manchuria Estate, and demonstrations of cocoa-bean processing, from fermenting, drying and roasting, right through to creating the finished bar. Chocolate tastings are included, and if in a group of five or more, you can combine the tour with a local lunch. A 'bean to bar' option forgoes the walk through the cocoa groves and includes just a demonstration of chocolate making at the company's HQ.

Hiking

There are some spectacular day hikes of varying lengths from Brasso Seco to waterfalls: Double River Waterfalls, Madamas Falls and Sobo Falls. The 13km trek to Paria Bay from Brasso Seco is one of the most gorgeous in Trinidad, passing the famous Paria Falls. You can make this hike into a fine coastal backpacking trip with camping on beautiful bays by continuing all the way to Matelot to the east. If you're a very hardy hiker, you might want to attempt the scramble up Cerro del Aripo, the tallest mountain in Trinidad (941m).

Guides, such as **Carl Fitzjames** (486-6059; www.brassosecoparia.com; hikes for groups of up to 6 from TT$600), can be arranged through the Tourism Action Committee.

Sleeping & Eating

Pacheco's GUESTHOUSE **$$**
(480-2271; www.brassosecoparia.com; s/d incl breakfast TT$350/700) You'll get a friendly welcome at the Pacheco's. Beside the church and surrounded by gorgeous flower-filled gardens, this is a neat and tidy house, with three bedrooms and a sitting area. It's basic and does the trick, and Mrs P's homemade meals and cocoa tea are delicious.

Information

Tourism Action Committee (718-8605, 493-4358; www.brassosecoparia.com; Brasso Seco Paria Visitor Facility, Paria-Morne Bleu Rd; tours TT$100;) As well as coordinating hikes, birdwatching and the the Brasso Seco Chocolate Company cocoa tours, this community tourism cooperative arranges fascinating village experience tours. Locals walk you through the village to learn about rural Trinidad living, from coffee and fruit cultivation to the traditional *brancas* used to smoke meats here before the village was connected to the electricity grid.

The Tourism Action Committee can also arrange local accommodations, home-cooked meals and transport to Brasso Seco. From the Visitor Facility (which has has public bathrooms), it sells ice cream and Brasso-made products such as pepper sauce and coffee. Book all visits in advance, especially if you want to eat.

Getting There & Away

Public transport isn't a viable option for getting to Brasso Seco; you can drive yourself in a rental car, most easily from Arima, though the road is winding and potholed. The Tourism Action Committee can arrange transport from Port of Spain and other points in Trinidad; alternatively, visit with Caribbean Discovery Tours (p758), which can also arrange hard-to-reach accommodations and local food options.

Grande Riviere

The closest the northeast gets to a resort town, Grande Riviere is still a far cry from most Caribbean holiday spots. It's a peaceful and magical place, rich in natural attractions from a stunningly rugged beach to the surrounding rainforest, speckled with waterfalls and hiking trails and offering fantastic birdwatching. A few small-scale hotels have sprung up to cater to lovers of the outdoors, and the village is a perfect place to get away from it all, but the big draw are the leatherback turtles that lay eggs on the beach between March and August. Grande Riviere is one of the world's major nesting sites, with hundreds of turtles visiting nightly in peak season; local guides lead turtle-watching trips. You can also immerse yourself in Trinidad's burgeoning chocolate industry: watching chocolate being made at the HQ of the Grande Riviere Chocolate Company or taking a tour of local cocoa estates.

Sights & Activities

Grande Riviere Beach BEACH

(Paria Main Rd) This long, wide beach is capped at each end by exuberantly forested headlands, with the ever-shifting lagoon of the eponymous river at its east end providing calm freshwater swimming. Scattered year-round with the broken shells of leatherback-turtle eggs, the coarse caramel-colored sand shelves steeply down to turbulent waters, best tackled by strong swimmers.

★Grande Riviere Nature Tour Guide Association ECOTOUR

(794-4959, 469-1288; grntga@gmail.com; Hosang St; turtle-watching incl permit TT$100, hiking from TT$120, birdwatching from TT$240;) As well as leading excellent turtle-watching excursions, where expert guides provide background information on the turtles and the laying process, this community-run outfit offers year-round hiking tours to waterfalls, swimming holes and seldom-visited natural wonders in the area. It also runs three-hour birdwatching excursions to see many local species, including the endangered piping gaun (pawi). The GRNTGA base is just off the road to the beach, adjacent to Mt Plaisir Estate hotel.

Grande Riviere Chocolate Company FOOD

(794-4959, 721-0406; www.facebook.com/destinationchocolatett; Hosang St; 1½-2hr Bean to Bar tour TT$120, 3hr Tree to Bar tour TT$240;) In the same building as the Grande Riviere Nature Tour Guide Association, this community-run chocolate company offers 'Bean to Bar' demonstrations of its chocolate production process, from fermentation and drying to the transformation of roasted beans to finished bars. You'll get to taste the sweet pulp from a raw cocoa bean and get a little history on the resurgence of the local cocoa industry, as well as sample its chocolate bars and enjoy a cup of cocoa tea.

Sleeping

Grande Riviere's cluster of hotels offers relaxed beachside accommodations; ask around for less expensive homestay options in the village. All options lower their rates outside of the March–August turtle-nesting season.

WORTH A TRIP

ASA WRIGHT NATURE CENTRE

A former cocoa and coffee plantation transformed into an 600-hectare nature reserve, the **Asa Wright Nature Centre** (667-4655; www.asawright.org; Arima-Blanchisseuse Rd; adult/child US$20/10; 9am-5pm, guided walks 10:30am & 1:30pm;) blows the minds of birdwatchers. Even if you can't tell a parrot from a parakeet, it's still worthwhile as you can see a great number of colorful specimens from the veranda viewing gallery, as well as lizards and agouti. Located amid the rainforest of the Northern Range, the center has a **lodge** (667-4655; www.asawright.org; Arima-Blanchisseuse Rd; d per person incl all meals US$235;) catering to birding tour groups and a series of hiking trails, open to day visitors via guided tours.

Bird species commonly seen here include tanagers, honeycreepers, oropendolas, motmots, channel-billed toucans, 14 species of hummingbird and numerous raptors. The sanctuary is also home to a natural swimming pool and a cave that holds a colony of the elusive nocturnal guacharo (oilbird). To protect the oilbirds, only in-house guests resident for three or more nights can visit the caves.

Tour companies such as Island Experiences (p758) can ferry you to Asa Wright as part of a half- or full-day tour.

★**Mt Plaisir Estate** BOUTIQUE HOTEL $$
(☎670-1868; www.mtplaisir.com; Hosang St; r incl breakfast US$150-185; P❄📶) The first hotel in the village, and still the best. So close to the sea that the waves will soothe you to sleep, the rooms open onto the beach or a wide wooden veranda. Sleeping two to six, rooms have just the right combination of shabby-chic and cool Italian design, with four-poster beds swathed in mosquito nets, handmade wooden furniture and local art.

Acajou BOUTIQUE HOTEL $$
(☎670-3771; www.acajoutrinidad.com; 209 Paria Main Rd; bungalows incl breakfast TT$1181; P📶) Set in riverside gardens, Acajou has five bungalows replete with rich wood and bright-white linens and cushions. French doors open to hammocked patios that look toward the ocean, and there's a path down past the river to the sea. No air-conditioning, TV or phones make this a fantastic retreat. There's a restaurant on-site.

Le Grande Almandier HOTEL $$
(☎670-1013; www.facebook.com/legrandalmandier; 2 Hosang St; s/d incl breakfast US$115/167; P❄@) Next door to Mt Plaisir Estate, the compact but decent rooms at Le Grande Almandier have quaint balconies overlooking the sea, and are a budget-friendly option. It also has a laid-back restaurant and bar.

Getting There & Away

Maxi-taxis are infrequent, so you'll need to hire a car or get a taxi; the fare from Port of Spain is about US$130. All the hotels can arrange transport.

Northeast Coast

'When you out, you out. When you in, you in,' is what they say about the remote northeast. Despite the ruggedly beautiful coastline, waterfalls, hiking trails and swimmable rivers – and leatherback turtles that lay eggs on the beaches – tourism remains very low-key here. Inaccessible from Blanchisseuse, where the North Coast Rd ends, this quiet region is bounded by Matelot in the north and Matura in the southeast.

But this delicious isolation is under threat. Plans to shorten inter-island ferry sailing times by building a port at Toco have resurfaced as part of a development incorporating a cruise-ship dock, yacht marina, hotels and facilities to service offshore oil and gas rigs, long-line fishing boats and fish processing. Widening the access road from Valencia is underway, and if plans are approved, the northeast's remote feel will be a thing of the past – as will Toco's pretty Mission Beach and much of the original village.

Sights & Activities

★**Rio Seco Waterfall** WATERFALL
(off Toco Main Rd, Salybia; 👪) Just past the bridge over the Rio Seco, a signposted trail leads inland to the Rio Seco Waterfall in Matura National Park. This stunning swimming hole and waterfall, with deep clear waters and a gorgeous canopy of rainforest overhead, is a 45-minute hike from the trailhead, and the path is signposted, well maintained and easy to follow without a guide, though it's best to go in a group.

Matura Beach BEACH
(Toco Main Rd, Matura) This wild, undeveloped beach with its coarse gray sand offers perfect conditions for leatherback turtles to lay their eggs, but it's far too rugged and windblown to throw down a towel for some beach time. This is one of the busier laying sites in the March–August season, when you need a permit to enter after dark. Turtle-watching trips are arranged through Nature Seekers.

Sans Souci BEACH
(Toco Main Rd) A short drive west of Toco, the small village of Sans Souci has several good beaches, though as they're all lashed by pounding waves most people come here to surf rather than swim. It's a quiet and truly scenic coastline, with the waves beating against the sand and the palm trees leaning drunkenly in the constant sea breeze. The best (and the largest) beach is Big Bay, a wide sweep of smooth yellow sand that's usually all but deserted.

Saline Beach BEACH
(Toco Main Rd, Salybia; ⏲lifeguards 10am-5pm; P👪) Salybia is dominated by two incongruous-looking resorts, popular with Trinidadians seeking a rural break, but the big draw here is just before the bridge spanning the Rio Seco, where a track leads down to Saline Beach, a popular locals' liming spot. The fine yellow sand meets relatively calm waters, protected by a barrier reef, and there's freshwater swimming in the river, which meets the sea here. There are lifeguards, a bathroom and kiosks selling drinks and snacks.

Galera Point LIGHTHOUSE

(Galera Rd, Toco; P) Beyond Toco's Salybia Beach, Galera Rd meanders through the countryside to Trinidad's extreme northeastern tip, capped by Galera Point lighthouse. Peek through the coastal trees at the edges of the grounds to see the waves crashing onto the rocks below, and the distinct line where the blue Caribbean sea meets the green Atlantic. Picnic tables dot the grounds.

Tours

★Nature Seekers ECOTOUR

(668-7337; www.natureseekers.org; Toco Main Rd, Matura; turtle-watching US$25, hikes from US$60) Matura is home to Nature Seekers, a nonprofit community organization that runs educational programs and evening turtle tours, where you can watch leatherbacks laying eggs close up – a magical experience. It also offers hikes to waterfalls and natural pools in the surrounding area, and kayak trips.

Sleeping

Suzan's Palace GUESTHOUSE $

(398-3038; Toco Main Rd, Matura; r TT$450) Basic and very local-style rooms right in Matura, all clean and well maintained, and in a convenient location for turtle-watching with Nature Seekers. Rooms sleep up to four. Meals are available.

★Leatherback Lodge B&B $$

(691-1188; www.leatherbacklodge.com; 70 Upper Rio Grande Trace, Matura; r incl breakfast US$125-140; P) Gorgeous B&B in a supremely peaceful location, a short drive inland from Matura Beach, with friendly owners who offer walks and waterfall visits in the surrounding area. The inviting rooms have ceiling fans and open out onto patios hung with feeders to attract hummingbirds and the many other bird species that frequent the area. Great local meals available.

Getting There & Away

The northeast is accessed via the busy little village of Valencia, a short way beyond the end of the Churchill Roosevelt Hwy, from where the Valencia Main Rd makes a T-junction with the Toco Main Rd, which hugs the northeast coast. Getting here is easiest by far in a taxi (around US$100 from Port of Spain) or with your own vehicle, as maxi-taxis are thin on the ground.

East Coast

Trinidad's east coast is wild and rural. The mix of lonely beaches with rough Atlantic waters, mangrove swamps and seaside coconut plantations creates dramatic scenery. It's very quiet most of the year, except for holidays and weekends, when people flood in to Manzanilla and Mayaro for beachside relaxation, packing coolers with food and splashing about in the gently shelving waters. Most visitors come here on a day trip bound for Nariva Swamp, with its protected wetlands and forest.

Running parallel to the sea, the Manzanilla–Mayaro Rd makes for a beautiful drive. It passes through the Cocal, a thick forest of coconut palms whose nuts are shipped all around the island, and which harbor some interesting birds, including red-chested macaws.

Sights

★Nariva Swamp WILDLIFE RESERVE

(Manzanilla-Mayaro Rd) Inland of the Cocal, the Ramsar-protected Nariva Swamp covers some 60 sq km of freshwater wetland inhabited by anacondas and a small population of elusive manatees. To fully appreciate the area's beauty, book a tour with Caribbean Discovery Tours (p758); trips include a walk into Bush Bush Wildlife Sanctuary to see howler and white capuchin monkeys, and sometimes kayaking on the waterways, as well as a home-cooked curry lunch. Take insect repellent.

Mayaro Beach BEACH

(Manzanilla-Mayaro Rd; lifeguards 10am-5pm) Around the headland to the south of Manzanilla Beach, expansive Mayaro offers calmer waters than its neighbor, and the beach scene is more genial. Locals play cricket on the flat sands at low tide. One of the busier spots is adjacent to Church Rd, south of Mayaro village.

Sleeping & Eating

Queen's Beach Resort HOTEL $$

(630-5532; www.queensbeachresort.com; Gould St, Radix Village, Mayaro; d TT$1035; P) The smartest and easily the most appealing of several laid-back hotels on this stretch of beach, with two pools, hot tub/sauna and a restaurant serving local food. Rooms are smart and modern if a bit box-like. You can also visit as a day guest (TT$150). To get there, turn off the Mayaro–Guayaguayare Rd onto Church St, then right onto Gould St.

★**Ranch** CARIBBEAN $$

(☎223-6798; www.facebook.com/theranchmayaro; Mayaro-Guayaguayare Rd, Mayaro; snacks TT$35-80, mains TT$65-160; ⏲11am-11pm Tue-Sun; 👪) Great little place past Mayaro village, with tables in an air-con indoor dining room and patio garden. Local food runs from chicken with Trini sides to shrimp and lobster, but the highlight is a whole grilled Mayaro snapper, seasoned to perfection. The snack fare, from crab backs to pepper squid, is equally lip-smacking. Great for a drink, too.

Getting There & Away

To drive to Manzanilla, Mayaro and Nariva, you have to go through bustling Sangre Grande ('sandy grandy'), from where signposted minor roads head down to the Manzanilla–Mayaro Rd. Most visitors arrive in a rented car or as part of an organized tour to Nariva.

West Coast

Trinidad's west coast allows you to dig deep into Indo-Trinidadian culture. The **Carapichaima** area is one of the heartlands of the island's Indian population, whose forebears mostly arrived between 1845 and 1917 as indentured workers to fill the labor gap when slavery was abolished. Today, there are endless restaurants and street stalls selling delicious roti, doubles and Indian snacks, and Hindu temples adding a splash of color to the landscape. The west also offers great birdwatching at the Pointe-a-Pierre Wildfowl Trust and at Caroni Bird Sanctuary.

Sights

Caroni Bird Sanctuary BIRD SANCTUARY

(Winston Nanan Caroni Bird Sanctuary; ☎755-7828; www.caronibirdsanctuary.com; Uriah Butler Hwy, Caroni; P 👪) This 5611-hectare estuarine swampland of dense mangrove thickets crisscrossed with tea-colored channels is best known for its scarlet ibis, T&T's national bird. Each afternoon, these bright crimson beauties swoop in to roost in their thousands, giving the trees the appearance of being abloom with brilliant scarlet blossoms. Even if you're not an avid birdwatcher, the sight of the ibis flying over the swamp, glowing almost fluorescent red in the final rays of the evening sun, is not to be missed. The sanctuary is off the Uriah Butler Hwy, 14km south of Port of Spain; the turnoff is signposted. Many guesthouses and hotels in Port of Spain arrange trips, as do tour companies such as Island Experiences. If you have your own transport or arrange a taxi (around TT$400 from Port of Spain), including waiting time, you can also book boat tours directly with the excellent Winston Nanan Caroni Tours.

Waterloo Temple HINDU TEMPLE

(☎681-4435; Waterloo Rd, Carapichaima; donation suggested; ⏲6am-6pm; P 👪) Beautifully situated at the end of a causeway striking off from the central west coast, Waterloo Temple was constructed almost entirely by indentured laborer Sewdass Sadhu, after his previous structure (built on state land) was demolished. It was a true labor of love, with Sadhu carrying each foundation stone on his bicycle to the water's edge. It's a beautiful place, surrounded by the shallow waters of the Paria Gulf at high tide and with prayer flags fluttering in the air.

Hanuman Murti & Sri Dattatreya Ashram HINDU TEMPLE

(☎673-5328; www.sridattatreyayogacentrett.com; Datta Drive, Orange Field Rd, Carapichaima; donations appreciated; ⏲ashram 9am-noon & 5-7pm; P 👪) Towering 26m over the Sri Dattatreya Ashram, the brightly painted Hanuman Murti is a potent icon of Trinidad's Hindu community. Devotees from all over the country come here to pray and walk devotional circles around the statue. Constructed by craftspeople from Tamil Nadu in India, the main temple is equally ornate, its rich exterior covered in statuary – an incredible sight to behold in the middle of a small Trinidadian town. Other smaller statues dot the grounds.

Indian Caribbean Museum MUSEUM

(☎673-7007; www.icmtt.org; Waterloo Rd, Carapichaima; ⏲10am-5pm Wed-Sun; P 👪) FREE Just inland from Waterloo Temple, this absorbing museum is dedicated to the Indian history and experience in Trinidad. Some gorgeous antique sitars and drums are displayed, as are photographs and informational displays about early Indian settlers. Other highlights include local art, traditional Hindi clothing, a display of a traditional Indian Trini kitchen (replete with a *chulha,* the earthen stove where roti is made) and photographs of Brits with Indian indentured servants.

Pointe-a-Pierre Wildfowl Trust WILDLIFE RESERVE
(ext 2512 658-4200; www.papwildfowltrust.org; PetroTrin Refinery, Southern Main Rd, Pointe-a-Pierre; TT$20; 9am-5pm Mon-Fri, 10am-5pm Sat & Sun, guided walks 9:30am & 1pm Mon-Fri, 10:30am & 1pm Sat & Sun;) A wonderful exercise in contradiction, this picturesque bird sanctuary covers 29 hectares of lake and forest within the incongruous setting of PetroTrin oil refinery (which ceased operations in 2018). It's home to some 109 bird species, including endangered waterfowl, colorful songbirds, herons and other wading birds, as well as a breeding colony of scarlet ibis. Ringed by a wheelchair-friendly boardwalk, the main lake is dappled with lotus plants and overhung by trees; guided tours help identify all the inhabitants.

Tours

★Winston Nanan Caroni Tours BIRDWATCHING
(645-1305; www.facebook.com/winstonnananecotours; 2½hr boat tours US$10;) One of the oldest Caroni boat operators, Nanan's are also the best; holding up to 30 passengers, its flat-bottomed motorboats are equipped with near-silent engines that don't emit the stinky exhaust of some boats here, and its guides offer expert commentary on the swamp ecosystem and its inhabitants. Tours pass slowly through the mangrove channels, stopping to afford a close look at the snakes and anteaters often seen in the surrounding trees, and mooring up to watch the ibis roost.

Sleeping & Eating

Petrea Place GUESTHOUSE $$
(658-5322; www.papwildfowltrust.org/petreaplace; 2 Petrea Rd, PetroTrin complex, Pointe-a-Pierre; r incl breakfast TT$1050-1470;) Run by the same team as the fantastic Freebird restaurant below the rooms, Petrea Place is named for the surrounding petrea trees, and offers a tranquil place to stay, perfect for enjoying early-morning birdwatching at the Wildfowl Trust or just for some serene downtime. Rooms are simple but appealing, with either queen or king beds and en suite bathroom.

★Freebird FUSION $$
(658-5322; www.facebook.com/freebirdtt; 2 Petrea Rd, PetroTrin complex, Pointe-a-Pierre; mains TT$105-150, afternoon tea TT$250, brunch TT$325; 3-6pm Thu, 11am-3pm Sat, to 4pm Sun;) Chic dining in a flower-wreathed building close to the Wildfowl Trust lakes, offering an enticing blend of exquisite presentation and truly memorable food. Flavors are delicate and each dish is perfectly executed: the lunchtime sandwiches, salads and burgers are anything but ordinary, though the highlight are the multidish tea and brunch spreads that take you on a culinary tour around the world.

Getting There & Away

From the Churchill Roosevelt Hwy, the well-signposted Uriah Butler Hwy swings south parallel to the west coast. You can also take the much slower Southern Main Rd from Curepe, which crosses over to the west side of the highway south of Chaguanas. A car is by far the best way to explore.

San Fernando

Trinidad's second-largest city, San Fernando is also the center of the island's gas and oil industries. Anyone looking for real cultural immersion will enjoy San Fernando, as few tourists come through the town. Most of the action happens at shops and stands around Harris Promenade and the main Coffee St, or you can find great views from San Fernando Hill. The spectacle of Pitch Lake is just a short drive to the south.

About 25km southwest of San Fernando, and just south of the small town of La Brea, the slowly bubbling, black **Pitch Lake** (651-1232; Southern Main Rd, La Brea; tours TT$30, museum free; 9am-5pm, last tour 4pm;) is perhaps Trinidad's greatest oddity. Once thought of by the Amerindians as a punishment of the gods, the 40-hectare expanse of asphalt is around 75m deep at its center, where hot bitumen is continuously replenished from a subterranean fault. One of only three asphalt lakes in the world, it has the single-largest supply of natural bitumen.

The lake's surface looks like a clay tennis court covered with wrinkled, elephant-like skin, interspersed with small pools ringed with reeds and water hyacinth; tour guides sagely take you across via the solid parts, poking a stick into the liquid areas to show you the fresh pitch. Flat shoes are recommended. During the rainy season, people bathe in its warm sulfurous pools, said to have healing qualities. A museum in the visitor center gives some interesting background on the history of the lake.

The Pitch Lake can be a fiercely hot place for a walk – try to arrive before 10am, and apply liberal amounts of sunscreen. Be aware that unofficial guides will approach you in the parking lot; most give a sub-standard tour, so it's far better to opt for the informative official guides, who wear name badges and red T-shirts. You can call ahead to book, but guides are always available during opening hours, via the visitor center. It's customary to leave a tip for them after the tour.

Looming over San Fernando, **San Fernando Hill** (Circular Courts Rd; ⌚9am-6pm; P) was once a sacred Amerindian site, but today its landscaped grounds are a great place to kick back and relax, dotted with picnic tables and offering sweeping views over the central plains. It has a cafe and a children's playground. You'll need a car to get here, as the access road is some way from the center.

Getting There & Away

The **water taxi** (☎652-9980; www.nidco.co.tt; King's Wharf, Lady Hales Ave; one way TT$25) between Port of Spain and San Fernando docks at Kings Wharf. The city is on the Uriah Butler Hwy, about 1½ hours' drive from Port of Spain. PTSC (www.ptsc.co.tt) runs express buses between Port of Spain and San Fernando, dropping off at the waterfront near the water-taxi terminal, which is also where maxi-taxis arrive and depart.

TOBAGO

While Trinidad booms with industry and parties all night, tiny Tobago (just 42km across at its widest point) kicks back in a hammock with a beer in hand watching its crystalline waters shimmer in the sun. Though Tobago is proud of its rainforests, fantastic dive sites, stunning aquamarine bays and nature reserves, it's OK with not being mentioned in a Beach Boys' song. It accepts its tourists without vigor, but rather with languor, and allows them to choose between plush oceanside hotels or tiny guesthouses in villages where you walk straight to the open-air bar with sandy bare feet, and laugh with the locals drinking rum.

Tours

Catamaran Picante BOATING
(☎620-4750, 369-8814; www.yachtpleasures.com; full-day cruise US$100) Super days on the ocean aboard this 42-ft catamaran, equipped with open-air covered seating area, bathroom and mats between the front hulls for sunbathing. Trips leave from Store Bay and head down the leeward coast for snorkeling and lunch at secluded Cotton Bay. Rates include pickup in southwest Tobago, plus lunch, snacks and beer, rum punch and soft drinks.

NG Nature Tours BIRDWATCHING
(☎754-7881, 660-5463; www.newtongeorge.com; tours US$50-120) Newton George is one of Tobago's best birdwatching guides, with many years of experience under his belt. Tours cover all the island's birding hot spots, from wetlands to Little Tobago and the Forest Reserve, and can be tailored to your requirements.

Peter Cox Nature Tours WILDLIFE
(☎751-5822; www.petercoxnaturetours.com; per person US$50-120) A good choice for serious birdwatchers, with avian-oriented trips island-wide, plus hiking, waterfalls, turtle-watching and general island tours.

Mountain Biking Tobago CYCLING
(☎681-5695; www.mountainbikingtobago.com; per person from US$50) Owner Sean de Freitas is a straight-shooting guide who provides solid rentals and cycling equipment. His Highland Falls ride is particularly awesome, ending at a splendid swimming hole and waterfall. He also guides road rides.

Getting There & Away

AIR

Most people get to Tobago by taking the 20-minute flight from Trinidad, or fly in direct from Europe. The ANR Robinson International Airport (p798), like Tobago, is small, relaxed and rarely rushed. Plans are afoot to rebuild and extend the complex, but the works are unlikely to commence for a few years yet.

BOAT

Passenger ferries, run by the Inter-Island Ferry Service (p767), shuttle between Port of Spain on Trinidad, and Scarborough on Tobago.

Getting Around

Getting around any of Tobago's small towns is easy on foot. For wider exploration, rent a car or hire a driver for the day. Buses are slow and infrequent but cover the whole island.

BUS

The Scarborough bus terminal is a short walk from the ferry terminal, off Milford Rd on Sang-

Tobago

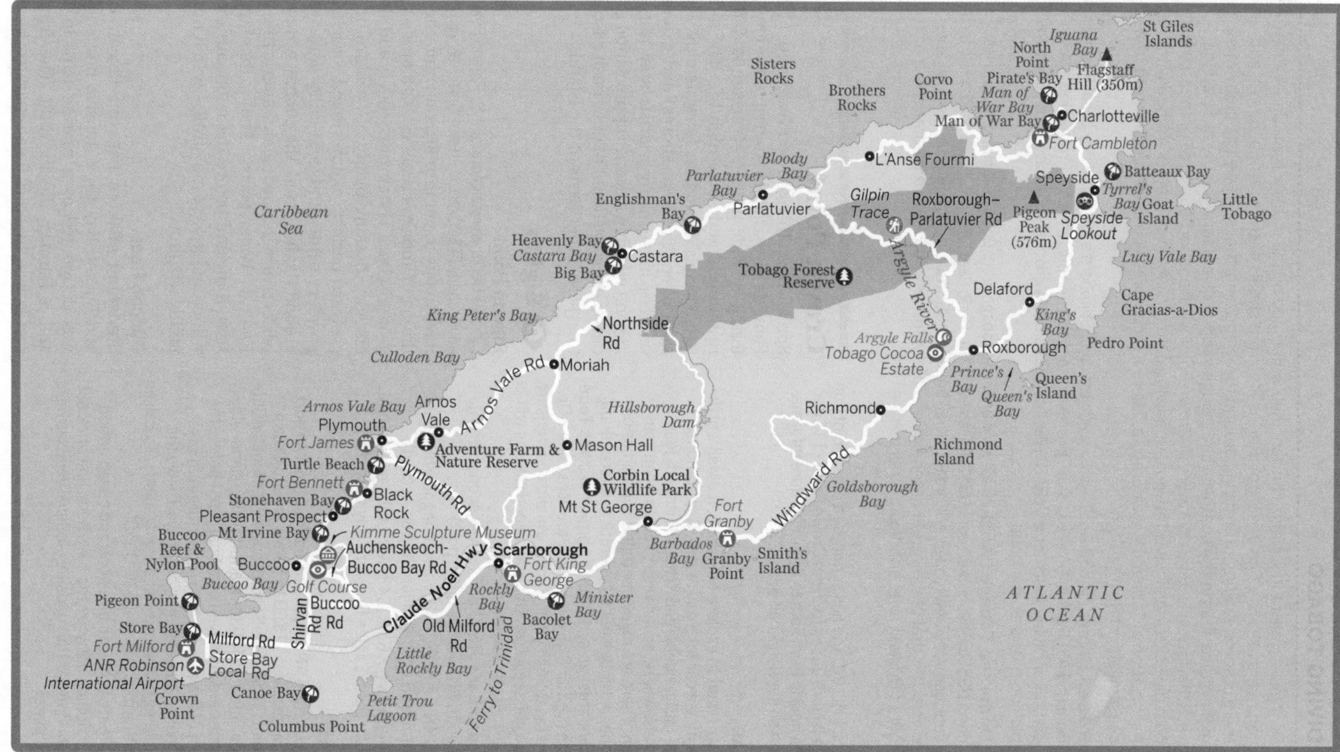
0 10 km
0 5 miles
St Giles Islands
Iguana Bay
North Point
Flagstaff Hill (350m)
Sisters Rocks
Brothers Rocks
Corvo Point
Pirate's Bay
Man of War Bay
Man of War Bay
Charlotteville
Fort Cambleton
Bloody Bay
L'Anse Fourmi
Batteaux Bay
Speyside
Tyrrel's Bay
Goat Island
Little Tobago
Parlatuvier Bay
Parlatuvier
Englishman's Bay
Gilpin Trace
Roxborough–Parlatuvier Rd
Pigeon Peak (576m)
Speyside Lookout
Caribbean Sea
Heavenly Bay
Castara Bay
Castara
Big Bay
Tobago Forest Reserve
Argyle River
Lucy Vale Bay
Delaford
Cape Gracias-a-Dios
King's Bay
King Peter's Bay
Northside Rd
Argyle Falls
Tobago Cocoa Estate
Roxborough
Pedro Point
Culloden Bay
Arnos Vale Rd
Moriah
Prince's Bay
Queen's Bay
Queen's Island
Arnos Vale Bay
Arnos Vale
Plymouth
Hillsborough Dam
Richmond
Fort James
Adventure Farm & Nature Reserve
Mason Hall
Richmond Island
Turtle Beach
Plymouth Rd
Corbin Local Wildlife Park
Fort Bennett
Black Rock
Stonehaven Bay
Mt St George
Fort Granby
Windward Rd
Goldsborough Bay
Pleasant Prospect
Mt Irvine Bay
Kimme Sculpture Museum
Buccoo Reef & Nylon Pool
Auchenskeoch-Buccoo Bay Rd
Scarborough
Barbados Bay
Granby Point
Smith's Island
Buccoo
Claude Noel Hwy
Fort King George
Buccoo Bay
Golf Course
Rockly Bay
Minister Bay
ATLANTIC OCEAN
Pigeon Point
Shirvan Rd
Buccoo Rd
Old Milford Rd
Bacolet Bay
Store Bay
Milford Rd
Fort Milford
Store Bay Local Rd
Little Rockly Bay
ANR Robinson International Airport
Ferry to Trinidad
Crown Point
Canoe Bay
Petit Trou Lagoon
Columbus Point

DIVING TOBAGO

Diving is excellent in Tobago. Nutrient-rich waters fed by the outflow from South American rivers attract a rich variety of marine life, from shoals of tropical fish to rays, and there is some exciting drift-diving around the island's northeast as well as many more mellow dive sites in the southwest. Although serious divers tend to stay at Speyside and Charlotteville, dive operators in Crown Point will transport you to all of the island's best dive sites. Visit www.tobagoscubadiving.com for lists of operators aligned with the Association of Tobago Dive Operators. There a recompression chamber in the southeast-coast village of Roxborough.

R&Sea Divers (☎639-8120; www.rseadivers.com; Shepherd's Inn, Store Bay Local Rd; dives from US$45) R&Sea Divers is safe, professional and friendly: this is a Professional Association of Diving Instructors (PADI) facility that's been around for a long time. Staff will pick up divers at any hotel.

Undersea Tobago (☎631-2626; www.underseatobago.com; Coco Reef Hotel, Milford Rd; dives US$50, 1hr snorkel tours US$20) Based at the Coco Reef Resort (☎639-8571; www.facebook.com/cocoreeftobago; Milford Rd; d incl breakfast US$510; P ❄ 🛜 ≈), this is a reliable dive outfit that places great emphasis on safety and uses top-notch equipment. It also offers Buccoo Reef snorkeling charters.

ster's Hill Rd, and has services to most points on the island. Buses to/from Crown Point (TT$2) run hourly from 5am to 8pm. For more information on services, call 639-2293.

CAR

If you want to explore the island, it's well worth renting a car for a day or two. Gas stations are fairly widespread in the southwest, less so elsewhere, so it's wise to fill up when you can. There are many car-rental companies on Tobago, though not all operate to international standards; going through a broker like **Yes Tourism** (☎357-0064; www.yes-tourism.com; 7 De Freitas Dr, All Fields Trace, Lowlands) will ensure you get a reliable vehicle at a good rate, as will the operators below.

Econo Car (☎622-8074; www.econocarrentalstt.com; ANR Robinson Airport)

KCNN (☎682-2888; www.tobagocarhire.com; cnr Alfred Cres & Dillon St, Bon Accord)

Sheppy's (☎639-1543; www.tobagocarrental.com; Palm Eagles Dr, Store Bay Local Rd)

TAXI

Taxis from ANR Robinson International Airport charge about TT$50 to hotels around Crown Point; TT$100 to Scarborough, Mt Irvine or Buccoo; and TT$450 to Charlotteville. Island-wide prices are displayed on a board just before the exit of the arrivals area (don't forget to take a look at current fares before you leave the building); drivers await arriving flights. To call an authorized taxi, dial 639-0950.

Route taxis can be a good and cheap option for zipping between the bays here; just stick out your hand at the roadside – official vehicles have 'H' plates.

Crown Point

Spread over Tobago's southwest tip, Crown Point is the island's tourist epicenter, offering a wide range of accommodations, restaurants and some nightlife. The attractive beaches (including Tobago's only white-sand uber-Caribbean shores) and extensive services make many tourists stay put, but anyone wanting a deeper appreciation of Tobago's charms should plan to push eastward to explore other parts of the island.

Sights

Pigeon Point BEACH

(☎639-0601; www.pigeonpoint.tt; Pigeon Point Rd; adult/child TT$20/10; ⏲9am-5pm; P 👪) You have to pay to get into Pigeon Point, the fine dining of Tobago's beaches, with landscaped grounds, bars, restaurants, toilets and showers spread along plenty of beachfront. The postcard-perfect, palm-fringed beach has powdery white sands and milky aqua water; around the headland, the choppy waters are perfect for windsurfing and kitesurfing with Radical Watersports. The palm-dappled stretch of sand before the main entrance is wilder and great for a stroll – watch out for falling coconuts!

Buccoo Reef BOATING

Stretching offshore between Pigeon Point and Buccoo Bay, the extensive Buccoo Reef was designated as a marine park in 1973 and a Ramsar site in 2006. The fringing reef boasts five reef flats separated by deep channels. The sheer array of flora and fauna – dazzling sponges, hard corals and tropical fish – makes marine biologists giddy. However, despite the efforts of conservation groups, some sections of Buccoo Reef have been battered by too much use and not enough protection.

The reef is too far offshore to swim to, so most people see it by way of a glass-bottom-boat tour from Store Bay and Pigeon Point. The boats pass over the reef (much of which is just a meter or two beneath the surface), stop for snorkeling and end with a swim in the **Nylon Pool**, a calm, shallow area in the middle of Buccoo Bay with a sandy bottom and clear turquoise waters. All the operators are pretty similar, charging TT$120 per person for a two-hour trip (you can often get a discount if you haggle), and playing loud soca and selling drinks on board; you'll be repeatedly approached by touts when on Store Bay and Pigeon Point beaches. Longer snorkel tours are available from **Zoe Snorkeling Charters** (www.snorkeltobago.com; Radical Sports, Pigeon Point Beach; 3hr tours adult/child US$80/40;) or **Pops Tours** (383-2348, 738-8226; www.popstourstobago.com; per person boat tours US$65-90, fun/sport fishing from US$75/150;).

Store Bay BEACH

(Milford Rd; lifeguards 10am-5pm; P) You'll find white sands and excellent year-round swimming at Store Bay, a five-minute walk from the airport and the seashore of choice for holidaying Trinis. It's also the main departure point for glass-bottom-boat trips to the Buccoo Reef, with hawkers offering these and rides on Jet Skis or banana boats, and renting umbrellas and sun loungers. Facilities include showers/bathrooms (TT$5) and, in the pedestrianized area above the beach, a cluster of craft huts, bars and a line of food outlets selling delicious local lunches.

Activities & Tours

★Radical Watersports WATER SPORTS

(728-5483, 631-5150; www.radicalsportstobago.com; Pigeon Point Beach; kiteboards per 2hr from US$75, lessons from US$190, windsurf rigs per hr US$45, lessons from US$70, kayaks/SUPs per hr US$22, sailing lessons US$65; 9am-5pm) Radical Watersports, at the northernmost end of Pigeon Point Beach, is *the* center for wind sports, providing quality rental and lessons. It also rents kayaks and SUPs that are perfect for exploring the mangrovey 'No Man's Land' and deserted beaches to the east. All options are also available for children.

★Stand-Up Paddle Tobago ECOTOUR

(681-4741; www.standuppaddletobago.com; Radical Watersports, Pigeon Point Beach; lessons US$60, bioluminescence tours US$60, full-day tours US$120;) The big deal here are fantastic night-time kayak or SUP tours through the bioluminescent waters of Bon Accord Lagoon; by day you can explore the Pigeon Point surrounds by SUP or take an adventurous full-day trip. Gear is top quality and the staff knowledgeable, professional and super-enthusiastic.

Friendship Riding Stables HORSEBACK RIDING

(660-8563, 308-7201; www.friendshipridingstables.com; Friendship Estate; rides TT$250-400) Near Canoe Bay, aptly named Friendship Riding Stables will take you on equestrian adventures through local woodland and down to the sea.

Sleeping

Crown Point has everything from inexpensive guesthouses to luxury resorts, and is a great base if you want to be close to the area's busy beaches as well as its restaurants and nightlife.

★Dimples Apartments APARTMENT $

(660-8156, 786-8134; www.dimples-apartments.com; Store Bay Branch Rd; apt TT$300;) Fantastic value, these appealing apartments come with dining room/kitchen and air-con bedroom, and are beautifully maintained by the Tobagonian/English owners, who are constructing a second complex with a pool nearby. Dimples is tucked away in a quiet residential area just off Store Bay Local Rd – a 10-minute walk from Store Bay Beach and the Crown Point restaurant strip.

Hummingbird Hotel BOUTIQUE HOTEL $

(635-0241; www.hummingbirdtobago.com; 128 Store Bay Local Rd; r US$60-75, with kitchen US$100; P) Friendly and efficiently run little hotel, with inviting rooms arranged around a central pool. All are immaculate, and breakfast is available. Store Bay Beach and the Crown Point bars and restaurants are a short walk away.

Bananaquit GUESTHOUSE $

(368-3539; www.bananaquit.com; Store Bay Local Rd; studios/apt from US$60/80;) The arrangement of these spacious studios and apartments around the courtyard garden creates a community feel. The upstairs lofts can sleep up to six people and are clean, comfortable and attractively decorated. It's a five-minute walk to Store Bay Beach and the Crown Point restaurant strip, and there's a restaurant for breakfast and snacks.

Surfside Hotel HOTEL $
(639-0614; www.surfsidehotel.online; Pigeon Point Rd; studios/apt TT$325/400; P) Right in the heart of the action on the road to Pigeon Point and surrounded by bars and restaurants, this is a good deal for travelers on a budget, and is very popular with visiting Trinidadians. The self-catering rooms are a bit dated but good value, with cable TV.

Sandy's Guesthouse GUESTHOUSE $
(639-9221; Store Bay Local Rd; r TT$300;) Stay with Valerie Sandy and you're a guest in a typical Tobagonian home. The rooms and shared kitchen facilities are basic but scrupulously clean, with air-con and cable TV, and rates are some of the lowest in the area.

Native Abode BOUTIQUE HOTEL $$
(631-1285; www.nativeabode.com; 13 Village St, Gaskin Bay Rd, Bon Accord; r incl breakfast US$145; P) On a tree-filled side street reached via Store Bay Local Rd then Gaskin Bay Rd, this is a lovely little place. Rooms are decorated to a very high standard; they're clean, modern and appealing, and have a kitchenette, though a full local breakfast is included. The owners' garden is a great chill-out spot, filled with fruit trees.

★Kariwak Village Holistic Haven HOTEL $$$
(639-8442; www.kariwak.com; Store Bay Local Rd; d incl breakfast US$225-250; P) Just a five-minute walk from Store Bay Beach, Kariwak feels incredibly peaceful despite its central location. The modern cabanas line paths that wind through flower-filled tropical gardens, past tinkling streams and a thatch-roofed yoga *ajoupa* (open hut). It's both rustic and refreshing. It has an organic herb garden, two pools (one with waterfall-fueled hot tub), yoga classes and a really excellent restaurant.

Eating & Drinking

Crown Point holds the majority of Tobago's restaurants, from buzzing Middle Eastern joints to Italian bistros and local seafood places. One of the best places to eat lunch is the row of food huts opposite Store Bay beach, which serve up delicious dishes like roti, curry crab and dumplings, and simple Creole plates (from TT$60).

Time to Wine BREAKFAST $
(639-7212; www.facebook.com/timetowinetrinidadandtobago; 281 Store Bay Local Rd, above Bananaquit Hotel; breakfast from TT$25; 7am-10pm;) An inviting breakfast option, with tables on a breezy balcony overlooking Crown Point and excellent service. You can get eggs any way, pancakes, grilled-cheese sandwiches and yogurt with seasoned fruits; and swap your morning coffee for a glass of white-wine sangria, too. It's also a great spot for wine by the glass or bottle, or a cocktail.

Yasraj Roti Hutt CARIBBEAN $
(332-5705; Crusoe's Village, Pigeon Point Rd; roti from TT$30; 6am-5:30pm, closed Wed;) You won't be disappointed by the curried goodness at this reliable roti shop, cooking up breakfasts of eggplant or tomato *choka* and *sada* roti, plus excellent rotis: fillings include chicken, duck, shrimp, goat and veggies. It also does pies and very moreish *pholouri*.

★Tobago Paradise Travel & Grill SEAFOOD $$
(344-1703; Pigeon Point Rd; lobster from TT$200; 5:30-10pm) With tables on a rustic deck just steps from the sea, beachfront dining doesn't get better than this. The specialty is lobster, grilled in garlic butter, but you can also get fresh shrimp and fish served with local sauces and sides. It's tiny and very popular, so book ahead; lunch is available with advance reservation. No booze, but you can BYO.

★Brown Cow FUSION $$
(324-2564; www.facebook.com/browncowtobago; Milford Rd; lunch mains TT$51-84, dinner mains TT$185-202, sushi from TT$85; noon-5pm & 6-10pm;) Brilliant little restaurant offering some of the most imaginative cooking in Tobago, featuring lots of local ingredients. Lunch offerings include soups (oxtail, fish or veggie), plus filling salads, from kale and grilled plantain caprese to roasted ratatouille and potato, plus lamb or shredded-steak sandwiches and pasta dishes. Dinner highlights include seafood pepperpot stew, chicken three ways and pan-roasted fish on a *dasheen* (taro root) rosti.

★Kariwak Village CARIBBEAN $$
(639-8442; www.kariwak.com; Kariwak Village Hotel, Store Bay Local Rd; breakfast TT$70-90, lunch TT$100-145, dinner TT$210-230; 7:30-10am, 12:30-2:30pm & 7-9:30pm;) Beneath the thatched roof and coral-stone walls of this open-air restaurant, enjoy masterpiec-

es of Caribbean cuisine made with fresh organic herbs and vegetables from the garden. Breakfast includes local specials such as fried fish, plus homemade yogurt and granola. The lunch and dinner set menus feature grilled fish, meat and seafood (plus a vegetarian option), and are cooked with plenty of love.

La Cantina PIZZA **$$**
(639-8242; www.lacantinapizzeria.com; RBTT Compound, Milford Rd; pizzas TT$109-175; noon-9:45pm Mon & Thu-Sat, noon-2:45pm & 6-9:45pm Tue & Wed, 6-9:45pm Sun;) Tucked into a bank compound off Milford Rd, with tables outside and in the air-con interior, this buzzing joint cooks up a huge range of authentically Italian pizzas in its wood-fired oven – you can watch the chef spinning dough and adding toppings. Good salads and fast service. Takeout available.

Pasta Gallery ITALIAN **$$**
(727-8200; www.pastagallery.net; Pigeon Point Rd; mains TT$75-115; 6:30-10pm, closed Tue & Wed;) Cute little pasta place with tables inside and on a deck out front. Cooked up by an Italian chef, the pasta is reliably good, with everything from fettuccine with smoked salmon or shrimp to spaghetti with seafood or classic carbonara sauce, plus beef lasagna; a nice bruschetta and house salad, too. Decent list of Italian wines, and gluten-free pasta is available.

★ **Bago's Beach Bar** BAR
(Pigeon Point Rd; 10am-late) Right on the sand where Pigeon Point Rd forks right, this cool little beach bar serves them cold and mixes a mean rum punch. Great for sunset-watching; the slip of beach offers decent swimming too.

Information

In Crown Point, there are banks at the airport and along Milford Rd close to Store Bay, all of which have 24-hour ATMs.

Tourist office (639-0509; www.visittobago.gov.tt; ANR Robinson International Airport; 8am-10pm) The staff provide only basic information, as well as supplying the useful free visitor magazines, *Discover Trinidad & Tobago* and *Ins & Outs of Trinidad & Tobago*.

Getting There & Away

International and domestic flights land at ANR Robinson Airport (p798), where taxi drivers line up to meet arriving passengers; there's a board listing fares island-wide just before you leave the arrivals area. Taxis are easy to find throughout Crown Point: you can expect drivers to slow down and ask if you need a ride whenever you're walking around the area. Route taxis run along Milford Rd and are a good option for short hops.

Buccoo

Though its narrow strip of white sand is monopolized by fishing boats at the village end, Buccoo's sweeping palm-backed bay is pretty spectacular, and completely undeveloped past the fishing facility, and the restaurants and bars of the looming concrete Buccoo Integrated Facility. Pretty though it is, Buccoo's beach is not really a place to throw down your towel and settle in for the day; there's no established beach scene here, but the calm, clear waters are good for swimming, and walking along the sand toward the headland is always enjoyable. First and foremost, this close-knit village offers a taste of true local flavor: friendly folks who define easygoing, breathtaking sunsets over the bay and the infamous Sunday School party every week, staged in and around the Integrated Facility. It's also the place to come for a fabulous laid-back horseback ride along the beach.

 Tours

★ **Being with Horses** HORSEBACK RIDING
(639-0953; www.being-with-horses.com; 14 Galla Trace; swim & trail ride US$100, being with horses session US$50;) This small-scale stable, home to an ever-growing herd of rescued horses, offers rides along Buccoo Point and beach, including a swim in the sea. Great for kids, with an intuitive, holistic approach to things equestrian, it also offers a Being with Horses option where you can groom the horses and have a short ride, and therapeutic riding for children with disabilities.

Festivals & Events

Goat Races SPORTS
(www.buccoo.net; Buccoo Integrated Facility, Buccoo Main Rd; 1st Tue after Easter Sun;) FREE Easter weekend is a huge deal in Tobago, and in Buccoo the festivities center on the annual goat races, an all-day event at the track and covered stands behind the Integrated Facility. Taken very seriously, goat racing draws more bets than a Las Vegas casino. A cut above your average roadside grazer, competing goats get pampered like beauty contestants – the champion is forever revered.

The races see the goats burst from the starting gates at the crack of a pistol, while their 'jockeys' run headlong beside them and attempt to coax them in a straight line by way of a long leash, often to hilarious effect. Smaller-scale crab races are also fun for kids, and the food and craft stalls that line the main road make for a festive atmosphere.

Sleeping

★Miller's Guesthouse GUESTHOUSE $

(660-8371; www.millersguesthouse.com; 14 Miller St; dm/s/d/tr US$30/40/65/70, apt US$80-120;) In a pretty location overlooking Buccoo Bay, the singles and doubles here are great for budget travelers; there are also bunk beds in a pleasant dorm with kitchen access. Rooms are decked out in bright colors and kept sparkling fresh and clean, and there's a shared kitchen. An excellent place for meeting people, and next to a restaurant, too.

Fish Tobago GUESTHOUSE $

(309-0062; www.fishtobago.com; 26a Buccoo Point; dm/s US$18/35, d US$40-100; P) Tucked away off the main road into the village, this is a good spot for travelers. It's efficiently run and has a range of rooms from dorms to apartments, some complete with hand-painted beach scenes on the walls. There is a communal kitchen, and snorkeling and fishing trips are available.

Seaside Garden Guesthouse GUESTHOUSE $

(639-0687; www.tobago-guesthouse.com; Buccoo Bay Rd; r US$44-58, apt US$100;) Friendly little guesthouse just stumbling distance from where the Sunday School street party is held. Its rooms and apartments are well cared for, and there's a pleasant communal patio for chilling out. The shared kitchen is well equipped, and guests can use a washing machine.

Eating

★Café Down Low CARIBBEAN $$

(475-0240; www.facebook.com/cafedownlow; Buccoo Bay Rd; mains from TT$60; noon-11pm Tue-Thu & Sat, to midnight Fri, to 10pm Sun) Cool little oasis, with a wooden bar serving up cold beers and cocktails, and a sunken garden lit up beautifully at night. Great for a drink as well as to eat excellent local food alfresco: traditional chicken, pork or fish lunches with all the trimmings, plus hearty soups on Saturdays. Everything is homemade and served with a smile.

La Tartaruga ITALIAN $$

(639-0940; www.latartarugatobago.com; Buccoo Bay Rd; mains TT$65-345; 6-9:30pm Mon-Sat;) It's surprising to find this authentic Italian restaurant with scrumptious homemade pastas and delectable wine (it has one of the largest Italian wine cellars in the Caribbean) tucked away in tiny Buccoo. But it's a treat, indeed. The ambience melds lively Caribbean colors and art with a candlelit patio fit for a romantic Italian cafe.

★Makara FUSION $$$

(340-9547; www.makaratobago.com; Buccoo Integrated Facility, Buccoo Bay Rd; mains TT$165-350; noon-3pm & 6-10pm, closed Tue;) On a balcony high above Buccoo Bay, with handsome ocean views, this fine-dining restaurant offers an upscale take on Caribbean cuisine: feast on Creole shrimp with cassava grits and wilted spinach, slow-grilled rack of lamb with couscous and tahini or blackened fish with coconut sauce and caramelized plantain. Great for a romantic dinner, or a perfectly made cocktail.

Entertainment

★Sunday School LIVE MUSIC

(Buccoo Integrated Facility, Buccoo Bay Rd; 8pm-3am Sun) Lacking any religious affiliation, Sunday School is the sly title for a street party held in Buccoo every Sunday night. Until around 10pm, partygoers are mostly tourists enjoying rum drinks, overpriced barbecue dinners and live steel pan. Later, folks from all over the island come to 'take a wine' or just hang out, with DJs spinning reggae, soca and dancehall hits.

Getting There & Away

A taxi to Buccoo from Crown Point will cost about TT$85. Route taxis run up and down the main coastal strip passing the Buccoo turnoff.

Leeward Coast

The stretch of coastline from Mt Irvine Bay to Arnos Vale has several lovely beaches, a few sizable hotels and a slew of fancy villas hugging the greens of the golf course. Like a sloppy adolescent propping its feet on the table in a fancy living room, Black Rock's tiny Pleasant Prospect community is right in the middle. It's a teeny surfer haunt, with inexpensive accommodations, some great restaurants and a happening bar.

Sights & Activities

★Mt Irvine Hotel Beach BEACH

(Grafton Rd, Mt Irvine Bay; P) Just south of the main Mt Irvine Beach, a turnoff from the main road leads to an adjoining swath of sand, where the swimming in calm emerald waters is even better than at the main beach; there's also good snorkeling just offshore and around the point. A hotel-run bar and restaurant sells snacks and drinks, and rents loungers and umbrellas at exorbitant rates, and you can hire kayaks and other gear from Mt Irvine Bay Watersports.

★Stonehaven Bay BEACH

(Stonehaven Bay Rd) Northeast of Mt Irvine, this fabulous sweep of coarse yellow sand, also known as Grafton Bay, offers some fabulous swimming and bodyboarding in clear emerald waters; the eastern end is calmer. A couple of large-scale hotels overlook the sand, one of which has a beach bar selling lunch and drinks. It's a great spot for sunset watching, too.

Kimme Sculpture Museum MUSEUM

(639-0257; www.luisekimme.com; Orange Hill Rd, Bethel; TT$20; 10am-2pm Sun or by appointment) At the Mt Irvine golf course, turn off the main road onto Orange Hill Rd and you'll see signs leading you to the blinged-out former home of Luise Kimme, a German sculptor who died in 2013 but who had lived in Tobago for many years. Some of her fantastic, 2m to 3m wood-and-metal Caribbean-themed sculptures are displayed inside, as are those of her artistic successor, Cuban sculptor Dunieski Lora Pileta, who now lives and works here.

The Kimme Museum isn't heavily visited, so it's best to call ahead even on a Sunday.

★Adventure Farm & Nature Reserve BIRDWATCHING

(639-2839; www.adventure-ecovillas.com; Arnos Vale Rd; US$10; 9am-6pm) Adventure Farm and Nature Reserve is a 5-hectare working organic estate that has retained about 1 hectare of wild area. This is home to a wealth of bird species, which flutter in en masse when a bell is rung to signify feeding time. The center is especially revered for its huge numbers of hummingbirds, which cluster around feeders at the main house; watching them up close is a wonderful spectacle. You can also take short hikes around the estate along marked trails.

Mt Irvine Bay Watersports WATER SPORTS

(771-9997, 682-2408; Grafton Rd, Mt Irvine Bay; s/d kayaks per hour TT$60/150, SUP boards per hour TT$120, sailboats per hour from TT$350) Great little water sports shack on the beach, with single and double kayaks, SUPs and sailboats, plus fun swim accessories, including a water mat with beer holders. Lessons and boat tours are also available. Find them on Facebook.

Sleeping

★Top O'Tobago BOUTIQUE HOTEL $$

(687-0121; www.topotobago.com; Arnos Vale Rd; cabanas US$120; P) In a fantastic hilltop location with views over the rounded eggbox-like crags and out to the sea, this flower-bedecked place is made special by its colorful, simple style and superlative service from friendly staff. The bright, breezy self-contained cabanas are beautifully decorated, and hammocks swing in the breeze. There's a lovely pool, and a trail down to Arnos Vale Beach.

Surfer's Paradise VILLA $$

(319-9394; www.surfersparadisevilla.com; 11 Glen Eagles Dr; 1-bed apt US$150, villa US$600; P) Aptly named, this splendid villa overlooks the Mt Irvine breaks, though it's hard to imagine the average surf bum hanging out in such luxury. Beautifully appointed and spanking new, the main villa has four bedrooms (including one Tree House unit), great indoor/outdoor liming areas and a lush pool. Downstairs, the one-bed apartment is equally appealing for those not in a group.

★Plantation Beach Villas RESORT $$$

(639-9377; www.plantationbeachvillas.com; Stonehaven Bay Rd; 2-person villas US$280; P) Right on Stonehaven Beach, this is the best of the villa resorts in the area, and one of the top options in all of Tobago. Enjoy tastefully appointed three-bedroom villas in handsome gingerbread style, equipped with everything you need and with spacious verandas for alfresco liming and dining. There's also a communal beachside pool with adjacent bar, and supremely helpful staff.

★Cuffie River Nature Retreat RESORT $$$

(660-0505; www.cuffieriver.com; Runnemede; d from US$210; P) Follow signs off the Northside Rd to this charming, secluded retreat at the edge of the rainforest. Designed for birdwatching fanatics, it has an excellent birding guide on hand to lead hikes around the area. The spacious, comfortable rooms, equipped with balconies, are flooded with natural light. It also has an ecofriendly swimming pool and there are several freshwater springs nearby.

Eating

Z's Grill Shack GRILL $
(www.facebook.com/zsgrillshack; Pleasant Prospect; lunch mains TT$45-55, dinner mains TT$90-145; ⌚11am-3pm & 6-10pm, closed Tue) Tucked away toward the back of Pleasant Prospect's semicircular main street in a rustic wooden building, Z's offers up simple and delicious food. Short and sweet, the menus change daily and consist of grilled lamb, chicken or fish lunches, and dinners like Mediterranean-rubbed steak or fish in herb butter. All dishes are perfectly executed and sides are generous and tasty.

★**Fish Pot** SEAFOOD $$
(☎635-1728; Pleasant Prospect; lunch mains from TT$50, dinner TT$160-275; ⌚11am-3pm & 7-10pm Mon-Sat; 👪) This laid-back restaurant specializes in super-fresh, simply prepared seafood (with some chicken and steak dishes), and has an open-air patio. Excellent homemade bread, and great starters from fish chowder to crab cakes. Don't miss it.

Seahorse Inn Restaurant & Bar CARIBBEAN $$$
(☎639-0686; www.seahorsetobago.com; Seahorse Inn, Stonehaven Bay Rd; mains TT$155-350; ⌚6-10pm) Sitting alfresco amid a tropical setting overlooking the water, with the sound of waves crashing below, this upmarket restaurant specializes in gourmet Creole cuisine. Think sesame-crusted tuna to rack of lamb with a port and guava sauce, plus to-die-for desserts. There's also a carefully curated wine list, and wonderful cocktails: daily happy hour is 5:30pm to 6:30pm.

Getting There & Away

From the airport, taxis to Mt Irvine are TT$80, TT$90 to Stonehaven Bay/Pleasant Prospect, TT$120 to Arnos Vale.

Castara

About an hour's drive from Crown Point, Castara is a pretty fishing village on the north coast that's popular with tourists who want to experience Tobago away from the inundated southwest scene. People love the wide, sandy beaches, relaxed atmosphere and picturesque setting, and the village is is a good base for a variety of tours and activities. Uniquely in Tobago, Castara has a real sense of tourism coexisting with village life, with visitors queuing up to buy bread and cakes from the clay oven just back from the main beach (order early on a Wednesday morning), or helping fishers pull in seine nets on Big Bay. The **Castara Tourism Development Association** (☎696-7957; Big Bay) is a true community effort, pulling together local businesses to beautify the village and promote sustainable tourism.

Activities

Wild Turtle Scuba DIVING
(☎766-8897; www.divingintobago.com; Depot Rd; dive from US$50) Wild Turtle is certified by the Professional Association of Diving Instructors (PADI) and is diver-recommended. It offers Open Water dive certification (US$450) in the waters of Heavenly Bay as well as refresher, advanced and Divemaster classes.

Sleeping

★**Boatview Apartments** APARTMENT $
(☎483-0964; www.boatviewcastara.com; Depot Rd; d US$70; P 📶) Fronted by a huge shared deck overlooking the ocean, and right over Heavenly Bay, these self-contained studio apartments have kitchen, ceiling fan, cold-water showers and a mosquito-netted double bed; the futon sofa can also pull out to sleep another person. Rates are great for the location, and the super-friendly owners offer fantastic hospitality and heaps of hands-on local expertise.

★**Castara Retreats** RESORT $$
(☎660-7309, 766-7309; www.castararetreats.com; Northside Rd; 1-bed apt US$120-272; P ❄ 📶) 🍃 Beautifully designed self-contained wooden villas on a lushly landscaped hillside that offers lovely views of the beach. Each is thoughtfully kitted out and quietly luxurious, and there are even sea views from some of the beds. Friendly, helpful staff and plenty of privacy, plus a fantastic restaurant and bar. It also has a scenic yoga deck, and massages are available.

Villas come with one or two bedrooms, and vary in terms of size and beach view –

but all are fitted out to the same high spec, and have outside areas.

★ **Alibaba's Sea Breeze** APARTMENT $$
(☎635-1017; www.alibaba-tours.com; Depot Rd; s/d US$80/90; P 📶) This well-run bunch of apartments has magnificent beach-facing balconies, full kitchens and comfortable rooms with bamboo and seashell details, plus four-posters draped with mosquito nets. All are beautifully maintained and very inviting.

Eating

★ **Caribbean Kitchen** FUSION $$
(☎687-7711; www.castararetreats.com; Castara Retreats, Northside Rd; mains TT$120-180; ⊙11am-10pm; 🌶 👪) In a beautiful setting on a fairy-lit all-wood deck overlooking the bay, this is a lovely lunch or dinner choice, with homemade carrot/spinach and ricotta ravioli, bean burgers and eggplant *involtini* (rolls) as well as curried lamb and excellent freshly caught seafood. The chocolate mousse, made with Tobago cocoa, is to die for. Great for fresh local juices and sunset cocktails, too.

★ **Cascreole** CARIBBEAN $$
(☎721-5700; Big Bay; mains from TT$85, set menu Thu TT$100; ⊙11:30am-3:30pm & 7-9:30pm; 🌶 👪) On a wooden deck built over the Big Bay sands, this is all you'd want from a beach restaurant: ice-cold beers and fresh and delicious fish, chicken and shrimp, cooked with love and served with tasty sides. Plenty of sea breezes and a Thursday night beach bonfire and feast, with a two-course set menu and a DJ playing Caribbean tunes.

Boat House CARIBBEAN $$
(☎483-0964; www.boatviewcastara.com; Depot Rd; bake & fish TT$50, lunch mains TT$75-95, dinner mains TT$125-135, pizzas from TT$80; ⊙9:30am-10pm Mon & Fri, to 5pm Tue & 1am Wed, 10am-5pm Thu & Sun; 📶 👪) Offering colorful decor, bamboo detailing and beachside ambience, this friendly bar and restaurant serves up sandwiches and burgers (including a great lionfish in beer batter option), as well as fish, chicken, beef, squid and shrimp mains with creative sides. There are good pizzas on Sundays, and lush homemade ice cream. A juice bar also serves bake and fish sandwiches.

Cheno's Coffee Shop CARIBBEAN $$
(☎704-7819; www.castaracoffeehouse.com; North Coast Rd; breakfast from TT$60, Sat BBQ TT$150; ⊙8am-1pm Mon-Fri, from 9am Sat & Sun, dinner by reservation; 📶) The best breakfast in town, from saltfish *buljol* and coconut bake to bacon, eggs and toast, plus decent coffee (and iced coffee). Local lunch and dinner (fish, chicken or curry goat, local-style) is also available with advance reservation. The excellent Saturday barbecue night usually features live steel pan, and a set menu of main meal, ice cream and rum punch.

Drinking & Nightlife

★ **Glasgow's Bar** BAR
(☎761-7755; Northside Rd, Parlatuvier; ⊙10am-10pm) Perched on the cliffside above Parlatuvier Bay, this friendly Tobago rum shop is a great place to kick back and enjoy superb views over a beer or a glass of rum.

WORTH A TRIP

TOBAGO FOREST RESERVE

A 20-minute drive east of Castara, at Bloody Bay, the Roxborough–Parlatuvier Rd strikes inland, meeting the windward coast at Roxborough. This smooth, paved road curves through the **Tobago Forest Reserve**, established in 1765 and the oldest protected rainforest in the Caribbean. The 30-minute drive through the reserve passes pretty valleys and mountain views, and is one of the most scenic on the island.

A number of trailheads lead off the main road into the rainforest, where there's excellent birdwatching. Three-quarters of the way from Roxborough, at Gilpin Trace, authorized guides such as **Fitzroy Quamina** (☎344-1895; hikes TT$160-300) can usually be found waiting for visitors, and charge TT$160 for a 1½-hour walk, or TT$240 for a two-hour hike to the Main Ridge lookout hut, which affords scenic views of Bloody Bay and the offshore Sisters Rocks. All guides provide interesting commentary on the forest ecosystem and inhabitants, and can rent you rubber boots when it's muddy. For the best birding, aim to arrive at 9am. Serious birders might prefer a specialist birdwatching trip with NG Nature Tours (p778) or Peter Cox Nature Tours (p778).

The adjoined cookshop sells local meals and fish-and-chips, too.

Getting There & Away

A taxi from Crown Point will cost about TT$300, and cars are available to rent locally from **Taylor's** (☎354-5743; www.taylorstobagoautorental.com; Depot Rd, Heavenly Bay).

Scarborough

Located 15 minutes' drive east of Crown Point, Scarborough is Tobago's capital, a crowded port with bustling one-way streets and congested traffic. Tobagonians come here to bank, pay bills or go shopping, and though there are some good places to grab a bite and a neat public market, most visitors will want to push onward after a quick trip to the scenic hilltop Fort King George.

Sights

★Fort King George FORT
(Fort St; P) FREE Atop a hill at the end of Fort St, this sizable fort was built by the British between 1777 and 1779, and is worth a visit to see its restored colonial-era buildings – one of which holds the Tobago Museum – and magnificent views. Benches under enormous saman trees allow you to gaze out over Rockly Bay, while cannon line the fort's stone walls, pointing out to sea over palm-covered flatlands below. Some of the buildings have plaques detailing their original use.

Tobago Museum MUSEUM
(☎639-3970; Fort King George, Fort St; TT$10; 9am-4:30pm Mon-Fri; P) The Fort King George officers' quarters now contain this small but worthy museum, which displays a healthy collection of Amerindian artifacts, maps from the 1600s, military relics, paintings, a small geology exhibit and a neat collection of domestic artifacts from Tobago's more recent history.

Botanical Gardens GARDENS
(Gardenside St; dawn-dusk) FREE A pretty place to duck out of the heat, with a variety of flowering trees and shrubs, including flamboyants, African tulips and orchids (in an orchid house) laid out over 3 hectares of a former sugar estate. The most convenient of several entrances is just back from Carrington St on Gardenside St. If you're in Tobago during the Christmas season, it's well worth checking out the outrageously extravagant fairy-light displays that deck trees and bushes throughout the gardens.

Sleeping

★Fort Cottage COTTAGE $
(☎680-1517; thefortcottage@gmail.com; Calder Hall Rd; cottage US$60; @) Totally unique and full of history, this gorgeous little cottage has the feel of a family home, with fantastic views over Scarborough Bay from the back porch, which also overlooks a garden dotted with fruit trees. It combines antique furnishings and appealing vintage-style decor with two air-con bedrooms, and an airy high-ceilinged living room with piano and Netflix on TV.

Sandy's Bed & Breakfast GUESTHOUSE $$
(☎639-2737; bluecrabrestauranttobago@gmail.com; cnr Main & Robinson Sts; r incl breakfast US$80;) Behind the Blue Crab Restaurant, and operated by the same family, the three rooms are pleasantly simple with pine floors, nice furniture and views overlooking Rockly Bay.

Blue Haven Hotel RESORT $$$
(☎660-7400; www.bluehavenhotel.com; Bacolet Bay; r incl breakfast from US$238; P) Robinson Crusoe supposedly was stranded at the beach below this romantic, tastefully done resort hotel with more than a hint of faded glamour. Amenities here include a beachside pool, tennis courts and kayaks, and each room has an oceanfront balcony. A restaurant and bar are on-site.

Eating

★Shore Things CAFE $$
(☎635-1072; www.facebook.com/shorethingstobago; Old Milford Rd, Lambeau; mains TT$60-115; 11am-6pm Mon-Fri, 8am-4pm Sat;) Just west of Scarborough, this is one of the most pleasant oceanside cafes on the island, serving quiche, pizza, filled crepes, salads, sandwiches and fresh juices, plus more substantial fish and meat dishes. The setting, overlooking the ocean, is lovely and breezy. Great for teatime treats including sublime lime cheesecake or coconut cream pie, and there's a kids' menu, too.

Blue Crab Restaurant CARIBBEAN $$
(☎639-2737; www.tobagobluecrab.com; cnr Main & Robinson Sts; lunch from TT$70; 11am-3pm Tue-Fri) A family-run restaurant with pleasant alfresco seating (and an air-conditioned dining room) and good West Indian food. You'll have

a choice of fresh juice and main dishes such as Creole chicken, fresh fish or garlic shrimp.

Information

There are branches of Republic Bank and Scotiabank just east of the docks, both equipped with ATMs. There's another ATM right outside the ferry terminal.

Scarborough General Hospital (660-4744; Signal Hill; 24hr) Just off the highway on the outskirts of Scarborough, this facility has an A&E and handles most medical issues on Tobago.

Getting There & Away

Tobago's **main bus terminal** (639-2293; www.ptsctt.com; Sangster's Hill Rd) is just behind the waterfront at Sangster's Hill Rd; buses and maxi-taxis to all points depart from here. The dock for ferries between Trinidad and Tobago, run by the **Inter-Island Ferry Service** (639-2417; https://ttitferry.com; Carrington St; adult/child one way TT$50/25), is on Carrington St, right in the heart of town. Taxis line up to meet foot passengers just outside.

In lower Scarborough, there are route-taxi stands: cars to Plymouth, Castara and Parlatuvier depart from opposite the market, and taxis to Crown Point leave from in front of the ferry terminal. In upper Scarborough, taxis to Speyside and Charlotteville leave from Republic Bank by James Park. Fares are TT$5 to TT$12.

Windward Road

East of Scarborough, the Windward Rd, which connects Scarborough with Speyside and Charlotteville, winds past scattered villages, jungly valleys and white-capped ocean dotted with tiny offshore islands. The further east you go, the more ruggedly beautiful the scenery becomes. Tobago's windward coast is the more rural part of the island, less appealing to tourists thanks to its rough dark-sand beaches and pounding Atlantic waves.

Sights & Activities

★Corbin Local Wildlife Park ANIMAL SANCTUARY
(327-4182; www.tobagowildlife.com; 68 Belmont Farm Rd, Mason Hall; tours TT$150;) Established by hunter turned conservationist Roy Corbin in Tobago's forest-covered interior, just inland of the windward coast's Hope Bay, this nonprofit sanctuary is home to most of the island's indigenous animals, from manicou (opossum) and tatoo (armadillo) to iguana, agouti and boa constrictors, housed in large enclosures between the trees; a lily-covered pond also holds a wild caiman. Guided walks (usually led by Corbin himself) offer a fascinating insight into Tobago's wildlife and forests, and are also great for birdwatching.

Argyle Falls WATERFALL
(Windward Rd; adult/child TT$60/30; 9am-5pm;) This 54m waterfall on the Argyle River is Tobago's highest, cascading down three distinct levels, each with its own pool of spring water, which you can swim in. From the parking lot, it's a 20-minute hike up. The entry fee includes an authorized guide who will lead the way and point out things of interest (it's usual to leave a tip). The path is easy to follow independently, though it can get slippery after rain (which also turns the pools a muddy brown).

Tobago Windward Chocolate Company FOOD
(298-5499; www.facebook.com/tgowindwardchocolateco; Louis d'Or Community Center; tours TT$60) Small and still developing, this community-based operation conducts Tree to Bar tours. Starting in the cocoa groves of estates along the Roxborough–Bloody Bay Rd, you can see cocoa trees, bean fermentation and the drying stage in a traditional cocoa house with its moveable roof. The chocolate production process takes place in the Louis d'Or community centre; tours include tastings.

Getting There & Away

Although much of the Windward Rd is narrow and curvy, with a handful of blind corners, it's easily drivable in a standard vehicle. Journey time from Scarborough to Speyside is about 1½ hours, then it's another 20 minutes or so to cross over the interior ridge to Charlotteville.

Speyside

The small fishing village of Speyside fronts Tyrrel's Bay, and attracts divers and birders. It's the jumping-off point for excursions to uninhabited Little Tobago island, a bird sanctuary 2km offshore. Protected waters, high visibility, abundant coral and diverse marine life make for choice **diving**, and Speyside is home to some renowned scuba sites. Several dive shops operate in the village and most visitors stay in diver-oriented hotels. Nondivers can take glass-bottom-boat/snorkel tours to Little Tobago.

Speyside has a quiet, end-of-the-road feel. Above town, the off-road **lookout** has panoramic views out over the islands and reef-studded waters.

Sights

Little Tobago ISLAND

Also known as Bird of Paradise Island (though it isn't home to any of the eponymous birds), Little Tobago was a cotton plantation during the late 1800s, and is now an important seabird sanctuary that offers rich pickings for birdwatchers. Red-billed tropic birds, magnificent frigate birds, brown boobies, Audubon's shearwaters, laughing gulls and sooty terns are some of the species found here. The hilly, arid island, which averages just 1.5km in width, has a couple of short hiking trails with captivating views.

Activities & Tours

Blue Waters Dive'n DIVING

(660-5445; www.bluewatersinn.com; Blue Waters Inn, Batteaux Bay; single dive US$66, PADI Open Water US$495) Well-run dive shop offering certification, refresher courses and recreational dives in and around Speyside.

Extra Divers DIVING

(660-4852; www.extradivers-worldwide.com; Speyside Inn, Windward Rd; 2-dive package US$110) Bilingual dive outfit popular with German travelers, attached to the Speyside Inn.

★Top Ranking Tours BOATING

(660-4904; Batteaux Bay; Little Tobago trip US$30, beach trip US$65; 10:30am & 2pm) Top Ranking Tours, departing from Blue Waters Inn, operates tours of Little Tobago aboard its glass-bottom boats. Guides identify bird species, as well as plants and animals. Masks and fins are provided so you can snorkel at Angel Reef. It also does a picnic trip to Indian Bay, a pretty beach reachable by boat only, with good snorkeling offshore.

★Frank's BOATING

(470-7084, 660-5438; Batteaux Bay; Little Tobago trip US$30; 10am & 2pm) Based at Blue Waters Inn, Frank's conducts glass-bottom-boat tours to Little Tobago. The trip includes birdwatching, with guides pointing out the various species as well as plants and animals of interest along the way, and snorkeling at the lovely Angel Reef, home to one of the largest brain corals in the world. Masks and fins are provided.

Sleeping & Eating

Speyside Inn HOTEL $$

(660-4852; www.extradivers-worldwide.com; 189-193 Windward Rd; s/d incl breakfast US$100/144; P ❄ 📶 🏊) This butter-yellow hotel houses bright balcony rooms looking over the ocean, and cottages nestled out back in the jungly landscaping. It's very much geared toward scuba business, with the Extra Divers shop on-site. There's a restaurant and a bar, and it's often the most animated spot in town (though that's not saying much in quiet Speyside).

★Blue Waters Inn RESORT $$$

(660-2583; www.bluewatersinn.com; Batteaux Bay; r incl breakfast from US$221; P ❄ 📶 🏊) Speyside's most upscale accommodations, geared to divers and birdwatchers, Blue Waters sits on aquamarine Batteaux Bay, the best beach in the area, and has a gorgeous seaside infinity pool. The rooms all have patios and great views. Guests get use of tennis courts, snorkel gear and kayaks/SUPs. It has a restaurant, bar and a full-service PADI dive center.

★Jemma's CARIBBEAN $$

(660-4066; Windward Rd; mains TT$90-150, lobster from TT$300; 8am-8pm Mon-Thu & Sun, to 4pm Fri;) Nestled in a seaside tree house, with tables on decks built up between the boughs and fresh sea breezes, Jemma's is a standard stop for tour groups. Offers reliable local food, including fish, chicken and shrimp dishes, and delicious sides such as breadfruit pie or tania fritters; sandwiches and burgers are available too. No booze, but you can bring your own.

Aqua MEDITERRANEAN $$

(660-4341; www.bluewatersinn.com; Blue Waters Inn, Batteaux Bay; lunch mains from TT$60, dinner mains TT$140-225; 7:30am-10pm;) Within the Blue Waters Inn, with tables on a balcony overlooking the beach, this is an excellent choice even if you're not a hotel guest. Lunch ranges from shrimp, fish or chicken salads to curry crab and dumplings, fish tacos, quesadillas and sumptuous steak sandwiches. Dinner mains include coffee-crusted filet mignon, blackened grouper or lobster in lemon-herb butter.

Getting There & Away

You can drive to Speyside from Scarborough, along the winding Windward Rd, in about 1½ hours. Taxis from Crown Point cost about TT$380, a little less from Scarborough.

Charlotteville

A delightful fishing village, Charlotteville nestles around the aquamarine Man of War Bay, a short walk from glorious Pirate's Bay beach. This secluded town accepts its trickle of off-the-beaten-track tourists with mostly jovial spirits and occasionally apathy. It's more lively than nearby Speyside, and tourist services include a sprinkling of places to stay and eat, and an ATM. This may all change, though, when the construction of a large new beach facility smack in the middle of the village's bayside main street is finally completed; local opposition and legal challenges have seen the works stalled for some time, however, and it's unclear as to whether it will ever be opened.

Sights & Activities

★Pirate's Bay BEACH
(Pirate's Bay Rd) Past Charlotteville's pier, a dirt track winds up and around the cliff to concrete steps that descend to Pirate's Bay, which offers excellent snorkeling and fantastic beach liming, with locals and visitors making a day of it with coolers and games of beach football. There are no facilities, so bring your own drinks and food. If you don't fancy the 10-minute walk, ask one of the Man of War Bay fishers to transport you there and back.

Flagstaff Hill HILL
(Windward Rd) Reached via a signposted turnoff from the main road between Speyside and Charlotteville, Flagstaff Hill is a popular spot to picnic and watch the birds circling St Giles Island. The coastal views and cool breezes are stupendous.

Man of War Bay BEACH
(Bay St; lifeguards 10am-5pm; P) The large, horseshoe-shaped Man of War Bay is fringed by a palm-studded yellow-sand beach with good swimming. Roughly in the middle of the beach, you'll find changing facilities (TT$1) and the Suckhole beach bar, adjacent to a swimming area watched over by lifeguards. The pier toward the eastern end is a nice spot for fishing or sunset-watching.

★ERIC DIVING
(788-3550; www.eric-tobago.org; Northside Rd; single dive US$65, snorkeling US$25-40, land tours from TT$60) The not-for-profit Environmental Research Institute Charlotteville is part dive shop, and part research facility dedicated to monitoring the health of Tobago's reefs and ecosystems. As well as PADI training, recreational diving, boat trips to secluded beaches, and snorkeling from the beach or from a boat with a biodiversity slant, it offers land-based nature tours and seasonal trips to see green and hawksbill turtles nesting.

Sleeping

Big Fish GUESTHOUSE $
(683-9723; thebigfishprestigesuite@gmail.com; Bay St; d TT$450;) This row of five rooms above Sharon & Pheb's (p792) restaurant are sparkling clean and meticulously maintained by the owners. Each has a balcony overlooking the bay, and a microwave, fridge and toaster; there's also a communal kitchen at the back. Friendly and with more of a vibrant feel than other Charlotteville accommodations options.

Man-O-War Bay Cottages CABIN $
(660-4327; www.man-o-warbaycottages.com; Campbleton Rd; 1-/3-bed cottages US$65/120; P) Plotted in a little botanical garden, with lots of tropical trees, ferns and flowering plants, these 10 simple cottages with kitchens and generous outdoor decks are very basic and a little rough round the edges, but have a fantastic location, open to the breeze and sounds of the surf. You'll find them beachside, about five minutes' walk south of the village.

Charlotte Villas APARTMENT $$
(660-5919; www.charlottevilla.com; Northside Rd; 1-/2-bed apt US$80/160; P) Close to the junction of Windward Rd and Bay St, in a pretty garden set just back from the inland side of the road (and within steps of the Man of War Bay beach facility), these three fully equipped, high-ceiling apartments are spacious, simple and relaxing, with verandas and tons of natural light flooding in.

Eating

G's CARIBBEAN $
(Bay St; mains from TT$50; 11am-9pm) This hole-in-the-wall eatery has a breezy seaside patio for enjoying simple, inexpensive meals of fish or chicken and chips, and more elaborate plates with all the local trimmings. Opening hours can be erratic.

★ Suckhole CARIBBEAN **$$**
(☎288-5820; Man of War Bay Beach, off Bay St; mains TT$80-180; ⏰10am-6pm Tue-Sun, lunch 11:30am-2pm) Right on the beach, with tables overlooking Man of War Bay, this enigmatically named place is a great lunch option, serving up burgers and huge portions of fried fish, ribs, chicken and shrimp. Great service and a knockout rum punch, too. Get there early as tables tend to fill up fast, especially at weekends.

★ Sharon & Pheb's CARIBBEAN **$$**
(☎660-5717; Bay St; mains TT$70-85; ⏰11:30am-4pm & 6-9pm; 👪) Doing great things with fresh fish, shrimp, beef, chicken and vegetables, chef Sharon cooks up delicious local cuisine, served up at tables on a covered veranda overlooking the town and the bay. Often open when other places are closed, and also a nice spot for drinks.

ℹ Getting There & Away

Most visitors get to Charlotteville in a rental car, as maxi-taxis and buses are sporadic. A taxi from Crown Point costs around TT$450.

UNDERSTAND TRINIDAD & TOBAGO

History

Early History

Amerindians were Trinidad's sole inhabitants until 1498, when Columbus arrived and christened the island La Isla de la Trinidad, for the Holy Trinity.

Initially, gold-hungry Spain gave only scant attention to Trinidad, which lacked precious minerals, but in 1592 a Spanish capital was finally established at San José, just east of present-day Port of Spain, and enslavement of the Amerindian population began in earnest. French planters descended en masse to assist the Spanish with development of the island, and enslaved West Africans were brought in to supplement the labor forces toiling on tobacco and cocoa plantations.

British forces took the island from the Spanish in 1797. With the abolishment of slavery in 1834, enslaved West Africans abandoned plantations; this prompted the British to bring in thousands of indentured workers, mostly from India, to labor in the cane fields and service the colony. The indentured-labor system remained in place for over 100 years.

Tobago's early history is a separate story. Also sighted by Columbus and claimed by Spain, it wasn't colonized until 1628, when Charles I of England decided to charter the island to the Earl of Pembroke. In response, a handful of nations took an immediate interest in colonizing Tobago.

During the 17th century Tobago changed hands numerous times as the English, French, Dutch and even Courlanders (present-day Latvians) wrestled for control. In 1704 it was declared a neutral territory, which left room for pirates to use the island as a base for raiding ships in the Caribbean. The British established a colonial administration in 1763, and within two decades slave labor established the island's sugar, cotton and indigo plantations.

Tobago's plantation economy wilted after the abolition of slavery, but sugar and rum production continued until 1884, when the London firm that controlled finances for the island's plantations went bankrupt. Plantation owners quickly sold or abandoned their land, leaving the economy in a shambles.

From Colony to Republic

In 1889 Tobago joined Trinidad as a British Crown Colony. Even though Trinidad and Tobago's demand for greater autonomy grew and anticolonial sentiment ripened, the British didn't pay attention until 1956, when the People's National Movement (PNM), led by Oxford-educated Dr Eric Williams, took measures to institute self-government. Independence was granted in 1962, and the country became a republic of the Commonwealth in 1976.

Frustration with the leftover colonial structure led to the Black Power movement, which created a political crisis and an army mutiny, but ultimately strengthened national identity. Bankrupt and without prospects, the country's luck changed in 1970 with the discovery of oil, which brought instant wealth and prosperity. During the 1980s, when oil prices plummeted, a recession hit and political unrest ensued. Accusations of corruption and complaints from an underrepresented Indian community led to the PNM's defeat in 1986 by the National Alliance for Reconstruction (NAR).

Corruption blossomed in a judicial system congested with drugs-related trials (the country is a stopover for the South American drug trade). In July 1990 members of a minority Muslim group attempted a coup, stormed parliament and took 45 hostages, including Prime Minister ANR Robinson. Though the coup failed, it undermined the government, and the PNM returned to power.

A Changing Political Landscape

Vast petroleum and natural gas reserves discovered in the late 1990s helped stabilize the economy. In 1995 Basdeo Panday of the United National Congress (UNC) beat PNM Patrick Manning in a controversial election, seating the first prime minister of Indian descent. A stalemated political process saw Manning win the 2002 and 2007 elections. With his popularity failing amid a slew of corruption scandals, Manning called an early election in 2010 and was trounced by the People's Partnership (PP), a coalition of the UNC and Congress of the People (COP) parties led by Kamla Persad-Bissessar, who became the republic's first female prime minister.

People & Culture

Of the country's 1.3 million inhabitants, some 60,000 live on Tobago. Trinidad has one of the most ethnically diverse populations in the Caribbean, a legacy of its checkered colonial history. The majority are of Indian (37.6%) and African (36.3%) descent; 24.4% are of mixed heritage, and there are also notable European, Chinese, Syrian and Lebanese communities, while a few hundred descendants of the Amerindian First Peoples live in the Arima area.

Trinidad and Tobago is most definitely not a secular republic: some 30% of its citizens are Protestant, from Anglicans and Methodists to Presbyterians and Pentecostals, and 21.5% Roman Catholic. Another 18% are Hindu, 5% are Muslim, and there are also followers of African syncretic faiths such as the Spiritual Baptists (5.7%) and Orisha (0.1%).

Cricket

Introduced by the British in the 19th century, cricket isn't just a sport in Trinidad and Tobago, it's a cultural obsession. International cricket legend Brian Lara – the 'Prince of Port of Spain' – hails from Trinidad and is one of the country's best-loved icons. And despite their failing fortunes, the arrival of the West Indies team for a test match still sees everything grinding to a halt as people stick to their TVs to capture the action.

The main venue is the **Queen's Park Oval** (☎622-2295; www.qpcc.com; 94 Tragarete Rd, St Clair; 👪), home to the Queen's Park Cricket Club, a few blocks west of the Queen's Park Savannah in Port of Spain. Originally built in 1896, with the northern hills as a spectacular backdrop, it's the site of both regional and international matches and holds 25,000 spectators who pack out the stands and create a party atmosphere at one-day tournaments or test matches. It also has a small museum dedicated to cricket heritage; call to arrange a visit.

Landscape & Wildlife

Formerly part of the South American mainland, Trinidad and Tobago have a rich natural environment that's quite different from the rest of the Caribbean. Lush rainforests harbor a huge variety of plants and animals, as well as spectacular birds, while the coral reefs around Tobago, fed by nutrient-rich currents from the Orinoco River, are some of the Caribbean's best.

AMERINDIAN LEGACY

Arima is home to a small First Peoples community, who still follow some traditional customs of their Carib ancestors. In the center of town, you can take a look at a few interesting displays at the **Santa Rosa Community Centre** (☎664-1897; www.facebook.com/santarosafirstpeoplescommunity; 7 Paul Mitchell St, Arima), where guides also relate the history of Arima's First Peoples and their efforts to establish a heritage village and living museum on land granted by the government in the hills north of town. Just west of Arima, the small and rather dusty **Amerindian Museum** (☎645-1203; Eastern Main Rd; ⏲8am-6pm; P 👪) FREE at Cleaver Woods displays some artifacts. The First Peoples' shaman **Cristo Adonis** (☎488-8539; tours from US$50) can show you around or take you on an educational hike to learn about the medicinal plants and spirituality of the Caribs in Trinidad.

The Land

Boot-shaped Trinidad was once part of the South American mainland. Over time a channel developed, separating Trinidad from present-day Venezuela. The connection to South America is noticeable in Trinidad's Northern Range, a continuation of the Andes, and in its oil and gas reserves, concentrated in southwestern Trinidad.

The Northern Range spreads east to west, forming a scenic backdrop to Port of Spain.

MUSIC IN TRINIDAD & TOBAGO

Stop for a moment on the streets of Trinidad and Tobago and listen. You'll likely hear the up-tempo beat of soca playing on a maxi-taxi radio, or the sound of steel drums drifting out from a panyard. Often festive, sometimes political or melancholy, music digs deep into the emotion of island life.

Although Carnival happens in February, there's always plenty of great live music, especially in the months leading up to Carnival.

Calypso

A medium for political and social satire, calypso hearkens back to the days when enslaved Africans – prohibited from talking whilst toiling on the plantations – would sing in patois, sharing gossip and news while mocking their colonial masters. Today, risqué lyrics, pointed social commentary and verbal wordplay are still the order of the day. Mighty Sparrow, long acknowledged the king of calypso, has voiced popular concerns and social consciousness since the 1950s, as did his contemporary, the late, great 'Grandmaster,' Lord Kitchener. Another famous calypsonian, David Rudder, helped revive the musical form in the mid-1980s by adding experimental rhythms, unearthing both the cultural importance and flexibility of calypso. Others to look out for include the inimitable Calypso Rose, whose international collaborations with acts like Manu Chao have brought worldwide success and an appearance at 2019's Coachella festival two weeks before her 79th birthday; and the great Winston 'Shadow' Bailey, who died in 2018 but whose distinctive voice still sings out on T&T's airwaves.

Chutney

This fast-paced, rhythmic music beloved by Indian Trinis is accompanied by the *dholak* (Northern Indian folk drum) and the *dhantal* (a metal rod played with a metal striker). It's a fusion of classical Hindu music with more contemporary soca, and can't fail to get you wiggling your hips; lyrics tend toward the lighthearted, often focusing on double entendres or the joys of rum-drinking. Notable stars include Rikki Jai and Ravi B alongside hot new acts like GI.

Soca

The energetic offspring of calypso, soca was born in the 1970s, and uses the same basic beat but speeds things up, creating danceable rhythms that perfectly accompany the Carnival season. Though soca is yet to break out internationally in the way of Jamaican dancehall, its biggest stars have collaborated with many international names, from Diplo to Pitbull, and many recent hits bring in elements of reggae, afrobeats and pop. Machel Montano is the reigning king of soca; other big names include speedy lyricist Bunji Garlin, Fay-Ann Lyons, Kes the Band, Destra, Nailah Blackman and Nessa Preppy.

Steel Pan

Rhythm and percussion are the beating heart behind Carnival. Traditionally percussionists banged together bamboo cut in various lengths, or simply drummed on whatever they could – the road, sides of buildings, their knees. When African drums were banned during WWII, drummers turned to biscuit tins and then oil drums discarded by US troops, which were shaped and tuned to produce a brand-new instrument. Today, steel pans come in a variety of sizes, each producing a unique note. Heard together, they become a cascading waterfall of sound. During Carnival, some bands are transported on flatbed trucks along the parade route. All bands aim to win Panorama, the national competition that runs throughout Carnival season.

BIRDWATCHING

Trinidad and Tobago are excluded from many Caribbean birding books because of the sheer magnitude of additional species here – about 480 in total. Torn from Venezuela, these islands share the diversity of the South American mainland in their swamps, rainforests, ocean islets, lowland forests and savannahs, and the birdwatching is some of the best in the Caribbean.

For references, try *A Guide to the Birds of Trinidad and Tobago* by Richard Ffrench, which has good descriptions but limited plates; or *Birds of Trinidad and Tobago* by Martyn Kenefick, Robin Restall and Floyd Hayes, newly updated in 2019.

The best birding spots in Trinidad are Asa Wright Nature Centre (p773), Caroni Bird Sanctuary (p776), **Yerette** (☎663-2623; www.yerettett.com; 88 Valley View, Maracas–St Joseph Valley; tours US$25-45; ⏲tours 8am, 11am & 3pm; 👪), Nariva Swamp (p775) and Mt St Benedict (p770). In Tobago: Little Tobago (p790) and Tobago Forest Reserve (p787).

The rest of the island is given to plains, undulating hills and mangrove swamps. Trinidad's numerous rivers include the 50km Ortoire River, and the 40km Caroni River dumping into the Caroni Swamp.

Tobago, 19km northeast of Trinidad, has a central range of hills that reaches almost 610m at its highest point. Deep, fertile valleys run from the ridge down toward the coast, which is fringed with bays and beaches.

Wildlife

Because of its proximity to the South American continent, Trinidad and Tobago has the widest variety of plant and animal life in the Caribbean: some 480 species of birds, 600 species of butterfly, 70 kinds of reptiles and 100 types of mammals, including red howler monkeys, anteaters, ocelots, agouti and armadillos.

Plant life is equally diverse, with more than 700 orchid species and 1600 other types of flowering plants. Both islands have luxuriant rainforests, and Trinidad also features elfin forests, savannahs and both freshwater and brackish mangrove swamps.

Environmental Issues

Water pollution is a huge environmental concern on Trinidad and Tobago. Agricultural chemicals, industrial waste and raw sewage seep into groundwater and eventually the ocean. Reef damage is due mostly to pollution, as well as damage from poorly placed anchors or careless snorkelers.

Quarrying (both legal and illegal) and unsustainable development are rampant in this ecodestination. Deforestation and soil erosion are direct results. Sand erosion is a special concern on the northeast coast of Trinidad, where leatherback turtles lay eggs.

So-called 'wild meat' such as agouti, deer, wild hog, armadillo and iguana is a hugely popular delicacy in Trinidad and Tobago, and though hunting is only officially allowed during the October to February open season, rampant unregulated hunting has had a devastating effect on the local animal population.

The Environmental Management Authority (www.ema.co.tt) is charged with monitoring environmental issues, but as in other developing countries, the pressure of 'progress' trumps preservation. Environment Tobago (www.environmenttobago.net) is an informative resource about issues facing Tobago, while Papa Bois Conservation (www.facebook.com/papaboisconservation) is a Trinidad-based environmental NGO.

SURVIVAL GUIDE

Directory A–Z

ACCESSIBLE TRAVEL

With tourist infrastructure already wobbly here, Trinidad and Tobago doesn't have extensive facilities for travelers with disabilities. However, the higher-end hotels and resorts are mostly accessible for those with limited mobility, with lifts and ramps, as are newer public buildings.

Towns and cities can be challenging if you use a wheelchair; dropped kerbs are rare and pavements are often nonexistent.

ACCOMMODATIONS

Both islands have good-value guesthouses and hotels. In Trinidad, these are concentrated in Port of Spain; and in Tobago around Crown Point, with other clusters around Buccoo/Mt Irvine, Castara, Speyside and Charlotteville. Aside from Carnival season in Port of Spain, when rates rise astronomically, Trinidad and Tobago is less

SLEEPING PRICE RANGES

The following prices refer to a double room with bathroom during high season (December to April). A 10% service charge and a 10% room tax (VAT) can add 20% more to your bill. Most advertised accommodations rates include the tax and service charge, but not always.

$ less than US$75

$$ US$75–200

$$$ more than US$200

expensive than elsewhere in the Caribbean, with budget options from US$45 a night.

ACTIVITIES

In addition to the usual beachside fare of swimming, snorkeling and diving, Trinidad and Tobago offer some of the best birdwatching in the Caribbean, especially rich in Trinidad's Northern Range hills, and the chance to watch the entrancing spectacle of giant leatherback turtles laying eggs in the sand.

CHILDREN

Kids of all ages flock with their parents to Tobago's beaches; Mt Irvine Bay Watersports (p785) at Mt Irvine beach has some fun water accessories that kids will love, while Radical Watersports (p781) on Pigeon Point offers kids' packages for all activities. Trinidad's **Skallywag Bay** (☎227-2469; www.skallywagbay.com; Williams Bay; adult TT$160, child TT$60-120, under 2yr free; ⊙11am-7pm Wed-Fri, to 8pm Sat & Sun; 👪) and **Five Islands** (☎612-5275; www.fiveislandswaterpark.com; Chagville Beach, Western Main Rd; nonriders TT$200, riders TT$120-200; ⊙9:30am-10pm Mon-Fri, 10am-10pm Sat & Sun; 👪) adventure parks in Chaguaramas offer lots for kids to do, from climbing and go-karting to gaming machines. During Carnival (p764), Kiddie Mas is a sight not to miss, whatever your age.

- Diapers (nappies), wipes, formula and baby food are available in all large supermarkets.
- Pharmacies stock accessories such as bottles.
- High chairs are available in some tourist-oriented restaurants.
- Nappy-changing facilities are nonexistent.
- Most hotels and many guesthouses can provide infant cots.
- Car-hire companies can provide child seats for a fee.
- Breastfeeding in public isn't common among local women, but if you use a cover-up, you shouldn't encounter any problems.

ELECTRICITY

Electrical current 115/230V, 60Hz; US-style two-pin plug.

EMBASSIES & CONSULATES

Embassies and consulates/high commissions in Port of Spain include the following:

Australia (☎822-5450; www.trinidadandtobago.embassy.gov.au; 18 Herbert St, St Clair; ⊙8am-4:30pm Mon-Fri)

Canada (☎622-6232; www.trinidadandtobago.gc.ca; Maple Bldg, 3-3a Sweet Briar Rd, St Clair; ⊙8-11:30am Mon-Thu)

France (☎232-4808; www.ambafrance-tt.org; 7 Mary St, St Clair; ⊙visits by appt only, phone lines open 9am-noon & 2-5pm Mon-Thu, 9am-1pm Fri)

Germany (☎628-1630; www.port-of-spain.diplo.de; 19 St Clair Ave, St Clair; ⊙8-11:30am Mon-Fri)

Netherlands (☎625-1210; www.netherlandsandyou.nl; Life of Barbados Bldg, 69-71 Edward St; ⊙8am-5pm Mon-Thu, to 2pm Fri)

UK (☎350-0444; www.ukintt.fco.gov.uk; 19 St Clair Ave, St Clair; ⊙9am-4pm Mon-Thu, to 1pm Fri)

US (☎622-6371; https://tt.usembassy.gov; 15 Queen's Park West, Newtown; ⊙by appt only 7:30-11am Mon, Tue, Thu & Fri)

EMERGENCY NUMBERS

Ambulance	☎811
Fire	☎990
Police	☎999

FOOD

The cuisine of Trinidad and Tobago is one of its undoubted highlights, an intoxicating blend of Indian and Creole flavors. Curried crab with dumplings is a Tobago specialty, while goat, duck, chicken, shrimp and veggies are also cooked up in a curry sauce to fill ubiquitous rotis. Fish and seafood are excellent, with kingfish, *mahimahi*, barracuda, carite and redfish such as snapper offered grilled, steamed or fried, and always delightfully seasoned.

Essential Food & Drink

Bake and shark – Seasoned shark steak, topped with salad and local sauces such as tamarind or cilantro-like *chadon beni*, served in a light fried bread; go for kingfish rather than unsustainable shark.

Buljol Saltfish cooked with onion, pepper and tomato, usually served with coconut bake (a flatbread infused with fresh grated coconut).

Callaloo Leaves of the *dasheen* tuber, cooked up with pumpkin, okra, coconut and plenty of seasoning.

Chadon beni Hyped-up relative of cilantro/coriander, this pungent green herb is ubiquitous in Trinbago staple dishes, and is made into a sauce that's slathered on doubles, bake and shark and corn soup.

Carib and Stag The national beers; always served 'beastly' cold.

Choka Breakfast dish of tomato or aubergine (eggplant; called *baigan* or *melongene* in T&T) sautéed with onion, garlic and seasoning pepper; and served with *sada* roti.

Crab and dumplings A messy and delicious Tobago specialty; small whole crabs in a curry sauce, served over thin flour dumplings; also made with conch.

Doubles Curried channa (chickpeas) in a soft fried *bara* bread; laced with spicy sauces.

Peas Local term for beans: usually pigeon, kidney, black-eye or green lentils, stewed with spices and coconut.

Pelau Chicken and pigeon peas cooked up with rice, pumpkin and coconut.

Pholouri Deep-fried chickpea-flour doughballs served with a spicy tamarind-curry dipping sauce.

Provisions Tropical tubers such as yam, *dasheen,* cassava and eddoes, served boiled as a carby side dish; also called ground provisions.

Roti Flatbread wrapped around curried meat and vegetables; the wrapping is called a skin and comes in lots of varieties, from *dhalpouri* (infused with ground split peas) to *buss-up-shut* (literally, 'busted shirt'), a thick, white-flour torn-up skin used to scoop up fillings. *Sada* roti is a plain, thick fried bread served at breakfast time with *choka*.

HEALTH

Trinidad and Tobago's public hospitals are oversubscribed and underfunded, though treatment is free; main facilities are Port of Spain's General Hospital (p767) and Tobago's Scarborough General Hospital (p789). Many locals opt instead for private hospitals such as the St Clair Medical Centre (p767) in Port of Spain, where costs are high – ensure your travel insurance has adequate medical coverage.

INTERNET ACCESS

Free wi-fi is almost always available at hotels and guesthouses throughout T&T, though it can be patchy in rural areas. Many cafes and restaurants, including the many branches of the Rituals (p763) chain, offer free wi-fi for customers, particularly in towns or tourist areas.

LEGAL MATTERS

If you are arrested in Trinidad and Tobago, you have the right to be told what you have been detained for, and do not have to give an oral or written statement unless you choose to. You have the right to speak to and to retain a lawyer to defend you. The police should inform the relevant embassy or consulate (where one exists) when a foreign national is arrested, who can in turn help with finding representation. If contact is not made on your behalf, you have the right to do this yourself.

Possession of drugs, including marijuana, is dealt with harshly here.

EATING PRICE RANGES

The following price indicators relate to the cost of a main meal:

$ less than TT$60

$$ TT$60–160

$$$ more than TT$160

LGBT+ TRAVELERS

Though more progressive than some other Caribbean islands, Trinidad and Tobago as a whole remains pretty closed to the idea of same-sex relationships. Nonetheless, in 2018 activist Jason Jones won a landmark victory in the first step of his legal challenge to T&T's buggery laws, when a judge ruled them unconstitutional. The hope is that these archaic laws will be permanently repealed, but the ruling was a controversial one in this religious and often conservative country. Homophobia remains quite rampant in T&T, and though there is a sizable LGBT+ community, it's not at all visible; being out and expressing affection is not the norm, and may draw negative repercussions, though these tend to be verbal rather than violent.

MONEY

The official currency is the Trinidad and Tobago dollar (TT$), but many goods or services are priced in US$. We quote rates as they are given.

ATMs, dispensing TT$ only, are widespread in towns and tourist areas. Many banks have drive-through ATMs.

Most restaurants, hotels, dive shops, car-rental companies and more established guesthouses accept credit cards. Contactless payment is available at large supermarkets and some service stations.

Exchange Rates

Australia	AS$1	TT$4.72
Canada	C$1	TT$5.18
Euro zone	€1	TT$7.59
Japan	¥100	TT$6.23
New Zealand	NZ$1	TT$4.49
UK	UK£1	TT$8.46
US	US$1	TT$6.76

For current exchange rates, see www.xe.com.

DRINKING WATER

Tap water is heavily chlorinated in Trinidad and Tobago, and tastes better boiled (preferably for 15 minutes) than fresh from the tap. It can still cause upsets for those unused to it, though.

Tipping

Tipping is not part of Trinidad and Tobago culture, though it's increasingly common.

Bars Not expected, but there may be a tip box.

Hotels TT$100 or more for cleaning staff.

Grocery stores TT$5 to TT$10 for shopping packers, and assistance wheeling trolley and packing vehicle.

Restaurants If no service charge, tip 10% to 15%.

Taxis Don't tip maxi-taxis or route-taxis. Not expected, but for decent service tip 10% in private taxis.

PUBLIC HOLIDAYS

Carnival Monday and Tuesday are unofficial holidays, with banks and most businesses closed.

New Year's Day January 1

Spiritual Baptist/Shouter Liberation Day March 30

Good Friday March/April

Easter Monday March/April

Indian Arrival Day May 30

Corpus Christi Ninth Thursday after Easter

Labor Day June 19

Emancipation Day August 1

Independence Day August 31

Republic Day September 24

Divali October, dates vary

Eid ul Fitr (Muslim New Year) Dates vary

Christmas Day December 25

Boxing Day December 26

SAFE TRAVEL

Tobagonians warn of rampant lawlessness in Trinidad, and Trinidadians say crime is increasing in Tobago. While such claims reflect a real crime increase, they tend to exaggerate the dangers of island travel.

- Avoid walking at night on Tobago's beaches and in Port of Spain, particularly downtown.
- Theft can be a problem, especially in downtown Port of Spain and at Carnival fetes; keep an eye on your valuables and don't bring them to the beach.
- The persistent tactics of souvenir hawkers or boat-ride sellers can be annoying. Be firm but polite and you'll usually be left alone.

TELEPHONE

The country's area code is 868. When calling T&T from North America, dial 1-868 plus the local number. From elsewhere dial your country's international access code, plus 868, plus the local number. Within the country, just dial the seven-digit local number.

To make an international call, dial the 011 international access code, followed by the country code for the place you're calling, and then the number, omitting the initial zero if there is one.

Public phones are rarely seen these days and often don't work. Your best bet is to get a local SIM card and use a cell phone.

Cell Phones

The main local provider is **bmobile** (☎824-8788; www.bmobile.co.tt), which offers prepaid SIM cards, compatible with most cell (mobile) phone brands, which you can load with airtime credit in TT$25 to TT$500 denominations; credit is sold at gas stations, supermarkets and lottery outlets. **Digicel** (☎399-9999; www.digicelgroup.com/tt) offers similar options; both providers also offer plans that include mobile data. You can buy SIMs and handsets at the innumerable communications shops and kiosks in malls and town centers throughout the islands; there's also a convenient bmobile kiosk just after the immigration desks in Piarco airport, which can hook you up before you leave the arrivals lounge.

TIME

Trinidad and Tobago is on Atlantic Standard Time (AST): four hours behind GMT/UTC in winter, five hours behind GMT/UTC in summer.

WOMEN TRAVELERS

Women travelers suffer a constant commentary from men, particularly if you are young. This might be anything from kissy noises, hissing or offering to be everything from your protector to your sex slave; expect lots of stares, too, and unasked for assistance when parking a car. Ignore it.

Getting There & Away

AIR

Piarco International Airport (www.tntairports.com; Golden Grove) in Trinidad handles the bulk of international flights; the rest fly into the much smaller **ANR Robinson International Airport** (www.tntairports.com; Crown Point) in Tobago.

A number of international airlines fly to Trinidad and Tobago. Caribbean Airlines (the national carrier) and LIAT are particularly useful for flights from other Caribbean countries and South America.

Caribbean Airlines (☎625-7200; www.caribbean-airlines.com) has flights between Trinidad

PRACTICALITIES

Newspapers There are three daily papers: *Trinidad Express* (www.trinidadexpress.com), *Newsday* (www.newsday.co.tt) and *Trinidad Guardian* (www.guardian.co.tt).

Smoking It's illegal to smoke in enclosed public spaces; most places also prohibit vaping inside premises. E-cigarettes are legal in T&T, but there are limited outlets selling liquids and devices.

Tourist magazines Helpful free magazines found at tourist offices and hotels include *Discover Trinidad & Tobago, Cré Olé* restaurant guide, and the *Ins & Outs of Trinidad & Tobago*.

TV & radio There are two local TV stations: CCN TV6 (channel 5) and CNC3 (channel 3). Cable channels include CNN and BBC World News. About 15 independent radio stations fill the airwaves with a mix of talk and music.

Weights & measures Trinidad and Tobago uses the metric system. Highway signs and car odometers are in kilometers; in Trinidad's Northern Range, you'll still see stone road markers that measure miles.

and Antigua, Barbados, Caracas, Cuba, Grenada, Guyana, Kingston and Montego Bay in Jamaica, Nassau in the Bahamas, St Lucia, Sint Maarten, St Vincent and Suriname.

LIAT (☎1-888-895-5428; www.liat.com) has flights between Trinidad and Antigua, Barbados, Dominica, Grenada, Guadeloupe, Guyana, Martinique, San Juan, St Croix, St Kitts, St Lucia, St Thomas, St Vincent, Sint Maarten and Tortola, though most flights involve a change elsewhere in the Caribbean.

SEA

Cruise Ship

In Trinidad ships dock at the King's Wharf, on Wrightson Rd in Port of Spain, from where you can walk onto Independence Sq and the downtown area. In Tobago, the cruise-ship terminal is adjacent to the ferry terminal in downtown Scarborough.

Yacht

South of the hurricane belt, Trinidad and Tobago is a safe haven for yachties. Chaguaramas in Trinidad has the primary mooring and marina facilities as well as an immigration and customs office. Tobago is an upwind jaunt, but a few yachts moor at Charlotteville, Castara or Scarborough. For more information, contact the **Yacht Services Association of Trinidad and Tobago** (☎634-4938; www.ysatt.com; Power Boats Marina, Western Main Rd).

Getting Around

AIR

Caribbean Airlines operates the 20-minute flight between Trinidad and Tobago (one way US$24); there are around 20 flights each way daily. The checked baggage weight allowance is one piece up to 23kg. While it's wise to book in advance online as tickets often sell out, it is often possible to buy tickets at the airport on the day of departure. Note that flights are often subject to delays and cancellations.

BOAT

Catamaran ferries make the trip between Queen's Wharf in Port of Spain, Trinidad, and the main ferry dock in Scarborough, Tobago; journey time varies between 2½ and four hours depending upon the vessel. It's a cheap, fairly comfortable way to travel, with the added bonus of not having to get all the way to Piarco airport, though the roiling waters of the Dragon's Mouth between northwest Trinidad and Venezuela mean that you're very likely to get seasick: travel-sickness pills are a good idea even if your sea legs are usually very sturdy. The ferries have a bar, cafeteria and outdoor area.

There are two to four departures daily from both islands, in the morning and afternoon. Tickets (adult/child TT$50/25) can be purchased from the Inter-Island Ferry Service (p767); do so well in advance around Christmas, Easter and in Carnival season. Ferries do carry cars, but none of T&T's car-rental companies allow you to take vehicles on board.

BUS

Run by **PTSC** (☎623-2341; www.ptsctt.com; City Gate, South Quay), buses offer travelers an inexpensive way to get around, especially on longer cross-island trips, but can be infrequent and unreliable, especially in Tobago. For shorter distances, travelers are better off taking maxi-taxis or route taxis. Check online for schedules. For bus information, call 623-2341 in Trinidad or 639-2293 in Tobago.

CAR & MOTORCYCLE

Cars drive on the left, and the car's steering wheel is on the right (as in the UK). Your home driver's license is valid for stays of up to three months.

Twisting, narrow roads and fast, horn-happy drivers can make driving on the islands an adventure; in Port of Spain, traffic, complicated roads and poor signage can be challenging. Your best bet is to study a map before you get in the car, take a deep breath and practice Zen-like patience. You will get the hang of it, and you'll find driving much easier if you simply relax a little and follow the flow. Be aware that fellow road users (especially maxi-taxis and route taxis) will stop suddenly to drop off a friend, say 'hi' to a neighbor or pick up a cold drink. Sometimes they'll simply stop, while other times drivers will flick on the hazard lights or wave an arm up and down to signal they are about to do something. Tobago's quiet roads pose much less of a challenge, though some are winding and potholed; you'll need to keep a lookout, too, for roadside-grazing cows and goats.

The (almost universally ignored) speed limit on highways is 80km/h, increased to 100km/h on some sections of Trinidad's highways, and 50km/h on city streets. Gas (petrol) is about TT$5 a liter for regular; pumps are self-service in most gas stations, and you often have to pay first. Road signage is good on the highways, less so in rural areas. The Waze app (www.waze.com) works well in T&T, though you'll need mobile data to use it.

TAXI

Regular taxis are readily available at the airports, cruise-ship and ferry terminals and at hotels. All are unmetered but follow rates established by the government; hotel desks and airport tourist offices have a list of fares, and there are boards detailing fares at the arrivals areas of the airports in Trinidad and Tobago. Make sure to establish the rate before riding off, and note that rates increase between 10pm and 6am.

Maxi-Taxi

Maxi-taxis are 12- to 25-passenger minibuses that travel along a fixed route within a specific zone. They're color-coded by route, run from the wee hours till late evening, are very cheap and are heavily used by locals. Rides cost about TT$5 to TT$15, depending on how far you go. You can flag a maxi at any point along its route, or hop on at the appropriate taxi stand. Keep in mind that, due to their frequent stops, maxi-taxis can take a long time to get from A to B, though in Trinidad maxis that take the Priority Bus Route can be pretty speedy.

On Trinidad, many maxi-taxis operate out of the maxi-taxi terminal adjacent to City Gate in Port of Spain. On Tobago, all maxis have a blue band, though services are a lot less frequent than in Trinidad.

For information about maxi-taxi routes, contact **Trinidad & Tobago Unified Maxi Taxi Association** (☎ 623-2947)

Route Taxi

Route taxis are shared cars that travel along a prescribed route and can drop you anywhere along the way. They look like regular cars, except that license plates usually start with an 'H' (for 'hire'); many private (P-reg) cars also run as route taxis. Route taxis run shorter set routes than maxis, mostly within towns and cities; fares start at about TT$5.

Turks & Caicos

☎649 / POP 31,500

Includes ➡

Best Places to Eat

- ➡ Coyaba (p809)
- ➡ Grace's Cottage (p809)
- ➡ Coco Bistro (p809)
- ➡ Bird Cage Bar & Grill (p816)
- ➡ Da Conch Shack (p808)
- ➡ Provo Fish Fry (p808)

Best Places to Stay

- ➡ Sibonné Beach Hotel (p807)
- ➡ Dragon Cay Resort (p812)
- ➡ COMO Parrot Cay (p811)
- ➡ Osprey Beach Hotel (p814)
- ➡ Salt Raker Inn (p814)

Why Go?

The Turks and Caicos Islands (TCI), hiding at the southern tip of the Bahamian Archipelago, elude most travelers' radars. Yet this sparsely populated string of low sand cays boasts some of the world's most spectacular coral reefs and beaches, and has built itself into a true luxury-tourism destination. The pace of life is easygoing, the local welcome genuine and the diving truly out of this world.

Providenciales is the bustling epicenter of all this, but beyond its flash beaches and world-class resorts, you'll find local festivals, jungle-wrapped ruins, perfect seaside bars and even traces of Europe's early journeys to the Americas.

Venture to the less populated islands, and you'll be enchanted by colorful postcards of fading colonial glories, gobsmacked by the annual migration of thousands of humpback whales, spoiled with your pick of deserted beaches and all but forced to abandon the pace of modern life.

When to Go

Dec–Apr High season, with warm, dry and settled weather coinciding with the annual humpback migration.

Apr–Jul Spiny lobster is prohibited on menus; college students converge for Spring Break early April.

Jun–Nov Hurricane season, with the severest storms typically from August to October.

Turks & Caicos Highlights

1. **Grace Bay Beach** (p803) Counting the luxury resorts fronting this legendary stretch of sand.
2. **Grand Turk** (p813) Wandering the salt-gritted streets of the islands' colonial heyday and diving the renowned 'Wall.'
3. **Iguana Island** (p811) Getting up close to the largest thriving population of the rock iguana.
4. **Whale-watching** (p815) Gasping at cetaceans from the comfort of a beachfront bar on Grand Turk.
5. **Mudjin Harbor** (p812) Feeling the might of the Atlantic batter the reef wall just off this stunning beach.
6. **Salt Cay** (p816) Relaxing on deserted North Bay beach and watching whales pass by.
7. **Provo Fish Fry** (p808) Joining the locals for conch salad, rum punch and music.

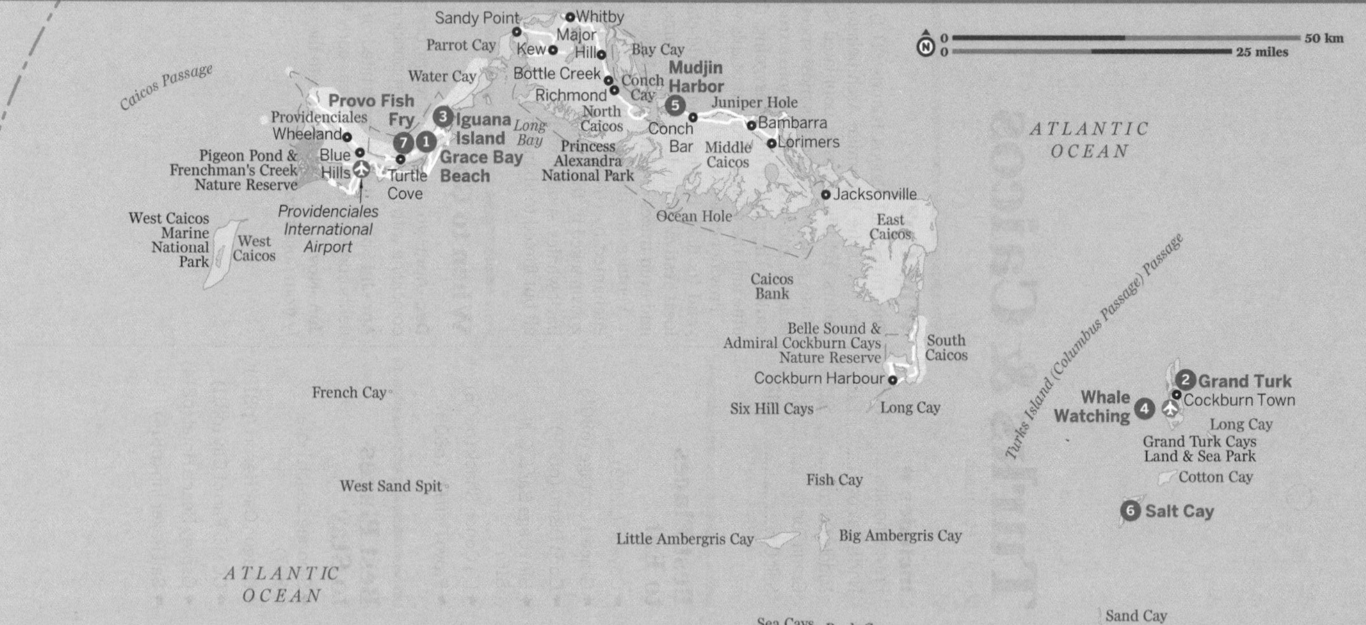

CAICOS ISLANDS

The fan of islands that forms the main landmass of this nation are the Caicos Islands, which range from the nearly uninhabited East Caicos to the condo-sprouting Providenciales.

Getting There & Away

The main point of entry for the Caicos Islands and the entire country is Providenciales International Airport (p810). For those arriving by boat, six of TCI's seven ports of entry are in the Caicos Islands: five on Provo, and one on South Caicos.

Getting Around

From Provo there are daily connecting flights to South Caicos Airport, but no regular, scheduled flights to North and Middle Caicos. You're reliant on the regular ferry, a tour or private charter to reach these islands, although once on North Caicos you can drive to Middle Caicos across a 1.6km causeway, built in 2007, almost immediately damaged by Hurricane Hanna, then repaired in 2014 and 2015. It survived the 2017 hurricanes intact.

The passenger-only TCI Ferry (p812) runs between Walkin Marina (off Leeward Hwy) on the leeward (west) side of Providenciales to Sandy Point Marina on North Caicos. There are five services a day, Monday to Saturday, and three on Sundays and public holidays; the 30-minute journey costs US$55 return for adults and US$30 for children. The TCI Ferry to South Caicos runs to the government dock two to three times a week. It takes 90 minutes and costs US$110/70 return for adults/children.

Providenciales

Providenciales, or Provo as it's locally and universally known, is the commercial and touristic capital of Turks and Caicos. By far the busiest and most populated of the islands, it's home to the country's major international airport and some relatively rampant development, from stunning all-inclusive resorts to rows of condos and the concrete shells of ill-considered ventures that never got off the ground. Its greatest attractions are kilometers of beautiful white-sand beaches, and the halo of reef that blooms in every direction. With that nature comes opportunities for diving, sailing, kitesurfing or just bumming on the beach.

Everything is modern and commercial because it's mostly new. There's no old town – just a few decades ago, this was all salt flats.

Sights

Grace Bay Beach BEACH

Several kilometers long – the frequently boasted '12 miles' (19km) only applies if you measure the entire northern coast of Provo, which is, admittedly, one unbroken beach – this world-famous stretch of coast is powdered with white sand and it's close enough to the reef wall to see the Atlantic breakers. Although it's studded with hotels and resorts, its sheer size means that finding your own square of paradise is not difficult.

Turk's Head Brewery BREWERY

(941-3637; https://turksheadbrewery.tc; 52 Universal Dr, Cooper Jack Bay Settlement; tour per person US$15; tap room 9am-5pm Mon-Fri, to 2pm Sat, tours 11am, 1pm & 3pm Mon-Fri, noon Sat) TCI's only brewery produces six excellent varieties, including the strong IPA 'Down Da Road' and a seasonal stout. Brewery tours are a popular way to see the process and taste a paddle of beers, but you can also visit the tap room and sample the brews outside tour times.

Long Bay Beach BEACH

This windy, less frequented beach on Provo's southern shore is ideal for kitesurfing.

Chalk Sound National Park NATIONAL PARK

Chalk Sound sums up Provo: a startlingly turquoise 5km lagoon studded with tiny cays sheltering Turks and Caicos rock iguanas, but marred by less-than-scenic development. It can be a delightful place to kayak (no powered craft are allowed) in the company of bonefish, barracuda, rays and lemon sharks, but isn't easy to access, as there are no launching places.

Head to Las Brisas Restaurant at **Neptune Villas** (www.neptunevillastci.com) to rent kayaks, paddleboards and canoes (US$35 for one hour and US$10 additional hours) or take a pontoon boat tour; it's ideally located at the southern end of Chalk Sound.

Village at Grace Bay Museum MUSEUM

(247-2161; www.tcmuseum.org; off Grace Bay Rd; US$10; tours 9:15am, 10:15am, 11:15am & 12:5pm Mon-Fri) The Providenciales location of the Turks & Caicos National Museum is located in the Village at Grace Bay development and features some heritage buildings and displays that can be seen on a one-hour guided tour.

Providenciales

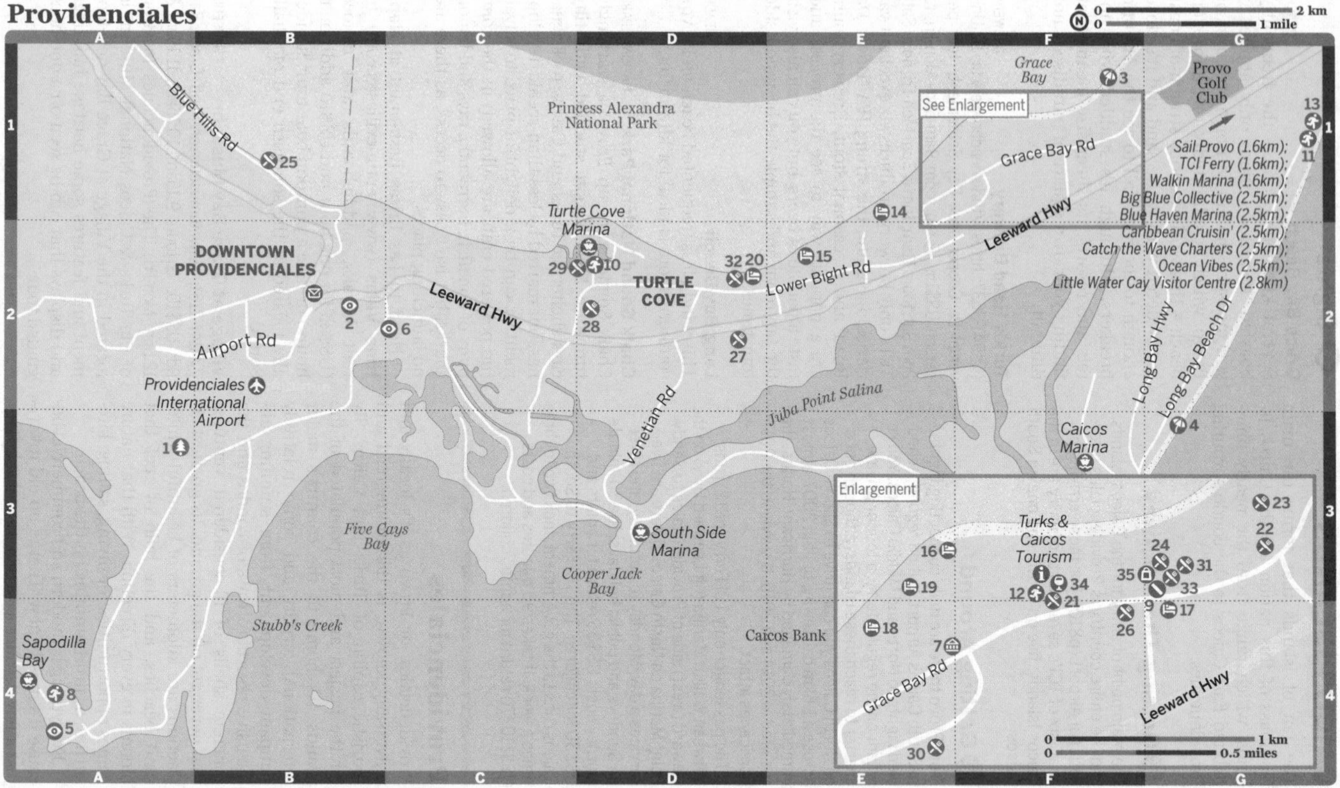

0 2 km
0 1 mile

Princess Alexandra National Park
Grace Bay
Provo Golf Club
See Enlargement
Grace Bay Rd
Leeward Hwy
Sail Provo (1.6km); TCI Ferry (1.6km); Walkin Marina (1.6km); Big Blue Collective (2.5km); Blue Haven Marina (2.5km); Caribbean Cruisin' (2.5km); Catch the Wave Charters (2.5km); Ocean Vibes (2.5km); Little Water Cay Visitor Centre (2.8km)
Blue Hills Rd
DOWNTOWN PROVIDENCIALES
Turtle Cove Marina
TURTLE COVE
Lower Bight Rd
Airport Rd
Providenciales International Airport
Venetian Rd
Juba Point Salina
Long Bay Hwy
Long Bay Beach Dr
Caicos Marina
South Side Marina
Five Cays Bay
Cooper Jack Bay
Stubb's Creek
Sapodilla Bay
Caicos Bank

Enlargement
Turks & Caicos Tourism
Grace Bay Rd
Leeward Hwy
0 1 km
0 0.5 miles

Providenciales

Sapodilla Hill HISTORIC SITE

TCI's long maritime history is etched into the limestone on Sapodilla Hill, where mariners have commemorated landfall by carving names, dates and pictures into the rock since the 1650s. Access to the hill is unsignposted: the trail starts near the entrance to Sul Mare Villas.

Cheshire Hall PLANTATION

(941-5710; Leeward Hwy; entry & tour US$10; 8:30am-4:30pm Mon-Fri;) Built in the late 1700s by a British Loyalist planter displaced by the American Revolution, Cheshire Hall was once the most important site on Provo, the hub of a 2023-acre cotton plantation. Now run by the National Trust, the remaining 15 or so buildings (including the Great House and kitchen) aren't in the best state of repair. Admission includes a 30-minute tour (8:30am to 11:30am and 2:30pm to 4pm).

Activities

Potcake Place VOLUNTEERING

(231-1010; www.potcakeplace.com; Salt Mills Plaza, off Grace Bay Rd; 10am-1pm & 2-4pm Mon-Sat;) This unique charity cares for Provo's many ownerless dogs (a small island breed named 'potcakes' for the practice of feeding them with the crust at the bottom of the rice pot). Visitors can help out, donate, take puppies for socialization walks on the beach (10am Monday to Saturday), and even adopt dogs they take a particular shine to.

Ocean Vibes WHALE WATCHING

(441-5938; www.oceanvibes.com; 3hr tour US$196) This Provo-based outfit runs three-hour whale-watching tours from Grand Turk in season (January to March). Tours are on a 48ft catamaran with a marine biologist on hand to explain whale behavior. They leave from just north of the cruise center.

Caicos Cyclery CYCLING

(431-6890, 941-7544; www.caicoscyclery.com; Salt Mills Plaza, Grace Bay Rd; 10am-6pm Oct-Aug, hours vary Sep) The place to go if you want to pedal around Grace Bay on something better than a clunky cruiser. Caicos Cyclery has high-quality road bikes, mountain bikes and hybrids, ideal if you want to take a bike over to North and Middle Caicos for some traffic-free touring. Cruisers/road bikes are US$25/80 per day, with discounts for three or more days.

After-hours returns can be made at the adjoining Big Al's Island Grill (p808).

Sky Pilot Parasail ADVENTURE SPORTS

(333-3000; http://skypilotparasailing.com; 9am-5pm) For US$85 per person (or US$65 for direct bookings, from 9am to 10am and 4pm to 5pm) this outfit will pick you up from your Provo hotel, strap you into a tandem parasail and drag you into the skies above Grace Bay at high speed.

LOCAL KNOWLEDGE

JOJO: A NATIONAL TREASURE

Since the mid 1980s, a 7ft bottlenose male dolphin called JoJo has cruised the waters off Provo and North Caicos. When he first appeared, he was shy and limited his human contact to following or playing in the bow waves of boats. He soon turned gregarious, however, and has become an active participant whenever people are in the water.

A local campaign in the 1990s resulted in JoJo being declared a national treasure by the Ministry of Natural Resources and he is protected by local conservationists, but his tendency to follow boats has inevitably resulted in propeller injuries.

Like any wild dolphin, JoJo interprets attempts to touch him as an aggressive act and will react to defend himself, so please bear this in mind if you're lucky enough to experience his playfulness and companionship.

Diving & Snorkeling

All the dive operators offer a range of dive and snorkel options, from introductory 'discovery' or 'resort' courses to Professional Association of Diving Instructors (PADI) certification (US$300 to US$800).

Most offer free hotel pickup and drop-offs. Dive sites include **Grace Bay**, **Pine Cay** and the famous, precipitous drop-off at **Northwest Point**. The reefs of North, Middle and West Caicos are also within striking distance, although you'll need a private charter to reach the stunning sites around South Caicos.

Provo Turtle Divers DIVING
(946-4232; www.provoturtledivers.com; Turtle Cove Marina; 2-tank dive US$160; 8am-5pm Mon-Sat) Going strong since the 1980s, this respected outfit offers two-tank and night dives, plus PADI courses from US$640.

Dive Provo DIVING
(946-5040; www.diveprovo.com; Ports of Call Plaza, Grace Bay Rd; 8am-5pm) Has one-/two-tank dives (US$83/165) at sites around the island, plus GoPro and camera rental.

Water Sports

A reef-sheltered shoreline combined with the steady trade winds that buffet the coastline of the Turks and Caicos between November and May make for a perfect combination for kitesurfing. An amalgam of stunt kite flying, wakeboarding and windsurfing, this sport has exploded in recent years and this is one of the top places in the Caribbean to do it. The warm TCI waters, especially those of Long Bay on Provo's southern shore, are firmly on the radar of the sport's elite – but don't be put off, it's also a great place to learn.

★**Big Blue Collective** WATER SPORTS
(946-5034; https://bigbluecollective.com; Leeward Marina; 7:30am-5:30pm;) Living by a sincere, ecofriendly ethos that's refreshing to see in TCI, Big Blue does it all: stand-up paddleboarding, kayaking, diving, snorkeling, kiteboarding, cultural and historic tours to North and Middle Caicos, and whale-watching in season. The staff is excellent, their equipment and knowledge top-notch.

Big Blue activities can also be booked through **Blue Turks & Caicos** (941-8670; Grace Bay Rd, Salt Mills Plaza; 9am-6pm Mon-Sat).

Turks & Caicos Kiteboarding KITESURFING
(442-2423; www.tckiteboarding.com; Long Bay Hills) An experienced team of instructors will get you up on Long Bay Beach. Beginner lessons start at US$392 for around three hours, rentals at US$230 per day and guided kite adventures at around US$112 per person per hour.

KiteProvo WATER SPORTS
(242-2927; http://kiteprovo.com; Long Bay Beach, Shore Club beach access; 8am-7pm) Operating on Long Bay Beach, one of the acknowledged epicenters of the sport, KiteProvo has multilingual instructors offering two-hour private lessons at US$175 per hour.

Sailing & Boat Tours

In many ways a sailor's paradise, the waters around Provo can nonetheless be treacherous, with shallow channels, sand banks and coral heads to negotiate. Boats can be chartered from the Blue Haven (p822), Turtle Cove (p822) and Walkin (p803) marinas, and most will be professionally captained to ensure you don't come unstuck.

Ocean Vibes BOATING
(242-4444; www.oceanvibes.com; Blue Haven Marina) This locally owned and run operation specializes in catamaran cruises and snorkeling adventures. Chartering a 14.5m catamaran to take up to 12 people on a skippered

half-day adventure costs around US$1500, but there are also snorkeling trips (US$120) and two-hour sunset cruises (US$120).

Undersea Explorer BOATING
(432-0006; www.caicostours.com; Turtle Cove Marina; adult/child US$70/60; hourly from low tide 10am/11am to 5pm Mon-Sat;) This moving underwater observatory, a big hit with kids and those with a phobia of getting wet, is a cool way to see three different sections of the reef. Pickup/drop-off at any hotel in Grace Bay. It also does Mermaid Adventure (with a real mermaid!) for kids.

Sail Provo BOATING
(946-4783; http://sailprovotci.com; Walkin Marina, Leeward Going Through;) There are many outfits and individual vessels keen to take you sailing around the island; Sail Provo is one of the better ones. Its sleek catamaran, *Arielle II*, plies the waters between Leeward Going Through, Iguana Island (and other cays) and the reef. Half-day excursions with snorkeling and lunch start at US$84/56 per adult/child, and private charters at US$875.

Fishing

The waters around Provo are noted gamefishing territory, with the 2000m deep just 15 minutes from shore promising tuna, wahoo, dorado and even sailfish and marlin. Bonefishing among the mangroves is another popular pastime for anglers in TCI. Boat charters and trips can be arranged from Blue Haven and Turtle Cove Marinas.

Grand Slam Charters FISHING
(231-4420; http://gsfishing.com; Lower Bight Rd, Turtle Cove Marina) Offers the biggest charter boat in Turks and Caicos for some serious deep-sea fishing. Group charters start at US$400 per person.

DB Tours Bonefishing Charters FISHING
(242-4327; www.turksandcaicosbonefishing.com; Harbour Club Villas & Marina; departures 7:30am & noon) Experienced local fisherman Captain Darrin takes anglers into the mangroves of Provo and nearby cays to hunt for the elusive bonefish. Catches of 4lb to 8lb are not uncommon, and the inedible creature is released. Half-/full-day charter is US$672/1064.

Catch the Wave Charters FISHING
(941-3047; www.catchthewavecharter.com; Blue Haven Resort, Marina Rd; 7:30am-5:30pm) Run by a North Caicos fisherman with decades of experience fishing on the reef, in the mangroves and in the deep sea, Catch the Wave has five charter boats of varying sizes. Bottom/deep-sea fishing costs US$1275/1475 per half-day, and the boats generally fit four fishers. They also offer island cruises, including a reggae-soca cruise on Wednesdays.

Sleeping

Most of Provo's places to stay are right on Grace Bay Beach, either condo-style, or resorts, all with a high price tag. Airbnb and similar services are starting to pop up – dig a little deeper online to find rooms to rent under US$150.

★ **Sibonné Beach Hotel** HOTEL $
(946-5547; www.sibonne.com; Grace Bay; d US$215-355, apt US$475;) Deservedly popular and occupying a divine stretch of sand on Grace Bay, Sibonné is a real anti-resort. It has a small pool and beachfront restaurant, and the vibe is very mellow – a steal at this price. The two cheapest rooms are small but the rest of the choices are roomy and comfy.

Ports of Call Resort RESORT $$
(946-8888; www.portsofcallresort.com; Grace Bay Rd, Grace Bay; d US$339-379;) If you're searching for an affordable resort and can accept that it isn't beachfront, this is a good central option. Clean and spacious rooms stack in three stories above the pool and chilled poolside bar. Nothing too special, but a reasonable choice if you're here to dive, lie on the beach (free shuttle) or not liquidate your finances.

★ **Wymara Resort Turks & Caicos** RESORT $$$
(844-5986; https://wymararesortandvillas.com; Lower Bight Rd, Grace Bay Beach; r from US$895; P) One of the slickest resorts along Grace Bay Beach, the Wymara brings the clean lines and minimalist chic of a big-city boutique to Provo. Its centerpiece is a vast palm-fringed infinity pool, while the rooms boast top-quality beds, 400-thread-count bedding and all the conveniences of life. The on-site restaurant, Stelle, is one of the best on the island.

Beaches RESORT $$$
(242-2437; www.beaches.com; Lower Bight Rd; d from US$1750; P) This all-inclusive

behemoth is a world unto itself, with four distinct 'villages' (the Caribbean, France, Italy and Key West), eight pools, a water park, 15 bars and 21 restaurants. Every conceivable diversion is available – diving, lawn chess, kids camp, even a DJ academy – making it ideal for a self-contained family vacation.

Day passes are available to nonguests who'd like to sample Beaches' myriad luxuries but the high price of US$520/180 adult/child (10am to 6pm) discourages most.

Point Grace BOUTIQUE HOTEL **$$$**
(941-7743; http://pointgrace.com; off Grace Bay Rd, Point Grace; d from US$560;) The 28 suites and penthouses at this tasteful beachfront hotel are sophisticated and luxurious, creating a retro fantasy of the colonial-era British estate (with far better plumbing). Units come in all sizes, amenities include a pool and thalassotherapy spa, and the sweet on-site restaurant, Grace's Cottage, is a wonderful place to wine and dine.

Caribique Villa Rentals ACCOMMODATIONS SERVICES **$$$**
(US/Canada toll-free 1-800-480-0941; www.caribiquevillarentals.com; villas from US$290) This rental service is a good place to find a self-catering villa in Provo.

Coral Gardens RESORT **$$$**
(941-3713; www.coralgardens.com; Penns Rd, off Leeward Hwy; d US$249, 1-/2-bedroom villas from US$449/549;) In the quieter environs of the Bight Settlement, on a sweep of Grace Bay protected by Princess Alexandra National Park, Coral Gardens is one of Provo's more understated and affordable resorts. It doesn't offer the range of activities that the biggest places do, but does offer diving, gym, cycling, fitness, free massages, clean-lined design and comfortable rooms.

The Sands at Grace Bay RESORT **$$$**
(946-5199; www.thesandstc.com; Grace Bay Rd; d US$420-700, ste US$700-930;) This mammoth place is a great family option with multiple pools, and kitchenettes in every room. The 118 suites cluster around the superb pool area or face onto the beach where there are tiki huts and the excellent Hemingway's Restaurant.

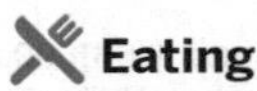

Eating

Provo has a huge range of eating options – the best in TCI. Some of the finest are run by young chefs and tucked away on resorts or away from the beach. Self-caterers should head to **Graceway IGA** (Leeward Hwy; 7am-10pm) or the more upmarket **Graceway Gourmet** (941-5000; www.gracewaysupermarkets.com; Allegro Rd, Grace Bay; 7am-9pm).

★ **Provo Fish Fry** CARIBBEAN **$**
(Lower Bight Rd; meals US$10-25; 5:30-10pm Thu) Locals and visitors alike flock to the weekly Fish Fry in Bight Park (next to Wymara Resort) for local fast food, drinking and entertainment. Makeshift stalls deliver fresh conch salads, jerked chicken, rum punch and the like, while live music plays. Arrive early as queues can get long.

★ **Da Conch Shack** BAHAMIAN **$**
(946-8877; www.daconchshack.com; Blue Hills Rd; mains US$16-20; 11am-9pm;) The quintessential Provo beach bar, Da Conch Shack is a cluster of clapboard huts and sturdier concrete buildings spreading out over the sand at Blue Hills, northwest of downtown. The cracked conch is the best on the island, they do a mean rum punch, and there's a beach party with live music (reggae, rake'n'scrape) from 7pm on Wednesdays and 1pm on Sundays.

Patty Place JAMAICAN **$**
(339-9001; Grace Bay Rd; patties US$3.50-7; 10am-8:30pm Mon-Wed, 10am-10pm Thu-Sat, 11am-10pm Sun) For a cheap, quick snack it's hard to go past these Jamaican-style beef, chicken or shrimp patties. Also excellent ice cream.

Big Al's Island Grill DINER **$**
(941-3797; http://bigalsislandgrill.com; Grace Bay Rd, Salt Mills Plaza; mains US$14-22; 7am-10pm;) It's mostly about the burgers at Big Al's, a relaxed American-style diner in Salt Mills Plaza. Burgers and sliders (mini burgers) include the pretzel burger and you'll also find wraps, paninis, steaks, pizzas, salads and a few veggie dishes on the menu. Take the slider challenge and get on the wall of fame.

Mr Grouper's SEAFOOD **$$**
(242-6780; Lower Bight Rd, Diamond Stubbs Plaza; mains US$17-24; 10am-10pm Mon-Sat, 3-11pm Sun) Aside from American standbys

such as breaded shrimp and seafood chowder, Mr Grouper's is all about the local *fruits de mer*: lobster (in season), blackened *mahimahi,* conch and the restaurant's namesake fish, either grilled whole or its meaty fillets fried to crispy perfection. The blue roadside shack doesn't look like much but it's a welcoming and popular venue.

Mango Reef INTERNATIONAL **$$**

(☎946-8200; http://mangoreef.com; Turtle Cove Marina, Lower Bight Rd; mains US$16-38; ⏰11am-10pm; 📶) The location in Turtle Cove Marina means you can tie up your boat right under the tiki lights and palm-decked terrace of this streamlined modern eatery. Enjoy snapper grilled with garlic, basil and lemon or a kaffir-lime-spiked lobster curry. Lunch specials are under US$25.

★**Grace's Cottage** INTERNATIONAL **$$$**

(☎946-5096; http://pointgrace.com; Point Grace Resort, off Grace Bay Rd; mains US$26-48; ⏰6-10:30pm Fri-Wed; ✎) Tucked out of the way from the main road, this 'gingerbread' cottage has tables spread out under trees and in romantic hidden enclaves. Crisp white-linen tablecloths and smart service complement a globe-trotting menu featuring inventive seafood dishes such as Caicos bouillabaisse, pasta and thoughtful vegetarian options. There's also a superb wine list. Reservations are usually essential.

★**Coyaba** FUSION **$$$**

(☎946-5186; www.coyabarestaurant.com; Caribbean Paradise Inn, off Grace Bay Rd; mains US$40-48; ⏰6-10pm Wed-Mon Nov-Aug) Coyaba ('heavenly' in Arawak) is a happy marriage of European technique and Caribbean flavors and ingredients. Alongside a diverse array of weekly specials (perhaps based around lobster in season) you'll find menu staples such as braised 'osso buccolettes' or local grouper with truffle fries.

Coco Bistro INTERNATIONAL **$$$**

(☎946-5369; www.cocobistro.tc; Grace Bay Rd; mains US$36-45; ⏰5:30-10pm Tue-Sun; P📶) Spreading out beneath the coconut palms surrounding an aggressively orange two-story house is this fine diner, one of Provo's best. A veritable army of waiters flutters from table to table, ferrying pesto-rubbed Atlantic salmon, West Indian shrimp curry and a much-lauded coconut pie to tables of well-heeled vacationers.

Magnolia Restaurant & Wine Bar INTERNATIONAL **$$$**

(☎941-5108; www.magnoliaprovo.com; 76 Sunburst Rd, Turtle Cove; mains US$30-46; ⏰5:30-8:30pm Tue-Sun; 📶) Sitting on the hill overlooking Turtle Cove, Magnolia is a great place for a romantic meal, with superb cooking and an equally lovely view over the lights of the cove. The fairy-light-rimmed balcony is the perfect setting for the signature dish, a cracked-pepper and sesame-crusted rare-seared tuna.

The restaurant has an ample wine list to choose from and the service is impeccable. Book ahead to get a table with a good view. The wine bar is open from 4pm daily, so this is also a great spot for a sundowner cocktail, even if you don't plan to eat.

Crackpot Kitchen BAHAMIAN **$$$**

(☎245-0005; www.crackpotkitchen.com; Ports of Call Plaza; mains US$27-44; ⏰11:30am-3pm Mon, Tue, Thu & Fri, 5-9pm Fri-Wed Nov-Aug) Run by TCI's only celebrity chef (Nikita O'Neil, who fronts the *Crackpot Kitchen Cooking Show*), this is one of the best places to try traditional island food. Conch fritters, curry goat, tamarind barbecue backs and blackened *mahimahi* don't get much better than this, and European-inflected dishes such as Guinness stew oxtails are excellent too. Live music on Friday evenings.

Drinking & Nightlife

Danny Buoy's PUB

(☎946-5921; www.dannybuoys.com; next to Salt Mills Plaza, Grace Bay Rd; ⏰11am-2am Mon-Sat, to midnight Sun; 📶) Provo's favorite drinking den has an English pub feel inside and a sprawling roadside terrace at the front. There's a menu littered with hearty, calorific bar food (eg battered shrimp with popcorn and smoked jalapeño mayo) and raucous entertainment Tuesday through Saturday nights (karaoke Thursdays get particularly hyped once the crowd from the Fish Fry pours in).

Shopping

Providenciales has a large selection of shopping malls spread out along Grace Bay Rd. These largely contain international-brand shops and prices aren't cheap, as everything has been imported. Locally produced items are generally of very little interest to travelers: there are few local arts and crafts, and most items on sale come far more under the heading of 'tourist tat' than genuine souvenirs.

Beachy items and souvenirs can be bought at a few places in Ports of Call Plaza, or most other shopping centers.

FOTTAC FOOD & DRINKS
(Flavors of the Turks and Caicos; ☎946-4081; Regent Village Plaza, Grace Bay Rd; ⊙10am-6pm Mon-Sat) Alongside the salts, spices and sauces on display at this high-end local grocer, you'll find noncomestibles such as soaps and locally made clothing, jewelry and handicrafts. Perhaps the most prominent line is Bambarra rum: you can taste different versions, or buy rum cake made from the local spirit.

Mama's Gift Shop GIFTS & SOUVENIRS
(☎946-5538; Ports of Call Plaza, Grace Bay Rd; ⊙10am-6pm Mon-Sat, 11am-3pm Sun) The longest-standing gift shop in the Ports of Call Plaza, and perhaps on Provo, Mama's has been run by Eleana Patrick since 1995. It's packed with souvenirs and beachwear, much of it locally made.

Information

Associated Medical Practices Clinic (☎946-4242; Leeward Hwy; ⊙24hr emergency) Has several private doctors. The clinic has a recompression chamber.

George Brown Post Office (☎338-3924; Airport Rd; ⊙8am-4:30pm Mon-Thu, to 4pm Fri) Provo's post office, in the downtown area near the airport, opened in 2019.

Police Station (☎941-5891, emergency 911; Salt Mills Plaza, Grace Bay Rd)

Turks & Caicos Tourism (☎946-4970; www.turksandcaicostourism.com; Ventura Dr, Regent Village Plaza; ⊙9am-5pm Mon-Fri) Brochures and useful information.

Getting There & Around

There is no bus service from **Providenciales International Airport** (www.provoairport.com). A taxi from the airport to Grace Bay costs around US$33 for two people (solo travelers pay the same). Some resorts arrange transfers.

BICYCLE

Both **Scooter Bob's** (☎946-4684; www.scooterbobstci.com; Turtle Cove Marina Plaza; ⊙8am-5pm Mon-Sat, to noon Sun) and Caicos Cyclery (p805) rent out bikes from US$15 per day.

CAR & MOTORCYCLE

There are a number of rental agencies on the island, with **Hertz** (☎654-3131; www.hertztci.com; Providenciales International Airport; ⊙8am-5pm) and **Budget** (☎946-4079; www.budget.com; Providenciales International Airport; ⊙10am-11pm) both represented at the airport. Local companies include **Rent-a-Buggy** (☎946-4158; www.rentabuggy.tc; 1081 Leeward Hwy; ⊙8am-5pm Mon-Sat, 9am-3pm Sun), **Paradise Scooters** (☎333-3333; http://paradisescooters.tc; 9 Grace Bay Plaza, Grace Bay Rd; ⊙9am-5pm), **Caicos Wheels** (☎946-8302; www.caicoswheels.com; Grace Bay Rd; ⊙8am-5pm) or Scooter Bob's.

TAXI

Taxis are a popular way of getting around the island. Most are vans; although unmetered, the pricing is consistent. It's best not to be in a hurry as they often take forever to come pick you up. Your hotel can arrange a taxi for you and they meet all flights at the airport. **Nell's Taxi** (☎231-0051) and **Presidential Taxi Tours** (☎246-8190; http://tcitaxi.com) are reliable.

Unlicensed taxis called jitneys roam the island looking for fares. Usually old cars driven by Haitians, they tout for business with short beeps of the horn: acknowledge them when they toot and agree a fare up front (US$10 should be the most you'll pay to reach any part of the island).

North Caicos

Despite its proximity to the wealth and flashy resorts of Provo, North Caicos feels a decade or two behind its neighbor, and is definitely more relaxing. Tiny settlements dot the northern and eastern parts of the island, while the south fractures into a maze of mangroves and shallow waterways. Inland lie historic plantation ruins, flamingo-filled waterways and small slash-and-burn farms growing corn, okra, peppers and other local staples.

Sights & Activities

★**Wade's Green Plantation** PLANTATION
(☎232-6284; http://tcnationaltrust.org/Wades-Green-Plantation; US$10; ⊙9:30-11:30am & 2:30-4pm Mon-Fri, Sat by appointment) Granted to Loyalist Wade Stubbs by King George III in 1789 as compensation for the loss of his Florida estate, this cotton and sisal plantation struggled on until 1814, when hurricanes, boll weevils and the harsh climate led Stubbs to abandon both the estate and his slaves. Quickly claimed by dry tropical forest, it's the best-preserved plantation anywhere in the Caribbean. Out-of-hours visits can be arranged (including Saturdays, but not Sundays) and guided tours are included.

Bring insect repellent: the forest is home to clouds of small-yet-utterly-ferocious mosquitoes.

East Bay Islands Reserve NATURE RESERVE

The beautiful, protected cays off North Caicos' northeast coast are a refuge for iguanas, birds and sea creatures. With sandy beaches and coral to the north, and mangroves to the south, they're delightful to explore in a kayak or boat.

Pumpkin Bluff BEACH

Much of North Caicos' shore is mudflats, but this beautiful spot on the northern coast has lovely fine sand, and is excellent for snorkeling. A foundered cargo ship adds to the allure.

Cottage Pond LAKE

This tropical blue hole (43m deep), formed by karst subsidence, is fed by the tides and connects to a much larger underground chamber. While it's not visually spectacular, it's interesting and a good place to spot West Indian whistling ducks, grebes, waders and other waterbirds. Look for the unobtrusive turnoff on Sandy Point Rd, about 1.2km from the T-junction with Kew Hwy.

Three Mary Cays NATURE RESERVE

While North Caicos doesn't offer the country's best diving and snorkeling, these three protected ironshore islets are surrounded by healthy coral, and can be reached from the shore.

Sleeping & Eating

Hollywood Beach Suites HOTEL $$

(☎231-1020; www.hollywoodbeachsuites.com; Hollywood Beach Dr, Whitby; ste from US$375; P❄📶) Four suites get prime position on an 11km beach that you'll often have to yourself. They have everything you need to unwind, and there are complimentary kayaks and bikes for guests. The swimming, snorkeling, diving and fishing are all fantastic too. Four-night minimum stay.

★Silver Palm Restaurant & Bar CARIBBEAN $$

(☎244-4186; Drake Ct, Whitby; mains US$10-30; ⏲8am-9pm Nov-Jun) Lobster and conch are the specialties here – all, of course, sourced locally, and sometimes caught to order (by prior arrangement). Informal and friendly, small and intimate, it's located in an old tropical Victorian house. The homemade conut ice cream is mandatory. Call a day in advance for dinner bookings.

Miss B's BAHAMIAN $$

(☎241-3939; Airport Rd, Major Hill; mains US$20-26; ⏲8am-11pm; 📶) One of North Caicos' best, Miss B's yellow house is a restaurant with character and charm. Forgo the pizza for Bahamian favorites such as conch, souse and lobster. Wednesday lunch is fish fry, Saturday night is karaoke.

THE CAYS

The smaller islands around Providenciales are known simply as the Cays, and most of them boast superb beaches and total isolation. They are only accessible by private boat charter.

Fort George Cay is home to the remnants of an 18th-century British-built fort. Now the only invaders are divers and snorkelers there to inspect the gun emplacements slowly becoming one with the sea bottom.

Little Water Cay is famous for its population of Turks and Caicos rock iguanas, which used to be common on the islands, but now thrive only here, thanks to conservation initiatives. Admission to the nature reserve on 'Iguana Island' is charged at the **visitor center** (☎941-5710). Visitors must stay on the boardwalks and refrain from touching or feeding the iguanas.

French Cay, south of Providenciales, is an old pirate hideaway now frequented by migrating birds. Just offshore the waters are teeming with stingrays. Nurse sharks gather here in summer.

Parrot Cay is home to one of the Caribbean's most luxurious and exclusive resorts, the eponymous **COMO Parrot Cay** (☎946-7788; www.parrotcay.com; d/ste from US$1080/2400; ❄📶🏊).

There are no scheduled public services to the cays. You can only visit as part of a tour or in a privately chartered boat. Big Blue Collective (p806) is one tour company offering kayaking and boat tours to the cays.

DON'T MISS

MUDJIN HARBOR

One of TCI's most beautiful spots is Mudjin Harbor. Near Conch Bar the rocky shore rears up to form a shrub-covered escarpment above the rolling Atlantic. Walking along the clifftop you'll be surprised to see a staircase appear out of nowhere, leading into the earth. Take it down through the cave and emerge on a secluded cliff-lined beach. Looking seaward waves crash into the offshore rocks in spectacular fashion. If you want to explore beyond Mudjin, walk the lovely Crossing Place Trail.

Information

There's a post office in Kew.

Bottle Creek Police (946-7116, emergency 911; Bottle Creek)

Kew Police (946-7261; Kew)

The nearest hospital is in Provo.

Bottle Creek Government Clinic (946-7194; Bottle Creek)

Kew Government Clinic (946-7397; Kew)

Getting There & Around

TCI Ferry (946-5406; http://tciferry.tciferry.com) connects Sandy Point Marina (p803) on North Caicos with Blue Haven Marina (p822) on Provo up to five times daily. Round-trip fare is US$55 for adults and US$30 for kids. Once on North Caicos you can rent a car for around US$80 per day. Try **Al's Rent-a-Car** (241-1276; www.alsrentacar.com; Sandy Point Dock, Whitby).

M&M Taxi & Tours (231-6285)

Middle Caicos

If you're really looking to get away from it all, Middle Caicos is remote-feeling but accessible. A causeway connects North and Middle Caicos, with stunning Atlantic coastline opening up to the north of the road, and vast mangroves stretching away to the south. There are only a few tiny settlements dotted along the island; Conch Bar and Bambarra are the largest, but there isn't much to them. However, Conch Bar Caves National Par and Bambarra Beach, two of the island's more worthwhile attractions, are nearby.

There are few services to speak of on the island, save the odd seemingly abandoned gas pump (which may or may not have gas). The proximity to North Caicos dictates that traveling over to the neighboring island is the way to go if you want to buy groceries or head out for a meal.

Sights & Activities

Bambarra Beach BEACH

Bring a picnic to enjoy at the tables provided on this broad, fine-sand beach. The water is shallow a long way out, and usually calm, so it's a good choice for families. The beach is reached by a 1km track from the town of Bambarra.

Conch Bar Caves National Park CAVE

(247-3157; US$20; 9am-3pm Mon-Fri) The largest cave system on dry land found anywhere in the Bahamian Archipelago, Conch Bar is accessible with National Trust guides on a pricey 30-minute tour. Call for access outside normal hours.

Crossing Place Trail WALKING

Following the historic route connecting Middle Caicos with North, this coastal trail is a fantastic way to see beautiful Mudjin Harbor, the island's dramatic Atlantic coast and the resident birdlife. Join the trail at Conch Bar or Mudjin Harbor, following the signs.

Middle Caicos Ocean Hole DIVE SITE

Thought to be the largest (but not deepest) yet discovered, this 76m-deep, 600m-wide blue hole is twice as wide as the more renowned Blue Hole off Belize and a paradise for hammerhead sharks. Divers wishing to meet them will need to charter a flat-bottomed boat, as it's bang in the middle of the shallows off Middle Caicos' southern shore.

Sleeping & Eating

★**Dragon Cay Resort** RESORT $$$

(586-354-3664; www.dragoncayresort.com; Mudjin Harbor; cottages US$406-825; Oct-Aug;) Formerly Blue Horizon Resort, this beautiful property at Mudjin Harbor boasts its own 670m stretch of private beach and a wonderful setting. The five individual cottages, all equipped with full kitchen and ocean views, are well spaced and sleep between two and eight people. The three-bedroom Solstice Villa offers sensational views. There's a restaurant but stock up in Provo for supplies.

Dreamscape Villa VILLA $$$

(946-6175; www.middlecaicos.com; Bambarra; per night/week from US$400/2240;) This fully self-contained villa is magnificently located on a pristine section of Bambarra Beach, just a few meters from the sea. With three bedrooms, filtered water, full kitchen and everything else you'll need, all that remains is to stock up, get here and unwind. The isolation, snorkeling, fishing, birdwatching and swimming make this a wonderful family-holiday option.

Mudjin Bar and Grill BAHAMIAN **$$**
(☎246-4472; www.dragoncayresort.com/dining; Mudjin Harbor; mains US$16-25; ⏲11am-3pm Oct-Aug; 📶) With peerless views over the limestone 'Dragon' to the reef wall and deep blue Atlantic beyond, the in-house restaurant at the Dragon Cay Resort could rest on its laurels. However, the food – conch fritters, lobster bites, grilled fish, burgers and more – matches the view. Dinner is available as room service to guests.

ℹ Getting There & Around

There are no direct flights or ferries to Middle Caicos, so you'll generally arrive by road from North Caicos via the causeway.

Arthur's Taxi Service (☎241-0730; Conch Bar)

M&M Tours (☎231-6285)

TURKS ISLANDS

The Turks group comprises Grand Turk and its smaller southern neighbor, Salt Cay, in addition to several tiny cays. The islands lie east of the Caicos Islands, separated by the 35km-wide Turks Island Passage. Both islands were significantly battered by Hurricane Irma in 2017.

ℹ Getting There & Away

Grand Turk JAGS McCartney International Airport (📶) Has multiple daily flights to and from Providenciales.

A government ferry runs three times a week from Grand Turk to Salt Cay. Arrangements can also be made with any of the Grand Turk dive companies to take you over to Salt Cay; costs vary depending on numbers.

ℹ Getting Around

BICYCLE

A few hotels on Grand Turk provide bikes for their guests, as they are the perfect way to get around the tiny island. On Salt Cay, Tradewinds Guest Suites (p817) has some very old cruiser bikes.

CAR, GOLF CART & SCOOTER

Car hire and taxi service is easy to arrange on Grand Turk, and on both Salt Cay and Grand Turk golf carts are a popular way of getting around. Expect to pay around US$70 per day. Ask at your accommodations or at the airport.

TAXI

Taxis are an inexpensive and reliable way to get around Grand Turk. A taxi from the airport to Cockburn Town will cost you about US$10, though prices vary according to distance; the entire island can be reached from the airport for up to US$25. Be sure to settle on a price before you head out, as the cabs are unmetered. Your accommodations can easily sort you a cab.

Grand Turk

Happily lacking the modern development that has enveloped Provo, Grand Turk is a step back in time. At just 10.5km long, this dot amid the sea is a sparsely populated, brush-covered paradise. Cockburn Town, the main settlement, has narrow streets frequented by wild donkeys and horses. Grand Turk is the port of call for most cruises coming to the Turks and Caicos Islands, thanks to a huge facility at the island's south end.

WORTH A TRIP

GRAND TURK LIGHTHOUSE

Standing on a bluff high above the notorious northeast reef, wrecker of many ships and nearly of the salt industry (cargo ships began to balk at the danger, demanding greater safety), this iron **lighthouse** (Northeast Point; adult/child US$3/2; ⏲Mon-Fri) was cast in England in 1852 and assembled in situ. The views out to sea are spectacular, and there's a high-rope course to add spice to your visit.

Chukka Caribbean Adventures (☎332-7169; https://chukka.com; Lighthouse Rd), the island's main adventure-tour operator, has an office at the lighthouse with a high-rope course and zip-lining (US$80), horseback rides on the beach (US$90) and other activities such as catamaran sailing and trips to Gibbs Cay.

On a busy day, two ships will be in port – off-loading nearly 7000 people.

Beaches rim the land and calm blue water invites you in for a refreshing swim. Grand Turk also offers excellent scuba diving and snorkeling close to shore.

Cockburn Town

It's hard to believe that sleepy Cockburn is the capital of the Turks and Caicos. But what it lacks in size and sophistication it more than makes up for in rustic charm. The town's historic waterfront suffered significant damage during Hurricane Irma in 2017 but is gradually getting back to normal. Cockburn Town is the ideal base for diving, with four operators and a dive resort.

Sights

The legacy of Grand Turk's salt-raking past survives in the salt-rotted Bermudan and Victorian architecture along Front and Duke Sts. Some are derelict (and reputedly haunted), some have been lovingly restored, several survive as inns, and some have been replaced by ugly, unfinished concrete shells, but the overall impression is of collapsing 19th-century charm, fringed with tropical foliage. Highlights include the **General Post Office** (Front St), Guinep House, housing the **Turks & Caicos National Museum** (946-2160; www.tcmuseum.org; Front St, Guinep House; US$10; hours vary, usually 9-11:30am Mon-Wed, 1-5pm Thu), and the old **HM Prison** (Pond St; adult/child US$7/3.50; cruise ship days, hours vary). To the south lies the grand 1815 home Waterloo, residence of TCI's governors.

Activities

Blue Water Divers DIVING
(946-2432; www.grandturkscuba.com; Duke St, Osprey Beach Hotel; 1-/2-tank dives US$90/170) Run by muso and longtime diver Mitch Rolling, this outfit uses international instructors and gets excellent feedback for its wall dives. PADI Open Water course costs from US$720. Dive-accommodations packages available.

Oasis Divers WATER SPORTS
(946-1128; www.oasisdivers.com; Duke St; 8am-4pm) Runs a huge range of diving and snorkeling tours (two tanks for US$115, night dives for US$75). Oasis also runs ecotours to swim with the stingrays on Gibbs Cay, spot humpback whales in February and March, and other memorable activities, and has dive-and-stay-package arrangements with local hotels.

Grand Turk Diving Co DIVING
(946-1559; www.gtdiving.com; Duke St; 8am-4pm) Local legend Smitty runs this excellent outfit with a team of local instructors. There are two-tank dives for US$130 and Discover Scuba courses for US$225, as well as snorkeling tours and boat charters. You can also hire a bike for US$23 per day.

Screaming Reels FISHING
(231-2087; www.screamingreelstours.com; Frith St; half-/full-day charter US$672/1092) Will take you out and help land the big one. Charters are based on a per-boat basis and the cost can be shared between up to eight people. They also have a guesthouse sleeping three adults or a family.

Sleeping

There are several sleeping options in both downtown Cockburn and elsewhere on the island. Everything is close enough that staying on one end of the island doesn't preclude you from enjoying the other.

Salt Raker Inn GUESTHOUSE $
(946-2260; www.saltrakerinn.com; Duke St; s/d from US$95/130, ste US$140-175;) Inviting, ramshackle Salt Raker is perfectly positioned on the seafront and is a welcome budget offering in Cockburn Town. The garden rooms at the back are comfortable and clean enough but much better are the ocean-view suites at the front. There's a rustic local restaurant in the rear garden.

Osprey Beach Hotel BOUTIQUE HOTEL $
(946-2666; www.ospreybeachhotel.com; 1 Duke St; garden/beachfront d from US$157/207;) This lovely boutique hotel and restaurant occupies a sublime waterfront niche with terrace pool. Nicely furnished rooms range from spacious beachfront suites with four-poster beds to the slightly cheaper atrium rooms surrounding a courtyard garden.

Island House GUESTHOUSE $
(232-1439; www.islandhouse.tc; Lighthouse Rd; d US$240;) Walking through the doors at Island House you'll be met with Mediterranean-influenced architecture, whitewashed walls and arched doorways. Further in you'll discover the inviting pool and opulent courtyard. The four one-bedroom suites are spacious, airy and nicely appointed, and

Grand Turk

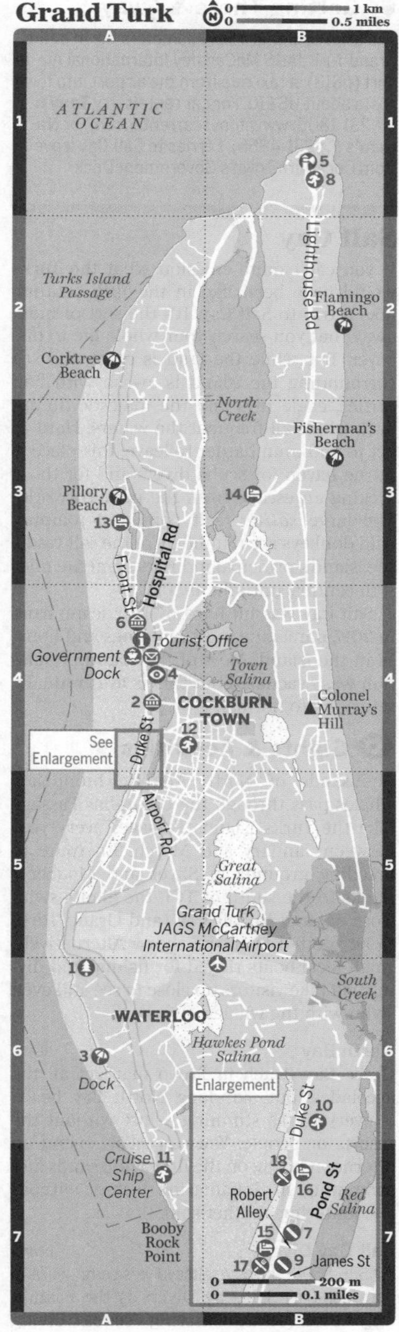

Grand Turk

Sights
1 Columbus Landfall National Park.......A6
2 General Post Office.......A4
3 Governor's Beach.......A6
4 HM Prison.......A4
5 Lighthouse.......B1
6 Turks & Caicos National Museum.......A4

Activities, Courses & Tours
7 Blue Water Divers.......B7
8 Chukka Caribbean Adventures.......B1
9 Grand Turk Diving Co.......B7
10 Oasis Divers.......B6
11 Ocean Vibes.......A7
12 Screaming Reels.......A4

Sleeping
13 Bohio Dive Resort & Spa.......A3
14 Island House.......B3
15 Osprey Beach Hotel.......B7
16 Salt Raker Inn.......B7

Eating
17 Bird Cage Bar & Grill.......B7
18 Sand Bar.......B7
Secret Garden.......(see 16)

there is a fully equipped kitchen. An unexpected bonus is free car hire.

Bohio Dive Resort & Spa RESORT $$
(☎946-2135; www.bohioresort.com; Pillory Beach; d US$270-297; ❄📶🏊) Bohio boasts a prime location right on a stunning stretch of sand, excellent-value dive packages and comfortable if unadorned rooms. There are kayaks, sailboats, snorkeling gear and other extras available, plus film nights, live music and an in-house restaurant, Guanahani. Week-long dive-and-stay packages start at US$2425.

Eating

Front and Duke Sts boast the best and most atmospheric places to eat.

Sand Bar PUB FOOD $
(☎243-2666; www.grandturk-mantahouse.com; Duke St; mains US$12-23; ⏰11am-1am; 📶) With a convivial open-air bar and decking stretching out over the water, Sand Bar is justifiably the most popular spot in town for an evening rum punch. The food – burgers, quesadillas and fresh seafood – is good, too. The quiz night every third Tuesday is legendary, as is the whale-watching when humpbacks pass close to shore in February and March.

Secret Garden BAHAMIAN $
(☎946-2260; Duke St; mains US$14-22; ⏱7-11am, noon-2:30pm & 6-9:30pm; 📶) You can rely on good old-fashioned Bahamian cooking such as grilled chicken with peas 'n' rice or eggs and grits, along with pasta dishes, at this simple open-sided restaurant bar at the back of Salt Raker Inn.

★**Bird Cage Bar & Grill** INTERNATIONAL $$
(☎946-2666; www.ospreybeachhotel.com; Duke St; mains US$18-25; ⏱7am-9pm; 📶) This terraced poolside restaurant is one of the fanciest places to eat in Cockburn Town. There's a legendary barbecue on Wednesday and Sunday nights: amazing seafood, poultry and beef are grilled before your eyes, paired with salads and served up to a happy throng. There are great ocean views and the house band keeps the energy levels up.

ℹ Information

National Hospital (☎941-2900; Hospital Rd)
Police Station (☎946-2299, emergency 911; Hospital Rd)
Post Office (☎946-1334; Front St; ⏱8am-4pm Mon-Thu, to 3:30pm Fri)
Tourist Office (☎946-2321; www.turksandcaicostourism.com; Front St; ⏱8am-4:30pm Mon-Fri) Located in the old shorefront customs house in Cockburn Town, this office is happy to dispense advice and historical knowledge to visitors.

OFF THE BEATEN TRACK

COLUMBUS LANDFALL NATIONAL PARK

This scrubby patch of **shorefront**, most popular with mosquitoes, commemorates Columbus' putative landing on the island in 1492. The park extends out into the water to encompass its true treasure: the reef and 7000ft wall beloved of divers.

Backed by the pines and low scrub of Columbus Landfall National Park and adorned by the picturesque (or ugly, depending on your view) iron hulk of a beached ship, **Governor's Beach** is a lovely place for a relatively quiet dip. It's also a scene of celebration during events like October's Lobster Festival.

ℹ Getting There & Away

The town center is a few kilometers north of the Grand Turk JAGS McCartney International Airport (p813); a taxi ride from the airport into town costs about US$10. For car rentals, try **Tony's** (☎231-1806; www.tonyscarrental.com) or **Nathan's** (☎231-4856). Ferries to Salt Cay leave from Cockburn Town's Government Dock.

Salt Cay

If you can't quite envision what the Turks would have been like in the 19th century, take a trip to Salt Cay. It's the sort of hideaway that you search your whole life to discover. But while the land is quiet, the sea surrounding the island is awash with life: turtles, eagle rays and the majestic humpback whale all frequent the waters. Hard to get to and even harder to leave, this place is a true haven for scuba divers and for those seeking an escape from the modern world. The large *salina* (salt pan) and roaming wild donkeys are reminders of the salt trade, the island's principal industry from the mid-17th century until the 1930s.

Salt Cay was hit hard by Hurricane Irma in 2017, damaging most buildings and houses in the island. Most of the island population was evacuated but things are gradually returning to normal.

👁 Sights & Activities

Thousands of North Atlantic humpback whales pass through the Columbus Passage (aka the Turks Islands Passage) every year between January and March. En route to breeding grounds in Silver and Mouchoir Banks to the south of TCI, the giants swim close enough to Salt Cay (and Grand Turk) to be spotted from the shore. Alternatively, small local boats rigged for fishing and diving will take visitors up close to see and even swim with the whales.

North Bay BEACH
Grace Bay Beach in Provo may get all the accolades, but 5km-long North Bay beach is every bit as stunning – just without the resorts or people. You can easily spend an afternoon lazing on the fine white sands and swimming in aquamarine waters without encountering another soul.

Salt Cay Divers DIVING
(☎336-8600; https://saltcaydivers.com; ⏱7am-5pm Mon-Sat) Salt Cay Divers is the island's only dive outfit, offering scuba diving

(US$90 for a single tank, Discover Scuba US$225), snorkeling and tours. The annual humpback whale migration (February to March) is a big draw, and this operation takes pride in showing off the whales but not disturbing them (US$180 including snorkeling gear).

Sleeping & Eating

Purple Conch Cottage COTTAGE **$**
(☎550-5235; www.purpleconch.com; North Side, Balfour Town; d US$150) This cute two-bedroom cottage is central and well appointed with a full kitchen. The sofa bed means it can easily accommodate a family or group.

Tradewinds Guest Suites RESORT **$**
(☎946-6906; www.tradewinds.tc; Victoria St; d US$190;) Tradewinds is fairly rustic but still a good spot to base yourself for an extended stay: there are weekly rates (US$1325) and the location is ideal – it's right on the beach, just a few steps from town. Complimentary bikes and dive packages are available. The rooms are tidy, ocean-facing and decent value for Salt Cay.

Pirate's Hideaway Guesthouse GUESTHOUSE **$**
(☎244-1407; www.saltcayaccommodations.com; Victoria St; d from US$220;) You can see the humpback whales from the upstairs rooms as they pass by, or just hang out in the tropical gardens with the parrots – it is a pirate's place after all.

Fresh Catch Lunch Inn CARIBBEAN **$**
(☎232-6009; South Side, Balfour Town; mains US$7-14; 7am-9:30pm Mon-Sat, from 6pm Sun) Join the locals for fresh-caught fish, chicken with rice or eggs and grits (breakfast). This rustic shack is the place for good-value local food or just a cold beer. Desserts include Salt Cay brittle and homemade ice cream. It pays to order in advance for lunch or dinner.

Oceanfaire CARIBBEAN **$$**
(☎341-3363; North Side, Balfour Town; 11am-2pm & 6-8pm Mon-Sat, 7am-3pm & 6:30pm-late Sun) This lovely local restaurant is the place to be for an intimate dinner of cracked conch or steamed snapper, or a relaxed fish burger or quesadilla lunch. Views from the rooftop terrace take in ocean and *salina*. Sunday is ribs night (US$25). Advance dinner orders recommended.

Getting There & Away

The twin-propeller planes operated by **interCaribbean** (http://intercaribbean.com) are the only ones making the 10-minute flight from Grand Turk to Salt Cay. There are twice-daily scheduled flights three times per week (Monday, Wednesday and Friday) to and from Grand Turk for around US$45 each way.

There's also the thrice-weekly community ferry from Grand Turk (return US$15), but it can often be thwarted by high seas. The ferry departs Salt Cay on Tuesday, Wednesday and Friday, returning from Grand Turk at 12:30pm on Wednesday and 2:30pm Tuesday and Friday.

UNDERSTAND TURKS & CAICOS

History

Taíno History

Discoveries of Taíno artifacts on Grand Turk and Middle Caicos have shown that the islands originally had much the same indigenous culture as their northern neighbors. Known as the Lucayans, this branch of the Taíno people probably began arriving here around AD 750, permanently settling most islands by around AD 1300. Sadly, this young society soon came into contact with European rapacity. While the local claim that Columbus made his initial landfall at Grand Turk in 1492 is unproven, what is certain is that within 30 years of that date the Lucayan civilization in these islands was gone, decimated by slavery and disease.

Salt & Cotton

The island group remained virtually uninhabited for most of the 16th and 17th centuries, passing between the nominal control of Britain, France and Spain. Permanent populations only developed from the 1670s, when Bermudian salt rakers settled the Turks islands and used natural *salinas* (salt-drying pans, still prominent features of Grand Turk and Salt Cay) to produce sea salt. Captured by the French and Spanish in 1706, the islands were retaken by the Bermudans soon afterwards. It was also around this time that piracy in the islands enjoyed its heyday, with famous outlaws such as Mary Read, Anne Bonny, Calico Jack Rackham, Captain Kidd

THE TROUVADORE

One of the most fascinating vignettes from TCI's history is the story of the slave ship *Trouvadore*. The slave trade had been abolished in Britain and its territories in 1807, with slavery itself fully outlawed in 1833. The *Trouvadore,* however, was Spanish. In 1841 it was carrying a cargo of up to 300 souls from the Portuguese African colony of São Tomé to the slave markets of Cuba when it ran onto the reef north of East Caicos. The crew of 20 and 192 slaves survived the wreck, and were carried to Grand Turk, where all were accommodated in the local prison.

Once a one-year 'apprenticeship' had been served in the salt works (ostensibly to pay for the cost of the rescue mission), 168 former slaves were resettled in TCI, primarily on Middle Caicos. Such an influx, equivalent to 7% of the islands' former population, represented a considerable alteration to their demographic makeup. The *Trouvadore* survivors went on to establish themselves in the islands, and many of today's so-called 'Belongers' (citizens) can trace their ancestry to this seminal event. It's thought that the place-name Bambarra, in Middle Caicos, indicates that at least some of the settlers were of the Bambara people of modern-day Mali, Guinea, Burkina Faso and Senegal.

The 1993 discovery of letters relating to the *Trouvadore* and its settlers revived interest in the story, and a search for the wreck itself. In 2003 archaeologists found a tell-tale ballast mound off the coast of East Caicos, becoming confident with further study that they had indeed found the ill-fated slave ship. Excavation and research continue, and can be read about at http://slaveshiptrouvadore.org and at the National Museum in Grand Turk.

and Blackbeard preying on wrecked and gold-laden shipping from the many hiding places the island group offers.

The French again took the Turks and Caicos Islands in 1783, successfully resisting the attempts of one Horatio Nelson to reclaim then for the British Crown (the Treaty of Paris, signed the same year, accomplished what he could not). British Loyalists dispossessed after American Independence were settled here, many attempting to make a go of cotton farming, until hurricanes, weevils and geopolitics wrecked their ambitions in the early 19th century.

Bermuda and Bahama, both British colonies, had spent much of the 18th century disputing control of the islands; in 1799 the Crown resolved the question in favor of the Bahamians. TCI enjoyed a brief period of independence from 1848 to 1873, when control passed to Jamaica, which administered the islands until 1962.

From Crown Colony to Island Paradise

Fast forward to the mid-20th century: the US military built airstrips and a submarine base in the 1950s, and US astronaut John Glenn splashed down just off Grand Turk in 1962, putting the islands very briefly in the international spotlight.

Administered through Jamaica and the Bahamas in the past, the Turks and Caicos Islands became a separate Crown colony of Great Britain in 1962, then an Overseas Territory in 1981. In 1984 Club Med opened its doors on Providenciales, and the Turks and Caicos started to boom. In the blink of an eye, the islands, which had previously lacked electricity, acquired satellite TV.

The Turks and Caicos relied upon the exportation of salt, which remained the backbone of the British colony until 1964. Today finance, tourism and fishing generate most of the income, but the islands could not survive without British aid. The tax-free offshore finance industry is a mere minnow compared with that of the Bahamas, and many would be astonished to discover that Grand Turk, the much-hyped financial center, is really just a dusty backwater in the sun.

Illegal drug trafficking, a major problem in the 1980s, has also been a source of significant revenue for a few islanders.

British Direct Rule

Relations between islanders and British-appointed governors have been strained since 1996, when the incumbent governor's comments suggesting that government and police corruption had turned the islands into a haven for drug trafficking appeared in the Offshore Finance Annual, and opponents accused him of harming investment. Growing opposition threatened to spill over into civil unrest.

Things were made far worse in 2009, when the governor of the Turks and Caicos imposed direct rule on the country following a series of corruption scandals that rocked the islands in 2008. The scandals concerned huge alleged corruption on the part of the Turks and Caicos government, including the selling off of its property for personal profit, and the misuse of public funds.

The imposition of direct rule from London was attacked by members of the suspended Turks and Caicos government, who accused the UK of 'recolonizing' the country, but the general reaction across the country was a positive one, as faith in the local political system had been extremely low in the years leading up to the suspension.

In 2012 a new constitution and general elections saw the return of the Progressive National Party (PNP) to power, despite the corruption scandals of three years prior. In 2016, however, the opposition People's Democratic Movement (PDM) took power, installing the country's first female head of government, Sharlene Cartwright-Robinson.

In 2017 twin hurricanes Maria and Irma had a particularly devastating effect on the Turks and Caicos Islands, including Providenciales, Grand Turk and Salt Cay. Many buildings and homes were extensively damaged with the bill estimated at US$500 million. As of late 2019 most tourism-related operations and island infrastructure were back to normal.

People & Culture

The culture of the Turks and Caicos is that of a ship that is steadied by a strong religious keel. There is a very strong religious core to these islands, and the populace is friendly and welcoming, yet a bit reserved. Native Turks and Caicos islanders, or 'Belongers' as they are sometimes locally known, are descended from the early Bermudian settlers, Loyalist settlers, slave settlers and salt rakers.

Unsurprisingly the Turks and Caicos, especially Provo, has a vibrant expatriate community: Americans because of the proximity; Canadians because of the weather; and Brits because of the colonial heritage. Some have come to make their fortunes, some to bury their treasure like the pirates of old, and others to escape the fast-paced life that permeates much of the developed world.

More recently hundreds of Haitians have fled their impoverished island and landed on the Turks and Caicos Islands; for some this is only a port of call on their way to America, while others are happy to stay.

Nightlife in the Turks and Caicos is of the mellow variety for the most part. There are a few night spots in Provo, and some beachside bars on the outer islands. Those seeking a roaring party of a holiday should look elsewhere – having said that, the local rake'n'scrape music can really get the crowd going. For those not in the know, rake'n'scrape or ripsaw (as it is locally known) is a band fronted by someone playing a carpenter's saw by rhythmically scraping its teeth with the shaft of a screwdriver; sometimes other household objects are used as percussion.

The art scene in the Turks and Caicos is slowly evolving. Traditional music, folklore and sisal weaving that evolved during early days have been maintained to this day. Paintings depicting the scenery are popular and the quality appears to be improving. The Haitian community has had a strong influence on the Turks and Caicos art scene.

Landscape & Wildlife

Much of the Turks and Caicos can be described as flat, dry and barren. The salt industry of the last century saw fit to remove much of the vegetation from Salt Cay, Grand Turk and South Caicos; low-lying vegetation now covers the uninhabited sections of these islands. The larger islands are in a much more pristine state, with vegetation and a higher degree of rainfall prominent on North, Middle and East Caicos. Small creeks, inland lakes – often home to flamingos – and wetlands make up the interior of these larger land masses.

A flourishing population of bottle-nosed dolphins lives in these waters. And some 7000 North Atlantic humpback whales use the Turks Island Passage and Mouchoir Bank, south of Grand Turk, as their winter breeding grounds between February and March. Manta rays are commonly seen during the spring plankton blooms off Grand Turk and West Caicos.

The wetlands and inland salt waterways of TCI make it fertile ground for birdwatching, especially on the uninhabited islands. The more remote islands will naturally require effort and expense to reach, but those who do visit may be rewarded with sightings of ospreys, flamingos, Cuban whistling ducks and other species. The *Birding in Paradise* booklet series, covering Provo, North, Middle and South Caicos, Grand Turk and Salt Cay, is a comprehensive guide to birdwatching in the major islands.

SURVIVAL GUIDE

Directory A–Z

ACCESSIBLE TRAVEL

Outside of the resorts little is done in TCI to make public spaces more accessible to those with disabilities or mobility issues, and there are no support or advocacy organizations. Individual hotels and resorts, especially the larger and pricier ones, should have accessibility provisions, but it's important to inquire before booking.

ACCOMMODATIONS

Accommodations in TCI are unavoidably expensive, reaching stratospheric heights at the plusher resorts. Aside from resorts, you can choose from hotels and self-contained villas/apartments. There's no official camping or backpacker hostels.

ACTIVITIES

TCI is an outdoorsy sort of place, and diving, snorkeling, sailing and fishing are the most popular pursuits. There's much more on offer though: kitesurfing, paddleboarding, hiking and other diversions are easy to organize.

Diving & Snorkeling

Diving highlights include Salt Cay and Grand Turk, with pristine reefs and spectacular wall-diving; and even built-up Provo, where you might get the chance to share the sea with JoJo the dolphin.

In the Caicos Islands a two-tank dive typically costs around US$160 to US$200 and a half-day snorkeling trip is around US$130. A two-tank morning dive in the Turks Islands, where dive sites are generally closer to shore, typically costs around US$130 and snorkeling around US$65 per half-day.

Fishing

Fishing is the big deal in TCI. With the islands' fringing reefs dropping away spectacularly, from around 9m to 2130m, the habitat of wahoo, tuna, *mahimahi*, dorado, sailfish and marlin is within easy striking distance of many of the islands. The hunt for the elusive silver bonefish among the saltwater channels of the Caicos Islands' mangroves is a local specialty. All anglers must hold a current fishing license (per day/month/year US$10/30/60), available from the marina office at Turtle Cove (p822).

Whale-Watching

The annual migration of 2500 to 7000 Atlantic humpback whales through the Columbus Passage, the deepwater channel separating the Caicos and Turks Islands, is one of the Caribbean's great sights. Moving through the channel (also known as Turks Islands Passage) between January and March, with the most reliable sightings in February and March, the mighty creatures are on their way to their breeding grounds in Silver Bank in the Dominican Republic, and Mouchoir Bank in TCI's southern waters. Local boats take visitors respectfully close to the action, and it's even possible to dive or snorkel with the whales. On land, with a pair of binoculars you can watch from the shores of Grand Turk and Salt Cay, as they pass close to the passage.

CHILDREN

TCI is a fantastic place to take kids. Although you may struggle to find specific programs and activities for youngsters outside major resorts, that's not such a problem when you consider the beaches, reefs, water sports and general freedom they'll enjoy. And all-inclusive megaresorts such as Beaches (p807) have so many diversions and activities for kids that the trick will be getting them to leave.

Kids not yet old enough to dive will be able to snorkel at reduced rates with outfits such as Big Blue (p806); those too young (or too timid) for that can still come face-to-face with reef life, riding the Undersea Explorer (p807).

One difficulty for those with infants in strollers is the scarcity of sidewalks. Beyond Grace Bay, Turtle Cove and similarly tourist-rich areas of Provo, sidewalks don't exist, and you can be forced to walk on the shoulder of the road. The

SLEEPING PRICE RANGES

Prices quoted are for pretax double rooms in high season. A 12% tax is levied on all services in TCI, including accommodations. Resorts and hotels (but not villas) incur an additional 10% service charge.

$ less than US$250

$$ US$250–400

$$$ more than US$400

good news here is that, Provo excepted, traffic is negligible throughout the islands.

Dedicated changing facilities won't be found outside modern resorts and one or two restaurants and transport hubs. Prepare to improvise.

Overall, any difficulties you meet will be outweighed by the pleasures of being in a warm, relaxed, beachy place where children are welcome everywhere (except at the swankiest 'adults-only' resorts and restaurants).

ELECTRICITY

Electrical current 120V, 60Hz. Sockets are two- or three-prong US standard.

EMBASSIES & CONSULATES

Only Jamaica, Germany, Haiti and the US have consular representation in TCI; the UK is represented by the office of the governor, on Grand Turk. Other countries are generally represented in Nassau (the Bahamas) or Kingston (Jamaica).

EMERGENCY NUMBERS

Emergency ☎911

FOOD

The locals might disagree, but between Bahamian food and TCI food, there's precious little difference. Nearly everything bar local seafood is imported, meaning price and quality part ways (in the wrong direction) and that the catch of the day is almost always the best choice. Conch is the staple protein, and lobster (not available between April and July) the star ingredient.

HEALTH

Providenciales and Grand Turk are the only places on TCI with larger medical facilities, although clinics are established in all settlements of any size. Visitors have to pay for medical care, and serious conditions will require relocation to Providenciales or Florida.

INTERNET ACCESS

Wi-fi is offered free of charge in nearly all hotels and most restaurants and bars, and phone coverage is more or less universal on the islands. It's a good idea to bring a smart phone or laptop with you to guarantee ease of access.

LEGAL MATTERS

TCI law derives largely from UK common law, with the limitations on powers of arrest and recognition of habeas corpus that entails. If you are arrested, you must be informed of the charge, can have your consular representative notified and are entitled to legal representation (at your own expense).

Recreational drugs are illegal to buy, sell or consume: any of these activities can result in fines and/or jail time. The blood-alcohol limit for drivers is 0.08, but there is little enforcement of this (consequently drunk drivers can be a real issue, especially in Provo, and especially on weekend nights).

EATING PRICE RANGES

The following price indicators are based on the cost of a main dish.

$ less than US$20

$$ US$20–30

$$$ more than US$30

LGBT+ TRAVELERS

As in most Caribbean destinations, the attitude toward LGBT+ travelers in the Turks and Caicos is not progressive. While legal, gay sex remains a taboo subject here, particularly with reference to gay men. As more visitors arrive, and brave locals challenge behaviors beyond the hetero-norm, some degree of acceptance has been forthcoming. However, there is still no openly gay scene to speak of, and LGBT+ travelers may decide to fly under the radar.

MONEY

The US dollar is the official currency. ATMs are found in Providenciales and Grand Turk; there are none in Salt Cay or Middle Caicos.

Exchange Rates

Australia	A$1	$0.70
Canada	C$1	$0.76
Euro zone	€1	$1.12
Japan	¥100	$0.92
New Zealand	NZ$1	$0.67
Switzerland	Sfr1	$1.02
UK	UK£1	$1.24

For current exchange rates, see www.xe.com.

Taxes & Refunds

All services incur a nonrefundable 12% tax. Many resorts charge an additional 10% luxury tax.

Tipping

Hotels Tip porters US$2.

Restaurants Tip 15% unless a service charge has been automatically added.

Taxis Tip 15%.

OPENING HOURS

Expect limited hours away from Provo or touristy areas.

Bars 11am to 2am

Businesses 9am to 5pm Monday to Saturday.

Restaurants Breakfast from 8am; lunch from noon; dinner 6:30pm to 9pm.

PRACTICALITIES

Magazines Key publications covering dining, accommodations and culture are *Where When How* (www.wherewhenhow.com) and *Times of the Islands* (www.timespub.tc).

Newspapers Weekly, digital and regional publications include *Turks & Caicos Weekly News* (http://tcweeklynews.com), *Caribbean News Now* (www.caribbeannewsnow.com) and TCI Enews (www.enews.tc).

Radio There are over 20 AM and FM radio stations throughout the islands, including 107.7 Radio Turks & Caicos FM, 99.9 Kiss FM and 93.9 Island FM.

Smoking Smoking is banned in public places in Turks and Caicos, including beaches and national parks. Bars, restaurants, casinos and other liquor-licensed premises can still provide non-covered smoking areas.

Television Aside from cable services from neighbors (particularly the USA), TCI is served by 4NEWS and Channel 8 from Provo, and Turks and Caicos Television from Grand Turk.

Weights & measures Imperial and metric systems are both in use.

PUBLIC HOLIDAYS

New Year's Day January 1
Commonwealth Day Second Monday in March
Good Friday March/April
Easter Monday March/April
National Heroes' Day Last Monday in May
Her Majesty the Queen's Official Birthday June 13 (or nearest weekday)
Emancipation Day August 1
National Youth Day Last Friday in September
National Heritage Day Second Monday in October
National Day of Thanksgiving Fourth Friday in November
Christmas Day December 25 (or nearest weekday)
Boxing Day December 26 (or nearest weekday)

TELEPHONE

The country code (649) isn't required for inter-island calls within TCI.

Phonecards of various values can be bought from Flow outlets, as well as from shops and delis.

Cell Phones

Most cell phones will work in the Turks and Caicos; you can either set your phone up for global roaming prior to leaving home or purchase a SIM card (for unlocked phones) once you get here.

Global roaming is both easier and more expensive in the Turks and Caicos; be sure to check rates with your phone company prior to dialing.

The best way to get set up with a local SIM card and prepaid account is **Flow** (https://discoverflow.co; Graceway Plaza, Leeward Highway; ⌚8:30am-6:30pm) in Providenciales, or **Digicel** (www.digicelgroup.com/tc) with offices in Provo, North Caicos and Grand Turk.

TIME

TCI is on permanent Eastern Daylight Time (GMT/UTC minus five hours).

Getting There & Away

AIR

While there are two other nominally international airports in TCI, you will certainly come through Providenciales International Airport (PLS). From there you can fly to the UK, US, Canada, the Bahamas, Antigua, Cuba, Jamaica, the Dominican Republic, Haiti and Puerto Rico. To get elsewhere in the region, you'll have to transit, most probably through Miami or possibly Fort Lauderdale.

SEA

While there are no international ferry services between TCI and neighboring islands, it is possible to arrive by private or chartered boat, and on the cruise ships that call regularly at Grand Turk.

Private boaters must clear customs and immigration within 24 hours of arrival, and should arrange this by contacting their chosen port of entry before arrival. Ports of entry to TCI are the **Blue Haven** (☎946-9910; www.bluehaventci.com; Leeward Marina), **Turtle Cove** (☎941-3781; www.turtlecovemarina.com), **South Side** (☎946-3417, 231-4747; http://southside-marina-tci.com; 26 Turtle Tail Dr) and **Caicos** (☎946-5600; www.caicosmarina.com; 1 Long Bay Hwy, Long Bay) marinas, plus **Sapodilla Bay** (all on Providenciales), and the government docks on South Caicos (p803) and **Grand Turk**.

If arranging clearance yourself, contact **TCI Customs and Immigration** (338-5493 in Provo; 946-1176 in Grand Turk; 946-3214 in South Caicos; https://customs.gov.tc) and a customs officer will visit, between 8am and 4pm from Monday to Friday (extra charges apply on weekends and public holidays). Until pratique is granted, vessels must fly the yellow Q flag and only the captain may come ashore.

Clearance costs US$50 and a cruising permit (US$300, valid for 90 days) is required for stays of more than seven days.

Getting Around

AIR

Air is the quickest and most convenient way to get from Provo to Grand Turk and all islands further than North and Middle Caicos. TCI's main carrier is **interCaribbean** (946-4999; http://intercaribbean.com; Providenciales Airport).

BOAT

TCI Ferry (p812), which has supplanted the regular short-trip planes to North and Middle Caicos, has two routes:

- **Providenciales to North Caicos** Several times daily (adult/child return US$55/30, 30 minutes)
- **Providenciales to South Caicos** Three times weekly (adult/child US$110/70, 90 minutes)

CAR & MOTORCYCLE

Driving is on the left-hand side. The lack of public transport means car and motorcycle hire is a common option for visitors. Provo has offices for international car-rental chains and local rental operations, all of which are easy to engage at airports and other major ports of entry. Grand Turk and Salt Cay can be comfortably explored on ubiquitous golf carts, which rent for around US$70 per day.

To rent a car, you need to be 25 or above, and hold a currently valid license. An international driving permit (IDP) is only required if your license is in a language other than English. The age limit is only 18 for scooters.

TAXI

Taxis are available on all the inhabited islands. Cabs are unmetered and pricing is set (but not cheap): confirm the price before setting out. Prices from the airport to the major resorts on Providenciales are advertised on the wall outside the airport taxi rank; it should be somewhere around US$25 to US$40 for two people. Also in Provo, taxis take the form of minibuses seating up to 12 people, allowing relatively cheap rides for a group.

US Virgin Islands

340 / POP 106,400

Includes ➡

Best Places to Eat

- ➡ Braata (p848)
- ➡ Harvey's (p843)
- ➡ Pizza Pi (p833)
- ➡ Rootz Cafe (p836)
- ➡ Longboard (p836)
- ➡ Daylight Bakery & Diamond Barrel (p829)

Best Places to Stay

- ➡ Fred (p848)
- ➡ Olga's Fancy (p829)
- ➡ St John Inn (p836)
- ➡ Estate Lindholm (p839)
- ➡ Virgin Islands Campground (p827)

Why Go?

Hmm, which of the US Virgin Islands (USVI) to choose for hammock-strewn beaches, conch fritters and preposterously blue water? Easy: any one, though each differs in personality. St Thomas has more resorts and water sports than you can shake a beach towel at and is the most developed island, with dizzying cruise-ship traffic. St John cloaks two-thirds of its area in parkland and sublime shores, ripe for hiking and snorkeling. It leads the way in environmental preservation and draws a more outdoorsy crowd. The largest Virgin, St Croix, pleases divers and drinkers with extraordinary scuba sites and rum factories. It's the furthest-flung island and offers the greatest immersion in local life.

Wherever you go, get ready for reggae rhythms, curried meats and mango-sweetened microbrews. These are US territories, but they feel a world away.

When to Go

Dec–Apr Dry and sunny high season, when activities are full tilt, culminating in St Thomas Carnival.

May & Jun Calmer waters and lower prices – perfect for sailors, swimmers and snorkelers, before the rainy season arrives.

Nov–Jun Conch season, after the August to September hurricane season, when the mollusks are widely available.

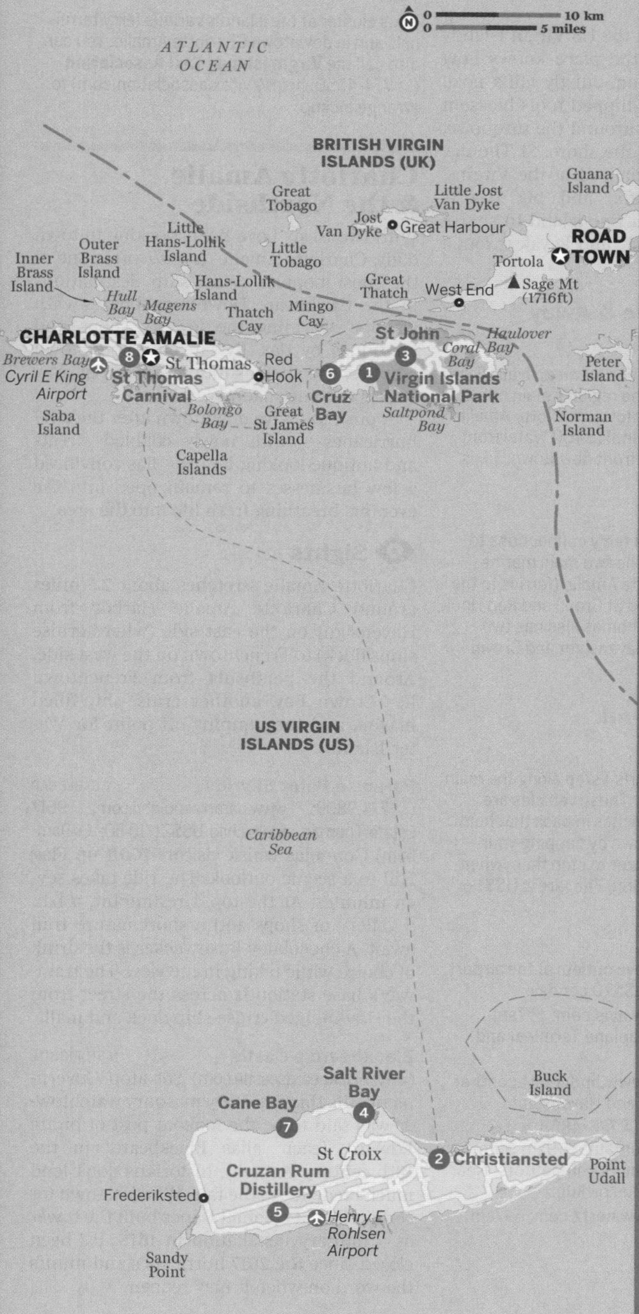

US Virgin Islands Highlights

1. **Virgin Islands National Park** (p834) Hiking to sugar-mill ruins, petroglyphs and isolated beaches rich with marine life.
2. **Christiansted** (p841) Sipping microbrews, exploring the cannon-covered fort and chowing down on traditional West Indian food.
3. **St John's North Shore** (p838) Choosing your favorite strand, from hike-in Honeymoon Beach to Maho Bay's turtle spotting to Leinster Bay's snorkeling with sharks.
4. **Salt River Bay** (p846) Seeing where Columbus landed by day, then kayaking the bioluminescent water by night.
5. **Cruzan Rum Distillery** (p849) Drinking the Virgin Islands' favorite attitude adjuster at its source.
6. **Cruz Bay** (p834) Raising a glass to happy hour in St John's fun-loving main town.
7. **Cane Bay** (p846) Diving the wall and peering into the deep.
8. **St Thomas Carnival** (p829) Dancing and dining at the second-largest Carnival in the Caribbean.

ST THOMAS

Most visitors arrive at the US Virgin Islands via St Thomas, and the place knows how to make an impression. Jungly cliffs poke high into the sky, red-hipped roofs blossom over the hills, and all around the turquoise, yacht-dotted sea laps the shore. St Thomas is the most commercialized of the Virgins, with cruise-ship traffic and big resorts aplenty, but it's also a fine island to sharpen your knife and fork, and kayak through mangrove lagoons.

Getting There & Away

AIR

The island has two facilities for air arrivals: Cyril E King Airport (p855), the region's main hub, a short drive west of downtown Charlotte Amalie; and the **Seaplane Terminal** (3400 Waterfront Hwy), right on the waterfront downtown. Taxis are easy to get at both.

BOAT

St Thomas has excellent ferry connections to the rest of the Virgins. The two main marine terminals are at Charlotte Amalie (ferries to the British Virgin Islands and St Croix) and Red Hook (ferries to St John). St Thomas also has two cruise-ship terminals: Havensight and Crown Bay.

Getting Around

BUS

'Dollar' buses (aka 'safaris') stop along the main roads around the island. These vehicles are open-air trucks with benches in back that hold 20 people. Flag them down by flapping your hand, and press the buzzer to stop them when you reach your destination. The fare is US$1 or US$2.

CAR

Most rental agencies have outlets at the airport. Prices start at around US$70 per day.

Avis (☎774-1468; www.avis.com; ⏲7am-7pm) At the airport, Seaplane Terminal and Havensight.

Budget (☎776-5774; www.budgetstt.com) At the airport, Crown Bay and Havensight.

Discount Car Rental (☎776-4858; www.discountcar.vi; 3308 Contant; ⏲9am-5pm) Often a bit cheaper than its competitors. Near the airport; staff provides pickup.

Hertz (☎774-1879; www.hertz.com; ⏲7am-9pm) At the airport.

TAXI

Taxis cluster at the island's various ferry terminals and in downtown Charlotte Amalie. You can also call the **Virgin Islands Taxi Association** (☎774-4550; http://vitaxiassociation.com) to arrange pickup.

Charlotte Amalie & the Northside

With two to six Love Boats docking in town daily, Charlotte Amalie (a-*mall*-ya) is one of the most popular cruise-ship destinations in the Caribbean. Downtown buzzes with visitors swarming the jewelry shops and boutiques by day. By late afternoon town empties, the shops shutter and the narrow streets become shadowy.

A push to revive downtown after the 2017 hurricanes – with newly cobbled streets and antique-looking lamps – has convinced a few businesses to remain open into the evening, breathing fresh life into the area.

Sights

Charlotte Amalie stretches about 2.5 miles around Charlotte Amalie Harbor from Havensight on the east side (where cruise ships dock) to Frenchtown on the west side. Around the peninsula from Frenchtown lies Crown Bay, another cruise-ship-filled marina and the jumping-off point for Water Island.

Paradise Point Skyride CABLE CAR

(☎774-9809; www.paradisepointvi.com; 9617 Estate Thomas; adult/child US$21/10.50; ⏲9am-5pm) Gondolas whisk visitors 700ft up Flag Hill to a scenic outlook. The ride takes seven minutes. At the top a restaurant, a bar, a gallery of shops and a short nature trail await. A chocolatey Bushwacker is the drink of choice while taking in the view. The tramway's base station is across the street from the **Havensight** cruise-ship dock and mall.

Blackbeard's Castle HISTORIC SITE

(www.blackbeardscastle.com) Set atop Government Hill, this five-story masonry watchtower was said to be the lookout post of pirate Edward Teach, alias Blackbeard, in the 18th century. Actually, historians don't lend much credence to the tale. What's known for certain is that colonial Danes built the tower as a military installation in 1678. It's been closed since the 2017 hurricanes and mum's the word on when it may reopen.

WORTH A TRIP

WATER ISLAND

Water Island – sometimes called the 'Fourth Virgin' – floats spitting distance from Charlotte Amalie's trafficky bustle. But with only about 200 residents and very few cars or shops, it feels far more remote. At 2.5 miles tip to tip, it doesn't take long to walk the whole thing. Most locals travel by bike or golf cart.

Honeymoon Beach is the palm-lined main attraction. It offers fine swimming and snorkeling in calm, shallow water. A couple of beach bars sell drinks, sandwiches and fish tacos. One, **Dinghy's** (227-5525; Honeymoon Beach; mains $10-16; 10:30am-9pm;), rents snorkel gear and kayaks (per hour US$15 and US$25 respectively). Expect peace and quiet – unless a cruise ship is in port, and then you'll have plenty of company. Honeymoon is a 10-minute walk from the ferry dock. Follow the road uphill from the landing; when the road forks, go right and down the hill to the sand.

Virgin Islands Campground (776-5488; www.virginislandscampground.com; Water Island; cottages US$195;) is the only option (other than villas) if you want to spend the night, but it's an eco winner. Each wood-frame-and-canvas cottage has beds, linens, electrical outlets and a table and chairs inside. Guests share the communal bathhouse, cooking facilities and hot tub. Captured rainwater runs through the sinks and showers; solar energy heats it. The cottages nestle into the surrounding trees, so it's a bit like sleeping in a breezy tree house. A three-night minimum stay is required.

The **Water Island Ferry** (690-4159; www.waterislandferry.com; 1-way US$5) departs roughly every hour from outside Tickle's Dockside Pub at Crown Bay Marina. The journey takes 10 minutes. Taxis from downtown to the marina cost US$4 to US$5 per person.

★ Magens Bay — BEACH

(www.magensbayauthority.com; adult/child US$5/free; 8am-5pm;) The sugary mile that fringes Magens Bay, 3 miles north of Charlotte Amalie, makes almost every travel publication's list of beautiful beaches. The seas here are calm, the bay broad and the surrounding green hills dramatic, and tourists mob the place to soak it all up. The beach has lifeguards, picnic tables, changing facilities, a taxi stand, food vendors, and water-sports operators renting kayaks, paddleboards and paddleboats (US$20 to US$30 per hour).

Hull Bay — BEACH

On the north coast and just west of Magens Bay, Hull Bay is usually a gem of solitude when Magens is overrun. The shady strand lies at the base of a steep valley and has a fun restaurant-bar but no other facilities. It's a locals' beach: fishers anchor their small boats here and dogs lope around. When there's a northern swell, Hull Bay is also the best surf beach around.

Brewers Bay — BEACH

This beach, located behind the University of the Virgin Islands, is beloved of students, local families and shell-spotters alike. There are restroom facilities, and snack vans serving *pates* (meat-filled dough pockets) and cold Heineken beers. It gets deserted fast come nighttime. Brewers is by the airport and accessible by taxi and public bus.

99 Steps — VIEWPOINT

These stairs lead from Kongens Gade up into a canopy of trees at the foot of Blackbeard's Castle. The steps, of which there are actually 103 (though you'll be too out of breath to count), were constructed using ship-ballast brick in the mid-18th century. The view at the top impresses.

St Thomas Synagogue — HISTORIC BUILDING

(www.synagogue.vi; 2116 Crystal Gade; tours by donation; 9:30am-4pm Mon-Thu, to 3pm Fri) The second-oldest synagogue in the western hemisphere (the oldest is on the island of Curaçao), peaceful St Thomas Synagogue is a National Historic Landmark. The current building dates from 1833, but Jews have worshipped here since 1796, from Sephardic Jews from Denmark to today's 110-family Reform congregation. The temple floor is made of sand to symbolize the flight of the Israelites out of Egypt and across the desert. There's a tiny **museum** in the back room.

Fort Christian — FORT

(Waterfront Hwy; adult/child US$10/7; 9am-4pm Mon-Fri) Red-brick Fort Christian is the

Charlotte Amalie

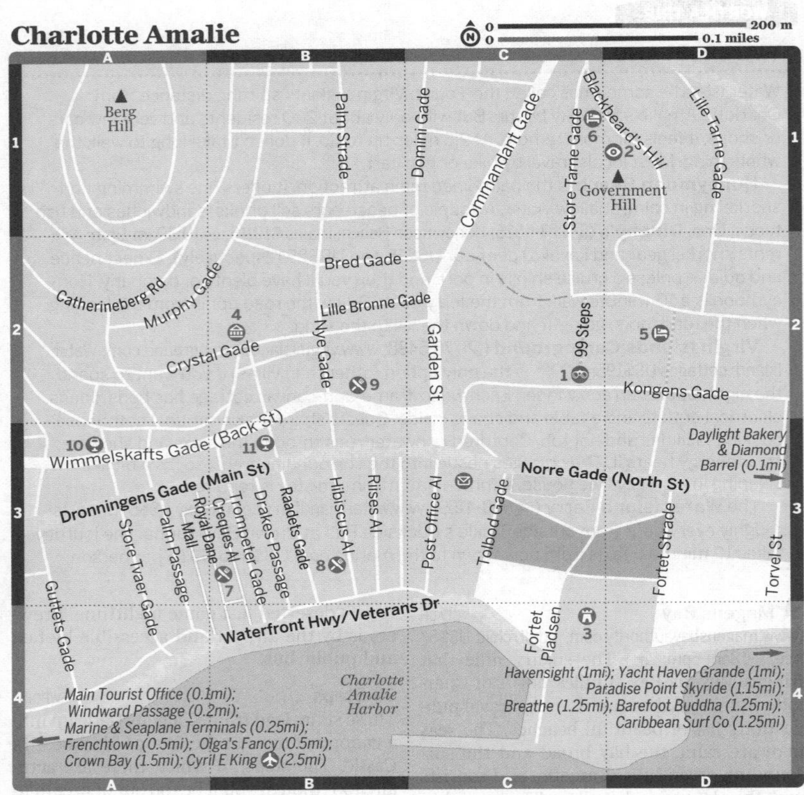

Charlotte Amalie

Sights

1	99 Steps	C2
2	Blackbeard's Castle	D1
3	Fort Christian	C4
4	St Thomas Synagogue	B2

Sleeping

5	At Home in the Tropics	D2
6	Green Iguana	C1

Eating

7	Gladys' Cafe	B3
8	Greengo's Cantina	B3
9	MBW Cafe & Bakery	B2

Drinking & Nightlife

10	ARC Vodka	A3
11	Taphus Beer House	B3

oldest Danish fortification in the Caribbean, dating to 1672. Over the years it has housed a jail, a governor's residence and a Lutheran church. The fort underwent a US$4-million restoration between 2005 and 2017, but there's not a whole lot to show for it inside, save the four occasionally functioning iPad information panels. To make the fee worth-while, join the curator's tour (10am daily, included with admission).

Activities & Tours

★ St Thomas Scuba & Snorkel Adventures SNORKELING

(☎ 474-9332; www.stthomasadventures.com; 10-1 Hull Bay) Located at Hull Bay, this company rents paddleboards and kayaks (US$30 per hour) and leads terrific night snorkel tours (US$65 per person). It also offers a slew of other snorkeling, diving, kayaking and hiking jaunts around the island. Reserve ahead.

Tree Limin' Extreme ADVENTURE
(☎777-9477; www.ziplinestthomas.com; 7406 Estate St Peter; 2½hr tour adult/child US$119/109) Guides whisk you through the jungle canopy here via zip line. The ride is relatively tame and provides great views of the island-dotted seascape. Tree Limin' operates via reservation only.

Festivals & Events

St Thomas Carnival CARNIVAL
(www.vicarnival.com; ⏲Apr & May) This is the second-largest Carnival in the Caribbean (after the one in Port of Spain, Trinidad). There's a full month of events at various locations, including calypso competitions, food fairs, beauty pageants, parades, fireworks and more.

Sleeping

Charlotte Amalie has smaller and more casual guesthouses than you'll find elsewhere around the island. The downside of staying here is that it gets pretty deserted come nightfall unless you head to Havensight or Yacht Haven Grande.

★ **Olga's Fancy** HOTEL $$
(☎643-4247; www.olgasfancy.com; Honduras 8; r with/without bathroom from $150/99; ❄≋) From the pattern-heavy textiles to the playful wallpaper and colorful artwork, it's the finer details that give this island-chic 17-room hotel a leg up on the competition. Budget rooms have exterior bathrooms but are a real value by St Thomas standards. The restaurants and nightlife of Frenchtown are just steps away along the seafront.

Green Iguana GUESTHOUSE $$
(☎776-7654; www.thegreeniguana.com; 1002 Blackbeard's Hill; r US$150-210; ❄📶) 🍃 Up the hill behind Blackbeard's Castle (p826), this welcoming place is set in lush gardens and overlooks Charlotte Amalie Harbor. The nine rooms come in several configurations, but all have speedy wi-fi, satellite TV, microwave and refrigerator; some also have fully equipped kitchen and private balcony. It's more plain than luxurious, but good value if you don't mind the steep walk.

★ **At Home in the Tropics** INN $$$
(☎777-9857; www.athomeinthetropics.com; 1680 (25) Dronningens Gade; r incl breakfast US$300-339; ❄📶≋) This oasis at the top of Government Steps, just above Charlotte Amalie Harbor, lies in a building erected in 1803 as barracks for the Danish governor's private guard. It's now a lovingly restored four-room inn with a beachy vibe and a panoramic pool deck where the Caribbean-inspired homemade breakfast is served each morning. Downtown action is a short walk away.

Eating

Downtown is good for breakfast and lunch, though dinner options are scarce as most places close by 5pm. Frenchtown holds several great restaurants that buzz in the evening. Havensight is touristy and chain-oriented by day but offers a fun, high-energy atmosphere come nighttime.

★ **Daylight Bakery & Diamond Barrel** CARIBBEAN $
(☎776-1414; 18 Norre Gade; snacks US$2-5, small/large meals US$8/12; ⏲6am-6pm Mon-Sat) It's mostly locals who visit this friendly spot at downtown's edge. If you can get past the guava tarts, sugar cakes and dum bread (flour sweetened with coconut and baked in a 'dum' oven), then pans of okra, fish stew, *fungi* (semihard cornmeal pudding) and more island dishes await. Point to your choice, and servers will heap it into a Styrofoam clamshell.

MBW Cafe & Bakery CAFE $
(☎715-2767; www.mybrothersworkshop.org; cnr Back St & Nye Gade; sandwiches US$6-13; ⏲7am-2pm) MBW stands for My Brother's Workshop, a nonprofit group that helps at-risk youth learn a trade. At the cheery cafe, teens bake the wares and run the place. The egg-filled breakfast sandwiches are a good deal, and the muffins and cake slices appease sugar addicts. Lots of locals hang out at the tables in back.

Greengo's Cantina MEXICAN $
(☎714-8282; www.greengoscantina.com; 34-35 Dronningens Gade; US$12-15; ⏲11am-5pm, to 9pm Fri) Join the boisterous young expat crowd chowing down on Greengo's tacos, burritos and quesadillas, and knocking back shots from the 150-strong array of tequilas.

Barefoot Buddha CAFE $
(☎777-3668; www.barefootbuddhavi.com; 9715 Estate Thomas; mains US$8-11; ⏲7am-4pm Mon-Sat, 8am-3pm Sun; 📶🖉) The island's yoga-philes hang out at yin-yang-decorated wooden tables, tucking into healthy specials such as the blackened-tofu wrap and the everyday list of toasted sandwiches (go for the hummus and rosemary goat cheese). The

Buddha is also popular for breakfast, thanks to the extensive range of organic coffee drinks and egg sandwiches. It's near Havensight's cruise dock.

★ Pie Whole ITALIAN $$
(☎642-5074; www.piewholepizza.com; 24a Honduras; mains US$13-24; ⏰11am-10pm) Six tables and 10 barstools comprise this cozy eatery, whose claim to fame lies with its 14in, brick-oven pizzas. Superfresh ingredients, eg spinach and ricotta or mozzarella and basil, top the crisp, hand-stretched crusts. Several house-made pastas and a robust beer list raise Pie Whole well beyond the norm.

Brooks Bar & Restaurant CARIBBEAN $$
(☎777-6871; 6200 Magens Bay Rd; meals US$20; ⏰7am-11pm; 📶) Here are three things you can count on at Brooks: old men playing dominoes in the corner, loud reggaeton music and gargantuan portions big enough for two. The whiteboard menu lists the proteins (pork, snapper, shrimp, conch) and sides (beans and rice, coleslaw, fried plantains). It's on the road to Magens (p827); stop in after the beach.

Gladys' Cafe CARIBBEAN $$
(☎774-6604; www.gladyscafe.com; 5600 Royal Dane Mall; mains US$11-25; ⏰7am-5pm Mon-Sat, 8am-3pm Sun; 📶) With the stereo blaring beside her, Gladys belts out Tina Turner tunes while serving some of the best West Indian food around. Locals and tourists pile in for her callaloo (spicy soup with okra, meats and greens), *fungi*, Ole Wife (triggerfish) and fried plantains. Gladys' homemade hot sauces (for sale at the front) make a fine souvenir.

Hook, Line & Sinker SEAFOOD $$
(☎776-9708; www.hooklineandsinkervi.com; 62 Honduras; mains US$17-32; ⏰11am-10pm) Though revamped after the 2017 hurricanes, this place still has a sea-shack vibe, where you smell the saltwater, feel the ocean breeze and see sailors unload their boats dockside. The menu mixes salads, pastas and seafood mains, such as the almond-crusted yellowtail, and there are plenty of Belgian beers to wash it down.

Old Stone Farmhouse AMERICAN $$$
(☎777-6277; Mahogany Run Golf Course; mains US$30-45; ⏰5-9:30pm Wed-Sat, 10am-2pm Sun) The 200-year-old farmhouse – once the stable for a nearby sugar plantation – sits high on a hill overlooking St Thomas' only golf course. The rustic, low-lit room impresses with its arched stone walls and mahogany ceiling. The menu changes, but local seafood (lobster, *mahimahi*) is always available, as well as a vegetarian option.

Drinking & Nightlife

★ ARC Vodka DISTILLERY
(☎646-573-4306; Store Tvaer Gade 2; ⏰5pm-2am Thu-Sat) Who makes vodka in the Caribbean? Two Virgin Islander brothers who were fed up with all the rum-guzzling pirate stereotypes. At their new bar, which at research time was soon to have food and a back patio, you can sample seven locally sourced, made-from-scratch vodkas (including flavors such as bay leaf or cinnamon) with fresh-pressed island juices.

★ Frenchtown Brewing MICROBREWERY
(☎642-2800; www.frenchtownbrewing.com; 24a Honduras; ⏰5:30-7:30pm Wed & Fri, 1-5pm Sat) This brewery is indeed micro: it's only open a few days a week, it only brews five beers, and they're only on tap here and at eight island restaurants. Beer buffs will want to seek out the Belgian-style Frenchie Farmhouse Saison and Hop Alley IPA. Tours available; call to make an appointment if you want to visit outside regular hours.

Taphus Beer House BAR
(www.facebook.com/taphusbeerhouse; 5120 Dronningens Gade; ⏰11am-8pm Mon-Sat; 📶) This low-lit beer house with exposed stone walls and a horseshoe-shaped mahogany bar is almost like a speakeasy on the back end of the Billabong store. Sample from a rotating list of six local and international craft beers, including a cream ale made by Frenchtown Brewing (p830) exclusively for Taphus.

Shopping

Jewelry is the big deal in town. Brands such as Rolex, TAG Heuer and Pandora are well represented, and there are diamond sellers galore. US citizens can leave with a whopping US$1600 in tax-free, duty-free goods.

★ Mango Tango ART
(☎777-3060; www.mangotangoart.com; 4003 Raphune Hill; ⏰9:30am-4pm Mon-Sat) The VI's top gallery is far removed in both quality and distance from its downtown brethren. Intricate Haitian metal pieces and contemporary paintings from Washington-based Mel McCuddin are on display alongside the work of the best local painters, potters and

photographers. There are monthly art openings from November to April.

Yacht Haven Grande SHOPPING CENTER
(www.igy-yachthavengrande.com; 5304 Yacht Haven Grande) Next door to Havensight (p826) is this marina and chic shop complex. Gucci and Louis Vuitton headline the tony roster, along with several waterfront bistros where you can sip cosmos and watch megayachts drift into dock. Among the monthly calendar of events is a **farmers market** (www.igy-yachthavengrande.com; Yacht Haven Grande; ⏲10am-5pm 1st & 3rd Sun of month) with produce and crafts.

Information

Waterfront Hwy and Main St in the town center are fine at night, but move a few blocks away and the streets get deserted quickly. Avoid the Savan area, a red-light district that surrounds Main St west of Market Sq and north of the Windward Passage hotel. In general, travelers who take reasonable precautions should have no problems.

Main Post Office (☎774-3750; 5046 Norre Gade; ⏲7:30am-4:30pm Mon-Fri, to noon Sat) Full-service facility by Emancipation Garden.

Main Tourist Office (www.usvitourism.com; 2318 Kronprindsens Gade; ⏲8am-5pm Mon-Fri) Near the seaplane terminal, with pamphlets, local guidebooks and staff eager to help. Also has kiosks at the airport, Havensight and Crown Bay.

Roy Schneider Community Hospital (☎776-8311; www.rlshospital.org; 9048 Sugar Estate Rd; ⏲24hr) On the east side of Charlotte Amalie, this full-service hospital has an emergency room, a recompression chamber and doctors in all major disciplines.

Getting There & Away

AIR

Cyril E King Airport (p855) is located 3 miles west of Charlotte Amalie. Taxis (ie multipassenger vans) are readily available. The fare to downtown is US$7; it's US$15 to Red Hook. Luggage costs US$2 to US$4 extra per piece, depending on the size.

The Seaplane Terminal (p826), where 25-minute flights to St Croix depart, is downtown next to the Marine Terminal.

There's an Avis outlet at the Seaplane Terminal. Otherwise, most rental companies are at the main airport.

BOAT

The **Marine Terminal** (Blyden Terminal; 3400 Waterfront Hwy) is a 10-minute walk west of downtown. It's a hub for ferries to St Croix, and Tortola and Virgin Gorda in the British Virgin Islands. A St John **ferry** (☎776-6597; www.interislandboatservices.com; 1-way adult/child US$20/10) departs from Crown Bay Marina at 3:30pm and 5:30pm daily. Crown Bay (1.5 miles west of downtown) is also one of Charlotte Amalie's two cruise-ship terminals. The other, Havensight, is 1.5 miles east of downtown.

BUS

'Dollar'/safari buses mosey along Waterfront Hwy.

TAXI

Taxis huddle around the Vendors' Plaza. The following are the set, per-person rates from downtown for two or more people:

Frenchtown US$4
Havensight US$5
Magens Bay US$8
Red Hook US$10

Red Hook & East End

The East End holds the bulk of the island's resorts. Red Hook is the only town to speak of, though it's small and built mostly around the St John ferry dock and American Yacht Harbor marina. Lovely beaches sprawl throughout the area, along with ace opportunities for diving, fishing and kayaking.

Sights

★**Lindquist Beach** BEACH
(adult/child US$5/free; ⏲8am-5pm) Part of protected Smith Bay Park, this narrow strand off Smith Bay Rd is a beauty all right: calm, true-blue water laps the soft white sand, while several cays shimmer in the distance. Hollywood has filmed several commercials here. There's a lifeguard, picnic tables and a bathhouse with showers, but no other amenities. It's low-key and lovely for a swim. Parking costs US$2. Cash only.

★**Tillett Gardens** ARTS CENTER
(www.tillettgardens.com; 4126 Anna's Retreat; ⏲11am-11pm Tue-Sat) This colorful artists' colony near Tutu Park Mall lures hippies, thinkers, musicians and outcasts with its good-times vibe and welcoming spirit. On any given day you might witness a concert on the outdoor stage, a play in the 150-seat Pistarckle Theater or artists at work in their studios. There are also bars, cafes, restaurants and a hostel (p832) for overnight stays.

Coki Beach BEACH
Coki is on a protected cove at the entrance to Coral World marine park. The snorkeling is excellent, with lots of fish action, and you can dive from the shore with gear from the on-site dive shop (p832). The narrow beach fills up with locals and tourists enjoying the eateries, hair-braiding vendors and loud music. A festive scene results. However, Coki is the one beach on St Thomas with touts – as soon as you arrive someone will quickly become your 'friend.'

Secret Harbour Beach BEACH
() Small and hammock-strewn, this west-facing beach in front of the eponymous resort could hardly be more tranquil. It's an excellent place to snorkel with equipment rented from the resort's water-sports operation. Kids like swimming out to the platform that floats in the bay. Bathrooms and food are available.

Sapphire Beach BEACH
Sapphire is among St Thomas' prettiest white-sand beaches, and accordingly it draws a big tourist crowd. Amenities include water-sports rentals (paddleboards, snorkel gear, kayaks), bathrooms and a bar-restaurant. There's good snorkeling on the reef to the right of the beach.

Activities & Tours

★Coki Dive Center DIVING
(775-4220; www.cokidive.com; Coki Point; 1-tank beach dive US$65, 2-tank boat dive US$110; 9am-3pm) Just steps from Coki Beach (p832), this outfit offers shore and night dives in addition to boat dives, plus PADI courses. Also rents snorkels (US$10 per day).

Red Hook Dive Center DIVING
(777-3483; www.redhookdivecenter.com; American Yacht Harbor; 2-tank dive US$130, 4hr snorkel tour US$79; 8am-5pm) Boat dives depart from here for all the fishy hot spots. There's a night dive every Wednesday (or by request), and guided snorkeling trips in the afternoons to two or three nearby reefs.

Ocean Surfari FISHING
(227-5448; www.oceansurfari.com; American Yacht Harbor) Runs private sports-fishing charters of between four and 10 hours (US$650 to US$1450) on a 37ft boat. It also offers half-day open-boat charters starting at US$150 per person for those not traveling in a big group.

Nate's Custom Charters BOATING
(244-2497; www.stthomasboatcharters.com; Compass Point Marina, 6300 Estate Frydenhoj 107a) Fishing, snorkeling, island-hopping: Nate's arranges boat, captain and gear to do any or all. Prices vary by group size and destinations.

★Virgin Islands Ecotours KAYAKING
(779-2155; www.viecotours.com; Mangrove Lagoon Marina; 3hr tour US$79; 8am-4:30pm) The company offers a three-hour guided kayaking-and-snorkeling expedition where you paddle through a mangrove lagoon to a beach, go for a short hike to a blowhole and then snorkel out to a small shipwreck. Birding and stand-up paddleboard (SUP) trips are available, too. The location is just east of the intersection of Rtes 30 and 32.

Festivals & Events

St Thomas International Regatta SAILING
(www.stthomasinternationalregatta.com; late Mar) World-class racing boats gather at St Thomas Yacht Club.

Sleeping

Resorts are the East End's primary option. Exclusive Resorts (www.exclusiveresortsvi.com) manages several local properties. Many units are privately owned condos, and they vary widely in quality. Savvy visitors say they have better luck booking through home-sharing websites where they deal with the condo owners directly.

Tillett Hostel HOSTEL $
(998-5993; www.tilletthostel.com; 4126 Anna's Retreat, Tillett Gardens; dm US$50, r US$100-150;) Located in a colorful artists' community (p831) within walking distance of Tutu Park Mall, this hostel is your spot for a local experience. There are two well-kept dorms (one for men, one for women), five private rooms (some with bathrooms), a communal TV area and kitchen, and a bar and stage for bands – all within the leafy grounds.

Two Sandals by the Sea Inn B&B $$
(998-2394; www.twosandals.com; 6264 Estate Nazareth; incl breakfast d US$190-310, q US$420;) Two Sandals offers a homey alternative to the East End's resorts. The rooms are nothing fancy, but each is modern and spacious, with a wood-beamed ceiling, crisp linens, dark-wood decor and a private bathroom. Enjoy the pastry-laden continental breakfast on the sea-view balcony. Secret

Harbour's beach is a five-minute walk away, Red Hook's restaurants a 10-minute walk.

Bolongo Bay Beach Resort RESORT $$

(☎775-1800; www.bolongobay.com; 7150 Bolongo Bay; r value/standard from US$175/250, all-inclusive from US$450; ❄🏊) Fun, casual, family-owned Bolongo offers a full array of water sports. The rooms won't win awards for size or decor, but who cares? You'll be outside. 'Ocean-view' rooms are on the 2nd and 3rd floors; 'beachfront' rooms are on the 1st floor. All have sea views and private patios. The 'value' rooms are in a building across the street.

★Point Pleasant Resort RESORT $$$

(☎888-619-4010; www.pointpleasantresort.com; 6600 Estate Smith Bay; ste US$325-450; ❄📶🏊) On a steep hill overlooking Water Bay, this resort with island-chic decor has lots of charm. The suites are in multiunit buildings tucked into the hillside forest. Each suite has full kitchen, separate bedroom and large porch. The grounds feature walking trails and three pools. It's about a half mile from Coki Beach.

Secret Harbour Beach Resort RESORT $$$

(☎775-6550; www.secretharbourvi.com; 6280 Estate Nazareth; ste US$325-990; ❄@📶🏊) Secret Harbour is a family favorite, with 48 suites filling four buildings right on the serene, palmy, same-named beach with water-sports opportunities. Suites come in three main sizes: studio (660 sq ft), one bedroom (935 sq ft) and two bedrooms (1360 sq ft). All have a kitchen and a balcony or patio prime for sunset views.

Pavilions & Pools RESORT $$$

(☎800-524-2001; www.pavilionsandpools.com; 6400 Estate Smith Bay; ste US$300-350; ❄📶🏊) The cool thing about this small property is that each of the 25 suites has its own pool – yeah, you read that right. Suites have full kitchens and separate bedrooms with sliding doors that open to your own swimmin' hole. Each unit is individually owned, so quality can vary. Sapphire Beach is within walking distance.

Eating & Drinking

★Pizza Pi PIZZA $$

(☎643-4674; www.pizza-pi.com; Christmas Cove; 16in pizza US$20-30; ⏰11am-6pm) Food trucks may now be a ubiquitous trend, but there are few parts of the world where a 'food boat' is the most popular eatery around. Such is the case with Pizza Pi, a floating restaurant in Christmas Cove with three seasonal menus of New York–style pies (including gluten-free options), plus creative cocktails by the pitcher.

XO Bistro AMERICAN $$

(☎779-2069; www.xobistro.net; 6501 Red Hook Plaza No 1; mains lunch US$11-16, dinner US$25-30; ⏰11am-2am; 📶) Low-lit XO mixes it up with casual salads, sandwiches and flatbread pizzas at lunch and more complex seafood plates such as crab-topped *mahimahi* and blackened tuna at dinner. Weekend brunches, two daily happy hours and one of the largest by-the-glass wine lists on the island add to the fun. Reserve in high season.

Iggie's Oasis SEAFOOD $$

(☎775-1800; 7150 Bolongo Bay; mains US$10-30; ⏰11am-11pm) Set in a large open-air pavilion overlooking the broad shore at Bolongo Bay Beach Resort, festive Iggie's is beloved for its conch fritters with Creole remoulade, grilled fish and rum-soaked Voodoo Juice (which is so potent a concoction it's no longer available by the bucket!). There's live music most evenings.

Duffy's Love Shack BAR

(☎779-2080; www.duffysloveshack.com; 6500 Red Hook Plaza; ⏰11am-midnight Sun, Mon, Tue & Thu, to 2am Wed, Fri & Sat) It may be a frame shack in the middle of a paved parking lot, but Duffy's creates its legendary, tiki-themed atmosphere with high-volume rock and crowds in shorts and tank tops. The people-watching is excellent and the cocktails are great fun, like the 64oz 'shark tank' or the flaming 'volcano.' The food is classic, burger-based pub fare.

Tap & Still BAR

(☎642-2337; www.tapstill.com; American Yacht Harbor; mains US$6-10; ⏰8:30am-midnight) This beyond-the-norm sports bar lets you sip a decent beer selection and cheap bourbon drinks while munching juicy burgers and thick, hand-cut fries in view of boats bobbing in the harbor. Also on the menu: funnel cakes (sugar-topped fried dough), a vastly underrated booze accompaniment. There are Tap & Still branches in Havensight and Cruz Bay (St John).

Getting There & Away

Red Hook's ferry dock bustles, with most traffic headed to St John; passenger ferries (US$8 one way, 20 minutes; cash only) to Cruz Bay depart on the hour. Ferries also go to the British Virgin Islands, running to Tortola's West End at least four times daily and to Road Town three times daily on weekends.

Taxis queue outside the marine terminal; it's US$13 to Charlotte Amalie. A taxi from Red Hook to the resorts runs about US$8 per person.

ST JOHN

Two-thirds of St John is a protected national park, with gnarled trees and spiky cacti spilling over its edges. There are no airports or cruise-ship docks, and the usual Caribbean resorts are few and far between. It's blissfully low-key compared to its island neighbors.

Hiking and snorkeling are top of the to-do list. Trails wind by petroglyphs and sugar-mill ruins, and several drop out onto beaches prime for swimming, with turtles and spotted eagle rays.

Two towns bookend the island: Cruz Bay, the ferry landing and main village that hosts a hell of a happy hour; and Coral Bay at the east end, the sleepy domain of folks who want to feel as though they're living on a frontier.

Getting There & Around

BOAT

All ferries arrive in Cruz Bay. Boats from Red Hook glide into the main ferry dock, while boats from the British Virgin Islands and Crown Bay Marina (near the airport in St Thomas) arrive at a smaller dock by the US Customs & Immigration building a short walk east.

BUS

Vitran (p856) operates air-con buses over the length of the island via Centerline Rd. Buses leave Cruz Bay in front of the ferry terminal at least four times daily. They arrive at Coral Bay about 40 minutes later.

CAR

St John rentals are all via small, independent companies. Most provide 4WDs and SUVs to handle the rugged terrain. Costs hover near US$85 per day. Companies typically have a three- to five-day minimum if you want to reserve. The other option – waiting to rent on the spot – is iffy. Most companies are in Cruz Bay; either they're walkable from the ferries or they'll meet you at the dock.

Courtesy Car Rental (☎776-6650; www.courtesycarrental.com)

St John Car Rental (☎776-6103; www.stjohncarrental.com)

Sunshine's Jeep Rental (☎690-1786; www.sunshinesjeeprental.com; Rte 10)

TAXI

Rates are set. From Cruz Bay it costs US$7 per person to Cinnamon Bay, US$9 to Coral Bay. Call the **St John Taxi Commission** (☎693-7530, 774-3130) for pickups.

Cruz Bay

Nicknamed 'Love City,' St John's main town indeed wafts a carefree, spring-break party vibe. Hippies, sea captains, American retirees and reggae worshipers hoist happy-hour drinks in equal measure, and everyone wears a silly grin at their great good fortune at being here. Cruz Bay is also the place to organize your hiking, snorkeling, kayaking and other activities, and to fuel up in the surprisingly good restaurant mix. Everything grooves within walking distance of the ferry docks.

Sights

Virgin Islands National Park NATIONAL PARK

(☎776-6201, ext 238; www.nps.gov/viis; ⏲visitor center 8am-4:30pm) FREE VI National Park covers two-thirds of St John, plus 5650 acres underwater. It's a tremendous resource, offering miles of shoreline, pristine reefs and 26 hiking trails. The park visitor center sits on the dock across from the Mongoose Junction shopping arcade. It's an essential first stop to obtain free guides on hiking, birdwatching, petroglyph sites and ranger-led activities. Green iguanas, geckos, hawksbill turtles and wild donkeys roam the landscape. A couple of good trails leave from behind the center.

Activities

Hiking

★**Reef Bay Hike** HIKING

(☎693-7275; www.friendsvinp.org/events/hike; per person US$40; ⏲9am-3pm twice weekly) Rangers from VI National Park guide you on a 3-mile downhill trek through tropical forests, past petroglyphs and plantation ruins, to a swimming beach at Reef Bay, where a boat runs you back to Cruz Bay (hence the fee). It's very popular, and the park recommends reserving at least two weeks ahead. Departure is from the park visitor center.

HIKING ST JOHN

St John is the premier island for hiking. Virgin Islands National Park maintains 26 paths, and any reasonably fit hiker can walk them safely without a local guide. Preview trails and download a map at the park website (www.nps.gov/viis). The Friends of the Park Store (p837) sells a terrific, more detailed map for US$4.

If you prefer guided jaunts, the park sponsors several free ones, including birding expeditions and shore hikes, but its best-known offering is the Reef Bay Hike (p834). Rangers lead the 3-mile trek that takes in petroglyphs and plantation ruins and ends with a swim at Reef Bay's beach. The tour fee covers a taxi to the trailhead (about 5 miles from Cruz Bay) and a boat ride back.

These other favorite trails are each less than 3 miles round trip; all have identifying signs at the trailheads and small parking lots.

Ram Head (p839) Rocky, uphill slog to a worth-every-drop-of-sweat clifftop view.

Lind Point (p835) Departs from behind the park visitor center and runs past donkeys and banana quits to secluded Honeymoon Beach.

Leinster Bay (p838) Goes from the Annaberg sugar-mill ruins to fantastic snorkeling at Waterlemon Cay.

Cinnamon Bay (p838) Easy loop trail that swings through tropical forest and mill ruins.

A taxi takes you to the trailhead. Book online or at the Friends of the Park Store (p837).

Lind Point Trail HIKING

One of the area's most accessible trails, this hike departs from behind the national-park visitor center and moseys for 1.1 miles through cactus and dry forest, past the occasional donkey and banana quit, to Honeymoon Beach. A 0.4-mile upper track goes to Lind Battery, once a British gun emplacement, 160ft above the sea. The lower track goes directly to the beach.

Water Sports

SolShine SUP WATER SPORTS

(☎850-371-0837; www.solshinesup.com; Westin Resort; yoga class/3hr SUP tour US$45/75, half-day SUP rental US$50) Let bubbly SUP and yoga instructor Thais take you into the water for some paddleboard yoga or a ride around Haulover Bay to the Lime Out taco joint (p840). Other tours include Chocolate Hole and Hurricane Hole.

Arawak Expeditions KAYAKING

(☎693-8312; www.arawakexp.com; Mongoose Junction; half-/full-day trips from US$75/120; ⏲10am-6pm) Well-planned kayaking and SUP trips depart Cruz Bay and glide around the North Shore to Henley Cay. Other trips launch from Coral Bay and head to Hurricane Hole. Arawak's shop sells all the water-sports supplies you may need on the island and also rents snorkel gear (US$7 per day).

Low Key Watersports DIVING

(☎693-8999; www.divelowkey.com; One Bay St; 2-tank dive US$145; ⏲8:30am-6pm) A great dive-training facility with some of the most experienced instructors on the islands. It offers wreck dives to the RMS *Rhone,* as well as night dives and dive packages. It also has day trips on 35ft speedboats that go to either the Baths (p254) or Jost Van Dyke in the British Virgin Islands through sister company **Ocean Runner** (www.oceanrunnerusvi.com).

Festivals & Events

St John Carnival CULTURAL

(www.stjohnfestival.org; ⏲early Jul) The island's biggest celebration falls around Emancipation Day (July 3) and US Independence Day (July 4). There's a food fair, a parade, beauty pageants, fireworks and more.

Sleeping

Inn at Tamarind Court HOTEL $

(☎776-6378; www.innattamarindcourt.com; Rte 104; s US$70; ❄📶) The 2017 hurricanes knocked out the main building at Tamarind Court, so at research time the inn was only operating its basic block with six single rooms sharing two bathrooms. Standard rooms, suites and apartments were forthcoming in 2020, as was a new restaurant.

MONGOOSES, DONKEYS & GOATS – OH MY!

Whether you're camping, hiking or driving on St John, it won't be long before you have a close encounter with the island's odd menagerie of feral animals. Hundreds of goats, donkeys, pigs and cats roam the island, descendants of domestic animals abandoned to the jungle eons ago. White-tailed deer and mongooses are two other introduced species that multiplied in unexpected numbers.

The donkeys are the big attention-grabbers. Often you'll see them on Centerline Rd, where they'll come right up to your car and stick their snouts in any open window.

Do not tempt the animals by offering them food or leaving food or garbage where they can get at it. And do not approach them for petting or taking a snapshot. While most have a live-and-let-live attitude and don't mind your stepping around them on the trails, they are all capable of aggression if provoked.

★St John Inn HOTEL **$$**
(☎693-8688; www.stjohninn.com; 277 Estate Enighed; r incl breakfast US$215-340; ❄📶🏊) The 14 rooms at this uberpopular inn feature bright-hued walls, tile floors and handcrafted wooden furniture. A homey atmosphere pervades, and guests grill fresh fish on the communal barbecue, laze on the sundeck or take a dip in the small pool. Evening rum punch and beach chairs are included in rates. Located up the hill from the ferry dock.

Cruz Bay Boutique Hotel HOTEL **$$**
(☎642-1702; www.cruzbayhotel.com; King St; incl breakfast r US$205-265, ste US$300-385; ❄📶) The closest lodging to the ferry dock, this place is right in the heart of Cruz Bay. The 14 tidy white rooms are located above an Italian restaurant, and are good value for the island, which is why they book up fast. There's also one larger suite with kitchen and living room. Breakfast features local pastries.

Garden by the Sea B&B B&B **$$**
(☎779-4731; www.gardenbythesea.com; 203 Enighed Rd; r US$195-300; ❄📶) B&B-ers swoon over this place. The owners live on-site and have splashed the three rooms, each with a sturdy, four-poster canopy bed and private bathroom, in bright hues of sea green, lavender and blueberry. Solar panels provide the electricity. Cash or traveler's checks only. Three- to six-night minimum stay.

★Coconut Coast Villas APARTMENT **$$$**
(☎693-9100; www.coconutcoast.com; 268 Estate Enighed; 1-/2-/3-bedroom apt from US$197/307/395; ❄📶🏊) The nine units in this compound – including single-room studios, two-bedroom suites and three-bedroom spreads when combined – stand right on the cobblestone beach at Turner Bay. Each apartment comes with local art, kitchen, private deck and wi-fi. The swimming pool, hot tub and barbecue grill are shared. Cruz Bay is a 10-minute walk over the hill. Three-night minimum stay.

Eating

North Shore Deli CAFE **$**
(☎777-3061; www.northshoredelistjohn.com; Mongoose Junction; mains US$9-13; ⏰7am-6pm Mon-Sat, 8am-3pm Sun; 📶) The morning spot in Cruz Bay, with an array of coffees, breakfast plates and baked goodies. The lunch sandwiches – all with meats slow-roasted in-house – are a cut above the norm. It's dark and highly air-conditioned, offering a welcome respite from the sun.

★Rootz Cafe CARIBBEAN **$$**
(Forward to Your Roots; ☎677-0950; Contant Point Rd; medium/large plates US$15/20; ⏰noon-6pm Mon-Sat; 🌱) This small food wagon whips up some seriously good Rasta food. The menu changes daily, but you can expect a wide array of healthy vegan bites, all piled high in a styrofoam to-go container. Tell owner Lance Brathwaite your ailments and he'll send you away with a herbaceous medicinal juice.

★Longboard CALIFORNIAN **$$**
(☎715-2210; www.thelongboardstjohn.com; cnr Prince & King Sts; mains US$16-35; ⏰3-10pm; 📶) Fresh, healthy, veggie- and grain-packed meals make this whitewashed, surf-themed spot stand out from the greasy, deep-fried pack. Enjoy raw fish as poke, ceviche or sushi, or munch on a fully loaded quinoa bowl. Your body will thank you!

Uncle Joe's BBQ BARBECUE **$$**
(☎693-8806; North Shore Rd; mains US$12-18; ⏰11:30am-8:30pm) Locals and visitors go wild tearing into the barbecue chicken, ribs and corn on the cob at this open-air restau-

rant across from the post office. The chef grills the meats outside, perfuming the entire harbor-front with their tangy goodness. Cash only.

Da Livio ITALIAN **$$**
(☎779-8900; www.dalivio.it; King St; mains US$22-44; ⏲5:30-10pm Tue-Sat) Fork into authentic Italian food lovingly cooked by a chef transplanted from the motherland. Staff members make all the pasta and gnocchi from scratch. The wood-fired, crisp-crust pizzas are a favorite, as are the hearty wines. Corks dot the ceiling, and the black-and-white decor gives the trattoria a sleek-casual ambience.

Lime Inn SEAFOOD **$$**
(☎776-6425; www.thelimeinn.com; King St; mains US$14-36; ⏲11:30am-9:30pm Mon-Fri, 5-9:30pm Sat; 📶) Lime Inn is a travelers' favorite for quality cuisine and top-notch service at moderate prices. Tables sit amid swaying plants, gently spinning fans and pops of bright-green paint on the walls. The New England clam chowder, seafood pasta and chocolatey desserts earn rave reviews. Reservations are a good idea.

★**Morgan's Mango** CARIBBEAN **$$$**
(☎693-8141; www.morgansmango.com; mains US$30-40; ⏲5:30-10pm) Take in a view of the harbor while dining on imaginative Caribbean recipes in dishes such as Haitian voodoo snapper or Cuban citrus chicken. The owners often bring in live acoustic acts (usually Wednesday through Friday), making Morgan's a good choice for a fun or romantic night out. It's by Mongoose Junction.

Drinking & Nightlife

★**Bajo El Sol Gallery & Art Bar** BAR
(www.facebook.com/bajoelsolgallery; Mongoose Junction; ⏲10am-7pm Mon-Sat) Just when you begin to lament the lack of cultural spaces in the USVI you find a place like Bajo El Sol, which showcases local painters, potters and woodworkers, screens Caribbean documentaries, and runs monthly events such as high-end rum tastings, pop-up dinners or book signings. Stimulate your mind as you sip fine wines or espresso coffees at the Art Bar.

★**Tap Room** MICROBREWERY
(☎715-7775; www.stjohnbrewers.com; Mongoose Junction, 2nd fl; ⏲11am-midnight; 📶) St John Brewers makes its sunny, citrusy suds here. Join locals hanging off the barstools and sip a flagship Mango Pale Ale, or try the alcohol-free options, including house-made root beer, ginger beer and Green Flash energy drink. Sample-laden tours (US$12) are available upon request. Sign up in the downstairs Brewtique, which has fun souvenirs for sale.

Good sandwich-y pub grub is available if you get hungry.

Woody's Seafood Saloon BAR
(☎779-4625; www.woodysseafood.com; cnr Prince & King Sts; ⏲11am-1am) St John's daily party starts here at 3pm, when the price on domestic beers drops precipitously (US$2 for a bottle of Coors). By 4pm the tanned crowd in the tiny place has spilled onto the sidewalk. Short-shorted bartenders pass beers out a streetside window. Woody's serves some reasonable nosh; try the shark bites (spiced fish pieces).

Shopping

Friends of the Park Store GIFTS & SOUVENIRS
(☎779-8700; www.friendsvinp.org; Mongoose Junction; ⏲10am-6pm) 🍃 Looking for paper made out of local donkey poo? Thought so. It's here, along with shelves of other ecofriendly wares and sea-glass jewelry. Proceeds go to the Virgin Islands National Park.

Information

There's a FirstBank branch with ATM in the Marketplace Building and a Popular (formerly Banco Popular) branch with ATM near the ferry dock.

Post Office (☎779-4227; cnr Henry Samuel & King Sts; ⏲7:30am-4pm Mon-Fri, to noon Sat) Across the street from the BVI ferry dock.

US Customs & Immigration (☎776-6741; ⏲10am-5:30pm) If you arrive on a ferry or on a yacht from the British Virgin Islands, you must clear immigration here (typically a hassle-free process) before you head into town. It adjoins the BVI ferry dock and was running out of a beige trailer following the 2017 hurricanes.

Visitors Center (Henry Samuel St; ⏲8am-5pm Mon-Fri) A small building next to the post office with brochures and whatnot.

Getting There & Away

BOAT

Boats from Red Hook, St Thomas, arrive at the busy main ferry dock, while boats from Crown Bay Marina (near the St Thomas airport) and the British Virgin Islands arrive at The Creek, which is beside the old customs building. Check Inter Island (p855) for Crown Bay and BVI schedules. Main routes:

Red Hook, St Thomas US$8.15 one way, 20 minutes, hourly (big pieces of luggage cost US$4 extra).
Crown Bay Marina, St Thomas US$20 one way, 45 minutes, two daily (big pieces of luggage cost US$5 extra).
Jost Van Dyke US$80 one way, 45 minutes, two daily Friday to Sunday.

BUS

Vitran (p856) buses pick up in front of the ferry terminal and stop along Centerline Rd en route to Coral Bay (a 40-minute trip). While they used to run almost hourly, the schedule was reduced to just four buses per day after the 2017 hurricanes. Check the website for the latest.

TAXI

Taxis hang out by the ferry terminal. From downtown it costs US$6 per person to Trunk Bay, US$7 to Cinnamon or Maho Bays and US$9 to Coral Bay.

North Shore

Life's a beach on the tranquil North Shore, where the national park's main attractions lie, including its most popular patches of sand and their swimming and hiking hot spots.

Sights & Activities

Snorkeling is the main event at the beaches. A couple of the larger strands rent gear on-site. For the others, it's best to rent gear from dive shops in Cruz Bay.

★Francis Bay BEACH

Francis Bay is home to one of the most serene stretches of sand on St John, with calm waters and fewer tourists than at any other beach of its size. It's also a prime spot for birdwatching, with an easy half-mile trail that circles around a salt pond over to the ruins of the Francis Bay Estate House. The best snorkeling here is along the rocky northern edge of the beach, by Mary Point.

★Annaberg Sugar Mill Ruins HISTORIC SITE

(www.nps.gov/viis; 9am-4pm, demonstrations 10am-2pm Mon-Wed) FREE Part of the national park, this site near Leinster Bay is home to the most intact sugar-plantation ruins in the Virgin Islands. A 30-minute self-directed walking tour leads you through the slave quarters, village, windmill, rum still and dungeon. The schooner drawings on the dungeon wall may date back more than 100 years.

Cultural demonstrations take place here at least three days a week and range from baking 'dum bread' to basketweaving.

Afterwards, tread the **Leinster Bay Trail** that starts near the picnic area and ends at, yep, Leinster Bay. It's 1.6 miles round trip.

★Leinster Bay BEACH

This bay adjoins the Annaberg mill ruins. Park in the plantation's lot and follow the trail along the water for 25 minutes. Some of St John's best snorkeling is at the bay's east end, offshore at **Waterlemon Cay**, where turtles, spotted eagle rays, barracudas and nurse sharks swim. Be aware that the current can be strong. There are no amenities and usually few people out here.

Maho Bay BEACH

The water here is shallow and less choppy than elsewhere (good for snorkeling and kids), and it's a good bet you'll see green sea turtles in the early morning or late afternoon, and maybe a stingray or two. There's a parking lot and a changing room, as well as a bar, a food truck and water-sports rentals. Maho can get crowded (especially after 11am), but never overwhelmingly so.

Honeymoon Beach BEACH

Honeymoon is a mile's hike from the park visitor center along the Lind Point Trail. The handsome, white-sand strand is often empty and quiet – except on days when charter boats arrive between midmorning and midafternoon. A hut sells snacks, and rents chairs, hammocks, kayaks and other water-sports gear. Snorkeling is good off the west side, where psychedelic fish and turtles swarm over the coral reef.

Cinnamon Bay BEACH

Mile-long Cinnamon Bay is St John's biggest beach and arguably its best. At research time, however, it was a sad sight: Cinnamon's archaeological museum, campground, restaurant and water-sports facilities all lay in ruins following the 2017 hurricanes. Plans were afoot to clean the area up and reopen the campground and other facilities by the end of 2020. Check the NPS website for the latest.

Across the highway, a half-mile hiking trail winds by the ruins of an old sugar factory.

Trunk Bay BEACH

(adult/child US$5/free) This long, gently arching beach is the most popular strand on the island and the only one that charges a fee. There are showers, toilets, picnic facilities, snorkel rental, a snack bar and a taxi stand. The sandy stretch is certainly scenic, but it often gets packed. Everyone comes here to swim the underwater snorkeling trail, though experienced snorkelers will likely not be impressed by the murkiness or quality of what's on offer beneath the surface.

Jumbie Bay BEACH
Jumbie is the word for ghost in the Creole dialect, and this secluded beach has a plethora of ghost stories. Look for the parking lot on North Shore Rd that holds only seven cars. From here, take the short trail down to the sand.

Hawksnest Bay BEACH
The bay here is a deep circular indentation between hills with a narrow ring of sand on its fringe. The beach is usually pretty quiet. Amenities include a bathroom, a picnic shelter and barbecue grills.

Tours

Virgin Islands Ecotours KAYAKING
(☎779-2155; www.viecotours.com; Honeymoon Beach; 3hr tours adult/child US$89/59) This groovy company, which also operates on St Thomas, offers several guided jaunts that include kayaking, snorkeling and/or hiking. Some trips are kid-friendly (Caneel Bay), some strenuous (Henley Cay). Most tours depart from Honeymoon Beach, but a few leave near the national-park visitor center.

Sleeping

★**Estate Lindholm** INN $$$
(☎776-6121; www.estatelindholm.com; North Shore Rd; r from US$265; ❄ 📶 🏊) This beautifully landscaped hilltop property less than a mile from Cruz Bay ticks all the right boxes. Each of the 17 rooms is tastefully appointed and has rocking chairs on the balcony to take in the view. There's also a serene pool and honor bar. More perks include complimentary ferry pickup on arrival and access to beach chairs and snorkels.

Getting There & Away

A rental car is the easiest way to see the area via North Shore Rd (Rte 20), which is full of scenic lookouts ripe for photo sessions. Taxis will also drop you at the beaches. From Cruz Bay it costs US$7 per person to Cinnamon Bay and US$9 per person to Leinster Bay.

Coral Bay & East End

Coral Bay, St John's second town, is a slowpoke frontier outpost. Located at the island's east end, the area is ripe for hiking and solitary beach walks.

Sights & Activities

Salt Pond Bay BEACH
Salt Pond Bay provides decent snorkeling in calm water. Keep an eye out for turtles. Two dandy trails take off from the beach's southern end: the Ram Head Trail rises to a tall cliff jabbing into the sea, and the Drunk Bay Trail leads to some crazy rock art. The beach has shaded picnic tables and a bathroom. It's located a few miles from Coral Bay town, down Rte 107 and a 10-minute walk from the parking lot.

★**Ram Head Trail** HIKING
This moderately difficult path climbs from Salt Pond Bay over switchbacks to Ram Head promontory, 200ft above the water at St John's southernmost tip, a grandly lonesome and windswept place. It's 2 miles round trip and exposed, so bring sun protection. Try to go for sunset or at night during a full moon.

Drunk Bay Trail HIKING
The easy footpath leaves Salt Pond Bay and follows the rim of the inland salt pond to a wild, rocky beach that faces east to the British Virgin Islands. The trade-wind-driven seas pile up on this shore, and the waves carry all manner of coral, fishing nets and other flotsam that locals sculpt into eye-popping artworks. It's 0.6 miles round trip.

Carolina Corral HORSEBACK RIDING
(☎693-5778; www.horsesstjohn.com; 16133 Spring Garden; 1½hr rides adult/child US$85/75; ⏱by appointment) Saddle up a trusty steed for a 1½-hour jaunt on rugged trails to a rocky beach. All the horses are rescue animals.

Eating

All lodgings on this quiet side of the island are private villas and cottage rentals.

Skinny Legs BURGERS $
(☎779-4982; www.skinnylegsvi.com; Rte 10; mains US$10-14; ⏱11am-9pm) Salty sailors and East End villa dwellers mix it up at this open-air grill just past the old fire station. Overlooking a small boatyard, Skinny Legs' focus isn't the view but the jovial clientele and the

lively bar scene. Cheeseburgers win the most raves, so open wide for one, or try a grilled-fish sandwich. Live music and dancing rock weekend nights.

★Lime Out VI TACOS **$$**
(☎643-5333; www.limeoutvi.com; Hansen Bay; single taco US$7-10; ⏰11:30am-5pm) What could be more gratifying than paddling into the turquoise sea, tying up your kayak or SUP to a floating solar-powered restaurant, swimming over to the bar and noshing on tacos packed with blackened tuna or rum-glazed ribs? Oh, and then there are the creative craft cocktails (served in reusable adult sippy cups). Make an afternoon of it!

Miss Lucy's CARIBBEAN **$$**
(☎693-5244; Rte 107; mains US$13-30; ⏰11am-9pm Tue-Thu, to 4pm Fri & Sat, 10am-2pm Sun; 📶) Miss Lucy passed away in 2007 at age 91, but her restaurant lives on, as famous for its Sunday jazz brunch and piña colada pancakes as for its weekday conch chowder and johnnycakes – all served at the water's edge under the sea-grape trees as the occasional pet goat wanders by.

Rhumb Lines FUSION **$$$**
(☎776-0303; www.rhumblinesstjohn.com; Rte 10; mains US$28-38; ⏰5-10pm Mon-Sat, 10am-2pm & 5-10pm Sun) Coral Bay's classiest joint is decorated in a tropical South Seas style and offers creative dishes melding Thai, Szechuan, Filipino and other Asian flavors. Try selections from the 'pu pu' menu, a mix of tapas-like treats, which are half-price during happy hour. Well-made cocktails accompany the food, while tiki torches and string lights give the patio a cheerful vibe.

Getting There & Away

Coral Bay is just over 8 miles from Cruz Bay, but it takes a good 30 minutes or so to drive it over the winding roads. The public Vitran (p856) bus also runs between the two towns. A taxi costs US$9 per person.

ST CROIX

St Croix is the Virgins' big boy – it's more than twice the size of St Thomas – and it sports an exceptional topography spanning mountains, a spooky 'rainforest' and a fertile coastal plain that, once upon a time, earned it the nickname 'Garden of the Antilles' for its sugarcane-growing prowess. Today the island is known for its scuba diving, rum making, marine sanctuary and 18th-century forts.

Perhaps because St Croix drifts by its lonesome 40 miles south of the other Virgins, the vibe here is noticeably different: it feels less touristy, less congested, and more 'lived in' by locals. It has two main towns: Christiansted, the largest, sits on the northeast shore; Frederiksted, its much quieter counterpart, resides on the west end, where an occasional cruise ship glides in and kicks up the pace.

Getting There & Away

AIR

Henry E Rohlsen Airport (p855) is on St Croix' southwestern side and handles flights from the US, some connecting via San Juan, Puerto Rico, or St Thomas.

Seaborne Airlines (p855) flies seaplanes between St Thomas and St Croix – a sweet little ride (one way US$90, 25 minutes). Planes land in Christiansted's downtown harbor.

BOAT

The cruise-ship dock is in Frederiksted on the island's west end.

QE IV Ferry (☎473-1322; www.qe4ferry.com) runs twice-daily ferries (US$60 one way, 2½ hours) between Gallows Bay on St Croix and Blyden Terminal on St Thomas. Ships don't run on Wednesday.

Getting Around

BUS

Vitran (p856) buses travel along Centerline Rd between Christiansted and Frederiksted. The schedule is erratic; buses depart roughly every hour or two in daylight.

CAR

Rentals start at about US$55 per day. Many companies have branches at both the main airport and the seaplane dock.

Avis (☎778-9355; www.avis.com)
Budget (☎778-9636; www.budgetstcroix.com)
Centerline Car Rentals (☎888-288-8755; www.stxrentalcar.com)
Hertz (☎778-1402; www.rentacarstcroix.com)
Olympic (☎718-3000; www.olympicstcroix.com; Northside Rd; ⏰7:30am-6pm)

TAXI

Rates are set. It costs US$24 to go between Christiansted and Frederiksted.

Christiansted

Christiansted evokes a melancholy hint of the past. Cannon-covered Fort Christiansvaern rises up on the waterfront. It abuts Kings Wharf, the commercial landing where, for more than 250 years, ships landed with enslaved people and set off with sugar or molasses. Today the wharf is fronted by a boardwalk of restaurants, dive shops and bars. It all comes together as a well-provisioned base from which to explore the island.

Sights

★Christiansted National Historic Site HISTORIC SITE
(☎773-1460; www.nps.gov/chri; Hospital St; US$7; ⊙8:30am-4:30pm) This historic site includes several structures. The most impressive is **Fort Christiansvaern** (1749), a four-point citadel occupying the deep-yellow buildings on the town's east side. Built out of Danish bricks (brought over as ships' ballast), the fort guarded against pirate onslaughts, hurricanes and slave revolts. Cannon on the ramparts, an echoey, claustrophobic dungeon, and latrines with top-notch sea views await inside. The fort entrance has brochures for self-guided exploration of the other nearby historic buildings.

Protestant Cay BEACH
(👪) This small oval cay, located less than 200yd from Kings Wharf, is a little oasis. It's the site of a mellow resort (p842) with a sandy beach and bar-restaurant that are open to the public. The **water-sports center** (☎773-7060; www.facebook.com/stcroixwatersports; ⊙10am-4pm Oct-May, by reservation Jun-Sep) rents out snorkel gear, kayaks and pedal boats. There's a decent amount of underwater life to see while snorkeling. It's also great for kids, with calm, shallow water. The ferry (US$5 round trip, five minutes) departs from the wharf in front of the **King Christian Hotel** (1102 Kings Wharf).

Danish West India & Guinea Company Warehouse HISTORIC BUILDING
(Hospital St) This three-story neoclassical building began life in 1749 as the headquarters and warehouse for the Danish West India and Guinea Company. The central courtyard was the site of one of the West Indies' most active slave markets until the abolition of the slave trade in 1848. The building is privately owned, so you can't go inside.

Activities & Tours

Christiansted is chock-full of operators that book Buck Island excursions and diving trips around the island.

Diving

Dive Experience DIVING
(☎773-3307; www.divexp.com; 2-tank dive US$115; ⊙8am-6pm) Owned by master instructor Michelle Pugh, this shop on the boardwalk at King's Alley has been around for 35-plus years and has a strong environmental commitment. Boats go out most days around 9am for a half-day trip.

St Croix Ultimate Bluewater Adventures DIVING
(☎773-5994; www.stcroixscuba.com; 81 Queen Cross St; 2-tank dive US$130; ⊙7:30am-7pm Mon-Sat, to 5pm Sun) An ultraprofessional company that offers dives all over the island. Also runs both introductory and technical PADI dive-training courses.

Boating

★Caribbean Sea Adventures BOATING
(☎773-2628; www.caribbeanseaadventures.com; 1102 Kings Wharf; ⊙8am-5pm) Half-day trips to Buck Island are aboard a glass-bottom powerboat; full-day trips are on a catamaran. Half-/full-day trips cost US$75/95.

Big Beard's Adventures BOATING
(☎773-4482; www.bigbeards.com; Caravelle Hotel, Queen Cross St; ⊙8am-6pm Mon-Sat, to 5pm Sun) Makes trips to Buck Island aboard catamaran sailboats. Half-/full-day trips cost US$75/105. Also does sunset sails (US$35).

Hiking

St Croix Hiking Association HIKING
(www.stcroixhiking.org) Sponsors a couple of guided hikes per month. They're in offbeat locales, are moderately strenuous and take three to five hours. The cost is US$10.

St Croix Environmental Association OUTDOORS
(☎773-1989; www.stxenvironmental.org; 5032 Anchor Way, Suite 4; ⊙9am-5pm Mon-Fri) Offers two-hour hiking, birdwatching, kayaking and snorkeling trips a few times a month. Many are free; some cost US$10 to US$50 depending on the activity. Departure points vary.

Tours

★Virgin Islands Food Tours FOOD & DRINK
(☎866-498-3684; www.vifoodtours.com; 23 King St; 3hr tour adult/child US$99/59; ⏱10:30am Fri & Sat or by request) Stroll the streets of downtown Christiansted with a local guide, stopping at six spots to enjoy an authentic Crucian lunch, Caribbean baked goods, bush teas and more. Along the way, you'll glean a wealth of information on St Croix' history.

Tan Tan Jeep Tours ADVENTURE
(☎773-7041; www.stxtantantours.com; 33 Queen Cross St; ⏱9am-4pm) Tan Tan goes four-wheeling to the Annaly Bay tide pools (p846), deep into the rainforest and to other hard-to-reach destinations. Tours range from 2½ hours (US$120 per person) to eight hours (US$200 per person). Book at least 48 hours ahead.

Festivals & Events

Jump ups (music-filled street carnivals) take place four times a year, usually in February, May, July and November.

Art Thursday ART
(www.facebook.com/artthursday; ⏱5-8pm, 3rd Thu of month Nov-May) Several painters, jewelry makers and photographers have galleries in town, and the third Thursday of the month from November through May they stay open late to party. Food and music are part of the hoppin' scene.

Taste of St Croix FOOD & DRINK
(www.tasteofstcroix.com; Queen Cross St; ⏱Apr) This annual fest has grown over the past two decades to become one of the finest food and wine events in the Caribbean. More than 40 restaurants, caterers and farms congregate on Queen Cross St for one epic night of fine dining.

Crucian Christmas Festival CHRISTMAS
(www.vicarnivalschedule.com/stcroix/; ⏱early Dec-early Jan) A month of pageants, parades and calypso competitions puts a West Indies spin on the Christmas holidays.

Sleeping

Christiansted's hotels are conveniently located downtown, walkable to bars, shops and restaurants.

★Hotel on the Cay HOTEL $$
(☎773-2035; www.hotelonthecay.com; r US$150-200;) The hotel sits offshore on its own little island called Protestant Cay (p841), accessible via a five-minute ferry ride (free for guests). It's good value for the spacious rooms with full kitchenettes and bright furnishings, even if they're a bit worn. Private balconies let you take in cool breezes and sea views. Access to the island's small beach and pool is included.

Company House Hotel BOUTIQUE HOTEL $$
(☎773-1377; www.hotelcompanyhouse.com; 2 Company St; r US$209-247;) Chris-

DIVING ST CROIX

If you are a scuba enthusiast worth your sea salt, you'll be spending lots of time underwater in St Croix. It's a diver's mecca thanks to two unique features: one, it's surrounded by a massive barrier reef, so turtles, rays and other sea creatures are prevalent; and, two, a spectacular wall runs along the island's north shore, dropping at a 60-degree slope to a depth of more than 3200ft.

The best dives on the north shore are at Cane Bay Wall and North Star Wall. The top west-island dives are at the Butler Bay shipwrecks (including the *Suffolk Maid* and *Rosaomaira*) and at Frederiksted Pier. While almost all dive operators offer boat dives, many of the most exciting dives, such as Cane Bay, involve beach entries with short swims to the reef.

The operators listed here go to the various sites around the island:

Cane Bay Dive Shop (p847) Recommended outfit located across from the pier in Frederiksted, though its boats depart from Salt River Marina.

Dive Experience (p841) Half-day trips departing most days from Christiansted.

N2 The Blue (p847) Specializes in west-end wreck dives and Frederiksted Pier dives (including colorful night dives).

St Croix Ultimate Bluewater Adventures (p841) Offers dives across the island.

WORTH A TRIP

BUCK ISLAND REEF NATIONAL MONUMENT

For such a small landmass – 1 mile long by half a mile wide – Buck Island draws big crowds. It's not so much what's on top but what's underneath that fascinates: a 19,015-acre, fish-frenzied coral-reef system, known as **Buck Island Reef National Monument** (www.nps.gov/buis), that surrounds the island.

The sea gardens and a marked underwater trail create captivating **snorkeling** on the island's east side. On land at pretty **Turtle Beach**, endangered hawksbill and green sea turtles come ashore. A **hiking trail** circles the island's west end and leads to an impressive observation point.

Most visitors glide here aboard tour boats departing from Kings Wharf in Christiansted, 5 miles to the west. Expect to pay US$75/100 (half/full day) per person, including snorkeling gear. Note that in winter the trade winds blow hard at Buck Island, which can result in rough water for newbies to the mask and fins. Recommended operators include the following:

Big Beard's Adventures (p841) Trips are aboard catamaran sailboats.

Caribbean Sea Adventures (p841) Half-day trips are aboard a glass-bottom powerboat; full-day trips are on a catamaran.

tiansted's one-time budget option got a revamp in 2019 and came out the other end a smart-looking boutique hotel whose design elements play off the main building's vibrant history. The 33 rooms may lack the sea views and private balconies of other area hotels, but they make up for it with modern amenities and regal furnishings.

King's Alley Hotel HOTEL $$
(773-0103; www.kingsalleyhotel.com; 57 King St; d US$179;) King's Alley has 21 rooms above a gallery of shops and restaurants right on the harbor. The setup imitates a 19th-century Danish great house, with colonial-style mahogany furniture and vaulted ceilings to match. The big, slightly dated rooms have French doors that open onto tiny balconies. It's the hotel many businesspeople use.

Club Comanche Hotel St Croix HOTEL $$
(773-0210; www.clubcomanche.com; 1 Strand St; r incl breakfast US$150-250;) This character-rich property, set in a 250-year-old Danish mansion, gives off a boutique-hotel vibe. The 27 rooms have West Indian antique decor, comfy beds, flat-screen satellite TVs and decent wi-fi, though the walls are rather thin. It's in the heart of Christiansted's entertainment district, right by the boardwalk, which means the area can be a tad noisy.

Eating

On one hand, there's imaginative, upscale dining at chic little bistros. On the other, you'll find local hole-in-the-wall places that specialize in budget-priced West Indian fare (King St offers a good row of these between King Cross and Smith Sts). Casual bar-restaurants that fall somewhere in the middle line the waterfront. Many eateries close on Sunday and/or Monday.

Singh's Fast Food CARIBBEAN $
(773-7357; 23 King St; mains US$9-14; 9am-9pm Mon-Sat;) When the roti craving strikes – and it will – Singh's will satiate it with multiple meat and tofu varieties. The steamy three-table joint also serves shrimp, conch, goat and tofu stews, all while island music ricochets off the pastel walls. Cash only.

Toast Diner BREAKFAST $
(692-0313; 81 Queen Cross St; mains US$8-15; 8am-2pm;) This teensy, brightly colored spot focuses on (belt-expanding) all-day breakfasts. Hash browns and rum-cake French toast are specialties, as are *arepas* (South American corn pancakes) with fillings such as pork and *queso fresco* cheese. The chalkboard menu splayed across the walls tells the story of these dishes and more.

★**Harvey's** CARIBBEAN $$
(773-3433; 11b Company St; mains US$15-20; 11:30am-6pm Mon-Sat) At breezy, 10-table

HAMILTON: THE EARLY YEARS

For 250 years, no one cared much about Alexander Hamilton, the guy on the US$10 bill. That he grew up in Christiansted elicited yawns. Then the musical *Hamilton* hit the stage in 2015 and became a Broadway smash. It won Pulitzer, Tony and Grammy awards for telling the historic figure's story via hip-hop tunes. Now visitors want to know more about his early days.

Hamilton was born on the neighboring island of Nevis in 1755 but spent his formative years in Christiansted. His was a hard-knock life – born illegitimately, orphaned by age 12, impoverished – but he worked hard and impressed the local merchants, who sent him to school in New York.

He flourished in the US and became a major voice during the Revolutionary War. George Washington appointed him as the architect of the new country's economic policies. In 1789 Hamilton became the first secretary of the treasury – which is what earned him the honor of being on the US currency.

Hamilton died infamously in a duel with Aaron Burr in 1804.

The entrance at Fort Christiansvaern has free brochures about Hamilton's time on St Croix, including a self-guided walking tour of places he frequented. Alas, most of the buildings from the era have been destroyed, so you'll have to use your imagination to see where young Alex lived and worked. One place that does still exist: the cell at Fort Christiansvaern where his mom, Rachel, was imprisoned for leaving her first husband.

Harvey's, a classic tropical cafe, you half expect Humphrey Bogart's Rick from *Casablanca* to walk in and order a drink. Conch in butter sauce, grouper, sweet-potato-based Crucian stuffing, rice and peas, and other West Indian dishes arrive heaped on plates. There's a mural outside of NBA star Tim Duncan; he was raised at the counter here.

Kim's CARIBBEAN **$$**

(☎773-3377; 45 King St; mains US$16; ⊙11am-4pm & 5-9pm Mon-Sat) No-frills Kim's is legendary for its flavor-packed island meals. Most plates feature seafood (the likes of conch or snapper), and all go down well with local juices such as sorrel (hibiscus) or maubi (made from a bitter tree bark). Yes, the service is slow, but it's well worth the wait.

Ital in Paradise VEGETARIAN **$$**

(☎713-4825; 22-20b Queen Cross St; veg/fish platter US$19/23; ⊙noon-9pm Mon-Sat; ✎) This tiny Rasta eatery serves two daily platters: one vegan (usually with tofu), the other fish. They come with sides such as collard greens, fried lentils and garden salads. Portions are big and delicious. You can eat in at one of the four cramped tables, but most people carry out. Cash only.

★Savant INTERNATIONAL **$$$**

(☎713-8666; www.savantstx.com; 4c Hospital St; mains US$25-45; ⊙6-10pm Mon-Sat; 📶) Cozy, low-lit Savant serves upscale fusion cooking in a colonial town house. The ever-changing menu combines spicy Caribbean, Mexican and Thai recipes; sweat over them indoors in the air-conditioning or outdoors in the courtyard under twinkling lights. Reservations recommended.

Drinking & Nightlife

★BES Craft Cocktail Lounge COCKTAIL BAR

(☎773-2985; 53b Company St; ⊙5pm-2am Wed-Sat) One of the hippest, sexiest and most urbane spots on St Croix, with a refreshingly high ratio of islanders to tourists. Let the bartender craft a cocktail to your liking using homemade infusions, bitters and island syrups. Then, slink into the barstool and let the silky beat of down-tempo hip-hop or melancholic reggae guide you into the night.

★Brew STX MICROBREWERY

(☎719-6339; www.facebook.com/brewstx; 55 King's Alley; ⊙11am-9pm; 📶) Right on the boardwalk overlooking yachts bobbing in the sea, this open-air brewpub is primo for sampling the small-batch suds cooked up steps away from the taps. Build-your-own salads and rice bowls provide a healthful boost before you squander it on the saison or pale ale.

Mill BAR
(www.facebook.com/themillboardwalkbar; 1 Strand St; ⊙noon-10pm) Set around a windmill at the water's edge, this spot is hard to miss. It hosts a crowd of grizzled regulars in the afternoon, then morphs into a younger scene at night. The windmill – now part of the bar – used to be the honeymoon suite for Club Comanche (p843).

Shopping

Riddims MUSIC
(☎719-1775; www.riddimsmusic.com; 3a Queen Cross St; ⊙10am-5:30pm Mon-Sat) Good source for reggae and *quelbe* music from the Virgin Islands, plus clothing, hats, incense and other Caribbean cultural items. The shop also helps sponsor occasional reggae/dub festivals around the island. Ask staff for the lowdown on the local scene.

Information

There are a couple of banks with ATMs on King St near Prince St.

Governor Juan F Luis Hospital (☎778-6311; www.jflusvi.org; 4007 Estate Diamond Ruby; ⊙24hr) About 2 miles west of Christiansted via Centerline Rd.

St Croix Visitor Center (www.usvitourism.com; King's Alley Hotel, 57 King St; ⊙10am-5pm) Located in King's Alley Hotel (p843); has pamphlets and island info.

Getting There & Around

Henry E Rohlsen Airport (p855) is 8 miles southwest of Christiansted. Taxis from the airport to Christiansted cost US$16 per person.

Seaborne Airlines (p855) seaplanes arrive in Christiansted's downtown harbor at the **Seaplane Terminal** (Christiansted Harbor). It's less than a 10-minute walk to most hotels.

CAR

Rentals cost about US$55 per day. The following companies are at or near the seaplane dock:

Avis (p840)
Budget (p840)
Centerline Car Rentals (p840)

TAXI

Rates are set. There's a taxi stand on King St near Church St. Rides between Christiansted and Frederiksted cost US$24.

Point Udall & East End

The scalloped coastline and steep, bone-dry hills of the East End beg for a drive. Rte 82 (aka East End Rd) unfurls along the beach-strewn northern shore, rolling all the way to Point Udall for sublime views and hikes to a turtle-inhabited nature preserve.

Sights

★**Isaac Bay** BEACH
This secluded beach off Rte 82 offers no shade or facilities, and you'll have to hike about 20 minutes through scrub to reach it, but you'd be hard-pressed to find a more beautiful stretch of sand. The Nature Conservancy manages the area as part of a preserve for green and hawksbill turtles, which are active from July to December. Snorkeling on the coral reef here is good, though be careful of the strong current.

To get to the beach, take the trail down the hill from the Point Udall car park. Isaac Bay is actually the second beach you come to on the trail (down the wooden stairs). From the western end of Isaac the trail continues to **Jack Bay**, which is also part of the nature preserve. Nudists sometimes hang out on the beaches.

Point Udall VIEWPOINT
(Rte 82) Point Udall is the easternmost geographic point in US territory. As you face into a 25-knot trade wind, the vista from the promontory high above the surf-strewn beaches is enough to make you hear symphonies. Hikers will like the challenge of taking the steep path down the hillside to isolated Isaac Bay, a nesting area for endangered sea turtles; look for the trailhead near the car park.

Sleeping & Eating

A few villas and big resorts – the kind with tennis courts and golf courses – dot the East End's shores.

There are relatively few restaurants out this way. Most are located at hotels or in condo complexes.

Divi Carina Bay Beach Resort RESORT $$$
(☎877-773-9700; www.diviresorts.com; 25 Estate Turner Hole; r all-inclusive from US$500; ❄@📶🏊) One of St Croix' splashiest resorts, this all-inclusive place on the southeastern shore draws visitors and locals alike. The former come to stay at the 180 mod, Caribbean-chic rooms. The latter come to win big at the island's only casino. Divi Carina underwent major renovations following Hurricane Maria but should be open again by the time you read this.

Cheeseburgers in America's Paradise BURGERS $$
(☎718-1118; www.cheeseburgersstx.com; Rte 82; mains US$12-18; ⌚11am-9:30pm; 👪) The setting is a roadside field with a small bar and kitchen building surrounded by a collection of open-air tables, all shaded by canopies. The ambience says 'picnic.' The menu revolves around beefy cheeseburgers, nachos and mahi Reuben sandwiches that taste best washed down with cold brews. There's a toy-filled play area for kids.

Getting There & Away

Hospital St in Christiansted morphs into Rte 82 (aka East End Rd) a short distance beyond downtown. A taxi to Point Udall costs US$18 per person.

North Shore

Luminescent bays, Christopher Columbus' landing pad and hot dive sites await along the north shore. Kayaking through the glowing water of Salt River Bay at night is a St Croix highlight.

Sights

Cane Bay BEACH
A long, thin strand along Rte 80 about 9 miles west of Christiansted, Cane Bay is deservedly venerated. It provides easy access to some of the island's best dives, and it's also the gateway to the rainforest's steep hills. The beach has several small hotels, restaurants and bars.

Salt River Bay National Historic Park PARK
(www.nps.gov/sari) FREE About 4 miles west of Christiansted, Salt River Bay holds prehistoric archaeological ruins and is the only documented place where Christopher Columbus landed on US soil. Don't expect bells and whistles: the site remains undeveloped beach. The 700 acres surrounding the Salt River estuary form an ecological reserve filled with mangroves, egrets, and bioluminescent life come nighttime.

Hibiscus Beach BEACH
Sand seekers hit palm-fringed Hibiscus Beach, 2 miles west of Christiansted off Rte 75/Northside Rd. There's good snorkeling at the beach's western end. Hibiscus has no amenities, but you can walk to neighboring Pelican Cove Beach, which has a small resort with a waterfront restaurant.

Activities & Tours

Annaly Bay Tide Pools HIKING
(Carambola Tide Pools) The 2.7-mile **Trumbull Trail** leads from a small parking lot at the gate of the Renaissance Carambola Beach Resort to remote Annaly Bay, famed for its secluded tide pools. The trail is mostly forested and shady, but check conditions before you set off as rough seas can make the pools at the end dangerous.

Caribbean Adventure Tours KAYAKING
(☎778-1522; www.stcroixkayak.com; 7a Salt River Marina; 2hr tours US$50; 👪) This outfit offers a terrific sunset paddle through the bioluminescent bay. There's also a history-focused daytime paddle that goes through the mangrove forest.

Virgin Kayak Tours KAYAKING
(☎514-0062; www.virginkayaktours.com; Salt River Marina; 2hr tours by kayak/SUP US$60/50; 👪) This company uses pedal-driven kayaks that are easy for novices to maneuver. By day, tours go through the mangrove estuary and stop on the beach where Christopher Columbus landed. By night, tours take in the bioluminescent bay. There are also female-only sunset SUP tours. Call or reserve online.

Sleeping & Eating

Divers and beachlovers can choose from a smattering of cool little hotels and B&Bs to be near the action. Properties are more casual than glamorous.

Cane Bay Campground CAMPGROUND $
(☎227-3856; www.canebaycampground.com; North Shore Rd; campsites/cabins from US$25/80) Choose from a bare tent site in a grassy knoll or a forest-green 'eco-cabin' (screened-in hut with bed, camp stove and kerosene lamp) tucked into the woods.

There's no electricity, and the bathrooms have cold showers only, but who needs trimmings when the idyllic sands of Cane Bay are just steps away?

★ Waves at Cane Bay HOTEL **$$**
(☎718-1815; www.thewavescanebay.com; 112c Cane Bay; r US$170-200;) Small, tidy Waves has big rooms painted in tropical pastels. All 10 units have balcony, kitchenette, cable TV and free wi-fi. And then there's the location: you can dive right off the rocks out front, lounge in the saltwater lagoon pool or dine just above the sea foam at AMA restaurant.

Arawak Bay Inn at Salt River B&B **$$**
(☎772-1684; www.arawakhotelstcroix.com; 62 Salt River Rd; r US$160-170;) The pick of the local litter for value, this peachy B&B has 14 bright rooms, each with individual color scheme and decor, and offers a cooked breakfast. It's best to have a car for stays here, as the peaceful hillside property is not walking distance to the beaches and eateries, though Cane Bay and Christiansted are a quick drive away.

★ Rowdy Joe's North Shore Eatery INTERNATIONAL **$$**
(☎725-5730; North Shore Rd; mains US$13-24; noon-midnight Thu-Mon;) Sit on the porch and order off the blackboard menu. The chef strives for 'good-mood food,' using ingredients from St Croix' farms and fishers. Dishes might include pulled pork, fish tacos or house-made pasta.

Eat@Cane Bay AMERICAN **$$**
(☎718-0362; www.eatatcanebay.com; North Shore Rd; mains US$12-25; 11am-9pm Wed-Mon) Located across from Cane Bay beach, this place serves burgers that are a cut above the norm, along with wine and cold Caribbean beers. Sunday brunch is popular for buttermilk pancakes or crab-cake eggs Benedict. Live music (often reggae) rocks the joint Monday, Wednesday and Friday nights and Sunday afternoon.

Getting There & Away

King St in Christiansted turns into Northside Rd (Rte 75) at the town's western edge and heads toward the north shore. North Shore Rd (Rte 80) then splits off toward Salt River and Cane Bay. A taxi from Christiansted to Cane Bay costs US$24.

Frederiksted

St Croix' second-banana town is a motionless patch of colonial buildings snoring beside the teal-blue sea. Other than the occasional cruise ship of visitors, it'll be you and that lizard sunning itself who will have this plucky outpost to yourselves. With its out-of-the-mainstream, laissez-faire ambience, Frederiksted is the center for gay life in the Virgin Islands.

Sights

Sandy Point National Wildlife Refuge NATURE RESERVE
(www.fws.gov/refuge/sandy_point; 10am-4pm Sat & Sun Sep-Mar) Created to protect nesting areas of the vulnerable leatherback sea turtle, this sporadically open wildlife refuge at the southern edge of Frederiksted, off Tranberg Rd, also harbors the most pristine stretches of sand on the island. Remember the final scene from *The Shawshank Redemption*? This is where it was shot!

Fort Frederik FORT
(www.nps.gov/places/fort-frederiksted-usvi.htm; EmancipationPark;adult/childUS$5/free; 8:30am-4pm Mon-Sat) The deep-red color of this fort at the foot of the pier is what most visitors remember about the little citadel. It's also where the island's enslaved people were emancipated in 1848. Exhibits inside explain the event.

Activities & Tours

VI Bike & Trails CYCLING
(Freedom City Cycles; ☎277-2433; www.vibikeandtrails.com; 4 Strand St; 2½hr tours adult/child US$60/25) Pedal past sugar-plantation ruins, beaches and tide pools with a guide; more difficult rides bounce over rainforest trails. Bicycle rentals (US$35 per day) are available for DIY adventures.

Cane Bay Dive Shop DIVING
(☎718-9913; www.canebayscuba.com; 2 Strand St; 2-tank dive US$125) One of the most well-regarded dive shops on the island, located across from the pier. Its boats depart from Salt River Marina en route to the Cane Bay Wall and wrecks on the west end.

N2 The Blue DIVING
(☎772-3483; www.n2theblue.com; 202 Custom House St; 2-tank dive US$110; 8:30am-4:30pm)

Specializes in small-boat trips for west-end wreck dives and Frederiksted Pier dives (including colorful night dives). It also runs PADI-certification courses.

Festivals & Events

Sunset Jazz Festival MUSIC

(www.facebook.com/SunSetJazzinFrederiksted; Verne Richards Veterans Park; 6pm 3rd Fri of month) Throngs of locals and visitors come to the waterfront with blankets and picnics in tow. The free concerts last about two hours.

Sleeping

Frederiksted is small and only holds a couple of options, the best of which cater to LGBT travelers (and their allies). Expect a subdued stay.

★Fred DESIGN HOTEL $$

(777-3733; www.sleepwithfred.com; 605 Strand St; r US$209-366;) When you enter the Cock Lounge (aka the lobby, which has huge rooster art), it becomes apparent that the Fred is fantastically over the top. Rooms in this flamboyant adults-only hotel are spread across five historic buildings, many of which boast Spanish-tile floors and vibrant decor. There's also a Jacuzzi, two pools, a bar and a spa for massages.

Sand Castle on the Beach HOTEL $$

(772-1205; www.sandcastleonthebeach.com; 127 Estate Smithfield; r/ste from US$184/264;) On the beach about a mile south of Frederiksted, the 24-room Sand Castle is one of the few gay- and lesbian-oriented hotels in the Virgin Islands. The vibrant, tropical-themed rooms come with kitchenettes; most have sea views. There's a good cafe on-site for easy eats.

Inn on Strand Street HOTEL $$

(772-0500; www.innonstrandstreet.com; 442 Strand St; r US$100-150;) The bright-blue Inn sits right downtown. Four floors are built around a courtyard, and many rooms have patios overlooking the pier. The 32 units each have tiled floors and standard hotel-style furnishings, plus a refrigerator. The common spaces are a bit rundown, but the rooms are perfectly adequate. Many still call it by its old name: the Frederiksted Hotel.

Eating & Drinking

Mosey along Strand and King Sts downtown near Frederiksted Pier, and you'll find the bulk of the town's cafes, sandwich shops and Caribbean restaurants. Note that many places close on Sunday and Monday.

Rhythms at Rainbow Beach INTERNATIONAL $

(772-0002; www.rainbowbeachstx.com; Hams Bluff Rd; mains US$7-15; 11am-7pm;) Chow down on the signature jerk pork and rice at a table overlooking the sea. Then, let the day turn to night as you toss back tropical cocktails and bounce to the beat of blasting reggae at this always-throbbing beach bar 1 mile north of downtown.

Polly's at the Pier CAFE $

(719-9434; 3 Strand St; mains US$9-13; 8am-3pm Mon-Sat, to 1pm Sun;) Polly's serves coffee, tea, sandwiches, omelets, waffles and cocktails a stone's throw from the pier. Savor it all in the cafe's open, airy, island-bohemian ambience. It's reliably open when many other places in town are not.

Turtles SANDWICHES $

(772-3676; 37 Strand St; mains US$12-15; 9am-5pm Mon-Sat;) Munch hulking sandwiches made with homemade bread or sip a fine cup of coffee at beachfront tables under sea-grape trees. Cash only.

Roots-N-Kulchah VEGAN $$

(513-8665; 67 King St; mains US$13-18; 11:30am-4pm Tue-Sat;) Chef-owner Kimba Kabaka cooks up authentic good-vibes vegan fare at this tiny four-table I-tal (natural food) restaurant with a strong Rastafarian vibe. The menu changes daily depending on what's fresh and typically includes juices made from tamarind, sorrel and other local fruits or herbs.

Lost Dog Pub PUB

(772-3526; www.facebook.com/LostDogPub; 12 King St; 4pm-1am) In a new location after the 2017 hurricanes, this breezy backyard bar and pizza parlor remains as popular as ever with welcoming expats. There's an upstairs art gallery that has rotating exhibitions and several weekly yoga classes (check Facebook for the latest schedules).

Getting There & Away

Taxis huddle near Fort Frederik. It costs US$24 to go to Christiansted and takes 45 minutes or so.

Greater Frederiksted

The area around Frederiksted has two distinct sides to its topography and character. First there are the wild mountains and beaches of the rainforest area in the island's northwestern pocket. Second, south of the mountains is the broad coastal plain that once hosted the majority of sugar plantations. Today the area is largely a modern commercial and residential zone where much of St Croix' population lives. But sprinkled along the land bordering Centerline Rd are some remarkable heirlooms from the colonial era. Oh, and rum factories.

Sights

★ Cruzan Rum Distillery DISTILLERY

(☎692-2280; www.cruzanrum.com; 3a Estate Diamond, Rte 64; tours US$8; ⏲tours every 30min 10am-2pm Mon-Fri) To find out how the islands' popular elixir gets made, stop by the historic distillery for a tour. The journey through the oak-barrel-stacked warehouses with their aroma of gingerbread (from the molasses and yeast) takes 20 minutes, after which you get to sip plenty of the good stuff. The Nelthropp family, Cruzan Rum's owners, have been perfecting the recipes since 1760. Cash not accepted; credit cards only.

Captain Morgan Rum Distillery DISTILLERY

(☎713-5654; www.captainmorganvisitorcenter.com; Rte 66; adult/child US$10/3; ⏲tours 10am-3pm Mon-Fri) Captain Morgan opened its shiny distillery on St Croix in 2010. The visitor center offers 30-minute tours. Expect multimedia films, self-guided information panels and, of course, samples of the Captain's happy juice.

Estate Whim Plantation Museum MUSEUM

(☎772-0598; www.stcroixlandmarks.com; Centerline Rd; adult/child US$10/5; ⏲10am-3pm Wed & Sat) Only 11 of Whim Plantation's original 150 acres survive at the museum, but the grounds thoroughly evoke the colonial days when sugarcane ruled St Croix. Damage from Hurricane Maria was extensive (the great house alone is in need of US$1 million in restoration), but you can still wander past the crumbling stone windmill or check out the library, archives and rotating exhibitions.

> **WORTH A TRIP**
>
> **CALEDONIA RAINFOREST**
>
> The island's wet, mountainous northwestern pocket is home to a thick forest of tall mahogany, silk-cotton and white-cedar trees. Technically, as only about 40in of rain falls here per year, the Caledonia Rainforest is not a true 'rainforest.' No matter – it looks the part, with clouds, dripping trees and earthy aromas. Mahogany Rd (Rte 76) cuts through the spooky woods; it's twisty and potholed, so be careful.

St George Village Botanical Garden GARDENS

(☎692-2874; www.sgvbg.org; 127 Estate St George; adult/child US$8/1; ⏲9am-4pm Mon-Sat) This serene 16-acre park is built over a colonial sugar plantation. More than 1000 native and exotic species grow on the grounds. Orchid lovers in particular are in for a treat.

Tours

Ridge to Reef Farm TOURS

(☎473-1557; www.ridge2reef.org; self-guided tour suggested donation US$10, guided tour US$25; ⏲dawn to dusk, guided tours 2pm Thu & Fri) Tour an organic farm in St Croix' rainforest, either on your own (with a map) or with a guide (reservations required). You can also work in the fields or stay overnight; lodging is provided in one of six rustic, though totally adequate, cabins (from US$65). Access is via a severely rutted dirt road off Rte 58.

Paul & Jill's Equestrian Stables HORSEBACK RIDING

(☎772-2880; www.paulandjills.com; Rte 58; 1½hr tour US$100) This outfit offers trail rides that lead through hidden plantation ruins and the rainforest to hilltop vistas. You'll also trot along the beach.

Sleeping

The area is more residential than touristy, so you won't find abundant accommodations. You will, however, find a few special, ecologically minded retreats in the rainforest that are the cheapest digs on the island.

Mt Victory Camp CAMPGROUND $

(☎201-7983; www.mtvictorycamp.com; Rte 58; campsites/bungalows/apt US$30/90/110; 📶) Pitch your own tent in the forest, or choose one of three bungalows (screened-in perma-tents on a wooden platform, each with electricity and a kitchen with cold-water sink, propane stove and cooking utensils). Guests share the solar-heated bathhouse, a pavilion with refrigerator and wi-fi, and sublime nature sounds. There's also an apartment (with en-suite bathroom) carved from an old schoolhouse.

★Northside Valley VILLA $$
(☎708-790-0558; www.northsidevalley.com; 2 Estate Northside; villas US$145-215;) The property offers eight concrete-and-tile villas, each with two bedrooms and a fully equipped kitchen, set amid jungle-like trees. It's wonderfully remote: no TV, air-conditioning or wi-fi (though the latter is available in the common area). It's near Butler Bay, across the road from the sea.

Ecofriendly features include solar panels and rainwater reuse.

Drinking & Nightlife

★Leatherback Brewing Company MICROBREWERY
(☎772-2337; www.leatherbackbrewing.com; Rte 66; 11am-7pm Mon-Fri, noon-7pm Sat, 10am-5pm Sun;) This new craft brewery opened in 2018 in the William Roebuck Industrial Park on the island's south side. Sidle up to the indoor-outdoor bar and order one of the six home-brewed beers on tap, including the signature trio: Island Life lager, Reef Life IPA and Beach Life blonde ale. There are also sandwiches, snacks and a popular Sunday brunch.

Shopping

St Croix Leap ARTS & CRAFTS
(☎772-0421; Rte 76; 10am-5pm Mon-Sat) Woodworkers transform chunks of fallen mahogany trees into all manner of art and housewares at this open-air studio set deep in the rainforest. Be prepared for bats fluttering above! Hours can be erratic, but if someone's there you'll likely get a personal tour of the space. It's a wild road to reach it.

Getting There & Away

The key sights lie south of Frederiksted around Centerline Rd (Rte 70). A taxi from Frederiksted costs US$10 or so. The main routes through the rainforest are Mahogany Rd (Rte 76) and Creque Dam Rd (Rte 58), both narrow and bumpy.

UNDERSTAND THE US VIRGIN ISLANDS

History

Early History to Danish Control

Folks have been living on the islands from as early as 2000 BC. The Taínos ruled the roost for a while, but the ruthless, seafaring Caribs eventually wiped them out.

Around this time, during his second trip to the Caribbean, Christopher Columbus sailed up to St Croix' Salt River Bay. It was 1493, and he gave the islands their enduring name: Santa Ursula y Las Once Mil Vírgenes, in honor of a legendary 4th-century princess and her 11,000 maidens. Mapmakers soon shortened the mouthful to 'The Virgins.'

The islands remained under Spanish control until the English defeated the Spanish Armada in 1588. England, France and Denmark were quick to issue 'letters of marque,' which allowed privateers the right to claim territory and protect their claims.

One king's privateer became every other king's pirate. Blackbeard (Edward Teach) operated in the Virgin Islands before 1720, along with a collection of other rascals.

The Danes and the English bickered over the islands, while each built vast sugar and tobacco plantations. The English held colonies on islands east of St John, while the Danes held St Thomas to the west. St John remained disputed territory. Finally, in 1717 the Danes sent a small but determined band of soldiers to St John and drove the British out. The Narrows, between St John and Tortola in the British Virgin Islands, became the border that has divided the western (first Danish, now US) Virgins from the British Virgins for nearly three centuries.

Plantation Slavery & its Aftermath

The West Indies grew rich producing sugar and cotton for Europe. In pursuit of profits, the Danish West India and Guinea Company declared St Thomas a free port in 1724, and purchased St Croix from the French in 1733. By the end of the century the number of enslaved Africans on the islands exceeded 40,000.

Harsh living conditions and oppressive laws drove enslaved people to revolt. Meanwhile, sugar production in Europe and American tariffs on foreign sugar cut into the islands' profits. The deteriorating economy put everyone in a foul mood. Something had to give and it finally did in 1848, when Afro-Caribbeans on St Croix forced a legal end to slavery.

However, they remained in economic bondage. Life on the islands was dismal. A series of labor revolts left the plantation infrastructure in ruins.

The Islands Change Hands

The USA, realizing the strategic value of the islands, negotiated with Denmark to buy its territories. The deal was almost done in 1867, but the US Congress balked at paying US$7.5 million (more than the US$7.2 million it had just paid for Alaska).

As WWI began in Europe, the USA grew concerned that German armies might invade Denmark and claim the Danish West Indies. Finally, the USA paid the Danes US$25 million in gold for the islands in 1917.

The US Navy then took control, which resulted in tensions with the local population. The USA tried to enforce Prohibition, an unusual concept for an economy tied to the production, sale and distribution of rum. In 1931 President Herbert Hoover traveled to the Virgins. He stayed for less than six hours and left unimpressed.

In 1934, however, President Franklin D Roosevelt visited and saw the potential that Hoover had missed. Soon, the USA instituted programs to eradicate disease, drain swamps, build roads, improve education and create tourism infrastructure.

Islanders received the right to elect their own governor in 1970. Though local politics brought its share of nepotism, cronyism and other scandals, the next four decades also brought unprecedented growth in tourism and raised the standard of living. Many USVI citizens have outwardly expressed a desire for greater self-determination over the years, but the government has tried and failed to ratify a Virgin Islands Constitution five times.

Marilyn, a Category 3 hurricane, took a chunk out of the islands in 1995, but they quickly got back to business. Two even larger Category 5 hurricanes, Irma and Maria, struck within two weeks of each other in 2017, causing catastrophic damage. Yet, as the USVI always does, it picked up the pieces, regrouped and bounced back two years later stronger than ever.

People & Culture

The US Virgin Islands are a territory of the USA, and the islands participate in the political process by sending an elected, nonvoting representative to the US House of Representatives. All citizens of the USVI are US citizens (and have been since 1927) with all the rights that entails, except one: they cannot vote in presidential elections.

Though the USVI wears a veneer of mainstream American life, with conveniences such as shopping malls and fast food, West African culture is a strong and respected presence.

Since 1960 the population of USVI has nearly quadrupled, although current growth has plateaued. Economic opportunities draw immigrants from other parts of the West Indies, along with US mainlanders who come to escape the politics and busyness of American life, or to retire in the sun. Tourism accounts for 60% of GDP and employment, and many locals work as hoteliers, restaurant owners, taxi drivers and shopkeepers.

According to the most recent census data, 76% of the population is black, 16% is white and the rest is a mix. About half the population was born in the USVI; another third hail from Latin America or elsewhere in the Caribbean; and about 16% were born in the US.

JUMP UP!

Reggae and calypso tunes blast from USVI vehicles and emanate from shops, restaurants and beach bars. *Quelbe* and *fungi* (*foon*-ghee, also an island food made of cornmeal) are two types of folk music. *Quelbe* blends jigs, quadrilles, military fife and African drum music with (often bitingly satirical) lyrics from the field songs of enslaved people. *Fungi* uses homemade percussion instruments such as washboards, ribbed gourds and conch shells to accompany a singer. The best time to experience island music is during the 'jump up' parades and competitions associated with major festivals such as Carnival on St Thomas and St John, or at St Croix' Crucian Christmas Festival.

Landscape & Wildlife

The Land

The US Virgins consist of about 50 islands and cays lying 40 miles east of Puerto Rico. They are the northernmost islands in the Lesser Antilles chain and, along with the British Virgin Islands, form an irregular string stretching west to east. The one exception to this string is the USVI's largest island, St Croix, which lies 40 miles south.

The mountain slopes are dense subtropical forests. All the timber is second or third growth; the islands were stripped for sugar, cotton and tobacco plantations in the colonial era. There are no rivers and very few freshwater streams. Coral reefs of all varieties grow in the shallow waters near the shore.

Wildlife

Very few of the land mammals that make their home in the US Virgin Islands are indigenous; most mammal species were accidentally or intentionally introduced over the centuries. St John has a feral population of donkeys and pigs, and all the islands have wild goats, white-tailed deer, cats and dogs. Other prevalent land mammals include mongooses and bats.

The islands are home to a few species of snake (none of which are poisonous), including the Virgin Islands tree boa. You'll also encounter native frogs, toads, iguanas, anoles, geckos and hermit crabs.

More than 200 bird species – including the official bird, the banana quit – inhabit the islands.

Environmental Issues

The US Virgin Islands have long suffered from environmental problems, including deforestation, soil erosion, mangrove destruction and a lack of fresh water. During the 18th century logging operations denuded many of the islands to make room for plantations. The demise of the agricultural economy in the late 19th century allowed reforestation, and in recent years locals (especially on St John) have begun several forest-conservation projects.

But population growth and rapid urbanization continue to pose threats. If it were not for the desalination plants (which make fresh water out of seawater), the islands couldn't support even a quarter of their population, let alone visitors. When a hurricane strikes, power and desalination facilities shut down. Islanders with enough foresight and money keep rainwater cisterns for such emergencies, but folks without them suffer.

Rising sea temperatures are another topic of concern, as they impact local reefs and cause coral bleaching. In 2005 a particularly 'hot' period killed about half of the USVI's coral. Another widespread bleaching event occurred in 2010.

Prior years of overfishing have put conch in a precarious situation. Currently, conch fishing is not allowed from July through October so that stocks can replenish.

The past decade has seen an increase in the resources and action dedicated to conservation efforts. Friends of Virgin Islands National Park (www.friendsvinp.org) is a local group that has pushed for environmental preservation, while the Nature Conservancy (www.nature.org) has made the USVI a focal point of its groundbreaking coral-restoration work. Even the local government has sounded the alarm, enacting a ban on plastic shopping bags in 2017 and taking aim at plastic straws in 2018. In 2019 lawmakers voted to ban common chemical-sunscreen ingredients that can damage coral reefs.

SURVIVAL GUIDE

Directory A–Z

ACCESSIBLE TRAVEL

While the *Americans with Disabilities Act* holds sway in the USVI, facilities are not accessible to the same degree as they are in the US. Click on the 'barrier free travel' link on the tourism board's website (www.visitusvi.com) for a list of accessible restaurants, resorts and attractions.

In general, St Thomas is best equipped to accommodate those with different abilities thanks to the heavy cruise-ship traffic and the availability of accessible transport. **Accessible Caribbean Vacations** (www.accessiblecaribbeanvacations.com) has tips and ideas for land- and sea-based excursions here.

ACCOMMODATIONS

Guesthouses, hotels, private villas and condo resorts are abundant on all the islands. High season is mid-December through April, when rooms are costly and advance reservations are essential. Three-night-minimum-stay requirements are common.

Be aware that while air-conditioning is widely available, it's not a standard amenity, even at top-end places. If you want it, be sure to ask about it when you book.

Accommodations Services

Carefree Getaways (☎779-4070; www.carefreegetaways.com; villas from US$1900 per week) St John–focused company that rents villas and condos around the island.

Caribbean Villas (☎800-338-0987; www.caribbeanvilla.com; condos from US$1000 per week) St John–focused company renting condos and villas around the island.

Catered To (☎776-6641; www.cateredto.com; villas from US$2000 per week) Rents villas and condos around St John.

CHILDREN

The islands are relatively child-friendly. While baby-change facilities and smooth pavements for prams are not ubiquitous, calm beaches and comfortable lodgings for families are.

Specific beaches that are good for children, with shallow water and minimal waves, include Secret Harbour and Magens Bay (St Thomas), Maho Bay and Cinnamon Bay (St John), and Protestant Cay (St Croix). Magens, Maho and Protestant Cay have water-sports centers that rent kayaks, paddleboards and more, so teens can enjoy these beaches, too.

St Croix' cannon-clad forts are cool for youngsters. Teens like dipping a paddle on tours with St Thomas' Virgin Islands Ecotours (p832) and St Croix' Virgin Kayak Tours (p846); the latter uses easy-to-maneuver pedal-operated vessels. Charlotte Amalie on St Thomas has the largest collection of kid-friendly attractions, including the Tree Limin' Extreme zip line (p829) and Paradise Point Skyride (p826).

All the islands offer rental villas and condominiums, which have lots of space and kitchens for DIY meals. Resorts offer similar amenities. St Thomas' East End is laden with such properties.

Even if most restaurants do not have a children's menu, they often serve burgers and pizza as part of their lineup. The ambience tends to be informal and relaxed wherever you go.

On St John, **Island Baby** (www.islandbabyvi.com) rents out gear such as high chairs (US$60 per week), baby hiking backpacks (US$50 per week), baby monitors and much more, which can lighten your travel load considerably.

EMBASSIES & CONSULATES

Danish Consulate (☎776-0656; www.dkconsulateusvi.com; Scandinavian Center, Havensight Mall, Bldg 3; ⊙9am-5pm Mon-Fri)

SLEEPING PRICE RANGES

The following price indicators refer to a double room with bathroom in peak season. Unless otherwise stated, breakfast is not included in the price, nor is tax (12.5%) or the energy surcharge (often 8% to 15%).

$ less than US$100

$$ US$100–300

$$$ more than US$300

EMERGENCY NUMBERS

Ambulance, fire, police ☎911

FOOD

Small, unadorned restaurants serving West Indian fare are common. Soups and stews are staples in local cooking. Meat (chicken, pork and goat) is primarily curried or barbecued with tangy spices. All manner of fish and shellfish (especially conch) make it to island tables. Roots such as yam and cassava are boiled, mashed or steamed and served as side dishes. Plantains and mangoes are popular fruits.

Essential Food & Drink

Callaloo Spicy soup stirred with okra, various meats, greens and hot peppers.

Pate (pah-*tay*) Flaky fried dough pockets stuffed with spiced chicken, fish or other meat.

Fungi (*foon*-ghee) A polenta-like cornmeal cooked with okra, typically topped by fish and gravy.

Mango Pale Ale Fruit-tinged microbrew by St John Brewers.

Cruzan Rum St Croix' happy juice since 1760, from light white rum to banana, guava and other tropical flavors.

HEALTH

St Thomas and St Croix have modern hospitals. You will find walk-in clinics and pharmacies on all three islands. Pharmacies sometimes run out of medications. If you are dependent on a particular medication, be sure to travel with it, and with a copy of your prescription. Without health insurance, care in the USVI is costly.

EATING PRICE RANGES

The following price indicators denote the cost of a main dinner dish.

$ less than US$15

$$ US$15–35

$$$ more than US$35

INTERNET ACCESS

Internet cafes are sporadic but do still exist, often near marinas and cruise-ship docks. Access generally costs US$5 per half-hour. Wi-fi is widely available, though service can be slow and fitful. Most lodgings have it for free in their public areas (though it's less common in-room), as do many restaurants and bars in the main towns.

LEGAL MATTERS

The blood-alcohol limit in the USVI is 0.08%. Driving under the influence of alcohol is a serious offense, subject to stiff fines and even imprisonment.

Open-container laws do not exist here, so you can walk around with drinks on the streets.

LGBT+ TRAVELERS

While a fair number of islanders are gay, you're not likely to meet many who are 'out,' nor are you likely to see public displays of affection between gay couples.

St Croix is the most gay friendly of the Virgins, with Frederiksted the center of gay life. Each June the island hosts a pride parade (www.stxpride.org) and a month-long calendar of events. While many bars and restaurants in Frederiksted proudly display rainbow flags, there aren't many structured outlets for meeting. One exception is Sand Castle on the Beach (p848).

PRACTICALITIES

Magazines *St Thomas/St John This Week* and *St Croix This Week* are free and widely available monthly (despite the name!) magazines.

Newspapers The *VI Daily News* (www.virginislandsdailynews.com) is the main paper. VI Source (www.visource.com), Virgin Islands Consortium (www.viconsortium.com) and VI Free Press (http://vifreepress.com) provide news online for free.

Radio WTJX (93.1FM) is the National Public Radio (NPR) affiliate, airing from St Thomas.

Smoking Banned in all restaurants, bars and other public venues.

TV Local stations include channels 8 (ION) and 12 (PBS).

Weights & measures The islands use imperial weights and measurements. Distances are in feet and miles; gasoline is measured in gallons.

MONEY

ATMs in main towns on all three islands. Credit cards accepted in most hotels and restaurants.

Exchange Rates

Australia	A$1	US$0.70
Canada	C$1	US$0.74
Euro zone	€1	US$1.12
Japan	¥100	US$0.91
NZ	NZ$1	US$0.65
UK	UK£1	US$1.27

For current exchange rates, see www.xe.com.

Tipping

Dive/tour-boat operators 15% of fee is reasonable.

Hotels US$1 to US$2 per bag for bellhops; US$2 to US$5 per night for cleaning staff.

Restaurants 15% to 20% of bill.

Taxis 10% of fare.

PUBLIC HOLIDAYS

New Year's Day January 1

Three Kings Day (Feast of the Epiphany) January 6

Martin Luther King Jr's Birthday Third Monday in January

Presidents' Day Third Monday in February

Transfer Day March 31

Holy Thursday and Good Friday Before Easter Sunday (in March or April)

Easter Monday Day after Easter Sunday

Memorial Day Last Monday in May

Emancipation Day July 3

Independence Day (Fourth of July) July 4

Labor Day First Monday in September

Columbus Day Second Monday in October

Liberty Day November 1

Veterans' Day November 11

Thanksgiving Day Fourth Thursday in November

Christmas Day December 25

Boxing Day December 26

TELEPHONE

USVI phone numbers consist of a three-digit area code (340), followed by a seven-digit local number. If you're calling from abroad, dial all 10 digits, preceded by the country code (1). If you're calling locally, just dial the seven-digit number.

Cell Phones

Be careful on St John, as phones can accidentally pick up British Virgin Island cell towers and lead to enormous roaming charges. It's a hassle to find local SIM cards.

AT&T and Sprint are the islands' main service providers. T-Mobile has limited (though growing) coverage. Other companies (ie Verizon) may also work without roaming fees, but check in advance with your provider to make sure.

TIME

The islands are on Atlantic Standard Time (GMT/UTC minus four hours). Relative to New York, Miami and Eastern Standard Time, the Virgins are one hour ahead in winter and in the same time zone in summer (due to daylight-saving time).

TOURIST INFORMATION

USVI Department of Tourism (www.visitusvi.com) Official tourism site with tips for planning a trip.

VOLUNTEERING

Friends of Virgin Islands National Park (www.friendsvinp.org) Volunteer for weekly trail or beach cleanups on St John.

Ridge to Reef Farm (www.ridge2reef.org) Stay on an organic farm in St Croix' rainforest and work in the fields.

St Croix Environmental Association (www.stxenvironmental.org) Help clean beaches where sea turtles nest.

Getting There & Away

AIR

St Thomas has the main airport; St Croix' airport is smaller. Each facility has an ATM, food concessions, car rentals and taxis.

Cyril E King Airport (STT; www.viport.com) On St Thomas.

Henry E Rohlsen Airport (STX; ☎778-1012; www.viport.com; Airport Rd) On St Croix.

American Airlines, Delta, JetBlue, Spirit Airlines and United Airlines all fly to the USVI. US hubs with nonstop flights include New York, Washington, Philadelphia and Atlanta. Many flights transit through Miami, or San Juan, Puerto Rico.

Regional airlines serving the USVI from around the Caribbean include the following:

Air Sunshine (☎954-434-8900; www.airsunshine.com) Runs flights between St Thomas and San Juan, Anguilla, Dominica, Nevis, St Kitts, St-Martin/Sint Maarten and the British Virgin Islands daily.

Cape Air (☎800-227-3247; www.capeair.com) Runs flights between St Thomas, St Croix and San Juan daily.

LIAT (☎866-549-5428; www.liat.com) Flights from St Thomas to Antigua two to three times weekly.

Seaborne Airlines (☎866-359-8784; www.seaborneairlines.com) The islands' busiest local carrier. Flights from St Thomas to San Juan daily, with onward connections to Dominica, St Kitts and Nevis. Also flies seaplanes between St Thomas and St Croix.

SEA

Cruise Ship

Cruise ships are big business in the USVI, especially on St Thomas.

Ferry

Ferry connections link St Thomas with Tortola, Virgin Gorda and Jost Van Dyke. You can also reach Jost Van Dyke from St John. **VI Now** (www.vinow.com) has schedules. For trips between the USVI and BVI, a passport is required.

Ferries between the two territories run until about 5pm only. Watch out for scheduling issues if you're trying to get from one to the other at night. Also, note that several routes in operation prior to the 2017 hurricanes are no longer available.

Taxes are not included in the fees below. There is a US$10 port fee to leave the USVI and a US$20 departure tax to leave the BVI. The BVI also charges a US$10 'environmental and tourism levy' upon arrival. Checked luggage costs US$5 per bag on many ferries. Arrive at least 30 minutes before departure time to buy tickets at the terminal.

Main companies and routes:

Inter Island (☎776-6597; www.interislandboatservices.com)

Native Son (☎774-8685; www.nativesonferry.com)

Road Town Fast Ferry (☎777-2800; www.roadtownfastferry.com)

Smith's Ferry/Tortola Fast Ferry (☎775-7292; www.bviferryservices.com)

Speedy's (☎714-5240; www.bviferries.com)

Ferries to/from Charlotte Amalie:

Road Town, Tortola one way US$40, 45 minutes, several daily; Road Town Fast Ferry, Smith's Ferry/Tortola Fast Ferry, Native Son

Spanish Town, Virgin Gorda one way US$40, 1½ hours, twice daily Tuesday and Saturday; Speedy's

Ferries to/from Red Hook:

Road Town, Tortola one way US$40, 30 minutes, three daily; Native Son, Inter Island

Jost Van Dyke one way US$80, 45 minutes, two daily Friday, Saturday and Sunday; Inter Island

Ferries to/from Cruz Bay:

Jost Van Dyke one way US$80, 45 minutes, two daily Friday, Saturday and Sunday; Inter Island

Yacht

If you're arriving by yacht in the USVI from another country, it must be at one of the following ports, which have customs and immigration facilities:

St Thomas Charlotte Amalie Marine Terminal
St John The Creek (Cruz Bay)
St Croix Gallows Bay (near Christiansted)

Getting Around

AIR

Seaborne Airlines (p855) operates seaplanes between the downtown harbors of St Thomas' Charlotte Amalie and St Croix' Christiansted. The flight takes 25 minutes and goes roughly once per hour in daylight. Cape Air (p855) goes between St Thomas' and St Croix' main airports twice daily.

BOAT

Frequent ferries run between St Thomas and St John. They go hourly from between Red Hook and Cruz Bay (US$8.15 one way, 20 minutes), and twice daily between Charlotte Amalie (Crown Bay Marina) and Cruz Bay (US$20 one way, 45 minutes). QE IV Ferry (p840) runs twice-daily ferries (US$60 one way, 2½ hours) between Gallows Bay on St Croix and Blyden Terminal on St Thomas. Ships don't run on Wednesday.

Check VI Now (www.vinow.com) for updated schedules.

BUS

Vitran (www.vitranvi.com; fare US$1) operates air-conditioned public buses along the length of St Thomas, St John and St Croix. Buses run daily between 5:30am and 7:30pm (approximately one bus per hour). Service isn't very reliable. St Thomas also has 'safari' buses: open-air trucks outfitted with benches.

CAR & MOTORCYCLE

Be prepared for challenging road conditions, including steep, winding roads and copious potholes. Chickens, cows, goats and donkeys often dart in and out of the roadway, to boot.

- Rule number one: drive on the left-hand side of the road.
- Seat-belt use is compulsory; children under age five must be in a car seat.
- Driving while using a handheld cell phone is illegal (but ear pieces are permitted).

Car Rental

To rent a car in the USVI you need to be at least 25 years old, hold a valid driver's license and have a major credit card.

Rental starts at around US$60 per day (higher on St John). If you're traveling in peak season, it's wise to reserve a couple of weeks ahead, as supplies are limited. Major international car-rental companies have branches at the airports and sometimes at ferry terminals.

TAXI

All the islands have taxis that are easily accessible in the main tourist areas. Most vehicles are vans that carry up to 12 passengers; sometimes they're open-air trucks with bench seats and awnings and room for 20 people. Taxis service multiple destinations and may stop to pick up passengers along the way, so rates are usually charged on a per-person basis. Rates are set, with prices listed in the free tourist magazines and at VI Now (www.vinow.com). Rates go down a bit if more than one person takes the taxi. Always confirm the price before getting in.

Survival Guide

Hurricane Planning

Caribbean hurricanes are born 3000km away off the west coast of Africa, where pockets of low pressure draw high winds toward them and the earth's rotation molds them into their familiar counterclockwise swirl. Though the weather patterns are no longer completely reliable due to climate change, hurricane season runs roughly from early June until the end of November. The strongest and rarest of hurricanes, Category 5, typically build up in July and August and pack winds that exceed 250km/h.

Before You Go

➡ Always check that your travel insurance covers hurricanes. This is inexpensive and must be purchased at least 24 hours before a hurricane is named; it will cover you for changes in your travel plans. Most airlines and hotels should also offer a rescheduled itinerary or refund if you have to amend or cancel your holiday due to a hurricane; check in advance before making bookings.

➡ If a storm is developing when you are due to travel, follow news from the US National Hurricane Center (www.nhc.noaa.gov) for updates and predictions on its passage. Embassies also usually post warnings on their homepages.

➡ If your trip is after a hurricane, it may or may not be appropriate to travel. Where widespread infrastructural damage has been done, your trip may not be possible or desirable. If your destination got off relatively lightly, sticking to your plans may be a good idea, as many islands affected by hurricanes have suffered a 'second disaster' through loss of tourism.

On the Ground

➡ If a hurricane develops when you are already in the Caribbean, but the storm is more than a day or more out, be sure to stock up on bottled water, nonperishable food and prescription medications, plus a flashlight and first-aid kit.

➡ Evaluate how safe your hotel or guesthouse is. Is it a beachfront property that might get hit by a water surge? Is it in an area prone to flooding or landslides? Is it a wooden building easily damaged by winds? Hotels often have windowless event spaces in which to shelter guests.

➡ Withdraw extra cash from an ATM. If driving a rental car, be sure the tank is full of gas.

➡ In assessing the danger, keep an eye on rain and wind speed forecasts. Let friends and family at home know where you're staying and what the conditions are like.

➡ When the storm approaches, be sure your mobile phone is fully charged, as well as any other devices you might need. Place your cash, passport and any important identification in a safe (and waterproof) place. Stay away from trees and power lines.

➡ Check updates online or on the radio frequently.

➡ Evacuate if told to do so by the authorities. Take refuge in designated storm shelters. If that's not possible, find an interior room and stay away from windows as flying debris and sudden pressure changes can shatter glass. Beforehand, be sure there are no lightweight objects just outside.

➡ Never walk, swim or drive through floodwaters.

➡ After the storm hits, have plenty of patience. Prepare to stand in line for hours for basic supplies or wait for aid to arrive. Don't expect comfort or electricity, and prepare to extend your trip. Airports reopen a day or two after hurricanes, but priority is first given to military and aid, then passengers with tickets for current flights, followed by standby passengers or those who'd had their flights canceled.

Directory A–Z

Accessible Travel

Travel in the Caribbean is not particularly easy for those with physical disabilities. Overall there is little or no awareness of the need for easier access onto planes, buses or rental vehicles. Notable exceptions include Puerto Rico and the US Virgin Islands, where compliance with the Americans Disabilities Act (ADA) means many sights and hotels have wheelchair accessibility.

Visitors with special needs should inquire directly with prospective hotels for information on their facilities. The larger, more-modern resorts are most likely to have the greatest accessibility, with elevators, wider doorways and wheelchair-accessible bathrooms.

While land travel may present some obstacles, cruises are often a good option for travelers with disabilities in the Caribbean. Many cruise lines can coordinate shore-based excursions in tour buses equipped for special needs.

US-based **Accessible Caribbean Vacations** (www.accessiblecaribbeanvacations.com) is a travel agency specializing in the Caribbean for disabled travelers. It has a particular emphasis on cruising, and its website has comprehensive accessibility information for region-wide ports of call and shore excursions.

Download Lonely Planet's free *Accessible Travel* guides from http://lptravel.to/AccessibleTravel, which includes resources for many Caribbean destinations.

Climate

Freeport/Lucaya

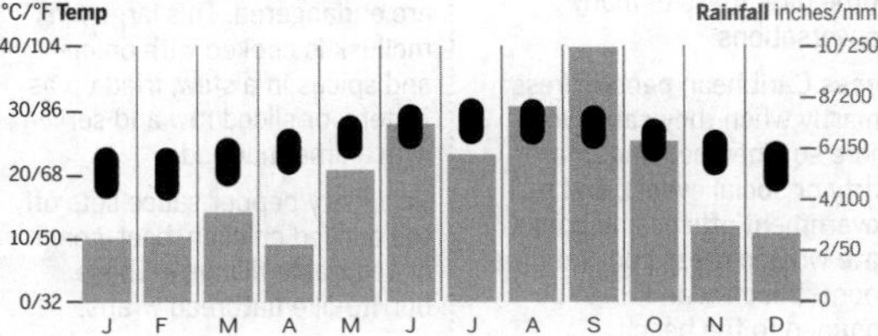

Kingston

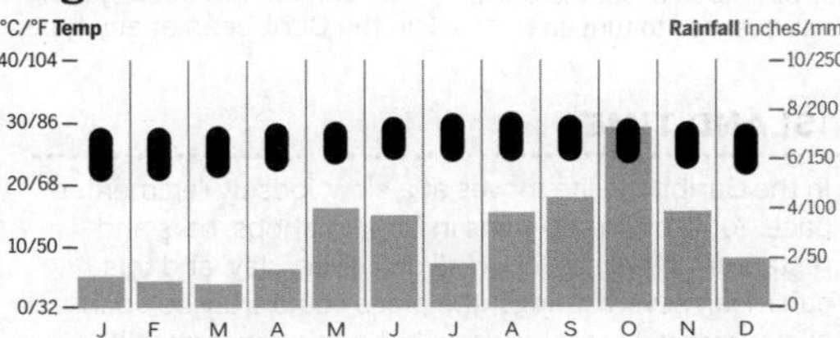

Port of Spain

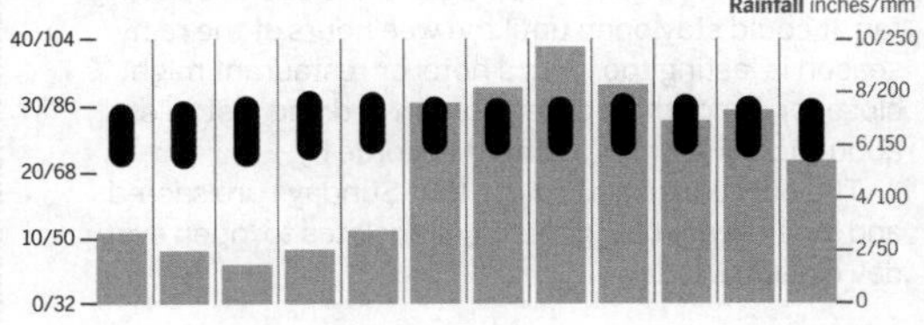

Customs Regulations

All the Caribbean islands allow a reasonable amount of personal items to be brought in duty free, as well as an allowance of liquor and tobacco. Determining what you can take home depends on where you're vacationing and your country of origin. Check with your country's customs agency for clarification.

Embassies & Consulates

Nations such as Australia, Canada, New Zealand and the US have embassies and consulates in the largest Caribbean countries. Check your government's foreign affairs website for locations.

Etiquette

The Caribbean is famously laid-back, but it's also a place that insists on good manners.

Greetings Always greet people properly, and treat elders with extra respect. Introductions done, don't be surprised at the directness of many conversations.

Dress Caribbean people dress smartly when they can (even more so when heading to a party or social event), and many government offices and banks have written dress codes on the door – beachwear should be confined to the beach.

Island time Even though locals may be relaxed about the clock, it's always wise to turn up to appointments at the stated hour (but be prepared to wait).

Food

Caribbean cuisine blends fruits and rice, seafood and spice. And it blends influences from around the world. Indian, Spanish, Italian, American and Asian influences are just some of the tastes and flavors you'll find. Beyond the bland buffets at all-inclusive resorts, there are plenty of reasons to seek out the best of the region. It's not hard to find.

Caribbean Staples

These dishes can be found across the Caribbean.

Callaloo A creamy thick soup or stew blending a variety of vegetables (eg spinach, onions, garlic, okra) with coconut milk and sometimes crab or ham. The base can be spinach-like.

Conch Look for farm-raised versions, as conch in the wild are endangered. This large pink mollusk is cooked with onion and spices in a stew, fried up as fritters, or sliced raw and served with a lime marinade.

Roti Fiery pepper sauce sets off the curried chicken, beef, conch or vegetable fillings in these burrito-like flatbread wraps.

Where to Eat

You can eat almost anything in the Caribbean at any type of restaurant. You'll rarely need to do more than turn up or book on the day, though some top-end places require advance booking.

Cafes and bars Cafes are good for a casual breakfast or lunch, or simply a cup of coffee. Bars often offer meals.

Hotels Many hotels have excellent restaurants open to nonguests. All-inclusives usually have a selection of restaurants, both buffet and à la carte.

Restaurants Caribbean restaurants run from casual beach grills to fine dining.

Insurance

It's extremely foolhardy to travel without insurance to cover theft, loss and medical problems. Check that your policy includes emergency medical-evacuation costs, and any activities deemed risky by insurers, such as scuba diving or other adventure sports.

Worldwide travel insurance is available at www.lonelyplanet.com/travel_services. You can buy, extend and claim online anytime – even if you're already on the road.

Internet Access

Internet access and wi-fi is generally easily found throughout most of the Caribbean.

Legal Matters

Due to the stereotype that pot-smoking is widespread in the Caribbean (it isn't), some visitors take a casual attitude about sampling island drugs.

Be forewarned that drug trafficking is a serious problem throughout the Caribbean and officials in most countries have little-to-no tolerance of visitors caught using. Penalties vary throughout the islands, but getting caught smoking or

ISLAND TIME

In the Caribbean life moves at a slow, loosely regimented pace. You'll often see signs in front of shops, bars and restaurants that say 'open all day, every day' and this can mean several things; the place could truly be open all day every day of the week, but don't count on it. If business is slow, a restaurant, shop or attraction might simply close. If a bar is hopping and the owner's having fun, it could stay open until the wee hours. If the rainy season is lasting too long, a hotel or restaurant might close for a month. In other words, hard and fast rules about opening times are hard to come by.

The only consistent rule is that Sundays are sacred and 'open every day' generally translates to 'open every day except Sunday.'

THE ART OF BARGAINING

Whether it's the beach vendor with the necklace you just have to have, the market stall owner with the charming sunset canvas, or the slick jewelry-store sales clerk, you will likely have a chance to try out your bargaining skills at some point in the Caribbean.

Note, however, that fixed prices are also common, especially at large stores and duty-free malls. Know that 'no bargaining' can mean just that and isn't a ploy.

Also note that it isn't just that bauble in the window that you can bargain for. Especially in the low season, almost everything, including accommodations, can be negotiated. Ask for a better room or a discount if you are staying for a few days.

Although many people are put off at the prospect, bargaining can be an enjoyable part of shopping, so maintain your sense of humor and keep things in perspective. Try following these steps:

- Have some idea of what the item is worth. Why pay more than you would at home?
- Establish a starting price – ask the seller for their price rather than make an initial offer.
- Your first price can be from one-third to two-thirds of the asking price – assuming that the asking price is not outrageous.
- With offer and counter-offer, move closer to an acceptable price.
- If you don't get to an acceptable price, you're entitled to walk – the vendor may call you back with a lower price.
- Note that when you name a price, you're committed – you must buy if your offer is accepted.
- Keep things in perspective. Is it worth aggravation to save one last dollar in dealing with a vendor who may only make a few dollars a week?

possessing marijuana (or any illegal drug for that matter) can result in stiff jail sentences. The notable exception is Jamaica, which has decriminalized possession of up to 2oz (57g; a small fine still applies).

LGBT+ Travelers

Parts of the Caribbean are not particularly LGBT-friendly destinations, and on many of the islands overt homophobia and machismo are prevalent.

People in the LGBT+ community generally keep a low profile, and public hand-holding, kissing and other outward signs of affection are not commonplace. Homosexuality remains illegal in some countries, most notably Jamaica and Barbados.

Still, there are several niches for LGBT+ travelers. Particularly friendly islands include Aruba, Bonaire, Curaçao, Guadeloupe, Martinique, Puerto Rico, Saba, St-Martin/Sint Maarten, and the British and US Virgin Islands.

Useful links:

Damron (www.damron.com) The USA's leading gay publisher offers guides to world cities.

Spartacus International Gay Guide (www.spartacusworld.com) A male-only directory of gay entertainment venues and hotels.

Money

US dollars are often accepted in lieu of local currency (and in some cases are the local currency). Several islands use the Eastern Caribbean dollar (EC$): Antigua and Barbuda, Dominica, Grenada, St Kitts and Nevis, St Lucia, St Vincent and the Grenadines, Anguilla and Montserrat.

ATMs & Credit Cards

ATMs are generally common on all but small islands (and increasingly available in Cuba). Many give out US dollars in addition to the local currency. Credit cards are widely accepted but watch for surcharges.

Cash

The US dollar is accepted almost everywhere, so if you have that it's not necessary to have local currency before you arrive. Carry smaller denominations to pay for taxis, street snacks or tips.

Taxes & Refunds

Value Added Tax is added on goods and services across the region. Rates vary from island to island. In some countries VAT is not included in menu prices, leading to unexpectedly inflated bills. Check whether quoted hotel rates include tax when booking.

It's sometimes possible for visitors to obtain VAT refunds on goods bought during a trip.

Tipping

Restaurants Varies in the region although 15% is average. Watch for service charges added to bills.

Taxis Not usually tipped.

Opening Hours

Opening hours vary across the region, although Sunday remains sacrosanct, with businesses and offices firmly shut throughout the Caribbean. Note that small and family-run businesses may close for a period between August and November.

Public Holidays

Regionwide public holidays:

New Year's Day January 1

Good Friday Late March/early April

Easter Monday Late March/early April

Whit Monday Eighth Monday after Easter

Christmas Day December 25

Boxing Day December 26

Safe Travel

In terms of individual safety and crime, the situation is quite varied in the Caribbean. Employ common sense.

➡ In big cities and tourist areas, take taxis at night.

➡ Avoid flashing your wealth, whether jewelry or blindly following your smartphone.

➡ Exercise extra caution in urban areas such as Pointe-à-Pitre (Guadeloupe), Fort-de-France (Martinique), Kingston (Jamaica), Port-au-Prince (Haiti) and downtown Port of Spain (Trinidad).

Telephone

Most cell (mobile) phones work in the Caribbean; avoid roaming charges with easily bought local SIM cards. The biggest operators in the Caribbean are Digicel and Flow. Puerto Rico and the US Virgin Islands are included in US plans.

Telephone Codes

ISLAND	COUNTRY CODE
Anguilla	+264
Antigua & Barbuda	+268
Aruba	+297
The Bahamas	+242
Barbados	+248
Bonaire	+599
British Virgin Islands	+284
Cayman Islands	+345
Cuba	+53
Curaçao	+599
Dominica	+767
Dominican Republic	+809 or +829
Grenada	+473
Guadeloupe	+590
Haiti	+509
Jamaica	+876
Martinique	+596
Montserrat	+664
Puerto Rico	+787
Saba	+599
Sint Eustatius	+599
St-Barthélemy	+590
St Kitts & Nevis	+869
St Lucia	+758
St-Martin/Sint Maarten	+599
St Vincent & the Grenadines	+784
Trinidad & Tobago	+868
Turks & Caicos	+649
US Virgin Islands	+340

Time

Only the Turks and Caicos and the Bahamas observe daylight saving time.

Eastern Standard Time (EST; five hours behind GMT/UTC) Turks and Caicos, Jamaica, the Cayman Islands, the Dominican Republic

Atlantic Standard Time (AST; four hours behind GMT/UTC) All other islands

Toilets

Except in major tourist areas there are usually few public toilets, and those that do exist are often best avoided. Most restaurants have restrooms, but may require you to make a purchase before you can use them.

Tourist Information

Travel information is often available by the kilo. Many free publications found in hotel lobbies are excellent, and most islands have a tourist information center in the main town and offices at the airport.

Visas

Requirements vary from island to island. Citizens of Canada, the EU and the US don't need visas for visits of under 90 days throughout the region (Cuba is one exception; most nationalities require a Tourist Card, which can be bought online ahead of travel).

Volunteering

Many volunteer programs in the Caribbean mix holiday fun with good intentions, and include themes such as 'learn to dive while saving the reef' (if only it were that easy). Some organizations don't provide a lot of value beyond the interesting experience for the traveler. Always ask hard questions of organizations as to who is really benefiting – the volunteer or the local beneficiaries of the program. Note that most volunteer organizations levy charges to take part in their programs.

Volunteer programs include the following:

Gapforce (www.gapforce.org)

Global Volunteers (www.globalvolunteers.org)

Habitat for Humanity (www.habitat.org)

Women Travelers

Although the situation varies between islands, machismo is alive and well. Men can get aggressive, especially with women traveling alone. On many islands local men have few qualms about catcalling, hissing, whistling, sucking their teeth or making kissy sounds to attract female attention. While much of this is simply annoying, it can make women feel unsafe.

Like it or not, some women may feel much safer if traveling with a companion. Women traveling alone should be more vigilant than usual – generally avoid any situation where you're isolated and vulnerable, such as picking up male hitchhikers. Wearing revealing clothing when you're not on the beach will garner a lot of unwanted attention, and also note that what might be considered 'harmless flirtation' at home can be misconstrued as a serious come-on in the Caribbean.

Work

The Caribbean has high unemployment rates and low wages, as well as strict immigration policies aimed at preventing foreign visitors from taking up work.

One good bet for working is to crew with a boat or yacht. As boat hands aren't usually working on any one island in particular, the work situation is more flexible and it's easier to avoid hassles with immigration. Marinas are a good place to look for jobs on yachts; check the bulletin-board notices, strike up conversations with skippers or ask around at the nearest bar. Marinas in Miami and Fort Lauderdale are considered good places to find jobs, as people sailing their boats down for the season stop here looking for crew.

You can also look for jobs with a crew-placement agency such as UK-based Crew Finders (www.crewfinders.com) or US-based Crew Seekers (www.crewseekers.net).

PRACTICALITIES

Smoking Banned in public places and hotels and restaurants in many Caribbean nations.

Weights & measures Some Caribbean countries use the metric system, others use the imperial system, and a few use a confusing combination of both.

Transportation

GETTING THERE & AWAY

Travelers, including all US citizens traveling to the Caribbean, will need a passport. For US citizens traveling by sea (eg on a cruise ship), you will need a passport or a passport card to reenter the US. The latter is essentially a wallet-sized US passport that is only good for land and sea travel between the US and Canada, Mexico and the Caribbean. In some circumstances you may only need a valid driver's license but confirm this carefully with the cruise line.

US citizens do not need a passport to visit Puerto Rico and the US Virgin Islands, which continue to allow established forms of identification like valid driver's licenses.

Flights, cars and tours can be booked online at lonelyplanet.com/bookings.

Entering the Region

Passport requirements vary from island to island, but visas aren't required for most nationalities.

Air

Flight options to the Caribbean will vary between islands.

Airports

Caribbean airports vary enormously, from huge modern affairs taking international jets to tiny affairs where small regional planes land on airstrips that don't look much longer than Band-Aids.

The most popular airports (by arrival numbers) in the Caribbean:

➡ Puerto Rico

Luis Muñoz Marin International Airport (SJU; San Juan; www.aeropuertosju.com)

➡ Dominican Republic

Punta Cana International Airport (PUJ; Punta Cana; www.puntacanainternationalairport.com)

Las Americas International Airport (SDQ; Santo Domingo)

➡ Cuba

José Martí International Airport (HAV; Havana)

➡ Jamaica

Sangster International Airport (MBJ; Montego Bay; www.mbjairport.com)

➡ The Bahamas

Lynden Pindling International Airport (NAS; Nassau; www.nassaulpia.com)

Airlines

FROM NORTH AMERICA

Most major airlines in North America fly direct to the more popular islands in the Caribbean. In fact such service is so widespread that even places as tiny as Bonaire have nonstop service

CLIMATE CHANGE & TRAVEL

Every form of transport that relies on carbon-based fuel generates CO_2, the main cause of human-induced climate change. Modern travel is dependent on airplanes, which might use less fuel per kilometer per person than most cars but travel much greater distances. The altitude at which aircraft emit gases (including CO_2) and particles also contributes to their climate change impact.

Many websites offer 'carbon calculators' that allow people to estimate the carbon emissions generated by their journey and, for those who wish to do so, to offset the impact of the greenhouse gases emitted with contributions to portfolios of climate-friendly initiatives throughout the world. Lonely Planet offsets the carbon footprint of all staff and author travel.

to major US cities. Generally, however, getting to the Caribbean from US cities without hub airports will involve changing planes somewhere. **American Airlines** (www.aa.com) has major hubs for its extensive Caribbean service in Miami and San Juan, Puerto Rico.

Also note that service to the Caribbean is seasonal. An island that has, say, weekly nonstop flights from Chicago in January may have none at all in June.

FROM EUROPE

You can reach the Caribbean nonstop from Europe.

Proving that old colonial ties linger, airlines from the UK serve former British colonies like Barbados and Antigua. French airlines serve the French-speaking islands; and Dutch carriers fly to Aruba, Bonaire, Curaçao and Sint Maarten. There are no direct flights to the Caribbean from Australia, New Zealand or Asia – travelers fly via Europe or the US.

CHARTERS

Charter flights from the US, Canada, the UK and Europe offer another option for getting to the islands.

Fares are often cheaper than on regularly scheduled commercial airlines, but you usually have to depart and return on specific flights and you'll probably have no flexibility to extend your stay. Such flights also often come as part of packages that include stays in resorts.

Sea

There are a handful of ferries to the Caribbean from the USA, notably from Florida to the Bahamas. Otherwise, the only way to reach the Caribbean by sea is on a cruise ship (or, for a few lucky people, on a yacht).

GETTING AROUND

Air

The Caribbean has an extensive network of airlines serving even the smallest islands.

Bicycle

The popularity of cycling in the Caribbean depends on where you go. Several islands are prohibitively hilly, with narrow roads that make cycling difficult. On others, such as Cuba, cycling is a great way to get around. Many of the islands have bicycles for rent. Bike shops are becoming more common. Most ferries will let you bring bikes on board at no extra charge; regional airlines will likely charge a fee.

Boat

Getting around the islands by yacht (p59) is a fantasy for many. Charters are generally quite easy.

Ferries link some islands within the Caribbean, including the following:

- Anguilla, Saba, St-Martin/Sint Maarten and St-Barthélemy
- British Virgin Islands and US Virgin Islands
- Dominica, Guadeloupe, Martinique and St Lucia
- Dominican Republic and Puerto Rico

Bus

An inexpensive bus service is available on most islands, although the word 'bus' has different meanings in different places. Some islands have full-size buses, while on others a 'bus' is simply a pickup truck with wooden benches in the back.

DEPARTURE TAX

Some airports may charge a departure tax that is *not* included in the price of the ticket.

Whatever the vehicle, buses are a good environmental choice compared to rental cars and are an excellent way to meet locals. People are generally quite friendly and happy to talk to you about their island. Buses are also a good way to hear the most popular local music tracks, often at an amazingly loud volume.

Buses are often the primary means of commuting to work or school and thus are most frequent in the early mornings and from mid- to late afternoon. There's generally a good bus service on Saturday mornings, but Sunday service is often nonexistent.

Car & Motorcycle

Driving in the Caribbean islands can rock your world, rattle your brains and fray your nerves. At first. Soon, you'll get used to the often-poor road conditions, slow speeds and relaxed adherence to road rules, and using your horn to punctuate any maneuver or passing thought on the road conditions.

Island Driving

Offer a lift It's common courtesy on many islands to slow down and offer pedestrians a lift (and is considered obligatory on some).

Beware of goats! Keep an eye out for stray dogs, iguanas, wild horses, chickens and goats, all of which meander aimlessly on the island roads.

Cede the right-of-way Drivers often stop to let others turn or pedestrians to cross even when you don't think it's necessary.

THREE FLYING RECOMMENDATIONS

Our writers learned from experience three things you should remember when flying:

➡ Try not to arrive on a regional flight in the afternoon, when most of the North American and European flights arrive, swamping immigration and customs.

➡ Keep anything essential you might need for a few days with you. Luggage often somehow misses your flight – even if you see it waiting next to the plane as you board. It may take days – if ever – to catch up with you.

➡ Check in early. Bring a book and snack and hang out. Even people with confirmed seats are often bumped once flights have filled with check-in passengers, and alternatives can be days later. A two-hour wait is not bad if you're prepared for it. In many airports you can check in early and then go someplace else like the incredibly fun beach bars near the Sint Maarten airport runway.

Avoid night-driving If possible, don't drive at night, when many cars are neglectful of using their headlights, and road-using pedestrians may be hard to see.

Driver's Licenses

You'll need your driver's license in order to rent a car, and frequently need to be over 21. On some of the former British islands, you may need to purchase a visitors' driver's license from your car-rental agent.

Rental

Car rentals are available on nearly all of the islands, with a few exceptions (usually because they lack roads). On most islands there are affiliates of the international chains, but local rental agencies may have better rates. Advance booking almost always attracts cheaper rates.

International rental agencies found across many islands in the Caribbean include Avis (www.avis.com), Budget (www.budget.com), Dollar (www.dollar.com), Europcar (www.europcar.com) and Hertz (www.hertz.com).

Road Rules

Road rules vary by island. In general, note that driving conditions may be more relaxed than you are used to.

Many Caribbean countries drive on the left (usually a sign that the British were once in charge). This can be confusing if you're island-hopping and renting cars on each island.

Hitchhiking

Hitchhiking is an essential mode of travel on most islands, though the practice among foreign visitors is uncommon. Hitching is never entirely safe, and we don't recommend it. Travelers who hitch should understand that they are taking a small but potentially serious risk.

If you're driving a rental car, giving locals a lift can be a great form of cultural interaction, and much appreciated by those trudging along the side of the road while comparatively affluent foreigners whiz past.

Health

Prevention is the key to remaining healthy while traveling abroad. Travelers who receive the recommended vaccinations for the destination and follow common-sense precautions usually come away with nothing more serious than a little diarrhea.

From a health point of view, the Caribbean is generally safe as long as you're reasonably careful about what you eat and drink. The most common travel-related diseases, such as dysentery and hepatitis, are acquired by consumption of contaminated food and water. Mosquito-borne illnesses aren't a significant concern on most islands, except during outbreaks of dengue fever.

Health standards in major resort islands, such as Barbados, Bermuda and the Cayman Islands, are high, and access to health care is good.

BEFORE YOU GO

Insurance

If your health insurance does not cover you for medical expenses while abroad, get dedicated travel insurance. Find out in advance if your insurance plan will make payments directly to providers or reimburse you later for overseas health expenditures.

HAITI

Many of Haiti's challenges are health related, due in part to the introduction of cholera by UN peacekeepers and the country's poor infrastructure. Malaria is also seasonally present. A higher level of health vigilance is required in Haiti than in the rest of the Caribbean. Always check reliable travel-health resources before travel to Haiti.

Note that Cuba requires proof of medical insurance to enter the country. On remote islands, such as the Grenadines, you will require transport to more developed areas for any significant problem, so be sure your insurance covers emergency medical transport and evacuation.

Recommended Vaccinations

At the time of writing there were no recommended vaccinations for the Caribbean, but check with your physician before traveling. If you are traveling away from major resort areas or going to places such as Haiti, however, it is vital that you consult a travel medical clinic at least three weeks before departure to check whether vaccinations are needed.

Medical Checklist

Bring medications in their original containers and clearly labeled. A signed, dated letter from your physician describing all medical conditions and medications, including generic names, is also a good idea. If carrying syringes or needles, be sure to have a physician's letter documenting their medical necessity.

Recommended items for a personal medical kit:

- acetaminophen/paracetamol (eg Tylenol) or aspirin
- antibacterial hand sanitizer (eg Purell)
- antibacterial ointment (eg Bactroban) for cuts and abrasions
- antihistamines (for hay fever and allergic reactions)
- anti-inflammatory drugs (eg ibuprofen/Advil)
- DEET-containing insect repellent
- steroid cream or cortisone (for allergic rashes)
- sunscreen.

Health Advisories

It's always sensible to consult your government's

MANCHINEEL TREES

Manchineel trees grow on beaches throughout the Caribbean. The fruit of the manchineel, which looks like a small green apple, is poisonous. The milky sap given off by the fruit and leaves can cause severe skin blisters, similar to the reaction caused by poison oak. If the sap gets in your eyes, it can result in temporary blindness. Never take shelter under the trees during a rainstorm, as the sap can be washed off the tree and onto anyone sitting below.

Manchineel trees can grow as high as 40ft (12m), with branches that spread widely. The leaves are green, shiny and elliptical in shape. On some of the more-visited beaches, trees will be marked with warning signs or bands of red paint. Manchineel is called *mancenillier* on the French islands.

travel-health website before departure, if one is available:

Australia (www.smartraveller.gov.au)

Canada/US (www.cdc.gov/travel)

UK (www.fitfortravel.nhs.uk)

IN THE CARIBBEAN ISLANDS

Availability & Cost of Health Care

Acceptable health care is available in most major cities throughout the Caribbean, but may be hard to locate in rural areas. To find a good local doctor, your best bet is to ask the management of the hotel where you are staying or contact your local embassy.

Many doctors and hospitals expect payment in cash, regardless of whether you have travel health insurance. If you develop a life-threatening medical problem, you'll probably want to be evacuated to a country with state-of-the-art medical care. Since this may cost tens of thousands of dollars, be sure you have insurance to cover this before you depart.

Many pharmacies are well supplied, but important medications may not be consistently available. Be sure to bring along adequate supplies of all your prescription drugs.

Infectious Diseases

You are unlikely to come down with an infectious disease in the Caribbean, especially if you are just visiting resorts and the most developed islands. Cruisers will find themselves sprayed with antibacterial hand sanitizer at every turn as the cruise lines seek to prevent mass viral outbreaks.

Dengue Fever

Dengue fever is a viral infection common throughout the Caribbean. Dengue is transmitted by *Aedes* mosquitoes, which bite mostly during the daytime and are usually found close to human habitations, often indoors. They breed primarily in artificial water containers, such as jars, barrels, cans, cisterns, metal drums, plastic containers and discarded tires. As a result, dengue is especially common in densely populated, urban environments.

Dengue usually causes flu-like symptoms, including fever, muscle aches, joint pains, headaches, nausea and vomiting, often followed by a rash. The body aches may be quite uncomfortable, but most cases resolve uneventfully in a few days. Severe cases usually occur in children aged under 15 who are experiencing their second dengue infection.

If you suspect you have dengue fever, seek out medical advice. There is no vaccine. As the cornerstone of prevention is protection against insect bites, always use repellent.

Hepatitis A

Hepatitis A is the second-most-common travel-related infection (after traveler's diarrhea). The illness occurs throughout the world, but the incidence is higher in developing nations. It occurs throughout the Caribbean, particularly in the northern islands.

Hepatitis A is a viral infection of the liver that is usually acquired by ingesting contaminated water, food or ice, though it may also be acquired by direct contact with infected persons. Symptoms may include fever, malaise, jaundice, nausea, vomiting and abdominal pain. Most cases resolve without complications, though hepatitis A occasionally causes severe liver damage. There is no treatment.

The vaccine for hepatitis A is extremely safe and highly effective. If you get a booster six to 12 months later, it lasts for at least 10 years. You should get it before you go to any developing nation. Because the safety of the hepatitis A vaccine has not been established for pregnant women or children under the age of two, they should instead be given a gamma globulin injection, which temporarily boosts immunity.

HIV & AIDS

HIV/AIDS rates across the Caribbean are estimated at 1.6%. More than half of those living with HIV in the region are in Haiti, followed by the Bahamas and Trinidad and Tobago. Most cases in the Caribbean are related to heterosexual sex, especially with sex workers. The exception is Puerto Rico, where the most common cause of infection is intravenous drug use. Be sure to use condoms for all sexual encounters.

If you require injections (or are getting a tattoo or piercing), always check that a sterile needle is being used.

Schistosomiasis

A parasitic infection carried by snails and acquired by exposure of skin to contaminated freshwater, schistosomiasis (also known as bilharzia) has been reported in parts of the Dominican Republic, Guadeloupe, Martinique, Puerto Rico, St Lucia, Antigua and Montserrat.

Early symptoms may include fever, loss of appetite, weight loss, abdominal pain, weakness, headaches, joint and muscle pains, diarrhea, nausea and a cough, but most infections are asymptomatic at first. Schistosomiasis is quickly treatable with a single dose of the drug praziquantel.

When traveling in areas where schistosomiasis occurs, you should avoid swimming, wading, bathing or washing in bodies of freshwater, including lakes, ponds, streams and rivers. Toweling yourself dry after exposure to contaminated water may reduce your chance of getting infected, but does not eliminate it. Saltwater and chlorinated pools carry no risk of schistosomiasis.

WATER

Tap water is safe to drink on some of the islands, but not on others. Unless you're certain that the local water is safe, don't drink it.

Note: if tap water is safe to drink – as it is on the major destination islands except for Cuba – then avoiding bottled water reduces the significant environmental impact of plastic water containers.

Traveler's Diarrhea

In places where tap water is safe to drink – much of the Caribbean – your risk of diarrhea is not high, though the sudden changes of temperature, diet and routine brought on by foreign travel can make your body more prone to stomach upsets. In places where the tap water is suspect, take the usual precautions: eat fresh fruits or vegetables only if cooked or peeled; be wary of dairy products that might contain unpasteurized milk; and be highly selective when eating food from street vendors.

Zika

Zika is present in many parts of the Caribbean, although outbreaks are currently on the decrease. The virus spreads through the bite of an infected *Aedes* mosquito. Common symptoms include fever, rash, joint pain and conjunctivitis. Most victims experience mild illness with symptoms that last for several days to a week. Since Zika may cause brain damage to a fetus in utero, pregnant women should seek medical advice before traveling to a potential Zika hot spot. The virus may also be sexually transmitted by an infected partner. Since there is no vaccine or treatment, the cornerstone of prevention is protection against mosquito bites.

For current advice, see www.cdc.gov/zika.

Environmental Hazards

A few things to watch out for:

Mosquito bites Caribbean mosquitoes and other biting/stinging insects come in all shapes and sizes, and are quite common. The biggest concern here, outside the few areas with malaria or Zika, is simply discomfort and hassle. Make certain you have a good insect repellent with at least 25% DEET.

Rabies Some islands do have rabies, so do as you would at home and avoid touching or petting strays.

Sea stingers Spiny sea urchins and coelenterates (coral and jellyfish) are a hazard in some areas. If stung by a coelenterate, apply diluted vinegar or baking soda. Remove tentacles carefully, but not with bare hands. If stung by a stinging fish, such as a stingray, immerse the limb in water at about 115°F (45°C) and seek medical attention.

Sunburn Wear sunscreen with a high SPF as the Caribbean sun is very strong and sunburn is common. Every day people have their trips ruined because they didn't apply sunblock, especially after time in the water.

Language

The rich language environment of the greater Caribbean is testament to the diverse array of people that have come to call it home.

From a colonial past that saw the dying out of virtually all traces of indigenous languages, there is the legacy of English, French, Spanish, Dutch and Portuguese. Outside these predominant languages, perhaps the most notable influences can be traced back to the slaves brought to the islands from West Africa. European tongues, creoles, patois, local accents and pidgins contribute to the particular linguistic mix of each island.

To find out who speaks what where, see the opening pages of each On the Road chapter.

FRENCH

The French used in the Caribbean is flatter in intonation, with less of the traditional French lilting cadence. Also, speakers of Creole pay less attention to gender; anything or anyone can be il (the French word for 'he').

There are nasal vowels (pronounced as if you're trying to force the sound through the nose) in French, indicated in our pronunciation guides with o or u followed by an almost inaudible nasal consonant sound m, n or ng. Note also that air is pronounced as in 'fair', eu as the 'u' in 'nurse', ew as ee with rounded lips, r is a throaty sound, and zh is pronounced as the 's' in 'pleasure'.

Basics

Hello.	*Bonjour.*	bon·zhoor
Goodbye.	*Au revoir.*	o·rer·vwa
Excuse me.	*Excusez-moi.*	ek·skew·zay·mwa
Sorry.	*Pardon.*	par·don
Please.	*S'il vous plaît.*	seel voo play
Thank you.	*Merci.*	mair·see
Yes.	*Oui.*	wee
No.	*Non.*	non

QUESTION WORDS – FRENCH

How?	*Comment?*	ko·mon
What?	*Quoi?*	kwa
When?	*Quand?*	kon
Where?	*Où?*	oo
Who?	*Qui?*	kee
Why?	*Pourquoi?*	poor·kwa

What's your name?
Comment vous appelez-vous? — ko·mon voo·za·play voo

My name is ...
Je m'appelle ... — zher ma·pel ...

Do you speak English?
Parlez-vous anglais? — par·lay·voo ong·glay

I don't understand.
Je ne comprends pas. — zher ner kom·pron pa

How much is it?
C'est combien? — say kom·byun

Accommodations

campsite	*camping*	kom·peeng
guesthouse	*pension*	pon·syon
hotel	*hôtel*	o·tel
youth hostel	*auberge de jeunesse*	o·berzh der zher·nes

Do you have a ... room?	*Avez-vous une chambre ...?*	a·vey·voo ewn shom·bre ...
single	*à un lit*	a un lee
double	*avec un grand lit*	a·vek ung gron lee
How much is it per ...?	*Quel est le prix par ...?*	kel ey le pree par ...
night	*nuit*	nwee
person	*personne*	pair·son

Eating & Drinking

What would you recommend?
Qu'est-ce que vous conseillez? kes·ker voo kon·say·yay

Do you have vegetarian food?
Vous faites les repas végétariens? voo fet ley re·pa vey·zhey·ta·ryun

I'll have ...	*Je prends ...*	zhe pron ...
Cheers!	*Santé!*	son·tay
I'd like the ..., please.	*Je voudrais ..., s'il vous plaît.*	zhe voo·drey ... seel voo pley
bill	*l'addition*	la·dee·syon
menu	*la carte*	la kart
breakfast	*petit déjeuner*	per·tee day·zher·nay
lunch	*déjeuner*	day·zher·nay
dinner	*dîner*	dee·nay

Emergencies

Help!
Au secours! o skoor

Leave me alone!
Fichez-moi la paix! fee·shay·mwa la pay

I'm lost.
Je suis perdu(e). (m/f) zhe swee pair·dew

I'm ill.
Je suis malade. zher swee ma·lad

Where are the toilets?
Où sont les toilettes? oo son ley twa·let

Call ...!	*Appelez ...!*	a·play un ...
a doctor	*un médecin*	un mayd·sun
the police	*la police*	la po·lees

Transportation & Directions

Where's ...?
Où est ...? oo ay ...

What's the address?
Quelle est l'adresse? kel ay la·dres

Can you show me (on the map)?
Pouvez-vous m'indiquer (sur la carte)? poo·vay·voo mun·dee·kay (sewr la kart)

One ... ticket (to Bordeaux), please.	*Un billet ... (pour Bordeaux), s'il vous plaît.*	um bee·yey ... (poor bor·do) seel voo pley
one-way	*simple*	sum·ple
return	*aller et retour*	a·ley ey re·toor
boat	*bateau*	ba·to
bus	*bus*	bews
plane	*avion*	a·vyon
train	*train*	trun

NUMBERS – FRENCH

1	*un*	un
2	*deux*	der
3	*trois*	trwa
4	*quatre*	ka·trer
5	*cinq*	sungk
6	*six*	sees
7	*sept*	set
8	*huit*	weet
9	*neuf*	nerf
10	*dix*	dees

SPANISH

While Spanish in the Caribbean is mutually intelligible with European Spanish, there are some differences, as migration and indigenous languages have left their mark on local vocabulary and pronunciation.

Spanish vowels are generally pronounced short. Note that ow is pronounced as in 'how', kh as in the Scottish loch (harsh and guttural), rr is rolled and stronger than in English, and v is a soft 'b' (pronounced between the English 'v' and 'b' sounds).

Basics

Hello.	*Hola.*	o·la
Goodbye.	*Adiós.*	a·*dyos*
Excuse me.	*Perdón.*	per·*don*
Sorry.	*Lo siento.*	lo *syen*·to
Please.	*Por favor.*	por fa·*vor*
Thank you.	*Gracias.*	*gra*·syas
Yes.	*Sí.*	see

WANT MORE?

For in-depth language information and handy phrases, check out Lonely Planet's *Latin American Spanish*, *French*, and *Dutch Phrasebooks*. You'll find them at **shop.lonelyplanet.com**, or you can buy Lonely Planet's iPhone phrasebooks at the Apple App Store.

QUESTION WORDS – SPANISH

How?	*¿Cómo?*	*ko*·mo
What?	*¿Qué?*	ke
When?	*¿Cuándo?*	*kwan*·do
Where?	*¿Dónde?*	*don*·de
Who?	*¿Quién?*	kyen
Why?	*¿Por qué?*	por ke

No.	*No.*	no

What's your name?
¿Cómo se llama Usted? (pol) — ko·mo se *ya*·ma oo·ste
¿Cómo te llamas? (inf) — ko·mo te *ya*·mas

My name is ...
Me llamo ... — me *ya*·mo ...

Do you speak English?
¿Habla/Hablas inglés? (pol/inf) — *a*·bla/*a*·blas een·*gles*

I don't understand.
Yo no entiendo. — yo no en·*tyen*·do

How much is it?
¿Cuánto cuesta? — *kwan*·to *kwes*·ta

Accommodations

campsite	*terreno de cámping*	te·re·no de *kam*·peeng
guesthouse	*pensión*	pen·*syon*
hotel	*hotel*	o·*tel*
youth hostel	*albergue juvenil*	al·*ber*·ge khoo·ve·*neel*

Do you have a ... room?	*¿Tiene una habitación ...?*	*tye*·ne *oo*·na a·bee·ta·*syon* ...
single	*individual*	een·dee·vee·*dwal*
double	*doble*	*do*·ble

NUMBERS – SPANISH

1	*uno*	*oo*·no
2	*dos*	dos
3	*tres*	tres
4	*cuatro*	*kwa*·tro
5	*cinco*	*seen*·ko
6	*seis*	seys
7	*siete*	*sye*·te
8	*ocho*	o·cho
9	*nueve*	*nwe*·ve
10	*diez*	dyes

KEY PATTERNS

To get by in Spanish, mix and match these simple patterns with words of your choice:

When's (the next flight)?
¿Cuándo sale (el próximo vuelo)? — *kwan*·do *sa*·le (el *prok*·see·mo *vwe*·lo)

Where's (the station)?
¿Dónde está (la estación)? — *don*·de es·*ta* (la es·ta·*syon*)

Where can I (buy a ticket)?
¿Dónde puedo (comprar un billete)? — *don*·de *pwe*·do (kom·*prar* oon bee·*ye*·te)

Do you have (a map)?
¿Tiene (un mapa)? — *tye*·ne (oon *ma*·pa)

Is there (a toilet)?
¿Hay (servicios)? — ai (ser·*vee*·syos)

I'd like (a coffee).
Quisiera (un café). — kee·*sye*·ra (oon ka·*fe*)

I'd like (to hire a car).
Quisiera (alquilar un coche). — kee·*sye*·ra (al·kee·*lar* oon *ko*·che)

Can I (enter)?
¿Se puede (entrar)? — se *pwe*·de (en·*trar*)

Could you please (help me)?
¿Puede (ayudarme), por favor? — *pwe*·de (a·yoo·*dar*·me) por fa·*vor*

Do I have to (get a visa)?
¿Necesito (obtener un visado)? — ne·se·*see*·to (ob·te·*ner* oon vee·*sa*·do)

How much is it per ...?	*¿Cuánto cuesta por ...?*	*kwan*·to *kwes*·ta por ...
night	*noche*	*no*·che
person	*persona*	per·*so*·na

Eating & Drinking

What would you recommend?
¿Qué recomienda? — ke re·ko·*myen*·da

Do you have vegetarian food?
¿Tienen comida vegetariana? — *tye*·nen ko·*mee*·da ve·khe·ta·*rya*·na

I'll have ...	*Para mí ...*	*pa*·ra mee ...
Cheers!	*¡Salud!*	sa·*loo*

I'd like the ..., please.	*Quisiera ..., por favor.*	kee·*sye*·ra ... por fa·*vor*
bill	*la cuenta*	la *kwen*·ta
menu	*el menú*	el me·*noo*
breakfast	*desayuno*	de·sa·*yoo*·no

lunch	*comida*	ko·*mee*·da
dinner	*cena*	*se*·na

Emergencies

Help!	
¡Socorro!	so·*ko*·ro
Go away!	
¡Vete!	*ve*·te
I'm lost.	
Estoy perdido/a. (m/f)	es·*toy* per·*dee*·do/a
I'm ill.	
Estoy enfermo/a. (m/f)	es·*toy* en·*fer*·mo/a
Where are the toilets?	
¿Dónde están los servicios?	*don*·de es·*tan* los ser·*vee*·syos

Call ...!	*¡Llame a ...!*	*lya*·me a ...
a doctor	*un médico*	oon *me*·dee·ko
the police	*la policía*	la po·lee·*see*·a

Transportation & Directions

Where's ...?	
¿Dónde está ...?	*don*·de es·*ta* ...
What's the address?	
¿Cuál es la dirección?	*kwal* es la dee·rek·*syon*
Can you show me (on the map)?	
¿Me lo puede indicar (en el mapa)?	me lo *pwe*·de een·dee·*kar* (en el *ma*·pa)

a ... ticket	*un billete de ...*	oon bee·*ye*·te ... de ...
one-way	*ida*	*ee*·da
return	*de ida y vuelta*	de *ee*·da ee *vwel*·ta
boat	*barco*	*bar*·ko
bus	*autobús*	ow·to·*boos*
plane	*avión*	a·*vyon*
train	*tren*	tren

DUTCH

While it isn't necessary to speak Dutch to get by on the islands of Saba, Sint Eustatius and Sint Maarten, these Dutch basics might help you make some new friends in the East Caribbean.

Note that aw is pronounced as in 'saw', eu as the 'u' in 'nurse', ew as 'ee' with rounded lips, oh as the 'o' in 'note', öy as the '-er y-' in 'her year' (without the 'r'), uh as the 'a' in 'ago', kh as in the Scottish loch (harsh and guttural), and zh as the 's' in 'pleasure'.

Basics

Hello.	*Goedendag.*	khoo·duh·*dakh*
Goodbye.	*Dag.*	dakh
Excuse me.	*Pardon.*	par·*don*
Sorry.	*Sorry.*	*so*·ree
Please.	*Alstublieft.* (pol)	al·stew·*bleeft*
	Alsjeblieft. (inf)	a·shuh·*bleeft*
Thank you.	*Dank u/je.* (pol/inf)	dangk ew/yuh
Yes.	*Ja.*	yaa
No.	*Nee.*	ney

What's your name?	
Hoe heet u/je? (pol/inf)	hoo heyt ew/yuh
My name is ...	
Ik heet ...	ik heyt ...

HAITIAN CREOLE

Here are a few basics to get you started in the predominant lingo of Haiti.

Good day.	*Bonjou.* (before noon)
Good evening.	*Bonswa.* (after 11am)
See you later.	*Na wè pita.*
Yes./No.	*Wi./Non.*
Please.	*Silvouple.*
Thank you.	*Mèsi anpil.*
Sorry./Excuse me.	*Pàdon.*
How are you?	*Ki jan ou ye?*
Not bad.	*M pal pi mal.*
I'm going OK.	*M-ap kenbe.*
What's your name?	*Ki jan ou rele?*
My name is ...	*M rele ...*
Do you speak English?	*Eske ou ka pale angle?*
I don't understand.	*M pa konprann.*
How much is it?	*Konbyen?*
I'm lost.	*M pèdi.*
Where is/are ... ?	*Kote ... ?*

GLOSSARY

ABCs – Aruba, Bonaire and Curaçao

accra – fried mixture of okra, black-eyed peas, pepper and salt

agouti – short-haired rabbitlike rodent resembling a guinea pig with long legs; it has a fondness for sugarcane

Arawak – linguistically related tribes that inhabited most of the Caribbean islands and northern South America

bake – sandwich made with fried bread and usually filled with fish

bareboat – sail-it-yourself charter yacht usually rented by the week or longer

beguine – Afro-French dance music with a bolero rhythm that originated in Martinique in the 1930s; also spelled 'biguine'

bomba – musical form and dance inspired by African rhythms and characterized by call-and-response dialogues between musicians and interpreted by dancers; often considered as a unit with *plena*, as in *bomba y plena*

breadfruit – large, round, green fruit; a Caribbean staple that's comparable to potatoes in its carbohydrate content and is prepared in much the same way

bush tea – tea made from the islands' leaves, roots and herbs; each tea cures a specific illness, such as gas, menstrual pain, colds or insomnia

BVI – British Virgin Islands

cabrito – goat meat

callaloo – spinachlike green, originally from Africa; also spelled 'kallaloo'

calypso – popular Caribbean music developed from slave songs; lyrics reflect political opinions, social views and commentary on current events

Carnival – major Caribbean festival; originated as a pre-Lenten festivity but is now observed at various times throughout the year on different islands; also spelled 'Carnaval'

casa particular – private house in Cuba that lets out rooms to foreigners

cassava – a root used since precolonial times as a staple of island diets, whether steamed, baked or grated into a flour for bread; also called 'yucca' or 'manioc'

cay – small island; comes from an Arawak word

cayo – coral key (Spanish)

chattel house – type of simple wooden dwelling placed upon cement or stone blocks so it can be easily moved

chutney – up-tempo, rhythmic music used in celebrations of various social situations in Trinidad's Indian communities

colombo – spicy, East Indian–influenced dish that resembles curry

conch – large gastropod that, due to overfishing, is endangered; its chewy meat is often prepared in a spicy *Creole*-style sauce; also called *lambi*

conkies – mixture of cornmeal, coconut, pumpkin, sweet potatoes, raisins and spice, steamed in a plantain leaf

cou-cou – creamy cornmeal and okra mash, commonly served with saltfish

Creole – person of European, or mixed black and European ancestry; local language predominantly a combination of French and African languages; cuisine characterized by spicy, full-flavored sauces and heavy use of green peppers and onions

dancehall – contemporary offshoot of reggae with faster, digital beats and an MC

dasheen – type of taro; the leaves are known as *callaloo*, while the starchy tuberous root is boiled and eaten like a potato

daube meat – pot roast seasoned with vinegar, native seasonings, onion, garlic, tomato, thyme, parsley and celery

dolphin – a marine mammal; also a common type of white-meat fish (dolphinfish; sometimes called *mahimahi*); the two are not related, and 'dolphin' on any menu always refers to the fish

duppy – ghost or spirit; also called *jumbie*

flying fish – gray-meat fish named for its ability to skim above the water, particularly plentiful in Barbados

fungi – semihard cornmeal pudding similar to Italian polenta that's added to soups and used as a side dish; also a Creole name for the music made by local scratch bands; 'funchi' on Aruba, Bonaire and Curaçao

gade – street (Danish)

gîte – small cottages for rent (French)

goat water – spicy goat-meat stew often flavored with cloves and rum

gommier – large native gum tree found in Caribbean rainforests

green flash – Caribbean phenomenon where you can see a green flash as the sun sets into the ocean

guagua – local bus; *gua-gua* in Dominican Republic

I-tal – natural style of vegetarian cooking practised by Rastafarians

irie – all right; used to indicate that all is well

jambalaya – a Creole dish usually consisting of rice cooked with ham, chicken or shellfish, spices, tomatoes, onions and peppers

jintero/a – tout or prostitute; literally 'jockey'

johnnycake – corn-flour griddle cake

jug-jug – mixture of Guinea cornmeal, green peas and salted meat

jumbie – see *duppy*

jump-up – nighttime street party that usually involves dancing and plenty of rum drinking

lambi – see *conch*
limin' – hanging out, relaxing, chilling; also spelled 'liming'; from the Creole verb 'to lime'

mahimahi – see *dolphin*
mairie – town hall (French)
malecón – main street; literally 'sea wall'
manchineel – tree whose poisonous fruit sap can cause a severe skin rash; common on Caribbean beaches; called *mancenillier* on the French islands, and *anjenelle* on Trinidad and Tobago
manicou – opossum
mas camp – workshop where artists create Carnival costumes; short for 'masquerade camp'
mento – folk *calypso* music
mojito – cocktail made from rum, mint, sugar, seltzer and fresh lime juice
mountain chicken – legs of the crapaud, a type of frog found in Dominica

négritude – Black Pride philosophical and political movement that emerged in Martinique in the 1930s

Obeah – system of ancestral worship related to *Vodou* and rooted in West African religions
oil down – mix of breadfruit, beef, pork, *callaloo* and coconut milk
out islands – islands or *cays* that lie across the water from the main islands of an island group

Painkiller – popular alcoholic drink made with two parts rum, one part orange juice, four parts pineapple juice, one part coconut cream and a sprinkle of nutmeg and cinnamon
paladar – privately owned restaurant in Cuba serving reliable, inexpensive meals
panyards – place where steel pan is practiced in the months leading up to *Carnival*
parang – type of music sung in Spanish and accompanied by guitars and maracas; originated in Venezuela
pate – fried pastry of *cassava* or *plantain* dough stuffed with spiced goat, pork, chicken, *conch*, lobster or fish
pepperpot – spicy stew made with various meats, accompanied by peppers and cassareep
plantain – starchy fruit of the banana family; usually fried or grilled like a vegetable
playa – beach (Spanish)
público – collective taxis; *publique* in Haiti

quelbe – blend of jigs, quadrilles, military fife and African drum music

rapso – a fusion of *soca* and hip-hop
reggaeton – mixture of hip-hop, reggae and *dancehall*
roti – curry (often potatoes and chicken) rolled inside flat bread
rumba – Afro-Cuban dance form that originated among plantation slaves during the 19th century; during the 1920s and '30s, the term 'rumba' was adopted in North America and Europe for a ballroom dance in 4/4 time; in Cuba today, 'to rumba' means 'to party'

salsa – Cuban music based on *son*
Santería – Afro-Caribbean religion representing the syncretism of Catholic and African beliefs
snowbird – North American, usually retired, who comes to the Caribbean for its warm winters
soca – energetic offspring of *calypso*; it uses danceable rhythms and risqué lyrics to convey pointed social commentary
son – Cuba's basic form of popular music, with African and Spanish elements
souse – dish made out of pickled pig's head and belly, spices and a few vegetables; commonly served with a pig-blood sausage called 'pudding'
steel pan – instrument made from oil drums or the music it produces; also called 'steel drum' or 'steel band'
SVG – St Vincent and the Grenadines
Taíno – settled, Arawak-speaking tribe that inhabited much of the Caribbean prior to the Spanish conquest; the word itself means 'We the Good People'
taptap – local Haitian bus
timba – contemporary *salsa*
T&T – Trinidad and Tobago

USVI – US Virgin Islands

Vodou – religion practised in Haiti; a synthesis of West African animist spirit religions and residual rituals of the *Taino*

zouk – popular French West Indies music that draws from the *beguine* and other French Caribbean folk forms

Behind the Scenes

SEND US YOUR FEEDBACK

We love to hear from travelers – your comments keep us on our toes and help make our books better. Our well-traveled team reads every word on what you loved or loathed about this book. Although we cannot reply individually to your submissions, we always guarantee that your feedback goes straight to the appropriate authors, in time for the next edition. Each person who sends us information is thanked in the next edition – the most useful submissions are rewarded with a selection of digital PDF chapters.

Visit **lonelyplanet.com/contact** to submit your updates and suggestions or to ask for help. Our award-winning website also features inspirational travel stories, news and discussions.

Note: We may edit, reproduce and incorporate your comments in Lonely Planet products such as guidebooks, websites and digital products, so let us know if you don't want your comments reproduced or your name acknowledged. For a copy of our privacy policy visit lonelyplanet.com/privacy.

OUR READERS

Many thanks to the travelers who used the last edition and wrote to us with helpful hints, useful advice and interesting anecdotes:

Blair Doyle, Hannah Hartley, Nicola Hartley

WRITER THANKS

Paul Clammer

Special thanks to Michael Becker in Kingston and elsewhere for being a great travel companion and fellow Caribbean history nerd. Bless up to David Scott as always. Thanks to Annie Paul, Emma Lewis, Susanne Fredricks, Andrea Dempster-Chung, Jan Voordouw, Kim Agerblad and staff at the UWI history department. Enormous shout out to fellow scribe Anna Kaminski, who helped scare off the duppies on the road to Alligator Hole. At Lonely Planet, thanks to Alicia Johnson. Finally thanks and love as ever to Robyn, who ensures there's always a home waiting at the end of the road.

Stephanie d'Arc Taylor

My home team: Xtine, Maya Gebeily, the Dzolomons, Alice Fordham. My Lonely Planet fam: Michael Grosberg, Paul Clammer (I'm not worthy), Alicia Johnson, Lauren Keith. In DR: Nicole Rodriguez, Molly-Ann Pereira de Cruz. In Haiti: Wyclef, Jacqui Labrom, Stephen Broege, Lolo & Sara for a great night out in Cap, Dillon Mangs & team Relaxo, and Bernie & Jean Edouarde for the education about Haitian creativity. Pa'lante!

Marc Di Duca

A huge thankyou to everyone who helped me out along the way on the ground in Puerto Rico, Martinique and Guadeloupe including the helpful staff at the Puerto Rico Tourism Company, tourist offices around all three islands and the staff at the DNRA in San Juan. Huge thanks must go to my wife Tanya for holding the fort during my long absences and to my co-authors Sarah Gilbert and Paul Clammer.

Alex Egerton

In Barbados, big shouts to Chrystabel in Bridgetown and Bryn in Holetown in addition to the staff at Andromeda. In Saint Lucia, Chris and Charlotte in Rodney Bay and Brandon down south. On the ground in St Vincent and the Grenadines Tabiah Regis, Jason, and Team Trudeau on Bequia. And finally in Grenada René and Nicole and the University gang. On the home front Nick and Olga and also Urs for the office.

Sarah Gilbert

Muchas gracias to all the *puertorriqueñas* that were so kind and generous with their time. Particular thanks go to Eddie Ramirez and Tisha Pastor in Old San Juan, Sylvia de Marco in Ocean Park, Carolyn Krupp and Jeff Ellison from El Yunque National Forest, Carla Arraiza and Carlos Guzmán in Luquillo, Alan DeLapp in Vieques and Keishya Salko in Punta Santiago. And, as always, thanks to my family and friends for their support.

Michael Grosberg

Thanks to Kim Bedall from Whale Samana, Nicolas and Monica from Flora Tours, Emily Wright, Esmelvin Vivas, Paola Montas, Indira Soltero, Francheska Oviedo, Bonnie Helena, Maurizio Bartezatti, Ashley Lagzial for all their help and insight; and to my co-author and collaborator Emily D'Arc Taylor. Most especially to Carly, Rosie and Willa for joining me for part of my time in the DR.

Paul Harding

Thanks to all the helpful people I met in the beautiful Bahamas and Turks & Caicos. In no particular order: Erika, Lynn, Debbie, Edward, Tom and Esther. Thanks to Alicia Johnson at Lonely Planet. Most of all thanks to Hannah and Layla at home for the phone calls and patience while I was living the island life.

Ashley Harrell

Thanks to: editor Alicia Johnson and my co-authors for making this a fantastic book, Tesh and Reena Chugani for the input and generosity, Simon and Louise Holder for the advice and hospitality, Erin Morris and Will Dunlap for the best vacay ever, Alexis Stranberg and Josh Buermann for tending to the vicious cur, and Steven Sparapani, for learning to scuba dive despite strong misgivings and providing endless entertainment. I'm sorry I lost your fin. I love you.

Mark Johanson

Thanks to all the people in the USVI and BVI who steered me in the right direction and helped me to navigate the post-hurricane recovery process. I owe a debt of gratitude to Heather Brewster, Jose Belcher, Michael Armendariz and Adam Quandt for being fountains of knowledge along the way. A special thanks to my partner Felipe Bascuñán for tolerating my long absences.

Anna Kaminski

Huge thanks to Alicia for entrusting me with half of Jamaica, plus my fellow scribe Paul and others who've helped me along the way. In particular: Bonz at Good Hope Estate, Sharon, David, Annabel and Lilith in Treasure Beach, Dr Connelly in Windsor, Lando and Allison in Black River, Marina and Kathy in Falmouth, Canute at Mountambrin, my guide in Accompong, Conrod and Rasta Ade in Negril, and assorted doctors in Kingston for patching me up.

Tom Masters

Many thanks to Clover Lee and family in Montserrat, the staff at Visit Antigua, Visit Dominica, Visit Montserrat and St Kitts & Nevis Tourism, Heather Archibald, Carol Ann Watson, Troy 'Poz', Rosemary Masters for joining me on the road in St Kitts and Dominica and all the brave people of Dominica and Barbuda recovering from Hurricane Maria.

Brendan Sainsbury

Special thanks to all my many Cuban amigos, especially Julio & Elsa Roque and Luis Miguel in Havana, Julio & Rosa Muñoz in Trinidad, Julio & Lidia in Playa Girón, Roberto in Viñales, Moreno & Mercy in Santa Clara, Yoel in Matanzas, and Carlos for his careful driving and excellent company everywhere. An extra gracias to my wife Liz for accompanying me on the road and enjoying La Isla de la Juventud.

Andrea Schulte-Peevers

Heartfelt thank yous to all the wonderful people in the islands who helped me with logistics, research and moral support. Special shout-outs to Glenn Holm, Crocodile James, Lynn Costenaro and Donna Cain on Saba; Kate Richardson in St-Martin; Donna Banks, Colwayne Pickering and Sharon Lowe in Anguilla; and Claudia Wichert and Ingrid Walter in Sint Eustatius. On the home front, a huge thanks to Sandy Peevers and Margarita Kurowska for keeping things under control, and to David for being with me in spirit.

Polly Thomas

Huge thanks to my Trini family for liming, love and support: Dexter, Lynette, Dale, Gillian, Dean, Sion, Aaron and Soleil Lewis, and Skye Hernandez, Mampuru Stollmeyer and Jillian and Jada Fourniller. To Gunda Harewood, Anna Carlsson and Faye Patrick for fabulous road trips; Mark and Zena Puddy for fantastic friendship and food; and Celia Rugg, Matthew Thomas, Imogen and Isabella Spencer, and Amanda and Beau Rolandini-Jensen for UK backup.

Wendy Yanagihara

My deepest gratitude goes to Diego and Rudens for uber-Cuban language lessons, unforgettable adventures (including the immigration office), and hiking beers. Muchas gracias also to Maité, Idolka, Nilson and Ramses for local insight and friendship, to Anna for sparkly companionship, to the many guides and patient taxistas who made this assignment feasible in two months on the ground, to Brendan and Carolyn for invaluable intel, and to the ones who always make my travels possible: Laura, Victoria, Jason and Jasper.

ACKNOWLEDGMENTS

Climate map data adapted from Peel MC, Finlayson BL & McMahon TA (2007) 'Updated World Map of the Köppen-Geiger Climate Classification', *Hydrology and Earth System Sciences*, 11, 1633–44.

Cover photograph: Flamingo Beach, Aruba, Kim Kaminski/Alamy Stock Photo ©

THIS BOOK

This 8th edition of Lonely Planet's *Caribbean Islands* guidebook was curated by Paul Clammer and researched and written by Paul and Stephanie d'Arc Taylor, Marc Di Duca, Alex Egerton, Sarah Gilbert, Michael Grosberg, Paul Harding, Ashley Harrell, Mark Johanson, Anna Kaminski, Tom Masters, Brendan Sainsbury, Andrea Schulte-Peevers, Polly Thomas and Wendy Yanagihara. The previous edition was written by Mara Vorhees, Paul Clammer, Ashley Harrell, Liza Prado, Brendan Sainsbury, Alex Egerton, Anna Kaminski, Catherine Le Nevez, Tom Masters, Carolyn McCarthy, Hugh McNaughtan, Kevin Raub, Andrea Schulte-Peevers, Polly Thomas, Luke Waterson and Karla Zimmerman. This guidebook was produced by the following:

Destination Editor Alicia Johnson

Senior Product Editor Martine Power

Regional Senior Cartographer Corey Hutchison

Product Editors Bruce Evans, Saralinda Turner

Book Designer Jessica Rose

Assisting Editors Janet Austin, Sarah Bailey, Bridget Blair, Lou McGregor, Charlotte Orr, Tamara Sheward, Gabrielle Stefanos

Assisting Cartographer James Leversha

Cover Researcher Brendan Dempsey-Spencer

Thanks to Bailey Freeman, Karen Henderson, Kirsten Rawlings, James Smart, Angela Tinson

Index

Map Pages **000**
Photo Pages **000**

Map Pages **000**
Photo Pages **000**

Map Pages **000**
Photo Pages **000**

Map Pages **000**
Photo Pages **000**

Map Pages **000**
Photo Pages **000**

N

Map Pages **000**
Photo Pages **000**

Q

R

S

T

U

V

Map Pages **000**
Photo Pages **000**

Map Legend

Sights
- Beach
- Bird Sanctuary
- Buddhist
- Castle/Palace
- Christian
- Confucian
- Hindu
- Islamic
- Jain
- Jewish
- Monument
- Museum/Gallery/Historic Building
- Ruin
- Shinto
- Sikh
- Taoist
- Winery/Vineyard
- Zoo/Wildlife Sanctuary
- Other Sight

Activities, Courses & Tours
- Bodysurfing
- Diving
- Canoeing/Kayaking
- Course/Tour
- Sento Hot Baths/Onsen
- Skiing
- Snorkeling
- Surfing
- Swimming/Pool
- Walking
- Windsurfing
- Other Activity

Sleeping
- Sleeping
- Camping
- Hut/Shelter

Eating
- Eating

Drinking & Nightlife
- Drinking & Nightlife
- Cafe

Entertainment
- Entertainment

Shopping
- Shopping

Information
- Bank
- Embassy/Consulate
- Hospital/Medical
- Internet
- Police
- Post Office
- Telephone
- Toilet
- Tourist Information
- Other Information

Geographic
- Beach
- Gate
- Hut/Shelter
- Lighthouse
- Lookout
- Mountain/Volcano
- Oasis
- Park
- Pass
- Picnic Area
- Waterfall

Population
- Capital (National)
- Capital (State/Province)
- City/Large Town
- Town/Village

Transport
- Airport
- Border crossing
- Bus
- Cable car/Funicular
- Cycling
- Ferry
- Metro station
- Monorail
- Parking
- Petrol station
- Subway/Subte station
- Taxi
- Train station/Railway
- Tram
- Underground station
- Other Transport

Routes
- Tollway
- Freeway
- Primary
- Secondary
- Tertiary
- Lane
- Unsealed road
- Road under construction
- Plaza/Mall
- Steps
- Tunnel
- Pedestrian overpass
- Walking Tour
- Walking Tour detour
- Path/Walking Trail

Boundaries
- International
- State/Province
- Disputed
- Regional/Suburb
- Marine Park
- Cliff
- Wall

Hydrography
- River, Creek
- Intermittent River
- Canal
- Water
- Dry/Salt/Intermittent Lake
- Reef

Areas
- Airport/Runway
- Beach/Desert
- Cemetery (Christian)
- Cemetery (Other)
- Glacier
- Mudflat
- Park/Forest
- Sight (Building)
- Sportsground
- Swamp/Mangrove

Note: Not all symbols displayed above appear on the maps in this book

Brendan Sainsbury

Cuba Born and raised in the UK in a town that never merits a mention in any guidebook (Andover, Hampshire), Brendan spent the holidays of his youth caravanning in the English Lake District and didn't leave Blighty until he was 19. Making up for lost time, he's since squeezed 70 countries into a sometimes precarious existence as a writer and professional vagabond. In the last 11 years, he has written over 40 books for Lonely Planet, from Castro's Cuba to the canyons of Peru.

Andrea Schulte-Peevers

Anguilla, St-Martin/Sint Maarten, St-Barthélemy, Saba, St Eustatius Born and raised in Germany and educated in London and at UCLA, Andrea has traveled the distance to the moon and back in her visits to some 75 countries. She has earned her living as a professional travel writer for over two decades and authored or contributed to nearly 100 Lonely Planet titles as well as to newspapers, magazines and websites around the world. She also works as a travel consultant, translator and editor. Andrea's destination expertise is especially strong when it comes to Germany, Dubai and the UAE, Crete and the Caribbean Islands. She makes her home in Berlin.

Polly Thomas

Trinidad & Tobago Polly has been writing about the Caribbean for 20 years, authoring guide books to Jamaica, Antigua & Barbuda, St Lucia and Trinidad & Tobago. Having lived for five years in Port of Spain, Trinidad, she's now back in her hometown, London, seeking out good roti and doubles whenever she can.

Wendy Yanagihara

Cuba Wendy serendipitously landed her dream job of writing for Lonely Planet in 2003 and has spent the intervening years contributing to titles including Vietnam, Japan, Mexico, Costa Rica, Cuba, Ecuador, Indonesia and Grand Canyon National Park. Wendy has also written for BBC Travel, the *Guardian*, *Lonely Planet Magazine* and lonelyplanet.com, and intermittently freelances as a graphic designer, illustrator and visual artist. Instagram: @wendyyanagihara

Sarah Gilbert
Puerto Rico Sarah Gilbert is an award-winning, globe-trotting freelance writer and photographer. Since 2014 she has covered a host of diverse destinations for Lonely Planet, including Morocco, Puerto Rico, Switzerland, Thailand, Bolivia and Uruguay. Sarah's travelled to 75 countries and counting, and feels equally at home in a city guesthouse, remote safari lodge or a wooden hut in the Amazon rainforest.

Michael Grosberg
Dominican Republic Michael has worked on over 50 Lonely Planet guidebooks. Other international work included development on Rota in the western Pacific; South Africa, where he investigated and wrote about political violence and trained newly elected government representatives; and Quito, Ecuador to teach. He received a Masters in Comparative Literature and taught literature and writing as an adjunct professor.

Paul Harding
The Bahamas, Turks & Caicos As a writer and photographer, Paul has been traveling the globe for the best part of two decades, with an interest in remote and offbeat places, islands and cultures. He's an author and contributor to more than 50 Lonely Planet guides to countries and regions as diverse as India, Belize, Vanuatu, Iran, Indonesia, New Zealand, Iceland, Finland, Philippines and – his home patch – Australia.

Ashley Harrell
Aruba, Bonaire, Cayman Islands, Curaçao After a brief stint selling day spa coupons door-to-door in South Florida, Ashley decided she'd rather be a writer. She went to journalism grad school, convinced a newspaper to hire her, and starting covering wildlife, crime and tourism, sometimes all in the same story. She traveled widely and moved often, from a tiny NYC apartment to a vast California ranch to a jungle cabin in Costa Rica, where she started writing for Lonely Planet. From there her travels became more exotic and farther flung, and she still laughs when paychecks arrive.

Mark Johanson
British Virgin Islands, US Virgin Islands Mark Johanson grew up in Virginia and has called five different countries home over the last decade while circling the globe reporting for British newspapers (the *Guardian*), American magazines (*Men's Journal*) and global media outlets (CNN, BBC). When not on the road, you'll find him gazing at the Andes from his current home in Santiago, Chile. Follow the adventures at www.markjohanson.com

Anna Kaminski
Jamaica Originally from the Soviet Union, Anna grew up in Cambridge, UK. She graduated from the University of Warwick with a degree in Comparative American Studies, a background in the history, culture and literature of the Americas and the Caribbean, and an enduring love of Latin America. Her restless wanderings led her to settle briefly in Oaxaca and Bangkok and her flirtation with criminal law saw her volunteering as a lawyer's assistant in the courts, ghettoes and prisons of Kingston, Jamaica. Anna has contributed to almost 30 Lonely Planet titles. When not on the road, Anna calls London home.

Tom Masters
Antigua & Barbuda, Dominica, Montserrat, St Kitts & Nevis Dreaming since he could walk of going to the most obscure places on earth, Tom has always had a taste for the unknown. This has led to a writing career that has taken him all over the world, including North Korea, the Arctic, Congo and Siberia. Despite a childhood spent in the English countryside, as an adult Tom has always called London, Paris and Berlin home. He currently lives in Berlin and can be found online at www.tommasters.net.

OUR STORY

A beat-up old car, a few dollars in the pocket and a sense of adventure. In 1972 that's all Tony and Maureen Wheeler needed for the trip of a lifetime – across Europe and Asia overland to Australia. It took several months, and at the end – broke but inspired – they sat at their kitchen table writing and stapling together their first travel guide, *Across Asia on the Cheap*. Within a week they'd sold 1500 copies. Lonely Planet was born.

Today, Lonely Planet has offices in Franklin, Dublin, Beijing and Delhi, with a network of over 2000 contributors in every corner of the globe. We share Tony's belief that 'a great guidebook should do three things: inform, educate and amuse'.

OUR WRITERS

Paul Clammer

Jamaica Paul Clammer has worked as a molecular biologist, tour leader and travel writer. Since 2003 he has worked as a guidebook author for Lonely Planet, contributing to over 25 titles, covering swaths of South and Central Asia, West and North Africa and the Caribbean. In recent years he's lived in Morocco, Jordan, Haiti and Fiji, as well as his native England. Find him online at paulclammer.com or on Twitter as @paulclammer. Paul also contributed the Plan and Survival Guide chapters.

Stephanie d'Arc Taylor

Haiti A native Angeleno, Stephanie has published work with the *New York Times*, the *Guardian*, *Roads & Kingdoms* and *Kinfolk Magazine* (among others), and co-founded Jaleesa, a venture-capital-funded social impact business in Beirut. Follow her on Instagram @zerodarctaylor.

Marc Di Duca

Guadeloupe, Martinique, Puerto Rico A travel author for over a decade, Marc has worked for Lonely Planet in Siberia, Slovakia, Bavaria, England, Ukraine, Austria, Poland, Croatia, Portugal, Madeira and on the Trans-Siberian Railway, as well as writing and updating tens of other guides for other publishers. When not on the road, Marc lives near Mariánské Lázně in the Czech Republic with his wife and two sons.

Alex Egerton

Barbados, Dominica, Grenada, St Lucia, St Vincent & the Grenadines A news journalist by trade, Alex has worked for magazines, newspapers and media outlets on five continents. A keen adventurer, Alex has hiked through remote jungles in Colombia, explored isolated tributaries of the mighty Mekong and taken part in the first kayak descent of a number of remote waterways in Nicaragua. When not on the road, you'll find him at home amongst the colonial splendor of Popayán in southern Colombia.

Published by Lonely Planet Global Limited
CRN 554153
8th edition – June 2021
ISBN 978 1 78701 673 6

10 9 8 7 6 5 4 3 2 1
Printed in Singapore